The Worlds of Lincoln Kirstein

The Worlds of Lincoln Kirstein

MARTIN DUBERMAN

ALFRED A. KNOPF · NEW YORK · 2007

THIS IS A BORZOI BOOK
PUBLISHED BY ALFRED A. KNOPF

Copyright © 2007 by Martin Duberman
All rights reserved. Published in the United States by Alfred A. Knopf,
a division of Random House, Inc., New York,
and in Canada by Random House of Canada Limited, Toronto.
www.aaknopf.com

Knopf, Borzoi Books, and the colophon are
registered trademarks of Random House, Inc.

Library of Congress Cataloging-in-Publication Data
Duberman, Martin B.
The worlds of Lincoln Kirstein / Martin Duberman.—1st ed.
p.   cm.
ISBN-13: 978-1-4000-4132-9 (alk. paper)
1. Kirstein, Lincoln, 1907–1996.   2. Authors, American—20th century—Biography.
3. Philanthropists—New York (State)—New York—Biography.
4. School of American Ballet—History.   5. New York City Ballet—History.
6. Arts—New York (State)—New York—History—20th century.
7. New York (N.Y.)—Intellectual life—20th century.
8. Gay men—New York (State)—New York—Biography.   I. Title.
PS3521.I74Z65 2007
792.8092—dc22   2006048732

Manufactured in the United States of America
First Edition

Again, for Eli—

and the blessings of continuity

CONTENTS

PART FIVE: MATURITY

PART SIX: DECLINE

PART ONE

Youth

Growing Up

(1907–1926)

WHEN ROSE STEIN told her family in the summer of 1893 that she wished to marry Louis Kirstein, she met with instant and strenuous opposition. The Steins, after all, were among Rochester's most prominent Jewish families, partners in the flourishing Stein-Bloch men's clothing company, pillars of the community—even if, but one generation back, their mother had been a wet nurse in Posen, Germany.[1]

Who was this Louis Kirstein? A nobody in the Steins' view, a large, coarse-looking man with limited education and income—and even more limited prospects. He did currently hold down a salesman's job for an optical firm, but though admittedly bright, congenial, and ambitious, he hadn't found work that genuinely engaged him or offered promise of a secure future. Nor did his history inspire confidence that he ever would.

Alarming tales had reached the stodgy Stein clan: Kirstein, it seemed, had only a grammar-school education, had left home at sixteen, ridden the rails as a hobo, worked as a janitor in a St. Louis brothel, and once been held in jail overnight for trying to peddle a worthless patent medicine. He had, though still in his late twenties, already gone bankrupt three times—once as part owner, player, and manager of a bush-league baseball team.

The words "sporting type," "maverick," and "outsider" clung to his name: he was said to like fine Cuban cigars (Corona Coronas) and well-tailored clothes, was a habitual (and lucky) poker player—and wasn't an observant Jew. Not that the Steins were, either, but somehow Louis *should* have been, given his otherwise unorthodox ways. No, Rose was told, the match was entirely unsuitable.

But Rose refused to yield. She felt certain that the man she'd fallen for couldn't be summarized by his hard-luck past, nor could his earlier missteps be taken as an accurate gauge of his character. The Louis Kirstein she knew was a charismatic man of integrity and generosity, a man of shrewd intelligence, unflagging optimism, and a tremendous appetite for life. Far from being a "sporting type," he believed strongly in the ideal of "service"—in using one's gifts and good fortune in behalf of those less fortunate. And, far from being a "fancy man," he adhered to standard middle-class values of hard work, civic-mindedness, and devotion to family. No, she would not give him up. (Nor would she be at all surprised when, within a decade, Louis would begin a rapid ascent to wealth and influence.)

Rose's obstinacy was not an entire surprise to her family. Though she'd grown up a conventional enough child, and was now seemingly content with the decorous confines of well-to-do womanhood—a keen interest in fashion, embroidery and lace, museumgoing, the arts and concerts—her six siblings had been warned at an early age, so one of them later remembered, "never to cross Rosie because she might have one of her crazy tantrums." Her daughter Mina would later write of her, "She was not given to revealing her feelings, only exploding when they were injured."

Ultimately Rose's parents gave their reluctant consent to an engagement. But they stipulated that marriage could not take place for three years, during which time they confidently expected their daughter to change her mind. She didn't. When the three-year waiting period was up, in January 1896, she and Louis quietly wed—and promptly moved to Boston. This further aggravated family disapproval. Rose's parents didn't cut her off, but when she gave birth to her first child, Mina, a year later, it was not her own mother who came down from Rochester to stand by but rather Louis's widowed mother.

Once settled in a modest rented apartment, Louis went to work for the well-established opticians Andrew J. Lloyd & Company, and began to spend considerable time on the road selling eyeglasses. His own father, Edward, had been a lens grinder in Jena, near Leipzig, a city that for a time had been a center of liberal thought and home to Fichte, Hegel, and Schiller. Edward and his wife, Jeanette, had been adherents of the revolutionary uprising of 1848, and in the wake of its failure, had fled Germany, along with hordes of like-minded social radicals, for the United States. There Edward had found work with the Bausch and Lomb optical company in Rochester, the same city where, some dozen years later, Rose's father, Nathan Stein, became a wealthy man—thanks to contracts he secured during the Civil War to make uniforms for the Union army (uniforms, it was widely rumored, that were cut from shoddy material).

The Steins' ongoing condescension to Louis dissipated somewhat with the birth of Mina, in 1897; to them it apparently signified seriousness and permanence. The renegade couple was invited to return to Rochester, and Louis offered employment with the family company, Stein-Bloch. He took his time accepting: the Steins had treated him as unworthy, and Louis had a settled sense of self-regard.

Still, he missed his mother, who'd remained in Rochester, living modestly in a small gray frame house in a decaying section of the city. Kindhearted, politically liberal, courageous (she was crippled with arthritis but never complained), and cultivated—her special passions were Goethe and Heine—Grandma Kirstein was the only religious member of the family;

she read the Old Testament in German, prayer books in Hebrew, and insisted that Louis attend synagogue on Rosh Hashanah and Yom Kippur. Despite her limited means, Grandma Kirstein (who died in 1914) would treat visitors to a spread of marzipan, pretzels, *Apfelstrudel*, and licorice sticks. Should Louis be in town, his favorite preserve, quince jelly, would be served, and should Mina accompany him, Grandma made her favorite—*Küchelchen*, little drops of sponge cake dipped in fat.

An additional reason for returning to Rochester was that Rose also missed her family, and especially two of her sisters, Molly and Jane. (She felt less close to her other siblings, and downright distant from her two difficult, somewhat showy bachelor brothers, one of whom summered in a palatial "cottage" and the other notoriously "not nice" to his female help.)

In 1901 the Kirsteins finally decided to return to Rochester, and Louis accepted a job with Stein-Bloch as a traveling salesman. They moved into a modest-size house on Portsmouth Terrace, around the corner from Rochester's most elegant street, East Avenue, which boasted the pillared mansion of George Eastman, inventor of the box Kodak camera. Louis had once worked for Eastman and became a personal acquaintance; it was rumored that he'd rejected Eastman's offer to join the Kodak firm, convinced that the new "toy" was a passing fad.

The Kirsteins' house was securely nestled within a cluster of Stein homes. Rose's widowed sister, Molly, lived next door with her daughter; sister Jane lived two houses down the street with her husband, Martin Wolff, owner of Rochester's prestigious Lyceum Theatre, and their two children. Young Mina Kirstein soon decided that her favorite neighbors were not her relatives but the firemen who lived around the corner, fed her pears from the tree, and lifted her up to pat the heads of their beautiful white horses.

Rose managed to give the interior of their home some distinction through a generous sprinkling of potted palms, large ferns, and a number of marble statues—a near life-size *Fisher Boy*, the bust of a Gypsy atop a twisted green marble pillar, and in the sitting room, a small *Cupid and Psyche*. She bought a big Morris chair for Louis, stocked the bookshelves (Rose was herself a devoted reader), and provided Mina, who'd early been labeled "precocious"—at seven she was reading Shaw's *You Never Can Tell*—with piano lessons, dancing school, a governess who spoke both French and German, and clothes imported from the fashionable New York stores Best and Peter Thompson.

Both of Rose's bachelor brothers, and a brother-in-law as well, worked in the Stein-Bloch business. Nathan Stein, the quick-tempered family patriarch, required (until his death in 1908) that all family members attend him daily at lunch in his impressive Gibbs Street brick mansion, with its ornate mirrors, cut-glass vases filled with fresh American Beauty roses,

superb Belter rosewood chairs—and *two* servants on duty behind his chair
to prevent his ever being kept waiting. After lunch the men would retire
for a game of billiards—which Nathan somehow always won. Though a
considerable despot, he had a soft spot for his grandchildren, and Mina
seems to have been a favorite. As an adult she would remember him as
having been "very kind" to her, sending her off every Saturday for a shampoo and manicure with a Mrs. Davenport (whom Mina, later in life, suspected had been Grandpa Stein's "special friend").

Rose Kirstein gave birth to a second child, a boy, on May 4, 1907, and
Louis (who was forty-one at the time of his son's birth) named the baby
Lincoln in honor of his idol, Abraham Lincoln. Ten-year-old Mina's reaction was less benign. "He looks like a lobster!" she screamed on first seeing him—and Rose promptly ordered her from the bedroom, into the
arms of her comforting father. The two loved each other deeply, and
Louis reassured Mina that her special place in his heart was inviolable.
The essential family alliances, never rigid, had been formed: father and
daughter, mother and son.

Mina quickly came round about the new baby, however and on the
nurse's day off, took to wheeling the infant, whom she now declared "ravishingly beautiful," along the street, demanding and getting admiring
exclamations from the neighbors. Mina would become Lincoln's closest
confidante when he was growing up, the person to whom he would turn in
distress—the "Dearest" of his youthful letters. When the Kirsteins' third
and last child, George, was born two and a half years later, Lincoln's initial
reaction was even more murderous than Mina's had been toward him;
allowed to watch baby George being bathed, Lincoln grabbed a tin of tal-
cum powder and tried to bash his brother's head in. But in the case of Lincoln and George, the relationship would never grow into anything
approaching a profound connectedness.

Though Louis and Rose were not observant Jews, he—unlike Rose—felt
deeply committed to his social obligations as a Jew and would later, in his
son Lincoln's affectionate words, become Boston's leading "bully and
blackmailer" in raising money for assorted Jewish causes and charities.
When in 1914, for example, Louis was denied, as a Jew, the right to play
golf at any of the area's country clubs, he began a yearlong fight to establish the all-Jewish Kernwood Country Club (and was promptly elected its
president). "True to our traditions," Louis said in his speech inaugurating
the club, "we were not discouraged. Rather, we were determined . . . [to]
show that we had the will, the force and the character to accomplish what
we deemed necessary for our development."[2]

Similarly Louis insisted all his life on adhering to a limited number of
Jewish rituals: he faithfully attended synagogue on the High Holy Days,

and he automatically assumed that his newborn son, Lincoln, should be circumcised. But instead of turning to the traditional religious specialist, a *mohel*, to carry out the procedure, the Kirsteins decided to let the family doctor perform it. He botched the job, septicemia set in, and Lincoln nearly died. To save him, the sweat glands in his groin were surgically removed, leaving physical and psychological scars, locker-room conceal-ments, and castration nightmares that would haunt Lincoln into adoles-cence; and leaving as well a small knot of loosely attached flesh that at age twelve he would—in what he subsequently described as "a fit of hysterical nervousness"—hack off with his mother's nail scissors. When George was born, he was left uncircumcised.

The terror of nearly losing her baby left Rose prone to panic every time Lincoln had a sniffle, hint of infection, or mood swing—and there were many, since he grew up a sickly child, given (in his own words) "to fits of anxiety . . . and despair." Late in life he laconically summarized the intertwined incitement to hysteria between himself and his mother: her "fathomless apprehension determined more of my character than was necessary."

In 1911, when Lincoln was four, the Kirsteins left Rochester and returned to Boston. The move was propelled by ongoing tension between Louis and several male members of the Stein clan; the persistent hint that he could never expect to become a full partner in Stein-Bloch had com-bined with the simultaneous beginnings of friendship between Louis and the Filene brothers, Edward and Lincoln. The Filenes had inherited their father William's clothing and piece-goods store in Boston and had begun to build it into what would become one of the world's largest—and most socially progressive—department stores. The friendship between Lincoln Filene, the more amiable and modest of the two brothers, and Louis had steadily deepened since its inception, and in 1911 he offered Louis a ju-nior partnership in the rapidly expanding company.[3]

For the next two years the family lived in the Hotel Ericson on Common-wealth Avenue, a prestigious Boston address. During that time Louis quickly consolidated his position at Filene's. He could be aggressively competitive and a bit of a bully who sometimes looked (though rarely was) formidably angry. But Louis also had a pronounced sense of humor, and his essential fair-mindedness and integrity made him popular with buyers and employees alike. He and the testy (as well as highly innovative) older Filene brother, Edward, never took to each other and at times were openly antagonistic. But the friendship between Louis and Lincoln Filene con-tinued to grow, and before long Louis became head of merchandising and was allowed to invest heavily in the company.

Rose's energy, meantime, remained centered on traditional household and cultural pursuits, but with a twist: she never bothered herself much with domestic chores or the routines of child care. Lincoln (and later, George) were turned over to the daily care of a full-time nurse, the kindly, ever-on-call "Bodie" (Helen Bodine). Rose herself, as a young girl, had gone for a time to a genteel finishing school in Manhattan, where she'd been taught the niceties of Continental deportment and speech and an appreciation for Parisian fashions and elegant furnishings (at one point she created a "Turkish" room for herself in the Kirsteins' home, and later, a Chinese one).

Rose decided that Mina should be given comparable advantages. But though patently intelligent and bookish, Mina for a time failed to gain admission to any of the well-regarded boarding schools. A number of headmistresses initially expressed enthusiasm—but then discovered that the family was Jewish. Finally Miss Capen, who ran her prestigious school for girls in Northampton, Massachusetts, agreed to admit her, assuring Rose (after Rose had said it was perfectly acceptable for Mina to go to church) that she herself had no prejudice whatsoever against "Hebrews," indeed admired the "race" for its many "geniuses." She had instituted a quota system, Miss Capen explained, only to satisfy the large number of parents who objected to their daughters being "over-exposed" to Jewish people. Fortunately, she added, the quota (which turned out to be 2 students out of 120) had not been filled for the upcoming year.[4]

Mina initially failed to appreciate her great good fortune. Miss Capen's School was strict and old-fashioned, and Mina was soon writing home about her unhappiness and her wish to leave. Louis (not Rose) wrote back a series of affectionately blunt letters admonishing her against quitting: "I really thought you had a real fighting spirit . . . you must not think of beginning so young in life to lay [sic] down . . . don't just think that Dad is only preaching again, as I try hard not to do too often." Mina, though hardly dutiful, decided to grin and bear it (actually, she later described her time at the school as "two happy years") knowing that she would be going to Europe in the summer and that in September 1914 she would be entering Smith College as a freshman.

That same month the Kirsteins moved into a rented, furnished five-story house at 506 Commonwealth Avenue. (Louis would all his life refuse to buy property, unconsciously haunted, perhaps, by his parents' ever-present fear in Germany of imminent persecution and the need for instant flight.) The house stood at the far—least fashionable—end of the street, near the Kenmore Square trolley station. Unlike many homes on Commonwealth Avenue, it had not been designed by the illustrious firm of McKim, Mead & White and was not architecturally distinguished.

Still, it *was* on Commonwealth, and it *did* have a number of special features, including an elevator. The unadorned limestone facade boasted a set of attractive bay windows, and the interior was made up of high-ceilinged, well-proportioned rooms—except for the raw pine cubicles on the fourth floor where two maids, a cook, and a laundress were installed. Some of the furnishings were of fine quality, including a few Louis XVI pieces, superb Lyon velvet portières and curtains, and a huge seventeenth-century Dutch painting by Melchior d'Hondecoeter that hung above the dining room sideboard.

But the house failed to meet Rose's standards as a dwelling worthy of Louis's newly acquired status as a budding merchant prince. She herself had, after all, grown up in luxurious surroundings, and it seemed the most natural—and comforting—thing in the world to try to reproduce them in her own home. Besides, it gave her an occupation. Though many middle-class and elite white women in Boston, including Jewish ones, were engaged in reform, philanthropic, and suffrage organizations, Rose was not among them. Unlike Louis, who by the onset of World War I would be widely active in the civic arena, Rose never involved herself, not even peripherally or behind the scenes, in public affairs.

Her personality had its quirks, but she did her best to conceal them in order to comport herself according to traditional standards of proper female behavior. Mina, whose relationship with her mother was often uncomfortably tense, and at times severely strained, thought her mother overly strict about what was or was not "suitable"; she refused to let Mina see the musical comedy *The Parisian Model* because its star, Anna Held, revealed too much of her anatomy on stage; and she expressed "horror" when Mina, as an adult, decided to become a teacher and to bob her hair. Mina felt that Rose had a gift and a penchant "for making scenes" and for controlling the household through headaches and histrionic attacks of "nerves."[5]

Mina tended to be her mother's harshest critic; in general Rose seems to have been viewed as affable and generous—though indeed given to occasional fits of temper or a bit of ostentatious display. The latter trait she now fully employed in upgrading the family's new house. She felt it was important for a Jewish family living in the very bosom of anti-Semitic Brahmin Boston to demonstrate that these outsiders could maintain a stylish home. With the help of a decorator, Rose covered the walls of the master bedroom with gold tea-paper, bought expensive black-and-gold lacquer furniture, and vermilion satin curtains and bedspreads. At night, bags were pulled over the curtains, and the bedspreads covered with yellow cloth to protect them from soot (two railroads ran a block from the house).

The living room was more welcoming: Rose bought warm blue velvet curtains, upholstered the chairs in grospoint, and built bookcases, topped with bronze busts, halfway up to the ceiling (with an entire section reserved for Louis's collection of books about Abraham Lincoln). But Louis, and later the children as well, tended to be pacers, not sitters—despite Rose's frequent injunction to "cultivate repose." In 1914, to complete the transformation, the Kirsteins bought a silver Rolls-Royce. In his son Lincoln's scornful later words, Louis Kirstein had begun "to fill the role of one of Boston's housebroken, token aliens."

The judgment was one-sided. As Louis once wrote about himself, "I was brought up in rather a hard school . . . where I had to fight . . . for what I got," and where, for a long time, success, or even its approximation, had proved elusive. Despite its arrival, Louis's values remained essentially egalitarian. Yes, he bought the Rolls-Royce, but after Sacco and Vanzetti were executed, he hired Sacco's son, Dante, to be his chauffeur. Louis enjoyed his comforts, but he remained largely indifferent to social status, and his acquisitiveness was pretty much confined to expensive suits, shirts, and golf clubs. Partly because he had limited visual acumen, he paid little attention to purchase and display.

Cost consciousness and budgetary restraint were second nature to him—character traits that would sometimes annoy his indulged children. Once chided by her father for having been insufficiently grateful for the gift of a car, Mina, then aged twenty-three, high-handedly responded: "I am sorry that you thought me so unappreciative that I needed to be reminded after the fashion of a small child, to say 'Thank you.' " She then proceeded to lecture her father for being so preoccupied with work that "you haven't always taken the time to analyze your personal relationships. They cannot be run like business. . . . We are both overwhelming egotists, and our virtues may to a degree make up for our outstanding fault of being self-centered."

Louis—who adored Mina—replied by thanking her for having "taken me into your confidence. . . . I do value your opinion and advice. . . . I sometimes treat people as I was treated"—harshly—"and there is no reason why they should like it any better than I did." But, he went on, "I don't believe anyone who accomplishes anything worthwhile can be anything but an egotist and to a greater or less extent self-centered." He emphasized, however, that he loathed selfishness.[6]

Though the Kirstein family, as Lincoln later wrote, was "remote from real piety," at age seven he was sent to Saturday Bible school at nearby Temple Israel. The "lessons" consisted of little beyond learning to draw maps of Palestine, and within a short time his parents relieved him from further attendance. For his elementary education Lincoln was sent to a well-regarded public school, Edward Devotion (named for one of the Puritan founders) in Brookline, an affluent Boston subdivision.

After graduating he was denied admission to the prestigious Boston Latin School because of poor grades, and his parents made the somewhat odd decision to send him instead to a YMCA-run school on Huntington Avenue. There Lincoln took at once to the daily singing of hymns. The music he'd been used to hearing at Temple Israel, he later wrote, was "little more than italic accompaniment by a faint choir and a reedy quasi-organ."

At the YMCA every school day began, after "a short religious observance of loose ecumenical informality," with what Lincoln would describe years later as the "massive glory" of "full ringing voices of boys and young men," to the accompaniment of a Steinway Grand piano, "declaring in words of elementary force, majestic metric and physical warmth, words that . . . had all the authority of truth and faith." "Onward, Christian Soldiers" became his favorite. Before the age of ten, Lincoln became attracted to "religious ritual," as well as "troubled" by the "peculiar problems" it raised.

The hymns propelled Lincoln into writing verse, and the "physical warmth" they induced became centered on the biggest of his classmates, Sonny Fitzgerald. Lincoln adored Sonny, the captain of Huntington YMCA's basketball team; saw him, in his "godlike proportions and massive maleness," as the epitome of the "Christian soldiers" they sang about each morning, part of the great clan of "Black Irishmen" who were "the tribal enemies of Henry Adams' Beacon Hill."

Though some felt otherwise, Lincoln was certain that Sonny was not to any degree a bully; he might occasionally snap a towel at him in the locker room, but Lincoln chose to view that as "recognition awarded." And surely Sonny wasn't responsible for an incident that happened when Lincoln was eleven: several of the older, bigger boys at Huntington pushed him, naked, into a steel locker and turned the handle, leaving Lincoln so "shocked with fright" that he made not a sound until, hours later, he got up the courage to pound his fist against the locker and was released by a watchman; Lincoln collapsed in his arms and cried his eyes out.

Attending concerts at Symphony Hall and going to the theater became his other fixations while he was still in his preteens. Under Rose's tutelage, music came to hold (he later wrote) "a prime place in furnishing my imaginative process." Not all music; he was too restless a youngster to sit raptly attentive through most concerts. A few special favorites emerged early on: Schubert's *Unfinished* Symphony, Tchaikovsky's *Pathétique*, and César Franck's Symphony in D Minor—these became "keys to how sounds could be manipulated towards theatrical splendor."

The theater itself was, in Mina's words, "an intensely immediate issue in our lives." When still in Rochester, Lincoln, by age five, had been allowed to attend performances at Uncle Martin Wolff's Lyceum Theatre. For a time, though, Rose drew the line at ballet, and she refused, when he was nine, to let him see the Diaghilev ballet during its U.S. tour: "You wouldn't understand it," she told him. Perhaps she was remembering how Lincoln had cried for hours after hearing the tragic finale of *Rigoletto*, and was protecting his easily overwrought nature.

When he reached the age of twelve, she relented, allowing him in 1919 to see his very first ballet—"The Dance of the Hours" from Ponchielli's *La Gioconda*. Far from keeling over from excitement, Lincoln pronounced the performance "disappointing," and he left unmoved. The following year proved a different story. Rose allowed him to go to New York, accompanied by his vaguely disreputable "sissy" cousin Nat Wolfe, then a junior at Harvard, to see Anna Pavlova. This time he was entirely smitten ("she was wonderful"); he and Nat went back five nights in a row—and the consuming passion of Lincoln's life was born.

With the onset of World War I, Louis—whom his son later characterized as "an American patriot in the old Fourth-of-July . . . style"—started making frequent trips to Washington to help the Quartermaster Department organize the distribution of uniforms; he was put in charge of clothing procurement for the army, a task he apparently performed "magnificently." He also joined a government mission abroad, headed by Bernard Baruch, to draw up plans for reviving European industry and would even have a chronic attack of "Potomac fever." His patriotic fervor rubbed off on his children, especially after the United States entered the war, with Lincoln conscientiously distributing canned goods and coal to the poor.

Mina—though she later described herself as a "political ignoramus" for most of her life—went quite a few steps beyond the acceptable parameters of family patriotism. She greeted the Russian Revolution of 1917 with vast enthusiasm and for a brief time became, as she herself put it, "a passionate if uninformed propagandist." While attending Smith College, she even wrote a piece for *Seven Arts*, a new literary journal that lasted only a year, denouncing the Justice Department for having arrested thousands of so-called Reds and deporting several hundred, including Emma Goldman.[7]

This managed to produce a considerable furor on the Smith campus. Mina was publicly satirized as "Mina Trotsky Lenine," and mocked for a revolutionary ardor that hadn't prevented her from wearing expensive, made-to-order clothes, dwelling in the grandest suite in her dormitory, and being the only undergraduate who owned an automobile. Mina soon agreed that the contradictions were "ridiculous," and after graduating from Smith, took a job as a research clerk in Washington, DC, for the British intelligence service. She worked first in the map room and then, after the November 1918 Armistice, for the Shipping Board. Her own leftist sympathies never disappeared, but for most of her life were reduced to a diluted, vague concern for those less fortunate than she. Her brother Lincoln, however, would in the early thirties develop a more sustained involvement with the Left, though it, too, would ultimately subside.

Rose had reluctantly agreed to let the twenty-one-year-old Mina live independently in Washington, but as a wartime measure only. She felt that

Mina's proper place was (so Mina described it) as "daughter-of-the-house until . . . [she] married a nice, socially eligible Jew and produced the grandchildren [her mother] . . . already longed for." One day early in 1919 Mina received a telephone call from Rose announcing that she was having a nervous breakdown and needed Mina to return home at once. Lincoln and George, Rose added, had no one to read to them at night, as Louis— who was in Europe—had regularly done.

Suspicious and angry, Mina did as she was bid—only to find the Rolls-Royce waiting for her at the Back Bay railroad station, with Rose in it, and showing neither symptoms of a nervous breakdown nor any awareness of the sacrifice she'd imposed. Furious, Mina exploded at her mother the moment they reached the house (much later in life, she remorsefully described her attack as ruthless and cruel). Rose retaliated: Mina's meals would henceforth be served in her room, and she was forbidden to read to her brothers.

When Louis returned soon after from Europe, he smoothed things over, but not before tactfully reprimanding Mina for the pain she'd caused her mother, who was, he said, her "best friend and always would be." He took Mina on a long walk and urged her, kindly, to make a concrete decision about what she wanted to do with her life. To her own astonishment Mina replied that she wanted to teach on the college level and, to achieve that, to get an MA at Columbia. "Well then, go ahead and do it," Louis said.

In early July 1919, coincident with his arrival for the summer at Camp Timanous in Maine, Lincoln started to keep a diary; he would maintain it, with occasional breaks and increasing detail, for nearly two decades. Still earlier, he'd begun a "drawing book" in which, for someone so young, he drew some remarkably elegant, lively sketches. As if in continuation, his Timanous diary is also filled with drawings, as well as tiny images that periodically substitute for a word itself. The centrality of visual imagery in Lincoln's life announced itself early in his diaries—accompanied by an equally long-lived penchant for misspelling.[8]

As for Camp Timanous itself, Lincoln's experiences there over two consecutive summers were for the most part commonplace. There were the usual number of treasure hunts, with the usual reward of ice cream; hikes to various nearby locales; masquerades, theatricals, and costume parties, swimming, boating, and mumblety-peg; blueberry pancakes and roasted corn; ghost and "dandy Jesse James stories" around the campfire.

On a few counts, though, Lincoln's camp experiences were atypical. For one, he could never learn to dive—though a relentless counselor kept him on the springboard for the better part of a day before yelling that Lincoln was a "Fimp" and marching off in disgust. Lincoln chose to blame himself; years later he traced what he described as his "hysterical tension" about diving back to an earlier experience when he was seven and an uncle, "fearing latent effeminacy" in his nephew, had thrown him repeatedly into the Rochester YMCA pool, where he'd "sunk to the bottom in a paroxysm of fear." At twelve, another uncle—Louis's difficult brother Henry—told Lincoln to his face that he was "a sissy"—and Lincoln "didn't like it either."

He tended in general toward self-recrimination: "The reason I am lonely is because I am bad company I suppose"; "I have too strong likes and dislikes"; "I am very very spoiled"; "am an awful bum sport"; am "absolutely self-disgusted." And as is often the case with someone afflicted with self-doubt, he sometimes compensated with over-assertion, telling himself (accurately) that though he never performed well on exams, his intelligence was in advance of his classmates'. At age twelve, when his class was reading *Julius Caesar*, which Lincoln loved, he grew impatient that the other students "didn't understand most of it" and that the pace of the reading had to be slowed down accordingly. In his diary he recorded a schoolmate's observation that Lincoln would be far happier if he would adapt himself "to the stupidity around me. Not that I am any better than the boys," Lincoln added, "just that I have a more questioning imagination."

He loved going on his own to the library, where he was able to devour, at his own pace, everything from Dickens to Molière to Hugh Walpole, as well as a large assortment of historical novels ("I have a romantic turn of mind"). He took instinctively, when at home, to art and piano lessons, wrote poetry and plays from an early age; delighted in going with his mother and aunts to museums, flower shows, and the opera; and often went alone to hear lectures at the Boston Public Library and concerts at Symphony Hall (Wagner was the one composer he disliked).

If to relatives like Uncle Henry, Lincoln's precocious interest in reading and the arts was dangerously "sissy," his class- and camp-mates seem not to have taunted him on that score (or at least he never recorded such teasing in his diaries), probably because of his large size and his physical exuberance at roughhouse play, tugs-of-war, shrieking water pistol battles, snowball and pillow fights—even, occasionally (though he described himself as "an awful coward") "fisticuffs." He was also known as an excellent horseback rider, and as a boy who loved to tramp through woods and frolic on the beach.

But he was too uncoordinated ever to enjoy gym; at fourteen he listed his "three pet abominations" as gym, Latin, and having to attend church services at school (apparently neither Rose nor Louis ever sought an exemption for him from the school's insistence on church attendance). Nor was he much good at team sports, though he played most of them, including hockey, baseball, and football. His younger brother, George, was much more of a natural athlete and far more of a sports fan; George and Louis shared a fascination with boxing and baseball, often attending Boston Red Sox games together.

Schoolboy crushes on their counselors are commonplace enough, but at Timanous, Lincoln developed such a passion for "Chief" Hamilton, the camp's young director, that whenever he dared, he'd beg Chief for a cuddle or a hug—which Chief would sometimes briefly allow. Lincoln also developed a passion, alone among his fellow campers, for dancing. Chief's girlfriend had studied with Isadora Duncan (whose company Lincoln saw perform at Symphony Hall in 1920—and "hated") and agreed to let Lincoln work out with her every morning. Still, she would teach him only "rhythmic exercises"(perhaps sensitive to the potential teasing he might otherwise get)—though she did tell him that the exercises bordered on "real" dancing. In any case they induced in Lincoln "rapture in bodily movements." She also encouraged him to believe that if he ever decided to, he could actually become a dancer. Chief, however, when handing out "diplomas" at the end of each summer for a variety of achievements, did not, pointedly, include "rhythmic exercises" among them. And when writing to Lincoln over the winter, Chief—though complimenting him on his "well-penned and artistic letters" as well as on his "art-work"—warned him that he needed to spend more time "outdoors," swimming, diving, and boxing.

Mina felt quite otherwise. She admonished her father for being more concerned with ensuring that Lincoln's hands were washed before meals than with his "mental and moral development," characterizing her then-thirteen-year-old brother as "far more complex and far wiser than you have any idea of. Lincoln will never be happy, any more than I shall ever be happy, for we both of us question too much for that." Louis thanked her for the advice and promised to try and make more time in his life for his son.

The profound bond between Lincoln and Mina while he was growing up would later, when both were accomplished adults, occasionally fray at the edges and lead to periods of minimal contact or overt antagonism. But as a youngster Lincoln viewed her as his emotional rock and was deeply reliant on her for comfort and advice. (Mina is "much the nicest person in the world," Lincoln wrote in his diary at one point.) He was already describing himself, at age fourteen, as a person of "moods and fancies," "disconsolate and lonely . . . like a person on a treadmill—walking and never getting anywhere." In another such mood, he wrote in his diary, "blue all day. Things look quite hopeless."

But when depressed, he was sensible enough to phone Mina, whose ability to make him feel better was very nearly a talisman: Mina "cheered me up a whole lot," Mina "lifted me to bliss above joy." Her magical power over his down moods seems to have centered on her shrewd ability to tell Lincoln convincingly that his "differentness" was a strength, a sign of superiority, even. As a subtheme of those pep talks, Mina constantly reinforced his artistic tastes and offbeat opinions (once, when asked what the most wonderful thing in life was, Lincoln had answered "the Jelly fish which although [it] has no back bone or brains manages to swim through thick and thin"). She plied him with books: Dos Passos and A. A. Milne, *Salammbô* and, among many others, "a dandy book on English Butter-flies." When he patronized his far more conventional younger brother ("George's one idea of bliss," Lincoln wrote in his diary, "is a movie, very sentimental, gum to chew during the performance and a soda after it"), Mina would confirm his assessment. After one heated argument between Lincoln and George about religion—George believed in God, Lincoln didn't—Mina told Lincoln that anyone who needed religion was trying to make up for "something lacking" in himself.

In the early years of the twentieth century, it was still exceedingly difficult for a Jew to gain admittance to any of New England's prestigious private schools—"unless," as Mina put it, "his name is Schiff or Warburg." The headmaster of Middlesex, for one, had refused even a preliminary meeting with the Kirsteins to discuss an application from Lincoln on the grounds that there were no openings at the school—only to have them learn of the instant admission months later of the scion of the prominent Bingham family.

Yet Louis's contacts would ultimately help. Even before World War I, his growing reputation as a businessman of acumen and fairness, as well as his work on behalf of multiple Jewish causes, had made him a number of influential friends, among them Louis Brandeis and Felix Frankfurter. As a result of his work for the government during the war and his increasingly prominent reputation in business circles, Louis's connections had proliferated to include such diverse and influential figures as the rising labor leader Sidney Hillman, the Boston politician James Curley, up-and-coming church figures like John O'Connor and Francis Spellman (who as a young man had very nearly become Lincoln's tutor), and even, by the early 1920s, Calvin Coolidge.

Louis was thus able to procure, through influential letters of introduction, first an interview for Lincoln and then his admission on a trial basis to Exeter Academy, the elite prep school of high academic standards, smug self-regard, and princely networking. Lincoln was one of four Jewish boys at the school at the time he was enrolled in the fall of 1921; they were housed together—not in a regular dormitory but in what Lincoln later described as "a rather dilapidated" private home that stood a considerable distance from the campus.[9]

He had difficulties at Exeter from the start. He missed Mina terribly, found the food "appalling," and promptly started flunking exams ("My work up here seems to be a succession of heroic failures"). Rose plied him with nearly daily packages of goodies, many of them from the fancy Boston grocer S.S. Pierce, and Louis sent him buck-up letters that alternated between affectionate encouragement and formulaic admonitions to persevere ("keep your courage up and go to it and I am sure you will come along all right"). Mina sent up her newly polished copper desk set, along with the poems of Shelley and Keats—and within weeks was visiting him. Rose followed soon after, laden with assorted treats; according to Lincoln they "had a very nice time together," and Rose took "savage pleasure" in neatly rearranging all his drawers.

Despite his discomforts and disappointments, Lincoln's time at Exeter was far from wholly negative. He liked several of his teachers (his English teacher described him as "extremely talented, little short of a genius for his age"), and in Howard Doughty—later the author of a well-regarded biography of the historian Francis Parkman—he found a friend who shared his interests and (being three years older) helped him toward developing new ones. He also found something more: a strong emotional attachment. "He's probably the nicest boy I ever met," Lincoln wrote in his diary, "He even swears well." The two became inseparable. They took long walks in the woods while "everybody else was in an ecstasy of school spiritism over a dull baseball game," walks that (as Lincoln later delicately put it) "often ended in wrestling matches, in which I fought with as much muscle as I could muster; intimacy of physical contact, for me hardly innocent, pleased both of us." ("I really am," he added in his diary, "a very affectionate fool.")

Howard introduced him to Aubrey Beardsley's drawings, encouraged his incipient interest in poetry, particularly in Oscar Wilde and Algernon Swinburne ("I don't try to get the meaning. It would spoil the lovely sound of the words")—and strongly confirmed what he already knew: the solace to be found in books. During his stay at Exeter, Lincoln buried himself for long hours in both the school and town libraries, often at the expense of completing prescribed assignments. He went through Exeter's entire run of the *Illustrated London News,* and later claimed that "from their wood-engravings I conceived a passion for England and the idea of Empire." He also managed to get a play published in the *Exeter Monthly* and joined the school's literary club (at Exeter, he later wrote, "I found a vocation in literature, such as it was").

But he continued to do badly in his official courses, consistently flunking math and Latin. Not even special tutoring made a difference. He became haunted by the fear of "disgracing" his father, since Louis had enlisted his influential friends in getting Lincoln admitted to the school. It didn't help that his father wrote him letters filled with mixed messages, telling Lincoln on the one hand that he was convinced the boy was trying as hard as he could ("I have no fault to find at all"), and on the other expressing exasperation over what he called Lincoln's "loss of nerve" when confronted with an exam paper: "It can't bite you and it hasn't any poisonous gas and no germs, so screw up your courage and make up your mind you can do it and I am sure you will." Not surprisingly Lincoln wrote in his diary that he found his mother more "generous emotionally" than his father.

In any case Lincoln's grades failed to improve, and by the end of the year, the Kirsteins were informed that their son would not be invited to return. Louis refrained from burdening Lincoln with additional recrimination and Lincoln later described both his parents as having been "quite extraordinarily understanding." Doubtless they took comfort in the opinions of "Chief" Hamilton (of Camp Timanous) that Lincoln was "of a type . . . too individual to shine in the average preparatory school," and also of Exeter's Recorder, a Mr. Cape, who felt the boy simply suffered from "nervousness" and expressed a "high opinion" of his intelligence and "literary ability." Lincoln himself claimed to have "expected . . . dismissal all along," and tried to deal with it through humor: "Home we'll go," he wrote in his diary shortly before leaving Exeter, suggesting as an epitaph, "He liked his prep school—It was such a nice place to get away from."

Soon after Lincoln returned home, Louis presented him with "a wonderful collection of stamps," and Mina gave him three pairs of silk pajamas: "yellow, brilliant orange and violet." Records were put on the gramophone, Lincoln donned the orange pajamas, and proceeded to perform "mad dances to the tunes of the 'Tinkers Chorus' from *Robin Hood.*" The paradoxical Rose, moreover, who had refused to send the sixteen-year-old Lincoln a copy of the "immoral" *Madame Bovary* because she thought it would "corrupt" his mind, that same year took him on a holiday trip to New York that included attendance at a Greenwich Village masquerade ball where, seated in a box, mother and son watched some 3,500 revelers until nearly three o'clock in the morning, searchlights on the balcony playing over their wildly gyrating bodies; Lincoln later wrote in his diary, "a man dressed as a priest, and I may add a very good looking man," climbed up close to their box and made "rather passionate love to a girl who was draped rather than dressed." Lincoln "looked libidinously" at them, until Rose, a bit belatedly, primly told him, "No, Lincoln, look the other way." So he did, shifting his focus to "the dancing below where . . . sluts were leaning lasciviously on their pleased partners."

An outwardly conventional lifestyle didn't quite cover over the occasional antics and dynamics of the Kirstein clan. Much later in life Lincoln wrote that although his mother was "quite without any sexual prejudice," she had told him that his father was "physically cold" and had "never liked" sex much—perhaps, she added, because as a young man he'd undergone painful mercury injections to cure venereal disease. (Many years later, Lincoln suggested an additional gloss: "After I left Boston Dad encouraged and even idolized a number of young men whom I also found attractive.") He further recorded in his diary that he, Mina, and George swam naked together in the reservoir, broadly hinting that he engaged in sex play of some sort with, separately, both of them, and that he occasionally tried on Mina's underwear (it's "nicer than mother's") or poured himself into her corset "and danced for her amusement." As Alfred Kinsey would reveal two decades later, such behavior and fantasies were far more commonplace than anyone would have believed at the time.

It was widely urged on the Kirsteins that Lincoln, for his next try, be enrolled in a smaller school where his hypersensitivity might be better appreciated. Mina asked President William Alan Neilson of Smith for suggestions, and he recommended the Berkshire School on the western border of Massachusetts. In the fall of 1922 Lincoln entered Berkshire as a sophomore. He stayed for a full two years, with intermittent trips home, one of them for an appendectomy. Rose went into a panic at the thought of her boy going into a hospital, and insisted that a surgeon they knew perform the appendectomy on the family dining room table. Yet another prolonged convalescence followed, further underscoring Lincoln's already well-developed antipathy to doctors.

Yet he was in fact a good patient, though in bed for two months. Aside from complaining about his nurse ("She did nothing but tell me of all the double headed embryos she had seen"), Louis reported to Mina, who was in London, that on the whole Lincoln "was a perfect brick about it"; he "laughed a good deal and didn't seem to be a bit scared." It helped that relatives showered him with presents, that he worked jigsaw puzzles for hours with Rose and George, and was allowed port before every meal. The operating doctor told Louis that his son "was one of the most remarkable boys" he had ever seen. For his part Lincoln expressed pleasure with his small scar—it was "nothing more than a raspberry bush scratch."

Various tutors, all of whom he pronounced useless, were brought in to keep his schoolwork up to par. One of them, on quitting, reported that Lincoln was "an affectionate boy . . . [but] fearfully scatter-brained and prone all too often to wander down imaginative bye-ways of his own devising." When he was finally pronounced well enough to return to Berkshire, Rose was "so tearful and sloppy" that Lincoln "hated to leave her." Though he knew that Mina and their mother were often antagonistic, Lincoln begged Mina to write to her more often: "She's really the world's loneliest person."[10]

The Berkshire School had only recently opened its doors, and it lacked the prestige of New England's top-drawer prep schools (despite which, during Lincoln's tenure, the student roster did include two Japanese boys of Imperial lineage). Lincoln found the food, at least, decidedly better than at Exeter, though he described his room as "unutterably vile" and his "corridor master" as "a sweet young thing out of Yale . . . [who] tries to combine the manners of a Marquis with the morals of a Methodist!"

There were only two tennis courts at Berkshire, and they could be used only on weekends; during the week gym was compulsory and football strongly encouraged. Lincoln thought the former "humiliating" and the latter "loathsome." During gym everyone had to wear a "pathetic little suit of white," which outlined the body, and Lincoln didn't think his was "a pretty one . . . to say the least," though "it looks all right with a suit of decent English Tweeds on." It didn't help when his gym teacher told another student, who promptly repeated it to Lincoln, that "I was or ought to be a prospective victim for the Ku Klux Klan."

His mood swings, he wrote Mina, continued "to veer between very happy or very depressed—there doesn't seem to be any halfway point." But Lincoln, from an early age, was given to theatrical exaggeration: his diary records many such "halfway" days. "I really think when I lay on bed at night," one entry reads, "that I get more pleasure out of life than lots of other people." And to Mina he confessed that "I've been having a very good time most of the time."

Mina, though traveling abroad, continued to send him packages of books, including "a huge gorgeous" one on the art of Java, from which he copied drawings. The school library, as always, became his "rock and . . . redeemer." Within days of arriving at Berkshire, he had devoured Sinclair Lewis's *Babbitt* and thought it the most enjoyable book he'd ever read. Soon after, he discovered William Blake and became "particularly crazy about him . . . I never saw any drawings which had such marvelous strength and double energy." He soon came to prefer Blake's poems to his drawings, and quickly added Blake to his short list of "favorite artists," which included Whistler, Botticelli, Sargent, Dürer, Watteau, Burne-Jones, and Beardsley (the works of Dickens, on the other hand, he was "not the least excited over").

His intense involvement with drawing and extracurricular reading did nothing for his grades, which, in his own words, remained mostly "deplorable." He found Latin somewhat easier than before, but still did poorly in algebra and thought geometry "incomprehensible." Louis, knowing how much Lincoln admired his sister, urged Mina to tell the boy "that he has got to make up his mind to try things that are worth while . . . he can't have the world made to order for him." Besides, Louis added, "I can't conceive that Lincoln would be happy at any school, unless he could choose the students and teachers himself."

But Lincoln did make at least a few friends out of some 125 classmates; their favorite pastimes were comparing views on books and poetry, walking in the "gorgeous" countryside, and listening to Chopin records on the roof of the dorm. As for the rest of the boys, he thought them "quite decent" but limited. When he felt lonesome and was advised by both his father and his teachers to "talk to someone," he countered that "there's no one to talk to"—except for those "who gasp over the possibility of Center beating Harvard."

There weren't five boys, he wrote his father, "whom I care a damn about. If I thought that I was unnecessarily snobbish, I would mend my ways," but the bottom-line truth, he felt, was that most of the boys simply weren't as bright as he ("This is not conceit, it's self-confidence"). Rose responded sympathetically, sometimes even tearily, to her son's complaints, but Louis was far tougher on him. When Lincoln announced, after completing his first year at Berkshire, that he had gotten all he could out of the school and didn't want to return, Louis let him have it. In a series of letters he berated his son for his "intolerant attitude," told him to stop being "a damn fool" and to make more of an effort to "enter into the spirit of things" at the school, adding, for toppers, that his refusal to participate "makes people think you are a one-sided gink."

Yet Lincoln doesn't seem to have been generally regarded by his Berkshire classmates or teachers either as a snob or as some sort of weird outcast. He indulged in the requisite number of roughhouses and pillow fights, designed and painted scenery for school plays, went to at least some of the dances ("I like dancing ever so much," he told his parents), wrote assorted pieces for the student publication, *The Dome,* and was elected its associate editor. At least once he took the heroine's role in a school production, performing in black wig and headdress, an orange-and-red sweater suit covered with flowered "Egyptian" chiffon lace, and got to kiss the hero "delicately on his small fat nose in the last act." He was unselfconscious enough to allow his father and brother to see the performance; Louis pronounced it very well done, despite the headdress falling off at one point and Lincoln missing a cue while chatting backstage.

Occasionally a classmate did tell Lincoln that he was "affected," "petulant," or "morbidly introspective." But far more often Lincoln was his own worst critic. He derided himself as not nearly as "complex and hard to understand" as some seemed to think he was, but rather merely "nervous, restless and irritable" ("my brain rushes about in mad crazy wheels"), and condemned himself as "too much of a 'sniveler.' " Nor did he hold his various drawings, poems, and stories in much regard, typically discounting them as "trashy, pseudo-sophisticated," and too "consciously clever." What he did know was that he had "a sincere desire to be a great artist," even while feeling deep in his gut that he never would be.

No, the role of class outcast was not assigned to Lincoln but to a student named George Platt Lynes. He was the true pariah among his classmates, who seem all but uniformly to have regarded him as some sort of foppish freak. Lincoln, too, viewed Lynes as "a sneering little bitch," a person whom he disliked "above all others," a boy who "never really gets below the varnish of anything whether it be poetry, drawing or talking . . . his life is a pose . . . he fancies he is pretty to look at and saunters through the post office, into the reading room to the library and back, waving his extremities, with the nonchalance of a [Fifi] D'Orsay [the actress]." Lincoln imagined Lynes, à la Oscar Wilde, "parading Piccadilly with a poppy or a lily firmly clenched in his not too medieval hand." Yet Lincoln was a great admirer of Wilde, as both a writer and a personage, which perhaps helps to explain why his distaste for Lynes gradually shifted to pity; seeing Lynes burst into tears one day, Lincoln felt bad for him and decided the boy was simply "sensitive" and "weak." The turning point seems to have come when Lynes, endlessly teased and bullied, one day "in utter desperation" (as Lincoln put it) "whipped out his knife and melodramatically stabbed" another student, who fortunately survived. Later in life Lynes, by then a prominent photographer, and Lincoln would become, in a limited way, friends, and would also develop a significant professional relationship.

Berkshire's founder and director, Seaver Burton Buck, apparently saw himself as a latter-day version of headmaster Arnold of Rugby, though the Victorian disciplinarian was sometimes subverted by a pixieish manner. Buck was much given to heart-to-heart talks with Berkshire students and seems to have singled out Lincoln for special attention. Overall Lincoln rather liked Buck, but the "heart-to-hearts" alternately annoyed or amused him. He wrote about his annoyance, naturally, to his parents, saving the humor for Mina. "I do mind Mr. Buck . . . pigeon-holing me . . . as literary," Lincoln wrote to Rose and Louis. "He has a favorite trick of indexing every one. Unfortunately human beings can't all be catalogued"— a rather sophisticated complaint for a fifteen-year-old, and this time his unpredictable father responded with sympathy: "I understand that the director hounded you a good deal and you stood it like a thoroughbred— so you see there is no reason for your being so dissatisfied with yourself all the time." When writing to Mina, Lincoln reported one meeting with Buck during which the headmaster, as usual, kept calling him "Louis," while reprimanding him for getting a 32 in Latin. No one can become a writer, Buck admonished, "unless they have Latin!" To which Lincoln, vastly annoyed, replied, "Oh? I daresay Mr. [Joseph] Hergesheimer . . . and [John] Mansfield don't know Latin."

On another occasion, after seeing the word "phallic" in the school weekly, the *Green and Gray*, Buck called in the boy who'd written the offending article and got him tearfully to confess that he wasn't sure what the word meant but believed it was a synonym for "significant." Buck felt sure that Lincoln could define it, and put the same question to him. "The phallus," Lincoln calmly stated ("I put it on thick," he later wrote Mina), "was the Roman symbol of the penis. It has come to be used as an adjective, as pertaining to the phallus, etc." "I suppose," Buck furiously replied, "you have read Oscar Wilde." Why yes, Lincoln said, "Quite a lot." Well, Buck stormed, "He was an *exotic* and do you know what he was sent to prison for?" Lincoln's response is unknown, but he did report to Mina that Buck proceeded to have the entire issue of the *Green and Gray* burned.

After completing his second year at Berkshire in June 1924, Lincoln warned Mina, with dramatic emphasis, that "should I have to stay here another year I'd go crazy." He wanted to join her in London for his senior year, after which he'd return to prepare for Harvard's admission exams. The proposition was presented to Louis, who made most of the final decisions for the family, though usually only after taking everyone's views, often discordant, into account.

Louis had periodically announced, sometimes with humor, sometimes not, that "the great thing in life is to finish what you start." He also strongly believed that Lincoln's education should be "primarily and fundamentally American." Yet given Louis's own youthful history of serial jobs and residences, plus his ingrained sportive streak, the Kirstein brood had learned that firm pronouncements were rarely unalterable. In the instance of Lincoln spending a year abroad, Louis preferred that he first pass his Harvard exams and then go to Europe for a year before actually starting college. But family pressure, along with Louis's own recognition that Lincoln was more "individualistic" than most boys and required "different treatment," produced a compromise solution: Lincoln would not return to Berkshire for his senior year, would spend the *summer* of 1924 abroad, accompanied by George and Rose, and would then return to Boston to prepare for the Harvard entrance examinations.

So off the three Kirsteins went to Europe for two months, Louis first stuffing his sons with admonitions about the importance of preparing themselves for "a life of service," and with loving caveats about treating their mother, who after all "had devoted her life" to them, with every possible consideration, putting her happiness above their own.[11]

Lincoln, Rose, and George had previously visited Mina in Europe, where, having gotten an MA at Columbia and studied for a term at Radcliffe, she was attending classes at London University and sharing a small eighteenth-century house off Fulham Road—and having an affair—with an ex-student, Henrietta Bingham (daughter of Judge Robert Worth Bingham, owner of the *Louisville Courier-Journal* and future ambassador to the Court of Saint James). Such sexual unorthodoxy made them take rather easily to the bohemianism of Bloomsbury. That connection, which would remain marginal, came about when, in 1922, the twenty-six-year-old Mina had stopped off one day to browse in the bookshop on Gerrard Street run by the tall, blond, and blue-eyed David Garnett, a novelist and

Bloomsburyite. Garnett had recently published his first and prizewinning novel, *Lady into Fox*, and had also, as Mina quickly learned, married and become a father. Throughout his life, Garnett had male lovers as well.

Garnett claimed that he fell in love with Mina at first sight. For her part—as she put it much later—"How could I, a romantic would-be writer, have found a more perfect embodiment of the ideal first lover?" Yet apparently the relationship never became sexual, despite Garnett's passionate wooing ("I . . . love the impetuous & free side of your nature. You are like the sea with tides rushing in & out"); another time, responding to Mina's complaint that they were being publicly linked as lovers, he wrote, "I can't help it if [Ralph] Partridge couples our names together. I only wish he could, like the panderer he is, couple our bodies." Garnett dedicated his second book to Mina, and they remained, for decades, deeply companionable friends. She blamed her own "strong if often inactive sense of Puritan morality" for keeping the relationship at what she characterized as an "uncomfortably platonic" level; she believed in the "sanctity" of marriage and couldn't overcome her scruples about Garnett already being a husband and a father.

None of which interfered with her readiness to take a female lover or to tolerate male homosexuality. She "accepted without any reserve" the additional information Garnett provided—which would have appalled a true "puritan"—that before his marriage, he'd been lovers with the painter Duncan Grant, and the two had shared a house with Virginia Woolf's sister, Vanessa Bell, who gave birth to Grant's child, Angelica. Years later, in a triple somersault, Garnett married Angelica; when the news reached Mina, she treated it as "unwelcome." Her warm feelings for Garnett himself never changed, but she subsequently realized that she had "never felt really comfortable" with her "fringily" participation in Bloomsbury.

At the time, though, she delighted in her daring, her enlightenment— and her contacts. Though she rarely got a glimpse of Virginia Woolf (when she did, Mina thought her "distinguished but not to my mind beautiful") or E. M. "Morgan" Forster, whose novels she adored. But she did see a fair amount of Duncan Grant and Vanessa Bell. Grant, in fact, painted her portrait; she spent long hours posing for him in the room that had once been Whistler's and Walter Sickert's studio. When the portrait was completed, she pretended that she liked it, but in fact chose never to hang the picture. After it had been in her attic some twenty years, "a young man, a passionate admirer of Duncan's painting," appeared on her doorstep one day and she impulsively gave the portrait to him; she later learned that the stranger became Duncan Grant's last lover and cared for him until his death at the age of ninety.

For the seventeen-year-old Lincoln, already a "passionate Anglophile" (as was his father), contact with Bloomsbury's luminaries further confirmed his devotion to England. A decade later he and E. M. Forster would become friends, but in 1924 Lincoln barely glimpsed Forster at the occasional festivity, and most of his other contacts with Bloomsbury proved glancing. The exceptions seem to have been the famed economist John Maynard Keynes, and his soon-to-be wife, the Diaghilev ballerina Lydia Lopokova. At one party, Lopokova went upstairs and roused George and Lincoln from their beds to join her in an impromptu, silk-pajamaed *pas de trois*—to much applause. "She was the first star I ever talked to," Lincoln later wrote, "the last I ever danced with."

For his part Maynard Keynes took Lincoln to several art exhibitions, including showings of Gauguin and Cézanne. Lincoln was already a great admirer of Gauguin's and was surprised at Keynes's insistence that some of Gauguin's canvases could be called better than others. With Cézanne, Lincoln had a more difficult time. A devotee of Burne-Jones and Beardsley—the kind of art Bloomsbury detested—Lincoln thought Cézanne's watercolors "clumsy, unfinished." Noticing his "wan response," Keynes, in his dispassionate way, tried to suggest that there were "different modes of describing form," as well as a "variable spectra of taste." He urged young Lincoln to "keep your eyes open, clean of received opinion and prejudice."

Lincoln at first thought Keynes was being dismissive, but soon came to feel that the older man's opinions had "launched a radical reformation in my naïve judgment." Yet as Lincoln wrote much later in life, "there would be limits I would not extend. Digital mastery and the accurate placement of the human face and form, supremacy in surface and texture, the seizure of exact retinal resemblance, were fixtures in my developing preferences. My ultimate criterion . . . [would be] portraiture, not only for its mirror imagery but for psychological anatomy. . . . I could never credit abstraction as anything past an admission of failed skill."

The empathy Rose and Lincoln felt for each other would always be more pronounced than the one she shared with George; he, on the other hand, was more deeply connected than Lincoln to their father. Thus, during the European vacation in 1924, George, nearly fifteen, wrote home to Louis angrily complaining about a seemingly trivial matter that represented deeper undercurrents: though Lincoln, George reported, didn't seem to care that Rose was still admonishing her sons about taking baths and cleaning their ears, he, George, decidedly objected to still being treated like a child.

Louis diplomatically replied that he could "understand perfectly" how George felt, but advised him to remember that "your mother is trying her best to instill in you the habits that are necessary to live the right kind of a life." He assured George that "mother is just as good a pal as I am," and suggested he talk with her in "man fashion" about his wish to assume full responsibility for his own behavior. George took his father's advice and Rose yielded—though George reported back that she was "rather bitter about it."

One area in which Rose and Lincoln's tastes did not coincide was music. Lincoln insisted all his life that although he had "a live eye" it was ill matched to his "tin ear." With the exception of sung voices, whose sound sometimes stirred him "romantically," music touched him only when it had some reference to dance, when he could hear it as a possible accompaniment. Rose, on the other hand, was passionately attuned to music, and in particular to the operas of Richard Wagner.

When the Bayreuth Festival announced that in the summer of 1924 it would, for the first time since the Great War, present Wagner's complete *Ring* cycle, a thrilled Rose arranged tickets for herself and her sons. Typically, the gesture ingratiated her more with Lincoln than George. Lincoln would later write that the Bayreuth experience "made a deep and lasting impression" on him, though not—again, typically—strictly on musical grounds. Since the operas were presented in much the style they had been since the 1890s, Lincoln found the mise-en-scène "superannuated and ridiculous." What did engross him was an unrenovated staging that provided "a very perfect picture . . . of what Wagner himself had wished for his presentation."

There were some troubling sidebars to the Bayreuth trip. On arrival the Kirsteins had gone to a recommended hotel, Der Schwarze Adler, only to be told that it was full and that they would doubtless be happier at the private home of a Frau Steinkraus, a "co-religionist." They left the hotel without protest, but the incident stayed with Lincoln. It wasn't the first time he'd "recognized the unhappy stink of ingrained prejudice"— "I had money, and racial prejudice barely touched me"—but he'd never before "experienced it in so public or official a dimension." Shielded for most of his privileged life from the more aggressive forms of anti-Semitism (and from much else), Lincoln got another whiff of the real world at a performance of *Die Meistersinger.* After the thunderous finale, the Jesuit priest who'd been sitting next to Lincoln "howled" in such an excess of "hysterical rage or joy" that the cords of his neck seemed about to burst through his skin. He was joined by the rest of the audience, which rose from its seats "in an explosion of patriotic ferocity," screaming in unison, "*Deutschland, Deutschland über Alles!*"

On returning from Europe, Lincoln set to work in earnest to prepare for the Harvard entrance exams. Private tutors were hired to spur him on, and all hands agreed that he was applying himself with determination. When he had spare time, Lincoln spent it sketching at Boston's Museum School, continuing to hope that he had the talent to become an "artist." The hope got a boost early in 1925 when one of the designs he submitted to a competition was chosen for a prize.

Despite his diligence over many months in preparing for the Harvard exams, when they came around in June 1925, Lincoln "lost his head" and failed to qualify. Deeply sympathetic though Rose was, she couldn't quite manage to conceal her profound disappointment. The unpredictable Louis, on the other hand, was all hearty encouragement. Trying to buck up Lincoln's sagging spirits, Louis leapt on the confidential news from a Harvard contact that the exams had been graded so severely that the college had ended up short of its goal of a thousand freshmen.

Still, even Louis privately confessed his bewilderment. So many people over the years, he wrote Mina, had commented on Lincoln's brilliance. "Everyone who knows him says what an extraordinary mind he has," and how much more knowledgeable he was, and on many subjects, than most boys his age. Unaccountably, however, he continued to panic under pressure.

And he did so yet again three months later, when Harvard reoffered the exams in order to get its full complement of freshmen. Though the grading was less severe than in June, Lincoln again failed to qualify. He was deeply disappointed and feared that he'd shamed his family—though Louis practically did handstands to make light of the failure, cheerfully announcing that he didn't "care a hang" and reminding Lincoln that he, Louis, hadn't amounted to much until he was twice his son's age: "I was stone broke when I was 36 and had a wife and family." To please his father Lincoln did his best to play the "good sport." A gratified Louis reported that he was neither "bemoaning his fate nor crying about his hard luck. . . . He is taking his disappointment standing up in man fashion."

A Harvard dean advised Lincoln to wait at least six months before preparing himself again for another try at the admission exams. Lincoln took the advice, and the immediate issue now became what he should do in the interim period. "The policy we have followed in our family," Louis wrote his disapproving brother Henry, "is to allow the children to pursue their bent," a policy he and Rose genuinely adhered to (though Rose was more permissive with her sons than her daughter; she had strongly objected to Mina taking a teaching position at Smith for more than a year or two: "It's too wearing," Rose declared. Besides, Mina should live "in a big city" where there were far more "advantages and relaxations").

Louis, after consulting various architect friends, came up with the idea of Lincoln working as an unpaid apprentice at Charles Connick's stained-glass shop in Boston, a place famous for its severe medieval aesthetic and for the important role the shop played in the Gothic revival centered on the architect Ralph Adams Cram. Louis thought the job at Connick's would help his son further explore and test his artistic talent. Lincoln would have preferred free time to continue with his drawing, but he agreed to his father's proposal.

Overall he found the experience worthwhile, though for the first few months he was kept at the tedious job of washing the heavy glass frames rather than designing cartoons for the actual stained glass that would be applied to the frames; eventually he was given some limited "artistic" work, lettering borders for the finished cartoons. What kept him from becoming entirely bored was his observation of the other men in the shop. They held him at a distance, well aware that he was a rich boy biding his time before going to college, with some of them suspecting that he was an informer.

Still, Lincoln got a whiff of what he called the "terror of poverty" and the "uneasy despair" that characterized the lives of the men. What made it all worse was his feeling that "with slight trouble to the boss" working conditions could be made far more palatable—an end put to unfair fines, the granting of sick-leave pay, and so on. There's some evidence that Lincoln tried, indirectly and without much effect, to plead the workers' case. He had associated "management," after all, with his own father's personal kindness and with the liberal labor policies he promoted at the Filene's department store. At Connick's, Lincoln got some insight into the odious conditions under which most people labored—and the experience would, within a few years, help to make him ripe for affiliation with left-wing causes.

In June 1926, on his third try, Lincoln finally passed the Harvard entrance exams. He later claimed that he'd succeeded only through the mindless strategy of memorizing the first five books of Euclid (geometry being his worst subject). He had just turned nineteen, two to three years older than what was then the average age for entering freshmen.

CHAPTER TWO

Harvard

(1927)

THE NUMBER OF Jews in the entering class at Harvard rose from 7 percent in 1900 to 21.5 percent in 1922. Simultaneously the country's immigration patterns underwent a marked shift. A far larger proportion of new arrivals now came from Eastern European countries—to the accompaniment of a mounting and indignant nativist outcry against admitting such "crude, desperate, unlettered" people, so unlike the educated, well-mannered, recognizably assimilable German immigrants—people like the Kirsteins—who had preceded them.[1]

Paralleling these developments, the previously fragmented and fractious Zionist movement in the United States became transformed as a result of the shifting alliances of World War I and the British government's 1917 Balfour Declaration, announcing its support for a Jewish homeland in Palestine. Supreme Court Justice (as of 1916) Louis Brandeis had been prominent in the American Zionist movement for a number of years, and he'd reached out with increasing success to other prominent Jewish Americans, including future Supreme Court appointees Benjamin Cardozo and Felix Frankfurter, as well as to the philanthropists Eugene Meyer—and Louis Kirstein. Louis had known Brandeis since at least 1911, when he joined Filene's, a firm Brandeis represented; by the following year the two men were friendly enough to pay a visit together in Rochester to Louis's aged mother. Before long Louis counted himself among Brandeis's greatest admirers and supporters, though socially the Kirsteins saw somewhat more of Felix and Marion Frankfurter.

Louis would not remain a committed Zionist throughout his life, but for a time he devoted himself zealously to the cause, donating money, traveling widely to make speeches on behalf of a Jewish state—and steadily broadening his own contacts and influence. In Boston by the early twenties Louis was widely regarded as one of the foremost representatives of the Jewish community, serving on a proliferating number of boards and committees, including the presidency of Federated Charities and membership on the socially prestigious Board of Trustees of the Boston Public Library—to which Mayor James Curley (another personal friend) reappointed him in 1924.

Louis's influence wasn't confined to Jewish circles. Due to his wartime service in Washington, he'd made many powerful friends. As early as 1923 he lunched at the White House with President and Mrs. Coolidge, along with only two other guests, and after lunch, he and the president walked alone in the garden, spending "quite a long time" discussing various matters. Coolidge told Louis that he especially enjoyed his company because "there is nothing you want [from me]," and he invited him to visit every time he returned to Washington. Yet Louis always kept a level head, repeatedly cautioning his children against seeking "special privileges" and urging them (as he once wrote George) "not to think of yourself alone, but also to think of others to the end that you may be of some service."

The mounting support for the Zionist cause led to accelerated protests against it, by Jews and non-Jews alike. The preeminent American Jewish Committee, dominated by some of the country's most prominent German-American Jews, including Jacob Schiff and Henry Morgenthau, argued that Zionism would promote dual national allegiances within American Jewry, and promote within the country as a whole an inflammatory image of Jews as unreliable, ambivalently patriotic citizens.

A. Lawrence Lowell, president of Harvard since 1909, was among many who felt rising concern about these assorted religious and ethnic developments. A descendant of one of the most distinguished Boston Brahmin families, Lowell took on the mission, in 1922, of reducing the number of Jewish students at Harvard. Lowell shared the fear—as did many members of Harvard's faculty and governing board—that the continuation of an admissions policy based on entrance exams and academic merit would irrevocably change Harvard's character, and he appointed a "Committee of Thirteen" to examine the college's admissions policies and to make recommendations for revision. Lowell's predecessor as president, Charles William Eliot, no less a Brahmin than he, but a liberal, open-minded one, spoke out forcefully (though in his late eighties) against any initiative to replace admissions procedures that paid no heed to distinctions based on race, religion, nationality, or color with quota systems. (During the long debate that ensued, no mention was made of discrimination based on gender.)

Louis Kirstein was among Eliot's close allies in the struggle that ensued. When Lincoln made some sort of disdainful adolescent comment on Eliot's "lack of humor" and his ignorance of art, Louis responded with sardonic anger: "Sometime, if you ever happen to have an opportunity, it might not be a bad idea for you to put him [Eliot] wise. You have failed to get the point at all." Not nearly as Jewish-identified as his father, Lincoln may well have been too offhand, but he was far from obtuse on the subject. While still at the Berkshire School, he'd written in his diary, at age fifteen: "I used to, when people teased me about being a jew [sic], ask them knowingly, if they knew what religion J.C. was. They were so utterly dumb that the remark fell flat. A case, much diluted with water, of pearls before pigs."

President Lowell's committee set to work. From the onset Louis, optimistic by nature, felt sure that it would reject the president's plans. But he believed, too, that rejection wouldn't settle the matter. He proved right on both counts. After long deliberation, the committee recommended that Harvard retain its traditional admissions policy, free of quotas based on religion or race. The Harvard faculty then approved the report on April 24, 1923. "It was a very great victory," Louis wrote Lincoln, "but it is only the first round in the fight. We will have to be very watchful to see that the will of the committee . . . is carried out."

For a time the victory seemed secure. But behind the scenes President Lowell remained determined to have his way. With the cooperation of the dean of admissions, Henry Pennypacker, who traveled to interview candidates in person, anyone whose name, history, or physiognomy suggested Jewishness became subject to rejection without explanation.

In addition Lowell saw to it, soon after his 1923 defeat, that a new application form was put into place that required the submission of a photograph and included for the first time questions regarding race. By 1926, just as Lincoln was entering Harvard, a vague but telling new admissions plan was instituted warning that "candidates should bear in mind that in all admissions to the University regard is given to character, personality, and promise, as well as to scholarly attainments."

Through the back door Lowell had gotten all the tools he needed: the admissions committee now had the authority to make an *intuitional* judgment of each candidate's fitness. As Oswald Garrison Villard asked in *The Gadfly*, a publication of the Harvard Liberal Club, "What constitutes character and personality and promise? Who can define them, and who agree on them?" Of course the aim wasn't to define but to give preference to those who were transparently "clubbable" and "assimilable." By the end of the decade, the percentage of Jewish students at Harvard had fallen from 27 percent to 16 percent.

Shortly before Lincoln entered Harvard, Mina, approaching her thirtieth birthday, married Harry Curtiss, a slightly older Yale graduate, dashing and wealthy, who headed A.G. Spalding & Brothers golf ball manufacturing worldwide. He lived in a beautiful 1840 white clapboard farmhouse with a huge attached barn in Ashfield, Massachusetts; it was near Northampton, framed by Pony Mountain, a great rocky cliff, and covered with vegetable and flower gardens, patches of arbutus, and woods full of virgin pines. Harry had a passionate attachment to the land, and Mina quickly came to share it.[2]

From the beginning Louis and Rose Kirstein had expressed opposition to the match: not only was Harry a divorced man but an Anglo-Saxon Episcopalian (his ancestors having arrived in Connecticut in 1642). Louis refused for more than a year even to meet Harry (though Rose, with little enthusiasm, did relent). When the couple married in 1926, Louis declared himself unable to face the ceremony, and he and Rose decamped for their annual trip to Europe a week before the wedding. Lincoln did attend, and the Kirsteins' friend, Judge Julian Mack, stood in for Louis.

Mina was angry—and puzzled. After all, her parents had sent her to overwhelmingly gentile schools, she could remember no significant discussions of religion in their household while growing up, and the family had joined a Reformed synagogue which Rose never attended and Louis solely on the High Holy Days. Mina decided that Louis's attachment to Judaism was much deeper than he acknowledged; its true depth was gauged by his dedicated fund-raising for Jewish causes and organizations (a dedication, after the rise of Hitler, that would become profound). Harry, sensitive and clearheaded, counseled patience. It paid off. Ultimately Louis and Harry became mutually admiring, sympathetic friends.

Lincoln had liked Harry from the start, but he was less enamored of the changes that he felt marriage had wrought in his sister's personality. "I don't find her as stimulating as I used to," he wrote in one diary entry; and in another, "Mina home from Northampton . . . she is perfectly adjusted etc. It's only I who am not to her." He was self-aware enough to add, "Although I won't really admit it, this . . . is part of the old resentment . . . at being kept intellectually subordinate to her for so long. I underestimate her." He was soon visiting Mina and Harry at Ashfield ("a place filled with high romance"), spending time with them on their periodic visits to Boston, and admitting, shamefacedly, that he felt stabs of jealousy—and erotic attraction—toward Harry.

Lincoln's freshman room in Gore Hall was, by his own estimate, "very pleasant"; plush and comfortable, it had blue glass in the windows, pewter on the mantel, and red woodwork painted with a Raoul Dufy chintz pattern. Nor did he fail to mingle among his classmates, though, as always, he proved finicky in choosing friends; of those he did decide to cultivate, he tended to be vigilantly critical. Within a few months of arriving, he was writing in his diary that he had found "an enormous amount of half baked people here—I eagerly look for bright faces—always disappointed. I crave intimacy but I can't afford it with people I don't like." But Lincoln reveled all his life in histrionic exaggeration and abrupt changes of mind. He had soon enough, in his freshman year, found a number of people, including several young faculty members, quite sufficiently baked to rival his own restlessly energetic, outsized, and demanding nature. He also found a fair number of sex partners, a few of them women, more of them men. They ranged, with the men, from romantic attachments to casual pickups in Widener Library or the Boston Public Gardens ("It was dark . . . a good many marines in pairs. I hunted about for a while—became interested in one figure in the ferns.").[3]

Even prior to Harvard he'd had a multitude of infatuations and, while still at the Berkshire School, at least one serious attachment—with the handsome Tom Mabry (who later worked at the publishing house Alfred A. Knopf, Inc., and as executive director at the Museum of Modern Art). "My mind," Tom wrote Lincoln in the spring of 1925, "is either waiting for you to come or [feeling] a great restlessness that you have gone." In other letters he repeatedly addressed Lincoln as "sweetest love," and wondered whether in five years Lincoln would still care for him; "perhaps what we have will be a thing we can lean on and go to for strength, for rest, for sympathy—there are so few in the world that find any of this." The two men would in fact remain friends for many decades.

Tom made reference in one letter to feeling "surer of the healthiness of our relationship"—which suggests the issue had surfaced for discussion between them; at another time Lincoln and two friends talked about whether "homosexuality is evil or not, otherwise than by convention"— and decided it "is not." More striking than these moments of apparent doubt is the comparative absence of torment or guilty self-consciousness when Lincoln recorded his various same-sex adventures, sexual or emotional, in his diary: "Met boy at Mass. Station. Conversation about sailors. He says they're not rough just playful . . . [feeling] general desire for a bedfellow"; "Bob . . . told me . . . [I was] considered in certain freshman circles as queer. This I daresay is nothing to weep over."

Perhaps his nonchalance was partly playacting or self-disguise, putting a more composed face on his sexual encounters with men than he actually felt—and there is some evidence for such an interpretation. Perhaps, as an Anglophilic, privileged young man well aware of the endemic homosexuality of upper-class English boarding schools, he simply assumed that his own behavior fell easily within the normal spectrum. Perhaps his "manly manner" and his simultaneous attraction to women ("refreshing dreams of . . . a golden beach with girls . . . all lying about to fondle"), made him feel it would be an inaccurate absurdity to label himself a "fairy"—the current term and category, one associated with the gender transgressions of effeminacy and cross-dressing. He saw himself as quite unlike that recognizable "type," and in his diary periodically disparaged "effeminate" men. He even, at one time, joined in baiting a classmate he described as a "horrible homosexual worm . . . distressingly affected . . . [with] a bad choppy walk."

In any case Tom Mabry had already left Harvard when Lincoln became a freshman, and had gone to live in New York; the two got to see each other only occasionally. Yet for some time Tom remained the touchstone:

"I seem to be lonelier for Tom now," Lincoln wrote at the end of his freshman year, "than ever before," even though "we often join in the eye of the
mind across the miles." They continued to exchange long letters, and Lincoln hid Tom's up the fireplace in his bedroom at home, unable to bring
himself to burn even a few.

Lincoln thought of himself as "endowed with a heart . . . full of affection . . . waiting to be spilled over." With Tom mostly unavailable, he
looked elsewhere for pleasure and connection. Along with periodically
prowling Widener Library, the Boston Commons, and the Esplanade (he
described himself as "ever the hunter"), he engaged in "elaborate flirtations," and occasional consummations, with classmates. When feeling
lonely he longed to "find someone where the rapport would be final and
close, for a space at least," but he recognized, too, that his "desire for being
bound is always echoed by the fear of it." In place of a "steady," he contented himself, during his undergraduate years, with assorted assignations.

There was Bryan, who hung around with a "sporty" crowd; he and
Lincoln "read most of the British poets to each other." There was Bob—
"he is the nicest boy I have found so far here." There was Bill, with whom
he did "a good deal of smoogling [sic] . . . impersonal but pleasant . . . fast
and loose." There was Howlands, who had that "bovine stubbornness
which I find so charming." There was Henry—"such a puppy dog." "Pup-
pin" was Lincoln's category of highest praise for a classmate he was physically drawn to. "The Lads," he called them collectively; they came mostly
from upper-class, Anglo-Saxon backgrounds, and were instinctively commanding and assured young men, marked by graceful athleticism, "depth-
less self-satisfaction," and an entire lack of interest in introspection.
Lincoln, by contrast, had reached nearly his full height of six feet three
inches and, despite a handsome head and piercingly intelligent eyes, felt
physically clumsy, overpowered "by a sea of people whom I cannot hope
to talk to even if I wished to—all fair and beautiful, etc."

The classmate he saw most of during freshman year was Varian Fry, who
lived on the floor above in Gore Hall. It was a friendship that veered
wildly between affection and dislike. They perhaps shared too many traits
to avoid a kind of mirror-image antagonism—each seeing in the other
qualities he disliked in himself. Both had had adoring, indulgent mothers,
and both had grown accustomed to getting their way (though Louis
Kirstein, unlike Varian's father, had served as something of a brake on Lincoln, periodically reining him in). Like Lincoln, Varian was unusually erudite for his age, and profoundly sensitive. Both compensated for bouts of
insecurity with aggressive intellectual one-upsmanship.[4]

Varian was more consistently arrogant than Lincoln, and much more
given to explosive temper tantrums. During one bootleg party, Varian
(according to Lincoln) "went nuts," ripped the telephone from the socket,

then threw it out the window—and "just screamed around." He could be so emotionally explosive that Lincoln became permanently leery, never feeling that Varian could be fully trusted. With brawl following brawl, it looked for a time as if Varian would be expelled; in the end he was only put on probation.

The two nineteen-year-olds also shared an erotic attraction to men. Varian (who would later twice marry) had a passionate affair with another Gore Hall freshman, Allen, who soon developed "a violent revulsion against him"; Varian, to no avail, got "emotional, posed, wept"—and "crumpled." All of which, in combination with what Lincoln called his "various indiscretions by word of mouth [and] a distressingly affected (although quite natural) manner when he is nervous," contributed to Varian becoming increasingly known on campus as "the Queen of the Fairies."

From the beginning Varian pushed Lincoln to have sex with him, despite his declared lack of interest. Yet when they finally did, it was Lincoln, feeling "emotional and affectionate," who initiated it. Afterward Varian claimed it "didn't mean anything," and Lincoln decided that he preferred "impersonal liaisons" to sex with friends; the experiment wasn't repeated.

The longer Lincoln got to know Varian, the more he found him "officious and tiresome." Lincoln accepted his share of blame for their mutual antagonism, acknowledging that he was himself sometimes "tense and hysterical" and not, at other times, "a gentleman." Still, what it came down to was that he simply "didn't like" Varian, even while admiring his intellect and his knowledge of the classics.

And yet Lincoln did hold on to the friendship, and he and Varian decided, early in freshman year, to start a literary journal together. Lincoln admitted in his diary that in his "dream of empire" he preferred to run the journal alone, wanted Varian "out of the way." But he sensibly realized that Varian's "practical brains" were essential to success and that "it could be fatal if I was given a free hand"—"he's an excellent sedative for me."

Originally the two had wanted to get on the board of the Harvard literary magazine, the *Advocate*, in the hopes of enlivening that stodgy publication and, ultimately, controlling it. Lincoln had early on published two pieces in the *Advocate*, one a parody of musical program notes (which, in turn, got a glowing review in the *Harvard Crimson*) and the other a talented poem, "March from the Ruins of Athens"—Conrad Aiken was among those who praised it—heavily influenced by T. S. Eliot, the poet Lincoln then most admired (" 'The Waste Land' burst on us as a revelation"). When the *Advocate* turned them away, Lincoln ascribed the rejection to Varian's "tart antagonism" and to his own "strident 'modernism.' "[5]

Determined in their quest to publish the literary avant-garde, they decided to start a competing magazine of their own. The chosen title, the *Hound and Horn*, came from Ezra Pound (" 'Tis the white stag Fame we're hunting / Bid the world's hounds come to horn"), and the model for a serious journal from T. S. Eliot's *The Criterion*. Rockwell Kent—whom Lincoln somehow managed to see as a latter-day version of his beloved William Blake—agreed to design a colophon.

Hound and Horn wasn't, of course, the first "little magazine" in this country to attempt to introduce avant-garde literature and commentary. Harriet Monroe had founded *Poetry* in 1912, Floyd Dell and Max Eastman had started the more politically minded *The Masses*, and Scofield Thayer and James Sibley Watson, Jr., had reinvigorated *The Dial* (with Watson the particular champion of James Joyce and Ezra Pound); it lasted, under Marianne Moore's editorship, until July 1929.

But whereas *The Dial* was international in scope, Lincoln and Varian aimed to focus above all on American writers, and preferably unknown or underappreciated ones. "We will try," Lincoln wrote his father, "to be the one standard of excellence in young American letters and the more American the better as far as I am concerned." As he wrote one potential contributor, "we must limit ourselves to the discussion of American milieu and American implications in general—except in very rare instances—when an international interest is general and important enough to be universally relevant."

Lincoln plunged ahead even though two of the people he admired most tried to discourage him. One was his faculty adviser, S. Foster Damon, the pioneering Blake scholar and one of the few Harvard instructors Lincoln respected. He told Lincoln that he thought the magazine "inadvisable"; even if he could pull it off, every vested literary interest on campus, Damon predicted, would dismiss or denigrate it. Though depressed by Damon's view, Lincoln refused to give up; he felt he'd "gotten too far into this now to step out easily."

Two days later he went to seek advice from Dick Blackmur, a young clerk in Maurice Firuski's celebrated Dunster House Bookstore, whose erudition and insight Lincoln admired. He was distressed when Blackmur told him that the magazine *might* be worth having, but only if its contents included subjects of "a much more general" nature than currently planned. Lincoln thought Blackmur was aiming too high too soon, but Blackmur's opinion, coming hard on Damon's, "shook the pins out from under me, causing a good deal of uneasiness."

Momentarily, that is. Though Lincoln could get flustered and overwrought, he had a core self-confidence that belied his outward agitation; as he wrote in his 1927 diary, "Whatever situation I may put myself in—given enough time—I feel sure my innate sense and past experience will pull me through." Sloughing off the negative predictions, Lincoln plunged ahead. He was soon "slaving every spare minute" on the projected new quarterly, neglecting his schoolwork and even Martin Mower's drawing class (among the few courses he thought valuable). "I have become terribly intense and energetic," he wrote in his diary. "I lose all sense of proportion . . . and get into a sweat about some unimportant detail in a second."

He spent most of his time racing around—soliciting articles, coaxing potential advertisers (a job he "hated most profoundly to do"), critiquing submissions, sending out editorial comments. Putting the magazine together became, in his own words, a "strange Frankenstein"—yet also, a hugely enjoyable one. Though he sometimes felt like a "wreck," more often the frantic pace energized and fulfilled him. "To me it's the stuff of life," he wrote in his diary.

But getting the first number launched proved "no easy dream." Individuals and businesses he'd felt sure would give him an ad or two, didn't—though Bennett Cerf, the head of Random House, unexpectedly came through. "How much is a page?" Cerf asked the two nineteen-year-olds. Lincoln deferred to Varian, who replied, "Fifty dollars"—though the actual rate they'd decided on was thirty. Varian's "practicality" was proving its worth.

Finding enough good material to fill *Hound and Horn* proved the most serious challenge. Lincoln felt sure that talented writers abounded—but "Where? Where? Where? Even their best friends won't tell." But as his contacts began to proliferate, so did his access to first-rate material. Through Mina he met Newton Arvin, the literary critic who taught at Smith; they got along so well that they became friendly, and Arvin contributed portions of a fictitious "Journal of Henry Marston" for the undersize trial issue of *Hound and Horn* that Lincoln intended to take to London during the upcoming summer in the hope that it could serve as an introduction to T. S. Eliot and other notables.

Lincoln also met the painter Maurice Grosser, four years his senior and already living with his lifetime partner, Virgil Thomson (an arrangement that astonished everyone who knew Grosser, since he'd initially disliked Thomson intensely). For the "advance" issue, Grosser offered three drawings, and Lincoln chose the one portraying another recent friend, the eccentric Brahmin/Trotskyist poet, John Brooks ("Jack") Wheelwright. "Jack and I get along very well," Lincoln wrote in his diary. "He is really a nice person, with a difficult exterior."

Wheelwright, from the beginning, proved an enthusiastic *Hound and Horn* booster. He made up a list of "200 of his literary friends" and urged Lincoln to send them the introductory issue of the magazine free of charge; grateful though Lincoln was for the ardent support, he pointed out to Wheelwright that "if I sent it we would be bankrupt." He asked

Wheelwright instead to become one of a hundred people (and to suggest additional names) who would each give a hundred dollars as "subscribers." Jack apparently joined up, but few others did.

Early in their friendship, Wheelwright read Lincoln "a sequence of very passionate love sonnets—homosexual," but Lincoln didn't much like them; he thought they were "not suggestive in a restrained, erotic way," and during the reading, he "began to feel embarrassed at their explicitness." But he was very much taken with Wheelwright's "Forty Days," a religious poem that Lincoln thought "extraordinarily moving"; he eventually secured it for *Hound and Horn*.

Lincoln admitted in his diary that Wheelwright was "slightly grotesque" in manner, speech, politics, and dress, but on the whole he thought him "a great comic character." Their artistic sympathies were similar, especially in regard to "the glories of the ballet," which Jack called "the only complete form of entertainment in the wide world." Occasionally they'd have a disagreement—Wheelwright insisted, for example, that Degas "was a greater artist than Cézanne," which view Lincoln "strongly opposed."

Overall Lincoln was, as he once wrote Wheelwright, hugely grateful to him "for all your many services of heart and hand." And his memories of Wheelwright would remain fresh; late in life Lincoln would write, "Through Jack, I inhabited a vivid landscape, a fair part of whose meadows extended lushly backward into the century before."

Contributions to *Hound and Horn* gradually trickled in. Lincoln's old love from Exeter days, Howard Doughty, sent an allegorical fable. And a newer friend, Henry-Russell Hitchcock (who would emerge as the country's foremost architectural critic), gave him an essay, "The Decline of Architecture," that later became the opening chapter of his celebrated book *Modern Architecture*. Lincoln once described Hitchcock as "that green dank puss. . . . He never washes and has a smell of dried wine and cockroaches ever about him." Periodically Hitchcock would so transparently court danger during one of his wilder homosexual binges that Lincoln, who was no slouch at sexual slumming, would worry about his friend's safety, and even sanity. Along with feeling real affection for Hitchcock personally, Lincoln greatly valued his brilliance, and the two would long remain friends.

In their frantic search for material, Lincoln and Varian changed the table of contents "20 times," and along the way made, perhaps inevitably, some poor choices. Lincoln committed the pardonable youthful error of including one of his own poems in the trial issue; later he shamefacedly described it as "damp." And he first accepted, then rejected, then finally published one of the weaker poems a Harvard graduate student named Stanley Kunitz—later renowned—submitted. (Lincoln didn't take to him personally, either; out of curiosity, he had Kunitz over for tea and decided he was "unattractive and difficult.")

In early May 1927, "after much fighting against inevitability," Lincoln and Varian decided to postpone publication of the first full issue until September. The disappointment was acute for two hours, but "a drunken tea" improved their mood. On May 4, his twentieth birthday, Lincoln "decided not to have a nervous breakdown on account of H & H as . . . a present to myself." Rose sent an extra birthday present: a check for a hundred dollars—roughly equivalent to a thousand today—to be applied to the *Hound and Horn* budget.

With Harvard just across the Charles River from Boston, Lincoln returned home fairly frequently. Louis was often away on a business trip (so often that Lincoln would later exaggeratedly tell an interviewer that his father "was never very real to me. . . . I never knew him very well, and on any intimate basis I had no connection with him"). Lincoln still felt closer to Rose at this point in his life and their relationship had become more "pleasantly casual and intimate" than before. Occasionally they went out to dinner together, usually at Boston's famed Parker House, and even took an occasional trip to New York City to visit galleries and go to theater.[6]

Rose still complained now and then that Lincoln didn't spend enough time with her. And she still tended to make a production out of everything—"she is never able to do anything easily," Lincoln wrote in his diary. He also objected to her having "far too much stuff around" and to her "horrible faculty of boasting about material things in what she thinks is a modest way." Lincoln claimed to have an "almost Freudian aversion to the subject of money" (and was aware it was an aversion only the wealthy could indulge); whenever his mother brought up the price of some recent purchase, he claimed that "a bell strikes in my heart." One notable exception was her purchase of six African sculptures from John Quinn's famed estate sale—even if she did then fuss about whether she'd been "gypped" and whether Louis would like them. Lincoln thought the pieces extraordinary and praised her taste. But she was right about Louis—he hated the sculptures on sight and never got used to them.

If Lincoln felt closer to Rose during his undergraduate years, he grew quite distant for a time from Louis. He thought his usually levelheaded father was beginning to succumb to flattery and self-importance (as part of his accelerated public prominence Louis had become president of the board of the Boston Public Library—in which capacity he defended John Singer Sargent's controversial murals and as a result got to know the painter). When Lincoln tried to talk to his father about *Hound and Horn*, he found him "neither sympathetic or interested"—he tended to pick up a newspaper or leave the room. Before long Louis would become the magazine's most important financial backer, but for the time being he'd grown exasperated with the way Lincoln kept shifting paths—writer, painter, publisher: wavering enthusiasms in pursuit of an unwavering ambition to achieve something of importance.

Nor was Louis enamored of the occasional friend or two his son brought home to dinner; he let Lincoln know that he considered them all "gutless and washouts." And that included the dapper, droll Eddie Warburg, the one Jewish friend Lincoln had made at Harvard (and the youngest son of Felix Warburg, a partner in Kuhn, Loeb, the prominent banking firm that handled Louis's accounts). With Rose compulsively chatting about interior decorating and Louis presuming his son's guests were self-indulgent wastrels, Lincoln laconically commented in his diary that it "would be rather nice to take people home more easily."

Not that he entirely disagreed about Eddie Warburg. He enjoyed Eddie's amiable presence and the ease with which he mingled socially with the coveted Lads ("I have always had a desire to mix in the glamour of sporty circles," Lincoln confessed to his diary, but "I become embarrassed and feel very strongly this is not my place"). But he recognized that Eddie was much more a social creature than he, preferring a good time to a serious talk. Still, they enjoyed each other enough to stay friendly and would, in the near future, become jointly involved in the worlds of painting and dance.

CHAPTER THREE

Hound and Horn

(1927)

THOUGH FEELING HIS father's current distance, Lincoln nonetheless asked him to finance three months abroad during the summer of 1927. And Louis, despite his current displeasure, agreed to do so. His son's reasons for the trip seemed valid: Lincoln hoped to advance the fortunes of *Hound and Horn* through introductions to T. S. Eliot, Ezra Pound, and other literary notables; and he hoped, for a future dissertation on El Greco, to wander the museums of Spain to study his paintings.

Just turned twenty and on his first trip by himself to Europe, Lincoln had little trouble finding his own way, artistically and sexually. The ocean voyage was the most difficult part; his "extreme nervous energy and . . . lack of power to relax" made for a tedious trip, enlivened only by his attempts to achieve a "chance" meeting with an attractive man who successfully eluded him, and by reading Virginia Woolf's "superb" new book, *To the Lighthouse.*

His ex-boyfriend Howard Doughty, who'd been studying abroad for the year, met him at the Southampton dock, and Lincoln hit the ground running. London filled him with "ecstasy . . . its alien air is crammed with lovely memories, familiarities, soft air. It excites me to walk the streets and hear passers-by talk. It does not change like N.Y. does." In a frenzy of excitement, he raced around the city, dragging along a resistant Howard, who (in Lincoln's words) had had a "fine homosexual year"—he'd fallen in love with Sergei, a Russian poet—was due to leave London shortly, and had long since had his fill of the "sights." Still, Howard did his best to keep pace.[1]

Lincoln's first stop was the National Gallery, where the Veroneses, Titians, and El Grecos deeply moved him, filling him "with great longing to paint immediately"; for that impulse he was willing to credit Harvard and all that Martin Mower had taught him over the past year. From the National Gallery the exhilarated young art lover dragged Howard directly to the Tate, where the Constables and Monet's "intoxicating" painting of a glass of peonies "frightfully excited" him—even while pointing out to Howard which lads wandering about the gallery he "would or would not like to go to bed with." He'd hoped, in advance, that Howard might be one of them. That expectation, he felt, had been "very conceited" of him; still, he took it hard that Howard only had eyes for Sergei.

Within three days of arriving in London, Lincoln was regularly attending what to him was already "the most satisfying spectacle of all"— the ballet. At this point in his life he'd seen, during his several summer visits, most of the Diaghilev repertory (in 1925 he'd watched George Balanchine dance the role of the wizard Kastchei in *Firebird* as well as two pas de deux he'd choreographed for Nikita Balieff's company, Chauve-Souris). By 1927 Lincoln considered himself "deeply addicted" to the ballet. He even entertained the periodic hope that he himself might yet become a dancer; it took a few more years before he'd finally become convinced that he was too old, too tall, too awkward.

During the summer of 1927 he caught a number of notable performances: the premiere of Léonide Massine's *Le Pas d'Acier* (he liked Prokofiev's score and some of the dancing, but on a second viewing decided that none of it was "much good"); and he saw the "lovely" new Sauguet–Balanchine *La Chatte*, which proved a milestone in Serge Lifar's career, and which Lincoln liked better each of the three times he saw it. But his favorite that summer, "the loveliest ballet of all" in his view, was Bronislava Nijinska's *Les Biches*, set to a Francis Poulenc score, with costumes and decor by Marie Laurencin. Nijinska (the sister of Nijinsky) herself sometimes starred in the leading role, but in 1927 Lincoln saw Lydia Sokolova perform it "in her superb ineffable way—ecstasy. The finest thing I've ever seen in the theatre."

"In my present ecstatic state," Lincoln wrote in his diary early in July, Howard's "complete willful indifference very much irritates me." And he became downright angry, while they were visiting with some "bawdy" new homosexual acquaintances, including the London *Times* reviewer Raymond Mortimer, when Howard casually talked about how easily Lincoln got an erection. Howard, in turn, had become "bored" with Lincoln's constant complaints about the "fairy" crowd—effeminate, campy men. Unlike the athletic, hard-drinking Lads he adored, Lincoln all but automatically equated the "confraternity of fairies" with being "catty," prone to "meannesses," and willing "to lower [themselves] . . . to any depth to get a laugh."

After Howard left for Paris, Lincoln turned to other people. He continued to see a good deal of Raymond Mortimer, who, Lincoln wrote in his diary, "on the surface is a bitch, but he has a good head and I respect his judgments." He also found him "much kinder than most of the Bloomsbury Buggers," though he became fond of Duncan Grant ("a very sweet, wise and sympathetic person"). Mina's old friend David Garnett saw Lincoln briefly and reported to her that "he is a very sensitive creature & has grown rather charming."

Lincoln also started to see a good deal of Bonamy Dobree, sixteen years his senior and a contributor to T. S. Eliot's influential *The Criterion*. Almost immediately Lincoln decided that Dobree was "the nicest person I've met in London." And the most attractive. Dobree sported a reddish beard "shaped in such a way as to suggest a past Elizabethan worthy." Bonamy was married, but it was he who initiated the subject of sex in such a way that Lincoln decided he was an "abandoned sentimentalist." Soon after, Lincoln met Bonamy's wife, Valentine, and thought her "wonderful"—which confirmed his sense that he shouldn't get "too damn much" involved, since he felt sure that Bonamy wouldn't.

Yet when Lincoln went to Paris for a few days, he soon got a telegram from Bonamy saying that he was coming over to join him. Lincoln was "amazed"—and delighted. To avoid the possibility of running into acquaintances, they holed up in the town of Sens for four days. Lincoln sensed from the beginning that the intense closeness would "prepare me beautifully" for going alone to Spain the following week; his previous involvement with Tom Mabry had made him something of a cynic about sustained relationships.

True to his own prediction, "feelings of peace, comfort and a kind of mitigated happiness" with Bonamy were soon followed by a conviction that his attraction was "momentary" and not comparable to the "absorbing passion" he'd felt (and in some moods continued to feel) for Tom. He could "pleasantly abandon" himself to the few days—"with the knowledge I prefer something else." He and Bonamy parted amicably, and would again see each other when Lincoln returned from Spain in September. "Bonamy was fun," Lincoln wrote in his diary, "but there was no mystery to him"—there was "nothing but surface meaning in it for me."

When still a student at the Berkshire School, Lincoln had, on a visit to New Haven, met a Yale man six years his senior named Payson Loomis. In physique and personality, Loomis was very nearly the opposite of the brawny, brainless athletes Lincoln ordinarily was attracted to. Loomis majored at Yale in Russian and Arabic, was severely intellectual, and had read, in Lincoln's awestruck view, "everything," and particularly everything that had to do with comparative religion. Lincoln, who "felt an anchored resistance to our Testaments, Old or New," was especially intrigued by Loomis's defense of the mystic Madame Blavatsky and by his growing involvement with the renowned George Ivanovich Gurdjieff.[2]

Loomis was in France during July, and at his urging Lincoln took the train out to meet him at Gurdjieff's "Institute for the Harmonious Development of Man," housed at Le Prieuré, the rundown country estate in Fontainebleau where Madame de Maintenon had in the late seventeenth century established an academy for girls. But when Lincoln arrived, Loomis failed to appear at their designated meeting spot. Lincoln momentarily thought of entering the mansion without him, but finally decided against it. Looking up, he thought he saw Gurdjieff at one of the windows: "The supposed Gurdjieff and I stared at one another interested for some minutes, then I drove away through a lovely tall alley of greenery." A more prolonged visit would soon follow, with lifetime repercussions.

A few days later Lincoln was off to Spain for two weeks. From the beginning the trip triggered a state of high excitement. His enthusiasm would waver now and then under the scorching heat, the unreliable food and lodging, and the omnipresent fleas, but Lincoln had thoroughly prepared himself to track down as many of El Greco's paintings as he could, and his passionate response to the artist brought him at several points to near-ecstacy.[3]

In Madrid's Prado Museum, El Greco's *Resurrection* moved him "more than any picture I've ever seen"; it was a "miracle," bringing such "ineffable pleasure" that he had an "emotional crise over it"; he felt he'd "never lived fully till I saw it today." The El Grecos in the cathedral at Toledo and in Philip II's Escorial ("the most wonderfully consistent building I've ever seen, even to the gardens and pissoir") produced other rapturous days. Lincoln felt literally swallowed up by the painter's "splendor," so completely lost in it that he once missed his train connection.

Goya, on the other hand, he thought "mostly very poor," while Velázquez left him arguing passionately with himself in his diary over the painter's merits, as if making a life-or-death decision about whether to continue an intimate friendship. He took himself back to the Prado several times "trying to decide about Velasquez," wanting to "give him a fair chance," "baffled" by certain characteristics, admiring others. Finally he triumphantly announced in his diary that the "mystery of Velasquez is solved": he liked him most "when he is least like himself." Lincoln was not your ordinary stupefied tourist, rushing dazedly past a limited number of certified masterpieces.

He missed not being able to share his emotional excitement: "If I only had someone to talk to about all this," he wrote plaintively in his diary after ten days of travel. His loneliness—and the heat—grew so keen at one point that he had "a sudden overwhelming feeling to chuck it all and go home." Instead he wrote long letters to his mother and to Tom. And he bought himself some fine vests, a dove gray sombrero, and, after "an anguish[ed] feeling . . . [of being] too extravagant, the most heavenly 18th century court suit which with a little tailoring will fit me beautifully."

On August 13, in Seville, he picked up a four-day-old Paris paper (his French was excellent, his Spanish nonexistent) and read "with feelings of horror" that back in the States, Sacco and Vanzetti had lost their final appeal. The two Italian immigrants had earlier been convicted of murdering a bank official and the case had become an international cause célèbre, with many—including Lincoln and his family—convinced that the men had really been convicted for their left-wing political views (the judge had actually boasted about what he'd done to "those anarchist bastards"). The previous spring Lincoln and Mina had participated in protest meetings, and over the summer Louis had twice written Lincoln deploring the injustice of the case. Two weeks later Lincoln learned that the executions had taken place in Boston's Charlestown prison. "They behaved superbly," Lincoln wrote in his diary, and wondered whether, if he'd been home, he could have gotten arrested along with other protesters.

From Seville, Lincoln decided, apparently at the urging of his friend Loomis, to spend a week in North Africa. What Loomis apparently had in mind was to induce a "feeling of intense remoteness from everywhere [Lincoln] had ever known." But most of the remoteness proved intensely uncongenial. On the very first day Lincoln's Berber guide offered to provide him "with boys and girls as far as I want," and when Lincoln made a deprecatory gesture, pressed ahead anyway: "May as well," the guide insisted. "Only 5 days ago in the Kursaal a lad like me fell dead after dancing." He brought a reluctant Lincoln to a bordello where young girls "with pendant breasts kept trying to make me have an erection by friction," and where he "had to literally fight" his way out. Lincoln decided that his guide, along with being handsome and charming, was "inhuman."

The insufferable heat added to his discomfort, Moorish architecture "bored" him, and his skin soon broke out in "horribly itchy irruptions." His one pleasant day was in the town of Ronda, which had an excellent hotel; as for the rest, the long patches of desert would "persist in my mind like the acid taste of grapefruit refusing to disappear." This may have been precisely what Loomis had hoped for. But for now Lincoln "panted" to get back to Madrid and to see if there were letters from home.

When he reached there on August 25, he rushed "in a frenzy" to his hotel, checked to see if the vests he'd bought had arrived (they had), devoured a batch of accumulated letters ("nothing from Tom"), and then raced straight to the Prado, where he all but camped out for the next few days. "I have learned an enormous amount in the Prado," he wrote on his last day in Madrid, "and I've worked as hard thinking about it as if I were at school. It has also brought my ambitions to a culmination. I know I must be a painter first of all." A mere two days earlier Lincoln had worried that his ambition was "unsystematized," and within another few days his seemingly fixed determination to become an artist would once more dissolve into doubt.

At the end of August he took a two-day trip to Barcelona. The city, he decided, "beats even its own photographs." But he saw little to admire in

Gaudí's much-touted architecture, characterizing his buildings as "heavily vegetable—like our hand drip castles on the beach . . . like the Grand Guignol."

In fact Lincoln had grown tired of travel. Needing the "assenting glance, the feeling of some sort of personal intimacy," he longed "for my old ways and conversation's balm. . . . I have a passion to talk to someone—anyone." His heightened loneliness sensitized him, and his nerve endings, thinly sheathed to begin with, became delicately susceptible. In Barcelona, seeing a woman on the street selling lottery tickets, he decided she was "desperate" and felt so overwhelmingly sorry for her that he became more "depressed . . . than I can say." When a car crashed into the side of the train he was on departing Barcelona, and its driver was killed, Lincoln, unlike most of the passengers, couldn't bear to look at the wreckage. An English boy on the train delightedly announced that the sight was "a jolly mess, thicker than blood," leaving Lincoln deeply shocked at "this astonishing impersonalization of mortality."

The incident reminded him of his two visits to the bullring. At the first he'd "almost wept." At the second, when a horse (to Lincoln, a beloved animal) was badly gored, he felt utter disgust and left. "It's a stinking sort of show," he wrote in his diary, and he had "a moment's feeling of intense hatred against everything Spanish; almost hysteria."

Back in Paris for a few days, on his way to London, Lincoln recovered enough energy to take on another round of museumgoing. His opinions, after an intense summer of looking at art, had become less hesitant: Manet's *Olympia* was "miraculous"; Rembrandt left him "completely cold" (though in Europe two years later, Lincoln changed his mind: "He really is a great painter. Veil after veil comes off my eyes"); he considered Cuyp the best of the Dutch painters; Turner suffered from "much the same dullness as beautiful light . . . always the same"; cubism was mostly "dull abstraction." He decided that he "should love to have a house" one day, which he could fill with a collection of favorite pictures. But he also decided that no amount of paintings or museum hopping could in the end compare to the satisfaction he derived from seeing the ballet.

While in Paris Lincoln once again went out to Le Prieuré, but Gurdjieff wasn't there and he quickly fled: the "atmosphere of [the] place completely terrifies me." The next day he had lunch with Payson Loomis, who revealed that he expected to spend the entire winter with Gurdjieff at Fontainebleau. "I distrust anything which depends so much on another's system," Lincoln wrote in his diary that same day, though admitting that the little he knew about Gurdjieff's system—and in particular, its focus on "the intensification of everything"—"sounds all right." He also continued to find Loomis a deeply intriguing figure who "interests and stimulates me more than anybody I know, intellectually. He puts new ideas into my head.

He takes me out of habits of thinking." Which is precisely what Loomis said about Gurdjieff.

Before leaving Paris for London early in September, Lincoln got a reassuring wire from Varian that *Hound and Horn* was moving steadily toward production. With that news in hand, he decided to stop in at Sylvia Beach's bookstore, Shakespeare & Co., to show her the abbreviated advance copy that he and Varian had cobbled together as an introductory offering, and to solicit her support. She did agree to take out a subscription—but only one, which disappointed him.

Once back in London, Lincoln again picked up with Bonamy Dobree: "We're fond of each other in an easy way and will find pleasure in spite of infrequent meetings." Bonamy had arranged a lunch with T. S. Eliot on the day Lincoln arrived from Paris, but the weather failed to cooperate; his plane was delayed, and he arrived too late for the appointment. Lincoln "regretted missing Eliot, but not," he claimed, "too much, since Eliot was "rather [a] fixture."

Despite Lincoln's youthful (and passing) hauteur, Eliot was to him (just as James Joyce was to Varian Fry) "the most important authority in the world for anything and everything that could occupy me." And when, two days later, Lincoln sent Eliot the introductory copy of *Hound and Horn*, his accompanying letter was elaborately humble: he was "painfully aware," he wrote, of the magazine's "literary shortcomings." Lincoln also included a list of first editions of Eliot's works that they hoped to publish in the magazine's forthcoming winter issue; he asked Eliot if—"without giving yourself too much trouble"—he would check the list to ensure that it was correct and complete. Eliot replied that he would be honored to have the bibliography appear, and suggested a few additions for it.

On one of his last days in London, Lincoln had supper with Alfred H. Barr, Jr. Apparently the two hadn't previously met, though Barr was a graduate student at Harvard and would become Lincoln's tutor in his junior year (by the late 1920s and early '30s they would be close associates during the founding years of the Museum of Modern Art). At dinner that night in London in 1927, Lincoln and Barr had a long talk about the future of painting, and they came away from it thinking well of each other. In his diary Lincoln described Barr as "a good sort," and Barr wrote to his mentor, Paul J. Sachs, the wealthy and well-connected associate director of Harvard's Fogg Museum, that Kirstein "seems to me a boy of considerable talent and of very great intelligence, taste and energy." Barr predicted to Sachs that because of Lincoln's "very modern interests . . . he may be looked upon with a certain suspicion in Cambridge," and he hoped that Sachs would be able "to give him careful and sympathetic direction." Sachs would indeed prove helpful to Lincoln, but their relationship would also develop some disagreeable overtones.

Lincoln sailed for New York on September 17, 1927, feeling "no regrets at leaving." The summer had been profoundly stirring, but he was eager to get home—to see the first full issue of *Hound and Horn*, which was due out, and once again to see Tom, who had written him "a very fine letter" explaining his long silence and whom Lincoln had "a most passionate desire to see." Tom's letter made him feel that he "was falling in love with him all over again."[4]

Louis, along with a business associate, met Lincoln's boat when it docked in New York—and, pleasantries dealt with, promptly reprimanded him for having gone to Morocco alone.

Two days later Lincoln was back in Cambridge—and holding in his hand a copy of the first full issue of *Hound and Horn*. It "looked lovely," was on all the newsstands and actually selling, and he was hugely excited. He had a "definite feeling of regret that it's not as good as it might be, but by God, it's actually realized," and for that he allowed himself to feel proud. The contents of the first issue were indeed strong, with the prose—which included Richard Blackmur's two-part critical essay on T. S. Eliot, Newton Arvin's "Henry Marston" diary, and Henry-Russell Hitchcock, Jr.'s, article on architecture—a good deal more distinguished than the poetry (by Howard Doughty, Tom Mabry, John Abbott, and Lincoln Kirstein).

Given the tradition of genteel "good taste" that still dominated Harvard's view of acceptable art, Lincoln took pleasure in the accusation that *Hound and Horn*'s first number was "full of bad taste." Both the Harvard undergraduate publications, the *Advocate* and the *Crimson*, patronized the new publication. (The notice in the *Crimson* was insignificant in size and nasty in tone. The *Advocate* wrote a negative review and, for good measure, a negative editorial.)

Harrison Parker, president of the *Advocate*, agreed to have supper with Lincoln in order to tell him, with maximum hauteur, how "very irritated" he was at *Hound and Horn*'s "preciousness," and (so Lincoln recorded the meeting in his diary) "how young pups like us should not meddle with our elders and betters"—meaning the *Advocate* staff—or "read anything but Keats and Shelley, and not much Shelley." Parker proudly announced that he himself "refuses to read anybody later than Browning . . . he wants to be sure of that which is approved by time."

Lincoln, in turn, managed to derive a "deal of pleasure" by alluding to the positive write-ups that *Hound and Horn* had received in the *Boston Herald* and the *New York Times*, and "in telling him how well we are getting along financially" (which they weren't). Their volunteer undergraduate "business manager," in fact, had proved a near disaster. Officious and sulky, he had managed, as of mid-October, to bring in only two ads—and soon resigned. Lincoln blamed Varian in part, accusing him of having bullied the young man and in general having an "inordinate amount of stupid pride." Lincoln *was* grateful to Varian for having, over the past summer, borne the brunt of getting the first issue to bed, but even so they remained testy associates rather than friends. Lincoln thought Varian was "in [a] terribly bad mental state . . . his lack of interest in his fellow men precludes any kind of fondness for him on their part." He took particular offense at the "horrid" way Varian treated servants: "He's lonely without people and abusive with them."

Lincoln's relationship with Tom Mabry, whom he'd been longing for, took several surprising turns. They saw each other within days of Lincoln's return, and (as he wrote in his diary) he could "hardly keep my eyes or hands off him." They took a long, long walk out to Fresh Pond, and Tom told Lincoln that he was quitting Knopf, leaving New York, and ultimately moving to Washington to try his hand at becoming a writer. They were due to see each other again two weeks later, but Tom cancelled the date for business reasons. Yet they did continue to correspond in "the old spirit," and Tom wrote Lincoln that he'd embarked on a biographical novel about John Donne—"a fine sign," Lincoln thought, that his friend was settling in well. But then came a long silence, followed by word from Tom that he'd been diagnosed with "incipient spinal tuberculosis." The news came over Lincoln "in a flood"—it was, he thought, "the most hideous thing that could have happened." Tom, in his mind, was "the one thing I can cling to for my lasting support." In his distress he confided in his mother, who reacted in a "sensible," supportive way, encouraging his loyalty.

What then followed were months of upsetting, contradictory feelings about just how much he owed Tom, and complicated, constant changes in plans for how best to fulfill his obligations to him. Initially Lincoln was certain that he'd spend the entire upcoming summer with him, and within twenty-four hours of receiving Tom's news, he was on a train to New York to see him. Lincoln wanted to believe that their relationship was as "strong as ever," but when they met, Tom told him that someone else was now in the picture, a man he cared about less than he did Lincoln "but who can be relied on entirely"—which, he said frankly, he didn't think Lincoln could be. Nor did Lincoln disagree, aware that his frantic energy and multiple activities constantly swerved him off an intended path.

Still, he felt wounded—and in his hurt, less committed. When Tom wired that "his third lumbar vertebrae is partly gone" but that he feared entering a sanitarium, Lincoln helped arrange the offer of a house in Millbrook owned by a mutual friend. But at the same time he felt that "my pity is uncommunicative and futile," and he was unsure what to do next. For a time he had trouble even writing to Tom, and by Christmas, when he'd planned a trip to see him, he let himself be guiltily persuaded by Rose and others that he was being "unsensibly overgenerous," and that his presence might create difficulties for Tom with his family.

He managed to convince himself ("I wanted to believe this anyway") that they "no longer emotionally cared" for each other to an extent that would warrant a visit. But he was sufficiently honest—and melodramatically self-indicting—to write in his diary that maybe the real truth was that "my capacity for friendship is nil—no friendship, only lovers, and when the emotion dies then everything else does. . . . I'm not sure this isn't as good a way of controlling personal relationships as any other, being in the last analysis always isolated."

He decided not to visit. Tom sent him a telegram saying that he understood. But he, too, had conflicted feelings, and the negative side soon emerged. He acidly let Lincoln know that TB could not be transmitted by mail, and then, after Christmas had passed, sent him a letter telling him he was "a fraud for not coming down." At first that made Lincoln "frightfully sore" but then, scrupulously introspective, he became "extremely repentant, thinking I probably lied to myself and incidentally to him." He had "wanted so much to do the right thing," but had managed in the end to get "terrifically mixed up in my motivation"; he decided, after all, that he'd "behaved badly." Eventually he and Tom would reconnect, though more on a professional than a personal level.

Lincoln turned his energies to recontacting other friends he'd made prior to his summer in Europe, and to making some new ones. One of his first stops was a visit to Northampton to see Mina and Harry. They were "in great form," deeply happy in their marriage, though Harry wanted children more than Mina did. But she was willing, and they were troubled by her inability to become pregnant. Harry blamed his periodic impotence on his being tubercular, but the doctor they consulted pointed the finger at Mina, diagnosing her as having "the reproductive organs of a child" and prescribing treatment with pituitary extract.

As much as Lincoln liked Harry (and was physically attracted to him), he felt that in some ways he and Harry "don't hit," and he chose to confide in Mina alone about his "increasing tendencies" toward homosexuality. Mina immediately recommended Freudian psychoanalysis as "the only way out." Among urban intellectuals especially, psychoanalysis had become fashionable in the postwar period (Mina herself would be analyzed by Freud's colleague and biographer, Ernest Jones)—at much the same time that a certain permissiveness about sexual contact between men had given way to a more condemnatory diagnosis of "pathology." "Normal" men were coming to be more tightly defined as men who had sex only with women.

Lincoln "hated" Mina's suggestion about analysis and told her that he had "no desire to change. . . . I feel if I was completely heterosexual I would lose a great deal of intensity." Mina insisted that he would lose nothing—"and gain everything." Such was the optimism—or was it the naïveté?—in those years about the wonders wrought by psychoanalysis that neither of them seems to have doubted for a moment that if Lincoln would present himself for treatment, he could readily enough "change"— and within a mere six months. To persuade him further, Mina pointedly added that in her opinion he had lately become "more nervous than ever."

Mina no longer had the profound influence over Lincoln that had earlier been the case, and he continued to resist her suggestion. But he also continued to brood about it. Her views made him feel "absolutely down" and deeply unsettled.

Nonetheless many of his strongest friendships continued to be with men who, without categorically defining themselves as "queer"—that designation was still mostly reserved for gender-nonconforming "fairies"— continued to have pleasurable sexual adventures with people of their own gender, often in a rather casual, uncomplicated way.

And that included his younger brother, George. He and Lincoln had sex together at least twice when they were seventeen and twenty, respectively. Lincoln wrote up the second encounter in his diary: "George over here in Cambridge and both of us feeling amorous, so we were incestuous for an hour enjoying ourselves intensely. The emotional stimulus however sapped me so that his plans for an all night bout such as we had in New York a year ago were wrecked."

It was a different era: effeminate "fairies" may have been regarded as distinctly "other," and vaguely repellent, but exclusive heterosexuality was not the automatic requirement and signpost of "normalcy," nor the required prerequisite for certification as a "real" man. George Kirstein subsequently became known as a considerable heterosexual stud, much married and often on the prowl.

Lincoln, on the other hand, increasingly had sex with men, though occasionally with women as well. Yet as early as his freshman year, word reached him that both he and Varian "were considered in certain . . . circles as queer." "This I daresay is nothing to weep over," he insouciantly wrote in his diary; "however, meaningless rumors often hold off nice people."

But as his worried conversation with Mina suggests, he wasn't consistently nonchalant about his erotic attraction to men. Perhaps his periodic concern centered less on the gender of his partner or the frequency of his escapades than on the fact that some of his involvements were decidedly *not* casual. Unlike many others in his circle who alternated between male and female sexual partners, Lincoln became deeply infatuated with particular men. During his sophomore year at Harvard, he "fell in love" several times over: with "Dick," who filled him "with all sorts of glowing emotion"; with "Bryan," who had "charm enough for any emergency" (and who, like many of the men he idolized, promptly fell "very much in love with a girl"); with Philip ("I seem to go around with my tongue out, panting. Rather revolting"); with Johnny ("I was surprised to learn I was the first . . . [he was] impetuous but unskilled").

All of these passionate devotions were played out over a mere three or four months, sometimes overlapped, were usually not fully reciprocal, and ranged in terms of sexual activity from dreamy talk to holding hands to "jiggling" to "acrobatics all over the bed and floor." It may well have been the romantic fierceness of Lincoln's attachments, more than the sex itself, that centrally accounts for his occasional bouts of uneasiness. Though he seems never to have wanted children, he'd long felt that eventually he would marry and settle down. He craved "the complete desirability of actually living with someone," the bonded security of a formalized relationship—a way to harness the emotional turmoil, even chaos, he sometimes felt.

So-called Boston marriages (two women devotedly settling down together) had long enjoyed a degree of social acceptability, probably because it was widely assumed that the relationships weren't sexual—since women supposedly weren't much interested in that sort of thing. But by the 1920s the concept of "lesbianism" as a singular and decidedly sexual identity had gained currency, and in direct proportion, an all-female household had grown more suspect.

The domestic coupling of two men had always seemed anomalous; a male was defined as sexually aggressive and uninterested in domestic (as opposed to wage-earning and political) matters. The celibate, upper-class Victorian bachelor, living in splendid isolation, may still have had a certain limited respectability—but were he to open his home to a live-in male partner who wasn't a relative or servant, his reputation would have deteriorated.

Thanks to the profound influence of Freud, an expanded range of sexual options and license had come into play by the 1920s, and as well, some softening of the gender guidelines: women were now viewed as more carnal than they once were thought to be, and homosexual contact as less morally fraught—at least within artistic and intellectual circles. But as always during periods of shifting social mores, the newer ideology continued to coexist and compete with the earlier one and, beyond the privileged classes, Victorian attitudes retained more authority (even as the actual behavior of the citizenry increasingly contradicted official morality).

Certainly in Lincoln's circle it became less and less of a rarity for two men to settle into live-in and long-term (if not monogamous or even enduringly sexual) relationships. Lincoln would soon come to know a number of such couples, including Virgil Thomson and Maurice Grosser, Glenway Wescott and Monroe Wheeler, Paul Cadmus and Jared French. But his own youthful romances with men had thus far proved truncated and unsatisfying—and with Tom Mabry, traumatic. He was still a very young man, at an age when few people "settled down," but he was an unusually sensitive one, too, and his experiences had left real scars. His romantic yearning for a loving male companion—and certainly his sexual drive—would persist, but now it had to compete with a certain cynicism about the likelihood of finding one.

No, heterosexual marriage seemed the more logical path to the stability he craved, and Lincoln began to feel—though the feeling would wax and wane—that the more ardently he pursued romantic involvement with a man, the more he might be jeopardizing the chance of finding permanence with a woman. In the middle of his sophomore year he abruptly announced to his diary "the necessity of becoming 'casual' almost at once." At another point he added: "I just see too many people. I am in the most highly accelerated state of nervous energy."

The resolution and the nervousness alike were further fueled by his realization that he was no longer doing much to fulfill his artistic ambitions. While in Europe he'd written some poetry and done a number of drawings, but since his return, he'd produced little of either. He was seeing something of his art teacher Martin Mower socially, but was no longer studying with him. Yet he insisted in his diary that he had a "very real desire to work hard at painting," and believed it was "the one thing I think I should do . . . [but] I have no time."

Not that he was spending much time going to classes or preparing for exams—as his middling grades attested. When not enveloped in romantic pursuit or staying up till dawn (as sophomores will) to drunkenly mull over the mysteries of the human condition, he was allotting the bulk of his time either to pursuing a hectic social round or working to ensure that *Hound and Horn* would have an ongoing life. The magazine's small office in Harvard Square was, at assorted hours of the day or night, abuzz with frantic (Lincoln's preferred style) activity—and argument. "Intrigue and pacification," Lincoln wrote obliquely in his diary, "are two half courses learned when one is connected with *Hound and Horn*."

Varian, despite being constantly provocative, continued to do yeoman work: he quickly found a new, more efficient business manager, and he was entirely conscientious about the tedious job of proofreading—as Lincoln was not; he preferred soliciting new material. That could have meant a constructive division of labor, but their personalities rubbed against each other like sandpaper. Lincoln blamed Varian for being unable to "do anything straight—he must always throw in some slight obstruction to maintain his own identity." Lincoln, for his part, tried to take on too haphazard a range of tasks, and then, failing to do everything at once, would sometimes blow up in frustration. But at least he could acknowledge, if irregularly, that "my capacity for intensity is perfectly astounding at times. It frightens me. It amounts to a kind of obsessional mania."

Financing the magazine was a constant struggle, yet one inherent to putting out a serious literary journal with a limited potential audience. That *Hound and Horn* survived at all was due almost entirely to support from both their fathers. Louis, unfortunately, had been "visibly unimpressed" by the magazine's first issue; on top of that Varian's father had decided at the end of 1927 to resign from his banking firm, which meant cutting back on his contribution. Nor could they find enough advertising to make up the difference. Nor, for that matter, enough good fiction to fill out the magazine's contents.

Soon after the second issue of *Hound and Horn* appeared in December 1927, Lincoln wrote his father a detailed letter describing their situation—and asking to borrow an additional two thousand dollars. To date, he wrote, they'd lost about a hundred dollars on the first issue. The second issue had been out only two months, but they'd already "gotten rid of"—he didn't say "sold"—1,529 copies out of 2,000, which, "if all goes well" would allow them to "about break clean." Lincoln interpreted that, not unreasonably, as "doing pretty well" for a new publication. They expected to gain still further on the third installment, due out in March 1928, and Lincoln felt certain "we stand to make a little money even this year."

Next came the pitch: "I wish you would lend me $2000, not to spend necessarily but to have in the bank." Their total expenditures, Lincoln reported, had thus far come to $3,100, and their total loss to about $780— and that included onetime costs of incorporation, stationery, and steel cabinets for the office. He solemnly offered to pay Louis "whatever rate of interest you usually allow in such matters," and promised to do so, moreover, on May 4, his twenty-first birthday, when he would come into a guaranteed annual income of $1,000. Varian, Lincoln concluded, intended to make a similar approach to his own father, and he himself was "going to work slowly on [Eddie] Warburg—he is a possibility I still think."

Then suddenly, in the midst of these literary/financial set-tos, tragedy intervened: Mina's husband, Harry Curtiss, not yet forty, suddenly died of unknown causes. Harry had been known to have tuberculosis, but although he had spit blood as recently as six months earlier, the disease had been considered under control. And up to the day he died, he'd led a vigorous, full life, tending to his well-run business, working hard on his beloved Ashfield farm.[5]

Mina was utterly engulfed, the entire family shocked and grieved. Seventeen-year-old George, who described himself as "not very emotional" by nature, "felt so like Hell" that he "just couldn't say anything comforting" to Mina. "Harry meant more to all of us," George wrote his parents, "than we knew, for he certainly was the whitest [the racist adjective was part of the everyday vocabulary of the times], kindest man I ever knew. I guess you don't realize all that till it's too late." Louis reassured his son that "you did entirely right to act naturally . . . I know that you had the same awful wrench that we all did."

As for Lincoln, though he had liked and admired Harry, the two had never entirely hit it off, their temperaments being too different for them ever to become close. Still, on Mina's behalf alone, Lincoln was deeply affected. He wrote a moving poem about Harry's death, and gave it to his sister.

> . . . *O let me stare well now*
> *And you look well at me. We must remind ourselves.*
> *In this splitting of air between us, the cold winds*
> *Mix what heat your virtue traces in my mind.*
> *Therefore, be not surprised if I pass by,*
> *Missing you at half way rock, for on the second lap*
> *When we shall cross again, or on the third or fourth,*
> *You eye me hard; you take my hand.*

CHAPTER FOUR

Brahmin Boston

(1928)

L INCOLN HAD OFTEN turned to Dick Blackmur for reading suggestions, and he "trust[ed] his poetical judgement more than anyone I
know." Blackmur was an ill-kempt, tersely formal autodidact, without
degrees or money—"spikey but agreeable," was how Lincoln later characterized him. Once *Hound and Horn* began, Lincoln had frequently asked
Blackmur for his opinion on this or that submitted poem or essay; and he
himself became an early and frequent contributor to the magazine (his
two-part essay on T. S. Eliot in 1928 was widely praised). Lincoln himself
preferred Blackmur's poetry to his prose, though he eventually decided
that the poetry wasn't "as good as Yvor Winters, nor [John Crowe] Ransom, nor Eliot."[1]

In the late 1920s Blackmur was living hand to mouth, his consuming
passion for literature substituting for ordinary creature comforts. (He
would end up as a renowned critic and professor of English at Princeton;
"I hated what Dick became," Lincoln would write Blackmur's biographer
more than forty years later: he "knew everything about literature and
withered accordingly.") As *Hound and Horn*'s reputation began to spread,
and as the relationship between Lincoln and Varian continued to deteriorate, Lincoln decided, early in 1929 to invite Blackmur to serve as "editing
manager." At the same time he asked a recent Harvard graduate, Bernard
Bandler, then working on a PhD in philosophy, to become an editor.
Bandler, who would later become a well-known psychiatrist, was primarily
interested in nonfiction and, in particular, religious and philosophical
issues. At the time he was deeply influenced by Harvard professor Irving
Babbitt, the leading figure in the moralistic Humanist movement, which
considered modern times degraded and aimed at making people "better"
than they currently were—meaning more rational and less emotionally
intense, more controlled, deliberate, measured. It was a movement that
interested the tempestuous, impulsive Lincoln not at all; he took Babbitt's
course, "Rousseau and Romanticism," and admired him as a teacher, but
came away untouched philosophically.

Varian Fry wasn't pleased with the arrival of Blackmur and Bandler on
the scene; he felt especially annoyed with Bandler and his high-toned,
programmatic attempts to "improve" humankind. Already harboring

years of resentment against Lincoln, Fry decided that *Hound and Horn* had gone seriously off track, and soon after Bandler's arrival he quit for good. In his place A. Hyatt Mayor and Francis Fergusson were invited to become involved with the magazine; Mayor would later become chief curator of prints at the Metropolitan Museum of Art (and author of the classic *Prints and People*), and Fergusson a renowned expert on the theater.

As for Blackmur, as soon as the offer of an annual salary of $2,340 arrived, he quit his bookstore job and went to work for *Hound and Horn* full-time. Just as rapidly he became essential to the magazine. Blackmur may have been young (though three years older than Lincoln), poor, and uncredentialed, but he was already well connected in the literary world. Many besides Lincoln—including Ezra Pound—had come to admire Blackmur's perception about contemporary literature, his uncommon ability to separate wheat from chaff in literary material not yet sorted out and certified by time. Later Lincoln would say of Blackmur, "I think he was the spine of the *Hound & Horn*."

It would be Blackmur who would accept Katherine Anne Porter's "Flowering Judas" for publication, who persuaded Kenneth Burke to submit his "Declamations," who relentlessly pestered his friend Malcolm Cowley to put him in touch with promising young writers. Over time, thanks to Lincoln as well as Blackmur, the likes of Allen Tate, Matthew Josephson, Edmund Wilson (though Wilson felt the magazine was "too abstract"), E. E. Cummings, Kay Boyle, William Carlos Williams, Yvor Winters, James Agee (his first published piece), and many other future well-known writers, would end up within *Hound and Horn*'s pages. The one major mistake Blackmur and Lincoln made, and Lincoln rued it long after, was rejecting the "Tunnel" section from Hart Crane's masterpiece, *The Bridge*.

After the stock market crash in 1929 and the deepening economic depression that followed, *Hound and Horn* could no longer afford a salary for Blackmur, which meant he could no longer afford to stay on full-time. His job went to Alan Stroock, a Harvard graduate who, thanks to family wealth, was able to waive any salary. Blackmur was deeply hurt—he must have felt that these rich Harvard boys could somehow have scraped together enough for him to live on—yet he continued to serve as a consulting editor and a regular contributor; and in 1932, after Bandler and Mayor had left, he once again became a chief mainstay of the magazine.

Given the accelerating economic depression, it was something of a miracle that *Hound and Horn* survived at all. The miracle had a name: Louis Kirstein. Due to the death of one of Filene's significant stockholders, a reorganization of the company had taken place in 1928, and Louis, along with the one other junior partner, were allowed to purchase additional common stock. Filene's sales reached an all-time high of more than forty-seven million dollars in 1929, and even during the worst years of the

Depression that followed the store never failed to show a profit or to take in less than thirty million a year.[2]

Still, some belt-tightening was necessary, both in the store and within the Kirstein family. In mid-1930 the *Hound and Horn* editors decided to try and save money by shifting printers from the Southworth Press in Maine, which had been "generous and kind," to the Rumford Press in New Hampshire. Southworth had been charging about sixty-five cents a copy for a run of 2,500, while Rumford's offer amounted to less than forty cents per copy for a run of 3,000. Since the magazine sold for fifty cents, and its advertising remained limited, the shift in printers was thought regrettable but necessary.

Simultaneously Lincoln and Bandler appealed to their fathers for additional yearly contributions of one thousand dollars each. In making his appeal to Louis, Lincoln emphasized what a pity it would be to shut down the magazine just as its reputation was spreading. "We are on sale," as of late May 1928, "at about 135 bookstores in America, 5 in England and 3 in France. Also Cuba, Mexico, Canada and Alaska—believe it or not." As well, extensive articles about the magazine had recently appeared in, among other places, the *World*, the *Christian Science Monitor*, the *New York Sun*, and the *Boston Globe*. "We feel very strongly," Lincoln wrote his father, "that we are doing something nobody else is at the present time . . . and that we can make a very important contribution to American art and letters."

Louis agreed, and fully, which perhaps came as something of a surprise given his lukewarm initial reaction to the magazine and his general lack of interest in literary and artistic matters. "I am quite as anxious as you are," he wrote Lincoln, "that the magazine should be continued . . . and agree that there is a place in the United States for it." But while providing the extra thousand dollars, Louis donned his hardheaded businessman's hat to remind his son—invoking Rose (who had now and then been privately sending Lincoln her own checks for the magazine) as if she were in agreement—that they expected him to repay the money, "although it may be in the dim and distant future." So distant, as Lincoln well knew, as likely to recede permanently over the horizon. Yet he dutifully agreed to Louis's terms, recognizing that in this instance, though certainly not always, paternal sternness was something of a pose.

His junior year at Harvard brought Lincoln pretty much everything he'd been hoping for and working toward. The classroom itself continued to hold limited interest for him, aside from an occasionally stimulating course—John Livingstone Lowes on Coleridge, Charles Grandgent on Dante—and his grades, accordingly, were never more than adequate (Alfred North Whitehead gave him a D+). But beyond the classroom Lincoln decidedly came into his own. Even his yearning to join the circle of those highly pedigreed, confident young men he so admired, and whose friendship he was convinced he'd never win, was realized.

It came about largely through chance. Standing in line for one of Harvard's ritual physical exams, he struck up a conversation with the undergraduate behind him. Both deplored their current off-campus living arrangements (the Harvard "house system" only came into existence in 1931, the year after Lincoln graduated), and the young man asked him whether he'd yet made plans for junior year. Lincoln said he'd leased an attic in an old house on Hawthorne Street and spontaneously asked him— he was exceedingly attractive, clearly one of the Lads—if he'd like to see it. The answer was yes. He liked the place, and the two agreed to room together starting in the fall of 1928. The young man's name was Francis Cabot Lowell. As Lincoln later wrote, "I no longer lacked a passport."[3]

Frank was the nephew of Harvard's president, A. Lawrence Lowell, and the personification of Brahmin high society. Lincoln greatly admired him, later writing that Frank was "a paragon, a three centuries' distillation of the best of Boston." Within a few months Frank took Lincoln home to Concord, and his parents soon put Lincoln's name on the roster of young men eligible for white-tie cotillions and debutante balls at the Somerset and Copley Plaza Hotels. Before long, he was being welcomed into the Beacon Hill homes of Boston's most exclusive clans—the Lowells, Shaws, Forbeses, and Ameses—and, when summer came, entertained at their private enclaves at Milton, Naushon, and Pride's Crossing.

Lincoln found Frank's parents "perfectly charming" and considered them "a great addition to my life." Father "Fred" Lowell, diffident and modest, would on rare occasions allow Lincoln to see his watercolors ("he has a great deal of talent," Lincoln wrote in his diary, "but lacks training and feeling for connection of planes"). Over time Lincoln became closer to the two Lowell daughters, Alice ("so self-possessed and cool") and the elegant Marianna, than to their brother, Frank. Alice was in fact Lincoln's first heterosexual bed partner.

Among the Lowells' weekend pastimes, horseback riding was a favorite and Lincoln, who'd learned to ride at Mina and Harry's place, became expert. He, Alice, and Marianna would sometimes ride for the entire day, once to the edge of Walden Pond, another time to the cottage in Lexington where Nathaniel Hawthorne had scratched his and his wife's names, and where the architect Jack Ames gave them tea while the horses cropped grass on the front lawn.

There were also archery contests, dancing in the moonlight, and assorted tea musicales. At one of them Alice and Marianna performed Elizabethan songs, and an aunt played a Bach concerto so movingly that Lincoln's "heart stood still and tears flowed" from his eyes—"a great and soft and somber moment." Apart from some traces of self-consciousness, and periodically feeling that he'd committed some gaucherie or other, especially when ice-skating or dancing, Lincoln invariably had "a lovely time."

Through his proliferating introductions, he also visited the Forbes family fairly often at Milton or Naushon. Cameron—"Uncle Cam"—Forbes had been governor of the Philippines after the Spanish-American War. He turned his front lawn at Milton into a closely mowed polo field, and took pride as well in composing music for the "Great Forbes Musical Comedy," which was, as Lincoln put it, "a sort of *vers de société musicale*."

At Naushon, Ralph Forbes headed a branch of the family that reveled in a far more strenuous life. They warmly welcomed Lincoln; as he wrote in his diary, he "never [had] a feeling in this dynastic dukedom of ever being anything but an honored guest, one having just slightly less claim on being kin than the rest of those present." And they included him in all their rugged outdoor activities, including sheepherding. At Naushon, Lincoln spent many days on horseback, riding along the shore to scare up sheep hiding among the boulders, forcing them into ravines where they could be counted as they passed in single file.

Some afternoons they would play "scout" in a mile-square plot in the woods, "tearing over the dead carpet of brown beech and oak leaves" lying on the ground, hiding, waiting—a repetition of rather than a respite from the rugged hours of herding. Even their after-dinner games of tag, played in the dark, involved breathless hiding and scuffling, sudden arms around the waist, tussles on the polar-bear rug, exhausting excitement. Lincoln loved all of it—"great relaxation of mind and spirit and body." He never felt bored, as he sometimes did with the Concord or Milton clans, where conversation could linger irritatingly long on such questions as "Why New York debutant parties were so much more stiff than those in Boston." Lincoln regarded the Naushon Forbeses as "friendly, simple folk approaching the vacuum of simplicity." Overall, Lincoln found life among the Brahmin upper class a great joy. As he freely confessed, he "savored every gilded moment up to its hilt," thoroughly enjoying the fact that he'd "successfully launched [him]self in Cambridge Society" and that he grew "from year to year in the *savoir vivre*."

His parents enjoyed it considerably less. They "adamantly refused" to meet Frank Lowell's parents because, as Lincoln chose to put it, "they maintained a shy superstition that no Gentile could ever be a 'real' friend to a Jew." Louis took Lincoln to lunch specifically to tell him, and "with some trace of rancor" (as Lincoln wrote in his diary), "how he expected that I would shortly forget I was a Jew boy. 'Jew boy' was his term." Rose even invited Lincoln to bring a friend home for "a Jewish dinner," in order, so Lincoln believed, "to offset the Lowell influence."

Lincoln sloughed off his parents' concern; they had, after all, brought him up to be non-observant, had sent him to schools that required chapel, and had raised no objection when he attended Midnight Mass with Christian friends or went caroling with them on Christmas Eve in Louisburg Square. Yet Lincoln would later claim that he'd felt all along that the gilded life was "a fictive veneer upon which I had no true claim. . . . I'd been hypnotized by a false position which I'd not dared define."

Yet this exculpatory hindsight may have been no less false: he'd liked and admired most of the individuals he'd met, not merely their social standing; and to have enjoyed being taken into their privileged circles was not, for a born outsider—a queer, Jewish intellectual—the worst of sins. In any case, soon after leaving Harvard, Lincoln would put Boston Brahmin society far behind him and would never look back. His hobnobbing with the elite, however—most of them far more crass and self-indulgent than the Lowells—would hardly cease; some of it would be the necessary and tedious adjunct of fund-raising for his assorted projects, but some would be, as it had been in Boston, the not-so-heinous pleasure of winning his way into aristocracies that birthright denied him but an aggressive ambition sought and his own charismatic brilliance validated.

On December 12, 1928, a memorable dinner meeting took place at Paul Sachs's splendid nineteenth-century home, Shady Hill, which had once been the residence of Charles Eliot Norton, the formidable earlier eminence in art history at Harvard whose influence still loomed large. Paul Sachs had moved into Shady Hill in 1915 after deciding to leave the family banking firm, Goldman Sachs, and devote himself full-time to a new career at Harvard in connoisseurship, teaching, and museum management. A combative, stocky man of great intelligence and occasional bombast, Sachs was equally well-connected in the worlds of art and finance and would become the mentor to a whole generation of upcoming scholars and curators.[4]

Lincoln had decidedly mixed feelings about Sachs, and felt, moreover, that Sachs personally disliked him. Yet he knew that Sachs's support would be essential if his latest brainstorm was to have a chance of success. Lincoln's tireless energy had remained unexhausted by a hectic social life, undergraduate course work, and the multiple demands of *Hound and Horn*, and he'd come up with a proposal to start a Society for Contemporary Art that would display modern works that neither the Boston Arts Society nor the Fogg had been willing to show. New York's famed Armory Show in 1913 had long since introduced Picasso, Cézanne, and other central figures in the modernist movement to the American public, but Boston's conservative art circles had continued to denounce modern art as "decadent" and to block its showing.

Having opened the pages of *Hound and Horn* to contemporary writing, Lincoln had become determined to find an outlet as well for contemporary art. Before approaching Sachs, he'd already enlisted two wealthy fellow undergraduates as allies: the ebullient, amusing, and (so Lincoln felt) essentially lightweight Eddie Warburg, already the owner of a Blue Period Picasso; and John Walker III, whom Lincoln had earlier enlisted to write reviews for *Hound and Horn* and who hung reproductions of Modigliani, Braque, and the like in his dorm room. Finally there was Agnes Mongan, in 1928 a recent Bryn Mawr graduate who was taking Sachs's "museum course" and would soon work as the cataloger of his sizable print and drawing collection, opening up a lifelong career at the Fogg. Walker, who would become Bernard Berenson's assistant at I Tatti, and later the director of the National Gallery in Washington, DC, fully credited Lincoln as the guiding spirit of the new enterprise, writing that he "was like a setter pointing out the coveys of genius."

Sachs was a close friend of Eddie's father, the financier and philanthropist Felix Warburg. But that wasn't the only reason he agreed to host the December 1928 dinner (to which Alfred Barr, Jr., already teaching a course at Wellesley called Contemporary Painting, was also invited). Both Sachs and Edward Waldo Forbes, the two directors of the Fogg, had come to feel embarrassed at Boston's insistent insularity. They weren't themselves strong adherents of modernism, nor were they eager to display its works on the walls of the Fogg, preferring to await the verdict of time. But they were feeling some pressure from a small group of undergraduates to show a friendlier face to modernism, as well as from a limited number of Boston Brahmins with a taste for the avant-garde—people like Lincoln's new friend Teddy Chanler.

The December dinner went well. After it Barr wrote Sachs that he'd been "much stirred by the discussion at Shady Hill" and was going to give "letters of introduction and various suggestions to Lincoln Kirstein. I shall do everything in my power to support this excellent scheme." And he did, though his teaching commitments at Wellesley made him unable to attend many of the innumerable meetings that followed. Still, Barr, as well as his close friend and longtime associate Jere Abbott, a young art historian, provided many leads and suggestions. As did Henry-Russell Hitchcock, already a close friend of both Lincoln's and of Barr's.

Compared with the turmoil that was an ongoing aspect of *Hound and Horn* (and perhaps its life's blood), setting up and running the Harvard Society for Contemporary Art proved a comparative cakewalk. Thanks to the active cooperation of Sachs and Forbes, a prestigious board of trustees was quickly put together; along with the two Fogg directors themselves, plus Sachs's banker brother, Arthur, the four additional members were John Nicholas Brown, a distinguished and wealthy collector and patron of medieval scholarship; Arthur Pope, a member of the Fogg teaching staff; Felix Warburg; and the affluent bibliophile Philip Hofer. By the second year, A. Conger Goodyear, the first president of New York City's Museum of Modern Art (Barr would be the first director) had also joined the board.

With so illustrious a group backing the Society, private collectors like

Chester and Maud Dale, Duncan Phillip, Samuel Lewisohn, Frank Crowninshield (the editor of *Vanity Fair*), and Lillie Bliss—shortly to become one of three founding patronesses of MoMA—as well as the cluster of avant-garde galleries and dealers centered mostly in New York City (including Downtown, Kraushaar, John Becker, Rehn, Valentine, and Weyhe), proved willing to loan works of art and to help in insuring, packing, and shipping them. And the Fogg helped on the receiving end. All this cooperation, as Lincoln would later put it, "was slightly disappointing, since the scandal we longed to evoke as daring pioneers eluded us."

Enough money was rapidly raised to allow for a quick start. For gallery space Lincoln and his friends rented two high-ceilinged rooms from the Harvard Cooperative on Massachusetts Avenue, decorated the walls with monk's cloth and applied "silver-paper squares set in alternating courses" on the ceilings. Each room was furnished with a large Monel metal-topped table that rested on four marble legs salvaged from a defunct ice-cream parlor. At the beginning of the second year, one of the tables, covered with modern Japanese handicrafts, jars, and vessels, crashed to the floor; it was then discovered that the exhibit had mistakenly been insured at its sales value—meaning that the Society earned a 100 percent profit on every broken item. (Some enterprises are mysteriously blessed from the onset.)

Within a mere two months of the dinner at Shady Hill, in February 1929, the Harvard Society for Contemporary Art opened its doors. Its first show, "Americans," was designed, as Lincoln wrote in the catalog, "as an assertion of the importance of American Art." It featured the works of fourteen older painters (including Ryder, Eakins, Henri, Bellows, Hopper, Sloan, Burchfield, Demuth, and Davies). A few of the lesser lights had never previously been exhibited in a public gallery, and none had been shown at either the Boston Arts Club or the Boston Museum of Fine Arts. Yet these were the artists who, in the opinion of the organizers, "have helped to create a national tradition in emergence, stemming from Europe but nationally independent."

Lincoln was well aware that these choices did not represent "allies of a genuine advance guard"; the possible exceptions were John Marin, Georgia O'Keeffe, and two of the three sculptors shown, the then virtually unknown Gaston Lachaise and the formally abstract Aleksandr Archipenko. During the Society's first year there would be more "revolutionary" shows—Calder's witty, now-world-famous *Circus* made out of wire, and an entire exhibit devoted to Buckminster Fuller's Dymaxion House.

Kirstein and his friends did feel themselves, in John Walker's words, "part of the new movement, discoverers and prophets of a new beauty." But they wanted to calm conservative fears and win an audience that could subsequently be introduced, as the Society soon made possible, to artists like Soutine, Noguchi, and de Chirico, to a wide range of modernist artistic expression—weaving, decorative arts, cartoons, stage design, photography, architecture, pottery—and to cutting-edge creative work being done in other cultures: by the second year the Society was offering shows on Modern Mexican Art (Rivera, Orozco) and Contemporary German Painting and Sculpture (Beckmann, Grosz, Klee, Kokoschka).

The temperate strategy paid off handsomely. The middle-of-the-road opening exhibit was praised by both the *Boston Herald* and the *Boston Globe*, as well as the *Harvard Crimson*, which patronizingly offered its approval of the organizers' "restraint." Yet as quietly contemporary as the opening show was, the *Boston Transcript* still managed to attack Hopper's painting of tenements: "By what pretense can such buildings have a claim on art, which, theoretically at least, is synonymous with beauty?" The depth of hostility to modernism in these years, with the partial exception of New York City, continued to be profound.

Yet thanks to the accessibility of the Society's initial choices, they did succeed in drawing considerable crowds. During the very first week, eleven hundred people viewed the exhibit, and attendance averaged 13,500 for the first two years. In 1929 alone, moreover, Lincoln and his friends managed to mount nine separate shows. When the Museum of Modern Art opened its doors in November 1929, with Alfred Barr, Jr., at the helm, it often reproduced, though in much expanded form, a number of the exhibitions inaugurated at the Harvard Society for Contemporary Art. At Hartford's Wadsworth Atheneum, too, Lincoln's friend A. Everett "Chick" Austin, Jr., the museum's modernist director, reproduced a number of exhibitions that had initially appeared at the Society. Lincoln's influence expanded still further when, in 1930, MoMA's trustees named him to its newly formed Junior Advisory Committee.

All told, Lincoln had compiled a remarkable record, made more so when placed in the context of simultaneously turning out *Hound and Horn*, of managing (somehow) to get passing grades in all his classes—and of being twenty-one years of age.

At the end of junior year, Lincoln allowed himself a two-month vacation in Europe—an active one, of course. His mother was traveling abroad with one of her sisters, and he promised that in August they'd meet up in Vienna. Prior to that he spent most of his time in London and Paris, looking up old friends, attending assorted cultural events, and making new contacts to advance his various projects. In London he went to see the Diaghilev ballet seven times in ten days, and had specially commissioned photographs taken of the company, later framing them in dark red mats to hang on the walls of the *Hound and Horn* office.[5]

He also had drawings made of the lead dancer Serge Lifar, who he saw perform that summer in several ballets: Massine's *Les Matelots,* and three Balanchine works: *La Chatte, Prodigal Son* (in which Lincoln felt the choreographer's "ingenuity" sometimes "ran away with him"), and the seminal *Apollon Musagète,* the last (now known as *Apollo*) with a score by Stravinsky. Lincoln intended the Lifar drawings to serve as illustrations for an essay, "The Diaghilev Period," that he began to write that summer; his first major piece on the dance, it would appear in *Hound and Horn* in its July–September 1930 issue. The impressive finished essay would become in turn the trial run for Lincoln's book-length history, *Dance,* which he would publish in 1935.

In several other senses the essay on Diaghilev echoed eerily into the future. Many besides Lincoln recognized by 1930 that George Balanchine was a brilliant choreographer, but Lincoln's analysis of the special nature of his gifts was unusually, if not uniquely, focused: not only, in his view, were Balanchine's "energy and invention prodigious," Lincoln wrote, "but he well understood the dangers attendant on the unintelligent if enter- taining implications of the 'clever,' acrobatic Massine. . . . [Balanchine's] dances had the spareness, the lack of decoration which is by no means a lack of refinement . . . in *The Cat* and in *Apollo* [he] was leading out of mere ingenuity into a revivified, purer, cleaner classicism . . . just as Stravinsky's music transcended Delibes and Tchaikovsky . . . so Balanchine has tran- scended Petipa."

The qualities, moreover, that Lincoln chose to emphasize in his description of Diaghilev's personality oddly echo his own: "His inherent gifts of taste, his consciousness of the chic, his appreciation of social snob- bery and his passion for the beauty of surprise and of youth—these in a combination of brilliant energies and practical qualifications made him the isolated genius that he was." Lincoln went on in the essay to express his fear that without Diaghilev, who had died from diabetes in 1929, "the future of the dance is very black indeed."

There was yet another remarkable tie-in during that same summer of 1929. While in Venice, Lincoln hooked up with Agnes Mongan, and they hired a car to drive along the Brenta Canal in search of a lost Tiepolo that Lincoln was hell-bent on finding. When they came to the last building on the canal, the Villa Foscari, Agnes offered to present the letter of intro- duction she had stating that she was a member of the Fogg staff. The owner of the villa welcomed them cordially but explained that friends from the Russian ballet were due shortly for tea, and that he himself was still greatly upset by Diaghilev's death and his burial the day before.

Lincoln and Agnes looked at each other dumbfounded. The previous day (August 19, 1929), they'd gone to a Greek church and had seen (in Agnes's words) "this fantastic funeral, all designed, we learned later, by Worth." Following the church service they'd watched the great black catafalque being placed on a gondola with a Greek cross in red, with the gondoliers all wearing black with red sashes. That cortège, they now realized, had been for Diaghilev.

The collapse of Diaghilev's company, the Ballets Russes, followed soon after his death. In his *Hound and Horn* essay on the Russian impresario, Lincoln, in an uncanny bit of divination, expressed his particular concern that should the Ballets Russes fail, prospects were dismal for Balanchine ever finding a venue in which further to develop his stunning gifts. Yet if the dissolution of the Ballets Russes was arguably a disaster for the dance at the time, it unexpectedly opened a door through which Lincoln would, in a few short years, step. Though he would never describe it this way, the dream he'd begun quietly, inchoately, to nurture—of himself taking on the role of an American Diaghilev—had now suddenly presented itself as not merely a possibility but, for someone who adored the ballet above all the arts, something of a vital responsibility.

Since 1927 Lincoln and T. S. Eliot had occasionally corresponded about matters concerning *Hound and Horn*. Now, in the summer of 1929, Lincoln finally met Eliot in person. Ezra Pound had warned him in advance by mail that Eliot was "crazy with dope & his wife," but Lincoln, as he reported to Blackmur, found him "charming and . . . very communicative—not only personally, but about the *Criterion* which has recently doubled its circulation."

Also while in London, Lincoln renewed ties with Raymond Mortimer and David Garnett, both of whom promised to write for *Hound and Horn*. Garnett told him that T. E. Lawrence's *The Seven Pillars of Wisdom* was "the greatest book ever written by a man of action"; Lincoln read it immediately and was "inclined to agree with him. Lawrence is the only person alive," he wrote Blackmur "I really would want to know—i.e. who is a character." Within a few years Lincoln would be corresponding with Lawrence, as well as writing about him, though the two would never meet.

During his time in Paris, Lincoln finally met Gurdjieff. His friend Payson Loomis, who was at work translating *The Herald of Coming Good* into English, had urged Lincoln this time around to take his courage in his hands and (as he had failed to do on two previous visits) actually stay for a few days at Le Prieuré, Gurdjieff's "Institute for the Harmonious Development of Man" at Fontainebleau. The experience proved "mysterious, wonderful and inexplicably terrifying," and would inaugurate, as it had for a significant number of other writers and intellectuals of the period, including Katherine Mansfield (who died at Le Prieuré), Jean Toomer (the African American writer), and Kathryn Hulme, a long-lasting and profound effect.

As a young man Lincoln had frequently announced himself as resolutely secular, an avowed atheist. Yet as early as 1923, when attending the Berkshire School, he'd written in his diary, "in chapel I prayed, which shows what a sniveling little coward I am. I go about bravely saying in my superb atheistical way, 'there is really no God you know.' And in reality I am too scared to believe it. I'm too weak to have nothing." (Already attuned, perhaps, to his potential instability, Lincoln found the authoritative appealing—whether it took an unconventional form, as with Gurdjieff, or a traditional one, as in the classical ballet.) Once, during a family dinner party a few years later, one of the guests told Lincoln that he was "too intellectual"; annoyed, and perhaps to parry the accusation as well as to indulge his penchant for hyperbole, he announced to the assembled guests that one day "I might become a Roman Catholic"—which, disappointingly, was let pass without comment or challenge.

But it wasn't mere bravado when, as a freshman at Harvard, he wrote in his diary, "I had an odd brainstorm—seeing myself completely catholicized—not to form but converted to idea of conversion—odd sensation." After further thought he "decided it was not so much catholicism as being under the influence of a man like [the French Thomist philosopher Jacques] Maritain or Gurdjieff. I seem to have a subconscious will to sink into that kind of domination; almost eager for it. And I am afraid of it, too . . . more will have to happen before this pimple is burst."

Ten months later he continued to mull over possibilities: "Conversation about mysticism as sentimentality. My distrust of it but leaning towards it . . . desire for authority tangible or intangible." Yet his ambivalence remained; he warned a fellow student who had become interested in Gurdjieff that "this Gurdjieff awareness business was pushing him to a destroying isolation"; that he was being "still very adolescent." Yet Lincoln (as he would later write) felt that "in a small way, I had been attracted, readied and was waiting."

Loomis, who was in residence at Le Prieuré when Lincoln arrived in the summer of 1929, helped him get his bearings, though his own unpredictable behavior—de rigueur for a Gurdjieffian—was sometimes disorienting. Over the next two days, as Lincoln experienced a seemingly capricious set of unexpected experiences, his emotions hopscotched from terror and depression to intense peacefulness and joy. First came "The Dance," then "The Bath," then "The Feast," then "The Goodbye."

Seated on a pair of tufted saddlebags in a large room with an earthen floor covered with layers of Persian and Central Asian carpets, which also draped the windows and walls, Lincoln and Loomis, along with a few children scattered about, watched what he initially thought was a "performance." Two dozen men and women, in pajamas belted around the waist,

moved "with mortal seriousness" through a set pattern of repeated movements, mutely counting off the precise measures. "Monotonous," Lincoln
thought for the first ten minutes. Then "the patterns became far more
complex," the sequence of hand signs and shifting steps "accentuated by a
steady rhythm." Then, after more than an hour, the dancers suddenly, "in
one thunderous surge . . . went berserk, and racing, with a startling jump
as from a catapult . . . came hurtling straight at" him—until a voice outside
his line of vision yelled out "*Stop!*" The dancers stumbled, then straightened up and quietly left the room. Lincoln felt severely jarred: "What on
earth was going on here? . . . the violent collective rush toward me . . . gave
me a theatrical shudder to which no dance or drama that I had seen could
compare. It seemed less of a game than a—what? An event? An inexplicable rite? A spectacle?"

"The Bath" further intensified his experience. When he entered the
steam room with Loomis, the first sight that greeted him proved a
shocker: on a slate slab "the raw body of an obese, dark-pink male, hairy
and with his belly down" was being stretched on either side by two adult
nude men. A little boy was gleefully "dancing a jig" on the back of the
man, who seemed to be enjoying it all. When he got up Lincoln saw that
he wasn't "as old or fat" as he had thought. But the man was no beauty
with "his Mongol features, moustaches of dank ferocity . . . [and] with
hairy epaulets and matted paunch."

It was Gurdjieff. He ordered tea, looked over at Lincoln, and asked,
"You? All right?" The voice sounded kind, and Lincoln nodded yes. Gurdjieff then stared at the naked Lincoln, his eyes raking him "with the
heartlessness of an X-ray." But rather than grow alarmed, Lincoln felt "a
superior sympathy from him. There was no negation in his inspection and
I felt no need to cringe." Gurdjieff turned to Loomis: "Let him dress."

That evening in the main-floor salon came "The Feast." Some thirty
people resident at Le Prieuré were present and mostly silent. Gurdjieff,
seemingly oblivious to them, sat in the middle of one side of a long table
covered with food, some of it recognizable and enticing, some of it, like
"the jerked bear's meat," repellent-looking "patent leather." The main
course was "garlicky and bloody" baby lamb—with the sheep's bare skull
still attached, and split down the center to reveal its glistening brain; at
one point Gurdjieff dipped his hands into the skull and extracted some of
the brain to give to one of the children, who apparently swallowed it down
without comment or protest. Suddenly Lincoln heard Gurdjieff speaking
to him: "You, Little Father. Take." A long serving fork, with two "black
raisins"—the sheep's eyes—abruptly appeared in front of Lincoln's face.
He took them and swallowed, "blinked, and survived." Gurdjieff smiled.

Huge layers of delicious brown pastry, soaked in brandy, followed. And
after that Armagnac—in immense quantities (Gurdjieff was "a firm
believer in the benevolent therapy of very strong liquor") and accompa-

nied by a series of toasts to assorted kinds of "idiots," to "ordinary" idiots, "zigzag" idiots, "square" idiots, "round" idiots, and, as the fifth or sixth toast—with Gurdjieff staring directly at Lincoln—"to compassionate idiots, and, incidentally, Monsieur, to you." Lincoln had often enough been drunk at Harvard, where the heavy consumption of bootleg liquor was the equivalent of a passport to acceptance. But he'd never been *this* drunk. Lifted up to be taken off to bed, he passed a smiling Gurdjieff: "Sleep well, Little Father."

Lincoln awoke with a dreadful headache and a sense of guilt "at what I might have done or undone." But that soon passed over into a delicious feeling of "swarming euphoria." Before returning to Paris, where he'd made an appointment for that afternoon to meet Ezra Pound for the first time, he asked to say good-bye to Gurdjieff. The interview turned into a befuddling cat-and-mouse game, with Gurdjieff ambiguously demanding payment for, among other things, the two sheep's eyes Lincoln had eaten, and casually letting him know, after Lincoln explained his return to Paris as necessary in order to meet Ezra Pound, that he'd known Pound for years and that Pound called his Persian melon soup "clean like Piero della Francesca, compare to shit-color Rembrandt."

Once Lincoln was on the train, he discovered, to his horror, that he'd left his address book back at Le Prieuré. Trying to conjure up Pound's address by memory, he careened in a cab all over Paris in an attempt to locate his apartment. To no avail. The two men would never meet face-to-face. Yet Pound soon became *Hound and Horn*'s international editor, a post he filled with a predictable fusillade of one-sided abuse—what Lincoln called his "tyrannical generosity." Pound cheerfully used his own substitute title, *Bitch & Bugle*, when referring to the magazine, and insistently demanded that the editors publish various of his followers and hangers-on: Adrian Stokes, Ralph Cheever Dunning, Basil Bunting, Joe Gould, and the like, a demand the editors usually resisted (Lincoln felt that Pound wanted to turn the magazine into his "personal house-letter"). *Hound and Horn* did publish in 1930, and gratefully, Pound's *Cantos XXVIII–XXX*—though Lincoln would later say that he "could never make head nor tail" of them.

There would be only a few subsequent meetings with Gurdjieff in later years, and none that replicated the impact of the initial one; the 1929 visit to Le Prieuré came at a time when Lincoln was feeling "at a peak of disorientation, when many choices appeared open while none commanded," when, as he put it in his diary, "my idea of disintegration and anarchy" had, during the preceding weeks, "been so strong." Nor would he ever find Gurdjieff's published writings (*Beelzebub*, *Remarkable Men*, and so on) a source of particular enlightenment; he could never manage to get through any of his books. Years later he would even write that "a vast mass of his verbiage can be read as a preposterous parody of quasi-scientific speculation" that in no sense amounted to a philosophical system.

But then, Lincoln had little taste for abstract thought of any kind and always found Western philosophical texts equally unreadable. If anything, he thought Gurdjieff's writings had the edge. He wasn't preoccupied with abstraction, epistemology, or semiotics; "his teaching was in the tradition of ambiguous, subsidiary and subliminal meaning." Lincoln willingly granted that his metaphysics was "nothing less than nonsense"—but in the same sense that the Sufi masters, and Sufi dancing, were what Western rationalists would describe as "pretentious obfuscation, impure poetry, or nonsense." Lincoln adored the fact that Gurdjieff primarily described himself as "a teacher of dancing."

He left Le Prieuré in 1929 "with a bundle of unanswered riddles," and without feeling that any of Gurdjieff's "cosmologies or metaphysical hieroglyphs [had] imposed themselves in any depth." Still, he felt "gravely impressed by concepts," as he wrote much later in life, that "stayed with me at instructive intervals ever since." Over time he came to feel that Gurdjieff was "a true magician," and "nothing will rob me of my conviction of his selflessness and benevolence . . . a personage who, of all of those I have ever met, defied licensing."

The "concepts" Lincoln left with, and that he would ever after retain, were an "amorphous load" of Gurdjieff's precepts that were peculiarly suited to his own temperament, "a few formulae" that he knew "sounded naive" when spelled out, but which he nonetheless found "saved time, worry, and waste motion"—like "never explain, never apologize." What centrally appealed to him was the view, which he'd often enough felt about those who surrounded him, that "most men are sleepwalkers, that most lives pass in mute, self-blinded somnambulism, that there is a factor which compels us to be pleased to exist passively without comprehension."

Gurdjieff offered a strategy for counteracting this condition: "systematic assaults on habitual response," along with an "endless, measureless responsibility" that aimed not at "perfection" but rather at the achieving of one's "God-assigned potential . . . this was as much salvation as one could expect." Which meant not sappy, content-free "happiness" but the realization that "freedom from unconsidered accretions of habit was the only real liberty; the salvation of consciousness . . . the process of self-questioning, was the sole stern pursuit."

What was critical, Gurdjieff had said, was "self-remembering," the awareness of one's core "idiocy," of "happiness" as "no more [of] a steady state than weather," of the needed "constancy of recognizing and enduring suffering," of the self as "a treacherous structure, never to be defined as a single unity, but braided of diverse strains responding to crises which alter, torment, or strengthen the forged centrality." In his own case, Lincoln felt that he'd specifically learned to accept "the onus of difference," to forgive himself for having been born "rich, privileged [and] what passed for 'well-educated,' " and to manage his "egotistical preoccupations with as little guilt as possible."

Though his formal ties to Gurdjieff and his followers would remain tenuous, Lincoln would, over time, come to regard Gurdjieff as "exerting more influence on my behavior than anyone, including my parents." As Lincoln wrote many decades later, "Under the influence of a force amounting to a revelation, I surrendered to whatever of his system I could grasp. The shock of his first impact would be tempered by time, but served, never wholly diminished, as a storage battery." Forty-five years after his stay at Le Prieuré, Lincoln, in 1974, urged his then-lover, the much younger Alex Nixon, to pursue his incipient attraction to Gurdjief-fian principles. But he warned Alex that "his teaching is . . . agonizing . . . he teaches conscious suffering. How to use disaster, mania, guilt, greed against themselves . . . [it] is material of transcendent energy. . . . But if understood in its essence [it] is very terrifying . . ." Payson Loomis, for one, ended up writing speeches for Norman Vincent Peale, the "vulgarian prophet" (as Lincoln called him), preacher to the very audience of som-nambulists that Gurdjieff had wanted to awaken.

Diaghilev and Gurdjieff. Two guides for ambition and survival. Two prophets of art and consciousness. Two molds into which Lincoln could pour his own youthful experiences to date and produce a figure hence-forth more distinctively himself.

Lincoln was now nearly ready. The jagged, unwieldy pieces from which he'd tried to create a satisfying persona—writer, entrepreneur, painter, editor, organizer, poet—could lose their fractious urgency and coalesce around an achievable, sustained, purposeful mission.

PART TWO

Beginnings

CHAPTER FIVE

New York

(1929–1931)

Fʀᴏᴍ ᴀʙᴏᴀʀᴅ the SS *Majestic* on his way home from Europe, Lincoln wrote his close friend Agnes Mongan that "a violent nervous breakdown I had felt coming on all summer" had been "arrested" and he was now feeling "pleasantly preoccupied with the state of my own soul." Similarly, when writing to Dick Blackmur in late August, Lincoln described his summer as "peeling off of the onion skins around myself—in the center will probably be a happy nothing"—and he particularly emphasized that he now saw clearly that he'd "been bound by my possessions, or interests that I have invented, to keep me off my proper track," the "track" unspecified. To neither friend did Lincoln mention Gurdjieff, as either catalyst or deterrent for his near-breakdown.[1]

Whatever plans and emotions were stirring internally, there was still one more year to get through at Harvard. Lincoln had long since given up hope of deriving much profit from formal class work. *Hound and Horn* and the Harvard Society for Contemporary Art, however, were together nearly enough to absorb his overabundant energy—along with his ongoing socializing among Boston's elite and his emerging involvements with both the Museum of Modern Art (which would open its doors on November 9, 1929) and the initial planning for what would become Rockefeller Center.

Of his two current preoccupations, the Society for Contemporary Art and *Hound and Horn*, the latter was by far the more difficult and demanding enterprise, given the constant clashes among the editors, the lurching shifts in personnel and philosophy, and the ongoing predicaments of raising money and of satisfying contributors hungry for acknowledgment—and cash (*Hound and Horn* paid a penny a word for prose, two for verse). Of the contending prima donnas who marched on and off *Hound and Horn*'s stage, none was more contentious than Ezra Pound. Though he served as foreign adviser for less than two years (1930–31), he managed to stir up enough trouble—along with offering a fair amount of shrewd advice—to keep Lincoln ricocheting between annoyance and gratitude.

Pound in 1930 was no longer at the influential center of the literary avant-garde or editorially connected to such seminal periodicals as *Poetry*,

The Egoist, Blast, The Dial, and the *Little Review.* Nor was he any longer close to such titans as T. S. Eliot and James Joyce or able to solicit unpublished material from other major writers of the period. By the time his connection to *Hound and Horn* began, Pound's contacts had greatly diminished—and his personality grown more cantankerous. From Rapallo, Italy, where he lived most of the time, Pound fired off a constant stream of acerbic, accusatory—and occasionally grudgingly admiring—letters to *H&H*'s editors, and to Lincoln in particular. The magazine, according to Pound, was guilty of publishing the wrong people, while ignoring or minimizing his own current candidates for immortality: Robert McAlmon, John Rodker, R. C. Dunning, Basil Bunting, Louis Zukovsky, and Wyndham Lewis—hardly the equivalents of Eliot or Joyce.

The relationship with Pound had initially begun when, in the spring of 1929, Blackmur wrote him to solicit a new, unpublished *Canto* for *Hound and Horn.* Pound had replied that none was currently available, and had gone on to ask whether the magazine was prepared to do more than either the recently defunct *Dial* (which Pound claimed had "gained not a damn thing by its excess of caution") or Eliot's *Criterion* (it had "printed in seven years about enough live stuff for one").

Over the next year and a half, Pound managed to be dismissive of just about everyone *Hound and Horn* published ("too much space allotted to discussion of trype [*sic*]. Slop 2nd rate"), and quite a few that it hadn't. Aldous Huxley was "largely blah," Matthew Josephson was a "waste of time," Archibald MacLeish—a neighbor of Mina's with whom Lincoln was becoming personally friendly—had "the disease of facility," Edmund Wilson and Gilbert Seldes did little but "float with the current," the Humanists Paul Elmer More and Irving Babbitt, along with Walter Lippmann, were "equally dead," St. John Perse was "pewk," Raymond Mortimer's reviews were decided on the basis of the "social connections of the reviewed," Dudley Fitts was "very nearly hopeless," and so on.

Lincoln, still only twenty-three years old, handled all this with quite remarkable grace and cogency. He thanked Pound several times over for being frank and outspoken, and frequently reiterated the editors' gratitude to him for his critiques and suggestions ("your recent letters . . . are of the utmost aid to us in every possible way . . . you really mean a great deal to us"). Lincoln also went out of his way to flatter Pound: "I need your advice very much"; "I am amazed that your influence has been as circumscribed in America as it is."

Lincoln did end up using an occasional bit of poetry or prose from one or another of Pound's favorites, but on the whole, impressively, he stood his ground and stuck to his opinions. He wrote Pound straight out that *H&H*'s editors "really don't much care" for Basil Bunting (in his poetry "echoes of yourself preclude its own integrity") or most of the other writers Pound had been pushing insistently. "I think Wyndham Lewis is a cuckoo," Lincoln wrote Pound. "If he had become a painter I'm sure he would have been first rate." As for Pound's special favorite, McAlmon, "I just can't agree with you. I do not think you can print a whole mass of, well, careless writing for the sake of a few pages . . . the criticism he sent us was lousy. And a short story was like Galsworthy. . . . I'm damned if I think his stuff is any good."

Lincoln also boldly defended some of the writers Pound had chosen to attack. He acknowledged that MacLeish "*does* want to please too much" and was "too sensitive to criticism." But he insisted that "underneath his slightly polished exterior beats an excellent heart & brain," and that his long epic poem in progress, *Conquistador,* was "a very ingenious and able and sustained piece of writing." (When the poem was published, in 1932, Lincoln reviewed it in *Hound and Horn,* calling it "the finest consecutive narrative since [Robert Browning's] *The Ring and the Book*"; the poem won the Pulitzer Prize that year.) As for Raymond Mortimer and the charge that he was a snob, Lincoln replied that Pound was "so suspicious of a certain kind of authority" that he tended to unfairly slap the label "snobbism" on it: "When I can find someone else who can give me the information about London better than he can, I will take it. I've looked, too. . . . Your dislike is only another sort of rough hearty snobbism."

Lincoln defended not only individual writers but the United States itself against some of Pound's more scabrous attacks. "You know," he wrote Pound in the spring of 1930, "you really ought to come back to America before it's too late. Your idea of it is absolutely not the right one." Lincoln claimed, with considerable exaggeration (one of the more deeply ingrained of his character traits), that New York publishers were "actually *crazy* to get their hands on *any* new work . . . it was *never* easier for the most avant-garde writer with an atom of something to get published." He added that three contributors to *H&H* had, on the strength of a single contribution to the magazine, already been signed up for books.

In general Lincoln also defended New York City—where he would soon settle—and with élan: "Something extraordinary is constantly happening to you . . . some excitement always tells you that the place is humming. . . . You can't deny it—because you don't know." Yes, the city's colossal energy was often misdirected; yes, many of its inhabitants were "loathsome people," but at least, Lincoln insisted (in something of a non sequitur) "we have not got anyway the lousy piddling drip of Surrealism (Chirico excepted), the Miros, late Picassos, Ernsts, etc.—in my mind the ultimate bunk." What New York, and the country as a whole, did have, he went on, in a burst of patriotic fervor that was far more characteristic of his father than of himself, was, among other things, "talking movies— 2 or 3 out of 365 are *swell*—a good average. Eisenstein is coming to Hollywood. . . . Hemingway writes . . . for *Fortune,* with pictures by Goya. Mrs. John D. Rockefeller, Jr. is commissioning Diego Rivera . . . it's not the Millennium, but it's the release of valuable interacting surfaces . . . if I've been over-emphatic it's only to try and make you see how much you miss."

To which Pound replied, with acumen, "I can only repeat my malediction: God eternally damblast [*sic*] a country that . . . can not support a single printing press which will print stuff that people like me want to read: i.e., regardless of immediate fiscal profit. . . . Even when some vague and good natured millionaire 'founds' something with allegedly cultural or creative intent, the endowment is handed over to academic eminences who are as incapable of picking a first class painter or writer as I shd. be of making a sound report on a copper mine."

Quite a dustup, with the twenty-three-year-old Lincoln standing toe-to-toe with a literary eminence twice his age and not giving an inch. Somehow their brusque give-and-take didn't lead to an immediate break. Still, with such divergent tastes and views, and with Pound in a state of perpetual irritability, the two men weren't destined to work in tandem for long. Pound soon enough built up, and in part invented, a sufficient number of grievances to produce, by the spring of 1931, his angry resignation from *Hound and Horn*.

The final break began when Bernard Bandler rejected out of hand Pound's "Terra Italica," a rambling commentary that veered from Italian publishing politics to the evolution of religion. Bandler's letter grandly announced that "I have no notion of what you are trying to do"; Pound's irascibility was then heightened by Bandler's failure to return the manuscript promptly. Lincoln had himself been developing something of a love-hate relationship with Bandler. He admired his intelligence, his "disarming, grinning ubiquity," and generally felt that Bandler's affinity for philosophical abstraction was a needed complement to his own distaste for such material. Yet he also felt that Bandler "refused to face his own personal shortcomings, and was completely incompetent to judge any poem or story"—which didn't prevent him from periodically intruding (as with Pound) into what Lincoln viewed as his own domain.

Early in 1931 Bandler would begin to lose interest in *Hound and Horn*, deciding first to devote himself to rabbinical studies and then to becoming a psychiatrist. But his departure from the magazine came too late to placate Ezra Pound—not that any one thing, including complete capitulation, could have. Pound and *Hound and Horn* no longer needed each other to the extent they once had. By 1931 Pound had become the associate editor of Samuel Putnam's *New Review*, and Lincoln had begun developing ties to two emerging, influential young Americans, Yvor Winters and Allen Tate.

Pound's grievances against *Hound and Horn* had by 1931 grown to include the magazine's rejection of his companion Olga Rudge's translation of Cocteau's "Le Mystère Laic (an appreciation of de Chirico's paintings)"; a mix-up about payment to him for the poems *Hound and Horn* had published (the check—for $82.50!—had indeed been sent but never received); and—the capstone to Pound's bitterness—Dudley Fitts's review in *H&H*'s January–March 1931 issue of his recently published *Cantos*. Fitts praised the *Cantos* as "memorable work [which] . . . should be universally read" but also characterized them as filled with "scatological invective," and as carrying "very little conviction."

That was it. Pound promptly wrote Lincoln that Fitts was a fool and that "IF by chance he understands ANYTHING he omits to manifest his understanding." In a final kiss-off letter, he wrote Lincoln that "It only remains for me to express sincere regret for the time wasted by me in correspondence with H & H. . . . I wish I had never heard of yr / magazine." In response Lincoln wrote that he "was shocked and horrified" to receive the letter, but if Pound felt the way he did, "That's all there is to say." He'd done his best, Lincoln added, "to take your suggestions and advice for which I have been very grateful always," but then noted, with a bit of justifiable tartness: "I am not particularly surprised that you should feel the way you do about us, since you generally behave this way about every magazine in which you have any initial interest." He closed with an even-tempered bit of statesmanship: "I am only glad that you held on to us as long as you did. If you ever have anything more that you want to say through us or change your mind in regard to us, it would be more than O.K."

Pound returned the courtesy by referring to Lincoln (in a letter to a third party) as "Stinkum Cherrystein, y'know," the anti-Semitic overtones obvious.

In 1930 alone Louis Kirstein contributed $5,250 to *Hound and Horn* and Rose gave $4,000; in today's inflationary terms that would amount to something like $90,000. On top of this Lincoln himself had savings accounts and securities that brought him nearly $2,500 in dividends in 1930, as well as a direct allowance from his father that amounted to an additional $4,275. And then there were the occasional "little gifts" from both parents—for car payments, garage costs, clothing, and books—that in 1930 alone amounted to the considerable sum of $3,652.[2]

All of which allowed Lincoln to treat money with casual indifference or, when temporarily short, impatient annoyance—attitudes that the mounting millions of Americans who were finding it increasingly difficult to put food on the table could hardly have imagined. In the early years of the Depression (which would hit new depths in 1932, and then again in 1937), the Kirstein family barely felt the pinch. After the crash, Louis Kirstein and Fred Lazarus led the forces in favor of an aggressive expansion that would soon eventuate in the successful holding company Federated Department Stores.

Even as he continued to prosper, Louis kept in mind the importance of community service and modeled that role for his children. In 1930 he gave $200,000 to the Boston Public Library, on whose board he served for many years, to create a branch library devoted to business. His philanthropic largesse led Harvard, three years later, to award him an honorary degree—an accolade he, a largely self-taught man, cherished above the many others he received during his lifetime. But he never rested on his laurels. As the plight of the Jews deepened in Germany, he worked hard, often alongside his friend Felix Frankfurter, to increase aid and awareness. And as the plight of American workers intensified during the Depression years, he staunchly defended trade unionism and, in his own Filene's bailiwick, kept wages higher than almost all his retail competitors.

There were some on the Left who denounced Filene's for running what was essentially "a company union," and there were others (including for a time, his own son Lincoln) who thought Louis's attitude toward the working class fundamentally patronizing, in essence a holdover from an earlier ethos that considered the sending of Thanksgiving turkey dinners to the tenements as the ultimate definition of "good works." But most of the labor leaders of the day would not have agreed. Sidney Hillman, for one, head of the Amalgamated Clothing Workers of America and increasingly a personal friend of Louis's, wrote him late in 1929, "to thank you for the very great assistance you have been to me . . . from the time when, over ten years ago we organized the Rochester Clothing Industry."

In that same year Louis, moving beyond a defense of trade unionism, gave a speech at Boston's Museum of Fine Arts in which he argued strenuously for extending museum hours in order to make them more convenient for working people; "no one class of society," he argued, "has a monopoly on 'good taste.' " And in some of the darkest hours of the Depression, he publicly insisted that "the underprivileged . . . find themselves in [a desperate] position not because of any inherent lack but because of forces entirely beyond their control, to maladjustments in the social and economic structure which [have] deprived them of the opportunity to be self-supporting and useful citizens of the community." As for the well-to-do, Louis bluntly asserted that "their favored position is just as accidental as is the tragic position of the under-privileged." The Socialist leader Norman Thomas couldn't have put it more succinctly. And when Louis called for "guaranteeing an annual wage or income to our employees," he was sounding a note that even today would be considered radical.

Despite these sentiments—and he announced them publicly in a variety of venues—Louis never developed even a remote interest in socialism. He'd simply been too deeply imprinted with mainstream ideology, including its structural assumption that "capitalism is an innately superior engine for economic progress." Indeed, in the early thirties, when Lincoln began to exhibit left-wing leanings, Louis would sternly lecture him on the perils of Bolshevism.

It was Louis and Rose's generosity that allowed *Hound and Horn*, almost alone among the "little magazines" of the day, to survive during the deepening economic depression. Even so, as Lincoln put it in May 1930, "we are as usual in a bad way financially," and "currently in need of finding an additional $4,000 a year in order to keep paying contributors and printers with reasonable promptness." Lincoln thought up several schemes for sustaining the magazine's solvency: combining *H&H* with another small magazine or with a printing firm; putting out a series of reprints or short books; shifting from a quarterly to a monthly. But none of these ideas panned out, for the same reason that had produced them: financial stringency. "It is a lousy job trying to run a magazine," Lincoln wrote, "I think I shall take up paperhanging. It goes on so smooth."

Lincoln also faced financial difficulty with his other baby, the Harvard Society for Contemporary Art. Paul Sachs ascribed the periodic shortfalls to bad management, but Lincoln rejected the charge and claimed that he'd written "hundreds of page-long personal letters" to prospective donors; he insisted that "people have not supported it as well now [late 1930] as in the beginning." Still, he gave some inadvertent credence to Sachs's complaint when he confessed to his diary that the Society now "bores me . . . it alone keeps me from New York." The novelty had apparently worn off and Lincoln's attention to the Society was slackening— probably because it hadn't produced the requisite amount of scandalous fireworks to suit his theatrical nature.

However, the Society had a much less difficult time sustaining itself financially than did the *Hound and Horn;* its patrons were more numerous than those of *H&H*, and drawn more from the ranks of the super-rich, those who tend to be merely brushed by mundane catastrophes like an economic depression. The Society had an additional advantage in being able to loan its shows to other museums and galleries—thus sharing original insurance costs while expanding the audience for modernist art. Chick Austin at the Wadsworth Atheneum proved particularly helpful. In 1930 he remounted four of the Society's shows after they'd completed their run in Cambridge: Buckminster Fuller's Dymaxion House, Modern Mexican Art, Modern German Art, and the pathbreaking International Photography, which aimed at demonstrating that photographs were as much an art form as painting or sculpture, and which included the work of Berenice Abbott, Walker Evans, Paul Strand, and Tina Modotti, among others.

Throughout his final year at Harvard, Lincoln continued to enjoy himself among the Brahmin elite ("Have been going out to parties, etc.," he wrote

in his diary, "and having a fine time"). His initial passport into high society, Frank (Francis Cabot) Lowell, spent his senior year in Germany, and
in any case (at least so Lincoln felt) preferred "his Concord frogs and
dogs" to people. But though Lincoln and Frank no longer roomed
together and rarely saw each other, Lincoln maintained his other contacts, often going out with Alice Lowell, Will Forbes ("The grave deliberation of his courtesy never fails to make a strong appeal to me"),
Prissy Fairchild, or Pauline Shaw. He continued to be especially drawn
to Ruth Forbes's husband, Lyman Paine, deciding at one point that he
was "absolutely gaga" about him and for some time nursing a profound, unrequited (though Lyman did once kiss him on the lips) passion.
Once in a great while Lincoln had sex with one or two of the women in his
social set, or began to: "She looked very fine in the dark room, her dress
down to her waist. . . . My excitement so conscious of itself as to hardly
merit the name. This wretched constant self-consciousness ruins literally
everything. . . ."

But by the time he graduated from Harvard in June 1930, life in
Boston had begun to pale, the feeling mounting in him that the place was,
ultimately, inbred and provincial, "easy and dead." In contrast to New
York City, where he began to spend increasing amounts of time and where
he felt "accelerated about 400%," his Brahmin friends appeared in a
diminished light; Will Forbes may well have been an appealing man, but
Lincoln doubted "more and more his sensibilities beneath his charming
silences." In New York he felt "constant emotional excitement," endless
stimulation—exactly the diet his frenetic temperament craved, even if
he'd occasionally recoil from the overstimulation.

Some of his non-Brahmin friends, and especially the architecture critic
Henry-Russell Hitchcock, underscored his mounting impulse to put
Boston behind him. Hitchcock, notoriously tactless (Lincoln thought the
trait related to Russell's "suicidal instinct for ruining himself with the
powers which he wants to give him prestige"), told Lincoln straight out,
and with his trademark Olympian snort, that if he still harbored any hope
of becoming a decent painter (he barely did), the move to New York was
essential. "Russell," Lincoln wrote in his diary, "always gives me a salutary
kick in my self-esteem." But though he was more than a little in awe of
Russell, Lincoln replied that he didn't yet feel ready to give up either the
gallery or *Hound and Horn*.

He spent most of the summer following his graduation from Harvard
in June 1930 keeping Mina company at her home in Ashfield, and writing
a good deal. Along with poetry, he tried his hand at a "moral tragedy," a
play that friends advised him was so dry and dull that he ought not to
bother revising it. He also began an autobiographical novel (which several
years later would be published as *Flesh Is Heir*), on which he steadily
worked, though his feelings about its merits fluctuated wildly. He thought

of the book, given his indecisive and multiple career lurches to date, "as a kind of dope to keep my self-respect up." He kept at it, too, because most of the friends to whom he showed sections of the novel made encouraging, if carefully hedged, noises. To Lincoln's surprise, when he talked to his father about the novel and its prospects, Louis "was very attentive, sympathetic, and generous"—though Rose, after reading halfway through, made only a single comment: "You use the word 'Christ' too often."[3]

It soon enough dawned on Lincoln that he could of course complete the novel just as easily in New York, where he'd also be at the center of the publishing industry, and that he could take the *Hound and Horn* with him as well. As of the fall of 1930, he shifted the magazine's business office to New York, preparatory to his own final decision, which didn't come until June 1931, to move there permanently himself.

Mina had already taken an apartment in Manhattan, having wanted to escape the loneliness of Ashfield after Harry's death (though she kept the house and would return there often). Both she and Lincoln had, on their multiple trips to New York, developed a considerable circle of mostly literary and artistic friends in the city, with Mina particularly close to the composer Roger Sessions and to the set designer Aline Bernstein—sponsor, lover, and then rejected lover of the novelist Thomas Wolfe.

In the fall of 1930 Aline was doing the sets for Herman Shumlin's production of *Grand Hotel*, but was nonetheless in desperate emotional shape, frequently (as Lincoln described it) "on the verge of suicide." Mina and he tried to cheer her up at assorted lunches and dinners; on one such evening Lincoln and several of his own friends "romped around and nuzzled and screamed and ate alligator pear [avocado] salad"—but even that night Aline "kept repeating herself and getting vague and looked as if she might cry." Another time, when the demolition of three blocks of midtown Manhattan had begun in order to make way for the creation of Rockefeller Center, Lincoln sounded Aline out about whether she thought there was a possibility of including a ballet company in the planning of Radio City Music Hall. In the next few years, as the center neared completion, the two would confer further.

Lincoln's feeling about Mina had become more complicated, less automatically trusting, than when they were younger and he'd viewed her as his dearest friend and confidante. After her husband's sudden death in 1928, Lincoln had felt deeply sorry for his sister and had spent considerable time with her at Ashfield. Two years later he still felt a strong attachment and allegiance to her, and when deciding about moving permanently to New York, stayed in her apartment for more than three weeks. They frequently went to the opera and the theater together, and they once took their father, who made periodic business trips to the city, to Tony's Speakeasy, their favorite hideaway, and to see the "good conventional musical comedy" *Girl Crazy*. ("It didn't bore me," Lincoln wrote in his diary, but "it never fills the demands of my heart and eye—nothing does like the ballet.")

On his infrequent visits to New York, Lincoln's brother, George, then finishing up as an undergraduate at Harvard, also stayed at Mina's apartment. George had never been particularly close to either of his siblings; he was, like them, smart, strong-willed, and opinionated, but unlike them, his interests focused on business, sports—and bedding down women. It came as a considerable surprise to Lincoln, therefore, when, for the first time in five years, George initiated sex with him one night at Mina's place. At least as surprising was (as Lincoln wrote in his diary) that the sex came off "with an ease and smoothness I would never have dreamt possible." Lincoln wanted to believe that "there was some affection in it," yet it quickly became apparent that for George the contact was simply for "the most obvious and superficial satisfaction."

But having sex did open up a rare and "considerable" conversation between them. George told Lincoln that he knew "the secret places" in his heart "very clearly" and that he "did not condemn . . . [Lincoln's] preponderant interest in men." Yet George went on to say that "from the point of view of ultimate satisfaction" he deplored that interest, even while believing that homosexuality was "so much more physically intense, imaginatively and actually considered, than normal intercourse." That his brother didn't "blame" him, came as a "great relief" to Lincoln, even though George adamantly refused to believe that Lincoln had had sex with a particular woman he himself had slept with; when Mina, the next day, confirmed Lincoln's story (and then bawled Lincoln out for having told him), George became "terribly upset."

Lincoln decided that his brother, who believed he could seduce any woman and lick any man in a fight, suffered in fact from "an intellectual inferiority" complex that led him to an "excess of enthusiasm" in the "expenditure of physical energy." He harshly judged George as a person who "causes pain through arrogance . . . a lack of power to see the implication and references of any action," and concluded that he was, all in all, "a good deal of a son of a bitch, that is a physically powerful, willfully blind person who bases everything on the premise of his own omniscience and omnipotence." He might have been speaking about how he viewed his father as well.

After their encounter Lincoln soon noticed, or chose to emphasize, that George was "considerably harder" toward him, "more contemptuous in his manner . . . his defenses solidify too rapidly into a sort of superficial toughness and a sardonic grin." The two brothers would, at later periods in their lives, think better of each other, though they never again had sex and never developed the kind of emotionally intimate bond that Lincoln and Mina had (however much it could waver). But Lincoln, with his lack of interest in business or money, would come to rely on George's financial acumen and would give him considerable control over investments.

The two would see little of each other over the next few years: after graduating from Harvard, and at exactly the same time that Lincoln moved permanently to New York, George headed for California, where he'd stay for a number of years trying to make his way on the production side of the motion picture industry. His father had a few years earlier added David Sarnoff to his long list of prominent friends, and with Sarnoff's help got George a job at RKO Studios. Louis thought Sarnoff "one of the most extraordinary men I have ever met," but George soon came to view him as a man who had "an excellent brain" but "absolutely no ethics whatsoever." On that score Lincoln sided with his brother. When Sarnoff came to dinner one night at Commonwealth Avenue, Lincoln summed him up in his diary as "piglike . . . [he] has interesting information but an utter lack of imaginative distinction."

As for Mina, it had now been nearly three years since Harry's death. Still a comparatively young woman of thirty-four, she'd gradually and bravely made herself rejoin the world, though her recovery was irregular and she now and then could still become (in Lincoln's words) "horribly upset." She tried psychoanalysis again, spurred this time by the attacks of nausea that overcame her when reading the manuscript of Lincoln's novel-in-progress, *Flesh Is Heir.* She did her best, also, to keep herself preoccupied with the joys and troubles of her friends, and to maintain her well-established interest in the arts, as well as in fashionable, expensive clothes.

Like her brother, Mina was a deeply serious person who wanted to write (eventually she'd publish several excellent books); for the time being, though, she couldn't manage more than a few halfhearted feints in that direction. She had, for a while, a rather elderly, devoted beau, but although grateful for his attentions, she knew the spark really wasn't there. As her spirits gradually improved, some of Lincoln's earlier sympathy became edged with impatience. "It annoys me extremely," he wrote at one point in his diary, "that Mina never for one moment doubts her way of life"—which Lincoln took to be, unfairly, "the small talk of personal relationships"—a pleasure in which he himself indulged at least as much as Mina did. And he once, as a confirmed modernist, patronizingly described her apartment in New York as having "the disarming qualities of a genteel extravagance on a limited scale: chintz and pewter and Victorian accessories."

But Mina was not a trivial-minded person, and most of the time Lincoln knew that. As they got older they could both be formidable, domineering, frighteningly grandiose presences. Yet Mina's devotion to Lincoln, unlike his to her, rarely wavered, even when she sometimes disapproved of his behavior or his choice of friends. And Lincoln knew that, too. When, one evening, he confided to Mina his passion for Lyman Paine, "she was" (as he wrote in his diary) "kinder to me than I ever am to her in such details."

The single factor that created the greatest distance between them was Mina's dislike and disapproval of the woman who had superseded her as the most important person in Lincoln's life: Muriel Draper. Mina and Muriel, probably for Lincoln's sake, maintained in public a tolerant truce, but in private they sometimes unleashed their mutual disdain. Mina characterized Muriel to Lincoln as a woman who "no longer has power over the people she likes and now can only handle those whose insanity she can augment . . . she makes up stories with a curious undiscriminating emotional excitement." For her part, Muriel tended to see Mina, although Mina was ten years her junior, as something of an uptight holdover from a benighted Victorian age.

Muriel ("Mools") and Lincoln had originally met in 1927, when he was twenty years old. During his trips to New York over the next few years he'd gotten to know her increasingly well, and before long they'd begun what would be a decade-long, periodically sexual affair that, by the time Lincoln moved to New York, had greatly intensified. From the very beginning of their relationship, Lincoln marveled at how Muriel "has all her barriers down all the time" and was "quite without conventional restraints." Even as a much older man, he credited her with having taught him "most of what I wanted to have known of people, politics, and principles." Throughout the thirties she was his "dominant companion and influence," often an oracle and compass—though Rose and Louis considered her a "menace," a disreputable older woman intent on leading their boy politically and emotionally astray.

She certainly did her best. The free-spirited, flamboyant Muriel, nearly twenty years Lincoln's senior, was a well-known, electric figure in New York's "high bohemia." Her evening salons and her afternoon teas in her loft above a coach house on East Fortieth Street were a magnet for the "smart set," and her friendships ranged across the arts—and the color line. She entertained, among many others, Carl Van Vechten, Alfred and Blanche Knopf, James Weldon and Grace Johnson, Paul and Eslanda ("Essie") Robeson, and the Stettheimer sisters; for her annual New Year's Eve party (as Van Vechten wrote in his daybook) "pretty nearly everybody turns up"—the horde of celebrities ranging from Cecil Beaton to Mabel Dodge Luhan.

Lincoln, age twenty-three, was there for the December 31, 1930, bash, which (he wrote in his diary) was full of "furs and feathers," and "extremely loud and gory." Alfred Barr and his wife, Margaret "Marga" Scolari, arrived looking (to Lincoln) "very snotty, hoity-toity," wouldn't drink—and soon left "in a huff." (Lincoln had liked Marga when they'd initially met but soon dismissed her as "horrible.") As for Van Vechten, he made a "sleepy entrance like a huge black pearl," while Muriel, with her circle of fellow Gurdjieffians, sat huddled in a corner "darkly and sweatily together." Philip Johnson made the mistake of being socially polite: "I have for so long wanted to meet the brilliant Mrs. Draper," he said; later, when he was leaving, Muriel—who, like Lincoln, could be as rude as she was charming—"waved gaily after him and said she probably would never see him again." Johnson winced.

Lincoln had met Philip Johnson only a few weeks before, and had taken an instant dislike to him as "a rather silly, gossipy, enthusiastic person." When he saw Johnson a month after Muriel's party, his opinion didn't improve: Johnson's "inferiority," Lincoln wrote in his diary, "renders his enthusiasm personally aggressive." Yet he accepted an invitation to tea at Johnson's apartment at 424 East Fifty-second Street (Alfred and Marga Barr lived in the same building), perhaps out of curiosity to see his much-talked-about flat. It had been recently renovated and furnished by Mies van der Rohe and his associate Lilly Reich, and was a showplace for their ideas and designs. Lincoln thought the rooms "magnificent . . . the utmost in luxe and utility," but he continued to find Johnson himself "a rather captious and disagreeable personality." He gave Lincoln "the impression that he is always trying to use me, so I return the same attitude." Unpromising though these early encounters were, the two men would have a long history—not always of friendship and without either ever losing his deep ambivalence about the other.

As Muriel's 1930 New Year's Eve party grew more heated, Lincoln had "an excellent time all evening racing around." By the early hours, general drunkenness and a sort of wild free-for-all set in. A Harvard history professor who Lincoln thought "looked like some horrible kind of wet skinned prick" made "lunging passes" at him; everywhere there was "more or less maudlin man-handling," and upstairs some flat-out screwing. The complicated Muriel, usually a champion of zestful eroticism, suddenly became inexplicably angry—"brusque and snappish"—and she and Lincoln stood in the hallway "rubbing bellies" while he tried to comfort her.

At about 5:00 a.m., the party still raucous, Lincoln decided to take a break and walk the neophyte photographer Walker Evans back to his shabby apartment. Lincoln had met Evans, four years his senior, only a month before, writing in his diary at the time, "His manner is one of great suppressed nervousness, of a colossal strain . . . however, his terrible nervousness was extremely appealing." Muriel shared Lincoln's fascination with Evans, and she and Lincoln often compared notes about him. Muriel spoke of the "very subtle and powerful influence that Evans exerted on all of us—mainly in the mysterious quality that he projected—did he know his own power, or not?" Lincoln thought that Walker was wholly conscious of the physical charm he emanated, and yet, because he was "uncertain, frightened," wasn't capable of employing it "to any satisfactory advantage." When Muriel laughingly asked Lincoln, "Which of us shall take him to bed?" Lincoln gave her the right of way; she was clearly the more erotically interested of the two.

Lincoln published Walker's early writings on photography in the October–December 1930 issue of *Hound and Horn*, and included him in the Harvard Society for Contemporary Art's pathbreaking exhibition of contemporary photography in November 1930 that featured, among others, Berenice Abbott, Edward Weston, and Alfred Stieglitz—as well as aerial photographs from the Harvard College Observatory.

By early 1931, Lincoln and Walker were seeing a fair amount of each other, often at mealtimes, with Lincoln paying because he was worried that the poverty-stricken Evans literally wasn't getting enough to eat. Evans expressed "great contempt for all other photographers in New York except Ralph Steiner" (who had taught Evans a great deal about photographic techniques and who shared his fascination with "ordinary" subject matter). When Evans showed him his own work, Lincoln was immediately impressed. Walker confided that he hated to sell his photographs, or even to leave them "where they might be seen, copied or have [their] ideas stolen from him." Lincoln, channeling his father, told Evans that "he submitted too easily to his terrors."

Before long Walker was taking photos of Lincoln, posing him as a convict and a gangster (when Lincoln saw the movie *Public Enemy*, he became a huge admirer of James Cagney—"an amazingly charming actor . . . the *ne plus ultra* of the baby gangster, my ideal"; a little later he would come to know Cagney slightly). Early in 1931 Lincoln suggested that Walker accompany him to New England to photograph various intact Victorian houses, a project that actually began with Lincoln's old friend John Brooks Wheelwright, who was interested in illustrations for a book he planned (but never wrote) on Victorian architecture. The three men, starting in the streets of Boston and ending up in Chestnut Hill and Arlington, spent five days photographing everything from "New Greek" to Italian and French Renaissance houses, many of them in danger of imminent destruction.

Along with trying to clarify their purpose—"did we want the best of the Romantic stuff, or the best and most eccentric, or a historical survey of the whole period?"—the technical process itself proved complicated: "The sun had to be just right," Lincoln wrote in his diary, "and more often than not we would have to come back to the same place two or even three times for the light to be hard and bright." Lincoln felt like "a surgeon's assistant to Walker, cleaning up neatly after him, and he [Walker] a surgeon operating on the fluid body of time."

The process could be tedious but was also deeply pleasurable. Lincoln felt that the Victorian houses they spotted and photographed were remarkable—the town of Salem, especially, was "a miracle of provincial grace and wealth"—and that he was "filling up the ledger of the indigenous past in recording these places." But he took much less pleasure in Walker himself, finding him "a considerable disappointment as a companion." He tended to see Evans as a phlegmatic, stone-faced contrarian, as well as something of a pessimist and puritan; one of Walker's convictions, Lincoln wrote in his diary, "is that nothing any good can happen except by mistake." His "carefully hedged equivocality" drove the impetuous Lincoln up the wall: Walker seemed to him "perennially bored, thin-blooded, too easily tired." Now and then Lincoln found it "impossible not to bully him by rushing him or telling him just what to do," whereas for his part, Walker felt that "he [was] only a paid photographer."

On their second expedition to the Boston area two months later, they concentrated mostly on houses in the city's South End but also made an excursion as far north as Newburyport. The photographing went well; the personal relationship continued to deteriorate. It was a case of temperamental oil and water: Lincoln's boundless energy and his huge enthusiasm for the "astonishing grace, breadth and dignity" of the architecture they were recording played off badly against Evans's laconic, resistant personality. At the peak of his annoyance at Evans's "tired, inert" ways Lincoln furiously characterized him in his diary as "a constipated and castrated bull dog, old and squatting before his time." But he made the Olympian decision not to blow up at him: that would invest Walker with far too much importance; he was, after all, little more than "a useful gnat." A week later, back in New York, Lincoln was surprised to hear from Muriel that the constantly exhausted Walker had made "a not inexpert attack on her virtue"; she'd put him off with the same speech she'd initially used on Lincoln: "Walker, go now. We mustn't spoil this, etc."

Throughout his life Lincoln was usually able to separate his personal feelings about a given artist from his assessment of the person's art. He believed strongly in Evans's talent and he promoted his work with a dedication most people reserve for the closest and dearest of friends. Lincoln's varied interventions on Evans's behalf would prove critical in establishing his reputation as a major figure. He did so at a time when, in Evans's words, "very few men of taste, education, or even just general sophistication, or any kind of educated mind, ever touched photography . . . it was a disdained medium."

Up through 1932 Evans had had only a single exhibit, a shared one with George Platt Lynes, at the recently opened avant-garde Julien Levy Gallery (Levy had introduced Eugène Atget's work to America), but the show, despite good reviews, sold only one or two prints. Thanks to Lincoln, a number of Walker's photographs were published soon after in *Hound and Horn*. He also made a concerted effort to persuade friends in the publishing world to put out a book devoted to Evans's photography and donated about a hundred photographs of the Victorian houses to MoMA, urging Barr to mount an exhibit of some of them. All these efforts would culminate in 1933, when Lincoln used his position as a member of the Museum of Modern Art's Junior Advisory Committee, and his friendships with the museum's codirectors, Alfred Barr and Jere Abbott, to mount the show that did more than any other to launch Evans as a significant talent.

"Walker Evans: Photographs of Nineteenth-Century Houses"—one of the first one-person photographic exhibits ever mounted in the country at a major museum—contained about a third of the pictures Lincoln had donated to MoMA. In addition, Lincoln wrote the introductory text for the exhibit (it was, importantly, published in the December 1933 *Museum of Modern Art Bulletin*). The show opened in mid-November 1933 and toured for a number of years. Five years later Lincoln, indefatigable, would write a striking and historically important essay on Evans's work for the catalog of MoMA's exhibition (and subsequent book) *American Photographs*. Lincoln's unstinting efforts in Evans's behalf were an early example of the dedicated, generous way he created opportunities and promoted the careers of artists he admired.

For his part, Evans wasn't nearly as bighearted, not only as regards Lincoln but also Muriel Draper, who'd done so much to introduce him to "high bohemia." In an interview late in life (1971) Evans did credit Lincoln with "having helped me a lot," and cited his essay for MoMA's 1938 exhibition as "a very bright piece of art criticism . . . and history-making, too." But that was about it for praise. He went on to describe Lincoln as "very untrustworthy; that is, you can't count on the accuracy of what he says; he just loves to throw things around." Which was true enough of Lincoln in certain moods, but Evans's limited, negative characterization hardly serves as a just summary of his character—or indeed his behavior toward Evans himself.

Nor was Evans remotely fair to Muriel. He did, in that 1971 oral history, refer to her as "a remarkable woman . . . [who] was very useful in the education of young men like me at that time." But he then went on to describe her salon as "imitation French," as "anything but a respectable house," and to refer to Muriel herself as always "putting on an act, and it was completely artificial and phony to the fingertips." A description, again, with elements of truth in it but harshly, ungratefully partial.

Muriel's life in New York was in fact her *second* cycle of notoriety. Prior to World War I, when married to the tenor Paul Draper, she'd presided over a remarkable musical salon at their London residence, Edith Grove, where such celebrated figures as Pablo Casals and Arthur Rubinstein (with whom she had an affair) performed late into the night for people like Lady Emerald Cunard, the conductor Pierre Monteux, and Nijinsky. In those years she'd gotten to know, among others, Henry James, John Singer Sargent, and the novelist Norman Douglas, attended the frenzied 1913 premiere of *Sacre du Printemps,* heard Chaliapin sing *Boris Godunov* and *Prince Igor,* saw Nijinsky dance in *Spectre de la Rose,* entertained the Sitwells, Langston Hughes, Mabel Dodge Luhan, Romaine Brooks, Mina Loy, Gertrude Stein and Alice B. Toklas, and become involved with Gurdjieff.

Paul Draper, increasingly addicted to alcohol and heroin (he died of an overdose at age thirty-eight), deserted Muriel in 1914 for the actress Jeanne Eagels. Soon after, Muriel had returned with their two young sons, Paul, Jr. (subsequently a world-famous tap dancer), and Sanders ("Smudge") to New York. Her life became shadowed by financial uncertainty; what limited income she had derived from irregular employment as an interior decorator and from writing occasional pieces on design for *The New Yorker.* Yet her social life remained frantically glamorous: she turned her bleak living space on East Fortieth Street into yet another salon, which, after some "terrible times with the Bailiffs," she continued at her new apartment, 312 East Fifty-third Street (Edmund Wilson lived next door).

And she remained agitatedly alive and restlessly sexual. Her tall, graceful figure was still intact, and her face, never classically beautiful (given her flat nose, high cheekbones, and full lips, many referred to her as a "blonde negress," others as "ugly"), retained its radically unique look. As did her dazzlingly eccentric sense of fashion, her remarkable insights into people, and her freewheeling, outspoken, bawdy conversation. As Lincoln described her, "she managed to dress on no cash with enormous elegance, and had a style of speech which mixed Jamesian detail with gutter immediacy." And she remained an omnipresent figure on the social circuit, even though her partying did take on a slightly rueful tinge in the context of unpaid bills, her inability to finish a second book (Lincoln published one section, "America Deserta," in *Hound and Horn*), the approach of her fortieth birthday, and the country's drastically deteriorating economy.

Muriel filled Lincoln with tales of her previous life (in his diary he described them as "never memoirs" but rather "incidents hot off the griddle of action"), and she threatened one day to write a book about her erotic adventures. When she plunged into the whirlwind of "in" parties, favored speakeasies, and Harlem hot spots like the Savoy Dance Hall and the Clam House, she often took Lincoln along with her. He sometimes found the outings "very dull and expensive" but more often enjoyed himself, especially when they went to the Clam House to hear the "great fat straight-haired tailor-suited" notorious lesbian Gladys Bentley hold forth in all her glory, singing "dirty" songs that got dirtier, "the night you told me those little white lies" progressing to "the night you unbuttoned those little white flies." According to Lincoln, Bentley "accepted dollar bills like a goldfish his food . . . never stopping singing."

As important as Muriel was to Lincoln as he shifted his base from Boston to New York, he'd earlier made friends of his own in Manhattan, and several people he'd been close to in Boston were simultaneously settling down for a time in New York: Eddie Warburg, for one, who continued to work with Lincoln on exhibitions for the Society for Contemporary Art (and whose father, Felix, continued to provide financial support), had, after graduation, temporarily returned to the family mansion at 1109 Fifth Avenue (today the Jewish Museum).

During their years at Harvard, Lincoln and Eddie had worked closely together, but they were an ill-fitting combination, akin to the pairing of an eagle and a hummingbird. Lincoln enjoyed Eddie's humor and admired his boyish disposition, but he felt constantly annoyed and hampered by Eddie's "inherent capacity to take nothing seriously" and tended to regard him as a superficial child blessed with "occasional instinctive penetration."

But in the context of living in New York, Lincoln had to revise his earlier view of Eddie as "joy personified." During one of their evenings out partying, Eddie (so Lincoln wrote in his diary) "got more and more low," and Lincoln decided to take him home; once there Eddie poured out his unhappiness—how his older brothers bullied him, how he suffered from "profound personal distrust," and how his homosexual inclinations worried him. Soon after, Eddie left to study art history in Germany and Russia in order to qualify to teach at Bryn Mawr. Lincoln felt that Eddie had "no real interest in anything like education or fine arts," and his judgment would prove accurate: after two years Eddie would give up teaching and return to New York, where Lincoln would enlist him (and his money) in trying to start up a ballet company.

Another old friend, Lincoln's ex-lover Tom Mabry, was then living in New York, free of problems with his tubercular back, and working at the avant-garde John Becker Gallery (Becker had fallen hard for him). Lincoln and Tom had remained deeply fond of each other even after their tumultuous affair had cooled, and Lincoln continued to admire Tom's "great penetration whenever he happens to be stimulated." But that was becoming rare, Tom's "psychic inertia" (as Lincoln put it) having markedly increased. He wasn't exactly unhappy at the Becker Gallery, but neither was he fully engaged. He'd been offered a teaching job at Vanderbilt University but couldn't decide whether to accept it. "His interest," Lincoln wrote in his diary, is "tenuous in anything"—which puzzled Lincoln, who was profoundly interested in so many things that he had trouble focusing full attention on any one of them for very long. Yet somehow Tom's indecisiveness, as Lincoln wrote in his diary, "never affects me at all, nor bores, nor irritates." For his part Tom felt he'd never commit to any worthwhile pursuit, and he'd persuaded his wealthy father to settle an income on him, arguing that if he was freed from the compulsion to do anything, he at least wouldn't drift into alcoholism.

Tom did manage to fall passionately in love with a black man known only as "Clifford," which made him think that maybe love was his one true career. Yet when Lincoln tried to tell Tom about his own current (late in 1930) passion for Lyman Paine, Tom was only "humorously interested" and (despite his own involvement with Clifford) went on to warn Lincoln, using the standard psychoanalytic vocabulary of the day, "that the great trouble with homosexuality was that it made one a slave to a pattern: one always fell in love with various examples of a central obsession of which oneself was the origin—a narcissistic repetition that allowed no free agency." If Lincoln offered a rebuttal, he didn't record it, but he and Tom did remain convinced that the two of them were "carnal indispensables and nothing we can ever do apart remains long hidden when we meet."

As for Lyman Paine, he and his wife, Ruth Forbes, had settled in New York and they often went out with Lincoln, producing a complicated roundelay that positioned Lincoln as the smitten romantic ("I could be absolutely drunk on people," he wrote in his diary), Lyman as the mysteriously simple, conventional Adored One, and Ruth as "a quiet, easy & persuasive" woman of "sleepy charm" who sometimes fell into self-doubt and depression. Lincoln's infatuation with Lyman mystified most of his intimates. Muriel tried to convince him that his affection for Lyman was "second-hand and indirect"; Tom Mabry thought Lyman nice but dull; and Mina was put off by his "naïveté."

Lincoln himself had trouble explaining his fascination: "I invest in [Lyman] an aura of mystery. He is still unaccountable to me . . . A stranger." Perhaps it was due to Lyman being, or appearing to be, "absolutely unself-conscious, naive, without a trace of affectation." In any case Lincoln was careful not to make any direct demands on Lyman's affection, or to attempt to convert their friendship into a sexual arrangement, accurately gauging Lyman's remoteness and unavailability. Lincoln felt a "terrific need . . . to directly love someone more than myself," but he was careful not to focus any such expectation on Lyman. Besides, he was sensitive to Ruth's insecurity; sometimes, especially when Ruth was feeling down, the two of them went out alone, and he'd try to provide what comfort he could. He turned elsewhere for his sexual needs and poured his intensity into his ongoing, multiple projects: finishing and peddling his novel, *Flesh Is Heir*, and keeping both *Hound and Horn* and the Harvard Society for Contemporary Art afloat.

His continuing penchant for what he liked to call "low life" sex with men (hanging out in dives, picking up sailors, cruising the streets and parks) once led him into a New York City office building and what he vaguely described in his diary as "a physical hell" that ended only with a "lucky release." The experience left him feeling "properly dazed" for several days. "The worst of it is," he wrote in his diary, "my mind is usually conscious of what the body is doing, even urging it away from . . . an interest in danger that amounts to insanity." This self-accusation was more than a bit strong, the knee-jerk reaction, perhaps, of his bourgeois upbringing. As Lincoln well understood in less frightened moments, undomesticated adventurous anonymity and risk-taking were central not only to intensified erotic arousal but to profound creativity of any kind. Had timidity and adherence to convention been the key components of Lincoln's personality, none of his high-flying, hazardous ventures would ever have gotten off the ground. His outside-the-law gangster fantasies— epitomized by his worship of James Cagney, by Walker Evans's photographs of him as convict and criminal, and by his profound responsiveness to Gurdjieff's formula "never apologize, never explain"—all represented and heightened the reprobate ingredients in Lincoln's temperament. His unorthodox behavior, his outside-the-law "immorality," was, to a significant degree, his saving creative grace.

"Two days without an occupation drives me frantic," Lincoln wrote in his diary early in 1931; "I'm always so frightened of being bored, of not being sufficiently occupied." Payson Loomis told him he was "wasting my powers by most of what I do—not really what I do, but the great friction of waste in the way I do it." Lincoln agreed: "So much energy expended, so little the margin of satisfaction at the result." But given all he'd accomplished before the age of twenty-five, and the multiple pleasures he'd recorded in his diary, Lincoln could only have been measuring "waste" and "satisfaction" by immoderate standards—as was his way. Plus the looming transition to living in New York may have brought to the surface the fear that his insatiable drive would consume him, given the city's multiple opportunities and excitements.[4]

Muriel tried to make him promise that he'd attend the meetings of her Gurdjieff group on Tuesday nights, and her friend, the painter Mark Tobey (whom Lincoln thought "a very nice man" and a gifted artist), strongly seconded the motion, telling him how "moving" he'd found the gatherings. But Lincoln rarely did anybody's bidding, and told Muriel that her suggestion irritated him. Yet he conceded that Gurdjieff's system held "the potential of great implication" for him, and when Gurdjieff himself arrived in New York in January 1931, Lincoln gave up his resistance and started to attend the sessions. When he arrived at his first meeting, Muriel, in an "ecstasy over my conversion," clasped Lincoln to her bosom. But "conversion," in the sense of surrender, was not assured.

The 1931 trip was Gurdjieff's third to the United States. On the earlier visits he'd drawn a flock of literary celebrities, including Sinclair Lewis, Theodore Dreiser, John O'Hara, and Hart Crane. But few stuck around for very long, the best-known exceptions being Jean Toomer, author of the highly regarded *Cane,* and the co-editors of the influential *Little Review,* Jane Heap and Margaret Anderson. The meetings Gurdjieff conducted in 1931, spread over several months; they affected Lincoln just as deeply as had his earlier experience at Le Prieuré, and he attended regularly.

As before, he was impressed that Gurdjieff's philosophical dialectic was conceived "in terms of human action, not in the technique of logic." And there was much in what Gurdjieff said that spoke to him directly: the view that contemporary values, dulled by tradition, had become meaningless, that "conditioned responses . . . bind in every way," that most people, including himself, led their lives as "sleep-walkers." Gurdjieff's principles, Lincoln felt, amounted to "the headiest, most insidiously right and suggestive philosophy" he'd ever known, and excited him "profoundly."

He went so far as to write in his diary that Gurdjieff was "probably the greatest intellectual stimulus and influence really in my life." He even felt that he'd already "been operating on this code of revaluation for some time, although I may or may not have attributed it to Gurdjieff." He also recognized that "the system was not any sort of easy release, a cure, or a diet, but a constant progressive regimen in one's own action." "One cannot," he wrote in his diary, "fall into its arms as . . . when one enters the church."

Now and then he felt the strong urge to return to Fontainebleau at once, "turning my back on the world and giving up all my dearest idiosyncratic delusions to follow this curious little island of anarchists in the middle of the world's deserted morass." Yet he drew back, telling himself that he was "too frightened of nihilism to give up the titillations which now satisfy me"; and also that he still "had certain jobs to do"—like editing *Hound and Horn*—and "could not devote all my time to . . . [the] discipline." He didn't feel "ready or willing," for the moment, to do more.

After Gurdjieff returned to Europe in mid-March, Lincoln made the decision not to go to any more meetings or readings ("I came back to my life in a dream, with a rush of appreciation") even as he retained all that he'd already accepted in Gurdjieff's teachings. When Lincoln told Muriel his decision, she responded that "it was better to sleep with one's eyes open than with them shut." Knowing that Lincoln's views could veer dramatically and abruptly, reversing from one extreme stance to its opposite, Mools seems to have sensed that Lincoln hadn't permanently opted out of the meetings.

And her intuition would prove accurate. Gurdjieff returned yet again to New York eight months later, primarily on a mission to raise money (he arrived with only twenty dollars in his pocket, or so he said). Muriel—

whom Gurdjieff called "his best friend in this country"—along with Payson and the actress Rita Romilly met his boat at the dock and negotiated his way through customs. At a meeting the very next night, Gurdjieff played some of his curious melodies on a hand organ, and read a chapter from a new book he was working on—and Lincoln was in attendance.

But thereafter he went irregularly, bothered by the assumption that since he was viewed as a "rich boy" with an unlimited amount of money and financial contacts, he was about to be called on as a contributor. In fact Lincoln was in one of those periods—which arose frequently when he was young and dependent on his father's fluctuating largesse—when he was feeling particularly strapped for cash. Often enough that was the result of his extravagant disregard for money and his claimed inability to take proper care of his accounts.

But in the fall of 1931 he was pressed for cash for a different reason. He'd recently met the sculptor Gaston Lachaise and, greatly taken by his work—and because Lachaise was at a low point in his life and periodically threatening suicide—had commissioned a head of himself, for which he'd been having regular sittings. All this had happened only a month before Gurdjieff's arrival back in New York, and the commission had actually left Lincoln in debt.

Just as he feared, at the next meeting he attended Gurdjieff addressed him as "Pater" and asked him to give his blessing on the gathering. Soon after, one of Gurdjieff's closest associates drew Lincoln into a side room and asked him to lend Gurdjieff three hundred dollars. Lincoln, as he wrote in his diary, "was more or less unsurprised," and awkwardly said he would see what he could do. He didn't feel he was being gulled but did feel acute embarrassment over his lack of funds.

In an effort to raise the money, he went to see several of his well-off friends, but all turned him down. To make matters worse, Rita Romilly whispered in his ear that he was "being prepared for something . . . they are testing you." Lincoln weakly replied, "I don't think so, possibly." Lincoln told Mools that he felt "confused," and he even said that if he did have extra cash he would rather give it to Lachaise than to Gurdjieff— "because Gurdjieff can get it and Lachaise couldn't."

Mools said she couldn't advise him, that he "had two thousand different, strangling impulses" in his head, and he had to make up his own mind. Lincoln told her that he'd "never been through such an anguish of distracted confusion of impulses and morally suppressed obligations." To which Muriel replied that "of course it was difficult," because he was "using part of [himself] . . . never exercised before, and as far as money went it is one's virginity in the particular world of evil and degradation we live in." Lincoln was so upset that he "went straight to bed, not eating . . . not jerking off"—and proceeded to have "a horrible, racking dream of the spirit of Gurdjieff [being] like a police inspector . . . exposing me to my social dependents and people I depend on in a terror of intimate detail and shame."

The next day he got *Hound and Horn*'s co-editor Bernard Bandler, with whom he'd renewed friendly relations—in one of his typical about-faces, Lincoln now decided that Bandler was "affectionate, perceptive and kind"—to write him a check for one hundred dollars. He then managed to scrape together one hundred dollars of his own, and gave the total amount to Gurdjieff's assistant. Payson, though hardly an apostate, told Lincoln that Gurdjieff had done the same thing "a thousand times," and not to invest the episode with so much importance.

At the next meeting Lincoln got drunk and told the assistant that he couldn't raise any additional money, but that Gurdjieff should regard his offering as a gift, not a loan. For the rest of the evening Gurdjieff proceeded to "make preposterous fun" of Lincoln "for being so easy & willing sheep to be shorn of cash." He also insisted that Lincoln consume a great deal of the food laid out and kept exhorting him to " 'eat, Pater, eat.' " On the way home Muriel told him that "one must steer a middle course between Gurdjieff and the old world of conditioning so as to be neither absorbed [nor] destroyed." The Gurdjieff system "was there for our use, not for it to use us."

Lincoln took the words to heart and thereafter calmed down, without feeling, in his extremist way, that he either had to abandon Gurdjieff's teachings or entirely capitulate to them. At the last meeting before Gurdjieff returned to France, Lincoln felt overcome with "terrific ennui"; he found Gurdjieff's words "incomprehensible" and thought the three hours were of "unparalleled & inconceivable boredom"—indeed he slept through two of them. The boredom, Muriel later told him, was "calculated, and always happens on his last meeting here." For a finale Gurdjieff announced that he'd raised forty-five thousand dollars during his stay, and that gifts with one zero he would distribute among the poor, those with two zeros he would give to the cook at Le Prieuré, and he would ask his secretary whether he should see the ones with three zeros.

There were no formal good-byes. Lincoln felt "enormous personal relief" that Gurdjieff was going: "I feel I am itching & pimply from him; as he says, some people who first fall in the salt water cannot stand it. I can't sleep from thinking. I need time to digest what all I've been exposed to."

Hound and Horn itself continued to be something of an irritant and trapeze act. During 1931 the magazine again went through a considerable shake-up, a result partly of its conclusive move to New York in June of that year, but also of various rivalries and new arrivals among the editors, with Lincoln remaining the one constant. No sooner was Ezra Pound out of the picture than tensions between Lincoln and Bernard Bandler once more arose. "I've learned things," Lincoln wrote vaguely to Jack Wheelwright, "he [Bandler] did & said that took the cake for a grotesque and fantastic idiocy—it's definitely killed any possible affection I could ever have for him." Lincoln never did itemize the purported crimes, but in any case Bandler had arrived at a point by early 1931 where he was losing interest in the magazine.[5]

As he withdrew, Bandler strongly urged Lincoln formally to take on his former Harvard tutor, A. Hyatt Mayor, as his co-editor. Lincoln himself had already had the idea. He had long held Mayor, six years his senior and later head of the print department at the Metropolitan Museum of Art, in high esteem, frequently turning to him for advice and, starting as early as 1929, publishing a number of his essays in *Hound and Horn*, as well as his fine translations from the Greek. Mayor formally became an editor of *Hound and Horn* in June 1931.

A few months earlier Lincoln had invited Yvor Winters to become *Hound and Horn*'s first regional (western) editor, and he had accepted. The astringent and contentious Winters already had a considerable reputation as a poet and critic. He could be difficult and dogmatic, but was more generous minded and less misanthropic than Ezra Pound. He was also a sounder judge of talent, despite a fair number of blind spots of his own. He and Lincoln shared a number of literary enthusiasms, especially for the work of Katherine Anne Porter, Hart Crane, Allen Tate, Wallace Stevens, and William Carlos Williams. They also shared a decided lack of interest in the Humanist movement that Bandler had promoted.

They further agreed that another new movement, Agrarianism, was essentially misguided. A group of Southern writers—principally Allen Tate, John Crowe Ransom, Merrill Moore, Caroline Gordon, and Donald Davidson (sometimes known as the "Fugitives") decried industrialism and advocated a return to the rural values of the Old South. Lincoln, like his father, had a pronounced interest in the Civil War, and was particularly intrigued by the romantic figure of John Pelham; for a time he even thought he'd write a book about Pelham, the Confederate "boy major" who died in his early twenties at the Battle of Kelly's Ford.

But Lincoln "never gave a damn" for the Southern Agrarians and— "more interested in people than notions"—thought "their economics . . . childish." Yvor Winters's antipathy was total; he once wittily wrote Allen Tate, "A farmer has no time to be a scholar or a poet. . . . And I'll bet a dollar that half you agrarians don't even raise your own milk . . . the industrial mess is with us, and . . . we'll simply have to learn to live in it and control it."

Lincoln would nonetheless decide, in 1932, to invite Tate to become the southern regional editor for *Hound and Horn*. He admired Tate's own poetry and coveted his contacts with other front-rank literary figures. Tate accepted the invitation, but the alliance would have its difficulties. Until the early thirties Lincoln had been essentially apolitical, but he would soon begin a serious flirtation with the Left, one that would spin itself out over the next few years—and put him in direct conflict with many of Agrarianism's core beliefs.

Even in 1932 he abhorred Agrarianism's retrograde views on race, its scorn for those (in Tate's words) who held to "humanitarian sentimentality about Negroes and the underdog." In one remarkably outspoken letter to Tate, Lincoln pointed out that "it seems to me a very significant and curious omission, that in all of our discussion about the South, the Negro is never mentioned. . . . This seems to me a most serious lapse somewhere. I would like very much to know what all your people think could be done in relation to black and white. It seems to me a paramount question in any attempt to understand or regenerate the South . . . and why [is] it . . . that sexual relations, however clandestine, between a white man and a Negro woman are tolerated, or at least not censured, as the reverse [are]."

Tate's reply was unambiguously racist: "The Negro race is an inferior race," he wrote Lincoln, and he added that "miscegenation due to a white woman and a Negro man" would compromise the Agrarian goal "to keep the Negro blood from passing into the white race." Tate's wife, Caroline Gordon, whose work *Hound and Horn* also published, was, if possible, even more racist than her husband, unabashedly declaring, "Niggers are unfathomable."

Gordon was a cousin of Tom Mabry's. But Tom, though southern-born, had a far different attitude toward race than his cousin, and for a time would teach at the all-black Fisk University. Decades later, Tate modified his views, even to the point of supporting Martin Luther King, Jr. But when the black struggle became militant in the 1960s, Tate reverted to hostility; as he wrote his daughter in 1967, "I am not moved by the Negro's demand for social justice and equality. . . . I am interested in order and civilization, which in a crisis take precedence over all other aims."

Lincoln himself, though never remotely sharing the coarse-grained racism of the Tates and other Agrarians, was not, at least in his early to mid-twenties, entirely free of ambiguity about black people. Yes, he frequently socialized at the unsegregated parties Muriel and Van Vechten threw, and without feeling any recorded discomfort or hesitation. And yes, he did regularly go to Harlem hot spots, along with any number of privileged white people who were in fact largely indifferent to improving the lot of "ordinary" black Americans. It's true, too, that Lincoln did directly question the Agrarians' bluntly racist views. Yet at the same time, he never broke with Tate or Caroline Gordon over those views, nor did he reject Tate's editorial counsel or close *Hound and Horn*'s pages to the Agrarians' poems, stories, and essays.

Still more puzzling, given Lincoln's growing involvement with the Left and his own later history (he participated in the march on Selma), is the singularly uncharacteristic remark he made in a 1933 letter to Tate: "Your attitude about the Negro as an inferior race seems to me pragmatically if not inevitably true." That could conceivably be interpreted as a cautious rebuke to Tate—that is, *if* one takes "pragmatically" to mean that the Negro's "inferiority" was the result of demeaning conditions, and understands Lincoln's denial of "inevitably" as a rejection of any inborn, genetic explanation for the Negros' oppressed state.

But what would still be left to explain is Lincoln's frequent use of the word "nigger" in his diaries for the late twenties and early thirties (thereafter the word gave way to "Negro"). After the storm in the black community over the title of Van Vechten's 1926 novel, *Nigger Heaven*, there could have been no doubt in subsequent years, as there might have been previously, that blacks considered the word "nigger" highly offensive. The black hostess A'Lelia Walker banished Van Vechten from her parties, and community leaders like Alain Locke and W. E. B. DuBois furiously denounced him for his use of the word. Today the term may be used in affectionate banter between African Americans themselves, but is never acceptable when spoken by whites. Like others after him, Van Vechten had to learn that truth. And so did Lincoln Kirstein.

Yvor Winters disagreed and argued with Lincoln much more vigorously than Allen Tate did. And over a wide variety of matters. When Lincoln, innovatively, introduced a "film chronicle" to the magazine in 1932 and hired the brilliant young Marxist Harry Alan Potamkin as its film critic (Potamkin would produce four remarkable essays—on René Clair, Vsevolod Pudovkin, G. W. Pabst, and Sergei Eisenstein—before succumbing to leukemia in 1933), Winters, whose interests were focused almost entirely on literature (and on raising and showing Airedales), announced that "the film chronicle bores me, but is probably competent in its field, a field of which I know little and care less."

But as Jay Leyda, who would become a prominent film critic and Melville scholar, emphasized in an interview late in life, "Lincoln's *Hound and Horn* was one of the few magazines that showed real and profound interest in both films and photographs." (Lincoln himself would shortly begin to write about movies.) When the left-wing Leyda asked Lincoln if he'd like to see some of the photos produced by the Workers' Film and Photo League, which had gotten scant public recognition, Lincoln leapt at the chance and published several of the photos in the magazine.

He and Winters also diverged sharply about the merit of certain writers. This was especially true in regard to two young Englishmen whose work Lincoln held in high regard and would soon meet—W. H. Auden and Stephen Spender. Winters announced that the two poets "do not interest me two cents' worth," they had "a little talent . . . but no knowledge of style and no desire to acquire any"; they weren't, in his opinion, nearly up to England's "two best poets, Elizabeth Daryush and Viola Meynell."

Almost from the day his editorship began, Winters started complaining that *Hound and Horn* was publishing too much "junk." And at the expense, Winters insisted, of passing up work by people like Howard Baker ("one of the half dozen best poets now writing"), Henry Ramsey, Rowena Lockett, and Achilles Holt—names that have, fairly or not, failed to descend to us as part of the literary pantheon.

By May 1932 Winters had become so angry over Lincoln rejecting "first rate" material he'd submitted "in favor of work that seems to me beneath contempt" that he was forced to doubt the "advisability of continuing formally as one of your editors." Lincoln managed to persuade Winters to stay on, and he remained in his post until *Hound and Horn*'s demise in 1934. But there was now an unspoken quid pro quo: Lincoln accepted more of Winters's submissions for publication, including a chapter from the novel that Winters's wife, Janet Lewis, was at work on, and some poems by a Winters favorite, J. V. Cunningham.

Though they often disagreed, overall Lincoln was exceedingly grateful to Winters for his help; as he wrote Allen Tate, "I admire and value Winters very highly. He has written me some letters which I consider the most instructive I have ever received." Lincoln had quickly learned that Winters was "no easy character to handle," and he was well aware that he sometimes made Winters "very angry with me." But he did his best "to be as tactful as I can," which for Lincoln required more self-control than he was sometimes willing to exercise.

CHAPTER SIX

Museum of Modern Art

(1929–1932)

H AVING SPENT a good deal of time in New York during the previous
year, Lincoln was already comfortably at home in the city when he
settled there permanently in June 1931. He left the Boston area—or as he
put it, "the late 19th century"—with few regrets. Even when it came to
finding an apartment, the move to New York proved easy: Lincoln simply
moved into the rooms his father Louis had long kept in the Berkshire
Hotel at 21 East Fifty-second Street.

Lincoln thought he might spend the upcoming summer in Europe, but
Louis quickly vetoed that plan. Having recently contributed yet more cash
toward keeping *Hound and Horn* alive, he told his son in no uncertain
terms that he expected him to stay in the city and devote himself to the
magazine, using his spare time to complete the novel he'd been at work on
for two years, and getting it published. Louis also reminded Lincoln that
he still hadn't drawn the panoramic mural of Boston he'd long promised
for the Kirstein Memorial Business Library, which Louis had given to the
city of Boston.

Lincoln never would complete the mural, but he did regard his father's
demand that he stay put and concentrate on the magazine as entirely justified. Still, he registered surprise in his diary at the "savage and noisy"
manner with which Louis made his wishes known: "I was interested to see
how he must carry his deals through by the weight and conviction of his
physical impact." Lincoln was well aware of the fact that his father's nerves
were beginning to fray. In early September 1931, when he and Mina went
to meet their parents dockside as they debarked from Europe, there was
an awful scene, and apparently not for the first time.

Rose came down the plank ahead of Louis and promptly burst into
tears, whispering frantically to Mina and Lincoln, " 'Don't tell your father
how dreadful he looks.' " As indeed he did. In Lincoln's diagnosis, Louis
had suffered another attack of "acute neurosis"; while abroad he'd had to
take drugs to sleep, which left him feeling horribly depressed and wanting
"to destroy himself in guilt" for having had to fire some Filene executives
in order to save money. He'd also been "subject to phantasy," fearing that
his fortune had dropped from seven million to one million, though in fact
his $100,000 annual salary had remained intact even if his Filene's stock

had somewhat declined in value. Further, he'd complained bitterly about "the constant society of women" during the trip and the "effete airs" of the crowd at Biarritz.

Once back in the Commodore Hotel, it was Rose's turn to become hysterical. According to Lincoln's account in his diary, she "railed at Mina for looking so ugly, for not writing sufficiently interesting letters," and for her extravagant expenditures. Then she turned on Louis for having paid three times as much duty at customs as he should have—though as Lincoln put it, "She herself brought in 3 times that much undeclared." Louis having awakened her while in Europe at six every morning in order to tell her that he hadn't slept all night, Rose was perhaps understandably unstrung.

After they both calmed down over the next few days, Mina insisted that Louis see her analyst, and this apparently helped him, if for no other reason (so Lincoln wrote in his diary) than that his father "loves to see doctors." Louis now decided that his panic attack was "a combination of a change of life & a break of routine." Lincoln's more Olympian diagnosis was that "what is now happening to father happens to everyone, usually in adolescence; what's amazing is that it happened so late in life to him." The analyst recommended that Louis have massages before bedtime. In Lincoln's words they "blessedly left for Boston" the following day. A week later Lincoln went up to Boston to check on what was happening and he reported his father "somewhat improved."

A few days after that, Louis was back in New York, investigating *Hound and Horn*'s financial problems, worrying that the editors "didn't know what they were doing," and then confessing to Lincoln over lunch that although his insomnia problem was improving, he still "had little interest in what he did and that his one great terror was that people should think he was losing his grip and feel sorry for him." But those fears quickly faded; within the month, he was again actively engaged in his business and philanthropic activities. Within a short time he even, in Lincoln's words, became "less hysterical about his income being cut," satisfied that he essentially remained on solid ground.[1]

Whatever the deep personal sources of Louis's temporary breakdown, the surface triggering mechanism may have been the economic uncertainty that continued to grip the country. Unlike most of Boston's business elite, Filene's executives called for increased federal spending on relief and for national unemployment insurance—leading most of the Boston establishment to denounce them as "socialists." When in 1932 Louis published an article, "Mind Your Own Business," in the prestigious *Atlantic Monthly* in which he suggested that business leaders were not, as many Americans believed, invested with special powers of insight and wisdom, and still further argued that the unchallenged reign of an indifferent plutocracy had to end, he deeply shocked the financial community—as he soon would again when, after FDR's election, he chose to work tirelessly in Washington on behalf of the NRA's Industrial Advisory Board.

Lincoln sent his father a letter of warm congratulation about his *Atlantic* piece, saying how "pleased and excited" he was, and suggesting that his father do a whole series of articles. By then Lincoln's own political education had considerably advanced. As early as the fall of 1930 he'd seen men selling apples on the street for a nickel apiece, and had felt their desperation "really terrifying." Then he started passing breadlines, and being stopped by well-spoken, even well-dressed men asking for money, and he had to turn away in mute despair.

Like so many intellectuals and artists of his generation, Lincoln began to get interested in the Soviet Union as an intriguing laboratory for creating a more just and equitable society. In 1932 he commissioned an essay review for *Hound and Horn* on a group of books about Russia, and started to feel increasingly excited, even "intoxicated," about what was going on there. New York suddenly seemed "thin in comparison," and when he heard that a travel agency called Open Road made traveling to Russia comparatively easy, he felt the impulse to go at once. He didn't, probably because Louis, who had himself been denounced, inaccurately, as a socialist, warned him against moving too far to the Left or ever signing his name to a political statement. But Lincoln's interest continued to grow, and by 1933 he would become still more deeply involved, if at a somewhat intellectual remove.

As for *Hound and Horn*, Lincoln's commitment remained firm, and he devoted considerable time and energy to promoting the magazine's solvency and reputation. Soon after arriving in New York he'd found, for a rent of seventy-three dollars a month, three "small but pleasant" rooms for the magazine in the old Hotel Lorraine at 545 Fifth Avenue, and had also hired two secretaries, one of whom, Doris Levine, became a managerial mainstay.

But though Lincoln continued his involvement with *Hound and Horn*, he didn't want to maintain responsibility, especially at long distance, for keeping the Harvard Society for Contemporary Art going. The Society was still solvent, but fewer and fewer people had been visiting the exhibits; it was time, Lincoln decided, to sever his connection, and he went to see Paul Sachs to tell him directly that he could no longer run the gallery. Less and less money was available to keep things going, and after four years of doing pioneering work in the visual arts, the Society had to close its doors permanently.

By the end of 1931 Lincoln had completed his thinly disguised autobiographical novel, *Flesh Is Heir*, and was faced with the job of getting it into print. He'd been apprehensive about the book's merit the entire time he'd been writing it, and he was also aware that the publishing world, due to the Depression, had cut back sharply on new titles. And in fact he did have a difficult time. Every publisher Lincoln sent the manuscript to— and that included Scribner's; Viking; Cape & Smith; Harcourt, Brace; and Harper's—disliked it in varying degrees. The editor who was nicest to him was also the best known: Maxwell Perkins of Scribner's. Lincoln had never met Perkins until he brought the manuscript to his office, but he was immediately grateful for Perkins's "kindliness and good humor." Unfortunately, he didn't care for the novel either, though he did read it twice.

Lincoln tried to hold his disappointment in check, humorously professing that "as a professional writer I don't fancy myself" either. But he acknowledged in his diary that the publishers' uniformly negative reaction left him profoundly discouraged, and also—because he thought much worse novels were published all the time—irritated. Fortunately a friend of Lincoln's, Joe Brewer, a partner in the small publishing house of Brewer, Warren and Putnam, had stood in the wings from the beginning with the offer of a contract should all else fail. All else had. And so it was that Brewer's firm ended up publishing *Flesh Is Heir* in February 1932.

Lincoln was unprepared for the almost uniformly lukewarm (or worse) reception the book got, both from his friends and from the reviewers. Lyman Paine thought *Flesh* was merely "O.K.," and he picked away annoyingly at a few technical details Lincoln had gotten wrong about sailing. Jack Wheelwright and Muriel Draper tried to emphasize the parts of the book they did like, but were unable to cite many. Russell Hitchcock told Lincoln that he liked the novel "a little but not much." Among his friends, Payson Loomis was the most positive, and while the book was still in manuscript, he'd helpfully pointed out assorted repetitions and grammatical errors. From London, David Garnett wrote Mina that he "liked the beginning but not the end" of Lincoln's novel: "It was too patchy—too much a cross-section." He decided not to send Lincoln his reaction, since "I loved Lincoln last time I saw him. He is one of the most charming creatures I know."

What most dismayed Lincoln were the reports he heard that the novel was bitterly resented by some of his Boston Brahmin friends, and in particular by members of the Forbes family, who thought they'd been thinly disguised—even caricatured—in the book. Their attitude, Lincoln claimed, was entirely "unexpected," since Will Forbes had written to thank him for the copy he'd sent and had called the novel "broadminded." News of the Forbes reaction made Lincoln feel "lonely and frightened," filled with a "curious fear of losing homeground," since he was well aware that now he "couldn't go back to Naushon," a place he cherished. It also made him feel "the necessity or inevitability of constant and complete isolation," but that proved a fleeting if desolating thought, since Lincoln knew perfectly well that he was incapable of being alone or unoccupied for very long.

But the greatest shock was the fiercely negative reactions from his own family. His father read the novel in galley proofs and declared himself "horrified." He thought the language was "too strong," the book filled "with a lot of irrelevancies," and, most important, the thinly disguised portrait of Mina ("Daphne") reprehensible. In the novel Daphne is portrayed as having made a good and quick recovery from her husband's death, despite occasionally feeling "low and depressed." She's further described as decidedly interested in remarrying, and not above playing the coquette now and then, which took the form of becoming overly "hostessy" and "artificial." But what may have bothered the family most was the passage in which the thoroughly admirable "Clay" (Harry Curtiss, Mina's late husband) is portrayed as delighting in Daphne's periodic "nervous and hysterical" moods: "The more excited she got . . . the better he liked it. He was wonderful that way. It never phased [sic] him." Overall the novel's narrator, "Roger" (Lincoln), is harder on himself than on his sister, and Daphne is often described as an appealing, likable woman. But the family didn't see it that way.

Egged on by Rose, Louis initially threatened to take steps to get the novel suppressed by buying up and burning every copy or, alternatively, paying the publisher to destroy the entire edition. In the long run Louis did neither, perhaps because, having vented his anger, he felt satisfied; perhaps because he thought Lincoln, bowing to the family's displeasure, might voluntarily withdraw the book.

When Rose and Lincoln had dinner one night just as the novel was about to be published, she asked him point-blank why he hadn't asked her directly how she liked his book. He said he'd been "busy," and so asked her now. Rose, with her penchant for histrionics, promptly burst into tears and said "she hated, hated it." How could he have been "so cruel & personal"? When Lincoln expressed surprise, Rose added that his brother, George, agreed with her, and she singled out for special condemnation the scene describing Daphne and Clay's wedding, calling it "horrible." *Why* she thought so, is somewhat mystifying. Possibly she resented Lincoln's inclusion of the fact that the bride's parents were in Paris at the time, thus revealing to the world that they had failed to attend.

Possibly she meant the description of Daphne as "terribly nervous" before the wedding ceremony, or Roger saying that the stunning wedding party Harry's family threw made him think of Newport in 1901—meaning, "the whiteness and freshness and flair, roses and white candles and silver." Beyond these seemingly minor lapses in taste (if that's what they were), it's difficult to know why Rose felt so aggrieved. Daphne, after all, is described as looking stunning and radiant, Clay as utterly happy, and the mother-in-law as convinced that "Clay and Daphne are just the people for each other." Oh, perhaps that was it: Rose and Louis hadn't exactly shared that opinion, certainly not initially.

Lincoln was astonished at his parents' reaction. He had, after all, showed Mina the manuscript of the novel and, according to Lincoln, she "didn't mind it when she read it." He was so upset that he sought out his friends Archie and Ada MacLeish, who were also Mina's friends. Archie essentially advised him to ignore his mother's outburst, telling Lincoln that when his own long poem *The Pot of Earth* (which associated women with the processes of nature) had been published half a dozen years earlier, "everyone went around consoling Ada for having such a horrible man for a husband, [a man] who thinks his wife is like an old flower pot."

Lincoln took some comfort from that, but he took it prematurely. The very next evening Mina herself finally let Lincoln know the true extent of her bruised feelings. She would never have dreamed, she told him, of saying or doing anything that might prevent his book from appearing, but now that publication was set, she'd decided to tell him that it had "cut her to the core." The novel, she felt, had "made her out such a bitch" that after it appeared she would have to leave Ashfield for good, since "she was disliked there enough already" (it was a prediction, or threat, she didn't make good on).

But it turned out that the novel was only part of what was bothering Mina. She went on to say (at least according to Lincoln's diary account) that until recently she'd always defended him but had now come to believe that he was "developing a powerfully split personality." She said, Lincoln wrote in his diary, that "I felt nothing. I merely knew sensation. . . . I had a false prestige due to a large vocabulary. I cared nothing for her who loved me very much . . . she realized just what kind of a person I was: how profoundly disinterested. My charm was just a weapon to use people." Then she added that she was deeply worried that if Lincoln continued along the same path, he was headed for "insanity."

Having delivered her indictment, Mina was apparently seized with guilt and began backtracking; perhaps, she volunteered, she'd spoken out of jealousy at Lincoln having published a book, when she herself was ambitious to write; or perhaps because he'd become so close to Muriel and been so disengaged of late from her. She told him again how much she loved him, how he'd long been to her "the child she'd never had by Harry," and how now, when she needed him most, it hurt her badly that he needed her less.

Lincoln chose not to respond directly and in kind because, as he put it in his diary (inadvertently confirming some of what Mina had said), "I felt on my part no interest, only the traces of a long-timed automatic affection & the fact that she would never, could never, admit the truth of my attitude & my real separation from her forever." An "exhaustive & unprofitable accusation [would] only . . . be a balm for her blindness, since she thinks, in the naïveté of her Freudian hierarchy, that since it is thus openly avowed, it is eliminated. The issue stands, and she may say that all she wants is to be good, a good little girl, but I know she never has known or will know anything about me except my apparently clinical symptoms. As Mools says, she is a precocious child."

This was harsh stuff—and they went at it until three in the morning. Mina had at least proved willing to consider that her motives in attacking her brother might have been, in whole or part, tainted. But Lincoln wouldn't yield an inch. He held stubbornly to the seemingly cruel position that he felt "merely sick" at Mina's "profound & willful deadness . . . her not dis-enjoyed dilemma of being dead since Harry died," and to the conviction that Mina "had no interest in me as me, but only as a part of her reflection."

There may have been some truth to this, at least at that particular point in Mina's life, but it was decidedly not the whole truth. In the years ahead, as in the past, she would prove time and again how deeply she cared for her brother, and not simply as some sort of mirror image or appendage of herself—no more so, at any rate, than sometimes occurs in all sibling relationships. And Lincoln would throughout his life, as one of his close friends put it, "run towards Mina when in trouble, away from her when not."

Histrionics, melodrama, and downright ferocity seem to have been recurrent components of the Kirsteins' tempestuous family dynamics. Louis and Lincoln were the most susceptible to these periodic bouts; George, the youngest, the least. If raging flare-ups were part of the Kirstein family culture, so too was the habit of putting them aside and moving on; the fallings-out and bruised feelings were not necessarily forgiven and forgotten, but they weren't allowed to disrupt family connections permanently. In Lincoln's case, and especially as he grew older, he'd blow up at people and then, when he next saw them, would act—often to their astonishment—as if nothing at all had happened, as if the relationship was entirely intact. Non–family members, less familiar with the pattern, would understandably be less prone to go along with such an emotional seesaw, would be permanently wounded and alienated. Lincoln would sometimes feel puzzled at why so-and-so, whom he'd recently denounced, would seem reluctant or unwilling to take up the reins of friendship or professional association again.

As was typical of them, within weeks of their blow-up Mina and Lincoln declared a "truce" over lunch. Lincoln characterized it as "two fencers afraid to make a lunge," but they did manage—and almost immediately—to start seeing each other again, and on a fairly regular basis. Mina was soon calmly sharing intimacies: how she planned to go to Saratoga (as she did) to try to find a suitable husband (which she didn't); and how their father's friend David Sarnoff, the president of RCA, had gotten an erection while talking to her.

Neither seems to have learned a thing from the blow-up, however. Lincoln wasn't, for the moment, at all interested in Mina's titillating news items; he was fixed instead on her manner (she "is so calm now," he wrote in his diary, "it makes me wild she had to create all her hysteria of 2 weeks ago"). Worse, Mina was soon back to pontificating about Lincoln's "bad neurosis," emphasizing, this time around, his relationship with their father. Lincoln, she announced, worked much too hard on trying to find ways to make himself productive and prominent in order to justify not having a regular job or income. What he failed to understand, Mina insisted, was that anything Lincoln did pleased Louis as long as he "took a definite stand." What worried their father, in other words, was Lincoln's vacillating between projects instead of steadily focusing on one.

Mina had a point—she almost always did, given her keen intellect and insight. But she lacked a sense of appropriate timing. Lincoln was in no mood at the moment for more of his sister's relentless psychologizing. Besides, her analysis of Louis's attitude didn't tally with his recent behavior. Though Louis had intensely disliked *Flesh Is Heir,* he'd already been urging Lincoln to try his hand at writing another novel, only this time a "popular" one that had a chance of selling. And Lincoln *had* started a new book (which he ultimately destroyed), just as he continued to make periodic passes at painting and at drawing the mural he'd long promised for Louis's business library. From Lincoln's point of view Mina seemed entirely unaware of the real pressures Louis continued to exert on him, even though she accurately pinpointed their father's ultimate concern: that Lincoln decide on a career and stay focused on it.

When Lincoln told Muriel "how sick my family conversations had made me," she decided to play it for laughs. She had a plan, she announced. She'd pay separate visits to Rose, Mina, and Louis. She'd tell Mina that her brother had gotten syphilis "from buggering little nigger boys" she, Muriel, had procured for him. She'd tell Rose that she must have money from her because she'd spent all of her own keeping Lincoln supplied with opium. As for Louis, who'd recently insisted that Lincoln tell him more about "this older woman" he was seeing so much of (Lincoln told him it was none of his business), Mools intended to don a dark suit, with a lace veil covering half her face, and dab nervously at her right eye while telling Louis that she was pregnant with Lincoln's child and refused to have an abortion—unless, that is, he purchased their love letters for ten thousand dollars in cash. Lincoln smiled at Muriel's fantasy confection but, still gloomy from the assorted family confrontations, felt his laughter was "joyless."

Decades later, Lincoln's memory either having failed or his preferred version of the fate of his novel having taken over, he'd claim that when *Flesh Is Heir* had been published in 1932, "the book was ignored." But in truth the novel received nearly a dozen notices, many of them in prominent publications, including the *New York Times* and *The Nation*, and many by well-known reviewers of the day, including Edward Dahlberg and Gorham Munson. To receive that much attention for a first novel, and at so young an age—he was still a few months shy of his twenty-fifth birthday—was a tribute to the reputation he'd already earned, thanks mostly to his work on *Hound and Horn*.

But the prominence of the reviews proved scant balm, given their content. Perhaps in deference to Louis Kirstein's public influence, the most polite notice ("will not be hailed as a youthful masterpiece . . . [but] merits attention") appeared in the *Boston Evening Transcript;* though Lincoln was able to acknowledge that the review was sympathetic, he also thought it was "very stupid."

A PRACTICE NOVEL was the dreary headline of Gorham Munson's review, and its contents proved still more offending: "The chief impression . . . is one of ineffectual willfulness." In his diary Lincoln characterized the review as "stupid and spiteful"; he knew Munson personally, intensely disliked him, and had rejected his submissions to *Hound and Horn*. Meeting Lincoln at a party the month after his notice appeared, Munson came up to him and apologized; Lincoln graciously "put him at his ease," but his dislike for the man deepened.

The review in the *New York Times*, unsigned, managed to speak well of the first section of the book, but of little that came after. And Edward Dahlberg in *The Nation* was savage: "egregiously stereotyped conversations, unimportant peregrinations . . . niggling, autobiographical mementos"—a nastiness that Lincoln again ascribed to his having rejected a Dahlberg submission to *Hound and Horn* (in this case, a not unlikely explanation, given Dahlberg's notorious reputation for vindictiveness).

Yet Dahlberg aside, the reviews weren't, on the whole, unfair: *Flesh Is Heir* is, in fact, an unengaging book, its "plot" devoid of any intrinsic interest or cumulative power, its characters blandly one-dimensional. The novel's protagonist, Roger Baum, wanders through a set of coming-of-age events that transparently reproduce, with little imaginative embellishment, Lincoln's own experiences, whether at boarding school, at work in the glass factory, at college, as a partygoer, or as a traveler abroad. Yet Roger Baum's personality, unlike his experiences, comes across, curiously, as very unlike Lincoln's own. Baum is an innocuous cipher, without any clear-cut, let alone compelling, personal identity, very nearly an inversion of Lincoln's own forceful, expressive nature. It's as if Lincoln had created a desired alter ego: calm, stolid, bland, the restful opposite of his own driven, nervous, intense self.

By the time *Flesh Is Heir* appeared in February 1932, Lincoln had "put the whole thing down as a bad job," and was, as always, already juggling a multiplicity of other projects. One of them now came to the fore: a mural show created for the Museum of Modern Art that had been on the back burner for some time.

Lincoln's connection to MoMA, which had opened in November 1929 in the Heckscher Building at Fifth Avenue and Fifty-seventh Street, went back to its precursor, the Harvard Society for Contemporary Art. The Society's bold modernism has often, and accurately, been credited with indirectly inspiring MoMA's formation; indeed, two of the museum's first four shows were reprises of exhibitions the Society had originated. But MoMA owed its actual formation to three remarkable women: Lillie Bliss, a pioneering collector of modern art whose father had made a fortune in New England textiles; Mary Quinn Sullivan, also a collector, and married to a wealthy lawyer; and the ebullient, dynamic Abby Aldrich Rockefeller, wife of the tersely reserved John D. Rockefeller, Jr., and mother of six children, only one of whom, Nelson, seems to have shared her sparkling, adventurous spirit, as well as her intense interest in modern art.[2]

MoMA's tiny staff of five was headed by twenty-nine-year-old Alfred Barr, Jr., as director (Paul Sachs had pushed his candidacy) and, as associate director, Barr's close friend Jere Abbott, a young art historian. Both men had served as Lincoln's tutors when he was an undergraduate at Harvard, and he'd come to know them reasonably well (Barr had frequently given him and the Society for Contemporary Art advice and guidance). Due to that connection, and in recognition of Lincoln's pioneering efforts, when MoMA formed an advisory committee, a sort of junior board of trustees, in the spring of 1930, he'd been invited to serve on it. The "Junior Committee," as it was often called, was small and prestigious. Among its early members, along with Lincoln, were Eddie Warburg; Philip Johnson (not yet an architect, but a close friend of Barr's); James Johnson Sweeney, then a fledgling scholar and later a leading figure at MoMA; and three wealthy young women, including Lillie Bliss's lively niece, Elizabeth "Betty" Bliss (whose widowed mother, in this tightly interconnected world, became the wife of A. Conger Goodyear, MoMA's first president). Nelson Rockefeller, after returning early in 1931 from his round-the-world honeymoon with his bride, the Philadelphia socialite Mary Todhunter ("Tod") Clark, became the Junior Committee's chair.

Of all these actual or potential movers and shakers, Lincoln was the most temperamentally akin to (though a more somber version of) the spirited, driven, and ambitious Nelson Rockefeller. But it was Alfred Barr for whom Lincoln would retain, over time, the most respect. Lincoln could grow wildly impatient with Barr's sometimes indecisive ways, his cautious administrative procrastinations, and his frequent bouts of illness, real and imagined. But if he could lose his temper at Barr, he could never (or never for very long) lose his affection for the man, for his shy decency, his modesty and melancholia, his loyalty, and his unshakable integrity.

During the first year and a half of MoMA's existence, Alfred often felt unhappy in his role as director, and he used Lincoln as something of a sounding board. Lack of funds particularly worried him, and he told Lincoln that "he wished to god his Trustees would put up or shut up." Alfred's "melancholy keenness" touched Lincoln; "he's all tight-up, packed, sweating inside," Lincoln wrote in his diary. He told Alfred that his true gift was scholarship, not administration, and advised him to think about resigning.

But by the early spring of 1931, Alfred began to feel more secure; the money situation had by then improved, and the trustees seemed more solidly behind him. The turning point was Lillie Bliss's death at sixty-six in March 1931. In her will she left MoMA a considerable portion of her splendid modern collection, though on condition that the museum demonstrate its financial stability by raising a substantial endowment. That lit a fire under the trustees, and within a few years the Bliss collection had been secured.

As for Alfred's wife, Marga, she plied Lincoln for a time with unwanted confidences, going so far one day over lunch as to tell him (so Lincoln recorded in his diary) that "she was miserably lonely, unhappy, hated housework, and hated to nurse Alfred who is constantly ill." Before she could say more, Lincoln interrupted; he told her that "she could do whatever she wanted to do" but that he "doubted if she wanted to do anything." According to Lincoln, Marga "loved" his forcefulness. For his part he felt "contemptuous of her proud body and little soul," and put her down as "a silly, pretty selfish, unimaginative woman."

Lincoln liked a few of the individuals on the Junior Committee, especially Betty Bliss, but he thought their meetings largely ineffectual. Yet he was pleased that the committee did consistently complain to MoMA's trustees about the early exhibits focusing too exclusively on European artists. Lincoln himself had been pushing for an American mural show at MoMA, keenly aware that the vast construction project under way in midtown Manhattan to create what was becoming known as Rockefeller Center, would soon be deciding on mural commissions to decorate the lobby of the RCA Building.

He wanted some of those commissions to go to American artists. Over the past year or so he'd met a number of them, admired their work, and—though his own funds at this point were limited—sometimes commissioned a portrait of himself to help them (and perhaps his own self-esteem) along. These would come to include, over time, Gaston Lachaise, Isamu Noguchi, Paul Cadmus, Pavel Tchelitchev, and, much later, Jamie Wyeth and David Langfitt. Lincoln had also been working hard to persuade far wealthier friends, like Eddie Warburg, to buy the work of artists he admired; Eddie did, after considerable pressure from Lincoln, purchase a Gaston Lachaise piece in 1932, thereby literally bringing the difficult sculptor back from the brink of suicide. Lincoln thought the best strategy for getting RCA commissions for American artists would be to mount a mural show at MoMA to showcase their talents.

When MoMA's trustees early in 1932 did finally give the go-ahead for such a show, Nelson Rockefeller saw to it that Lincoln was put in charge. He was delighted; tired of coping with MoMA's difficult personalities, Lincoln leapt at the chance to produce an actual exhibit and write its catalog. He titled the show "The Post War World" and invited various easel painters—a good half of whom were barely known, and only three of whom had ever previously attempted to cover a large space—to participate. The show was not designed as a competition, but Lincoln did ask each artist to prepare sketches for his or her suggested mural and some fragment of a realized design. Some of the best known among the invitees, including Charles Burchfield, Thomas Hart Benton, Boardman Robinson, and John Sloan, expressed interest in the idea but declined to participate because of the limited space and time allotments.[3]

Lincoln individually pursued some of the artists he was most eager to have in the show, especially those he wasn't already acquainted with personally. Of those, Georgia O'Keeffe proved the most antagonistic; "she was nasty," Lincoln wrote in his diary, "about all the other Americans I told her were in the show, except Stuart Davis." He thought her "a spoiled prima donna," yet he somehow managed to persuade her, against the wishes of Alfred Stieglitz, her exceedingly difficult husband, to participate.

Lincoln's own favorites, when the murals began to arrive, were those done by Franklin Watkins, Hugo Gellert, William Gropper, Ben Shahn, and Philip Reisman, though he found elements to admire in the work of a number of others, including Jane Berlandina, Louis Bouché, Philip Evergood, Stefan Hirsch, and Henry Varnum Poor. But when MoMA's trustees were given an advance look at the show, most of them found little to praise and several of them, including Conger Goodyear, Samuel Lewisohn, and Stephen Clark (the Singer sewing machine magnate), expressed outrage at the "Communistic" political content of the Shahn, Gellert, and Gropper murals in particular. Shahn's *The Passion of Sacco and Vanzetti* showed the stuffed-shirt Lowell committee and Judge Webster Thayer, those responsible for sealing the fate of the two Italian American anarchists, staring into their coffins. (Exactly a year later Shahn would serve as Diego Rivera's assistant in a mural scandal at Rockefeller Center that replayed, with remarkable similarity, the earlier events at MoMA.)

An alarmed Alfred Barr told Lincoln that the Shahn, Gellert, and Gropper murals, at the very least, could not be included in the show, and then called a meeting with Lincoln, Nelson Rockefeller, and several of the affronted trustees. That gathering so angered Lincoln that he hinted at canceling the show and then paced silently up and down the room. Nelson, according to Lincoln, "as usual relied on his boyish charms" to calm matters down for the moment. That evening at dinner, Archie MacLeish reprimanded Lincoln for his behavior. He had no right, Archie told him, to be "vindictive"; he could resign if he chose, but he could not take the show with him.

Thus admonished, Lincoln went the following morning to see Abby Aldrich Rockefeller. He tried to persuade her to use her influence to see that the embargoed murals were allowed to stay in the show, insisting that "it would be far better for the Museum." He later wrote in his diary that "Mrs. Rockefeller's attitude was liberal." She told him that "she had always considered herself a revolutionary . . . but she saw no reason why people had to indulge in bad taste, particularly Ben Shahn . . . because she had helped him originally." Lincoln responded (or so he wrote in his diary) "that she couldn't hope to control or take the responsibility for Ben Shahn's future & that he painted with no intent to annoy—so she had no legitimate reason to be disappointed in him." Mrs. Rockefeller, in turn, told Lincoln that it would be "cowardly to resign & that Nelson was so impetuous that he would resign too." And that, she went on, would be "a great shame," as it would hurt his usefulness, inasmuch as (at twenty-three) he'd been made a trustee of the Metropolitan and might be able to influence that museum's willingness, limited until then, to buy American pictures.

Lincoln left Mrs. Rockefeller's house certain that he had "convinced her," even though he thought her "so remote from actuality as to make a plan on my part difficult." But it quickly became clear that plan or no, Conger Goodyear and Stephen Clark would remain "adamant" about rejecting the offending murals. Given their implacable position, Lincoln went to see Ben Shahn to tell him that his mural would not be hung ("it was a nasty thing to have to tell him"). Shahn said that the whole controversy had worn him out, that he'd completed the mural while ill (and with an ice pack on his head), that though he'd done the mural "merely as a social record," the refusal to show it might "yet make him 'class conscious.' "

The day after giving Shahn the bad news, Lincoln had to do a repeat performance with William Gropper, whose mural had depicted J. P. Morgan riding on a bear "with a floosie around his neck." Lincoln was more upset than Gropper, who told Lincoln he'd "quietly expected it." Lincoln viewed Gropper as an uncommonly "sweet" man, "very calm and naive," who was "more interested in painting than in Communism"—though Gropper would have denied it.

As for Lincoln, he was in anguish, finding it hard to keep straight whether he was, or should be, acting on behalf of MoMA's trustees, the mural show itself, or the painters. His anguish intensified when Shahn told him that a committee was being formed by some of the other painters aimed at withdrawing their work as a gesture of solidarity with the three artists—Gropper, Shahn, and Hugo Gellert—whose work had been excluded. When Lincoln passed that news on to Barr, he tersely remarked, "Now we are being threatened."

At Shahn's suggestion Lincoln went next to see the civil-liberties lawyer Philip Wittenberg, who told him he'd try to get a temporary injunction against MoMA, forcing it either to hang the excluded work or to cancel the entire show. Wittenberg admonished Lincoln for being "entirely confused" about his loyalties, and Lincoln freely admitted that he was—though he added that Shahn "was satisfied I had acted in good faith."

After leaving Wittenberg, Lincoln went to confer with Gropper and Gellert at a nearby Child's cafeteria. They told him that Reginald Marsh had decided to head the artists' committee of protest, that Boardman Robinson and Diego Rivera were backing him, and that the intention was to achieve "a universal secession" from the show. Lincoln told the two men straight out that his loyalties were "very mixed" but that he felt he should refuse to let them have the total list of participating artists (which hadn't as yet been published), feeling as he did that "most of the artists would feel called on to ruin their own chances and yet they had no idea of the political implications when they accepted the Museum's invitation to show." Lincoln thought both men were "better-tempered and more genuine, but no easier to work with or talk to, than the capitalists up at the Museum."

Alan Blackburn, MoMA's assistant treasurer, took the attitude of "threatened sabotage"; and Barr, according to Lincoln, told him that if the artists intended to "mix themselves up with an imposed political ideology, they will lose all the values of a Bohemian laissez-faire which up to the present they have desired." Nelson, in turn, asked Thomas Debevoise, the Rockefeller family's imperious counsel ("lip-curling" is how Lincoln described him), to go up to MoMA himself and have a look at the murals in question. After completing his inspection Debevoise asked Lincoln point-blank whether, if called upon, he would be willing to affirm publicly that the Shahn, Gellert, and Gropper panels were "offensive." Debevoise "tightened" when Lincoln promptly replied no.

Yet another lengthy conference followed with Stephen Clark and Lewisohn, after which Nelson was dispatched to get J. P. Morgan's opinion. "Of course hang them!" Morgan told him, and Ivy Lee, the Rockefellers' publicist, agreed. Lincoln immediately informed Gropper and Gellert, who were jubilant; the next step, they told Lincoln, was for him to resign from the museum. He refused but let the artists think that the victory had been entirely due to their unyielding defiance; in the privacy of his diary,

Lincoln confessed—seemingly overconfessed—that he viewed his own actions as having been "as unscrupulous as possible" toward *both* sides in the name of getting the show on "as it was intended."

The "victory," it soon became apparent, was not yet secured. No sooner had J. P. Morgan sanctioned the show than Conger Goodyear returned from vacation, declared his "furious" opposition to "the Communists," and threatened to resign as MoMA's president if the decision wasn't reversed. The whole day of April 27, 1932, was spent in what Lincoln called "cross machinations." Lincoln himself manned the barricades, dispatching runners in all directions. He sent Betty Bliss to persuade her father, Cornelius Bliss, guardian of Lillie Bliss's collection (which MoMA desperately wanted to secure), to intercede with Goodyear. He got from Gropper an actual count of how many artists were really prepared to secede (probably twenty-five, Gropper reported). He called Wittenberg "to make sure of an attempt to get an injunction to stop the show" should the three artists be excluded. He advised Nelson to try to *make* Goodyear resign; Nelson "was mad enough," Lincoln wrote in his diary, "to do anything." And finally, he tried, with limited success, to ascertain just how many trustees stood behind Goodyear.

People were in and out of conferences for the better part of the next two days. When, at one of the meetings, Goodyear angrily banged his fist on the table while insisting that MoMA's policy "must protect from offense," Debevoise, representing the wishes of Nelson and his mother, calmly stood firm, insisting that *all* the murals must be hung. Goodyear finally backed down, but as a rearguard action, did his best to delay the show's catalog long enough to keep out reproductions of the Gropper and Gellert panels—though Lincoln somehow succeeded in "forcing" in Shahn's *Sacco and Vanzetti*.

Lincoln drew a sigh of relief—but then nearly choked on it. The show's thirty-odd paintings barely got hung (and not very well) in time for the next day's press opening, and the day after that, as the notices began to appear, it became clear that the show was in for a severe drubbing. Lincoln himself acknowledged that only a few of the panels were of any real distinction, but he also felt that those few, along with the experimental nature of the effort, fully redeemed the enterprise.

The critics disagreed. Every single reviewer lambasted the show. The *New York Times* critic haughtily wrote that the show contained "violations of even the most catholic conceptions of good taste"; he further claimed that his objections to "the class struggle orgies" was due not to their theme but to "the childish or generally uninspired way in which they are handled." Royal Cortissoz, the prominent and highly conservative *Tribune* critic, announced that "in sheer, dismal ineptitude the exhibition touches bottom." And so it went, with the *Evening American* suggesting that MoMA "could not do better than to close at once the American Mural exhibition."

Instead, MoMA—which had just moved to expanded quarters in a Rockefeller-owned town house on West Fifty-third Street—parked the exhibit on the fourth floor, making it difficult for visitors to find; overall attendance, not surprisingly, would be only half that of MoMA's other exhibits in 1932. Lincoln himself was singled out for special blame, and Nelson exonerated, though he'd backed Lincoln to the hilt and was the actual chair of the Junior Committee, which had initiated the show.

Lincoln played out the disaster with bravado and humor. As he wrote Agnes Mongan, then the Fogg Museum curator, "The mural show was a shattering failure & ruined my, er, reputation with all those to whom reputation counts. . . . But I was delighted at the universal irritation & the general feeling of betrayal everyone seemed to feel that I provided, I who was so charming & bright, etc. No longer. Now I'm only an, er, Jewish Bolshevik with shocking bad manners."

Though several trustees resigned in the wake of the show, Lincoln's fiercest antagonist was the headstrong Mary Hoyt Wiborg, an amateur playwright and the daughter of wealthy financier Frank Wiborg (another daughter, Sara, married Gerald Murphy of Lost Generation fame). Lincoln already knew "Hoytie" and thought her "the world's nastiest woman"; she was, among much else, openly anti-Semitic. Outraged at the mural show, she immediately resigned from MoMA's membership committee, saying that "the Communist propaganda on the walls" would corrupt schoolchildren entering the museum. And she denounced Lincoln, to his face, as "a parlor Bolshevik."

Lincoln's politics were becoming a matter of interest to a number of people, of concern to his parents, and of considerable confusion to himself. His friend Archie MacLeish, then working for *Fortune* magazine but himself moving leftward and soon to produce a number of significant essays criticizing capitalism, nonetheless cautioned Lincoln about his interest in the Soviet Union; Archie worried especially about the role of the artist in a bureaucratic state like Russia, fearing that talent would be drafted for purposes that were "purely propaganda." In the spring of 1931 Lincoln himself still felt that "the system of individualism" remained worth defending. " 'Every man a Morgan,' " he wrote in his diary; capitalism as an ideology still seemed to him "to have less flaws, in ratio to our present information, than Russian communism."

Lincoln even suggested to Sherwin Badger, editor of the *Wall Street Journal* (he frequently saw Badger socially) that he, Lincoln, might be interested in putting together for the *Journal* "a symposium of articles in defense of capitalism." Badger was interested, but nothing came of that particular idea—perhaps because Lincoln freely acknowledged that he knew nothing of economics and had "no talent for abstraction."

Or perhaps because Lincoln was occasionally having sex with Sherwin's freewheeling wife, Mary, who may well have told her husband about it. What we do know is that she told Lincoln that he "didn't really like women," that (as Lincoln recorded her words in his diary) "she found that out when she went to bed with me. That she enjoyed it but she could see my affections were elsewhere. For two hours," Lincoln commented, "I felt castrated by her perception but generally speaking pleased at having found not a lover but a friend."[4]

During this same period, and for a much longer time, Lincoln was also regularly seeing and having sex with (once as part of an orgy) another of his "smart set" friends, the fledgling actress Margot Loines, and it was Margot, not Lincoln, who eventually put a stop to the sex. When one of Muriel Draper's friends, Rita Romilly, heard that Lincoln was having "an affair with some girl," she expressed surprise to Muriel because "she had always understood" that Lincoln was "on the other side." "If you mean queer," Muriel replied, "he screws who he pleases. He's probably had her clothes off ten times already . . . she's his girl, Margot is Lincoln's girl."

Lincoln in fact liked Margot so well that he introduced her to Muriel "as [a] possible wife for me." It was an idea he'd been toying with for some time (he'd earlier talked marriage with Alice Lowell as well), and he actually asked Margot to consider the possibility. When Jack Wheelwright heard of the proposal he berated Lincoln for making it—not because he liked sex with men but because he had no guaranteed income at all except for eight hundred dollars a year from his grandfather. Ultimately Lincoln and Margot decided against marriage, but as late as the spring of 1932, he wrote in his diary, "I like her better than any girl I've ever known & yet except in the most direct physical contact, she doesn't deeply move me. She is so open and uninhibited, her mind is so unabused, that no perception can lodge there long, and her sympathy which is burning is somehow too welling constantly for satisfaction."

If Lincoln's suggestion to Sherwin Badger of a symposium on the defense of capitalism implied a lingering attachment to the existing economic order, that view increasingly alternated with the sense that capitalism had outworn its usefulness. Over the next two years he would now and then lurch back toward a more conservative position (reading *Fortune*'s issue on Russia in February 1932, for example, made him momentarily feel that the Soviet Union "is by no means the paradise of undiluted energy" he had thought it was). Yet in general, Lincoln's shift leftward, like that of so many other modernist intellectuals of the day, continued to solidify. But even during 1932–33, the high-water mark of his pro-Soviet sympathies, he never (other than as a momentary fantasy) considered adopting the

The Stein family, c. 1897. Back row, farthest left: *Rose Stein Kirstein;* fourth from right: *Louis Kirstein, holding Mina;* seated center: *Rose's parents, Mina and Nathan Stein*

ABOVE: *Louis, Mina, and Louis's mother, Jeanette, c. 1898.* RIGHT: *The Kirsteins with Lincoln and Mina, c. 1907.* BELOW: *Rose and Lincoln, c. 1905.* BOTTOM RIGHT: *George, Mina, and Lincoln, c. 1913*

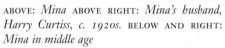
ABOVE: *Mina* ABOVE RIGHT: *Mina's husband, Harry Curtiss, c. 1920s.* BELOW AND RIGHT: *Mina in middle age*

Young Lincoln

ABOVE: *Lincoln in his early teens in France*
LEFT: *Lincoln at Harvard, age twenty*

RIGHT: *At Harvard,
c. 1929*
BELOW: *Lincoln in
1935, age thirty-one*

With Mina, 1936

Wall of portraits of family and friends in Lincoln's house on Nineteenth Street in New York. At the top left corner: *Fidelma by Paul Cadmus, c. 1926;* and to its right *Lincoln by Pavel Tchelitchev, c. 1935*

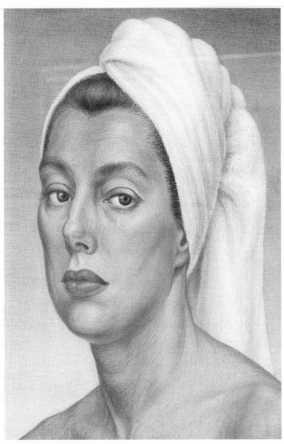

Portraits of Fidelma and Lincoln by Fidelma, early 1950s

Lincoln in and out of uniform, 1940s

An elderly Lincoln looking at George Platt Lynes's photograph of himself as a young man

self-label "Communist" let alone (unlike Muriel, the person he trusted most in the world) actually joining the party and becoming a functionary. The FBI did open a file on him, but it remained thin and contains no evidence of any sustained radical involvement, beyond signing a few "calls" and protest letters.

Still, within a mere month after suggesting the pro-capitalism symposium to Sherwin Badger, Lincoln was drinking beer for three hours in a Greenwich Village speakeasy with Mike Gold, editor of the *New Masses* (a mutual friend, the left-wing poet Norman MacLeod, brought them together). Lincoln listened raptly as Gold, with "great energy, directness and real charm," denounced "*New Republic* liberalism" and hailed "communism as the only panacea." Among many other things, Gold told him that all the current talk among capitalist countries about arms reduction was a facade for a new military buildup, and in any case would remove "none of the basic fundamental evils of capitalism." Lincoln came away from the speakeasy feeling that Mike Gold was *wonderful*.

In February 1932 Lincoln began to write occasional pieces for *Arts Weekly* magazine, as well as a weekly column (which he would continue for nearly a year) called "Books and Characters" for the *Boston Evening American*, the newspaper with the largest evening circulation in New England. Those articles and columns were filled with his newfound left-wing convictions. Reviewing the Soviet film *The Road to Life* for *Arts Weekly*, he acknowledged that "it is propaganda," but "only in the best sense of that word: It increases one's interest and confirms one's sympathy with a policy, here shown as regeneration. . . . Russia seems the last, the only, frontier left in the world."

The following month, he chose to review Leon Trotsky's *History of the Russian Revolution* in his *Evening American* column, and in it he characterized the czar's court as "rotten and inert . . . functioning blindly on the brink of an abyss, ignoring the smoldering, servile millions that were to become the triumphant Russian proletariat." Two months after that, Lincoln was announcing in print that the current depression "held behind its mask . . . fantastic potentials . . . those who can afford not to be frightened by a violent shift, both in the scale of our private lives and also in the standard of the whole social system, eagerly await something which we vaguely generalize under the term 'revolution.' "

In late May 1932 Lincoln was the youngest member (he'd just turned twenty-five) of a small group of intellectuals who gathered at Edmund Wilson's apartment on West Fifty-eighth Street to listen to William Z. Foster, the Communist Party candidate for president, explain his philosophy. Among those present were Matthew Josephson, then an assistant editor at the *New Republic*; Laurence Dennis, author of the highly influential *Is Capitalism Doomed?*; the critic Gilbert Seldes; and John Dos Passos (whom Lincoln had met previously and had found "the essence of kindness & sweetness"; he might have changed his mind had he been able to read Dos Passos's private letters, filled as they were with anti-Jewish and racist remarks).

In his just-published book, *Toward Soviet America*, Foster had expressed his distrust of the multitude of intellectuals who were suddenly discovering their consciences, and he predicted that only those with proletarian backgrounds would continue with the social struggle for very long, with most of them becoming "social fascists." Nothing that transpired at Edmund Wilson's that evening would have led Foster to moderate his position. Lincoln was among those who made various objections during the evening to Foster's views. Yet he did conclude in his diary that "the main thing I got from the evening was the fact that I disagreed with nothing that he either said or advocated"—though adding that "I don't propose to surrender my interests in the basic standards during that time when . . . other standards are being formulated for use."

What particular "standards" Lincoln may have been thinking of remains unclear, but the co-existence in his mind of seemingly opposite views, the disjunctive appeal both of chaos and order, of sympathy for the newness in tandem with an insistent defense of tradition, was a defining ingredient of his personality (and the central reason, perhaps, for the contemporary feel of his character). If Lincoln was attracted to "low life" and erotically turned on by sailors and the like, he equally loved playing "scout" or "pin-the-donkey" with the Brahmins of Naushon. His class membership—whether defined by income, job status (the prestigious editor of *Hound and Horn*), or education—landed him somewhere in the higher echelons; but he lacked pedigreed antecedents, and being Jewish and queer (his word) further limited his acceptability in high society—as well as his wish to be part of it.

Lincoln did feel genuine empathy for the suffering he saw around him among those less fortunate, and he even (if irregularly) believed that systemic structural changes were needed in American institutions. But what he didn't feel in his gut—not in any sustained way at least (and few Americans ever have)—was that the lowliest should be automatically raised up to share equitably in social wealth; there was always the lurking, elitist suspicion that a classless society was incompatible with his highest priorities: the production of "art" and "taste." Foster was right: Lincoln's attraction to socialism would not last, though he'd remain politically liberal (if largely inactive) all his life.

But in 1932 Lincoln's left-wing tendencies were strong enough to alarm his father. Louis decided that the time had come to reintroduce his son to the "glories" of Western-style democracy. And so it was that Lincoln was reluctantly dragooned into accompanying his father to the Democratic National Convention in Chicago at the end of June. Louis was in no sense one of the major players at the convention, but he did know several people who were, and they shared with him the swirling rumors, and even some of the real information, to which they were privy. Arriving in time for the convention's opening gavel on June 27, Louis and Lincoln had dinner the first night with Bob Norton, Washington correspondent for the *Boston Post*, who told them that for the time being at least, Franklin Delano Roosevelt's candidacy had been stopped in its tracks; John Curry, the leader of New York City's Tammany Hall, added that he had 507 votes locked up against FDR.[5]

Louis was glad to hear it. His preferred candidate was Al Smith, whose losing run for the presidency he'd supported in 1928. Smith, disliking Roosevelt intensely, had come out of political retirement to challenge him for the nomination, and was the overwhelming favorite son of Massachusetts, having trounced Roosevelt by three to one in the recent state primary. Smith seemed to have a fair shot at ending up as the convention's choice, since party rules required a two-thirds vote for nomination.

Much as he liked Smith, Louis was in fact less interested in the national election than in the upcoming state one. Governor Joseph Ely, who'd been chosen to nominate Smith at the convention, was himself running for reelection in Massachusetts, and Louis not only knew him personally but had worked closely with him on a number of occasions. Ely had just pushed through the nomination of Felix Frankfurter to the Massachusetts Supreme Court; Frankfurter declined the nomination but in the postconvention period would be instrumental in persuading FDR and Ely to reconcile. The shrewd, pragmatic Louis had also been careful all along to maintain ties as well with Boston's mayor, James Michael Curley, the declared enemy of both Ely and Al Smith.

Chicago's mayor, Anton Cermak—who *was* a major player at the convention (and would be assassinated within months by a bullet meant for FDR)—personally warned Louis that there could be riots in the city during the convention. The Depression had hit Chicago with special fury: half the city's banks had failed, the local government was on the verge of bankruptcy, schoolteachers hadn't been paid in eight months, and upwards of a million citizens were unemployed, with thousands sleeping in the streets. Cermak went so far as to prophesy actual revolution.

It didn't come to that, and Louis was able contentedly to indulge his penchant for hobnobbing with the great and near-great. "We met everyone who was worth meeting," he later wrote his son George, "and had one of the very best boxes in the convention" (the box was courtesy of his friend Albert Lasker, the well-known advertising whiz, who chaired the convention's committee on arrangements). Another friend, the department store head Bernard Gimbel, brought the boxer Gene Tunney to Louis's hotel room for an hour's chat. The famed Arctic explorer Adm. Richard Byrd, whose brother Henry Flood Byrd was one of the long shots for the presidential nomination, approached Louis with a moneymaking scheme to exhibit some items from his polar expeditions at Filene's (in his diary Lincoln described the admiral as "like a gull around the possible refuse of the convention pies").

Father and son also briefly met Bernard Baruch, who Lincoln thought "was humorous, seemed steady, even attractive, and with authority." Baruch allowed Louis to read the platform, typewritten on two sheets of paper, prior to its presentation to the convention, probably because he'd given a minor assist to Massachusetts senator David Walsh in writing up the Prohibition repeal plank (which ended up being passed). Louis happily wrote George that he'd participated "in some of the inside stuff." Lincoln had a somewhat different gloss: "I was informed," he wrote in his diary, that "I had been in a smoke-filled room at last. I know how power works, how Presidents are made. . . . I tried to get father to admit it was all lousy and had nothing to do with policy as government" but, he added sarcastically, Father was "kinder, or knew more."

By the second day of the convention Lincoln already felt that the proceedings were "sickening," that he couldn't take too much more of the "sodden organ playing," the "heavy movie-tone bright lights," and the duplicative, endless speechifying—"protracted tedium," is how he put it. "We had a marvelous time," Louis would write George after the convention was over and they'd returned to the East Coast, but the use of "we" constituted a major liberty. Lincoln did his best to amuse himself during the convention by chatting up the male ushers and ogling assorted bellboys, taxi drivers, and attendants, all of whom he decided were more attractive than their New York counterparts. But by his own account he soon turned surly, glowering "at anybody who tried to be conversationally friendly about Franklin Roosevelt's chances," and that included FDR's son Jimmy Roosevelt, who acted surprised at what Lincoln admitted was "my nastiness." Louis suggested that if anything was "at fault" in the convention proceedings, it wasn't "the lousy political system" but "merely human nature," to which Lincoln responded that he was "not at all interested in this chapter of my education."

To spare everyone Lincoln decided that he'd stop trying to sit still and would take himself off for various outings. He went twice to Chicago's Art Institute, where he lingered over an El Greco "immeasurably superior to anything else in the museum." He went to the planetarium, the movies (where he saw his beloved James Cagney, for the second time, in *Winner Take All*) and to the grounds of the upcoming World's Fair, where he took a picture to give Lachaise of the sculpted gate that he'd earlier been commissioned to do.

Louis reprimanded his son for being "so selfish and thoughtless," and for "sulking generally"—and Lincoln agreed with his father's criticism. But though displeased, Louis also had a decided sense of humor. At night, he and Lincoln shared a twin-bedded room; as Lincoln lay awake listening to his father's snoring and to assorted party noises, he debated "various genital considerations" as a way of easing himself off to sleep. Could he risk masturbating with his father nearby? As a "filial experiment in infantile regression," he went ahead and started to play with himself on his bed. After a time Louis called out, "Why don't you get a machine to play with?" They both chuckled.

When California shifted to Roosevelt on the fourth roll call, thus securing his nomination, the woman sitting next to Lincoln told him, in reference to FDR's crippling polio, that "they were merely substituting a man dead from the waist down for a man dead from the neck up." Lincoln apparently agreed, since he thought the remark worth recording in his diary. When FDR flew in from Albany to deliver his acceptance speech, Lincoln decided he'd heard enough and went horseback riding instead.

Once they were back home Louis pronounced the Democratic convention "the greatest spectacle" he'd ever seen, and characterized Massachusetts Governor Ely's nominating speech for Al Smith as the "greatest speech since Bob Ingersoll." Lincoln wrote sardonically in his diary that his father apparently had "neither seen or heard much." He didn't risk saying that to his father's face, but he did devote a whole column in his *Boston Evening American* series to his experiences at the convention. Louis could hardly have been pleased with the way Lincoln publicly characterized the experience. "We sat on the hard red seats," he wrote, and "listened to the limp yards of inert oratory spun out into the warp and woof of threadbare praise . . . were we surprised, or interested, or aroused? We were not . . . we were irritated, exhausted, amused, sickened and hopeless." The entire proceedings, the column concluded, were a "mixture of a rodeo, a revival meeting and a riot."

Nor did Lincoln change his left-leaning views or cease to express them in his newspaper columns. He devoted an entire piece to reviewing William Z. Foster's *Toward Soviet America*, in which he characterized Foster as "no monster to meet. He gives the impression of being a very quiet, convinced and concentrated member of his own working class." He did go on in the column to characterize Foster's prediction of an inevitable revolution in this country as "naive," but primarily on the grounds that "sentiment of the average middle-class could be quickly stirred into a violent nationalist sentiment," and "government arsenals and barracks," as had happened before during the Pullman strike, would "crush revolts for many years to come . . . [and] would turn the country into a Fascist State."

Lincoln had been to Chicago, but his left-wing views had barely been dented.

CHAPTER SEVEN

Nijinsky

(1931–1933)

In the years preceding World War I, when Muriel's famous Edith Grove salon in London was at its peak, she'd known Diaghilev personally, had seen Vaslav Nijinsky dance in *Spectre de la Rose*, among other roles, and, after his performances, had watched him as he "moved unnoticeably from room to room at Edith Grove, smiled without meaning, and spoke rarely." So when Lincoln came bounding into Muriel's apartment late in the fall of 1932, wild with excitement after the long lunch he'd just had (as arranged by a mutual friend in publishing) with Nijinsky's wife, Romola, Muriel was comparatively cool to the news. She'd always felt that Romola's marriage to Nijinsky, now schizophrenic and a patient in a Swiss sanitarium, had "undermined him"—and she said as much that day to Lincoln.[1]

But for the moment nothing could restrain his enthusiasm. He couldn't then know that his first impression of Romola would be his most positive; he thought of her, he told Muriel, as "an uncomplaining, tragic woman"—tragic not simply because of Vaslav's illness but because U.S. immigration was threatening to deport her before she could complete several tasks she'd set herself. One was to arrange for a benefit performance for Vaslav; the Swiss sanitarium, she told Lincoln, would soon deport him to the Soviet Union unless she came up with more money for his care—and the great Russian bass Chaliapin had warned her, she said, that the Soviets "will let him die."

She also wanted to write her husband's biography, for which she'd been making notes, in the hope that royalties from the book would serve as a source of financial support for Vaslav, herself, and their two daughters (who were living in Hungary with her mother and stepfather). Her third task, Romola told Lincoln—along with announcing that she was a lesbian—was to fulfill a promise she'd made to her lover Frederica Dezentje, a young married Dutchwoman whose recent death had alternately been ascribed to suicide or pulmonary tuberculosis, to bring her ashes home to Europe. (Another of Romola's lovers, the actress Lya de Putti, had died earlier, purportedly from swallowing a chicken bone.) Frederica lay in a receiving vault in New York's Woodlawn Cemetery, and Romola made frequent trips there to weep over her casket, but she'd not yet succeeded in making arrangements for its transport.

"I liked her genuinely," Lincoln wrote that night in his diary, "and would do anything I could to help her." Since Lincoln adored drama, his fervor over Romola could be attributed to her considerable histrionic skills but—since he was also a quick and penetrating study—it was probably more centrally linked to his eagerness to find a way into the world of classical ballet. Before long he and Romola would begin work together on Vaslav's biography.

Lincoln's interest in the ballet went back to his childhood attendance at the Chicago Opera Company's performance of "The Dance of the Hours," from *La Gioconda* and the performances by Anna Pavlova he'd seen with his cousin Nat; his interest quickened on his various trips as a teenager to Europe, where in 1929 he'd seen Diaghilev's Ballets Russes. He'd even taken some ballet lessons in 1931 from Edward Duburon, a member of the comparatively short-lived (1922–31) Pavley-Oukrainsky Company.

For some time Lincoln had also been regularly attending dance recitals, had begun to write critical articles about various performers, and had himself been thinking up possible themes for new ballets (sometimes as many as five a day). He also started to ponder possible venues for forming a ballet company or school—perhaps at MoMA or in one of the new Rockefeller Center buildings. He'd even, a mere two weeks before meeting Romola, and in what he would have been entitled to view as a transcendent coincidence, started to take classes with Michel Fokine, one of ballet's most celebrated pioneers.

By now, Fokine's glory days as dancer and choreographer were far behind him. He and his wife had lived in the United States since 1919, and two years after arriving had opened a successful school in a nineteenth-century French-style mansion at 4 Riverside Drive; at the top of its broad staircase Fokine hung a full-length self-portrait (in Lincoln's opinion, Fokine's paintings, which were all over the walls, were "exceptionally proficient"). Their students would become some of ballet's brightest stars, but Lincoln wasn't destined to be one of them. As Fokine made clear early on, Lincoln would be wasting his time if he held out any hope of becoming a performer—he was too big, too awkward, too old. But—though the occasional fantasy lingered—Lincoln already knew that. He was there primarily, as he later wrote, "to learn the structure" of Fokine's work, having finally realized (an awareness he credited to Muriel) that what he wanted to do more than anything else in life was "something connected with dancing." And the time he spent in Fokine's classes (he attended regularly for more than four months) allowed him, he later wrote, to learn from the

barre exercises "a modicum of what is necessary in the schooling of profes-
sionals. I learned the consummate logic in the progression of academic
exercises from first steps to ultimate virtuosity."

When he first appeared for class in mid-November 1932, and got his
first look at the master himself, Lincoln described Fokine in his diary as
"bald and grey, very Russian and charming." Twelve girls and two other
boys—one of whom Lincoln described as "fairy, small" and the other as "a
rather burly Russian [with a] tough guy attitude"—were in his class. He
found Fokine "a very swift and exacting teacher"—and found himself
"baffled trying to follow the . . . long, difficult routines." The Russian student told him that he was wasting both his time and that of the class. (Lincoln told the other students, who'd apparently assumed that he was "a
college boy," that he was in fact a reporter for the *New York Sun*, which
nobody questioned.) Despite his awkwardness Lincoln felt "enormous
excitement seeing them all dance, and of dancing," and wondered why in
God's name he hadn't done it before.

At his next class he saw to his delight the well-known dancer Patricia
Bowman finishing her lesson. He'd met her once at one of Muriel's
"evenings," but though she looked over at him several times, she didn't
seem able to place him. She was, Lincoln wrote in his diary, "exquisitely
made up and danced with great grace"—unlike "one heavy, fat, pitiful girl
in big black bloomers." He thought Fokine was "divinely kind and sympathetic to everyone." Many years later, perhaps as the result of subsequent
experiences between the two, or perhaps because Fokine could be charming one day and moodily difficult the next, Lincoln would describe him as
"a vain, resentful, disappointed veteran who could see nothing in any work
save his own, and whose restricted taste was that of his early youth." But
initially, at least, he was enraptured with his teacher and looked forward
eagerly to class.

The two men soon began exchanging a few words after class, and then
to have longer talks—all of which would eventuate in Lincoln writing (at
the suggestion of the English ballet historian and critic Arnold Haskell,
who was editing a series of short books) a sixty-seven-page monograph,
Fokine. Not surprisingly, Fokine had firm opinions about all aspects of the
dance, and he gave Lincoln a copy of his mimeographed lectures on the
subject. Among much else, he told Lincoln that Nijinsky, not one of his
favorites, "often made the error" in *Sacre* "of imitating the rhythm of the
music itself rather than creating his own tunes"—music should come from
the dance, not vice versa. He also chastised Lincoln for having said, in his
article "The Diaghilev Period," that Nijinsky invented contrapuntal
rhythms in dancing; no, Fokine told him, there had been "6 or 7 separate
groups in different times in 'Prince Igor' & all national dances have contrapuntal rhythm."

Fokine highly praised his own two star students at the time, Patricia

Bowman and Paul Haakon, and also told Lincoln that he should go and see the "very great artist" Uday Shankar, whose popular concerts distilled Indian dances for Western audiences. On the other hand he denounced— and Lincoln would soon come to agree—"the horror" of the modern dancers Harald Kreutzberg and Martha Graham. On an entirely different level he asked Lincoln to please stop whistling during class; his wife, the imperious Madame Vera Fokine (Lincoln described her as "a dragon- lady . . . who guarded Fokine as if he were a beleaguered fortress"), "thought it unsuitable for a Russian house."

Lincoln attended a mounting variety of dance recitals: Harriet Hoctor, Charles Weidman, Léonide Massine, Mary Wigman, Agnes de Mille, and, several times over, Martha Graham. Because of the extremely limited opportunities then available in the United States for classically trained ballet dancers, he was able to see only Harriet Hoctor (who he felt was "America's premiere ballerina"); she performed as part of a vaudeville bill at the Palace Theatre on a program that included the comedy team of Clayton, Jackson & (Jimmy) Durante, and the Hainault Brothers (who spoke to each other in bird sounds). Despite the context, Lincoln could see that Hoctor's technique was "out of the ordinary," though he regretted that she showed "the horrible traces of Mary Wigman," the vanguard German expressionist whose harsh, angular, "ecstatic" choreography Lin- coln loathed.

In one of the first articles he ever wrote on the dance, when he was only twenty-four years old, Lincoln had crucified Wigman as a "destruc- tive dancer" whose influence he considered "dangerous." Acknowledging that she could do "astonishing things with her body," he insisted that her contortions represented "the complete and pitiful exhaustion of the imag- ination." The terms Lincoln employed in the article reveal that the kernel of his lifelong resistance to most "modern dance" was already securely in place: Wigman, he wrote, did not "understand the restrictions and limita- tions of the body, [how] to control the body as a medium of expression— rather than of self-expression." Classical ballet, in contrast, centered on "the dignity of the universal, the anonymous, the interest inherent in the *object* of expression"; ballet "does not crush individuality except when the individual is an exhibitionist." There it was, the enemy of "true" dancing spelled out and flayed: "self-expression."

Given the particular set of standards Lincoln employed for judging excellence, it was predictable that he would see little of value in the cre- ations of Weidman, de Mille, or Graham. Weidman had been a soloist with the Denishawn company but had left in 1928 and opened a school with the dancer and choreographer Doris Humphrey. When Lincoln first met him in May 1932, he and Humphrey were participating in the coop- erative Dance Repertory Theatre, along with the well-known performer Helen Tamiris.

Lincoln had asked for the meeting in order to suggest to Weidman that Melville's *Moby-Dick* would be a wonderful scenario for a ballet. Weidman had never heard of Melville or the book (the writer's reputation was in fact at a low ebb in those years), but anticipating that, Lincoln had brought along a copy for him. Lincoln's impression of the man himself was favorable: he liked Weidman's "humility and common sense," his "self-effacing" attitude, and he admired Weidman's "lack of sentimentality about himself or his dancers."

But he wasn't hopeful that Weidman would take to his idea—and indeed nothing came of the project—given how uninterested he seemed in classical ballet. Watching Weidman and his company rehearse in his studio on West Eighteenth Street, Lincoln found several dancers to admire, especially the comparative newcomer José Limón, who would later form his own company. And the technique Weidman taught seemed to Lincoln "as good as you can get without real ballet training, but there is no elevation, if some physical dexterity & precision."

After rehearsal Lincoln tried to argue with Weidman "about the necessity for a ballet training," but Weidman replied that classical ballet "only developed a part or parts of your body, leaving the middle weak. He also claimed (as did many proponents of "modern dance") that ballet "crippled individuality—a ballet was just a machine for an idea." "Exactly!" Lincoln exclaimed—"That's what it should be!" He feared that Weidman had "inoculated all his dancers with the virus of personal individuality—they all want to be 'concert dancers.' " When he showed them some photos he'd brought along of the Diaghilev company, some of them seemed "thrilled—though skeptical." Lincoln left Weidman's studio dispirited, but at least he'd seen some better dancing than he'd recently been able to find elsewhere. "How hungry I am," he wrote in his diary, "for a speck of good dancing."

He thought he might have found at least that speck when he first encountered Agnes de Mille (Cecil B. DeMille's niece) at a party in January 1933. Lincoln initially found her a "very forthright Californian & on to herself. She said her own dancing in Paris, from which she'd just returned, bears the same relation to art as chromolithography" (an inexpensive colored picture popular in the late nineteenth century among those who couldn't afford to buy oil paintings). For now, she told Lincoln, "she wants to do only formal or comic things until she is big enough to be emotional." Though he thought her appealingly "frank and forthright," he "liked her less" as he talked to her more.

They subsequently had tea together a few times, and Agnes talked a lot of "California chi-chi," seemed suspicious of Lincoln's ideas about the need for a ballet school, and claimed that Tamara Geva, Balanchine's ex-wife, "had bitched" her out of choreographing the dances for Geva's Broadway show *Flying Colors* (her third in a row soon after she immigrated to the United States). Yet Lincoln did go to see Agnes dance on the tiny stage of the Arts Club on West Eighty-fourth Street, where he sat next to "her awful mother" and didn't care for her dancing: "She likes a few gestures too well. Not much." A few days later he had tea with her again and, being at least as frank as she was, tried to tell her (so he wrote in his diary) "how I didn't like her dancing." Nonetheless she soon invited him to a party where he met Louis Horst ("big, fat, white-haired"), adviser and accompanist to Martha Graham.

Lincoln had first seen Graham and her company back in December 1931. By then she already had a devoted following, though she'd only started to perform some five years earlier; her fans had come to include the *New York Times* dance critic, John Martin, whom Lincoln had recently met. But while Martin was writing by 1931 that Graham "already touched the borderline of that mystic territory where greatness dwells," Lincoln, after seeing her perform that same year, expressed unadulterated outrage: "The horror of her dancing," he wrote in his diary, "a cross between shitting and belching." Seeing her perform again a year later, his opinion remained unchanged: "She retched and belched and the audience screamed—and I fear their taste is so corrupted they won't know good dancing when they see it."

Over several lunches with Martin, Lincoln tried to bridge their very different perspectives on several matters, Martha Graham included. When Lincoln told Martin of his dream to establish classical ballet in the United States, the critic had a mixed response. At their first lunch he told Lincoln that he thought such a dream was "physically possible" but that it "would take years to do it and quantities of cash." But when they discussed the matter a second time, Martin came down on the negative side, saying (according to Lincoln), that "no such ballet was possible in this country. We have no feel for the monarchical discipline or patronage it demands." When Lincoln brought up Fokine as a possible participant, Martin called him "a tragic case of arrested development," though he did think people might be ready to attend—yet another idea Lincoln had put forward—a "revival of 1914," a Fokine season, using all the old ballets with their original Léon Bakst and Alexandre Benois sets.

As for Martha Graham, Lincoln wrote in his diary that John Martin thinks she "is the greatest woman alive and that the future of the dance lies in her direction," whereas Lincoln was convinced that the future of dance hinged on the successful establishment of classical ballet in the United States. Martin admitted that Graham had her faults but claimed that "she was developing, and was young, & her present attitude of harshness was merely a reaction from the over-sweetness of the Denishawns, where she received her training."

Martin and Lincoln were, for the moment, stalemated about Martha Graham's merits and potential. Lincoln would himself have a long, complicated relationship with her, and for a time would greatly modify his assessment of her work and become something of a champion. But the two were born to be antagonists, their aesthetics too much at odds for permanent reconciliation, their personalities too dominant to entertain much respect for opposing views.

By 1931 Lincoln's long-simmering search for a way to establish a classical ballet company in the United States picked up steam and intensity. When he read one day in the newspaper that E. Ray Goetz, a Broadway producer, had acquired all the scenery and costumes of Diaghilev's Ballets Russes and was purportedly planning to bring what remained of the company's available artists to the United States in the fall of that year, Lincoln wrote excitedly in his diary that he wanted "somehow to get hooked up with it all," get to be Goetz's right-hand man—"and then displace him."

Nothing came of that, but three months later Lincoln tried to persuade Eddie Warburg's older brother, Gerald, who was passionately devoted to music and the only one of Eddie's siblings to share his artistic interests, to form a collaboration consisting of ballet, a repertory of Mozart operas, and a string quartet or chamber orchestra. But Gerald wasn't interested; his goal was to become a professional cellist, not an impresario. Thwarted again in his ambition and deeply frustrated, Lincoln dismissed Gerald as "vague and crazy in a way that exasperates without being at all seductive . . . [he is] a happy, wandering, useless person." That characterization was not only harsh but inaccurate. Gerry Warburg was in fact a sensitive, insecure man whose financier father, Felix, constantly double-binded him about his talent and the "appropriateness" of an artistic career.

Lincoln's next candidate as a potential conduit for creating a ballet company or school was Mrs. Frances Flynn Paine, whose considerable involvement in the arts scene of the day has been all but forgotten. For the better part of three years she'd be involved with Lincoln in trying to pull off a variety of enterprises, including the establishment of a ballet company, and her extensive connections—she advised Abby Aldrich Rockefeller and served for a time as Diego Rivera's New York agent—made her seem to Lincoln a promising ally. Soon after they met late in 1931, Frances Paine enlisted Lincoln's help in working over the scenario, "until some fairly decent choreographer would know what was meant," for the ballet *Horse Crazy*, which, conducted by Leopold Stokowski, opened early in 1932 in Philadelphia, with sets and costumes by Rivera and a score by the Mexican composer Carlos Chávez. For Lincoln this seemed a promising beginning for advancing a broad alliance with Mrs. Paine.[2]

By then he'd met Rivera. Jere Abbott had taken him to the artist's studio in December 1931, and Lincoln had immediately liked the artist, characterizing him as "very gentle, considerate & informative" (an estimate he would revise). Yet Rivera's painting, Lincoln wrote in his diary, "had really no effect on me. I only was moved by his technical mastery" and the fact that he was "the only first rate decorator in America. By his pre-eminence I gauge our poverty." Lincoln also disliked the "abstract" elements in Rivera's work. It was the same objection he'd had to aspects of modern dance: "Abstraction in the long run was a subjective enterprise"— meaning a discreditable one. That conviction, fixed early and centrally in Lincoln's aesthetic, would remain relatively though not totally unwavering, whether in regard to art or to dance.

Himself sympathetic to the Left, Lincoln also thought Rivera had unnecessarily limited his artistic themes: "I feel," he wrote in his diary, that "his Revolutionary subject matter is no longer a conviction but a repetition." In this Lincoln may have been echoing the sharp criticism of Rivera currently being heard on the Left; Mexico's Communist Party would soon expel him for having accepted commissions from prominent capitalist institutions, including San Francisco's Pacific Stock Exchange, and for his friendly personal relations with assorted Yankee millionaires, preeminently the Rockefellers.

By early 1932 Lincoln and Frances Paine were conferring regularly on assorted schemes to push through their mutual interests. Initially they talked over the likelihood of trying to get a theater established in Rockefeller Center devoted to the arts and "perfectly equipped for ballet"; among other productions, they hoped to produce a *Billy Budd* ballet, with scenery by Rivera and a scenario by Lincoln and Jere Abbott, who'd already been at work on it.

Lincoln shared Paine's penchant for outsized, unrealizable schemes. When she claimed that her very *lack* of alliances put her "in a key position" to tap the Rockefellers' "huge source of income" and thereby "finance all our experimental ballet, movies & music," the only fear Lincoln expressed was that John R. Todd's powerful management team at Rockefeller Center would "take all her ideas and chuck her out." Because he wanted to believe, she was able to reassure him easily. When he repeated that his "first and foremost" heart's desire, all that he personally wanted from their work together, was a ballet school, she confidently replied, "If we both live, you'll have it"—allowing Lincoln to write exultantly in his diary, "I feel like a spy, pirate and an incipient conqueror . . . [we] both feel . . . like we were making history."

Her next move, Mrs. Paine confided to Lincoln, would be to "tell Nelson how fantastically careless he's been in delegating responsibility." That planned confrontation, even ignoring its effrontery, should have revealed to Lincoln her profound ignorance of who was in fact manning the controls. At that point in his life Nelson's appetite for power was no match for the actual amount he wielded. His ambition was towering, but he was still struggling for a foothold in his family's various enterprises. Even in relation to MoMA, where he became a full-fledged trustee in 1932, Nelson was unable to push through his suggestion for a Decorative Arts building. Yet Lincoln, who already knew Nelson reasonably well, thought the problem lay in his "laziness." He told Frances Paine that Nelson and his brother John D. Rockefeller III had "absolutely no idea of what potential they control"; "it is our task," he added, "to instruct them." Lincoln advised her, in this escalating *folie à deux*, to bypass Nelson and "go straight to the source of power"—Nelson's father, JDR Jr.

A more accurate estimation of both Nelson and Frances Paine dawned on Lincoln slowly. One night when he was the sole dinner guest at Nelson and his wife Tod's apartment on East Sixty-seventh Street, they had a long talk about Mrs. Paine, and Nelson said "there was no way to connect her to Rockefeller Center as he had no money to hire her and she has antagonized so many of the big businessmen down there by her long conversations."

Lincoln tried to persuade him that "people with less gifts" were being hired, but Nelson said that Lincoln "had an exaggerated idea of his power." Lincoln replied (at least so he recorded the conversation in his diary) that Nelson "could have as much power as he wanted if he was only strong enough with the staff." To which Nelson said, " 'My God, I have to spend my whole life being nice to people!' His wife, Tod, smiled sweetly & said: 'Except to me.' " Lincoln privately clung to the view that Nelson was too "naturally friendly" and conciliatory ever to "really risk anything." But he did come away from the dinner with a budding awareness that "there was little chance that a ballet company would take root at Rockefeller Center."

On a different matter—the need to decide which artists should be invited to create murals and other artworks for Rockefeller Center—Nelson invited Lincoln to a high-level, two-hour conference where his opinion, despite his youth and lack of a staff position at the Center, does seem to have carried some weight; Nelson was able to persuade the others to add Reginald Marsh, Yasuo Kuniyoshi, and Charles Burchfield to the list. Even so, Lincoln decided it would be premature to bring up the ideas he and Frances Paine had been nurturing for an arts theater. That, he hoped, would come later. In the meantime, he was pleased at having been included in a meeting with some of Rockefeller Center's top brass. "I saw all the plans and models for Radio City," Lincoln excitedly wrote his father, "and I asked every question I wanted to know about it. I think I may be able to do quite a lot. . . . Nelson is so tactful and agreeable that he paved the way for me pretty clearly."

Over the next few months the plan to get some sort of arts center incorporated into Rockefeller Center gradually came to focus on the notion that MoMA should take the lead in trying to push the scheme through, and that perhaps MoMA should itself house the as-yet-undefined center. A lengthy series of consultations and memos culminated in Lincoln and Alfred Barr having lunch together on June 20, 1932. Alfred "outlined plans for a movie department at The Museum of Modern Art," something that he'd intended from MoMA's inception. He also said that he wanted to put Lincoln in charge of the department. Lincoln somewhat hesitantly agreed to the offer, "but then wondered for the next three days" if he really wanted "more of that kind of work."

On June 24 Lincoln, Frances Paine, Nelson Rockefeller, and two MoMA people, assistant treasurer Alan Blackburn (a close friend of Philip Johnson's) and Board President A. Conger Goodyear, held another meeting. Coming a mere month after Lincoln's "disastrous" mural show at the museum, which had purportedly disgraced him, he was probably surprised when Goodyear, his recent antagonist, announced that he and Barr agreed that work should begin on "a correlated plan" for including "drama, motion pictures, music, ballet, et cetera, with the purpose in mind of establishing these activities in the Museum of Modern Art."

Having accepted Barr's "movie department" offer, Lincoln agreed to participate in discussions for a "correlated plan," privately hoping that he could delegate most of the responsibility for the movie side of things to other people, and especially to Jay Leyda and Harry Alan Potamkin. Potamkin was already *Hound and Horn*'s film critic, and he and Lincoln had become two of the eight directors (Dwight Macdonald was another) of the newly formed nonprofit Film Society, whose aim was to show avant-garde, experimental, and European films (which at the time were subject to a high import duty) to those who signed up as subscribers.

At the end of June, Nelson invited Lincoln to the Rockefeller family estate at Pocantico, overlooking the Hudson River, for two days. Lincoln may have anticipated the visit as designed to explore further the possibilities of an "arts center," but if so, he was disappointed: most of the time was devoted to swimming, croquet, riding ("the stables," Lincoln wrote in his diary, "are enormous, Mycenaean"), and light chatter. He stayed with Nelson and Tod in their (comparatively) small colonial house on the estate, one Nelson himself had done over with antiques and with his mother's fine collection of American primitive paintings.

For most of the time conversation remained casual and superficial. Nelson did share a few "intimacies" with Lincoln, ranging from the confession that he'd wanted to become an architect but that "family affairs could not afford him that indulgence" to considerable detail about the intractable "jock itch" he'd had for eight months prior to his marriage, and how his mother had wrongly thought he'd contracted a venereal disease.

Lincoln met several of the Rockefeller clan for the first time, including Nelson's younger brothers, Winthrop (who Lincoln thought had "more physical charm than the rest") and Lawrence, who'd just graduated from Princeton and seemed shy and detached. Abby joined them for tea, and was "very affectionate with Nelson" ("I noticed," Lincoln wrote in his diary, "how really very long her nose is"). Their talk ranged narrowly from the movies—Abby said she'd seen only two "talking pictures" because "the sound of voices was so distasteful to her"—to Alfred Barr's hypochondria, with Abby revealing that she'd had her own doctor examine Alfred and he'd found "nothing organically wrong with him."

On the second day they went up to the Lodge for lunch with Abby and her husband, John D. Rockefeller, Jr. (whom Lincoln thought "a very quiet, shy, almost timorous man"), and the atmosphere in general continued "pleasant and really simple," so much so that Lincoln couldn't help wondering whether the Rockefellers weren't somehow longing for "some disease, or terror, or tortures of richness." Nelson and Tod did manage to express regret that they lacked religious faith, and Nelson revealed that he felt the desire "to believe in some order" so strongly that he'd consulted Dr. Harry Emerson Fosdick, the well-known minister, who told him there wasn't any prescription for acquiring it.

Bemused at the aura of sustained contentment that Nelson emanated (despite bewailing his "bad skin" along with his lack of faith), Lincoln tried to start an argument by declaring that consciousness was preferable to happiness. But Nelson declined the challenge, ignored the implied insult, and suggested a rigorous game of water polo. And thus the two-day holiday passed harmoniously, a state Lincoln couldn't usually tolerate for long, or fully approve. The Kirstein household, populated with prima donnas of varying styles, had provided no precedents for such amiable proceedings.

But Lincoln at least came away from the visit with a firmer understanding of Nelson's lack of decision-making power in the affairs of Rockefeller Center; Nelson told him that the family mostly kept him occupied with being a kind of liaison officer to the restoration work the Rockefellers had underwritten at Colonial Williamsburg, and with leasing office space at the Center. And if the two days had failed to provide Lincoln with any additional clues about the prospects for an arts center, he did feel pleased with himself for having deepened his connection to the family. In time, he felt sure, "Nelson could be valuable"—unless, that is, "the Revolution comes quick."

The prospects of finding a permanent home for the arts center at MoMA soon soured. Barr's offer to put Lincoln in charge of the new "movie department" led to widespread annoyance with Barr at MoMA. Philip Johnson, for one, said that the creation of the Film Society had had the effect at MoMA of "knocking them all of a heap." And Frances Paine told Lincoln privately that he'd made a dreadful mistake and acted "disloyally"; his only option now was to resign from the Film Society or bring it into the museum. Lincoln chose to do neither, deciding that his own "instinct [is] worth 1000 considerations" in regard to becoming a "force" at MoMA. At a meeting with Frances Paine, Nelson, and Alan Blackburn to discuss the issue, Lincoln told them that he felt no conflict of interest whatsoever in regard to the Film Society, but that if *they* did, he was fully prepared "to get out of the Museum altogether." That took them by surprise, since a voluntary surrender of potential power was an unfamiliar strategy, and they tried to smooth things over by telling Lincoln that he was being "too sensitive."

But nothing could persuade him to withdraw his resignation from MoMA. Lincoln had firmly concluded that he'd been "wasting my time in vain hopes" of an arts center and that what he "wanted to do" most in the world—to find a home for ballet—"can best be done single-handed and apart from Nelson or his dependencies." As he wrote in his diary, with rather remarkable self-assurance, "I work . . . with a faith that the probable concatenation of events to land me where I want to be is just about equal to the effort of remaining in an organization like the Museum of Modern Art." On the other hand he felt no need to break off personal relationships with anyone, and that included Nelson, Frances Paine, and Alfred Barr. In the upshot Barr would, in the summer of 1933, appoint the English-woman Iris Barry, who'd been a film critic at the London *Daily Mail*, to head up a film library, which in 1935, thanks to a gift of $100,000 from the Rockefeller Foundation, would become a separate corporation.

The indefatigable Paine tried to assure Lincoln that if plans for an arts center at MoMA had collapsed, there was still a live prospect of setting one up at Rockefeller Center. She insisted that no less a figure than S. L. "Roxy" Rothafel was entirely on their side. The flamboyant, imperious Roxy was in charge of running the various theaters planned for Rocke-feller Center, and Frances Paine tried to persuade Lincoln that Roxy was fully committed to the idea of housing a ballet school and a "large experi-mental theatre"; she even claimed that "the money is all available" to bring their elaborate "vision of a cooperative creative paradise" to life— that "Napoleon was nothing to us."

But Lincoln was no longer listening. He'd finally realized that "all I wanted was a ballet, that the only reason I did any public committee work at all was because I thought it might lead to the solidification of that. . . . I don't want to be connected to anything any more." His sole concern, he told himself, was to concentrate his energy and to preserve his "free agency." But if he now had his priorities in order, he remained tempera-mentally incapable of focusing exclusively on a single project.

Indeed, during all the time he'd been working with Frances Paine and wooing other potential allies, Lincoln had been active on a variety of other fronts. He'd continued to edit *Hound and Horn*, and was particularly excited about a special Henry James issue planned for the following year. Then there was his ongoing work with Romola Nijinska on her husband's biography, which had expanded to include an assortment of errands and tasks designed to get her visa extended, to cope with her frequent bouts of depression and hysteria, and to keep her grounded until the project could be completed. Beyond all that he somehow managed to dredge up enough additional energy to complete a second novel (which went nowhere), to attend Fokine's ballet classes regularly, and to juggle a social life that in season could mean three or four parties a night and, when he was in search of sex, haunting until dawn the various speakeasies, Harlem hot spots, Turkish baths, and "lowlife" hangouts that might provide it.

He'd even recently added to his frantic schedule an additional project, joining forces with others (including Mrs. Paine) in trying to rescue Sergei Eisenstein's film *Que Viva Mexico!* Eisenstein had come to the United States late in 1931 under contract for $3,000 a week to Paramount but his unwillingness to modify his own ideas to comport with Hollywood's had led to the cancellation of his contract. Accompanied by his renowned associates, the cinematographer Eduard Tisse and the editor Grigori Aleksandrov, Eisenstein had left for Mexico to make his own film. But by December 1931, with the film nearly completed, he still needed to raise an additional $25,000.[3]

Lincoln's own involvement with Eisenstein started with a special-delivery letter he received from a Seymour Stern declaring that "Eisenstein's Mexico film had been butchered" by a commercial cutter hired by the left-wing novelist Upton Sinclair and his wealthy wife, Mary Craig Sinclair, who had an investor/ownership position in the movie. Lincoln called Edmund Wilson for advice. Wilson told him that Stern was "a crook," but he urged Lincoln not to "go off half-cocked" (implying that he habitually did)—a comment Lincoln didn't appreciate; he didn't like Wilson anyway, characterizing him in his diary as "sententious"; Muriel told Lincoln that he and Wilson "are both so intelligent & informed that ... [it all] came out in a great mist and ... [they] couldn't see each other at all."

In the meantime Jere Abbott arranged a lunch so that Lincoln and Eisenstein could meet in person. Eisenstein told them that his contract with the Sinclairs, to which he'd apparently given only a cursory reading, awarded world rights (except for the USSR) and both positive and negative copies of the film to Mary Sinclair. Eisenstein made "preposterous fun" of Sinclair's "socialism," describing him as a man without "guts or wits" who'd been unable or unwilling to raise the additional sum needed to shoot the final episode.

On his side, Upton Sinclair claimed to have learned that the Soviets distrusted Eisenstein and felt little interest in his film—and so had decided to cut off funding and stop production. Eisenstein told Lincoln that he hoped to return to Moscow to cut the footage himself, but feared that the Sinclairs, who retained the negative, would refuse him the right and would allow the footage to be cut up for newsreel clips and truncated travelogues that would destroy the film's integrity. Eisenstein's fears would prove warranted, though Lincoln, among others, tried to forestall the grim outcome.

A week after the lunch meeting, Lincoln was invited to the small Amkino projection room to see the rushes of the film. Eisenstein, Aleksandrov, and Tisse were all there, and none of them had previously seen the footage. For Lincoln it all proved hugely exciting. He thought "the pictures . . . fantastically beautiful, the most rich & historic camera work" he'd ever seen, making "every other movie look like a disease." He watched for four hours, the experience so "intensely powerful" that he could think of nothing else for the rest of the day.

Lincoln decided to take advantage of his father's contacts as a board member of RKO to try to prevent Eisenstein's film from being dismembered or misappropriated. Louis set up appointments for Lincoln both with David Selznick and David Sarnoff. Selznick quickly brushed him off, but Sarnoff at least gave him a hearing—a perfunctory one. When Lincoln tried to press his case, Sarnoff, perhaps grown tired of the relentless young man, laid out impossible terms before RKO would even consider buying the film—including world rights for $100,000 and the promise by both the Mexican and Soviet governments of full cooperation. As Sarnoff was doubtless aware, not even someone with Lincoln's formidable drive and wide set of contacts would be able to meet such requirements. Sarnoff had successfully managed to take himself out of the picture without jeopardizing his friendship with Louis Kirstein.

At some point during their talks, Eisenstein mentioned to Lincoln that he'd been amused by "a small drag" show he'd seen in Harlem, and also asked him why it was that all "sex books" in New York drugstores were priced at sixty-nine cents. Obviously the two had earlier referred to their shared erotic interest in men, and within two weeks of the Amkino screening, Lincoln, Jere Abbott, and two other friends were giving Eisenstein a tour of New York City's queer "lowlife," of which Lincoln had considerable knowledge. They went first to the notorious Sand Street YMCA in Brooklyn and asked a sailor if any new places had opened. He pointed them around the corner, where they walked through a dark passageway and emerged "into a dive full of sailors and a few tarts." Three people were singing and playing the piano, and there were vestiges of crepe paper hanging down, suggesting a recent opening.

They ordered a pitcher of beer, and before long "a very large, very drunk & quite attractive gob" headed across the room and aggressively slammed his "two great paws" on their table. Eisenstein was, as Lincoln put it, "semi-comatose" through all this, preoccupied with worry about the undecided fate of his Mexican film. The sailor's anger soon simmered down, and before long he was calling Eisenstein "a rocky mountain goat" in reference to all the hair on his head. Lincoln could feel that Eisenstein was bored, and they toured several more queer speakeasies, including Tante Matilda's at Forty-second and Sixth, where someone warned them not to drink the beer, and from there headed up to the Metropolitan bar in Harlem, where they spoke a few words to Clinton Moore, "the great Queen procurer of Harlem." One of their party next suggested an "exhibition" as something "extra special" to wake Eisenstein up, but he said he'd already seen enough of those and was ready to call it a night. Lincoln felt that on the whole it had been "rather a waste of the evening for Eisenstein," though the filmmaker graciously protested otherwise. At dawn, they dropped him off at the Barbizon Plaza, and he asked Lincoln "to keep in touch" with him.

Soon after, Eisenstein returned to Moscow, and the two exchanged an occasional letter while Lincoln continued his efforts to rescue *Que Viva Mexico!* from the Sinclairs. As late as February 1933, just weeks before a truncated, mangled version *(Thunder Over Mexico)* sanctioned by the Sinclairs opened in Los Angeles, Lincoln and Frances Paine were still trying to get the job of cutting the film for Eisenstein himself. Nothing worked; the Sinclairs were adamant, and what Lincoln was convinced would have been a cinematic masterpiece was permanently lost.

Lincoln added his name to a protest denouncing *Thunder Over Mexico* as "a cheap debasement." Other pieces of footage or partial, uniformly wretched versions later appeared—but never a version cut and completed by Eisenstein himself. When *Thunder* had a special showing at the New School for Social Research in New York City in early September 1933, Lincoln distributed leaflets outside the school declaring, "Upton Sinclair, you have butchered a great work of art." When a friend of Sinclair's started to give a short speech just before the showing began, Lincoln jumped up from his seat and yelled that he "wanted to ask a question." Two ushers grabbed him before he could say another word and deposited him on the street outside—an incident written up in several newspapers.

During this same period Lincoln became deeply infatuated with one of his pick-ups at the YMCA, a French-Canadian cashier at the Hotel Pennsylvania named Jack Hamilton. He was "a close cropped blonde with a blank face, animal ears and small blue eyes," a penchant for dope, and a cut under his upper lip from a razor fight in Harlem; "[my] gangster dreams come true," Lincoln wrote in his diary. For a time he was wildly turned on by the potential danger and "the possibility of surprise" Hamilton represented and by his special combination of attributes: "his perfect body and his fucked-out spirit"; the fact that he was all at once "passive, strong, dead-hearted, but with a specific gravity of maleness . . . [that] went to my head like liquor." Lincoln told Muriel all about Hamilton, and she assured him of the "essential normalcy" of the affair. But Muriel, if flamboyantly sex positive, also had a level head, and she made a point of warning Lincoln "to be careful about practical details," to be "cautious" in how he handled Hamilton. She also told him, Lincoln wrote in his diary, that she "didn't think I was really promiscuous, only I had certain bad sexual habits; sometimes my mind got separated from my body and the two went off uncontrolled."

In the spring of 1933 Lincoln and Frances Paine became involved together one last time. Raymond Hood, the leading architect for Rockefeller Center, following the example Donald Deskey had set as head of design for the Radio City Music Hall by filling it with sculpture and wall paintings, decided to commission a series of murals from various artists to decorate the lobby of the RCA Building. Mrs. Paine was still Diego Rivera's agent in New York, and Lincoln was still an admirer of both the painter and his politics; thus both became entangled in the enormous brouhaha that would develop over Rivera's mural.

Commissions for the side walls of the RCA Building were given to the Englishman Frank Brangwyn and the Spaniard José María Sert; both were in every sense traditionalists (indeed, Sert would become a supporter of Franco and fascism). They could be counted on to produce works of uninflected tribute, if limited artistic merit (though Lincoln, to his own surprise, would end up thinking better of Sert's wall paintings than he'd expected to: "They looked satisfactorily efficient, rich, competent & expensive"). Thanks largely to the influence of Abby and Nelson Rockefeller, Rivera was given the $21,500 commission for the lobby's centerpiece of more than a thousand square feet.

He began work in mid-March 1933, assisted by an international group of some half-dozen left-wing artists, including Ben Shahn, the most militant among them. Rivera had made no secret of his intended anticapitalist message, and he included depictions of policemen on horseback clubbing striking workers, idle society women drinking and playing cards, and a floating encirclement of what looked like syphilitic germs. All these had been described in Rivera's written synopsis of the mural's contents, and had been approved in advance, with Raymond Hood reportedly merely glancing at an accompanying sketch before signing off on it.

Nor did Nelson or his mother, when visiting the site as the mural unfolded on the wall, express anything but enthusiasm. Abby arrived with a friend, and Rivera asked a workman to "pull up chairs for the ladies"; the workman didn't know who they were and, wanting to protect Rivera from visitors, managed (according to Lincoln) "to find the most intolerably uncomfortable chairs they could." Rivera told Lincoln that he considered Abby Rockefeller "the most ardent Communist he knows," but that hardly seems the likeliest explanation for her subsequent reaction to the mural. Abby's failure to find anything to object to in the work-in-progress was more likely a case of willed blindness to the evidence in front of her eyes.

Lincoln himself paid several visits to the lobby and found, in mid-April, "a general feeling of exhilaration." The union had sent its very best men to do the plasterwork, and young children scampered over the scaffolding while workmen from the building stood below admiring the portraits of themselves that Rivera had painted into the crowd of demonstrators. Ben Shahn had been assisting on the project for several weeks, and he told Lincoln that Rivera worked on twenty-four, thirty-six, and forty-eight-hour shifts, with only two-hour breaks in between, during which he'd often fall asleep over his soup. Shahn was filled with enthusiasm for Rivera's composition, but Lincoln frankly told him that he felt it was "too particularized, too thin," and "the symbolism a bit heavy and obvious." In Lincoln's view Rivera was at base "an Italian post-Renaissance artist." When Lachaise arrived for a look at the mural, he agreed, as did Jean Charlot, a Mexican artist Lincoln had earlier championed. Charlot told Lincoln that he thought the mural was Rivera's "worst," that he "had always been influenced by inferior men," and that in this instance it seemed "he had been fatally influenced by [Thomas Hart] Benton in the literalism of types."

On Lincoln's second visit Rivera asked him to pose in "a student group," along with two young African Americans. He did—until seven in the evening; during the hour break for lunch, he went up on the roof with Rivera's wife, the artist Frida Kahlo, who was dressed like a workman, except for her leather cap, her Indian jewelry, and a silk bandanna; as they stood there, pressed against the stone, they could actually feel the building sway. Lincoln found Rivera's finished portrait of him "bold, accenting the Semite." Ever after he would say that he'd posed for Diego Rivera as "the eternal Jew."

His stint of posing completed, Lincoln went straight to a party at the architect Wallace ("Wally") Harrison's, with the sole intent—he was always tenacious in promoting people whose gifts he admired—to again argue the case with Wally for giving Lachaise the commission for a coat of arms on the French building. That done, even Lincoln felt exhausted. When he got home he wrote in his diary that "the world is revolving too fast for me: broken dates, hopes raised & shattered, jitters, and no love." As if by telepathy Muriel called him the next morning (they'd been a bit on the outs of late) to say with conviction how much "we love each other," even if, she said, "some part of [your] . . . heart is dry."

He needed that reassurance, however diluted; Muriel "knows what I feel really," he wrote in his diary—he "owed her more than anyone in the world." He'd been spinning in so many directions, had "so many ideas trembling in my mind," that he'd been having "violent nightmares." And the day following Muriel's call, he had to head off to Bryn Mawr to speak to Eddie Warburg's class on the "classical ballet." The lecture went off "O.K.," though Lincoln felt he'd bunched words together and mumbled. More important, he and Eddie spent a longer time together than in quite a while; Eddie often "doesn't hit on all 4 cylinders," but at times "his charm is real, spontaneous, independent of self-justification." When Eddie complained about wanting to move back to New York but felt he lacked an excuse, Lincoln used the opening to "hint" that they might collaborate on something to do with ballet. "He will be my Dimitri Gunsbourg yet," Lincoln confided to his diary; Baron Dmitri de Gunsbourg had been a leading Diaghilev patron: Lincoln had tellingly revealed the role model he hoped to pattern himself on. (Ironically, Gunsbourg, to promote his own ambitions, is thought to have centrally engineered Nijinsky's marriage to Romola.)

And Lincoln wasn't relying on Eddie alone to make that future a reality. In mid-May 1933 he went up to Hartford to see his friend Chick Austin and his wealthy wife, Helen. Chick, the youthful head of the prestigious Wadsworth Atheneum, gave Lincoln a tour of the half-completed new International Style addition to the museum; Lincoln noted in his diary that "his little auditorium is perfect for small ballets." They then went out to the large house, with a Palladian facade, that the Austins had built for themselves. Unlike almost everyone else, Lincoln was unimpressed; to him the house looked like a flimsy "pastiche." Nor did he take much to Helen, whom he hadn't previously met. A member of the socially prominent Goodwin clan, she struck Lincoln as "unattractive, suppressed . . . frightened . . . [but] nice with their sweet month old baby David."

Lincoln knew (though Helen didn't) that Chick's erotic preference was for men, and Chick privately told him "how hopeless his marriage was . . . how confined he was, how inferior, jealous & envious Helen was." He hinted to Lincoln about having indulged in "some highly irregular pleasures," and said he would tell him more some other time. Most people saw Chick Austin as a charming, engaging, outgoing man, but Lincoln had a far different take on him. He intuited "glimpses of acute hysteria, like lightning in his conversation; a person of many splits whose energy could collapse at almost any moment, I think, if he was either confined or pressed. Really vicious: that is, unimaginative, morally repetitious & lazy."

None of which mattered much to Lincoln. His chief interest in Chick Austin was to get him involved in some way, somehow, with his ballet plans. Lincoln suggested that the Atheneum host a "Ballet Demonstration," which he thought he could arrange for the following year with Fokine and Serge Lifar (who had recently emerged as director of the ballet at the Paris Opéra). It was an idea that Chick apparently "warmed up to." Lincoln told him that he'd provide more details soon.

By early May the public was finally admitted to the RCA lobby to see the Rivera mural in its nearly completed form. All hell immediately broke loose. Prominently displayed in the most recently completed section of the wall was a large, benign head of Lenin—which had *not* been part of the synopsis and sketch Rivera had originally submitted to the powers-that-be. Nelson at once sent off a letter to Rivera, his tone temperate and complimentary, but the underlying steel behind it unmistakable. Lenin's portrait, Nelson wrote, "might very easily seriously offend a great many people," and "I am afraid we must ask you to substitute the face of some unknown man where Lenin's face now appears." Nelson flatteringly added, "You know how enthusiastic I am about the work which you have been doing and . . . to date we have in no way restricted you in either subject or treatment," but the family "will greatly appreciate your making the suggested substitution."

That same day, May 4, which also happened to be Lincoln's twenty-sixth birthday, Lincoln told Ben Shahn that he thought "Diego was to blame . . . that he had put [the Rockefellers] . . . in an embarrassing situation willfully." Shahn replied that "Diego should not be touched by the fact that Nelson is nice or Mrs. R. is kind." He revealed that a faction of the Communist Party USA had urged Rivera to remove the head in order to save the mural, but that Diego would refuse. To which Lincoln predicted, wrongly, that "they'd never dare take the panel down; it would be too much of a black eye for a place that's had enough already."

The very next day Lincoln went over to the RCA lobby to see Rivera, who gripped his hand firmly; Ben Shahn had apparently told him that in Lincoln's opinion he should stand firm, that the Rockefellers would never have his mural taken down. When Lincoln heard that Frida, Shahn, and the other assistants were planning "some kind of a strike," he promptly told them he thought the idea "preposterous."

Three days later Shahn showed him a copy of the letter he'd written in Diego's name to Nelson. It was just as polite as Nelson's letter had been—and just as adamant. He would not remove Lenin's head, but offered instead to add a portrait of Abraham Lincoln for "balance," and possibly some others as well, including John Brown and William Lloyd Garrison. That offer carried no appeal at all for Nelson or for his mother. Nelson promptly left town, and Diego's letter was answered by Hugh S. Robertson, John R. Todd's management partner. It said, in essence, that Rivera had no moral or legal grounds for refusing to make the required changes in the mural. Rivera, egged on by Frida and Shahn in particular, simply ignored the letter and went back to work on the mural. In Lincoln's view Diego was "delighted with the quarrel; he is in his element; surrounded by proprietary Communists, he despises their mediocrity but . . . encourages them." He told Lincoln he was in fact a Trotskyist "and his head of Lenin is an affront to the Stalinists."

That did it. Robertson, accompanied by uniformed guards, entered the lobby, handed Rivera a check for the full amount owed him, and ordered him off the premises. The scaffolding was wheeled away and the mural covered. Protests of various kinds instantly erupted. Ben Shahn called Lincoln and asked him why he hadn't been around. Lincoln went immediately to the Barbizon Plaza hotel, where Diego and Frida were staying, in order to show (as he wrote in his diary) "that I did not entirely sympathize with the Rockefellers." The hotel room was filled with indignant sympathizers, yet Lincoln had the gumption to tell Rivera that he himself had precipitated the outcome. When the group tried to enlist him in the protest, Lincoln said that he would instead try to persuade Nelson to arrange some sort of compromise. Ben Shahn scoffed at the notion, telling Lincoln "there was no use fooling with the Crown Prince; he couldn't be changed."

Shahn's assessment proved accurate. Both Abby and Nelson Rockefeller tried to get MoMA to accept the fresco for its collection, but MoMA argued that no technique existed for separating the mural from the plaster, and nothing came of the suggestion. Nine months later hammers smashed into Diego Rivera's mural, reducing it to dust. He did later re-create a version of it for a wall in Mexico City's Palacio de Bellas Artes; Lenin's head shines in an even more saintly light, portraits of Trotsky and Marx have been added, and John D. Rockefeller, Jr., is pictured, cocktail in hand, close to the swarm of syphilitic germs.

Abby Rockefeller felt that Diego had personally betrayed her, and she never saw him again. Nelson, on the other hand, went right on collecting Rivera paintings, and he even occasionally saw Diego and Frida socially. Lincoln's relationship with Nelson remained intact and would span many decades.

Lincoln had begun to work with Romola Nijinsky on her husband's biography late in 1932. "Please believe me when I say," he'd written her on December 20, that "I am more interested in helping you with your book than anything I have ever done. . . . I am sure we can make a splendid thing of it." That they continued their collaboration through the winter and spring of 1933 was a testimony to Lincoln's determination, since Romola quickly proved herself to be among the most difficult of the many difficult people he'd ever known.[4]

Born Romola de Pulszky, the socialite daughter of Count Pulszky and Emilia Markus, a famous Hungarian actress, she'd inherited a flair for drama but not the talent for turning it into a professional career—though on a personal level she was a match for any of the stage's reigning divas of

the day. Lincoln early on recognized her essential unreliability and sometimes hysterical manipulation but, while gnashing his teeth, held the partnership together and resourcefully met her frequent, shifting, and taxing
demands. His ambition strapped him to the mast: he felt that the biography could prove a critical stepping-stone toward becoming a force in the
world of ballet and toward that end he proved willing to put up with the
kind of outrageous exactions for which he ordinarily had little tolerance.
It helped that Romola, on occasion, could also be "great fun and very
brave," and that her life (or the way she described it) of "fantastic survival"
and "desperate ploys" fed his own appetite for heightened theatrics.

The two began to work together in earnest early in January 1933,
though Lincoln could never be sure that Romola wouldn't cancel an
appointment at the last minute, selecting (it often seemed at random)
from a grab bag of overwrought excuses that focused heavily on "exhaustion," "boredom," or "despair." She would periodically announce that
she'd lost all interest in the book, regularly threaten to kill herself, and
kept Lincoln on a constant tightrope so that he didn't know from day to
day whether the project would continue.

Then there were those occasions when Romola would suddenly claim
an urgent need to commune with Frederica's ashes at Woodlawn, sometimes demanding that Lincoln accompany her. Or she'd rush off for a
session with the English trance-medium Eileen ("Ma") Garrett, her constant adviser, who used an ancient Persian mullah and a sprite known as
"Little Blue Bell" as her "controls." At Romola's insistence, Lincoln sat in
on several of the séances, but he soon found the stereotypical tabletop
tappings, gusts of cold air, and wandering trumpet candlesticks "silly."
During one séance, a voice said, "Harry, Harry," and Lincoln, on the
assumption it was supposed to be Mina's dead husband, Harry Curtiss,
"finally spoke up." "The trumpet banged around my head," he later wrote
in his diary, and he dutifully "asked him how it was. He said he was continuing his studies." Since "Harry Curtiss didn't do much studying," Lincoln
"lost interest." Despite Romola's displeasure, he managed to beg off from
further attendance.

But he wasn't wholly skeptical about psychic phenomena, and he asked
Muriel for her opinion. In Europe, she said, she used to sit with Chaliapin,
but after weeks of it, the only "manifestation" she ever got was seeing a
light suddenly glow, growing brighter and brighter; it turned out to be a
cigarette stub someone had thrown into the wastebasket. She told Lincoln
that spiritualism "was really for people who can't take it. She would hate to
think of the dead returning on the particular sphere that people seem to
wish them to. It relegates death to such an unimportant experience." Lincoln's sister, Mina, surprisingly (given her rational approach to life) said,
"It didn't seem in any way unnatural to her. Harry often came back to
speak to her. The only thing she wouldn't ever do is attempt to explain it."

Lincoln and Romola's usual routine was to meet at her apartment at the Hotel Montclair on Forty-ninth Street; for Romola to talk her recollections aloud (filling any lacunae in her memory through sessions with Ma Garrett, who would retrieve the needed data from the spirit world); for Lincoln to take notes on what Romola said, add whatever material she had herself put on paper, and then recast the whole into drafts that Romola would correct. Initially, with Lincoln still not sure how far he'd gotten his foot in the door, he heaped praise on Romola's efforts—at least to her face; his diary is filled with frustrated complaints about her—while Romola, fully aware that she held the whip hand, would typically declare that she "didn't much like" his drafts, sending him off to make additional revisions, often many times over.

He did all this work for three months without a contract of any kind. But then he managed to pull off a sort of minor miracle for Romola that solidified her confidence in him, made her momentarily grateful—and brought forth at least a semiformal agreement. The "miracle" involved her visa. Romola had already had two extensions, and Immigration now seemed intent on deporting her when her passport expired on March 1— one of several reasons she continually threatened suicide. Understandably fearing that if Romola returned to Europe, she'd find a different collaborator, Lincoln did everything in his power to get her a long enough reprieve for them to finish the book.

He managed this largely through his father's friendships with Felix Frankfurter and Massachusetts senator David Walsh, though his own determination—he went several times to consult with immigration authorities in New York City and Ellis Island—contributed greatly. Eventually he succeeded in getting Romola a two-month extension, and after the news came through, she made a handwritten, brief (and unwitnessed) "last will and testament" in which she declared that should she die and should Lincoln finish (underlined twice) her memoir and also live up to his promise to look after [Vaslav] "as well as I did," he'd be given Vaslav's "book of notations and the rights of all his ballets."

That "book of notations" nearly produced a permanent rift between the two. Romola showed him Vaslav's small, handwritten notebook early on and Lincoln, convinced that it was of immense value and fearing that Romola might make good on her suicide threats and the notebook be lost to posterity, surreptitiously had the notations photostatted. Romola somehow discovered what he'd done, hysterically denounced him, called him a thief, said she could never trust him again, and screamed abuse.

The rift was only mended when Lincoln gave her the photostats and apologized profusely several times over. At which point the unpredictable Romola, who had her charms (earthly and otherwise), kissed him on both cheeks, "roared with laughter," and told him affectionately that he was "a silly, enthusiastic boy." Though he'd apologized, Lincoln continued for many years to believe that he'd done the right thing, that Nijinsky's notations were "amazing . . . incredibly precious and exciting," and "a language of time-space which could be read to revive the entire past or present repertory." He later came to understand that the notations were simply "an extension of the Stepanov method, taught at the St. Petersburg Academy as an *aide-memoire* to ballet masters"; Nijinsky's own errors in trying to expand the method (the notations have never been fully deciphered), moreover, made it essentially unusable even to him.

Romola did have her better days, especially after she'd found a new girlfriend ("Romola says she needs a girl like she needs oxygen," Lincoln wrote in his diary). Trying to extend her briefly renewed cheerfulness, Lincoln would take her out for an occasional dinner, movie, or social event. Once they went to Radio City Music Hall, which did amuse her. Another time, he took her to see Uday Shankar; she declared him "the first dancer since Vaslav" whom she'd actually liked (Lincoln found him "very monotonous and beautiful"). He even took her to Constance and Kirk Askew's fashionable salon—Kirk ran the New York branch of the Durlacher gallery—and to Agnes de Mille's for tea (where he decided, once and for all, that "Agnes is a crashing bore and I'll be amazed if she ever does anything worth looking at").

During these more relaxed occasions, Romola would share various confidences with him. Muriel tried to warn Lincoln that Romola "lies unconsciously," but he was more worried, he told Muriel, that his own "instinct for the dramatic" might "have falsified my interpretation" in writing up Romola's recollections. Muriel wasn't persuaded, and said that she hoped he'd at least keep his name off the book, lest he be held accountable for what she felt certain (the prediction proved accurate) would be its many distortions.

Romola did indeed fill Lincoln's ears with "scandalous" tidbits which, she said, were not meant for publication. But Lincoln's sense of history was strong, and he duly recorded those tidbits in his diary, without, however, passing judgment as to their veracity. Among her "revelations" was that the great ballerina Tamara Karsavina, whom Nijinsky had often partnered in the glory days of Diaghilev's Ballets Russes, "never washed, sweated & stank; Vaslav said she was afraid to wash the success off." She also denounced Diaghilev's "ruthless perversion," and claimed that she'd gotten Vaslav's "feet in the ground & he never got them off afterwards"— a somewhat idiosyncratic view of his subsequent madness.

She told Lincoln, too, of her "great admiration for Rasputin, whom she adores . . . talked of a friend of his, a doctor, 'not unlike Mesmer in Petrograd' "; how "years later Diaghilev wanted to take Vaslav to see him [the doctor], but he couldn't be found"; how Vaslav's sister, the dancer and choreographer Bronislava ("Bronia") Nijinska, was "against it, as she thought it was black not white magic." Romola further confided that she'd just (January 1933) gotten a monthly report from the sanitarium at Kreuzlingen saying that Vaslav "was getting on very well: that after 14 years he was actually dancing a little." ("Whatever that means," Lincoln sardonically commented in his diary, sounding a note of skepticism about Romola's tales; he also wrote that the more he heard from her about Vaslav, "the more of a saint he becomes, a Blake or D. H. Lawrence of the Dance.")

She also confided intimate details about her own life. She said that she "hates animals of any kind & of people prefers Mongolians: the eyes & bony structure around them attracting her most." She described her late lover Lya de Putti as "god's most fiendish sadist," who had forced her to St. Moritz when Vaslav went insane, telling her further that she and Vaslav's two daughters, Kyra and Tamara, "were nuts" (why the willful Romola had put up with such treatment went unexplained). She revealed, too, that Ma Garrett had refused to put her in a trance because "in a previous reincarnation" she'd been "insane." Since childhood, Romola said, she'd known that she was "a repository for psychic energy," that "she has some alien power which she never could control & which has proved largely destructive."

As examples, she cited having, "in a fit of desperation," prayed for Lya de Putti's death—and she indeed did soon die. She claimed further that she'd kept Frederica alive "for 17 days by force of her own will and then she had to relax, as she would have died too." As yet another example of her psychic power, she told Lincoln that it was he who'd been chosen "to take care of the ruins of the Russian ballet as well as its future." But she warned him "how hopeless [it would be] ever to revive the Russian ballet, nothing could ever be done twice"; instead, he should import from Moscow the USSR state ballet, with its "fine new dancers" and present them at Rockefeller Center. Lincoln momentarily thought the idea "brilliant," that is, until the next day, when, at the Askews' salon, Romola told Kirk that *he* should import the state ballet, leaving Lincoln feeling "betrayed."

By this point in their relationship, Romola's passport extension had nearly run its course, and she booked passage for England on May 5, 1933 (*with* Frederica's ashes on board). They had a "charming" farewell dinner, at which Lincoln presented her with two beautiful white-and-purple orchids and she made him promise that he'd soon follow her to Europe. It turned out that Romola had bade an equally affectionate farewell to her French maid—but neglected to pay her; when the woman protested, Romola wrote her a check ("I hope it's good," Lincoln commented in his diary).

If the formalities of friendship between Romola and Lincoln had been preserved, a number of matters remained unresolved. The biography was unfinished, and they hadn't succeeded in getting a firm commitment from a publisher—though Lincoln had gotten Roger Dodge to lend his extraordinary collection of Nijinsky photographs for use in the book. Viking, initially interested, had backed out, Dutton remained uncertain, and Scribner's, though expressing interest, had refused to meet the demand for a thousand-dollar advance.

Romola had several times presented Lincoln with batches of her bills to be paid, usually claiming that she was bankrupt and would kill herself if she couldn't clear her debts. Rather than go to his father yet again, Lincoln persuaded Eddie Warburg to lend him the thousand dollars that no publisher would provide. He finally got Romola to sign a formal agreement promising to return the money out of her first royalties (but not out of any advance she might receive). To make matters more tenuous still, Romola's lawyer told Lincoln privately that she still remained "very suspicious" of him because of his having photostatted Vaslav's notations, that she'd thought of suing him "to protect herself" but had finally decided not to go to court. The news infuriated Lincoln, since Romola had let him believe that she'd long since accepted his apology about the notations. The lawyer's comments so unnerved him that he threatened to stop work on the book altogether.

But he didn't; seeing the project through to completion seemed too important for his own future.

CHAPTER EIGHT

Ballet

(1933)

"Business here does not show any signs of improvement," Louis Kirstein wrote his son George early in 1933. In the preceding year Filene's had had its poorest showing at any time since Louis had been with the firm, and the company was paying nearly a million dollars more in taxes. The coming year, he predicted, would be at least as bad. Louis was particularly upset at the number of layoffs Filene's had had to make, and he "wasn't sleeping too well nor feeling so chipper." The Kirsteins, however, were hardly in desperate straits compared with most of the citizenry, and, cognizant of that, Louis asked his entire family to remember that "this is a time when everybody should give thought to those around them and to the fact that they are so much worse off, and not think of themselves alone." He warned them not to believe the constant boosterism in the newspapers about how better times were just around the corner; it was all "ballyhoo," he said, and the entire family would have to cut back on expenses. He urged Mina to trim her household expenditures, and he told Lincoln that he could no longer promise to support the *Hound and Horn* to the extent he had been. To cut back on his own expenses, Lincoln moved, late in 1932, to a small unfurnished room on Minetta Lane in Greenwich Village.[1]

Nonetheless, as Louis wrote George, "as long as you don't squander money . . . I am perfectly willing to advance some until you are able to take care of yourself." And all three of his children knew that their father's word was his bond; he would continue to help them financially to the best of his ability. When Lincoln told him how urgent it was that he spend the summer of 1933 in Europe to ensure that he and Romola Nijinsky complete their work together, Louis agreed to the importance of the project—and to the added expense, though he did hold Lincoln to a tight budget. Having gotten Louis's approval, Lincoln sailed on the *Ile de France* for Europe on May 26, 1933. The night before, he dropped by Muriel's house on East Fifty-third Street and left her "a note of equivocal farewell." He knew she was visiting friends in the country, but had decided not to phone her. She was herself due to leave soon for the Soviet Union, having become increasingly intrigued by its possibilities, and Lincoln thought there was a chance she might stay for years. He wanted to avoid making "a special goodbye out of it"—that would have been too painful, given all that Mools had come to mean to him.

There was no one in the world Lincoln trusted more or felt more attuned to ("She is the only person who knows what I am talking about," he once wrote in his diary). He felt from the beginning that he could be "franker" with Muriel "than anyone else I know, and the question of discretion never enters into it." Muriel had become his touchstone, her freedom from cant and her personal bravery in the face of shifting fortunes his guideposts for behavior. He'd come to believe that her instincts about people were close to infallible, which meant that when she criticized him, he had to take heed.[2]

That went for every aspect of their relationship, including the erotic. Sex between them had never been frequent, and by the time Lincoln left for Europe in May 1933, had apparently all but stopped—even as their intimacy had continued to deepen. The choice seems to have been mostly Lincoln's; as he put it in a diary entry: "I found I don't want to when I can & when I can't I do, & that when I do, it is always less than I expect & that is no one's fault but mine." Occasionally, though, it would be Muriel who wasn't in the mood, leaving Lincoln angry—"she's not so choosy with her other men," he once wrote in his diary.

Both of them did regularly sleep around, gossiping together in engrossing detail about their various experiences—and sometimes about their experiences with each other. Lincoln described one of their erotic encounters: lying on Muriel's "ratty" bed, they "joked and lay still and rested and joked, and her knee somehow was on my crotch and there was some flirting between the control of my loins and her knee . . . she had no more qualms than I, and she tore off her necklace, Woolworth coils of coral beads, which spilled all over the bed and floor. She ripped the ugly pink satin dress down the side. When I was coming she said, 'This is you, Lincoln. Lincoln, this is you!' "

That murky cry is unlikely to have meant that Muriel thought Lincoln was basically heterosexual—all along she'd been entirely accepting of his adventures with men, and had treated them as part of his nature. (She believed he took more "emotional responsibility" in his affairs with men than with women.) Mools once asked him what his "best pick-up" had been. "Jack Hamilton of course," he said. And hers? "An Italian with red trousers"—though a close second was the night in pre–World War I Europe when she and a baroness friend decided to go out "whoring" one night and had a whole series of encounters.

In the same spirit of frankness, Lincoln told her about his occasional experiences with women as well as men, and in particular (during the early thirties) with Margot Loines, a "fine looking" young socialite with whom he sometimes got more passionate ("we made love to each other indiscriminately") than was usually the case with Mools. Lincoln never pre-

tended that sex with Muriel, even at its best, was much more than "a pleasurable exercise . . . just quite a lot of fun . . . [there's] great pleasure at
being able to find a whole man, or a whole woman."

But sex was the least of what bound Lincoln and Muriel together. By
1933 they'd come to share a great deal: a passionate devotion to the arts; a
commitment to left-wing politics (though as Muriel's, by 1933, intensified, Lincoln's was becoming more attenuated); a firmly held belief in the
importance of Gurdjieff's teachings, including the conviction that one had
to reject social convention and the trancelike state it induced in the name
of mobilizing one's own latent idiosyncratic force.

The two moved, moreover, in many of the same artistic and social circles, and tended, though not always, to hold similar opinions of individuals, about whom they loved to exchange gossip. Mools would tell him
stories about her "horrible" sister-in-law, the well-known monologist
Ruth Draper, or regale him with anecdotes about the famed saloniste
Mabel Dodge Luhan, with whom she shared a mutual if sometimes
strained affection.

Sometimes, though, Lincoln and Muriel disagreed about people, at
least initially. Muriel had no use for Payson Loomis, whom she viewed as
"a petulant bitch . . . tight and prim," who "has only the strength to be
alone." Lincoln protested the description but later came to agree with it.
And that was usually the case; in disagreeing about a given individual's
personal qualities or gifts, Lincoln would generally come to believe that
Muriel's intuition was keener than his. To acknowledge that kind of ultimate deference sometimes bothered him: "I found myself repeating
everything she said," he once wrote, "and all my articulateness ground
itself out."

Another case in point was Mools's friend, the tall, physically unattractive, loquacious Esther Murphy Strachey, whose father owned Mark
Cross and whose brother Gerald was the model for Scott Fitzgerald's Dick
Diver in *Tender Is the Night*. Lincoln couldn't understand, at first, what
Muriel saw in her. In his opinion, Esther talked and drank too much and
was often a bore. But before long he grew to appreciate her tenderheart-
edness, intelligence, and loyalty, and when he was in Europe in 1933,
where Esther would also happen to be, she would prove a generous source
of contacts and introductions.

As for Estlin "E. E." Cummings, Muriel and Lincoln agreed from the
start about his talent, with Muriel going so far as to call him a genius. But
she had far less tolerance for him as a person than Lincoln did; she
thought Cummings too quick to put all other writers down, too eager to
shock, to play Peck's bad boy, and to adopt a style that was "a mockery of
courtesy." Lincoln saw all those same traits in Cummings, but for a time
found his stimulating, brilliant conversation more important.

Muriel had met Cummings first, through their mutual acquaintance the novelist John Dos Passos. Lincoln would often see Cummings at parties, but the two didn't actually meet until early in 1932. That initial encounter was a near disaster. As Lincoln summed it up in his diary, Cummings "was withdrawn & I was silent." The problem was apparently Estlin's wife, the notoriously rude Anne Barton, whose marriage to Estlin was about to end. During that first conversation she landed on Lincoln like a ton of bricks, telling him that *Flesh Is Heir* was "puerile, disgusting . . . a cross between Krafft-Ebing & a school girl gush," and she advised him to get psychoanalyzed; to top things off, she threw in some vaguely anti-Semitic remark (a number of people thought Estlin himself was both an anti-Semite and a racist). Feeling as if he was "about to weep," Lincoln quickly left the party. Mools comforted him with a story about how Anne, some years before, had tried to seduce her young son Paul when he was dead drunk.

A month later, when Lincoln and a friend were at Tony's on West Fifty-second Street (the "in" crowd's favorite speakeasy), Lincoln saw Cummings seated alone and invited him to their table. He accepted, but was, according to Lincoln, "extremely difficult & affected," though "he got better as he got a little lit." Until, that is, they got onto the subject of politics. Cummings announced that there was no difference at all "between the despotism of Fascism & Communism," and he and Lincoln got into an argument about it, with Lincoln defending the Soviets and denouncing the Fascists and with Cummings pointedly calling Lincoln "Keershtein." The only thing that mattered, Cummings finally, haughtily announced, was art, not politics.

None of which stopped Lincoln from publishing several of Cummings's poems in *Hound and Horn;* soon after their argument about the Soviet Union, Cummings told him that the fifty-dollar check for the poems was "the first decent thing that had happened to him in six months." From that point on the two started to see more of each other; Lincoln found Cummings's conversation, even when he disagreed with its content, "enchanting" and his face "beautiful," though he described Cummings's eyes as "scared or mean."

Cummings had picked up on Muriel's distaste for him, and with "cold malice" (as Lincoln put it), denounced her to Lincoln as someone whose "histrionics" he despised and whose worst vice was wanting "to change people." But then again, as Muriel had warned, Cummings found a way to denigrate nearly everyone; among others he characterized Dos Passos, who'd been a loyal friend to him, as "just goddamned clever" and announced that the main trouble with Archie MacLeish's poetry was that it wasn't "somehow a part of him, but a thing that he does very well" (a shrewd if ungenerous estimate).

Cummings brought up the subject of homosexuality a number of times. He told Lincoln that during World War I he'd seen a great deal of it, that men had been "practically thrown into each other's arms in an ecstasy of fear, terror and desire for love & protection." But the men, he added, were "always wrong, and in homosexual contact one's own precious psyche" got "spilled out and [was] never returned." Married men were always, he said, "trying to make him," but they were all "bastards who give nothing, who wish to devour your surrender." The only homosexuals he liked were "regular fairies." It wasn't long before Lincoln noticed that "the only question that . . . [Cummings] has not asked . . . is whether I personally prefer men, women or horses." Nor did Lincoln volunteer the information.

Yet he persisted in seeing Cummings, even while describing him in his diary, in terms that Muriel might have used, as someone who "behaved like an incredibly spoiled but precocious child," and whose "most apparent emotion is surely hate." With each meeting Cummings managed to find someone or something to denounce to Lincoln, apparently eager to "shock" him. The boxer Max Schmeling, Cummings said, was "queer"; "all painters were anal erotics"; "all actors were exhibitionists," and so on.

In the spring of 1933, Cummings won a Guggenheim Fellowship, which stipulated that he spend the year abroad. He and his new girlfriend (who would soon become his wife), Marion Morehouse, a stunning fashion model, would both be in Europe when Lincoln arrived there for the summer.

As in any intense relationship, and particularly when the two people speak their minds as spontaneously, even indulgently, as Muriel and Lincoln did, there had all along been spells of misunderstanding, moodiness, and mutual disappointment between them. In one of her more irritable moods, Muriel berated Lincoln for his inability to be alone, even to have a meal by himself. When Lincoln was on the outs with Mina, Mools told him that he wasn't being sufficiently humane, "that the only thing to do about Mina was to try to continue . . . [the relationship] so that she would find it possible to proceed from her present predicament."

As for Lincoln, he found that Mools could sometimes get in what he described as "a dangerous mood with a kind of hard detached gaiety that chilled" him. He could also openly disparage qualities in her sons that annoyed him; he told her that the older boy, Paul, was much too pleased with himself, "too god-damned facile," and that her younger son, "Smudge," was "self-indulgent" and drinking far too heavily.

They took turns accusing each other of being distant and distracted; Mools once told him that she'd been avoiding him lately because "we were spinning around too close together in the same circle." But at the end of another evening, when Lincoln felt "too tired and nervous . . . [to] really keep my mind on her," she simply laughed and said that he'd been seeing too much of her, that he was understandably "good and bored."

Despite their occasional spats Lincoln and Muriel basically remained "linked souls," deeply attuned to each other, far more supportive than critical and quick to express sympathy for the other's struggles. When Muriel would get depressed about her inability to complete her second book, *America Deserta*, Lincoln would read over what material she had and suggest strategies for moving forward. When she worried about how her sons were developing, Lincoln, quietly reversing himself, would pronounce them both essentially sound.

When he was torn by indecision in mid-1932 about what path to take in life, or whether indeed he had a path, and confided to Mools that he sometimes felt "impelled by terror," she proved a wellspring of comfort. She told him that he was going through the process of becoming a more "ordinary person" (not one of her more acute insights) and that he had at least "more or less stopped . . . [his] blanket-tossing of activities," which was a needed prelude to getting his goals in focus.

And she often gave him shrewd, even predictive, advice. She thought he should give up *Hound and Horn*, that it had served its purpose, and that it stood in the way of his deciding whether he wanted to devote himself to becoming a writer; if so, he could become "a superlative" one. But she added that in her opinion, his "true forte was as an organizer and a catalyst," and that it was only because he was "frightened of being bored" that he continued to paint and to try and write fiction. She even predicted that he "would have a lot of power one day" and that he would get married "as the next inevitable step" in his development. It's no wonder that Lincoln once wrote in his diary that he marveled at the way Mools "always guesses and she always guesses right."

As it turned out, Muriel wouldn't stay in the Soviet Union for as long as she'd initially intended, and after Lincoln returned from Europe, they'd again become part of each other's lives. But the summer of 1933 would prove a momentous one for Lincoln, and would come to mark a decisive turn of direction. He and Muriel would continue to see each other and would sometimes be as intimate as in the old days. Yet both would soon come to realize, however regretfully, that the intensity of their relationship had cooled and that they were no longer unquestionably at the center of each other's lives.

When Lincoln arrived in Paris on June 3, 1933, he tried to locate Romola, but quickly discovered that she was at The Hague seeing to the deposition of Frederica's remains. They'd been out of touch since she left for Europe the month before, and he hadn't given her advance notice of his arrival. Nor did he immediately get in touch with her at The Hague. He later explained that he'd wanted to "surprise" her, but in fact he waited nearly two weeks, trying to make up his mind about how and even whether to proceed. He may have felt angry at not having heard from her, or perhaps thought, given Romola's quixotic nature, that she'd abandoned the book—as she'd often threatened to do—or found a new collaborator to work with. Or he may simply have needed a breather from the turmoil and demands that seemed always to surround her, wanted time for renewing ties with old friends and for attempting to win entrée into the émigré world of Russian ballet artists then centered in Paris.

In terms of old ties he was particularly eager to reconnect with Virgil Thomson and his likable, even-tempered companion, the painter Maurice Grosser. The two had been living in Paris off and on for years, and seemed to know everyone in its artistic circles. Lincoln and Virgil had originally met some three or four years before (among other things, Lincoln had asked him to do a "Letter from Paris" for *Hound and Horn*), but until the summer of 1933 they'd seen little of each other and were not—and would never be—close friends. As recently as six months earlier, after running into Virgil in New York, Lincoln had described him in his diary as "an awful deprecatory little man whom I sort of like." And he did like him, particularly his wit and "serpentine charm," his unsentimental, brilliant intelligence and his "uncommon common-sense." What he found far less appealing in Virgil was his occasional testiness and impatience, and his tendency to bully those around him—perhaps because Lincoln recognized comparable traits (except for the bullying) in himself. Virgil would prove a "cold-eyed," comprehensive guide to a glamorous Parisian cultural world infested with malice, envy, and corruption.[3]

Even before arriving in Paris, Lincoln had written Virgil to report the "long, serious talk" he'd had with Chick Austin "about the possibility . . . of a ballet demonstration" the following year at Hartford's Atheneum. On arriving, he gave Virgil more details. What he had in mind, Lincoln said, was "a Fokine ballet demonstration" to be performed with "music of the period," which he wanted Virgil to choose or compose. Virgil said he'd take it under advisement, but he didn't seem at all keen about the idea. Nor, for that matter, about the way Lincoln continued to toss around his trunkload of imagined schemes and scenarios.

After Lincoln had been in Paris for ten days, Virgil and Maurice sat him down for a severe talking-to; Lincoln called it "a grand attack on me." The gist of their joint lecture was that the role of entrepreneur Lincoln seemed hell-bent on creating for himself was "too easy," was based on a misconception of where his real talents lay. He was, Virgil announced, "a creative not an appreciative soul," and "the only thing that linked up . . . [his] preferences were painting." He then went on to declare that Lincoln "had no mind," was "by no means a man of taste" (in comparison, say, to the "interior decorator" Philip Johnson), but was "a worker," just as Virgil was a worker in music. Lincoln must become a "worker in paint"; what was needed was "a steady professionalism."

Lincoln wrote in his diary that he'd "been thinking this independently for some time"—but that simply meant he'd had the periodic but fleeting sense over the past five years that painting might indeed be his métier. He tried to argue with Virgil and Maurice that, as an appreciator of painting, his only interest "was in subject matter, the restoration of the atmosphere of a period." No, Maurice said, his interest "was entirely technical"; he liked Lachaise, for example, "purely for his technical gifts, and sculpture was merely an extension of painting." Virgil emphasized that what Lincoln needed at the moment was to submit to the *discipline* of becoming a painter—"not in any competitive way, but purely to amuse himself; it would all put him in a much better position to be an entrepreneur like Diaghilev at the age of 45."

"Shit," Lincoln wrote in his diary—a fairly accurate summation of what on all counts seems a remarkably peremptory and wrongheaded set of career directives. How many of Lincoln's drawings (there were no paintings to speak of) had Virgil and Maurice actually seen? The number couldn't have been substantial, for the simple reason that Lincoln had never completed many; those that he had, show talent but nothing approaching a distinctive style—and that was Lincoln's own ruthless self-assessment. Though Virgil was a decade older, and to that degree presumably wiser, Lincoln decided to resist everything that Virgil and Maurice had said to him, though he did write in his diary that "maybe I will become a painter after all." But that afterthought was a hedge, a function of fear, a possible role to fall back on should the many irons he'd put in the fire go cold one by one.

Though Virgil may have been, at least in regard to Lincoln, an inept career counselor, he was a magical social doyen: keen on gossip, acquainted with many of the important figures in Parisian artistic life, and a shrewd appraiser of their personalities. He magisterially mapped out the major players and their assorted intrigues for Lincoln, and generously saw to it that he got to meet a fair number of people. Soon after his arrival, Virgil took him to lunch at the home of Romaine Brooks, the portrait painter and prominent figure in the Sapphic artistic circle (which now included Esther Strachey) centered on the famed 20 rue Jacob salon of Brooks's longtime lover, the wealthy writer Natalie Clifford Barney. Brooks was in her late fifties when Lincoln met her, not much given to socializing, and sometimes unpleasantly sour. But on the day of his visit Dolly Wilde, Oscar's niece (she sometimes dressed like him), was also present, and she livened things up considerably—though Lincoln didn't much take to her; he thought her basically "nasty," "snobbishly rude," and a drug addict to boot.

It was Esther Strachey who introduced him to Natalie Barney herself, taking him to tea at rue Jacob. Barney, then fifty-seven, was a legendary, free-spirited figure; she'd long insisted that sex be divorced from sin and guilt (her many lovers over the decades had included the most famed courtesan of the time, Liane de Pougy), and she'd set as her personal standard of conduct "to live openly, without hiding anything." Barney cherished friendship and loyalty, and helped to support a considerable number of artists (including Virgil Thomson). She gave Lincoln a personal tour of her home, and also the "enchanting" Temple d'Amitié, a small pavilion on her property devoted to readings, contemplation, and dance. Lincoln liked her from the start and admired her "brash courage." After his initial visit he saw her a number of times, and invariably found her "charming" (even after Esther confided to him that Mools had known Barney in the prewar period and had "hated" her).

Thanks to Virgil, Lincoln also met the "never-boring" though sometimes insufferable Christian "Bébé" Bérard, the gifted painter and distinguished ballet set designer. Slovenly, overweight, and opium addicted, when at home Bébé usually wore a soiled white bathrobe and was most likely to be found lying in bed or on the sofa. In either setting he always needed a shave (until he finally grew a beard), and was often munching on bonbons. Lincoln saw him in both of his preferred settings, "lying big, grey and apologetic," but far from being put off found him "quite charming."

Bébé was full of fascinating gossip about the ballet world and talked intimately about the sexual history of Diaghilev and others. He recalled visiting Diaghilev in the company's rooms at the Continental, big, "entirely empty room after room except for the one pot of vaseline"; Diaghilev, according to Bébé, "buggered them all." (According to the pianist Allen Tanner, Diaghilev's "sexual capacity increased with his age: his hypnotic charm, his domination"). Romola had earlier told Lincoln that Diaghilev "never liked anything but sucking," so Lincoln didn't know who or what to believe. Bébé also told him that Massine "was the real love of S. P. D.'s life: not Nijinsky nor the dancer Serge Lifar." He also passed on "some story about Cocteau and Vaslav being surprised by Diaghilev," but Lincoln didn't record any additional details in his diary.

Bérard praised Massine as "a magnificent worker," but he warned Lincoln about Romola's daughter, the dancer Kyra Nijinsky. Though the composer Igor Markevitch was "dying of love for her" (the two would soon marry), and though she was "a very fine character dancer, beautiful with her father's fire," Kyra had, Bébé said, "a bad character" (Romola tended to agree, but didn't, of course, blame herself). When Bérard talked of Boris Kochno, who'd been Diaghilev's general factotum in the last years, Bébé described him as "desolate" ever since Diaghilev's death, "worn out by it." He promised to introduce Lincoln to Kochno, Cocteau, and others, which threw Lincoln into a stew of excitement.

Within a week of arriving, Lincoln was writing home to his parents that "Paris is real grand . . . [it's a city] arranged for people to live in—plenty of breadth—not like N.Y. which seems from this window more barbarous than ever. Maybe it was kings we needed." He also reported that "the streets are full of the cars of German refugees. There are posters against Hitler all over and some really incendiary ones like, 'France has been invaded 4 times in the last 100 years. Arm.' " He noted, too, that a French fascist party had come into existence, with its own set of posters: " 'The Jewish question is not a question of religion: It is a question of race, of Nation.' "

On a related matter, the defining characteristics of "Jewishness," Lincoln and Virgil got into something of an argument. During the thirties, Virgil frequently wrote for Minna Lederman's influential periodical, *Modern Music*, and his first essay (in 1932), on fellow composer Aaron Copland, included a few comments that could be construed as mildly anti-Semitic. Virgil was apparently convinced, and in his frank way said so, that a definable "Jewish School of Art" existed, "practical, of action," directly reflecting "the sorrowful story of the race," with an emphasis on home and family rather than, say, "war, nationalism, love."

Lincoln resisted Virgil's emphasis on the specialness of Jewish culture. Virgil, in turn, told him, in his Olympian, patronizing way, that he was in denial; the reason he "fought so hard the idea of a separate, definite Jewish art" was that he'd been "brought up in the first generation without persecution" and wanted to "prove the Jews are just as good as—i.e. just like—other people." Virgil may have had a point in general but it didn't apply especially well to Lincoln himself. He had a considerable sense of entitlement, felt sure that he was smarter than most people, and was hardly interested in being "just like" everyone else. He did have spasms of self-doubt about the extent of his artistic gifts, did long to make some special mark, and went through considerable self-torture about the direction and limits of his talent. But he also had a realistic sense of himself, especially for so young a man. It is true, though, that—unlike his father—he didn't consider Jewishness *the* most salient feature of his identity.

Along with his introductions from Virgil and Esther Strachey, Lincoln made a number of new friends on his own, including Katherine Anne Porter and the English writers Peter Quennell and Stephen Spender. He also discovered that a surprising number of people he'd known in New York happened to be in Europe that summer, including E. E. Cummings and Marion Morehouse, the art gallery owner Julien Levy and his wife, Joella, Philip Johnson, Jere Abbott, Glenway Wescott and his companion, Monroe Wheeler (at the time the publisher of Harrison of Paris, a line of exquisite and distinguished books).

Lincoln saw them all, some of them often. Social frenzy had become more or less second nature to him, and for the first few weeks he enjoyed the energetic round of dinners and parties, even if he found some of the New Yorkers less appealing abroad than at home. He thought Julien Levy "infantile," with his repetitive "dirty French puns"—but was thrilled when Levy invited him to Brancusi's studio. Brancusi himself amiably showed them around and Lincoln found him "more than anyone I've so far met here a really angelic and noble character." And he adored Brancusi's sculpture: "All the work [is] in the realm of the essential . . . pure, rich and the core." Later Lincoln would be branded an "enemy" of abstract art—and he would give his antagonists plenty of ammunition with which to make the charge. But he never fit neatly into simplistic categories, with regard to art or anything else, as his admiration for Brancusi (*and* Picasso) and his inclusion of a variety of modernist artists and writers in *Hound and Horn* and the Society for Contemporary Art abundantly demonstrates.

In these early years he even championed Le Corbusier. Philip Johnson turned up in Paris and told Lincoln that Le Corbusier's most recent building, the Swiss Pavilion, demonstrated once and for all that the architect had "gone mad." Lincoln had seen the building and he told Johnson that he found it "astonishing" and a "superbly satisfactory whole." Philip further annoyed him by constantly announcing how much Paris "depressed" him in contrast to Berlin, and he spent most of his time, according to Lincoln, "running around to find German [male] whores."

Far more infuriating to Lincoln were Philip's periodic expressions of admiration for Hitler. At first Lincoln thought he was perhaps being provocatively playful, but he soon concluded (as he wrote in his diary) that Philip "is a real Nazi and hates Jews. He likes me but I resent his attitude. Told him I'd knife him quicker than he could me." As late as 1939, after Johnson had purportedly seen the error of his ways, Lincoln still referred to him as "my Fascist friend"—but thought he was "too much of a fool to worry about."

Some of Lincoln's other acquaintances held up better. Cummings could be, as in New York, cantankerous and belligerent, but on the whole seemed "really entirely happy" (for which Lincoln credited Marion), and moreover expressed interest in Lincoln's idea that Cummings write a ballet based on Harriet Beecher Stowe's *Uncle Tom's Cabin.* Lincoln also enjoyed Monroe Wheeler (who would later become head of publications at MoMA) seeing more of him in Paris than he had in New York. Increased contact led to heightened admiration: he found Wheeler "charming and delightful," full of information about ballet, and shrewd in his assessments.

He had quite the opposite opinion of Wheeler's companion, Glenway Wescott; Lincoln thought him "chi-chi" and "a great boy." During one dinner party Glenway talked disapprovingly of Russia and "of Communist leanings for the young." He sidled up to Lincoln and coquettishly asked if Marx was a "good writer" ("Must I read Marx really?"). Lincoln may have been edging away somewhat from his political radicalism, but the fey coyness of Glenway's approach was sufficient by itself to anger him—

especially since, in Lincoln's view, he'd "pettishly applied" for a Guggenheim award, and then "disdainfully received" it. According to Lincoln, over the course of the evening the two became "violently engaged in a row," and on the way home Monroe managed to convey to Lincoln that emotionally he'd sided with him throughout.

Monroe and Glenway, especially the latter, were already good friends of Katherine Anne Porter's; Porter had even told Glenway that she wished she could somehow turn *Hound and Horn* into a vehicle for him to edit, and Monroe's Harrison of Paris press was just then publishing *Katherine Anne Porter's French Song Book*, which she'd compiled and translated. By the time Lincoln first met Porter in Paris that June, the two had already corresponded about her contributions to *Hound and Horn*. Just a month before Lincoln left for Europe, she'd sent him, at his request, a chapter from her biography-in-progress of Cotton Mather. Lincoln had loved it and published a section that winter. The chapter had even given him another possible idea for a ballet scenario (he was constantly coming up with them); he called it " 'Doomsday': the essentialized New England graveyard with one of those Cotton Mather angels cracking tombstones."

When he finally met Porter in person that June of 1933—he was surprised at her white hair, not having realized that at forty-three she was nearly a generation older than he—he mentioned the ballet possibility to her (Porter had written a ballet, *Xochimilko*, for Pavlova in 1923 that had been performed in Mexico). According to Lincoln "she loved the idea," and said she'd think about doing it. Over a long tea on the Boulevard St. Germain, Porter's intimate gossip bordered, since she was talking to a stranger, on the indiscreet. Among much else, she told Lincoln "how feminine" Glenway had become "and what an endless flirt he was"; she also gave a telling description of Hart Crane's last six months in Mexico preceding his suicide—how he took younger and younger boys and finally said that the only thing that excited him was blood. Porter said he was just the same as Jack the Ripper, that his insanity was "without dignity."

Lincoln listened with some skepticism, and in his diary characterized Porter's long story about Crane as "somehow unconvincing & boring." He'd had some slight experience of his own with Crane, seeing him now and then at parties in New York, but Lincoln would usually steer clear of the poet's drunken, chaotic behavior, which sometimes included brawls. He was once accused of having been rude to Crane, at a party at the MacLeishes', but Archie assured him that it was difficult not to be.

Nor had Lincoln ever been much drawn to Crane's poetry. Back in 1931, through Walker Evans, Lincoln had met and fallen for (but apparently never had sex with) a tough seaman friend of Crane's, a would-be writer named Tommy Thompson. In his memoir, *Mosaic*, written late in life, Lincoln devoted the better part of a chapter to Tommy, giving him the name "Carl Carlsen" and including a fake picture of him from a gay physique magazine. When, in 1932, news of Crane's suicide had arrived, Lincoln had felt "a sickening feeling" and soon went to call on Tommy, who "was all broken up." He told Lincoln that Crane "was the greatest man he'd ever met." He also confided that when the critic Yvor Winters had found out that Crane was homosexual, it had "changed Winters' [and also Allen Tate's] attitude . . . toward his verse" and "terribly upset" Crane. Both critics began ascribing Crane's "failure" to develop as a poet to his homosexuality.

After the initial few weeks of incessant socializing, his spare hours spent in prowling the museums, Lincoln decided he needed a change of pace. Virgil, for one, had been getting on his nerves. In Lincoln's current mood, fixated on trying to find a way to get a foothold inside the ballet world, his interest in sex had all but vanished. Yet Virgil and Maurice "became increasingly solicitous" about his "not having gotten a piece of tail" since arriving in Paris, and kept urging him to go to a male bordello. When Virgil then proceeded to go on and on about how, sexually, he "could never any longer take anyone of his own class . . . suddenly something went snap" in Lincoln. He was fed up with "miscellaneous fucking," and the endless talk about it, and fed up, too, with all the "purely social" aspects of trying to do something "in relation to the production of art."

"I've had too long a vacation from . . . 'real work,' " he wrote in his diary, "I get seedy & remote." He was back to thinking about trying his hand again at a novel, but decided that "I really do want to work with Romola if possible." He'd been putting off making a decision about going to The Hague to see for himself what the actual state of the manuscript was, and after his spat with Virgil would have left Paris immediately had it not been for the ballet season in progress. But he did write Romola for the first time since arriving.

She responded warmly in her somewhat fractured English: "I most certainly want still very much that you should come. The book I think means to [*sic*] much of us that now at the last minute we should fail." Lincoln wrote back that he couldn't come immediately but that he would definitely arrive before the end of June. She tried, in a second letter, to coax him to come earlier, pleading the double urgency of arranging a benefit for Vaslav ("unless within the next six weeks something is done he will be put out of the sanatorium"), and of her own desperate depression ("I can not stand it longer"). But Lincoln had grown familiar with her wiles; Vaslav's security, he'd learned, was not her top priority, and her mood swings, while real enough, had never yet dictated emergency proceedings. Even when, in yet a third letter, she claimed that "the book . . . is almost completed. I must make some defenit [*sic*] arrangement without delay," Lincoln felt confident that as usual, she was exaggerating for effect. No, he would go to her soon, but not until he'd seen his fill of the extraordinary ballet season, with two separate companies vying for attention and supremacy.

In the wake of Diaghilev's death in 1929, the ballet world had become rent by factions. A number of émigré artists had been trying to lay claim to his mantle, and to find venues, patrons, and, they hoped, companies that might make their existence less precarious. By the summer of 1933, Col. Vasily de Basil's Ballets Russes de Monte Carlo had emerged as the leading new configuration. It had originated in 1931 with René Blum, director of the theater at Monte Carlo. Blum had hired, among others, Georgi Balanchivadze (George Balanchine), Diaghilev's last major choreographer, as ballet master; the designer Bébé Bérard; the painter André Derain; and, as the company's artistic adviser, Boris Kochno (Bérard's live-in companion). Balanchine, in turn, hired what the press was soon referring to as the "three baby ballerinas" he'd discovered in Paris: the virtuoso prodigies Irina Baronova, Tamara Toumanova, and Tatiana Riabouchinska, who ranged in age from twelve to fourteen.[4]

Colonel de Basil, a powerful personality and something of a genius at manipulation, soon managed to persuade Blum to take him on as a partner in the new enterprise. Born Vasily Voskresensky, de Basil had been a captain in the Cossacks and had briefly managed the tour of a small fly-by-night ballet company. Despite his limited experience and taste, he nonetheless succeeded, step by step, in gaining control over the Ballets Russes de Monte Carlo, and he reshaped it, giving commercial success precedence over artistic experimentation. That emphasis put him automatically at odds with Balanchine and Kochno, who were soon protesting de Basil's encroachments on artistic policy.

Not that de Basil cared. In 1932 he quietly replaced Balanchine as ballet master with Léonide Massine, the better known of the two as both dancer and choreographer; conveniently Massine also owned a significant number of costumes and sets originally created for the Diaghilev company. The dancer Roman Jasinski, a member of the troupe, has additionally suggested some sort of antagonism between Balanchine and Massine that prevented them "from working well together."

Balanchine and Kochno resigned. Soon after, they succeeded in putting together a group they called Les Ballets 1933, a young company of some fifteen dancers, including Toumanova. Derain and Jasinski also joined up. None of this would have come to pass had it not been for the events of a decade earlier, when Vladimir Dimitriev, a former baritone in the Maryinsky opera company, successfully engineered exit visas from the Soviet Union for a small group of artists, the so-called Soviet State Dancers. Among them were Balanchine, Tamara Geva, his first wife, and Alexandra Danilova, who would become his "unofficial" second wife.

Soon after they arrived in Europe, Diaghilev hired them, and Balanchine had ever since regarded Dimitriev as his most trusted adviser. "This man," Roman Jasinski has said, "really took care" of Balanchine after he left Russia.

Les Ballets 1933 could never have gotten off the ground, however, had it not been for yet another man: Edward James, a wealthy English socialite who put up the money to secure a try-out season for the new company. He did so in an effort to entice his estranged wife, the dancer-actress Tilly Losch, to return to him; delighted with the gift, Tilly ended up divorcing him anyway. But James's money did enable Balanchine to do far more with Les Ballets 1933 than would have otherwise been possible. For the company's performances in Paris and London that summer, Balanchine was able to gather together an extraordinary group of collaborators, including the dancers Diana Gould and Pearl Argyle, the painter-designers Derain, Bérard, and Pavel Tchelitchev, and the composers Kurt Weill, Darius Milhaud, and Henri Sauguet. In a remarkably short period of time Balanchine managed to create six new ballets, including *Errante*, *Songes*, and *Mozartiana*.

Within a week of arriving in Paris, Lincoln had heard about the splits and rivalries within the ballet world; thus far he'd met few of the actual players, but he'd become thoroughly familiar with their histories. On his very first night in Paris, he'd seen Serge Lifar (who'd been Diaghilev's lover and star) dance at the Paris Opéra. Although sitting at the top of the balcony, Lincoln was impressed: Lifar's dancing "was a great pleasure," though he thought both the music and decor "very bad." But when he went back the following week to see Lifar dance the Nijinsky role in *Spectre de la Rose*, he was greatly disappointed. He "danced well" but "was no dream . . . it was merely perfunctory" and left Lincoln "absolutely unmoved."

The opening night of Les Ballets 1933 took place during the same week, on June 7 before a posh audience at Paris's Théâtre des Champs-Élysées (site of the first, riot-provoking performance in 1913 of *Rite of Spring*). Lincoln, along with Esther Strachey, Natalie Barney, Virgil Thomson, Romaine Brooks, and Dolly Wilde, were in attendance, and Lincoln himself "in a fever of excitement." The first offering was *Mozartiana* with Toumanova and Jasinski in the leading roles, choreography by Balanchine, decor and costumes by Bérard. For Lincoln the standout was Balanchine's "very lovely choreography, witty and Mozartian," though Virgil assured him that it wasn't up to Balanchine's work of the previous year.

During intermission Lincoln ran into Agnes de Mille, fresh from a concert triumph in London where Arnold Haskell, the prominent critic (soon to figure importantly in Lincoln's work with Romola), had given her a laudatory notice. Agnes and Lincoln did a quick kiss-kiss, swore to get together soon, and then didn't; their budding antagonism must have been apparent to both. Lincoln also spotted Edward James, who looked to him like what he was purported to be: the illegitimate son of Edward VII— that is, "strained through a sheet" and somehow "extremely offensive-looking."

The Seven Deadly Sins was next on the program, performed to Kurt Weill's "familiar haunting delayed music" (as Lincoln put it in his diary), with Tilly Losch and Lotte Lenya heading the cast. Lincoln thought it was "boring, but intense like a nightmare . . . Lotte being a perfect sign for it"; overall Lincoln liked it, thought it had a "deliberate, shabby elegance," and "applauded wildly at every opportunity." There was some whistling from the audience, but it was drowned out "in cultivated applause."

The final offering was *Songes*, with Toumanova and Jasinski again in the leads, and with music by Milhaud (which Lincoln thought "very dull and boring"). As for the rest he "often thought [it] was dull but was not bored," reserving his highest praise for Toumanova's "fine dancing . . . [she] is amazingly strong in her extension, agile and brilliant." As for Balanchine's choreography overall, Lincoln thought the three ballets were too much for one man "to do perfectly," and concluded in his diary that "he's no Fokine." Yet he was hugely excited by the evening, confirmed in his view that the medium of ballet "is one of the miracles of life."

The next day he went to the Théâtre du Châtelet to get tickets for the competing company, Les Ballets Russes de Monte Carlo. On his way he stopped off at Notre-Dame Cathedral, where he "lit a candle and offered a prayer for everybody I know"—a gesture that, in true Gurdjieffian style, he recorded in his diary but made no effort to explain; Lincoln's Jewish identity was a real, if attenuated aspect of his personhood, but lighting those candles was no token tourist gesture, devoid of spiritual significance. Lincoln would always travel between various belief systems—Judaism, Christianity, Gurdjieffism, Bolshevism—picking and choosing, emphasizing this aspect or that, depending on the exigencies of a given period in his life. Indeed, that same day he had a conversation about the Soviet Union, which interested him so much that he gave renewed thought to going there—the official home of atheism.

On June 9, thanks to a French friend, Lincoln got to sit in on the final rehearsal for *Errante* and *Fastes*, both due to premiere the following night. For *Errante*, Tchelitchev had done the decor and costumes and also coauthored the libretto with Balanchine; Tilly Losch and Jasinski were to dance the leads. For *Fastes*, Henri Sauguet, a contemporary composer, provided the music and Derain the decor and costumes. A third premiere, *Les Valses de Beethoven*, was also scheduled for June 10, with Losch, Diana Gould, and Jasinski in the leads. Balanchine had choreographed all three pieces.

At the rehearsal Lincoln sat next to Bébé Bérard, who plied him with "coarse" and funny remarks. All the principals involved in *Errante* and *Fastes* were, of course, in the theater, and Lincoln found them all friendly—that is, with the exception of Kochno, who Lincoln thought "disdainful . . . and in a way, horrid," but without specifying why. Sauguet struck him as "like some sort of bird," perhaps because of nerves over the pending opening. Lincoln had met Milhaud once before, at Lincoln Filene's house in Boston; Milhaud remembered and was cordial. In his diary Lincoln mentions only seeing Balanchine "miming" with "a little girl." He was not introduced.

Lincoln saw *Errante* as "very much a motivated Tchelitchev painting," and though he found "some nice passages" in the choreography, he wasn't ecstatic about it; what he did comment on was "Balanchine's tragic ideas of the relations between men & women: always broken up by someone jumping between." He again thought Toumanova was "fine" but dismissed Tilly Losch as having "a music hall style I don't like." From the "general overtone" he picked up from those present, the apparent consensus was that *Songes* had been "a great flop" and that *Mozartiana* hadn't "been praised highly enough." Virgil, who was also at the rehearsal, said, "that's all right: it would be."

That same evening, Lincoln went to see the Ballets Russes at the Châtelet. Back in 1929, he'd seen Lifar dance the lead in Massine's *Les Matelots* but in 1933 Massine himself (with Lifar sitting in the front row) danced the role. Lincoln thought he was "fine" and found the ballet itself "nearly as charming as ever . . . thrilling to see again." Two other Massine ballets completed the evening. One was *Les Présages*, to the music of Tchaikovsky's Fifth, which Lincoln thought "a wonderful choreographic thing"—but with such terrible costumes one could hardly see it; he complained, too, about the "often ragged" corps de ballet. During the intermission following *Présages*, Lincoln saw Tilly Losch and Kochno leave the theater, perhaps because the audience (according to Lincoln) had been so "enthusiastic" in its response. Lincoln thought the third ballet, *Le Beau Danube*, "a continued enchantment" and Massine's own dancing "lovely"; after the performance he and a friend "fell into each other's arms in ecstasy over Massine." At this point in his ballet going, in other words, Lincoln was more enthusiastic (and by a considerable margin) about Massine's work than about Balanchine's.

The next night, June 10, he was back at Les Ballets 1933. This time around a number of changes had been made in both the staging and choreography of *The Seven Deadly Sins*, and though Lincoln thought no better of Tilly Losch, he liked the "speeded up" ballet more than at first viewing. The premiere of *Errante* was also on the bill; in his diary comments, Lincoln heaped praise on the music and orchestration, and had some admiring words for Tchelitchev's decor—but, obviously underwhelmed, he wrote not a single comment on Balanchine's choreography. Nor did he make any observation about the third ballet, *Fastes*, which had also premiered that night.

Dining with Maurice Grosser the following evening, Lincoln complained that "the sensibility of Tchelitchev and Berard" seemed to him "thin, an echo." Maurice protested that "there was a virtue in sensing & directing the mode, like Berard," and added that he himself "wants to be a good bourgeois painter who sells a picture occasionally." Maurice then returned to his preferred topic of sex, and extolled "the educational virtues of promiscuity." As Lincoln thought he'd made clear earlier, this wasn't at the moment on his list of priorities. Just the day before, Marion Morehouse had told him of her "great concern" about his lack of a "love life," advising him to "get a ballet girl for a mistress." Lincoln's terse reply was that "no woman would have me." He obviously hadn't spelled out his erotic preference to Marion or Estlin, but it seems curious they hadn't picked up on it, since Lincoln made no special effort at concealment and traveled in notably queer circles.

Alfred Barr turned up in Paris in mid-June, and Lincoln had dinner with him. A variety of subjects came up: "possibilities" at MoMA, past and future; Alfred's ideas for "ethnographical shows"; a promised exhibition for Lachaise (whose "decorative" works Alfred did not like and whose portraits he thought weren't, as Lincoln had suggested, "Roman"). When talk turned to "our queer friends," including Jere Abbott's "ostrich in the sand" discretions, Alfred asked Lincoln "point blank how I get along. I said I thought all in all I proceeded, which I hope [I] do," and he was touched at Alfred's solicitous question. "He is very sweet and kind," Lincoln later wrote in his diary, "and knows more than any of us."

As the competition between Les Ballets 1933 and Les Ballets Russes de Monte Carlo raged on, Lincoln was constantly at the Châtelet or the Théâtre des Champs-Élysées. His third exposure to the James/Balanchine Company again left him with mixed reactions—*Songes* looked "even worse than before," and *Errante* (except for Tilly Losch) "better," while he continued to enjoy *Mozartiana* "very much"—whereas his follow-up visits to the Ballets Russes provided undiluted pleasure. Fokine's *Les Sylphides* he "enjoyed . . . beyond anything—beautifully danced," and he thought *La Dame de Pique* was "absolutely lovely."

"It's an excellent troupe," he wrote in his diary, and went on and on to a friend about "the high standards of the ballet at the Chatelet." He felt that "never such extreme satisfaction have I seen on the stage" as when Massine danced "*The Blue Danube*. . . . He was adorable and such a magnificence of style. Absolute perfection." Lincoln had obviously come to prefer Les Ballets Russes to Balanchine's Les Ballets 1933, as did the Parisian critics and public; they gave de Basil's company far more acclaim, with the press commenting on how much it had improved over the previous year, when Balanchine had been ballet master.

But he continued to attend performances of Les Ballets 1933 and certainly found much to admire in them. *Mozartiana* delighted him at every viewing; he "adored it," thought it the "perfect complement in dancing for the music." He told Bérard as much, who reciprocated by introducing him briefly to Kochno; they made an appointment to meet a few days later. *Errante*, too, continued, in Lincoln's opinion, to improve; "as spectacle," he found it "more brilliant and touching" with each exposure, and he had the thought that it would look "superb" on the stage of the Radio City Music Hall. His fourth time watching the James/Balanchine company proved the best, "a marvelous evening" for him. Les Ballets 1933 had slowly risen in his estimation.

The day after that epiphany, Esther Strachey's sister-in-law, Noel Murphy, took him to the studio of Pavel "Pavlik" Tchelitchev, the designer of *Errante*, who'd been painting her portrait. Tchelitchev would prove, in terms of future friendship, a far more important figure in Lincoln's life than all the Virgils and Bébés put together. More than two years earlier Lincoln had seen Tchelitchev's work, already widely hailed in Europe, in a group show in New York, and it had caught his eye. At their first introduction, that June day in 1933, Tchelitchev had a number of guests in his studio, including George Platt Lynes and Glenway Wescott. According to Lincoln's diary, "Tchelitchev was a little fancy, but charming to me when I told him how much I'd loved *Errante*."

He regaled his guests with tales of how the chorus girls in *Errante* had deliberately spiked the long, glittering green silk train on Tilly Losch's dress, producing a large tear; Tilly had later screamed at them in German, but at the time she made a quick recovery, appearing within minutes in her rehearsal costume. And he railed against "the horrible" Bérard, the designer of *Mozartiana* and his archrival at the moment, saying he was "without talent, a pig." As Lincoln would soon enough learn, Tchelitchev, for all his charm and liveliness, was a cauldron of hyperbolic exasperation; at some point or another he ended up railing ungratefully at nearly everyone in his life.

Tchelitchev also brought out various portfolios of his drawings and showed a few of his paintings as well. Lincoln felt they showed "extraordinary manual dexterity" as well as "a gift of likeness and glamorous romance that is quite wonderful." He liked the drawings better than the paintings, though he thought some of the paintings "had . . . a kind of essential truth as visualized by his personal nostalgia and piteous sympathy of perennial adolescence." (In years to come Lincoln would become Tchelitchev's leading champion; when his reputation faded, even before his early death in 1957, Lincoln would almost single-handedly attempt to resurrect it.)

Tchelitchev was due to leave shortly for London with Les Ballets 1933, but he invited Lincoln to visit him again before he did so. Eager to solidify the contact, Lincoln reappeared in the painter's studio three days later. This time only two other people were there: Tchelitchev's devoted sister, Alexandra Zaoussailoff, and his longtime lover, the pianist Allen Tanner (soon to be replaced by Charles Henri Ford).

Once again Tchelitchev was full of animated talk, generously sprinkled with inventive denunciation. Edward James was merely "an adorable child, delighted to be able to spend money." Kochno "had his uses as a stage man" but was otherwise negligible. There was "general hatred" for Bébé Bérard. Roman Jasinski "was very stupid, but he could be told what to do." Lifar was "impossible." Diaghilev in his last years "was tired and didn't supervise the way he had before." And so forth. Only one person was exempted from censure: George Balanchine. He was, Tchelitchev said simply, "a great man." According to Tchelitchev, the Schubert music for *Errante* was originally suggested by one of the ballet accompanists. When Tchelitchev heard it he rushed to Balanchine, "who took fire at once and it was composed in the rough in 24 hours."

Lincoln made it a point to bring up his earlier thought that *Errante* would be seen to splendid advantage on the large stage of Radio City Music Hall, "where wonderful things could be done." Immediately picking up the cue, Tchelitchev said he wanted "to work for lots of masses of people—not for just snobs," and he had "many other wonderful ideas for huge stages." He was tired, he claimed, of all the intrigues and rows of the European ballet scene; New York was the hope of the future, even though he was afraid of the place because "he adored Anglo-Saxons so" and "didn't know how he could control himself with them." Lincoln delicately added one final drop of icing to the cake: in New York, he said, "one could do pretty much as one pleased" (as if he didn't know better), and he felt confident that Tchelitchev "would be sure to have a great success" there. When Lincoln said that he, too, would be headed for London in July, Pavlik suggested that he look him up there.

Other new acquaintances also poured ballet gossip into Lincoln's ears. Monroe Wheeler warned him that Tchelitchev was "lazy and captious," emotionally unreliable. He described Kochno as "by no means strong enough to direct anything: he doesn't care enough, and they are all too bitten by society to work really well"; what they needed, according to Monroe, was a Diaghilev "to crack their heads together and tell them to go to hell." Lincoln idealistically told Monroe that through the ballet, he hoped it would be possible "to restore to the world the human scale again"; they both felt "it could be done in America," and that Lincoln "was the person to do it."

He got another sort of earful of ballet tattle from the American journalist Janet Flanner, who was part of the Natalie Barney circle. At lunch she told Lincoln that David Lichine, the other male star (along with Massine) of de Basil's Ballets Russes, was "a great cocksman, having had everyone at the Opera *and* at the Châtelet." She described Kyra Nijinsky, who had rudely failed to answer Lincoln's letters and was currently "practicing" with the Châtelet crowd, as "fattish and sulky." Kochno and Massine, according to Flanner, were not on speaking terms, and Kochno and Balanchine had "a contract keeping them together for some years" (a rumor without any apparent basis in fact). She also reported that the Princesse de Polignac (Wineretta Singer of the sewing machine millions) had been so angry at the refusal of de Basil's Ballets Russes to perform an Igor Markevitch ballet that she gave a huge party on the evening of the company's opening "and spoiled the Massine debut."

It certainly hadn't spoiled it for Lincoln, which made him somewhat leery of Flanner's reliability as a source of information—fortunately, or he might have assumed the truth of a binding long-term agreement between Kochno and Balanchine. Besides, Lincoln knew from firsthand experience that Flanner sometimes cheated on her sources. When at Tchelitchev's studio, the painter had specifically asked Lincoln what Flanner had thought of *Errante*, because he thought she "had great good taste." Lincoln had told him that she "adored" it, when in fact she hadn't seen it—it had been Lincoln who had described the ballet to her "in great detail" so that she could write it up for her regular "Letter from Paris" in *The New Yorker.* No, he and Janet Flanner were not destined to become good friends; when they went out together one night, she expressed annoyance that he hadn't dressed, told him that he "had passion" (which Lincoln interpreted as meaning he was naive), and insisted that "everything had been much better before." Which may well have been true, if one had lived through the glorious twenties in Paris. But the twenty-six-year-old Lincoln preferred to look forward, to believe that the future would be more glorious still.

During the final week of the ballet season, during intermission one evening, Lincoln spotted Serge Lifar ("small, dark, slightly oily and compact") talking in front of the bar to a smaller, aging man, "roving-eyed, gray haired, rather strong but feminine-faced"—who turned out to be Picasso, whom Lincoln greatly admired. Lincoln had earlier written to Lifar asking for an interview but had gotten no response. He hovered until Lifar was alone, then went up to him and introduced himself. According to Lincoln's account in his diary, Lifar replied, "Oh it is you, who wrote me." He added that "he'd been terribly busy," but that Lincoln should come around to his hotel the following morning at 10:00 a.m.

Lincoln could hardly believe his good fortune, since he'd been feeling discouraged of late at not having had more success in meeting key ballet figures. Just the day before he'd written in his diary, "depressed & low in my mind because no one seems willing to see me about the ballet. I feel either they don't care to discuss it out of competitive jealousy or they all hate Romola," and knew of his connection to her.

Lincoln arrived promptly the next morning at Lifar's hotel and was ushered into a surprisingly small room, made smaller still by the presence of a manservant. Lifar, who struck Lincoln as "more Latin-looking than Slav," lay in bed wearing a red bathing suit; as Lincoln sat down, Lifar pulled the corner of a yellow puff "out of modesty up to his chin." Lincoln had brought along photos of Nijinsky that he'd been collecting and showed them to Lifar, who scornfully referred to them as "only" copies. "Screw him," Lincoln later wrote in his diary; "He was either extremely tired, or nasty. Maybe both." They talked in French; Lincoln had a good command of the language, Lifar spoke "with a thick Russian accent." The entire interview lasted half an hour: "I found he would be of no use to me at all," Lincoln wrote in his diary.

Lifar did tell him a few anecdotes, mostly negative ones, about Nijinsky. He said Vaslav "was afraid of him. Something about being afraid of being shaved." He insisted that Vaslav was "crazy in 1912; that Fokine was once good, but was now impossible—a flat statement [said] without animosity." He further told Lincoln that he'd be dancing in concert in London on July 3 and suggested he come and see him there. "Peut-être," Lincoln said, smiling, as if to suggest that Lifar was "far too grand to see me." "Non, assurement," Lifar responded. He even "half apologized for being so dopey" and said, fixing Lincoln "with a semi-hypnotic eye," that "he could tell me a few stories some other time." The manservant reappeared, and Lifar sank back on his pillows.

The next day Lincoln went for his prearranged appointment with Boris Kochno at the apartment he shared with Bébé Bérard. Kochno was unshaven but "agreeable" and looked at Lincoln's Nijinsky photos "in ravishment & delight." He had little time to talk, though, since they were getting ready to leave for London, where Les Ballets 1933 was due to open at the Savoy on June 28, four days thence (de Basil's company would begin performing at London's Alhambra on July 4). But Kochno did invite Lincoln to come and see them again on July 26, after they'd returned to Paris. In the meantime he gave Lincoln a note, written in elaborate Russian script, to Walter Nouvel, a Diaghilev intimate of some forty years.

Lincoln went to see Nouvel that same day. He found an "oldish man with sharp, saggy bags under his eyes," who told him that he "could remember little or nothing about anything" (Tchelitchev had told Lincoln that Nouvel "does nothing now but . . . flirt with little boys on the Boulevards"). Nouvel did give him the address in Paris of the set designer Alexandre Benois, another prominent associate of Diaghilev's, as well as coauthor with Stravinsky of the libretto for the daring 1911 production of the Fokine/Stravinsky ballet *Petrouchka.*

Lincoln decided not to use the letter to Benois for the present, nor the one he'd been given to Cocteau. He was feeling "pretty low in my mind as what to do next." A few doors had begun to open, but all of the Russians he'd met had warned him that his connection to Romola could ruin his chances "of getting any dope at all." They uniformly described her as "a terrible liar" and cautioned him "not to trust her."

Even so Lincoln decided that he would go to The Hague for at least a brief visit. The entire ballet world, it seemed, was about to decamp for London. He had nothing tangible to do. "I'm fed up with everyone," he wrote in his diary; Julien Levy was irritated with him for not thinking Dalí was a genius, and Virgil was in a general sulk because a check due from Chick Austin (*Four Saints in Three Acts* was scheduled to open at the Hartford Atheneum early in 1934) hadn't arrived. Lincoln felt so out of sorts that he failed to enjoy the final performance at the Ballets Russes: he thought Lichine danced badly (he "seemed to be bored"), and paid Balanchine's *Cotillon* the backhanded compliment of being "a pretty kind of headache, but . . . ingenious."

In his gloom Lincoln decided that, after all, he disliked the French. It was time to clear out. Romola, with all her liabilities, represented a chance for doing something concrete, making some definable mark in the ballet world. He left for The Hague on June 28, "relieved to leave Paris; felt I could hold its beauty in my memory for some time to come and that I had learned all I wanted of its bitchery."

He went straight to Romola's hotel. He'd "expected her to be hysterical with misfortune," but found her cheerful, if full of complaints. She'd successfully seen to Frederica's interment, had no money (or said she had none), had no idea where to go or what to do in the future—her "terrible" stepfather had refused to let her return to Hungary, and she had no hope of regaining entry to the United States. She'd been ill and was alone, and lamented that she'd "had no girl since N. Y." But she'd decided that "it's all funny [and] she laughed & laughed." Lincoln couldn't help feeling sympathetic, but he was used to her wiles and remembered the warnings about her unreliability. He kept waiting for her to present him with unpaid bills.

Since they'd last seen each other, Romola had written five new chapters, which, in Lincoln's opinion, were "not inspired but a skeleton at least. . . . O.K. to work on." He spent the next five days revising the chapters, with time out for museum excursions and for visiting the local dancing school. He spent some time with a young instructor there, a dancer from Kiev named Igor Svetzov, who had toured with Bronia Nijinska in South America and elsewhere, and had known Fokine. The two talked and talked about the current ballet scene, disagreeing about Lichine (Svetzov thought he had "more chance than any of the younger dancers to improve & develop") but agreeing "that Balanchine was far less serious than Massine."

Lincoln also took time off to visit the Frans Hals Museum in Haarlem and the Rijksmuseum in Amsterdam. But aside from admiring several Rembrandts and recognizing the "excellence" of room after room of Metsus, Terborchs, and Vermeers, he decided he had "no interest in ever seeing any of them again." And he felt the same about Holland itself. As he wrote his parents, "The Dutch are God's deadest folk. They have no memories, they're incredibly insular & slow and one waits eagerly for an earthquake. . . . I will go scary cuckoo and smash all the clean tiling . . . if I have to stay here one more day."

Besides, the ballet season had begun in London. He talked over with Romola the possibilities for arranging a benefit there for Vaslav, and they agreed she'd follow within a few days; but he did tell her "as tactfully as possible" that she was widely distrusted within Russian ballet circles and that winning cooperation for a benefit would be tricky. Romola made plans to arrive in London on July 3, and Lincoln said he would meet her boat train.

On the morning of the third, he was dutifully at dockside at 8:00 a.m. And there he stood until 9:30. No Romola. Returning to his hotel, Lincoln found a wire from her that he'd been anticipating all along: she had no money to pay her hotel bill and needed him to send her one hundred dollars immediately. Angry but resigned, he went down to the American Express office and sent her the money. Instead of Romola promptly appearing, another wire followed two days later requesting still more money, and without any explanation for why the first hundred dollars hadn't sufficed. Lincoln was depressed to find that he now had "comparatively little money" left. But he sent her the additional sum anyway. Once again Romola neither responded nor appeared.

Lincoln felt decidedly put out but wasn't one to sit around cooling his heels. He looked up some old friends, made some new ones—and was in constant attendance at the various ballet performances that had by then begun. He went to see his and Mina's old friend, David Garnett (the three of them had taken a brief vacation trip to Virginia together three months earlier), and David took him to a gathering at Roger Fry's, the critic and Bloomsbury luminary; several of the Sitwells were there, and also Virginia Woolf (whom Lincoln mistook for Vanessa Bell), looking "very gaunt in a lace cap, and frightening." Constance and Kirk Askew were also in residence in London, and Lincoln went several times to their fashionable soirées.[5]

He also sought out A. R. Orage, whom he'd earlier met, editor of the *New English Weekly* and for a time a close associate of Gurdjieff's; through Orage he was introduced to two South African writers, William Plomer and Laurens van der Post, who, in quite distinct ways, would become good friends. He also began to see a good bit of the then highly regarded English poet and critic Peter Quennell, about whom he kept changing his mind, finding him one day charming and the next "exceedingly cantankerous."

Most important, given his primary interest in the ballet, Lincoln arranged to meet with Arnold Haskell, the well-known English dance critic, who he described in his diary as "a tiny, black-moustached little creature of great shyness and suppressed intensity." At lunch together they talked nothing but ballet, and Haskell was full of wonder at the young ballerina Tamara Toumanova; she "is really the works," he told Lincoln excitedly, she had "restored his faith in the future of classic dancing." According to Lincoln they "agreed on all subjects"—with the exception of Agnes de Mille; Haskell felt that she "was such a good artist, however limited," but Lincoln insisted he'd yet to see the evidence.

Three days later Haskell arranged a lunch so that Lincoln could meet Toumanova and her notoriously protective mother (Lincoln thought her "a caution"). The four of them talked at length about the history of Tamara's troubles with de Basil, director of the Ballets Russes de Monte Carlo, including his demand that she sign a ten-year contract, and the additional problem posed by the second of the three "baby ballerinas," Tatiana "Tania" Riabouchinska, who was wealthy and helped to support the company—and therefore expected all the big parts for herself. Lincoln felt that "the most important part of the narrative"—why Tamara had defected to Les Ballets 1933—was being "tactfully left out" of the discussion, with just a hint given that de Basil had tried to get Tamara into bed.

Both mother and daughter expressed their satisfaction with having shifted to Les Ballets 1933. Tamara "adored" Balanchine and thought he was himself "a magnificent dancer," though she felt that given his medical history (several years before, Balanchine had been diagnosed with tuberculosis and had spent a number of months in a sanitarium; the bacillus had been dormant since then), he ought not to be dancing at all. As for Roman Jasinski, often her costar, Tamara described him as "a charming boy . . . acutely modest and sensitive" who practiced constantly and was "desolated" by his mistakes. Unfortunately he was not, she said, a good partner; "he gets a little stage fright when he comes on" and "is terrified of dropping her." Lichine, by contrast, she considered "a beast" to dance with; when they performed *Sylphides*, Tamara said, Lichine "told her to support herself and let her fall." She found Edward James, the company's main financial backer, also a problem; he could be "nervous, hysterical," and "terrible" about programming, suddenly deciding to star "obscure British girls," leaving everyone uncertain what he would do next.

Lincoln had started attending ballet performances the day after he arrived in London, beginning with Serge Lifar at the Savoy Theatre. He thought the program awful ("Faun without the nymphs; Spectre with a lot of jumps"). But Felia Doubrovska, the elegant Diaghilev ballerina who'd danced in several of Balanchine's early creations, did "a superb variation" and in the "Blue Bird" *divertissement* he thought Lifar was "splendid"— "his magnificent instrument and his lousy conceit." The following evening he went with the Askews to the Ballets Russes, which he again thoroughly approved, singling out the "fine performance of Fokine's Les Sylphides," and deciding, this time around, that Massine's *Les Présages* was a "really monumental" work. The next night he saw Massine's *Jeux d'Enfants* and was again entranced, finding it "really delicious." Thus far at least, Massine could do no wrong in Lincoln's eyes, whereas his reactions to Balanchine were more mixed, his enthusiasm more tempered.

And then on July 7 who should finally arrive but Romola—without advance notice, and while Lincoln was shaving. She was, as usual, full of excuses, the real and imaginary impossible to disentangle. And again, as usual, she was tired, depressed, "convinced" she should "never have made the effort." She took a room on the floor below Lincoln's at Batt's Hotel, and while she rested, Lincoln dashed over to see Arnold Haskell. He laid out the whole situation to Haskell, explaining the necessity for a publisher's advance, since he was running out of money and Romola had made it clear that she intended to rely on him wholly. Haskell immediately called up Victor Gollancz, of the prestigious Gollancz publishing house, who asked for a copy of the manuscript to read over the weekend.

After lunch Lincoln went back to Haskell's, this time to enlist his help in achieving a rapprochement between the warring ballet companies and personnel in the name of putting on a benefit that would secure Nijinsky's care in the Swiss sanatorium. Having learned that de Basil's Ballets Russes had made definite plans for an American tour that would begin in the late fall, Lincoln also made a plea to Haskell to use his influence to get "an American ballet" into the company's repertory. Haskell replied that de Basil didn't have "much sense," but he would suggest the idea to him.

Lincoln decided that Haskell was "a touchy little man," but for the best of reasons: he was "so full of heart it sometimes silences him." When Lincoln thanked him for all his efforts on Nijinsky's behalf, Haskell turned away and quietly said, "It's nothing; it's for the dance." But he clearly took to Lincoln, since he invited him to return the next day, this time to accompany him to the sculptor Jacob Epstein's studio. Having seen and liked Epstein's recent show, Lincoln was delighted to accept, and he found Epstein "nice: detached . . . innocent like Brancusi and Lachaise . . . intent and kindly." Epstein gave them a tour of his studio, and then they sat and talked for a bit, mostly in shared deprecation of the sculptors Aristide Maillol, Antoine Bourdelle, and Charles Despiau.

That same evening Lincoln took Romola to the Savoy Theatre to see Les Ballets 1933: *Mozartiana, Songes,* and *Errante.* It made him feel "awfully nervous to have her see it: as if I had some personal responsibility involved." On the whole she was unimpressed. Toumanova, she said, "was too heavy ever to dance well" (in truth she still had a bit of baby fat, but was rapidly losing it). As for Balanchine, Romola liked his "ideas" but said she "kept seeing [the] sources" behind them: they were "a real Russian salad"—in other words, not particularly original.

Nonetheless they went around to the stage door after the performance and sent a note in to Balanchine, who came out "for a second & spoke a word to Romola" (in his diary Lincoln recorded no exchange between himself and Balanchine). Romola, inimitably, told Balanchine that "he made even the scenery dance," which she implied was a good thing since "he had no dancers"; "Old Pa Diaghilev," as she so tactfully put it, "would be pirouetting in his grave." They left quickly. Lincoln thought Balanchine "looked ill." And indeed he was; he'd again been showing symptoms of tuberculosis. Besides, he'd had to dance that night, stepping in (despite having a bad knee) for Jasinski in *Errante.*

It wasn't until three days later, on July 11, that Lincoln and Balanchine can actually be said to have "met." After a performance at which Lincoln saw Balanchine's 1932 ballet *La Concurrence* for the first time (and liked it —"very 1900 and sweet, pretty to look at"), he and several friends went back to the Askews' for drinks. When they had been there a short time the young choreographer Frederick Ashton, along with Diana Gould and Balanchine, arrived. Lincoln found Ashton "agreeable if a little fancy." But he thought Balanchine "wholly charming," and the two had "a long and satisfactory talk" in French. He looked even more ill than when Lincoln had seen him a few days before, and "aspired through his teeth as if he really had T.B."

Lincoln recorded a full, if staccato, account of the conversation in his diary, and it portrays an unusually voluble and frank Balanchine, a man ordinarily known for maintaining a discreet reserve, especially when talking to strangers. According to Lincoln, Balanchine told him "how difficult it is to make good French dancers. Too lazy, always take out time for lunch. Take nothing seriously . . . how he worked day & night for years with Lifar who at first was modest, worked hard, wanted to know all he could. Now you can't tell him a thing. Jasinski . . . is slow witted but good material: perhaps in 2 years something. How dancing is like *Papillon* [butterfly], a breath, a memory gone. One must never revive anything. Even if he was doing 'Fils Prodigue' [*The Prodigal Son*] now, he would do it differently."

Balanchine went on to say, according to Lincoln, that "the conventions of Petipa [were] intolerable for the present. Should be restudied. Taglioni an inferior technician to any well trained modern dancers. . . . Fokine could no longer compose. He can teach sitting down but no one can compose long after they forget the actual movement through their own bodies. Dancers can rarely compose as they always think only of themselves—never of the others. Lifar hates competition—didn't want to give [the great ballerina Olga] Spessivtseva a thing in Giselle even. Massine was trained by a Spanish dancer for 'Tricorne' and the style has left its strong imprint on him. He is unmusical. . . . How he [Balanchine] wants to come to America: with 20 girls & 5 men he could do wonders. Particularly in the classical style or his adaptation of it. . . . How Americans have great potential—but they are often dead from the waist up. They must be made to *love* the music & to *love* dancing. But they have spirit and could be touched off into fire . . . He was willing to talk—very expressive in the gestures of his body. . . . He seemed intent, convinced, not desperate—but without hope. [He said that] dancing is for a few people. Difficult to get intelligent patronage and an audience at the same time."

It came time to leave, but contact, real contact, had been made. Within two days Lincoln was using Romola as a sounding board for his ideas about how to get Balanchine to America and "founding a small company slowly." Three days after that, Balanchine came to lunch.

CHAPTER NINE

Balanchine

(1932–1933)

BALANCHINE ARRIVED on July 16 for lunch with Lincoln and Romola, nattily dressed in a gray flannel suit, "his strong, delicate Caucasian face very animated" but, as Lincoln wrote in his diary, "slightly drawn." As they began to talk, Balanchine told them that he was having a "row" with Edward James and that Tilly Losch, whom he described as "hysterical and useless," was "through with him." He said that de Basil constantly falsified his books and was, moreover, suing him for having left the Ballets Russes. He and Lifar, Balanchine revealed, were "in a temporary rapprochement" and were trying to raise the money to do a week's run, without Edward James, of *Songes, Mozartiana, Faun,* and *Spectre de la Rose. Errante,* Balanchine said, "is already dead," but he described the pas de deux in *Les Valses de Beethoven* (which he'd created in just three days) as "perhaps the best thing he ever did." (Lincoln confessed in his diary that he didn't remember it.) Balanchine said that "he wants next to do a big erotic ballet."[1]

They then went on to talk in some detail "about the possibility of an American ballet," a conversation Lincoln briefly recorded in his diary: "I put it with Chick Austin's Museum at Hartford. He [Balanchine] wants to bring Jasinski and Toumanova with him . . . her mamma has to come. We got frightfully excited about it all. I visualized it so clearly. He wants so much to come . . . says it has always been his dream. He would give up everything to come. Mme. Toumanova could cook for them." Romola, ignoring the unlikelihood of ever getting a new visa, said she would come as well and could "give lectures with the dancers' demonstrating." She promised them "the rights for all Vaslav's ballets."

After Balanchine left, Romola told Lincoln that Ma Garrett, her spiritualist guide, had predicted that Balanchine "will not live longer than two years. He is consumptive." To which Lincoln said, "But two years work will be a lot out of him, a real start." He then got "frightfully worked up" and, able to "think of nothing else," sat down and wrote his now-famous sixteen-page letter to Chick Austin at the Hartford Atheneum. It began with a grand theatrical flourish: "This will be the most important letter I will ever write you . . . my pen burns my hand as I write: words will not flow into the ink fast enough. We have a real chance to have an American ballet within 3 years time. When I say ballet, I mean a trained company of young dancers—not Russians—but Americans with Russian stars to start with." Years later Lincoln claimed that he'd deliberately chosen "an optimistic style" in writing to Chick. But "calculated optimism" doesn't begin to capture a tone that singes with intensity; ardent, touchingly zealous, Lincoln's words leap off the page with an almost libidinous passion. "You will adore Balanchine," he tells Chick. "He is, personally, enchanting-dark, very slight, a superb dancer and the most ingenious technician in ballet I have ever seen." Then, knowing his audience, Lincoln appealed to Chick's homoerotic side by describing the likely male star, Roman Jasinski, as "extremely beautiful—a superb body." And oh yes—he's "by way of becoming a most remarkable dancer."

But Chick, like Lincoln, was interested in far more than pulchritude; he was a serious advocate of the arts and an audacious innovator. As director of the Wadsworth Atheneum, he'd transformed Hartford's reputation as the stodgy headquarters of the insurance business into an important center of cultural ferment, acquiring works by such radical figures as Balthus, Max Ernst, Piet Mondrian and Alexander Calder, and broadening the Atheneum's offerings to include photography, music, film, and architectural design. He himself created a splendid small theater as an adjunct to the Atheneum, where, in 1934, he would mount the premiere of Gertrude Stein and Virgil Thomson's *Four Saints in Three Acts*.

There had been earlier attempts to find a home for ballet in the United States, but although Anna Pavlova (from 1910 to 1925) and a few other internationally famous stars, as well as Diaghilev's Ballets Russes on its 1916–17 tours, had successfully drawn audiences, there had been few opportunities to study classical technique and a scant tradition of indigenous choreography. Adolph Bolm, a leading dancer with Diaghilev, did, after he settled in the United States, choreograph a jazz ballet, a "machine" dance, and several others that may have contained American themes—but none of his work has survived. As for teachers of classical ballet, isolated figures, like Elizabeth Menzeli and Louis Chalif, did appear from time to time, and Fokine's school survived in New York for many years—though he seems to have concentrated mostly on his own ballets.

No, as Lincoln emphasized in his letter to Chick Austin, "we have the future in our hands. For Christ's sweet sake let us honor it." And he argued eloquently that they could, that in Balanchine, Toumanova, and Jasinski, they had all that was needed to make a start, and in Hartford, distant from the distractions of New York, an ideal atmosphere for concentrated work. (Balanchine, Lincoln reported, though "socially adorable," in fact hated society.)

The plan, according to Lincoln, was first to establish a school of dancing. Initially Balanchine would accept as students "4 white girls and 4 white boys, about sixteen years old and 8 of the same, *negros*," all of whom would be taught "in the classical idiom—not only from exercises but he would start composing ballets at once so they would actually *learn* by doing. As time went on he would get younger children from 8 years on." Lincoln then went on to rhapsodize, in the vaguely racist if commonplace terms of the day, about why Balanchine wanted to include blacks: their "combination of suppleness" and their superb "sense of time . . . they have so much abandon—and discipline." (Forty years later, Lincoln would lament not only the lack of black dancers in the company but also express the "wish we reached more blacks, Porto-Ricans [*sic*] and underprivileged citizens . . . we must strive to push . . . [our] limits.")

No tuition fee would be charged, but the dancers would have to sign contracts "to prevent them from appearing anywhere else, except in the troupe for 5 years." In the meantime Balanchine, Toumanova, and Jasinski would "serve as demonstrators and models" of what it meant to be "artists of conviction." At the same time he himself, along with Romola Nijinsky, would charge a hundred dollars to lecture at these demonstrations, which would take place at various educational institutions in New England (and maybe "3 or 4 times in N.Y."—but never at a commercial theater).

Lincoln estimated the start-up costs at six thousand dollars, enough to guarantee one year's work plus passage money back and forth. He confessed to being "glib" in suggesting that Chick could raise that sum from people like Lincoln himself, Philip Johnson, MoMA's Jim Soby (the scion of a wealthy Hartford family), Jere Abbott, the Lewisohns, and so on. To forestall hesitation or paralysis, Lincoln perhaps needed to exaggerate the likely ease of raising money, but he was also skirting fantasy, since (except for Johnson) he hadn't approached any of those named, not even his own father; and curiously he'd omitted from the list the one person—Eddie Warburg—who would come through as a major benefactor.

Lincoln insisted that the original six thousand dollars would not be a dead loss because "by February you can have four performances of wholly new Ballets in Hartford." Balanchine had indeed proved, with Les Ballets 1933, that he was capable of that kind of productivity, but there he'd been working with a seasoned troupe and performing in sophisticated European capitals. When Lincoln further claimed that "Balanchine is willing to devote all his time to this for 5 years," he was moving beyond exaggeration to untruth. Balanchine *was* enthusiastic about coming to America, but he'd made no time pledge; the arrangement was on a trial basis only—thus his insistence in advance on money for a return passage.

In another enthusiastic overstatement, Lincoln wrote Chick that Romola Nijinsky had already given him all the rights to her husband's *Sacre du Printemps, Jeux, Afternoon of a Faun, Tyl Eulenspiegel,* and "4 unproduced Nijinsky ballets," along with "the benefit of his *untried* system of training dancers." Romola *had* promised to do so, but Lincoln by then surely knew the worth of her promises—to say nothing of the likely legal complexities those rights entailed, or the fact that the brief *Faun* was the only Nijinsky ballet still in repertory.

Lincoln was also overelaborating when he wrote Chick that he'd already discussed with Balanchine seven ballets with American themes that they would produce, and further, that he'd enlisted the ardent cooperation of a number of gifted writers, musicians and designers, including Katherine Anne Porter as the librettist for *Doomsday*, E. E. Cummings for *Uncle Tom's Cabin*, and Virgil Thomson as the composer for *The Defense of Richmond*, a ballet set during the Civil War. All three artists had indeed been willing to listen to Lincoln's proposals, but with varying degrees of enthusiasm and commitment. Besides, precisely when, where, with what dancers, and thanks to whose bankroll were such productions going to take place?

This was a wing and a prayer with a vengeance. And Lincoln soared into silver-tongued flight: "This school can be the basis of a national culture as intense as the great Russian Renaissance of Diaghilev. We must start small. But imagine it—we are exactly as if we were in 1910. . . . Please, please, Chick, if you have any love for anything we do both adore, rack your brains and try to make this all come true. . . . It will mean a life work to all of us [and] incredible power in a few years." He assured Chick that he was not being "either over-enthusiastic or visionary."

But of course he was being both. Drunk on possibilities, perhaps feeling it might be now or never, Lincoln couldn't help throwing caution—along with absolute truthfulness—to the winds. Even if he'd been capable of a more modulated tone, it might not have appealed to Chick's own audacious nature. Bravado and amplitude were mother's milk to both men. If Chick was going to bite, the nervier the vision, the better.

And bite Chick did. Immediately and passionately. But, as Lincoln had already assumed, it would take Chick a week or so before he could secure the support of various bankers and Atheneum trustees and be able to send Lincoln any news. It would be a difficult waiting period, made still more so by the fact that Balanchine, to keep afloat, had to accept an offer to teach for a few weeks and left London on July 21. But before leaving he and Lincoln managed to spend another four hours together, along with Romola, talking about "the American project." To help familiarize Balanchine with the country, Lincoln pointed out various places on a map of the United States, and also showed him some Walker Evans photographs of Victorian houses and some MoMA catalogs on American painting.

For his part Balanchine honorably provided a full account of his health. As Lincoln recorded the conversation in his diary, Balanchine said that the TB had started in his thigh and at one point he'd "almost lost a leg; how one lung is OK, the other is not." He then shifted topics. He said that once in the States he wanted "to start a class also for Maitres de ballets," that he "has not a single photo or clipping of a single ballet he's done: he has no interest at all in recording his life or what he has made. He said music was much more important than dancing anyway, but that's because he's a professional dancer & an amateur musician." Lincoln, in turn, told him that when word arrived from Hartford, he would instantly notify him.

While Chick was hard at work in Hartford, Lincoln, in London, stayed as frantically busy as possible. Fortunately he was a practiced hand at filling in every spare minute of his time. He raced around to museums, went constantly to the ballet, intermittently worked with Romola on the biography, saw a steady stream of friends both old and new—and nonetheless would periodically fall into gloom.

He often took Romola with him to the ballet and she, predictably, thought poorly of almost everything they saw; but she was at least an equal opportunity detester: Lifar had "no elevation nor was he an artist"; Massine's troupe had "no joie de vivre" *and* she "hated" Balanchine's *La Concurrence*. Lincoln himself had become less enthusiastic about Massine as a choreographer than he'd once been, and he ascribed the change to his talks with Balanchine; having heard him analyze the limitations of *Les Présages*, for example, when Lincoln next saw that ballet he came away feeling that it had "hardly any good points." There isn't a shred of evidence to suggest that Balanchine had deliberately set out to sabotage a possible competitor for a job in the United States; he was too honorable to stoop to that. And besides, Massine was far better placed than he. With the Ballets Russes as his home base, he'd found great success both with the public and the critics, and de Basil had already scheduled an American tour for the company, with the New York opening set for December 1933. Massine admired Balanchine but had no wish or need to trade places with him.

Coming home one night to Batt's Hotel, Lincoln found a note from Romola under his door: "Lot of interesting dirt I have. Look my picture in tomorrow paper: am divorcing and marrying Lifar." When he saw her soon after, she insisted that Lifar had actually proposed and that she was genuinely interested (the latter being only slightly more plausible than the former). She admitted that Lifar was "a frightful snob," but claimed that *"au fond"* he was "a very nice boy, a baby in fact." What held her back from accepting, she said, was the fear that people might lose their sympathy for her if she divorced Vaslav; and she soon decided not to. Within days she was announcing a new scheme, claiming it had been suggested to her by Karsavina: she would go on the stage. But that prospect, too, rapidly evaporated; what she *really* wanted to do, she told Lincoln, was to return to New York and design costumes.

Given his impatient nature, Lincoln was remarkably forbearing of

Romola's shifting fictions. To some extent he seems actually to have grown fond of her, or at the least found her continuing theatrics enlivening. He also, of course, maintained their contact out of calculation: he wanted to remain associated with Vaslav's biography. And in that regard prospects took a promising turn toward the end of July. Arnold Haskell reported that Gollancz did want to publish the book, though only after substantial cuts. Lincoln was "very much against" making the cuts too deep, but basically he felt "an enormous sense of relief" that the project was drawing to an end, that the biography was assured publication, and that, if all went well on Chick's end, he could finally turn his energies to what was far closer to his heart: working to establish an American ballet. He was willing to put in a few more weeks of work on the manuscript and then turn it over to Haskell for a final set of revisions.

But word had yet to arrive from Chick, and along with intermittent work on the biography, Lincoln filled his days by alternating manuscript revisions with a renewed round of socializing that was hectic even by his standards. Through David Garnett he saw more of the Bloomsbury crowd than he had previously. He found Duncan Grant "as charming as ever" and once again "got on well" with Vanessa Bell. He took Romola along to one party, where he got reacquainted with Maynard Keynes (characterizing him as "a curiously satyrized man") and his wife, the ballerina Lydia Lopokova, who he thought was "falsely sweet to Romola." He had a long talk with the art critic Roger Fry, who told him that he disliked any art "with utility as an aim."

On another day Lincoln drove down to Cambridge with Garnett, along with Duncan and Vanessa in their own car, to see Virginia and Leonard Woolf. Leonard's hands were "very shaky," and he was "stooping a little," but Virginia was "fine-looking with her spaniel bitch Pinka." They all decided to go for a picnic, loaded crates of cider and beer into the cars, and drove some five miles away to a pleasant pasture with a stretch of clear water. The food, alas, was "horrible"—cold coffee, four pounds of cherries, and twenty-four "soggy and rubbery" pork pies, of which twenty remained uneaten.

Lincoln thought Leonard Woolf "a nice, intelligent man," and they talked together about "the negro question" and lynching (Leonard was reading a book about it). Virginia and David sympathized aloud with each other about having been forbidden to bring anything to read or to write with on the picnic, and Virginia, whom Lincoln found "aquiline and . . . affected," got into a long conversation about "maggots, worms, butterflies and moths." She and Lincoln, whether from disdain or timidity, "never spoke a word to each other." Before long it began to "pour torrents," and as they started to leave, the Woolfs' Lancaster got mired in the mud, which gave Pinka the opportunity to roll in some nearby manure. The plight of the Lancaster got Leonard and Virginia into "a heated discussion about various merits of different makes of autos," which Lincoln felt sure "wasn't going to break up for some time." Fearing he might be put in the same car with them for the drive back to Cambridge, Lincoln got David Garnett to drive him to the railroad station and caught the train to London.

So much for Bloomsbury. Lincoln turned elsewhere for amusement. And he found it primarily in a budding new friendship with Stephen Spender and his lover, Tony Hyndman. They'd first met during an intermission at the ballet that summer; in his diary Lincoln described Stephen as a "great big blonde boy. Slightly wet behind the ears I thought—with a troupe of admirers . . . although he didn't seem to pay them much mind." Despite that lukewarm appraisal, the two men had lunch just a few days later and were soon trading intimacies. Stephen told him "how badly Bernard Berenson had behaved to him," inviting *him* to his villa, I Tatti, but not Tony (who was the son of a Cardiff pub keeper), even though Stephen had "made it quite clear he was inseparable." Berenson then relented, but only on condition that Tony take his meals separately.

Spender, at that point in his career, was already considered a rising star. In a privately limited edition, he'd published *Twenty Poems* and had completed a somewhat racy autobiographical work, "The Temple," which went unpublished in his lifetime. Spender gave Lincoln a copy of his story "Burning Cactus" for possible inclusion in *Hound and Horn* (Lincoln read it the same day and thought it "remarkable"). Both T. S. Eliot and Virginia Woolf had already taken Spender under their wing. South African novelist William Plomer told Lincoln that he thought Eliot was a "suppressed homosexual" and "in love" with Spender. Eliot certainly did boost Spender's career: as early as 1930 Eliot had expressed admiration for some of his poetry, and for years he'd serve as Spender's editor at Faber & Faber. Initially Spender got a less favorable response from the Woolfs; when he submitted his first novel to their Hogarth Press, Virginia advised him to destroy it; but she did recognize Spender's talent and drew him into Bloomsbury's social circles.

Stephen was a close friend of William Plomer, whose first novel, *Turbott Wolfe*, the Hogarth Press did publish (in 1926); though Plomer at the time was a youngster of twenty-three, the book, a remarkably early denunciation of South Africa's brutal racial policies, caused a sensation, and he quickly followed it up with other well-received fiction. Spender lamented to Lincoln, perhaps shedding a few crocodile tears, "that Plomer so much desired to be normal and substantial that much of the juice had gone out" of his more recent work. Showing still a bit more of his spiteful side, Spender characterized his good friend Christopher Isherwood as "a small man whose jealousy and intrigues rise from his height" and said that Auden, who'd been something of a mentor to him, had "fallen in love with a 13 year old pupil at his school—and how his verse sounds more and more as if it were written for schoolboys."

Lincoln hadn't yet met either Isherwood or Auden (though he'd read Auden's *The Orators* and thought it the greatest poem in English since *The Waste Land*), but he'd gotten friendly with William Plomer, who invited Lincoln to have lunch with Morgan Forster and his married policeman lover, Bob Buckingham. He found Forster a "shy" man with "a small chin" and Buckingham "rather heavy, slightly cow-like" but charming. Lincoln talked to Forster about coming to America to lecture and to Bob about the varying police systems in the United States and England, agreeing that both were "rackets." Lincoln wrote in his diary that "Bob was the same type in a way as Tony Hyndman."

Lincoln's friendship with Spender had rapidly solidified, and he'd come to see a lot of Tony as well. He took to him immediately, felt he was simple, frank ("and yet cunning"), and "entirely male," a man who loved life—and adored Stephen. Tony had, in Lincoln's view, "a strong, almost fiery, passionate quality of being feminine-affectionate, the frankness of whose avowal" Lincoln found "thrilling." He also, to Lincoln's apparent relief, showed "not a trace" of his class origins. Lincoln often denounced snobbery in others but could sometimes be capable of it himself; in this instance, though, the "relief" seems to have been a function of not wanting his new friends to face even more social difficulties than they already had.

Both Stephen and Tony considered themselves socialists, but Lincoln, while still sympathetic to the Left, told Stephen (in a voice that echoed his own father's advice on politics) "to keep away from preaching." He added that he "feared as much from Fascism as from Communism." Lincoln had recently met the writer and editor J. R. "Joe" Ackerley, who'd told him that fascism was "inevitably coming to England" and that Jews were already being beaten up nightly in Whitechapel and Soho. He further predicted that the English fascist leader Oswald Mosley would use "the symbolic, modest phantom figure" of T. E. Lawrence ("Lawrence of Arabia," author of *Seven Pillars of Wisdom*) as a "rallying point"; Ackerley felt that Lawrence already had "Mosley memoranda in his pocket." These assessments got Lincoln so worked up that he took himself to fascist headquarters on Regent Street and, to learn more about the movement, signed up for a year's subscription to *The Blackshirt*. At a party at Plomer's, Morgan Forster told Lincoln that he suspected Lawrence of "fascist leanings."

Lincoln started to fantasize about shooting Lawrence and began to write a play, *The Leader*, about the rise of an American Hitler, which was based on Lawrence as the villain and himself as his assassin. Nonetheless Lincoln remained a worshipful admirer of T. E. Lawrence's writings, and when David Garnett lent him one of the few manuscript copies of

Lawrence's "The Mint" (which wouldn't be published until after his death in 1935), Lincoln found it overwhelming, a "masterpiece," an even "greater work of art" than *Seven Pillars*.

The more Lincoln saw of Stephen and Tony—and they now saw one another frequently—the more Lincoln fell (as he wrote in his diary) "acutely in love" with their relationship, with "their life together." But in fact Lincoln greatly romanticized it, a function of his own sometimes acute sense of aloneness ("I felt depressed at all the lacks in my own existence—and my accumulating & intensifying loneliness & passionate desire for exactly the same relationship"). In truth there had been difficulties between Stephen and Tony from the beginning, though Lincoln, even when witness to a blatant quarrel, preferred to ignore or downplay their problems with each other.

Finally, on July 26, the long-awaited cable from Chick Austin arrived: GO AHEAD IRONCLAD CONTRACT NECESSARY STARTING OCTOBER 15 SETTLE AS MUCH AS YOU CAN BRING PUBLICITY PHOTOGRAPHS MUSEUMS WILLING CAN'T WAIT. Lincoln was elated and immediately wired Balanchine in Paris. But Balanchine failed to reply. Had he received other offers? Had he fallen ill again? In a panic Lincoln thought of rushing off immediately to Paris. Then he remembered: Balanchine wasn't in Paris; he was visiting French friends in the countryside for a fortnight, near a village whose name, Negrepelisse, Lincoln recalled only later. He delayed plans to go to Paris until August 8, when he knew Balanchine would be there.[2]

In the meantime he wanted to clear up loose ends with Romola. From her vacation in Birchington, Kent, she wrote him to send at once the four chapters he'd been working on, as she and Haskell (who was also at Birchington) "had nothing to do" and Lincoln was "holding up Haskell." She further accused him of having "put a lot of falsifying into" the manuscript already. Her peremptory tone bewildered Lincoln. "Don't understand this," he wrote in his diary, "unless she is sore that I've not come down there . . . [and] is using this as an excuse to break off before I go—or to punish me—God knows she could do anything." Even though Lincoln hadn't gone to see Gurdjieff that summer (in a letter Muriel, curiously, had advised him not to), he now tried to remind himself of one of Gurdjieff's basic principles: "Work without reward—towards consciousness."

But he finally decided after all to go down to Birchington and have lunch with Romola; as a surprise he brought along some of the pictures he'd been collecting of Vaslav, including a large one of the first scene in *Petrouchka*. Romola "screamed with joy" at the sight of them, and also expressed pleasure at the various peace-offering gifts Lincoln gave her, including a flacon of the perfume L'Aimant, and a loofah bath glove. Yet she still managed to behave "like a spoiled child," complaining bitterly that "Haskell had cut the book to bits: butchered it."

That aspect of her grousing did worry Lincoln. He felt that "the book must come through untouched" and told Romola that if Haskell insisted on his cuts, she should take the manuscript elsewhere. At that point Haskell himself arrived and took Lincoln to the cottage he'd been renting nearby. They went through the manuscript together and aside from "4 or 5 notable omissions," Lincoln "was greatly relieved that, on the whole, he had done such a good job." Haskell also told him that on the first of September, Romola would get a thousand dollars in advance. Lincoln bade Haskell "an affectionate farewell, promising eternal cooperation," and went back and told Romola his good opinion.

She was "furious" with him for having "changed" his mind, and threateningly said, "You don't know Romola Nijinsky. I just let everyone talk, I say yes and then I get tired of the whole thing and I give it up—like with Tamara and Kyra [the daughters she'd abandoned]." At that moment Lincoln "hated her cordially" and felt she was being grossly ungrateful. Sensing his anger, Romola said she'd be mentioning the help he'd given her in both the preface and the epilogue to the book. Lincoln simply changed the subject, bade her good-bye, and left, feeling that his summer "was really over."

Or rather, that he was now entirely free to concentrate on the Balanchine project. And in the nick of time. No sooner had he returned to London than another telegram arrived from Chick Austin: he'd already succeeded in raising three thousand dollars from some dozen people, with Philip Johnson (five hundred dollars), Jim Soby (five hundred dollars), and Eddie Warburg (one thousand dollars) giving the largest sums. Muriel Draper was also trying to raise money for the enterprise, though she confessed in a letter to Lincoln that she was having trouble envisioning the "poor Russians" in Hartford, "stopping for a Western at a lunch wagon"; nor did she think "the educational-museum chi-chi" was any better than "the Broadway chi-chi." Her letter upset Lincoln because he knew she was "the best adversary one can have," and because he felt her concern was at least "half true" about the cultural disjunction between the cosmopolitan Russians and the conservative business elite of Hartford.

Muriel also urged Lincoln to give up *Hound and Horn,* with which he was now only marginally connected anyway, in order to devote himself entirely to the ballet project. Again her advice tied in with what Lincoln had himself been feeling; he immediately wrote Bernard Bandler to say that he intended to see the special "Henry James issue," due early in 1934, through to publication, but would thereafter withdraw from any further connection with the magazine; he wondered if Bandler knew of anybody who might want to take over *Hound and Horn* and carry it into the future.

On August 9 Lincoln left for Paris in order to be there as soon as Balanchine arrived back from the country on the eleventh. Suddenly idle after a frantic few weeks, he soon felt his spirits sink: "I feel lonely if I don't see someone every 2 minutes. I'm as bad or worse than Cecil Beaton." Off he went to call on Katherine Anne Porter, who was in an unhappy state, lamenting her inability to "get anyone to take her work seriously." Lincoln then went on to see E. E. Cummings and Marion Morehouse, and brought along some of Spender's and Auden's poetry for them to read (Cummings liked Auden, not Spender).

The next day Lincoln was cheered up by another telegram from Chick saying that he could now guarantee living expenses up to six thousand dollars. Still, it wasn't at all clear what the next step should be, or exactly who would make up Balanchine's entourage. Lincoln worried that Toumanova and Jasinski might not want to go to the States, at least not immediately, and he wondered why Balanchine had earlier mentioned his friend Vladimir Dimitriev as a necessary addition. Lincoln went to a movie, stopped in at the Renoir exhibit ("a little thin"), had a Cinzano at—where else?— the Deux Magots, and worked himself up "into a tense calm." And then word came: Balanchine and Dimitriev had arrived at their hotel, the Élysée Palace, and were waiting for him. Lincoln raced over.

It was the first time he'd met Dimitriev, a former baritone with the Maryinsky opera and the man who'd gotten Balanchine, Danilova, and Tamara Geva (among others) out of the Soviet Union. Lincoln was immediately impressed with Dimitriev's solidity and shrewdness. A man of forty with considerable experience, he could be a formidable ally—or antagonist—depending on whether he felt Balanchine's interests (and his own) were being sufficiently protected. Almost at once Dimitriev raised objections as to the ultimate control of the company and what pay scale Lincoln had in mind. Lincoln said that he'd "never thought definitely" how the six thousand dollars would be specifically divided and under what auspices. He thought it might be wise to found a new corporation that would be under the umbrella of the Atheneum but independent of it. Perhaps the best thing, he suggested, was for Balanchine to come over first and, depending on what he found, either return to Europe or send for the rest of the group.

Dimitriev flatly rejected the suggestion. Balanchine, he said, was not known in the United States; it was therefore necessary that he should arrive with dancers, " 'as befitted him,' to show what he had done and could do," especially since dancing was impossible to talk about and had to be seen to be understood. Lincoln could tell, he wrote in his diary, "how afraid they are to be left high and dry." Edward James's "caprices," and the critical and commercial failure in London of Les Ballets 1933, meant that Balanchine was feeling particularly tender at the moment. He insisted that he did want, above all, to come to the United States, but as everyone agreed, it would be "a big risk and . . . very difficult to actualize."

Besides, though he claimed a lack of interest in them, Balanchine had recently received several offers to stay in Europe, including an invitation to go to Copenhagen as *maître de ballet*, and to stage for Ida Rubinstein, the well-known and wealthy actress-mime, a Stravinsky–André Gide work for the Paris Opéra. Lincoln fully understood and largely shared Balanchine's apprehensions; after their meeting concluded that day, he wrote Chick Austin another lengthy letter telling him it was "extremely difficult to come to any definite agreement."

Dimitriev, Lincoln wrote, felt that the project fell into two distinct parts: a school to train dancers and a ballet company to perform; and at first "everything should be centered around the foundation of a *school* . . . nothing at all should be mentioned about a company or ballets"; it was essential "to emphasize the non-commercial aspects of the venture." Not until mid-January could any actual ballet performances be scheduled, at which time, Lincoln reported, Balanchine "would have to be paid on a sliding scale according to the ratio of receipts—as is his due and as he would be paid in Europe."

Lincoln urged on Chick the formation of a private corporation, arguing that *it*, and not the Atheneum trustees, must hold "the whiphand." He reiterated that "such a chance as now presents itself comes but once in a lifetime," and lamented that it should be at a time of such general economic distress. "When I think," he wrote Chick, "of the cash spent on the bushes and shrubbery of the Philadelphia Museum, of the people who collect stamps and matchboxes, I go mad. This will be no collection, but living art—and the chance for perfect creation."

The next day Lincoln, Dimitriev, and Balanchine had another session together. Balanchine "let fall [that] the Julliard [*sic*] had offered him some sort of job," Lincoln wrote in his diary, "but he didn't want it. Why not, I can't see. I have offered him nothing definite." Needing additional rest, Balanchine left that same day to finish his vacation at Monte Carlo. Lincoln thought he looked better than he had been, and he described him to Chick as "God's nicest man." All three "parted amiably" and expressed the hope that they would soon "see each other in America." Lincoln himself was due to leave for the States shortly, and he warned Chick that he'd promised Balanchine and Dimitriev "to telegraph them yes or no by September first, as they have to live."

Hearing that negotiations were in progress, Romola sent Lincoln her congratulations, but warned that if "Russian-American plans" proceeded without her presence as "intermediary" that "within 4 weeks—there will be nothing left—I fear so many complications." She also instructed Lincoln again to contact Senator Walsh so she could come to the States to "jointly lecture" with him—which Lincoln, feeling well rid of her, had no intention of doing. Romola also dared, for the hundredth time, to ask him to wire cash since "I have no money now at all." But Lincoln already knew from Haskell that within days she'd be getting a thousand-dollar advance, and for once did not rise to the bait.

He lingered on a few more days in Paris. "If the ballet goes through," he wrote in his diary, "I won't be in Europe for a long time." He also wanted to say good-bye to various friends, including Laurens van der Post, Stephen and Tony, Katherine Anne Porter (who cooked him a farewell meal), Monroe Wheeler and E. E. Cummings, with whom he talked about the *Uncle Tom's Cabin* libretto and who told Lincoln "how close" he thought Harriet Beecher Stowe came "to being a great writer."

One unexpected good-bye resulted from last-minute shopping. After buying various gifts to take home, including some junk jewelry for Muriel, he stopped off at the Russian bookseller Povolovsky's to purchase some ballet books and another copy of Gurdjieff's *Beelzebub's Tales*. It turned out that Povolovsky had been the book's publisher, and they talked together enthusiastically about "the most remarkable man we'd either known." At that very moment, Povolovsky told him, Gurdjieff was sitting in the Café de la Paix. It was startling news.

Although he had decided not to visit Gurdjieff that summer, Lincoln immediately took a taxi to the café, instantly recognized Gurdjieff, and then had "to screw up my courage to greet him." When he did, Lincoln expected "some painful surgical observation" about his character, but the conversation was brief and bland. Gurdjieff told him that he had finished "all the writing he would ever do," and would soon be reopening the institute at Fontainebleau. He asked after Muriel: "Every year she say she come over. She never come." Gurdjieff said to tell her that if she did, he would take her to a "very fine" restaurant "and they would have much Armagnac." He also told Lincoln that "he was having a very hard time about money. No one ever sent him any." Lincoln "felt the 900 francs burning" in his pocket. "Would they burn their way through? They didn't." Gurdjieff took out some papers and began to go through them; Lincoln said good-bye.

Before leaving for the States, Lincoln went to consult with the American consulate as to the terms required to assure that Balanchine and the others would be admitted to the United States on an emigration passport. He was told "it was all a question of cash"; ten thousand dollars would make everything easy. Perhaps in alarm at the amount, Lincoln wrote to Balanchine (as he summarized the letter in his diary) "asking him, as nicely as possible what the Hell Dimitriev did anyway: was he necessary?" Balanchine at once cabled back: ATTENDONS VOTRE DECISION PRESENCE DIMITRIEV EST NECESSAIRE. The message left no room for doubt: if Lincoln wanted Balanchine, he had to take Dimitriev too.

The news exacerbated his anxiety. Where could he raise additional money? What if the whole scheme fell through? What could he fall back on? He decided to convert his play-in-progress (*The Leader*), about the rise of an American Hitler, into a novel, but feared he wouldn't have any success in interesting a publisher; he hoped he could sell it, because it would "please father—not the theme, but the publication."

He worried, too, that he'd acted prematurely in telling Bandler that he intended to give up *Hound and Horn*, especially if it turned out that Louis could continue to afford spending eight thousand a year on the magazine. He consoled himself with the thought that he, Philip Johnson, and Frances Paine had had preliminary discussions with Nelson Rockefeller about running a high-toned art reproduction postcard concession at Rockefeller Center. But the discussions had been far from conclusive, and should the ballet fail to materialize, Lincoln didn't know where he could turn for a job or how he would "ever settle down." During the worst of his gloom, he decided he was "no writer, nor editor," and wrote cryptically in his diary, "Deepest night. No sounds. Rocking horse itches of power and suicide: observation: consciousness: repetition."

On August 18 he left for home.

PART THREE

Launching

CHAPTER TEN

Balanchine

(1933)

Within twenty-four hours of arriving back in New York, Lincoln managed to touch a number of bases. Since Muriel (having postponed her trip to the Soviet Union) was on an extended visit to Mabel Dodge Luhan in Taos, Mina met his boat and over breakfast caught him up on family news. Brother George had decided against trying to carve out a career in the movie industry, and was headed for a management job at Bloomingdale's (it had helped that Louis was on the board of Federated Department Stores). Louis himself had been spending a great deal of time in the capital as a high-level consultant for the National Recovery Act (NRA); he was now prominent enough to have become a target of the press. Mina herself had recently completed *In the Midst of Life*, a novel based on her marriage to Harry, and she was eager to have Lincoln's opinion of it.[1]

After breakfast Lincoln headed over to his apartment at 16 Minetta Lane and while he was still unpacking got a phone call from Chick Austin, who was in New York and asked him to come at once to his room at the Murray Hill Hotel. When Lincoln arrived, Chick filled him in on the latest developments: "The Museum Trustees were suspicious, but said if he could raise the money o.k." After talking with Chick, Lincoln returned to his apartment to find a cable from Balanchine asking if he'd come to a decision. That was something of a surprise, since Lincoln had already promised to cable definitive word by September 1, four days thence. He worried that Balanchine might be pressing him because either Copenhagen, Ida Rubinstein, or Juilliard had sweetened their offers and he was now more tempted to accept. Lincoln delayed a day, then wired Balanchine "making it pretty near definite." But he continued to worry: "Would he come—really? Wouldn't Dimitriev try to dissuade him—to accept an easier berth?"

Lincoln next stopped in at the *Hound and Horn* office to find that Doris Levine had matters well in hand, as had been true for some time, but that masses of manuscripts did await final decisions and the suggested changes in the magazine's typography also needed work. Lincoln postponed those chores for a few days longer, feeling it more urgent to check in with Nelson Rockefeller and the others involved in the pending "postcard conces-

sion" at Rockefeller Center. He put in a call to Nelson, who'd just returned from Mexico (where Frances Paine had served as his guide), and
talked to Alan Blackburn at MoMA, who encouragingly told him that
postcards by Sheeler, Steichen, and Margaret Bourke-White were already
in the works.

He then had lunch with Philip Johnson and Chick Austin, at which he
learned from Philip that Eddie Warburg had given him five thousand dollars to design his apartment in Mies van der Rohe modern. With edgy
humor Lincoln wrote in his diary that he "might be forced to cut his
[Philip's] throat & Virgil Thomson's Opera [which Chick was scheduled
to produce at Hartford] to get the cash to bring over Balanchine." Holding off on the knife for the moment, Lincoln instead went to see Eddie,
who was living with his family, and did "propaganda work for some 3
hours." He concentrated less on Eddie than on his father, Felix, a noted
connoisseur and benefactor of the arts; Lincoln ended up feeling that
Felix "got the point very well."

The following day, with Nelson "driving like a fiend," he motored out
to the Rockefeller estate in Pocantico, along with Philip and Alan. They
wandered the grounds, had dinner, and then settled in for a serious two-
hour discussion of the postcard project. Nelson "seemed loath to incorpo-
rate but we rather forced it." It was decided that Blackburn would be the
business manager and Lincoln and Philip the "artistic consultants"—
though Nelson surprised and disturbed them by insinuating a Mr. Darling, the ex-head of the Playland amusement park in Rye, New York, as
the overall "boss" of the project.

Lincoln's next stop was Hartford, where he again inspected the
museum with Chick and again decided it would "be superb for the ballet."
But both men still worried about whether they had enough money to proceed if Eddie Warburg didn't come through with additional funds. As a
possible fallback, Chick introduced Lincoln to some moneyed Hartford
people, and he gave them his impassioned ballet pitch; one of them was
persuaded enough to volunteer the information that the Junior League
had an unearmarked eight thousand dollars in the till that might be drawn
on. Though the money hadn't been formally offered, a delighted Lincoln
decided that he had "no doubts now that it will work." In high spirits he
went back with Chick to his house, where Chick "amused . . . [him] endlessly" with stories of his summer adventures out West: "The sailor's bundle he undid . . . to try on his clothes . . . the cowboy with the smallest cock
in the world, etc."

On September 1, Lincoln drove up to Mina's home in Northampton to
await further word. It came almost at once. Telegrams from Eddie Warburg and from Balanchine arrived almost simultaneously: Eddie *would* let
him have more money—at least five thousand a year, as it would turn
out—and Balanchine confirmed that all was "O.K." and he was "only

waiting for the cash." Lincoln got so excited he burned his tongue on the tea he'd just poured. To try and calm down, he read all the summer issues of *The New Yorker* that he'd missed. When that didn't work, he turned next to the manuscript of Mina's novel and managed to read it through ("not bad," he decided, though she "identifies every woman with herself").

Together with Mina he rendezvoused with his parents and brother in nearby Beverly, and found them all in "excellent spirits." Louis was downright jubilant about his work with the NRA, announcing that he had "a grand crush" on Gen. Hugh S. Johnson, its head, and expressing "great excitement" over the future of young Edward Stettinius (who would later become secretary of state). Brother George had a new home, a new girlfriend—and a raise at his job; he, too, felt "fine." Absence had made the heart grow fonder, and a rare harmony ruled the day.

That is, until the topic of Hitler and the Jews came up. Though Lincoln identified less with Judaism than his father did, and wasn't remotely as involved in community good works, he took the more radically activist position in regard to the Nazi threat. Louis argued that the United States government shouldn't attempt to intervene more than it had (which was scarcely at all) on behalf of the Jews. He said, so Lincoln recorded in his diary, that "he had no doubt if a secret ballot were taken here in the U.S., the Jews would come out lousy . . . they were bound to be a marked people. . . . As far as a world plot goes, the Jews have never stayed together since Solomon. They can't even decide what to do in relation to Hitler." Louis was accurately describing current divisions within the Jewish community over what strategy to pursue, but Lincoln "got sore at his self-assurance" and his putting the onus for inaction more on the Jewish community than on the U.S. government. What made him presuppose, Lincoln angrily asked his father, that "the U.S. *wanted* to do something" about the plight of the Jews—"which they don't." Lincoln decided that hobnobbing with the big boys in Washington had gone to Louis's head.

He was still angry when he saw Philip Johnson the next day, and Philip once more "confessed" to him "an unreasonable Jewish prejudice," saying however that Lincoln himself "was not included." Not wanting to deal yet again with Philip's bias, Lincoln shifted the discussion to "postcards & Nelson & balls & life," but didn't find Philip any more cogent on those subjects than on the Jews. It turned out that Philip's "idea of Heaven" was having a simultaneous orgasm with another man, a notion Lincoln found "plain screwy." In Lincoln's opinion Philip's "only real passion was to exert power [and] to tell people what they want." He acknowledged that Philip had "some natural sweetness," but "any long discussion" with him was difficult and any serious exchange about the ballet "impossible—he thinks it's just another interest of mine, like postcards."

As for *that* enterprise (now tentatively called "Art, Inc."), Lincoln began to have serious second thoughts. Now that Nelson had put "Dar-

ling of Playland" at their head (Mrs. Paine told him that Darling was suspected of being involved with racketeers), he had the growing feeling that
he, Philip, and Alan were giving away a lot of ideas free of charge and that
they were being "bitched & stuffed up Mr. Darling's asshole." In his diary
Lincoln confided his concern that "no one had ever worked with the
Rockefellers and come out of it unhurt."

He had a frank talk with Nelson about his uneasiness, so frank that he
said outright that he disapproved of business practices at Rockefeller Center and "couldn't possibly afford to be a party to the kind of blackmail
methods they use." Nelson calmed him down, assured him that they
would make a lot of money quickly, and told Lincoln that he was eager for
him to remain involved in any capacity he chose, whether as partner or
employee. Lincoln decided that for the time being he'd stay with it, but he
remained concerned that if Darling did turn out to be a shady character,
his own reputation for integrity could be jeopardized, to say nothing of
"some toy of a shop" eating up time and energy better saved for organizing the ballet.

Some positive developments on that front helped to boost Lincoln's
spirits. Eddie Warburg, as promised, wired three thousand dollars to Balanchine, and Lincoln, on September 6, wrote to urge him "to try and sail
as soon as possible, as we eagerly await your arrival." He also suggested,
with the planned Hartford "demonstrations" in mind, that Toumanova
and Jasinski bring along costumes. He was caught off guard ten days later,
when Balanchine cabled him to say (as Lincoln summarized the contents
in his diary) that he now felt "the presence of Toumanova and Jasinski was
not necessary: that he would commence with Dimitriev; that they would
or would not follow." This upset Lincoln "a good deal," because he felt
sure Hartford "wants dancers to look at—at once."[2]

Balanchine's cable threw his mood into reverse; he went back to wondering, "Would any of them ever come here?" The following day a three-
page letter from Balanchine arrived reiterating his view that the two
dancers weren't necessary and saying that he had understood that Lincoln
"wanted a school to train American dancers" and had been worried about
the expense of bringing over Toumanova, her mother, and Jasinski. If
more money *was* available, Balanchine suggested it would be better spent
in hiring Pierre Vladimiroff, once a *premier danseur* at the Maryinsky and
with Diaghilev, as well as "a first-rate teacher." If Lincoln felt differently
Balanchine thought he should come at once to Paris or he, Balanchine, to
the States—unaccompanied. Lincoln wired him to come over as soon as
possible. It was only later that Lincoln learned that de Basil had somehow
persuaded or pressured Toumanova (or her mother) to stay with the Ballets Russes de Monte Carlo; as for Jasinski, he joined Lifar's company,
which that same fall of 1933 came to New York—and to a disastrous
reception.

Meanwhile Romola once more began to hound him. She sent him a series of hectoring letters, full of complaints against Haskell and Gollancz, of her usual lamentations about poverty and illness (with a slightly new twist to the latter: "I still could not find a nice girl and am on the verge of getting crazy"), and of insistent demands that he contact Senator Walsh so she could come over and help start "our" school. She even sent over a trunk, for which Lincoln had to pay a sizable duty and had to find storage space in *Hound and Horn*'s crowded office.

Over a period of several months Lincoln skillfully held her at bay, mixing placation with outright fabrication. He commiserated with her about the cuts made in Vaslav's biography and assured her that "some day we will really issue it as it should be issued." But as for coming over, he strongly advised against it. For one thing he claimed not to have had word from Balanchine. For another, he emphasized—even after Eddie Warburg had made his pledge—that "there doesn't seem to be any money."

When he finally did acknowledge that Balanchine seemed likely to come, Romola congratulated him for being on his way "to become the American Diaghilev," then sarcastically added that he had "already developed his mannerism of dropping and kicking out those who were instrumental in the realization or conception of ideas. . . . I refer to my little self, who is cast out of the whole school plan." Lincoln dropped placation and let the steel show: "Listen, dearie, I'm no Diaghilev casting out my old friends. If I was, I would have cast you off long ago. . . . I'd be a bad friend to you if I told you to come over, without any hopes of doing anything." A week later he'd softened a bit, writing her that when the biography was published in the United States "I hope you can come over. . . . By that time I hope to have enough money to be able to give you something regular in regard to the school. Of course I can't promise anything."

And Lincoln did try to facilitate the biography's publication in the United States. After the book finally came out in England in November 1933 and had (as Romola wrote him), "a success which sincerely amazes me, as it has been crippled by the cutting beyond recognition"), Clifton Fadiman, then an editor at Simon & Schuster, called Lincoln up to say he'd received a copy of the English edition (which was more than Lincoln had) and "was very displeased with it"; he thought that "it was a terrible job, and would never go in America." Fadiman asked to talk to him about it, but Lincoln, wanting to avoid a potential row with Romola or Haskell, told him that he had no authority to act in their behalf. Yet he did offer Fadiman some suggestions for publicity purposes should he decide to proceed with publication. And he also successfully discouraged the publishing house of John Day Co. from putting out a potentially competitive biography by Anatole Bourman (Nijinsky's classmate at the Imperial Ballet School).

On September 19 Balanchine cabled that he and Dimitriev were working out passport difficulties with the American consulate and clearing up other odds and ends; they expected to arrive in New York in mid-October. A few days later, hoping to spur them on, Lincoln mailed off one-year contracts. And there matters stood, with minimal communication, for a number of weeks—more weeks than Lincoln could easily tolerate, given his temperamental impatience and his need for perpetual motion. An enforced apartment move helped absorb some of his time when his place in Minetta Lane became infested with bedbugs and rats; he took a new apartment uptown, at 320 East Fifty-third Street.

But he felt too unsettled to be able to do any writing, though he still held out some hopes for his novel-in-progress, *The Leader*. While awaiting further word from Balanchine, he occupied himself with renewed vigor in the management of the *Hound and Horn*, even as he continued to waver about whether or not to close it down permanently. The magazine's future, Bandler rightly told him, depended entirely on his own interest in it, which Lincoln confessed was "not over-intense." If he did decide to continue, Bandler advised that he "keep out politics except as they are related to literature." Lincoln thought Bandler's "scolding" was "constructive," but postponed any final decision until he had a better handle on the likely prospects for the ballet and for Art, Inc.

Meetings and side intrigues about Art, Inc., had been proliferating, and heightened contact hadn't endeared Alan Blackburn to him. Lincoln objected to his grandiosity and the "selfish game" he was playing; he had no doubt that Blackburn would "stick me in the back without a qualm." It had also become increasingly clear to him that Alan and Philip Johnson had found in fascism common grounds for a deepening alliance. Yet Lincoln decided not to bother Alfred Barr with his distrust of the two men since Barr, after returning from Europe in 1933, still remained seriously unwell. He couldn't sleep at night, and he said outright that "he wished he was dead." Lincoln didn't hold Marga directly accountable for Alfred's deplorable condition, but continued to feel that she was "really a fiend." He pitied Alfred and decided that "if he doesn't kill her, she'll kill him."

By early October Art, Inc., had produced mounting opposition from some of the top brass within the Rockefeller organization, and especially from John Todd of the powerful management firm Todd, Robertson & Todd. He first reduced the proposal for two shops to one, then shifted the site to an undesirable location, and finally (as Lincoln put it in his diary) rejected "most of our ideas . . . either in fact or principle." Lincoln absolved Nelson of personal responsibility for the debacle. At the time he was hors de combat with appendicitis, and in any case didn't yet have the power within the Rockefeller organization to move the Todd mountain.

By that point Lincoln hardly cared whether he got to sell art objects and souvenirs or not: Balanchine had wired him on October 2 to say that he'd turned down all other offers and, accompanied by Dimitriev, was definitely on his way to the States. Thrilled at the firm commitment, Lincoln moved into high gear. He went up to Hartford a number of times to discuss details with Chick and to view progress on the completion of the Avery Memorial addition to the museum. By October 1, scaffolding on the building had come down, and Lincoln felt sure that its state-of-the-art theater would be "perfect for our purposes."

When in Hartford Lincoln usually made side trips to Ashfield to see Mina, his recent antagonism to her having receded (at least for the time being); she told him she'd grown bored with teaching at Smith and was disappointed that her old friend David Garnett had been unable to place her novel with an English publisher. While in the area Lincoln sometimes saw Archie MacLeish as well. Mina said she thought Archie's mind "has gone to hell," but Lincoln thought he'd merely turned into "the worst intellectual snob I ever knew." On one visit Archie attacked Spender's pro-Communist views, and then asked Lincoln if it was true that Stephen was a "homosexualist." Annoyed, Lincoln decided "to release Archie from several of his preconceived ideas on this & other subjects," and so he "sailed in and made Stephen & Tony seem as rosy as I could, which was never hard for me." On another occasion, Lincoln introduced Archie to Chick Austin, but Archie said he wasn't "drawn to him" and mumbled something about "pansies." Lincoln applauded Chick, who could be a world-class charmer, for not making any attempt to act agreeably toward Archie.

Lincoln also paid a calculated visit to Mina's neighbor William Bullitt, whom he'd known casually for years and who was about to take up his position as the first U.S. ambassador to the Soviet Union (FDR having decided to extend formal recognition). He talked to Bullitt about Balanchine's imminent arrival and his plans for inaugurating an American ballet. Bullitt seemed enthusiastic and even suggested that he might be able to secure some government funding for him, as well as helping to smooth over any visa or passport difficulties that might arise. (Chick, simultaneously, was working toward the same end through his local congressman.)

On October 11, Balanchine wired Lincoln asking him to notify Tamara Geva, his first wife, of his imminent arrival. That worried Lincoln. Geva had come to New York six years earlier to star in several productions of Nikita Balieff's Chauve-Souris, a group that mixed cabaret and dance. She had been a big success, had gone on to a show-stopping appearance in Ziegfeld's *Whoopee* (which starred Eddie Cantor and Ruby Keeler) and then to stardom on Broadway in *Three's a Crowd* and *Flying Colors*. Lincoln viewed Geva as a threat, fearing she "might poison" Balanchine "away from us into Hollywood or N.Y. and ruin all our lovely plans."

But ready or not, the day of Balanchine's arrival was suddenly upon them. In the early evening of October 17, Lincoln, Chick, Eddie War-burg, and—at Chick's insistence—a reporter and photographer from the *Hartford Times* gathered dockside to await Balanchine and Dimitriev's debarkation from the *Olympic*. Lincoln recorded the event in his diary: "For the longest time I could find no friendly face on that boat. Had they come first class or third? Finally I spotted Balanchine in Tourist—with Dimitriev. Amid the roar of unloading, he told me that they couldn't land—had to go to Ellis Island in the morning—must stay on the boat all night."[3]

Chick tried to get permission to see the inspector of immigration on the dock, but was told that was impossible. Suddenly Eddie disappeared and then reemerged some minutes later to say that he'd made use of Felix Warburg's magical name and everything, after all, was all right. The prob-lem had been "a lousy immigration officer" who'd somehow raised an objection to the disparity between the Russians' six-month visa and their yearlong contract. There was a brief delay at the top of the gangplank—Balanchine had misplaced his landing card—but it was soon located and they passed through customs easily. The first of what would become a rapid-fire string of crises had been weathered.

Following a quick *Hartford Times* interview and a few photos, Lincoln immediately took Balanchine and Dimitriev to the duplex apartment he'd rented for them on the thirty-fourth floor of the Barbizon-Plaza at Fifty-eighth and Sixth; he'd decided to splurge on the steep twelve-dollars-a-night rental to help create a favorable first impression. As he'd hoped, the two arrivals "gasped" at the view out of their window. After a brief rest Chick and Lincoln (Eddie had a prior engagement) took them to dinner in the hotel's grill. Light pleasantries predominated, though Lincoln told them he knew that both the Juilliard School and the Russian-born Leon Leonidoff, associate producer at the Radio City Music Hall, had made offers to Balanchine. But Balanchine "shushed" him: "Swell, OK, Keed etc." He also said that "he didn't want to see any Cathedrals."

After dinner they walked the short distance to Kirk and Constance Askew's for a drink, and it was there that Lincoln had the first of what would be many "heavy" talks with Dimitriev about plans for the school, Dimitriev telling him firmly that the importation of Vladimiroff was "a necessity." After a short walk that impressed the two arrivals "with the width of the streets and the airiness of the city," the three returned to the hotel and talked until two in the morning about money and about what in Dimitriev's view was an unacceptable contract that made them "slaves."

He reminded Lincoln that Balanchine had *also* had offers from Copen-hagen and from René Blum (who wanted "to separate from de Basil") as well as a two-ballet commission from Ida Rubinstein—"all jobs which . . . [would have] paid him a lot had he accepted them." Lincoln boldly replied that he "knew Balanchine's services were not to be named in mere figures, but if it was money he wanted he wouldn't be here." More boldly still, Lincoln suggested that "it might be a good idea to accept the Music Hall job to see what it would be like," and to allow Balanchine to "keep his hand in." At that point Balanchine spoke up, saying, "No: it didn't interest him." He added that "he would produce something by April or would go back to Paris." Well, Lincoln told himself, "at least they are here and it's something accomplished along the road to a National School."

The next morning he reported the previous night's conversation to Chick, who felt "very strongly [that] a star is needed," and thought maybe they should bring over Felia Doubrovska. Then they got to worrying together about Balanchine's "high color" and what it indicated about his health; he'd had a coughing spell during dinner and Chick had observed Dimitriev forbidding him another cigarette. After breakfast Chick had to get back to Hartford for an appointment, and Lincoln went off to the Barbizon-Plaza.

He found Eddie Warburg already there, who told Lincoln that he liked the two Russians "very much" and thought Balanchine was "one swell guy." Lincoln was relieved that Eddie soon had to leave; as he once wrote in his diary, "when Eddie tries to talk ballet, I nearly crawl out of my skin—but I'm getting better keeping cool." Lincoln took Balanchine and Dimitriev to see Grand Central Station, and the Chrysler and *Daily News* buildings, and then left them with Tamara Geva while he went off to meet John Martin, who was planning to do a feature story on Balanchine's arrival for the Sunday edition of the *Times*.

He and Martin talked freely. Martin was "persistently tactless" about Geva (who Lincoln had already decided was "really a sinister bright bitch"), mocking her preference for "being glorified as a Ziegfeld Beauty" over being an artist. Lincoln had observed that Dimitriev "obviously adores her . . . she was his best friend"—which if true, Lincoln thought, "argues badly for us." Martin told him to remember that Russians "are not interested in money but they are interested in things that money can buy"—a remark Lincoln found "terrifying." Back at Geva's apartment she advised Lincoln to "get a lot of $20 a week dancers, keep them for 3 months . . . [and] put on a kind of advertisement performance at the Town Hall." Lincoln flatly rejected the suggestion, and was relieved that both Balanchine and Dimitriev thought the idea a bad one. Still, Lincoln came home that night feeling "good and depressed about the whole undertaking. . . . It seems impossible now. After Hartford, it might be best if they went back to Europe. I don't know."

The next morning they wandered around the streets for a while and ate in one of the many Horn & Hardart Automats: "The cascade of nickels on the marble plate, the clearness and cheapness of all the food filled them with acute rapture," Lincoln wrote in his diary. And then it was off, by car, to Hartford. On the way they talked politics, with Balanchine and Dimitriev expressing their grave fear about "the coming of communism" to the United States, and how no Russian "has any civil rights anywhere." Dimitriev described how he'd refused to join the Red Army and had been constantly forced to hide out. Balanchine interjected that "he hoped some day to do a Jewish ballet with liturgical music," and Lincoln suggested that the compositions of Ernest Bloch might serve him well.

Arriving in Hartford at Chick and Helen Austin's house, they were soon told that the *Hartford Times* article about them had produced a storm of protest from local dancing teachers, up in arms about godless Bolsheviks being invited to open a free ballet school that would drive good Americans out of business. The protest would rapidly become beside the point: after seeing the museum's new theater, the Russians declared that it was "a big disappointment; there is no height; they couldn't use any scenery in it . . . the floor is too hard for dancing, the whole thing too small," that no more than twenty-four people at most could be put on that stage. Dimitriev said it might do well enough for rehearsals, "small ballets," or school performances, but no more than that.

Balanchine and Dimitriev told Lincoln privately that from now on they wanted to talk to him alone, leaving Chick out until the three had agreed on their decisions. Chick had made the mistake of (as Lincoln put it in his diary) "jumping up and down like a child with pleasure" when they'd arrived, and the Russians had quickly dismissed him as a person of no substance. Lincoln had by now been around Dimitriev enough to know that he was a "hard, wise, bear-like . . . distinguished character, fearless, patient and accustomed to (ultimately) just what he wants." Lincoln went to bed that night feeling "tired, suspicious, nervous—fretful of the morrow."

The next morning Dimitriev asked to see Lincoln alone in his room, where they sat on the unmade beds and talked. Lincoln had such "a terrible weight of fear" that part of his "thinking apparatus" felt deadened. Dimitriev came quickly to the point: Hartford was impossible. It was too far away from New York, the facilities were unsuitable, the cost of living too high, and Chick's dilettantism (he'd made the mistake of remarking at one point that he himself would paint whatever scenery was needed) boded ill for a serious venture. Chick, moreover, had in conversation referred to himself as "Director of the American Ballet," and "Balanchine couldn't bear . . . criticism from anyone like" him. Lincoln tried to explain that Chick had simply meant director of the Atheneum's trustees, but Dimitriev wasn't convinced and added that the mere thought of having to be polite to "important people" in Hartford was insupportable. He and Balanchine did want to work with Lincoln, but a new plan needed to be formulated.

After dinner at Chick's that evening, a long conference followed. Dimitriev suggested that the original idea of a free school give way to charging fees, and that a corporation be set up under the auspices of the museum under which he and Balanchine would be included as prominent shareholders. That amounted to creating a commercial venture, a notion that filled both Chick and Lincoln "with utmost horror." Chick said "the whole idea had changed; it was no longer a modest affair"; they were now indulging "delusions of commercial grandeur."

It dawned on Lincoln that it had been "preposterous" of him up to now to have had "no idea of the gravity or scope of the undertaking" the Russians had in mind—and he found it "horribly frightening." This was a curious reaction for a man who had himself long been harboring lordly plans for the establishment of an American ballet of potentially national, even international, significance. Now he was suddenly in full flight from his own large-scale dream and felt "relieved," as the meeting inconclusively broke up after midnight, that the project had probably "failed," that the "enormous" responsibility had been lifted from his shoulders. He had the strange sensation "of being drugged, intensely tired beyond hope of, or interest in, success or failure—yet without any ensuing disillusionary wisdom."

What had caused him to pull back so abruptly? Was it the intrusion of "commerce"—of the possibility that making "art" might be accompanied by making money—that had so unnerved him, conjuring up as it did an uncomfortably familial, stereotypically "Jewish" activity that threatened his self-image as someone unconcerned with (and superior to) such unappetizing, demeaning activity? Was this an eruption of the buried self-disgust that is so often the unacknowledged underbelly of bravado? Lincoln "slept fitfully, feeling it all absolutely at an end."

He awoke the following morning "with the same dead feeling of hideous responsibility." But he made "a very brave face of it" at breakfast, saying he "was fuller of courage than ever." Then they all sat down again at the same card table, still covered with the yellow papers on which they'd scratched definitions and numbers the night before. Dimitriev began by saying that he'd come up with a new plan: Instead of trying to find a way to stretch the money they had to cover a year's work, which had proved impossible, why not spend it all in six months? Vladimiroff could be brought over at once from Paris, dancers could be auditioned from the surrounding New England area, and several pre-existing Balanchine ballets put into practice (they already had the costumes and scenery for *Mozartiana* and *Songes*, which Vladimiroff could bring over). Then, utilizing the Atheneum's much-larger Bushnell Auditorium, they would invite "people in the theatrical world" to come up from New York to view the productions. Following that they would play a week in Manhattan, and then in the spring would tour various university towns. The tour would bring in enough money to allow them to open the desired school in New York the following fall.

Both Chick and Lincoln thought the new idea "a perfect solution of all our difficulties." With everyone in seeming agreement, Lincoln, Balanchine, and Dimitriev left Hartford and drove to Mina's house. Once comfortably ensconced in Ashfield—before the Russian Revolution, Dimitriev had owned 200,000 acres, and Mina's wonderful books and furniture, the birch trees and dogs, filled him with nostalgia—the "new plan" just put in place began to come apart. Was Hartford really a needed preliminary? Why waste six months in a provincial backwater, and allied with a dilettante like Chick? Perhaps they could open the school straight off in New York under the auspices of MoMA—especially since Eddie Warburg had just given the museum a hundred-thousand-dollar check. Mina told Dimitriev that "Chick was wholly unimportant," and she told Lincoln that they "never could work with him." Jere Abbott, who lived nearby, dropped in and said he thought neither Barr nor Blackburn at MoMA would object to becoming the school's sponsor. Lincoln expressed his feeling that they had to have some sort of a sponsor in order to convince the public that this was not just another dancing school. The more everyone talked, the more Hartford faded into the background.

The next day Lincoln drove back to Hartford to see Chick alone. Chick knew at once that "something was in the air"; he "may be a dilettante," Lincoln wrote in his diary, "but he was not a fool or insensitive." Chick begged Lincoln to *talk*. Lincoln said that he, Balanchine, and Dimitriev had come to believe that "more talk was useless." Chick reminded him that all three of them had agreed to return in a few days to meet Stokowski, who was due in town; but Lincoln told him they wouldn't return because they had no intention of working with Stokowski anywhere, much preferring the Russian émigré conductor Serge Koussevitsky. Chick said flat out that Lincoln was "double-crossing" him, and politely asked if he minded his phoning Eddie. Lincoln said, "Of course not." He tried to joke with Chick, but Chick was having none of it. Lincoln left.

On their ride back to New York, Balanchine, Dimitriev, and Lincoln whistled, sang songs, and talked about almost everything *but* Hartford. Balanchine spoke of the possibility of creating a ballet based on The Song of Solomon, and reminisced about Diaghilev: how he only attended rehearsals once a week, how the one thing he ever changed in Balanchine's choreography was the ending of his 1925 ballet *Barabau*. They also talked about Fokine and why it was that he "gave out." As Lincoln recorded their exchange in his diary, Balanchine said that Fokine had "done much in a short time" and "now was too old. A man can't compose after his body can no longer dance itself. He has to think in real terms of actual movement." He added, "my own Fantaisie [*sic*] will give out. Who can tell? One never knows." Lincoln hastened to offer reassurances that were perhaps, given Balanchine's adultness, quite unneeded; "this was of course," Lincoln said, "the artist's greatest . . . fear"; yet if he was "always sure of his invention he wouldn't be a great artist."

While they were still at Mina's, Balanchine had suggested she invite some "pretty girls" to come by (which Mina did), but Balanchine felt that Lincoln was "not as interested" as he "should be in them." Now, as they passed through Harlem, Balanchine asked him if he'd "ever screwed a negress." Lincoln said, "No, but [he] had always wanted to"—which would have come as surprising news to any number of Lincoln's closest friends. *"Alors,"* Balanchine responded, "we will go together." Obviously Lincoln hadn't yet brought up the subject of his sexual preference, nor had Balanchine surmised it for himself or heard about it from the many others who knew. Either that or Balanchine was playing cat and mouse. Dimitriev later confided to Lincoln that he "really didn't understand" Balanchine, that he "had no sentiment, liked casual fucking . . . no heart"; he was of "another generation." At the same time Dimitriev didn't feel that Eddie Warburg appreciated Balanchine sufficiently, "either his talent or his position."

The following morning Lincoln headed straight up to 1109 Fifth Avenue, the Warburg mansion. Chick had indeed called and according to Eddie was "in a panic," saying he'd been "cut out of the whole thing" even though the Atheneum's imprimatur had been responsible for getting the Russians into the country. Eddie might have contested that claim, since his own intervention, at least at dockside, had proved critical. But in a larger sense he felt, and Lincoln didn't disagree, that Chick's hurt and anger were justified. Eddie made it clear to Lincoln, with more force than he could usually muster, that he was unwilling to guarantee his support "indefinitely." He wanted to see "an exact budget" drawn up.

So did Lincoln. But he also wanted to draw up a prospectus for the school that would simultaneously attract students and a potential institutional sponsor. And taking priority over everything else, was securing Balanchine and Dimitriev's visas in case Chick decided to pursue a vindictive path. Having carefully ingratiated himself earlier with Bill Bullitt, Lincoln headed down to Washington on October 26 to see him in his State Department office. "Realizing how much flattery had already done" for him with Bullitt, Lincoln began the visit by "gratuitously" complimenting him on the soon-to-be-announced recognition of the Soviet Union.

He then cleverly sought Bullitt's advice on several peripheral matters on which he'd already made up his mind, thanking him profusely for his sagacious counsel. The ground having now been carefully laid, Lincoln finally brought up the matter of the visas. Bullitt fell into his hands like a predrugged lover: *yes of course* he would see to it that the two Russians got immigration visas after their current six-month ones expired. And surely Lincoln realized how "interested" he himself was in the ballet—why, he'd just seen Walt Disney's cartoon *The Three Little Pigs*, and felt confident Lincoln would agree that the choreography for the song "Who's Afraid of the Big Bad Wolf?" "had recaptured for us the spirit of the Russian Ballet." Lincoln agreed, doubtless dropping Bullitt into his already stuffed file of educated barbarians.

Next up on his agenda was finding an institutional sponsor and a space for school rehearsals. Felix Warburg thought the Juilliard School of Music might be interested, but it wasn't. As for MoMA, Alfred Barr read the prospectus Lincoln drew up "with great sympathy," and made several useful suggestions for improving it still further. But he told Lincoln frankly that he thought the whole idea was "utopian," that "no Americans could submit to the necessary discipline" for creating an American ballet; in addition Barr emphasized his belief that "European sources" were responsible for *all* American art—that there was "no possibility of calling anything primarily American."

On the other hand, John Martin also read the prospectus and told Lincoln that he thought "our program was stimulating and our curriculum excellent." Frances Paine chimed in with her opinion: Lincoln "needed no sponsorship by anyone." And Mina said much the same; it was "ok to put all my eggs in one basket," she told her brother, "if it was as strong as B & D." Lincoln decided they were right, and set out at once to find a suitable and affordable rehearsal space.

In the meantime, in another phone call to Eddie, Chick had "exploded" with resentment, and Eddie felt that "a definitive meeting" with him, without the Russians present, was necessary. Lincoln agreed and the two headed up to Hartford. The meeting *was* definitive—but hardly pleasant. Chick had already decided to save face by telling the local press that the venture had unexpectedly turned commercial and that the Atheneum could not possibly lend its good name to that sort of enterprise. He intended to announce publicly that he was voiding the contract with Balanchine and Dimitriev, apparently not realizing (or caring) that the contract was already void, since neither man had as yet signed it.

When face-to-face with Chick in Hartford, Lincoln could feel his "just resentment." He told Chick how sorry he was that things had turned out the way they had, and made "several polite attempts to engage" him in conversation. They failed. Chick told him "bitterly" that he'd "hypnotized Eddie and betrayed him." Within twenty minutes the meeting was over. Lincoln wired Dimitriev: EVERYTHING O.K. WORK STARTS MONDAY. He then took the train to Boston to spend the weekend with his parents.

He spent more time with his mother and with a few old friends, like Agnes Mongan, who still mattered to him, than he did with his father, since he and Louis had already had lunch several times recently in New York and Louis was almost wholly preoccupied with politics, revealing to his son that he was giving serious thought to running for governor of Massachusetts. He thought Rose would like that, and David Sarnoff had advised him to go ahead, but only if he could win by a large majority— which Louis thought he might. In the end, however, he would decide not to seek the nomination actively; it would have to come to him—which it never did.

Lincoln, still sympathetic to the Left, wasn't a particular admirer of FDR's, and he sometimes grew impatient with his father's starry-eyed adoration. During one of Louis's panegyrics, Lincoln told him about an article he'd recently read describing the terrible conditions in the mines. Unquestionably terrible, Louis agreed, yet "it was less bad here . . . [than] anywhere else in the world." Lincoln let the matter drop, but sounded a militant tone in his diary, "the terror of the mineowners will be automatically equivalent to the terror of the miners when the revolution comes."

On returning to New York, Lincoln went with Balanchine and Dimitriev to see Eddie Warburg's new apartment, designed by Philip Johnson, at 37 Beekman Place. Balanchine thought it was "perfect, except that it lacked a piano and *sept filles*, four for him and one a piece for us." He insisted (from Lincoln's point of view) on "showing how rutty he was by making obscene drawings, which Eddie carefully destroyed." Lincoln was puzzled; usually he found Balanchine "gaily quiet" and rather enigmatically remote, but now he was acting "more and more captious." Lincoln suddenly realized that Balanchine was unwell.

Not that he would give in to it, or even willingly discuss it. As Lincoln and Dimitriev sat around the hotel room in the Barbizon-Plaza, trying to figure out budgets, the details of incorporation, or possible sites for the school, Balanchine would lie on the bed, yawn "with intense boredom," and finally fall asleep; some of that was due less to illness than to a lifelong aversion to anything relating to administrative detail.

Nor would Balanchine heed Dimitriev's stern demand that he rest more. He gladly agreed not to accompany the other two men as they scoured the city searching for a suitable space, but he rarely turned down a party or an opening. When Pierre Vladimiroff arrived from Paris, they took him to an oyster bar for a celebratory welcome. When the Edward Hopper retrospective opened at MoMA, Balanchine was in attendance. When his close friend, the composer Nicolas Nabokov (cousin of the novelist), who had done the music for Massine's *Ode* in 1928, appeared in New York, Balanchine frequently went out with him (Lincoln thought Nabokov "nasty"). When Balanchine insisted that Lincoln take him to the Savoy in Harlem, he did so, but for only half an hour. (Balanchine thought they should sleep with one of the "hostesses" and also thought "it would be fine to do a classical ballet with negresses in tutus of gold and silver *paillets* and white bodices.")

And when the Kurt Jooss Ballet Company, which specialized in a combined form of modern dance and classic ballet, opened in New York on October 31, Balanchine, Dimitriev, and Lincoln were all on hand for several performances. And all agreed that the company was a disaster. Lincoln thought that Jooss's most famous creation, *The Green Table*, "had 2 or 3 good ideas in it," but that the other works were "without the slightest interest whatever." Archie MacLeish, who sat in front of them, thought it all "wonderful." Which perhaps partly accounts for Balanchine's negative reception the next day when Archie presented him with the idea for his ballet, *Union Pacific*; Balanchine told him it "would make a better film."

They were all present, too, when Serge Lifar debuted a few nights later. Lincoln thought he'd never performed "so abominably," never "made such narcissism chichi and rot." Roman Jasinski also danced, and in Lincoln's opinion, "with a lot more distinction than Lifar." Among the ballets on the program was Balanchine's *La Chatte*, and he was "simply wild" with Lifar for bringing over "such a poor company," and "furious" that "the entrance of the young men, entirely pederaste, was greeted with roars of laughter." He insisted that he "never realized how queer it all was" and demanded that his name be taken off the program. At the party afterward, Misia Sert, Diaghilev's longtime confidante and patron, who had "put up a fortune" for the occasion, said that she thought "Serge had a succes personelle," and Lifar himself announced that "all New York" was at his feet. But Balanchine and Dimitriev thought the more accurate description was that he was suffering from "a malady of self-love."

Lincoln asked Dimitriev if Balanchine ever liked anybody else's ballets—Massine's, for instance. Only Massine's *Le Tricorne* and parts of *Jeux d'Enfants*, Dimitriev replied. He went on to warn Lincoln that Balanchine was "often like a child, intractable . . . he would disagree, waste hours in argument, and finally agree." Balanchine was a Georgian, Dimitriev explained, and therefore "extremely heartless"; he would think nothing of screwing another man's wife, he had "the folly of genius," was "an entirely difficult character" whom he "[didn't] understand at all."

The latter may well have been true, but "entirely difficult" was quite another matter. Lincoln had already decided for himself that Balanchine was both "simple and deep," too remote and undemonstrative to match up well with his own temperament, but not someone he thought (as Dimitriev repeatedly suggested) would prove difficult to work with. Like every significant artist, Balanchine could stubbornly hold his ground in defense of his own vision, but he was almost always—at least when feeling well—calm, concentrated, and generous, not at all similar to a petty, flamboyant, demanding narcissist like Serge Lifar.

Yet on other grounds entirely, Lincoln was beginning to worry that the school would never get started. Though they had looked and looked, they had yet to find a suitable space. It was clear, moreover, that Eddie Warburg lacked any profound interest in ballet and it was questionable how long he would stick. Then there were all those people, from Archie MacLeish to Alfred Barr to the dancing teachers of Hartford, who believed the project was misguided from its inception. And perhaps worst of all, despite a printed notice soliciting applications, no students were banging down the doors seeking instruction. That is, with one exception. A "boy" named Erick Hawkins, whom Lincoln remembered seeing in Harvard Yard, came by to say he'd already studied with the modern dancer Harald Kreutzberg and now wished to learn ballet from Balanchine. This was the same Erick Hawkins, of course, who would subsequently shift his allegiance to Martha Graham, become her lover, and play an aggressive role in her company before going on to found his own.

Then, just as Lincoln's gloom again began to thicken, he and Dimitriev finally found "a dream place" for the school at 637 Madison Avenue, a space "better than anything [that] could be imagined." That same day they signed the papers for incorporation that they'd long been working on, with parity for all four participants: Lincoln, Eddie, Balanchine, and Dimitriev. A further boost to their spirits arrived in the form of a letter of inquiry the following morning from a fifteen-year-old girl named Ruthanna Boris, who'd been studying the Cecchetti method with Mme. Rosina Galli at the Ballet School of the Metropolitan Opera, and had read a mention in John Martin's *New York Times* dance column that a "School of American Ballet" was being formed and potential dancers interviewed. As Boris remembers it, she had a "cordial, courtly, welcoming, enthusiastic" response from Lincoln "within the week." When he interviewed her, she reminded him of Toumanova—"a fresh little creature, but sweet"— and she was accepted into the school. When she told Mme. Galli, who disliked Russians and their dances, that she'd be leaving, Galli shook her fist in Ruthanna's face and denounced her as a "traitor." Ruthanna Boris would become a company mainstay and a well-known choreographer in her own right.[4]

But these encouraging developments were paralleled by a sudden, sharp decline in Balanchine's health. On November 7, Dimitriev told a frightened Lincoln that "Balanchine should see a doctor for his T.B.," that he wasn't eating enough and was further risking his health, "now that he has no girls to 'baiser,' " by going out nights "searching for company chez Nabokov." Ill though he felt, Balanchine insisted on keeping an appointment in Philadelphia with Dorothie Littlefield, sister of the budding choreographer Catherine Littlefield, and apparently a potential inamorata.

When he returned the next day, he was running a fever. At this point Lincoln decided that "the worst has finally happened." He called up Eddie Warburg's physician, a Dr. H. Rawle Geyelin, and got Balanchine out of bed and down to his office. ("I had visions," Lincoln wrote in his diary, "of Saranac [Saranac Lake in the Adirondacks, the location of a string of T.B.

sanatoria] and quick death to all of us.") But Geyelin said that Balanchine merely had a bad cold, though he added that there was "a 40% chance some tubercular activity was evident." Balanchine was sent for X-rays to another doctor, and Lincoln was allowed in the room during the process, where he peered at "the healed ravages of the old T.B." The radiologist said "there might be something, he couldn't tell: It didn't look terribly serious."

In order to throw a scare into Balanchine and keep him reasonably quiet, Lincoln lied to him, telling him the doctor had said he "was very ill" and must get a good amount of rest for six months. To Eddie Warburg, their chief benefactor, Lincoln "passed it off jokingly" over the phone. The lie, alas, soon turned out to be the truth. After viewing the X-rays Dr. Geyelin came over to the hotel and said, in front of Balanchine (who was now running a high fever), that they had shown "an active tuberculosis spot" and he would have to go to the Presbyterian Hospital for at least two weeks. Then, out of Balanchine's hearing, he notified Lincoln and Dimitriev that there was "another darker spot on his lung which might be a really serious thing. If so, he would have to go away for six months perhaps." In any case, "he could not live much longer than ten years, if that long." In response to Lincoln's direct question, Geyelin advised them not to sign any lease for the school—which, of course, they had already done.

After Geyelin left, Dimitriev said that he "had no faith" in him, that the TB, as in the past, would "heal itself." Ignoring him, Lincoln insisted they get Balanchine into the hospital at once; Geyelin had already reserved a room in the exclusive (and expensive) Harkness Pavilion. But Balanchine refused to go, saying he would "rather die in the streets." He told Dimitriev to "make a Russian potion for him like he'd been given before and he would be OK." Lincoln felt "desperate," shocked at "how primitive their ideas were about our doctors."

Balanchine's fever rose still higher and Dimitriev called up a Russian drugstore. They sent over "a kind of midwife" who said Balanchine had pneumonia, not TB, "cupped" him, and took off "a great deal of water." Balanchine looked green and said, ominously, that "it had never been like this," that he was going to die. At that point Serge Lifar abruptly entered the hotel room, not saying how he'd learned the news. He immediately phoned Misia Sert and a Russian doctor named Silverstein.

Lincoln left the room and paced the corridor. Later he recorded his thoughts in his diary: "I thought B. would die. . . . End of the American Ballet, but no, I would call a meeting of all interested persons to keep it going, in spite of no choreographer, no drawing card. Impossible. I would return to my novel, 'The Hero.' Explanations to Warburg. I would wait for the next chance. This was the end here . . . many terrible and trivial thoughts. Dead feeling in my belly. Gurdjieff objectivity devoutly to be desired."

Suddenly Lifar appeared in the corridor and told Lincoln that the Russian doctor, who'd rushed to the hotel, said Balanchine had "a bad grippe," not pneumonia, and that he'd be "O.K. in two days, he was sure." Lincoln almost kissed Lifar but quickly thought better of it, since he'd just ferociously denounced him in an article for *Vogue* magazine, calling him an "athletic young man who made up in an excess of endearing narcissism what he lacked in technique . . . the most striking thing he's done since the old days is to appear as an usher at the Hutton-Mdivani wedding." Yet Lincoln felt Lifar had been so "sweet" to Balanchine that he apologized to him for what he'd written. Lifar, rising grandly to the occasion, said "in his excessively loud voice" that Lincoln was entitled to his opinion but that he, Lifar, knew he'd been dancing better over the past four years than ever before. They shook hands and Lifar left, tragedy and farce having become delicately intertwined.

Nothing had actually been settled about the state of Balanchine's health, however. Though Dimitriev was "jubilant," Lincoln could see no grounds for believing the Russian doctor over Geyelin, especially since his sole prescription was for an enema bag. They'd now had three separate and contradictory opinions, and Lincoln felt "so shattered . . . [he] didn't know what to do." Could Balanchine work or not? *Of course*, said Dimitriev—"tomorrow."

But on the following day the Russian doctor, still not having seen the X-rays, started to hedge his bets. He thought maybe Balanchine ought to go to the hospital after all, just in case. Lincoln felt his stomach—and his raised hopes—plummet: "This was too much"; the doctor had been so sure yesterday and now he suddenly "didn't know." In the meantime Balanchine's fever had come down somewhat, and he was feeling better. And arriving visitors helped provide a distraction. Roman Jasinski, whom Lincoln thought a "nice rather sweet boy" and whom Balanchine liked and considered "a perfect machine," diverted them with a description of his costume for the *Sylphides* pas de deux.

Vladimiroff, before leaving to tour with Lifar, came to the hotel frequently, and after having initially turned down the offer to teach at the school, now accepted for at least a limited period. Tamara Geva also said, though "not with a hell of a lot of enthusiasm," that she, too, would be willing to lend her name, and perhaps to teach. Eddie Warburg, who they feared had been wavering, pledged his ongoing support. And the hiring of a part-time publicity man, along with an ad in the Jooss playbill, began to bring in additional inquiries from potential students. The decision was made to charge tuition, though Lincoln, his Left-leaning lobe to the fore, told a friend that he "intended to enlist the masses, cut the social bias entirely except for the cash they would pay for tuition."

Everyone's spirits took a turn for the better. But the question of Balanchine's health remained unresolved. His temperature, to Dr. Geyelin's surprise, continued to come down, and as it did Balanchine became more irritable and started to complain about being idle and "sex-starved." He accused Dimitriev of having "made up the whole business about his illness"; he didn't have TB or anything else. Dimitriev shouted that after Balanchine was well, "all their friendship is off; he will see him only in the school." And he told Lincoln privately that he "could no longer support Balanchine's stupidities." Lincoln calmed him down with the advice that he was "too close to it all," that he should "put the weight of responsibility on Balanchine, let him do everything: temperature, etc."

More consultations with more doctors made it clear, even to Balanchine, that he *was* ill and needed a period of recuperation. The Russian doctor, Silverstein, now concurred that there was "an active tubercular liquid spot in Balanchine's chest," and Balanchine finally agreed to be transported to the Harkness Pavilion. Lincoln had told him that the hospital was "like a grand hotel," but Balanchine's room turned out to be "small and mean," and, now ravenous, he had trouble getting any food. "It was all farce," Lincoln wrote in his diary, "like a nightmare. . . . Hospital like a prison. Black despair. Perhaps worse than ever before."

A few days later, Lincoln had a brainstorm: perhaps Mina would agree to let Balanchine come to Ashfield and recuperate there in peace and comfort. Mina immediately expressed her willingness, and on November 25 they took Balanchine by train to Northampton. Mina had prepared a buffet dinner, and they settled in. A firm diagnosis for Balanchine remained elusive, but at least a refuge from weeks of turmoil had been found. Lincoln returned to New York and tried to pick up various other threads in his life.

Throughout the previous month, he'd managed, as only the fearsomely energetic Lincoln could, to snatch an hour here and there to pursue an assortment of other engagements and projects. He saw the latest issue of *Hound and Horn* to press; called on Henry Allen Moe of the Guggenheim Foundation to tell him (in the hopes of getting a future grant) all about the pending school of ballet; listened several more times to his father's stories about Washington; and met with both Clifton Fadiman and Arnold Haskell to discuss the American edition of Romola's book. He didn't take to Fadiman ("a shifty bastard") at all, and he could see that he wasn't interested in the suggestions and additions that Lincoln nonetheless offered (when the book was in proofs, Lincoln volunteered to go over it and caught some 129 errors). Haskell told Lincoln that Romola had initially refused to make any reference to Lincoln's help on the book, but that Haskell had insisted he be credited. As it was, the credit was minimal and perfunctory, and Romola failed even to send Lincoln a complimentary copy. He also had a great deal of trouble extracting the return of Roger Dodge's valuable collection of Nijinsky photographs, which Lincoln had persuaded him to lend for the book—and had promised to guard with his life; only a threatened lawsuit finally produced the photos.

Furious at Romola's ingratitude, Lincoln wrote her a scorching letter, saying in essence that he'd done his best to be a friend to her but no longer had "any illusions" and wanted nothing more to do with her. Yet "in spite of everything," he wrote, "I felt it a privilege to work for Vaslav, and I would do as much and more again—for him." The ever self-righteous Romola replied in a six-page letter that Lincoln's tone had been "insulting and rude," and she accused him of going around New York "telling people you are writing my book . . . [you] merely wanted to use our association for your own benefit." She reiterated her claim that she'd "encouraged and helped you with advice, how to make a school of ballet; and it was supposed to be done by us both," and further, that had she not introduced him to Balanchine, all his hopes would have been dashed. "I must realize the fact," she concluded, "that you are my enemy."

Lincoln refused to let her distortions be the final word, and in yet another letter answered them one by one. He denied that he'd ever gone around New York "saying I wrote your book, nor have I ever taken any credit for it over the last few months, when God knows I could have." If anything the reverse was true, since Haskell "told me . . . that you had said rotten things about me all along." He honorably owned up to her accusation that he wanted "to advance myself in a position of authority about dancing," but he insisted that although that was an "important" reason for his helping her with the book, it was hardly the only one: "My motives in helping you write the book were because I wanted it written, and I knew perfectly well that if someone didn't take the emotional and personal responsibilities for you, it would never get done." As to her claim that she'd given him advice about founding the ballet school, he flatly declared that "you gave me absolutely none." Yes, she'd introduced him to Balanchine, but she was hardly the reason why he'd come to know him well and to work with him. "Whether you believe it or not," Lincoln concluded, taking the high ground, "I have a real affection for you . . . and only hope that you can do what there is to be done for Vaslav." So ended their operatic duet, though there would be intermittent letters for another twenty years, mostly relating to Romola's unceasing requests for various kinds of assistance.

By the end of November, Lincoln had also managed to put the finishing touches on his short book about Fokine. Just before Balanchine landed in New York ("I'm so scared he [Fokine] won't speak to me after Balanchine arrives that I must work fast"), Lincoln had spent nearly an entire day asking Fokine additional questions for the book, during which Fokine "particularly was bitter against Diaghilev" and "expressed contempt" for both Balanchine and Massine, "saying it was his innovation which made them possible, but they were no good." Lincoln's *Fokine*, published in London in 1934, was a straightforward and largely appreciative account of the choreographer's career; both Dimitriev and Vladimiroff had fed him negative tales about Fokine, but he put those into his diary, not his book. Dimitriev had told him that Fokine was "all inconsistency," and that with the exception of *Sylphides* and *Prince Igor*, his contribution to ballet would prove impermanent. Vladimiroff called him "a mercenary beast" and referred obliquely to his "bitcheries at the Marinsky during the Revolution." Balanchine had briefly joined one such conversation in order to broaden the indictment to include Diaghilev, who he said was overall "a bad influence in dancing: in his last ten years nothing was accomplished of importance aside from its period interest. . . . There was never any underlying idea." On another day Balanchine did an imitation of Diaghilev "to perfection"—"sputtering, monocle, blurting at Lifar to take the buttons off his trousers."⁵

By early December, Balanchine was decidedly on the mend. Though "plagued by wet-dreams," his appetite was good, he'd put on weight, and "seemed happy," and had, as Lincoln put it, turned "quiet and well-behaved." Strangely, given how supportive his father had always been, Lincoln had still not been able to bring himself to tell him about the pending school, having decided to wait until it was so thoroughly established that Louis "can do nothing against it. Not that he would," Lincoln quickly added in his diary, "but he keeps trying to get me to get Eddie Warburg to give to H & H [*Hound and Horn*]." But Lincoln was well aware that his father "was no fool," and before long Louis "finally got it out of" him about the school. His initial reaction was apparently lukewarm, since Lincoln wrote in his diary that Louis "would understand all of it if he should stop to think of it for a second."

The sticking point seems to have been the fate of *Hound and Horn*, in which Louis had invested heavily over the years, and not just financially; though he rarely read the magazine and had sometimes complained to Lincoln that *no one* could understand it, he did value the *Hound and Horn* as the likeliest vehicle for securing his son's literary career. But with Balanchine's arrival and planning for the ballet school, Lincoln finally made a definitive decision to end his connection with the magazine.⁶

That couldn't, of course, be accomplished overnight. He had already set in motion what would become *Hound and Horn*'s final issue in 1934—a significant symposium on the then-underappreciated Henry James—an issue that he would come to regard as "definitely our masterpiece." And that meant a considerable amount of effort was still required. Doris Levine, who was still running the *Hound and Horn* office, had for some time done much of the heavy lifting and almost all of the detail work, with Lincoln investing "less and less" time and interest. Still, he did have to put in a certain number of hours dealing with contributors and editing their pieces.

Most of which he did on the run, "with scarcely a morsel of attendant guilt," and with a fair amount of high-handedness. He cleared up his mail by leaving much of it unread and unanswered, and when he did respond, he was often snappishly succinct. He wasted little more than five lines telling the poet Winfield Townley Scott that he didn't care much for his latest work: "There is so much extra writing in it. . . . I feel the diffusion impedes the real impulse." To the young poet Muriel Rukeyser, later considered a major figure, he commented in regard to her submitted "Satire to Decay," that "I think you have got a kind of bastard vocabulary which comes from reading too much." Even to an old friend like Jack Wheelwright, Lincoln could be unceremoniously blunt: "The proofs of your poems came, I think you have overdone the introduction. . . . I have read it several times and every time the smugness grows."

As news began to get out that the magazine's days were numbered, Lincoln made numerous expressions of regret over its coming demise and several suggestions for prolonging its life. Alfred Barr, who cared little for ballet and thought Lincoln's idea of setting up a school "utopian," wrote him that "of all the things . . . you have been interested in, I think the *Hound and Horn* is by far the most important . . . it would be a great shame if you were to let it go now when it is as badly needed as ever." And Monroe Wheeler was among those who seemed "very much interested in keeping" the magazine alive, "with the possibility of Glenway Wescott as editor." But Lincoln was as unmoved by the pleas as he was indifferent to the schemes for salvage (none of which, in any case, came to fruition).

For the first time in his life, Lincoln knew in a profound and sustained way, and one that didn't rely on his hoped-for rather than actual gifts, where he wanted to concentrate his time, talent, and formidable energy. Indeed, he'd known for some time that the ballet mattered to him more than anything else, yet it had taken until now for him to put together the pieces that might make his dream come true. But "might" was still the operative word. The obstacles remained formidable, and for some time the odds for success would shift on a near-daily basis.

CHAPTER ELEVEN

School of American Ballet

(1934)

Tʜᴇ ʟᴇᴀsᴇ ᴍᴀʏ have been signed for rehearsal space at 637 Madison Avenue, but getting the needed furnishings installed—from mirrors and lights to *barres* and lockers—brought a whole new set of headaches that kept postponing the school's actual opening. The workmen showed up irregularly, and when they did, managed to make a series of excruciating mistakes, like installing the *barre* in the wrong way.[1] A brouhaha over the lockers became especially upsetting for Lincoln. He had given the job of designing them to Philip Johnson without consulting with Dimitriev, who, once he learned of the commission, made a "great row" about it. Worse, Lincoln discovered that Philip "had been gypping us terrifically"; he had a "brief, cool talk" with his erstwhile friend, ending with Johnson giving up the job; between Philip's anti-Semitism and his petty embezzlement (why, with his sizable income, he would bother is itself a mystery), it's difficult to fathom why Lincoln didn't simply break off the friendship—but he didn't, even though he kept Philip at a considerable distance. After World War II, Philip Johnson—in what Lincoln would call an "amende honorable"—contributed a considerable sum of money to Louis Kirstein to use for Jewish charities; the gesture went a long way towards allowing Lincoln to maintain the friendship.

By mid-December, with renovations on the rehearsal space finally nearing completion, the focus of Lincoln's anxiety shifted to worrying about whether they'd get enough students to fill it. He kept vacillating between "thinking we'll have lots of students and that we'll have none." Balanchine was inclined, as always, to shrug at the workings of fate, while Dimitriev told Lincoln to simply stop his "nervous masturbation." Despite feeling in the grip of an emotional roller coaster, Lincoln had a chrome plate, reading "The School of American Ballet," affixed to the front door on December 19.

Five days after that a total of twenty-two students actually began classes—with Lincoln "so nervous" he "could barely watch them." The "girls" were taught from 11:30 to 1:00, the "boys" at 4:30. Dorothie Littlefield from Philadelphia led the beginner's class, though "always with the supervision of Balanchine and Vladimiroff." When Lincoln saw Vladimiroff in action, he was amazed: the Russian became "an entirely different person: strong and masterly on the dancing floor," a "superb teacher."

But Lincoln's unease resurfaced when Arnold Haskell arrived in New York and explicitly "warned" him that Dimitriev had a reputation for manipulation and capriciousness. Initially Lincoln had characterized Dimitriev as "simply a darling," but of late he'd become more and more irascible and exacting—perhaps because, as an equal partner and the formal "director" of the school, Dimitriev was determined on securing his financial interests, especially since he saw no future for himself apart from his ties to Balanchine. But his treatment of Lincoln had become increasingly "malicious and tigerish," constantly tangling with him over everything from contracts to the "useless" soundproof curtains Lincoln had dared to order without "the director's" consent—and in the wrong color (black) no less!

Dimitriev's ferocity wasn't confined to Lincoln, though Jews did seem a special target of his venom. The teenage student Ruthanna Boris recalls Dimitriev angrily telling her, out of the blue, that she was finished, to pack up her things and leave at once. When she asked why, Dimitriev yelled, "You are Jew. Not be here. Go! . . . Jew no good! Out! Out! Out!" The feisty Ruthanna was not one to crumple and burst into tears. She protested that she had every right to be there, that being a Jew had nothing to do with being a dancer. And when Dimitriev held his ground, she went to Lincoln's secretary, Doris Levine, who told her that Dimitriev was "an anti-semite from the old school" and to just show up for classes the following day. Which she did, passing Dimitriev on the way; "he didn't look at me, just went on as if I were not there." Later in the day Balanchine sat down next to her on a bench and, according to Ruthanna, said, "It is good you are here. I want to say to you something. I envy you because you are Jew." He touched his heart: "Jews have here something warm, like the sun. I have here something sharp, you know, like dagger I keep in boot when I was son-of-a-bitch little Georgian boy." Ruthanna remained enrolled in the school.

Additional students, ranging from total novices to several with advanced training, continued to trickle in. The most promising was a young man named William Dollar, who'd been dancing for two years at Radio City and had earlier attended classes with Lincoln in Fokine's home. Lincoln thought Dollar was "ugly and feminine," as well as "difficult to handle," but did recognize his talent. Initially Balanchine wasn't so sure; Dollar reminded him of a dancer he'd known who "is admirable in class and nothing on the stage." But Vladimiroff, who had himself been a *premier danseur*, was impressed with Dollar; in two months, Vladimiroff declared, he could make him a better male dancer "than any in the Ballets Russes de Monte Carlo."

Lincoln regarded the Ballets Russes, which under Sol Hurok's management was about to open in New York, as their "mortal enemy." He understood that the European company could help to build a much-needed audience for ballet in the United States, and he further recognized that the School of American Ballet was hardly prepared to give public performances (though he, Balanchine, and Dimitriev did nurture the hope that by spring they could do a series of "demonstrations" on college campuses—and to that end the advanced classes had, nearly from the beginning, started to rehearse both *Errante* and *Mozartiana*).

Lincoln's overriding fear was that the Ballets Russes would "steal" from the school any dancer who showed unusual promise, a fear confirmed almost immediately. Charles Laskey, another promising male dancer who'd showed up for classes, was less well trained than Dollar but in Lincoln's view "more male and [with] a better body." Yet within a week of the Russians' arrival, Laskey received an offer from Massine and shifted to the Ballets Russes, expressing deep regret at "having to make a living." But the defection proved brief. Laskey returned to the school within a few weeks, his decision probably helped along by Lincoln secretly providing the penniless dancer with five dollars a week for food.

Lincoln had trouble "asking the pupils for their paychecks," but Dimitriev had no such compunction. He and Balanchine also stepped in and vetoed Lincoln's proposal that they place an ad in the Ballets Russes playbill. Dimitriev said that "it was a question of principle not to," since de Basil had made a point of leaving out any mention of Balanchine's name from the company's advance advertising, even though it would be performing his 1932 ballet *La Concurrence*.

The Ballets Russes formally opened on the night of December 22. De Basil had enlisted a remarkable group of dancers for his company, including Alexandra Danilova, Tamara Toumanova, Tatiana Riabouchinska, Irina Baronova, Leon Woizikovsky, Yurik Shabelevsky—and, of course, Massine himself. The company opened with *La Concurrence*, the program crediting Bérard's costumes but not Balanchine's choreography. It was the first time Balanchine had seen the piece from the audience, and afterward he said that "he was through forever with that kind of stuff," that he was now "full of new ideas." But a "thrilled" Lincoln thought Toumanova had "danced divinely" in it; he also thought Massine's *Les Présages* "brilliantly" performed, and he very much admired Shabelevsky in Massine's *Le Beau Danube*. There was nothing small-minded about Lincoln; he may have felt "at war" with the Ballets Russes, but that was a separate matter from his appreciation of excellence.

In fact Lincoln went back often to see additional performances, and though he felt none measured up to opening night, he was more generous in his overall appreciation of the company than the critics and the public. John Martin wrote a sharply negative review in the *New York Times*, a review that infuriated Arnold Haskell, who told Lincoln that Martin had "killed the Monte Carlo Ballet season" though "the future of ballet depended on its success." Whether or not due to Martin's review, New Yorkers failed to turn out in large numbers for the Ballets Russes, and its season was widely considered a failure. Martin, for his part, confided to Lincoln that he was fed up with the "deceits and bitchery" of the company and felt outraged that Sol Hurok had succeeded in getting some critics fired from their newspapers "for ripping up *Présages.*" He added that Balanchine's *La Concurrence*, "even if it was slight, was the only thing that showed any originality in the whole repertory."

Hurok came up to Lincoln in the lobby one night after a Ballets Russes performance and accused Balanchine of trying to recruit Woizikovsky, Toumanova, and Riabouchinska. The accusation was false, as Lincoln "hotly" told him, adding that in truth Massine "had taken Charles Laskey from us." Hurok's "sheer gratuitous nastiness upset" him for days, and he felt "further unnerved by stupidly allowing him to see the extent and innocence of my righteous indignation."

Lincoln believed that Hurok's attack was entirely "a compensation for their lack of success." But it was more likely inspired by an article Lincoln had written for *The Nation* that came out at the time of Hurok's confrontation. Lincoln had written that the Ballets Russes consisted of "uneven" younger members and "overworked older stars" from the Diaghilev era, and claimed that "the troupe is without any real spirit save a commercial one." By contrast he praised Balanchine's "touching and witty dances" in *La Concurrence*, and then used the remark as a lead-in for an overblown bit of press agentry: "America at last has the possibility of gaining a complete education in dancing with . . . The School of American Ballet, under M. Balanchine. . . . [it] offers to any interested person all the perfected materials of a dancer's craft." Given this combination of understated appreciation of the Ballets Russes (whose performances he'd in fact admired) with an overstated description of the advantages of his own new school, it should have come as no surprise to Lincoln when Hurok singled him out for attack.

In truth the future of the School of American Ballet was far from secure. For one thing Balanchine's health remained problematic. Lincoln took him to Dr. Geyelin's office for a checkup early in January 1934, and Geyelin pronounced himself "well pleased with his improvement." But when Lincoln brought over Balanchine's X-rays two weeks later, Geyelin found two "active" tuberculosis spots and said that Balanchine wasn't "nearly as well" as he'd believed. After reexamining him, he told Balanchine, in Lincoln's presence, that "there were from 100 to 200 bacilli of T.B. in the microscopic range of vision," and that a 100 percent recovery hinged on complete rest. If Balanchine continued activity at his present rate, Geyelin said, the chances of recovery were only 80 percent. Balanchine chose to continue at his regular pace.[2]

Then there was the ongoing problem with visas, a responsibility Lincoln took on almost single-handedly and which involved a considerable amount of irritating and demeaning legwork. Dimitriev and Balanchine, never having acquired any national status but Russian, had initially traveled on so-called Nansen passports, which were essentially certificates of identity. In October 1933 the American consul in Paris had issued them twelve-month visas as non-immigrants, and they'd been admitted to the United States for a six-month visit, due to end on May 1, 1934. Vladimiroff, too, was in need of an extension. Lincoln went down once more to Washington to seek Bill Bullitt's help in arranging for immigrant visas that would allow for permanent admission to the country. One roadblock in the way was that the only record of their birth was locked away in churches in Russia; the Soviet ambassador in Paris had turned down their applications for formal birth certificates. Lincoln's hope was that the Department of State would accept their personal affidavits in lieu of the required birth certificates.

This time around, a frantically busy Bullitt had to shunt Lincoln off to someone in the Visa Division, who was "fiercely official" and came up with several new questions that Lincoln felt were designed to *prevent* the Russians from ever being able to settle in the United States. At that point his father decided to intervene and sent Lincoln to his old friend Charles Wyzanski at the Department of Labor. As Lincoln reported back to Louis, Wyzanski (later a federal judge) was "extremely kind," and after a series of worrisome delays, Balanchine and Dimitriev finally received, just before their six-month visas ran out, "the confirmation of their first papers." The fact that they were able to remain in the United States and to create a foothold there for ballet owed a great deal to the efforts of Lincoln, his father, and Charles Wyzanski.

Then there was the overriding problem of lack of money. Though the number of students continued to climb, by the end of 1933 only some seventeen of them (by Lincoln's estimate) were paying fees, which in total were projected to bring in about $10,000 during 1934. In the sketchy budget the four partners had drawn up, expenses came to roughly $22,000, with rent ($94 dollars a week) and salaries the major items; Vladmiroff topped the list at $150 a week, and Balanchine and Dimitriev each got $100. (All these figures, in today's terms, would be approximately nine times higher.) That left a considerable projected deficit, even without factoring in any of the much-desired and discussed plans for performance and expansion.

Eddie Warburg's pledge of twelve thousand dollars a year and Lincoln's of eight did, theoretically, cover the deficit. But Eddie would one day declare himself "satisfied with the way everything was going," and the next privately tell Lincoln that he was "consumed with apprehensiveness about the future finances of the ballet school," that he was wary of committing himself to what seemed like a bottomless pit, and that he doubted if Balanchine "understands American taste sufficiently to give them what they want."³

Lincoln constantly had to play nursemaid to Eddie, reassuring him about everything from the school to his hemorrhoids to the endless crises attendant on his endless psychoanalysis with the brilliant but unscrupulous Russian émigré Gregory Zilboorg (George Gershwin was another of his patients). Lincoln thought Eddie essentially "soulless" and without any real commitment to anything. But out of both self-interest and friendship (at his best Eddie could be a charming companion), Lincoln played out his role of concerned confidant—half the time wanting to strangle him. One night, when Eddie had a bad cold, Lincoln stayed overnight in order to administer steady doses of tea and lemon. On another, Eddie asked Lincoln to talk him to sleep, and as he did (so Lincoln recorded in his diary), Eddie "became amorous and over a long sleepy period gradually worked himself down and me up"—but Lincoln, "moist," stopped him. That seems to have been the only time Eddie attempted sexual contact, though Lincoln occasionally recorded other instances of Eddie's homosexual escapades.

Lincoln had no significant financial resources of his own, or none he could touch, anyway, in order to meet his pledge to the school of eight thousand a year; in truth, as he wrote his father, "I have no idea how much money I own myself, that is, in my own name." He'd grown accustomed to his father paying his bills and providing him with a monthly allowance to cover incidental expenses. Louis constantly hectored Lincoln about his financial irresponsibility, but it was he who'd set up the framework that perpetuated it: he'd kept Lincoln in the dark about his own assets, even after he'd turned twenty-one, and then, from his own pocket, had indulged his son's constant overdrafts. As a result Lincoln had become incorrigibly inept at keeping reliable financial records and had long since learned, when pressed, to turn to his parents to bail him out; he'd occasionally borrow money as well from friends (including Eddie), or even dip into *Hound and Horn*'s minimal reserve.

But in regard to expenses relating to the new School of American Ballet, Louis proved far less indulgent than in the past. Lincoln did manage to coax his father into seeing a rehearsal at the school (Rose had already gone and had seemed pleased), and he declared himself impressed—that is, with "the atmosphere of work" and with Balanchine's "authority." But not sufficiently impressed to open up the Kirstein coffers. Over the winter of 1934, Lincoln several times arranged to meet his father for lunch or dinner, practiced his pitch in advance—and met with indifference. As Lincoln put it in his diary after one such encounter, "My carefully prepared speech . . . was in competition with the financial section of the paper . . .

my praise or rather defense of the school rather petered out in the face of his lack of comprehension or attention." Alternatively Louis would redirect the conversation to his own adventures among the high and mighty in Washington, DC (where he was deeply involved at the time with drawing up the Retail Code under the NRA).[4]

Throughout his life, Lincoln occasionally complained about his father being emotionally "distant." But Louis had never been detached in overseeing Lincoln's behavior or advising him on his professional commitments—which made his studied indifference to the school highly atypical. Perhaps Louis was angry at Lincoln for deciding to close down *Hound and Horn* (even as he raided its remaining coffers).

Or his attitude toward the school may have resulted from uneasiness over the standard equation of ballet with homosexuality—and what that might say about his son. Lincoln had talked openly about his sexuality with Mina, but not with his parents; and there's no evidence that Mina had passed the news on to them. What may also have contributed, if less importantly, to Louis's resistance to helping the school, was one consequence of his past indulgence that had recently surfaced: Lincoln had been caught in an overt lie. He'd told his father's secretary, Miss Beverley, that he was "absolutely clean as far as my debts go," and had then proceeded to submit a hodgepodge of outstanding bills for payment.

Incensed, Louis wrote him—while enclosing yet another check to cover his personal expenses, thereby diluting his own message—that "I hope to heaven you keep straightened out! . . . Credit is a very sensitive thing—once you lose it, it is difficult to get back." Louis also instructed Miss Beverley to read Lincoln the riot act. "Personally," she wrote Lincoln, "I think you are not only unfair to your Dad but disrespectful as well . . . it grieves [him] that you are so careless about financial matters."

Lincoln knew just how to play the squabble: he wrote Miss Beverley that she was "perfectly right" to reprimand him, and he acknowledged that the allowance he regularly got from his father (which in 1933 totaled $3,150), the occasional gifts from Rose, and the periodic small dividend checks were most certainly "enough money to live on." (This was at a time when *skilled* male workers earned less than fifty cents an hour and a teacher's yearly salary hovered around $2,000.) Lincoln then went on to point out that with his apartment rent at fifty dollars a month, he was not, like Eddie Warburg, living in extravagant luxury. He was, in fact, "continually broke." Moreover, he wrote, he had some "special" expenses that he hadn't previously revealed. Two in particular. One was his long-standing support of Gaston Lachaise, whom Lincoln considered "a very great artist" as well as a friend, and to whom he both gave money and found commissions (he persuaded Eddie Warburg, for one, to sit for a portrait head in alabaster). More recently Lincoln had also been giving small sums to a poverty-stricken young sculptor whose talents he admired; even after he lost faith in him, he still provided him with enough money ("extremely necessary for my peace of mind") to head off actual starvation. Lincoln's sometimes rude and heated exterior concealed a brusquely tender-hearted, generous man who usually made his donations anonymously and tried to avoid being thanked.

Early in the new year money concerns at the school reached crisis proportions, producing frayed nerves and a round of nasty personal quarrels. Two weeks after telling Lincoln that "he would find him a firm friend always," Dimitriev (so Lincoln recorded in his diary) "gave me a bitter scolding for wasting my time and his by hanging aimlessly around the school, not trying to get more pupils—not helping Balanchine." Two days after that, the usually pliant and people-pleasing Eddie Warburg delivered a comparably humiliating message. He airily referred to "the curious reversal of position" that had taken place; how he, Lincoln, "was now the most unimportant member of the crew—having no money to put in and being psychologically stopped."

The latter charge was partly a case of Eddie grinding his own ax; he'd been trying to convince Lincoln that he should begin psychoanalysis with his doctor, Gregory Zilboorg, who managed to keep Eddie in profitable *daily* therapy for more than twenty years. Lincoln knew nothing of Zilboorg's behavior, yet resisted seeing him on generic grounds; as he wrote in his diary, "I don't need any analyst to get where I want to get, if, in the Gurdjieff sense, I can overcome an insufficient desire to live"—a poignant, unelaborated glimpse into the terrifying emptiness that sometimes engulfed him. This was not melodrama but fact.

More hurtful still, Eddie repeated Balanchine's remark that he feared Lincoln would "turn into another Edward James," the wealthy English dilettante. That was deeply wounding and left Lincoln feeling "cursed . . . cheated . . . vengeful and sorry for myself." He'd seen himself as something of a co-creator, and for months he'd been dreaming up ideas for new ballets based on American themes—*Flying Cloud* (about the clipper ships), *Custer's Last Stand*, *Pocahontas*, and (one that did interest Balanchine) a ballet based on the Rover Boys books. Still, Lincoln fully understood Balanchine's "righteous fear of dilettantism" and had no doubts about who the chief creative force was. But Dimitriev and Balanchine's combined remarks, cruelly overstated, now made him feel like some sort of incompetent office boy, someone incapable of carrying out even the minor tasks assigned him.

It rendered Lincoln upset and resentful. He tried to harden himself against feeling bitter toward the Russians, though (as he put it in his diary) "their iron lack of emollient words" did nothing to help his hurt pride. Lincoln had a habit, when feeling emotionally wounded, of believing that his current mood would be permanent ("I will *never* meet Balanchine or Dimitriev on friendly terms again," and so on), but he vowed to break the habit this time around, to work himself through his resentment. Yet the wound went deep, and he had trouble adjusting to what their harsh words had revealed about the diminished esteem in which they held him and the peripheral role they saw him playing in future plans.

Lincoln was quite abruptly forced to conclude that his "place in the picture of the school and company" was "increasingly remote" and would never fully absorb his time. He thought yet again of turning back to his unfinished novel, *The Leader,* or to his new idea for a popular book on dance history. In his diary he gloomily wrote that "perhaps the personal touch I would choose to give it [the school] as a spirit is unnecessary, inefficient, even dangerous. Resolve to be cold-blooded and careful both about Balanchine and Dimitriev."

Yet even during the worst of his pain, Lincoln recognized that he remained "influential," saw clearly enough that "Balanchine can be ably and efficiently influenced, if it is sufficiently indirect, flattering, and if the suggestions are validly imaginative. What my role would have been had I not been, as now, disappointed, I have, now, no idea. As a matter of fact I thought hardly at all of what I'd do, imagining only consecutive and charming collaboration." Yet instead of holding to his decision to be "cold-blooded" and coolly aloof, while concealing his resentment, Lincoln in fact lurched quite quickly in the opposite direction, turning his anger inward, blaming himself for all that had gone wrong, indulging an orgy of lacerating self-recrimination and a humiliating outburst of apologetics.

It was as if he couldn't manage to sustain an emotional middle ground, couldn't simply acknowledge where he may have made some mistakes or come up short, even as he justifiably held to account those who evaded their own inadequacies by trying to blame them on him. Instead he tended to lurch between fierce denunciation and savage self-blame. Always a man of extremes, he dealt all his life in hyperbole, crudely lashing out at others or holding himself infernally culpable and damned. What he called his "demons" rarely allowed, in personal relations, for a cool appraisal or for more than a fleeting sense of inner peace.

Whatever the source of his indecipherable "demons," whatever proportion was familial or genetic, they drove him relentlessly, and kept him during the first few months of 1934 in a state of tortured self-doubt. He even told himself that perhaps he no longer had any "particular place in the school," that "the effort of establishing it seems to have wrecked my interest in it." And for "crimes" unreal or imagined, he ended up making an abject apology to Dimitriev for the "stupid vanity and lousy manners" he'd displayed, agreeing that he *had* been behaving like a benighted Edward James. Instead of accepting the (misguided) apology, the ungracious Dimitriev—who'd been far guiltier than Lincoln of "lousy manners"—proceeded to accuse Lincoln of a damning instance of "non-cooperation." Dimitriev had earlier complained to Warburg (who'd glee-fully told Lincoln) that Lincoln "had a secret urge for publicity" and was determined "to carve a niche" for himself—unlike, presumably, the rest of them. Now Dimitriev had proof positive: *Stage* magazine had come out with an article about Lincoln that had failed to mention either Dimitriev or Balanchine. Lincoln tried to explain that the fault was that of the "lousy reporter," not him, but that only slightly mollified Dimitriev.

The Russian's grossly unfair attack helped Lincoln recover a more accurate sense of himself. He now sensibly reassigned the ineffectiveness he'd been feeling to a "natural letdown after some nervous strain . . . [about] Balanchine's health [and] the disposal of the *Hound and Horn.*" His feelings of self-worth were further burnished as a result of lectures he'd started to give, both at the school itself and at various colleges, on the his-tory of dance. At first he disliked doing it and felt his performance poor ("spoke too fast and made little impression"). But by the spring of 1934, after talking to an enthusiastic audience of more than four hundred at Vas-sar, he wrote exuberantly to his father that "I have completely cured myself once and for all of stage fright. After this I know I can talk almost anywhere."

It helped, too, to see that not even Balanchine, who once described himself to Lincoln as "like water," was immune to the tense atmosphere currently pervading the school. Balanchine and Dimitriev themselves got into "a savage fight" following Dimitriev's accusation that Balanchine "never takes any pains with any but the Philadelphia girls [sent to him by the Littlefield sisters] whom he considers his own." It took a few days before the "coolness" between the two men started "gradually patching up."

But Balanchine still felt "desperate about not doing ballets this year, the first time in ten years he would be showing nothing." In Lincoln's view his desperation was partly the result of failing to have "fully perceived the idea this was a school, only a school, and no company." Dimitriev encour-aged that misperception. He'd earlier pushed for the idea of starting out with a performance of *Errante* at Radio City, and told Lincoln that "if he [Dimitriev] was running our school he'd do it the other way around, i.e. spend $10,000 on a ballet performance: *then* open the School." Yet both Dimitriev and Balanchine agreed with the recent decision to give up all plans for a spring tour of college campuses. They recognized that there hadn't been enough time to risk a public performance, with Balanchine adding that he hadn't had sufficiently "finished artists to work with."

But at just this low ebb, a number of unusually promising, even estab-lished, students began to appear at 637 Madison Avenue to sign up for classes, enough of them to raise again the hope that some sort of public showing might well be possible by summer. Among the newcomers who, in the first two months of 1934, joined the already enrolled William Dollar, Charles Laskey (who Lincoln had by now decided was "vain and conceited . . . and too nervous to learn"), Erick Hawkins, and Ruthanna Boris, were the tiny, technically brilliant Leda Anchutina; fourteen-year-old Marie-Jeanne Pelus (for whom Balanchine would later create *Concerto Barocco* and *Ballet Imperial*); the Radio City and Ziegfeld Follies dancing star Patricia Bowman; Gisella Caccialanza, who'd been schooled by her uncle, the great Italian teacher Enrico Cecchetti; Annabelle Lyon; Elise Reiman; and Paul Haakon (who Lincoln thought was "as delicate and exquisite as a Cartier watch"—and was soon complaining that he thought Balanchine "a very bad teacher"). And finally, in February, the two Christensen brothers—Harold and Lewellyn ("Lew")—arrived, after having performed in vaudeville for a number of years. As Lincoln wrote in his diary, "a really agreeably fresh spirit" took hold "in all the students."[5]

Simultaneously the twenty-five-year-old Eugenie Ouroussow, an exiled Russian aristocrat, joined the staff as secretary of the school and, less formally, as a kind of liaison between what Lincoln would later call "two brash Americans and half-a-dozen Russian theater-people unaccustomed both to their perplexing manners and amateur attitude towards professional business." Ouroussow would remain with the school for decades, her (as Lincoln put it) "superior tact, extraordinary kindness and strength" long serving as a cohesive force.

Simultaneous with the arrival of Ouroussow and the highly talented cadre of new students, there was a general spurt in enrollment (by May the school boasted some sixty students). Additional good news came from Dr. Geyelin; after examining Balanchine over the winter, a surprised Geyelin announced that he "might be the case to refute the old idea one could not get well from T.B. while in New York and working."

All of which helped to dissipate months of gloomy apprehension and backbiting—though hardly ushering in an uninterrupted reign of harmony and sunny satisfaction. The School of American Ballet was, after all, a newborn; as with most infants, peaceful interludes were all but guaranteed to give way to some rude wailing and sudden spitting. Within weeks of the general rapprochement, Eddie Warburg was sitting Lincoln down for yet another lecture about his shortcomings, and a renewed insistence that he go to see his analyst. "You aren't exactly mean," Eddie said, "but your nervous jumpings-about and your shortness with people gave a bad impression."

Eddie had figured it all out: laying down the standard Freudian boilerplate of the day, he ascribed Lincoln's "difficulty and tension" to the two "bugbears" of money and sex. His specific attraction to tough guys, he told Lincoln, was the result of trying to convince himself that he *was* a man "in spite of the fact" that he "never earned [his own] . . . living." (As someone who lived on inherited wealth, Eddie, apparently, never paused to apply the same diagnosis to himself.) Lincoln dutifully agreed with everything Eddie said (he *did* need his money)—and continued to resist seeing Dr. Zilboorg.

Besides, Lincoln had become infatuated with one of the new students and became briefly oblivious to the ongoing undercurrents of acrimony. The object of his affection was one Harry "Bosco" Dunham, who'd simply appeared at the school one day, "a small blonde from Ohio" already in his early twenties. Lincoln had no sooner laid eyes on Bosco than his passion flared, though he'd been celibate for some time. (As he somewhat sadly put it in his diary, "Streets full of sailors and marines. I keep my eyes neatly averted, forcing on myself what I know and have known too long to be true, that it's no use.")

But he was instantly infatuated with Bosco and felt he could be developed into "a splendid hero" for the troupe (and, by implication, for his own life). Lincoln soon learned more about Harry Dunham from the composer/writer Paul Bowles, whom he'd recently met and whose music he thought would interest Balanchine (at the time it didn't, though two years later, Lincoln would again suggest Bowles for a project). Over lunch, Bowles told Lincoln enough about his own relationship to Harry Dunham to make it clear that the seemingly bland blond had a decidedly wild side. Bosco's family had some money and he'd graduated from Princeton. According to Bowles, he'd seduced Bosco while they were traveling together in the South of France and in Africa.

Dunham had generously shared his money with the nearly destitute Bowles, and in 1934 was still helping to support him. Lincoln said that he thought Bosco had "a fine dramatic gift." Bowles said that "he was nuts, and that sitting down in a chair was drama to him." To press home his point, he told Lincoln about some of Bosco's escapades when they were abroad, including dashing over the rooftops of Fez, picking up with an Arab boy, and getting a girl pregnant in Dresden.

The fact that Bosco apparently had an unpredictable, dangerous side seems to have heightened his appeal for Lincoln—at last another "gangster" type had come along to feed his long-standing James Cagney fantasies. "I felt strong and stronger inside me," Lincoln wrote in his diary, "the unmistakable solar plexus pains of strong attraction and longing which I have not felt since I can't remember and which I thought up to now were forever dulled by jacking off and concentration . . . he is wholly charming and I gauge my snatched moments in the dressing room so that Dimitriev will not suspect me" (though Dimitriev quickly did).

Just as Lincoln's infatuation with Bosco was peaking, he received a telegram from him saying MANY APOLOGIES CIRCUMSTANCES MAKE IT IMPOSSIBLE TO BE IN BALLETS. At first Lincoln hoped the decision was reversible, but it turned out that Bosco had indeed left the school for good. Lincoln, who had his own penchant for drama, moodily felt for a time that Bosco's defection "was a symbol for the dissolution of all we did." But Dimitriev quickly cut through the sentimentality: "We could lose ten dancers and never know the difference." Lincoln wrote to Bosco, urging him to reconsider, but in his reply, Bosco confessed that he wanted to marry a girl whose parents refused consent until he had a steady job. This was apparently a barefaced lie; Bosco soon married a fifteen-year-old girl and took her for a few months to Trinidad, after which they divorced. He then resurfaced in New York, where Lincoln continued to see him from time to time through the summer of 1934, his passion still alive even as he became more and more aware of Bosco's "eccentricity"—which Lincoln once characterized in his diary as his "combination of truthful deception and mannered truth." Muriel explained it differently: she told Lincoln he liked Bosco "on account of his disintegration—since I resisted my own so hard." Later Bosco turned his hand to making movies, completing several, including the atrocious *Bride of Samoa* (for which Bowles did the score), a leering travelogue that played for years in semiporn theaters along Forty-second Street. Bosco was killed in World War II.

Dimitriev, shockingly, had taken to opening Lincoln's mail; he read Bosco's letter and promptly "made fun" of Lincoln's affection for him. Lincoln decided on the spot that henceforth "no intimacy . . . [would be] possible" with Dimitriev and that their relationship would be confined to "an efficient working school and business basis." It hadn't helped that Dimitriev had made "preposterous fun" (as had Balanchine) of Gurdjieff's *The Herald of Coming Good*, which Lincoln had given both men as gifts (his friend Stephen Spender, to whom Lincoln also sent the book, was more politely nonplussed; he found it "occult").

Lincoln suffered over Bosco, mostly in silence, for some time; months later he still had "acute dreams of Harry Dunham, as if I was with him and he in my arms." In the past Lincoln would automatically have turned for comfort and advice to Muriel, but when he finally did broach the subject of Bosco with her, he did so guardedly, well aware that their relationship had undergone a considerable shift from what it had once been.

"Maybe her mania has not increased," Lincoln wrote in his diary after first seeing Muriel again after her return from Taos, "but it startled me to see how intense it was." She seemed "more remote and exaggerated," and they were "nervous" with each other. It didn't help that when Muriel showed him the partial manuscript of her book "America Deserta," he made "a rather elaborate criticism of it, saying its . . . vocabulary [was] too . . . subjective and corroborative, but never evocative." It helped even less when a series of publishers, confirming Lincoln's estimate, turned the book down, driving Muriel into considerable despair.

Nor did it improve their relationship when Muriel, grown more tactless than ever, declared that Balanchine was *not* "a genius" but that

Diaghilev had been; she predicted that "in two or three years time" Lincoln "would no longer be interested in the ballet." This remark particularly rankled because Lincoln for some time had been having intermittent bouts of feeling "superfluous"—though even at his low points he felt he had ten more years of work to do to put the school on a permanent basis, not merely two or three. He decided that Muriel "hurts as much as possible to relieve herself" over the failure of her book. But Lincoln, too, could be hurtful. He once told Muriel flat out that he "no longer derive[d] pleasure, as such, from her company," easing the blow somewhat by adding that it was he, not Muriel, who had changed.

The intuitive Muriel, who retained her ability to "guess" what was bothering Lincoln most, abruptly asked him when he'd "been loneliest"—and it was then that he finally told her about Harry Dunham, whose abrupt disappearance had made him become, Lincoln said, "nervous with" himself. His "heart and belly were full of Bosco" and he'd been "taken unawares in the waste places of . . . [his] heart." Muriel said, "accurately" in Lincoln's view, that he hadn't "learned even as yet how irrelevant" such seizures of passion and pain were. He asked her "how one could change the quality of an emotion." "Not by the will," she answered. Lincoln said he realized that ultimately it wasn't Bosco who'd caused his pain but rather "some mechanical . . . re-echoing of a blond narcissism [the Lads at Harvard, perhaps], which will only be exhausted when I can take the responsibity of its renunciation." But Muriel interrupted him: she "didn't want to know," she said, about his "psychological states (they're familiar enough)"; what she did want to know was whether Bosco was "pretty—the flesh is all that counts." Lincoln refused to answer.

And there they left it. But later that night Muriel called him up, sobbing: "I just wanted to say . . . to hell with everything except what you create and what I create, and I love you very much." Then she rang off. Then she called back: "I don't care, and all I do care is that (sob) I'm alive and you're alive. . . . Forgive my bad manners." Her ardent weeping helped to close the distance between them, though they'd never be as close as they had been. Still, they were able to talk more intimately again, and Lincoln was able to express to mutual friends his growing concern about Muriel's future.

He thought she was "looking old in the jaw" (though having accidentally seen her naked recently, he was astonished at how "incredibly young" her figure still was), and he worried about what she would find to do in Russia. Perhaps, he thought, she should start to write "extremely entertaining novels based on her own life," which would at least provide her with enough money to live on—but that wasn't a suggestion Muriel took to. For his part Lincoln told her about the recent reappearance in his life of his sometime girlfriend Margot Loines, how they often went out together and occasionally had sex, and how she'd finally taught him how to kiss in a way that she liked. He'd come to feel, Lincoln said, that Margot "really trusted and loved" him. Maybe they ought to marry. He told Mools that he felt "ready and willing . . . not through any love but for a focus and a family." All the women he knew, except for herself and Margot, had a "general chi chi that has to be gone through." "Yes," Mools agreed, "at least with a man you can go into a pub and talk." Lincoln continued to see Margot but never proposed marriage to her.

Muriel came up to the school for the first time in mid-February and liked what she saw—though she told Lincoln that Patricia Bowman had a "chloroformed diaphragm." She told Eddie Warburg that psychoanalysis, about which he talked incessantly, was "a harmless diversion"; Eddie declared Muriel "dangerous." The school itself, meanwhile, continued throughout the winter of 1934 to generate a roller coaster of emotions. And Lincoln continued to suffer various admonitions from Dimitriev, which he tended to internalize and which no amount of drudge work on his part seemed to diminish.

He continued to do what was essentially promotional and fund-raising work, very little of which he found gratifying. At one point he waited for more than an hour to see the lone headmaster who'd responded (out of eighty-nine) to his letter announcing the school's existence and soliciting student applications—only to be told that it was his wife who was interested in ballet. On his way out of the school, Lincoln extracted a screw from the flag's standard, "so it would collapse if touched."

Even when he had success, his efforts were more often faulted than applauded. Though he struck out with *The New Yorker*, he did get five articles on the school placed—in *Town and Country*, *Stage*, *Vogue*, *Vanity Fair*, and the *Tribune*; they created little pleasure or congratulation. But when the sixth, in *Harper's Bazaar*, came out in early March, "hell broke loose with Dimitriev and more mildly with Balanchine" because neither was mentioned by name (Balanchine, according to Lincoln, fell into "a very depressed humor on account of *Harper's Bazaar* being seen in Paris kiosks, etc."). Since it was the third article of six that had failed to feature the two men, Lincoln was covered with embarrassment and he agreed with them that he'd been "negligent" and "incompetent." Perhaps he agreed too readily. After all, he'd never billed himself as a professional press agent, and he hardly had the clout to demand that the reporters submit their articles to him for pre-publication approval.

When it came to the important task of pursuing permanent immigrant status, Lincoln's considerable efforts were more often than not belittled and disparaged. In mid-March he went to Montreal personally to consult with the consul general, who said there'd be "no difficulty" with Balanchine, but with Dimitriev there were "certain considerations of contract waiver from the department of labor." Returning home with the news, he got not thanks but an angry upbraiding from Dimitriev for having failed to "put him across with the authorities as a teacher or an artist." Lincoln dutifully wrote a long letter to the Montreal consul trying to make the case that as an "artist," Dimitriev wasn't subject to any contract-labor clause, and he also went to see the Canadian trade commissioner, a man he knew casually. In addition, he enlisted Mina's help with her influential Washington friends, Bill Bullitt and Dean Acheson.

Yet despite all Lincoln's efforts, which the Russians treated as their due, Eddie once again berated him for his "incompetency," and reported that neither Balanchine nor Dimitriev "had any faith in what . . . [he] could do for them through the government" and wanted to appeal directly to President Roosevelt; Dimitriev had become convinced that Lincoln was "trying to get Balanchine into the country without him." Eddie, for his part, rejected Dimitriev's suggestion that he himself go to Bermuda and use the Warburg name to get them into the country through that route; Eddie said he wasn't in the mood to leave New York. Even Vladimiroff had begun to "act up," complaining about the extra rehearsals that had been scheduled and, in Lincoln's view, conducting his classes "automatically" and while sitting down—though there's no question that generally speaking Vladimiroff was highly regarded as a teacher. "It is all," Lincoln wrote in his diary, "exhaustingly precarious," though he alone seemed bent on self-blame. It took a toll; he had barely enough energy, he concluded, to "see everything through," but he "no longer [felt] any extra to be exuberant or enthusiastic about the future or what we're doing now."

It hardly helped that Dimitriev, having picked up on Lincoln's infatuation with Harry Dunham, decided to have the conversation that Lincoln had long been "dreading." He "couldn't understand Americans," Dimitriev announced to Lincoln when the two were alone one day early in April. "He'd been here five and a half months and he'd only met Pederasts: Eddie and I never went out into the country, etc. with young girls: Were all Americans queer?" Lincoln told Dimitriev he was right: "We are the nation of the great intermediates." (Lincoln had been reading Havelock Ellis.) "I was not apologetic or ruffled," Lincoln wrote in his diary, "but resentful at the arrogance with which he stated his position of . . . limitless normality."

Where Dimitriev could be openly abusive, Balanchine could be coolly dismissive. As Lincoln wrote in his diary, Balanchine could be "suggestible in small doses, in cafeteria intervals," but "a formal conversation tires him." After one talk between them about legal and financial matters, Lincoln could feel "Balanchine's slight contempt" and it left him all "loose and worried" and prone to nightmares; in one bad dream, "Balanchine a murderer; myself shipwrecked. Disaster and guilt all around."[6]

During the winter of 1934 Lincoln and Balanchine did have at least a few discussions involving "creative" issues, mostly centered on the suitability of the composer George Antheil and the writer Francis Fergusson collaborating together on an American-themed ballet. Lincoln liked both men personally, and their work as well. But Balanchine decided against Fergusson and hesitated over Antheil. He thought his music had "many potentials," but he kept hearing echoes of Puccini and Ravel in it. Yet he did think Antheil "had it over all the other American composers" in that he could write jazz (nobody seems to have considered Duke Ellington, among a number of other black composers), and Balanchine did eventually want to compose a jazz ballet. The following year, 1935, Balanchine would settle on Antheil's music for the ballet *Dreams* and his orchestration of Liszt's music for the ballet *Transcendence*.

But in 1934 such discussions with Lincoln about creative matters were rare. What was primarily wanted from him was not creativity or collaboration, but small-task efficiency—and large sums of money. Lincoln was perfectly willing to sweat and toil in the trenches, and did so prodigiously, but efficiency at niggling detail work was not well suited to his off-handed nature, his baronial sense of consequence, and his stirring dreams. Being relegated to treadmill routines amounted to an insulting misreading of his temperament and talent, of his high intelligence and genuine artistic sensitivity. Lincoln had envisioned himself as sitting at the helm of an ocean liner, not working the ropes on the assisting tugboat. Feeling unappreciated and underutilized, he turned increasingly to the ego-soothing pursuits of writing ("my bitterness against Balanchine and Dimitriev conveniently keeping me in my room"), lecturing, and socializing.

But he did recognize that some of the ongoing deprecation was justified; he had not, after all, come through on his original pledge of eight thousand dollars a year to help support the school. It hadn't been for want of trying. Despite Louis's studied indifference, Lincoln had remained determined to get the eight thousand that his father had always freely given to *Hound and Horn* reassigned to the School of American Ballet. But thus far it had been "like prying the lid off a can."

Finally, in mid-March, Lincoln decided to go directly to Rose. Though blaming himself for being "shifty" and for "riding down" his mother, she immediately agreed to give him four of the needed eight thousand, adding only that she thought he might have shown "more grief" at the demise of *Hound and Horn*. He told her that he simply didn't, and couldn't pretend otherwise. Three days later he got his father and brother to go with him to a Ballets Russes performance, at which, conveniently, Balanchine and Dimitriev also "happened" to be in attendance; they issued Louis a personal invitation to visit the school.

He appeared the very next day. Balanchine got Charles Laskey and another promising student, Holly Howard, to do the pas de deux from *Mozartiana* for Louis's benefit—and lo and behold, "he seemed genuinely impressed and interested," declaring that the pair had done "damn well."

It turned out later that what had impressed him the most was how "really hard" the two dancers had worked. Since Lincoln's attempts to engage his father directly about money issues had been largely evaded, he decided early in April to write him a long letter explaining his position in detail.

He shrewdly began the letter by soothing Louis about the demise of *Hound and Horn* ("what little reputation I have in New York comes from it alone") and itemized the various attempts he'd made, to no avail, to keep the magazine going. He also reiterated his determination to continue with his own writing, citing his book-in-progress on dance and his articles for various publications. The work of placation done, Lincoln then proceeded to tell his father, whether he wished to hear the news so starkly put or not, that "I have a very definite calling in relation to the School of the American Ballet."

He enclosed the school's budget and painted an exaggerated picture of how well it was doing: even though "we have as yet never presented anything publicly," sixty students were currently enrolled, and "we are taking in more money, hence our loss is less"; Balanchine and Dimitriev were now "sure of the success of the School"; the Theatre Guild was thinking of taking over its management (a fleeting notion the guild had quickly discarded); and they'd had an offer to appear at the Chicago World's Fair (in actuality, the *hint* of an offer that never materialized). All that was needed to complete this rosy (and unrealistic) picture, Lincoln wrote, was to take from Eddie Warburg's shoulders the school's entire financial burden.

Eddie, Lincoln went on, had grown ever more resentful about being the school's sole supporter and their personal relationship had become "increasingly difficult—he feels very strongly that all I want out of him is his money." The school's expenses ran to about twenty-two thousand dollars a year, of which Eddie was putting up the bulk. Lincoln was convinced, as he wrote his father, that if he was able to contribute eight thousand dollars, "it would solidify my position with Eddie . . . and exactly clarify my position with Balanchine and Dimitriev."

It took yet another month and another awkward lunch before Louis finally agreed to send Lincoln a check for the remaining four thousand dollars pledged. (Filene's revenues, fortunately, had improved over the winter, even while Boston's retailers in general continued to lag behind most urban centers in the marginal national recovery of 1934–35.) Lincoln was hugely relieved and grateful. As he wrote in his diary, "I could scarcely believe my great fortune and the enormous weight lifted off my shoulders of ceaseless self-recrimination." To Louis he wrote, "Your generosity to me is so great that I never could even start to thank you for it." He added that "Mr. Dimitriev is extremely pleased by how everything is going, and so are Eddie and Balanchine." He was, of course, again exaggerating—needfully, to protect a fragile enterprise.

CHAPTER TWELVE

The Warburgs

(1934)

A s HITLER CONSOLIDATED his grip on Germany, polarized feelings about Jews began to surface in the United States as well, and sometimes in startlingly unexpected ways and places. Stopping off one day to see Mools, Lincoln found her upset and crying fitfully. It turned out that the night before, her good friend, the famously intelligent and civilized Esther Strachey—who was once more living in New York—had, as usual, gotten drunk at a party, turned on a Jewish fellow guest and screamed, "You live on corruption! . . . you all ought to be extirpated!" (Ironically, Esther's ex-husband, John Strachey, had recently published *The Menace of Fascism*, one of the first full-throated outcries against Hitler.)[1]

A witness to Esther's outburst, Muriel was for once nonplussed. It was only the next day that the full impact hit her; she "wept for the human race" and warned Lincoln that "this is what might happen here in America; that it must not; that she was not able to do it herself, but this was something to do." She said, too, that "Jews knew how Christians felt about them in a way no Christian ever knew how they felt about Jews."

None of this was news to Lincoln; his parents may have been assimilationists, but Louis had retained a strong sense of Jewish identity and had become increasingly upset of late over the rise in American anti-Semitism. On one occasion he showed Lincoln a sheet "gotten out by an Edmonton [Alberta] economic survey bureau called 'The Deadly Parallel,'" which on one side portrayed "Good Americans," with not a Jew among them, and on the other side printed portraits of Louis, Felix Frankfurter, and other prominent Jews. Louis and his friend Felix had in fact been consulting about how "to map out a plan to stop the Nazis in the U.S."

It was also clear to both men, earlier than to many, that the plight of the Jews in Germany had become desperate. Frankfurter went so far in the spring of 1934 as to write that "there is no doubt that the Jew in Germany is doomed." For his part Louis spoke widely and gave generously. He typically urged American Jews to "think of ourselves not as so many individuals, but as a Jewry, as a Jewish community that has a special role to play in this crisis in Jewish history . . . giving with all our heart and all our might."

Lincoln would later describe himself during these years as "a sort of false gentile," but his dormant sense of Jewishness did come to life when confronted with the blasé attitude (or worse) of friends. He asked Nelson Rockefeller at lunch one day if he'd noticed the recent rise in anti-Semitism. Nelson said that he had, but wasn't concerned about it because "the country was too diffuse" to allow for a large fascist movement to develop here; he pointedly added that "the Rockefeller family's stand had always been for tolerance."

Lincoln's Left-leaning sympathies resurged in tandem with his renewed sense of being Jewish, and he let Nelson know that he regretted the recent efforts to block unionization in the oil industry, emphasizing that "labor was and had been badly treated . . . in the mines." Nelson agreed, but then remarked that the miners, "even after years of unemployment [and] after only a month of re-employment," were "buying cars on the installment plan." To which Lincoln sardonically replied that they had "not had a great deal of chance to learn thrift."

During another lunch Nelson referred to his brother Winthrop's "marvelously democratic manner with the Working Man"—why, he could go into their homes and "dandle their babies"! When Lincoln tried to focus the conversation on the relationship between capital and labor, Nelson said "he [couldn't] afford to think very much about the status of the world at present." Lincoln concluded that for the time being, Nelson "skims the surface of his accidental power." Nelson, for his part, felt that his friend's "prowling opportunism and . . . frankness" were something of a "threat." Committed to a centrist position, he placed his faith on neither capital nor labor but on "the technicians," which meant that for now the two men weren't particularly compatible. Lincoln had recently told the left-wing artist Hugo Gellert that "there was nothing about Communism I didn't agree with—only the means of affecting it bothered me"; by "means" he probably meant seizing the state by force. In any case, after the lunch with Nelson, Lincoln wrote in his diary, "I won't be seeing him for some time," naively assuming that the choice was all his.

In fact, despite some fallow periods, the two would long remain friends, and Nelson, over many decades, would prove himself a very good one to Lincoln. And the two would come closer politically over the years, as Lincoln's ardor cooled and as Nelson, once he found himself in a position of real power, proved himself a staunch supporter of Jewish organizations (at one point he assumed the chair of the United Jewish Appeal [UJA]) and—at least in the opinion of established labor leaders like George Meany and David Dubinsky—a generally sympathetic friend to labor.

Loyal to her friends, Muriel had tried to excuse (even while deploring) Esther Strachey's shocking behavior by unconvincingly attributing it to her frustration at failing to bed down Lawrence Dennis, whose 1932 book, *Is Capitalism Doomed?*, had made him a considerable celebrity. Lincoln considered Dennis "a great Fascist fool," but others, and especially Philip Johnson, had come to hold him in awe. Lincoln had seen little of Philip of late. They'd maintained a nodding acquaintance, and Lincoln had continued to think of Johnson as essentially fatuous. When Philip and Alan Blackburn stopped in to watch a rehearsal at the school one day early in March 1934, Lincoln characterized them in his diary as "two buzzards . . . envious and gushy." Lincoln did go to see Johnson's MoMA exhibition, "Machine Art," but while granting that it was "beautifully arranged," dismissed it as merely "decorative," though the show was widely praised in the press.

Lincoln's lack of interest in Johnson gave way to a more active antagonism when he discovered early in May 1934 that he and Blackburn, with Lawrence Dennis as their mentor, had launched a new venture: the organization of a fascist group called The Gray Shirts. That, Lincoln wrote in his diary, "set me off . . . [I feel] very sore and hating about this." He dreamed that he "threatened to kill Phil Johnson and scared him dreadfully out of his Nazi activities." Louis advised his son "to do nothing official" about Johnson and Blackburn's pro-Nazi propagandizing at MoMA.

But Lincoln rejected the advice and sent a letter directly to Alfred Barr. "I am more and more troubled," Lincoln wrote, "by the possibility of the Museum . . . [being] a center of a lot I hate. . . . The presence of Philip and Alan in the Museum seems to me the harboring of paranoia and prejudice." He'd therefore decided to "exert the only authority I have"— namely, merely to loan rather than to give the Museum (as previously promised) Lachaise's sculpture of his head. This wasn't quite the equivalent of a shot across the bow, but for the moment it was all that Lincoln could think of to announce his determination to serve as a counterforce at MoMA to Johnson and Blackburn.

Lincoln also had a long talk over lunch with Nelson Rockefeller about Johnson's activities, advising that the entire Rockefeller family stay "strictly clear of the pair, that otherwise both his family and MoMA could become tarred with the Fascist brush." As yet, Lincoln said, Johnson and Blackburn's activities had amounted to little, but "they would later on have to make some kind of public utterance" about the formation of the Gray Shirts, and before that they should be forced to resign from the Museum of Modern Art. Nelson told Lincoln that he had "an accurate idea of Alan and Philip," but Lincoln believed that his "idea" was little more than a "hangover" from the notion "that power was in the hands of the rich, the well-born and the able"—could easily resist any fascist threat.

Lincoln soon decided to confront Philip directly. He went to his apartment and, with "demonstrated anger and intensity," asked him for an explanation of "his Gray-Shirt Fascist activities." Philip made light of the whole thing and, lying, said he'd already "abandoned" the idea. Besides, Philip insouciantly added, their "barely organized" group (which seconds before he'd declared abandoned) was "not anti-Semitic" and indeed he "even hoped" (so Lincoln rendered Philip's words in his diary) "that nice Jews like Warburg and myself would join them. They were merely a group of young men interested in 'direct action' in politics, who believed in a totalitarian state and leadership, instead of democracy." He once more insisted that he was not anti-Semitic. To which Lincoln retorted, "Not yet."

In fact well before 1934, Johnson had been making assorted anti-Semitic remarks; in a letter to Alfred Barr in 1931, for example, while discussing possible financial contributions from Europe for a MoMA show on the International Style featuring Mies van der Rohe, he'd written, "the patrons of Mies are Jews and do we want them?" Far from "abandoning" his fascist activities, moreover, Johnson now set about pursuing them with vigor.

After Lincoln's confrontation with Johnson, the two didn't see each other again for several months. When they did finally have lunch, Philip told Lincoln that he simply couldn't understand either his attraction to "communism" (Philip tended to equate any left-wing stance with Bolshevism) or his failure to see that Blackburn was "a great man"—a "new and humane Napoleon." That same summer of 1934, Lincoln did have lunch with Blackburn after he and Philip had returned from their cross-country trip to "feel the pulse of the country." It was "morally sick," Blackburn told Lincoln. He also told him that he was concerned about Nelson's "personal coldness" toward him. Lincoln assured Blackburn that he knew nothing about it (though as he wrote in his diary, "I was at least, of course, partly responsible for it"). Blackburn, in turn, assured Lincoln that both he and Philip weren't fascists and were against "race-hatred as a weapon." Lincoln wasn't buying any of it. Blackburn, he wrote in his diary, is "a cheap, smart little rat." As for Johnson, Lincoln concluded that Philip's future course would be based "on chance"—and "on a private army like the Heimwehr."

Blackburn and Johnson would finally resign from MoMA in December 1934 and head south to sit at the feet of Huey Long and to learn more about his "methods." In 1937 they would change their organization's name to Young Nationalists, suggestive of Hitler's National Socialists, and in both 1936 and 1938, Johnson would make trips to Germany, where, by his own account, he was overcome—romantically "transported"—at hearing Hitler speak at the Nuremberg rally. By 1939 Johnson would be writing articles for Father Charles Coughlin's anti-Semitic publication, *Social Justice*, and, in relation to the *American Mercury*, declare in a private letter that "the Jews bought the magazine and are ruining it, naturally."

Yet as late as 1985, when interviewed by a fellow architect, Robert A.

M. Stern, Johnson blithely remarked in regard to his fascist leanings in the 1930s, "Everything was called Fascist, of course, by the Communists." And he would still, even then, refer to Lawrence Dennis as "a real intellectual" whose books "were regarded even by the leftists then as being very, very good"—an inaccurate characterization of how Lincoln and most of his left-wing friends regarded Dennis. Yet unlike so many other well-known figures persecuted to the point of ruin for their youthful pro-Bolshevik leanings, Johnson remained Teflon-coated for his fascist and anti-Semitic sympathies until the late 1980s, when a few muckraking journalists finally managed to extract a sort of vague apology from him for his "youthful foolishness." When Johnson died in 2005, even the obit writers tended to downplay or ignore his sordid past. Not even Lincoln, despite his fury at Johnson during the mid-thirties, ever broke with him fully; if anything, their friendship years later would solidify, a fact that Johnson would ascribe to their shared view that "elitism is the only proper philosophy." There's some truth to that explanation; Lincoln did believe in an aristocracy of taste and talent. His elitism, however, unlike Johnson's, was shot through with democratic impulse and with sympathy for the oppressed. In 1934 he remained "confused" in his attitude toward Communism, unwilling to align himself too closely (unlike, say, Muriel). Yet he'd show considerable left-wing fervor over the next few years, going so far as to declare that "revolution [was] inevitable." For the May Day Parade of 1934, he went to Union Square to watch and found it "very moving"—in contrast to the Socialists, who were simultaneously marching on Fifth Avenue and whom Lincoln found "much more sedate and dead."

During those tumultuous months the American School of Ballet was moving at last toward its first public performance. Temperamental outbursts had become, for the time being, less frequent and the affairs of the School less precarious. The unpaved road still had plenty of bumps in it, but in Lincoln's view anyway, a positively "angelic atmosphere" prevailed among the students. But it didn't help morale when the well-known journalist Marya Mannes, whom Lincoln knew socially and actively disliked, returned the compliment by attending several rehearsals at the school and then publishing an article in *Vogue* that dismissed the women in the company as "unimaginative" and the men as "fairies."[2]

Nor were the students—vying, after all, for attention and glory—quite so uniformly angelic toward one another as Lincoln sometimes chose to believe. This was particularly true of Erick Hawkins, who was considerably older than the others and seems to have been widely disliked by them—"an overbearing pain-in-the-neck," as Ruthanna Boris put it. Nor did they seem to have thought much of him as a dancer. Ruthanna, for one, couldn't understand why he was kept on, since he was "bulky, cumbersome and awkward," and "seemed to go *at* steps instead of dancing *into* and *through* them . . . as Mr. Balanchine and Mr. Vladimiroff showed us." She suspected that it was mostly due to Lincoln that Hawkins was allowed to stay (and was even, before long, given some limited teaching duties).

Lincoln in fact did go out of his way to be helpful to Hawkins. The two were nearly the same age, and Lincoln, as he rarely did with students, occasionally had a meal with him. Hawkins told him that he knew he had a "serious handicap" in starting so late as a dancer, but he had confidence in his own "brains and perseverance" and resented the fact that Vladimiroff didn't give him enough personal attention in class. He complained, too, about how "piddling" the talk was in the male dressing room and how annoyed he got at Charles Laskey's determination to be "the star." Lincoln found Erick's earnestness, so in line with his own temperament, appealing; and he was also prone to his own seizures of annoyance with the erratic Laskey. (He once talked directly to him about his tendency as a dancer to "rigidity"; Laskey replied that he feared losing "any trace of his maleness," but Lincoln assured him that he "could very easily afford to.") Lincoln went so far as to tell Hawkins that he "hoped I could make some kind of place for him in our affairs" though (as he noted in his diary) "I felt a little guilty being so encouraging."

The students generally seem to have found Lincoln congenial; they brought out what Ruthanna Boris has memorably called his "planting propensities" (for a while he gave Holly Howard, considered among the most promising of the dancers, private lessons in English literature). But the students did call him "Mr. Kirstein," and he "wasn't talkative" around them; Eddie Warburg's efforts to make them into his "pals" drove Lincoln into near-apoplexy, since he believed, like Balanchine, that hierarchy and discipline—without being dictatorial or unapproachable—were important elements in their training.

By the spring of 1934, the advanced students had been working steadily on a number of Balanchine ballets, in particular *Errante, Songes, Mozartiana,* and two new works-in-progress, *Dreams* (to George Antheil's music) and *Serenade.* It was generally agreed that the time had come to show some of the work publicly. Dimitriev came up with various possibilities: giving Sunday performances at the school, trying to arrange with Radio City Music Hall for an occasional appearance, having a "public day" once a week (this last designed in part to keep guests from disrupting rehearsals on all other days). But it was finally decided that the best venue for an initial showing would be an invitation-only event at Eddie Warburg's family estate, Woodlands, in Greenburgh, New York, to take place in mid-June. Eddie's parents agreed to host the event as a birthday present to him.

Balanchine only began choreographing *Serenade* (to music by Tchaikovsky) in mid-March, while simultaneously still "doing new things" to

Errante. He told Lincoln, on that first day of preparing his first ballet in the United States—which would prove one of his most enduring and beloved—that "his head was a blank," and he asked Lincoln "to pray for me." Ruthanna Boris recalls that Balanchine dismissed the boys and then lined up the remaining seventeen girls according to their heights, picking them one by one. She and Annabelle Lyon, the two shortest, were left unchosen—and terrified that they'd be excluded—but then, to their huge relief, Balanchine put them in the front.[3]

Lincoln sat on the side and watched as Balanchine began by slowly composing "a hymn to ward off sin." He "tried two dancers breaking the composition, first in toe-shoes, then without; without won. The gestures of the arms and hands," Lincoln wrote in his diary, "already seemed to me to have Balanchine's creative quality. When I ebulliently suggested this to Dimitriev, he said 'Je ne sais pas,' dampening my too excessive and ready admiration."

The great ballerina Alexandra Danilova, who'd left Russia with Balanchine, been his lover, and remained his friend, was also present that day. After the initial *Serenade* rehearsal, Balanchine showed her part of *Mozartiana*, which she'd seen in its inaugural performance in Europe by Les Ballets 1933. She confided to Lincoln afterward that in her opinion, "Holly Howard was far better than Toumanova in it, but not to tell her so."

As rehearsals for *Serenade* proceeded day after day, Dimitriev, having earlier dampened Lincoln's enthusiasm, became excited himself, declaring that "Balanchine has now hit his stride and style; for years he was doing trick stuff, hoping for surprise . . . now it was pure Balanchine." But Dimitriev being Dimitriev, he couldn't bear to sustain a positive note; that very same day, he had a row with Balanchine after accusing him of giving too much time to Marie-Jeanne (she'd dropped "Pelus" from her name)—who, as Balanchine had doubtless already sensed, would become one of ballet's brightest stars.

At the end of March, Tatiana Riabouchinska came by to see how *Serenade* was progressing. She'd been performing in New York with de Basil's Ballets Russes (which, to Lincoln's delight and relief, was faring poorly at the box office). By then, Balanchine had composed a brilliant pas de trois for Charles Laskey, Kathryn Mullowny (another of the more promising students), and Balanchine's current lover, Heidi Vosseler (who would subsequently become the wife of Muriel's son Paul). Watching the rehearsal, Riabouchinska declared herself amazed; she couldn't believe, she told Lincoln, that Balanchine "could do anything so tender." With *Serenade* progressing so well, the Broadway designer Jo Mielziner was hired to do the lighting (as well as the sets for *Mozartiana*).

Filled with creative energy, Balanchine wanted to start work as well on a jazz ballet and he also began to cast a more interested eye toward Lincoln's long-standing idea of a ballet based on *Uncle Tom's Cabin*, with a scenario by E. E. Cummings. Again being treated as part of a collaborative process did wonders for Lincoln's spirits; he became much more positive about the school's chances for survival and far less gloomy about the value of his own contributions. But he'd learned not to expect any consistent level of artistic consultation and, wisely for his self-esteem, reserved time for writing and other independent activities. He continued to do research for his popular history of the dance, and sifted through his poetry until he had enough—and enough encouragement from friends—to submit a volume's worth for publication.

But both Scribner's and the Yale University Press turned down the collection, and on rereading the poems Lincoln agreed, with rather remarkable objectivity, that they weren't worth much after all: they "don't seem very good," he wrote in his diary. "I lack in relation to verse a kind of concentrated vision or continuous structure; it's all too rhetorical and the emotional content is not very interesting." Although Lincoln would continue to write poetry, it would be years before he thought they were of high enough quality to warrant publication.

As for the ballet *Tom*—as E. E. Cummings had been quick to rename it—it moved forward with considerable enthusiasm. Cummings was currently living on the edge of poverty. His adverse circumstances had made him more cantankerous than ever, and Lincoln had been finding him "petulant and fractious." But Cummings had long been a knowledgeable fan of ballet and he considered the Stowe novel a "great" book. Lincoln's offer of a fifty-dollar advance further sweetened the pot, and Cummings embarked with enthusiasm on writing the scenario; he even agreed that nothing in the ballet would be sung or spoken—according to Lincoln, "a great concession for him."

For *Tom's* decor Lincoln proposed the painter Franklin Watkins, whose recent show he'd found "very impressive"; to compose the music, he approached Virgil Thomson. Both men were interested, but Virgil made it clear that he'd need enough money to live on and announced, as well, that he "didn't propose to 'try out' for Balanchine." Yet Virgil was at least willing to play his String Quartet for Balanchine, who liked it; he also thought Watkins's show, which Lincoln took him to, "better than any other American painter he has so far seen."

There was even some preliminary talk about casting, with Gisella Caccialanza the likely candidate for Eliza and Balanchine willing to consider dancing the role of Tom himself. (There's no evidence that black dancers were considered for the roles, despite Lincoln's idealistic early announcement that he wanted to create a company that was 50 percent black; but then again, few blacks trained in ballet were then available, opportunity having long been closed to them.) Adding to the excitement about *Tom*, Muriel, after reading Cummings's draft of the scenario, said that it "seemed to her already a classic" and that Cummings was American literature's "only trace of fragmentary genius." Lincoln, too, thought the script "very brilliant," and believed that *Tom* "could run a year in New York." Even Dimitriev joined in the general enthusiasm, though when Eddie was shown the initial scenario, he said the weather "was too hot for him to concentrate on such difficult writing."

Yet the entire project, despite all the fanfare and promise that initially attended it, ultimately foundered. Balanchine, disagreeing with the others, found Cummings's scenario merely literary, exemplifying a writer's concern for words, not a dancer's for movement. Cummings deeply resented the rejection but took comfort the following year in the scenario's publication as a well-received book.

Six weeks before the scheduled mid-June event at the Warburg estate, and just as preparations for it went into high gear, Gurdjieff arrived in New York. He'd been rumored for some eight months to be leaving Europe for good, but when he did finally appear at the end of April, the timing, from Lincoln's point of view, could hardly have been worse; as he wrote in his diary, "I've just about enough energy to concentrate on the Ballet and I can't afford to get into any new crises at this point." Gurdjieff's old disciple Payson Loomis, now disaffected, had been back in New York for some time and had again become friendly with Lincoln, telling him that he no longer had "interest in any cosmic system which depended upon the accidental possession of a certain amount of money for its survival."[4]

But Lincoln still felt greatly indebted to Gurdjieff and still very much under his influence. Though frantically busy, he tried to show up at least occasionally at the Child's cafeteria in Columbus Circle, which Gurdjieff, somehow fittingly, was using as a kind of office. At first sight of the old man, Lincoln, despite his annoyance, felt his depression giving way to "a swelling of emotional elevation," which he ascribed not personally to Gurdjieff but "to his energy."

He also went reluctantly to a number of "long and tedious" meetings at Gurdjieff's apartment in the Henry Hudson Hotel, where several dozen people listened to Gurdjieff's lengthy lament about money. He said that anyone who wanted any further association with him had to sell seven copies of his book, *The Herald of Coming Good* (a work he repudiated several months later, calling in all copies)—that is, everyone except for Muriel, "his oldest friend in America." Lincoln dozed through part of the meetings and yet felt "all of it was of the greatest interest"; in the same paradoxical Gurdjieffian spirit, he felt such "infinite agony of boredom" that he didn't want to be there—yet "surely [didn't] want to be anywhere else more."

During their first meeting alone at Child's, Gurdjieff told Lincoln that he found him "very sympathetic—and had need of $1,000 at once." Lincoln said it would be "impossible" for him to get it, that he was sorry but he was broke (which was true) and could do nothing. To which Gurdjieff replied that "he needed $300 at once." Again Lincoln said he "could not let him have it," but he would try and secure whatever he could. That ultimately turned out to be twenty-six dollars, one dollar more than he'd promised himself (in advance of Gurdjieff's arrival) to offer. Lincoln did worry "for thirty minutes about my obligation to him" and then "decided to hell with it."

Yet, still feeling guilty, he conferred with Payson Loomis. Both agreed they felt "respect and affection and exasperation" all at once for Gurdjieff, citing an earlier comment of Muriel's that he was "a person about whom it is fascinating but useless to conjecture." But even Muriel thought that Gurdjieff had become "more difficult," and none of the three "felt any particular desire in seeing him." By June, Gurdjieff was off for an extended visit to other disciples, Olgivanna and Frank Lloyd Wright at Taliesin in Wisconsin. But he would return to New York the following winter.

It was now only weeks before the scheduled performance at the Warburg estate. By mid-May *Mozartiana* was looking very promising in rehearsals, though Lincoln heard through a third party that Virgil Thomson was telling people that originally Bébé Bérard's "sketches entirely directed Balanchine," who therefore deserved little credit for the ballet's success. "Virgil is so wicked, so malicious," Lincoln wrote in his diary, yet he was also "unaffected and kind, hard as nails but gentle. He is still an egg with a feather on it but I like him just the same."

As Balanchine polished *Mozartiana*, he also continued to work on *Serenade* (as he would for years), while *Dreams*, rather than a revised *Songes*, began to emerge as the likely candidate for the third ballet, even though it was still very much a work-in-progress. At rehearsals various guests would insist on giving Lincoln their usually dogmatic, often contradictory opinions. When John Maynard Keynes and Lydia Lopokova dropped by, she offered a more encompassing analysis than anyone had invited, telling Lincoln that Balanchine "never finishes anything; not quite a genius; yes, a touch; oh, George? I love him." Then turning to Muriel, who happened to be present that day: "You ever tasted his borscht?" Balanchine himself, curiously, confided to Lincoln one day that (so Lincoln wrote in his diary) "ballet in the Diaghilev, Petipa idiom is dead. *Serenade, Mozartiana, Songes,* all that with him is only commercial, of no interest. One must find new ideas," he said, "although the exercises are valuable in themselves."

By late May, Balanchine also had started working on a new ballet, *Alma Mater,* based on a Yale-Harvard football game. Eddie Warburg had suggested the idea, and ended up being credited with the "scenario." His relative-by-marriage, Kay Swift, composed the music. In 1930 Kay had been the first woman to do a score for a Broadway musical comedy, *Fine and Dandy*, which had run for some 250 performances. High-spirited and gifted, she was well-traveled on the celebrity circuit and had become an intimate friend of George Gershwin's. (It was Gershwin who'd first been approached to write the score for *Alma Mater*, but pleading a heavy schedule, he'd suggested Kay Swift in his place.) She'd started on the score early in May, and everyone exclaimed that it was turning out "better than we'd dared hope," everyone that is but Lincoln, who thought it was "not good enough."

Eddie himself, meantime, had started to make waves again, proudly crediting psychoanalysis for his loud-voiced, heightened demands. At the school he even dared to go over Balanchine's head once and "correct" some of the students' steps, which Lincoln found "extremely objectionable." Then, as wrangling began over a new set of contracts, Eddie announced that as the chief investor he had no intention of sharing any potential profits with the others. This drove everyone else into their lifetime postures for managing stress: Dimitriev flew into a towering rage, Balanchine into a trance state of indifference, and Lincoln into exhausted despair over his own unspecified inadequacies (and Eddie's "selfishness").

Eddie claimed that Balanchine and Dimitriev were "quite well paid," and pointed to the fact that Balanchine had just bought himself a new Dodge car. At the same time Eddie began to make various budget cuts for the upcoming performance at the Warburg estate, some of them on essential items like pianos and lights. Then came an unexpected showdown over *Dreams*. Dimitriev said it wasn't ready and shouldn't be shown, especially since William Dollar was having trouble with his leg and ankle. But Eddie insisted it be part of the program. A compromise of sorts was eventually reached: they would present substantial excerpts from *Songes*, *Dreams*, and *Serenade*—and *Mozartiana* in its entirety.

On June 4, just a few days before the scheduled presentation, new contracts were also completed—with Balanchine and Dimitriev for three years, with Pierre Vladimiroff for two. During the signing, Lincoln felt extremely nervous: "It seemed to me like an incredible assumption of responsibility on everybody's part." Two days later Lincoln accompanied Balanchine to Bloomingdale's, where they spent hours, "more or less fruitlessly," while Balanchine tried to make up his mind about the men's costumes for *Serenade*. "He has a spoiled boy's vanity," Lincoln wrote in his diary, "which makes him at once refuse any given suggestions. One must approach him always from behind: even this [is] no cinch as there are always more than two alternatives. Dimitriev says he was not this way until London, 1930 and Copenhagen, where he made a great deal of money and spent all of it."

Eddie Warburg, meantime, had already bought ready-made garments for $2.50 apiece, which, when they arrived, were "adjudged absolutely hopeless." But there was no time left to ask Helene Pons, their new costumier, to come up with anything. Lincoln, on his own, finally found suitable shirts for the male dancers at Abercrombie's. At 3:00 p.m. on the afternoon of June 7, the entire school left for Woodlands, the Warburg estate. Lincoln took Dimitriev and his recently arrived wife, the dancer Kyra Blanc, in his car, and they talked anxiously about the threatening weather and the likelihood that the Warburgs would provide very little food and that it would be very bad. And who would actually show up in the audience? Would the Rockefellers really appear, as they had said they would?

When they arrived at the Warburg mansion, no one seemed in residence; it had the air, Lincoln wrote in his diary, "of a castle deserted before the onslaught of invaders." Eddie, they were told, was off delivering a speech at the Westchester County Center. Then the weather abruptly turned colder, and they "ransacked" the house for overcoats, sweaters, and bathrobes. After that they unpacked and hung up the costumes. Finally a photographer from *Vogue* appeared and took pictures of the cast of *Dreams* in costume. Then one of the girls started to cry, another hurt her foot, and Caccialanza tripped and fell.

Some food eventually appeared, but it was, as predicted, "not nearly enough and very poor." The students "looked cold and peaked and were hungry," and Lincoln feared "a revolution." Balanchine, who rarely lost his temper, became very angry. He said later that he would "invite Eddie to a Russian restaurant, and show him how one eats." Dimitriev cautioned him not to: it would "cause a scandal." At that point Eddie himself finally appeared, and, according to Lincoln, "was furious with all of us," for reasons unspecified.

By then it had gotten dark and they did a run-through in full costume of *Mozartiana*, after which everyone's spirits turned around. The lights didn't go very well, due, apparently, to Eddie's last-minute budgetary spasm, but the flooring on the outdoor stage that had been erected proved excellent, and the ballet, in Lincoln's view, "looked heavenly; very brilliant, and the kids were superb." Vladimiroff was so enthusiastic about Marie-Jeanne's dancing in the "Ave Verum" that he said he was reminded of the debut of Pavlova. And Lincoln thought Erick Hawkins was not only "sweet" and "enthusiastic" but downright "inspired" in his dancing.

Among the few disappointments, at least to Lincoln, was Holly Howard in the pas de deux: she was "accurate" but "without a trace of emotional warmth." The other disappointment was Felix Warburg, who watched some of the rehearsal, but seemed to Lincoln "pre-occupied and absent—as if he'd received secretly some bad news." But Balanchine said he was "pleased enough," and that was what counted. They headed back to New York.

The next morning dawned gray and threatening, though when they called the weather bureau, it kept predicting "fair and warmer." So they headed off again for the Warburgs' home in Greenburgh. But an intermittent drizzle set in, and after they arrived, the weather—and the decision about whether to proceed—kept changing. Three separate times tarpaulins were put over the pianos and the stage and then taken off again. Balanchine, according to Lincoln, seemed "wholly indifferent" and went off in his car to get some decent food. Suddenly the weather turned fair again, and Balanchine couldn't be found. Vladimiroff started the rehearsal, but then it suddenly began to rain again. When Balanchine reappeared he calmly said, "God's will be done."

By this time, guests had started to arrive and finally, at 8:40 p.m., the decision was made to go forward with the performance. Eddie Warburg made a little speech of welcome that Lincoln found so embarrassing that he moved out of earshot. The dancers did manage to get all the way through *Mozartiana* and though Lincoln thought it "looked lovely," the unresponsive audience was "ridiculously stupid." He was especially annoyed with Mina, E. E. Cummings, and Marion Morehouse, who sat in the first row and, apparently drunk, were "very objectionable." Anyway, Lincoln felt grateful that they'd been "permitted to finish one complete thing," and the dancers began to prepare for *Serenade*. But then the rain started up again, this time in earnest, and the guests were hurried into the house.

The guests, but not the company. Eddie, by deliberate intent, not oversight, had decreed that the dancers would not mingle with his family's distinguished friends, but would instead take their dinner in the cement garage. The Russians, who'd been wined and dined by royalty and the smart set throughout Europe, took this, understandably, as a grave offense. Vladimiroff, who apparently thought the garage doubled as a stable, said that Eddie "must be crazy," that he had "never yet eaten with the horses and didn't propose to now." To make matters more difficult—and nearly causing Lincoln to faint—Mina got so drunk that she stuffed three initialed Warburg towels in her bosom and pranced about extracting them for one and all to see. Cummings, too, had tied on one of his "screaming anti-social" drunks, and Marion was unable to control him.

Now it was Eddie's turn to become furious. He told Lincoln to remove his guests from the house, saying that "the servants were going to have another hard day tomorrow." As soon as the dancers had gotten something to eat (in the garage), they all headed back to New York. On the ride down Dimitriev said "he hoped to God it would pour with rain tomorrow," when they were scheduled to perform a second time at the Warburg estate. Lincoln tried to persuade him that "Eddie was not mean or nasty," that his domineering, difficult mother, Frieda, had been responsible for their mistreatment. Dimitriev seemed unpersuaded. At 3:00 a.m. Mina, still drunk, called Lincoln to apologize for her behavior; though he could often be hard on Mina, Lincoln decided (perhaps because he himself had gotten rowdy-drunk often enough at parties) to forgive her.

By the next morning Lincoln had managed to recast the bizarre events of the previous night as "comic," though when he met the Russians for lunch, Eugenie Ouroussow said that it had all reminded her of the enforced travels she'd endured after the Bolshevik revolution: "waiting on boxes in harbors for steamers to come in," and the like. At 5:00 p.m., though the weather again seemed threatening, they all headed back up to Greenburgh, this time bringing their own sandwiches. The "wondrous" flooring on the stage was now "sticky," but they went ahead and started to rehearse. At the last minute it was decided to open the program with *Dreams*, though everyone agreed it wasn't ready, and to follow with *Serenade* and then *Mozartiana*. As the performance began, it again started to rain and the piano keys became so wet that the two accompanists could barely play. Yet taken as a whole, the evening came off well enough. Lincoln thought *Serenade* looked "very lovely," with Marie-Jeanne outstanding and "the boys OK in red pants and brownish polo shirts." *Mozartiana*, too, was beautifully danced except for a brief mishap during the ending. Despite the difficult conditions all around, "everybody behaved extremely well."

The audience was larger than the previous night and included Alfred Barr, Julien Levy ("as disagreeable as he could be"), and Nelson Rockefeller, who "seemed impressed." Alan Blackburn looked over at Lincoln as if to say "I had deflected the Warburg millions from the Museum of Modern Art." The previous evening, Chick Austin had turned up, been "very sweet," and had generously invited the fledgling troupe to perform at Hartford in December. He and Lincoln had for some time been gradually feeling their way back to a rapprochement. Immediately after the debacle in the fall, Lincoln had written to say that Chick's resentment was "more than justified." At the time Chick wasn't ready to resume contact, but by late April the two had spoken and by mid-May Chick had dropped in to watch a class for the first time, thereby cementing their reconciliation.

After the performance, members of the company left "speedily" for New York and had their own "noisy and amiable" banquet at Chesney's restaurant, where they toasted one another and even the weather, and Balanchine "made a little speech sober and comic ending up with 'we only have one Dollar [William] but soon hope to have many dollars.' " Eddie Warburg appeared, which was in itself a conciliatory gesture, and Lincoln succeeded in persuading Dimitriev to be agreeable, on the grounds of "general utility." Lincoln himself felt that some additional financial support would result from the two performances, and he was glad that at least a few people had been able to see what they'd been up to—and "doubly glad it is over."

CHAPTER THIRTEEN

The Left

(1934)

IN THE MONTH following the performances at the Warburg estate, the
four principals—Eddie, Lincoln, Dimitriev, and Balanchine—had an
intense round of talks about future plans, with the usual leitmotif of angry
accusations and flaring tempers, mostly between Eddie and Dimitriev.
Eddie announced that he might want to set up a production company with
himself as its director general that would be completely independent of
the school. Dimitriev made it clear that he wouldn't participate even if
asked; he had no intention of doing the difficult, behind-the-scenes work
while Eddie reaped the public acclaim. Both Dimitriev and Balanchine
already resented Eddie's habit of going around town talking about "*my*
ballet school*"; nor were they exactly pleased when a *World-Telegram* story
appeared with the headline WARBURG'S BALLET. When they confronted
him, he insisted that *he* was news but that the school was not.

That aside, Dimitriev simply didn't believe that they were ready to
form a company. He urged instead that they concentrate on reworking
Mozartiana, *Dreams*, *Serenade*, and *Errante*, on completing *Alma Mater*,
and then perhaps starting on Balanchine's idea for a ballet based on Josef
Lanner's waltzes, with Lincoln as the possible librettist. In Dimitriev's
view they could still consider doing single engagements, if offers came in,
but for the moment he felt they had "nothing overtly remarkable to
show," that it would take another year before they had a repertory and
troupe actually ready for anything like a "season" or even a truncated
tour.[1]

But Eddie persisted, and would darkly threaten that if he didn't get his
way, he would withhold further financial support, even though he was
under contract to provide twelve thousand dollars a year for another three
years (and Lincoln eight). Lincoln could barely contain his anger at
Eddie's "impossible" behavior, at how "blind" and self-serving he could
be. But some evidence does exist that Balanchine may have subtly encouraged Eddie in his wish to form a separate company—a company that
might, after all, provide him with the opportunity to create new ballets.

Balanchine told Eddie at least once (according to Lincoln's diary), that
"he must show some work and if there is no chance of doing the ballets
then he must get other work." This was conceivably a ploy, encouraged by

Dimitriev, to extract more cash from Eddie in order to polish and perform the ballets they already had, rather than designed to encourage his scheme for creating a production company. But more likely Balanchine was feeling frustrated at not being able to create and show more new work. He'd been getting an increasing number of outside offers, including one to direct the dances for a new Paramount picture starring the comic Jimmy Savo, and also to create movement for two operas that Stokowski was scheduled to conduct in Philadelphia. According to their recently signed three-year contracts, Balanchine required permission to take outside work, but that would almost certainly be given—not solely to keep him content and committed but also to enhance the reputation of the school by building up his public prestige.

The antagonism between Lincoln and Eddie wasn't a one-sided affair. Eddie felt just as aggrieved as Lincoln did, although, or so it appears, with less justification. At one point he got so upset with Lincoln that he complained to—of all people—Muriel. "I wish I could figure out," he sententiously wrote her, "what is going to happen to Lincoln . . . it seems the more business that has to be done, the more useless he becomes"—this, at the very time when Dimitriev was complaining that "Eddie does nothing," and soon after Eddie had gone abroad for several months. Eddie professed to Muriel that he was "as fond of [Lincoln]. . . as ever and [I] appreciate his mind, his enthusiasm and his artistic integrity. But all these qualities are useless if they cannot be brought down and adjusted to existence." "I wish," he added, with a touch of sanctimony, "it were possible for him to figure out his place and his responsibility in this organization."

This particular complaint from Eddie might have been more applicable at an earlier point, when Lincoln had felt hurt at being consistently sidestepped on artistic matters and had been having trouble carving out a suitable role for himself at the school. But recently he'd been much more involved with the creative process, frequently suggesting composers, set designers, and possible scenarios for ballets, several of which seemed, however briefly, to catch Balanchine's attention.

Recently, too, Lincoln had taken on a whole new responsibility: getting individual donors to sponsor individual scholarship students. Dimitriev confidently predicted an enrollment by the end of 1934 of some hundred students (many of them paying thirty dollars a month), but even so, his eye forever fixed on the profit margin, he argued for reducing the number of full scholarship students from twenty to ten. Lincoln "hated to do this," but Dimitriev insisted that "too many people thought it was easy to get into the School," which affected its prestige and future potential.

With Balanchine in agreement, Dimitriev's scholarship cuts were scheduled to go into effect in the fall. Ruthanna Boris and Erick Hawkins were among those henceforth denied scholarship money (though both continued on, Hawkins with financial help from Lincoln and by taking a tutoring job in the mornings). Others lived in poverty; one girl fainted in class after not having eaten in two days. Lincoln became determined to find a way to provide more aid for them. He came up with a list of twenty-three people, hoping he could persuade at least ten to "adopt" a pupil for three hundred dollars to cover them for a ten-month period (and he set aside most of his lunch dates to achieve that goal). He also decided to give a new series of lectures at the school on the history and development of classical dancing, charging twelve dollars for the set or $1.50 at the door, with all receipts going to the scholarship fund.

The tangled set of relationships among the school's principal players continued to evolve and shift. Between Lincoln and Balanchine there was the least overt friction, and almost never raised voices; polite distance became their standard modus operandi. Nonetheless, even between those two tensions did sometimes accumulate, though remaining mostly buried—a strategy that came much more naturally to Balanchine than to Lincoln. Balanchine was temperamentally "cool" and concealed, whereas Lincoln was very nearly his opposite, hyperbolic (and hyper), given to the sort of passionate, exaggerated outbursts that would have been anathema to the emotionally remote Balanchine.

As for Balanchine and Dimitriev, they, like Eddie and Lincoln, had been drifting still farther apart. Dimitriev had never hesitated in the past to make harsh remarks in private about Balanchine's "laziness and selfishness," but he now told Lincoln that he "sees nothing of Balanchine," that he "is always out with his car and new friends," that he was "insufferable and would listen to no criticism"—another reason, so Dimitriev claimed, that he "had no interest in producing ballets." Lincoln caught wind of a rumor that may further explain Dimitriev's mounting resentment: his wife, Kyra Blanc, who was considerably younger than he, apparently loved sex—"she is young, why not?" Lincoln wrote in his diary—and also a variety of sexual partners. She'd apparently developed an attraction for Balanchine himself, who, so he told Lincoln, "keeps strictly away from her."

In contrast, Dimitriev and Lincoln had recently become somewhat more cordial, each more willing than in the past to credit the other's talents and contributions. They now, as Lincoln wrote in his diary, often "plotted our policies" together. That shift may have owed a lot to Louis Kirstein's high opinion of Dimitriev; during his occasional visits to the school, and his active participation in the most recent round of contract negotiations, Louis had come to view Dimitriev as a positive influence, a man who, despite his irascibility, was reliable, hardworking, and basically honorable. Louis's assessment may have helped to soften Lincoln's attitude toward Dimitriev, allowing him better to appreciate the central contribution he'd made toward holding the school together. The two would never become real friends, or even firm allies, and periodically they'd fall back into acrimony. But at a minimum, something like mutual respect had begun to develop.

Early in July the school closed its doors for six weeks to allow for studio renovations and expansion, and people scattered in various directions on vacation. On July 12, Lincoln and Balanchine were driving up toward the theatrical designer Aline Bernstein's place in Armonk, and talking about not doing a ballet based on the Lanner waltzes after all, because of *The Great Waltz* extravaganza due to open soon at the Center Theater—when suddenly, just as Lincoln had turned off the road to head to the Bernstein place on the lake, Balanchine gripped Lincoln's arm and became "rigid and red." For an instant Lincoln thought he might be playacting or, possibly, that he'd been stung by some bug. But then Balanchine's eyes glazed over, he started slavering at the mouth, and tried "to stiffen himself out of the car."

Lincoln shouted out of the window to two boys passing by to ask directions to a hospital, but the boys got frightened and ran off. Lincoln drove frantically on and turned up a hill that he thought led to the Bernstein house, but in the turmoil he'd lost his way. To make matters worse the car suddenly stalled, Balanchine turned violent, and looked as if he were dying or going insane. Lincoln "fought him wildly in the car"; Balanchine broke Lincoln's glasses, cut him on his hand and arms, and destroyed the hand brake with his foot. A maid appeared from a nearby house, and a distraught Lincoln yelled for her to get help. But she apparently thought the car had been stolen and promptly called the state troopers. In the meantime Lincoln "tried to hobble [Balanchine]. . . with his belt; he fell out of the car into the dirt-road, barking his shins."

Then, blessedly, the state troopers arrived and took Balanchine into the nearby house. A doctor was quickly called and he administered morphine, breaking the needle in Balanchine's arm as he struggled. At this point Mina had somehow been notified, and she, too, arrived on the scene. The doctor said "it might be epilepsy," but "it looked more like hysteria." He had to leave almost immediately for another appointment, but Aline Bernstein, who'd also been called, sent over a Dr. Irving Clark, and she herself appeared soon after. Balanchine then had a second but less violent attack, turned yellow and gray, trembled, and then seemed rigid. He was unable to speak and didn't recognize Lincoln or the others.

By then an ambulance arrived from Mount Kisco and "tore back" to the local hospital. There Dr. Clark said "it could be [a] brain tumor . . . [or] possibly meningitis." Lincoln was at least grateful that the attack hadn't occurred in New York or during a rehearsal; this way it could be kept secret from nearly everyone. But he did call Dimitriev, vacationing on Lake George, who said that "nothing had ever happened like it before to Balanchine," nor were comparable symptoms part of his family history.

The day after the attack Balanchine seemed "sane and unparalyzed." But its origin was still a mystery. What exactly had gone wrong? If the cause of the seizure couldn't be determined, how could a recurrence be prevented? When Dimitriev and Vladimiroff arrived the following day, "they corroborated the theory of hysteria," blaming the episode on the fact that Balanchine "keeps everything to himself, has no intimates." But the assorted specialists who were now called in believed the attack had a primarily physical, not emotional, basis—though as before, their diagnoses conflicted.

One prominent specialist felt, before seeing Balanchine, that he "unquestionably" had "a very serious brain disorder." But then after examining him and noting no serious aftereffects, promptly shifted the diagnosis to "toxemia and auto-intoxication"—essentially meaningless terms equivalent to saying, "he has toxic substances in his blood." The specialist did make one optimistic suggestion: the seizure may well have been induced by the "health" injections Balanchine was currently getting, on the recommendation of his close friend, the wealthy Lucia Davidova, of parathyroid and adrenaline; such injections were known to have a convulsive effect on dogs. Everyone seemed delighted with that explanation, since injections could be stopped and the problem permanently solved.

But Balanchine had spit up some blood in his sputum, and Dr. Clark, while not entirely ruling out an emotional or toxemic component, wasn't satisfied that a full diagnosis had yet been made (nor, needless to say, was Lucia Davidova, who insisted that Balanchine suffered from epilepsy). To make matters still more confounding, Eddie Warburg, who paid no visit himself, sent up Balanchine's previous physician, Dr. Geyelin, who announced that they were dealing with "a brain disease," possibly an "incipient tumor." Throughout those days of competing diagnoses and authoritative pronouncements, Balanchine somehow managed to remain more or less "cheerful," though worried about a recurrence and "confused" at all the conflicting advice. Orders were given to prevent any additional people from seeing or telephoning him.

In the meantime Dr. Clark sent him for new X-rays, and what they showed was "a dark spot on his head, possibly a thinner bony structure . . . [which could] cause pressure," as well as two active TB lesions. Clark advised rest in a sanitarium and pneumothorax treatment (meaning collapsing a lung, then a standard procedure for treating TB). When Dimitriev went to talk to Balanchine about the latest medical recommendations, Balanchine, according to Lincoln, was "disagreeable" with him. Yet later he talked "gently" with Lincoln and Mina, telling them that he thought Clark was a "fool," that the blood in his sputum came from his teeth, not his lungs, and that—having seen people die from the pneumothorax treatment while at a European sanitarium—he absolutely refused to have the procedure. He would, however, agree to a prolonged rest if a suitable place could be found.

The reasonable attitude Balanchine adapted toward Lincoln and Mina contrasted sharply with his contentious one toward Dimitriev, who reacted with anger of his own. He irately announced that Balanchine was "spoiled," that he, Dimitriev, and only he, had stood by him in all his illnesses and crises, and that this current "ingratitude" was simply "too much"; he was "finished," he said, and forever. He wasn't; everyone was familiar with Dimitriev's outbursts of temper, and everyone knew that they passed. But both Mina and Vladimiroff separately warned Lincoln that he had become too "good-humored" with Dimitriev and needed to be more on his guard against him. Mina shrewdly predicted that Dimitriev's insistent focus on the school and his refusal to encourage plans actually to produce ballets for public showing had made Balanchine determined to become free of him.

Vladimiroff confirmed her view. He told Lincoln that in Paris, Dimitriev had been known as "Rasputin," that he had had a "sinister" influence on Balanchine, thwarting many of his plans and turning him against Diaghilev—an accusation difficult to assess since Vladimiroff and Dimitriev had been antagonists. But what does seem clear is that by mid-1934, Balanchine had reached the point where he "wants to breathe alone . . . to be independent." Lincoln had already begun to sense that Balanchine was "determined to split with Dimitriev," and he took both Mina and Vladimiroff's words seriously, vowing to put himself back on guard against Dimitriev's assorted machinations.

The immediate concern, now that Balanchine felt and looked better, was to find a nearby health farm where he could recuperate. Balanchine told Lincoln that "he wanted a wife to take care of him," but at the moment he was between wives and girlfriends. They first tried a hilltop rest camp near Mount Kisco, but Balanchine was refused admittance because of his active tuberculosis. Their second choice, Cranker's Health Farm, on the opposite side of Mount Kisco, struck Lincoln as fairly primitive, with iron bedsteads and grimy mattresses and Cranker himself "a kind of unprofessional male nurse." He himself wouldn't have stayed there, but Balanchine was willing to. The doctors at least agreed about the length of time needed for rest: four to eight weeks, depending on how quickly he improved.

Lincoln, with great relief, went off to recover for a week at Ashfield, all the while expecting a telephone call saying that "Balanchine had escaped or something." While staying at Mina's, Lincoln had a conditional reconciliation with Archie MacLeish, her neighbor. Lincoln had been feeling alienated from him for some time; he'd decided (as he put it in his diary) that MacLeish lacked "greatness in his poetry or person." As Lincoln's own politics moved further left, moreover, he'd come to disdain Archie's "smug" centrism.

On top of everything else, Archie had the previous spring done the scenario for a de Basil ballet, *Union Pacific*, that Lincoln had found "of no conceivable interest of any kind." In one of his spasms of bluntness, he'd told Archie his opinion in nearly those exact words—except for adding "pointless and vapid." Archie had defended the ballet as "a good show—vulgar and brash," and had said at the time that "it took the taste of 'Three Saints in Four Acts' out of his mouth," presumably the taste of "effeteness." Mina, soon after, told Lincoln that Archie was being "jealous and nasty" about both the ballet and him, and had said "he can't imagine anyone taking the ballet seriously as a form of art." Lincoln had decided he didn't "ever want to see" Archie again.

But during his stay at Ashfield in late July, Archie called him up and they agreed to meet. Archie made it clear that given fascism, he felt "one must be unequivocally on the side of socialism." That helped soften Lincoln up. Then, as they were parting, Archie asked him "not to get him wrong ever, or get mixed up about him." He loved him very much, Archie said, and always respected his opinion. As Lincoln wrote in his diary, "he made my heart melt."

By early August, Balanchine was looking "very fine" and feeling "extremely cheerful." He continued on at the Cranker place for several more weeks, and Lincoln, along with others (including Eddie, once), continued to visit, to check on his progress, and to worry over whether the new burst of good health could sustain itself. Balanchine acknowledged privately to Lincoln that before the seizure "there were some things that were troubling him, private things," but though Lincoln tried, he couldn't get Balanchine to say *what* things.

Once back in New York, Lincoln and Dimitriev had a long talk about making changes in school policy when it reopened in late August. Dimitriev wanted to retain only the fewest possible number of scholarships, a policy Lincoln rejected. But he was more willing to accept Dimitriev's view that henceforth "the Ballet be entirely in the hands of Balanchine and separate from the School, if and when he can do it," while he, Dimitriev, would reorganize the school around "the most elaborately instructive lines"—details unspecified.

At just this time Muriel was making her final preparations to leave, at long last, for an extended visit to the Soviet Union. Over the past few months, as if reading from her will, she'd been delivering herself of oracular opinions (not that she'd ever been shy about offering her views) that Lincoln was finding more and more grating. She told him that over the past three years he'd been "man-to-man haunted—not queer," and she dismissed his infatuation with Bosco Dunham as "a weakness of character." She also insisted that he was "so idea-ridden that a simple impulse never got through." Yet in truth, she went on, his personality was at base "emotional rather than intellectual," though most people, and in particular Eddie Warburg, believed the opposite. Muriel had hit on a salient element in Lincoln's personality. Wishing to be an artist and equipped with enough talent to make the wish seem plausible, he'd also been blessed/cursed with an intellect so keen that analysis rather than creation seemed to come more spontaneously to him, dividing his attention, preventing his diffuse gifts from maturing.

Two weeks before her scheduled departure, Muriel told Lincoln "how glad everybody would be" when she was finally gone, since "no one would have to feel, think, love or hate any more with the stimulus of her presence removed." Lincoln agreed with her, but thought that was no excuse for her recent "footloose philandering, her impatience and monomania." "I more than love or hate her," he wrote in his diary, "yet I'll be glad enough when she's gone—at least a year's vacation, not from her but from my dependence on her as a point of reference."

On the evening of August 7 Muriel gave herself a farewell party, a "pretty lugubrious" affair, according to Lincoln, because of all the painful good-byes. After it was over and he was back home, his phone rang at 4:30 a.m.; picking it up, he heard only Muriel's "faint, faint 'goodnight.' " The next morning he had a late breakfast with her in her garden: "She was weeping steadily and uncontrollably." Lincoln ran out and got some champagne and Muriel put on a black dress and a new yellow hat with three feathers in it. They took a taxi, in silence, to the boat, where some twenty friends had gathered. Lincoln waited until nearly everyone had left, then kissed her good-bye. She told him "not to get married until she was back with me on the same continent. Only after I'd left the dock did I realize how much I would miss her."

A month after his attack Balanchine announced he was now well and wanted to leave the Cranker Health Farm. He was persuaded to stay just a bit longer—and the very next day, had another attack. Lincoln left at once for the farm, his blood "completely chilled and fearing the worst." But the attack turned out to be much milder than the first. Still, Drs. Clark and Geyelin had earlier agreed that should Balanchine have a recurrence, brain X-rays would be necessary, though the disagreeable procedure then involved removing brain fluid. Dimitriev argued against that tack, convinced it would lay Balanchine out flat. He was already, Lincoln wrote in his diary, "frightened and whipped," and would, for once, "do anything that he was told to do." But Lincoln agreed with Dimitriev, and they decided to take Balanchine instead for examination at the Neurological Institute at Broadway and 168th Street.

At the institute a Dr. Ehrlich told them that Balanchine might have tuberculosis of the brain—yet another diagnosis to add to an accumulating pile. "Everyone says something different," Lincoln wrote disconsolately in his diary. Dimitriev took the reins decisively: He told Balanchine that there was nothing wrong with him, and that they would take him the following day to Spring Lake, on the Jersey coast, where Vladimiroff and his recently arrived wife, the dancer Felia Doubrovska, were vacationing. Dr. Clark agreed to the plan; he said that given how dangerous brain surgery was, they could afford to wait (the various other doctors were on vacation and unreachable).

The next day, on their way to the Vladimiroffs', Dimitriev, Balanchine, and Lincoln stopped off in Manhattan to inspect the enlarged quarters for the school that had been constructed over the summer, and Balanchine declared himself delighted with what he saw. In a further effort, perhaps, to normalize a difficult situation, the three then went out to dinner and to see a performance of *Faust*. Balanchine said he "adored bad music," that "it's a great relief to be bathed in its familiar sounds." They stayed for two acts, with Lincoln keeping his eyes glued on Balanchine throughout the performance; when he scratched his arm at one point, Lincoln steeled himself for the imminent arrival of another attack; but it was only an itch.

Lincoln thought that Balanchine's second attack may well have been induced by "hysteria," since Balanchine had admitted to him that he "hideously feared a recurrence." He found further comfort in the knowledge that both attacks had been pre-signaled by numbness in Balanchine's hand, and that he now carried luminol in his pocket, which could quiet him immediately. Through Eugenie Ouroussow, Lincoln heard that a rumor was already making the rounds in London that Balanchine, like Nijinsky before him, had gone mad and been institutionalized.

After an overnight in the city, they headed out to the Vladimiroffs' at Spring Lake. Lincoln, still on the alert, noticed that Balanchine couldn't recall a name at once "and seemed to be slow" in general; he also thought "his gestures are much more extravagant and prolonged when he is mimicking someone in conversation." Since "slowness" and "extravagance" seem somewhat at odds, the recorded symptoms may well have reflected Lincoln's own supersensitive state more than any significant change in Balanchine's behavior.

Arriving at Spring Lake, Dimitriev told Balanchine to "leave behind all thoughts of illness." But Lincoln, for one, remained "jittery"; he feared Balanchine's "inevitable incapacitation" and "racked" his head, should the worst happen, for a way that would allow the school and the incipient troupe to continue. "O Lord," he wrote in his diary, "spare us one good year. Yours gratefully."

———————

Such fears went on the back burner when the school reopened at the end of August. Balanchine appeared looking "well and happy, a changed and healthy man." To Lincoln he seemed to have "obviously forgotten or put away from his mind most of what happened." But Balanchine confided to a friend (who then told Lincoln) that every so often he still heard Lincoln's voice screaming at him in the midst of his first seizure. Once told, Lincoln made a conscious point with Balanchine of "trying to be off-hand and not hold his glance over-long"—especially since Dr. Geyelin told Eddie Warburg that another attack "will happen again undoubtedly." It was only in early October that the generalized anxiety subsided: Dr. Geyelin examined Balanchine and said that he was "amazingly improved and quite OK."

Everyone went back into high gear. But with this contentious crew, that didn't necessarily mean high spirits, at least not for long. Too many axes were waiting to be ground, ruffled egos to be soothed, antithetical visions for the future to be sorted out. High on everyone's list of priorities was the unresolved issue of whether or not some sort of producing company should be attempted, and if so, how soon and under whose direction.

Early in September, Balanchine "gravely" stopped Lincoln in the lobby of the school and sat him down for a talk. It took Lincoln quite by surprise; he felt Balanchine had been avoiding him ("He has refused to go out with me ever since we returned from vacation, night after night, on one pretext or another"). Even now Balanchine sought not an intimate conversation involving an open airing of health concerns or thanks for Lincoln's devoted ministrations, but rather a professional one. "He told me," Lincoln later wrote in his diary, "what I could do if I had a lot of money; that is, a great season at the Metropolitan [Opera]: Stravinsky, Hindemith, Kurt Weill; all new works; Braque, Tchelitchev, Picasso. I listened, amazed at the obviousness of his idea, and the intensity of his tone. [I] became frightened that he was sickening because he had no chance to produce on his own."[2]

In a sense Lincoln was already a step ahead of him. Though he personally loathed John Erskine, the head of the Juilliard Foundation and musically one of the most powerful people in the country, Lincoln had been trying to cultivate him as a possible entrée to the Metropolitan's management. He also, the day after he and Balanchine talked, set up a meeting with Alexander Merovich, the Russian concert agent who handled, among others, Vladimir Horowitz and Nathan Milstein. Lincoln told Merovich point-blank that he "wanted Balanchine to be *maître de ballet* at the Metropolitan." How could that be accomplished? What did he need to do?

They concluded that Balanchine, still not well known in the United States, needed to be put in a position of sufficient prestige for the Metropolitan to decide to choose him. Merovich suggested that Balanchine somehow connect himself to the Philadelphia Opera's pending productions of *Carmen* and Gluck's *Iphigenia in Aulis*, or that Lincoln arrange an evening of ballet one night a week at the Hippodrome—both plausible enough ideas but hardly easy to carry off.

They also talked about Broadway as another possible route to prominence. Balanchine had recently been approached to do the dances for the Broadway comedy *Revenge with Music*, music by Arthur Schwartz and Howard Dietz and scenery and costumes by Aline Bernstein, but opinions varied as to whether he should accept the offer. Dimitriev, uncharacteristically, was favorably inclined, since it was agreed that all publicity would include, "of the School of American Ballet." But when Lincoln solicited Virgil Thomson's opinion, Virgil said they should "by no means" become involved with Broadway—or, for that matter, with the Metropolitan Opera or John Erskine.

Lincoln didn't think Virgil got the picture: "It was a question about Balanchine doing something; personally, he must do it." Virgil agreed that Balanchine had become ill because "he was thwarted." More than ill, Lincoln said: "He nearly died." "Oh yes," Virgil airily replied, "they sometimes do." In his opinion Balanchine should forgo Broadway and keep busy with doing "lots of small things." A disgusted Lincoln wrote in his diary that Virgil "didn't at all understand the situation."

Throughout these assorted pow-wows, Balanchine (so Lincoln wrote in his diary) was "as usual in such discussions, a little vague." But of course it was Balanchine who ultimately made the decision not to accept the Schwartz-Dietz offer, while characteristically failing to volunteer any particular reason for his decision.

Lincoln couldn't shake off Balanchine's words during their earlier talk: "What I could do if I had a lot of money." Tired of having to cater to the quixotic Eddie, still deeply worried about Balanchine's health and convinced that active ballet production would go a long way toward sustaining it, Lincoln decided to make a strenuous appeal to his parents for access to his own trust funds. Before doing so he'd already consulted with his brother, George, who was far more knowledgeable about family finances and about business matters in general. George told him that "we will all have a lot of cash one day and if a mere matter of $10,000 is holding me down from producing, I could perfectly easily take it from my principle without any bad effect."

With that assurance under his belt, Lincoln sent his parents a long letter that began by emphasizing that the school had now created "the nucleus of a splendid company—the best talent, one can fairly say, anywhere around"; it was time, he strongly implied, to show them off. But that would of course take money, even for a limited tour of a few colleges. To help make that feasible, and for assorted other expenses as well (like continuing to give handouts to five or six artist friends), "I must," Lincoln wrote, "have some money in my own name," and he asked for permission to use at least a portion of his capital. He insisted that the money would not be used simply as a stopgap measure, but rather would be put toward creating "a more and more stable foundation for a continuous institution." In his mind, he assured his parents, "we will come through with flying colors if we are given a tiny bit of chance. But up to that time I live in constant nervousness due to the fact that there's all the gasoline we need but damn little grease."

In response Louis paid another visit to the school and asked Dimitriev to send him all the incorporation papers as well as two budgets: their current one and a second that projected into the future. Dimitriev complied the very next day. Louis, acute businessman that he was, then proceeded to ask a variety of questions, ranging from who was authorized to sign checks to whether Lincoln was sufficiently protected in his shareholding rights. All of which made Lincoln exceedingly nervous: "Neurasthenically," he wrote in his diary, "I always think in my great guilt father will find some hideous flaw in the whole fabric of my enterprise and cease his support." Lincoln's affection for his father had always been threaded with dread of him; ironically, and perhaps predictably, he would himself, as a mature adult, inspire a comparable mix of affection and fear in others.

But in this instance, anyway, Louis was apparently satisfied that affairs were, thanks to Dimitriev, pretty much in order. He seems nonetheless to have decided—the evidence here is sketchy—that he would himself pay for most of Lincoln's increased obligations to the school rather than release any significant sum to Lincoln from his own trust funds. That included paying for Lincoln's previously promised but still unpaid contribution toward some new costumes, as well as his share of the summer's construction costs (which together came to about $1,500). Louis also bought his son an expensive forty-volume library of reference books on dance history, and a new projector and set of slides for his planned series of sixteen lectures, the income from which would go entirely to the school. And Rose, as she'd often done in the past, sent along an additional check of her own.

Lincoln appreciated his parents' continued generosity, but failure to gain access to his own money meant that the creation of any sort of producing company would still have to rely primarily on the unpredictable largesse of Eddie Warburg. And Eddie was still determined to run any show that got on the road. As they again began to toss around possibilities for setting up a ballet company and performing in public, Eddie remained insistent that he be its director general.

Lincoln thought that a bad mistake. He tried to persuade Eddie that it would cost him a great deal less money if he would utilize Dimitriev's skills and experience. But Eddie (as Lincoln wrote his father) "can't stand"

Dimitriev's "hard-boiled" ways, his "constantly talking about money, forcing hard terms, and being very strict." Lincoln further deplored the fact
that Eddie's assumption of the title director general had "managed pretty
thoroughly to discredit Mr. Dimitriev in the eyes of the students," which
in turn "has a bad effect on the School."

For his part, perhaps to save pride, Dimitriev declared himself totally
uninterested in producing ballets anyway. His focus, Dimitriev said, was
on the school, on consolidating its position and maximizing its profitabil-
ity. He began to make noises, as well, about starting a second school in
Hollywood, where he thought he could make a great deal of money. Yet
privately Dimitriev told Lincoln that he *did* want to put on ballets, "but
not until the moment something was certain."

And it was Balanchine's fault, he claimed, that that moment hadn't yet
arrived. He repeated to Lincoln a conversation he'd had with Balanchine
the previous day, when Dimitriev had purportedly berated him for having
"wasted everyone's time last year" by listening to Lucia Davidova, who
"told him he was a genius, he got a mania of genius and nothing happened." He also accused Balanchine, once again, of being "merely lazy: he
gave correct lessons, but without a trace of enthusiasm . . . he seemed to
have no interest in his work." Lincoln, in fact, had been feeling much the
same of late about Balanchine's teaching (and "it worries me," he wrote in
his diary). However, he ascribed Balanchine's seeming lack of interest not
to "laziness" but to his feeling frustrated at his lack of creative outlets. But
in Dimitriev's view, Lincoln and Balanchine were "very alike," in the sense
that both "would start something very hot and enthusiastic and then let it
drop."

Dimitriev told Lincoln that Balanchine had taken his stern lecture "all
in good part," and they were once again working together harmoniously.
More likely, Balanchine had simply retreated to a lifetime strategy of
seeming to acquiesce in order to avoid confrontation. But at least Dimitriev felt better, and he in fact now joined, despite his stated lack of
interest, in what became a running set of discussions about whether or not
to form a production company. He even worked out a tentative budget for
a possible "season," and one that wasn't, in Lincoln's view, "too damned
expensive." But Dimitriev continued to feel that Eddie was unreliable and
he therefore remained "bitterly realistic" about prospects; Lincoln did his
best "to hold him off Balanchine so as not to dash him too much."

Yet Lincoln, too, thought their prospects daunting—"very tough"
going, even if they forswore scenery and dropped the most expensive of
the potential ballets, *Errante*, from consideration. The Russian concert
agent, Merovich, agreed with him: besides, it was simply too late, he said,
to think of securing any bookings for 1934. And so after the prolonged
round of discussions, it was decided that the most feasible plan for the
moment was to rehearse three ballets in preparation for possible single

engagements, while letting Balanchine take any outside work that appealed to him—even though that risked Balanchine's temporary absence from the school and a possible split in their own incipient company.

Through his lawyer Balanchine learned that de Basil and Massine, who had returned with the Ballets Russes for another season in New York, were interested in talking to him about a possible reconciliation. Eager though Balanchine was for a creative outlet, he ignored the feeler—a gauge of his unrelenting anger at how badly they'd treated him earlier. Simultaneously, and apparently with Balanchine's knowledge, Lincoln published an article in the left-wing *New Theatre* magazine that burned all possible bridges to the Ballets Russes, mercilessly trashing both the company and Massine himself. He referred to the Ballets Russes's "unscrupulous direction"—meaning de Basil—"its overworked dancers, its second-hand repertory [and] its intense commercialism." As for Massine, Lincoln, having left his high esteem of a few years earlier far behind, dismissed him as "an intellectual rather than a spontaneous or musical composer . . . very conscious of what is good theatre, he often misses what is good dancing." Lincoln's enthusiasm for Massine when a younger man had fallen victim to his fervid allegiance to Balanchine.

Having destroyed any prospect, never very likely, of cooperation with the de Basil forces, Lincoln turned back to his onetime ally Chick Austin. The two men had been gradually growing closer again, and in October, they even shared a rowdy queer night out on the town—these days a rare indulgence for Lincoln. They went first to the Barrel House, a sailor hangout on Forty-second Street with (in Lincoln's words) "some nice-looking trade" in it. Then it was on to Jackie's, a dark little bar with a dance floor; Lincoln described the owner as a "made up screaming queer with a transient Canadian-Oxford accent . . . jangling with nerves." Chick called him "Pearl" and said "it was a real pleasure to hear someone . . . camp in the good old 1925 way." The night ended with a stop at a large queer bar on West Fifty-sixth Street, populated, as Lincoln put it, by a "new kind of thicker set and quieter fairy."

Chick offered Lincoln the Avery Memorial Theater at Hartford for the public debut of the new "producing company"—a generous offer, given how badly bruised Chick had felt the previous year. Grateful though he was, Lincoln initially thought the Avery's stage would prove too small and that not enough cash would be available to make a decent impression. But he was "afraid everything would be off if we didn't have at least one engagement," and after a round of discussions it was agreed that four performances would be given over a three-day period, December 6 through December 8. The program would consist of *Serenade* and *Mozartiana*, already shown to an invitation-only crowd at the Warburg estate, plus two world premieres of ballets on which Balanchine had been working: *Alma Mater* and, most recently, *Transcendence*.

Lincoln himself wrote the scenario for *Transcendence*, based on the life of the virtuoso Niccolò Paganini; it would be performed to music by Franz Liszt, as orchestrated by George Antheil, and with costumes designed by Franklin Watkins, who had just won the Carnegie International painting prize. Lincoln took Balanchine to Schirmer's music store on West Fifty-seventh Street, where he bought almost all of Liszt's published scores. A renewed sense of energy took hold all around. Warburg was to have his *Alma Mater*, Lincoln his *Transcendence*, and Balanchine, at last, his new ballets.

Pleasing though it was to have something tangible in the works, and for Lincoln personally to feel an active participant in the creative process, he was still prone to fits of anxiety about being "useless" and underemployed. "I've such a sense of guilt and disaster," he wrote in his diary, "that I think everything will stop at the drop of a hat." Both Dimitriev and Eddie were more than happy to feed Lincoln's insecurity. Eddie kept taunting him about his failure to carve out any particular role or set of responsibilities in the organization, while Dimitriev patronizingly told him "to bury . . . [himself] with publicity in the provinces"—which Lincoln dutifully promised to do, since in his own estimate he'd proved "inefficient" in his most recent project of securing a significant number of scholarships for students (though Alice de la Mar, a wealthy lesbian and a loyal friend to the school, did come through with two).

Lincoln's sometimes brusque, commanding outward presence would always make it difficult for people to give credence to his inner contradictions and conflicts. There was a comparable disconnect between his bouts of guilty self-accusation and his nonstop activity on a wide variety of fronts—though these traits are often two sides of the same coin. As powerfully energetic as Lincoln was, he often felt that he wasn't doing "enough" or not doing it well enough. This central conflict in his personality had long been in place and had multiple sources.

Despite the many ways his father had always encouraged him, Louis's drumbeat admonition over the years that a man who didn't earn his own living wasn't really a man was surely one significant ingredient in Lincoln's conflicted self-image. Perhaps, too, his sexuality played a role; within the circles of "high bohemia," where lusty sexual adventuring was, in these years, practically de rigueur, Lincoln usually carried off his bisexual attachments with aplomb; yet he was hardly secure enough about his erotic preference for men to discuss it openly with his parents—let alone be casually explicit about it with Balanchine.

What perhaps also contributed to Lincoln's periodic fits of deep self-recrimination was his plaguing inner struggle between wanting to be an "artist" and fearing he lacked sufficient talent in any single field to become one. A diary entry from early October 1934 succinctly conveys the fissure:

"Same split as usual: do I want to do something myself, i.e. write, paint—or collaborate? How much," he went on, "does the School actually mean to me? Relieved to find it means less in one way than I thought, in so much as I feel it is more stable. But I have little or no connection with it basically. Do I want to have? Yes."

Yet at the same time he wanted to write his poems and prepare his lectures, to plot possible novels and occasionally sketch, to complete his history of the dance (now well advanced), and—once more of mounting concern to him—to become more active in left-wing politics. He'd recently been more drawn than ever to the concerns of the Left—while trying not to put both feet firmly inside the Communist Party door. Yet by late 1934 Lincoln's flirtation with the party deepened; it was neither trivial nor did it much partake of romantic posturing. He told Payson Loomis at one point that he preferred the "efficacy of the Communist doctrine over all other policy." And during this period he went a number of times to Communist-sponsored meetings, especially to those called by the International Labor Defense to disseminate information about the spreading textile strike.[3]

He also became friendly during this period with Herbert Kline and Leo Hurwitz of the radical publication *New Theatre*, and they suggested that the best way Lincoln could help the movement would be to organize "a big pageant ballet with massed workers' groups," to be called *Red Hydra* and performed, they suggested, at the Civic Repertory Theater. Lincoln was "elated" at the idea of a ballet "full of revolutionary and comradely zeal," and devoted himself to making it happen.

For a time, that is. Not only were the logistics and cost overwhelming, but opposition to Lincoln's involvement in the project arose within party ranks. In particular Edna Ocko, a dancer as well as the dance critic for *New Theatre*, found a major flaw with his scenario: he'd failed to show Communism "growing parallel with the growth of Social Democracy." Ocko had in fact been against him "as an intruder" from the start, and others within the party also criticized him for being too "personally attached" to his own script. Lincoln soon decided to back out, but he didn't give up the hope of using dance "as a revolutionary medium . . . to enlarge a rapprochement with the audience . . . to set Balanchine on a more apocalyptic idea."

While the pageant still seemed a possibility, Lincoln told Balanchine about it—a surprising move, given the Russian's well-known bitterness toward revolutionary politics, and the tacit way he and Lincoln had previously avoided all such discussions. Predictably Balanchine responded to the pageant idea by telling Lincoln that the subject would be appropriate for the Soviet Union but not for the United States, and he advised Lincoln not "to get mixed up with" politics.

In the arts, of course, Balanchine was audacity itself; the censorship of artistic experimentation that he'd earlier experienced under Soviet authorities had been a paramount force leading him to seek exile. Nor was

Balanchine indifferent to human suffering; a little later in life, he would dedicate performances to Italian earthquake relief and would personally buy bulletproof vests for New York policemen. But after his experiences in Soviet Russia, Balanchine was hostile to any and all encompassing political ideologies—though not to religious ones.

Lincoln's father could hardly have agreed more with Balanchine's advice to his son about avoiding politics. Louis angrily disapproved of his deepening left-wing activities, and during one of their discussions (as Lincoln described it in his diary) he warned him in no uncertain terms "against being a Communist . . . You're not one of those bomb-throwing people, who want to overturn everything." Lincoln replied that "the difference was merely in our point of view": Louis "didn't think you could change human nature," and Lincoln did. Louis said he "would get over it." Lincoln assured his father that he "wouldn't disgrace him." When, soon after, Lincoln had dinner with Mina, she said their father had, in every sense, aged: he'd shriveled in stature, lacked energy, and had grown fearful of any "principled stand," even to turning away somewhat from his long-standing support for labor.

Rose cautioned her son privately that his "Communist activities . . . musn't involve Father"; besides, she told him, "nobody can do anything about it anyway—you shouldn't make yourself unhappy by thinking about it." Lincoln did vow to himself that he'd arrange his "future, if any, Communist activities so as to give no inconvenience to Dad. Must not have my address found on persons of Communist organizers or let the School be used for Communist meetings." For a time he thought of using a pseudonym for his articles, so he "could write free of bother from Father."

But he continued seriously to mull over "how best to serve" left-wing causes. His diary during this period contains many entries along the lines of "[We] talked about the inevitable revolution, how one could not afford to be anything but on the side of the workers. How it would benefit the country." And he published his growing number of reviews and essays almost exclusively in left-wing periodicals, particularly in *New Theatre* (to which he also gave money), *The Nation*, and the *New Republic*—though for all three he usually wrote on non-political topics relating to dance, film, and photography. He even came close a few times to direct participation in marches or strikes, though in the end he always held back.

Lincoln's circle of friends also shifted somewhat. He now saw a good deal of committed left-wing activists like Leo Hurwitz and the "social realist" artists Ben Shahn and Philip Reisman (he made several suggestions to Reisman of radical subject matter for paintings, including one about the Rhode Island textile strike). Ben Shahn took Lincoln to the new prison on Rikers Island, in whose hall he was currently trying to get his murals on prison reform installed. Lincoln thought they were "much too good ever to be put up anywhere under this regime," though Ben thought he might pull it off. Shahn "started working" on Lincoln to join the Communist Party, telling him "how it would make me 'happy,' how I was confused now"—just make the break, Shahn insisted, and he'd be "surprised what a clarifying process it was." But Lincoln told him that "as yet I was not prepared to accept discipline, nor was I sure it was the only revolutionary agency."

Lincoln also drew closer to some radical-minded activists whom he'd previously known more casually—for one, Jay Leyda, a photographer, filmmaker, and critic active in the pro-Soviet Film and Photo League. Among his entirely new contacts, Lincoln was taken most of all with a young Communist from Birmingham named Wirt Taylor. The Party in Alabama had for a number of years been spearheading the effort to improve conditions of work and relief for blacks, and Taylor had been arrested and jailed several times for his involvement. Lincoln first heard Wirt talk at a meeting called by the International Labor Defense, itself active in the struggle. Out on bail from a thirteen-month sentence, Wirt spoke, the first night Lincoln heard him, with what Lincoln described as "a very limited vocabulary, a southern accent and some vehemence."

As he got to know him, Lincoln found Wirt "an extremely nice person—sweet-tempered and indignant," but "not the type from which leaders are made. Not the Lenin material." Yet in his simplicity and dedication—and his description of the horrors of the chain gang (to which he'd been sentenced for "obstructing traffic")—Wirt moved Lincoln profoundly: "I found myself extremely emotional. . . . My heart beat through my vest." On another occasion Wirt showed Lincoln a copy of *Southern Worker*, the underground CP paper he was trying to keep alive by raising money. Lincoln quietly managed to round up enough cash for the purpose. When Wirt decided in mid-December 1934 not to go back to Alabama to serve out his sentence on the chain gang, feeling sure he'd be killed, he was sent to a new organizing assignment in Norfolk, Virginia. Lincoln said good-bye with deep regret.

His infatuation with and admiration for Wirt Taylor brought Lincoln as close to joining the party as he would ever come. But with Wirt gone, Lincoln slowly drew back. He would ultimately persuade himself that to actually join the Communist Party would be "impracticable," that as someone involved in the arts, he could make a "better" contribution in that way. When he talked it over one day with his old friend A. Hyatt Mayor, the two men concluded that "we had work we wanted to do"— goals to achieve that they feared could be slowed or blocked by submitting to any sort of political discipline. They were hardly alone; like most Americans, Lincoln had ingested with his pabulum the notion that individual "identity" and "achievement" rightly took precedence over collectivist enterprises aimed at the common good.

But in drawing back from actual party affiliation, Lincoln didn't simultaneously surrender all interest in working for social justice. He even approached Balanchine again with the outlines of an idea for a ballet he called *Procession*, describing it as "a Communist ballet of continuous, fluid, inevitable movement"—hardly a concept richly enough detailed to excite even a committed party member, let alone a fierce anti-Communist like Balanchine. In response Balanchine simply said, "It would be OK in Red Square, but it was not for a theatre: It should be filmed." Elaborating a bit further, he let his hostility show: "Masses of men filmed from on high: they would be like an army of ants; there should be seas of blood bathing the sun and moon."

Lincoln had thought of suggesting as well "a hobo jungle ballet" to Balanchine, but he didn't. He'd gotten the message.

CHAPTER FOURTEEN

Hartford

(1935)

As the time approached for the December engagement at Hartford, Dimitriev kept repeating that he was indifferent to anything but the school. Yet he'd been the one recently arguing for at least a few performances over the coming winter in a New York City theater (as would indeed happen in early March). Lincoln finally told him straight out that he was overplaying his "indifference," that everyone knew he *was* interested in the production side though furious at Eddie for having anointed himself director general of a new company that would be entirely separate from the school—and from the possibility of Dimitriev playing any major role in it.[1]

Lincoln also let Dimitriev know that he agreed with him at least in part: he, too, believed that the Russian's experience and discipline (and Eddie's lack of them) made him the logical choice for at least a co-directorship in the proposed company. At the same time Lincoln felt (as he wrote in his diary) that Dimitriev was using him "as some kind of solvent agent on Eddie to make Eddie offer him the director generalship of the School *and* Producing Company." Dimitriev denied that he wanted such an outcome, but Lincoln felt sure he did.

Lincoln predicted that in any case Eddie's interest in forming a company would soon wane, since it wasn't rooted in any genuine involvement with ballet as an art form. Eddie's only real concern, Lincoln felt, was in being seen (especially by his dismissive older brothers) as someone involved in An Important Enterprise. (Later, as a leading figure in Jewish philanthropy, Eddie would prove that Lincoln underestimated his ability to work more or less disinterestedly for a common good.)

But Lincoln was unquestionably right that Eddie lacked any profound interest in ballet, and he told him so to his face. Eddie's response was that Balanchine's ballets were too technically difficult: "Why make it so hard? Look at the Rockettes." Lincoln, astonished at such philistinism, "tried to speak of the necessities of high standards." He also gave Eddie "an earful" for going around town telling people that he'd "edged him out, wrested control" of the American Ballet from Lincoln, and shunted him off to the sidelines—"when as a matter of fact," Lincoln said, "it was he who was least occupied." Eddie asked him to "lay off him," that "he was passing through a very difficult time in his analysis."

Lincoln, Dimitriev, and Balanchine huddled together over the puzzle of what Eddie really did want. They agreed that above all he wanted "to figure." Beyond that he wanted "to get his money back and a little over." Dimitriev felt that Eddie "has no interest in anything" and "will never give a lot of money." But Lincoln pointed out that Eddie had recently pledged twenty-five thousand dollars toward production costs, and that his money had not only kept them afloat but remained all-important to their future plans. And that, in turn, meant that he somehow had to be placated. At least for the time being.

In the six weeks or so that preceded the Hartford performances, jangled nerves on all sides produced a bumper crop of collisions. Dimitriev had long been grousing to Lincoln about Balanchine's purported "inadequacies," and he now filled his ears anew with various complaints: Balanchine was "impossible to work with"; he "worked for a week and only ten minutes of ballet" would be composed; he "never thinks of practical details"; "we would never arrive anywhere with this lack of system."

Lincoln knew perfectly well that such accusations were at bottom those of a hardheaded administrator against the unpredictabilities of a creative artist. Still, this time around, Lincoln listened. He'd been developing some doubts of his own—not about Balanchine's choreographic brilliance but about his character. They clustered around what Lincoln referred to a number of times in his diary as Balanchine's "sadism." In one entry he characterized him as "tyrannical and silent"; in another he recorded Balanchine's "playful sadism" in abruptly shifting a role from one dancer to another; in a third he described a rehearsal in which "Balanchine got into one of those repetitive sadistic things he sometimes can't pull himself out of. Made them repeat the same step for an hour . . . [said] if they were tired they could go home, and abruptly left himself. Up to rehearsal time today he spoke no word to anyone of the company." Similarly, just before Hartford, "Balanchine got into one of his insistent moods, and started to torture" one particular student, "reducing her to tears." Having witnessed the scene, Lincoln wrote in his diary, "Sadism or exactness, it's equally difficult to support."

On yet another occasion, a month later, when a touring agent who was considering taking them on as a client insisted he wouldn't proceed unless they fired Dorothie Littlefield and Gisella Caccialanza, Balanchine "in his bright way" (as Lincoln put it) immediately told Caccialanza, who "wept ceaselessly"—and needlessly, since neither the connection with the agent nor the firings went forward. Both the leading male dancers, Charles Laskey and William Dollar, came to Lincoln with grievances against Balanchine. Laskey complained that Balanchine's classes were "lax, had no snap, were too involved, not enough technique in them. I told him to speak to Dimitriev about it. More corroboration for him." William Dollar, after badly twisting his ankle, complained to Lincoln that Balanchine had been (in Lincoln's words) "running him ragged," that he had a "crazy way of either ignoring you or killing you with work."

Some of Balanchine's behavior may have been centrally related to his unsettled health during this period; certainly over the years the overwhelming bulk of testimony from dancers who studied with him comes down on the side of adoration and gratitude. Even at the time, William Dollar, when complaining to Lincoln, made a point of telling him as well that "all the kids love" Balanchine (though "the kids" might conceivably be interpreted as younger students in the school, "those who don't have much to do with him or who don't know any better").

Balanchine's quiet unease about his health does seem to have affected his teaching. Dimitriev claimed that Balanchine had never enjoyed conducting classes and tolerated them only because they provided an opportunity to compose. Lincoln himself, who often sat in on classes and rehearsals, concluded at one point (as he wrote in his diary) that Balanchine "doesn't like to teach"; Lincoln felt that "little discipline [was] left and no morale. It's all too fanciful in the exercises. He wants to compose all the time, even in class."

Lincoln and Dimitriev began to talk seriously of hiring Anatole Vilzak, a leading dancer of the day, as a teaching member of the staff, especially since Vladimiroff had been threatening to leave. Lincoln also told Dimitriev that although he "saw our company as a great institution in the future . . . it would be unthinkable as entirely dependent on Balanchine." By which Lincoln unquestionably was referring neither to the occasional complaints about his classes nor to his character but rather to his precarious health. As Lincoln wrote in his diary, "Every time he's out of my sight I think he's either gotten sick again or has been killed."

On December 2, a "dress-parade" took place at the school of all the costumes they'd be using for the Hartford performances. Lincoln thought the dancers looked "pretty sweet flopping around in their big skirts," but Balanchine was "furious" that the costumes for *Transcendence* were made of heavier material than he'd asked for—all because, it turned out, Eddie, without consultation, had decided to save a hundred dollars. Balanchine was more upset still at how badly the pianists ("one dead ogre and his meek boyfriend," in Lincoln's phrase) played during the rehearsal.[2]

Before lapsing into what Lincoln described as "a frenzy of silence," Balanchine plaintively asked what the use was of good choreography, sets, and costumes when the most important ingredient, the music, was poorly done. Dimitriev, who'd grown used to solving last-minute crises, managed—despite having declared his indifference to the Hartford proceedings—to get hold of an old friend, the onetime *chef d'orchestre* at the Maryinsky, to lead the two piano players, who *did* improve.

On the morning of December 4, a hired bus, with the complete troupe, left for Hartford in "a general air of gaiety." Baskets marked "Les Ballets 1933" were fastened on the roof and filled with the costumes. Lincoln drove up the next day with Mina; Rose would arrive the following evening in time for the first performance. On arrival, problems arose almost at once. The headdresses for *Transcendence* hadn't been finished in time and had to be sent up later by parcel post. The chief electrician, from Yale, had to go back and forth to New Haven. The stage crew had been slapped together from a group of what Lincoln called "excessively unprofessional" Trinity College students—who kept disappearing to go to classes.

The first lighting rehearsal at the Avery Memorial confirmed earlier fears that the stage would prove too small, especially for *Serenade* (which, along with *Transcendence*, was having its world premiere). The ballet shoes, thanks to Eddie again skimping on costs, caused the dancers "great pain," which made Lincoln "furious." None of the four scheduled performances had sold out; many thought the tickets too expensive, and poor Chick Austin had been selling them himself in the lobby of the Boston Opera House during intermissions. Even so Eddie refused, in yet another misguided effort to cut costs, to give out any complimentary tickets; Lincoln went temporarily broke when he had to spend seventy-seven dollars on tickets for friends he felt had to be there.

The pink-and-yellow flies for *Transcendence*, which Frank Watkins had been painting all day, were at the last minute ruled out and Chick and Lincoln spent much of that evening painting two large wings to mask the ballet's side. Eddie would later claim, quite unfairly, that "Chick was gushing all over the place, but unavailable when any real work had to be done." If anything, Chick had been knocking himself out being helpful, while Eddie was busy giving interviews to the papers about "his" ballet company, and effusively greeting arriving "social notables."

Despite all the annoyances, inevitable in any theatrical presentation, the dress rehearsal the next morning looked generally "OK," and Lincoln thought *Transcendence* came across as "unbelievably superb." Though he'd worked hard on the ballet's scenario (in the process dropping the focus on Paganini), the printed playbills didn't list him as its author—apparently at his own request. Nor did Dimitriev's name appear anywhere in the playbill. Balanchine, appropriately, was listed in boldface letters as responsible for "Direction and Choreography," and Eddie Warburg's name appeared twice: as the "book" writer for *Alma Mater*, and as "Director General" of the School of American Ballet. At dinner with Mina several days later, Lincoln was taken to task about his penchant for anonymity, his sister telling him that he "always repeated a [pattern of] self-effacement and tended deliberately to underestimate" his own achievement; she thought it represented a wellspring of "recessive guilt" that could prove "dangerous" to his future.

On December 6, a Pullman car festooned with BALLET SPECIAL signs and filled with New York luminaries (including George Gershwin) set out from Grand Central Station for the opening-night performance in Hartford. The formally dressed audience that night also included Salvador Dalí, Russell Hitchcock, the modern art collectors James Thrall Soby and Katherine Dreier, Sol Hurok, Thomas Hart Fisher (husband of the dancer and choreographer Ruth Page, who'd recently been appointed director of the Chicago Grand Opera), Tod Rockefeller, Ellen and Wallace Harrison, Alice de la Mar, Lucia Davidova (who came by plane), Constance and Kirk Askew, MoMA's A. Conger Goodyear, and Pavel Tchelitchev, who'd recently arrived in the country and would soon become one of Lincoln's intimates. Chick Austin had refused to unionize the Avery Memorial Theater, and the bejeweled crowd was greeted at each performance, much to Lincoln's chagrin ("I wondered what Wirt Taylor would say," he guiltily wrote in his diary) by "two cold and orderly pickets" in front of the door.

Opening night began with *Mozartiana*. It went only moderately well. The ballet shoes squeaked on the stage, and Marie-Jeanne, as feared, got tangled up in the elaborate set of ropes and wept a good deal afterward. Still, the performance was respectable enough, and the second ballet, *Alma Mater*, was better received—though some thought it closer to Broadway than to ballet. The final ballet, *Transcendence*, proved the evening's triumph; Lincoln thought it went "marvelously well," and the Hartford critics agreed. Even Dimitriev, though silent, seemed pleased. Eddie went around saying, "Tops! Tops!"

After the performance, almost everyone went off to a party at James Thrall Soby's house in West Hartford, but Lincoln took off his tails, Rose handed him a steak sandwich, and he worked with others—including, for a time, Eddie—until 2:30 a.m. to put up the set for *Serenade*, so they'd be ready for the morning's rehearsal. The second performance went less well; Lincoln found it "something of a let-down; not enough snap to it," and the audience, this time mostly "a conservative Hartford group," wasn't "very wild about it."

Afterward, when garaging his car, Lincoln came across Balanchine, alone; he "seemed contented though he said nothing to show his approval of any recent events." Together they went to a party, mostly for the dancers and their friends (plus "salesmen standing by their doors with lust in their eyes") at the Hotel Bond Annex. There, according to Lincoln, Balanchine was "in his element, mildly lascivious with Elise Reiman and Heidi [Vosseler], seeing how strong their knees were by forcing his in between." There was some drinking and some "mildly improper stories retold from the French." Lincoln, his Boston background peeking out, found it all "curiously naughty and uncomfortable."

The next day both a matinee and a final evening performance were scheduled. Though the premiere of *Serenade* had been announced, it was decided at the last minute not to give it; the rehearsal had gone badly, with the stage simply too small to accommodate the large cast and the costumes (designed by one William B. Okie, Jr.) looking "impossible." There was "no use in trying to fool ourselves," Lincoln wrote in his diary. "It would ruin an otherwise good ballet by getting it set off on the wrong foot."

The matinee itself was "a nightmare; full of substitutes and all bad." Erick Hawkins proved a particular problem. Just the week before, Dimitriev had given him his first chance to teach at the school, for which he'd been pleading, but "after all his talk" (as Lincoln wrote in his diary), he "wasn't very eager for it," announcing that he was "set on being a dancer, not a teacher." Lincoln had been finding Hawkins "slightly uppity and fractious" of late, and he now added "hard-headed, thick and even dumb." During the matinee performance Hawkins was so full of his own importance that he took it upon himself to make several changes in the choreography and demanded that various props be taken offstage during his big scene with Caccialanza in *Alma Mater*, "to better show off his mimicry." It all made Lincoln feel "sick."

The evening performance set all to rights. Lincoln thought it was "by far" the best of the four; everything went "extremely smoothly" and *Transcendence* proved a "knockout." Merovich, the agent, had come up from New York and was "very enthusiastic," and Archie and Ada MacLeish were also there, and "very sweet." No less a celebrity than Katharine Hepburn showed up, wearing "great furs"; she was "extremely enthusiastic and charming" and later went backstage to meet Bill Dollar. Afterward Balanchine drily said of her, "Pas mal; une peu grande." To top the evening off, Rose Kirstein outdid herself by throwing a party for the cast and guests in the lobby of the Avery Theater. Eddie left early due, in Lincoln's view, to it being "too much of a Kirstein occasion."

One might have thought, in the aftermath of the company's successful if imperfect debut, that a period of mutual congratulation and reduced friction would ensue, however briefly. But no. The troupe was no sooner back in New York City than discord among the four principals was again front and center. The arguments and accusations among them had by this point become repetitive: Dimitriev was angry that Eddie continued to get most of the publicity, and that he remained rigidly insistent on going it alone with the new production company (with the sole help of a man named Jack Birss, whom Eddie hired as its business manager). Dimitriev predicted that Balanchine would himself "stand only so much of it, and then would sock Eddie as he almost did Edward James."[3]

Lincoln sided with Dimitriev. He was angry, for starters, that Eddie, in his pennywise way, had tipped the Hartford bus drivers a miserly fifty cents each. And he was convinced that Eddie, "thick-skulled and superficial," would in short order run the new company into the ground. He found it mystifyingly stupid of Eddie not to see the necessity of a symbiotic connection between the company and the school, and predicted that eventually he himself might have to start another company which *did* emanate directly from the school.

In the meantime he kept trying to find a way of persuading Eddie to share the reins of power in the new company with Dimitriev, emphasizing, among other things, that he could save Eddie a good deal of money. At one point Lincoln wrote in his diary that Eddie "seemed to mull it over in his mind [and] reserved judgment," but Lincoln could see that Dimitriev's "discipline" irritated him so much that he felt Eddie "will try his best to do it alone—if so, woe to all of us." He thought there was even a chance that Eddie, once he faced up to his own inadequacy, would "farm the whole thing out to Hurok, or anyone who will take it. His meanness is becoming accentuated with his sense of power."

As for Balanchine, he wanted to get on with things, wanted to compose, not confer. He kept himself more or less aloof from the contentious squabbling that swirled around him; he knew that Lincoln was a more serious man and a far more committed balletomane than Eddie, but he also knew that Eddie, like Edward James before him, held the purse strings. But if Balanchine tried to remain above the fray, Dimitriev did his best to drag him in, railing at him both in front of others and behind his back. At various times he openly denounced Balanchine for refusing (as Lincoln summarized Dimitriev's accusations in his diary) "to believe he could do any wrong" and for always giving "excuses for his errors." He seemed to believe that "no one else ever did anything till he was born." Yes, Dimitriev acknowledged, Balanchine was "a genius in choreography," but not, as he seemed to think, infallible in set design and music as well. In fact he'd made some serious mistakes, the most recent being the totally inappropriate costumes and decor he'd insisted on for *Serenade*.

Balanchine, Dimitriev declared, "is in his seventh heaven of delight because he is unchecked." But in Dimitriev's view that was precisely the problem, and he suggested at one point that all four together become "artistic director," with Balanchine pledged to "abide by *our* decision." Neither Eddie nor Balanchine paid the slightest attention to the suggestion. An angry Balanchine said that he "could not be nailed down with any definite plan. Only Massine could work like that." He would not have anyone over him. The choreographer had to arrange everything. To which Dimitriev shot back, "for ten years you've had always someone over" you, and he accused Balanchine of "being loath to let anyone new come in . . . he wants it to be not the American Ballet, but the 'Ballets Balanchine 1935.' " True, Balanchine had spoken of inviting the young English choreographer Frederick Ashton to do a ballet, but that was only "because he is bad Balanchine, the way Lichine is bad Massine."

Lincoln reacted to these angry exchanges with "universal apprehension," writing in his diary that he wasn't "sure" that any of Dimitriev's accusations were true, and pointing out to him that whereas Balanchine had done only ten ballets for Diaghilev over a period of five years, in one year he'd already worked on seven for the American Ballet. To Lincoln the real obstacle to moving ahead wasn't the supremely gifted Balanchine, who Lincoln felt "always wants to proceed to new works," as did he, but rather Eddie Warburg. Eddie was due to leave shortly for a conference in England on Jewish repatriation, and Lincoln hoped that as he increasingly replaced his ailing father, Felix (who would die in 1937), as a leading figure in the movement to save European Jewry, he would proportionately lose interest in heading a mere ballet company. Eddie, Lincoln wrote in his diary, wants to be "King of the Jews"—a peculiarly graceless comment given his own marginal contribution at the time to the work of Jewish rescue.

As it became increasingly certain that the company would perform in New York City in late February or early March at the Adelphi Theatre, Balanchine was eager to develop a number of new ideas, as well as to revise some of his earlier pieces; he'd already started to re-work *Transcendence* and *Dreams*, and to start rehearsing *Errante* (in which Tamara Geva had agreed to star). He was especially keen to work on two new ballets, a classical piece to music by Benjamin Godard that would ultimately become *Reminiscence*, and a ballet he tentatively titled *The Master Dancers*, which he envisioned as a series of staged competitions among the best dancers in the company.

Lincoln, too, was full of suggestions for new work. Still toying with the notion of directing and producing the *Red Hydra* spectacle for *New Theatre*, he also wanted to insinuate more "revolutionary" content into the company's own repertory. He suggested a ballet about the Paris Commune, and pressed for his earlier idea of a "hobo ballet: The Jungle," which Balanchine, despite his lack of interest in politics and his distaste for left-wing ideology, said he liked. Lincoln was still pushing, too, for the now-long-standing possibility of doing *Tom*, the adaptation of *Uncle Tom's Cabin*; Balanchine had already rejected E. E. Cummings's libretto as unsuitable for dance, but Lincoln wanted to try his own hand at writing a new scenario and asked Virgil Thomson to consider doing the score and Ben Shahn the sets. Cummings was furious when he heard the news, yet he wrote Lincoln a note saying he'd found a publisher for his own *Tom*, and suggesting that they remain friends. "I can't really see why," Lincoln wrote in his diary. "I'll never have anything better from him than what I've already had, and the explanation of his long alienation, or the lack of it, would be too difficult, too tedious to go into."

Simultaneously Tchelitchev tried to get everyone excited about a "wholly new idea [of a] great spectacle" based on *Medea*. Dimitriev was enthusiastic—"Voila! Votre Renaissance!" Eddie said "he had no idea what it was, but he thought he might do it." But Balanchine, who was an old friend of Tchelitchev's and had worked with him on various projects, including *Errante*, cautioned that they "mustn't go too fast." Lincoln, too, was initially uncertain about working with Tchelitchev. When the two men first met, Lincoln had found him "very difficult" (and indeed, despite his abundant charm, Tchelitchev was often quick-tempered and would himself boast about being "impossible"). There was also a real question as to whether Tchelitchev would be allowed to work on the stage of a unionized theater. Besides, too little time was left before the scheduled performances at the Adelphi Theatre (now set to begin on March 1) to prepare both *Medea* and *Tom*, and Lincoln strongly preferred the left-oriented *Tom*.

Lincoln's commitment in general to the Left still remained strong. He hoped to get to the Soviet Union in the near future for at least a short visit, and Muriel sent him a long letter from Moscow with "practical instructions" for the journey. To get a rise out of Philip Johnson and Alan Blackburn, Lincoln told them shortly before they left New York to sit at the feet of Huey Long that he'd joined the Communist Party (which he hadn't). Philip said "it was a great pity; such a good man lost." Blackburn said "he'd know where to shoot," and threatened to have Lincoln beaten up before he left New York. "You live in the Village, don't you?" Blackburn asked. Yes, Lincoln replied, and gave him his old address, 16 Minetta Lane—which Blackburn wrote down. Philip insisted to Lincoln that Huey Long was "the greatest and most loveable man in the world," and that Long and he were *not* fascists but "believers in democracy"; their only interest, Philip claimed, was "the happiness of the American people." Lincoln was skeptical. He began an article for the *New Republic* in which he aimed "to be as insulting as possible without seeming to take them seriously, which I find I do." He heard someone ask Julien Levy what he thought would become of Philip Johnson; Levy answered, "Oh, I guess he'll come back with Alan Blackburn's tail between his legs."

Then came the news from the Soviet Union of the assassination of Sergei Kirov, the popular head of the Leningrad party, a murder that served as prelude to and excuse for Stalin's Great Terror of 1936–39. Kirov's death deeply disturbed Lincoln, as it did many other leftists. He'd recently written in his diary that of late he'd been "considering my role, if any, in the Revolution," and had been "drawing nearer . . . to the necessity of active participation," by which for now he meant "only . . . picketing and organizing." But Kirov's assassination seems to have been an important marker in Lincoln's gradual retreat from pro-Communist sympathy. Muriel wrote him that Stalin was "hideously unpopular," and when she followed up in March with news of the "heavy false witness and terror and lack of privacy," Lincoln, though reluctant "to strike my colors," took down the hammer and sickle he'd been displaying in his office and decided against a trip to the Soviet Union.

He was able to find some relief from ongoing tensions, political and professional, through various other activities. He gave periodic assists to Alfred Barr in mounting MoMA's Lachaise retrospective, wrote various articles, prepared a collection of his verse for publication in 1935 as a ninety-nine-page book, and completed his *Dance: A Short History of Classic Theatrical Dancing* (which would appear toward the end of that same year). He filled in much of his remaining time with what he characterized as "lecturing, taking lessons and fucking."[4]

Lincoln's old friend and mentor Hyatt Mayor often looked over Lincoln's lectures (which were based on various chapters from his history of the dance) and was infallibly helpful in shaping them. Nonetheless, Lincoln, typically, was more often than not dissatisfied with his performance: "perfervid guilt due to the general ruggedness of my lecture"; "acutely conscious of my very limited vocabulary when I am speaking" (and so on).

Along with taking a series of ten lessons in public speaking, Lincoln also took instruction in ballet for several months, this time with Erick Hawkins as his teacher. Lincoln wasn't entertaining any renewed hope, as he approached his twenty-eighth birthday, of actually becoming a dancer, but he did wish further to familiarize himself with the vocabulary of the dance. "It's all too hard for me," he wrote in his diary, "but I do get increasingly a sense of understanding out of it I never have had before." During one lesson Balanchine happened to come into the room when Lincoln was attempting a plié—and promptly fell over, "much to Erick's chagrin."

The "fucking" was pretty much confined, give or take the occasional sailor or gas station attendant, to his longtime female companion, Margot Loines, now an aspiring actress, and to "Joe," a seventeen-year-old male student at the school whom Lincoln mentored, advising him among other things against becoming "exclusively queer."

Much more often than not, Lincoln turned down offers from various friends to be taken to this or that sailor hangout. But he did at least twice go with Jack Birss, who Lincoln thought "a crazy bastard, cross-stitched with little fixations on the U.S.N.," to a private house on Fulton Street run by (in Lincoln's words) "an ex-chorine of 50, motherly, fat" George

Barnum. His home was a gathering spot for soldiers and sailors looking for male sex and/or the chance to make a few dollars. "Though unaccustomed to the atmosphere," Lincoln found it "easy enough and fun too." Barnum sat him next to "a tired boy called Chuck Peters off the [naval vessel] Tuscaloosa." Lincoln was "not exactly drawn" to Chuck, but—and this speaks volumes about Lincoln's sensitivity—"didn't wish to hurt his feelings, he being shy and friendly"; so they did retire to the front room together and Chuck was "o.k." Lincoln, as advised, put two dollars in Chuck's jacket pocket. The two then sat in the kitchen, drank, and talked about the navy. Apparently in reaction to Lincoln's considerateness, Chuck, a seaman first class, showed him "his efficiency ratings, explained the uniform," and invited him for a tour of the *Tuscaloosa*, which Lincoln took him up on.

As for "Joe," he roomed at the time with Eugene ("Gene") Loring, who'd been a student at the school for some six months and whose talent Lincoln had spotted early on and supported, pushing him for roles in several ballets and giving him money for living expenses (in the 1940s, Loring would emerge as a leading choreographer, particularly with *Billy the Kid*). At first Lincoln found Joe very sweet and smart, but after a few months he got bored with what he called his "gentility" and decided that although Joe was a "nice enough little boy," he guessed that after all he "didn't much like little boys."

His short-lived affair with Joe didn't compare in seriousness to his relationship with Margot. They'd now known each other for several years, and as far back as September 1934, Lincoln had confided to Joella Levy (wife of Julien) that "she was the first to know I was to be married in the near future to Margot Loines." But that was as close to the altar as they ever got. A mere two weeks later, when Margot returned from an acting job in the South, Lincoln decided he "was not as glad to see" her as he'd expected. They continued to go out regularly, and also to have sex, but the erotic charge (as Lincoln once wrote in his diary) was "like a warm bath" compared to the excitement he often felt with men. Perhaps, he thought, he and Margot saw too much of each other and he was "too sure of her." Certainly he was always honest with her; she knew that he slept with men and knew, too, about his affair with Joe.

None of that seemed to bother her, or at least she was shrewd enough to tell Lincoln that she "wasn't trying to hold me or to own me." "She is," Lincoln wrote in his diary, "a miracle of tact and good sense; I feel guilty that I offer her no more for expecting so little from me." He further acknowledged that "she puts up with lots; I haven't an unselfish bone in my body." But Margot did ask him to be a little "nicer" to her, less "rude." To which he replied, "Perhaps I could but I doubted whether I would or not"—a prime example of how Lincoln, good Gurdjieffian that he was, in his determination to be "frank" could sometimes blind himself to the attendant hurt his remarks or behavior could cause; the examples would multiply as he grew older.

At least he did tell Margot, honorably, that he felt "confused." In the privacy of his diary he asked himself, "Should I never see her again or get married or take Joe and anyone else I want?" or would his "hard-pressed moral integrity dissolve to pieces" if he continued to try to satisfy all his contradictory needs simultaneously? What made him feel especially guilty was his clear realization that Margot "merely completes my idea of myself as I want to appear publicly. . . . Is this the permanently dry feeling about my heart [that] Muriel used to frighten me" with? The "idea of Romantic Love [is] as remote to me as the Berkshire School; I once adored the idea."

Then one night in January 1935, "the god-damned sheath broke" when he and Margot were having sex, putting Lincoln "in a sweat of fear." They went and bought "a whirling syringe" from a helpful drugstore clerk, tried to laugh the episode off and ("with terror in my balls") settled in to wait. That month Margot skipped her period, and Lincoln felt "fatalistic mortal apprehension." But finally "the curse" (as many called it at the time) did arrive, and Lincoln, who in all likelihood would have felt compelled to marry Margot had she been pregnant, could now breathe again. The two continued to see each other for a while longer, but within a few months Lincoln told Margot straight out that he "could not love her," and they decided to call a halt. Margot, no longer sure that she was in love either, wasn't crushed.

Lincoln was afraid that she might try to contact him, but she didn't— and that, he wrote in his diary "is why I respect her." When she finally did phone several weeks later, "her voice chilled me with guilt and . . . I'm afraid I was too abrupt. But there's no use for me to see her." Margot had become "unessential" and Lincoln had become determined to "disembarrass myself of all unessentials." Yet for a while longer he would often think about her, would have trouble concentrating, and sometimes felt he'd "explode, nearly scream or swoon." Eventually he wrote to her, if only to say that he couldn't see her, couldn't see any point in talking about what had happened, or not happened, between them. Lincoln had turned his back on Margot, but not on the idea of marrying someday. As for Margot, she pursued for a time a career in the theater but got no further than a "female chorus" role in Archie MacLeish's 1935 play *Panic* (which ran for only two performances, despite boasting Orson Welles in the cast). In 1937 Margot married D. W. Morrow, Jr., son of the ambassador to Mexico and brother to Anne Morrow Lindbergh. But that marriage ended in divorce and Margot later remarried and had two daughters.

In preparation for the engagement at New York City's Adelphi Theatre, set to begin on March 1, two tryout performances were given at Bryn

Mawr on February 7 and 8. The first of them could hardly have gone worse. Dorothie Littlefield's mother refused at the last minute to let her appear, feeling that her daughter should have been featured as a principal, and *Serenade*, according to Lincoln, "was ruined." *Alma Mater* went somewhat better, but *Transcendence*, due to the poor lighting, could barely be seen. The company was plunged into "general gloom," but Balanchine seemed unfazed; he was, Lincoln wrote in his diary, "as usual . . . wholly calm and without interest, apparently." But he did tell Lincoln over dinner a few days later that he was angry with Littlefield for "refusing" to dance in the corps.

The second performance, on the following evening, saw a considerable turnabout. With the lighting greatly improved, *Transcendence* could now be appreciated, and the company in general performed well—despite Balanchine having told Heidi Vosseler, just before the dancers went on, that she'd gotten too fat. He later confided to Lincoln that Vosseler was "impossible" in *Serenade* and he intended to replace her. The other sour note came when the dancers dragged Balanchine onto the stage at the close, which, according to Lincoln, made him "furious."[5]

The week before Bryn Mawr, Balanchine had again come down with a fever and had felt so ill one night in late January that Lincoln had had to take him home and put him to bed. Dimitriev, according to Lincoln, was "triumphant," declaring the illness inevitable, given Balanchine's "stupidity" in not taking care of himself. Dr. Geyelin was called in and said it was merely a case of the grippe, that there was "small sign of T.B.," which made everyone feel relieved, at least temporarily.

Balanchine's friend the dancer George Volodin (whom Lincoln described in his diary as a "funny little modest if campy Russian") came in to nurse him. Several of his other close friends, nearly all Russian, were also attentive; they included the school's rehearsal pianist, Nicholas Kopeikine, Tchelitchev, and the composers Nicolas Nabokov and Vladimir Dukelsky, who later, under his new name, Vernon Duke, became a successful stage and screen composer. Still, Balanchine's recovery was slow. On one visit Lincoln found him out of bed and "banging out" music on the piano, behaving, in Lincoln's words, "like a child." He "wouldn't be a bit surprised," Lincoln wrote in his diary, "if Balanchine had presently another nervous attack." It didn't help *Lincoln's* nerves at all to hear Dimitriev predicting that "everything will be a failure," and announcing his intention of selling his own stock in the school to Lucia Davidova.

From his sickbed Balanchine did manage to do some of the preparatory work for the public performances. He'd earlier insisted, over Lincoln and Dimitriev's objections, on hiring Serge Soudeikine to design the sets and costumes for *Reminiscence;* now, during one of Lincoln's visits, Balanchine showed him Soudeikine's sketches for the first time. Lincoln was horrified; he thought them badly drawn and "vulgar." On the spot he quickly drew his own sketch of how he thought the stage should look. Balanchine liked it and said he'd show it to Soudeikine as his very own suggestion. But he wouldn't budge on his choice of designer ("another triumph for Dimitriev," Lincoln dryly wrote in his diary). Soudeikine's revised sketches, in Lincoln's view, "erred on the side of being too academic."

Balanchine did manage to attend the Bryn Mawr performances, but within a few days was back in bed. Worse news soon followed. Dr. Geyelin, once again reversing his own initial diagnosis, phoned Lincoln on February 14 to say that Balanchine was, after all, "fuller of T.B. bacilli than last year at this time." He said that Balanchine "could work for two or three weeks possibly," but at the end of that time, would require complete rest. "I think," Lincoln wrote in his diary, "that will more or less permanently remove him from the School for this year, and Dimitriev plans next year merely to give him [Balanchine] classes specially for himself. Danse Moderne"—not, that is, *danse classique.*

At dinner soon after, Tchelitchev told Lincoln that he was "very worried" about Balanchine's ongoing "row" with Dimitriev. He said that "in the old days . . . Dimitriev had George under his thumb, as if he were hypnotizing him or blackmailing him." Pavlik (as Lincoln now started to call him, their intimacy deepening) said that in the old days they all used to joke that Dimitriev would threaten Balanchine with revealing that he, or the two of them together, had killed someone. But now, Pavlik said, it was no joke: "Without a guide or check Balanchine is lost. Here he's been in New York a year and more [and] who are his friends?—that foul, vulgar whore Davidova, that bastard Dukelsky [whom Lincoln also "hated"], Volodin a crazy nice Russian, Kopeikine, Soudeikine. That's all. He lives on flattery: it will be his undoing. He has no mind and no taste," yet was a "great genius when directed."

Pavlik was notorious, as Lincoln well knew, for his supercharged, reckless invective, for opinions that were a mix of scurrility and truth and delivered, circus-barker-style, at full hyperbolic pitch. Yet taking all that into account, Lincoln nonetheless worried that Pavlik, who after all knew Balanchine well, was somewhere near the mark when he talked of Balanchine "committing every conceivable kind of suicide." Lincoln's consolation was that the school was now "stable enough without Balanchine, if we have Vladimiroff." He felt encouraged, too, that Eddie Warburg had stepped up to the plate and generously offered to lend Balanchine enough money to pay his outstanding bills and to go south, after the New York performances, for a complete rest.

Balanchine, as was his way, kept his own counsel and surprised the gloom-and-doom-sayers by suddenly getting out of his sickbed (Geyelin, in yet another shift, now pronounced him free of TB). He appeared at the school on February 17 and promptly composed a new polka for *Dreams*, which, along with *Errante*, he'd decided to resurrect from Les Ballets 1933 and revise for the New York run.

In Tchelitchev's opinion *Errante*, for which he'd done the original decor and costumes, wasn't worth reviving. He told Lincoln it had been "flung together to confound the Bérard coterie, because both Balanchine and he were hopelessly in love, and this was an exteriorization of private grief, not to be repeated." It was nothing more than "a revue fantastique pour les gens riches . . . subjective and of no value"—though he thought "perhaps it would have success here because it was so neurotic." To underscore his point, Pavlik revealed to Lincoln that the day before *Errante* was due to debut for Les Ballets 1933, both Dimitriev and Balanchine had wanted to have it taken off the program; it was he, Pavlik, who'd resisted, saying, "I will take the responsibility—and there were eighteen curtain-calls."

But now, Pavlik said, something "absolutely revolutionary" was required instead. Ballet as previously known was "dead." "New forms" were required, something "huge," like his own prior suggestion for a vast spectacle based on *Medea*. Unlike *Errante*, he said, the spectacle would not be "sentimental" but rather "cold and cruel and exhausting." It was a project Tchelitchev would continue to push for, but although Lincoln had by now become convinced that Pavlik was a "master of his métier" and full of rich "invention and surprise," the *Medea* never won Balanchine's approval, perhaps in part because Dimitriev was also enthusiastic about doing it.

For the revival of *Dreams*, George Antheil recomposed his music, but both Lincoln and Balanchine felt the score was "still *merde*." To perform his new polka for *Dreams*, Balanchine decided to cast Gisella Caccialanza and Paul Haakon as principal dancers, Haakon, along with Tamara Geva, having recently agreed to appear as "guest artist" during the New York run. Lincoln had been instrumental in procuring Haakon's services; he liked and admired him ("genial, elegant and easy") nearly as much as he disliked Geva. Haakon had studied with both Fokine and another esteemed teacher and dancer, Mikhail Mordkin, and he had a contract with the *Follies* that was scheduled to begin in May. Currently, though, he was free, and although Eddie Warburg offered him a salary that in Lincoln's opinion was "next to nothing—like the rest," Haakon agreed to perform for the Adelphi Theatre run.

Watching him during rehearsals, Lincoln thought he was "possibly more acrobat than dancer," yet "splendid, tight" (he managed to acknowledge, despite his personal distaste for her, that Geva was "very good" as well). As part of his new ballet, *Reminiscence*, Balanchine, wearing three jackets and sweating, composed material for Haakon that incorporated the use of a hoop (Balanchine had graduated from the Maryinsky in 1921 with a similar dance); seeing Haakon struggle with the hoop during rehearsals, Mina whispered to Lincoln, "The sicker . . . [Balanchine] gets, the more difficult his choreography will be." Lincoln felt that Haakon "dispels such joy" that he'd "like to have him always around." Yet when Eddie, who was equally smitten, suggested that Haakon "head the Company on the road" during the "tour" he was planning for fall 1935, Lincoln advised that Haakon "is not old enough and hasn't enough sense."

In the ten days preceding the New York City opening, the usual melodramatics prevailed, attended by some illness. An angry Volodin told Lincoln that he'd no longer nurse Balanchine, that he was fed up with his "selfishness and ingratitude." Dimitriev became bedridden for a time with painful gallstones, though he rallied long enough to underscore Volodin's complaints, telling Lincoln that Balanchine "is sick in mind and body and should be kept away for six months." Tchelitchev, too, in bed with "liver disorders," raged against Balanchine for "countermanding" his ideas, and rhetorically asked Lincoln "who was designing *Errante* anyway?" Yet thanks to Lincoln's pleas Tchelitchev did come through with a drawing for the souvenir program that Lincoln was almost single-handedly preparing.

While shouldering all this, Lincoln was having his own fits of gloom, writing at one point in his diary, "I am in a delicately superstitious condition now and see chimeras of blackmail and death everywhere; however, courage." And courage he continued to show, even while feeling "excessively nervous." He more than deserved the unexpected compliment that came from Erick Hawkins: "everyone" felt that Lincoln had become "the bulwark."[6]

Some of the dancers were also acting up. A number of them had been unhappy ever since the importation of Geva and Haakon as guest stars became known—it "broke the idea of the School's importance in relation to the Company." William Dollar became "difficult and irritable," Haakon got uncharacteristically angry when he had to give up his dressing room to the conductor of the orchestra, and Geva, in general, seemed "furious at everyone." Perhaps for a bit of comfort, Lincoln started to see somewhat more of his own family, though his brother, George, didn't exactly cheer him up with the news that Filene's was "in a bad way," with a number of good men being fired to cut costs. But Lincoln and Mina "were getting on better than in a long time," and his parents tried their best to be supportive, though Rose, thanks to Eddie's reluctance to give out complimentary passes, was decidedly put out at having to spend eighty-five dollars for family tickets.

On February 25, just a few days before opening night, there was a cocktail party/rehearsal at the Adelphi Theatre for friends and some of the press. A number of "notables" also attended, including Mrs. William K. Vanderbilt, Aaron Copland, Conger Goodyear, Cecil Beaton, the painter Walt Kuhn (whom Lincoln described as a "half-assed phony . . . the Sandy Calder of his day"), and no less a figure than the famed bass Fyodor Chaliapin, who posed for a picture with a delighted Balanchine and declared that "civilization would perish without the ballet." Eddie Warburg "restrained himself from saying a few words," which to Lincoln was "a triumph." Reactions to the rehearsal itself were mixed; Lincoln thought both *Reminiscence* and *Transcendence* were well danced, but that Charles Laskey should look "the best of anyone on the stage" came as a surprise.

The orchestra rehearsal two days later was still more of a surprise. It was the first time the musicians had played together, and Lincoln thought that they "sounded like hell." Sandor Harmati, the conductor, seemed second rate, and to add insult to injury, his dog ate up seven pages of the score of *Transcendence*. Lincoln thought that Henry Brant's orchestration for *Reminiscence* was "worse than the orchestra," and Antheil's orchestration for *Transcendence* "so bad" that it couldn't be used (yet with some adjustments, it had to be, given the lateness of the hour).

At the dress rehearsal on February 28, John Martin of the *New York Times* showed up. Afterward he didn't mince words with Lincoln. He told him he'd liked *Reminiscence* but (passing over *Alma Mater* and *Errante*) came down hard on *Serenade:* the costumes were "frightful," the choreography "bad." "He's wrong," Lincoln wrote in his diary. But he could have predicted Martin's essentially negative response.

He and Lincoln had now known each other for some two years, and Martin had rarely been encouraging. As early as November 1933, after Lincoln had invited him to give a lecture at the school, Martin had replied with a lengthy statement of his views on ballet and on the dance in general, that essentially threw down the gauntlet: "I do not consider . . . [ballet] the foundation of dancing, any more than I consider the methods of the actors of the 17th and 18th Centuries the foundation of acting. . . . I believe heartily in the creation of totally new forms . . . the ballet in its outlook and its technical principles was designed to meet the social requirements of an aristocratic society in a period radically different from our own . . . the ballet technique and point of view are excellent and delightful—as far as they go; but I can never concede them the whole ground."

He did visit the school in October 1934, and told Lincoln he was impressed with "the way everyone was dancing," that they showed "some kind of similar style." Though he hinted at the time that he'd be doing an article on the school, it was only in a column two months later that he addressed the "New Company," and then in the form of an open letter. In it, he extended "hearty greetings" to the American Ballet and wrote that thus far he saw "every evidence of your sincere and almost passionate purpose." But he warned that there were three enemies to future success: "glamour, snobbery and provincialism," making reference to the conspicuous amount of "ermine and diamonds" that had attended the Hartford debut.

Martin went on to say that he understood the necessity of choosing the "greatly gifted" Balanchine as ballet master—"no American has had the necessary experience" to head an organization devoted to the "classical tradition." Yet Balanchine, Martin asserted, would ultimately "constitute a problem"; that is, if the company hoped to do more than revive the great ballets of the past (a purpose Martin disapproved) and aimed instead at evolving a contemporary approach that would *derive* from classical dance but find its essential "material and its technical means in its own scene"— about as succinct a description as possible of Balanchine's eventual accomplishment.

Lincoln thought Martin's piece was on the whole "excellent," but he remained rightly cautious, referring to him at one point in his diary as "John Martin, the unaccountable," and writing at another that he didn't "trust him for a second, i.e. [for] a favorable review . . . [though] he's honest enough." And when they did now and then talk, Lincoln would try and keep the conversation "restricted"—"to impart as much information as I can without seeming to push too much."

The antipathy to Balanchine that Martin voiced in his open letter would soon become more strenuous—as his write-up of the Adelphi Theatre performances would shortly demonstrate. On the other hand, his openness to a variety of dance expression had already made him the most influential proponent of "modern dance," and a particular champion of Martha Graham and Agnes de Mille. As early as 1929 Martin, though never an uncritical partisan of Graham's work, had greeted her first performance of *Heretic* in the *Times* as "strikingly original and glowing with vitality." And early on he'd proven himself a staunch supporter of Agnes de Mille's work—though in 1935 he wrote a blistering review of one of her recitals, sending her reeling for comfort into Martha Graham's arms. "They never raised a statue to a critic," Graham cheerily told her.

Lincoln first met Martha Graham at an April 1935 meeting called by John Martin to protest pending legislation aimed "by Dance Commercialists" to weed out small groups like the Workers Dance League. By then, he'd already seen her perform several times and by 1935 had decided that she "is phonier than I even thought: a lot of repetitious, unimpulsive Romanticism." He also unhesitatingly denounced her in print. In an article on the dance for *The Nation* in February of that year, Lincoln wrote that he was "blind to . . . [her] aesthetic," though admiring of her "personal integrity . . . and her talent for composition." In his diary he went further, writing that in terms of the dance, he regarded her as "a bitter antagonist of mine, with a good deal of talent." When he took Balanchine to see her perform, he, too, "thought she had a certain talent, superior to Massine's," but felt she'd seen too much Mary Wigman and not enough ballet.

With de Mille, Lincoln was on friendlier terms, at least during the mid-thirties (though even then he thought her "a trace of a pain in the neck)." The two would occasionally meet for tea and talk, and he attended her dance recital in early February 1935 (the same one John Martin panned), writing in his diary that "Aggie" had "worked hard" and the recital "was not boring or cheap"; but he also thought that half would have been plenty, since she had "only about three moods."

Yet he felt she "could be well used as a choreographer," and he told her he "hoped she could teach one day at the School"—even while knowing that Balanchine had seen her perform in Paris and been dismissive of her gifts. Aggie seemed to like the idea not only of teaching but also taking classes at the school, though she told Lincoln that she "disapproved" of Warburg and didn't think Vladimiroff was a good teacher. But for now all that remained in abeyance, since Aggie was headed for an extended stay in California.

Advance sales for the Adelphi Theatre engagement had gone above a thousand dollars, which in those days was thought to be very good. Stopping by the box office three days before opening night, Lincoln encountered Fokine buying tickets, a sight that left him feeling "very sheepish," probably because he had no complimentary tickets to offer but possibly, too, because Fokine, no fan of Balanchine's (or of Massine's, for that matter), may have been smarting at not being invited to choreograph. Lincoln guessed that Fokine had brought himself to buy seats because he wanted to see some of his old pupils dance (and indeed, on the second night of performance, Lincoln spotted him in the audience applauding Paul Haakon "vigorously").

Opening night on March 1 brought out what Lincoln called "a brilliant audience," though it trickled in late and the curtain didn't go up until after 9:00 p.m. Balanchine, "not dressed, unshaved and unslept," stayed backstage and as *Serenade*, the opening ballet, began, cursed Harmati, the conductor, for taking the pace too slowly. *Alma Mater*, which Lincoln had grown tired of, followed to "factitious applause." Then came *Errante*, which Lincoln thought "was a great success," though Geva was off stride and there was some unexpected audience laughter in the middle and some hissing, mingled with cheers, at the end. The closing ballet, *Reminiscence*, also went off well, though poor Paul Haakon did get caught in his hoop. Lincoln gave the dancing honors to William Dollar: "He looked marvelous in a white Nijinsky-like costume [and] danced divinely . . . he stole the show." (Carl Van Vechten, John Martin's predecessor as dance critic on the *Times*, agreed about Dollar, praising him in a letter to Gertrude Stein and remarking that "the VERY American Ballet . . . is almost as American as the steppes and chalets of Rome. But it is quite delightful.")

When the curtain came down at 11:30 p.m., the audience responded with twenty-two curtain calls. Lincoln went backstage and kissed everyone he saw. He couldn't find Balanchine, who'd apparently ducked out. Erick Hawkins seemed "beside himself with joy" and told Lincoln, "It's all you, Lincoln, it's all you." Vladimiroff said, it is "true they dance better in Russia, but nowhere else in the world."

Mina gave a large party afterward at which she herself got drunk and though at the time she was having an affair with the theater director John Houseman, expressed annoyance that no one was flirting with her. Aggie de Mille told Lincoln that "she must do a ballet"; Pavlik "was in all his states"; and Virgil Thomson announced to Lincoln that "in spite of Eddie Warburg being a cunt, etc., he managed it very well on the business side," adding that he also thought well of the Benjamin Godard score; Lincoln refrained from responding on either count. He got to bed at 3:30 a.m., feeling in a "prayerful mood" but also worried about John Martin's review.

It arrived the next morning—and enraged Lincoln. Though *Serenade* was not yet the ballet that would become a beloved worldwide favorite, it already had merit enough to deserve more than Martin's dismissive comment that it was "serviceable rather than inspired." He was even more negative about *Errante*, and at lunch that day Balanchine told Lincoln that in fact he agreed it was a "silly" ballet in the sense of being "entirely simple, like a dream"; it didn't "mean" anything, and it annoyed him that "Americans always have to see meaning in everything." Martin thought the one "real delight of the evening" (an opinion echoed in the *New York Post*) was *Reminiscence*, a crowd-pleasing concoction for which Balanchine had never made any great claims and which Lincoln had come to actively dislike (later in life he called it "banal, compromising and retardative . . . [a] betrayal of Diaghilev's *avant-gardisme*").

But overall the notices were good enough for Eddie to confirm the full two-week run. The remaining performances ran a predictable gamut, with one ballet or dancer on a given day topping the others, and the usual mix of tantrums and triumphs. An exhausted Bill Dollar (John Martin accused the management, in print, of "overworking" him) seldom matched the heights of opening night, Haakon had periodic problems with his wretched hoop, Holly Howard nearly turned her ankle (but "brought down the house by her pluck"), and Tamara Geva, who seemed unable to hit her stride, plaintively asked Balanchine why "she felt no pleasure in anything," why she was finding "no happiness from her work." Balanchine, who throughout the run looked "terribly ill" to Lincoln and whose nerves were raw from lack of sleep, sharply told Geva that "the reason was [that] she thought only of herself, nothing of others."

In the course of the run, two other ballets, *Dreams* and *Transcendence*, were added to the repertory, and various friends and eminences caught performances and pronounced verdicts. Lincoln himself thought *Dreams* was "a bad ballet," not helped by the fact that Haakon, in a black costume against black velvet curtains, could hardly be seen (though Annabelle Lyon "had a great personal success"). *Transcendence*, too, was so poorly lit that an upset Franklin Watkins, ordinarily mild-mannered, accused Tchelitchev of having "ruined his lights." John Martin weighed in with another review in the *Times;* he wrote, in essence, that *Dreams* wasn't worth doing and that *Transcendence* was hopeless. Since Martin had seen each ballet only once, Lincoln doubted if he was "as careful a student" as he'd previously thought. The *Tribune* review, in any case, was more positive. Over dinner Pavlik told Lincoln to calm down and to stop being "such a barometer." He further advised that Lincoln "must always be friends with Balanchine," that Dimitriev was "frequently unjust," and that if Eddie Warburg "didn't have his money, he'd be selling newspapers." All of which, Lincoln felt, was "good advice" indeed—and especially since he'd come to realize that Balanchine felt he unjustly tended to side with Dimitriev during their quarrels.

As for eminences and their verdicts, the variation was so great as to defy consensus—or comfort. Lincoln's old friend from his Boston days, Marianna Lowell, "bubbled with excitement," and his father "seemed to like it a lot," though Lincoln thought he was primarily impressed by the size of the theater and the fact that it was nearly full the evening he came (on other evenings they sometimes had to paper the house to create the semblance of an "event"). Anne Lindbergh, a former pupil of Mina's at Smith whom Lincoln had also gotten to know and like, was also appreciative of the performance; her husband didn't attend because Lincoln had left tickets for the couple at the box office, reporters were tipped off—and Charles was "scared away."

Few of the other celebrities who attended various performances—including Leslie Howard, Tallulah Bankhead, Bea Lillie, and Claudette Colbert—left any record of their reactions. But Igor Stravinsky—who under Diaghilev had collaborated several times with Balanchine (most notably on *Apollo*)—came on March 10 and said that with the exception of Charles Koechlin's "dreadful" orchestration of Schubert (*Errante*), the rest was *très gentil*. Lincoln hadn't met Stravinsky before but would soon get to know him well; his initial impression was of a "strange little rat-like man" who was "sweet with Balanchine."

There was an abundance of negative reaction, much of it delivered to Lincoln flat out, with no apparent regard for hurt feelings. His left-wing friend Leo Hurwitz of *New Theatre* told him bluntly that he "abhorred" the entire thing, that ballet amounted to little more than a "form of narcissism and sexuality and rigidity." The critic Edna Ocko and the dancer-choreographer Anna Sokolow fully concurred; themselves active in socialist struggles, and Sokolow in the currently popular Workers Dance League, they deplored the ballet's lack of social consciousness. Arguing with them over beer, Lincoln hotly defended ballet as a form of expression, yet given his own wish—and failure—to produce ballets (like *Tom*, *Red Hydra*, and *Hobo Jungle*) with more political content, he felt the criticism deeply.

More so than he did the complaints reported to him by third parties from his antagonists in the world of modern dance. He was told that Louis Horst, Martha Graham's influential friend and adviser, had "hated all of the ballet," and that Graham, though "interested in Balanchine's work," thought "the turns are unnecessary and the costumes embarrass the girls." Lincoln refrained from passing the comments on to Balanchine, but in fact Balanchine found Graham's choreography much more interesting than Agnes de Mille's, and Lincoln did talk to Graham's manager, Frances Hawkins, about the possibility of her doing a ballet for them, but not using her own group; Hawkins said that Graham "plainly disapproved of ballet." Ironically Hawkins herself would soon put her managerial skills at Lincoln's service.

At the final performance at the Adelphi Theatre on March 17, Léonide Massine, freshly returned from the de Basil Company's national tour, and long estranged from Balanchine, came onstage and a public rapprochement between the two took place. Massine said that "he admired the corps de ballet and was glad Balanchine was starting such an important thing." It was, Lincoln wrote in his diary, "like Washington meeting Cornwallis," implying that some sort of surrender and triumph of the underdog had taken place.

The close of the engagement left Lincoln feeling "terribly let down," whereas Balanchine seemed calm and contented. He was "very affectionate" with Lincoln, held his arm, talked of next year, and told him to regard their survival thus far as a "victory." But a temperamentally gloomy Lincoln wrote in his diary that Balanchine doesn't "seem to me to be worried enough."

CHAPTER FIFTEEN

The Metropolitan Opera

(1935)

T HE MONTHS AFTER the Adelphi Theatre engagement resembled the strange sort of calm that follows a squall (or in the case of this contentious group, a series of hurricanes). A kind of uneasy detachment reigned. There was still the familiar scurry of meetings and negotiations, new contracts drawn up, plans for the future under constant discussion. But the atmosphere was curiously lethargic; something like a slow-motion waltz replaced the frantic lindy hop that had preceded.[1]

None of the four principal figures in the American Ballet seemed eager for quick decisions or instant commitments. Dimitriev was the possible exception; he, more than the other three, seemed concerned about clarifying future plans as soon as possible. Eddie, though often paralyzed by indecision, was also, if to a lesser degree, concerned about restructuring current arrangements. It was Dimitriev and Eddie who presented most of the plans, aware that their prospects as gifted individuals were less promising than those of Balanchine and Lincoln. Eddie had little except money to fall back on, and Dimitriev, though still talking of opening a ballet school in Hollywood, had been, despite all his complaining, deriving a secure and growing income from the increasingly stable School of American Ballet.

On the other hand Balanchine and Lincoln seemed, throughout the spring of 1935, to have turned inward (Balanchine's usual place of residence), mulling over the comparative appeal of other outlets for their gifts and in search of some countervailing respite from the exhausting, all-consuming entanglements of the American Ballet. Balanchine had already made it clear that he wouldn't be teaching much at the school during the upcoming year, and as a result Muriel Stuart, who'd been a dancer with Pavlova, was asked in the spring of 1935 to give a demonstration class for Vladimiroff, Balanchine, and Lincoln. It was "unanimously appreciated," and she was immediately hired, at first as Vladimiroff's assistant; she quickly gained everyone's admiration and would for many decades remain a mainstay at the school.

Balanchine rejected Dimitriev's post-Adelphi plan for "restudying" the repertory they already had in order to make *Errante, Transcendence, Reminiscence,* and *Alma Mater* "perfect" for the road. No, Balanchine said, "nothing more can be done with them," he was "bored with it all and wants to go on with something new." He also let it be known that he'd been getting feelers to choreograph the *Ziegfeld Follies*, and once he had a firm offer intended to take it.

Lincoln, for his part, turned down a nervous Eddie's unexpected offer to become co-director of his long-gestating production company. Lincoln felt that Eddie would soon enough fail or get bored; he'd let the company "get out of his hands," and Lincoln felt he could "pick it up or start another," one directly linked to the school and focused on developing American themes and choreographers. Dimitriev tried to interest him in doing so immediately, but Lincoln was content to wait: basically he trusted neither Dimitriev nor Warburg and counted "only on the chance that's made whatever's happened possible, and also vaguely on Balanchine." "Having seen something actually produced this year," Lincoln wrote in his diary, "I'm less impatient, less apprehensive of disaster."

But Eddie had become so skittish about his ability to exercise the total control over the production company he'd earlier insisted on that he began to turn increasingly to his once-scorned antagonist Dimitriev for advice; this, in fairly short order, brought Dimitriev into a position of authority with the company that he'd once denounced and from which Eddie had sworn to bar him.

Lincoln neither disengaged from discussions involving plans for a fall tour nor devoted much of his time to it. For the next few months he rearranged his priorities, putting primary emphasis on completing his history of the dance—which meant as well finishing up his current series of lectures drawn from the book's chapters. He also devoted some incidental energy to trying to promote his just-published book of verse, *Low Ceiling*, perplexed at the lack of reviews. But a few reviews is more than most poets ever get, and Lincoln not only got a decent number, but they were largely favorable. The first notice, a pleasing one by the well-known poet Babette Deutsch, appeared in the *Sun*, and Lincoln thought it "very discerning and fair—only I'm sure my line is not as monotonous as she said." Subsequently the *Herald Tribune* published a review that was approving overall ("Mr. Kirstein has an extraordinary sense of the color, texture and anatomy of words") but suggested—just as Lincoln had predicted—that he'd come under the influence of Stephen Spender in regard to vocabulary and verbal mannerisms.

When Lincoln found time to socialize, the person he now sought out most for companionship was Pavlik Tchelitchev. Pavlik was all at once volatile, charming, and ferociously opinionated. He tended to talk with brilliant passion, his conversation sometimes so relentlessly forceful that it made Lincoln "tired and nervous."

With his wide range of acquaintances, Tchelitchev was among the great gossips of the day, a joyful scandalmonger with effusive views on everyone and everything. Among much else, he told Lincoln that Ben Shahn was currently "the only good young American painter," and a likable though weak man who needed Communism to feel strong. He further told Lincoln that he'd talked with Massine after the final performance at the Adelphi Theatre, and the choreographer had told him that he "must kill de Basil or be killed by him," that he was "exhausted and his nerves ruined," that he had to stop trying to create things like his recent ballet *Jardin Park* (which Lincoln had seen and found "boring and vulgar"), until he had something to say: he should leave experiment to Balanchine "with a new company in a new country."

As early as April 1935, Lincoln was writing in his diary that "next to Muriel Draper . . . [Tchelitchev] is, humanly speaking by far the most wonderful person, most understanding and helpful I know." The two men were trusting enough to talk together with the utmost frankness. Pavlik, unlike most Russian émigrés, to a degree shared Lincoln's left-wing views, telling him, "We cannot make fun of the Communists: they are *quand même*, the only hope." Beyond politics, Tchelitchev, nearly ten years older than Lincoln, played something of a mentor role with him. He told Lincoln that he'd been "dominated too long" by Dimitriev's "grossness," that Dimitriev was "bitter and coarse," and that he himself would no longer speak to him. Pavlik also insistently encouraged Lincoln to demand for himself "a position equivalent to . . . [his] capacities." Pavlik's admonitions gave Lincoln (in his own words) "considerable strength," made him feel "bucked up" and more determined to "assume the importance of [his]. . . position: just nurse the School, see that it is well fed and well kept up."

It was not a one-way relationship. Tchelitchev also confided in Lincoln, especially about his problems with Charles Henri Ford. Although satisfied with him as a lover and companion (though he worried that Charlie didn't work harder), Pavlik knew that his friends found him far too fey and effeminate for their taste. Due to leave for Europe shortly, Pavlik asked Lincoln's advice about what to do; he couldn't "bear" to leave Charlie behind, he said, but his closest friend in England, Edith Sitwell, and his frequent patron, Edward James, could not stand having Charlie around. (In the end he took Charlie with him.)

On this subject Lincoln decided against candor. He himself had little respect or patience for Charlie Ford. "Fairies" and their campy ways had long disgusted him (though he was quite capable, with intimates, of camping himself, the more so as he got older). Nor was he predisposed to appreciate what Ford had already achieved in his young life. Still only twenty-six in 1935, Charlie had, as a teenager, published a poem in *The New Yorker* (and would eventually publish more than a dozen volumes of verse); had in 1929 edited a significant little magazine, *Blues*, which in its eight issues had given first publication to, among others, Paul Bowles,

Harold Rosenberg, and Erskine Caldwell; and in 1933 had coauthored (with Parker Tyler) *The Young and the Evil*, which many consider the first (if undistinguished) novel to portray gay characters in a positive light. Charles Henri Ford would never become anything like a significant literary figure, but Lincoln's distaste for "effeminacy" would always prevent him from acknowledging whatever accomplishments Charlie did manage.

Lincoln was delighted that Balanchine, before starting in on any new work, decided to take a two-week holiday in Florida at Alice de la Mar's place. "I get such a pleasure of relief," he wrote in his diary, "when I see Balanchine lazy, rested and amusing." But after returning from Florida in April, Balanchine told Lincoln that although he felt well he did constantly worry about falling ill again. As a preventive measure, he decided to take a series of "injections" designed to ward off tuberculosis; he had his first one (ingredients and doctor unknown) on April 8. Balanchine also confided to Lincoln (who wrote the conversation into his diary) that currently "he doesn't screw much, mainly to save his energy, not because he's frightened of transmitting the disease." He told him further that Tamara Geva had let him know that she'd marry him again, "but he didn't want to."

Lincoln, in turn, reported Dorothie Littlefield's defection during Balanchine's absence. She'd abruptly left for Europe to join the Monte Carlo Ballet, and had done so, as Lincoln put it, "very cavalierly, without a word of goodbye to her late lover Mr. Warburg" (she and Eddie had been having an on-again, off-again affair). The news came as a shock to Balanchine. He said that since she'd "gone over to the enemy" he'd be against her ever being allowed to return to the school.[2]

Despite his fear of falling ill, Balanchine felt ready to begin new work. Lincoln revived the idea of *Uncle Tom's Cabin*, this time with Ben Shahn doing scenery and costumes. Shahn hadn't wanted to start working up sketches without some assurance that *Tom* would actually be produced. Balanchine now said that he did want to do the ballet, and Lincoln told Shahn to go ahead and wrote excitedly to a friend that *Tom* would be "the first really revolutionary ballet that's been achieved in this country." Balanchine even seemed willing for a time to reconsider the possibility, after all, of mounting Tchelitchev's *Medea*. A delighted Lincoln quickly sketched a story outline, and he, Balanchine, and Tchelitchev had several long discussions on ways in which the plot might be further elaborated. But in the end Eddie would refuse to provide the money for a production.

In the midst of all this, Fokine sent a letter/article to the school in mid-April that caused, in Lincoln's words, "considerable excitement." Written in Russian, the article asserted that "nothing has been done in choreography for the last 25 years except representations of abnormal love." He mentioned no names, but Balanchine asked, "What the hell had . . .

[Fokine] done in the last 25 years himself?" When Dimitriev translated the article, it emerged that Fokine traced the present-day "pornography" in ballet to Nijinsky's *Faun,* and singled out the "stretcher scene" in *Errante* as a prime example of the endemic obscenity.

Mid-April brought a second surprise: an invitation to Lincoln from Bronia Nijinska to work with her on her memoirs. The two had met the previous month at Vladimiroff's, and Lincoln had found her intelligent, charming—and very deaf. She told him—with Felia Doubrovska translating between them—that Romola's book, on which Lincoln had worked long and hard, was "cross-cut with lies." Among those she cited was Romola's claim that Pavlova regretted that Vaslav didn't injure himself; wholly false, Bronia said. She insisted as well that "Vaslav was all right until he married Romola."

On the subject of her own ballets, Bronia told Lincoln that nobody, including Diaghilev, had initially liked or understood *Les Noces,* except for Vassily Ivanovitch, a Russian peasant who served as a bodyguard and whom Romola had denounced in her book. Bronia also made it clear to Lincoln that Fokine "hates" her, and that for her part she "[wouldn't] speak to Balanchine," had had "a row with Hurok" and "[couldn't] work for de Basil now." She showed Lincoln pictures of her ballets, and sketches she'd made of Vaslav at school, but wouldn't allow him to make slides from them.

Bronia said she'd require any publisher to provide a thousand-dollar advance for her memoirs, but Lincoln thought she'd have a hard time getting it; he tried to explain to her that the publishing world was currently beset by economic woes. He also told her that until a publisher was assured, he needed to concentrate on completing his own history of the dance. But he did promise to do what he could for her and, true to his word, approached Henry Hart, his poetry editor at Putnam's. Hart said the firm might be interested in Bronia's memoirs, but that she would first have to submit a prospectus. Since she was due to sail for Europe in a few days, the matter was put off.

As Eddie Warburg and his chosen agent, Merovich, continued to mature plans with Balanchine for the production company's early fall tour, Lincoln devoted his energies primarily to the completion of his book. Having turned twenty-eight on May 4, 1935, he was more intent than ever on carving out an individual reputation apart from his behind-the-scenes role as the promoter of the talents of others.

Throughout the spring and summer of 1935, he bent his energies toward producing what would become the first comprehensive study in English chronicling dance history from ancient times down through the choreography of Balanchine. He succeeded brilliantly, producing an erudite work of wide-ranging commentary that placed dance performance within the cultural and political contexts from which it emerged. In her introduction to the book's most recent re-issue in 1987, the distinguished dance historian Nancy Reynolds pointed out that *Dance* appeared at a time when scholarship on the subject was "virtually nonexistent"; she further asserted that in its "quality of thought and powers of synthesis" it has still not been superseded.[3]

Perhaps the book's most remarkable feature, given Lincoln's tempestuous personality, is the evenhanded tone he managed to maintain throughout; this despite his passionate partisanship for classic ballet and his antipathy to most of "modern" dance. In *Dance*, Lincoln somehow managed to modulate his partisanship and create a decent approximation of fair-mindedness. Though he made his admiration for Balanchine clear enough, he also referenced what were then standard complaints that the choreographer "has not been responsible for any new genre of ballet." And though Lincoln referred to Massine as being somewhat too "intellectual," he also included high praise for his recent *Choreartium*, elevating it above Balanchine's *Serenade* or *Cotillon* in its grander, "nobler scale" of "spiritual evocation."

Typically, Lincoln focused on what was *wrong* with his book, writing a friend soon after publication, "I realize very bitterly the errors in it, not only in regard to proof errors, alas, but also there are some errors in fact . . . it was written too quickly." In truth he'd labored long and hard on it; there was no other way a man of such opinionated intensity could have brought off a work of such skilled restraint. Lincoln also thought the book read "somewhat awkwardly" (it doesn't), and he worried further that he'd "left out any aesthetic judgments or any standards by which dancing can be judged"; *Dance* is in fact rife with judgments, if happily free of codified "standards of judgment."

Over the summer of 1935, as Lincoln was winding up work on his book, the prolonged series of negotiations about the school's future also drew to a close. He'd always been more or less indifferent to matters of profit and loss, except when he found himself unexpectedly broke; he cared only that the school survive and, unlike Dimitriev, not at all about lining his own pockets. But his father cared more, and had long been indignant that the original contracts setting up the school had failed to provide Lincoln with a salary or with what he considered an equitable share of stock. Louis intervened directly with Dimitriev during the new contract negotiations, and a formula was drawn up whereby Lincoln, starting September 1, 1935, would get a salary of fifty dollars a week and in return would earmark 50 percent of the income from his subsequent writings to the school; also the percentage of shares was, "in a manner more favorable" to Lincoln, redistributed.

In early July it was decided that the accumulated profits from the school would be divided up (Lincoln received nearly two thousand dollars)—but that for the next three years profits would be allowed to accumulate and no further division would take place. Eddie Warburg, however, felt that the school should simply "finish up," since it "had fulfilled its function of forming his Company." Henceforth, he told Dimitriev, he wanted "no further responsibility in the School, and would cede his stock." But Eddie was known to change his mind about as often as the weather, and no one knew whether to take such pronouncements seriously. Nor were Dimitriev and Lincoln at all alarmed; they felt that the school could go on "perfectly well" without Eddie.[4]

Whether the production company could get along *with* Eddie now became the big question. Early in June a meeting was held at his lawyer's office to discuss "a possible settlement of all our frictions between School and Company." It boiled down to a question of "equalization or complete separation." Lincoln and Dimitriev held out for the right to produce on their own, which raised the specter of a competing company and greatly upset Eddie, whose confidence in his own ability was, at best, unsteady. His immediate response was to take Lincoln out to lunch and suggest that the two of them should run everything themselves, cutting Dimitriev out entirely or reducing him to the level of an employee. Knowing the idea was preposterous, indeed suicidal, Lincoln turned him down cold.

By the end of June an agreement of sorts had been patched together: the school and the production company would be separate entities, with Eddie given leave to employ dancers trained in the school but denied the right to advertise his enterprise as "the Company of the American School of Ballet." Dimitriev was pleased with the outcome, Eddie "furious" that his archenemy would continue to exercise authority in the school and draw a substantial income from it, and Lincoln resigned and biding his time. Dimitriev may have thought of Lincoln as his "ally," but Lincoln thought otherwise; he "visualized a break with him, similar to the break with Warburg" as soon as the time was ripe.

Two months later Eddie reiterated to Lincoln that "the School offers him nothing" and that—again reversing himself—Dimitriev would "have absolutely no part of the ballet productions" given by "*his* Company." He shed a few crocodile tears over the "necessity" of cutting Lincoln "out of it" as well, but felt it necessary in order to avoid the appearance that he was discriminating against Dimitriev. Since Lincoln had scant confidence in Eddie's abilities, and expected the production company, despite Balanchine's participation, to fail, he took Eddie's patronizing attitude in stride. Keeping his own counsel, Lincoln continued to see himself as a bridge between the school and the company. He himself had no intention (as he wrote in his diary) of being "split from Balanchine"; he felt, however, that "George *is* suggestible."

Lincoln's positioning of himself in this complex set of personal alliances soon proved his shrewdness. In late September, when the com-

pany's initial tour, arranged by the agent Alexander Merovich, kicked off
in White Plains, Lincoln dutifully attended. But he found the performance "simply dreadful": the lights went wrong, Annabelle Lyon injured
herself, and Holly Howard was not at her best. "It was all too grisly," Lincoln wrote in his diary, but "Balanchine was imperturbable." The disaster
gave Lincoln no pleasure; in fact he felt "awful about it," said nothing, and
slipped quietly away at the end. A few days later, though, he told Eddie
how "wrong" he felt the White Plains performance had been. Eddie didn't
agree but was "very nice" about what he called Lincoln's "hysteria." Balanchine, for his part, told Lincoln that "a better company did not exist in
the West, save for the men; perhaps in Russia but nowhere in Europe."

Despite the proclaimed general optimism, the company ran into trouble even before it left on tour. Merovich started to lose his temper and yell
at the dancers for acting as "individuals" rather than as a collective. Eddie
cautioned him against treating them as if they were grown-ups—they
were, after all, "children," and it was impossible "to be democratic."
When Merovich, out of nowhere, abruptly asked Eddie for a twelve-
thousand-dollar loan, he became further disconcerted—and turned him
down. Lincoln took the role of onlooker, deciding he "couldn't afford to
let . . . [himself] become involved"; but he chalked it all up to "experience
for the future."

On October 15, the company, with Balanchine and Eddie on board the
bus, set off on what was supposed to be a three-month tour. Pictures were
taken, Lincoln kissed everyone good-bye—and privately told Eugene
Loring "to report to me at all occasions." Some twenty of the school's students were part of the tour, but classes continued as before. Not only was
Muriel Stuart working out splendidly as a teacher of classic technique, but
after much hemming and hawing, the dancer Anatole Vilzak was finally
hired in early October and proved, to Lincoln's "great relief," immediately
impressive and popular (though Lincoln considered his wife, the well-
known dancer Ludmilla Schollar, "a bitch").

A mere two days after the company departed, Eddie called Lincoln at
midnight from New Haven to say that Merovich "had been behaving outrageously, calling everyone names, screaming at the kids." Eddie (Lincoln
wrote in his diary) "was in a panic" and was convinced that the whole tour
was lost. Lincoln thought he sounded "scared to death" and ready to cede
the touring organization to Merovich, a refusal of responsibility that made
Lincoln "sore." But he took the high road, told Eddie there was "no question but to continue," and tried to calm him down by reminding him of
Diaghilev's "disaster" just before his first Paris season.

The next day Eddie returned to his New York apartment on Beekman
Place and Lincoln, picking up Dimitriev along the way, went there and
found Eddie in "an acute state of panic." Sandor Harmati, the tour conductor, had called to say he couldn't get any work done at all, that

Merovich had locked himself away, refusing to talk to or see anyone. Dimitriev felt sure that the whole thing was a calculated effort to terrorize Eddie into giving him the twelve-thousand-dollar loan. The troupe was due to perform that night in Allentown, Pennsylvania, and both men urged Eddie to proceed.

Somehow the company did struggle on for a few more days, the audiences small, the dancers unpaid, and Balanchine "tired and worried." Lincoln felt the tour would manage to lurch forward a bit longer, but he was wrong. On October 21 the company reached Scranton, Pennsylvania, where all hell broke loose. Merovich announced that he had guns, would launch an attack against the "enemy," annihilate all "spies," and kill Balanchine and Warburg. He terrorized the troupe so thoroughly that they could hardly dance, yet somehow they did manage a performance on the twenty-second. The next day, however, a closing notice was posted, and the company folded. They'd been "on the road" exactly one week.

Once they were back in New York, ramifications from the disaster multiplied. Eddie became "terrified of the publicity of failure," whereas Lincoln was more concerned that Balanchine might be on the verge of a breakdown. He'd grown fearful on the road that he was about to become ill again and as a result, his nerves frayed, had (so one of the dancers reported to Lincoln) acted "dreadfully" to Holly Howard—badly upsetting her by publicly saying that Elise Reiman danced much better than she did.

Some twenty-five years later, Eddie claimed in an interview that Merovich had "declared himself insane and ran off with all the money and left us stranded." But that was an exaggerated version of what had happened, since Merovich continued for a time to appear at the school and to make demands. In the aftermath of the tour's collapse, Eddie further asserted that he'd "had sixty-eight lawsuits thrown at me by every manager across the country for the expenses they'd incurred"; when told by Lincoln that he "had to settle with them because if we ever want to tour again we'll need them," Eddie purportedly replied, "The hell I will."

Whatever the full truth of the matter, all sides agreed that the tour's failure could seriously jeopardize negotiations currently in progress with the Metropolitan Opera, talks that had begun several months earlier. Lincoln had for some time casually known the Met's new general manager, ex-tenor Edward Johnson, and thought him a warm, sympathetic man. The previous spring Johnson had come to watch a class at the school and had spoken in a vague way about rethinking the role of ballet at the Metropolitan. Until recently Eddie Warburg's father, Felix, had been prominently involved with the Met, but Lincoln thought that the long-standing Italian dominance at the opera house would continue to hold sway, with little likelihood that Johnson would make the American Ballet any sort of offer.[5]

As a result of his pessimism, he took seriously overtures from the dancer-choreographer Ruth Page, director of the Chicago Grand Opera, and her husband, Tom Fisher, that they combine forces in order to gain control over the ballet at the Met. In May, a month after Edward Johnson visited the school, Fisher invited Lincoln to dinner, telling him that the Met's previous administration "had fixed it up pretty much" with Ruth to take over the ballet there, but that with the appointment of Johnson as general manager "the situation was entirely changed"—though Ruth "was still in the running." In order to block other possible contenders, in particular the people at Juilliard, Fisher suggested that a combination of his wife and Balanchine be proposed to Johnson; both of them knew opera and could "fill that lousy stage."

Lincoln's initial response was enthusiastic, since he thought it highly unlikely that the American Ballet would itself be asked to become the resident company. But then, a mere two days later, Lincoln and Eddie Warburg were asked to come to Edward Johnson's office. On their way in Eddie told Lincoln that he thought Tom Fisher "protests too much," that in his opinion they didn't "have to play with Ruth Page at all." Lincoln told Eddie he was crazy, that there was so much prejudice against Balanchine as a Russian that only an alliance with an American choreographer would allow them to get a foot in the door. As it would turn out, and as Lincoln freely acknowledged, "irresponsible" Eddie had read the situation "just right."

At the ensuing meeting Johnson was attended by his chief assistant, Edward Ziegler. Lincoln—whose delicate antennae seemed temporarily on the blink—put Ziegler down as "an amiable old dodo," but he would soon learn that Ziegler was a very able manager and to a significant degree the power behind the throne. Johnson, without hesitation or qualification, told Lincoln and Eddie that he did want the American Ballet to become the Met's resident company, and that "in no circumstances did he want Tom Fisher on their necks," or Ruth Page, whose ambition "he couldn't bear." If Lincoln and Eddie felt they needed an associate, Johnson said he'd prefer Agnes de Mille. Lincoln said they didn't; he sang Balanchine's praises and emphasized his considerable experience with opera houses.

After the meeting concluded, Johnson asked Lincoln to stay behind to meet his daughter, and once they were alone told him "how pleased he was with the results" of their talk and how confident he felt that "something could be worked out." But Lincoln—who temperamentally required something to worry about—privately expressed concern to Eddie that the Met's governing board, and in particular John Erskine ("who does not love Balanchine") would throw up barriers to Johnson's offer. He also complimented Eddie on his acumen about Fisher and Page, acknowledging that Fisher "had completely fooled" him as to the absolute necessity of having his wife aboard. Lincoln said he now felt "both betrayed and betrayer."

In the event, the complications came from Eddie, not the Met's board. He told Lincoln the following month that he couldn't afford to sponsor both the Met ballet and his then-pending company tour. Dimitriev argued that the Metropolitan Opera was the far greater opportunity, but even if the advice had come from someone less antagonistic to him, Eddie stubbornly opted for the tour—and disaster. In making his choice, Eddie cited his analyst Zilboorg's view that if his "beautiful mind . . . can only have the shit taken off it," Eddie would go far—as far, it turned out, as Scranton, Pennsylvania. At the time, a dumbfounded Lincoln decided not to argue; he simply made the decision that the school, from which Eddie had separated himself, would itself take up the Met's offer—and despite the fact that Dimitriev insisted the school wasn't ready for such an assignment. Lincoln and Balanchine conferred about whether or not to take on Agnes de Mille as "second in command," but Balanchine worried about her "in relation to intrigue at the Met," and also didn't want her to dance. He intended to invite the experienced European-trained dancers Felia Doubrovska, Leon Woizikovsky, and his once common-law wife, Alexandra Danilova, to serve as guest artists.

In August the press announced that it was official: Balanchine was to be the new *maître de ballet* at the Metropolitan Opera. John Martin immediately protested. In a *Times* column that declared "it is deeply to be regretted that once again American artists have been passed by for a high artistic post for which at least half a dozen of them are eminently fitted" (though he failed to specify who, he probably had de Mille foremost in mind). Martin didn't dispute the fact that Balanchine was "a gifted artist" and would "grace his new position," but he had doubts on several fronts.

He had little confidence, first of all, in the American Ballet company Balanchine would take with him, calling it "an apprentice group rather than a company of artists" (an assessment with which Dimitriev, and possibly even Lincoln and Balanchine, might have agreed). In addition Martin pointed out that the American Ballet had been originally formed with the intention of creating dance that would evoke "the full flavor of American life and culture," with "the technical tradition of the academic ballet as nothing more than a framework." Instead the company had taken "a different turn almost from the start." Martin insisted that Balanchine had "no experience whatever" of "American possibilities." (Actually Balanchine had immediately felt at home in the United States, though it was true that he—unlike Lincoln—hadn't shown much interest in creating ballets with homegrown themes.) His compositions to date, Martin argued, reflected "the type of audience he already knew in Europe"—the same sort of audience "of social position and wealth" that largely dominated the Metropolitan, which would encourage, if not insist, that the American Ballet continue along traditional lines.

Martin was making a fair point: though Lincoln had pushed hard for the creation of ballets like *Tom* or *Hobo Jungle*, Balanchine had shown limited interest, and the only American-themed ballet that had as yet made it into production was the slight *Alma Mater*. But in a letter to the *Times* responding to Martin's column, Lincoln leapt to the defense. Challenging Martin as an authority of what was or was not "American," Lincoln sarcastically commented that although ballet wasn't indigenous to America, neither were violin or piano playing: "In these times of aggressive nationalism," he expressed sardonic gratitude to Martin for not limiting his definition of "American" to Anglo-Saxons alone.

Lincoln further argued that "sound training" in classic ballet technique was as essential for "modern dance" practitioners as for ballet dancers themselves. That was a shaky point. Most of those involved in modern dance (Louis Horst was a partial exception) saw nothing of value in the inherited forms of classic ballet and were bent on inventing their own, oppositional, dance vocabularies. In his letter Lincoln also revealed a prior conversation with John Martin in which he'd expressed the hope "that the ballet would be in America a popular, widely loved institution," and not just the property of the rich.

Be that as it may, Lincoln's rejoinder entirely ignored Martin's essential points: that the American Ballet was a risky choice because it was relatively new and inexperienced; that an art originating in an aristocratic culture might not flourish in a democratic one; and that George Balanchine had, thus far at least, seemed uninterested in American themes and American forms of expression in dance. Lincoln avoided those issues because—in 1935—no cogent response to them was yet possible.

These months of turmoil surrounding the American Ballet were paralleled by various jolting developments within Lincoln's private circle. In late May, Mina had discovered that she was four and a half months pregnant with John Houseman's child. The news created mixed emotions in her; she was pleased that she *could* conceive, since doctors had long since told her that she couldn't, but she was apprehensive about the abortion she felt it wise to have, since Houseman's affections had turned elsewhere. The head of Mt. Sinai Hospital proved willing to perform the operation, but only for the startling sum of twenty thousand dollars; it didn't help that brother George blew up when he heard the figure. Ultimately, the abortion was done at Mt. Morris Hospital for a much-reduced fee. The procedure proved more difficult than expected, and it was a week before Lincoln could take Mina home to Ashfield; she remained unsteady for some time, but her health was basically intact.

There was agitation, too, surrounding Lincoln's political activities.

Despite his disillusion following Kirov's assassination, he'd remained a committed left-winger. He accepted with pleasure the invitation from Herb Kline of the Communist-oriented *New Theatre* to chair a fundraising dinner, concerned only that he spoke at it "so badly." And he also joined a committee formed to raise money for the *Southern Worker*, the only Communist organ in the South. Moreover, it was Kline he turned to when he learned from the American consul in Hamburg that a new anti-Semitic campaign was about to be launched in the United States linking "Jew" and "Communist" as much as possible. A concerned Lincoln discussed strategies with Kline for combating the linkage and he also asked him how he could be of further service, short of contributing funds that he didn't have. Kline advised him "to shut up," not to write under his own name for Communist publications, and to "give all information to only one person."

Kline also told Lincoln that he'd spoken about him to Earl Browder—then editor of the *Daily Worker*, later head of the Communist Party USA. *What* Kline said to Browder, Lincoln failed, perhaps deliberately, to record in his diary. But he did mention an earlier meeting when Browder had asked him for a loan for the *Worker* and Lincoln had turned him down "on the grounds I was an avowed capitalist." He now read Browder's *Communism and Religion* for the first time, and thought it "excellent." He also had another talk with Browder and explained to him "in detail" why he wasn't a party member.

As late as mid-November 1935, Lincoln got so angry at his old friend and mentor, Hyatt Mayor, for cynically saying that he thought the Communists were "boy scouts," that he doubted he could continue to see him. In regard to another old friend, Lyman Paine, Lincoln was "very much" moved when Lyman told him that he'd given up architecture and "had found his stability in his part of the Revolution" as a Trotskyist. Here, Lincoln wrote, was Lyman as he should be: "intransigent, articulate, puritanical and courageous. . . . The more I am swayed, the more deeply I feel the necessity of my own complete independence at least at this period." All of which sounds far less like a man who'd lost his revolutionary ardor than one whose commitment to establishing ballet in the United States had—temporarily, he apparently thought—taken precedence over all else.

In the meantime, Muriel Draper had returned to New York from the Soviet Union. "It's wonderful having her back," Lincoln wrote in his diary. He'd "never seen her look so marvelously well," and that first night the two of them talked until five in the morning, catching up on news, delighting in their restored companionship. Among much else Muriel told Lincoln that "everything is ultimately OK" in the Soviet Union, which was what he had "hoped" to hear. Within weeks she had started a campaign to raise $750 to buy a press for the *Southern Worker*.

Muriel and Lincoln were soon going everywhere together and consulting on everything from politics to the ballet. But, as had been true in the
past, their tempers would periodically flare at each other and their relationship run temporarily aground. The first serious problem came when
Lincoln moved to a new apartment at 971 First Avenue, and Muriel
decided to take a flat in the same building, two floors below him. Lincoln
wasn't pleased; "I don't intend being interrupted," he wrote sternly in his
diary, and he was afraid she'd become too reliant on him. But it was
Muriel, not Lincoln, who slammed the first door, which he took, with
considerable relief, as a sign that she wanted him "to keep away most of
the time."

His father somehow conflated the new living arrangements with a
1928 letter to Lincoln that he'd discovered when going through a safe
deposit vault; the letter included the word "syphilis." Greatly agitated,
Louis asked his son if he was "keeping a woman" or (a suspicion triggered
by Lincoln having recently asked his father for additional money) "being
black-mailed." Louis demanded to know if anyone "had a hold" on him.
Lincoln refrained from itemizing the assorted Bosco Dunhams who'd
recently held a grip on his emotions, and tried to reassure his father that
all was well. Taking Lincoln aside, Rose confided to him that Louis's fears
were due to his "change of life."

During these same tumultuous months, several deaths occurred that
deeply upset Lincoln. His hero T. E. Lawrence ("he is my standard of the
best writer and the best life") and the sculptor Gaston Lachaise died
within a short time of each other. Lincoln had never met Lawrence, but he
had long been a patron and friend to Lachaise. Soon after the sculptor
died, Madame Lachaise sent word to Lincoln that her husband had
thought of him "like a son." Lincoln had seen to it that Lachaise's insurance policy remained paid up, with the result that his widow could count
on at least a modest income—though a year later he had to speedily solicit
funds to prevent a dispossess notice served on her from being carried out.
For many years to come, Lincoln would continue to play an active role in
placing Lachaise's remaining work with well-regarded institutions and
collectors.

Following the collapse of the Merovich tour, Eddie, in mid-November,
took himself off to Mexico for a month's vacation. As Lincoln wrote his
father, "I am doing the best I can to give the impression that I am outraged, and accuse him wildly of all sorts of laziness and so on . . . [but as]
you can quite well imagine . . . we are all delighted that he is going to be
gone for a month. Rehearsals start at once and I really think that we will
have a chance to redeem the last disaster." Told by the Met that he could
have a company of fifty to fifty-five dancers, Balanchine held open tryouts;

according to Lincoln, they auditioned "about forty dreadful dancers, out of whom about two were possible."

Little time remained to get ready for the Met's season. The American Ballet was expected to make its bow at the opening night performance of *La Traviata* on December 16, 1935, quickly followed by performances in *Faust* and *Aida*. Then, on Friday afternoon of the same week—and for the first time since 1927—the Met decided to present a ballet independent of that evening's opera, on a double bill with *Hänsel und Gretel*. All this loomed as a formidable amount of work, not made easier by the whispered resentment of some of the dancers at rumors that Balanchine again planned to feature guest artists in leading roles.

Vladimiroff also contributed to the state of uneasiness. He'd been restive for some time, partly due to anxiety over the pending expiration of his and Kyra Blanc's visas in September, partly because of his displeasure at the recent additions of Muriel Stuart and Anatole Vilzak to the staff. Lincoln himself made trips to Canada and to Washington, DC, to try and get visa extensions for the couple, but Vladimiroff continued to be difficult and at one point Lincoln decided he was a "bastard." Perhaps seeing the handwriting on the wall, Vladimiroff suddenly changed his tune, declaring "his great love for us all" and his intention to work at the school "always." But then he made the mistake of demanding that the school pay for his vacation in Cuba *and* continue his salary while away. That did it: Dimitriev and Lincoln decided not to rehire him for the following year. But Balanchine intervened, saying the students preferred Vladimiroff's classes to Vilzak's, and if they fired Vladimiroff they might "as well shut up the School." As a compromise Vladimiroff was offered half the teaching and salary he currently had; furious, he threatened to defect to de Basil, but then decided, after all, to stay put.[6]

It was time now to get to work in earnest. Starting in mid-September Lincoln devoted considerable effort to preparing the libretto for *Tom*, though knowing it would have to await the Met's spring season. He, Balanchine, Ben Shahn, and "Nicky" Nabokov (who was to do the score) collectively outlined the first act, with Ben and Nicky determined to keep Balanchine "away from religious or mystical or 19th century" themes; they were bent instead on producing a work of social import. When he'd initially met Nabokov, Lincoln had actively disliked him, but recently Nicky had helped Lincoln "a lot" with *Dance* and had also turned out— rare among the Russian émigrés—to have pro-Communist sympathies. Still, their friendship remained limited; Lincoln found Nicky "cunning like a fox, a poorly disguised failing that is not attractive." Muriel, whose opinion continued to count with Lincoln, thought Nabokov a "second-rate careerist," out to exploit him. When Lincoln took her to hear some of Nabokov's compositions for *Tom*, she thought "the music was useful enough but that he is emotionally very underdeveloped and it shows, in spite of his skill."

Balanchine himself took on a workload heavy enough to have challenged the health of someone with a less compromised medical history. Simultaneous with preparing for the Met's winter season, he signed with a Broadway agent, Milton Bender—often called "Doc" because he'd previously been a dentist—and accepted a commission to prepare choreography for the forthcoming *Ziegfeld Follies* debut of the international sensation Josephine Baker. When walking with Balanchine in the street one day, Lincoln unexpectedly met Baker, who remembered Balanchine from Europe but not his name, and invited them back to what Lincoln called her "meager" rooms. She told them she had her food sent in from a delicatessen, and Lincoln thought her isolated and "poignant." Balanchine pulled out a chain she'd given him in Berlin and said "it had brought him good luck." Later he told Lincoln that she'd once cooked spaghetti for him without a stitch of clothing on, and that she was "sweet and domestic" in her big Paris flat.

In the belief that Edward Johnson would soon expand the Met's offerings of ballet, Balanchine expressed interest in choreographing Ernest Schelling's *Victory Ball*. Though Lincoln disliked the idea, he accompanied Balanchine to Schelling's apartment to discuss it. He found what he expected: a "stuffy man in a stuffy antique shop apartment" and thought him so "full of bad ideas" that he was "amazed that George kept on talking to him." Nothing, to Lincoln's relief, came of *Victory Ball*, but Balanchine had been energized by what he thought would be a true creative home at the Met, and he came up with a number of new ideas for ballets. Neither he nor Lincoln seems to have digested Edward Johnson's early warning that "the ballet must lay low for a while and just be opera-ballet."

The first opera Balanchine worked on extensively was *Carmen*, and he straightaway composed for it what Lincoln—marveling at the way he "controls the whole thing so quickly I can't see"—called a "brilliant" farandole for the fourth act. Yet at the same time Lincoln worried about the "frightening" amount of work Balanchine faced in having to compose, and swiftly, so many dances for so many different operas—to say thing nothing of his simultaneous commitment to the *Ziegfeld Follies*. Balanchine seemed "eager to work," but he struck Lincoln as "frail and separated"; it filled Lincoln with "apprehension and tension" (and perhaps provided a temporary focus for the anxiety that was his constant companion).[7]

Balanchine, despite his workload, insisted on reworking *Reminiscence* (throughout his life, he constantly rethought his creations). While Lincoln dug around the Met's dusty costume wardrobes—"a chamber of horrors from way back"—for possible material that their fine seamstress, Maria Stepanova, could recut, Balanchine created a new mazurka and waltz for *Reminiscence*. When Edward Johnson saw them in rehearsal, as well as the two new dances for *Carmen*, he was "duly impressed." He "will not be hard to work with," Lincoln wrote in his diary. He was aware that Johnson "has his troubles with his trustees," but not of the depth of those troubles. Under financial constraints from the Depression, the Met's board in the mid-thirties was further inhibited by its own devotion to the tried and true; tradition-minded, it had little appreciation for ballet and less tolerance for innovation of any kind. Like guardians of a museum, the board saw its mission as maintaining the standards of a past age.

Balanchine soon started in on *Aida* but "hated" the music. By early December he was at work as well on creating a new "acrobatic Adagio" (as Lincoln described it) for *Lakmé*. Lincoln kept fearing that he would "collapse" from the strain of so much work, "but he doesn't seem to"; Doc Bender kept a close eye on him, and insisted he drink a daily "pep" cocktail of orange juice with an egg. Balanchine wasn't nearly as pleased with what he was turning out as Lincoln seemed to be, and he "hated" his work at the *Follies*. The week before opening night, the ballet company of fifty-five rehearsed for the first time on the Met stage, and Balanchine "unenthusiastically" began to prepare dances for yet another opera, *Coq d'Or*, as well as creating a "Bacchanal" for *Tannhäuser*. Being onstage, the company now had to deal as well with the notorious arrogance of the stage director, Désiré Defrère, and with an occasional opera diva instructing Balanchine on exactly when the singers should come in.

Nerves began to fray. Dimitriev did another reprise of "I resign forever," and Lincoln got into a row with Tchelitchev for saying that Balanchine had been "sleeping" ever since they worked together on *Errante* in 1933—the one ballet, according to Tchelitchev, responsible for getting them invited to the Met in the first place. To compound his provocation Pavlik badgered Lincoln about his "restricted" sex life and told him he needed to "fuck freely"—it would make him "happy." In retaliation, Lincoln accused Pavlik of never having had any real interest in the ballet and claimed that he'd failed as a friend to "give us any help to maintain our position, which is based on how we dance." The two would reconcile within days, but not until the mounting pressures of the opening-night *Traviata* had been surmounted.

The week preceding the opening was unusually difficult: long rehearsals, constant disagreements, costume fittings that took "hour after hour." Balanchine at one point pricked his finger on a pin, and Lincoln, "sure he'd get blood poisoning," raced off to a drugstore for iodine. He became so unstrung that he ended up, by his own admission, "being rude to everyone," including the "imbecilic" stage director Defrère and, alas, Edward Johnson himself.

Lincoln became so distraught that he came close to skipping opening night altogether, but finally did attend. He thought "the kids danced well enough" and looked well trained, and that Stepanova's costumes were "beautiful" (Lincoln had himself successfully brought down two dozen tutus in a taxi during a pouring rain that threatened to make the tarlatan limp). A "good deal of decent enough publicity" about the dancers in the press helped to cool everyone down. Lucia Davidova called Lincoln "faun" and (as Lincoln saw it) "slavered over George." While standing in the back of the house, Lincoln saw Ruth Page brush by him and chose to interpret her look as "haggard and devoured with rage and jealousy"— adding "harridan" for good measure.

Once opening night was behind him, Lincoln took to his bed for several days; he had intermittent fears of having contracted TB or spinal meningitis, and continuous ones about the "grand inconclusiveness" of the ballet's standing at the Met. Muriel told him that his illness "was an elaborately evasive process which preceded the ultimate assertion of . . . [his] own direction." She may have had a point. Lincoln had become downright "frightened" of Dimitriev, who continued to hold aloof from doing any administrative work at the Met unless given "supreme" control—which Balanchine continued to refuse him, "pretending" (in Lincoln's view) that Dimitriev essentially "threw him out" of the school, and asserting that he had no intention of letting him do the same at the opera.

Lincoln "couldn't see any way out," though he regretted Dimitriev's defection and thought Balanchine's "egotistical demands" were "wrong." Eddie's return from Mexico a few days after opening night clarified nothing. Lincoln had prepared "a great blast to make him feel guilty but was too fatigued to deliver it." When he tried to discuss the future, he found Eddie "elusive" and "basically unchanged." Lincoln decided that he "must stay in with all three for the sake of the future," and felt that he could himself perform the tasks Dimitriev refused to do at the Met. Rousing himself from bed, Lincoln helped Stepanova get the costumes ready for the first of two performances of *Reminiscence*.

It went reasonably well, even though the conductor, Wilfrid Pelletier, was "slow on the uptake" and one of the dancers fell on her entrance. Still, the audience seemed "enthusiastic" and Balanchine looked "pleased." Tchelitchev, not the most trustworthy witness, told Lincoln that Balanchine "adored the house and thinks of himself as a fixture for years and years, like Petipa at the Maryinsky." At intermission Lincoln said a brief hello to E. E. Cummings—their first exchange of words since Balanchine had turned down his scenario for *Tom* a year earlier. Lincoln also chatted, this time at some length, with the anthropologist Margaret Mead ("one dumpy little woman"). He asked her to explain to him "the inertia of civilizations—the separation of ritual and belief"; though hardly the usual fare of entr'acte chitchat, Mead jumped right in and described her theory that "every culture creates a surplus, then lives on it until it is exhausted." It was a message Lincoln agreed with—though he may well have wanted to add, with Balanchine's reinvention of classic ballet in mind, "unless the surplus is poured into new channels."

A whole series of operas—and new dances for them—now followed in rapid-fire order. First up was *Aida*. Lincoln regarded the Met's production, with its "horrible" costumes and broken-down supernumeraries pretending to be Egyptian dignitaries, as simply "preposterous." But he luxuriated in the "madness and freakishness" of backstage life and "frankly gloried in being alone there without Dimitriev." The dances in *Aida* starred a "nearly nude" Bill Dollar and Daphne Vane, which produced considerable tongue-clucking from opera patrons still wedded to turn-of-the-century notions of modesty. Yet when Lincoln ran into Edward Johnson, he professed himself "delighted" with the dances and repeated, in what Lincoln had now come to regard as his "active, vacant, vegetable way," his pleasure with the troupe's "youthfulness . . . [and] vitality—great stuff, etc."

But that same week Johnson told Eddie Warburg that he'd received "much criticism" about both the dances and costumes for *Aida*, as well as for *Lakmé*, which had soon followed. Since Johnson had himself been recently hired and served at the pleasure of a crusty board, he understandably retreated a bit, letting Lincoln know that for now at least he couldn't take up Balanchine's recent suggestion that he create a ballet for Gluck's *Orpheus and Eurydice*; his singers, Johnson explained, simply didn't know the music. "If I was director," Lincoln wrote in his diary, "I'd make them, by God."

Lincoln decided that Muriel had been right: it was time he moved himself more openly into the foreground, overtly took on the prominent role, managerial and artistic, that his talent and intelligence warranted. True, he lacked the personal financial resources simply to separate himself from Eddie, just as it was also true that he lacked Dimitriev's depth of managerial experience or Balanchine's creative brilliance. But Lincoln had enough of all three attributes to assert himself more fully than he had been, to do less nervous placating and backstairs maneuvering and to come forthrightly into his own.

There would be hesitations and backslidings, but the new year, 1936, saw, rather abruptly, an emergent new Lincoln. The instances rapidly multiplied. He "raised such a row" with Pelletier, the conductor, about an undesirable scheduling reshuffle at the Met, that he ended up getting his way. When, soon afterward, Dimitriev started in on one of his harangues about Balanchine's inadequacies, Lincoln told him outright that he was sick of hearing about what was "wrong" with George when in truth so much was supremely right. And when the company began work on Jacques-François Halévy's opera *La Juive*, Lincoln personally designed Vilzak's costume—black velvet, chains, and silver—and pronounced it "beautiful." He also, or so he maintained, "criticized and changed absolutely everything I didn't like," and claimed responsibility "for many ideas and even gestures" in *La Juive*'s dances.

And he also blew up at Eddie (*that* wasn't new), told him that he was "lazy," that as the official "director" of the company he needed to press Edward Johnson about letting Balanchine do the ballet based on Gluck's *Orpheus*. Under pressure Eddie did have a talk with Johnson, who said "he [was] a good friend of the American Ballet" but could not, for the moment, make any further commitments to it. "No security ever," Lincoln wrote disconsolately in his diary, adding that Johnson "is as weak as Warburg and will force nothing." Balanchine privately told Lincoln that "if nothing happens at the Met he will go back to Russia and do something there, as all of his friends and father are in important positions."

But then, quite unexpectedly, John Erskine of the Met's board, rumored to be an enemy of the ballet, along with Lucrezia Bori, one of world's most admired sopranos, told Eddie at a meeting of the Met's Spring Opera Committee that they "are crazy for us" and would, after all, push to have *Orpheus* scheduled for the spring, and possibly even *Tom* as well. That seemed to Lincoln a stunning, and therefore not wholly to be trusted, turnabout. But the very next night he, Balanchine, and Tchelitchev (who was to do the decor for *Orpheus*) had dinner together and talked all night. Tchelitchev, "despondent over the music," at first declined the offer. But Balanchine said "we musn't refuse this chance as it is given us," and he played Gluck's score over and over until all three of them started to come up with ideas.

Two days later an apparently overexcited Lincoln made the bizarre misstep of sending Edward Johnson a five-page letter enumerating what was wrong with the Met. "Am I too fresh?" he asked himself in his diary. "Maybe I shouldn't have sent it." Maybe, indeed—especially at a moment when things seemed to be turning their way. Lincoln quickly came to his senses and felt "ashamed" at what he'd done; apparently his newfound assertiveness could easily enough become confounded with a more destructive impulsiveness. Remarkably, though, there were no immediate repercussions, though Johnson did tell Balanchine about the letter, making it clear that he found it not only "fresh" but "irrelevant."

The three men met that same day, and (as Lincoln melodramatically put it in his diary) "horror chilled me." But Johnson, overall, took the high ground. He complained less about Lincoln's letter than about Eddie's too-talkative, "dilettante" ways. He even proved willing to discuss, though without entering into specifics, prospects for the following year, and said he hoped to "do things for the ballet"—that is, if they could "be backed by a benefit audience of special evenings" to ease financial constraints. Lincoln credited Johnson with being "sweet," and acknowledged that his own letter had been "unnecessary, however well intentioned."

That seemed to be that. Except that the ground beneath the ballet's feet kept morphing into quicksand. Less than two weeks after the conference with Johnson, Eddie was reporting a far less sanguine meeting with him. He quoted Johnson as saying that the American Ballet was "adequate and youthful" but that it had not made "the great hit we should have." But the problem, as Lincoln heatedly pointed out, was that they still hadn't "been given a chance." Besides, in the interim between the two meetings, Balanchine unexpectedly accepted an offer to do the choreography for a Broadway show in which Tamara Geva and Ray Bolger would have the leading dance roles—the historic Rodgers and Hart musical *On Your Toes*. It was due to open on April 11, 1936.

Though under intense work pressure, Balanchine had no intention of resigning his role as ballet master at the Met, especially since *Orpheus* began to loom as a real possibility for May. But he, Lincoln, and Warburg had a series of long, difficult talks about the future of the American Ballet, and in particular about the problem of keeping the troupe together over the coming summer. Lincoln had been hearing reports that the company's morale was sinking, and that a number of their leading dancers were talking about returning to their previous jobs at Radio City Music Hall and elsewhere. Perhaps, Lincoln thought, they could take the company to California for the summer, perform in the Hollywood Bowl, return by way of Chicago. Perhaps, perhaps . . .

CHAPTER SIXTEEN

Ballet Caravan

(1936)

Balanchine was as angry during the meeting as Lincoln had ever seen him. They'd done their best, along with Nabokov and Tchelitchev, to explain to the Met's "Spring Season Committee" what they had in mind for *Orpheus*. Nabokov had brought along his score, and Tchelitchev his superb sketches for the ballet's decor. And Nabokov made what Lincoln felt was a "courteous and excellent speech," though Juilliard's John Erskine, a committee member, characterized it as a patronizing "lecture." The proposed plan to put the dancers on the stage and the singers in the orchestra pit—elevating an "insignificant" art form above the majesty of the opera—struck Erskine and others on the committee as the height of absurdity. Lincoln tried to explain that the ballet was meant to complement, not compete with, the music, but his words fell on deaf ears.[1]

Tchelitchev proceeded to make matters far worse with what even Lincoln called a "catastrophic" exposition of his ideas; he kept talking vaguely of making constructions of chicken wire and cheesecloth, conjuring up henhouse images that hardly comported with Erskine's inflated sense of the Met's stately mission. After a half hour he got up and abruptly left the meeting. If Balanchine was furious, Lincoln was nearly beside himself with disgust. He raged against Erskine in his diary as "the shit of all time," a "life-hater" who reeked of "smug inertia" and whose "sideburns of pubic hair" made him look like "the big bad wolf."

The following day Edward Johnson explained to Pavlik, Lincoln, and Balanchine—in what Lincoln described as his "best false frankness"—that the possibility of a spring season remained in doubt and that he felt they were pushing him too hard for an immediate commitment he could not give; he further reminded them that "they could get along without the ballet if they had to." After Johnson left, Pavlik suggested, with Nabokov later seconding him, that they separate from the Met and either turn to Edward James, who'd bankrolled Balanchine's Les Ballets 1933, or form a committee of "rich old ladies" to raise money for a season on their own featuring *Orpheus* and *Tom*. But Lincoln (and Dimitriev) felt they needed the Met for another year "to build up publicity for a tour the year after." In the meantime Lincoln suggested they explore, with the help of Balanchine's agent, Doc Bender, additional venues in California. Lincoln felt he was "really swimming in nervousness, apprehension and fear," yet he "instinctively sensed a decent resolution of our problems."

His instincts were right. Despite all the apprehension and miscommunication, the Met not only decided, in the end, to have a supplementary "spring season" but to include *Orpheus*. The positive news came as a considerable shock. From what Lincoln could gather, Erskine hadn't changed his mind but had been outflanked when it became clear that a bare majority of the committee was (hesitantly) willing to move forward. Nonetheless, with a vacant summer looming just ahead, Lincoln decided to make the trip to California after all, accompanied by Bender. He hated to go and feared that he'd be unable to secure any summer venues for the American Ballet. Still, as Lincoln wrote his father, "I am seizing the opportunity to take what control I can of the company."

He and Bender flew to Los Angeles on March 15, 1936. The flight was "a real nightmare"; Lincoln had earlier come down with a case of trench mouth (a painful bacterial infection of the mouth's mucous membranes), and he got "hideously sick" on the plane, "trying to throw up with nothing left to throw up." Los Angeles itself provided no compensation: he found "the streets, weather, people, everything detestable . . . Hollywood [is] without exception, the nastiest place I've ever been in." He tried to comfort himself with Gurdjieffian boosterism: "In pain, work better: am more concentrated and cynical and hard-boiled." And he had at least a somewhat pleasant time visiting Agnes de Mille at the Culver City movie lot where she was finishing up work on the dances for Irving Thalberg's film *Romeo and Juliet;* she showed Lincoln some of the dances and he thought them "very charming" and "imaginative." (Yet when de Mille later saw the drastically cut version, she left the projection room, lay on the grass "and was very, very sick.")

Bender proved of little help in providing introductions or opportunities, and Lincoln soon decided that he was "a small-time guy and a lousy salesman." Isabel Morse Jones, the influential dance critic of the *Los Angeles Times*, urged Lincoln to pay a call on the prominent agent, Merle Armitage, who'd earlier secured four thousand dollars' worth of bookings for the Merovich-Warburg tour and had lined up positive publicity for the company with the Hearst press. The "tour," of course, had never come within shouting distance of Ohio, let alone California, but Armitage didn't seem to hold any grudge. However, he did advise Lincoln not to think of coming out to the West Coast until 1937–38. Lincoln flew back to New York on March 21, and was again "hellishly sick" on the plane. The trip to California, just as he'd feared, had proved worthless.

In mulling over other possibilities for the summer, Lincoln took to bouncing his ideas off Doug Coudy, a member of the troupe. Over the past six months, thanks to Coudy's persistent, discreet pursuit of Lincoln, the two had carved out a relationship that straddled friendship, sex, and company business, and Coudy had come to serve as Lincoln's chief source of information about the fluctuating moods and intrigues among members of the troupe. Lincoln had allowed Coudy's "courtship" to proceed, but had maintained control over its boundaries; after the two had dinner one night early in their relationship, Lincoln wrote in his diary: "He was respectful and warm and I was warm and distant." He was soon inviting Coudy up for a drink but continued to maintain his distance, leading Coudy to say that "he was sorry I wasn't interested."

But Lincoln was sufficiently interested to let Coudy's campaign to insinuate himself into his life continue. They were soon being seen together often enough for Joe Lane, another of the dancers Lincoln sometimes saw socially, to warn him that Coudy was "dishonest, treacherous . . . could not be trusted." When Lincoln pressed Joe for evidence, he spat out, "Personal!" That wasn't good enough, and Lincoln went on seeing Coudy, who continued to tell him "many things I wanted to know about the kids and the Company."

Lincoln decided he liked Coudy: he was "nicely mannered" and exuded a "manly bearing." He recognized that Coudy "gravitates toward power and responsibility, and while denying his ambitions . . . would like to run the works, really." The inconclusive evidence suggests that their relationship occasionally included sex but never became romantic. That sort of attachment was a fate reserved for another member of the troupe, Gene Loring, a promising young dancer-choreographer whose career Lincoln pushed and whom he occasionally saw socially.

Gene, unlike Lincoln, *did* fall passionately in love with Coudy, a passion that went unrequited. A disconsolate Gene started missing rehearsals and dancing less well than usual. He finally sought Lincoln's advice, and they talked for some two hours, Lincoln feeding him "dilute Gurdjieff" and worrying that the thus-far-unnamed love object might be himself or Lew Christensen (who'd been steadily emerging as the troupe's leading male dancer). But no, Gene eventually blurted out Coudy's name.

Apparently Lincoln provided little comfort, since Gene was soon missing rehearsals again. At one point Lincoln became alarmed, fearing a suicide attempt. When he went looking for Gene and discovered he wasn't in his room, Lincoln felt "acute fright"—less for Gene than for the farewell letters and diaries he might have left behind, which would provide disastrous fodder for the scandal sheets. When Gene did finally appear, drunk, a relieved Lincoln became "wildly irritated," chewed him out, and "refused to let him weep." Gene eventually got over his passion for Coudy, and within just a few months began to prove himself a gifted choreographer.

The other company member Lincoln was most drawn to was Lew Christensen. But where Coudy was something of a confidant and down-to-earth co-conspirator, Christensen served Lincoln as a kind of platonic ideal. As a Mormon, Westerner, and heterosexual, the unpretentious, even-tempered Christensen was too foreign to Lincoln's temperament to become an intimate. But he did become something of a *beau idéal*, a resuscitated, reincarnated fantasy of the Harvard Lads he'd adored as a younger man. Unlike the Lads, though, Lew was neither sophisticated, privileged, nor well educated; yet somehow that added to, rather than detracted from, his luster for Lincoln: he was an innocent angel, "gentle, simple and firm."

When Lincoln invited Lew and his brother Harold (also a member of the company, but less gifted) to dinner one night, they arrived "very clean and in blue suits . . . like honor students at the headmaster's." Lew called him "Mr. Kirstein," and Lincoln found his "frankness" decidedly formal. He thought of Lew as "in a kind of perennial suspension . . . elusive, self-content and quiet, an animal that only does well on the stage with movement; otherwise he has little existence." Yet every so often he'd surprise Lincoln with "an unexpected flash of positive interest or opinion." Lincoln was eager to help him, and to that end consulted Balanchine, telling him that "it was useless to try to educate . . . [Lew] but one could give him large general ideas about philosophy, art, etc., which he lacks—although he can express them instinctively in his dancing."

Lincoln soon got to the point where he wanted to "see as much of Lew as I could," and in April 1936 invited him, along with Coudy, to spend the weekend in Ashfield. Mina wasn't yet in residence, the weather was cold and rainy, and the roads still muddy, but Lincoln was determined on magic: the three of them hunkered down in the blacksmith's shop, got their provisions in Northampton, and let their beard stubble grow. Lew "is a source of endless delight to me," Lincoln wrote in his diary. "I cannot believe my ears when he talks; he is the so-called 'Normal' artist . . . his experience is so exotic to me, plus his diction, that I keep having the feeling it's all made up."

It wasn't. Nor was Lew's talent, which became more and more apparent. Once the Met gave its final go-ahead for *Orpheus* (after Eddie generously agreed to foot the bill for Tchelitchev's elaborate designs, and Tchelitchev succeeded in getting certified as a member of the set designers' union), Balanchine chose Lew over Charles Laskey for the leading role. (He picked Daphne Vane and William Dollar for the other two principal parts.) But just as rehearsals were due to begin, the dancer George Volodin, who periodically served as a kind of nurse to Balanchine, secretly let Lincoln know that over the past two weeks George had had three "attacks," screaming in the night that "death was coming." Since Balanchine also had a bad cough and had been looking tired and eating little, Volodin's news seriously upset Lincoln. He took comfort in the fact that

even before starting on *Orpheus*, Balanchine had been "brilliantly" composing dances for *The Bat* (an overture to *Die Fledermaus*, with a libretto
by Lincoln) four full hours at a time.

When rehearsals for *Orpheus* finally began, a mere two weeks were left
before the scheduled opening on May 11. Johnson's chief assistant,
Edward Ziegler, understandably concerned about the tight schedule, kept
pressing Tchelitchev to speed up his work on props and costumes, but
Tchelitchev, as usual, followed his own timetable and indulged in his usual
melodramatics—screaming at the workmen, telling Lincoln "it's all quite
hopeless," that there was no way he could finish in time. But he did, and
the end result of the nerve-racking process was a striking production
design, with light, not paint, the chief ingredient, the "scenery" a shifting
efflorescence of three-dimensional effects, and the costumes a wisp away
from nudity.

Lincoln and Balanchine were both pleased with the opening performance: "It was a great effort," Lincoln wrote in his diary, "and considering the circumstances was brought off remarkably well." He did feel that
Dollar was disappointingly "campy and weak" and, to his surprise, that
Lew Christensen's nervousness led to a much chillier *Orpheus* than he'd
shown in rehearsal, where Lincoln had been so overwhelmed at his "heartbreaking combination of virtuosity and tenderness" that he felt confirmed
in his view that Lew was the "ideal dancer" he'd always "imagined in fantasies about the American Ballet."

Though there'd been some disconcerting laughter during the performance, Lincoln had chosen to read the general reaction as enthusiastic.
And afterward, at the party Eddie threw in the lounge, there was "a
tremendous state of excitement," with the performers (as well as Johnson
and Ziegler) being greeted with applause as each arrived. Even Dimitriev,
"sour as ever, admitted Pavlik's enormous theatrical gifts" and conceded
that *some* of Balanchine's work was also impressive. Lew took Lincoln
aside at the party and "thanked me for what I'd done for him. I told him
how much I loved him and what work we'd do together in the future."

Lincoln hardly slept that night and rose early to get the morning newspapers. Given the cordiality and excitement of the night before, he was literally stunned at the nearly unanimous virulence of the reviews. Olin
Downes, the powerful music critic of the *New York Times* set the tone with
his denunciation of *Orpheus* as "the most inept and unhappy spectacle this
writer has ever seen in the celebrated lyric theatre . . . pretentious dilettantism." *Time* magazine was no less brutal: "The most inept production that
present-day opera-goers have witnessed on the Metropolitan stage."
Eddie Warburg was as "staggered" as Lincoln, but Balanchine said he
"was not surprised, said he knew that either the critics would be marvelous
or lousy." And Tchelitchev pronounced himself "delighted"; he'd never
gotten "so much space" before. Edward Johnson, remarkably, continued

to be "agreeable," and he assured Eddie that the negative reception would not affect his decision to invite the company back for the following year. Nor did it; within weeks Johnson signed the ballet to a new contract to run from nineteen to twenty-five weeks, or roughly from the end of December 1936 through the spring of 1937.

Within days of the *Orpheus* disaster, Lincoln turned his attention, this time in a concentrated way, to creating a viable prospect for the summer. Balanchine had continued to run an intermittent fever throughout May, and he planned on taking a prolonged rest. It dawned on Lincoln that his ill health, much as it was to be regretted, at the same time offered an opportunity to allow some of the budding young choreographers in the company—especially Gene Loring, Erick Hawkins, and Lew Christensen—a chance to try out their wings. Lincoln had decided that although Balanchine was "a very great composer" of ballets, "any extensive repertory by a single person unavoidably seems monotonous, showing always his style and his alone."

A crucial talk with Eddie Warburg helped to solidify Lincoln's plans. Over lunch one day Eddie "finally admitted" what Lincoln had long known: "that he is sick to death of the ballet," that it was like "being screwed without pleasure." He felt he'd been a "continual sucker," was "sick of making mistakes" and tired of the responsibility. He would quit at once, he told Lincoln, were it not for the obligation he felt toward the company, and particularly toward Balanchine. Besides, as the company's official "director," he'd just signed a contract with the Met for the following year. Lincoln cagily urged Eddie to stay until the contract expired, but then to put the ballet entirely behind him. Eddie expressed a desire to work at the Rockefeller Foundation dispensing money for education, and Lincoln promised to speak to Nelson. (He did, but Nelson wasn't interested.)[2]

Lincoln was delighted with Eddie's pending withdrawal. He felt he could now clarify his plans for the future and look ahead to a time when he could finally take control of the company. Exultantly he wrote his father that he intended "to use next year at the Met to achieve a transition whereby an excellent group of our dancers, with Balanchine, will be permanently engaged"—only not under Eddie's directorship. And the company would finally focus on "encouraging new talent in *composition* (the most important angle)" and in "offering an *entirely* American program." Lincoln felt that he was at last "on the right track for my whole future."

The wild card was Balanchine. Should his health hold, he now had, following the enormous success of *On Your Toes*, a continuous flow of commercial offers. Besides, it wasn't at all clear that he'd be willing to continue with the Met even for the following year; Lincoln was fearful of Balanchine's "supreme disinterest in the Met operas, which disinterest is transmitted to the dancers." He now felt that both he and Eddie had "spoiled" Balanchine all along, and that if the American Ballet had "no tours and no brilliant prospects," Balanchine and Massine, now reconciled, would "combine in an international company to replace Basil."

It was a prospect he, for one, "would not very much regret," since he felt that Balanchine would "always be available for special productions and I would be free on my own to do as I pleased with new musicians and new choreographers." Lincoln felt confident that once the company was reorganized and under his control, new choreographers would emerge. He continued to value Balanchine no less than in the past, but henceforth he would "criticize and be harsh with him when I feel like it . . . instead of being scared by his uniqueness and genius."

In regard to the upcoming summer, a re-energized Lincoln hit on the idea of choosing twelve of the troupe's best dancers, five men and seven women, to form a small but "completely American" company that would tour the New England states for two months; he named it the American Ballet Caravan, and gave Doug Coudy the title "company manager." Lincoln immediately let Balanchine know his intentions, and Balanchine seemed to feel that it was "a good idea"—that the traveling group would provide at least some of the dancers with part-time work until the new Met contract went into effect in December. Yet Lincoln thought he detected some "mental reservations" on Balanchine's part, and particularly as to whether "the boys can do choreography." Later on it became clear to Lincoln (though he found it "difficult to realize") that Balanchine "really detests the idea of the Caravan and will do nothing to help it." The realization made Lincoln feel that he'd all along been "naive" about Balanchine, that he was basically "jealous and suspicious."

Balanchine was never easy to read, and Lincoln may have misinterpreted his attitude. But with Eddie Warburg, who pretty much wore his heart on his sleeve, there was no mistaking his negative reaction to the Caravan idea. He accused Lincoln of "founding a rival company" and—in giving three young, untried choreographers (Hawkins, Loring, and Christensen) a chance—"encouraging an over-ambitious project." Eddie also felt that those in the troupe not chosen for the Caravan would feel hurt at being passed over, and morale in general would suffer. Lincoln acknowledged that, and was himself soon hearing rumblings of discontent; yet that unhappy side effect seemed unavoidable.

Dimitriev, unlike Balanchine and Eddie, was "very enthusiastic" about the Caravan; if kept small, he told Lincoln, it would have "a great future" and he gave considerable practical advice in getting things started. Yet given Dimitriev's limited availability and Coudy's limited experience, Lincoln realized that he also needed the services of a professional manager. He turned to Frances Hawkins, Martha Graham's expert business agent, hoping she'd take on the job. There were abundant reasons for her not to:

little time remained to get summer bookings; she herself had never seen an American Ballet performance; and she was well aware that Graham (as well as another of her clients, Harald Kreutzberg) regarded Lincoln as an "enemy."

On the positive side Lincoln could point to the number of "enthusiastic inquiries" he'd received in response to a batch of "feeler" letters he'd already sent to assorted summer theaters and colleges. He could also demonstrate to Frances that expenses were likely to be minimal. The twelve dancers had volunteered their time free of charge for a month's worth of rehearsals (Lincoln scraped up ten dollars a week for those literally destitute); costumes could be borrowed from the company's extensive wardrobe (though Eddie initially grumbled about it); the troupe would perform without scenery—and Lincoln's father had come through with a $2,500 contribution, thus guaranteeing all the foreseeable rock-bottom costs of travel expenses, basic room and board, stationery, postage, photographs, and the like.

Still, Frances Hawkins not only hesitated but consulted John Martin about the advisability of proceeding. Ardent "Americanist" that he was, Martin urged her to go ahead; he told her the Caravan was "an excellent idea" and that if anyone could pull it off, it was Lincoln Kirstein. That clinched it for her; for a fee of 20 percent over and above Caravan costs, she accepted the role of business manager. When she repeated to Lincoln what John Martin had said about him, he was flattered, but—being Lincoln—he immediately started to worry that Martin might write something to the effect that "Thank heavens!—they've kicked out the Russians and the rich men and we will finally have an American Ballet!" (In fact Martin simply wrote a brief, encouraging notice in the *Times* that helped to advertise the Caravan's pending tour).

Both Frances and Lincoln worried that the formation of the Caravan might suggest that a secession had taken place from the American Ballet, thereby potentially damaging both groups. She came up with the clever idea of issuing a news release in which Lincoln would announce that the Caravan was neither a secession nor a part of the American Ballet, and would further claim (falsely) that the Caravan had resulted from a group of twelve dancers coming to *him* with the idea and asking for his aid. Frances told Lincoln that although it was very late for booking a summer season, she felt reasonably confident that she could get them at least six weeks of work. She intended to try and get a three-hundred-dollar-a-night guarantee and would aim at three performances a week. If successful, that would mean all fifteen members of the Caravan (Lincoln, Coudy, twelve dancers, and a piano accompanist) would be able to draw salaries of forty dollars a week.

Throughout June, as the dancers rehearsed and the three young choreographers started composing their new ballets, Lincoln, now wholly in charge, was "in seventh heaven," supervising details and completing arrangements. Pursuing his determination to focus on American themes and artists, he spent two days at Ashfield talking to Mina's friend Elliott Carter about writing music for a ballet based on the story of Pocahontas. The composer agreed to take on the assignment, and Lew Christensen was commissioned to do the choreography; early in July, Carter came down to New York to supervise the *Pocahontas* rehearsals. Meanwhile the "chosen three"—Hawkins, Loring, and Christensen—were turning out choreography of decidedly uneven quality.

Hawkins was composing a ballet to music by Anton Webern, and initially Lincoln felt that "there is no question about his inventive talent or his power to use the classic manner." Lincoln also thought that Lew Christensen's piece *(Encounter)*, based on music by Mozart, was proceeding well. Gene Loring, on the other hand, had started his *Commedia* ballet but had then fallen into another "love sick" stupor over Coudy. This time around, feeling his own future at stake, Lincoln showed little patience or sympathy; as he wrote in his diary, "It all bores the hell out of me as I refuse to consider any more suicide attempts this summer." He chewed out Coudy as well, accusing him of flirting with Gene—which Coudy denied.

Before long, though, it became obvious that Erick's ballet was the most problematic of the three. Overcomplicated, it became (in Lincoln's view) "impossibly difficult and complex, and the kids hate to do it"; what made the situation worse was that Erick was "so fucking stubborn." Lincoln asked Muriel Stuart to have a look, and her verdict was that Erick's ballet "should be scrapped," that "nothing can be saved from it." Lincoln wasn't quite so sure—but then Balanchine came to watch a rehearsal of all three works. Afterward he told Lincoln that Erick's work was "too confused," though he believed he would ultimately "be an excellent choreographer." Balanchine further said that he didn't like Loring's piece but thought it might well be a popular success. On the other hand he thought that Lew's Mozart ballet had "taste and brilliance and was complete" (wedded to the classical style, Lew was having a much harder time with *Pocahontas*, though Lincoln "loved" the portions he'd completed).

By early July, shortly before the Caravan was due to leave New York, Lincoln had come to agree with Muriel Stuart that Erick's ballet "was a hopeless mess." When Erick briefly went to Boston, the other members of the Caravan told Lincoln they didn't want him back, that he was "too egotistical and unreliable." Only Lew Christensen argued that Erick should be given another chance. Lincoln had agreed to let the troupe decide all "personal" matters, while he reserved control over artistic and financial considerations. With Erick, the "personal" and the "artistic" seemed intertwined, but Lincoln bowed to the wishes of the troupe. It all made him "rather sick," though, since he felt that despite Erick's stubbornness and rigidity, "the value of any creative person is a love discipline."

Behind the scenes Lincoln continued, through Coudy, to exert pressure for a reconsideration. The troupe did finally come up with a compromise: Erick would be allowed back as a dancer, but his ballet would be thrown out. Erick accepted the terms and set to work on a new idea, this one based on the Minotaur legend. To ensure additional new "American" works, Lincoln invited William Dollar, whose choreographic talents Balanchine had earlier encouraged, to try his hand at making a ballet; he quickly turned out *Promenade*, based on music by Ravel. Lincoln also encouraged Coudy to try composing, and his piece, *The Soldier and the Gypsy*, to music by Manuel de Falla, was frequently performed during that first summer tour (the *Hartford Courant* called it "a sparkling fusion of the Spanish and the classic").

By the time the Caravan was ready to leave for its opening engagement, a two-performance stint at Bennington College, Frances Hawkins had managed to sign up seventeen dates for the troupe. Some places had refused the hoped-for three-hundred-dollar nightly guarantee and she'd had to settle for a percentage of the box office, but in Skowhegan, Maine, she'd secured a nearly six-hundred-dollar guarantee. Lawrence Langner of the Theatre Guild came to see the troupe rehearse and promptly offered them three performances at his theater in Westport, Connecticut. The choice of Bennington College—which in its short history had already become a citadel of modern dance—for their opening performance on July 17 was an artistically risky decision; in forming the Caravan, Lincoln had emphatically emphasized American themes and artists, but the troupe's technique was rooted in classic ballet, which the modernists scorned as European and rigidly elitist. Lincoln anticipated that there might even be "heckling."[3]

Though Gene Loring, years later, would remember the atmosphere as "very strange and unfriendly," Lincoln, writing at the time, felt that the Caravan's reception was far more cordial than he'd expected: "Everyone was extremely generous . . . and all their numerous facilities were put at our disposal." Martha Graham herself went backstage after the first performance and singled out Erick Hawkins (who would shortly become her lover and a pillar of her troupe) for special praise. Lincoln himself found Martha "charming and demonstrative"; she told him (according to what he wrote in his diary) that they "were in different worlds, but she firmly believed in our destiny and in the vitality of the classic form." John Martin, who was also present, particularly praised Bill Dollar's *Promenade*.

After Bennington the hosting sites varied widely: in Burlington, Vermont, they performed at the city hall; in Middlebury, under the sponsorship of the summer school for French, to a capacity crowd in the gymnasium. Lincoln found the mechanics of traveling far easier than he'd expected, thanks mostly to Frances's efficiency and to Coudy's industry; he found the life of an "ambulatory troupe" very much to his liking. Except for opening night at Bennington, he was able to watch the performances "quite easily"; instead of being overcome with nervousness, he could derive pleasure from them. And he himself did whatever mundane chores were needed—including dressing the dancers and sewing.

Though already known as someone who could be (à la Gurdjieff) abruptly rude, Lincoln saw himself, at least in regard to the Caravan troupe, as eager to please, "to be thought well of by everyone" (as he put it in his diary). And with the members of the Caravan he seems to have succeeded. Gene Loring even recalled, much later on, that the famously excitable Lincoln was, during this initial tour at any rate, "very calm, and very spare with words . . . he was not verbose, he was very quiet actually." Lincoln himself (with Gurdjieff perhaps whispering in his ear) worried that he wasn't being sufficiently forceful when it came to handling the dancers. He thought Harold Christensen, for example, got "worse daily" as the tour proceeded, but when he asked him to dance "a little stronger," he let Harold get away with the reply that it would "spoil his certain Romantic quality."

During a brief break in New York, Balanchine "very sweetly" took him to task for being "so loose-mouthed about plans with the dancers," warning him that people would use the information "for their advantage." As the summer progressed Lincoln did stay more apart, became "more separate and hard-boiled," less casually egalitarian. He also started to exercise his artistic authority more vigorously, at one point simply cutting Erick Hawkins's latest ballet in half, and allowing performances of only the last movement of Lew Christensen's Mozart piece, *Encounter.* He also started to show occasional irritability with Coudy, with whom he shared living quarters; toward the end of August Lincoln wrote in his diary that although it was difficult "living with Coudy all the time, without [him]. . . I would be lonely: a not unvicarious relationship . . . but [I] frequently wish he were someone I like better—anyone." Lincoln wasn't alone during the latter part of the tour in allowing himself an occasional outburst; Loring had "a fit of temperament" over some last-minute rescheduling, and even the "angelic" Lew got into a "fury" with Lincoln for "pressing them too much" and threatened to resign as the Caravan's ballet master.

All of which was within the predictable range of behavior for an untried, youthful, underpaid company confined over a two-month period to close-quarters living and subject to an unpredictable, wildly varied reception: in Easthampton, the audience was "cold and Republican"; in Keene, New Hampshire, only a few people showed up for the performance; in Ogunquit, Maine, they got "splendid" publicity, a nine-day engagement, and "enthusiastic" audiences. In the end there was plenty of reason for self-congratulation: they'd created a repertory of five ballets, had held together as a troupe despite occasional injuries and tantrums, and had never missed a scheduled performance. John Martin agreed that they had a right to feel pleased with themselves; in a column he wrote soon after the troupe returned to New York, Martin called the Caravan, which had succeeded, "with very little advance preparation," in giving twenty-five performances in seven weeks, "a courageous venture" that had uncovered as well possibilities for others in the field: the Caravan had made it "apparent that there is an extensive summer territory for dancing to be opened up, and profitably."[4]

The school itself began its new term with a significant rise in applicants; it was doing so well that it was no longer necessary to call on Louis Kirstein for any contribution. Balanchine himself returned to teaching twice a week—and showed renewed interest in it. Muriel Stuart remained, as she had been all along, popular and effective. Vladimiroff and Vilzak, on the other hand, had become problematic. Vladimiroff set off a series of rows with his shifting and escalating contract demands and his threats to start a rival school of his own.

But Balanchine—and many of the students—staunchly defended his teaching, with Balanchine going so far as to insist that Vladimiroff is "All—the whole works at the School; it is impossible to limit him in any way; he should give lessons when he wants to." Lincoln tried to get Balanchine to see that such a haphazard arrangement would make any sort of order or discipline impossible; but he made little headway, and for the time being Vladimiroff remained. Vilzak, on the other hand, had few defenders as a teacher; Lincoln thought he had "no mind or system, and his combinations are uselessly difficult." But in Vilzak's case, too, no immediate action was taken.

Balanchine himself was entering a period of stable health and extraordinary activity. Simultaneous with teaching, he signed on to do the choreography for a new Rodgers and Hart Broadway show, *Babes in Arms*, and also began negotiations with the Met for a Stravinsky festival (financed by Eddie Warburg), to consist of a double premiere, *Le Baiser de la Fée* and *Jeu de Cartes*. The Broadway show and the Met production would open within weeks of each other in the spring, leading to escalating fame and income for Balanchine—and an elegant new apartment in the Essex House.

But that lay months ahead. During the fall and winter of 1936–37 Lincoln kept as busy as Balanchine, juggling school affairs (mostly attended to by Dimitriev), the new season at the Met, and future prospects for the Caravan. Of the three the Caravan took most of his time. With the immensely competent Frances Hawkins handling the business side, Lincoln was able to focus on artistic matters, and he was full of ideas for the coming year. Among the earliest was a ballet he called *Yankee Clipper* (the "atmosphere of [the] first part of *Moby Dick*"); he envisioned himself doing the libretto, Gene Loring the choreography, and Paul Bowles the music, a quadruple bolt of "Americanism"—not that that was any guarantee of quality, as Lincoln himself soon acknowledged: "I behaved as if to be native was to be enough. No Nazi could have been more zealous." *Yankee Clipper* would prove to be the most successful offering of the 1937 summer Caravan.

Since rehearsals for the new nineteen-week season at the Met didn't begin until December 1, the Caravan continued during October and November to make a number of appearances. The most important was its two-performance New York City debut in the Kaufmann Auditorium at the YMHA. The first of the two went badly; in Lincoln's opinion "everyone was too scared to dance well," and afterward he "rode around the Park with Elliott Carter in a suicidal postmortem." But the second-night performance, to which Lincoln brought Nelson and Tod Rockefeller as his guests, went "a lot better." Dimitriev, Vladimiroff, and Vilzak all liked it, and Eddie Warburg "was nice" and the critics friendly (Balanchine, on the other hand, "was quite nasty," though Lincoln left no record of his specific comments). Financially the Caravan broke even, and the YMHA made nearly a thousand dollars.

The troupe's fall engagements were as far away as Montpelier, Vermont (where the total gate from a small but enthusiastic audience came to $129), and also included Hartford, Danbury, Amherst, and Smith College. Though Smith was known as a stronghold of sympathy for modern dance, the Caravan actually had to turn people away at the door. Perhaps word had gotten around that Lincoln had recently become more sympathetic to the modernists. Or to some of them: he pronounced the preview he attended at Martha Graham's studio of four new Agnes de Mille dances "shatteringly frightful"; nor was he alone: Louis Horst referred to de Mille that night as "The Eternal Amateur."

Yet early in October, Lincoln did join with Graham, Doris Humphrey, and Charles Weidman in an expedition to look over Madison Square Garden as a possible site for a February 1937 municipal dance festival; "all differing factions," Lincoln wrote in his diary, "we were very amicable." Within the same week he, Graham, Frances Hawkins, and Balanchine lunched together to discuss Graham doing something at the Met "if a formula could ever be worked out." Lincoln thought she had some good ideas, including a Civil War–themed dance "when the battle-scarred regimental flags are returned and no one is left to receive them."

Graham herself was "charming" during the lunch, and she and Balanchine "got on well." After further meetings Lincoln wrote in his diary, "I like her a lot personally . . . we get on like a house afire." He subsequently had a long talk with her after she saw a rehearsal of William Dollar's ballet-in-progress, *Concerto;* she told him that she felt "the kids danced well, but without fire and with little conception of what they were doing. It worried her about what work she would do in the future with us (if any); could she get cooperation from Balanchine and the company?" Lincoln felt confident that something would emerge from their ongoing discussions, even if not during the current year, and that their cooperation would mark "a first step in our united front towards success [*sic*] policy for the Ballet."

It was also in the fall of 1936 that Philip Barnes, director of the New York WPA Theatre Project, asked Lincoln if he'd be interested in taking over "the dance part, including modern dance." He was interested enough to enter into serious discussions that came to include Hallie Flanagan, the Theatre Project's national head. Balanchine, Dimitriev, and Eddie Warburg all advised Lincoln to proceed, though Martha Graham and Frances Hawkins both thought it would be a waste of his time. After some consideration, he recognized the difficulty that lay ahead, and after a week, he told the WPA administrators that he couldn't go ahead with the project in the state it was in. When, three weeks later, Lincoln attended a Humphrey-Weidman concert, he felt confirmed in the wisdom of parting company: "Dreadful, dreadful stuff they do . . ."

Despite his busy schedule, Lincoln found time, sometimes accompanied by his old boyfriend Tom Mabry (now, thanks largely to Lincoln's pushing for his appointment, an executive at MoMA), to begin boxing lessons at the YMCA. Where once, as outsider and supplicant, Lincoln had ruefully disciplined himself to assume the role of an awkward, embarrassed beginner in ballet classes, his shift to lessons in boxing nicely represented, at least as metaphor, his recently recast role in life. Having spent some four years in the essentially subservient position as Dimitriev's assistant at the school and Balanchine's gofer at the American Ballet, Lincoln had now emerged, with the Caravan, as the director of his own company, the man in charge, giving orders, determining careers. Like his long-standing gangster hero James Cagney, he could learn to punch rather than please, to discipline rather than defer to less-quick-witted opponents. Like his other hero, T. E. Lawrence, he might even "self-effacingly" release from within a masterful ability to manipulate uprisings, overturn established empires.[5]

Tom Mabry was among the few old friends Lincoln saw with any regularity. Muriel Draper was of course another. But in her case the relationship had lost some of its once-electric edge. Muriel turned fifty in 1936, and her deteriorating fortunes were sadly out of sync with Lincoln's ascending ones. Muriel was essentially without work, as well as "desperately poor," though she tried to maintain a good front and rejected aid. Her older son, Paul Draper, was becoming an acclaimed tap dancer, but her younger one, Smudge, was unhappily married and living in Europe.

Lincoln was relieved when Muriel decided to sail for England to spend some time with Smudge. He didn't like feeling sorry for her—it somehow felt patronizing—but didn't know how not to.

He also saw his family with some regularity. When his parents were staying in New York—Lincoln rarely went to Boston anymore—they had periodic dinners that tended toward admonition (from Louis) or admiration (from Rose) but rarely included any intimate exchange. Lincoln did visit Mina fairly often at Ashfield, though he usually brought along friends as a buffer; deeply bonded as they were, theirs was a seesaw relationship, with Mina far more constant in sharing confidences and affection than Lincoln, who kept veering from intimacy to annoyance. He knew that he could always count on Mina but wasn't sure he wanted to, and he often complained about her "grand" domineering ways and her "instinctive jealousy."

His relationship with his brother, George, on the other hand, was merely perfunctory. He thought of him as "cold-blooded" and as having "no real interest" in anything—meaning he loved sailing and did not love ballet, was pro-labor but not pro-Soviet. Lincoln regarded George as some sort of boring "business type," and minimized his abilities (except when needing his advice on money matters); George, in turn, felt Lincoln's patronization keenly.

Most of Lincoln's social life was an offshoot of his work life. He spent the bulk of his time with people from the world of ballet or the associated arts, and dining out usually revolved around arranging a Caravan engagement or putting together the pieces of a ballet-in-progress. But if Lincoln's socializing had become more subdued than earlier, there was still the periodic breakout event—like a party at Elsa Maxwell's or Cecil Beaton's drag ball, where, amid much carrying-on, Cecil "implored" Glenway Wescott to undress; when Glenway loudly whispered that his body was "ugly," Cecil said, "My dear—every cubic inch of it's divine, I'm sure." Glenway held his ground.

Lincoln also managed to find time to pay a call at George Barnum's new sailor bordello at 93 Washington Street. Since he'd failed to telephone in advance, Barnum proved "disagreeable" and a put-out Lincoln told him he'd never return. "Suit yourself," Barnum tossed over his shoulder. Lincoln later regretted his hasty ultimatum and thought of calling back—but didn't.

If less socially available than earlier in his life, Lincoln did begin a new friendship during this period that would become even more important to him than the recent closeness he'd established with Pavlik Tchelitchev. The new friend was a young painter named Paul Cadmus. Having seen some of Cadmus's work, Lincoln invited him to dinner to talk about the possibility of his designing one of the new ballets he had in mind (*Bombs in the Ice-Box*) for the summer 1937 Caravan tour. Cadmus brought along his lover of six years, Jared ("Jere") French, another gifted young painter. The two had recently rented a studio together in Greenwich Village, and French, six years older than Cadmus, had had his first show at the Julien Levy Gallery in 1935. Lincoln much preferred Cadmus, and especially the fact that he didn't indulge in the easily bruised feelings or require the sensitive stroking that so many of his artist friends seemed to. He also liked the set of sketches that Cadmus quickly completed—thought them "excellent, efficient."

Thinking that Pavlik would also be impressed, Lincoln took him down to the studio Cadmus and French shared to look at their work. Never shy about expressing his opinion, Pavlik disdained all but Paul's early drawings and pronounced the rest merely "anecdotal, immediate and caricature." In addition, Pavlik told Lincoln that he'd "hated" Jere French, and thought him "a bad influence" on Paul. Pavlik's views carried weight with Lincoln, and may have influenced his reaction to a public showing of Cadmus's paintings several weeks later; Lincoln sharply criticized Paul for not having demanded more space than a single room and for hanging his pictures badly. Cadmus became "very upset."

Whether or not Lincoln's criticism was warranted, his overcharged manner of delivering it wasn't appreciated. In his diary he recorded a curious explanation: "Any display of weakness, even if I understand it, dangerously arouses all my sadistic instincts." The comment seems doubly strange. Lincoln was certainly given to periodic outbursts of impatience or irritability, but he was not, by any standard definition, "sadistic." Now and then, like most people, he could deliberately inflict pain on others and derive pleasure from their wounded feelings—but this was hardly his routine or preferred way of dealing with people. As for Cadmus, Lincoln—at least in this instance, when he barely knew the painter—seems to have equated his new friend's laid-back temperament with "weakness."

Lincoln was similarly off the mark when, a few weeks later, he wrote in his diary that Paul "is very much like me emotionally, but lazier." Yet the two men could hardly have been more different emotionally (that was part of their mutual appeal)—unless one views volcanic intensity, which Paul never showed, as the buried flip side of "placidity." But if Lincoln's initial perceptions of Paul were skewed, what he knew for certain was that he was drawn to him, and the two began to see each other with increasing frequency. Lincoln cherished their evenings together as (to use his own words) "comfortable and quiet encounters always."

Paul's gentle nature was soothing to Lincoln's immoderate spirit, even though Paul was in fact not, at this point in his life, feeling particularly content with himself. The sale of a self-portrait to the Metropolitan Museum, which he had thought settled, unaccountably fell through and seems to have triggered a generalized distrust, even dislike, of much of his own previous work. He feared not only for his artistic future but for the security of his relationship with Jared French, who'd been talking increasingly of wanting to marry—a woman, that is—which Lincoln thought would be "an excellent thing for them both."

Lincoln's important new friendship with Paul Cadmus coincided with his meeting a twenty-year-old student at the school named José ("Pete") Martínez, who would become one of the great loves of his life. Pete was from Texas, of Mexican parentage, a handsome, life-loving, vigorous, and affectionate young man—he was known as "Tarzan" among the students—who could also be willfully self-directed. When Tom Mabry first met him, he warned Lincoln that Pete's "independence was against him as a steady companion." But Pete's lively company delighted Lincoln from the start; he thought him "generally an angel" and was prepared to let the future take care of itself.

PART FOUR

Expansion

CHAPTER SEVENTEEN

Ballet Caravan

(1937–1938)

Despite Igor Stravinsky's personal importunings, Pavlik refused to get involved in the upcoming Stravinsky-Balanchine gala at the Met. The event, he insisted, "should be entirely an American tribute to the great man." This was a curious logic, given the national origins and provisional citizenship of several others involved in the enterprise, but Pavlik was a curious man. He'd begun a decisive shift from theater design to easel painting and held firm to his decision not to participate.[1]

Nonetheless excitement over the pending gala, due to have two performances in April 1937, built steadily. Thanks to Eddie Warburg's generosity, Stravinsky was offered five thousand dollars to compose one entirely new score, thus guaranteeing a world premiere; the ballet would become known as *Jeu de Cartes* (or *The Card Party*). The second ballet, *Le Baiser de la Fée*, Stravinsky's tribute to Tchaikovsky, had originally been commissioned by Ida Rubinstein in 1928 and choreographed by Bronia Nijinska; Balanchine's new version, if not the score, would constitute a second premiere. And the same would be true for the evening's third ballet, Balanchine's revised choreography for the 1928 Balanchine-Stravinsky *Apollo* (originally titled *Apollon Musagète*), which had been a revelatory experience for the young Balanchine. The April gala was destined to be both the high point and the swan song of the American Ballet.

Stravinsky's completed score for *Jeu de Cartes* arrived on December 2, 1936. On December 5 Holly Howard, pregnant with Balanchine's child, had an abortion. On December 10 Lincoln wrote in his diary that the entire week had been "a nightmare" due to an anonymous denunciatory letter to the Immigration authorities that led to a "mysterious investigation by agent of Immigration into Balanchine's private life—to whom he lied, implicating Danilova and God knows who. He was so frightened he might have said anything . . . the whole School, the Caravan and Company [could be]. . . wrecked on a whispering campaign . . . everything dimmed by Balanchine's possible deportation—even for T.B. (the denunciation said syphilis and making passes at the boys as well)."

That one horrific diary entry stands alone, except for Lincoln scrawling in the margin: "Letter I think sent by father of Ruthanna Boris who has done similar things in the past." Earlier Lincoln had characterized her father in his diary as a "crook"—an allegation Ruthanna insists is as mystifying as it is untrue. And there the entire bizarre incident must stand—essentially unexplained. No additional clarifying evidence has surfaced, nor any further information from Lincoln's diary. A few days of recorded terror give way to a silent blank. All that can be said is that the terror did pass, Balanchine was not deported, and soon work began in earnest on Stravinsky's newly arrived score.

From the very start Balanchine was clearly in top form; Lincoln thought his initial variations for *Jeu* were "heavenly"; "he adores the music and is even behaving well" (a veiled reference, perhaps, to his recent reaction to the immigration investigation). Irene Sharaff started to prepare the costumes and decor for *Jeu de Cartes*, and Stewart Chaney the decor for *Apollo* (Lincoln regarded Chaney as a "self-indulgent, spoiled boy . . . like Chick Austin, more interested in having 'fun' than in the theatre as such"; Chaney would surprise him).

As for *Le Baiser de la Fée*, Balanchine wanted the painter-poet Florine Stettheimer (who'd done the decor for *Four Saints in Three Acts*) to design the costumes; Eddie Warburg may initially have suggested Florine, since they were distantly related. Florine was one of three avant-garde and personally odd sisters, whose stage setting of a home had until recently been one of the city's most cosmopolitan salons. Lincoln, who'd been to the Stettheimers' several times, considered all three sisters "cuckoos," and he tried to dissuade an insistent Balanchine from his choice. As it turned out, Florine proved "shy, had to be courted" (Pavlik suggested to Balanchine that he marry her)—and ultimately decided against the assignment.

Balanchine then chose his casts: Lew Christensen would star in *Apollo*, William Dollar and Annabelle Lyon in *Jeu*, and there would be six principals, including Dollar, Lyon, and Caccialanza (who'd become romantically involved with Lew) in *Baiser*. Between rehearsals for the Stravinsky tribute, Balanchine was not only juggling *Babes in Arms*—which would open on April 14 (a mere two weeks before the gala) to great acclaim and a run of nearly four hundred performances—but was also, with less enthusiasm than ever, preparing dance interludes for various Met operas. Conditions at the Met remained so deplorable for the dancers, and they were given so little rehearsal time, that during one performance the orchestra suddenly stopped playing while the dancers were still in midair: cuts had been made in the score, but neither Balanchine nor the dancers had been told about them.

Given the ineptitude of the Met's administration and the fact that it was contributing nothing to the Stravinsky festival other than an empty stage, it was decided to hire the Philadelphia Orchestra for the gala, with Stravinsky himself conducting. He arrived on February 1 to oversee progress on *Jeu de Cartes*. On the whole he liked what Balanchine had thus far done but thought (as Lincoln put it) "the gestures were too small for the opera house"—an observation both Dimitriev and Lincoln had earlier made—and that there was "too great a prodigality of choreographic invention."

Then he dealt with the designer, Irene Sharaff. Using a set of medieval playing cards, she'd already completed the sketches for forty costumes and all the scenery. Stravinsky insisted that everything be changed, that her designs placed the work "in a definite period and evoke a decorative quality not present in his music." Sharaff was understandably upset. She complained to Lincoln that she'd "received enough different orders and ideas to make her go crazy." Lincoln was unmoved: "I don't love her or feel sorry for [her]."

A few days before opening night, Sharaff was (so Lincoln wrote in his diary) "green with frustration, rage, envy, etc.," and Stravinsky remained "furious," saying that "the Kings look like 'Ivan' not like Kings." Lincoln would claim, in his 1937 retrospective article, "Working with Stravinsky," that "the creation of *Jeu de Cartes* was a complete collaboration." Yet during rehearsals he'd felt quite the opposite, writing in his diary that "none of the Stravinsky ballets, except possibly *Baiser de la Fée* has been in the least collaboration: just [a] job like any other."

Lincoln agreed with Dimitriev that *Jeu* was "a crashing bore," and he wrote in his diary that "the Stravinsky ballets, except for *Apollo*, don't make any great difference to me." The little he found to admire centered on Alice Halicka's scenery for *Baiser* ("divinely well done"), Stewart Chaney's "brilliant" set for *Apollo* (which came as an absolute surprise to him given his earlier dismissal of Chaney as a lazy "boy"), and on Lew Christensen's "wonderful" presence as Apollo. (Watching Christensen from the wings, Lincoln was startled to come upon the hard-nosed Erick Hawkins crying, his handkerchief wet with tears.)

Despite Lincoln's view to the contrary, the Stravinsky gala most certainly did involve "collaboration"—but it centered on the partnership between Balanchine and Stravinsky. And that may have been the chief source of Lincoln's disgruntlement: he felt left out of the artistic deliberations. He couldn't reasonably have expected otherwise, given the long-standing relationship between those two giant creative figures—to say nothing of the fact that most of Lincoln's energy had recently been focused on what Eddie definitely, and Balanchine possibly, considered a "rival" enterprise, his own Ballet Caravan. Lincoln had yearned to become his own master, yet apparently still hankered to remain at Balanchine's side, serving his needs *and* being at least a junior partner in the work at hand. The role of "suffering servant" (one of Lincoln's durable self-images) who confusedly, guiltily, longed to be in charge wasn't a recipe for contentment.

If the Stravinsky gala brought Lincoln little gratification, it pleased both audiences and critics. Some hundred guests attended the dress rehearsal on April 26, including the enthusiastic cast of *Babes in Arms*. Lincoln's verdict was that "even *Apollo* was tedious" and *Jeu de Cartes* "insufferable (if improved)." But he heard a variety of opinions from others; Mrs. William Vanderbilt, whom Lincoln had been trying to interest in backing the Caravan, called him the next day to complain that Daphne Vane's "breasts bobbled up and down, and [Kathryn] Mullowny looked pregnant." Virgil Thomson and Muriel, however, pronounced themselves "ravished."

Going backstage the following evening, opening night, Lincoln found a nervous Lew Christensen; his leg straps "didn't work" and on top of that he'd stepped through the china washbowl in his dressing room and cut his toes (Lincoln leapt for the worst-case scenario: Lew would come down with blood poisoning). During all this, Volodin was busy curling Lew's hair (which Muriel later said made him look like Yves Tanguy). But once the curtain rose, all came right. Lincoln later wrote in his diary that "it was a very brilliant house and a superb performance." Even *Jeu de Cartes* seemed to him "bright and clean," and "success was everywhere in the air."

Though Lincoln had felt disconnected from the gala, he was delighted at how well everything went. Even Muriel, Mina, and Rose all got along (Muriel ascribed this strictly to the excitement of the occasion). Lincoln presented Lew Christensen, who he thought "did well and looked superb," with a stainless steel watch that had "*Apollon* 1937" engraved on it—and then got very drunk at the opening-night party. The second and final performance the following evening also went well. Lincoln thought *Jeu* was "less brilliantly done, but *Apollo* was better"; even *Baiser*, thanks to improved lighting, "went smoothly."

And, miraculously, John Martin's review in the *New York Times* was largely favorable. He began it by announcing that "The American Ballet covered itself with honor . . . the young dancers have grown greatly in proficiency and in projection . . . [and] more important . . . George Balanchine has begun to depart markedly from his previous absorption in seeking for strangeness and novelty and has turned his hands to reasonably straightforward composition." But as if shocked at his own compliment, Martin promptly took it back, declaring that "Balanchine has assumed a surface of studied simplicity, but underneath it there is none of the essential nobility of the classic style."

As for the three ballets, Martin dismissed *Apollo*—subsequently the longest-lived and most admired of the three—as the "least notable." He found *Jeu*—with the exception of Sharaff's "stunning" set—"cute, if nothing more," and proceeded to declare *Baiser de la Fée* "far and away the best work of the bill . . . by all odds the best ballet [Balanchine] . . . has made in America." *Time* magazine's critic, on the other hand, declared that the company was still too "short of a finished ensemble" to do justice to the "sophisticated" *Apollo*, had little to say in favor of *Baiser*, and chose *Jeu de Cartes* as the most fully realized of the three.

Long familiar with the vagaries of the critical fraternity, an undaunted Balanchine actually took a bow onstage with Stravinsky after the curtain came down on the second performance—the first time Lincoln had ever seen him do such a thing. Lincoln was inclined to agree with the enthusiastic Russian in the audience who said, "All, all, all is due to Balanchine." Afterward Mrs. Vanderbilt hosted a party in the Met's restaurant; high spirits reigned, and glasses were raised in a long series of toasts. The one sour note came when the party members applauded Alice Halicka at her entrance, which (according to Lincoln) made Irene Sharaff "leave the room in fury."

Within a matter of weeks Balanchine departed for Hollywood, having been hired by Samuel Goldwyn (at twelve hundred dollars a week) to stage the dances for his new film *The Goldwyn Follies*. As part of the terms of his contract, Balanchine had stipulated that he could hire twenty-five members of the American Ballet Company *and* that Goldwyn would build a complete ballet studio for them. Several of the Caravan's leading dancers went with Balanchine to the West Coast, and several others decided against doing a second Caravan tour; in all, Lincoln lost William Dollar, Charles Laskey, Gisella Caccialanza, and Annabelle Lyon. Laskey frankly said that he thought the Caravan would never become a permanent organization, and that the American Ballet would in the long run offer more work; he would prove right on the first count, wrong on the second.[2]

But Lincoln did manage to hold on to Doug Coudy (who would, unlike the prior summer, dance a good deal as well as remain company manager), Eugene Loring, Erick Hawkins, Ruthanna Boris, and, most important, Lew Christensen, whom Lincoln designated ballet master; together the two watched rehearsals at the school and decided which of the young dancers to choose for the corps (Balanchine and Dimitriev also gave their advice). There was also one major new addition to the Caravan: Marie-Jeanne, an appointment that, as Lincoln wrote in his diary, "is not pleasing to those dancers who stayed over from last year."

Now came the hardest part: money. Louis had recently told his son that a $24,000 savings account existed in his name, and Lincoln now told his father that he wanted the money set aside for Caravan expenses, both immediate and in the future. Louis was willing to give him access to the money, but before releasing any portion of it wanted to see an itemized budget. With the help of various hands, including Dimitriev, Hawkins, Levine, Coudy, and his own brother, George, Lincoln worked up a carefully detailed and persuasive set of figures (not the sort of thing he was ordinarily good at). The major items included costumes ($1,500), dancing shoes ($1,000), and salaries. The highest-paid Caravan member ($75 per week) was the unionized piano accompanist. Coudy and Christensen, at

$55 each, got the next-highest pay; the rest of the dancers ranged between $20 and $45, for a company total of $805 per week. Louis thought the itemized expenses might be underestimated, yet in general seemed realistic; he immediately sent Lincoln a check for $4,000 and promised the balance as needed.

A great deal hinged, of course, on how many bookings could be procured. Through mid-April 1937 Frances Hawkins was on tour with Martha Graham's troupe, but she and Lincoln stayed in frequent touch. Along with detailed correspondence about matters relating to the Caravan, they also discussed at length Lincoln's latest idea of putting together a subscription series for the following year of eight to fifteen "collaborative" evenings in New York City; he saw it as "an inevitable development towards the establishment of our own theatre for dancing." As the main participating artists, he had in mind Martha Graham, Paul Haakon, Lehman Engel's Madrigal Singers, Paul Draper and, of course, the Ballet Caravan, with an orchestra conducted by Leon Barzin and with additional artists to be added subsequently. On behalf of both the Caravan and the collaborative evenings, Lincoln raced around the city trying to enlist the desired artists and financial backing.

By late March he was writing Frances that "nobody to whom I have shown our possible collaborations . . . has not been interested and extremely enthusiastic. Barzin was convinced we would have a sell-out, and he thinks in two years time we can do it much more consistently, and have a larger orchestra." Lincoln's old friend (and Mina's ex-lover) John Houseman, who was currently director of the WPA Federal Theatre Project, offered him the Maxine Elliott Theatre, which seated eight hundred people and had a whole new lighting system, for the low figure of $150 a night, plus stagehand salaries—and threw in use of the box office and ushers free of charge.

Lincoln saw Martha Graham as the linchpin of the collaborative evenings, and through the mails he and Frances Hawkins mulled over her possible participation. Lincoln and Martha had recently become far friendlier than earlier, and Lincoln's letters to Frances are filled with variations of "my best love to Martha." Privately, in his diary, Lincoln could sometimes still harbor reservations about her work ("her *Chronicle* is in many ways effective, but she is so limited by creating always for herself in her own vocabulary").

But publicly he praised her to the skies. In a series of four articles on the dance that he wrote for *The Nation*, Lincoln devoted an entire one to hailing Graham's *American Document* when it debuted at the fourth annual dance festival at Bennington the following year, 1938. Where John Martin, Graham's early champion and close personal friend, gave the performance a tepid review in the *Times* (when it later came to New York he was far more receptive), Lincoln, who'd earlier been neither champion nor friend, gave the Bennington performance an unstinting rave, calling it "the most important extended dance creation by a living American."

Even so, neither Martha nor Frances was exactly swept away by Lincoln's tidal-wave enthusiasm for his new scheme. Martha did write him "an absolutely angelic letter" and, further, sent word through Frances that she was "very interested" in the idea, liked the Maxine Elliott Theater, and thought his offer to her of $250 a performance was fine—that is, if meant for herself alone (the twelve members of her company would in addition each get $10 a night, and Louis Horst $100). She humorously added that if Lincoln promised to marry Helen Tamiris, the modern dancer, "the entire group would dance at your wedding with . . . abandon and bare feet."

Frances joined the effort to expose division within the modernist ranks: she reported that she'd seen Ted Shawn dance in Seattle, and had found the performance "slightly obscene; Ted is far too fat and far too forty, but the audience being what they were, loved him dearly, and it was very discouraging." She added that Martha, after reading Shawn's "souvenir booklet," had said that "she seriously considered taking up dancing on her points." Picking up the mood, Lincoln wrote back that he "would have given anything to see Ted Shawn's program; I like the kind of Camembert cheese that runs by itself."

Frances did try to be encouraging about the collaborative evenings, telling Lincoln that she *had* liked the proposed prospectus he'd sent, even though she thought the notion of fifteen concerts was definitely excessive; committing in advance to so many successive Sunday evenings "will *frighten* people." And she advised Lincoln, before he got too carried away, to discuss the whole idea with John Martin ("if John gets wind of them through someone else and if he thinks that his advice is overlooked when you are out advice-hunting, he'll be down on the project from the first curtain").

Following Frances's advice, he dutifully trooped off to see Martin at the *Times*, and afterward wrote her an amusing account: Martin was "most agreeable, as always. He had that particular glint in the eye which from long practice I recognized as a combination of resentment, terror, dislike, sympathy, interest, dissatisfaction, frustration, doubt, and kindness. I think he would often like to kill me. His eyes wander. He answered the telephone on seven separate occasions, and I was with him for thirteen minutes."

When it came to his opinion of the collective evenings, Martin said that he thought the idea a good one, if it could be brought off, but doubted it could be. Audiences, he shrewdly told Lincoln, "didn't like to combine—they like all fish or all meat." If Lincoln did decide to go ahead, Martin warned, there would have to be a strong hand at the helm; "democratic ventures didn't work." As a result of his experience with the Caravan, Lincoln had already come to agree; he'd started out determined not to indulge in "Dimitriev's ukases" (or, he might have said, Diaghilev's), and had insisted on treating the company members as friends, not serfs. But—or so he later claimed—the dancers themselves protested: they were dancers, they purportedly told Lincoln, not administrators. They wanted a leader, not a buddy.

By the end of his meeting with John Martin, Lincoln felt that the *Times* critic was determined to give him "very little satisfaction." Throughout, Lincoln wrote Frances Hawkins, "I was angelic, earnest, desperate and 'frank.' You remember Frank—he is Earnest's brother." If Lincoln came away with minimal encouragement from Martin, the meeting neverthe-less left him in high spirits: "After I leave Martin I always feel that I have swallowed unwittingly a peach pit, a large wad of gum, sausage rind, and that stuff they wrap cheese in. It's not particularly unpleasant, but some-how disturbing." He was at least grateful, Lincoln wrote Frances, that Martin hadn't asked him "why Doris [Humphrey] and Charles [Weidman] were not included, but if I am a trace of a mind-reader, the question was on his thin lips. Well, we will see."

Lincoln continued, though less zealously, to explore the possibilities for a collaborative series, but for now, most of his energy shifted back to the Caravan's upcoming six- to eight-week summer tour. That meant drawing up contracts; exploring ideas for new ballets (he had almost too many of his own to prioritize); commissioning choreographers, musicians, and designers; and helping Frances Hawkins maximize the number of engagements that could be secured.[3]

For one of the new ballets that were actually begun, James Agee (who Lincoln had known since their days together at Phillips Exeter) started writing a scenario—the piece was something they called *Bombs in the Ice-Box*. Agee worked on it for a while, but by mutual agreement it was soon abandoned; Agee lost interest and Lincoln thought the material he'd already produced was "too literary and not theatrical." Glenway Wescott came to Lincoln with the idea for a ballet he called *The Dream of Audubon*, but Lincoln didn't want to touch it; he thought it "very old hat and full of nonsense."

Among the few ballets to make it through the screening process was *Yankee Clipper*, which had a plot line that followed a young man on a sea voyage to worldwide ports of call, thus allowing for a wide assortment of dances—the tango in Argentina, and so on. Lincoln assigned the music to Paul Bowles and the choreography to Gene Loring. Lincoln didn't much like Bowles, once describing him in his diary as "weak, anemic, vague, petulant and not quite right." Elliott Carter (who was at work on *Pocahon-tas*) told Lincoln that he was too "harsh" about Bowles, but when Lincoln replied, "O.K. let him collaborate with you on *Ball Room Guide*" (yet another ballet under consideration), Carter was less than enthusiastic.

Bowles proceeded to write a piano score for *Yankee Clipper*, but then himself realized that it "was practically incapable of being orchestrated." At that point Lincoln called in the young composer Henry Brant to compose the shipboard scenes while Bowles concentrated on the ports of call. The end result *was* orchestrated ballet music, though Bowles always preferred the piano version. The other new ballet that emerged for that summer's tour was, unexpectedly, Erick Hawkins's *Show Piece*, to music by Robert McBride. It was designed to be a technically flashy piece that would show off what the company dancers could do.

As planning proceeded Frances Hawkins tried to rein Lincoln in a bit. He'd been flying a little high in his letters to her, mentioning his expectation of a performance at Lewisohn Stadium in New York and then, in the spring, his hope of arranging for a season in London. Dimitriev was keen to expand the reputation of the school (from which his income derived), and assured Lincoln that "inside of two years the Caravan will be as successful as the school is"; and he put him in touch with the European agent Meckel. But Frances gave Lincoln a far different and more realistic estimate, telling him that he was being over-optimistic about bookings while at the same time low-balling his estimate of expenses (his father had said the same).

Frances believed she could get the Caravan three to five bookings a week during July and August, for an average of four hundred dollars a performance. By the end of June she'd succeeded in arranging for some thirty engagements for the summer, from New Jersey to Maine, a figure that would eventually grow to fifty-two performances at forty-one different venues (among them two prestigious performances with the Philadelphia Symphony Orchestra). Lincoln confidently wrote his father that he was moving toward "the establishment of a permanent company and a permanent theatre," thereby freeing him from both the Metropolitan Opera and the American Ballet. He thought neither organization had been "aggressive" enough, and he felt Warburg's American Ballet "is a one-man company which I feel is much too limited in its scope, since it banks entirely on Balanchine who, while he is a very great man, is nevertheless only one man." He added that he and Balanchine "are on the most friendly" terms and that "he highly approves of what I am doing." Since Balanchine had earlier been lukewarm at best about the Caravan, Lincoln may well have been exaggerating to keep his father favorably disposed.

Just before the Caravan began its summer tour, Louis turned seventy, and in honor of the occasion the Harvard Medical School established a fellowship in his name; it was an honor that Louis valued "first of all the good things that have happened to me." His friend Felix Frankfurter assured him "that 70 did not mean one was an old man" and added the compliment that Louis retained "the same outlook on life as his youngest friends." He certainly maintained very nearly the same level of business and philanthropic activity as when younger.[4]

To retain the services of the principal dancers in the Ballet Caravan, Lincoln felt he had to guarantee them full salaries for twenty-six weeks—"and hope to Christ we can find work." He also told Frances Hawkins not to book more than four nights during a given week, except when the company was in one place; he felt that the standard practice followed by most dance troupes of six performances a week was "crippling for the dancers," and he refused to put that burden on them. Two distinct tours were planned for 1937, one during July and August, and then a second from October to November.

The summer tour began with a week's engagement in Saybrook, Connecticut. Although the audiences were "quite small," the eight performances gave the company a chance to deal with a variety of problems, ranging from makeup to stage fright. Since the very next stop on the tour was the two-performance gig with the Philadelphia Symphony Orchestra, its well-known conductor, Alexander Smallens, came up to see the company dance in Saybrook. Liking what he saw, he volunteered an additional (and expensive) orchestra rehearsal "so that he could do full justice" to the dances and music.

Unfortunately the train schedule proved so tight that the company only had a total rehearsal time of three hours for five ballets. In addition the overcast weather kept people away, and the orchestra's costs weren't met. Still, there was a considerable amount of publicity, which helped spread the Caravan's name, and the critics were kind enough (though irritated at the lack of a "star," they played up Lincoln more than he liked; he felt that the focus on him was "bad for the company"). Overall he thought the engagement "quite successful"—and for good measure there was a whole page of photographs of the Caravan in *Newsweek*.

Lincoln felt, too (as he wrote his parents), that "every engagement we play is an education for me. I realize that managing this company is like any other business, and the problems involved are largely organizational." On the whole their equipment, which included a convertible cyclorama that could be adjusted for almost any size stage, "worked out wonderfully well." From Philadelphia, the Caravan headed up to New England, with a variety of engagements in town halls, movie houses, school gymnasiums, and small theaters. The longest stop (four performances) was at the American Legion Hall in Gloucester, Massachusetts,where the company offered two separate programs, each performed twice; along with *Yankee Clipper* and *Show Piece*, the ballets included Dollar's *Promenade*, Coudy's *Folk Dance*, and Christensen's *Encounter.* By the time the troupe reached

Bar Harbor, Maine, funds had been exhausted and that week's payroll had to be delayed. But an accountant hired to audit expenses to date confirmed that they'd been justified and shouldn't be cut further; the dancers, for example, were already working at salaries lower than the American Ballet paid, with Coudy and Christensen, at fifty-five dollars a week, at the top, and Marie-Jeanne at forty-five dollars the next highest. After receiving the accountant's opinion, Louis immediately released additional funds.

The summer tour was completed by late August, after additional engagements in New York, Pennsylvania, Connecticut, and New Jersey—and a single one farther south in Cumberland, Maryland. For July cash receipts (with expenses deducted) came to a grand total of $2,096.88. The top-grossing date by far ($700) came from the two performances with the Philadelphia Orchestra; all the other engagements, with the sole exception of the $240 taken in at Manchester, Vermont, brought in less than $200, with the low mark hit in Montpelier, Vermont ($40.80).

To keep the Caravan alive while operating in the red required a heavy financial investment on Lincoln's part. He estimated to his father that it would cost him some fifty thousand dollars (nearly half a million in today's terms) to put the Caravan on its feet, to make it the kind of permanent organization that could, in order to "preserve the integrity of its troupe," offer contracts three years in advance for a ten-month season and be able to accept engagements abroad as well.[5]

During the summer of 1937 Lincoln received a "substantial" (his term) offer from Europe. Meckel had written to Frances Hawkins proposing a tour for 1938–39 that would include France, England, Belgium, and Scandinavia and might potentially stretch to South America and Australia. Meckel felt able to dangle this wildly ambitious schedule to Lincoln because the terms he offered would make Lincoln, not Meckel, responsible for the company's salaries.

Hungry for international status, Lincoln was tempted to take the plunge, but he held off, reluctantly acknowledging that he didn't have sufficient capital to take on so large a financial risk, and that the Caravan was still an experimental young troupe without box-office stars or more than a few budding potential choreographers. Louis had given Lincoln a certain amount of access to his own financial holdings, but had done so reluctantly, often preferring simply to provide the Caravan's periodic shortage of funds with money out of his own pocket. Yet Filene's had not of late been providing the income it once had; now that it was part of Federated Stores, stock dividends had been cut in half, which (in Louis's words) "reduces my income tremendously and makes money pretty awful tight." All the Kirsteins had been forced into some belt tightening.

Lincoln told his father that he felt "continually embarrassed by not being able to show you even a moderate rise in my income" (he was currently getting about three thousand a year in income from the school, plus occasional small fees for his articles). Yet he continued to press for the chance to further invade his own capital, offering "in every way to diminish the scale of my living, even to the extent of half." But Louis resisted Lincoln's importunities, unconvinced that he yet knew the full value of a dollar and fearing he might dissipate his own inheritance.

Europe—and additional funds—were for now out of the question. Yet Lincoln continued to ply his father with predictions that were more sanguine than he actually felt, aware that Louis needed to hear (not least because of his own ambition) Lincoln's conviction that he was finally on the right path and that the Caravan's ultimate success was all but assured: "It is increasingly clear to me," he wrote his father, "that all I want to do is the work that I am now doing. . . . I am trying to plan now not for one year or two years, but for the rest of my natural life. In ten years' time I want to be in a position to have had experience and enjoyed the prestige which would entitle me to the kind of power I hope to be able to wield."

At the age of thirty his prestige was already considerable, the result not only of the Caravan and his own mounting number of books and articles but also of the ever-increasing success of the school. Its yearly budget was now forty thousand dollars, and from August 1937 to February 1938 alone, the school took in more than thirty thousand dollars—a third better than during the previous term; plus there was a reserve fund of thirty thousand. Dimitriev unexpectedly decided late in 1937 that he wanted to reduce his hours as the school's working director and also to safeguard his share of the accumulated profits; toward those ends he suggested that Lincoln buy his five hundred shares of stock (one-half the total) in the school. Lincoln was eager to make the purchase since he would thereby come into undisputed control. But the issues at stake were complex, and negotiations (with Louis Kirstein and his lawyers and accountants centrally involved) took the better part of a year to complete.

Many difficult questions needed to be addressed: how much cash would Dimitriev expect up front and how much in installments; who would assume the burden of taxation on the sums that changed hands; what sort of ongoing role would Dimitriev play at the school, and would it be as a salaried employee or as someone who was paid on a percentage basis from incoming profits. As was expected, Dimitriev "had fits of emotion storm" during the protracted discussions, but an agreement did finally emerge in October 1938.

It contained a number of critical points. Initially Dimitriev had been offered an immediate payment of twenty thousand dollars, but he successfully held out for twenty-five; he would himself, however, be responsible for whatever tax liability followed, and moreover Lincoln would immediately gain control over his voting rights—which was tantamount to gaining control over the school. To ensure Dimitriev's "unswerving devotion to the School's interests" (and, not incidentally, to avoid the necessity of Lincoln having to step in at once and manage daily affairs), Dimitriev would continue to be employed on a profit-sharing basis until October 1, 1941. On that date he'd receive a sum equal to what was then the book value of his stocks, but until then he was restrained from forming any new school or organization within fifty miles of New York City that might compete with the school.

By the time agreement had been reached, the Caravan was in the midst of its third year of touring, and the American Ballet and the Metropolitan Opera had severed all connection between them—a severance that marked both the demise of the company itself and of Eddie Warburg's connection to the world of ballet. The Met's director, Edward Johnson, in an interview he gave to *American Dancer* for its September 1938 article "What Is Wrong with Opera Ballet?" exercised his usual "good taste" and never once mentioned the American Ballet by name.

But Balanchine, for his part, let loose with an uncharacteristically furious tirade against the Met's misuse and mistreatment of his dancers, its refusal of needed rehearsal time, its lack of decent facilities, and its encompassing stodginess. Lincoln, too, in the polemical pamphlet he published that year, *Blast at Ballet*, pulled no punches, accusing the Met of a litany of misguided policies, among them "contempt for American singers and composers of our generation" and giving less thought to dance than to the design of new uniforms for its ushers. The press, to Lincoln's surprise and delight, overwhelmingly came down on the side of the American Ballet, and the Met became so embarrassed that they called up and asked an amused Lincoln to "lay off."[6]

As for the Caravan, its third year of touring involved somewhat fewer performances, but they were spread over a far wider geographic area, reaching across the continent to California. Previously Frances Hawkins had to book ahead almost week to week, but with the reputation of the Caravan growing, she was now able to fix engagements much farther in advance—including, for the spring 1938 tour, performances in Canada and Cuba. And that, in the opinion of Louis Kirstein, was not necessarily a good thing, given the additional outlay of money that would likely be involved. He advised Lincoln to confine the troupe to New York City and its immediate environs, and he characterized Lincoln's proposed budget as "altogether too optimistic." To placate his father Lincoln professed "complete agreement," and promised that unless he had substantial guarantees he would in the future curtail the Caravan's touring—that is, *after* Havana.

But Louis wasn't so easily reassured. Giving vent to his bullying side, he told Frances Hawkins directly that her 20 percent commission, considering the small-scale nature of the operation, was too high, and he told Lincoln that the Caravan should look for higher-powered representation. In essence Louis was challenging Frances's professionalism, and she refused to let him get away with it. She sent him a lengthy letter that was at once dignified, pointed, and conciliatory. She outlined for him in detail her training and experience, reminded him that the Caravan had "come a hell of a long way since the start two years ago," and offered henceforth to take 20 percent only when the Caravan receipts were above sixteen hundred dollars a week—not because she felt she'd overcharged in the past but because of her conviction that the Caravan would soon be making money for Lincoln *and* herself and she didn't want to "kill a goose that might some day lay golden eggs for me."

Even before Louis issued his complaints, Lincoln—with Frances's help—had been seeking additional sponsorship from some major institution or promoter, as well as from moneyed individuals. Nelson Rockefeller, whom Lincoln had continued to see fairly regularly (and whom he continued to find "charming and cagey"), had gotten the Caravan a three-performance engagement late in 1937 at the Center Theater in Rockefeller Center. Lincoln had also tried to enlist the support of, among others, his father's friend David Sarnoff, who was pleasant to him but made it clear he had "absolutely no interest."

Frances and Lincoln finally had to settle for help with bookings, especially in the Mid- and Southwest, from Paul Stoes, who ran a small operation but nonetheless did a good job for them. The Caravan's winter 1938 season began, thanks to Chick Austin, with a double performance at Hartford's Avery Theater that consisted of Erick Hawkins's *Show Piece*, Loring's *Yankee Clipper*, and the premiere of *Filling Station*, one of the Caravan's two new ballets that year (*Billy the Kid* would be the other). *Filling Station* was the collaboration of Lew Christensen (choreography), Virgil Thomson (music), Paul Cadmus (costumes and set), and Lincoln himself (libretto). Christensen danced the leading role of Mac, a gas station attendant who has assorted run-ins with patrons ranging from truck drivers, a family, a gangster, and The Girl—and danced it with brilliant virtuosity, utilizing all his vaudevillian acrobatic skills. Lincoln, pressing his "American" mission, liked referring to the characters in *Filling Station* as representing "an actual facet of American civilization . . . a recognizable social type."

The ballet, in any case, proved a huge success for the Caravan and from the first was critically acclaimed; one of the country's toughest, most astute critics, B. H. Haggin, hailed it as a "classic of American Ballet," and the piece is still performed today. The Hartford premiere was "absolutely jammed" both nights, and the small theater brought the Caravan some eight hundred dollars in receipts. Lincoln wrote his parents that the event had been "a triumph."

Word of the success spread quickly, and some especially good offers came in, including an engagement with the large WPA orchestra at the Federal Music Theatre in New York, a sixteen-hundred-dollar guarantee for two performances in Havana and, for the fall, two full weeks in Canada at twenty-nine hundred a week. On top of all that, *Life* magazine expressed interest in giving a three-page spread to the Caravan's 1938 spring tour. Lincoln cheerily (and perhaps with just a touch of I-told-you-so) informed his father that "by weathering this winter at a considerable cost [he'd spent some forty thousand dollars on the Caravan during 1938], we will be in an independent position next year . . . a paying proposition."

He further predicted "that at the end of that time I can very easily go to Nelson with a definite proposition for a large capitalization." Lincoln's optimism even led him to reassure Louis that he felt certain he'd never again have to call on him for any subsidy for the Caravan, nor have to invest any further sums of his own: "If it doesn't go on the strength" of the current year's forty-thousand-dollar outlay, "it will never go." Time would soon tell.

Lincoln again accompanied the Caravan on its spring and fall 1938 tours. Earlier he'd greatly enjoyed the traveling and camaraderie and to some extent still did, but by this, the third year, it had all become a bit more taxing and prosaic. Not that there wasn't still much to enjoy, including riding cross-country on a bus (and later, on a special railroad car) and getting to see so much of the nation close-up. As they headed farther west, Lincoln found the scenery "becoming more and more beautiful every second, vista after vista. . . . Mount Shasta is really glorious even if you don't ski." And the people fascinated him. As he wrote home to the "Dear Ones" (Paul Cadmus and the newly married Jared French and Margaret Hoening), "the cowboys here are all designed by Jared . . . such elegance, little hippy heels and nice faces." It helped that Lincoln found the bus driver "a fine specimen of American manhood . . . chock full of southwestern lore and . . . friends with the state troopers and all the *very* corrupt cops in Phoenix."[7]

Even more exciting than the scenery and the people was the great success of the Caravan's newest ballet, *Billy the Kid*, which premiered during the fall 1938 tour. Lincoln had handed Eugene Loring a copy of Walter Noble Burns's *The Life and Times of Billy the Kid* and said, "See if you can make a ballet out of it." Loring took it from there, doing (in his own words) "a great deal of research about the settling of the West." It was he who came up with the scenario, which Lincoln then gave to the composer Aaron Copland (whom he'd originally met through Virgil Thomson). To complete the creative team, Lincoln assigned costumes and backdrop to Jared French, sending him, for inspiration, Theodore Roosevelt's memoirs of the far west, with Frederic Remington's illustrations.

When Copland completed the score in September 1938, Lincoln not only immediately sent him a $250 check but wrote him that "it is the best music we have ever had." He added his prediction that *Billy* would also be

"the most successful ballet we have ever had." Before leaving to perform
it on tour, Lincoln gave *Billy* a dress rehearsal performance before an
audience of four hundred people in New York. It came off "wonderfully
well . . . everybody was crazy about it." And "everybody" included Martha
Graham as well as Serge Lifar of the Paris Opéra—very nearly as broad a
spectrum of the dance world as could be imagined. Lincoln felt especially
delighted that the ballet "couldn't be any more American."

When *Billy* opened at the Chicago Opera House in October, it proved
an immediate hit, and on the fall tour, audiences everywhere, and most
critics, "adored" it (*Billy* "has been a great success wherever it's given and
the dancing gets better at each performance," Lincoln wrote home to "the
dear ones"). Marie-Jeanne alternated the leading female role of the
Sweetheart with Leda Anchutina, a new addition to the Caravan, and Lew
Christensen performed the part of the noble sheriff Pat Garrett. Loring
thought Lew epitomized "the straight-laced, good person," preferring
him in the part to John Kriza, who danced Garrett in a celebrated later
revival. Lincoln was tremendously proud of *Billy;* he thought Loring's choreography "intense and evocative," Copland's score done with "extraordinary finesse and tenderness," and the entire ballet not the story of the
Wild West done as some "stylized Dumb-Show" but a "bare and haunting" re-creation.

If *Billy* marked the high point of the 1938 Caravan (or even, arguably,
of its entire history), there were some less happy aspects to the tour that
year. For one thing Lincoln missed his new boyfriend, Pete Martínez, terribly. "I am insanely lonely," Lincoln wrote Monroe Wheeler. "Pete has
put me through the paces. . . . Please call him at the Y.M.C.A. He adores
you and beat him up for me." Lincoln thought of Pete as "like a wise
child . . . not shrewd . . . but able to take care of himself." He well understood that Pete, some five years younger than he and "on the verge of a
considerable field of experiment and physical release," was "scared" of
anything like a commitment, even though Lincoln "felt the reverse."

He'd told Pete to use his apartment while he was touring, but Pete
hadn't taken him up on the offer. Nor did he, for the longest while, even
write. "Has someone offered him a platterful of tiaras and has he
accepted?" Lincoln asked the "dear ones," in that ironically campy tone he
never used when writing to family and only rarely with heterosexual
friends. He added, "My heart is perforated already and can crack on the
dotted line." But then he finally got a few letters from Pete, sweet and sad,
expressing the wish that he'd gone home to Texas, yet making Lincoln feel
that "he still loves me, I guess (I hope)." In the interim Lincoln made do
with "some heavenly boys, particularly cowboys, whom I hate to have to
quit as soon as I get to like them. There never have been any people so
heartbreakingly handsome as these kids in cowboots, blue riders and flat
hats."

Among the other downsides of the cross-country fall tour was boredom. The long stretches of travel and the intervening time between performances involved a good deal of tedious "waiting around," which grew increasingly irksome. The company went to the movies to blot out the boredom but not as often as they would have liked: the film *Angels with Dirty Faces* seemed to be on the same circuit as the Caravan and followed them around for two weeks. When on the bus (or subsequently the train), there were hours and hours to kill. Gisella Caccialanza, who'd rejoined the troupe, knitted sweaters for "her Lew," Erick Hawkins determinedly plowed through the basic writings of Freud, Doug Coudy put together poker games, and Trude Rittman, recently arrived from Germany and one of the Caravan's two pianists (and later a well-known dance-music arranger), sat reading Schiller's *un*published work.

When given a layover at a bus stop or railroad station, Lincoln dutifully carried out an assignment Paul Cadmus had given him to check the scribblings on bathroom walls. He found them generally uninspired, though Oklahoma provided something of a Renaissance: "I want to meet a nice middle aged man with a big cock to suck" (Oklahoma City); "Question: Where can you get your prick sucked in this fucking town? Answer: Try the Union Depot" (Tulsa); "Oh! Oh! Oh! Oh! Show it . . ." (Emporia, Kansas). The marbled toilet walls, to Lincoln's regret, failed to yield more than an occasional half-obliterated drawing.

Some of the troupe's lodgings also proved a problem. When they played in Las Cruces, New Mexico, they were housed in what Lincoln called "the wackiest hotel in the western world." Seated in a lobby chair was a wax dummy dressed in a bullfighter's costume. The walls were hung with "silk mantillas in flaky rags," Japanese carvings, and bad paintings of the Virgin Mary. None of the plumbing worked, and the walls were as thin as paper. Las Cruces itself was "a real dusty wild frontier town," except that it had a state mining school—which was where the company performed, on a postage-stamp-size stage "to raucous howls of success."

Still, after weeks on the road, the troupe was (in Lincoln's words) showing "signs of weakening, becoming . . . recalcitrant, uninterested and tiresome." Lincoln wrote Monroe Wheeler that "the kids dance *very* well really, although I am, er, a little bitsy bit insanely wildly frantically bored with their god-damned bottoms." Yet, some forty years later, Eugene Loring would recall Lincoln on tour as not at all irritable or prone to playing the petty despot.

If nerves occasionally got frayed—an inevitable side effect of protracted travel and close-quarters living—the cross-country tour in 1938 met almost everywhere with enthusiastic audiences and well-disposed critics. In Austin, Texas, seven thousand students watched the performances in the university's huge gymnasium "and the applause rolled around in the rafters like detonating dynamite." In Fayetteville, Arkansas, the football team noisily arrived smack in the middle of Dollar's elegant *Promenade* and proceeded to whistle and cheer whenever a male dancer touched a female one. In Toronto the audience, which included the lieutenant governor-general, was far starchier; Lincoln thought it "would have preferred some white tarlatans and Russian music."

The most consistently favorable audiences and notices came in California. The San Francisco and Los Angeles reviews "were really marvelous," and elsewhere in the state the Caravan's reception was better "than I could have hoped for," Lincoln reported to his parents. "In fact it is better I feel than the Caravan at this stage in its development really warrants . . . people are so eager to see something approaching American dancing that they are eager to forgive our smallness and lack of spectacular display" (which the large-scale Ballets Russes touring companies were noted for, along with their lack of originality).

Lincoln would often struggle to define what he meant by "American dancing." When one critic (John Henry Rogers in Dallas) accused him of being overly insistent on "100% Americanism in the ballet," Lincoln pointed out to him that the Caravan's program included music by Ravel *(Promenade)*, Scarlatti (Loring's *Harlequin for President*), and Mozart (Christensen's *Encounter*), and he insisted that he wasn't interested in "nationalist prejudice or blind chauvinism." But he *was* interested in what he called the "unique, indigenous and creative style" of American dancers, choreographers, and composers.

In an April 1938 column in *The Nation* he focused on the dancers: "Instead of setting a stereotype of remoteness, spectral grandeur and visionary brilliance [that is, the Ballets Russes], the Americans are volatile, intimate, frank. . . . The most important thing about American dancers is the retention of their amateur status and their nearness to the audience . . . the frontier spirit of spontaneous collective entertainment where everybody got up and danced as they could, still persists. But with a difference. Our dancing artists have selected and amplified all that is most useful in the amateur spirit to make of it a conscious and brilliant frame for their individual theatrical projection"—and he explicitly included not merely ballet or "modern" dancers but also the can-do "hoofers" Fred Astaire, Paul Draper, Ginger Rogers, Eleanor Powell, Buddy Ebsen, and Ray Bolger. "Volatile, intimate, frank" were shrewd if contestable definitions of the American essence (certainly in dance, "energy" and "athleticism" might just as easily serve), yet at the very least Lincoln had put his finger on some recognizable, canny half-truths. Throughout his life he'd continue to hone his definition of "American."

While in California, Lincoln heard a great deal about a woman who had taken as her mission in life "to unqueer queers"—a sort of secular Aimee Semple McPherson (whom Lincoln referred to as "Jesus' little bitch"). The heterosexual missionary's "scientific" technique was to ex-tract semen from "100% butch normal males like firemen, lifeguards, truck drivers," grade the semen (90 percent, 80 percent, and so on) and then inject it into "queers whose corresponding . . . [quotient] is only, say, 5% or 10% or 15%"—and "voila! they're even butchier than the other non-bitches." *How* she extracted the fluid remained a mystery Lincoln was unable to penetrate, though he entertained a string of fantasy scenarios. The woman missionary had managed to persuade the Pasadena chief of police and a judge to let her inject queer prisoners in the local jail—"over their furious protests." "A nastier business," Lincoln wrote home to the "dear ones," "I never heard of." He assured them that he'd remained out of her clutches and was having a lovely time at the San Diego and Long Beach marine bases: "Such nice pocket-sized ones, all friendly as one o'clock, as they say in Hollywood."

Despite all the good reviews and the cordial receptions, Lincoln came to realize that it would be difficult in the upcoming year to expand the Cara-van's number of bookings. And the realization made him angry. He blamed the near-monopoly of concert engagements held by CBS's Columbia Concerts Corporation and NBC's National Broadcasting and Concert Bureau, the latter including impresario Sol Hurok, manager of the two leading, and intercontinental, Russian companies—de Basil's Bal-lets Russes and Serge Denham's new (1938) Ballet Russe de Monte Carlo. Between them, CBS and NBC controlled 90 percent of bookings and were known to suppress—sometimes ruthlessly—potential competitors. Local managements that had come to admire the Caravan were often afraid to invite them back for fear that the two media giants would deny them access to major artists.

Yet in 1938, deeply concerned about the Caravan's future and realizing that it—or rather, Louis Kirstein—couldn't continue to bleed money indefinitely, Frances and Lincoln tried to make peace with the enemy. Frances initiated contact with both Columbia and NBC, seeking some sort of mutual arrangement. Columbia did briefly express interest, but only if the services of Paul Haakon could be procured as the Caravan's "star"; Haakon, however, was unable to secure release from his current contract with the Shubert office, and Columbia concluded that without him the Caravan was too negligible an enterprise to warrant their involve-ment. Lincoln also explored some possible arrangement with Sol Hurok, even while fearing that the Caravan wasn't "in a position now to stand absorption in a subordinate position in any Russo-American organiza-tion." He needn't have worried; though Hurok made some vague feints in their direction, Frances soon discovered that behind the scenes he was using his considerable weight to get bookers to turn down the Caravan and replace it with the dancer Argentinita, whom he already represented.

AGMA (the American Guild of Musical Artists) threatened to bring antitrust action against CBS and NBC, and in 1942 the Federal Communications Commission (FCC) would in fact rule that a "conflict of interest" did exist in that both networks were simultaneously buying and selling artistic talent. The ruling was expected to force the networks out of the booking business, but they managed to circumvent it by selling off stock to insiders who proceeded to set up new agencies (for example, Columbia Artists Management), with approximately the same high-level personnel and market power as the old organizations.

Even if the FCC ruling had managed to produce a different result, it wouldn't have come in time to help the Caravan's immediate prospects. Lincoln claimed that during the Caravan's 1938–39 tours, NBC especially "has done everything in their power to black-leg us. They have said that I pay to have the troupe perform, that I bribe critics with untold Warburg millions, etc., etc." (Eddie Warburg, of course, hadn't shown the slightest interest in the Caravan, nor invested a penny in it.) The NBC office in California, Lincoln wrote his parents, proved particularly ruthless and in his opinion was "full of the slickest bunch of crooks I ever met. The only reason for our slight success is in the fact that they let us get in a few dates."

Yet he refused to accept the situation without a fight. He contacted local arts committees, women's clubs, and even the Sons and Daughters of the American Revolution to try to persuade them that democratic fair play was at stake. And he had lunch with nearly every dance and music critic on the West Coast; "there's not one," he reported, "that hasn't been completely in my favor." Still, by 1939 Lincoln had become seriously concerned that the "big boys" might try to kill the Caravan outright; up until its cross-country tour, the troupe had seemed a minor-league effort of no real consequence. Now that people on the West Coast had actually seen the Caravan, NBC could no longer simply wave off local managements with a "don't bother with it, we've seen it and it stinks." Now the managements themselves had seen it, and they wanted it back. To which NBC said, in essence, "By all means re-book the Caravan—if you're willing to forgo Marian Anderson." "It works," Lincoln wrote home, "you bet it does."

Yet at the same time, he felt "there is absolutely no question that the country wants and will pay well for a moderate-priced ballet company with American themes." That conviction led him, some four months after returning from the cross-country tour, to write an extraordinary letter to George Balanchine that began with Lincoln claiming that after three years' experience with the Caravan, "I am convinced that there is an enormous chance all over America for a permanent traveling company." Part of the reason was that various international companies (de Basil; Mikhail Mordkin's long-standing troupe, and Serge Denham's 1938–39 Ballet

Russe) had, whatever their artistic shortcomings in Lincoln's eyes, done a great deal to educate the American public about ballet; there was now scarcely a city with a population of more than one hundred thousand that hadn't seen a ballet company over the past few years.[8]

"The era of pioneering," Lincoln wrote Balanchine, "is over." And the public, he argued, had grown weary both of repetitive "foreign attractions" and of the Caravan's too-small company of twenty, which "cannot possibly interest [those] . . . who have already seen the eye-filling spectacle of the Monte Carlo Ballet." The time was now ripe for "a permanent fair-sized American company—say, about forty dancers. "If you and I can work together," Lincoln wrote Balanchine, "there is already a basis of an excellent repertory": combine four of his ballets with four that had emerged from the Caravan. If, further, Balanchine would create two new ballets ("particularly for New York"), they could then, Lincoln believed, travel successfully for two seasons at least.

Lincoln even had a name picked out—the New American Ballet Company—and the time and place for its opening: early in 1940 in Boston; Stravinsky was scheduled to teach at Harvard that year, and Lincoln felt that the conductor Koussevitsky (who "has the greatest respect for you, and . . . happens also to be a very good friend of my father") would direct the Boston Orchestra in a Stravinsky festival. Lincoln was also able to report to Balanchine that he'd already spoken to Nathaniel Saltonstall, president of the Boston Institute of Modern Art, and he'd agreed to sponsor a ballet festival.

The Caravan, Lincoln told Balanchine, *would* go back on tour for ten weeks, from October through December 1939; thereafter, Lincoln proposed, he would like to place his company "at your disposal . . . the dancers I have are already well known to you, since all of them have come out of our school, and many of them have worked with you." He offered Balanchine the role of artistic director and proposed that he himself "be general director and supervisor of detail and of the company; and . . . I will always accompany the troupe on tour."

But Balanchine, for reasons unrecorded, apparently turned Lincoln down out-of-hand—even though he would soon return to teach at the School of American Ballet (SAB). Personal antagonism doesn't seem to have played a significant role in his decision, since he and Lincoln continued to see each other when Balanchine was in New York. Yet it can't be wholly discounted either; Balanchine may well have seen a June 11, 1938, piece in *The New Yorker* entitled "Americans Dance, Too," in which Lincoln had purportedly whispered to the reporter when they ran into Balanchine, "he's a Georgian . . . Stalin's type. He seems as soft as silk but he's like steel. He's really rather sinister."

Early in 1939, moreover, Lincoln, disheartened and apparently angry at Balanchine's defection to Hollywood and Broadway, had referred, in a letter to Tchelitchev, about the "rogue's gallery" of people George was now hanging out with; "I don't think that George's genius is an eternal value. He has it only when he works with great collaborators." As for himself, he wrote Pavlik, "I am absolutely divorced from George both professionally and emotionally. When I talk to him I feel I no longer know him." The two men, of course, had never been personally close, but neither, so far as is known, had Lincoln ever previously spoken quite so negatively about Balanchine.

But if personal antagonism did play a possible role in Balanchine's rejection of Lincoln's proposal, other factors seem of more importance. Lincoln, after all, had yet to put the Caravan on a sound financial footing; the idea of starting all over again with a new company twice the size of the old had all the earmarks of pie in the sky. It wasn't that money was ever of paramount importance to Balanchine; when he made large sums he spent them, assuming that the future would somehow take care of itself.

Yet he wasn't cavalier enough to give up the financial, if not artistic, security he'd found in the world of film and theater for the outside chance that Lincoln's risky new scheme might succeed—even though Balanchine would probably have preferred to be making new ballets, and even though he'd begun to have his share of theatrical flops (*Keep Off the Grass*, *The Lady Comes Across*, and *Dream with Music*). Besides, on Christmas Eve 1938, Balanchine had married Vera Zorina, his leading lady in *The Goldwyn Follies*, and the marriage, given Zorina's somewhat distant affection for her husband, consumed a fair amount of his emotional energy. It isn't even certain that Balanchine during this period was eager for the chance to recenter his artistic life in the world of ballet. He did have other offers during the years 1937 to 1941, and did accept a few. But among the occasional ballets he created during this period, none proved of any lasting importance.

A new company did debut early in 1940, but it was the wealthy Lucia Chase (herself a dancer) and Richard Pleasant's well-financed Ballet Theatre, not Lincoln's New American Ballet. In Ballet Theatre's extraordinary first season (rumored to have lost its backers some two hundred thousand dollars), it produced some fifteen ballets, eleven of them composed by contemporary choreographers, including the young Antony Tudor, Agnes de Mille, and the Caravan's own Eugene Loring and William Dollar. Lucia Chase had invited Balanchine to participate as well, but he declined, which further suggests that for the time being his attention was focused elsewhere.

Lincoln's years of tireless work trying to create an American ballet company had painfully eventuated in someone else coming out of left field and capturing the flag. It hardly helped that the *Herald Tribune* pointedly hailed Ballet Theatre with the declaration that "here at last is a solidly American organization." But Lincoln was shrewd enough to keep his hurt to himself and to swallow his pride; in a magnanimous if calculated gesture of support, he sent Lucia Chase a congratulatory telegram: GREATEST RESPECT FOR YOUR COURAGE, ENTERPRISE AND FAITH IN THE BALLET. BEST WISHES FOR GREAT SUCCESS.

By this point the Caravan had already embarked on its fourth (and as it turned out, final) year of touring, and the tour would have its high points. Not the least of its incidental pleasures for Lincoln was the fact that Pete Martínez joined the company as a nondancing member (he'd had a foot injury), thus providing Lincoln with built-in companionship—*and* Pete agreed to Lincoln's suggestion that they live together once back in New York. Almost simultaneously Lincoln would, in 1939, meet Paul Cadmus's sister, Fidelma, a talented painter and a great beauty, and would start once more to think about the possibility of marriage (though not of "settling down," at least not in any traditional sense).

Despite these new possibilities, the end of the decade found Lincoln discouraged. As he wrote Cadmus, "The tour has been very disheartening. I've lost a lot of money and guess it's the end of the Caravan for good—although we've had excellent notices and receptions." He sent Nelson Rockefeller much the same sort of dispirited account: "My tour has been rather heartbreaking . . . the monopoly system in the entertainment business has me stopped. I'm alone, as you know, and pretty well washed up. I know it could go in time, but pioneering has never been a paying proposition."

Another disappointment during this discouraging interregnum was the eventual reduction of a feeler from the world's fair in Flushing Meadow to direct "a large dance production" into something considerably less than that: helping to mount a minor art exhibit and putting together an eighteen-minute middlebrow revue-ballet (*A Thousand Times Neigh!*) for the Ford Pavilion which mostly embarrassed him. "Our work," he wrote Frances Hawkins, "goes ahead with reckless extravagance and general horror. I have the general impression that I have sold out to big business, but underneath it all comes the feeling that I hate what I am doing to such a degree that I hope I won't get sick before the rehearsal is over." He felt that the Ford people thought they'd gotten something good—"which they [had] not." He wished only that he could have spent the large sums of money they threw at the "spectacle" for something worthwhile—"but that is never the way." He was at least pleased to have been able to give six months' work to some forty dancers, including Caravan members William Dollar and Trude Rittman.

To top off this downturn in prospects, Lincoln's hard-hitting pamphlet *Blast at Ballet*, which he'd expected to strike like a thunderbolt, had a more limited impact. Lincoln had published it himself, and both the sales figures (the print run of two thousand never sold out) and the number of reviews proved disappointing. Among the few prominent notices *Blast* received, Jacques Barzun's in *The Nation* was the most important. In his review Barzun credited Lincoln with considerable courage for his various provocations in the pamphlet and found much of his analysis "both witty and true." But in general he characterized *Blast* as "a battery of insulting comparisons, thundering scorn, and personal allusions." Well, yes, but that had been precisely Lincoln's intention; the real point was whether his insulting remarks about, say, the Metropolitan Opera ("a specimen of inert survival . . . a diverting relic"), were warranted. Barzun bypassed that debate and simply concluded, inaccurately, that "there is strictly speaking no argument" in the pamphlet.

Even the school, after a sustained period of growth, took a temporary downturn in 1939. With enrollment off, Lincoln felt he should forgo taking any salary for six months. That meant a personal income loss of $2,400, which in turn necessitated a renewed attempt at belt tightening. Essentially he remained as oblivious as ever to what his father called "the value of a dollar"; for him, money was for use—and overall he used his well, used it for beneficent purposes rather than mere self-indulgence. He did at least try—with mixed success—to put some mechanical measures in place, limiting himself, for example, to no more than ten dollars a day for his immediate cash needs.

But he refused outright to stop helping friends who came to him for a "temporary" loan (few of whom ever paid him back); in 1939 that included Pete Martínez, his old friend James Agee, and a recent acquaintance, Christopher Isherwood. Justifying these loans to his father, Lincoln argued that "on an absolute basis, I can't afford to do this, but since I live in a certain way, and I am known to be your son, it is almost impossible for me to blankly say no to everybody. Hence I say yes to a few people." In response Louis played out a classic case of "the schizophrenic parent": he sharply admonished Lincoln for his extravagance—and then increased his allowance by a hundred dollars a month.

By the end of 1939 the school was doing much better business than it had at the start of the year, perhaps helped by the return of both Vladimiroff and his wife, Kyra Blanc, to the teaching staff, and by the somewhat premature departure, due to a heart condition, of Dimitriev. Lincoln also asked Martha Graham to teach at the school; she took the offer seriously and was flattered by it but finally decided that her schedule was already too crowded.

By early 1940 Lincoln had entirely taken over as head of SAB. And that proved to be, as he wrote his father, "quite a job." He felt that an additional reason for enrollment falling had been the "disdainful" atmosphere Dimitriev had created, squeezing every nickel, acting the strict martinet, creating the reputation that the school was so hard to get into that a number of potential students had decided not to try. Lincoln was determined to change all that. He tried to be "aggressively friendly to everybody in every ballet company, and on every possible side." He also decided to do some advertising (Dimitriev hadn't wanted to "waste" the money), and to begin a campaign to solicit foundation support.

Before the close of the year, the school had the highest registration in its history. The shoestring publicity campaign had brought in sixty new pupils (a nearly 50 percent improvement over the preceding year), and the school had become more national in scope—some 40 percent of the students now came from outside the Greater New York area. Lincoln felt entitled to reward himself with a steady salary of five hundred dollars a month.

For several years Lincoln had been well aware (as he wrote his father back in 1938) that "compared to the events in the great world"—Hitler had by then already seized Austria and the Sudetenland—"my own affairs seem increasingly tiny." He found the rapidly unfolding events in Europe "so awful" that "anything one does from day to day seems almost pointless." With the looming possibility of a world at war, he found it difficult to focus on making plans "for next year or even next month. And trying to imagine what it must be like in Barcelona or Vienna at the present moment practically cripples your imagination."

As the Caravan's 1939–40 tour proceeded toward its close, international events moved toward an accelerated climax. In March 1939 the Spanish Republic gave way to the fascist dictatorship of General Franco. Lincoln, in *The Nation*, denounced Neville Chamberlain's policy of appeasement and the English government's "dissembling with Hitler and Mussolini," excoriating its "modest and resilient stupidity." In August 1939 Hitler and Stalin signed a nonaggression pact. On September 1 Hitler's battalions marched into Poland, plunging Europe into war. In 1940 the U.S. Congress passed its first peacetime military draft.

CHAPTER EIGHTEEN

South America: Ballet

(1939–1941)

THOSE WHO KNEW Fidelma Cadmus in her middle-aged, timorous
years would have been unlikely to guess that as a young woman she'd
shown considerable independence, bordering on rebelliousness. After her
mother's death and her father's remarriage, she'd left the family apartment
rather than live with a difficult stepmother with whom she frequently
quarreled. She was, to be sure, twenty-six at the time, but in 1932 it wasn't
common for a single woman to strike out on her own.[1]

It infuriated her father, Egbert Cadmus, whose Jutland ancestors had
immigrated to the American colonies back in the early eighteenth century.
"I may seem old-fashioned to you, Fidelma," he wrote her, "but you have
imbued many modern ideas that to me seem false, even hideous . . . and I
am saddened by the thought that you may have to suffer before experience
teaches you her lesson." Egbert thereafter all but stopped seeing his
daughter.

The high-strung Fidelma, nicknamed Fido, had had "nervous troubles" even as a young girl and as a teenager had gone through a traumatic
operation for what was apparently an ovarian cyst, though the doctor did
tell her that she'd be able to bear children. In 1933, within a year after
leaving her father's house, she had some sort of "breakdown" and was
briefly hospitalized (stories later circulated that she'd been raped during
her stay). Thereafter she went to live with her aunts, entered art school,
and scraped together a living designing wallpaper. It would be decades
before she'd again be seriously troubled with emotional problems.

Fidelma and Paul's parents, Egbert Cadmus and Maria Latasa (whose
family was Basque), had met as students at the National Academy of
Design. Neither their subsequent marriage nor their careers (his primarily
as a watercolorist, hers as an illustrator) met with much success. The
family lived at the edge of poverty, with Egbert bringing in a meager living working in a commercial lithography shop. The children initially
grew up in a tenement on 103rd Street and later moved to a somewhat
more spacious apartment on West 152nd Street and Convent Avenue.

At a time when most adults had no more than eight years of schooling,
Fidelma and Paul did attend high school, but Paul quit at fifteen and was
allowed by his parents to enroll at their old school, the National Academy

of Design. Though widely read, they didn't consider themselves "literary" or "intellectual."

Paul inherited the fairhaired Danish looks of his father, Fidelma the olive skin and statuesque beauty of her mother. Her elegant appearance and graceful bearing suggested a sophisticated self-assurance that she in fact lacked. The few surviving letters from her youth are sprinkled with apology and self-doubt: "I feel dreadfully ashamed . . . I've been feeling rather stupid . . . he [a current date] seems to like me—so of course I like him . . . feeble-minded Fido . . . forgive me for neglecting you," and the like.

Yet she was popular with most of her fellow art students, and this despite the fact that she often dressed, due to poverty, out of a sometimes bizarre ragtag bundle of hand-me-downs. Though she and her brother had numerous friends, Fidelma and Paul, only two years apart in age, would remain each other's close confidants. When Paul and the painter Jared French met in 1929 and became lovers soon after, Fidelma, though nonjudgmental about homosexuality, advised her brother to have a variety of experiences before settling down. Paul, in love with Jared, ignored her advice. But he always felt that Fidelma was a person of enormous empathy, as well as wide democratic impulses: There was nothing of the snob about her.

Lincoln and Fidelma first met at a George Platt Lynes party in 1939. Though living at the time with Pete Martínez and deeply attached to him, Lincoln seems to have made an almost instantaneous decision to court Fidelma. They began to see each other often, and within weeks of their initial meeting, Lincoln told Paul that he intended to marry his sister someday. Taken aback, Paul pointed out that they hardly knew each other and that Lincoln was involved with Pete, who hadn't been at all pleased with Fidelma's sudden appearance on the scene (though they would soon become mutually adoring friends). Paul had the sense that Lincoln intended the two relationships to run simultaneously, though in separate apartments.

The historical record, so full on nearly every aspect of Lincoln's life, is utterly blank about how much, if anything, he explicitly told Fidelma about his history of attachments to men or his current feelings for Pete. Many years later Paul could recall no conversations of his own with his sister about Lincoln's sexual proclivities, nor any confidential request for advice and guidance on the subject. But Paul did have the lifelong sense that Fidelma "understood" early on, decided that Lincoln simply needed his close relationships with men—and that was that; whether she ever managed to settle the matter quite so definitively within herself is another matter; some scattered later evidence suggests that she had at least occasional qualms and, now and then, an outburst of anger.

It was Paul's further impression that Lincoln's instant courtship wasn't the result of having fallen madly in love, though like everyone else who knew the couple well, Paul was certain the two did care deeply for each other and would remain intensely devoted throughout their long marriage. Paul felt certain, too, that the match was sexual for the first few years. It's been suggested that the source of Lincoln's fevered pursuit of Fidelma derived from family pressure to marry, now that he'd reached the age of thirty-two (Fidelma was a year older). Yet Louis and Rose seem initially to have disapproved of her—she was poor and not Jewish—and to have treated her coldly at first.

Such pressure as Lincoln may have felt to produce a wife was more likely social than familial in origin. As he entered the junior ranks of cultural movers and shakers, an open and exclusively homosexual lifestyle (even assuming that was what he wanted, though his past "bisexual" history suggested less mutually exclusive possibilities) would have sat badly in the starchy world of fund-raisers and foundations. The cynical conclusion would be that Lincoln married in order to foster his career. Yet that seems *too* cynical, given how little he would bother to cover up his homosexual activities—and how much he genuinely cared for Fidelma.

The couple didn't actually marry until April 1941, but when they did, neither set of parents, nor Lincoln's siblings, attended the wedding ceremony—though "ceremony," in any case, is too elaborate a description for what was simply a classic dash to city hall. The entire wedding party consisted of Lincoln and Fidelma, Margaret French (she and Jared had by then also married), and Paul, who handed Lincoln the ring. The four then had an unexceptional lunch near city hall—and that was that. Frances Hawkins, who was on the road with Martha Graham, brought back with her to New York one of Lincoln's presents to Fidelma: an Afghan hound puppy named Taimur. Frances felt that Fidelma was bound to love him since he was just like Lincoln: "as wild and shy and untouchable with strangers as an unbroken colt." Fidelma was enraptured.

Frances was also instrumental in helping Lincoln close down the Ballet Caravan. Its fourth and final tour in 1939–40 involved fewer performances (forty-one) and venues (thirty-five) than in any year but the first, though the troupe did once again appear in both Canada and California and in most places got excellent notices. Lincoln had continued "wheedling for money" to avoid having the significant investment to date go for nothing, holding on to the hope that "some genuinely equipped concern" could be found to take over and manage the Caravan. But none of his feelers to Sol Hurok and others brought forth a sponsor, and by late 1939 Lincoln reluctantly concluded that "to go on waiting for an eventuality which may not transpire" simply wasn't feasible.[2]

But the Caravan at least went out with something of a bang. Once Lincoln made a definite decision to close down the company, Frances ar-

ranged a mini-festival for the last week in December 1939 at the Adelphi
Theatre in New York City. The original plan had been to feature three
attractions—the Caravan, Martha Graham, and Harald Kreutzberg. But
the German government at the last moment refused to allow Kreutzberg
to leave the country, and so the bill was eventually made up of the Caravan
(four performances), Martha Graham (three), and a single appearance by
Kreutzberg's replacement, Sai Shoki.

Lincoln and Martha Graham had remained on affectionate, even intimate, terms. Theirs had decidedly become a mutual admiration society. In
a series of (unpublished) letters, Graham delicately and shrewdly analyzed
him: "I have wanted love for you—not happiness, particularly—because
you are too aware for happiness . . . you are often so impatiently sure . . .
[but] you are really a lamb yourself, Lincoln . . . you are a little 'scared'
too—yes you are darling . . . you have so much, darling—only you are so
damned afraid . . . you are difficult to come near to at times—at the times
when you want it most yourself . . . what I do not think you know is really
how much people can and do love you, feel your warmth and your great
dearness, which you try too hard to hide."

The sales and reviews of their joint appearance at the Adelphi were
good enough to provide a decent close to the Caravan adventure. After it
was over, costumes and scenery were put in storage in the hope (later
borne out) that at least some of the ballets created during the Caravan's
life, particularly *Filling Station* and *Billy the Kid*, would have a future.
Lincoln later summed up, perhaps too modestly, what he felt was the Caravan's overall accomplishment: "The echo . . . gave other local organizations courage and a certain impetus . . . home groups formed themselves
into rudimentary ballet troupes, gave performances, embarked on tours,
pleased a certain public, and instructed themselves." The Caravan had
also done pioneering work in focusing on American music, dancers,
themes, librettists, costumers, set designers, and choreographers. The
resulting quality may have been uneven, but opportunities had been given
and taken, talents showcased, careers launched. A start had been made.
There were grounds in that for genuine self-congratulation.

Surveying the ballet scene as a whole in 1940, Lincoln found little to
admire. He initially, somewhat calculatedly, praised the advent of Ballet
Theatre, but soon developed mixed, and then negative, feelings about it.
The dominant companies in this country were still the international Russ-
ian ones represented by Sol Hurok. De Basil's Ballets Russes de Monte
Carlo (rechristened in 1939 as the Original Ballet Russe) had successfully
crisscrossed the country from 1933 to 1937 and then, after several years in
Australia, again returned to the United States in 1940.[3]

Beginning late in 1938, de Basil had to face the competition of Serge
Denham's Ballet Russe de Monte Carlo, which from 1938 to 1942 was
under the artistic direction of Léonide Massine. It, too—and for a quarter

of a century—traveled across the country giving some two hundred performances a year. Lincoln politely contacted Denham asking him to
release Alexandra Danilova from her exclusive contract so that she could
teach at the school, which she'd agreed to do, but Denham refused—and
that liberated Lincoln to express in print his real views of Denham's company. Linking it with de Basil's troupe, Lincoln denounced both for letting
"convenience and expedience" dictate their repertory . . . the direction of
both Russian companies is either unimaginative and recklessly extravagant
or unimaginative and cannily conservative . . . they are enemies to anything that is really fresh."

Lincoln was not being entirely fair, since Denham had in 1939 commissioned a ballet from the young Frederick Ashton and in 1940 had
incorporated three Balanchine works—*Serenade, Jeu de Cartes,* and
Baiser—into his company's repertory. Even de Basil, from whose company
Balanchine had long ago defected, now commissioned him to make a new
piece for his tired troupe. To Stravinsky's Violin Concerto in D, and with
decor and costumes by Tchelitchev, Balanchine's *Balustrade,* starring
Tamara Toumanova, debuted in January 1941. Badly received by the critics, skewered in the *New York Times* by John Martin, it had only five performances; but more than thirty years later, Balanchine would produce an
entirely new ballet, *Stravinsky Violin Concerto,* to the same score.

After many years of juggling multiple commitments, Balanchine, like
Lincoln, found himself more or less at liberty. Lincoln still had the school,
and Balanchine would never be at a loss for long (Ringling Bros. and Barnum & Bailey's Circus commissioned him that same year to create a ballet
for—literally—elephants; and he did). But neither man had a major new
commitment or project at hand. That would soon change, thanks to Lincoln's old friend Nelson Rockefeller.[4]

Nelson and Lincoln had remained on cordial terms since they'd first
met back in 1931, and their friendship, in Lincoln's words, was both
"extremely agreeable" and had "done me a considerable amount of good
in making contacts." Early in 1939 Nelson had confided to Lincoln that
he currently felt "extremely isolated and left out in the cold, not on a
financial but on a moral basis." Passionately interested in South America,
Nelson felt that the Roosevelt administration had been neglecting its own
vital interests in the area in order to concentrate on the accelerating crisis
in Europe. Throughout much of 1939 he'd been trying, without success,
to find a way of utilizing his expertise about the region to become "dollar-
a-year" consultant in Washington.

Frustrated by the closed doors, Nelson had accepted the post of president of MoMA. That decision had delighted Lincoln; he called it "the
virtual triumph of a younger and more liberal spirit in the museum." At
the same time he let Nelson know that should he find a way of entering
the Roosevelt administration, he himself "would like to be sent down

there" to South America "because dance was the perfect medium for art, since it did not even involve speech."

The way finally opened up in the spring of 1940, after Nazi Germany had invaded and quickly subdued one Western European country after another and, simultaneously, reports of mounting pro-Nazi sympathy throughout South America had begun to flow into Washington. It suddenly became obvious to the Roosevelt administration that its own strategic interests on the North American continent were at stake, and that improved relations with South America had to become a top priority. A host of compensatory proposals, economic and cultural, suddenly appeared on the front burner, and with four different government departments—State, Treasury, Agriculture and Commerce—each trying to make up for lost time and to some extent contradicting one another's efforts, the need for an overall coordinating agency became apparent.

Nelson had in 1939 submitted a detailed analysis of what needed to be done in South America, and his memo now finally worked its way onto President Roosevelt's desk. He immediately ordered the secretaries of the four competing government departments to present a joint proposal to him; they complied, though with considerable reluctance and grousing. At the end of June 1940 Roosevelt appointed James Forrestal as his special assistant on Latin American affairs. Forrestal had little interest in the region and would soon become undersecretary of the navy, but he did come up with the idea of appointing a coordinator for the government's various efforts in regard to Latin America, someone who would work with previously existing departments yet be independent of them. FDR offered the post to Nelson Rockefeller, who was given the official title "Coordinator of Inter-American Affairs," a budget of 3.5 million dollars, and an encompassing mandate that included finance, exports, and cultural relations.

Nelson's expansive vitality had finally found an appropriate channel, and he exuberantly set to work on a wide variety of fronts. On the cultural side he asked Lincoln to prepare a proposed six-month ballet tour to every Latin American country save for Paraguay and Bolivia—an opportunity Lincoln leaped at. He immediately secured Balanchine as the new company's artistic director, and together they decided on ballets and casts for what they called the American Ballet Caravan—a name that combined their two preceding ventures. They signed an official contract, effective March 17, 1941, that outlined in detail the formal arrangements agreed upon and created a budget of ninety-five thousand dollars for the tour.

But because the company was due to depart the States at just the time Nelson was presenting his office's budget to Congress, and because he feared the ballet subsidy might become a focal point for conservative attack, he withheld funds for an initial publicity campaign about the tour in the U.S. press. The decision would have some unfortunate consequences: the lack of advance publicity suggested a lack of official enthusiasm for the ballet tour, thus providing a number of conservative U.S. embassy officials in South America with a built-in excuse for failing to support the company when it reached their locale, and for failing to encourage resident North Americans, usually ultra-conservative, to buy tickets. As it would turn out, the company would find sympathetic North American colonies only in Caracas, Bogotá, and Lima.

But all that lay in the future. For now Lincoln found himself happily back in harness and he plunged ahead at the frantic pace which made him happiest. He and Balanchine chose thirty-five dancers, many from the recently defunct Caravan but a number of others chosen from various companies as well as from the school. The four principals were all Caravan alumni: Giselle Caccialanza, Marie-Jeanne, William Dollar, and Lew Christensen, who was named ballet master. Among the soloists were two newcomers who would become international stars: Alicia Alonso and Nicholas Magallanes. In addition the troupe included Todd Bolender, Doug Coudy, John Kriza—and Pete Martínez (still suffering from an injury, he danced only occasionally during the tour). Hired as well were Trude Rittman as one of two pianists, the conductor Emmanuel Balaban, a technical supervisor, a stage manager, and a wardrobe mistress. A "guest of Mr. Kirstein's" was also listed—Fidelma, whom he'd married some six weeks before the company departed in June, thus turning the tour into a honeymoon.

Fourteen ballets were chosen, including the three outstanding hits from Ballet Caravan—*Filling Station, Yankee Clipper,* and *Billy the Kid*—and seven of Balanchine's earlier compositions (including *Serenade, Orpheus and Eurydice,* and *Errante*). Additionally, in a burst of creative energy unlike anything he'd had for several years, Balanchine created four new ballets, among them two of his masterworks, *Concerto Barocco* and *Ballet Imperial* (later renamed *Tchaikovsky Piano Concerto No. 2*). Ultimately the tour would consist of four complete changes of program, with at least one and frequently two North American works included on each. The company was given a paid two-month rehearsal period preceding departure, as well as three dress rehearsals before invited audiences in the Hunter College auditorium from May 27 to 30.

Five weeks before leaving, Lincoln issued a formal memo to members of the company warning them that "traveling in South America is extremely difficult," with abrupt changes in temperature, "very rude" living accommodations, and "uncertain diet and water conditions." He advised the troupe to think of the coming experience as "much more in the nature of an army expedition than it is of an ordinary ballet tour." Lincoln's warning about likely difficulties would prove more accurate than not. In further preparation, all members of the company were given a wide variety of inoculations and shots. Balanchine himself was sent off to a specialist who reported a lesion on his lungs but not an active one; he was therefore "of no danger to people in contact with him." However, the specialist added, "an exacerbation of his disease might very well occur under the arduous conditions of the proposed tour." Balanchine predictably shrugged off the warning; he would remain healthy throughout the tour, despite its many rigors.

At midnight on June 6, the company embarked on the liner *Argentina* for Rio de Janeiro, with both Balanchine and Fidelma aboard. Lincoln himself had to stay behind a bit longer to ensure that the affairs of the school were in good order; he put Eugenie Ouroussow in charge during his absence, and hired his old friend Tom Mabry, who'd been fired the year before from his position at MoMA, to manage the school's publicity and advertising on a part-time basis. Lincoln flew down to Rio on June 15, accompanied by Philip Barbour, whom the State Department had appointed, in Lincoln's words, as "a guide and also a male nurse"; Barbour in fact would prove himself a knowledgeable and conscientious manager. The two men arrived in Rio three days before the *Argentina* docked.

The hotel accommodations were "tacky" but had the advantage of being opposite El Teatro Municipal, the theater where the company was scheduled to open on June 25. He wrote his parents that "since I pretend to have no connection with our government, I'm accepted as just another commercial traveler, which is what Nelson wants." The Caravan, in other words, was not meant to be seen by South Americans as an official "goodwill" tour, of the sort they'd long since become cynical about; but Lincoln's choice of words also suggests that, at least secondarily, he was on a sort of private mission for Nelson, doing informal intelligence work that centered on reporting the effectiveness of the United States' ambassadorial and consular representatives—and Lincoln's private letters to Nelson do contain a number of detailed assessments of various North American officials.[5]

In the first flush of arriving in Rio, Lincoln found everyone "really frightfully kind and helpful," though his initial impression (especially in regard to U.S. officialdom) would certainly not be his final one. And even initially, not everyone was in fact kind or helpful. The Teatro Municipal was leased to an Italian fascist, Silvio Piergili, who proved "consistently unfriendly." On one occasion he threw a cordon of police around the theater to prevent Lincoln's invited guests from witnessing a dress rehearsal that he'd hoped would stimulate interest in the company's work. When Lincoln brought up the incident with an official at the U.S. Embassy, he acted as if it were Lincoln who had misbehaved, and ordered him never to mention the matter again.

During the week of rehearsals that preceded opening night at the Teatro Municipal, the language barrier (no one in the troupe spoke Portuguese) also presented difficulties, especially in relation to certain technical aspects of the staging, like lighting. The orchestra, moreover, was in Lincoln's opinion "very poor" and the theater itself badly run, with no stage crew to speak of. Then there was the matter of delayed luggage; no one had told them in advance that customs and baggage declarations were required at *every* stop in Brazil. But at least Balanchine, Lincoln reported to his parents, "has worked marvelously and we really owe him every-thing. He gets $100 a week and he's worth $2,000. He never complains and is a life saver."

It was decided that the opening-night bill in Rio would consist of *Serenade*, *Filling Station*, and *Ballet Imperial*. Lincoln had earlier met the Brazilian painter Candido Portinari while working at the World's Fair and admired his work; "down here," Lincoln wrote Paul Cadmus, "Portinari seems like Michelangelo," but the artist had been given "a hard time" because he insisted on painting people living in poverty and was therefore considered "decadent and anti-Brazilian." Lincoln hired him to do a new backdrop for *Serenade* and thought the result "extremely effective."

Lew Christensen performed brilliantly in *Filling Station* despite an injury incurred during rehearsal and a bad case of nerves just before the curtain went up. The ballet itself found its admirers, but Lincoln reported to Virgil Thomson that his score had suffered from an inability to find proficient jazz musicians. (In general, he wrote Virgil, "we've had a terri-ble time with orchestras . . . there are no horns or percussion available . . . which makes the North American things sound dismal and weak.") Balan-chine composed the closing piece, *Ballet Imperial*, in less than a week, and in Lincoln's view the company pianist, Simon Sadoff, performed it "amaz-ingly" and Marie-Jeanne danced the lead role "incredibly well" (as part of her costume she wore two "egg-sized" aquamarines given her by an ardent female admirer).

Lincoln felt that the opening-night performance was the least good of the seven they gave in Rio, yet it got eighteen curtain calls, and the stage was covered with so many orchids that Lincoln thought it "looked like a state funeral." The critics were enthusiastic and also proved, somewhat to Lincoln's surprise, deeply informed about American music and dance. But it was the audience response, despite all those orchids, that became the sticking point during their Rio stay.

In Lincoln's perceptive analysis there simply wasn't any "general" pub-lic; instead there were the masses, "society," and professional people. The Teatro's management had priced the tickets far too high for the masses or even for young professional people. As for "society," Lincoln felt that its general orientation was far too traditional to appreciate the company's more innovative and contemporary work; it much preferred the classi-cism, however tired, of Denham's Ballet Russe de Monte Carlo, which had successfully toured South America the previous year. Besides, in Lincoln's opinion the upper class went to the theater "for their entrance" and "for social intercourse during intermissions." He thought Rio society, as he wrote Nelson, "of a silliness and idleness you can't believe." (Later, in Buenos Aires, he was asked to lengthen the intermissions so that society would have sufficient time "to promenade.") Yet Lincoln consistently found that whenever a theater management provided cheap seats in the upper galleries, they would be filled—even though the rest of the house might be half empty. And he also found that it was primarily in the galleries that any real enthusiasm could be generated for contemporary work.

Lincoln wrote his parents that "there are lots of very nasty Germans around"; attending an English-language film, he was startled at the amount of hissing in the audience. And he reported that censorship extended to a ban on sending any photographs of Rio's slums out of the country, to prevent awareness that most of Brazil is "very poor and backward . . . all the nice people one meets are in a terrible hurry to get out of the country just as fast as they can. So am I."

As for the ballets themselves, *Errante* and particularly *Apollo* enjoyed genuine success. Lincoln reported to Nelson that the audience "nearly tore the house down" over *Apollo*, and everyone told him "it was a recognition unheard of here." However, the American ambassador, Jefferson Caffery, was less than pleased. He called Lincoln into his office and upbraided him for "not establishing social contacts with the correct people—i.e. people who bought boxes"; Caffery further told him that had he had more advance notice, he would have "forbidden us to present the American scores" entirely, in particular Copland's *Billy the Kid* (which generally failed to find much favor). Yet those members of the public who managed to afford tickets, as well as many South American artists, musicians, and newspaper critics, singled out for special praise several of the ballets that Ambassador Caffery denounced, and especially those with jazz elements, like Bill Dollar's *Juke Box*.

Caffery "really turned on the project," Lincoln wrote Nelson, and was so hostile to the company that not a single representative of the embassy, not even a low-ranking one, attended any of the three parties given for the troupe. Caffery let his negative opinion be known far and wide, which in turn led the Brazilian international set further to withdraw its support; they "stopped coming [and] were cold in the elevators *en passant*." Yet ticket sales—probably due to the ongoing raves in the press ("we didn't deserve them frankly," Lincoln wrote Nelson)—did manage more or less to cover costs.

Lincoln had from the beginning refused to draw his own salary, foreseeing possible difficulties ahead. He wanted to keep a decent-sized reserve and also—since the official budget provided no money at all for this—to be able to offer commissions to some local painters and musicians; he was able to give work to four Brazilians: Portinari; Santa Rosa to do the decor for *Apollo*; Eduardo Biarco to provide the decor and costumes; and Francisco Mingone to compose the music for *Fantasia Brasileira*. But he warned Nelson that thanks to the hostility of Caffery and other U.S. officials, he should expect to receive "very bad marks from the State Department" about the Caravan. It pleased Lincoln to learn from his father that during a recent trip to Washington he'd had a long talk with Nelson, who'd told Louis that his son "had done an extraordinarily good job . . . he was very pleased . . . and considered you one of his very best friends."

The troupe's next stop after Rio was São Paulo, and Lincoln flew ahead to meet with the press. In contrast to Rio (in his final dismissal of the city, he called it "as beautiful as Woodlawn" cemetery), he adored São Paulo. He thought the people far more agreeable personally, and "some rich, homicidal maniacs" even took him and some members of the troupe to witness several "hidden pagan ceremonies." Still, even in São Paulo, a clear preference existed for classical dance along the lines of the Monte Carlo ballet, and some of the troupe's contemporary pieces, like *Billy the Kid*, were considered "shocking."

Unlike Lincoln, Fidelma generally (as he wrote home) "loved" the Brazilians, even those in Rio. It helped that her Spanish was "quite good"; she not only "met a lot of nice people" but accepted invitations, despite "her terrific shyness," to give talks at the American Women's Club and at the University Club on "The Dance"—and in Lincoln's view did "amazingly well." But she increasingly shied away from attending ballet performances; like Lincoln, she'd become so nervous about possible or actual mistakes that she preferred not to watch. She spent quite a lot of time instead wandering around with Pete Martínez.

After the engagement in São Paulo was completed, the company was scheduled to leave for Buenos Aires. But the war caught up with them. Boat schedules were generally abandoned and the particular vessel they'd been due to sail on cancelled its voyage entirely. Finally an unscheduled and run-down Spanish refugee ship from Bilbao arrived, and they were forced, forty-six strong, to book first-class passage—which added four thousand dollars to their costs and brought them to Buenos Aires a week after they'd been scheduled to arrive; that, in turn, cut into the number of performances they'd planned. Not only was the boat trip itself wretched, but several of the younger members of the company were detained for hours by the authorities, since the official age of consent to work was twenty-two; the signed consent forms they'd brought along from their parents finally secured release.

Still, once safely arrived, the troupe found much to like in Buenos Aires: the water was good, the weather cool but not, as in Rio, wet, and the food cheap and delicious—though as a group they passed over what Lincoln called the "darling little octopuses and young sheep's' brains in oil." Lincoln thought the shift in cities did the company good; they were now, in his opinion, "working much better here than ever before. It resembles more of a company . . . everyone is surprised how strong they are technically."

Still, having now been away for nearly two months, an outburst of theatrical hysterics was overdue. When one male member of the company became ill and fainted, Lincoln described the aftermath in a campy letter to Paul Cadmus: "Mother Coudy just protected and protected him. I ran back like a kind father. Miss [Todd] Bolender started screaming, said 'this is too much; they have poisoned [him]. They have spread glass on the stage to ruin my bourrées'. . . . Kriza had hysterics." As you can see, Lincoln concluded, "it's the same old Caravan under all its trappings of gold lace and good will."

Lincoln felt great respect for the professional journalists he met. Of the half dozen he got to know well, not one, he notified Nelson, "actually believes our Government is *really* serious about South America; they felt . . . that we [that is, the United States] are ultimately, beyond a few tokens or palliatives, uninterested. The South Americans," he added, viewed "good-will" missions as "so much bunk." The correspondents from *Life* and *Time* took special pains to warn him that Argentina was probably the most blatantly pro-Nazi country in South America, and that scorn for all things North American was widespread. Not only was pro-German feeling strong, but the Nazi newspaper, *Pampero*, was popular and prospering. They added that a pro-Allies group did exist but that it shouldn't be confused with being pro-American; North Americans, in the dominant view, could neither dance nor paint nor "do anything but sell." The American colony in Buenos Aires responded to such disdain in kind; every American Lincoln met told him that they lived their lives apart and felt no connection to Argentina itself.

Taste in music and art was as conservative in Buenos Aires as in Rio, and Lincoln was warned to try and arrange the ballet programs in a way that led gently "into our new things," since modernism was not generally admired. ("Tell Martha [Graham]," Lincoln wrote Frances Hawkins, that "she should never come here. It would kill her. It's just the place for the Ballet Theatre. And they can have it.") The reigning cultural arbiter, Ignacio Pirovano, "hated our native American works," announcing that "jazz is not music." Once again neither the American colony nor the American Embassy proved supportive, and ticket sales were much worse than in Rio or São Paulo. The "smart" people, Lincoln reported home, were predominantly guided by French taste circa 1930, and were pro-Vichy. Had he been able to buy pictures and commission more music and scenery from local artists, he felt that he might have made a greater dent in improving the negative climate of opinion—but unexpected expenses like the delayed boat trip had made serious inroads into his limited budget.

The company gave its Buenos Aires performances in the renowned

Teatro Colón at, for American dancers, the disconcerting though typical Latin times of matinees at 6:00 p.m. and evenings at 10:15 (which meant finishing at about 1:30 in the morning). Lincoln found the Colón "much grander" in scale than New York's Metropolitan Opera, but also "riddled with a most inept and hidebound bureaucracy"; it was run entirely, Lincoln wrote his Mexican composer friend, Carlos Chávez, by "Senators who keep 40 year old red-headed ballerinas." Yet it was at the Colón that Lincoln saw a "wonderful" performance of the Verdi Requiem, conducted by Toscanini, and a rendition of *Carmen* that was "1000 times better than the Met."

The reception of the American Ballet Caravan, which gave nineteen performances in twelve days, was greatly aided by the advocacy of one of South America's leading literary figures, the wealthy Victoria Ocampo, who published *Sur*, the most important literary review in Latin America at the time, and the left-wing writer Maria Rosa Oliver, translator and champion of Eugene O'Neill, Sherwood Anderson, Theodore Dreiser, and other North Americans. Though confined to a wheelchair as a result of childhood polio, the indomitable Maria Rosa Oliver appeared at the ballet every single night and introduced Lincoln to a wide circle of artists. Ocampo, though friendly, was more reserved in her enthusiasm; she told Lincoln that she was disappointed that the company didn't have more French music and decor and deplored the fact that it had only a single Stravinsky score. Lincoln grew to dislike Ocampo's grand manner and pronouncements, but he would remain friendly long after with Maria Rosa Oliver.

In Buenos Aires *Billy the Kid* again failed to win much approval, primarily, Lincoln thought, because Copland's music was "almost incomprehensible to them" and they had little success in "getting a good reading of the score." Although ticket sales remained generally poor throughout the two-week engagement, several of the company's offerings were well-received, in particular *Apollo, Errante, Filling Station*, and *Juke Box*. There was also one surprise hit: *Pastorela*, a new piece by Pete Martínez based on the Mexican Christmas play *Los Pastores*, with music by Paul Bowles and choreography by Lew Christensen. Balanchine, in the meantime, was working hard on his final new ballet for the tour, *Fantasia Brasileira*, to lighthearted, effectively showy music by the Brazilian composer Francisco Mingone; it was due to be performed in Chile at the end of August.

The company made a brief side trip to Montevideo, where they gave five performances in four days, and were, for once, kindly entertained by the U.S. ambassador, William Dawson. The audiences were thin, though "more sympathetic" than usual. From Montevideo the company headed for the Argentine provinces of Rosario, Córdoba, and Mendoza, where the theaters were not good but the box office receipts surprisingly high and the press reception excellent. Lincoln and Fidelma stayed in Buenos Aires until it was time to rejoin the troupe in Mendoza, but Balanchine was with the company throughout. He had, according to Lincoln, been selfless during the entire trip, repeatedly accepting the worst accommodations, content to be paid last, "the first to come into a theatre, the last to leave."

Balanchine was apparently enjoying the tour enormously, but by early August, Lincoln's own enthusiasm had plummeted. "It's hard as hell making this tour," he wrote Virgil. "The facilities of producing our type of show are very limited and everything is backward and dreary." The unpredictable audience reactions had gotten him down; it's "like performing in a half-filled house," he wrote Virgil, "at 11 o'clock in the morning for a ladies club . . . in Detroit." To Frances Hawkins, Lincoln wrote that he had "a deep personal love for New York City at this point amounting to physical passion. Once home, I will never even go as far as Jones Beach. . . . I have turned into the most rabid imperialist son of a bitch you ever met," he humorously added. To his parents Lincoln swore that he'd never again (though he would) "take the responsibility of a tour. . . . I'm not good at it and I hate it . . . someone else, anyone else, could manage the mechanical side better than me. The effort expended in "putting the performances across," he concluded, "seems incommensurate with the results."

The worst, however, lay ahead. When Lincoln and Fidelma rejoined the company at Mendoza in order to cross the Andes to Santiago de Chile, a blizzard unexpectedly hit the area. The railroads were damaged and the highway closed, leaving the company marooned in Mendoza for six days while they tried to figure out whether to go back to Buenos Aires or to wait out the storm. The weather finally cleared and—sending their equipment and luggage ahead through Bolivia—the company was able to board four Pan-Air Boeing transport planes and fly through the two highest peaks in the Western Hemisphere. The view was spectacular, but several of the dancers were far too frightened to enjoy it.

The ten days in Santiago de Chile provided a decided boost to Lincoln's spirits. Among other things the U.S. ambassador proved unexpectedly friendly and helpful, and the city's orchestra turned out to be far better than any they'd thus far encountered; it even included brass, woodwinds, and percussion. The company's conductor, Emmanuel Balaban, whom Lincoln considered not only very gifted but something of an uncomplaining saint, could for the first time play North American music, thus far little appreciated on the tour, in the way it deserved. In contrast to Buenos Aires, Lincoln found Santiago "infinitely more alive and intelligent . . . the people have much more self respect—they don't continually apologize for not being Paris." Moreover, Balanchine's new ballet, *Fantasia Brasileira*, was well received at its premiere in Santiago (though Lincoln thought it was "about as Brazilian as *Prince Igor* is early Russian"), with Olga Suarez, a Latin American member of the company, winning especially high praise in the lead role.

Another cheering aspect of the stay in Santiago was that he finally received a mis-routed letter from Nelson. Lincoln had begun to worry that the troupe had "been forgotten," though he understood that official Washington was preoccupied with far larger matters concerning the war in Europe. Yet he couldn't help worrying that the State Department, in response to potentially negative reports about the company from hostile U.S. embassies in South America, had been thwarting Nelson's efforts and might even cancel the remaining portion of the tour. Feeding that fear was the fact that the company's original budget had been drawn up without sufficient information about local conditions and hadn't taken into account the possibility of unexpected disasters—like the blizzard in Mendoza.

In truth there *had* been something of a dustup in DC and serious discussion within the State Department about cutting off the tour after Chile. Fortunately the matter was turned over to Lincoln's old friend, the architect Wally Harrison, now doing some work for Nelson's Inter-American Affairs office, and Carleton Sprague Smith, another acquaintance of Lincoln's and head of the agency's Music Committee. After studying all the reports and reviews, issued a sizzling defense of the American Ballet Caravan, blaming whatever inefficiencies had occurred on lack of communication from Washington, and "emphatically" insisting that the prestige of the United States was directly involved in the completion of the tour.

As a result the company continued straight on until November 6, performing in Lima, Manizales, Medellín, Bogotá, and Caracas—though it did so without Lincoln and Fidelma. Lincoln had decided—"quite suddenly" according to Fidelma—that he needed to fly home after Santiago in order to consult with Nelson in Washington and also to be present at the opening of the school's fall term in September. Since no known crisis existed at the school (both enrollment and tuition fees had increased over the prior year) and no urgent conference with Nelson followed on Lincoln's return, he'd probably used those reasons as pretexts for leaving a tour that he'd grown heartily sick of ("How Fido puts up with my sour puss," Lincoln wrote Frances, "is remarkable"). Once Lincoln made the decision to leave, his gloom dissipated, and, according to Fidelma, he turned "quite gay and happy."

She herself was "a little disappointed to be missing the most interesting part of the West coast," and she finally decided to go with the company as far as Lima (which she adored). By doing so she was present at what may well have been the high point of the entire tour: Copland himself, who was in Lima at the time, conducted *Billy the Kid*, and a host of dignitaries, including the president of Peru and his family, attended the brilliant premiere. After Lima, Fidelma returned home by ship.

In evaluating for Nelson the overall impact of the tour, Lincoln honorably pointed out that his own objectivity was open to question and that Nelson should solicit additional perspectives from both South American and U.S. embassy representatives. But in fact his several reports to Nelson contain very little gilding of the lily. He made no bones about the fact that financially the Caravan "was not so successful." But he was able to point to the overwhelmingly positive press reception that the company received throughout the tour and to the obvious contribution made in demonstrating what South Americans had long doubted—that the United States was capable of a pronounced contribution to the arts. Proof that many South Americans had become convinced was the fact that the company was invited for return engagements in Rio, São Paulo, Montevideo, Santiago, and Lima. And Balanchine himself was offered the position of *maître de ballet* at the Colón Theater in Buenos Aires.

Lincoln seems to have been proudest of the fact that he'd managed to offer commissions to a number of artists in Brazil, Argentina, and Chile. He pointed out to Nelson that although various Russian Ballets, as well as the Jooss Ballet, had made extensive tours in South America, only the American Ballet Caravan had ever "collaborated with native painters or musicians, or interested themselves seriously in native folk-lore or popular dance expression." Lincoln's account, far from being idle boasting, was a concise and accurate picture of what the Caravan had (and had not) managed to achieve.

CHAPTER NINETEEN

South America: MoMA

(1942)

WITHIN A FEW weeks of returning home Lincoln, ever restless and driven, had several new prospects in the works ("he had more arms than Shiva," one acquaintance has said). Back in late 1939 he'd donated to MoMA his private collection of some two thousand books, fifteen hundred prints, and several thousand programs, clippings, and other documentary materials on the dance, thereby establishing the first such scholarly resource in this country. John Martin, in the *New York Times*, had hailed the establishment of the Dance Archives as "a collection of distinctly serious import . . . an extremely fine nucleus." Lincoln had gotten MoMA to hire Paul Magriel, the American correspondent of the Archives Internationales de la Danse in Paris who'd been helpful to him on earlier projects, as curator of the archives, and agreed to pay half his meager annual salary of some fifteen hundred dollars. (It would only be much later, after the materials had been transferred to Lincoln Center, that the archivist Genevieve ("Gigi") Osborne first put them into any kind of working order.)[1]

Now, in the fall of 1941, Lincoln invited Magriel, along with Baird Hastings, music editor of the publication *American Dancer*, to join him as co-editors in establishing a new journal, *Dance Index*, to appear monthly beginning in January. Designed as a non-commercial enterprise, *Dance Index* announced from the beginning that it would accept no advertising, would carry no current criticism of dance performances or reviews on books relating to dance, and would focus instead on publishing scholarly articles by leading authorities. While the editors insisted (at twenty-five cents a copy) that the publication was aimed at the general public, not the "trade," some of its announced monographic titles—such as "Romantic American Dance Lithographs" and "European Dance Teachers in America"—hardly seemed designed to appeal to popular taste. Nor did they. But *Dance Index* (which would survive until 1949) would become the cornerstone of American dance scholarship, making a major contribution to the establishment of a fledgling field.

Among the very first people Lincoln turned to as possible contributors to *Index* was his old acquaintance Carl Van Vechten. He'd been a pioneering, if under-appreciated, figure in dance criticism, writing from 1906 to

1913 in the *New York Times*, and for two decades thereafter producing various articles and books on the subject. As Lincoln wrote to Van Vechten, "Those wonderful articles you used to write about the Spanish dance or about the Diaghilev seasons . . . really started me off." As it happened, Lincoln would, to Carl's great pleasure, end up devoting an entire number of *Dance Index* to reprinting Van Vechten's early reviews.

Lincoln was also absorbed for a time in negotiations with Serge Denham and his Ballet Russe de Monte Carlo to facilitate some sort of a merger. Conceivably Denham was unaware that Lincoln and Balanchine's American Ballet Caravan had immediately disbanded following the South American tour (though it might have been quickly reassembled in whole or in part if necessary). But Denham was probably mostly attracted to the fact that Lincoln had long been focused on attempting to create ballets out of American source material and through the talents of American artists. Denham, too, had from the inception of his company in 1938 been actively interested (unlike de Basil) in producing work based on American themes, even though the Ballet Russe continued to rely on Russian staples. Indeed in 1942 Denham would give an out-of-work Agnes de Mille, and the composer Aaron Copland, an opportunity to create what would turn into a major and long-lasting hit—the ballet *Rodeo*.

The turn to de Mille may have come about as a result of the ultimate (and mysterious) failure of Denham's negotiations with Lincoln. From November 1941 through February 1942, those negotiations had seemed alive and promising. From the beginning Lincoln, speaking for Balanchine as well, had made it clear to Denham that they had no wish to become embroiled in any unpleasantness with Léonide Massine, who at the time was still the artistic director of the Ballet Russe and had broad powers (though he was going through a discouraging dry spell that ended with his resignation in 1942).

In the draft agreement that was drawn up in December 1941 but never signed, Denham formally expressed his desire "to adopt a new policy" by which the Ballet Russe "will become more Americanized [someone crossed out those two words] in personnel and in repertoire, feeling that this is most essential to keep up the interest of the American public in the art of Ballet." For a period of one year, commencing in October and ending the following September, the Ballet Russe and the American Ballet (which currently existed only on paper) would become merged and be considered as one working organization, "though both corporations would retain their officers, board of directors and properties." Lincoln, as "Director General" of the American Ballet, would receive a regular salary of two hundred dollars a week.

Almost immediately word arrived that Massine had heard about the negotiations and was "terribly upset," in particular about the rumor that

Balanchine was to replace him as artistic director of the Ballet Russe. Massine insisted that given his broad contractual rights, nothing could be decided without his prior approval. On hearing of Massine's reaction, Lincoln felt deeply embarrassed and assured Massine that there had been no intention of proceeding behind his back, or of replacing him with Balanchine; it was apparently a case of Denham failing to keep his promise of notifying Massine from the beginning about a possible merger. Kirstein offered at once to fly to Chicago or St. Louis to meet personally with Massine, but the offer wasn't taken up.

Instead silence descended. No written response to the draft agreement ever arrived (though possibly some unrecorded meetings took place), either from Denham or from David Libidins, the Ballet Russe's business manager. All negotiations simply ground to a halt. Precisely why, is unclear. Perhaps Massine had threatened legal action (he did later sue Denham for certain rights in his own ballets). Perhaps, given Massine's angry response to the proposed merger, Denham simply dropped the whole idea as too hazardous. Perhaps Lincoln and Balanchine themselves broke off the proceedings after hearing of Massine's displeasure—though that seems highly unlikely, since letters from their representative exist that plead for some word, any word, from Denham or Libidins. Massine's autobiography, *My Life in Ballet*, fails to make the slightest mention of the contretemps, and instead confusingly insists that Denham (or, technically, the Ballet Russe's board of directors) had fired him in the fall of 1941— meaning *before* the draft agreement between the two companies had even been drawn up. Whatever the truth of this curious interlude, one thing is clear: Denham never lost interest in Balanchine, who, from 1944 to 1946, would mount no fewer than ten of his own works for the Ballet Russe.

If Lincoln was sharply disappointed at the outcome, he had little time to brood over it. Within weeks of the collapsed negotiations with Denham, the Museum of Modern Art asked him to return to South America and purchase works that would augment the museum's holdings. The money came from Nelson, who, when stepping down as president of MoMA to focus on his job in Washington, had established "the Inter-American Fund" to buy Latin American art. Nelson wanted Lincoln back in South America for a second reason as well. He'd received a memo from one of his aides lambasting the U.S. diplomatic corps in South America as grossly ineffective when compared to the efficient political apparatus established by the Axis powers—a memo that confirmed the private reports Lincoln had sent Nelson during his 1941 trip. As a result of the memo Nelson decided to set up a corps of his own operatives throughout Latin America who would be independent of the official U.S. embassies and would report directly to him, not to the State Department. He now enlisted Lincoln, incidental to his art mission, to report confidentially to him about the political situation.

In early 1942 that situation was clearly not favorable to the Allies. After the attack on Pearl Harbor and the U.S. declaration of war, only seven Latin American countries followed the United States' lead, though a number of others did break off diplomatic relations with the Axis powers. But Argentina and Chile, known to harbor powerful pockets of fascist sympathy, refused to do even that; and in Brazil, where the army was dominated by profascist sympathizers, dictator Getúlio Vargas rejected any policy that might threaten his alliance with Argentina. When the so-called Rio Conference took place in January 1942, the failure to create a united inter-American front against the Axis proved a severe embarrassment to the U.S. State Department.

Lincoln had expected to be in the army by spring 1942; he'd already unsuccessfully attempted to enlist in the Naval Reserve and been turned down for a commission in Naval Intelligence (its policy of accepting only third-generation Americans effectively barred, among others, almost every Jewish applicant). Lincoln had then applied for a petty officer's rating in the Coast Guard but been rejected for faulty vision. Now, thanks to Nelson's direct intervention and influence—by mid-1942 his work in South America had landed him on the cover of *Life* magazine—Lincoln was granted a temporary deferral.

MoMA gave him a $5,000 salary, allotted him $12,500 to spend on art, paid his travel costs, and added $3,500 for expenses. Through Jock Whitney, the new president of MoMA, Lincoln was also given various letters of introduction. The plan was for him to spend a month in Brazil, six weeks in Argentina, three in Chile—in other words, the leading fascist hot spots—and to be gone roughly five months, from late May to mid-October 1942. In a confidential letter to Nelson, Lincoln wrote, "You know how grateful I am personally to you to have made this work possible."

Pleased though Lincoln was with his new assignment, he did "hate" to leave Fidelma behind; after much consideration they'd agreed it was the most advisable course, and she was "wonderful and generous" about it. He also hated leaving Pete Martínez and "the benefit of his blind love and essential wisdom"; Pete and Fidelma decided to live together while Lincoln was away. And finally he hated leaving behind "Bob," his newest inamorato; Monroe Wheeler told Lincoln that Bob was "just one more" of his "blondes," but Lincoln assured Glenway Wescott that the loss of Bob, "at the moment when everything was 100% OK, produced a shock that I didn't know I could actually respond to"—even though it did comfort Lincoln to know that "that old sand-filled bag of mine which for years has done service as a heart is really of quite good valve quality. It pumps." It pumped so wildly as the time for departure approached that Lincoln apparently created something of a scene at his farewell party and had to send off a round of apologetic letters ("forgive me for my lousy, weak, self-indulgent behavior last night . . . I was drunk and tired").

Soon after arriving in Rio, Lincoln sent Nelson a gloomy initial assessment. After seeing "a great many people here" (Lincoln spoke Spanish
well and could also navigate in the criollo dialect), he concluded that
"there is a very profound suspicion of eventual betrayal" by the United
States. For this he placed a portion of the blame on his old antagonist
Ambassador Jefferson Caffery: "I have heard no one here say a good word
for him. Our own people . . . loathe him . . . from the representation here,
there is *nothing* to prove we are essentially friendly." Yet Lincoln felt that
there wasn't anything wrong that "guts and steel and love can't cure. Up to
now we haven't enough of any," which he felt was a great pity since the
people, though "isolated and lonely," had a "natural sweetness" and "impressive" capacities.[2]

Soon after, he provided Nelson with a more detailed evaluation. By
that point Lincoln was seeing some ten people a day, ranging from artists
to politicians to "young patriots who believe in democracy so much they
are willing to endure prison for it and who look to us for a meaning that *so
far*, they have found in *no* representative of ours." He didn't claim to know,
Lincoln wrote Nelson, "how important Brazil is in the world picture, or as
far as your work goes," but he did have "a certain fortunate talent of establishing quick intimacies," and as a result he felt confident in reporting that
many of Nelson's initiatives and representatives alike were not faring well.

"I cannot overemphasize," he forcefully told Nelson, "the gravity of
your position here . . . [and] I only regret that you are separated by a wall
of glass from the whole situation." Lincoln felt that "in a small way" he
knew what could be done to improve the situation, and although he had
"no right to make recommendations" he decided to go ahead and make
them anyway, hoping that Nelson would remember that "of all the people
who work for you, I want nothing but to have the creative impulse fur-
thered."

He then proceeded to make some tough assessments and pose some
difficult questions for Nelson to consider. A case in point was Orson
Welles. Nelson had asked Welles, whom he knew through his family's
connections with RKO (the company that had produced Welles's early
films, including *Citizen Kane*), to make a film about Rio's famed Carnival.
Welles had accepted the offer as a means of resuscitating his earlier idea to
produce an "anthology" film consisting of different segments of Latin
American life—of which Rio's Carnival could serve as one sequence. Once
in Rio, Welles began to spend money with his usual extravagance, and initially he was known in the streets (according to Lincoln) as a "cry-baby."

But the Rio public soon changed its mind about him, perhaps in part
because Welles made waves with the Vargas dictatorship by skirting the
censors and filming the city's shantytowns, thereby providing a *real* taste
of life in the country. Lincoln was on Welles's side from the beginning; as

ABOVE: *George Ivanovich Gurdjieff*
BELOW: *Muriel Draper*

ABOVE: *Nelson Rockefeller*
BELOW: *Pavel Tchelitchev*

ABOVE LEFT: *Chick Austin* ABOVE RIGHT: *Eddie Warburg*
BELOW LEFT: *Paul Cadmus and Jon Anderson* BELOW RIGHT: *Jensen Yow*

On Fire Island, 1940s. ABOVE: *Fidelma*
BELOW: *Lincoln and Fidelma*

Fidelma. ABOVE: *In her late forties, by George Platt Lynes*
BELOW: *In her late twenties, by Paul Cadmus*

The house in Weston

Lincoln on Fire Island, 1940s

Lincoln at Harvard, framed by a mural he painted

Exhibition of soldier art organized by Lincoln at Fort Belvoir

From Lincoln's art collection. ABOVE: Diana, *by Augustus Saint-Gaudens, c. 1890 (designed for the top of Madison Square Garden)* BELOW: Dancing Female Nude, *by Gaston Lachaise, c. 1917*

ABOVE: *Couple dancing by Elie Nadelman*
BELOW: *Bust of Lincoln by George Grey Barnard, c. 1912–1913*

Promenade of New York State Theater in Lincoln Center with Elie Nadelman sculptures at either end

he wrote Glenway Wescott, "I feel he is conscientious and unlucky" (one of his leading actors died in a drowning accident in Rio). After attending two of Welles's press conferences, which Lincoln found "masterly," he became an outright advocate and saw quite a bit of Welles. He also strongly defended him to Nelson, concerned about rumors that David Sarnoff would persuade Nelson to cancel Welles's picture.

There wasn't any doubt, Lincoln wrote Nelson, that Welles could behave badly at times, but he argued (with perhaps himself in mind as well) that "people love our *failings* . . . love to feel we have done something to make us human." On the whole, Lincoln reported, Welles was "very calm, self-assured, realistic and practical," and had won "enormous prestige" for himself. (He added that Welles always stayed at the Mexican Embassy, since "ours takes no cognizance of him"). Sounding much as he had nearly a decade earlier when defending Sergei Eisenstein, Lincoln insisted to Nelson that "the picture *must* be saved," that it would justify the "whole dismal flop of the movie program," which he considered "the biggest defeat we have suffered." Whereas the Germans never hesitated to buy off the South American censors and show films that highlighted their military successes, the United States couldn't even manage to get *The March of Time* through, except occasionally. The kinds of American films that did get shown—the life of fishermen on the Maine coast, and the like—Lincoln assured Nelson might be of some interest in the provincial towns of Uruguay but had absolutely no appeal in cosmopolitan cities like Buenos Aires.

Even while urging Welles's case, Lincoln admitted to Nelson that he was disturbed at the insolent way Welles's staff—*not* Welles himself—tended to treat the "enthusiastic, idealistic kids" who had wanted to work on the film, even while employing people who in Lincoln's view were "a lot of second raters." The larger moral, Lincoln emphasized, was embedded in a definition he'd recently heard of a "good neighbor." It was someone who "gives you a loaf of bread, some butter or sugar when you're out of it. It's not someone who gives you the champagne you don't want."

Although Nelson sent Lincoln a number of cables expressing confidence in his opinions and gratitude for having received them, he did, after Welles had gone way over budget, eventually withdraw his backing from the film. It was an act that helped to consolidate the growing view of Welles in the movie industry as undependable—thereby limiting his future options and forever embittering him against Nelson.

If Lincoln defended Welles, he rarely had a positive word for the network of operatives Nelson had set up throughout South America. Lincoln acknowledged that the "Coordinator's Office" in Rio was on the whole "impressive," but in Buenos Aires and elsewhere he found these offices dominated by men "who are instinctively and habitually closer to their own corporate interest than to their countries." He doubted, Lincoln audaciously wrote Nelson, that "your aim was to create a super Rotary Club of antique dullards . . . they live in the American Club, read *Time*, *Life* and *Fortune*," and "feel nervous about the British . . . they are, to my way of thinking, uniquely unexceptional and uniformly mediocre. . . . The Germans in every way are more imaginative, serious and realistic."

Lincoln was at least as scornful of the glossy magazine *En Guardia* (On Guard), which Nelson had set up in the summer of 1941 to counteract Axis propaganda. The magazine was popular and Nelson was proud of it—but that didn't stop Lincoln from lambasting the publication as "a digest of weeks old news" which everyone already knew, and little more than a slicker version, if that was possible, of *Life* magazine. Again he contrasted it with the kind of information the Germans turned out, with its emphasis "on the laboring conditions of the average local working man" and on plugging the "nationalist proletarian angle."

Lincoln himself, both in 1941 and 1942, made the acquaintance of a significant number of pro-democratic professional people. He was stunned one day to see that many of them had signed a "manifesto" printed in three of Rio's morning newspapers attacking the reactionary elements in the Brazilian army and denying that the United States, "under the guise of the war effort," was positioning itself to secure its long-range "imperial interests." Among the signers was the painter Candido Portinari. The very next morning all three papers were suppressed. Lincoln himself took part in several subsequent strategy meetings among the signers of the manifesto, but a fair number ended up imprisoned for various lengths of time on the island fortress of Das Cobras.

In São Paulo, Vice-Consul John Hubner, the embassy contact Lincoln had made the previous year, gave him—even though Lincoln made it clear he'd be reporting everything to Nelson—an insider's view of police operations. It turned out that Hubner ran a local and secret-police unit made up of "men from the North who are," Lincoln wrote, "notoriously brutal and who have no local 'sentimental' attachments." Lincoln was unable to figure out who employed or sanctioned Hubner, whose activities seemed to include the harassment of both pro- and anti-Axis adherents. Was Hubner's protector Ambassador Caffery? Or Vargas himself? Or the U.S. government?

For reasons of his own, Hubner showed Lincoln secret-police records for the prior three-month period, told him that he'd personally ordered a number of arrests, including a reporter from "a major U.S. newspaper syndicate," and implied that Lincoln himself was under continual surveillance and his mail regularly opened. Lincoln found the whole situation frightening and mysterious, and it made him eager to leave São Paulo. But before moving on he did make contact, as he had in Rio, with several leading Left intellectuals, including Dr. Rubem Borba de Moraes, head of the municipal library, who soon after was jailed; and Mario de Andrade, the well-known musicologist. He kept these contacts secret from Hubner.

Without claiming to understand all aspects of the political information he gathered, Lincoln simply sent it on to Nelson, accompanied by the bold assertion that "sufficient information does *not* penetrate to you for you to be able to act efficiently." For Nelson's further enlightenment Lincoln included some sharply pointed political conclusions of his own, among them that "our ridiculous, simple-minded good neighborliness is one of the big reasons why there has been a pretty complete German victory in Argentina," that "the opposition (revolutionary) generation" considered the United States, "far more than the German or the Japanese," the "real (not the apparent) enemy of local national autonomy," and that the revolutionary opposition, as Lincoln put it, "when ripe to break" would be found to consist of several disparate groups, primarily "a really popular (socialist)" cohort and its opposing force, "a national-socialist (demagogic)" group bent on preserving class divisions and emphasizing "chauvinism."

What was needed, Lincoln emphasized, was "a real, not a fictitious, collaboration" between antifascist elements and the United States. It was essential, in his view, to take advantage of the hostility felt in South American democratic circles to the *terra-tenientes* (the landowning class), which had set itself against industrialization and denounced as "Communist" any development that might threaten their rents.

Neither in Argentina nor anywhere else in South America, Lincoln argued, was there any real awareness of "our technical supremacy," and he recommended that it was far more important to send down scientific attachés than cultural ones—and to send as well "an economic and political weekly" and "a monthly technical summary" *in Spanish*. As matters currently stood North American representatives—"and particularly yours—" he wrote Nelson, are "a loutish gang of dead heads . . . my contempt for Embassy usefulness on these matters is boundless."

For a neophyte in Latin American affairs who claimed not to understand part of the information he was forwarding, Lincoln had in fact sent Nelson what amounted to an emphatic series of broadsides attacking U.S. policy and personnel in South America. Nelson may have had mixed feelings about Lincoln's strenuous set of opinions, but he was impressed enough to urge that he send a copy of his final report to Capt. William Harding, chief of operations at the Pentagon. Lincoln did so, along with a modest covering note that again stressed his "confusion" about some of what he'd seen, and declaring his own report "inadequate."

Lincoln's humble-pie attitude was something of a masquerade. He may have been perplexed now and then over what he'd seen, but not to the extent he claimed. In general he was confident of his powers of observation and the accuracy of his conclusions. His diffident posture when addressing Harding, and to a lesser extent Nelson, represented to a degree his genuine modesty, but it also reflected a certain amount of calculation. Though Lincoln would not withhold his blunt assessments, he did want his views to be treated seriously, and not dismissed as left-wing ravings. He also wanted—and there's nothing inherently dishonorable in self-protection—to safeguard his own standing and future prospects. The mask of the blushing maiden suited his several purposes, as well as reflecting the manifold impulses of his temperament.

Intrigued as he was by the political situation in South America, Lincoln was well aware that his primary mission was to secure works of art for MoMA, and during most of his five-month stay, he busied himself more with seeing artists and buying pictures than with untangling the machinations of a John Hubner or a Jefferson Caffery. As he summed up a given day to Glenway Wescott: "At lunch I have one hour of coffee economics, Amazon development and São Paulo politics, [but] morning and afternoon [is] spent in looking at naivist painting and a sculpture cooperative . . . at 4:30 I have a go at the Propaganda Division to let me get a film made of the Naval Academy, which is spectacularly beautiful . . . at 6 I meet an honest academician folklorist poet who teaches me Brazilian verse. I dine with a composer who plays me recent works till 10. . . then for a short tour of bars and sincere cultural establishments."[3]

Lincoln greatly admired Brazilian architecture and took copious photographs—especially of the work of the "brilliant" Oscar Niemeyer (whom Lincoln also credited with encouraging Brazil's younger generation of architects). By contrast he thought Brazilian art was impoverished. Yet he made a few exceptions: Rossi Osir's tiles, Lazar Segal's recent large paintings, and the "first-rate" sculpture of an émigré Polish count, August Zamoyski, who ran an artists' cooperative.

Still, Lincoln managed to buy some twenty paintings from some dozen artists (he mostly liked the "primitives") and to commission three others. His purchases were almost all in the range of $25 to $150—though Candido Portinari, Brazil's most prominent painter, complained that this was "so insanely high" that Lincoln "was ruining the market." Lincoln also bought a good reference library and was careful to collect full documentation on the artists and their works.

But Lincoln disliked the general atmosphere in Brazilian art circles, regretting that Portinari was so insistent on maintaining dominance that most of the local artists, some of whose work Lincoln admired and bought, "have no chance." And he "loathed" the general feeling in the country—"the disgusting backbiting, laziness, talentless, grasping, boring officialdom." He predicted that "if I don't get out soon I'll be *persona non grata* anyway."

He felt homesick from almost the first day of his arrival: "I am really terribly lonely for all the people I love in the U.S.," he wrote Monroe Wheeler. "Not only does there seem an awful lot of them, but I love them much more as time goes on. I think I'll have to be handcuffed by the time I get to Peru in September." He hoped, and urged, that Pete Martínez would continue to stay on with Fidelma (he did) and that Monroe and other friends would create some sort of social life for her (they did).

Lincoln wasn't much happier in Buenos Aires, but at least he found more art that appealed to him. His friend from the previous year, the painter Horacio Butler, was in Lincoln's opinion "one of the nicest people I've ever known," and he thought his new pictures "very beautiful." He felt that Butler was the one painter in Argentina "who has come to terms with the local material . . . he has done a service similar to Hopper and Burchfield"—which was why, in Lincoln's view, he wasn't particularly well regarded; his work was represented in three public collections but not a single private one. Lincoln bought one landscape from Butler for five hundred dollars and offered him a thousand for a second canvas Butler decided he didn't want to sell. "Until Argentina forgets the Ecole de Paris," Lincoln wrote Alfred Barr, "they will have no intellectual autonomy."

In Buenos Aires, Lincoln also had the comfort of George Balanchine's company. Balanchine had been there since May, having accepted the offer the Teatro Colón had made during the Caravan tour of the previous year to become their *maître de ballet* for the summer (New York's winter) season. They paid Balanchine handsomely, allowed him to hire Tchelitchev to do scenery and costumes, and agreed to mount the new Horacio Butler–Alberto Ginastera ballet, *Estancia*, that he and Lincoln had commissioned the year before.[4]

From the beginning Balanchine had felt "overwhelmed" by his reception. The Teatro Colón was one of the world's great theaters, and they laid out the red carpet for him. Everything he asked for he immediately got, including some improvements in the orchestra. Once Lincoln arrived in Buenos Aires in mid-June, he, too, "was received like visiting royalty," and was even asked to reorganize the Colón's teaching program. Among the ballets Balanchine mounted—brilliantly, in Lincoln's opinion—were *Apollo* and the premiere of *Concerto* (Mozart); Lincoln thought that Pavlik's decor was also "stupendously beautiful and marvelously executed." Balanchine was such a sensation that at the end of the brief season, he was given a tremendous banquet and invited to return the following year "in complete charge of an augmented ballet season." As pleased as Lincoln was by Balanchine's success, he himself, as he wrote Nelson, "essentially wanted to get home and do something useful besides crabbing."

But he still had a long trek ahead of him. He ultimately decided that

Argentina, unlike Brazil, did have some "quite good" painters besides But-ler, and he ended up, after visiting the studios of fifty-four artists, buying some thirty canvases from some dozen painters, as well as monotypes, lithographs, and aquatints from a dozen others; they ranged in price from twenty-five dollars to the five hundred he paid Butler. Lincoln refused to buy anything from the cubist Emilio Pettoruti, whom he considered "an arrant fascist" and mostly purchased, in his words, "the more advanced and independent members of the younger school."

At the suggestion of Wally Harrison, now serving in Washington as assistant coordinator of inter-American affairs, Lincoln also assembled material for a supplement on contemporary South American buildings for the magazine *Pencil Points*, a New York architectural monthly. As well, he bought a huge seven-hundred-volume reference library about Argentina, in line with his hope of getting MoMA to establish a department of Latin American art. In all his work Lincoln tried to avoid the curators and offi-cials of the museum establishment. And to prevent artists from jacking up their prices, he also avoided letting people know (though the word did get around) that he represented MoMA, whose prestige in Latin American artistic circles was, in Lincoln's words, "fantastically high."

Throughout his stay in Argentina, Lincoln kept running into Francis Henry Taylor, director of the Metropolitan Museum of Art, who was also on a purchasing mission, though interested primarily in colonial and viceregal art—"Death and Tombs," as Lincoln put it. He disliked Tay-lor intensely, thought he was "all piss and vinegar (and something else too) . . . [and] not as bright as other boys." He characterized Taylor to Monroe as "bumbling about in an agony of boredom, giving lectures on Italian primitives in American Collections—which is just what he should do. He misses everything and I have a lovely time embarrassing him."

Arriving in Chile in mid-July, Lincoln thought some of the work of the architectural students at Catholic University in Santiago "extremely inter-esting," but he found most Chilean painting "conservative . . . there is little representative of any national attitude" and, deplorably, "no connec-tion with the Araucanian Indian." But he did buy work from a few out-standing exceptions: Israel Roa (whom he considered "the best of the teachers and painters of this generation"), a piece of Raúl Vargas's sculp-ture (one of the few works of sculpture Lincoln purchased, since he feared the wartime difficulties of transportation), and a canvas, *The Painter's Birthday*, by Roberto Matta Echaurren (later known simply as Matta).

But what astonished him far more than any of these works was the Mexican David Alfaro Siqueiros's murals-in-progress at Chillán. He saw a lot of Siqueiros during his stay and told him, and everyone he wrote to, that the murals were "magnificent" and "thrilling." Having been under-whelmed throughout his trip, Lincoln had now finally found the wonder-ment he craved. The Siqueiros murals, he wrote Paul Cadmus, "are very marvelous. . . . I think he is the best of the people around these parts." To Monroe, Lincoln declared his belief that "next to Pavlik, I feel [Siqueiros is] the greatest painter in the Western Hemisphere." He also urged Monroe, who was then director of exhibitions at MoMA, to give Siqueiros a one-man show, which, Lincoln reported, "he wants desperately" and most assuredly deserved.

By mid-to-late August Lincoln's exhausting journey had taken him as far as Peru (where his single enthusiasm was for José Sabogal's painting) and Ecuador, where he found the people and their extraordinary clothing "very beautiful" but found, too, "a basic misery I'm sure exists only in Greece and China. Maybe India . . . you feel drunk, sadly drunk, all the time." He did admire the work of Lloyd Wulf, a non-Ecuadorian transplanted to Quito, and especially the painting of Oswaldo Guayasamin, who Lincoln believed was "his country's most gifted artist in spite of his youth."

The lengthy trip was taking its toll. "I feel lost and miserable on this hateful continent," Lincoln wrote Monroe. "I hope that I will learn a lot from the discipline of exile. I've never been so continually uncomfortable or dis-eased or dis-pleased in my life. . . . Not that there aren't charming people and even good work, but it's a prison entire. Some of the prisoners don't know they are jailed, some like jail, but the ones who do the best work know it, loathe it, and are helpless. The local political situations crush my desire or faith in our power to do much." To Frances Hawkins (now, thanks to Lincoln, employed as secretary to MoMA) he bawled: "Do I want a little clean vice, gossip, liquor, and screams and yells! I've been so good for so long it *hurts*. It's bad for me."

But at least the end of the trip was finally in sight. And Lincoln's last full stop, Mexico, filled him with delight: "the people are so alive [and] . . . incredibly rich in all the things I like." By now, he spoke Spanish fluently, though, as he put it, "with no grammar and a charming greco-jewish accent." There was some talk of Fidelma joining him on the last leg of the journey, but Lincoln was so eager to get home as fast as he could that he wanted to avoid even the minimal amount of sightseeing, socializing, or shopping which he knew Fidelma would want. So he plowed ahead alone, arriving back in New York early in October, full of ideas on how to make the most out of what he'd gathered—and of apprehension that he'd be drafted into the army before he could inaugurate any of his elaborate plans.

Those plans included setting up a department of Latin American art at MoMA, helping to mount and write the catalog for a planned exhibit early in 1943 that would show off his acquisitions and begin to acquaint the public with a South American artistic culture of which it was abysmally ignorant; doing a series of lectures at the museum recounting his five-month trip that would then be published as a book; and pressing to get financial support, gallery shows, and funded trips to the United States for some of the individual artists he'd been most taken with. Lincoln's formidable energy went into overdrive; he dashed off a dozen letters in a single day, raced back and forth to Washington to drum up additional sponsorship (since MoMA itself was in the midst of a financial crisis and recently had to drop a number of staff members), wrote a whole series of reports, and wined and dined collectors, art gallery owners, and prospective donors.[5]

At the center of Lincoln's missionary zeal was concern for the well-being of Latin American artists themselves. As he put it in one of his letters, MoMA could "make a start to do a job that 25 divisions of soldiers and all our embassies can't do: to stir their own gifts for their own uses . . . helping them to help themselves to assert what is best in them." South Americans, in Lincoln's view, "will *never* like us. But they will like us more when they see we innocently want to get their best exportable product, which is their popular art and music." Among his characteristically inflated ambitions was "to train Indian kids in the U.S. and send them back as leaders of their own people . . . the Museum is, with luck and money, going to do the first scientific job in Cultural Relations to equal the great health projects of the Amazon, the financing of Peruvian cotton and Brazilian rubber. . . . This is very important work, although it may not seem so to a draft board."

For a time it did. Lincoln's deferment, due to expire on October 15, 1942, was extended, at MoMA's request, for four months, expiring in mid-February 1943. During that grace period, he worked like a demon to accomplish as much as possible before his induction. South American cultural affairs had recently been shifted from Nelson's coordinator's office to the State Department, yet knowing Nelson's long-standing personal fascination with Latin American art, Lincoln continued to turn to him for advice and intervention in regard to various projects, particularly his elaborate plans to set up folk art museums in both Latin America and the United States. Lincoln also worked closely with René d'Harnoncourt, who in 1939 had put together an impressive exhibit of American Indian art at the San Francisco World's Fair; an expanded version of the show opened at MoMA two years later and marked the beginning of d'Harnoncourt's long association with the museum. Within just a few years, he'd become MoMA's director, a post he would hold with distinction for more than two decades.

Lincoln was determined to do what he could to foster the prospects and reputations of many of the South American artists and cultural workers he'd come to admire most during his trip. He wrote dozens of letters on their behalf, badgering galleries, museums, and foundations to provide exhibition space, travel grants, and funding for them. Those efforts produced some distinct successes. For one of his favorite people, the Argentine writer Maria Rosa Oliver, Lincoln helped find employment with Nelson's office. She was delighted to come to the States but wasn't notably happy in Washington, feeling that she was too often "used like a guinea pig to try out ideas on," with many of the most appealing of the ideas never taken up. Lincoln himself often consulted her on the accuracy and comprehensiveness of the assorted reports, articles, and catalogs on Latin American art that he had under preparation. He further enlisted her help in writing the catalog for a one-man show he arranged and did most of the preparatory work for, of Demetrio Urruchua's monotypes (prints achieved by a graphic process of applying paint to a glass or stone slab).

The Urruchua show marked one of Lincoln's most noteworthy successes in advancing the careers of South American artists. Urruchua's bold antifascism had closed off most opportunities to him in his native Argentina, and he'd received little recognition and few commissions. His show, in Lincoln's words, made "a great impression" and it was subsequently turned into a traveling exhibit that toured the country. Alfred Barr told Lincoln that he thought Urruchua was "the one big discovery I made."

Lincoln also made special efforts on behalf of a number of other South American artists, including Lloyd Wulf, José Sabogal, Horacio Butler, Oswaldo Guayasamin, and David Siqueiros (who was unable to attend his MoMA exhibit because the State Department refused him a visa). Further, Lincoln used his acquaintance with Henry Allen Moe, director of the Guggenheim Foundation, successfully to urge on him the need to bring Victoria Ocampo and Gregorio Hernández de Alba, the able director of the archaeological museum in Bogotá, to the United States.

In the midst of this hurricane of activity, terrible news suddenly stopped Lincoln in his tracks: his father, having recently turned seventy-five, had unexpectedly died of pneumonia. The funeral services in Boston were private, but at a memorial ceremony at Temple Israel on December 14 nearly a thousand people braved a snowstorm to pay their respects. Among those who spoke at the memorial were many of the most prominent figures in Massachusetts political life: Governor Leverett Saltonstall, Boston mayor Maurice J. Tobin, U.S. Representatives James M. Curley and Christian Herter, and federal judge Charles E. Wyzanski. One of the speakers, Ben Selekman, head of Boston's Associated Jewish Philanthropies, wisely said of Louis, "He could always forgive those who were weak, but never those who were shoddy. He understood human frailty, but despised human cant. He could lend a hand to men who occasionally might falter, but he could not tolerate those who shirked."

The obituaries, especially in the Boston press, were extensive, complete with pictures and often full-page coverage. Several of them spoke of Louis's prominent role in improving labor conditions in the clothing industry, others of his hard and difficult youth, his uncompromising integrity, and his lifelong reverence for learning. Prominent individuals from various walks of life sent letters of condolence to the family, including Felix Frankfurter, Mayor La Guardia of New York City, and President Roosevelt, who'd invited the Kirsteins to the White House on a number of occasions and consulted privately with Louis on others. FDR now wrote Rose, "A life of singular usefulness in many fields of activity has closed with the passing of your devoted husband, who was my friend and counselor through many years."[6]

Mina, who'd always been close to her father, felt uncomplicated sadness over his death and made plans (never carried out) to write his biography. Rose, suppressing the deficiencies of her marriage, played out a conventional hand: she wrote to commiserating friends that Louis's passing had been "very hard" for her, but she felt grateful to have had "such a marvelous companionship for nearly fifty years. The children are wonderful. I am their only consideration."

As for Lincoln, he left no record of what he felt at his father's death, at the passing of a man who'd been all at once his severe taskmaster and his indulgently generous supporter. Along with undoubted feelings of gratitude and loss, Lincoln almost certainly felt as well a sense of relief from having constantly to justify himself (and his expenditures), from the repetitive, treadmill effort to win approval from a man who, for all his surface warmth and sociability, wasn't, ultimately, emotionally available. In that regard, the aloof Balanchine had proven himself a chillier, less combustible version of Louis. Lincoln never stopped trying to win the endorsement of either man, but neither Louis nor Balanchine shared Lincoln's self-flagellating search for approval, nor—despite his confident dynamism and forcefulness—his contingent sense of self-worth, his tortured, chaotic, guilty inner world. They did not share it and they did not understand what lay beneath: Lincoln's deeply affectionate, tender need for connection.

Once back in New York, Lincoln used his remaining time before his scheduled February army induction to tie up as many loose ends as he could (MoMA's Latin American exhibit wasn't scheduled to open until March 30, 1943, after Lincoln's departure). A number of those loose ends simply had to be abandoned or, for lack of time, given short shrift. His intended full-scale history of South American painting, for example, got condensed into a ninety-six-page catalog for MoMA's exhibit. His planned eight-part lecture series was reduced to four—and then cancelled altogether. The elaborate three-year plan Lincoln had been strenuously at work on to support the arts in Latin America—which had included everything from aiding the nonfascist review *Forma* in Chile to supplying individual artists with needed materials, new galleries, and art organizations—went on hold for the duration.

Even though Lincoln had ultimately concluded that "Latin-American art is in most cases not a source but a tributary," and felt that "there are few painters who are of real importance," he had done a vast amount to increase consciousness in the United States about Latin America culture. As Alfred Barr wrote him, "You certainly did wonders . . . you should be proud."

Remarkably, Lincoln had somehow found the time during these hectic months to write a short "novel," *For My Brother: A True Story by José Martínez Berlanga as Told to Lincoln Kirstein,* closely based on the many stories Pete had shared with him about his early life in Mexico and Texas. Lincoln worried that he hadn't gotten Pete's "essential quality into it—it's entirely physical, and . . . defeated," but the book did perceptively and sympathetically recount the tribulations and joys of Mexican American life; it was also suffused with a tenderness that simultaneously revealed the depth of Lincoln's affection for Pete (without ever once mentioning homosexuality) and the deeply sweet, compassionate side of Lincoln's nature that, especially as he grew older, he seldom allowed to surface in his professional life.

Lincoln sent the manuscript to, among others, Muriel Draper, of whom he'd seen little of late; she knew and liked Pete and wrote Lincoln a winningly evasive note about the book. *For My Brother* does lack the imaginative invention characteristic of a true novelist, and American publishers were quick to reject it. Christopher Isherwood, with whom Lincoln was becoming friendly, then took the manuscript in hand and cut it drastically, omitting most of the second half (which had centered on southern white prejudice against blacks and Chicanos). Isherwood had Lincoln send the new version to John Lehmann at the Hogarth Press in London, who accepted it for publication just weeks before Lincoln left for the army.

"Why no U.S.A. publisher would take it," Lehmann wrote Isherwood, "beats me," but Lehmann himself did have "an awful struggle with the Mexican words . . . which proved to be full of mistakes (Lincoln's or the typist's?) and several corruptions (or Americanisms?) in the text which had to be settled without reference to Lincoln himself, as time pressed." Once the book was announced for publication in July 1943, advance orders were so heavy that Hogarth ordered a second impression even before the first one reached the bookstores.

Few of the books ever did. Both printings, stored in a warehouse prior to distribution, were largely destroyed during a Nazi air raid on London. To compound that disaster, most of the reviews (apparently done from galley proofs) were unfavorable, though the most distinguished reviewers—

Elizabeth Bowen, L. P. Hartley, and Philip Toynbee—liked it. In comforting Lincoln, Isherwood reminded him that English reviewers were "much more reserved and snooty" than in the United States, "especially toward first appearances of foreign writers, and most especially American."

Before reporting to Fort Dix, Lincoln gave over "complete control" of the School of American Ballet to Eugenie Ouroussow, asking only that she consult with Balanchine in regard to scheduling classes, hiring teachers, and enrolling students. Later, when Lincoln was about to go overseas, and anticipating the possibility of being killed, he wrote Ouroussow that on his death the school would legally go to Fidelma who, "although she loves it as much as I do . . . is not capable of doing anything" about the actual management of the place. Lincoln would therefore instruct her to give Ouroussow "anything you wanted, short of ownership, for the rest of your life." Should Balanchine die, Lincoln asked Ouroussow to consider the possibility of Lew Christensen as the new chairman of faculty: "In spite of his lack of cultural background, he is . . . a lovely person, and one whom I trust implicitly. He is not imaginative but has been poor, and hence has a sound instinct for survival."

Then, less than a week before his departure and pressed with a thousand tasks relating to it, he took the time to write Henry Allen Moe of the Guggenheim Foundation, expressing how "disturbed" he felt "about Martha Graham and how she will survive the war. I feel that she is one of America's greatest artists and that her individual survival is most important"; he hoped Moe would find a way to be helpful. It was a gesture beautifully illustrative of the generosity of spirit that was an essential, if not always visible, part of Lincoln's nature.

On February 23 Lincoln was inducted into the U.S. Army at Fort Dix.

CHAPTER TWENTY

The Army
(1943–1945)

"I AM AN OLD man," the thirty-six-year-old Lincoln wrote a friend after being in the service a few weeks, "and find the going very hard. I guess the first part is always toughest, but I have nothing to complain about. . . . The boys are Arkansas squirrel shooters and . . . are helpful and sympathetic. I am so tired I can't sleep but I believe they only care if you get 4½ hours. . . . I learned (almost) to shoot and disassemble a rifle, roll away from a not very big tank, do very slow an awful obstacle course and fall into assorted water hazards. I don't think its fun—though most do." Or as Lincoln put it in a letter to Alfred Barr, "I feel both ancient (my bones) and infantile (my dexterity)."[1]

The humorous stoicism of most of his letters home barely conceals the real hardship he felt. Isherwood, who'd settled in Los Angeles, heard from Paul Cadmus that Lincoln's spirits were "gruesome," and immediately wrote him several buck-up letters. Lincoln himself confessed to Archie MacLeish that "at 36 I did with difficulty what wouldn't have been so tough at 26, and fun at 16."

Homesickness heightened the physical hardship; "I can't help admitting that I miss you terrifically," he wrote Fidelma, and then playfully added, "If you could get an eyeful of your brown and brawny husband, you'd be more lonesome than ever." Over the course of basic training, Lincoln dropped forty-five pounds in ten weeks, and his waistline, which had been expanding, went from a thirty-eight to a thirty-two. Given a brief leave, he was able to spend a few days with Fidelma in New York, and then subsequently in Washington. She, too, was unhappy ("she misses you awfully," Pete Martínez wrote Lincoln), and after Pete returned to Texas to await induction, Lincoln got Frances Hawkins to move in with Fidelma, offering to pay the rent.

Once basic training was behind him, Lincoln hoped to get assigned to the War Department division of counterespionage. He was sent instead (with the army's usual logic) to train as a combat engineer at Fort Belvoir in Virginia and initially attached to a unit that wrote training manuals, a job that was soon reorganized out of existence. Advised to apply for Intelligence, his application was swiftly turned down. Oh well, Pete wrote him from Texas, "You've never been happy unless you have something to worry about." Pete himself was eager to join up: "I won't be near you and it's too much to hope for, but at least we'll be doing the same thing. . . . I don't think I want to go back to N.Y. if you are not there." (Pete signed his letter "Goop"—one of the variant nicknames, strictly confined to the *inner* inner circle, which included "Goozlie," "Gloop," "Goosie," "Goopie," "Gooper," "Glooper," and the like.)

While awaiting a long-term assignment, Lincoln was kept busy enough at Fort Belvoir doing routine tasks that ranged from rifle practice to cutting the grass and hauling beef carcasses, watermelons, and garbage. After he'd been in service some three months he still didn't "feel like a soldier" and thought he probably "never will." What he usually did feel was "hot, horrid" and "numb." He waggishly enumerated his daily life: from 5:00 a.m. to 4:00 p.m. he'd mechanically perform menial jobs; at 5:00 p.m. he'd shave, shampoo, shower, and consume large amounts of ice cream with syrup and nuts, leaving him "slightly nauseated," until it was time for a Bing Crosby movie, which left him feeling "more nauseated." He'd then have a Coke, go to the library, and be in bed by ten. Of his tentmates, who were mostly fifteen years or so younger, he playfully wrote, "If someone tried hard no doubt they could all be taught to read and write. As it is, they curse with a not unpleasing druglike monotony which I find soothing."

Fortunately Fort Belvoir was in easy striking distance of Washington, DC, and Lincoln tried to spend every Sunday there; he'd have two old-fashioneds at the Willard bar, indulge in what he called an "orgy of luxury" and "feckless talk," occasionally see a friend—Maria Rosa Oliver, say, or Archie MacLeish (then Librarian of Congress)—and visit art galleries. All of which left him "not unhappy, just subnormal and unmoralized." What he needed (as he well knew) was total immersion in an ambitious project.

Before long he managed to invent one: gathering and documenting soldier art—initially among the Corps of Engineers at Fort Belvoir itself, but eventually branching out (as was Lincoln's way) into an elaborate set of plans for surveying U.S. "battle art" through time, plans that would come to include a large-scale exhibit *and* a book, tentatively entitled "Artists Under Fire." By late summer, thanks to the cooperation—and in some cases the enthusiasm—of his commanding officers, he'd moved briskly ahead on varied fronts, gathering materials at Fort Belvoir itself; researching the extensive archives at West Point, the Library of Congress, the War College, and elsewhere; writing up scores of proposals to win the support of influential people in both the military and art worlds. The proposals were a masterful mix of real scholarship, eloquent and deftly exaggerated advocacy, and a clever approximation of unassuming modesty.[2]

Lincoln's tactics, along with his strenuous hard work, paid off handsomely. By the fall of 1943, he'd succeeded in establishing an ambitious Art Project at Belvoir, which itself resulted in the creation of an "album" of some thirty-five of the best wartime paintings and sculpture, nine of which *Life* magazine reproduced in a large color spread. Lincoln then moved on to enlist the support of his many prominent contacts in creating a still more elaborate set of exhibitions and publications. That process continued for the better part of a year, and its culminating events, on July 4, 1944, would take place after Lincoln himself had already been sent overseas.

Among the eminences whom Lincoln managed to cast in leading roles for his interlocking set of stagings were Jim Soby, Monroe Wheeler, and Alfred Barr at MoMA, Archie MacLeish at the Library of Congress and, at the National Gallery of Art in Washington, DC, its director David Finley and his high-level associate, John Walker (who nearly twenty years earlier had helped his fellow undergraduates Lincoln and Eddie Warburg establish the Harvard Society for Contemporary Art).

Over the course of nearly a year, Lincoln worked simultaneously on producing exhibitions of American Battle Art at the National Gallery of Art (paintings and drawings) and the Library of Congress (prints and lithographs), with a smaller-scale follow-up exhibit at MoMA. For a long-range encore Lincoln also began drumming up support for a National War Art Museum either in Washington, DC, or at West Point, based on London's Imperial War Museum in South Kensington. As his old friend Agnes Mongan of the Fogg Museum, whom Lincoln also enlisted to track down various items, put it: "I am perpetually staggered to find that you have so much energy to do what you do." The War Museum proposal (of which he'd sent her a copy) "in itself would have represented in any other person several months' unbroken effort. I think it is excellent in all points." No commercial publisher was interested in Lincoln's plans for a large-scale book on battle art, but he was able to extract from his work-in-progress a three-part series for the *Magazine of Art*, as well as a fifty-nine-page catalog for the exhibition at the National Gallery of Art.

Just as these interlocking ventures were peaking in the spring of 1944, Lincoln—after having had his various applications for transfer, most recently to the Signal Corps, turned down—was unexpectedly offered a master sergeancy in the Air Corps. By then David Finley of the National Gallery had already recommended that he be assigned to an overseas post with the U.S. Arts and Monuments Commission, of which Finley was vice-chair. Initially Finley's recommendation was turned down, since (as Huntington Cairns, the secretary-treasurer of the commission, explained to Lincoln), there was an "apparently absolute rule against the employment of Privates in arts and monuments work." But Finley and Cairns pressed the case; they went together to the War Department to argue for Lincoln's special qualifications and, since the ten-person advisory board to the commission also included MacLeish, Paul Sachs, and John Walker, Lincoln did finally get his assignment—but not a commission. The Air

Corps job might ordinarily have appealed to him; it would have primarily involved editing the service newspaper, *The Shutter*, and would have allowed Lincoln to stay, risk free, in Washington. But the appointment to the monuments commission appealed far more.[3]

Before leaving the United States in early June, Lincoln sent off "parting salutes," as he called them, to Jim Soby and Alfred Barr. He himself characterized his letters as "of an insolent arrogance that even surprised me," but they seem a good deal less than that. To Barr, who'd recently been asked by MoMA's board of trustees to step down as director and to concentrate more on his scholarly articles, Lincoln sent in his resignation as consultant on Latin American art, announcing that the museum "is becoming increasingly official"—which Barr could have read as an act of solidarity. To Soby, a wealthy, charming man who over the years had held various positions at MoMA, Lincoln denounced the museum for having become "really reactionary" and having "retired from the position of imaginative pioneering," risking less and less, intent instead on giving the public more of what it already liked.

Lincoln freely acknowledged that he himself wouldn't "last two minutes" if he held Soby's job, since he'd "show ten Pavliks, ten Picassos, four Hoppers and a few others" (he specified, among them, Yves Tanguy, Rufino Tamayo, and Ben Shahn)—he would, in short, show "those painters . . . of the rank of seminal gifts," which would in turn "open the museum to such attacks as not even its worst enemy would relish." He closed the letter to Soby: "I honestly agree with you about almost everything, only I roar and scream more. Also am a horrid character and you are a sweet one." Lincoln signed the letter "Pvt. Parts."

Accompanied by four other non-commissioned art specialists, Lincoln left in June 1944 for England. Unfortunately no one seems to have been notified that the group was arriving, with the result that (as Lincoln wrote Monroe Wheeler) "with our exalted rank we have not, shall we say, fared very well." Six months earlier a number of distinguished British and American experts had drafted a set of directives for protecting and preserving important historical sites, but SHAEF (General Eisenhower's Supreme Headquarters Allied Expeditionary Force) had rejected their plan as too extensive. When Lincoln presented himself at SHAEF he found it "had other things" on its mind, and he got shunted off into serving as "an interpreter with nothing to interpret."

It wasn't that Lincoln particularly minded being a private; as he wrote Mina, "I would be a lousy officer. . . . I would have been automatically separated not only from the associations I prefer, but I would have been bored to screaming sobs by a forced congeniality with people of no interest at all . . . the ordinary soldier (who does not exist) is much easier to get on with, essentially more interesting." But Lincoln did mind being at loose ends. He wandered around a blitz-shattered London for a month and then, thanks to the kindness of his commanding officer, got transferred to a unit in France where at least the possibility existed of his being put to use by some public works or monument officer.

By that point the war in Europe had shifted decisively in the Allies' favor, but it was hardly over (in December would come the frightening reversal of the Battle of the Bulge), and even in the Paris environs, Lincoln would every so often see "little hints of horror which make me realize this is not an enforced vacation in the Maine Woods." But overall he was delighted to find so much of Paris (unlike London) essentially undamaged, and "never felt such exaltation." He was particularly thrilled, as he wrote Agnes Mongan, that "the French national patrimony of art is untouched," a feat of preservation for which he fully credited the French themselves. To Monroe Wheeler, Lincoln reported that "except for the rifled Jewish collections, as you doubtless know, the loss to French national monuments is not great, as for example and alas, in Italy."

Though there were shortages in Paris of everything from paper to food, the city was "seething with intellectual activity." In Lincoln's opinion the political and literary weeklies were greater in number than before the war, and most of them "young, vigorous, independent." The theaters, too, though unheated, were alive with remarkable productions that included the brilliant Jean-Louis Barrault's performance in Paul Claudel's four-hour *The Satin Slipper,* and Jean Anouilh's new *Antigone.* Lincoln wrote an article about French theater for *The Nation* and as well sent Virgil Thomson newsy letters about musical life in the capital to use for his regular column in the *New York Herald Tribune.*

Lincoln was not, however, an admirer of every aspect of France's reemergence. He thought the "classe moyenne" was "pretty grim," and he regretted that "the horrors of the salons are all being revived and that the Academy and the rotation of prizes are all to have their way again." But he felt pleased that Serge Lifar had been (briefly) imprisoned for having had the lights of the Paris Opéra turned on—after all the workmen on the premises had refused to do so—in order to give Hitler a personal tour.

When Archie MacLeish implied that the Free French forces contained some unsavory elements, Lincoln took offense and wrote him that they "are *not* hoodlums or 'Communists' " but rather the soul of France . . . they are marvelous." Lincoln had for a long time been ambivalent about Archie, both as man and poet. Lincoln's recent (and permanent) poetic hero had become Wystan Auden, with whom over the past few years he'd begun a friendship that would prove lifelong. Lincoln felt Wystan was "the greatest English poet of our time"; by comparison, Archie (and Stephen Spender, too) was demoted into "a curious, disappointed category . . . where talent is not enough."

Pleased though he was to be back in Paris, Lincoln couldn't stand being comparatively idle for long. He made himself a desk out of a packing crate, got up earlier than anyone else, and fired off, along with the occasional article, dozens of letters to a wide variety of correspondents. He also began to write verse again (which would later be published in book form as *Rhymes of a PFC*) and sent it out to a few friends for their opinion. "Chris" Isherwood, for one, was not impressed. "I can accept the verses as 'communication,' " he toughly responded, "but when you ask what I think of them from a *literary* point of view, then I can't just be kind or polite." Poetry, Chris stated flatly, "isn't really your medium," and he expressed the hope that "for your sake, you won't publish these verses. You will regret it." But Isherwood was being overly harsh, too glibly equating the poetry's sometimes crabbed convolutions and singsong meter with all there was to Lincoln's sometimes ironic, witty, urgent verses. From an autobiographical viewpoint alone, his poetry provides invaluable insights—for example, to his anger over the endemic racism in the armed forces. In the poem "Black Joe," he wrote of dazed, exhausted black troops arriving at their campfire:

> We whites, with gummy eye, but brave, as our blond blood stirs to its round
> Stare hard the dark intruders down to stand our own usurped ground.
> With psyches sound, but half-awake, we keep possession of our pyre,
> Warding the somber soldiers off; this shall remain a white-man's fire.

Still, Isherwood's reaction upset Lincoln, since he suspected that Chris was right; "poetry is after all, and first of all, song. . . . I wanted to do what Kipling did. . . . I wanted to express, in a combination of exalted and colloquial language a common experience, that is the war." Lincoln took comfort in Isherwood's further opinion that he was not merely meant to write prose but that there was "nothing to stop [him] . . . becoming one of the best we have."

Isherwood's negative view of Lincoln's poetry kept him for a time from writing any verse at all. But it didn't check his need to stay busy. Before long he was proposing to Monroe Wheeler that the two of them—that is, MoMA and any army or government agency Lincoln might entice— mount a show at the essentially empty Jeu de Paume museum, from which Göring had long since handpicked an assortment of treasures for shipment to Germany, and which had subsequently been the object of other lootings. Lincoln wanted the show, which he called Revive France!, actually to be done by the French themselves, with him and Monroe contributing their services behind the scenes; it would be "our homage and appreciation," he wrote Monroe, "of France's persistence and sacrifice."

Lincoln recognized from the beginning that his proposal was "rather a pipe dream," and indeed nothing came of it. Nor, for a while longer, could he find any other compelling outlet for his energy and expertise. But he did at least manage to become friendly with a number of like-minded and like-positioned servicemen: Lamont Moore, a man who had previously managed the National Gallery's education program; John Skilton, who soon after the war would write *Défense de l'art européen;* and Sheldon Keck, an art conservator. Lincoln already knew George Stout, who'd been chief conservator at Harvard's Fogg Museum, and whom Lincoln would later come to regard as the main hero of the effort to preserve and recover European art. By September, Lincoln had also contacted 1st Lt. James Rorimer, who'd been a curator at the Cloisters in New York, had entered Paris soon after its liberation, and had immediately become active safeguarding the Tuileries and Versailles; within weeks Lincoln got off a letter to Rorimer: "I suppose it's too much to expect that Monuments can use Keck, Skilton, Moore or me."

Yes, for a few months longer it still was too much. Lincoln took out his frustration in two familiar ways: he wrote an article, "Letter from France," for the *Magazine of Art,* detailing the surprisingly limited amount of damage he'd found in Paris ("actual damage to the face of the capital was skindeep"); and he got off one of his famously blistering letters, this one to Huntington Cairns, vice chair of the Arts and Monuments Commission—the man who, along with David Finley, had originally gotten Lincoln his assignment.

In his letter Lincoln bluntly stated that "the behavior of the Commission has been, to put it mildly, callous and insulting," and he insisted that unless he was put to work doing the job he'd been assigned to do, he "had absolutely no desire to remain on your lists." Lincoln sent copies of the letter to Paul Sachs and Archie MacLeish. Two months later Lincoln wrote Archie that he regretted "the nasty letter" to Cairns, "but being treated like a baby for 23 months has only one sinister result, you get to act like a baby." He continued to feel that neither Finley nor Cairns understood that "the civilian hierarchy is inoperable in the army . . . they can mean well, but they can do literally nothing. So let's forget about it."

He did have a compelling personal assignment from his friend Tchelitchev: to locate his sister Choura, last known to be living somewhere in Paris. When Lincoln failed instantly to find her, the testy Pavlik ungratefully denounced him as an example of what was wrong with the United States: "People of this country only think of themselves." (At exactly this time Martha Graham described Pavlik in a letter as "a devil, but he opens whole areas of magic life because of his very anguish and perversity.") Yet Lincoln did locate Choura, and in fairly short order; he found her "divine and saintly . . . a sort of Russian holy woman, as gay and heartless as a bird." The two spent one whole evening together going through all the material Pavlik had left behind in Paris, including "a complete set of all his Berlin theatrical designs of great brilliance"—and also "reams of dirty drawings" that were "absolutely stupendous."

He wrote at once to Pavlik to tell him that his sister was safe, and Pavlik's gratitude overflowed in the same exaggerated way his earlier denunciation had; in sending Lincoln his thanks Pavlik waxed on about how much he "adored" Fidelma, how she was spending several weeks with him and Charles Henri Ford at Wellfleet, where she continued to work on her own drawings, and how they "all became big friends." Pavlik added that he deliberately hadn't invited her brother Paul to join them "because then it becomes family visit and Fidelma wouldn't be as free and unselfconscious as she is now."

Meantime Lincoln's initial thrill at being back in Paris had begun to wear off. Pavlik's sister was but one of many who began to tell him in hairraising detail about the true horrors of the occupation, about the nights "when all you heard was a knock at the door, not even very much talking and you'd never see your friend again, and you would never be sure who informed on him or you, or what was about to happen." Lincoln also began to feel some distaste for the rapidity with which Paris, after all that it had been through, so quickly returned to many of its less attractive habits, including "the familiar signs of new scandals" and factional literary squabbling, libel suits, and mutual recriminations. It all "only enhances my already violently stimulated sense of evil," Lincoln wrote Paul Cadmus. "I used to think suffering . . . in itself, beneficial . . . but I can see that certain people have a talent for suffering as well as indignation, and that terror is not necessarily a cure-all, or even a cure-anything."

Though he still basically adored Paris, he was relieved when, at the end of September 1944, he was assigned to a more active role as an official interpreter. Able to "think in French and talk very fast," he enjoyed "racing around the countryside on various assignments." One of them took him, along with his colonel, up to General Patton's headquarters, and he wrote admiringly of "Blood & Guts looking eleven feet high, walking up a new road, unarmed . . . it was as casual as nothing at all." In his short poem "Patton" Lincoln later wrote:

> *Patton's informal entrance seems some sort of booby trap,*
> *But his easy stoic manner is devoid of any crap,*
>   *So I stick right in my car.*

Lincoln now found himself stationed not far from the army unit Pete Martínez had been assigned to, and the two were finally able to meet again. They'd planned to get "roaring and screaming," but Pete had a bad cold and was confined to quarters. Still, they had a wonderful time catching up; Pete did full theatrical justice to his escapades in England among the officer corps, all "needless to say" (as Lincoln repeated the adventures in a letter to Isherwood, who had met and was crazy about Pete), "unhappily married, separated for the time being from their misunderstanding wives." Pete was still having a "wonderful time" despite the white southerners in his unit "who call him a no-account greaser Mexican." The question of what Pete would do after the war, since he was growing too old and unpracticed for ballet, bothered Lincoln but not Pete. "I daresay," Lincoln wrote Isherwood, "he will come and live with Fido and me, which we would both love."

In early January 1945 Lincoln was finally—after "seven months bucking the entire system, and in spite of my well-known charm"—assigned as assistant to the monuments officer of Patton's Third Army. He thought it was "the best possible assignment, because we are in the field, that is we follow combat troops." Then, late in January, he was promoted, along with nearly everyone else in his unit, to the rank of PFC ("Oh fuck," he wrote Paul. "I have now been in the army 24 months and they can stick it"). But he was delighted at last to be doing the work for which he felt best equipped.

For three months Lincoln was primarily based in the city of Nancy ("certainly one of the most lovely in France, not only for its monuments but for its people"), and from there he moved about the eastern, more remote parts of the country. Much of his daily work continued to be mundane: "I iron out petty difficulties with the prefecture," he wrote Frances Hawkins, "see that the man comes to fix the pump in the flooded basement, get a (oilcloth only) muzzle for the colonel's dog," contact the local gendarmerie about an arrest, and travel by jeep to a village that for some unaccountable reason had an abundant supply of otherwise unavailable plywood.

On one expedition into the countryside Lincoln and his companions "heard a lot of sound-effects," which they assumed were coming from one of their own units; in fact it was hostile fire, and they had to take temporary refuge in an old mill. At another time Lincoln found himself in a town where two thousand Jews had once lived; four remained, and the synagogue, which the Germans had used as a warehouse, had been badly smashed up. Yet one of the four survivors intoned "the ceremonies of the High Holy days," with the congregation made up entirely of GIs.

In between these excursions, Lincoln served meals at mess, dug latrines, volunteered to paint backdrops for an army production of *AWOL in Paris*, wrote and directed a play designed to show "how an American detachment behaved in the face of a dam breaking, shells flying and an actual retreat." The latter concept displeased his superiors. During dress rehearsal the unit's colonel announced "in no uncertain terms that the American army NEVER retreats," and the script was adjusted to show the U.S. Army *advancing*—at exactly the time the Germans broke through during the Battle of the Bulge.

By early February 1945, Lincoln's unit left France and, moving through Luxembourg, crossed over into western Germany. For some time he'd been preparing for this moment by buying paperbound guidebooks to Germany and spending hours in travel bureaus collecting photographs, travel brochures, and maps. By now Lincoln felt "quite instructed" on German folklore and history and believed he could "travel anywhere in Germany and know in advance what historic monuments to look up first." His stored-up knowledge—not simply, of course, from guidebooks and the like, but from his own long-standing immersion in the world of art and artists—was now, finally, about to find its application. Fidelma (whom he missed "more and more") further bolstered him with a package containing long underwear and his leather jacket, Rose sent several hundred chocolate-covered mints, each in its own glassine envelope, and Abby Aldrich Rockefeller, a comb and nail file. Thus fully equipped, Lincoln began his explorations.[4]

It was immediately obvious to him that the Arts and Monuments Commission's "official list," though helpful, was inadequate. The commission's members, moreover, "are not in uniform and do not understand military problems"; their instructions and desires carried "little weight" with the U.S. Army. Not that Lincoln automatically sided with the army. "Awful things," he wrote Archie MacLeish (who was now assistant secretary of state) in February 1945, "have been done by mistake, and by intent, in the last six months, things which there were no need for." When he heard people express delight that the German cities were being flattened, it hardly pleased him—"because the Roman gate at Trier, and similar monuments, aren't just German."

Since his grandfather had fled as a political refugee to the United States in 1848 and "had a gospel against Prussia," Lincoln had grown up "terrified of anything German." To return to Germany in his current capacity as occupier and as a Jew was more than irony, it was semi-sweet revenge. Lincoln regarded the Germans as "worse than anyone can ever believe," and felt that objectively "we are better." He fully agreed with François Mauriac, who had written in *Le Figaro* that the God currently ordaining revenge was not the Christian God of mercy but Yahweh, God of the Hebrews, "the Jews' best friend and severest critic, extracting all the teeth and all the eyes, murdering not so much people as cities." At first Lincoln thought it was the border towns only that had heavily suffered, but the further he went into Germany the worse the destruction got.

It turned out that Lincoln's monuments officer, Capt. Robert Posey, a New York City architect, was someone he'd known slightly at Harvard, and the two worked well together. Their first major discovery had come in late February, while they were still in France. The Priory Church of Mont

Saint Martin, an eleventh-century Rhenish-Romanesque structure, stood on top of a hill overlooking the Luxembourg border. The Germans had bombed the hill in May 1940, destroying the church roof but not the interior vault. During an inspection tour on February 24, 1945, Posey gained entrance to the long-locked church, and he and Lincoln noticed traces of color under the plaster on the side walls.

Made damp from years of rain pouring in, the plaster easily peeled away, revealing underneath a large and (in Lincoln's words) "absolutely glorious" wall painting in tempera of the Annunciation "as fresh as the day it was done, almost"—it was "like finding a new Canterbury tale," Lincoln wrote MacLeish (or as he put it to Agnes Mongan, "I believe in Santa Claus"). George Stout, the monuments officer with the Twelfth Army and an expert in the chemistry of pigment and plaster, was called in to confirm the dating of the painting; he put it at 1350–75. Since there were few comparable paintings in France from that period, the Signal Corps immediately took pictures of the recovered work, and both a restorer and a copyist were sent out to the site.

Other discoveries followed in Germany. One day Lincoln found himself trapped down a mine shaft he'd been exploring; power had suddenly gone out and for seven hours—"rather than walk up the height of 2 Empire State buildings"—he explored what turned out to be a vast Luftwaffe uniform depot. Another time, in the town of Hungen, Posey and Lincoln found eight buildings crammed with the archives of what seemed like "all the Jewish congregations in Europe," and with anti-Semitic clippings stockpiled for apparent use by Nazi bigwigs Alfred Rosenberg or Julius Streicher in their "research" studies. They also went to examine the homes of both Streicher and the Görings. Streicher had long been one of Hitler's leading "theorists" of anti-Semitism and had filled his influential newspaper, *Der Stürmer*, with vitriolic denunciations of "the Jewish beasts." His farm was a large, "three-winged, barn-like factory of a place sitting in the middle of nowhere." The following day Lincoln rummaged through *Der Stürmer*'s office in Nuremberg, and found in the basement a huge collection of ancient Jewish texts, including vellum rolls from Prague and Amsterdam, as well as Streicher's own private police files— "like a memory book," is how Lincoln put it.

He and Posey took something of a risk in going to Göring's home, Schloss Veldenstein, at Neuhaus. There were no American troops in the immediate vicinity, and Lincoln felt torn between "the fear of seeming silly and the essential interest in coming home for supper." (They later learned that the day following their visit a still-combative SS officer had terrorized the citizens of one of the towns through which they'd driven.) With two MPs accompanying them in separate jeeps, they decided to make the trip, but the jeeps drove at a sixty-yard interval from each other, in case one should be hit.

Schloss Veldenstein sat alone on a craggy peak. Trains from Berlin had a few months earlier carted off most of the pictures and sculpture that Göring had been "acquiring" since 1938, often from museums or wealthy Jews who'd been deported to the camps. A few items of interest still remained, in particular some wooden Gothic carvings, several large Gobelin tapestries (which fitted their uneven wall spaces poorly), and three of Emmy Göring's Tanagra figurines. As an officer, Posey could place a given site off-limits and remove artworks; he immediately arranged for military guards to be posted at the Göring home, and removed the Tanagra figurines. Lincoln, as a private, could do none of these things, but he let himself swipe some of Goring's stationery (as he had from *Der Stürmer*), with DER REICHSMARSCHALL DES GROSSDEUTSCHEN REICH emblazoned at the top, and delightedly used it to write to friends.

As for the figurines, Lincoln thought the prettiest one was a fake, but "one can never be sure about terra-cotta." So now, he wrote Cadmus, "What does one do with them?" It was the classic question faced by monuments officers throughout the war. In this case Lincoln's uncompromising answer was, "Pack them carefully and save them until they can be legally proved to have been bought in 1935, the property of Epernheim [Hermann von Epenstein, the previous owner of the castle, and Göring's godfather], or were given by an old Greek called Helianos to Goring's papa. Yer takes yer cherce."

It was Lincoln's theory that the Nazi hierarchy was so incapable of envisioning defeat that they never made sufficient protective arrangements for their own monuments. The result was that "a very great number of churches, and particularly Gothic civic and domestic architecture" were lost beyond repair. For some Americans the desolation became a source of pride; for Lincoln, of regret: he could never, as he wrote Cadmus, "get entirely case-hardened to the remains of large churches, the least of which is better than anything in our beauty-tost country, being gutted and lying in expensive ashes." The builders of such superb structures as the Kurfürstliches Palais or Schinkel's great houses "were not," in Lincoln's view, "the executioners of Buchenwald or Dachau."

He took comfort in the fact that despite the terrible architectural losses, and "with certain very sad exceptions" in painting and sculpture, "what was in Germany that we loved," as he wrote Agnes Mongan, "is still there." Agnes wept quietly when she got his letter, wept with relief "that so much I thought gone forever has been saved," and with joy that Lincoln was at last using his "extraordinary gifts where they can do real service."

Baroque art had never held much appeal for Lincoln, but early in May he came across one vast castle from the early eighteenth century that stupefied him with its "great shell grotto inlaid with fish scales, mirrors, shells, Venetian glass," all intact except for a few fish scales; someone, and he hoped it wouldn't be him, would have to see "that us conquerors don't

piss on the Gobelins and bathe in the horse troughs." As the army continued to press forward, it became clear that in many areas the local aristocracy remained ensconced in their enormous, largely untouched baroque
castles. Arriving at one such *Schloss*, Lincoln was told that the countess, its
mistress, had taken to her bed at the appearance of the "Russian-Jewish-
Negro-American army." "That witch in her bed," Lincoln later wrote in
his poem "Das Schloss,"

> *Smothered in covers up to the chin, shamming dead*
> *Her boots sticking out black below, tightly laced . . .*
> *Dull thuds suggest she has several uniformed men*
> *Upstairs or down who can make beds, murder, or cake.*

She told Lincoln that she'd been "ill, oh so ill" and that she'd been
using her castle as a hospital for "lightly" wounded Germans. As it turned
out, the countess was harboring "a whole slue [*sic*] of art dealers, young
'sick' counts and barons . . . and my," Lincoln caustically wrote Fidelma,
"my, have they had a terrible time—they almost didn't get out of Paris . . .
and them with their weak lungs."

The countess showed Lincoln pictures of her two "lovely boys," who
just happened to be SS officers (Lincoln agreed that they *were* "wildly
pretty"), and expressed her gratification that they had been "privileged to
surrender to the Americans, rather than to "the un-democratic and dirty,
awful, Russian-Jewish-Polacks"—whom, the countess advised, "we
MUST fight quickly." She had one other "little insignificant request";
that the American soldiers cease to shoot the deer in her park, because it
was out of season and her chief forester was becoming most upset. It was
all, Lincoln wrote Fidelma, "frightfully comic and sick-making."

Day after day Lincoln found himself consumed in one "mad activity"
after another; he'd rarely in his life felt "so entirely occupied"—and also
"amazingly adaptable," even when it came to being able to sleep at night.
In the smaller towns Lincoln felt more tension and dislike from the inhabitants than he had in the cities. His German was not nearly as good as his
French or Spanish, yet he could "scarcely help wanting to be agreeable to
children and older people"; he was well aware, though, that "there are
monstrous types still around, and I could kill a lot of people I've seen with
real pleasure."

Besides, "unlike others," Lincoln wrote his secretary, Doris Levine, "I
am not a kiss and make up boy. I do not feel cooperative towards our late
enemy." "Germany is detestable," he wrote the painter Honoré Sharrer
(whose career he helped launch). "They take no responsibility of any sort
and spend all the time flattering us and saying how we are 'good sports'
but of course we will all join the big game against the dreadful Russians."
When he wasn't feeling active disgust for the Germans, Lincoln felt

bemused: "Frankly," he wrote Agnes Mongan, "I understand nothing about them . . ." But after a while, he developed what he liked to believe was "a manner of extreme professionalism" with the locals, "like talking to a problem child who is a habitual liar. Your politeness indicates that you believe nothing they say."

Lincoln had heard that Archie MacLeish was developing a plan for the re-education of Germany. "Well, I suppose someone should," Lincoln laconically commented, but he thought it might better be Wystan Auden, "who knows the country, and not the great poet [MacLeish] who thinks he knows fascism." Anyway, Lincoln wrote, "it really makes very little difference, as the future is so accidental it is of no interest what plans are made." He added that "I cannot begin to indicate my lack of hope for the future aside from my personal amusement and luxurious adventures which are as irrelevant as everything else." His bout of radical pessimism included himself. He claimed the war had not "improved my character or mellowed me in any way. On the contrary, if I was intolerant of idiocy before, I am a thousand times worse now."

Mina, who knew the eruptive, impatient side of her brother as well as anyone, and had sometimes suffered from it, begged to differ with his overall self-assessment. "I wonder," she wrote him, "if you have any idea how proud I am of you, and how magnificent I think your attitude has been throughout . . . not only the way you have taken the official nonsense, the discomforts and dangers, but the superb way you have never for one instant let down in your preoccupation with and expression of the interests that you have always had. If ever I have seen an example of inner discipline, you are it." Mina had it exactly right.

In April came the news of FDR's death. Mina reported that Rose "cried more even than when Father died," and Mina tried to convince her mother that as incoming president, Harry Truman "will have some of that rude, earthy, honest force we like to think of as essentially American." Roosevelt's passing came as something of a shock to Lincoln himself. He thought the army newspaper, *Stars and Stripes*, put it best: "Mr. Truman is said to be a kindly man with a sense of humor. He'll need it, and so will we."

As Lincoln and Posey followed in the footsteps of the combat units, moving into southern Germany, sporadic fire continued (two monuments officers were killed by mortar rounds). Lincoln felt that it would take another five years before even a "half-peace" could be achieved, and he resigned himself to at least one more year of active duty. Told that his field record and age (in May he turned thirty-eight) meant that he could eventually expect a commission, Lincoln expressed indifference—"the food's no better and the company is infinitely worse"—though he did recognize that an officer's commission would have made it easier for him to get around.

Lincoln and Posey were now on the verge of the most thrilling of all their achievements: the recovery of the *Adoration of the Lamb*, the so-called Ghent Altarpiece. The famous polyptych had been done by the brothers Hubert and Jan van Eyck between 1426 and 1432 and had been stolen in 1942 by the Germans from its temporary storage place, the Château of Pau. They had sent the *Lamb* to Paris, then still under Nazi control, but in recent years its whereabouts had become unknown. Posey, like all the army monuments officers, carried around with him photos of the Van Eyck painting, and also of works seized from the Church of Notre-Dame at Bruges, including Michelangelo's early marble piece *Madonna and Child*. Contradictory rumors as to the *Lamb's* present location had been circulating for some time; it was said to be everywhere from the fortress at Ehrenbreitstein (near Koblenz), the vaults of the Berlin Reichsbank, Hitler's retreat at Berchtesgaden, or Göring's estate outside Berlin. From various museum directors in Luxembourg, Posey and Lincoln heard the additional rumor that the Ghent Altarpiece was in fact hidden somewhere in a salt mine.

Early in their stay in Germany, Posey, who had a toothache, went to consult a dentist in the town of Trier. It proved an epochal stroke of good fortune. Posey asked the dentist, as he did nearly everyone, "Have you heard anything about the 'Lamb'?" The dentist nervously said that Posey should talk to his son-in-law, a scholar named Herman Bunjes who had worked before the war with Harvard's Kingsley Porter at Cluny and had then come under Göring's patronage and been made director of the German Institute in Paris. The dentist volunteered to drive with Posey and Lincoln to Bunjes's home in a remote valley. As the trip lengthened, the Americans began to fear some sort of fraud or trap, but they did eventually arrive at Bunjes's cottage, where he lived with his wife and child.

The agitated, distressed Bunjes talked to them freely, with a minimum of prodding; he claimed that he now wanted to work with the Americans and longed to return to Paris, which he'd evacuated just twenty-four hours before its liberation, to complete his book on twelfth-century sculpture. Whatever Bunjes's motives, words poured out, and before the day was over Posey and Lincoln had learned not only that the *The Adoration of the Lamb* was in a salt mine but where the mine was located—at Alt Aussee, near Salzburg in Austria, where the Germans had long been storing hoards of art in preparation for the construction of the Führer Museum at Linz. Concealing their excitement, they politely thanked Bunjes and left. Soon after, he killed himself, his wife, and his child.

Alt Aussee had only recently come under the control of Allied forces, and the mountainous area was known to be harboring remnants of the SS and the retreating German Sixth Army. Though VE-day—"peace" in Europe—had officially been declared on May 7, 1945, danger didn't disappear with the stroke of a pen: that very same night Lincoln's unit was "inconclusively strafed," and another nearby outfit lost more men than during the previous six-month period. Yet Posey and Lincoln, galvanized by their new information, set off the next day for Alt Aussee. After passing through areas of "travel poster beauty," when they reached the mining town they found it already abuzz with contradictory rumors: the mine had already been blown up; the mine was intact but no one was allowed to enter. Carrying small acetylene lamps, Lincoln and Posey walked nearly half a mile into "a horizontal gallery" of the mine; it was, as Lincoln later wrote Cadmus, "deep dark and wet" and as he moved his hand along an interior wall he got shocked twice by live wires. He also "felt something" that, thanks to his engineer combat training at Fort Belvoir, he recognized as undetonated dynamite.

In the morning they were told that it would take from seven to fifteen days to clear away the blocks to the main entrance. Some of the Austrian mine workers had been part of the anti-Nazi Resistance, and they told the two Americans that the previous month several large wooden cases had arrived at the Alt Aussee mine marked MARMOR; NICHT STÜRZEN (Marble, Don't Drop). The cases contained not marble but explosives designed to trigger flooding from the backed-up accumulation of mountain snow. The fulminating devices had been placed in the six mine caverns containing the art deposits: clearly the Germans had intended to blow up their stolen treasures rather than allow them to fall back into enemy hands—just as the SS had burned Himmler's extraordinary collection of stolen paintings before the British could stop them. But the anti-Nazi miners at Alt Aussee foiled the Germans' plan. Before the detonators could be hooked up, the miners, working secretly at night, removed almost all the explosives and hid them along the road under piles of fir boughs.

The morning after they arrived, Lincoln and Posey managed to enter the mine through a narrow passageway off the main chamber. They opened two padlocks on an iron door—and there at their feet, unwrapped, lay the eight panels of *The Adoration of the Lamb*. As Lincoln wrote Fidelma a few days later, they gasped at the sight—it was "incredible in every sense of the word, literally unbelievable, and it was like all the detective stories coming true." Remarkably, still further astonishments lay directly ahead. Not only did they find the Ghent Altarpiece but also, over the next few days, a multiplicity of other treasures that included paintings by Fragonard, Watteau, Gerard Terborch, and Adriaen van Ostade, masterpieces like the Vermeer self-portrait in his Delft studio, four Louvain panels by Dierik Bouts and, lying on a mattress covered with a piece of asphalt paper, Michelangelo's marble Madonna from Bruges.

Posey immediately called in the specialist George Stout from the Twelfth Army Group, who declared conditions in the mine, from a conservator's point of view, safe enough to allow for gradual removal and storage. Lincoln greatly admired Stout: "The nicest man in the world," he was

Lincoln's nominee for "the greatest war hero of all time—he actually saved all the art that everybody else talked about saving." With Stout remaining for a time at the site, the explorations—and the miraculous findings—continued.

Within a few weeks, a second Vermeer *(Astronomer)* was found, as well as a Leonardo and numerous Brueghels, Rembrandts, Raphaels, and Veroneses. The number of recovered works grew to staggering proportions. In the final count some 6,500 paintings, almost all of them works of significance, were brought out of the mine—to say nothing of truckloads of etchings, watercolors, drawings, engravings, statuary, armor, tapestries, and furniture. "There was never anything like this," Lincoln later wrote, "in scale or quality." He summed up the experience in one of his wartime poems, "Arts and Monuments":

> *Presupposing virtuoso vision—scratched, fragmented, or hacked,*
> *Art's intention is barely marred. The residual artifact*
>   *Glimmers steady through years or blood . . .*
> *It's been often observed before: objects we choose to adore*
>   *Don't prevent war but survive it and us.*

Back in New York, Fidelma devotedly saw to it that Lincoln, who was often bitterly cold when working in the mines, got numerous packages of warm clothing. She also sent him magazines and other items in which he'd expressed interest, and spent considerable time, especially during the summer, with members of their inner circle—visiting Pavlik at Wellfleet or staying at the house Jared and Margaret French shared with her brother, Paul, in the Fire Island community of Saltaire. Fidelma enjoyed the atmosphere of serious work that pervaded both places, and still continued, at this point in her life, to turn out drawings and paintings; the others viewed her as a gifted artist, as she unquestionably was, judging from her few surviving works. She was also a gentle presence, quick with sympathy and kindness, though often enigmatic, absorbed in her private obsessions, silent and abstracted. She adored animals and felt attuned to their suffering (when she finally consented to mousetraps at home, she made it clear that she regarded their use as a form of murder).

In her letters to Lincoln or to her brother, Fidelma spoke only vaguely and briefly about her art ("We are about to set off on a sketching expedition"; "I've made a very painstaking study of a dead tree with its branches collapsed about the trunk," and so on). Paul, on the other hand, often sent Lincoln detailed descriptions of his work-in-progress, along with photographs designed to solicit his comments. On one occasion he got a great deal more than he bargained for. In 1945, while still in Germany, Lincoln received pictures from Paul of his new painting, *Lust*, the first in what became a famous series, *The Seven Deadly Sins*.[5]

Lincoln looked at the photos and, typically, pulled no punches in giving Paul, whom he loved and admired, his reaction: "It is a really terrifying and horrible picture. There is not much to be said about it. It is so full of hate and disgust, in an active way, that it is quite paralyzing." But it turned out that Lincoln had a great deal to say—not about anything as trivial as Paul's estimable technique, but about his psychology and values. "I do not understand," he bluntly began, "your aching agony about the flesh. I suppose it partly comes from hating being queer, and partly from [the] curdled catholicism of your nasty youth. I think it is a romantic and immature attitude. . . . I don't think anything as impermanent as flesh is corrupt. . . . Lust isn't so bad, it lasts no time at all and is not destructive. . . . maybe the nicest thing about all of us is our poor half-stiff peters and stretched, hungry cunts."

When Paul defended himself as having achieved in the painting what he set out to do, Lincoln agreed that it was "monstrously well done." But he wouldn't yield the moral ground, insisting that the painting was Paul's "excuse of a personal pathology"; the representation of lust as destructive, Lincoln reiterated, "does not connect with anything in me." Lincoln had grown far beyond the priggish indoctrination of his youth.

Lincoln would be back in New York to continue the argument much sooner than he'd expected, and for the unhappy reason that his mother was suddenly diagnosed with cancer and told she had only a short time to live. (Rose did have cancer, but would in fact survive for a good number of years.) The army granted Lincoln an immediate discharge (as the navy did his brother, George), but several months of bureaucratic delays prevented his instant return. By then he'd become "extremely fed up," loathing Germany more and more. "The war," he wrote Virgil Thomson, "wasn't so bad but the peace is awful."

While awaiting discharge, he kept busy writing articles and continuing to participate in the work of the monuments commission, including setting up Munich's Central Collecting Point for looted art. It helped that his friend Wystan Auden, who, with the rank of major in the U.S. Air Force, was in Europe during the summer of 1945 on some "modest little" government mission relating to bomb damage and that Wystan—at least according to Lincoln—"likes the Germans, he understands them." They were able to see each other only occasionally, but he thought Wystan "quite a curious spectacle in GI uniform and bedroom slippers, being saluted by amazed MPs."

Even so, what others viewed as Lincoln's "glamorous assignment" had for him become "insanely boring." Coming upon a set of "atrocity pictures" during one foray, he felt that he could now "understand Kafka completely"; he thought it might be a good idea to send the pictures throughout the American South, as an antidote to "LIFE's smugness about how awful the Nazis were," with a caption reading "What's wrong with this picture? Nothing, except they were white." He never sent out the "atrocity" photos, but he did mail $275 to Clark Foreman's Southern Conference for Human Welfare to help in its 1946 drive to secure the rights of African Americans, then voting in large numbers for the first time since Reconstruction in the Democratic primaries of five southern states.

Consistent with Lincoln's continuing left-wing take on events, he also let Nelson Rockefeller know what he thought about the role he'd been playing as assistant secretary of state, in pleading the Perón government's case for letting Argentina participate in the United Nations Conference in San Francisco. He was as blunt with Nelson about politics as he'd been with Cadmus about art: "I was personally very upset about the Argentine deal." It could mean, Lincoln insisted, only one thing: "the clear statement of a consistent anti-Soviet policy, the clear support of Perón, the dragooning of the hemisphere."

By way of further provocation, he included the observation that having worked with the Russians of late, he found himself liking them "a lot," as well as finding them "politically aware in a way that their opposite numbers in our armies are not." It took Nelson a month to reply, and when he did, he sounded a vague, cagey, note: "I am terribly anxious to talk to you about so many things. I was very much interested in your comments concerning the Russians, and hope that as time goes by, I will have the opportunity of coming to know them better myself. . . . When you get back, I will give you the whole story on the Argentina situation." If Nelson ever did, Lincoln didn't find the "whole story" persuasive: once back in the States, he signed a protest demanding that the UN expel Argentina because it had become a pro-Nazi refuge.

As the time finally approached for Lincoln's release from the army in September 1945, he summed up his wartime experiences in a letter to Cadmus: "There is my guilt, the guilt of not having faced enough danger, and the pissy gratitude to have my little collection of souvenirs to talk about." As usual Lincoln was being hard on himself, minimizing the hazards he'd faced and the daily hardships he'd lived through, though no longer a youngster, with a minimum of self-dramatizing complaint. He was also making light of his contribution toward the recovery of a significant portion of Western Europe's cultural heritage, a contribution he never, unlike others (John Walker, say, or Francis Henry Taylor), used for glamorous self-promotion. He claimed to have learned only a single lesson from his time in the army: "that one wants almost nothing, and that one can adapt oneself easily to almost anything, and there is nobody to talk to, and so what."

He knew what he wanted to do after he got home, though some unpredictable developments would reshape his priorities. He wanted to write a series of articles, or a book, about the Boston sculptor, painter, and anatomist William Rimmer (1816–79), a man whose work he'd excitedly discovered just before going overseas. He also wanted to do a book on Pavlik's recent paintings. And he wanted, as he cheerily wrote Fidelma, "the largest possible income. . . . I will spend all I can, I promise you, on the wildest things too. I will have a manservant, 2 Afghans, 2 cars, 4 horses, and I will produce 2 ballets every year."

The ballet, of course, was where most of his money—never a large enough amount to match his plans—would go. During the war, his passion for dance, though painfully on hold, hadn't diminished. "I miss the horrors of the ballet world more than I ever thought I could," he wrote Paul, and while still in Europe, he offered Aaron Copland a commission for a new musical score, one that Balanchine would choreograph and Pavlik design. "I won't be able to have my own ballet company," he wrote Aaron, but he thought that perhaps Denham's Monte Carlo (with whom Balanchine had been working and traveling for two years) might provide a home. As it would turn out, he would, after all, again try to build an independent company.

Ballet Society

(1946–1947)

I FIND NEW YORK rather hard to get accustomed to," Lincoln wrote soon after returning home. "With so much choice of activity, you hardly know where to begin." So Lincoln began where he usually did—by doing everything simultaneously. He plunged back into his research on William Rimmer, started work on a slew of articles on varied subjects, rejoined the social whirl, took on his old job as director of the School of American Ballet and—his main preoccupation—began plotting assorted strategies for allowing him to produce ballets again. *En passant,* he accepted membership on MoMA's Board of Trustees, applied for the art critic's job on the New York *Herald Tribune* (they backed and filled, then passed), and proposed to Harvard's Fogg Museum that he edit a "series of classic texts on American art"—an idea that got an enthusiastic response from Agnes Mongan and Paul Sachs but ultimately foundered on the unwillingness of John Walker of the National Gallery, which had a publishing fund, to cosponsor the project. (Walker may have heard that Lincoln had criticized him for inflating his role in the recovery of European art.)[1]

In the midst of this whirlwind, Gaston Lachaise's widow again turned to Lincoln for help. Seventy-five and desperate for funds, Madame Lachaise asked Lincoln to help find buyers for some of her husband's remaining work. More, she wanted him to get a gallery to display the work, to write the catalog for any show that might emerge, *and* to write Gaston Lachaise's biography. Lincoln, his three hands already fully engaged, promptly grew a fourth to cope with Madame's difficult set of assignments—which, as Nelson Rockefeller wrote him, is "typical of your thoughtfulness and loyalty to old friends." In trying to sell Lachaise's *Heroic Size Woman,* priced at ten thousand dollars, he turned first to Nelson, who in Lincoln's view had been the sculptor's "most generous and disinterested friend." But family members talked Nelson out of the purchase. Still, he *did,* through Lincoln, anonymously send Madame Lachaise some money. Lincoln next approached the firm of Knoedler, and under his persuasion they agreed to become Lachaise's agent and to do a show early in 1947 of his work (one that, in Lincoln's view, was "magnificently installed and lit").

The manic pace took its toll. Lincoln gave out the story that he was having serious problems with his eyes, and, accompanied by Fidelma, went off to Williamsburg, Virginia, for a rest of several weeks. He'd had earlier depressive episodes, but this one seems to have been the most severe to date. Subsequently, the doldrums would appear with greater frequency and in darker, more destructive form.

But he and Fidelma were soon enough back in New York and Lincoln back to pursuing a multiplicity of projects, with perhaps a slightly less ferocious pace. During much of 1946 two projects commanded most of his attention: putting together a new production unit for the ballet and finishing up his research on William Rimmer. The second of the two projects would be completed before the end of the year; the first would increasingly take center stage—and stay there.

The volume of Rimmer's surviving work was small—less than a dozen pieces of sculpture (one of which is the statue of Alexander Hamilton in the public gardens on Boston's Commonwealth Avenue), and some score of paintings. Nor could a great deal more be turned up about the artist's personal life, though that little proved intriguing. William's father, Thomas Rimmer, claimed he was the lost Dauphin, son of Louis XVI and Marie Antoinette, and his son entirely supported the claim. William himself—born in 1816—was educated at home and as both a practicing physician and an artist, self-taught. He married, had children, got an occasional commission, and was nearly always wretchedly poor.

Lincoln's championing of Rimmer isn't easily accounted for—it even puzzled Lincoln sometimes. As he once plaintively wrote Agnes Mongan (who dug up a number of Rimmer's drawings for him from deep storage at the Fogg Museum), "I can no longer determine whether he is a monster, a curiosity, or just trash." But that was only a temporary seizure of doubt. Overall Lincoln was deeply committed to the view, surely hyperbolic (as Agnes kept telling him), that Rimmer was a "far more important artist" than William Morris Hunt or Daniel Chester French, that his work "almost prophes[ied] certain American expressionists" and investigated anatomy and "psychological gesture" thirty years before Thomas Eakins. He saw Rimmer as the "type of blasted genius of the American 19th century, as Ryder . . . and Melville," as a man who ultimately failed "to exteriorize his revelation, because he did not live in a workable tradition."[2]

Rimmer's surviving work shows a powerful mastery of form (the granite sculpture *Saint Stephen*, for example) linked to subject matter that was highly melodramatic and full of contained, unexploded violence, with catastrophe and disaster perceptively in the wings and with a heavy emphasis on the nude, muscled male body that decidedly verges on the homoerotic; one drawing, *The Call to Arms*, even sketchily suggests, in the background, a male couple embracing, and the sculpture *Falling Gladiator* can easily be read as camp.

The qualities Lincoln emphasized when writing the catalog for the 1946–47 Rimmer shows at the Whitney and at Boston's Fine Arts Museum themselves make the argument. Lincoln chose to underscore particular aspects of Rimmer's art: "his lifelong moral obsession with the animal nature of man . . . his lifelong obsession with the nude . . . [and an] imagination [that] teemed with equestrian battles, wild charges, the rush of banners, armies sweeping up dizzy parapets, the fall of angels, the thunder of demon wings."

All this—the inflamed, sometimes self-conscious exaggeration, the homoeroticism, the melodrama—were aspects of Lincoln's own multilayered personality. In his private correspondence, he provided still other hints of Rimmer's appeal: "the real tenderness and excitement of his male nudes"; his "cranky, lonely and isolated" character; his "unresolved sensuality and curiously pornographic" tendencies.

Lincoln actually bought one Rimmer painting, *Lion in the Arena*, for himself, describing it to Agnes as "madly beautiful. Or mad." It depicted a corseted male gladiator, sword drawn, confronting what Lincoln tellingly called "a snarling lion which seems to be stuffed, except for the head, and the head is saying GO AWAY YOU HORRID MANS." Writing to Cadmus, Lincoln was still more explicit: "I think he was and did, don't you? That corset and that Queer lioness making paddy paw noises. What a KAMP, but quite alarming. Rimmer was the Jared French of the nineteenth century. His pictures are all sex and the fear of not getting too much or enough of it. Glenway [Wescott] would feel very close to him."

Within four months of returning from the army, Lincoln had worked out a lengthy proposal for a new organization, Ballet Society—right down to the dates, programs, and venues for its first performances. In sending a copy to Virgil Thomson, Lincoln described the proposal as one he'd "adopted after realizing I don't want to tour, or do old works, or take the money that would stop me from working in the way I want to." In thinking through his ideas, Lincoln consulted from the beginning with Balanchine, as well as with the conductor Leon Barzin. But the scope of the concept was (according to the skeptics) ambitious enough to border on the grandiose.[3]

The production of new ballets was only part of Lincoln's overall scheme. He also intended Ballet Society to produce and distribute a series of books on the dance, the first to be a collection of new essays on Vaslav Nijinsky, followed by a collection on Isadora Duncan, a volume of Edwin Denby's dance criticism, and the first "year book of the Ballet Society," an annual that would include documents and designs from the first season, along with commentaries.

As for the ballet itself, Lincoln was dead set against star vehicles or vintage and popular favorites. "We are hungry," he wrote, "for an adventurous taste," and he no longer thought it sufficient merely to "exploit" national themes. Further, Lincoln intended that Ballet Society would produce not solely ballets but "ballet opera" and "chamber opera," create and circulate documentary dance films, publish record albums containing the music used in its performances, award fellowships to gifted young dancers and choreographers, and cooperate with other cultural institutions to produce exhibits and performances "difficult or impossible for one to accomplish alone"—a stately and sublime not to say protean set of goals. What portion of them, if any, the real world would accommodate, remained to be seen.

For Ballet Society's initial performance on November 20, 1946, Lincoln's princely dreams were reduced to modest proportions. Though he'd emphasized a goal of "freshness, care and elegance," none were much in evidence at the chosen site for the first performance—the auditorium of New York City's High School of Needle Trades on West Twenty-fourth Street, a large, bleak space lacking an orchestra pit or clear sight lines, with a shallow stage and hideous murals covering the walls. The program itself seemed more promising: Balanchine's new *The Four Temperaments* (which would become a seminal work), to music by Paul Hindemith that Balanchine had himself commissioned back in 1940, and a new version of the Ravel-Colette *L'Enfant et les Sortilèges* (for which Lincoln and Mina's old friend Aline Bernstein did the decor and costumes). The casts combined "old-timers" like Gisella Caccialanza, Lew Christensen, Pete Martínez, and William Dollar, with a scattering of brilliant newcomers, several of whom—including Tanaquil Le Clercq and Francisco Moncion— would become world famous.

A colossal amount of work went into putting together the November performance. When it was over Lincoln's official stance was that it had gone "as well as I had hoped, and far better than I had feared." But he let Virgil Thomson know privately that he was in fact "very upset" over the general reception; Pavlik, among others, told Lincoln to his face that "with people starving in Europe, it was a disgrace to do anything like" the Ravel piece, and Monroe Wheeler called it "a betrayal"—though of what he didn't say. Lincoln himself thought the Ravel looked "dowdy"; he and Balanchine had "wanted it to look like a children's performance at graduation, which in a way it was . . . it should have been clearer and simpler." Virgil, not given to sweetness, sent Lincoln a comforting note, explaining that the Ravel, wherever performed, was usually "a flop" because it was so difficult to stage convincingly. All the same Virgil regarded it as "beautiful" and told Lincoln he was "delighted that you gave it."

The Four Temperaments got a more favorable response, though the range of reaction was wide. Leonard Bernstein "hated" it and called it "such corn" ("a specialist, he should know," Lincoln remarked). And, according to Lincoln, "many of the avantguardists" of MoMA also "loathed" it; "I suppose," Lincoln scornfully noted, "I should have had decor by Stuart Davis or Georgia O'Keeffe." There were many (justified) complaints about the Kurt Seligmann costumes, which were so elaborate that, as one viewer put it, "It took all of Mr. Balanchine's genius, which is certainly inestimable, to hold them down, so to speak." Within the month, Balanchine decided to change what Lincoln called the "music-hall ending" of *The Four Temperaments*, and over the next few years, he stripped away the costumes and further reworked the ballet.

But there were some who immediately recognized the brilliance and importance of *The Four Temperaments*, including Edwin Denby, regarded by many as the best dance critic of the day, as well as the French cultural attaché, Claude Lévi-Strauss, later a major figure in the world of anthropology, who wrote Lincoln that "it is the most magnificent ballet I have seen since the great days of Diaghilev." Lincoln himself thought the Balanchine work "miraculous," "indescribably brilliant," though also "insanely difficult to dance . . . the only justification I have," he wrote Lucia Chase of Ballet Theatre, is to enable Balanchine "to do exactly what he wants to do in the way he wants to do it." But it was left to Martha Graham, who was present as Lincoln's guest at the performance, to strike the warmest note: "Have courage, dear heart, do not let the ice bergs armored in ermine touch you. Let them reduce themselves to tinkling cubes."

The initial performance proved more expensive than Lincoln had intended—but that was a predictable given for him. He justified the extra outlay as being necessary—a "supreme effort to get the thing launched"— and confided to Tom Fisher, husband of Ruth Page, that over the two-year period 1946–48 he expected to invest one hundred thousand dollars. Lincoln didn't have that kind of capital at the time but seems to have felt he could raise it. Possibly he arrived at the figure by assuming that Ballet Society's fifty-dollar membership fee (it also had a cheaper fifteen-dollar rate, with fewer privileges) would sell widely. But it would take twelve hundred such subscriptions to make a go of it, and as of late 1946, he hadn't secured nearly that number.

His brother, George, with understandable impatience, tried to make Lincoln face the reality of his financial situation. The major part of his holdings, George pointed out, was some fifteen thousand shares of Federated stock (then selling at about twenty-five dollars a share), which George estimated would bring Lincoln about twenty-two thousand dollars in dividends during 1947. In addition he owned fifty thousand dollars' worth of securities, which Rose had put into a trust fund for him back in 1941. Finally he had thirty-nine thousand dollars in a "personal account" of cash and securities, the only sum free of any restrictions.

George strongly urged him not to dip into that account, no matter how rough things got in trying to balance the Ballet Society books: "Any kind of prudence would indicate that you keep this fund available . . .

against that inevitable rainy day where a crisis in your personal affairs may make unencumbered funds indispensable." Taking out a loan from *any* source would be preferable, George advised, to invading the limited amount of available capital he had. Yet a mere six weeks after George offered his well-considered advice, Lincoln told his brother that in order to sustain Ballet Society's commitments, he intended to cash in twenty thousand of the thirty-nine-thousand-dollar "personal account."

Convinced that Lincoln was about to make a terrible mistake—the securities in the portfolio were underpriced at the moment—George turned to his mother for help in staving off his brother's impetuosity. Rose's health had been improving of late; having lived for a time with George and his wife, dutifully attended to by Lincoln (and even more so by Fidelma), she'd recently moved into a place of her own and was feeling up to a more active life. Lincoln had earlier decided he couldn't, in conscience, again ask Rose for money, given how generous she'd always been to him in the past. But George bypassed Lincoln's scruples, went directly to his mother and advised her that in order to forestall Lincoln's decision to sell securities, she simply had to loan him the needed twenty thousand dollars (and to equalize it, in terms of her other two children, had to write a codicil to her will). Rose, of course, went along with George's advice, and for 1947 at least, Lincoln, though personally embarrassed at once again being bailed out by one of his parents, was able to continue Ballet Society's activities.

He did curtail some of the Society's planned subsidiary activities, like books and annuals, but continued to offer commissions to a multiplicity of artists that came to include (some of them not well known at the time) Dorothea Tanning, Morris Graves and Alvin Colt, Esteban Francis for scenery and costumes, Jane and Paul Bowles for a one-act opera, Elliott Carter, John Cage and Virgil Thomson for musical composition, Merce Cunningham, Todd Bolender, William Dollar, and Lew Christensen for choreography—and for the ballet score that became *Orpheus*, Igor Stravinsky. The five-thousand-dollar Stravinsky commission, by far the largest offered, came from the School of American Ballet's surplus funds—the only commission the School had ever given. *Orpheus* was scheduled for Ballet Society's 1947–48 season.[4]

Ballet Society's next event took place in mid-December 1946 in MoMA's attractive auditorium, and consisted of an ambitious evening of dance films and dance photography. Less than a month later, this time in the auditorium at Hunter College, Lincoln produced a second evening of ballet. Three works were shown: *Pastorela*, with a book by Pete Martínez, choreography by Lew Christensen, and music by Paul Bowles; the first American stage performance of *Renard*, with music and book by Stravinsky, choreography by Balanchine, and decor by Esteban Francis; and finally, Élie Cartier-Bresson's Javanese dancers, led by, in one critic's appraisal, the "altogether remarkable" Ratna Mohini. The program was repeated twice, apparently with some variation, on January 13 and 14, 1947.

Renard was the big hit. Stravinsky attended on both evenings and, according to Lincoln, said "he had not ever had a better performance since Diaghilev." Esteban Francis's costumes and scenery were much admired; Lincoln called them, with trademark enthusiasm, "staggeringly and fantastically good." He was also delighted with the dancing of Mary Ellen Moylan, the company's new ballerina (though she was soon performing primarily with Ballet Theatre), and he also thought Lew Christensen— "though not up to his old slimness"—did "very well" in *Pastorela*.

But Pete's ballet wasn't generally well received. He'd again been living with Fidelma and Lincoln and had worked hard on *Pastorela*, recognizing, following a knee injury that had recently forced him to retire as a dancer, that if it proved successful, a new kind of career in ballet might open up for him. But it was not to be. Pete would manage to spend his life in the world of dance, but in the teaching and administrative areas. At the close of 1947, he went to live for a time in Norfolk, Virginia, where he taught ballet to (as Lincoln put it) "the local queens . . . and about 100 children." Pete had never been equipped to become a major dancer or choreographer, but he'd always been a superior human being and lover, a charming companion, "kind . . . madly funny and cheerful"—and his friendship with Fidelma and Lincoln would continue, long distance, for many years.

Fidelma had always adored Pete, and she greatly missed him after he left the city. But in the late forties, she still had her art for consolation and still worked at it with a fair amount of consistency. Lincoln thought she was making "enormous progress" in tempera; at the moment he particularly liked a self-portrait in progress and "quite a large" Nantucket landscape. Sometimes Fidelma would go off without Lincoln for several weeks on a working vacation. He almost always joined her at Fire Island, where they consistently summered, but she sometimes spent time in Provincetown or Nantucket along with Jared and Margaret French, her brother, Paul, and (in the late forties) his then-lover, the brilliant young painter George Tooker. These were serious working vacations, with most socializing confined to mealtimes.

Reginald Marsh, Tooker's main teacher (as well as good friend), had urged him to work not in oil but in egg tempera—the favored medium not only of Fidelma and Paul but of most of the painters in Lincoln's circle. He thought especially highly of Tooker and from the beginning of his career bought his paintings. He described the young artist in these years as "thin and amethyst . . . full of reverence for Italy, and reservations about art and life." Tooker's personality was gentle, grave, and somewhat reserved. He "adored" Fidelma and also admired her talent; he thought she and Margaret French were both "very gifted" and regretted that neither seemed to have "much drive," both sharing the view that their husbands' work was "the more important."

"It was always lovely seeing Fido," Tooker has said, especially away from New York, where she seemed less relaxed due to her assorted "hostess" obligations (these, in time, would become a painful source of anxiety). Tooker found Fidelma's graceful simplicity a welcome relief from the company of Jared French, who could be surly and morose (he once refused even to shake Tooker's hand, which was never again proffered). Jared, as Tooker well knew, was still sleeping with Cadmus, though they were purportedly *ex*-lovers. Margaret French, whom Tooker thought "an attractive, appealing person," knew in general outline, as did Fidelma, all about the various Bloomsbury-like sexual configurations. According to Tooker, Margaret, who was wealthy, was very much in love with Jared and chose to play the role of "a devoted wife" not given to commenting on or complaining about her husband's behavior. In that regard she and Fidelma had much in common.

Other occasional guests during the Provincetown summer of 1947 included Isherwood and his current lover, Bill Caskey. In New York, Lincoln and Fidelma saw them often; Lincoln thought Isherwood "really quite wonderful; he is not easy to be with; he is extremely, tinglingly nervous, but in dashes he is wildly funny." E. M. Forster was also in the States that summer, and they saw a fair amount of him as well; they found him "very sweet" and Forster, in turn, wrote them effusive thanks for their hospitality.

Lincoln's overheated social life was matched, and then some, by his professional enterprises. He managed, between dealing with the countless details of Ballet Society performances—arranging for venues, dealing with unions, coaxing out scenarios, scores, and subscriptions, arguing over designs—to simultaneously put together for publication a book of Pavlik's drawings and silverpoints, complete with an introduction, plates, biographical notes, and a reproduction of the catalog James Thrall Soby had done for Tchelitchev's 1942 show at MoMA. In the 1940s Tchelitchev was still regarded as a major figure (and as a modernist), the battle between realism and abstraction not decided until the 1950s in the latter's favor. Lincoln's work on the book was made doubly difficult by having the ever-dissatisfied and contentious Pavlik constantly looking over his shoulder. Up to that point, nothing Lincoln had written about his friend had pleased Pavlik. Still, despite his disgruntled obstructionism, Lincoln, in as rare a disinterested fashion as any writer can be expected to summon, pressed ahead and saw the book published in the fall of 1947.[5]

By this point Balanchine was no longer on the scene. Along with his new bride, the twenty-one-year-old dancer Maria Tallchief, he'd left for Paris some months earlier to take up a six-month engagement as guest ballet master with the Opéra. It was Balanchine's first trip to Europe in more than a dozen years, and during his stay, he created, to music by Bizet, *Le Palais de Cristal* (later known as *Symphony in C*), one of the choreographic high points of his career. Yet on the whole he wasn't happy with conditions at the Opéra, or with Paris itself. Though never a letter writer, Balanchine sent half a dozen to Lincoln while away, filling them, uncharacteristically, with complaints and worries, and signing them, no less uncharacteristically, "Love, George."[6]

Balanchine's complaints were varied but interlinked. He found Paris "very provincial," and devoid of "*decent* choreographers." Serge Lifar, still under suspicion of having collaborated with the Nazis, had not yet been returned to his post at the Opéra, but he soon would be and people discussed him continually; that mystified Balanchine, who regarded Lifar's "so-called choreography" as not "worth talking about." It didn't help that when Balanchine staged *Apollo* at the Opéra, several critics—"friends of Lifar"—wrote hostile pieces; Balanchine even heard "that they have gone so far as to intimate that every step was stolen from Lifar's ballets." He claimed not to "have the time to listen to or read such petty 'stuff' "—yet the charge rankled enough for him to repeat it to Lincoln.

The people who actually worked at the Opéra were in fact "really very nice" to Balanchine, and invariably called him "maître." But that didn't help in getting serious work done in a timely way. Paris, of course, was still licking its wartime wounds, and there were shortages of all kinds. But more was involved. Balanchine saw Lincoln's sister, Mina, several times— she was on an extended research trip preparatory to putting together a collection of Proust's letters—and they shared their frustration (in Mina's words) that "Paris is much too small, too full of gossip, too inefficient . . . that the excessive politesse with which people promise things they never do, is enough to drive one mad." (Or as Balanchine himself more succinctly put it, "Lives are arranged carefully around 'the restaurant.' ") Mina assured Lincoln that he needn't "have the slightest worry of George's ever wanting to work here again"—not even piano scores were available, making him unable to "try out music to use."

But Balanchine's worries focused more on New York than on Paris. "I don't understand very well what is going to happen with our Ballet Society," he plaintively wrote Lincoln in May 1947. Did they have a future? During Balanchine's absence the Society gave two more performances. The first, in the gruesome Needle Trades auditorium on March 26, had been marked by a triple premiere: Elliott Carter and John Taras's *The Minotaur*, the Todd Bolender–Esteban Francis *Zodiac*, and William Dollar's *Highland Fling*.

The other performance took place on May 18 in the prestigious Ziegfeld Theatre and consisted of a somewhat daring two-part program:

Lew Christensen's *Blackface* and the Cage-Noguchi-Cunningham collaborative effort, *The Seasons*. *Blackface* featured the splendid black dancer Talley Beatty (trained by the pioneering Katherine Dunham); Lincoln had earlier tried to persuade an uninterested Virgil Thomson to compose music for a new work he wanted to commission with Beatty as choreographer.

The world of modern dance had led the way in the 1940s in training and hiring nonwhite performers. This was especially true, of course, with the black-led companies formed by Dunham, Pearl Primus, and Wilson Williams, but a few white dancers and choreographers, like Helen Tamiris and, in particular, Martha Graham, also advanced the multicultural cause. By way of contrast, the world of ballet was (and to a considerable extent remains) a mostly white enterprise. It says a good deal about the state of Lincoln's political consciousness that he put *Blackface* on the boards and made a place for Talley Beatty in the august precincts of Ballet Society.

As for *The Seasons*, Lincoln had previously known all three of the artists he commissioned. He didn't much like Noguchi, and didn't know Cage and Cunningham well (Cunningham had been a pupil at SAB and would later teach there briefly). But of the little he saw of both men, he found them agreeable enough; the problem, as he wrote Cadmus, is that "I wish I believed in them more." Of the five new pieces presented in the March and May programs, none had much of an impact, though *The Seasons* did have its admirers and would be presented again the following year.

In Paris, meanwhile, Balanchine was witness to the alacritous rise and fall of companies at a pace that seemed alarming even for the unstable world of the ballet. Of the recent new companies, two had seemed especially promising. The "Ballets des Champs-Élysées," which resulted from the combined effort of Boris Kochno, Christian Bérard, and Jean Cocteau, prominently featured the youthful choreographer Roland Petit. In 1948 Petit would break away to form his own "Ballets de Paris," and even before then, the "Champs-Élysées" came to New York in March 1947, with (according to Lincoln) "no theatre, contract, money or prospects." The French consulate called on Lincoln for help, and he found that Kochno and Petit—as a result of the Hollywood producer Mike Todd having given them a bad check—had "about $25 between them and strict hunger." But Lincoln was deep into his own financial problems (in 1947 Ballet Society had brought in only twenty thousand dollars from membership fees, plus an additional fifteen thousand from contributions); he extended his sympathy to Kochno, but decided not to involve himself in the "Champs-Élysées' " affairs.

The other potentially promising new company was the creation of the immensely wealthy Marquis de Cuevas. He'd immediately succeeded in hiring, among others, Toumanova, Rosella Hightower, and André Eglevsky, and many predicted that with his millions de Cuevas would sweep the field. Even Balanchine thought the de Cuevas company might "turn out to be very good . . . but knowing the Marquis' usual way of confusing matters—no one knows what will happen." Besides, among de Cuevas's stars, Toumanova, in Balanchine's opinion, was "no longer the same person she used to be. She is primarily interested in making money and glorifying Toumanova." (Even so, a year later Balanchine created the second movement of *Le Palais de Cristal* for her.)

In regard to developments back in the States, Balanchine expressed his concern and confusion to Lincoln about conflicting rumors he'd heard regarding the relationship between Lucia Chase's Ballet Theatre and Ballet Society. The rumors had run the gamut: Lucia (a) was about to disband for lack of funds, (b) was going to be backed by "a new elaborate corporation with lots of prominent men," (c) "wants to replenish her repertoire with our works," and (d) had reached an agreement with Lincoln to merge their two companies. "Are we going to exist," Balanchine ruefully asked Lincoln, "or will it be Ballet Theatre?" He felt "it would be a pity to give everything to Lucia," and couldn't understand why "everyone helps that organization which doesn't really exist." Besides, he personally felt "very strongly against Nora Kaye and Alicia Alonso," two of Ballet Theatre's stars, "dancing my ballets," characterizing both as "mythical ballerinas." (But again, Balanchine would create *Theme and Variations* for Alonso in 1947, and a few years later would welcome Kaye into the company.)

Balanchine's own strong preference, as he wrote Lincoln, was "to try and make a go of our previous plans"; he wanted, from now on, "to devote all my time towards making a good American company." After what he'd seen in Europe, "one can only realize how many centuries they are behind us." If, he wrote further, "financially, this is impossible then let us try and make the best of the arrangement with Ballet Theatre so that, at least, we will be independent." While still in Europe, Balanchine talked to Mina about her helping to raise money for Ballet Society. She said she wasn't very good at that sort of thing but would try. The two agreed, as Mina conveyed to Lincoln, "that by far your best bet for a backer for the ballet is a Jewish business man." She shrewdly advised Lincoln *not* to try raising money himself: "You make the most convincing things sound questionable . . . deep down you are a person of sure direction, wisdom and patience, but chemically you are . . . too much influenced by the inevitable discrepancy between the perfection of the idea in the mind and its execution."

Lincoln's lack of success at fund-raising was precisely why he'd become involved in negotiations with Lucia Chase—and they were just as tangled and murky as Balanchine, even from a distance, had perceived. By late 1947 Lincoln was (as he wrote Virgil) "having a very hard time about money for Ballet Society . . . nobody cares about what we do; it has no chic and I don't know whether to try to get a 'Committee' of people on or not."

He decided not, but that left the money issue unresolved, and Lincoln feeling somewhat desperate: "I've bitten off more than I can really chew this year," he wrote Ruth Page, "and I have to fight like hell to survive."[7]

Lucia Chase had been having considerable problems of her own. The early success of Ballet Theatre—which, remarkably, had included a well-received engagement in England in the summer of 1946—declined so precipitously thereafter that the company would have to disband for most of 1948 to save money. At the height of her initial triumph Chase had seemed indifferent to SAB and Ballet Society (though she did become a subscription member), and even, at times, hostile. It got to the point in the fall of 1946 when Lincoln had to formally express his concern over "the marked unfriendly feeling which has been directed against our school by various choreographers and dancers of the Ballet Theatre."

Publicly Lincoln several times declared—in language more exaggerated than he felt—his sense of "the great service that the Ballet Theatre has made" and his desire "to cooperate in every possible way" with the company. Privately he was more candid: "I find her [Chase] temperamentally unsuited to work with me; she has never been conscious of the real lines of contemporary creative art; her taste was formed by [Mikhail] Mordkin and never changed" (Chase had earlier danced with Mordkin's company and been his chief financial backer). But Lincoln's criticism was somewhat unfair; for at least some portion of its early history, Ballet Theatre had been distinctively open to contemporary dance and to the work of a variety of choreographers, including Eugene Loring, Agnes de Mille, and Antony Tudor.

But, as financial problems deepened for both organizations during 1947, the sense grew that they needed each other to survive, and *politesse* now became the dominant mode of discourse. In June of that year, Chase wrote to Balanchine, who was still in Paris asking him to do two ballets for her—one of which would be his Ballet Society piece *Divertimento*. Balanchine asked Lincoln to serve as intermediary and instructed him to say "I could do something for her with the condition that I would receive lots of money—otherwise, the artistic part of it, does not interest me at all. I have all the 'soul' satisfaction I want working with our own organization." Balanchine saw no reason, though—"if it's agreeable to you"—why they shouldn't let her do *Divertimento*.

Lincoln carried out Balanchine's instructions to the letter. He relayed Balanchine's willingness to work with Chase on "one or two ballets, but at the moment he cannot say which, because he does not know in detail what you need, or what music is available." As for *Divertimento*, Lincoln made sure she understood that the ballet was only twelve minutes long, "is most difficult to dance," and would be "useless as a vehicle for [Igor] Youskevitch," her leading male dancer. Lincoln also made clear that Balanchine had two offers for Broadway shows in hand, as well as an appeal from

Boris Morros of United Artists to return to Hollywood. "If you seriously want him to work," Lincoln delicately warned Chase, "he would have to get an equivalent security." Lincoln further added that Balanchine was about to go to Monte Carlo to talk with the Marquis de Cuevas, who, Lincoln cheerfully added, "must be mad, as he has paid for Bill Dollar, Yvonne Patterson and four of our kids to go over."

Soon after this exchange Lincoln received a "puzzled" letter from Igor Stravinsky. He, too, it turned out, had in July 1947 gotten a letter from Chase, and now quoted it to Lincoln: "I have talked a great deal with Lincoln [Chase wrote], who has been most enthusiastic in helping us, and he has even said he might let us do your new ballet [*Orpheus*] for him next spring." If Lincoln had said any such thing, there's no record of it, though there's the off-chance that in one of his splurges of excess enthusiasm he'd in fact offered Chase the Stravinsky piece. But Lincoln reassured a mystified Stravinsky that Ballet Society, not Ballet Theatre, would be the producer of *Orpheus*. Stravinsky reported being "entirely absorbed" by the new ballet and "anxiously awaiting George back from Paris."

Balanchine returned the very next month, in late August 1947, looking, Lincoln thought, "rather thin but very handsome, and is quite happy with Maria Tallchief." Balanchine left almost immediately for California to work with Stravinsky for a week on *Orpheus*. On his return he and Lucia Chase came to terms on a new ballet—*Theme and Variations* (to music by Tchaikovsky) which had its premiere in late November 1947 and starred none other than Alicia Alonso, the ballerina Balanchine had earlier discounted as "mythical." It proved a great critical and public success, marking the moment, in Lincoln's opinion, when Balanchine finally achieved his due after nearly fifteen years of work in the United States. Ironically Lincoln and Pavlik agreed that *Theme and Variations* "is not at all a first-class work."

Meanwhile Lincoln and Chase continued to assure each other—a certain air of unreality surrounding their sugarcoated words—of their utmost mutual regard and their eagerness to find some way for their companies to cooperate. Lincoln solemnly asserted that he "would like to think we are friends, in spite of being professional rivals," and expressed the hope that in the future they could discuss ways in which "some combination could be effected." Chase was equally insistent as to her interest in discussing some possible joint arrangement. Included in the fancy footwork between the two were apologies on both sides—Lincoln for a *Telegraph* article assigning negative remarks to him about Ballet Theatre that he claimed "were not mine" (though they almost certainly were), and Chase for "a wrong impression" Lincoln had "somehow" gotten that she'd made unfavorable comments about Ballet Society in public (as she almost certainly did).

The delicate minuet between the two, as well as several serious proposals, would continue throughout 1948 (when Ballet Theatre went on a forced sabbatical) and well into 1949. Lincoln did emphasize to Chase that in any joint enterprise he "could not attempt to assume a penny of risk," as he had "no money, except what we get from box-office." This was not precisely true, since the Society had taken in fifteen thousand dollars from membership subscriptions during the first year of its existence, and during the second, twenty thousand, plus an additional twenty-five thousand in contributions. Lincoln had to contribute a total of sixty-five thousand dollars of his own money during both years in order to keep Ballet Society afloat (never a truly rich man, he gave away a larger proportion of his total wealth than most patrons of the arts ever do), and even so, the Society had an ongoing deficit of nearly forty thousand dollars.

George Kirstein continued to warn his brother against his free-spending ways, yet when George was asked to approve a newsletter to Ballet Society's membership that included the phrase "Mr. Kirstein has again contributed $65,000, which completely depletes his resources," he protested the exaggeration. "It seems to me," George remarked, "that such a strong sentence makes it appear as though Lincoln were seeking entrance to a charitable institution, which fortunately is far from the facts."

After the Society's disappointing first season in 1946–47, Lincoln knew the odds were slight that he could make a success of the venture. Yet he felt a renewed determination to try and make a go of it. He fired the company's general manager and replaced him with his old friend Frances Hawkins, who'd earlier proved a marvel of efficiency when handling the affairs of Ballet Caravan. Frances is "sensational," Lincoln reported, and he felt "for the first time, some sort of assurance that if I drop dead, at least the idea can go on."

For the Society's fifth presentation in November 1947 (which included the premiere of Balanchine's *Symphonie Concertante*, starring Tallchief and Le Clercq), Lincoln was tempted to rent the Metropolitan Opera. But he had the sense to back away from their fifteen-thousand-dollar fee, realizing that all the unions involved in the production would, in the face of such seeming affluence, have demanded substantial wage hikes and pushed the budget far beyond what was feasible; as Lincoln put it, booking the Met would have amounted to "an ostentatious display of cash that we really have not got." He decided to rent instead the New York City Center. It was a seemingly inconsequential decision, yet one that would have profound consequences.[8]

City Center was a large mosquelike building on West Fifty-fifth Street in Manhattan known as Mecca Temple that had been erected in 1924 by the Shriners. During the Depression the Shriners had fallen far behind in mortgage payments and real estate taxes, and in addition, the building had deteriorated badly. The city had finally foreclosed in 1942, after which it held formal title to the property. No one, however, seemed to know what to do with the white elephant. Mayor La Guardia gave Newbold Morris, president of the city council, scion of a wealthy family and a man interested in the arts, the general assignment of putting idle city-owned properties to constructive use.

Enter a middle-aged lawyer named Morton Baum, who had earlier served on the city's Board of Aldermen and was himself much drawn to the performing arts. He and Newbold Morris together inspected City Center and found, amid dilapidation and debris, an impressive (though rather hideous) theater. It had a wide proscenium and a well-equipped stage. It also had a seating capacity close to that of Carnegie Hall (2,700) and comparable to the largest theater in the city, the Metropolitan Opera House (3,400). The sight lines, moreover, were then (though not currently) splendid; the broad stage could be seen from nearly every seat in the house. Morris and Baum more or less simultaneously had the same idea: Why not have the City of New York itself operate the theater for the benefit of the public?

And so it had come to be—a city center devoted to cultural events that included opera, ballet, music, and drama, and with low ticket prices within the reach of all. Within a mere three years City Center was a going enterprise, offering a wide variety of performances to near-capacity audiences. During its initial few years Leonard Bernstein served as director of the New York City Symphony and Laszlo Halasz headed the City Center Opera (the two men, however, soon came into conflict—Halasz was an old-school task master with the orchestra, "Lenny" its indulgent pal—and by 1947, Bernstein had resigned).

As for ballet, the City Center had earlier served as the New York home for Denham's Ballet Russe de Monte Carlo. During the 1944–45 season, Balanchine had worked with the Denham company and had brilliantly revitalized it. But after he departed, the company had again become dispirited, the corps sloppy, and the repertory reliant on warhorse classics, with no new ballets offered. By the 1946–47 season Baum—who now chaired the center's executive committee—had become unhappy with the Ballet Russe. At just this time Sol Hurok gave up managing Lucia Chase's Ballet Theatre and booked de Basil's company into her slot at the Metropolitan. That left Chase without an obvious space to perform, and she accepted Baum's offer to present Ballet Theatre at the City Center—though she did so reluctantly, since it meant a drastic cut in ticket prices (from a $4.80 top at the Met to $2.50 at the Center), with a parallel drop in revenues.

Ballet Theatre's twice-a-year three-week seasons began in May 1946 and proved popular with both critics and audiences. It looked as if a successful new partnership had emerged. Then, one day during the winter of

1947–48, Baum by chance wandered into a Ballet Society rehearsal. Lincoln had rented the Center for the company's second season, planned as a series of four Monday evenings; when Baum happened by, the Society had already given (on November 12, 1947) its inaugural program, featuring *Symphonie Concertante*, as well as the season's second performance (on February 9, 1948), the highlight of which was the premiere of Balanchine's *The Triumph of Bacchus and Ariadne*, with a remarkable cast that included Magallanes, Le Clercq, Marie-Jeanne, Moncion, and old-timers Lew Christensen and Charles Laskey. Lincoln had been happy with both performances, and particularly with the first one: "It was heavenly, and Balanchine's new ballet [*Concertante*] is unreal it is so lovely."

The rehearsal Baum happened to witness was for the final two programs: *Symphony in C* on March 22 and the long-awaited Stravinsky-Balanchine *Orpheus*, due to premiere on April 28. Watching the dancers, Baum (in his own words) felt overwhelmed, "enthralled by the artistic beauty" of what he saw. He would later describe the experience as something of an epiphany: "the thought flashed through . . . [my] mind. There was the nucleus for a great ballet company—the Center's own company," a concept he'd discussed inconclusively with John Martin and Agnes de Mille as far back as 1944.

At this point Baum and Lincoln had never met, but Baum immediately made an appointment to go to Lincoln's office the next day. When he arrived he found Lincoln himself, Frances Hawkins, and Lincoln's new secretary, Betty Cage (who would soon become a dominant force in the ballet's affairs). Lincoln impressed Baum as an "energetic personality of tremendous vitality and artistic dedication." For his part Lincoln would later describe Baum as "a man of consummate warmth, toughness, political sagacity, and sterling integrity." Clearly it was a match. At least for the time being.

Baum was somewhat taken aback, though, at Lincoln's "bitter mood of complete despair and frustration." Though the two men talked at length, it's doubtful that Lincoln confided all the elements contributing to his current distress. He almost certainly shared with Baum an ongoing concern about finding the money to keep Ballet Society going. ("If I cannot raise my deficit this year," Lincoln had recently written Tom Fisher, "I shall dispose of my properties to whoever will pay most for them, and devote myself to raising pigs and chickens.")

But it seems unlikely that he would have told Baum, ecstatic at what he'd just seen of *Orpheus*, that Tchelitchev had recently thrown a sizeable monkey wrench into plans for the ballet. Pavlik had initially refused to do the decor for *Orpheus;* he'd decided to focus entirely on painting and drawing and to have nothing further to do with ballet, where (as Lincoln paraphrased Pavlik's attitude) "the score lasts and can be performed in concert, [but] the stage designer's work is lost." Stravinsky had succeeded in getting Pavlik to change his mind and by the summer of 1947 he'd been hard at work and full of ideas about how *Orpheus* should look.[9]

Even so, Lincoln remained concerned. Pavlik was in the midst of one of his negative phases about Balanchine—"he doesn't care a bit what I have to say, neither do I care to tell him because he is like myself a sort of 'obsessed machine.' " Also Pavlik was in one of his hectoring moods in regard to Lincoln: "I am very fond of you . . . but there are moments of confusion in you on account of too much enthusiasm. It is a most wonderful quality and comes from goodness only—from the best in a human being. But it mustn't be wasted on nonsense." The particular "nonsense" Pavlik had in mind was Lincoln's attempt to persuade the painter Dorothea Tanning to do the decor for a ballet *(The Favorite)* centered on the racetrack—what she and Pavlik referred to as "the horsey ballet." It would never reach the starting gate.

Beyond Pavlik's general negativity, Lincoln was also worried about the ideas for *Orpheus* that he'd begun to send back East. Tchelitchev apparently felt (as Lincoln wrote Stravinsky) that "the essence of the *Orpheus* legend is understood only by him," and he was fixed in his notion that the story centered on the fate of the artist, on the creative figure who "penetrates the mysteries of life" and, because of that, is destroyed. "I am terrified," Lincoln wrote Stravinsky, "lest he dream up a whole production which has nothing to do with your score; he is quite capable of so doing, and then you would not want it, or he would not, and then the wonderful collaboration that Balanchine imagined goes to pieces." Lincoln was right to worry. By the fall of 1947 Pavlik had angrily backed out of the collaboration.

After considering various replacements, including the French designer André Beaurepaire, the collaborators decided not to approach another painter but to concentrate on "lights and certain sculptured forms." Lincoln had previously worked with both the lighting designer Jean Rosenthal, about whom he was enthusiastic, and the sculptor Isamu Noguchi, about whom he was somewhat less so. But as Lincoln wrote Stravinsky, for this assignment Noguchi seemed perfect: "He has a charming delicacy and justice of handling forms; they are not wildly original, but he creates space and airiness, and this is what Balanchine wants." With Stravinsky agreeing to conduct, the team was in place for what would be the most important event in Ballet Society's history.

The Art World

(1948)

Throughout the two-year-long preparation for the premiere of *Orpheus*, Lincoln, never happy without a multitude of simultaneous projects, was active on a number of other fronts, professional and personal. When, later in life, he would say that 1948 marked the decisive turning point for him, the clearing in the woods, he centrally had in mind the new connection with Morton Baum and the City Center. No other development during this period was of comparable importance. But several other enterprises and commitments made a distinctive contribution to his sense that, having just turned forty, he'd entered upon the determining period of his life.

On the personal side there were several watershed exits and entrances. Lincoln's beloved Pete Martínez, accompanied by his current boyfriend, had by late 1947 already left the New York City area, to settle, eventually, in California. Pete and Lincoln would remain in touch for many years, but inevitably the relationship became attenuated. Even before Pete's departure Lincoln had begun seeing something of a handsome young man with the arresting name of Jensen ("Jens") Yow. The name belied his look; Jens was Asian neither in feature nor family background, but rather a classically sturdy, blond, likable, all-American type—though a thoughtful, quiet, independent-minded version thereof and, as Lincoln described him, "very shy, he simply evaporates in official atmospheres." Growing up on a farm near Henderson, North Carolina, Jensen had shown an early artistic bent and had come to New York in 1946 specifically to study at Cooper Union and the Art Students League.[1]

At the League he'd met Paul Cadmus, who introduced him to Lincoln and Fidelma. "I *adore* Fidelma," Jensen wrote Paul soon after first meeting the pair; "she's so like you." As for Lincoln, Jensen reported back to Paul that "we got along quite wonderfully together. I think your description of him," Jens admonished, "was a little harsh, but then of course you've known him a long time. Anyhow, I like him very much and *very* much enjoy his enthusiasms. The way he raves on about you and Jerry [French] and Pavel is wonderful." When Lincoln took Jensen to meet Pavlik, Jens had a less enthusiastic response: He "talked incoherently for the hour we were there about Gertrude Stein, the artistic aristocracy, the Universe, the ballet, etc."

Jens would not become simply another of Lincoln's "blond young men" but rather, after the romantic phase of their relationship ended ("sex was minimal with people he loved," Jens has said of Lincoln), a loyal and devoted friend to Lincoln throughout his life. In the late 1940s Jens had an apartment on Bethune Street in Greenwich Village, but after Lincoln, in 1951, bought a house near Gramercy Park on Nineteenth Street (which would become his permanent home), Jens lived with him and Fidelma until 1958. He then took an apartment of his own and would eventually buy a house in New Jersey. But he never lost touch with Lincoln and Fidelma, and many years later, beginning in 1985, he'd use a room in their house as a studio.

In the late forties, as a poor student worried about a job and money, Jens was grateful when Lincoln got him work at the Pippin Press, a silkscreening firm he'd originated some years back. The press had by then reproduced, in limited editions, works by, among others, Picasso, Tchelitchev, and Ben Shahn, but it still hadn't turned a profit, and so early in 1948 began to accept commissions from selected educational organizations. Lincoln had never much involved himself in the daily workings of the press; the ballet absorbed most of his time in the late forties, and what remained was invested in assorted projects relating to the art world, to activities at MoMA and, in particular, to resuscitating the reputation of Elie Nadelman.

The Polish-born Nadelman had been an instant sensation after his first show in Paris in 1909, had moved to the United States during World War I, married a wealthy socialite in the 1920s, and lived in a mansion overlooking the Hudson staffed by a retinue of servants. His gilded life came to a halt when the couple lost most of their money during the Depression; but even before then Nadelman had grown contemptuous of the art world, had refused dealer representation and invitations to participate in group shows (his last solo exhibit was in 1927), and had retreated ever further into isolation. A nearly forgotten figure, he died a suicide in December 1946.

Lincoln never met Nadelman, but he'd been fascinated by his sculpture ever since seeing reproductions of it in *The Dial* in the 1920s; when still an undergraduate he, together with his cohorts at the Harvard Society for Contemporary Art, had invited Nadelman to exhibit there, but he'd declined. Lincoln had remained intrigued with the artist's work and, reading of his death, immediately sought out his widow; she quickly agreed to cooperate with Lincoln's two (never less than two) projects: to research Nadelman's life, with a full-scale biography ultimately in mind, and to campaign for a retrospective show of the artist's work at MoMA.

Viola Nadelman was herself imminently due to leave for a trip to Poland, but she gave Lincoln what amounted to free run of the mansion in Riverdale—jammed from attic to cellar with Nadelman's work, much of it in disrepair: bronzes corroded, wooden figures split, ceramics broken. Lincoln immediately had the more important pieces photographed, and persuaded a recent friend, Henri Cartier-Bresson, to produce a pictorial record of the house itself. Just as rapidly Lincoln started to invite key MoMA staffers up to the mansion, starting with Monroe Wheeler and René d'Harnoncourt, both of whom were impressed (d'Harnoncourt was "dazzled"). His enthusiasm was of critical importance. D'Harnoncourt, a man all but universally liked and admired, had recently emerged as the central figure in MoMA's operations.

As early as the fall of 1947, the powers that be at MoMA decided to schedule a Nadelman memorial show for September 1948. Already juggling the complex affairs of Ballet Society, Lincoln simply threw another ball into the air and, in the true tradition of a circus professional, proceeded to perform the impossible. Having also taken on the job of preparing the Nadelman catalog, Lincoln plunged ahead, simultaneously managing affairs at the Nadelman estate and undertaking the needed research on his life. He wrote scores of letters asking for help from people who'd themselves known the artist or might provide leads and introductions to those who had. These prominently included the aged Bernard Berenson, who tartly dismissed Lincoln's inquiry, to Alice Toklas, who warmly lent her assistance (Leo and Gertrude Stein had been among Nadelman's early champions).

Lincoln bombarded Toklas with questions ranging from Nadelman's disputed influence in originating cubism to particulars about the role Leo and Gertrude Stein had played in his career. Toklas responded to his inquiries in detail, and also provided introductions to Leo Stein's widow and to Tadée Natanson, who in the pre–World War I period, while co-editor of *La Revue Blanche*, had taken André Gide to Nadelman's studio. Natanson, in turn, sent Lincoln page proofs of his memoir, which contained a description of the young Nadelman at the turn of the century. Through Toklas, Lincoln was also given access to the Stein-Toklas correspondence on deposit at Yale, and the distinguished curator Donald Gallup spent days expertly guiding him through Nadelman-related materials. In gratitude Lincoln gave Gallup, along with Carl Van Vechten, a tour of the Nadelman house; both were "very much touched and impressed."

When Viola Nadelman returned from her trip to Poland, she, too, proved warmly cooperative. Lincoln thought her a charming woman, "an angel . . . selfless, so modest as to efface herself," he wrote Toklas. Sensitive to Viola's loneliness, Lincoln tried to see her at least twice a week. She apparently trusted him completely, even confiding that her husband had killed himself, a fact not publicly known for many decades. Lincoln was deeply puzzled by the revelation. He knew that Nadelman had a worrisome heart condition, but decided that his suicide was more the result of "spiritual isolation, a lack of appreciation which he himself did everything to augment by his refusal to show, to accept commissions or to talk about his work." Given Nadelman's enigmatic personality, Lincoln wasn't surprised to find during his research "the most savage contrasts of opinion" about him; he was as adored as he was hated.

Along with everything else, Lincoln helped Viola Nadelman sell some of her husband's works in order to ease what had become her "desperate financial situation." In the process he managed, as often in the past, to get into yet another tangle with Alfred Barr. Lincoln was in point of fact among those, in a deeply divided school of opinion, who valued and appreciated Barr. Even in the midst of their current spat, he described him to Agnes Mongan as "a man of extraordinary qualities," including "his incorruptibility and trueness to his own best nature, which is all any of us have." But Lincoln also thought that Alfred "has the tenacity of an octopus, and he masks his muscle with a piteous appearance of wounded innocence." Worse—and he had said all this many times to Alfred's face—he considered him "a prince of procrastination" and personally responsible for MoMA's permanent collection being, in Lincoln's view, "full of unmitigated truck . . . school-pieces of debased school-pieces." Lincoln knew perfectly well that Barr "considers me his enemy, and as a matter of fact, I am"—meaning that he would not, though admiring Alfred's "merits," soft-pedal his complaints against him.

For the moment Lincoln's antagonism toward Barr was to the fore. Among his grievances was the way the museum had treated his recent gift of Tchelitchev's *Hide-and-Seek*, discarding—without consulting either artist or donor—the frame Pavlik had specifically made for the painting and replacing it with a "white mat in a beat-up stock frame." An additional grievance centered on the "absolutely lousy" way MoMA's Department of Theatre Design, headed by George Amberg, had been handling Lincoln's large-scale donations of dance archives. Barr dealt with both of Lincoln's complaints out of hand. He did acknowledge that Lincoln *might* have a point about the reframing of *Hide-and-Seek*, but he responded to the disparagement of the theater collection summarily: "Your complaint about Amberg should go to René [d'Harnoncourt] and Monroe [Wheeler]."

This dismissive rejoinder may well have contributed to the retrospective outrage Lincoln managed to work up over the fact that MoMA had never, during Nadelman's lifetime, bought a single piece of his work; the sole offer the museum had ever made was four hundred dollars for one of Nadelman's now-famous stags, an offer that succeeded only in upsetting the artist, since he'd priced the work at eight hundred. Faced with Lincoln's accusatory anger, Barr stiffened: "You keep reminding me (by implication)," he wrote Lincoln, "about our not having bought Nadelmans during his life time. I went out twice to see them during the '30s . . . when I asked about his sculpture he would not show it to me."

Barr then proceeded to anger Lincoln further by admonishing him to take care that his "great service" in rediscovering Nadelman not be disfigured and discredited "by exaggerated partisanship." He accused Lincoln, with some justice, of being misled by his "humanistic esthetics" into equating good art with "a preoccupation with the human body in its ideal or perfect form," and into dismissing other kinds of art as inferior. "This leads you," Barr gratuitously added, "into cant on the one hand and critical slander . . . on the other."

Ignoring the provocation, at least for the time being, Lincoln returned to his original complaint: if in the thirties Nadelman refused to show you his sculpture, why not buy something *now*, when the work *is* available and Madame Nadelman is in such difficult financial straits? Barr wouldn't budge; he might well be interested in making a purchase, he wrote Lincoln, but he preferred to "wait until the time of the exhibition." In contrast, Nelson Rockefeller, ever responsive to Lincoln's enthusiasms, stepped up to the plate and bought, at a generous price, a whole collection of Nadelman's figurines.

In preparation for the MoMA show in September 1948, Lincoln devoted himself to restoring both the mansion and the artwork, along the way uncovering, as he put it, a continual series of "marvels." By June 1948 Lincoln was able to report to Alice Toklas that "all the marbles have been beautifully cleaned which were covered with soot and paint; the cellar has been cleaned out and we discovered a mass of drawings and even woodcarvings thrown there years ago." Lincoln saw to it that some of the plaster figurines were cast in bronze and all the wooden figures repaired. Then came the difficult job of choosing eighty pieces, out of some two thousand housed in the mansion, for the memorial show at MoMA. "When you present a man before the world virtually, both for the first time and as a whole," Lincoln wrote Toklas, "the responsibility to present him clearly and definitively is great."

Somehow the choices were made, and the show proved a success both with the critics and the public. Not everyone, of course, applauded Nadelman's restored visibility or agreed that he was an artist of the first rank. Lincoln got an outraged letter from George Bellows's widow for claiming in the catalog that Nadelman had had an influence on her husband's work, and an additional letter of outrage from the irascible Madame Lachaise "saying worse." The already well-known art critic Meyer Schapiro wrote Lincoln that in his opinion Nadelman "could not utilize in his art the conflicts and imperfections of his own nature; there is a lack of real struggle, such as we find in his greater contemporaries." He felt an excess of "compromise" in Nadelman's sculpture, "a lack of energy and wholehearted-ness, a reliance upon his charm"—overall rather a shrewd assessment.

Nor did the show convert Alfred Barr into an ardent Nadelman fan. A month after the opening, he informed Lincoln that MoMA's acquisitions committee did not share Lincoln's "enthusiasm or . . . interest in Nadel-man" and had limited any purchase from the show to twenty-five hundred dollars. Lincoln had long since come to believe that Barr used the com-mittee as a front to avoid taking public responsibility for decisions he himself had made—even while presenting himself as the committee's "vic-tim." In any case, for the proffered twenty-five hundred dollars, Viola Nadelman, out of need and generosity, gave Barr his declared wish list: two of her husband's masterworks, *Man in the Open Air* and *Man in Top Hat*, along with a number of drawings.

The transaction did not end, and may have further fueled, the roller-coaster relationship between Lincoln and Barr. Within weeks of the Nadelman opening, Lincoln published a major article in *Harper's Maga-zine*, titled "The State of Modern Painting." The timing and the contents of the piece can be read as a strategic reply to Barr's general characteriza-tion of Lincoln's taste in art, as well as to MoMA's acquisition policies. Lincoln centrally positioned himself in the article as opposed to those who "defend inertia by invoking patriotism, social responsibility, or normalcy in the arts"—to "Philistia." Implicitly denying Barr's character-ization of him as solely wedded to "humanistic esthetics" and a "preoccu-pation with the human body," Lincoln insisted in the article that he did *not* oppose "the use of unhampered imagination, experiment in new method or material, or what is loosely called distortion . . . there is no question here of the artist's prerogative to paint whatever he wants to paint; there is no intention to limit his freedom."[2]

But he did place himself among those critics who opposed "improvisa-tion as method [and] deformation as a formula." He insisted that many of the painters from the emergent school of abstract art basically lacked "general culture, historical and scientific," and viewed their "decorative improvisation" and "lack of stable technical processes" as positive virtues. Without naming Jackson Pollock or any of his fellow practitioners, Lin-coln deplored their elevation of "chance into a canon" and their pretense that "every lucky accident of the brush . . . [was] a sort of extra dividend of creation." Spontaneity and immediacy were not, in his view, prime virtues—not, that is, when compared to "mindfulness" and technical mastery.

Lincoln's own public record, as well as the flexibility of taste he often exhibited in private, belies the categorical judgments of his *Harper's* piece. Lincoln was, after all, *the* champion of Balanchine's "abstract" choreogra-phy, of Lachaise's "distorted" female torsos, of Tchelitchev's painterly experiments with wax, sand, and coffee grinds; he would invite the uncategorizable artist Joseph Cornell to design decor for the ballet, and would later delight in (and financially support) the explosive physicality of Paul Taylor's dance inventions. Even into old age, Lincoln would remain open to the unexpected—he adored *E. T.: The Extra-Terrestrial*. Though he declared himself in *Harper's* as opposed to improvisation, within just a few years he would hail that same quality as quintessentially, valuably American. These "contradictions," rejecting as they implicitly do, binary assumptions and value judgments, along with Lincoln's own personal ability to contain presumed opposites (seriousness and playfulness, self-doubt and self-assertion, etc.), is precisely what makes his sensibility, with its eclectic cultivation of varied modes and moods, feel so contemporary.

Turning directly, in his *Harper's* piece, to Alfred Barr and MoMA, Lincoln proceeded to damn with faint praise. He characterized the museum's catalogs of past exhibits as a record of the past five decades "not balanced by the publications of any other influential museum." But—out came the fist from the velvet glove—MoMA had done its job "almost too well": thanks to the museum's publications many younger painters had come to feel "that the past fifty years are more important and worthy of imitation than the past five hundred."

Lincoln also blamed—and here he explicitly implicated Barr—MoMA's permanent collection for its unacknowledged bias; the collection, he wrote, represented after all "just one kind of picture selected [as] . . . a significant body of tendencies." But their actual significance, Lincoln argued, was in doubt. Too often, he claimed, what the museum bought and hung "are infrequently good models, too often charts of dead ends, unselective and feeble imitations."

Whether MoMA's permanent collection did or did not represent what was currently the "best" work and the most significant trends in art production was a subjective judgment open to endless debate—in 1948 and ever since. What *is* certain is that any group of curators (or for that matter, any collectivity of designated "experts") inevitably makes its judgment calls within the context of a particular cultural climate, influenced, consciously or not, by transient cues, enthusiasms, and mind-sets that subsequently give way to a quite different set of social imperatives. Lincoln's own hierarchy of artists, after all, has hardly been immune to shifts in taste and subsequent challenge; he once predicted confidently to Agnes Mongan that the work of such current art-world favorites as Derain, Matisse, Soutine, Beckmann, Ernst, and Dalí would end up in the cellars currently occupied by previous "stars" like Adolf Schreyer, Mihály Munkácsy, and Ernest Meissonier—a prediction that hasn't, as yet, come to pass, despite tremors of debate about the comparative standing of this or that artist in the hierarchy. Nor have some of Lincoln's own enthusiasms—artists like

Dean Newman, William Brice, Henry Koerner—enduringly (justly or not) entered the pantheon.

Besides, as several of those who responded to the *Harper's* article pointed out—and the piece inflamed a good many people—Lincoln had essentially stacked the deck. MoMA's specific mission, after all, *was* to collect and exhibit the work of the last fifty—not five hundred—years. Further, Lincoln had drawn his indictment in terms that were far too broad: he'd dualistically separated intellect from improvisation without defining either or entertaining the possibility of their interconnection; he'd damned most abstract expressionist painters as mere decorators, and assumed, wrongly, that they all lacked mastery in the techniques of their craft and were ignorant of historical and cultural tradition. Still, at a time when abstract expressionism had begun to sweep the field, relegating many representational artists to the sidelines, Lincoln's oppositional voice, however polemical, helped somewhat to redress the balance. Today, some fifty years later, with a significant number of art historians and artists again championing representational work, Lincoln's views have come to seem far more acceptable, even prescient.

By this point in his life Lincoln had become widely regarded as a consequential, if controversial, figure in the art world. His influence was about to increase still further. Early in 1949 the *New Republic* invited him to write a regular column for them, "Lincoln Kirstein: The Fine Arts." He immediately accepted the opportunity and would continue, irregularly, to produce columns for the magazine through 1951. The bulk of the dozen articles he wrote over the three-year period consisted of book reviews, sometimes composite ones, and they were marked by a real talent for compressed, if occasionally opaque, writing and by a remarkable, if not always deep, range of erudition.

His excellent editor at the *New Republic*, Robert L. Hatch, proved no pushover; he rejected one of Lincoln's pieces outright and asked for extensive revision in others. But because Hatch's manner was diplomatic and his criticism keen ("I think you should take care to make clear that you object, not to novelty of communication, but to the failure of communication") Lincoln adopted most of his suggestions, leading Hatch to comment, "Editing, a dog's life, is made endurable when a writer will not only listen but actually profit by the editor's sour objections."

Still, there would be periodic complaints from the *New Republic*'s readers about Lincoln's stern, sweeping judgments. The most serious came from Lloyd Goodrich, associate director of the Whitney Museum of American Art. Their spat arose after Lincoln reviewed Goodrich's book on Max Weber, calling it "an uncritical monograph" and summarily dismissing Weber as an unimportant artist. Goodrich sent Lincoln a copy of the letter he'd written in protest to the magazine, and Lincoln responded, as he often and genuinely could, like the gentlest of his adored pussycats. The two men subsequently had a friendly, informative exchange over their differing views on "modern" art. "As for personal favorites," Lincoln wrote, "we all have them . . . your[s] include Weber and Hopper. Mine include Hopper and Tchelitchew. But do you actually think that I am irresponsibly prejudiced against 'modern' art? I am sure that we both share an admiration for Ben Shahn, Lachaise, Nadelman and a number of others. My attitude is merely against the idea of improvisation, decoration, fragmentation and stylization."

Goodrich thanked him for "the pleasant tone" of his letter, and in a cordial spirit the two pursued their differences. "Some of what you say about the faults of modern painting I agree with," Goodrich wrote back, "but it seems to me that you have carried your criticism to such an extreme that . . . you disregard the positive virtues of modern art," insistently, and unnecessarily, positioning "mindfulness" against "spontaneity," when both qualities are invariably at work. He praised Lincoln's "unusual gifts as a critic" but was concerned that "by too sweeping condemnation you can do great harm to artists and to the public's relation to all living art." There the two men left it, and Goodrich graciously withdrew his letter of protest from publication.

In Lincoln's other major *New Republic* piece, a combined review of Bernard Berenson's *History and Aesthetics in the Visual Arts* and a general summing-up of his "imperial" influence, he eschewed "sweeping condemnation" for a sly rebuke. Lincoln in fact detested most of Berenson's writings ("embarrassingly horrible and tacky," is how he once described a portion of them), and deplored his mandarin dismissal of almost all art that wasn't Italian painting up through the Renaissance. Yet fearless though Lincoln nearly always was in his criticism, he sprinkled his *New Republic* piece, perhaps in deference to Berenson being in his mid-eighties, with a number of guileful "compliments," remarking, for example, that Berenson had "clarified the semi-science of attribution."

But that left plenty of room for forthright complaint, and Lincoln filled it. He characterized Berenson's taste as at base "a fanciful, if neither an unseductive nor modest display of whim," and called his current book "neither carefully written nor edited." Lincoln also made a point of referring to Berenson, who'd never embraced his Jewish origins, as "the child of an ancient Jewish house in Riga," and insisted that he had essentially a "dandy's mind" (Agnes Mongan, for one, thought the "dandy" characterization "exactly" right). Berenson himself, especially given his advanced age and iconic stature, responded with several haughty corrections but also with considerable grace: "I do regret," he wrote Lincoln, "that you take up so much of the skimpy space allotted to talking about the relatively private B.B. and so little about the contents of his book."

During the same time that Lincoln was embroiled in art-world scuffles, he remained more deeply involved than ever in Ballet Society's ongoing struggle to stay afloat. Morton Baum may have declared his enthusiasm for the company, but City Center had no governmental subsidy or endowment of any kind, and private donations accounted for no more than one fifth of its yearly budget; indeed, the Center itself was some sixty thousand dollars in debt in 1948. It stayed alive primarily through box office receipts and rental fees. But if constantly strapped financially, City Center had begun to develop a real following, with total attendance averaging half a million a year for its varied events, and a mailing list that had grown to ninety thousand.[3]

In 1948, just as Baum was expressing interest in Ballet Society, City Center was hit by a series of crises. The first, in early March, was Leonard Bernstein's resignation as conductor of the New York City Symphony. Bernstein had been only twenty-seven when appointed in 1945, and by introducing a number of contemporary scores hardly known in the United States—including Alban Berg's *Wozzeck*—had developed a loyal and young following (though Virgil Thomson, the *Herald Tribune*'s music critic, wasn't among his fans: "With every musical season his personal performance becomes more ostentatious, his musical one less convincing"). Thomson aside, the loss of Bernstein and the subsequent abandonment of the New York City Symphony Orchestra meant a dip in ticket sales and income.

Then in swift succession came Serge Denham's announcement that after the current year, Ballet Russe would no longer perform at City Center, and Lucia Chase's decision that Ballet Theatre would not fulfill its contract for a three-week engagement during the coming winter. Baum called the latter "an arbitrary cancellation," either not realizing or not crediting the dire financial circumstances that would force Ballet Theatre, as of July 1948, to close down its operations for nine months. An angered Baum forced an arbitration hearing, during which he claimed that "the real reason for the withdrawal was disclosed: if the center would abandon the idea of a New York City Ballet, Ballet Theatre might fulfill their engagement." Baum was more prepared to credit that motive because he learned that Denham, too, had acted in part out of "a desire to stop the City Center from forming the proposed new Ballet Company." It was Baum's view that "the New York City Ballet had started war among the ballet companies. They certainly feared the emergence of this embryo."

More bad news soon followed. José Ferrer, who'd headed the New York City Drama Company, also decided to quit; the Theatre Guild had offered him a leading role in a new play, and he felt the need to replenish his finances. The final blow came when the popular team of Paul Draper (Muriel's son) and the harmonica virtuoso Larry Adler, who'd provided the Center's profitable Christmas attraction, came under fire from a congressional investigating committee as "Communists," and their bookings were cancelled. The so-called cold war had begun—and would speedily deepen.

That left, for the moment, only the popular New York City Opera Company, plus a three-week engagement by the Paris Opéra Company forced on Baum by Grover Whalen, head of the city's planned jubilee for the fiftieth anniversary of the consolidation of the Greater City of New York. Baum had tried in vain to resist booking Serge Lifar's company, knowing Lifar had been accused as a Nazi collaborator, and having heard that the company (except for its premiere ballerina, Yvette Chauviré) was "old-fashioned" and second rate. The Paris Opéra engagement did, at Whalen's insistence, take place, but left-wing groups picketed several performances.

Realizing that City Center was in a precarious position and that the possible formation of a New York City ballet company therefore uncertain to the point of being unlikely, Lincoln continued to try to bolster Ballet Society's income and prospects. His siblings, George and Mina, refused, for Lincoln's own good, to let him further invade his trust funds. With no bonds of his own left to cash in, he decided to embark on a lecture tour during the winter of 1948, assigning all fees to Ballet Society. The tour was fairly extensive (from Boston to Chicago), and though Lincoln found it "a hard business," he met "some charming boys" along the way and managed to enjoy himself at least some of the time.[4]

At Harvard he met a "funny and cute" young instructor whom he liked well enough to introduce to his New York extended "family" (according to Lincoln the instructor was fascinated with the group's free-love "atmosphere of *l'amitié amoureuse*"). In Chicago, Lincoln met "Woody," the son of a cop—"an affectionate and a nice boy"—currently feeling "alienated from the bitch-Chicago big apartment society of the refined queens." In Detroit, Lincoln himself saw something of the "rich-bitch set," and also mixed with the crowd at the School for the Arts at Cranbrook—where, except for the weaving, he found little of value. "I am too much of a New Yorker," Lincoln decided, "ever to leave even for a day, but it is good for me to get around. After all, at forty, youth is gone and the only thing to do is to keep in contact with it by the cultivation of the young."

The lecture tour may have helped in that regard, but it didn't produce nearly enough money to solve Ballet Society's financial problems. Lincoln told Nelson that he was "desperate," and begged for his help. The two had lunch, and Nelson offered to contribute ten thousand dollars; he sent Lincoln half the money that same day. In gratitude Lincoln made him the gift of one of his own Nadelman sculptures. Lincoln was hopeful that other donors might be attracted through Ballet Society's varied activities.

He presented two performances (in the Hunter College auditorium) of the opera *Far Harbour*, with music by Baldwin Bergerson and text by William Archibald. Lincoln preferred to call it a "lyric drama," which he defined as a marriage of words, music, and choreographed action. He'd commissioned the piece himself and had closely supervised it during the period of gestation. Balanchine told him the music "is very bad" and Auden warned him that "it is hopeless to create in the tradition of *verismo*," but Lincoln remained convinced that the work had "considerable theatrical power." In that, he stood nearly alone; *Far Harbour*, whether viewed as an opera or a "lyric drama," was widely dismissed. Agnes de Mille, for one, told Lincoln (who'd sent her free tickets) that she liked some of the music but thought the text "puerile."

But among the few fans of the piece was John Marshall of the Rockefeller Foundation, who sent Lincoln a lengthy, enthusiastic commentary. He seized the occasion to ask Marshall whether the Rockefeller Foundation might be interested in supporting one of Ballet Society's subsidiary efforts, the *Dance Index*. Since he and Marshall were already well acquainted, Lincoln hadn't overstepped the bounds, but Marshall responded that the time was not yet ripe to try to win the foundation's support.

Fortunately David and Alice (Astor) Pleydell-Bouverie, among Lincoln's recent acquaintances, were more immediately responsive. Like Nelson, the Bouveries sent Lincoln ten thousand dollars, even while expressing doubt (as had Nelson) whether the sum would prove of much help, given the Society's overall yearly budget of $150,000. But both Lincoln and Frances Hawkins rushed to reassure them that their contribution (in Frances's words), arriving at a desperate point, had literally meant "life or death for the Society." Without these emergency funds, they might have been forced to cancel at least one of the two performances imminently due for March and April.

As it was, it took all of Morton Baum's magician-like juggling of funds to allow the lights to go up at all. On March 22, 1948, Ballet Society did manage to mount a revival of *The Seasons*, along with Todd Bolender's *Capricorn Concerto* (to Samuel Barber's music) and Balanchine's *Symphony in C*; a fourth ballet, long in the works, had been announced as part of the program—the premiere of Balanchine's *Beauty and the Beast*, with music by Alexei Haieff and decor by Esteban Francis—but it had proved too expensive to complete (and indeed would never be mounted). *The Seasons* was moderately well received, but Bolender's *Capricorn Concerto* was mostly dismissed as derivative. On the other hand, *Symphony in C* got an ecstatic reception—except, predictably, from Balanchine's longtime antagonist, John Martin of the *New York Times*.

A little more than a month later, on April 28, Ballet Society presented the much-anticipated Stravinsky-Balanchine collaboration, *Orpheus*. Three other ballets were also on the program—the premiere of *Élégie*, and two revivals: *Renard* and *Symphonie Concertante*. All of which went well, or as well as could be expected, given that the audience was distractedly focused on the premiere of *Orpheus*. There was much to anticipate. It was known that Stravinsky himself would be on the podium—he'd arrived in New York a full three weeks before the premiere in order to work closely with Balanchine, Lincoln, and Noguchi on every detail of the production— and that the cast would include a stunning group of emerging young principals: Tallchief, Le Clercq, Magallanes, and Moncion. In honor of the occasion Stravinsky forswore his usual staggering fee and charged Ballet Society $750 for conducting the premiere performance—quite staggering enough for the poverty-stricken company.[5]

When Stravinsky mounted the podium a wave of applause greeted him. He acknowledged the crowd, briskly tapped his baton, and the ballet began—the classic tale of a grieving Orpheus led into Hades to retrieve his beloved Eurydice, only to see her again perish after he disobeyed instructions and turned to glimpse her. Stravinsky's remarkable score, Balanchine's exquisitely spare, poetic choreography, brilliantly danced, and Noguchi's perfectly attuned sculptural design combined to produce a memorable evening. The audience responded with tumultuous applause, and Edwin Denby was so overcome that he remained motionless for some time in his seat. The reviews that followed—even John Martin's— matched the enthusiasm of the opening-night audience.

Probably no one was more thrilled than Morton Baum. His gamble had paid off, his confidence in Balanchine and Kirstein resoundingly justified. The premiere had been confined to Ballet Society subscribers, and it was music to Baum's ears when the City Center's phones started ringing off the hook with pleas from the public for additional performances; some half a dozen were promptly scheduled, with the tickets quickly snapped up.

Soon after the premiere Baum called a meeting in his office with Lincoln and Frances Hawkins and, after congratulating them on *Orpheus*'s success, asked if they'd be interested in forming a ballet company for the Center—the New York City Ballet. He offered, during the upcoming winter season, to set aside Monday and Tuesday evenings for ballet performances, and also expected the new company to provide whatever dancing the New York City Opera Company might need for its Thursday-to-Sunday performances. Baum told them frankly that opposition to the notion of a ballet company at City Center had already risen on the board of trustees, and particularly from Eddie Warburg's older brother, Gerald, who'd long blamed Lincoln for earlier involving Eddie in the ballet world's costly affairs. Still, Baum had the backing of the board's chair, Newbold Morris, and felt confident that the trustees would accept his proposal. But he warned Lincoln that Ballet Society would still be responsible for its own deficit; City Center could only pick up the incidental (though not inconsiderable) costs of an orchestra, stagehands, advertising, and front-of-the house personnel.

Lincoln was excited at the prospect of having a more secure home for the ballet than ever before and told Baum that "we have liked working with you so much that it would be indeed a deprivation to leave." Yet he wasn't at all confident that he'd be able to find the needed funds. "I owe so much money," Lincoln wrote Glenway Wescott, "that unless I can clear it by July 1st, we cannot accept the City's kind offer, and even if we did, it means raising that much again."

Balanchine, too, was eager for the proposal to go through. He'd long felt concern about how to keep his dancers in top physical condition when the company was so frequently idle. Dancers need regular rehearsals and performances to stay in shape; they can't, like opera singers, keep tuned up by going over scores, nor can they sustain their spirits and commitment while doing part-time sales work at Macy's. Balanchine decided that he'd join the fund-raising effort, specifically to try to raise enough money to provide his dancers with a year-round stipend, however minimal. He came up with the figure of fifty dollars a week, for a total of twenty-six hundred a year, to maintain a single dancer, and felt that if he could raise enough money to support ten dancers, the company would be assured continuity.

With Betty Cage's help, Balanchine worked hard to compose a letter to prospective donors outlining his plan. But his attempts at fund-raising were apparently inept, and Frances Hawkins ended up having to apologize to an annoyed Morton Baum; when Balanchine "is not at work in one way or another," she explained, "he is miserable and depressed." Perhaps fortunately, Balanchine soon had to leave for Europe to fill a contractual engagement with the Marquis de Cuevas's company.

For a brief spell in the spring of 1948, Lincoln came close to closing up shop for good and forgoing Baum's offer. Then, in early June, Nelson Rockefeller's promised second five-thousand-dollar check arrived and provided breathing space. "I hardly know how to thank you," Lincoln wrote Nelson. "With some sort of psychic intuition you knew I was in a bad spot. I did my best not to ask you, since you had already helped me . . . you always seem to think that what you do in these cases is of slight value; I can tell you that in this particular instance, it was a question of life and death."

During that very same week, Lincoln met again with John Marshall of the Rockefeller Foundation. Marshall was a great admirer of Lincoln's, but in the foundation world new initiatives progress slowly. Marshall had hired Virgil Thomson to try to find a formula whereby the foundation "would be justified in awarding music money," and Lincoln hoped that, eventually at least, "music means me." But as Marshall made clear to him, for now the Rockefeller trustees would consider only requests "which fall in fields in which they and we have agreed to work"; all he could offer Lincoln at the moment was his own "very keen interest in what you are doing."

Lincoln had also held out the hope that MoMA, as part of its twentieth-anniversary year, would broaden its mandate and form an alliance with City Center to foster the performing arts in general. But that initiative, too, proved stillborn. The Art Commission of the City of San Francisco did sound Lincoln out about the possibility of Ballet Society participating in its annual festival, and the prospect provided a temporary shot in the arm—but the high costs involved soon doomed the project.

Yet other more positive prospects did slowly begin to emerge. Lincoln conferred with Henry Allan Moe of the Guggenheim Foundation about Ballet Society's "general organizational problems" and found Moe "sympathetic and interested," though he, too, was unable to offer any immediate support. More tangible results came from the willingness of Alice Astor Bouverie to introduce Lincoln to some of her friends among the super-rich; he assiduously cultivated them all, and with some success. Yet as Wescott pointed out to him, "the financial assistance you have had from Rockefellers & Astors et al, as it compares with your own ruinous generosity, has been absurdly & pitifully little." Balanchine's commitment to the company was probably the biggest morale booster of all; thanks to his lucrative Broadway shows (currently the mammoth hit *Where's Charley?*), he'd long since waived any salary from Ballet Society.

Somehow Lincoln did gradually make some financial progress. Whereas in mid-May he'd despaired of the company's chances of survival, by mid-September its indebtedness had been cut from thirty to fifteen thousand dollars. That was enough progress, all sides agreed, to establish (literal) credit and to allow Lincoln to enter into negotiations with City Center. He, Frances Hawkins, and Morton Baum came up with a fall-winter schedule that called for ballet performances each Monday and Tuesday evening, at an approximate budget of nine thousand a week. Theoretically the City Center theater, when playing at capacity, could take in more than eleven thousand dollars, but Monday and Tuesday were the two worst attendance nights, and Lincoln knew they wouldn't come close to that mark. No, it was going to be a high-wire act all the way. The company had no reserve funds at all (Lincoln had again tried, and again failed, to borrow further on his inheritance), and a single week's deficit could, in Lincoln's words, "tumble our whole structure."

On the positive side, the incipient New York City Ballet had no competition at the moment: Ballet Theatre had temporarily ceased operations, and the Ballet Russe was scheduled to produce only one new ballet. But Baum did promise that if the company did "fairly well," City Center would assume part of its deficit for the spring season. "This is really our critical year," Lincoln wrote John Marshall in mid-September 1948. And the outcome was by no means assured.

The company couldn't afford any new productions for its inaugural program on October 11, but what it did offer were three proven Balanchine masterworks: *Orpheus*, *Symphony in C*, and *Concerto Barocco* (with the scenery and costumes Eugene Berman had designed for the 1941 Latin American tour, never before seen in New York). Happily the program got a rapturous reception; *Newsweek*, for example, described the company as having put "its best foot foremost" and hailed *Orpheus*, in particular, as "breath-taking"—"one of the most important ballets given in the last ten years." The magazine also accurately reported that "the New York City Ballet must support itself or leave the boards. This season, appealing to a broader public at popular prices, is Kirstein's final stand. 'This,' he says, 'is the last formula I can think of.' "[6]

Despite the excellent notices, the demand for tickets remained modest, though each week's gross did improve somewhat on the previous one. Lincoln tried to remain sanguine by reminding himself that the City Center Opera, when it had begun performances five years earlier, did even less well at the box office—yet now sold out on a regular basis. Still, as Lincoln wrote Lucia Chase, he felt "rather more than less grim about a future of any sort. Simply, I cannot see a feasible way of making the thing work without continual priming of the pump."

He decided to appeal yet again to Nelson Rockefeller, and outlined his plight in detail: for the fall season he'd guaranteed City Center that he would meet any deficit not covered by box office receipts, but unfortunately, subscriptions and ticket sales by late October (*after* the splendid notices) had brought in only fifteen thousand dollars. He'd already had to borrow ten thousand dollars from the School of American Ballet's reserve fund (SAB, fortunately, was doing well, with some five hundred students currently enrolled), but Lincoln didn't feel he could turn to that source again without jeopardizing the school's future. The good news was that Morton Baum had been so pleased at the enthusiastic press that he now made the definite promise that City Center would assume financial responsibility for the ballet's future seasons *if* the company proved able to get through this first one by itself. That meant, in Lincoln's figuring, that he had to raise an additional fifty thousand dollars.

This time around Nelson proved unreceptive. He sent Lincoln a brief note saying that "unfortunately, I am way over on present commitments and am sending under separate cover the best I can do." That "best" turned out to be a couple of thousand dollars. Lincoln, shrewdly, made much of the gift; "Again," he wrote Nelson, "you literally saved our existence. . . . The City Center had its cancellation announcement ready for the press." *If* Baum had ever considered issuing such an announcement— Lincoln was known for exaggerating—he withheld the cancellation not because of Nelson's small gift but because the day following its arrival, John Marshall told him that the Rockefeller Foundation, after all, was "seriously interested in the entire music and lyrical theatre picture." Support might not be rapidly forthcoming, Marshall said, but the foundation

did feel "some responsibility towards the future." In an internal memo circulated among the foundation's higher-ups, Marshall reported that he
"came away from this interview with a high regard for Baum. He is both
practical and artistically discriminating."

In the meantime, determined that the show would go on even as he
searched for the needed financial support and tried to damp down his pessimism, Lincoln again made overtures (but to no conclusion) both to
Lucia Chase and to Tom Fisher, about possible combinations and collaborations. He also started negotiating a loan on his last life insurance policy,
feeling certain that another, and larger, deficit crisis lay directly ahead.
With the beginning of the new year, the entity still known as Ballet Society (even as it teetered longingly toward the goal of becoming the New
York City Ballet) tried to hold on to its declining subscriber base by offering several nondancing programs—Ballet Society Member Nights—open
only to members.

The most notable, attended by considerable press, was a reading by
Edith and Osbert Sitwell, who were currently on a triumphant U.S. tour,
with Osbert accompanied by his companion David Horner. During the
Sitwells' stay in New York, Lincoln and Fidelma wined and dined them,
and Pavlik (a close friend, off and on, of Edith's) also took them in hand.
Pavlik's companion, Charles Henri Ford, found Edith's company "witty
and pleasurable," but Pavlik (of course) took a grumpier view, professing
himself "bored with Edith's preoccupation of who is a lady, who is well-
bred and who isn't." Nor was Lincoln particularly drawn to Edith, though
he liked Osbert a good deal, and a real friendship sprang up.

But David Horner apparently got a bit pouty at having to stand so constantly in the wings. To give him some diversion, Lincoln kindly took him
along on a two-day trip to Boston (Lincoln had accepted appointment to
the Fogg Museum's Visiting Committee), where he introduced Horner to
a number of people, including his old friends Agnes Mongan and Henry-
Russell Hitchcock. In thanking Lincoln for the trip, Horner got in a few
perceptive digs: "You are a pearl of an angel, and yet Mephistopheles as
well—it is an ideal combination. . . . [I had] a divine time . . . except when
you were kinda ornery, which frightened me." "Mephistophelian angel"—
not a half-bad summary of Lincoln's now well-formed and unpredictably
bifurcated personality.

At the start of the new year City Center, thanks largely to some sizable
donations from board members, was in better economic shape than it had
been. At the same time Lincoln managed to fulfill his earlier pledge to
Baum personally to guarantee any deficit that might accrue from the ballet's fourteen performances during its 1948 season. Attendance at those
performances, unfortunately, had never reached more than one-third
capacity—the American ballet-going public, such as it was, still preferred
the traditional offerings of de Basil's Ballets Russes, which had recently

had a successful engagement in New York. As a result of the poor attendance, the accumulated deficit from those fourteen performances reached the rather staggering sum of $47,000 (more than $300,000 in today's terms). It would have been higher still had Ballet Society not already owned all its needed scenery and costumes, and had not the dancers' salaries been jointly paid by the New York City Opera Company, which profited from the dancers' services.[7]

Lincoln's ability to fulfill his pledge was due not to the Rockefellers or Bouveries (though they'd been far more generous than most of those to whom he'd appealed), but rather to a more devoted supporter still—his mother, Rose. Apparently overriding the advice of trust managers and lawyers alike, she once again picked up the tab, thus allowing Lincoln to make good on his promise to Baum. As a result, some of the ongoing wariness of City Center's board further dissolved (though Gerald Warburg's hostility remained unremitting).

It thus finally became possible for Baum to take the action he'd long been wanting to: he officially invited Ballet Society to change its name to the New York City Ballet Company and to become City Center's resident dance unit. "The artistic quality of the performances has more than exceeded our anticipations," Baum formally wrote Lincoln. "You will be gratified to know that in the future ballet season the City Center will assume all the running expenses and meet any deficits." Baum, with his usual foresight, predicted that "in a short time," the company "will have achieved international fame." To speed that day he came up with a revised schedule for the new year: the ballet would no longer be confined to Monday and Tuesday performances, but would have a two- to three-week season of its own, spread over late January and early February 1949; the company would also be given six weeks of paid rehearsal time. Thereafter it would continue to serve the opera, thus providing the dancers with some, if not enough, additional paid work.

A true milestone had been reached. (Indeed, 1948 could be called epochal in other regards, ranging from Jackson Pollock's breakthrough show at the Betty Parsons Gallery to the rapid escalation of the cold war.) For Lincoln and Balanchine, the deal with Baum meant that after fifteen years of unending struggle, of crises, moratoriums, and frequent despair, they'd finally found a home base. Yet the achieved goal would prove, almost immediately, a mixed blessing. Lincoln himself, finally released from the overall financial responsibility for the ballet, hardly knew "how to get used to . . . such an overwhelming change." He felt, quite suddenly, that he'd aged "a good deal," and "was less enthusiastic about everything." A deflation of spirits often follows on the achievement of a long-pursued goal, but Lincoln's decline in energy foreshadowed something more. Over the next few months, his mood would fail to pick up in any consistent way, and a serious emotional crisis lay directly ahead.

The long-sought dream of finding a permanent home had other potentially undermining aspects; like most realized dreams, this one fell short of utopian expectations. It soon began to sink in that Baum had agreed to underwrite the ballet's future expenses *only* for the current repertory; he couldn't afford to underwrite new works. City Center, in other words, had offered basic lodgings; if additional furnishings were desired, someone else would have to foot the bill. The production of a single new ballet, in Lincoln's estimate, would cost—*apart* from commissioning music, copying parts, paying for rehearsal space, choreographers, and designers (Balanchine himself continued, as before, to refuse any salary)— about $15,000.

There were other unnerving repercussions. With all ballet performances now open to the public, Ballet Society no longer had any special identity or—after the decision was made to close down the long-valued *Dance Index*—any special membership privileges to offer. The Society remained a legal entity, primarily to serve as a pass-through for potential donations, but its operating expenses were reduced in 1949 from $28,000 to $7,000. That paid for a tiny office and an equally tiny salary for the capable Betty Cage, who now became a staff of one, the once-indispensable Frances Hawkins having budgeted herself out of a job. (Typical of her conscientiousness, she stayed on an extra month, without compensation, in order to clean up some loose ends; in 1950 she would briefly return to help out with a crowded schedule.)

Her departure was a serious loss. Frances had played a major role throughout Ballet Society's existence (even lending it $600 from her own meager savings during one crisis). But more, her down-to-earth practicality and unimpeachable integrity had served as a calming counterweight to Lincoln's volatile temperament and sometimes pie-in-the-sky excesses. He'd trusted Frances completely (rare for him), adored her personally, and relied heavily on her sensible judgments. After leaving the company, Frances was for a time unemployed and nearly penniless, and had to live for a while with her sister in Colorado. Lincoln sang her praises to Nelson and pressed him to find a place for her ("she beats most men") somewhere in the Rockefeller empire. She did finally, thanks in part to Lincoln's connections, land a job at Fleur Cowles's slick new art/fashion magazine, *Flair*, but after developing lung cancer in 1951 was forced to return to Colorado where for a time she made a good recovery but missed New York. ("I miss you and Fidelma horribly," she wrote Lincoln, "but it's quite likely now that I can never live in the east again.")

The problem of how to finance new ballets was linked to the issue of how to provide enough paid work to the dancers to hold the company together. Both Lincoln and Balanchine approached the Rockefeller Foundation's John Marshall yet again, but much to Marshall's own regret, he had to reply, yet again, that the Humanities Division he represented was still not in a position to provide the desired money (he did, however, manage to get through a $2,500 grant to help prepare a text, "A Model of the Classic Dance," for which Muriel Stuart, the stalwart SAB teacher, would assume primary responsibility).

Balanchine himself tried to do more for his dancers. Without Lincoln's knowledge, he even wrote directly to the much-approached Nelson Rockefeller. The United States, Balanchine declared in the letter, "is in a position to become the cultural and artistic leader of the world, and our company is now one of the finest in the world. I think it is very important to keep the company together . . . we must be able to guarantee to at least the leading dancers an income which will enable them to live between periods of performances." His letter, Balanchine added, "perhaps . . . will annoy you. If it does, please tear it up." He had his answer in three days, not from Nelson but from one of his secretaries: "He does not feel he can make another contribution at this time."

Morton Baum, too, was eager to do more both for the dancers and for the production of new ballets, though hamstrung by City Center's lack of money. He sent a proposal, in the name of the Center, to the Rockefeller Foundation that included a request for $75,000 for the production of new ballets. But, like all previous pleas to the foundation, it was declined. Nor was there any chance that Lincoln could, or that his mother would, come up with additional funds. As he wrote to Chick Austin in February 1949, "I am desperately hard up. . . . I won't have any money until the first of May in my own checking account."

Yet somehow, for the brief three-week season early in 1949, the company did manage one premiere: Jerome Robbins's *The Guests*. The thirty-one-year-old Robbins was already a well-known figure, a successful triple threat as dancer (he'd been a soloist with Ballet Theatre) and as choreographer both of ballets *(Fancy Free; Interplay)* and Broadway shows *(On the Town; Billion Dollar Baby)*. It was Robbins who approached Lincoln and Balanchine about doing a piece for the New York City Ballet. He knew Lincoln only slightly, but had already worked with Balanchine on Broadway and, recently, had been stunned at the brilliance of his *Symphony in C*. The two men gave Robbins the go-ahead to compose a ballet on the socially conscious theme of intolerance, in collaboration with the composer Marc Blitzstein (whom Lincoln knew well). *The Guests* premiered on January 20 to mixed reviews. But if the ballet itself was no landmark, the association of Robbins with the New York City Ballet would prove of enduring consequence.[8]

The January-February season was a considerable artistic success (it also featured Antony Tudor's *Time Table*, new to the United States, and several Balanchine revivals, including *Four Temperaments* and *Serenade*). Financially, to everyone's vast relief, the season was more successful than the previous one and produced only a modest deficit. Yet the company's future still hung by a thread; opposition to any permanent arrangement continued to simmer on the Center's board of trustees, and as a further complication, both Balanchine and Lincoln (like Leonard Bernstein before them) frequently clashed with Laszlo Halasz, head of the opera.

There also remained the unresolved issues of how to raise money for new ballets and how to retain dancers who—however deeply loyal to Balanchine—needed, for their art, to perform regularly and, for their survival, to have an income more dependable than unemployment and odd jobs. Several of the company's principals—including Tallchief and Magallanes—found work during the long hiatus that followed the January-February season with other ballet companies, but Lincoln and Balanchine remained deeply worried about which and how many of their dancers would stay on board and whether City Center would ever provide them with sufficiently long seasons to ensure stability—especially since, unlike Ballet Theatre or Monte Carlo, the company couldn't provide continuity by touring the country. That would necessitate cutting down the size of the troupe (it now had a roster of some fifty dancers), which in turn might jeopardize showing it off to maximum advantage; besides, the company's avant-garde reputation held limited appeal for regional booking agents. Nor was the alternate option promising: much as Baum himself might wish to extend the ballet's runs at City Center, the New York market, for the moment, seemed saturated; the Sadler's Wells Ballet was due to arrive soon from England, and with Ballet Theatre back in business and Monte Carlo's traditionalist approach still drawing big crowds, it seemed highly unlikely that New York's limited ballet-going public could be further expanded.

Given his long struggle to reach this point, and having glimpsed light at the end of the tunnel, Lincoln found that the deflating uncertainty about the company's future had a crushing effect on his spirits. Already predisposed to depressive disorder (he'd recently described himself to Alfred Barr as having "an anxiety obsession")—its origins, finally, as mysterious as its eruptions were unpredictable—he now gave way under the long-accumulated pressure. Curiously, Fidelma, too, just a month before, had "had a nervous crisis," which Lincoln attributed, simplistically, to difficulty over finishing a painting.

Both Kirsteins were sufficiently distraught to have to leave the city for a time, first for a country retreat some fifty miles outside New York, and then, as their moods lightened, to Fire Island for the entire summer. While still in the country, Lincoln wrote Nelson that he'd found that "enforced rest is a good thing, particularly for me. . . . I've thought more than at any time in my life. It's been a painful but salutary experience."

Part of what Lincoln was dealing with, as he wrote his old friend from Buenos Aires, Maria Rosa Oliver, was the sense of staleness he felt about the ballet; perhaps he'd gone on with it too long after his initial passion had somewhat faded; besides, he felt growing disgust with those aesthetes who believed that art is superior to life. Oliver agreed with him, and put a positive gloss on his disenchantment: "You are growing. . . . You have lived for too many years in the world of aesthetics, not in the real one, although, in a very strange and moving way [she was referring to his left-wing sympathies, which she shared], you always knew that the real world—with its misery and pain—existed."

Lincoln also confided to her that he felt an emerging attraction to Roman Catholicism. On that score Oliver severely rebuked him: "You say you believe by instinct in supernatural powers. Well, so do I. But why seek in an earthly orthodoxy your contact with them? . . . mysticism yes, my darling, but not as an escapism . . . call God what helps you to live, but don't mention Him too much. First one must achieve inner unity, then comes the sense of Wholeness with everything that exists."

E. M. Forster had much the same reaction to Lincoln's incipient attraction to Catholicism. Forster was on a visit to the States that spring and saw Lincoln in New York shortly before he and Fidelma left for their rest in the country. "I saw of course," Forster later wrote him, "that you were very ill, and you are not well enough in your letter for my taste and hopes." Forster himself had had an acute depressive episode in the fall of 1948, and provided what comfort he could. He felt that Lincoln's financial worries had played a "much larger" role than he himself supposed. "You were so overtired and accused yourself [in a previous letter] of things that did not exist." Like Rosa Oliver, Forster told Lincoln plainly that "I certainly do mistrust Catholicism (for those who did not grow up in it)," and thought that "its assertion that it has worked, that it is a success, ought to be rejected in the realm of the spirit."

Mina's response was more pointed still. Her longtime Bloomsburyite friend David Garnett assured her that "Lincoln's aberration . . . would prove temporary; I have known people to become [Catholics] for 2 or 3 years & then completely recover." She herself had longed all her life, and especially in the period following her young husband's death, for the capacity to "believe" and, without feeling fraudulent, to pray. But she was denied that comfort, that ability, as she wrote Lincoln, "to find an opening in myself which would have permitted a faith . . . a path to follow." Still, she tried her best to convey empathy for his "spiritual experience," for what he described in a letter to her as an "excessive and almost insupportable clarity where everything seems to be an illumination of normal order."

But his description of the "God father" he'd found, a God of "terrible mildness—the God who is not necessarily good but who is also terrible"— sounded to Mina "much more like the Jewish than the Christian God," as well as their own father, Louis, whose death she sometimes thought Lin-

coln had "never fully faced." They both, Mina added, had in their different ways, experienced extreme suffering, in part a punishment for their
shared "sin of pride." But she felt confident, she wrote her brother, that
given his "quality, power and depth of conscience," he'd "rise above all
this agony"; her faith in his "ultimate victory is complete."

Nelson Rockefeller urged Lincoln not to "put yourself under too much
pressure, as there's a lot of time ahead." But that, of course, was like telling
an alcoholic to *just stop drinking*. Temperamentally Lincoln was incapable
of suddenly (or ever) becoming prudent and low-key. Even while recuper-
ating, he continued to jump back up now and then on his multitasking
trampoline. Some of his renewed activity was modest—an article for the
New Republic, an introduction to a small book of Nadelman's drawings—
but he also began hatching more grandiose schemes, including an elaborate proposal for a "Newport Festival" that envisioned, among much else,
erecting a permanent opera house; the project, unsurprisingly, found no
takers.

Fidelma, too, gradually revived as the summer progressed. Unlike Lincoln, her depressive disorder seems to have lacked much of a manic
component—that is, any over-the-top outbursts of rabid activity. But in
her quiet, reserved way, she did begin to socialize again and even started to
think about resuming her painting. In August she felt well enough to
travel to Naushon, wanting to revive her memories of the place for a
painting she had in mind. And her engagement with her natural surroundings, always profoundly important to her, resurfaced. Writing "from
Sodom by the Sea" (Fire Island), Lincoln described to Cadmus and Tooker
(who were still together, but not for much longer) Fidelma's gentle ministrations to an ailing spider crab, stuck in the sand. She managed to work
the crab free (she'd been reading Albert Schweitzer, Lincoln campily
explained) and tossed it back into the sea. "God recognized this act of
mercy," Lincoln wrote, by rewarding them with still more spider crabs,
along with their fiddler and soft-shell relatives, blowfish, and an abundance
of sea moss; those that failed to revive were moved indoors, thus turning
their house into "a Museum full of . . . Bosch views of undersea life."

"Cherish Fidelma," Maria Rosa Oliver wrote him passionately from
Buenos Aires: "I'm sure you need nobody so much as you need her. She is
the most understanding person I have ever met, and you must have such a
person near you." Lincoln well understood Fidelma's centrality to him;
only a few months later he'd write, "God has at a crucial point in my life
sent me an angel, whom I married ten years ago and with whom I have
always been much too happy for my deserts . . . she is far nicer than me."
But now and then the problem of "the boys" *would* prove difficult for
Fidelma, though most people, then and since, have assumed that she
always took Lincoln's "proclivities" in unbroken stride.

On this score Rosa, who was entirely unjudgmental about Lincoln's attraction to young men—indeed, she admonished him for sometimes feeling guilty about it: "Au fond, it is the puritan in you. . . . My God, Lincolncito, why don't you admit to yourself that it is no sin to love a young body or a young spirit." Yet she also had some cautionary advice for him. She reminded him that although Fidelma was able to ignore his casual male pickups and to turn some of his longer-term male partners, like Pete Martínez and Jensen Yow, into personal friends, what was not supportable was "to hear the person one loves talking continually or being obsessed by a third person; then one not only feels useless but *de trop*. And when discretion and dignity prevents us to complain or protest, one gets innerly poisoned."

Rosa believed Fidelma incapable of bitterness, but she did warn Lincoln to guard against "the need to tell." She wisely considered the typical "outburst of sincerity" to "the person we love or loves us" as a covert device for helping oneself decide whether the current obsession was significant or not; "the child's cruelty goes on in us when we are no longer children, it is persistent though camouflaged." Rosa felt certain that Fidelma would and must remain the most important person in his life: "You cannot imagine future years without her. Yes, she has patience and understanding because she loves you deeply. It must be difficult to be your loving wife. Your luck has been great to have such a wife. . . . *She* is the gift of Heaven, be sure of it."

As their depressions lifted in tandem, Lincoln and Fidelma began to invite a few select visitors out to Fire Island, Paul Cadmus and George Tooker among them; Lincoln thought Tooker looked "thin" but the two "had lovely talks" together. The longest-staying guests that summer were a male couple Lincoln had known casually for a year or so: the wealthy young art gallery owner Ed Hewitt and his on-again, off-again lover, Dan Maloney, a promising and handsome art student, outgoing and full of life, with an entertaining, generous spirit. Lincoln would grow increasingly disenchanted over the years with Ed but increasingly entranced by Dan, who would become an integral, even essential, part of Lincoln's life for more than two decades.

At the end of October 1949, rehearsals began for the ballet's three-week season at City Center, with opening night set for November 20. Lincoln and Fidelma continued to spend time on Fire Island through October but then shifted their residence back to New York and once again plunged, a bit more diffidently than in the past, back into the maelstrom.

City Center

(1948–1950)

I T WAS NONE other than the impresario Sol Hurok, a man Lincoln disliked and distrusted, who made it possible for Balanchine to restage the Stravinsky-Fokine *Firebird* (originally created for Diaghilev's company in 1910) for the ballet's new season in late November 1949. There had been other versions in the years between, most recently Ballet Theatre's 1945 production for which Hurok (then managing the company) himself put up $25,000 to commission new sets from Marc Chagall. The sets had remained Hurok's property and, as a personal friend of Morton Baum's, he now offered to sell them to City Center for the nominal sum of $4,200.[1]

Morton Baum found the needed money, mostly from the coffers of City Center's successful new drama company, led by the British actor Maurice Evans. The resurrection of *Firebird* was one of several unexpected events that together contributed to holding the not-yet-stabilized ballet company together. During the long hiatus that preceded the new season, there was considerable fear that a number of principal dancers might defect. Yet with the single exception of Marie-Jeanne, all returned. Joining them was a new roster of established dancers increasingly attracted to Balanchine's work and to the company's growing reputation for innovative classicism—including Janet Reed and Melissa Hayden of Ballet Theatre. In addition, Balanchine's old friend, the superbly gifted designer Barbara Karinska, knowing the company couldn't afford her high fees, offered to costume a second new Balanchine ballet, *Bourrée Fantasque*, strictly for cost—forty-two costumes in all, which Lincoln thought the most "spectacular" designs he'd seen "since Bérard's for *Cotillon*."

Like Karinska, Jerome Robbins would have a long, notable history with the company. Still dancing as well as choreographing, he would be one of the principals in the December 1 premiere of *Bourrée*. Despite the mixed reception *The Guests* received, Balanchine felt certain that Robbins was unusually talented and late in 1949 made him associate artistic director of the company. Lincoln, too, regarded Jerry as "a clever boy, really gifted," and thought his appointment "a smart move" on Balanchine's part, not least because it would help to "de-Russianize the City Center."

Despite these upbeat signs, the company's future remained clouded. In the months preceding City Center's new season, both Ballet Russe and Sadler's Wells had, with their traditional programming, completed successful runs in New York and, it was feared, saturated the limited market—especially since enthusiasm for Balanchine's innovative ballets in these years was still confined to a limited cognoscenti with a taste for the unexpected. The mainstream American audience had never yet, even when overseas competition wasn't in town, lined up in droves at the City Center box office.

The deepening resistance in the United States to the avant-garde reflected the spreading equation by the late forties of that which was "different," that which departed from traditional American behavior and values, with deviation from a growing national consensus that "communism" represented a profound menace (when defined at all, communism was simplified to mean Soviet-style authoritarianism). In a country grown rapidly, and even rabidly, conservative, to stray from mainstream values was to become an object of suspicion and scorn.

Such reflexive orthodoxy was less apparent in the arts, though the decade that ran roughly from 1947 to 1957 saw considerably less innovative work than in the earlier part of the century. There were pockets of creative ferment—bebop in jazz, the insistent subjectivity of action painting, the "spontaneous flow" of the Beats—and islands of radical communalism existed from San Francisco's North Beach to New York's Greenwich Village (even if few blacks were seen and though women of ambition and talent were routinely belittled). Such pockets of Bohemia were largely underground in these years. Above ground, it was Herman Wouk's runaway best-seller *Marjorie Morningstar* (in which the heroine finally has the "good sense" to forgo rebelliousness in favor of middle-class security) that encapsulated dominant values of the day, along with the macho white male triumphalism of John Wayne's movies. They, far more than Allen Ginsberg or Charlie Parker, typified the era.

Doubtless many artists of the day would have denied that they'd retreated, consciously or otherwise, from experimentation; most artists, after all, proudly self-define as pioneers of newness. Yet the reckless, hotheaded witch hunts of Senator Joseph McCarthy and his minions unquestionably changed the country's cultural climate. It was difficult, after all, to escape the relentless hammering of the House Un-American Activities Committee (HUAC); Hollywood alone endured 135 investigations between 1946–54, and HUAC's wrecking balls mindlessly enforced anti-Communist dogma, successfully squeezing the film industry into a conformist straitjacket and destroying, in the process, numerous careers.

As for Balanchine and Kirstein, they were barely within shouting distance of each other's political views. Supreme innovator in the dance, Balanchine was conservative both in public affairs and in religion. Generally he held himself aloof from anything to do with politics, though he was

known to be resolutely anti-Soviet; in religion, too, he was a strict traditionalist, adhering firmly to the Russian Orthodox Church of his youth.
Lincoln, as he grew older, grew closer to Balanchine's attraction to religious orthodoxy, or at least to its theatrical rituals. But politically the two
remained far apart.

During the cold-war period, Lincoln continued to hold on to his long-
standing left-wing views, but with less vehemence—and far less public
expression—than earlier. There were times, though, when he let loose
without restraint, as when, dining with an old friend in 1949, he "shrieked
against the atom-bomb." Both his siblings, Mina and George, also felt
strongly about the country's conservative turn. As early as 1947 Mina
denounced James Pope-Hennessey's "disgusting" new book, *America Is an
Atmosphere*, for droning on about the romantic glories of the Old South
"without suggesting, except in one place, that the negroes are anything
but the happiest of body-servants."

As for George Kirstein, when the prominent State Department official
Alger Hiss was indicted for perjury after denying that he'd been the leader
of a secret Communist cell during the 1930s, he played a leading role in
raising money to help defray Hiss's legal expenses; he claimed to have "no
fixed opinion as to whether Hiss is guilty or not," yet he himself contributed five hundred dollars toward Hiss's defense. Later, from 1955 to
1965, George would serve as publisher of the liberal magazine *The Nation*.

Lincoln had one vulnerability that Mina and George did not: his
highly irregular sex life. Homosexuality was endemic in Lincoln's circles,
shared by most of the male dancers in his company and a great many people of accomplishment whom he knew—Virgil Thomson, Philip Johnson,
George Tooker, Paul Cadmus, Leonard Bernstein, Paul Bowles, Tchelitchev, Auden, Spender, and Isherwood—to name but a few. But in the
cold-war years homosexuality became far more suspect than during the
preceding decades, and subject to far more official scrutiny; "queers," like
"Reds," came to represent a subversive nonconformity that was thought to
imperil the "American way."

When Alfred Kinsey published his two pioneering volumes on sexual
behavior in 1948 and 1952, declaring (among much else) in the first volume that 37 percent of the adult male population in this country had had
at least one homosexual experience to orgasm (a statistic since confirmed),
an onslaught of outrage nearly buried him and his work. Queer bars
(mostly Mafia-owned) continued to pay off the police but were more frequently raided and with more dire consequences: arrests, extortions, publication of names in the press, followed by loss of jobs and apartments.
Federal agencies, and particularly the State Department, inaugurated
secret probes of their employees' personal lives, leading to dozens of firings, public disgrace, and ruined lives.

Lincoln had never put much effort, even as a younger man, into concealing his sexuality; nor had he ever gone out of his way to announce it. His marriage to Fidelma may secondarily have provided protective covering, but that wasn't his intention in marrying her. Nor is there any evidence that in a deepening conformist climate he readjusted his private life; he continued to be as homosexually active as before, he would never have considered the notion of shunning unmarried gay friends, limiting the sexy references that dotted his sometimes campy letters and conversations, or ceasing to vacation in Fire Island's notoriously gay resort. He and Fidelma continued to spend a good deal of time during summer and early fall in their house (the ex–Coast Guard station) just east of Cherry Grove. He had "an anthropomorphic passion" for Fire Island, but even before the heightened cold-war crackdowns, he and Fidelma had "never . . . [gone] to the bar, except on off-nights, and we never see all the fascinating Fauna which makes FIRE Island Firey." The fact that Auden and his boyfriend, Chester Kallman, had, in these years, a beachfront shack in Cherry Grove was an added source of pleasure.

Sadler's Wells's four-week engagement at the Metropolitan Opera House ended just two weeks before the City Center season began. The English company had broken all attendance records and (unlike the Ballet Russe) had been given a delirious critical reception, with special praise heaped on its dazzling prima ballerina, Margot Fonteyn. Lincoln went to see Sadler's Wells often during its New York run, and he regaled his new epistolary friend, the English dance critic Richard ("Dickie") Buckle, with his candid opinions of the company. Buckle, nearly a decade younger than Lincoln, had started the periodical *Ballet* in 1939; then, following World War II (during which he served in the Scots Guards), restarted it in 1946. Buckle was, as well, an influential and acute dance critic, known for his wit and occasional flippancy; from 1948 to 1955 he was the ballet critic for *The Observer* and from 1959 to 1975 for the *Sunday Times*. Buckle was entirely open about his homosexuality at a time when such acts were legal crimes.

His friendship with Lincoln began when Buckle invited him to write up Sadler's Wells's New York engagement for *Ballet*. Lincoln thanked him but declined, not wanting to complicate the British critics' reaction when, as he hoped, the City Center ballet might one day perform in England. But the two men continued to correspond, exchanging down-to-earth, undiplomatic confidences. They would meet in person the following year, and thereafter they (in Lincoln's words) "cruised into intimacy at several thousand miles distance and several hundred miles an hour cruising speed"; their letters thereafter became even more forthright, and were often hilariously campy (Lincoln sometimes addressed Buckle as "dear Dickie von Meck" and signed himself "Hideola" or "Horrorpants"). Superficially at least the two had much in common: both were sexually attracted to handsome young men, had sharp wits, were conspicuously opinionated, could sometimes be socially difficult—Lincoln the more rude and argumentative of the two—and both were subject to serious depression.

But they were also very different: Buckle lacked Lincoln's generosity of spirit and his muted self-display; his range of interests and breadth of knowledge; his piercing intelligence, self-awareness, animal energy, and—though he liked to disguise it—his talent for intimacy. Lincoln told Buckle that he was "entirely unromantic" and insisted that he didn't permit himself "the possibility of a continuous emotional relationship with ANYBODY." But this was pure bunkum (unless meant as pure camp), since Lincoln already had long-standing relationships with, among others, Fidelma, Mina, Auden, Pete Martínez, Tchelitchev, and Paul Cadmus. And he would have others, including long romantic ones, with Jensen Yow and Dan Maloney. (Not that longevity is ever a reliable gauge of quality, or that his attachments weren't sometimes marked by periods of angry alienation.)

Buckle and Lincoln also had somewhat contrasting takes on Sadler's Wells. Buckle had certain complaints about the company; he thought the choreography of its director, Ninette de Valois, "deadly" (he referred to her *Checkmate* as "the most boring ballet in the world"), and he disliked David Webster, general administrator of Covent Garden, the company's London home. Buckle described Webster as "bland and self-satisfied," a "complacent eunuch" who "should have been a bishop." Lincoln himself thought Webster "a police-inspector, commissar, culture-gangster." But he decided "there's no point in being mean to him if you want something," and Lincoln did—an invitation for the New York City Ballet to perform at Covent Garden.

Overall Buckle was a decided fan of Sadler's Wells and predicted that Lincoln would become one as well. And to some extent that proved true; Lincoln liked many of the individual dancers, and found much to admire in certain performances. But whereas Dickie had predicted that Lincoln would adore Margot Fonteyn, his actual reaction to her, while admiring, was compromised: he thought her "a lovely dancer"—and in *Swan Lake*, "exquisite"—but a "muted" one, her full powers unawakened.

Lincoln already knew many of those connected to Sadler's Wells and met most of the others at a party he and Fidelma gave for the company. Champagne flowed, spirits were high, and the last of the guests, David Webster, lingered on and on; "He WOULDN'T go home," Lincoln reported to Dickie. During the height of the party, Webster got into "a nice frank row" with Virgil Thomson; the part of the argument that Lincoln overheard had Virgil saying "the trouble with you is you don't give a damn about music," with Webster replying, "I am interested in the maintenance of a great institution, of which music is a part."

Lincoln excused himself and went to talk to Michael Somes, a leading Sadler's Wells dancer. He'd thought Somes *looked* "ravishing" in *Swan*

Lake—"he is a beautiful boy [with]. . . a pleasing princely elegance"—but alas (Lincoln wrote Dickie) "he don't dance very hot, but then who does? [Anton] Dolin? Mercy, mother!" Subsequently Lincoln raised his opinion of Somes as a dancer and liked him "enormously" as a person. But for another Sadler's Wells principal, Robert Helpmann, he felt mostly contempt. He acknowledged that Helpmann was "intelligent," and thought him "fine" as the clown sister in *Cinderella*. Yet he recoiled from what he described as "a sort of dwarfish, vengeful narcissism [that] explodes into little nodules of unlove."

As for Frederick Ashton, the company's leading choreographer and a Buckle favorite, Lincoln liked him personally but feared that theirs was "a friendship that should have started twenty years ago; we're both too old and set now." He thought Ashton "rather sad": He "needs new excitements." To that end Lincoln invited him to do a ballet about Rimbaud for City Center, to music by Benjamin Britten (it would be performed in 1950 as *Illuminations*). Ashton was still occasionally dancing, but Lincoln found his "Carabosse" in *The Sleeping Beauty* to have "a rather limited repertory of denunciatory gestures; there are six in all."

Further, he thought Ashton's choreography for *Symphonic Variations* (which Dickie found "charming," and which many continue to view as a masterpiece) was "to say the least, naive." But he reported to Buckle that "everyone but me loved it, and I must say I am practically the only carping voice; only I don't carp aloud." As for Balanchine, he thought Ashton "has a real gift for individual variations and the invention of point steps, but little for large concerted organizations." Balanchine agreed with Lincoln that "the real hero" of the Sadler's Wells company was its conductor Constant Lambert: "He is a genius of tempi," as Lincoln put it, "absolutely on the nose in every variation . . . he whipped people up into applause, purely by sound." Balanchine also felt that English training was "better for the AVERAGE dancer than any he has seen," but he disliked "a certain emphasis on primness." "Don't quote him or me," Lincoln warned Buckle, "or it will be the END."

Seeing the work of Ashton and other English choreographers convinced Lincoln more than ever that Balanchine was "the only genius of the dance since Petipa," and it angered him that he'd still "not been properly seen except in his Stravinsky works." But he supposed that was part and parcel of Balanchine resisting "popular interest and acceptance," and he admired him for it: "he is ONLY a dancer; he hates painting; he dislikes pantomime, and hence the dramatic and spectacular elements are left out of our repertory, with a few major exceptions" (the upcoming revival of *Prodigal Son* being one).

A mere two weeks after Sadler's Wells concluded its acclaimed New York run, it was the New York City Ballet's daunting turn at bat. For this new season, Lincoln's initial plans were cautious; "my idea," he wrote Virgil Thomson, "is to try to establish ourselves modestly this year and have little deficit, and hope for something later." But Lincoln's diffidence gave way, as it often did (especially in fantasy) to outsize display. Though the company had only four weeks of rehearsal time, it ended up reviving ten ballets and producing four new ones: Christensen's *Jinx*, to music by Benjamin Britten; the William Dollar–Vivaldi *Ondine;* Balanchine's *Bour-rée Fantasque* to music by Emmanuel Chabrier; and the Balanchine-Stravinsky *Firebird.*

A week before the November 23 opening of the new season, the ballet had a $25,000 advance sale; that wasn't spectacular but it was higher than ever before. Due to run through December 11, the season was a week longer than previous ones, and its sixteen performances would play from Wednesday through Sunday rather than simply two days a week. All of which seemed a good omen and generated considerable excitement within the company. Happily, an omen for once proved accurate.[2]

The high point came with the premiere of *Firebird* on November 27. The audience gave it a clamorous reception, and the critics—including John Martin—hailed everything from Jean Rosenthal's lighting to Maria Tallchief's dancing. Additional performances were immediately added (four in all), and Martin warned his readers to "get your order in early." The day after the premiere Lincoln wrote Stravinsky that they'd had an "extravagant success," and he praised Tallchief as "absolutely miraculous, really a bird-of-fire."

A few days later, after Balanchine's second new ballet, *Bourrée Fan-tasque,* debuted and received only a slightly less rapturous reception, Lincoln sent Dickie Buckle a far giddier account. According to Lincoln, Balanchine had choreographed *Firebird* "with his tongue in his cheek, because everyone says we are so highbrow, and that I am such an art snob; we don't care about the PEUPLE Alright [*sic*], Buster, we give 'em *Fireboid* and *Boury Fantcy;* and they respond like sulphur and molasses."

Neither Christensen's *Jinx* nor Dollar's *Ondine* fared nearly as well as the new Balanchine ballets, though Moncion, Janet Reed, and the upcoming Herbie Bliss were highly praised for their dancing. *Jinx* had more fans than *Ondine,* among them Sadler's Wells's director, Ninette de Valois, who, along with David Webster, attended often during the season. Webster told Lincoln that if the company continued to improve he would invite them to Covent Garden in 1951. "In 1951," Lincoln wrote Dickie, "we won't need to come. But I would adore to come in 1950." De Valois, however, didn't think they were ready. Lincoln blamed that opinion on her having seen the "wrong" performances, but though he wouldn't know it for some months, the case for Covent Garden in 1950 wasn't closed.

In the meantime Lincoln and Balanchine turned, with Baum's encouragement, toward planning yet another four-week season, to begin a mere two months hence. The company had yet to turn a profit, but the final two performances in December had sold out, the critical reception had been splendid, de Valois had declared the company the most important in America—and Baum was more convinced than ever that he had a tiger by the tail.[3]

Plans for the February 1950 season moved ahead rapidly. Stravinsky agreed to come in from the West Coast to conduct the opening performances of both *Firebird* and *Orpheus*. Jerome Robbins would do a new ballet based on Auden's seminal poem "Age of Anxiety" and would collaborate with Balanchine (as well as dance in) a second new ballet, the lighthearted *Jones Beach* (swimsuits by Jantzen and Leonard Bernstein conducting.) Freddie Ashton, for a fee of two thousand dollars, agreed to the world premiere of his major new work, *Les Illuminations*, based on Benjamin Britten's setting of the Rimbaud text. Balanchine would revise his 1929 *Prodigal Son* (the final ballet he created for Diaghilev) and would also create *Pas de Deux Romantique*, to music by Carl Maria von Weber, for Janet Reed and Herbie Bliss. An additional eight ballets would be revived. It was quite a lineup; "ambitious" would be an understatement.

Baum still insisted that the cost of new productions remained Lincoln's responsibility, and Lincoln estimated their overall expense at twenty-five thousand, with the Balanchine and Robbins ballets costing little (Jantzen cheerfully picked up the tab for the free swimsuit ad *Jones Beach* would provide). But *Les Illuminations* would eat up a full fifteen thousand, since Ashton was nervously unwilling to sanction anything less than a fully dressed production, including decor by Cecil Beaton. With considerable effort, Lincoln managed to piece together ten thousand dollars each from a variety of individuals, including Mrs. W. K. Vanderbilt, Oliver Jennings, and Alice de la Mar; and Alice and David Bouverie paid for the entire cost of the Ashton ballet.

In the midst of the hectic preparations for the February season came the barely-hoped-for news that David Webster had changed his mind (apparently other arrangements he'd been working on had fallen through), and the City Center ballet was invited to perform at Covent Garden for five weeks that summer. Additionally (this had been agreed upon earlier) Balanchine would go over in April to stage his 1941 *Ballet Imperial* for Margot Fonteyn and Michael Somes. For Lincoln the Covent Garden invitation was both a dream come true and a source of nervous apprehension. As he would later write, "To an important degree, an alien audience establishes the artistic, economic, and political importance of a luxury export. Acceptance by a foreign public affixes a convincing seal of prestige for home approval." Whether the City Center company would gain that seal gave Lincoln many a sleepless night.

But first up was the February-March 1950 season in New York. With an advance sale of some fifty-five thousand dollars, more than double that of the preceding season, the company opened on February 21 with *Firebird*, Stravinsky conducting. Two days later saw the revival of *Prodigal Son*, and then, in rapid succession, the premieres of *The Age of Anxiety* and (the gala opening, attended by the British ambassador) of Ashton's *Les Illuminations*—it got fifteen curtain calls. The following week *Jones Beach* debuted. In between these major events, eleven other ballets were also danced.

It was more than breathless—it was highly successful. Overall the critics warmly approved, with John Martin edging ever closer to becoming an outright Balanchine fan, calling *Prodigal Son* a work of "irresistible emotional conviction." Lincoln could hardly have been more pleased at the outcome. The season ended with another deficit, but an insignificant one, the smallest yet. And he adored nearly everything new that they'd done; he thought Robbins's *Age of Anxiety* "very impressive . . . nervous and brilliant" and "close to Auden's intention, but not illustrative" (Auden himself "hated" it); he also thought that Robbins was "sensational . . . a remarkable dramatic dancer" as the lead in *Prodigal Son*. And he was delighted with *Jones Beach*; its "sort of celestial musical comedy atmosphere" was like nothing else in the company's repertory and could serve as a charming final ballet for a given evening.

The success of *Les Illuminations* came as something of a relief. During rehearsals Lincoln had worried that Ashton, "very sweet and frightened," was "so much in awe of Balanchine that he is flying in the other direction and wants to produce something never seen before on land or sea." Besides, Freddie was having trouble with his lead dancer Nicholas Magallanes, who, as Lincoln described it, was "so unpredictable, by turns so cat-like and so passive, so fierce and so soft that Fred is bewildered" and, Lincoln initially feared, somewhat paralyzed. But Ashton had come through with what Lincoln thought was at least (thanks in part to Cecil Beaton) a "wildly pretty" piece, "a sort of child's version" of Rimbaud.

The season's success, after fifteen years of formidable effort, was to Lincoln "as gratifying as it is disconcerting. I feel like the Irish sweepstake winners who fall dead from the shock of joy. Everything has opened up for us." Above all he came away with, if possible, a still more heightened sense of Balanchine's "great difference from other masters" and a keener sense of what made him so special: his "sharp, abrupt, jazzy" style "combined with an ironic courtesy and a very intense physical tenderness, a provocative physicality, an overture to love." Lincoln felt that even in the section of the minor-key *Jones Beach* where mosquitoes disturb the corps of dancers, he could detect the essence of Balanchine's aesthetic: that "divine providence" can interrupt all plans, "that nature is balanced and that God, not art, is divine"; as Balanchine himself said, "c'est une question morale," which meant, in Lincoln's gloss, that his choreography was "never decorative, never anecdotal, never small-scale. It always refers to possibility; its limits and extremities."

Dickie Buckle predicted to Lincoln that the London season of the New York City Ballet "will have a great success." Lincoln was less convinced. "Our repertory," he wrote Dickie, "is right odd, you know." By "odd" he meant peculiarly "American." And what did he mean by "American"? Shortly before the London engagement began, Lincoln spelled out his definition in a particularly brilliant and contested two-part article, "Balanchine and American Ballet," published in Buckle's magazine, *Ballet*. How did an American style differ from other forms of national expression? Lincoln thought improvisation was the essence, in contrast to the European grounding in authority. "Frontiersmen made our country," Lincoln wrote, "and while we have long conquered our physical frontier (bypassing many moral ones), frontiersmen have few rules and slight precedent to go by. We are continually improvising our physical success on a basis of individual performance."

As for the "classic" American style, Lincoln emphasized "a leanness, a visual asceticism, a candour, even an awkwardness which is in itself elegant, shared also by some of our finest Colonial silver, the thin carving on New England grave slabs and in the quicksilver of Emily Dickinson's unrhymed quatrains. And sometimes there is a galvanizing, acetylene brilliance, a deep potential of incalculable human strength which, particularly between all our wars, is a novel and hopeful promise. . . . Our democracy is based on a hope of infinite possibility, whose symbol is a permanent post-adolescence. . . . We are boys, neither men nor princes. When we get older, too often—alas—we don't grow up: we become old boys, but there are wasteful rising generations to take our place."

In terms of the dance itself, Lincoln provided some specific examples of how he felt our distinctive national ethos expressed itself: "It is hard, if not impossible, for an American male dancer to bow without shyness or servility . . . few Americans can accept homage simply, as if it were their personal due . . . few Americans have any comprehension of time, or its passage—that our own time depends upon time past, that there is any continuum of accumulated manners. . . . The European ballerina is queen. The American ballerina . . . must perforce be queenly enough to claim her calling, but more on the basis of physical (or sexual) prowess, or of mysterious intensity (like a film star), than from an ideal of authoritative virginity or inaccessibility (like Taglioni or Pavlova)."

All of which was prelude to Lincoln's claim that no American choreographer better represented the singular American national character than the Russian-born Georgi Melitonovitch Balanchivadze—George Balanchine—who in his sixteen years of creative work in the United States, ranging in various forms from classic ballet to musical comedy to film, had found, even if he had not invented, this dominant American style. What fascinated Balanchine "was the human body's instinctive, yet scarcely unconscious, expression of its era—our corsetless, all but skirtless, princeless era, where good social and theatrical manners are more a problem of individual obligation and affection than the reflection of the devotion for, or authority felt resident in, sovereign or system."

This was a remarkable summation, acute and even courageous ("older boys") in some sections, debatable in others. And debate it got, far more than Lincoln anticipated or wanted. What upset him most was the reaction of some of his own dancers to the two-part piece. He claimed that Tallchief for a time refused to speak to him and that Magallanes cut him whenever they crossed paths. Apparently they and others felt that Lincoln had written out of a "slavish and servile bid for the flattery of the English dancers," preferring them to American ones. In fact he decidedly had not; he thought Sadler's Wells was run "like a girls' finishing school" and found most English dancing "weak and thin," prim and precise rather than, like the Americans, quirkily alive; English dancing in 1950 needed, in Lincoln's opinion, "a trace of hysteria."

He blamed himself harshly (as was his wont) for the misunderstanding, for having been "so irresponsibly analytical," for not having realized that his own company might take his comments personally. "I do not know whether to apologize," he wrote Dickie Buckle, "or attempt to explain; I hate to hurt people's feelings, particularly those of whom I'm fond." Lincoln realized that few members of his company would have studied the article carefully; more likely most had simply scanned the pages looking for their names and, finding Fonteyn and Somes instead, had taken umbrage, assuming that Lincoln thought little of them. He also realized that the tempest would soon pass, that most of the company was well aware of his respect for them, and they returned it (there were exceptions, to be sure; some dancers, as Lincoln approached his mid-forties, found him distant and intimidating). In the end what was most telling about the entire episode was that Lincoln—whom some, especially later in his life, saw as insensitive and harsh—anguished over the dancers' hurt feelings and repeatedly blamed himself for having been "so obtuse and thoughtless" in his remarks.

At the end of March, Lincoln decided to accompany Balanchine to London for the Sadler's Wells production of *Ballet Imperial*. The point wasn't to hold Balanchine's hand—no one would have welcomed it less—nor to bask in his glory, but rather to use the occasion to negotiate final terms with David Webster for the New York City Ballet's forthcoming summer visit to Covent Garden. Frances Hawkins also came along; she'd agreed to return to the company for a brief time to help out with the press of business, and her presence would again prove indispensable.[4]

Webster had held off, somewhat mysteriously, from signing the final contract, which called for a six-week engagement at $5,600 per week, plus one-half the transportation costs (Baum picking up the other half). For a number of days after their arrival, Webster—as Lincoln wrote home to Betty Cage—"has not had the decency even to see" Balanchine, and his "lousy behaviour" in regard to the summer contract continued into the second week. Lincoln's guess was that Webster wanted to renege on transportation expenses, but he was determined to hold him to point, knowing that no other possibility existed for raising the needed money. "I would adore to come here," Lincoln wrote Betty; "the theatre is heaven; the audiences are apathetic but vast and we could electrify them into spasms." But he was immovable about Webster paying for half the transportation costs.

Lincoln lived at Buckle's house during his three-week stay in London and before arriving had sent him an astonishing letter of warning (it would be the first time the two men had actually met) that painted himself in the most ferocious possible terms: "There are several things you must know about me. . . . I am not rich; that is, I was. In the last three years I have spent a quarter of a million dollars. . . . I own no real estate, live in three rooms, and that is *all*. . . . I do not trust anyone, neither you, nor myself. By trust, I mean, the delicious relaxation of the merged immersion. . . . I gather you are not very kind, but then neither am I. I try to learn kindness, to suppress vanity and to pray, and while I do not credit the divinity of Jesus Christ, I believe in God. . . . I violently disapprove of any possessions save pictures, and believe that pictures are merely granted one's stewardship for a few years, on their way to the museums. . . . The pastiche, the decorative, the baroque [Dickie's house was filled with baroque paintings and assorted, mostly elegant, bric-a-brac] I find vanitous and uninteresting. The Baroque is the art of the Impersonator. . . . My taste is recklessly austere and resolutely stoic. I HATE refeenment [*sic*]. . . . I hate good taste, parties, divine people, historical personages, rising celebrities, promising artists, interesting personalities, etc. . . . The initial intimacy is a frequent convenience for me, but I take no responsibility for it, and often people are WOUNDED and BETRAYED when I turn around and never recall them; this is not being horrid, it's being busy. I am essentially only interested in my work, on a narrow basis, and I believe in Auden and Tchelitchew and they govern my life.

"Well, mother, was that a divine aria."

Dickie wasn't at all sure. "I have a feeling," he wrote back, that "you were afraid I was expecting we should have a love affair! . . . I know quite well we are not *at all* each other's types!—if that means anything." He went on, despite Lincoln's fierce warnings, to reiterate his invitation to move in. And when Lincoln did arrive at Victoria Station—Freddie Ashton had gone there to meet Lincoln's train from Southampton, but somehow missed him—Lincoln took a cab immediately to Dickie's house on the eastern edge of Chelsea, where Ashton and Balanchine joined them that first night for dinner. That is, when they could persuade Lincoln to get up off the floor where, even before unloading his luggage, he'd been displaying, and enthusiastically commenting on, George Platt Lynes's latest photographs of the company.

Dickie, a shrewd observer, gave Lincoln a quick once-over: "About six foot three and sturdy. His close cropped head had little back to it, but he had a powerful forehead, a jutting nose, and dark eyes, beneath well-marked brows, peered at the world through gold-rimmed glasses." Lincoln did an equally quick study of Dickie's house. He'd painted the paneled walls of the drawing-room crimson and hung the walls with seventeenth- and eighteenth-century Italian paintings by such artists as Sebastiano Ricci, Giovanni Pittoni, and Giovanni Pellegrini that depicted assorted Saint Sebastians and "Women Taken in Adultery." Lincoln soon began urging Dickie to sell them.

The very next evening the same group dined in the kitchen of the effervescent Lady Keynes—Lydia Lopokova, Diaghilev's former ballerina—in Gordon Square, Bloomsbury. After leaving, Dickie spotted a cat on the street and called out to it, "pooza-pooza"—an expression Lincoln ever after used for the cats he (as well as Fidelma and Balanchine) so adored; he sometimes called Dickie "pooza-pooza" as well. On the whole, their living arrangements worked out fine; Lincoln recognized Dickie's frivolous and somewhat malicious side, but liked him anyway. It helped that Dickie was away in Holland for part of the time; when he was home, Lincoln later campily complained, "I sweated alone some nights listening to the bells from the window and the grunts from the other side of the wall."

Lincoln decided early on not to see David Webster himself and to leave the negotiations entirely to Frances, suggesting she tell the Englishman that Lincoln "was a dangerous lunatic whom she was sent over to protect against any commitment of any sort." While Frances worked her considerable magic, Lincoln kept himself busy attending rehearsals for *Ballet Imperial*, making various business decisions by mail with Baum and Betty Cage, and taking side trips to Paris and Rome (the latter to attend Pavlik's new show of drawings, which he, and Auden, too, admired, but the critics did not).

Lincoln found postwar London itself "pretty uninteresting and grim . . . everyone hating Americans. . . . The theatre was poor; there is no real writing; painting is non-existent." He did see a number of friends, in particular Osbert Sitwell ("a sweet old incarnation of the last of the British

Empire, a kind of monument of memories, but very frank and open"), and Morgan Forster. Lincoln adored Morgan, and he in turn seemed pleased whenever Lincoln visited, though he denied someone's suggestion that Lincoln and Bob Buckingham, Forster's companion, had similar personalities: Lincoln, Morgan announced, was shy. Through Buckle, Lincoln also made a new acquaintance, the painter Lucian Freud; Lincoln thought him "very disorderly in his life, but magnificently orderly in his art."

Balanchine and Frances Hawkins had their different sorts of triumph. Balanchine's *Ballet Imperial* enjoyed a considerable success, and that in turn helped to soften up David Webster for Frances. She ended up getting better terms than Lincoln had thought possible, including the guarantee of thirteen thousand dollars for one-half the costs of transportation—and despite the fact that (at least according to Lincoln) Sol Hurok "tried to sell us down the river." Lincoln praised Frances to the skies and wrote to Baum that it was now "responsible to believe that we will have a success here, due to the fact that we dance the pants off the British. They know it and resent it . . . there is a real problem of admitting to themselves the excellence they know we have." He felt it more important than ever that their company not "look poor," because "the splendor of the spectacle is half the battle" with the British.

To ensure that end Lincoln was no sooner back in the States than he plunged into preparations for a ball at the Waldorf-Astoria on April 20 to raise money for new costumes. Six ballets were in special need, with four looking "pretty desperately shabby": *Symphony in C, Divertimento, Prodigal Son,* and *The Guests;* Balanchine himself had made the costumes currently being used in *Prodigal Son,* and both *Symphony in C* and *The Guests* were still performed in practice clothes. The Waldorf ball wasn't exactly a flop, but society (with a few exceptions, preeminently Mrs. W. K. Vanderbilt and Alice Bouverie) continued to prefer traditional ballet and withheld its wholehearted embrace of New York City Ballet. The ball ended up raising only enough money ($4,000) to enable Karinska to costume *Symphony in C;* Ashton's suggestion to change the clothes for *Serenade* to flowing robes was also adopted. "We won't look exactly poor" at Covent Garden, Lincoln wrote Buckle; "it will be neat but certainly not gaudy." He turned his efforts to seeking funds for a program book that would feature George Platt Lynes's theatrically elegant ballet photographs.

Simultaneously—Lincoln remained the master of multitasking, whether feeling manic or well—he set about organizing a show for London's Institute of Contemporary Arts to run at the same time the ballet company was performing. Even as his central focus remained on the all-important Covent Garden appearance, he didn't neglect his painter friends, still largely—in a world dominated by abstract expressionism—underappreciated, and some still unknown. The Institute exhibition was

scheduled to open in mid-July, would be titled American Symbolic Realism, and would feature (along with several artists Lincoln didn't personally know—Alton Pickens, Henry Koerner, Kenneth Davies) a number of
his old friends, including Paul Cadmus, George Tooker, Bernard Perlin,
Jared French, Ben Shahn, and Tchelitchev, as well as several recent
acquaintances, among them Andrew Wyeth and Honoré Sharrer, whose
polyptych *Tribute to the American Working People* would make an especially
strong impression.[5]

Lincoln's initial plan had been for him and Fidelma to share a house
with Balanchine and Tallchief, but when Buckle advised against the plan,
arguing that working and living together constantly could prove an irritant, Lincoln decided he was right. Dickie had suggested—"much as I dislike you"—that he and Fidelma simply stay with him. He'd generously
offered them the two bedrooms (he would sleep in the garden room), but
begged to be allowed to use the single bathroom in the house once a day.
If they had money to spare, they could pay ten guineas a week, half of what
Buckle charged when he rented out the whole house. Lincoln insisted on
twenty guineas. He predicted that Dickie and Fidelma "will love each
other . . . she is fascinated by hell, horror and guardsmen just as I am, and
has no recriminations, and after all she is Notre Dame de Sodome."

Lincoln and Fidelma flew to London in late June; the rest of the company, including Morton Baum, followed a week later. Lincoln confessed
to Dickie, "I dread our ordeal; I am frankly frightened. . . . I simply trem-
ble to think what will happen if the City Center has to bail us out; it means
we lost our position in New York, and there is nothing else left. But
Courage, whatever that means."

In the weeks preceding the Covent Garden opening, Lincoln tended
to various official duties (he led a panel on "Symbolic Realism in American
Painting"; he and Balanchine gave a talk at the London Ballet Circle)
while Fidelma spent most of her days happily visiting one museum after
another. Occasionally she'd go along with Lincoln on a social call ("I am
completely in love" with Bob and May Buckingham, she wrote home to
Paul), and in general greatly enjoyed herself. She and Dickie did get along
well, as Lincoln had predicted, but then again, Fidelma almost never spoke
negatively about anyone, whether to their faces or behind their backs.

Lincoln, on the other hand, was disgruntled from the first. Along with
the forebodings he'd brought with him, he found London a great bore—
"the deadly dullness and conventional behaviour and the furtive vice and
the awful slow rot." He was "very much entertained by Dickie Buckle's
life, and the procession of characters that wend their lightsome way
through this charming old Regency house." And as always, Forster and
Osbert Sitwell held up. But Lucian Freud was another matter. Lincoln
found him entangled in various sorts of improvised, competing relation-

ships between his Catholic-convert wife, assorted girlfriends, and three children (two "illegitimate").

The reception of the Symbolic Realism show Lincoln organized at the Institute of Contemporary Arts did nothing to improve his mood. The critic in the *Sunday Observer* spoke for the majority: "Most of these paintings have been worked over again and again with fine and feeble brush-strokes, in the manner of late Victorian anecdotal art, and it is disheartening to find so much labor expended to produce the mildest electric shocks." The anthropologist Geoffrey Gorer, whom Lincoln knew, wrote a complex piece for *The Listener* in which he praised the "superb technique" on display but thought it mostly misused in the service of "superficial sensuousness"; the one exception he made was for Paul Cadmus's "haunting and original symbolizations of evil" in his paintings *Sloth* and *Envy*, two of the *Seven Deadly Sins* project still in progress.

Lincoln responded with a strong letter of objection to *The Listener*, but Auden told him he was "wrong to take offense at Geoffrey's article . . . which, for him, was extremely friendly." Fidelma, whose lifetime strategy for muddling through was to present a politely pleasant face (a useful counterpoint to Lincoln's characteristic stance of gloom), wrote her brother that "the exhibition looks divine," then offhandedly added that "some people even like the pictures—though I believe most don't." After someone from the Tate Gallery saw the show and expressed interest, Lincoln offered to give the Tate three paintings (by Pickens, Koerner, and Perlin) as a gift; typically he made the gesture not in his own name but as coming from the Institute of Contemporary Arts. The gallery trustees accepted one of the three, Perlin's *Orthodox Boys*—the first contemporary American painting admitted to the Tate.

Balanchine and Lincoln decided that the opening night program at Covent Garden would consist of *Orpheus*, *Age of Anxiety*, and *Symphony in C*. Buckle felt that they were making "a great mistake," that although *Orpheus* was an "amazing" ballet, its pace was "too slow" and, coupled with Robbins's *Anxiety*, too innovative for the traditional-minded British critics; he urged instead that they start with *Firebird* and close with *Bourrée Fantasque*. Ashton, too, thought it was "madness" to open with *Orpheus* and suggested *Serenade* for the opening work. But Balanchine and Lincoln stuck with their original plan, perhaps in part because they felt the premiere audience would have a fair-size contingent of genuine balletomanes. The well-disposed critic Edwin Denby was coming from Italy, the dancer-choreographer John Taras from France, and the journalists Anatole Chujoy (editor of *Dance News*) and John Martin of the *New York Times* were due from the States. Lincoln's "angel," Morgan Forster, who hadn't been well recently, would also be attending as his personal guest.

Buckle and Ashton proved prophetic about the English critics and *Orpheus*. As Lincoln wrote Stravinsky, "They said it was acrobatic, nervous, not LYRICAL, not soft, Why don't they do *Giselle* and *Swan Lake*? Why don't they do *Sylphides*? Finally, why do they DANCE so much? Because they *can*, and because they like to dance and because Balanchine has the naive idea that the ballet is about dancing and not about revolting pastiche or self-pity."

Fidelma had quite a different take on the critical reaction. She reported to her brother, Paul, that the press notices were "excellent" and the company "a big success"—but that was more a reflection of her determined (and poignant) optimism than of the actual reviews. In truth very few of the notices for any of the ballets—*Serenade* was the chief exception—could be characterized as enthusiastic, though a number were sympathetically mixed and several dancers, especially Tanaquil Le Clercq and Janet Reed, were highly praised. The critical complaints varied: there wasn't enough scenery or "decoration"; too many of the ballets lacked "stories," were cold and "abstract," athletic rather than poetic, and, in the case of Robbins's two ballets, were "opaque"—though T. S. Eliot wrote Lincoln to say, "I was much impressed by 'The Age of Anxiety,' " and went on to compliment him on "a very remarkable achievement to have built up such a company in less than a generation"; Eliot parenthetically added: "I wish there was a 'Hound and Horn' still; the Partisan Review is so inadequate from the point of view of art and letters."

The company's chief public champion turned out to be Dickie Buckle himself (he was the only critic, for example, who unreservedly admired *Firebird*), and he later wrote a piece in *The Observer* rebuking his fellow reviewers for their fossilized response to Balanchine's dazzling inventions. Not even the country's native son, England's renowned choreographer Freddie Ashton, fared especially well when the American company presented his *Les Illuminations* during the second week of performances. The lukewarm response to Ashton so angered Lincoln, already mystified and overwrought at what he considered British "provincialism, ignorance, insularity, envy" (as he put it in a letter to Stravinsky), that in consultation with Morgan Forster, he wrote an indignant response to the anonymous London *Times* reviewer.

Lincoln's special effort on Ashton's behalf may have been partly due to a recent—and to Lincoln disturbing—estrangement between them. A few months before, while still in New York, Lincoln had written Freddie a letter urging him to "grow up out of romanticism into a position of classical responsibility and authority," and had even suggested that he take over Sadler's Wells from "Ninetter de Valore" [*sic*]. Ashton had apparently taken offense and failed to respond to that or any of Lincoln's several follow-up letters (which had also requested a needed answer to his invitation to choreograph a second new ballet for NYCB). Lincoln thought Ashton might additionally be angry with him for having commissioned a new ballet *(The Witch)* for the London run from the promising young choreographer John Cranko.

Lincoln became convinced that Freddie was "livid" with him, and he had rather plaintively asked Buckle to intervene: "I do love him [Ashton], for himself alone, but I wish he'd not sulk." Eventually, through Buckle, Freddie finally sent word that (as Dickie phrased it) "he loves being buffeted by your sound advice, and loves you dearly, longs to talk to you, but cannot exert himself to write letters"—though earlier he'd written Lincoln any number of them. In any case their friendship was sufficiently patched together for Ashton to resume communication and to attend the opening night of *Les Illuminations*. He'd predicted all along that his ballet would flop in England and that the critics would prefer Cranko (on that last count, he proved wrong; Cranko's *The Witch*, performed at the very end of the run, and a minor work, was in general disliked more than *Les Illuminations*).

At the opening-night party for Ashton's ballet that Lady Anne Rothermere gave (Lincoln described it as a "perfectly awful crush . . . like a salesman's convention in Ottawa"), he, Freddie, and Cecil Beaton got stuck for a time in the Covent Garden cellars when a door slammed behind them as they attempted to take a shortcut. When they finally arrived, the Duchess of Kent angered Lincoln with her gratuitously outspoken distaste for what she'd seen onstage, his anger temporarily appeased by George Lascelles, the Earl of Harewood, who was quick to express his enthusiasm for the company.

Lincoln already knew Harewood and his magazine, *Opera*, knew that he was "genuinely devoted to music," and that he and his wife were themselves good musicians. Harewood was also a man of insight and humor. When Lady Rothermere dropped him a curtsy, Harewood turned to Lincoln and said, " 'She must be mad; noble I may be, but royal I am not.' " Lincoln and Harewood would stay good friends over the coming years. Along with greatly liking him, Lincoln considered Harewood "very ambitious" and predicted that "sooner or later he will turn up in a very responsible position."

The London audiences seem to have enjoyed the American company far more than the critics did. Lincoln implausibly claimed that "no one cares a damn about the press; they have neither prestige nor power." But whatever the case, box office receipts did reach 75 percent of capacity, and performances were often greeted with extended applause and numerous curtain calls. This was not due to any special effort on the part of David Webster, who met with Lincoln exactly once for lunch (Lincoln paying the bill), or to Covent Garden–generated publicity for the American company. Webster "aided us in no way," Lincoln wrote Stravinsky.

Webster did decide to extend the company's run an additional week, though that proved a serious miscalculation, since it coincided with London emptying out for August vacation—and with a drastic falling off in ticket sales. Worse still, Webster insisted that the extension be followed by a four-week provincial tour to include Manchester, Liverpool, Croydon, and Kilburn, which did even worse business, and which, in the absence of a general manager (Frances Hawkins had returned to the States in mid-August), drove poor Betty Cage to twelve-hour days seven days a week. Not that her efforts helped much. Everyone had told them that Manchester especially "was a wonderful ballet town," but in the first week alone they lost a thousand pounds. What no one told them was that minimal advance publicity had been done and that even if they had sold out every performance, the theater's limited capacity would have allowed for a total profit margin of only five hundred pounds. In Betty Cage's opinion the company would never be able to tour successfully with a repertory that required so many dancers and so large an orchestra.

By the time the tour began, Lincoln and Fidelma had already left for New York. Lincoln had gradually fallen into another state of "nervous tension" (Buckle's phrase), sleeping poorly, feeling gloomy and rundown, yet at interludes still charging around, talking with breathless contradiction about how the British were living solely on outworn artistic capital even while proposing elaborate schemes for a grand Anglo-American cultural alliance—and occasionally getting off a line like, "I have always wanted a male secretary who was both a marine paratrooper and male nurse. In this I must be indulged. All else I have given for ART."

To make matters worse, Lincoln and Dickie Buckle had become increasingly snappish with each other. At one point Lincoln ordered Buckle to paint his crimson drawing room white, and to "SELL ALL THE BAROQUERIE AT ONCE AT AUCTION!" Lincoln put most of the blame for these peremptory outbursts on himself, on "the terrific weight of my vanity and speedy reckless energy." Despite his frequent expressions of remorse and shame to Dickie for his eruptions, Lincoln's apologies didn't prevent Buckle from becoming increasingly cross—and showing it. He took particular exception to Lincoln's coziness with his charwoman; finding her full of "common-sense" and "decency," Lincoln would slip her extra money, which, according to Dickie, was "destroying the standard of wages for such service."

Lincoln also got into a number of nasty tangles with other people that made his exchanges with Buckle and with the Duchess of Kent look like playful frolics. Two of the worst were with Lady Aberconway and Lucian Freud. Lady Aberconway had come calling on Lincoln to ask that he reconsider his earlier refusal to let another member of the English aristocracy give a second, smaller party for the ballet company. Lincoln had originally turned down the offer when it became clear that *he* would be expected to pick up the costs, and when Freddie Ashton expressed concern that Lincoln would (as he put it) invite "a lot of *louche* characters." Lincoln replied he'd had no such intention; he wanted only to ask Morgan Forster's friends, Bob and May Buckingham, that May was "a marvelous woman" and Bob not an "exotic cop" but "a most distinguished human being." When Freddie persisted in claiming that the Buckinghams wouldn't "be 'happy' in such elegant surroundings," Lincoln had blown his top— "the top," he later admitted, "was quite lightly screwed on by that time anyways." Lady Aberconway, for her part, explained to Lincoln "how democratic she was"—at which point he snapped, behaving, as she said, "like a GORILLA." He later agreed, acknowledging that he'd been "brutal."

The eruption with Lucian Freud was even uglier. He'd been squeezing in sittings for a portrait by Lucian without really having the time for it, and had grown increasingly annoyed at the painter's "disgusting campy impersonation of Bébé Berard," heightened by the "abominable" way Freud treated his wife. But because he thought Lucian "wildly gifted," he'd suppressed his antagonism. Lincoln's frayed nerves finally gave way one day when they were driving, at Lucian's insistence, to his favorite pub, the Prospect of Whitby, in a jazzed-up 1936 American Cadillac, and Lucian kept whipping up the driver to go faster and faster; the car skidded and scraped a lamppost. Lincoln exploded and, in a fistfight with Lucian, ended up knocking him to the ground. His portrait of Lincoln, needless to say, was never finished, though Lucian sent him a telegram poem that could conceivably be read as conciliatory:

> *he who after a sudden skid*
> *jumps out into an east end street*
> *before his portrait is complete*
> *may from posterity be hid*
> *love lucian.*

Frightened at his own behavior, Lincoln sought counsel with Morgan Forster, who was ill with prostate trouble. "Sick as he is," Lincoln later wrote Osbert Sitwell, "imagine anyone being inflicted with me, in my state. . . . I cannot begin to tell you what Morgan did for me." What he did, first of all, was to try to get Lincoln to see that there was a difference between hysteria and madness, strongly implying that Lincoln belonged in the former category and had simply become overwhelmed with the demands and disappointments of the London engagement. Forster urged that he surround himself with "more dull people"; he'd apparently noticed that Lincoln, without realizing it, had been clawing away at his palm, tearing open a wound on his left hand. As Lincoln wrote Osbert, Morgan "is so mild, so quiet, so learned in passivity . . . that I was shamed out of my theatrical violence into the simulacra of clarity, and I hope that I can temper my natural gifts for drama by restricting their uses to the stage . . . rather than mixing them up with life. . . . [Morgan] really saved my mind . . . his character is a slender monument of loving yet truthful analysis."

Back in London, Lincoln told Fidelma that he yearned more and more for the peace, quiet, and anonymity of Fire Island. She readily agreed to leave. On the whole she'd enjoyed London, but her own work—as would increasingly become the case—had had to be put on hold; as she wrote Paul, "I have made exactly 5 drawings" during the entire trip, "but I have at least one painting in my head." Certainly Dickie Buckle was ready for their departure. "Much as I liked Kirstein underneath," he later wrote, "I began to dislike him on the surface, and I wished he would go." He did, abruptly. He and Fidelma moved to a hotel in South Kensington on August 7 and a week later, after stopping in for a sheepish farewell visit with Dickie, flew home. He and Buckle would renew their correspondence almost immediately, and their friendship, though continuously subject to strain through the years, would last for many decades. As Buckle put it several years after the 1950 visit, "Even to this day I believe he thinks me deficient of a heart," while Dickie, on his side, had learned to be cautiously alert to Lincoln's unpredictable, exhausting "electricity."

PART FIVE

Maturity

A Home

(1951–1952)

WITHIN TWO WEEKS of being back on Fire Island, weeks of sun, ocean, and not seeing people, Lincoln felt "no longer exhausted but bright and interested." To Betty Cage he allowed that "I have still a couple of untamed wild horses waiting for the attention of the Holy Spirit," but he also felt that unlike mid-August, when "I thought I had better see somebody," he was no longer in need of psychiatric attention. He and Fidelma avoided seeing various people they knew at nearby Cherry Grove, including Marc Blitzstein, the designer Oliver Smith, and Jane Bowles.[1]

By the third week of isolation and rest, they began to invite out a few guests. The first, on Labor Day weekend, were Dan Maloney and Ed Hewitt. "I hope to get off alone with Dan, at least for a walk," Lincoln wrote Cadmus. "I think Ed hopes he can get off alone, at least to the bars." Lincoln was rarely judgmental about other people's sexual habits, but eventually he'd come to disapprove of Ed's incessant sexual adventuring— mostly because it increasingly interfered with other aspects of his life, like running an art gallery, which he felt Ed genuinely cared about. Live and Let Live was usually Lincoln's guiding principle; when he disliked some- body's behavior he didn't try to change it—he simply stopped seeing the person. Fidelma, too, had a kind of aristocratic obliviousness toward mainstream standards of behavior. She nonchalantly watched Danny and Ed walk, stark naked, around the porch at the Fire Island house, and amusedly wrote Paul that the unmarried sister in the one house that adjoined theirs had strategically placed herself on the side of the fence through which "she gets a good clear view."

Following Dan and Ed, a limited number of other guests were, at dif- ferent times, invited out, including intimates like Auden, as well as people from the ballet company like Ed Bigelow (a dancer who'd become Balan- chine's indispensable general assistant). Then there was "Buster"—a recent Mr. Pittsburgh—who came along with Butch Melton of the Pippin Press. Buster had apparently been confined for a time in a psychiatric ward, but had a sweet disposition and a gorgeous body ("neither muscle- bound nor weight lifty," was how Lincoln described it). He could be "insanely boring" but was also full of tales of past adventures: a man who paid him to pelt him with oranges; a man who gave him $150 to tickle him to orgasm with a peacock feather, and the like.

Fidelma agreed that Buster was "perhaps the most beautiful object" she'd ever seen and that he had "a nice character" as well, always striving to please. She suggested Buster become an apprentice cobbler; Lincoln thought he should get a job in construction. A nocturnal type, Buster would get up in the middle of the night and go out to the Cherry Grove bars; he said it soothed him to look at the television, and he would call up Butch every hour to let him know that he was thinking of him and would be home soon. Lincoln found it all "madly fin de siecle."

Most of the time, however, there were no guests at all. Lincoln read, did some writing, and started to make plans for the fall. Fidelma began to draw again, beginning with a series of sketches for a planned oil portrait of Lincoln. She also adopted a stray family of cats, and began writing a small book about them; the mother, Christabel, would become one in a long line of felines to whom the Kirsteins became extravagantly devoted. Fidelma initially fed the "poozas" a diet of steak, then started to worry that they lacked a sufficient range of choice, and so added plates of salmon, warm milk, and servings of brand-name cat food. The hovering concern over feedings and formulas had an obsessive aspect to it, an early symptom of a compulsive disorder that would later become a serious condition.

The more Lincoln's health and confidence returned, the more he started hatching plans for the coming year. They soon burgeoned into an elaborate set of schemes likely to produce exactly the sort of frenzied activity that Morgan Forster, among others, had cautioned him against. Starting with a long letter to Stravinsky, Lincoln laid out a potential schedule for ballet production that stretched ahead nearly two years, and even included a return engagement at the Teatro Colón in Buenos Aires. Stravinsky, hard at work with Auden on *The Rake's Progress*, put a quick damper on those aspects of the agenda that involved himself: "Too busy right now to be able to go through all the fascinating things you mention." Lincoln immediately backtracked: "I am too impatient. Thank you for slowing me down."[2]

But the pause was momentary. Within days he was writing to John Rothenstein, director of the Tate Gallery, proposing, as part of the Festival of Britain in 1951, "a really representative showing" of American painting; to prevent the show from becoming loaded down with his own preference for "symbolic realism," he suggested that MoMA's James Thrall Soby choose five painters to complement his own five. Rothenstein politely but definitively replied that "next year would not be the best time for the kind of exhibition that you have in mind."

The Sitwells were next up. Lincoln proposed to Edith that her "very great theatrical gift . . . not be restricted to the confines of Women's Clubs" and that she come to the States "to speak dramatic verse in a dramatic frame," a masque of some kind, a "danced-scene" in which she, gowned as an "Elizabethan queen-figure," would read bits of poetry and prose with "imperial authority" while a gorgeously costumed Unicorn and a Lion performed dance works around her. This time Lincoln got a *thrilled* response. Edith eagerly embraced the scheme, especially since she and Osbert were due to come to the States anyway in the fall.

In the event, the elaborate masque would never happen, and Edith would substitute a set of poorly received readings from *Macbeth*, herself playing Lady Macbeth and various literary friends alternating as her lord. Lincoln attended a rehearsal for the combination of Edith and Glenway Wescott (of whom he'd seen very little of late), and found it breathtakingly awful: "Edith thinks Lady Macbeth was a sort of old maid aunt; Glenway thinks Macbeth is . . . Rabbi Stephen Wise. She uses a microphone; he uses his, er, natural voice. The combination is not to be described. One's averted eyes will never re-avert."

The main item on Lincoln's agenda continued to be the New York City Ballet. Morton Baum had expected the Covent Garden engagement to produce a deficit of about twenty thousand dollars, but due to the failure of the provincial tour, the actual amount came closer to forty thousand. It filled Baum with gloom about the company's future. When he and Lincoln had their first meeting post-London—though it was "without hysterical manifestations on either of our parts," Lincoln wrote Betty Cage—Baum made it clear that the company would not return to England in 1951, nor could its fall program, if there *was* a fall program, include any new works. But Baum was aware that an increasing number of established dancers, including Hugh Laing and Diana Adams, stars of the Ballet Theatre, had been asking to join the City Center troupe, and word had also increasingly begun to filter through that despite the critics, the Covent Garden engagement had had a significant impact on the dance scene in London (Dickie Buckle, for one, predicted to Lincoln that "during the next year Balanchine will become a hero in England").[3]

And so Baum went ahead and scheduled a three-week season of twenty-six performances to run from November 21 through December 10. At the same time he made it clear that the greatest economy had to be exercised. "We have to do what we can do," Lincoln explained to Stravinsky; "we cannot do much." They already had the decor for a revival of *Jeu de Cartes*, and Balanchine managed to secure from Serge Denham the scenery and costumes for a reworked version of *Baiser de la Fée*. For novelties, Baum sanctioned a pas de deux from Delibes' *Sylvia* for Tallchief and Magallanes, as well as a *Mazurka* to music by Mikhail Glinka that would require no scenery and in which Balanchine himself would dance. To offset the minor costs of the new works, Baum raised ticket prices from the previous top of $2.50 to $3.00, and to attract a larger attendance, he suggested that four, rather than the customary three, ballets be performed on each program—a practice soon adopted elsewhere as well.

The Kirsteins remained essentially based on Fire Island through late October, with Lincoln making occasional trips into the city. Balanchine and Tanaquil Le Clercq, who'd become increasingly devoted to each other, came out for a visit in the fall, as did Herbie Bliss, who Lincoln believed had the makings of a very great dancer should he be able to get his self-destructive and melancholic temperament under control. Just three weeks before the new season was to begin, an unexpected financial shortfall hit City Center and it looked to Lincoln, often given to hyperbole, that "with no home and no future," they were finally finished as a company. In the nick of time the City Center Opera Company's production of *Meistersinger* proved a big hit, providing just enough surplus funds to permit the ballet season to go forward.

Still, the episode was another reminder that after all the years of struggle, and after having finally secured what seemed a safe home base, the company remained in a precarious position, subject to last-minute shifts in fortune—subject even to abrupt dissolution. Yet this time around, perhaps as a result of his sustained isolation on Fire Island, Lincoln claimed not to care very much. As he wrote Maria Rosa Oliver, "My curiosity and ambition both have dried up quite a lot, and I don't really want to go anywhere or see anybody. I still have the relics of an attraction for the theatre, but it's automatic."

The attraction would revive—though the "not too hot" (Lincoln's words) fall season that began in November wasn't the cause. With the chief exception of Tallchief's brilliant performance in the *Sylvia* pas de deux, Lincoln found little to admire: *Baiser* merely "looked pretty"; Balanchine was "cute" in the *Mazurka* ("but we all feared he would drop dead afterwards"); Hugh Laing was "awful" in *Les Illuminations*. Still, box office receipts were a little better than they had been, the company remained alive, and Baum decided to go ahead with plans for another four-week season to begin in February 1951.

He made clear, though, that it had to be conceived as a season with virtually no capital expenditures. Borrowed sets and costumes alternated with practice clothes for most of the program. For novelties there were Balanchine's *Pas de Trois*, Antony Tudor's *Lady of the Camellias* (music by Verdi), and the revival of *Jeu de Cartes*. Tudor had only a few weeks in which to compose *Camellias*, and it was generally considered one of his minor works. The one significant event of the winter season was Balanchine's *La Valse*, done without scenery but with brilliant costumes by Karinska and with a cast that stunningly featured Tanny Le Clercq. Lincoln thought *La Valse* "really very remarkable," and it proved a great success with both critics and audiences.[4]

The box office got a further boost from the first-time presence in the company of two international stars, the guest artist André Eglevsky, widely regarded as the premier *danseur noble* of the day, and Nora Kaye, the intensely dramatic dancer who'd recently defected to NYCB from Ballet Theatre, her home base for more than a decade. Eglevsky's debut was a great success; Lincoln characterized him to Buckle as "that great hunk of flying butt" and linked him with Igor Youskevitch, the other prominent *danseur noble*, as "elder statesmen, and pretty static at that, although Eglevsky's *cabrioles en avant* stop the breath of me and all." Nora Kaye's debut (in *Symphony in C*), on the other hand, was much more coolly received; many thought that her previous work with Ballet Theatre in mostly dramatic roles had ill prepared her for the intricate technical requirements of a Balanchine ballet.

Kaye had left Ballet Theatre, in Lincoln's opinion, because she'd been "stupidly handled" by Lucia Chase. Whether or not that was the case, Kaye's departure, following hard on the defections of Diana Adams and Hugh Laing, left Chase (according to Lincoln) "embittered personally," and she was rumored to have "forbade" her Ballet Theatre associate Oliver Smith (who'd earlier designed Robbins's *Age of Anxiety*) from working on Balanchine's *La Valse*. Nora Kaye, for her part, wasn't easily integrated into the City Center company. Since she hadn't been schooled in his style, Balanchine had difficulty finding appropriate roles for her. Additionally there was the issue of (in Lincoln's words) "displacing loyal persons." When Kaye and Eglevsky were together given a separate line on program billings, displeasure among the company's principals rose further.

One day somebody sent Kaye a dead snake in a box, an act of hostility that "created quite a commotion." Lincoln felt sympathy for her: "She is the new boy at school and she is very brave; I hope she stays because Balanchine can do a lot with her if she has the guts to stop being the Duse of the Dance" (the nickname she'd gotten at Ballet Theatre). Kaye had another strong ally in her close friend Jerome Robbins. The two had an affair for a time, and it became rumored in 1951 that they would shortly marry. Given the intimacy of their friendship, a live-in marriage might have worked, despite the fact that Robbins's sexual energy was focused on men; but in fact the two never actually wed.

As a result of the drawing power of Kaye and Eglevsky and the success of *La Valse*, the four-week winter engagement grossed nearly $150,000 and—*mirabile dictu!*—produced a small profit for the first time. Before the season had even closed and the usual worries could set in about keeping the dancers employed and raising funds for producing new works, the Chicago Civic Opera House offered the company a two-week spring engagement. It was at once accepted, though a second offer for a week's tour of Richmond, Washington, Baltimore, and Philadelphia, was turned down; it would have involved, unlike Chicago, too great an effort for too little a financial guarantee.

In the period immediately preceding the Chicago engagement, Balanchine, in need of money, went to work on what would be his last Broadway musical, the folksy, square-dancing *Courtin' Time* (based on William Wycherley's *The Country Wife*), which would prove a critical and commercial failure. Lincoln, in turn, decided to return to painting, a symptom, perhaps, of his lingering disaffection from the world of theater. He worked up his artistic muscle by doing small still life exercises, and loved being back at the easel. But he didn't love what he saw there. His still lifs, he decided, resembled those of "a fifth-form boy who will go far if he gets that scholarship to the Slade [the famed London art school], ca. 1910 (he won't get it)."

Lincoln accompanied the troupe to Chicago, and everyone was rather nervous about the engagement. It would mark the company's first appearance in the United States outside New York, and the Civic Opera was a huge house. Chicago was known, moreover, as a sophisticated ballet town, and Lincoln heard that Lucia Chase had already told the all-powerful critic Claudia Cassidy that he'd "raped her of the Duse," Nora Kaye. Besides, Lincoln was convinced that Chicago hated New York (just as he hated Chicago) and would be badly disposed toward the company before the first ballet shoe touched the stage.

His prediction proved pretty much on the mark. The reviews were indeed mixed (though several critics, including Claudia Cassidy, wrote raves), and Chicago audiences were thin. This was in distinct contrast to the way they had always flocked to see the Ballet Russe and other large touring companies, all of which regarded the city as a reliable cash cow. But the New York City troupe lost a cool twenty thousand dollars on the Chicago engagement. Having prepared himself for a disappointing result, Lincoln took it in stride, even insisting that the engagement had been "good for prestige."

Given how tight the City Center was for money, it came as an enormous vote of confidence when, soon after the company's return to New York, Baum offered Lincoln and Balanchine an unprecedented three-week summer season, even while suggesting that the troupe might wear out its welcome with the city's still limited ballet-going audience. Despite the lack of preparation time, the company managed to offer, in this its seventh season at City Center, three new works: Balanchine's quickly whipped-together *Capriccio Brillant*, one of his short, minor works; the premiere of Ruthanna Boris's lively *Cakewalk*, using the set from Ballet Society's *Blackface;* and Jerome Robbins's striking new ballet, *The Cage,* which gave Nora Kaye her first opportunity at NYCB to display the full intensity of her dramatic powers. Robbins's innovative, savage piece was widely hailed, though it repulsed some people; Kaye got unanimous raves. *The Cage*, Lincoln reported to Buckle, "was a sensational success." It was performed no fewer than a dozen times during that June.

Even so the engagement produced a deficit of some twelve thousand dollars. At this point Baum, who deeply believed in the company and had played a critical role in sustaining it, told Lincoln frankly that he feared the point had been reached where the City Center Board might seriously curtail, if not entirely cut away, the ballet unit; to prevent that from happening, Baum said, some additional outside help had to be found. According to Baum's later account, Lincoln bluntly asked him "how much did he have in mind" and Baum replied, "About $25,000."

Lincoln purportedly hesitated a moment, then said he'd find the money—but only on condition that the board agree to another full year for the ballet and to sponsor a tour in Europe in 1952. The board (led by Newbold Morris), despite some strenuous opposition, agreed to the terms. And so yet another of the ballet's hairbreadth escapes from the jaws of extinction was accomplished. But where Lincoln found the money remains a mystery. (The likeliest guess is that he borrowed against the considerable sum he was due to receive from his trust funds on his forty-fifth birthday in May 1952.)

Further amazements were waiting in the wings. Thanks to the company's mounting prestige, Sol Hurok, the country's leading impresario, offered to arrange an extended American tour for the company. Despite Balanchine's desire to have his work seen more widely, Lincoln turned Hurok down. After Baum crunched the numbers, he agreed with Lincoln: the costs of such a tour would be high, and given the company's non-traditional repertory, audiences might not turn out in large enough numbers to offset those costs. Lincoln later recalled that disappointed pro-tour people asked him what had happened to his earlier, near-doctrinaire commitment to all things American. He replied (or so he later chose to remember) that his "nationalism was alive and fairly well at the City Center. But now we knew for sure that we were not American in general, but specifically New Yorkers."

Both Baum and Lincoln were more disposed to take their chances on a European tour—not with the wily Hurok but with the prominent European impresario Leon Leonidoff. He initially wanted a guarantee that Eglevsky and Kaye would be part of the touring company, but Betty Cage explained that NYCB contracts with its artists were always made for a single season at a time, adding that she saw "no reason for us to suppose that they will not be with us" for the tour, as would Balanchine himself, though he might have to leave for a time to fulfill an engagement with La Scala. That apparently satisfied Leonidoff, and he proceeded to solicit bookings.

By early August 1951, he'd set up engagements for the Holland Festival, Portugal, Spain, Italy, and three weeks at the Champs-Élysées theater in Paris.

During the summer break, Lincoln and Fidelma returned to Fire Island, where she produced a few drawings and mastered the art of putting up peach jam, and Lincoln, in turn, completed his long introduction to a textbook on the basic techniques, movements, and positions taught at the School of American Ballet that he and Muriel Stuart (mostly Stuart) had been at work on for four years. In 1952 Knopf would publish the volume, *The Classic Ballet* (with illustration by Paul Cadmus), to fine reviews, and it would run through many editions (the most recent in 1998).[5]

One curious sidebar to that book was an acknowledgment in it to David Vaughan for his "aid in the final revisions of this text." The description was a good deal off the mark, and in trademark "Lincolnesque" ways. Lincoln had met David Vaughan back in 1950 during the company's Covent Garden engagement and had been impressed with the budding choreographer's idea for a ballet based on an E. M. Forster story. Lincoln had long been trying to get Forster to write a ballet scenario, and immediately got excited. He told Vaughan, "You'd better come to America. I'll arrange it."

And he did. Lincoln told Betty Cage to send Vaughan a hundred pounds and to give him a scholarship to the School of American Ballet, adding "I feel sure he has more sense, and at least as much gift as Cranko; I am not wrong about things like that." Lincoln, fueled by his intense Anglophilia (an inheritance from his father), had been spinning an elaborate plot in his head for a grand cooperative enterprise between Britain and the United States. Vaughan struck him, almost apparitionally, as the likely first candidate for a series of exchange dancer-choreographers, and sent out enthusiastic letters about him to Dickie Buckle, Osbert and Edith Sitwell, and even Morgan Forster ("I hope he is not one of my shrieking enthusiasms that turn out dreadfully"). At Lincoln's request Morgan agreed to meet with Vaughan and talk about the prospective ballet, to which he gave a rather tentative okay.

Once Balanchine got wind of Lincoln's offer to Vaughan, he sent for the young man, with discouragement decidedly in mind. As Vaughan recalls their interview, Balanchine did everything possible to dissuade him from taking up Lincoln's offer, telling him, reasonably enough, that he himself was the only choreographer who could really make ballets quickly, at least at a certain level, and that they couldn't possibly take a risk on somebody wholly unknown. Feeling that Lincoln had handed him the opportunity of a lifetime (and to this day he blesses him for it), Vaughan decided to proceed anyway.

Arriving in New York two months later, he produced a scenario in short order and gave it to Lincoln, who read it, said, "Thank you, it's very nice"—and never referred to it again. He did continue to assist Vaughan financially and also paid for him to start work on another ballet for the New Choreographer's Workshop. But that was pretty much that. Vaughan's new ballet was not taken into the repertory (nor did he himself think it good enough), but Lincoln did hire him to do much of the final editing on *The Classic Ballet*. Vaughan went on to become an admired performer, administrator (and later the archivist) of the Merce Cunningham dance company, as well as the author of well-regarded studies of both Cunningham and Frederick Ashton.

The entire episode with Vaughan was emblematic of certain aspects of Lincoln's personality—of his impulsive enthusiasms, of his well-intentioned if sometimes scattershot generosity, of his reckless embraces and abrupt disappearances, of his flooding, commanding visions, so initially convincing, so often destined to peter out in harum-scarum forgetfulness or high-handed disregard—or to be overtaken by a new seizure of phantasmic dimension and promise. But if Lincoln's overall record included a fair share of washouts and duds, they were a necessary by-product of his imaginative ambition. Few could match that imagination, nor Lincoln's conviction and drive. The impressive fact remains that a high ratio of his undertakings did come to fruition.

After a bare six-week summer break, the company began rehearsals for the opening of its eighth City Center season on September 4. The advance sale of some fifty thousand dollars was the largest to date, yet it wasn't a season of particularly notable premieres. Balanchine quickly put together a charming trifle entitled *À la Françaix* after Tanny Le Clercq sprained her ankle and was unable to appear in the planned revival of *Apollo*. The only other new piece was Todd Bolender's *The Miraculous Mandarin*, which Lincoln hated ("No one knew what he meant," Lincoln wrote Cadmus, "except that fucking corpses is fun"). To make matters worse, Bolender (according to Lincoln) "got so hysterical at the dress rehearsal that I almost slapped his face which is, I believe, the way to handle bitches in heat. Anyway, he will not work for me again for a *long* time."[6]

The critics were somewhat kinder to Bolender than Lincoln, and they particularly applauded Melissa Hayden's performance in *Mandarin*'s lead role—just as they delighted in Tallchief, Adams, and Magallanes in the company's revival of *Concerto Barocco*. The three-week engagement played to 70 percent of capacity and brought in a slight profit. Baum, who'd struggled so faithfully in the company's behalf, was exuberant, convinced that NYCB was at last "catching on" with the New York public. He promptly gave Lincoln and Balanchine the go-ahead for another season only two months thence, a four-week, thirty-two performance engagement for which he sanctioned a number of ambitious new works.

That November 1951 season would prove epochal. For several years Baum had been arguing, even pleading, with Lincoln and Balanchine to produce one "bread and butter" ballet that would guarantee larger crowds. And for years they'd said no, insisting that NYCB's mission precluded "old hat" revivals. But in response to Baum's magnanimous plans for the November season, Balanchine finally agreed to provide a new version of *Swan Lake*'s second act (the only interesting one, in Lincoln's opinion)—but on condition that Baum hire Cecil Beaton, whose fees were high, to do the decor. Baum agreed, and the company was soon (in Lincoln's words) "madly producing and making scenery and costumes of unparalleled magnificence"—not solely for *Swan Lake* but also for an ambitious new Balanchine work, *Tyl Eulenspiegel* (music by Richard Strauss, decor by Esteban Francis); a new Robbins ballet, *Pied Piper* (to Copland's Clarinet Concerto); and a revival of Antony Tudor's masterwork, *Lilac Garden*, starring Nora Kaye.

It all looked dauntingly expensive, but cutting a few corners kept costs to a relatively modest level. Practice clothes were utilized when appropriate, and *Pied Piper* was done on an empty stage. Lincoln himself took an exceptionally active hand in production design. He diplomatically steered Beaton away from his penchant for overly elaborate, even saccharine, decor and successfully moved him toward a much more austere design for *Swan Lake*. He also, for *Tyl*, did considerable archival research, feeding Esteban Francis book after book of background material to help him create an appropriately medieval, Bosch-like setting.

All this effort proved justified. *Swan Lake*'s premiere on November 20 was greeted with an enormous ovation; it was "heaven," Lincoln wrote Dickie Buckle, "the loveliest stage spectacle I ever saw." And *Tyl* also got a fine reception, even though Balanchine himself, at the end, felt considerable frustration over the brevity of the Strauss score. Robbins's *Pied Piper* and Tudor's *Lilac Garden* proved more than icing on the cake. The Robbins work had a few critical detractors but overall was favorably received (Lincoln thought it "charming"). And the revival of *Lilac Garden* was wildly successful: the costumer, Karinska; the set designer, Horace Armistead; and the lead dancers, Nora Kaye and Hugh Laing, were all resoundingly hailed. Despite all this the company's season ended with yet another deficit—but of "only," as the thrilled Baum put it, twenty thousand dollars.

Lincoln was due to receive trust fund money on reaching his forty-fifth birthday in the coming spring, and in preparation he and Fidelma started looking for a town house to buy. They had long since grown tired of cramped apartment living but hadn't previously been able to think about more spacious quarters—not with Lincoln's frequent outlays to support the ballet, as well as steady gifts (which were *not* tax write-offs) of survival money to assorted artists. Now that NYCB had finally achieved a certain status and security, Lincoln felt that they should entertain more and that Fidelma should have enough physical space to draw and paint in comfort.[7]

Initially they thought of looking in Manhattan's East Seventies and (since they would still not be rich-rich) of renting out one or two floors. But they finally decided to buy the 1845 stable- and coach house (once owned by the railroad magnate Stuyvesant Fisk) on Nineteenth Street near Gramercy Park. It had a tiny garden and a largish terrace, but was basically a large old barn badly in need of renovation. In a mock version of what he planned, Lincoln described the refurbishing to Buckle: "all the furniture teensy to make it look emptier. And just a few absolutely horrible pictures for which I am already famous; a sprig of thorn; one perfect spike of cactus and a dead crow." The end result would prove grander by a good bit. Lincoln bought a mass of "beat up but beautiful" French Empire mahogany-veneer furniture with brass appliqués from a second-hand furniture dealer and, partly giving way to the familial habit of luxurious living, started eyeing rock-crystal chandeliers and framed malachite mirrors.

During the first six months of 1952, as the house was being torn apart, Lincoln's beloved Jens Yow provided essential help. He did all sorts of odd jobs to get the place in shape, from designing murals to importing manure from New Jersey to plant an ivy garden. Renovations continued through the summer, but when the Kirsteins finally took occupancy in late July, Jens had become not only a family member but a sort of "houseman," tending to the furnace and polishing the brass. Jens had his own room on the top floor, decorating it in what Lincoln called "High Thrifte Gothicke Shoppe." The Kirsteins' longtime cleaning woman also moved in and tended to most daily chores.

In the year and a half since Lincoln and Jens had first met, Jens had gradually become an integral part of Lincoln's life. But Lincoln didn't believe in keeping anyone, including himself, on a leash. Jens had his own set of friends and lovers, even as Lincoln openly continued his attachment, though no longer sexual, to Dan Maloney, along with several brief flirtations on the side and trips now and then to the orgiastic Turkish baths, where he tended, shyly, mostly to wander around and watch. Lincoln did sometimes feel jealousy over Jens's serial love affairs, but carefully controlled any expression of it. He once, though, expressed his feelings in an unpublished poem:

> . . . *His hot young friend is his.*
> *I am no part of their pact.*
> *Try to deserve their goodwill.*
> *How fast must high bonfires be fed:*
> *All hungry boys are starved until*
> *You bring them their breakfast in bed.*

Jens "is a wonderful course in discipline sent to me by the Heavenly Father," Lincoln wrote Cadmus. "I am nicer than ever before, I think, although no one seems to notice it." He offered to pose for Cadmus's canvas *Jealousy* (one of his *Seven Deadly Sins* series-in-progress): "I will add a new angle of expression that has not been caught to the intensity that it deserves. Its mouth is an asshole developed into a sanctimonious well-wishing smile, and its eyes are cataracts in reverse."

The love between Lincoln and Jens became profound, long-lasting, and always physically affectionate if less and less sexual. By early 1951 Jens had already been ending his letters to Lincoln with "I love you," or "There just isn't any substitute for *you*!" Lincoln, in turn, thought Jens "an angel," his "happy nature" a blessed addition to his life. Jens soon became, as Lincoln put it, "incorporated to such a degree in our hearts" that when he went off to Philadelphia for a few days, Lincoln felt he'd lost "the focus from my life." Jens and his current boyfriend once made the mistake of telling Lincoln how intrinsically "kind" they thought he was: Yeah sure, was Lincoln's comment to Cadmus; "wait till they find out *what* kind"—a typical bit of brutal self-putdown.

Lincoln introduced Jens around widely, and everyone seemed to take to him, including Fidelma, who according to Lincoln was "always kissing him hello and goodbye," and Mina ("the first success in years," Lincoln wrote Cadmus). Returning from a visit to Glenway Wescott and Monroe Wheeler—the former never a favorite of Lincoln's; the latter, in recent years, alienated by Lincoln's continuing disparagement of MoMA—Jens announced that he'd found Glenway "a fascinating conversationalist, full of wonderful if cynical ideas." As Lincoln wrote Cadmus, "I did not speak, I did not speak, I did not speak. But I am afraid Fido did, a very little; also, I LOOKED."

At one point Lincoln took Jens on a tour of New England museums, stopping off in New Haven to see a production of *Billy Budd*, coauthored by one of his recent protégés, Bob Chapman (whom Lincoln, through his old friend Harry Levin, chair of Harvard's comparative literature department, had gotten a job teaching and producing theater); and also stopping off to see the returned and restored Pavlik Tchelitchev. Pavlik had been in Europe much of the preceding two years and had been having a difficult time. His shows had been unsuccessful, his health poor, and his financial resources low. He grew so morose and difficult that Edith Sitwell wrote despairingly to Lincoln, as "a true, loyal and devoted friend of Pavlik's," for advice and intervention to save "a *very* great genius."

Deeply concerned about Pavlik and knowing (as he wrote Jim Soby) that his "megalomania has developed past most people supporting it" and that he might be headed for a schizophrenic break, Lincoln had responded immediately to Sitwell's plea, and she blessed him as "the best friend Pavlik ever had . . . you work *endlessly* on his behalf." Pavlik gradually improved; before long, Edith was writing to Lincoln that he seemed "like his old self" and "spoke with the greatest affection of you . . . said you are one of the only people in the world on whom he can rely."

Yet a few months later, when Lincoln had himself become desperately ill in London and Balanchine sent Tchelitchev a personal plea for help in getting him home, Pavlik replied (as he recounted his reaction to Edith), "I am sorry to be of no avail. I am ill myself [and]. . . I am not a good nurse." Lincoln probably never learned of Pavlik's refusal to help; even if he had, it would have been characteristic of him to have brushed it aside, aware of his own abrupt shifts in attitude toward people and not expecting anyone else to behave better than he himself did. Lincoln was soon again promoting Pavlik's work and even trying to re-enlist his interest in designing ballets.

He even wrote the catalog for Pavlik's 1951 show, which had a great success: Pavlik sold twenty large drawings and both *Life* and *Time* did articles about him. He became, for a time, less overwrought and self-absorbed, even downright benevolent, and took a house in Connecticut. When Lincoln brought Jens around for lunch, Pavlik was affectionate and funny, though Lincoln embarrassed Jens by bragging to Pavlik about his "real gift for portraiture."

The description was true enough, and Jens also became a skillful restorer of the works of others, including Nadelman; he brought a large number of Nadelman's wooden figures, with which Lincoln supplied him, back to their original paint. Jens also did some lovely drawings, including one of Lincoln, who thought it "very good . . . me as my father, around 65, with dewlaps, jowels, no hair and a hard cruel look that I am afraid is the REAL me. He [Jens] is very talented I think; his hand is sure and he has lots of taste, no trace of flattery—indeed the reverse."

Meanwhile, a considerable upheaval was under way at City Center. Laszlo Halasz, head of the opera company, had long been belligerent towards the ballet, doing his best to force it out of the Center. He not only antagonized Lincoln and Balanchine but also Maurice Evans, then director of the Center's theater unit: Evans told the board that he found Halasz impossible to work with. The climax came when the Musicians' Union joined the chorus of complaint, presenting Baum with an ultimatum: its members would no longer work at the Center while Halasz remained head of the opera. As a result the board dismissed him in 1952.[8]

A "new spirit," according to Lincoln, now settled over the Center, "a smoothness of operations has come into being wholly different from the Halasz regime." Balanchine, who had worked all this time at the Center without salary—even as Halasz was drawing up to twenty thousand a year—was now belatedly given royalties on performances of his ballets (Baum offered him a fixed salary of ten thousand a year, but Balanchine immediately turned it down). Lincoln himself began to be consulted about matters beyond the ballet, particularly as regarded the opera; as early as 1952 he was centrally involved in the production of Gian Carlo Menotti's *Amahl and the Night Visitors*. And before the end of the year he was formally elected to the Center's board of directors. As he wrote Dickie Buckle, "Our star is in the ascendant." The next ballet season, he felt, "will solidify our position."

That season was soon upon them. During February and March 1952 the company gave forty performances over a five-week period (its longest engagement up to that point), which included five new works. Two were by Balanchine: *Caracole*, to Mozart's Divertimento 15, and *Bayou* to Virgil Thomson's *Acadian Songs and Dances* (with sets by Dorothea Tanning). The other three premieres were Robbins's *Ballade*, Tudor's *La Gloire*, and Ashton's *Picnic at Tintagel* (designed by Cecil Beaton). In Morton Baum's opinion only *Tintagel* could be called a success; he thought *Caracole* "repetitious," *Bayou* distinguished only by its sets, *Ballade* "unrealized," and *La Gloire* "overwhelmed" by its music. Baum's uncharacteristically jaundiced view of the season was probably influenced by a financial loss of some forty thousand dollars.

Yet the season had grossed nearly half a million dollars, and more than two hundred thousand people had attended performances—exceeding all previous records at City Center. Besides, not everyone was as disappointed in the new offerings as Baum. *Life* magazine did a full-color spread, and Lincoln himself thought Balanchine's *Caracole* was "his greatest ballet and the loveliest thing ever seen by human eyes"; he sent Buckle the opinion of the critic from the *World-Telegram:* "If Mozart were alive today his name would be Balanchine." Lincoln acknowledged that Tudor (whom he referred to as "the eminent neuropathic choreographer,") had had "a terrible flop" with *La Gloire* ("he is finished I am sadly afraid," Lincoln wrote Buckle). On the other hand he was a fan of *Bayou*, though he thought it needed revision and feared that Balanchine himself didn't "take it seriously." But he made no effort to defend Robbins's *Ballade* (which Edwin Denby liked but Balanchine didn't); Lincoln's decidedly mixed feelings about Jerry Robbins—the person, not the talent—would soon grow more negative still.

Lincoln did agree with Baum, though, about the merits of Ashton's *Tintagel*, even though he continued to think that Ashton was too "damn British" in the way he viewed the dance as "direct drama." Lincoln was especially taken with the performances in *Tintagel* of Diana Adams (she is "our rising star; she has a chance to be the American Margot") and the seventeen-year-old newcomer, Jacques d'Amboise, in his first big role with the company (he'd been studying at the school for seven years). In Lincoln's opinion d'Amboise was a "Pluto the Pup type"—"sweet, big and strong . . . quite marvelous, not alone as an acrobat." Lincoln thought d'Amboise was the first male dancer since Lew Christensen who was "fresh and touching" and predicted that the youngster was going to "forge ahead."

By the time the season closed in March 1952, Leonidoff, a great admirer of Balanchine's and the sort of thoroughly honest, decent man rarely found in the crafty impresario world, had succeeded in lining up a prestigious European tour for the company. It began within weeks of the New York closing and would extend for five months, with David Webster finally agreeing to a return engagement at Covent Garden. For Paris, Leonidoff secured an official invitation from the French government (much to Lifar's fury) for performances at the Opéra—an honor accorded to a foreign company only once before, when Diaghilev performed there in 1911. He'd also gotten an additional two weeks in Paris at the Théâtre des Champs-Élysées, as well as substantial bookings for Barcelona, Florence, Amsterdam, Lausanne, Copenhagen, and Edinburgh—and even the Allied-occupied sector of Berlin. The tour would be filled with more than the usual amount of drama, bickering, misunderstandings, and mixed receptions.[9]

Trouble started even before the company left the States in mid-April for its opening engagement at Barcelona's Teatro Licea. Baum claimed that he and Lincoln had both tried to eliminate fascist Spain from the itinerary, but had reluctantly bowed to Leonidoff's insistence that the financial guarantees were too high to forgo. But neither seems to have tried very hard. The reactionary political climate in the United States, with McCarthyism rampant and congressional investigating committees hunting down left-wingers of all stripes, doesn't seem to have had any direct effect on Lincoln's views. Yet his interest in public affairs had been declining now that he'd clarified his "real" mission in life: "The energy or talent needed even tangentially for devotion to valid causes," he later wrote, "was incommensurate with what energy I had to keep our company working."

Yet if Lincoln was no longer inclined to active participation in social protest, he'd never become less than "liberal" in his sympathies. In the 1952 election he voted for Stevenson over Eisenhower and in the sixties would personally participate in the Selma civil rights march. When Jerry Robbins (who'd briefly joined the CP in the mid-forties) testified before HUAC in 1952, Lincoln privately made clear his disdain for the way Jerry had spilled out, with little hesitation or prompting, the names of others he'd seen at meetings, some of whom had not been named by previous witnesses.

But if Baum and Lincoln found it acceptable to put Barcelona on the schedule, others did not. Veterans of the Lincoln Brigade who'd fought against Franco picketed City Center; the Spanish Refugee Appeal asked (to no avail) the president of City Center, Vincent Impellitteri (the future

mayor of New York City), to cancel the engagement, and the two labor
members of the City Center board resigned in protest; one of them, Jacob
Potofsky, had been Louis Kirstein's good friend and was currently president of the International Ladies Garment Workers Union (ILGWU). In
response Chairman Newbold Morris issued a rather lame statement
emphasizing the importance of keeping open "the lines of communication
between . . . the people of other countries whose governments we
deplore." Lincoln expressed regret that Potofsky had resigned and scoff-
ingly passed on to Baum the opinion of dance critics John Martin and
Walter Terry that the protest against appearing in Barcelona was being
engineered by the Communist Party.

Balanchine had already left for Europe on March 1, 1952, to stage his
ballets at La Scala, and he met the company on its arrival in Spain in mid-
April. Lincoln and Fidelma, however, had decided against joining the
tour. Not only were they still preoccupied with making their new house
habitable, but Lincoln's mother, Rose, had recently fallen seriously ill
again. Having nearly succumbed to cancer back in 1945, she'd unexpectedly gone into remission and had not only fully resumed her life but
seemed "in excellent health and excellent spirits." After the recurrence
Lincoln thought it would be "heartless" to leave her for any length of
time, and throughout the next few months, as Rose's health deteriorated,
Fidelma especially became her devoted and tender daily companion.

It fell to the shrewd, efficient Betty Cage, now company manager, and
her two assistants, to deal with the often-overwhelming details of managing the logistics of the European tour. From New York, Lincoln and
Baum made decisions on large policy issues, such as whether or not to
extend the tour to Germany. Between Lincoln and Betty the lines of communication were open, cordial, and mutually affectionate. Occasionally,
Betty would scold him when she felt he'd made a mistake, but he took her
rebukes in stride, convinced that her judgment was keen and that, as he
put it to Baum, "her resourcefulness, ability, devotion and grace under
extreme pressure" remarkable.

Betty's relationship with Baum wasn't nearly as close or respectful; for
one thing he mostly ignored her letters from Europe, rarely responding to
her assorted questions, which both mystified and angered her. Those
questions needed answers if she was to resolve the pressing on-the-ground
complications that arose from nearly the first day of the tour and thereafter seemed never to end.

The complications were often predictable and insignificant, but not
always. Among the more predictable: intermittent complaints from
dancers in the corps about unfavorable exchange rates or cramped living
quarters. Among the far less expected and potentially more serious problems were Sol Hurok's backstairs intrigues against the company, Balanchine's insistence on making cuts against Ruthanna Boris's wishes in her

Cakewalk, and his annoyance about the tour being extended to include Berlin but not La Scala. In addition a sizzling set of bruised egos among some of the company's leading dancers developed, which for a time posed a serious threat to the company's future.

On one side of the division between the principal dancers were Nora Kaye and her close friend Jerry Robbins, and on the other ballerinas Tallchief, Janet Reed, and Melissa Hayden. Betty reported to Lincoln that the three felt far too much emphasis, in regard both to roles and publicity, was being put on Kaye. Balanchine himself agreed, according to Betty, "that we must in the future consider very carefully what dancers are to be used when new ballets are done." Yet at the same time Balanchine didn't feel he could dictate to Robbins, Bolender, or Agnes de Mille (all three of whom were about to set to work on new pieces for NYCB) as to dancers they could or could not use.

Balanchine thought the way out of the dilemma would be to shift casts for some of the works already in the repertory, to let "Millie" Hayden, for example, take over the lead role in *Age of Anxiety* from Nora. This could well mean, Betty predicted to Lincoln, that both Kaye and Robbins would leave the company—but she added that "George is quite willing to see them go. He has fortunately taken a new interest in the company and he wants to keep it, and keep it in its original form with its original policy."

"Original" was a murky concept. Surely the maintenance of obscurity, poverty, and the constant fear of dissolution wasn't what either Balanchine or Betty had in mind. The reference was probably to the feeling that had previously dominated that the company was a unit, a community with a common goal, rather than what might currently be called a vipers' nest of warring egos. "The sort of thing that Nora does," Betty wrote Lincoln, "is new to this company. The private press-agenting that goes on with her, the cocktails with all the right people, the interviews which she and Jerry manage to give with no mention of anything but *The Cage* and themselves. There is no one else in the company who acts that way. And that is what Maria and Janet are upset about. With Milly, it's a problem of roles as well, but now that she has had *Firebird* and George admits that she is improving, that should be all right." As for Robbins, both Balanchine and Betty were convinced that he simply couldn't be counted on. "One day he protests," Betty wrote Lincoln, "that he wants to help, the next day he says he wants to go to New York and do a show, and every day he says that no one gets any publicity except George and that the tour is solely for the purpose of adding to George's personal fame."

As they tried to work their way through the crisis, Betty implored Lincoln not to commit to a new ballet, whether by de Mille or anybody else, that mandated Nora's centrality. Lincoln was content to follow Betty's lead; as he wrote Buckle, "I'm tired, and I can't take on the emergencies and rows of the tour, particularly since I can do nothing about avoiding them." He was already overextended in other directions, including his absorption in working out a ten-year plan for the company that envisioned a new building to house a theater-opera-ballet complex. Simultaneously, he was actively participating in City Center board meetings ("it's an awful gang") and had begun personally to handle most of the opera's affairs; that included commissioning Auden's companion and sometime collaborator, Chester Kallman, to do a new version of Bartók's *Bluebeard's Castle* and hiring Rouben Ter-Arutunian (who would become a close friend) as staff designer, and maestro Tullio Serafin as the conductor for Italian opera.

As of July, Lincoln also had to mull over a formal invitation from the Board to take over as managing director of City Center from Baum, who'd grown tired of the place and wanted to run for the state senate in order to try to push through a bill to fund the arts. Lincoln thought he might accept the position (though Betty strenuously advised against it), but preferred the title "Coordinator"—"out of respect for the other unit directors" (opera and theater), and because he intended to remain general director of the ballet.

Preoccupied though he was, Lincoln did closely follow the ongoing row over Nora and Robbins, and eagerly read the assorted reviews and reports he was sent about the tour's general progress and reception. Occasionally he would even, despite his decision not to intervene, send Betty bits of advice. He thought it essential, for example, that *if* Jerry or Nora decided to leave the company, they be allowed to do so gracefully and without anger; minimizing recrimination would facilitate their later return, should all parties wish it. Betty entirely agreed, though she clearly disliked Robbins: "He will be with us," she wrote Lincoln, "when he has nothing better to do." But when Robbins did decide in mid-July to leave the company and accept an offer to choreograph a revue for the movie star Bette Davis, Betty Cage handled him "very carefully," telling him that everyone loved him, didn't want to tie him down, and entirely understood his need to make money.

Once back in New York, Jerry for a time avoided Lincoln. That was fine with him: Jerry "obviously wants to see me as little as I essentially want to see him." Lincoln did put in one call to Jerry soon after his return, but when it went unanswered he made no further attempt. Even after hearing reports that Jerry "talks disgustingly about us," Lincoln kept silent, since he wanted a new ballet from Robbins for the upcoming 1953 season. Finally, three weeks after returning from Europe, Jerry contacted Lincoln, asking for a meeting.

In advance of it, Lincoln decided "to be as agreeable as possible." For the first hour Jerry, according to the account Lincoln sent Betty and Balanchine, "wept with rage" while Lincoln humored him, agreeing that "the company was such a disastrous flop, so badly run, no artistic integrity. . . .

Balanchine . . . at once the cause of the company's greatness and its ruin, etc." Yet when Lincoln asked Jerry if he wanted to leave the company and not do a new ballet for them in 1953, Jerry promptly answered no (though his close friends, the duo-piano team of Arthur Gold and Robert Fizdale, as well as the dance critic Edwin Denby, had been urging him to form his own company). Jerry also explained to Lincoln his need to make lots of money quickly, since he'd been "denounced" and would have to appear before HUAC, with the likely result that his ballets would be banned from performance. (As it would turn out, Robbins freely "named names" before HUAC—and his ballets were not banned.)

Lincoln reassured Jerry, in words similar to those he'd written him the year before, that "you are the only choreographer alive who can take George's place," and counseled him not to be "terrified by the responsibility: fulfill it; if I can help you as I have him, you can count on me." Lincoln wisely concluded that what Jerry most wanted was "to be loved more deeply and more personally." The fact is, Lincoln reported to Betty and Balanchine, Jerry "is a complex combination of vanity, guilt, fright, inadequacy, talent, viciousness, sweetness, ambition, greed and gifts—like most of us, only he has more gifts." What Lincoln understood was that internal cohesiveness was one of the more recent myths about the human personality, a regrettable offshoot of the Descartian revolution whose either-or distinctions ("good" versus "evil") had long since found their warmest embrace in a shallow American psyche bent on pragmatics over close analysis. Lincoln's embrace of complexity, ambivalence, and contradiction as central to "human nature" had often made him seem, in his own country, more European than American, just as they had also earlier predisposed him to Gurdjieff, and would later set him on the path to Roman Catholicism.

The kid-glove treatment worked with Robbins. In 1953 he'd create not one but two new ballets for the company. As for Nora Kaye, Betty Cage had a long talk with her and came away from it persuaded that "she is completely devoted to NYCB," though she "would like to have more roles" and wanted to go "on leave" to appear in Jerry's revue for Bette Davis. Lincoln's confidential response to Betty was that he'd "entirely changed my mind about Nora; I am urging her to take the show with Jerry. Only I want her name not to be missing from our roster as everyone will crow and she can perfectly well do a couple of CAGEs . . . then she is out and we have Melissa [Hayden], Janet [Reed] and Maria [Tallchief]. . . . I met Janet and we had a good heart to heart and I saw everything quite clearly. Please urge Nora to go, but nicely." During 1953 Nora Kaye would put in only infrequent appearances with the company on Sunday programs.

Despite all the internal turmoil, the tour itself marked a significant overall advance in the company's international reputation. The three-week spring engagement in Barcelona proved a huge success with critics and audiences alike; at the closing performance there was an astonishing, elaborate display of enthusiasm, with a cascade of flowers thrown from the rafters, doves released from the balconies, and gifts presented on the garlanded stage to every member of the company. Balanchine himself was given an enormous ovation and begged to stay and establish a school (he'd already had the same offer from Milan). The sole problem in the engagement related to differing cultural habits: the Spanish audience would straggle in throughout the opening ballet, talk continuously yet applaud little, stay out a full half hour during intermissions, and tend to leave shortly after the curtain fell.

From Barcelona it was on to Paris for a single opening-night performance at the Opéra as part of the current Masterpieces of the XXth Century International Exposition of the Arts, and then a week-long stint at the Théâtre des Champs-Élysées. Betty reported to Lincoln that the opening at the Opéra was "a triumph . . . unbelievably warm," with the critics generally laudatory (*The Cage* and *Bourrée Fantasque* were the special favorites), though the reviews expressed some standard uneasiness about the company's devotion to "abstraction."

The high point of the tour was the two-week engagement at Florence's Teatro Communale. The 4,500-seat theater was sold out for the entire run, and Robbins's *The Cage*, as well as his *Pied Piper*, were once again singled out for special praise. Glenway Wescott, who attended the glittering opening night, reported to Lincoln that it was "a triumph," with Tallchief dancing "ecstatically" in *Swan Lake*—"never nobler, never more accurate and fiery in her love of the music. After that, all evening, they could do no wrong." The sole problem, in Wescott's opinion, was that the hastily assembled orchestra hadn't had sufficient rehearsal time. Performances in Lausanne and Zurich were no less successful, critically and commercially, and the week at The Hague was sold out too. "The whole tour," Betty wrote Lincoln, "has been a series of triumphs. We are considered the greatest thing that has hit Europe since Diaghilev."

Yet her assessment proved premature. The company opened its seven-week engagement at London's Covent Garden on July 7 (the night before Betty wrote her jubilant letter)—and the English critics were about to deliver the company's comeuppance. The best that could be said for the English reviews of the opening-night performance was that they were (for the most part) polite. But with a very few predictable (Buckle and Haskell) exceptions, the critics, in a near rerun of 1950, once again lamented the American troupe's penchant for technique over "warmth," and its lack of narrative plots and plush decor.

Part of the disappointing reception was a result of Balanchine's choice of the opening-night program. Betty called him (in a letter to Lincoln) an "idiot" for having thought he could wait until the troupe got to London before deciding on programs for the run; on top of that he (in the opinion not only of Betty but of Buckle, the dance critic Anatole Chujoy, and Lincoln himself) had ended up making a disastrous last-minute choice for opening night: *Serenade, The Cage, Firebird*, and *La Valse*. It was an ill-advised offering for an English critical fraternity not used to a four-ballet evening and already on record as disliking *Firebird* and having a general distaste for modernist works like *The Cage*; the difficulty was further compounded by choosing *La Valse*—refined rather than resounding, and lost on the huge Covent Garden stage—for the closing ballet. Nora Kaye, ironically, had, in *The Cage*, a great personal success, even though the ballet itself was generally disliked. Balanchine, in turn, declared himself (in a letter to Lincoln) as "very angry that nobody told me about seven weeks in London. It is terrible idea."

Despite the tepid opening-night reviews, the rest of the London run was reasonably well attended (though more in driblets than droves), and many individual performances were enthusiastically applauded. Still, it was not what had been hoped for, not within shouting distance of the sort of ardor that had greeted the company elsewhere in Europe (and would again in the Netherlands, Edinburgh, and Berlin). The London letdown, moreover, seems to have exacerbated pre-existing tensions within the company. Not only was it widely felt, according to Betty, that Nora Kaye was like some member of "the Royal Family . . . they don't really mix or allow themselves to be grafted or drawn into this body politic," but other principal dancers were feeling underused.

Betty reported to Lincoln that she'd taken Melissa Hayden to supper to listen to her complaints. Hayden confessed that Lucia Chase had been courting her for American Ballet Theatre, but insisted she preferred to remain with NYCB. Yet she *was* "unhappy." She was "dying to do a *Swan Lake*" and "would give her eye teeth for a classic ballet by Balanchine." But although she had "a certain seniority" in the company, she felt it was "not being respected by Balanchine." Betty felt that Hayden was "right in many respects," and that "it was too bad that Balanchine does not like her." Hayden did promise not to take "any drastic steps" in the immediate future, but Betty knew how tricky the situation was. Balanchine didn't take well to complaints from company members, and Betty felt he misunderstood most of those that did reach his ears. But she somehow managed to keep all of the simmering pots from boiling over during the tour. "How you have been able to do what you have done, I'll never know," Lincoln wrote her, "it is really remarkable and you deserve all the praise that you'll certainly never get."

By mid-July, Lincoln's attention had shifted elsewhere: his mother took a drastic turn for the worse. She'd lived gallantly with cancer for a number of years, but it now metastasized to the brain; by late July she sank into unconsciousness, though occasionally rallying and becoming (in Lincoln's words) "amazingly clear." A devoted Fidelma was in constant attendance during Rose's last days, and Mina, whose relationship with her mother had become far more loving than it had once been, was also steadily at her bedside. Rose died in early August, age seventy-nine, plunging the immediate family into grief. Soon after her death, Lincoln wrote Pavlik, "I had no idea of the involuntary and unconscious effect on the imagination; it is as if I had very little self-confidence all of a sudden."[10]

Rose died on the very day Lincoln and Fidelma had been scheduled to move into their new home on Nineteenth Street. Fidelma retreated to Fire Island, and Lincoln briefly went up with Mina to her home in Ashfield. The first stage of the move was left to Jens Yow, but Lincoln returned by mid-August, and serious work was begun on putting the place in order. Some of Rose's comfortable furniture from Boston was moved in, along with Lincoln and Fidelma's own elegant pieces and art collection; the well-known lighting designer Richard Kelly installed track lighting with dimmers. Jens worked especially hard on the backyard, turning it into a lovely, inviting garden. On the second floor Lincoln and Fidelma both had large bedrooms of their own, hers with a small terrace; she insisted that each of the many doors in the house have a working cat entrance in the baseboard to facilitate access for their beloved felines.

On the third floor Jens had his own bedroom, studio, bath, and small kitchen. Close-quarter living always breeds some irritations, and Lincoln would occasionally become annoyed with what to him was Jens's occasional "laziness" and his frequent changing of lovers. But the irritations were few, and his love and admiration for Jens remained deep; as he wrote Cadmus, "Everyone finds him irresistible, and he seems a lot more skilful than anyone else . . . he amazes me; everything is well-worked and no nonsense." In fact the entire household, including the live-in maid, Elise, was remarkably harmonious; they were all utterly delighted with the new home (when both Elise and a later maid became chronic invalids, Fidelma and Lincoln assumed responsibility for their bills).

The double trauma of Rose's death and the shifting of residences was further compounded just a few weeks later by the death (at sixty-five) from a paralytic stroke of Muriel Draper, Lincoln's early love and mentor. In recent years the two had rarely seen each other. As Lincoln became depoliticized, Muriel associated herself increasingly with pro-Soviet causes, becoming especially active, along with Paul and Essie Robeson, in the National Council of American-Soviet Friendship, where she headed the Women's Division, and the Congress of American Women, of which she became president. HUAC cited both groups and denounced Muriel herself in 1949 for her assorted "Communist-front" activities. In 1952, the final year of Muriel's life, Lincoln joined a group of her friends in raising a small pot of money that had yielded her a monthly $110 cashier's check.

Ever since the Spanish civil war, Muriel's and Lincoln's views had been diverging. In Lincoln's opinion she'd become over time "wildly political," "obsessed," and he came to feel that it was "impossible to talk seriously about the world as I think it is any more with her; her world is some exaggerated prefiguring of some time never, I hope, to come." As a result the relationship had disintegrated from deep intimacy to an infrequent, casual encounter. His ultimate view of Muriel was that she was "essentially a New England eccentric." This denigration of her values and intelligence was perhaps primarily a measure of the political distance he himself had traveled.

By 1952, the year of Muriel's death, Lincoln had abandoned socialism and voted in the presidential election for Adlai Stevenson, whom he called "the greatest American since Abraham Lincoln." Which left Lincoln standing pretty much on the same liberal—decidedly not radical—political ground once occupied by his father, Louis (though unlike his father, Lincoln was much more private about the causes, institutions, and individuals to whom he gave money). Yet some vague radical sympathies remained and would occasionally surface. Even in 1952, the year of Muriel's death, Lincoln reported to Maria Rosa Oliver, with intimations of regret, that currently "there is no advance-guard party or progressive movement of any interest or power" in the United States.

Despite the political chasm between them, and the diminished contact during Muriel's final years, Lincoln continued until the very end to "adore her." Indeed her death upset him, somewhat mysteriously he felt, "almost more" than his mother's; "it's part of my life gone," he wrote Pavlik—that youthful, passionate, earnest life that had fed on issues of social injustice.

Lincoln attended Muriel's funeral and sent a splendid spray of white mums. In thanking him, her son, the dancer Paul Draper—who'd gone into self-imposed exile in Switzerland after his denunciation by HUAC—wrote to tell him, "I think about how very much you loved her." He did indeed. Some years after her death, Lincoln wrote Carl Van Vechten that "she stays with me much of the time; she educated me and focussed me and I am forever grateful."

Managing Director

(1953–1954)

W HEN LINCOLN WAS offered the job of "managing director" of City Center in September 1952, an important factor in his acceptance was Morton Baum's reiterated assertion that he was tired of the center and wanted to turn over the reins. John Marshall of the Rockefeller Foundation had the same impression; as Marshall put it in an inter-office memo, Baum "is gradually withdrawing from his work there."[1]

But if so, Baum subsequently changed his mind. When Lincoln resigned his post two and a half years later, Morton Baum was still very much the dominant force at the center. Much of what went wrong in the intervening period was the direct result of Lincoln's duties and powers as managing director never having been closely defined—in large measure because Baum had advised him not to press the board of trustees for precise parameters lest they end up binding him too tightly. What Lincoln came to realize only gradually, and with mounting bitterness, was that his control over artistic matters—all that really interested him—was no more than marginal. He increasingly came to find himself ever more submerged in administrative and fund-raising matters that bored him to death and failed to employ his essential abilities.

When Lincoln accepted the job, for which he took no salary, he believed, as he wrote Benjamin Britten, that he would be a "sort of an artistic coordinator, responsible for visual aspects and production." And he'd expected his duties, in short order, to be defined along those lines. In his very first memo to the center's board of directors, Lincoln said as much, expressing the hope that "the policy of improvisation" that had long characterized staff duties and created duplication and overlapping of functions would be ended.[2] But the board, partly absentee and largely inactive, continued for the next two and a half years to rely on improvisation and to leave artistic decisions primarily in the hands of Morton Baum—with the sole exception, of course, of NYCB, where Lincoln maintained his post as artistic director and, along with Balanchine, his firm control over policy.

That City Center had survived for a decade was itself a considerable miracle, and one for which Baum deserved a large share of the credit. The Center had put on some fifty seasons of opera, ballet, drama, symphony, and dance without benefit of government or foundation subsidy, and with scant support from wealthy individual donors—who continued to avoid the vaguely déclassé Center, preferring to be associated with more socially prestigious museums and institutions. (Over the years Lincoln himself gave about one hundred thousand dollars, making him the Center's largest single contributor.)

City Center catered mostly to a middle- and working-class audience and kept its ticket prices affordable; the downside of its unique and essential mission was that appeals to its base for contributions usually brought in less than five thousand dollars (much of it in one-dollar bills). Survival had been possible only through endless juggling of limited funds, a few unexpected windfalls, and more than a few heedless plunges. In 1952 City Center—not for the first time—was virtually without cash.

Yet Lincoln dived with zest into his new job; as he wrote Cadmus (soon to return from living several years, on and off, with Jared and Margaret French in Italy), "I love having all the mud puddles to get up to my ass wet in." He was dedicated, as always, to the visionary possibilities inherent in a project, with self-aggrandizement—and his own health—of limited concern. He told a *Variety* reporter that he envisioned an entire new building complex, fully equipped to present opera, ballet, and theater; the complex, he added, might not come about for ten years, but it would come (Lincoln Center would in fact be constructed in the sixties).

Even if Lincoln refused to pay much attention to his health, some of his friends, as he plowed ahead, expressed concern. One of them was the poet Marianne Moore, who wrote, "I am dazed, Lincoln, by your pouring out strength and exercising resourcefulness, persevering, till you might die of exertion. Give that last, some thought. I *beg of you.*" He would—but only when necessity demanded, when a full-scale collapse loomed; the idea of a voluntary slowdown was unimaginable.

Lincoln much preferred giving money to raising it. As he ironically wrote Andy and Betsy Wyeth (with whom a friendship had been steadily growing over the past few years), "I've had a happy summer raising money; this is at once relaxing and sexually stimulating. If you really think so, you're as crazy as I've become, doing it." The immediate problem was finding enough money to cover traveling expenses for the ballet company to return to Europe in 1953.

Due to the expenditures on the Nineteenth Street house, Lincoln himself had scant discretionary funds of his own to offer. He tried appealing to John Marshall, but sympathetic though Marshall was, he made it clear that the Rockefeller Foundation would never respond favorably to any request for touring money; he did confide, though, that before very much longer he believed the foundation's trustees would make a significant award to the Center for commissioning new works in opera and ballet.

Exciting though that prospect was, it did nothing for the Center's current financial circumstances, which, in the fall of 1952 were in Lincoln's opinion "never so shaky as now." Ticket prices were held to a $3.60 high (roughly half what the Metropolitan Opera and Broadway theaters charged), while labor costs remained fixed by contract, and the cost of materials and other services had doubled and in some cases tripled.

Despite the desperate financial situation, Lincoln continued to spin ambitious fantasies for City Center. His initial focus was on the sorry state of its theater offerings; he dreamed up the idea of organizing a permanent drama company based on the model of England's Old Vic, complete with production and training facilities. With that in mind he had a series of conversations with Robert Moses, the city's building czar, about the possibilities of finding better space for the Center, and he also held talks with William Schuman, Juilliard's director, about moving the school from Columbia to the midtown area, thereby allowing for collaborative ventures.

Neither set of discussions bore fruit, but Lincoln continued to plan for a new theater season. Within two months of becoming managing director, he'd rounded up leading players for a season tentatively consisting of *A Midsummer Night's Dream*, *Six Characters in Search of an Author*, and *Major Barbara*. But if Lincoln was still under the illusion that he had enough artistic clout to carry out such a plan, he was quickly shown otherwise. The Center's board of trustees, at Baum's urging, cancelled the drama season, citing, plausibly, a lack of operating expenses.

If Lincoln felt humiliated or deflated, he showed little sign of it. He simply shifted his energy back to the ballet, where his authority was uncontested. In the same month that the trustees rejected his plans for a theater season, NYCB, fully rehearsed and funded, presented two major new Balanchine works, *Scotch Symphony* (music by Mendelssohn) and *Metamorphoses* (based on a Hindemith symphonic work). Because of the cancellation of the drama series, the ballet was extended from its originally scheduled six-week season to nine and then to twelve, marking the longest continuous run for a ballet company in U.S. history—and throughout, surprisingly, it played at two-thirds capacity.[3]

As if to mark the ballet's unprecedented success, Balanchine (who had divorced Tallchief) and Tanny Le Clercq, who'd already been living together, were formally married the day before New Year's, followed, at midnight, by a gathering at the Stravinskys' for what Lincoln called "a rather gloomy coupe de champagne"; as more and more Russians continued to troop in, Tanny leaned over to Lincoln and whispered "Oh God, what Have I got Myself IN FOR?"[4]

The extended ballet run produced an unprecedented profit of some thirty thousand dollars, making it possible to start thinking about reviving theater at City Center for the spring of 1953. Lincoln was somewhat active in the planning, but in a much more limited way than earlier. His biggest contribution was in successfully pushing for the noted director Albie Marre to head the season; Lincoln considered Marre a great find ("he has taste, courage and real brilliance," he wrote Pavlik. "He has not the vanity or silliness of Jack Houseman"), and his production of *Misalliance* at the Center in 1953 actually moved to Broadway, though for a modest run.

Lincoln also had a hand in preparations for the spring opera season, which featured Rossini's *La Cenerentola*, which hadn't been produced in the United States in nearly a century, and proved a tremendous success with critics and audiences alike. The same season saw a revised (less decor, more music) version of Marc Blitzstein's *Regina*. Blitzstein was a close friend of Mina's (she paid for the new sets); Lincoln knew him as well, though he had more mixed and changeable feelings about the composer (he told Newbold Morris that the low morale of the cast of *Regina* was due in part to Blitzstein's persistent "needling" of them: "They have come to me over Rosenstock's head to ask for extra 'protection' and 'consideration' ").

Joseph Rosenstock had replaced Halasz as head of the opera company, and from the beginning of his tenure Lincoln had regarded him as second-rate and a provocateur. The lack of regard was mutual. The dislike between the two men broke into the open during the dress rehearsal for *Cenerentola*, when Rosenstock for the first time saw the costumes, scenery, and John Butler's choreography for the ballet. Lincoln had had a hand in choosing all three, and Rosenstock now declared them "grotesque," demanding that the ballet be removed from the opera. Lincoln, by his own account, "savagely defended" the dancers. Rosenstock "lost his temper" and told Lincoln that he had no authority whatsoever over him— which was true, since Lincoln's vaguely defined power as managing director hadn't given him any right to interfere with decisions made by the three unit heads (opera, ballet, and theater). Butler quickly whipped up an entirely new ballet, which Olin Downes, music critic of the *Times*, singled out for praise; Lincoln himself thought the music chosen "poor" and the ballet "too long."

The tug-of-war with Rosenstock wasn't over. He accused Lincoln to his face of plotting to replace him as head of the opera unit (Rosenstock's contract ran out early in 1953). Rosenstock's accusation made Lincoln furious and he took his anger directly to Baum, telling him, among other things, that he had the right to know precisely the state of negotiations with Rosenstock. That was a miscalculation. Baum took Lincoln's query as an interference with his own authority and used it as an occasion to vent his own long-suppressed anger at Lincoln for assuming powers (like signing contracts) for which he lacked authority and for his repeated refusal to abide by agreed-upon budgets, thereby jeopardizing the Center's financial future. Baum cited *La Cenerentola* as the most recent and flagrant example of Lincoln's extravagance: the widely heralded production of the opera had landed the Center seventy thousand dollars in the red. An infuriated Baum put "a great deal" of the direct responsibility for the high costs on Lincoln's head, and he made it clear to the board that Lincoln was incapable of being "restricted by financial considerations."

Apparently Baum also said something to the board about Lincoln being in one of his "hysterical" states, even hinting that he might be "crazy." Several friendly members passed Baum's remarks on to Lincoln, and in writing up the whole destructive interaction to board chair Newbold Morris, Lincoln straightforwardly acknowledged that he *had* been "nervously upset," though "by no means 'hysterical.' " He revealed to Morris that in the last four years he'd had four "periods of over-exhilaration," as he characterized them, but had "never *broken down* (whatever that means)."

"Up to this time," Lincoln continued in his lengthy account to Morris, "I had considered Morton Baum my friend; I had been absolutely frank with him. I discounted his animosity. I believe now I was in error." In summarizing his grievances to Newbold Morris, Lincoln accused Baum of "continuing to do his calculated and experienced best to destroy my position, authority, integrity, and peace of mind," and he closed with a semi-ultimatum: he would stay on as managing director, but "only if I am actively supported by the Board of Directors without the open and harmful opposition of Morton Baum."

Morris, in response, wrote Lincoln a brief letter in which he tried to get clichés ("I do not know of any organization which amounts to anything where there is not a clash of personalities," and so on) to do the hard work of grappling with the issues at hand. He was no less bland in assuring Lincoln that the majority of the board supported him—a dubious claim, given its loyalty to Baum. A sort of armed truce was pieced together, and Lincoln did stay on at the Center for more than a year.

Lincoln wrote Pavlik, who was again living in Europe, that he'd "had a frightful battle with Mr. Baum. . . . Its been very hard on Fido as I got terribly over-wrought through sleeplessness, and behaved more or less out of control; rather, I utilized hysteria towards constructive ends, but I can't ever afford to do this again, because the border-line between hysteria and sanity is so close that one could really go out for good. Fido recognized the symptoms and since she has been there herself she guided me across the trapeze."

Life had become harder for Fidelma than Lincoln was able, or perhaps willing, to recognize. "Guiding" him through his depressive-hysterical periods was indeed difficult. But when he was over them and in an expansive, baronial mood, it was—for someone of her shy, essentially unsociable personality—at least as difficult being his hostess and the person centrally responsible for running their new domain on Nineteenth Street. True, the house before long became fully staffed: a cook, a daytime maid, a cleaning woman once a week, a laundress, a man available for repairs and upkeep— and the handy live-in Jensen who, besides maintaining the garden, was able to fix the furnace and the plumbing.

For Lincoln the new home was a pure delight; "it's lovely to entertain in this house," he wrote Cadmus. But for Cadmus's sister, Fidelma, it meant being in charge of a far larger household and far more socializing than she'd previously known in their relatively cramped apartment. It wasn't that Lincoln wanted Fidelma to run their home like some round-the-clock grand salon; as a writer, scholar, and omnivorous reader, he had his own need for considerable "time out"—for quiet and solitude. The problem was that professionally he now and then did have to entertain potential foundation grantors and the like, as well as to throw an occasional party following a ballet premiere or to put together a congenial gathering in honor of visitors and friends like the Sitwells or Auden. And sometimes, too, he simply wanted, as he himself once put it, to parade around like "one of Napoleon's less[er] marshals."

Fidelma struggled to meet the new demands put on her, but they were at odds with her temperament. She and Lincoln were near opposites characterologically; that could often serve the relationship well—but not in regard to socializing. Fidelma lacked Lincoln's charismatic social skills, his conversational brilliance, his forceful, dominant presence. Above all she lacked his ability to flourish in a whirlwind of activity. Fidelma's energy was limited (and unlike Lincoln, she never learned to devote the bulk of it to herself). Essentially a meek soul, she had trouble managing an enlarged staff, let alone the occasional feast for fifty.

Over the years, in Jensen's firsthand view, these assorted responsibilities would end up "crushing" her spirit. Among the symptoms she developed over time, according to Jensen, was a tendency, when feeling overwhelmed, to "talk compulsively and repetitively" at home—in curious contrast to her difficulty in talking at all in public. These "chattering" spells would, as Jensen recalls, "drive Lincoln crazy and he'd sometimes speak sharply to her: 'Goosie, goosie [their nickname for each other, and for a few intimates as well], stop talking, you've said all that already.' " But, Jensen adds, "they did love each other, and Fido, when reprimanded, was often able to more or less hold her own: 'How can you tell me to stop talking, goosie, when you know I have to talk, I can't stop talking just because . . . ,' " and the like.[5]

Fidelma's emotional difficulties developed gradually over a long stretch of time. For several decades after Lincoln's rise to prominence as a cultural force, she (mostly) succeeded in holding up her end, in meeting Lincoln's multiple social demands, thankless and difficult though she found them. But by the 1950s the toll on her had clearly begun to show. Her painting was among the early casualties. The long summers on Fire Island had always been a respite for Fidelma, a time when minimal domestic distractions allowed her to get back to her art in a concentrated way. But following the spate of hurricanes in 1953, Lincoln decided they should give up the beach house and look for a place in the country. They soon enough found one near Weston, Connecticut, a lovely house, spacious but not grand, close by the homes of Balanchine, Pavlik, and Alice de la Mar.

Fidelma was fond of the country and as she grew older would spend increasing amounts of time there. But initially she missed Fire Island fiercely, missed the sunlight and sand, the starkness and simplicity, missed the seamless connective link to that earlier time when, surrounded by her brother, Paul, Margaret and Jere French, and buoyant, gifted young friends by the boatload, they'd let carefree day after day slip away, and in the evenings would spin tales together of the glories that awaited all. Weston, Connecticut, represented a very different phase: not youth, but middle and then old age, a time that for Fidelma was accompanied by foreshortened dreams, diminished experience, and restricted companionship—and then toward the end a landslide of devastated hopes, a flood of grief.

Fidelma's last substantial painting was completed late in 1953, soon after she said good-bye to Fire Island. Thereafter it was the occasional drawing; then it was nothing (or nothing that has survived, at any rate). That last painting was of Lincoln and was meant to complement the portrait that she'd earlier completed of herself. When placed side by side, the two images can be read in various ways, but the reading that seems the most obvious—and startling—is also the most poignant. The portrait of Lincoln is the smaller of the two, and is diminished in other ways as well: the figure is middle-aged and vaguely unattractive, the brow furrowed, the expression somewhat suspicious, even threatening. If (consciously or not) the portrait was meant to express Fidelma's buried anger, serving as a kind of clandestine revenge for having been diverted from art to domesticity, Lincoln failed to get the message. He widely praised the work, writing Andy Wyeth that "it is very lovely, her best picture, and the sense of form and character is very full and firm."

Fidelma's portrait of herself, in contrast, shows a strong, confident, vibrant woman—perhaps the image she retained in her mind of her younger self, of the person who'd rebelled against her authoritarian father, leaving his house to join New York's bohemian art scene; it was a Fidelma perhaps still alive in 1953 but buried deep within, no longer available for public display: those who encountered Fidelma at a Nineteenth Street party or a social event during the fifties invariably describe her as still glamorous looking but in manner distant, subdued, and uncomfortable.

There's no question that Fidelma adored Lincoln. But adoration doesn't exclude the presence of other, contradictory emotions, like resentment and fear. There's no evidence that she consciously blamed Lincoln for her failure to develop as an artist. She might well have failed, through lack of talent or drive, even had they lived a peaceable life that would have given her all the unencumbered time she needed. Yet the least that can be said is that the high-powered existence they in fact led created a set of devouring demands and an atmosphere of endless static directly at odds with what she needed in order to pursue her own work. Emotionally fragile and increasingly obsessive—even under the best of circumstances it took her a long time to complete a single painting—she found it difficult (and later impossible) simultaneously to meet her own high standards for successfully performing the role of Lincoln's wife and to reserve the needed solitude and time for becoming her own person.

In the 1950s, of course, traditional gender roles were at their sanctified peak in this country. Though Lincoln was different from most men of his generation in that he actively encouraged Fidelma's desire for an independent career, he was like them in assuming that his wife would be responsible for running the household. Lincoln had grown up, after all, in an essentially traditional home where, without any notable difficulty arising (though one wonders about Rose's occasional "nervous fits"), Louis had the active public career and Rose managed their domestic life. In Fidelma's generation somewhat more women managed successfully to combine the demands of a career and the home. But Fidelma wasn't one of them; the Nineteenth Street house, with its high-pitched activity and the attendant stress, was hardly an ordinary one—and Fidelma had far less energy and confidence than the ordinary person. She rarely complained to Lincoln about her difficulties, usually blaming herself for any household problem or for her failure to pursue her painting.

Part of her confusion was that Lincoln persistently encouraged her to spend more time on her art. And he did so with more than words. At one point Fidelma wrote her brother, Paul, "Goosie is desperately anxious to help and photographs for me every day on the week-end." Lincoln also urged her to spend time at Naushon, a spot they'd often visited and which seemed to stimulate her ability to paint. He also pressed her, during the years when they were still summering on Fire Island, not to come into the city for the fall ballet season, but to remain on the island and continue to work. This was, without question, meant lovingly, but it didn't help resolve Fidelma's intrinsic dilemma. Given her emotional fragility, she was unable to break out of the double bind her life had become (and which the cultural climate of the fifties strongly underscored): her prime obligation was to support her husband's activities; whatever free time and energy remained beyond that—minimal and diminishing in Fidelma's case—belonged legitimately to her.

Lincoln remained at his post as managing director of City Center until the winter of 1955, but 1953 marked the high-water mark of his artistic, as opposed to administrative, involvement. In the spring of that year Balanchine was fulfilling an engagement at La Scala, and Lincoln was left entirely free to plan the ballet season. NYCB now had a repertory of some fifty works, most of them outside the standard offerings of other troupes. The company's emphasis on dance itself, rather than on surrounding theatrical elements like scenery, costuming, or pantomime, also set it apart. Further, Balanchine and Lincoln had always been intent on creating new works, however difficult that was to accomplish working within the budgetary constraints of City Center.

The spring 1953 ballet season was the first in thirteen seasons at City Center in which Balanchine didn't offer a new work. But there were two by Robbins (a version of *Afternoon of a Faun* and *Fanfare*, in honor of the coronation of Britain's Princess Elizabeth), and one by Todd Bolender. The six-week engagement began in early May and also featured Jacques d'Amboise in a revival, supervised by Lew Christensen, of *Filling Station* (in Lincoln's opinion it made d'Amboise "a star overnight," and he declared him "the first real male dancer for years"). Lincoln hated Todd Bolender's piece, privately calling it "a really stupid thing," but he loved both of Robbins's ballets, even if the critics were divided.[6]

In advance of the season, Lincoln had assured Baum (or so the latter claimed) that any new ballet productions "would all be on a small scale and would, if necessary, be done in practice clothes." If Lincoln did make such a promise—and given his past history of extravagantly exceeding agreed-upon budgets, he probably did—he broke it with a flourish. During rehearsals the costs for *Fanfare* began to rise alarmingly, and at one point Baum actually threatened to cancel the production. Lincoln responded with a sharp carrot-and-stick letter that pointed to his own significant fund-raising efforts of late and threatened to cancel the last two weeks of the ballet season if *Fanfare* wasn't done. Baum rescinded the threatened cancellation.

But tempers would soon flare again. Despite good attendance, at the end of the season the deficit for the ballet reached seventy thousand dollars. Lincoln himself either personally contributed or raised more than half the needed funds, but that didn't appease Baum. He angrily insisted that "the responsibility . . . be placed directly on Kirstein, who could not be restricted by financial considerations when he was in control . . . [and who] had precipitated the Center into heavy deficit financing," bringing it "to the very verge of disaster."

As yet another eruption and crisis threatened, two events occurred, almost miraculous in their simultaneous timing, that sharply eased tensions: Governor Thomas E. Dewey of New York signed a bill that reduced City Center's rent from approximately twenty-five thousand dollars a year to one dollar; and Lincoln received a confidential phone call from John Marshall telling him that the Rockefeller Foundation's board of trustees had approved a grant to City Center of two hundred thousand dollars to commission new works in opera and ballet. Credit for that triumphant outcome, as even Morton Baum acknowledged, was Lincoln's alone. He'd worked for years to produce the desired result, greatly aided by a sympathetic John Marshall's advocacy within the foundation itself.

One clause in the grant made it clear that the foundation had decided on its gift largely out of confidence in Lincoln himself: it not only designated him as administrator of the grant but specified that it would remain in effect only as long as he was managing director at the Center. Thanks to that clause, Lincoln was henceforth able to exert more control, though still constrained, over artistic decisions relating to the opera and drama at City Center. When Baum, for example—his commercial eye ever cocked—insisted that the center put on *Show Boat*, Lincoln firmly informed him that no Rockefeller money could be used toward the production, that the grant had been designed strictly for commissioning new works. Various foundation officials subsequently corroborated Lincoln's position, but Baum, as usual, got his way: *Show Boat* was mounted in 1954 out of other funds entirely.[7]

The Rockefeller grant was apportioned equally between opera and ballet and spread over a three-year period. The sum was hardly sufficient, of course, to transform City Center into, say, a significant rival to the Metropolitan Opera, but the grant did help to ease financial tensions all around. And it was certainly enough to propel Lincoln into his favored orbit of fantasy planning. He was soon drawing up "experimental surveys" for creating "an ideal City Center" that would contain a "monumental opera house [and] a triple academy of music, the drama and the dance serving the city, the nation and the hemisphere."

The terms of the Rockefeller grant didn't give Lincoln the sole right to make awards for new works, but did give him a large leg up by providing that the money would be withdrawn should he cease to be the Center's managing director. From an early age Lincoln had formed decided views, sometimes subject to change, as to who was or was not worthy. He'd already, out of his personal funds, given the Mexican composer Carlos Chávez and Auden's longtime companion, the talented and tempestuous Chester Kallman, seven thousand dollars to produce, respectively, the music and libretto for a new ballet, *The Tuscan Players*. He now upped the ante to double that amount and got the Center's board to approve it.

He also decided that the Center *had* to produce the world premiere of

Menotti's *The Saint of Bleecker Street* and *had* to have a new opera from
Aaron Copland, both warranting commissions of seven thousand dollars
each—which both received. But Lincoln lost the struggle (since no Rockefeller funds were at issue) over whether to create an exhibition space for
art at the Center, even though René d'Harnoncourt, the director of
MoMA, joined him in expressing opposition; both men feared that a lot of
third-rate material would get chosen by jurors of limited experience in the
art world. Their shared fear proved justified.[8]

Buoyed by a resurgent wave of energy, Lincoln prematurely accepted a
host of European offers for the ballet company before he'd secured the
needed fifty thousand dollars in travel expenses. As contract deadlines and
dates for departure drew near, Lincoln found himself in a frantic, increasingly desperate search for funds. With only a few days' leeway remaining,
Nelson Rockefeller stepped into the breach—though he and Lincoln had
seen each other only irregularly in recent years; serving as intermediary to
the Rockefeller Brothers Fund, Nelson got the money needed to allow the
NYCB company to depart for Europe, thereby once more saving Lincoln
from major embarrassment. When he gratefully wrote Nelson, "I hardly
know how to thank you," the phrase, for once, was not hyperbole.

The tour itself, fortunately, was (in Betty Cage's words) "a terrific success." At La Scala the audience stood up to applaud, which was unheard
of, every performance was sold out, and the critics wrote long essays of
praise about "the magnificent American group" rather than the brief paragraph or two usually allotted ballet performances. The engagement in
Rome that followed again produced an ecstatic press ("luminous picture
of an ensemble perfect in every part") and "endless ovations and thunderous enthusiasm." And so it went throughout Italy and on into Belgium,
the Netherlands, and Germany. Only Bologna provided a negative note:
the men in the audience insisted on smoking throughout the performance, and by the fourth ballet (so Tanny Le Clercq wrote Lincoln), the
cast was choking and "you couldn't see anyone, the haze was so thick."

The major dissenting voice on the triumphant tour was an utterly predictable one: Pavlik Tchelitchev. He and Charles Henri Ford happened to
be in Milan, saw one NYCB performance, and after it told Eddie Bigelow
that the only thing he liked was Jean Rosenthal's lighting. Bigelow, in
turn, told Lincoln, who, in an otherwise newsy, appreciative letter to
Pavlik, sent him a head-on rebuttal: "I don't think you've had a good word
to say about him [Balanchine] since 1933. . . . I certainly haven't the
energy or desire to disagree with you or justify what I have to do." Lincoln, now in his late forties, had found a way to go on honoring Pavlik's art
even as he held him to point about Balanchine's accomplishment (and his
own).[9]

Given the ballet tour's financial success, Morton Baum wanted the company to stay longer in Germany and also accept Italian invitations for the company to extend its stay or to return at a later date. His persistence infuriated Betty Cage, who now joined Lincoln as a committed antagonist of City Center's chief officer. "He must realize," Betty wrote Lincoln, "that we are not primarily a touring company. The only reason for our existence is that we have a home and can work most of the year in NY and prepare new works." She predicted that if Baum insisted on having his way, among those who would immediately resign from the company would be herself, Balanchine, and Maria Tallchief. Baum desisted.

The ongoing antagonism between Baum and Lincoln was basically a struggle between a financially (but not artistically) astute accountant determined to safeguard the Center's future, and a high-flying visionary of extraordinary discernment and ambition, coupled with a scornful impracticality. If Baum was prone to belittle some of Lincoln's grander schemes, Lincoln was repeatedly guilty of refusing to heed financial realities. The latest issue between the two arose out of Baum's decision (which the board could almost always be expected to accept) to put José Ferrer back in charge of reviving drama at City Center.

Lincoln had nothing against Ferrer personally, but considered his taste middlebrow and worried that the Center would simply repeat the box office orientation of commercial theater rather than creating a much-needed alternative to it. He'd already been talking to an interested John Marshall at Rockefeller, as well as to Bob Chapman at Harvard, about the need to set up some sort of academy to train actors in a classic tradition that stressed diction and comportment and would present an alternative to what he considered the slovenly habits of American actors.

If Lincoln was dismayed over Ferrer's appointment, he was outraged by his choice of plays: *The Shrike, Cyrano de Bergerac, Charley's Aunt,* and *Richard III.* Lincoln wasn't alone in thinking that Ferrer had taken the easy way out: he'd already done three of the four plays on Broadway, and their very limited literary merit (except *Richard III*) hardly seemed to warrant such instant revival. Although he lacked any power in the matter, Lincoln did angrily protest to Newbold Morris: "If we are to classify as anything but a subsistence house, we have to make the effort to establish some sort of artistic integrity rather than the most bald-faced expediency." His disdain for Ferrer's planned season somehow got leaked to *Variety,* angering Ferrer, who (according to Lincoln) accused him of "trying to drive him back to Hollywood." Baum promptly got the board of directors to issue a statement in strong support of Ferrer's season, and the advance sale for the plays quickly went over the two-hundred-thousand-dollar mark. "I hope to spend it," Lincoln wrote Bob Chapman, and he voluntarily took the veil of silence. But both he and Jean Rosenthal withdrew from any participation in the drama season.

Defeated on that front and essentially still a mere adviser to Rosenstock on opera (Baum had, over Lincoln's objection, renewed Rosen-stock's contract), Lincoln at least had the ballet to fall back on as a creative outlet. For the 1954 winter season, plans were well under way for present-ing two new Balanchine ballets: the difficult, intricate *Opus 34* to music by Arnold Schoenberg, and the long-incubating production of what would be the roaringly successful *Nutcracker.*

Lincoln's life wasn't entirely consumed by professional involvements, angry entanglements, or controversial plans for future projects. He also attended and hosted (to Fidelma's mounting consternation) an ongoing round of elegant social events, many obligatory, some for pure enjoyment. And he also maintained a more intense, semi-paternal involvement with a small number of younger men, many of them artists whom he supported in various ways, some of whom had once been lovers or part-time sexual partners (he also still had the occasional "quickie"—in 1953 with a mar-ried Harvard student). He agreed completely with some lines Auden had recently sent him from Ischia: "All we homosexuals dream of one day being married to a comrade in arms. Our affairs, however, continue to be affairs between officers and enlisted men. Necessarily. Homosexuality is a feudal relationship." And it's probably true that in the fifties and early sixties cross-class sexual contact between men was more common than subsequently; later, the modern gay movement, initially radically anti-bourgeois, became more centrist in its values, with "ideal" relationships being defined in a manner close to "official" mainstream views.[10]

Jensen Yow and Dan Maloney continued to be the two younger men of most emotional interest to Lincoln (neither relationship was any longer sexual). Jens was helping Fidelma complete the decor of her bedroom (which included a silk velvet carpet that had belonged to Lincoln's mother, as well as Göring's bedspread, which Lincoln had "commandeered" dur-ing the war); and, after he finished fixing up the exterior garden as well, Jens constructed a mammoth "Wardian Box"—an interior garden of sol-dered brass filled with orchids and houseplants ("Mercy!" Lincoln wrote Cadmus, "what a production"). Jens also continued to work at the Pippin Press (which he helped to reorganize), and had been getting a number of mural commissions on his own. Lincoln thought Jensen "entirely profes-sional; he amazes me; everything is well-worked and no nonsense."

Dan Maloney had preceded Jensen in Lincoln's life. The two never much warmed up to each other, but almost everyone but Jensen fell for the handsome, black-haired, volatile Irishman. Lincoln found Dan end-lessly fascinating and saw deeply into his complex character. It didn't sur-prise him at all when his "slightly mad" tough friend revealed enormous empathy for Osbert Sitwell, whose health was deteriorating from Parkin-son's disease and whose longtime companion, David Horner, proved increasingly unavailable; when Osbert was in the U.S., Dan filled in faithfully as his helpmate, giving up his own painting for a time to do so.

If neither opera nor theater at City Center was operating to Lincoln's satisfaction, he could take pride in the mounting prestige and financial security of both the ballet company and the independent School of American Ballet. During the summers of 1953 and 1954, NYCB had highly acclaimed tours of the West Coast, and plans for another European tour were well advanced. The *Tribune*'s critic, Walter Terry, confided to John Marshall that by this point the company's only serious rival was Sadler's Wells—but was quick to add that he found the English company "tight and unimaginative" and felt "its dancers simply cannot do what even members of the corps de ballet of the New York City Center Company do easily." The British liked to dismiss NYCB's prowess as "mere acrobatics," but it was better ascribed, in Terry's view, to "technical and physical strength."[11]

The high-water mark for NYCB during Lincoln's tenure as managing director of the Center came early in February 1954 with the premiere of *The Nutcracker*. Its creation had spanned a three-year period, during which costs had climbed into the stratosphere (eighty thousand dollars, double the planned budget); "it took genius to acquire" such a debt, Lincoln insouciantly claimed, but Baum thought it simply took gargantuan irresponsibility. He reluctantly changed his mind after the rave reviews were in (John Martin was one of the few critics to express regret at the lack of much actual dancing in *Nutcracker*), and the box office stampede began; even when the run was extended, every performance was sold out, and the first week in February saw a house record of fifty-two thousand dollars (more than fifty years later, *Nutcracker* continues to be a box office bonanza for NYCB). One of the happiest aspects of the production was the use of thirty-five children from SAB; in tandem with the recent emergence of Jacques d'Amboise and Tanny Le Clercq, the first wholly SAB-trained Balanchine stars, the school's students would henceforth feed the company at every level.

Lincoln's discretionary power over the use of the Rockefeller grant ensured his ongoing involvement during 1954 in certain aspects of opera production at City Center. He and Rosenstock continued to tangle (and Baum once again saw to it that the conductor's contract was extended for yet another year), but at a more polite distance than previously, since Lincoln, thanks to the wording of the Rockefeller grant, indisputably had the final say over commissioning new works. Menotti cooperated eagerly with *The Saint of Bleecker Street*, but Lincoln had to work hard to persuade Aaron Copland to accept an opera commission. Copland finally did agree, and *The Tender Land*, directed by Jerome Robbins, was the result.

Even during rehearsals Lincoln developed strong doubts about the opera's viability; as he wrote Carlos Chávez, "While the musical value of the work is considerable, the theatrical elements are rather pallid . . . it worries me very much that none of our composers here, except for Menotti, believe in the roaring, impassioned, whole-souled melodrama; the drama of the released voice." The critics, as feared, were lukewarm, with Olin Downes treating the opera as an inconclusive tryout rather than a finished product. As a result audiences were thin and the financial loss considerable. After the run was completed Lincoln, characteristically, told Copland exactly what he thought: "The music is lovely . . . but the dramatic dynamics are faulty; there is no real climax and an elegiac mood is ineffective on an operatic stage."[12]

Due to the financial failure of *The Tender Land* (and also of Rosenstock's production of Gottfried von Einem's *The Trial*), Baum got the center board to declare a moratorium on all new opera productions for the foreseeable future. Stymied at the Center, Lincoln had to take *The Saint of Bleecker Street* elsewhere. He went to Chandler Cowles, who'd successfully produced previous Menotti works and now did so again. City Center owned a piece of *The Saint* and profited from the arrangement; its new light opera company had a simultaneous hit with a revival of *Carousel* and the financial cycle turned once more.

But this constant see-saw between brimming coffers and yawning ruin was no way to run an institution—unless one wished to parallel Lincoln's own personal suffering with manic-depressive disorder. For City Center to have survived a dozen years was on some level a decided triumph. But for it to survive much longer, the house had to be put in some sort of managerial order. A serious crisis over precisely that issue emerged in 1954 when John D. Rockefeller III, whom Lincoln had long been cultivating as a potential board member and patron for City Center, came within a hairbreadth of saying yes—but then decided against.

Prior to making that decision, John D. had had a number of discussions with Baum, Newbold Morris, and Lincoln, during which he urged that the Center hire a paid business manager, have a management survey done of its internal operations, and actually implement the authority of the managing director (Lincoln) so that he no longer felt managed and directed by others. Lincoln was grateful for, and had strongly favored, all of John D.'s recommendations; he, in turn, had advocated the importance of raising a "working capital reserve," which John D. and his advisers had agreed was not only desirable but could be done with "little trouble" once "a sound appeal" had been lined up.

But these suggestions didn't appeal to Morton Baum (nor, to a lesser degree, to Newbold Morris). And Baum had little trouble persuading the

Center's essentially inactive board to go along with the decision respectfully to decline John D. Rockefeller's recommendations. In Lincoln's view the board had thrown away the opportunity of a lifetime; had Rockefeller come on the board, other wealthy New Yorkers would have flocked to join up, opening their coffers and thus securing the Center's future. He let Newbold Morris know in no uncertain terms that "John's presence would have meant a new balance of power, and one that neither you nor Mr. Baum were prepared to countenance." Their refusal, in Lincoln's view, meant the continuation of policies that guaranteed "a fifth-rate opera company and a drama-company which triumphs on warmed-up hits."

What Lincoln didn't know was that he himself had played an unwitting role in John D.'s decision not to accept membership on the Center's board. Dana Creel, head of the Rockefeller Brothers Fund, had warned John D. in a confidential memo that Kirstein's disposition was essentially artistic, not managerial, that he was not "either by temperament or by training, a person who goes about things in a particularly logical or analytical manner, nor does he have a Board which forces him to do so," and that he "is dreaming of a cultural center" with "far broader facilities for teaching and training classical techniques than City Center would or could provide." Creel felt that Kirstein "should be pulled out of the clouds . . . and that his attention should be focused on first things first, namely, getting the Center's present program on a firm basis."

But to Lincoln, "pulling his head out of the clouds" was tantamount to settling for what he felt was City Center's "declining mediocrity." He decided that he'd had enough. On January 5, 1955, he abruptly submitted his resignation as managing director. As he wrote Pavlik, "I am bored to death with people defending and attacking me, and it is of no interest, and I never want to hear the name of the City Center mentioned again. . . . I just never want to think about raising money or horrible German operadirectors, etc. . . . It was all intensely disagreeable, and in a way still is; but in time it will pass. I had no idea people would care so much—either way."

But of course Lincoln had cared as much as anyone, and no one had been as impassioned as he during the previous few years. Besides, he was not yet finished with the Center, nor could he possibly be, since it remained the ballet's continuing home. And all parties wanted it to remain so. The company had, for the time being at least, no other place to go. From the Center's point of view, NYCB had been operating in the black for the past two years and was no longer a drain on its finances; besides, the company now had a worldwide reputation and brought the Center far more prestige than any of its other units.

In the name of NYCB and the Center maintaining their connection, Lincoln, Baum, and Morris were all careful to observe the proprieties in dealing with Lincoln's resignation. Lincoln, "for the record," wrote Newbold Morris that Morton Baum had been "uniquely responsible [which was true] for getting Balanchine and myself into the City Center and, against opposition from the Board, for keeping us here . . . however much he may have exasperated me, I hope I have not been too ungrateful in word or deed."

Morris, for his part, initially rejected the resignation and appointed a committee of five "to explore the problem." But Lincoln refused to meet with the committee, making it clear that his position was irrevocable. He was already on to other things. Throughout the summer of 1954, he'd been having preliminary discussions with Lawrence Langer of the Theatre Guild, and Joseph Verner Reed, a wealthy Broadway producer, about the planned Shakespeare Festival and Academy to be created at Stratford, Connecticut. Lincoln had agreed to serve on the board, and he and Jean Rosenthal had been advising on the design of the permanent theater. They'd already succeeded in moving the original plan of a small summer house to a large permanent one that would serve year round as what Lincoln called "a home-base for a great classic repertory company" as well as a potential site for concerts, opera, and ballet. Though Dana Creel may have regretted the fact, Lincoln had neither been "pulled out of the clouds" nor given up "dreaming of a cultural center."

Lincoln Center

(1955–1957)

The turmoil that attended Lincoln's association with City Center exacted a terrible toll on him. During the final, tumultuous six weeks of his tenure, as accusations flew, a deep sense of guilt and failure ("a belief I could be God and settle all problems in one swoop") settled in on him. Able to sleep only a few hours a night, he hoped a change of scene might help, and he and Jensen went off to his brother George's lakefront home in Mamaroneck, New York. But there he worsened rather than improved; years later Jensen recalled hearing Lincoln "howling" in the woods surrounding the house and at another time standing precariously at the end of the pier, looking as if he would jump.

After returning to Weston, Lincoln became wilder still, wrecking his room and becoming generally unmanageable. Jensen barely left his side ("he is the son I never had," Lincoln later wrote), but finally, as he himself acknowledged, "it was too much": in May 1955 Fidelma had to hospitalize him. Because Lincoln was physically powerful, he injured himself during his frenzied struggles and frightened the nurses. Put in a straitjacket for forty-eight hours, he was then given a series of electric shock treatments. Only limited drug options existed in the mid-1950s for treating severe bipolar disorder (lithium, one of the first in what has become a large chemical arsenal, wasn't introduced until the sixties). At the time Lincoln was hospitalized, electroconvulsive therapy (ECT) was the preferred treatment for major depressive illness (and still remains a leading, though controversial, option when drug therapies fail).[1]

During one of the electric shock treatments, the gag slipped from Lincoln's mouth and he badly bit his tongue. He also suffered some temporary memory loss from the ECT, repeating himself in conversation and not recognizing people; but no permanent damage ensued. The doctors initially thought he might have to remain hospitalized for six months, but he responded so well to the treatments that they released him in six weeks. During his hospitalization the person Lincoln wanted to see above all others was Father William Lynch, a priest at Fordham University. Lincoln had never found life, as one friend commented, particularly "satisfying or fulfilling," and he had a profound longing for "immersion or revelation." "I shall never be catholique," he once confided in a letter to Pavlik, "mais je crois que j'étais vraiment sauvée par l'intercession du Bon Dieu . . . certainly prayer is the only possibility . . . the mercy of God or the order in nature . . . is so clear to me now."

The doctors urged Lincoln, after his release from the hospital, to seek treatment with a psychoanalyst, even though the then-dominant view was that "talk therapy" works better with people suffering from standard neuroses rather than major mental disorders. Still, psychoanalysis was among the few treatment modalities available in the mid-fifties that offered any hope. As recently as the year before, Lincoln had expressed his contempt for psychiatry to Jerry Robbins (who sought treatment at various times in his life), writing him that "it is supposed to adjust you and make you 'happy' and 'well.' . . . I feel about psychoanalysis very much like I feel about the weather. No one can hope for equilibrium of sunshine and lovely weather all the time. Unhappiness is part of the human condition and it's not a valid category. . . . The only thing of importance is consciousness."

Yet his ordeal had been terrifying enough to overcome his scruples about the efficacy of psychiatry; he did agree, for a period of time, to see a Dr. Fine five days a week and even thought that "he does me good." But it's doubtful that Lincoln lasted very long; overall he found the sessions "a terrible bore" and constantly felt he should be at rehearsals in Stratford. He settled, early on, for his own rather pat explanation for the breakdown. Writing to Carlos Chávez, Lincoln emphasized that "the reason was that I had smothered the failure at the City Center in my mind, that I minded leaving it more than I admitted and that my guilt about failure was more intense than I could consciously support." Others had their own theories. Osbert Sitwell's was one of the more persuasive: "I am sure," he wrote Lincoln, "that your psyche must turn on you for not giving your purely creative gifts enough scope. That is the worst of being both a born impresario and a born writer."

Lincoln vowed that "all this has changed my life." He would, he swore, never again work as hard or engage as intensely. But momentarily stalled tornadoes don't remain stationary for long. Within a mere month of his hospitalization, Lincoln was eagerly preparing for the July opening of the Shakespeare Festival at Stratford, Connecticut, and as well (thanks to John D. Rockefeller III) had been added to the small group of powerful movers and shakers gathering regularly to discuss plans for the cultural complex that would eventually become Lincoln Center.

The American Shakespeare Festival, spearheaded by leading figures in the Broadway theater, and in particular Lawrence Langner of the Theatre Guild, had been incorporated by the Connecticut legislature as far back as 1951. That same year Langner had approached the Humanities Division of the Rockefeller Foundation for financial assistance, but both John Marshall and his boss, Burton Fahs, had been unimpressed with Langner's "amateurish" and "pretentious" presentation, and had discouraged an application. Marshall later characterized Langner as "a promoter, even a wheedler," with scant "discrimination or taste."[2]

Thereafter, the project languished until Langner turned to Lincoln for advice. Once he became involved, "our picture" of the Shakespeare Festival (Marshall later said) "quite changed . . . more particularly when it became evident that Langner was listening to his advice." In the end the foundation approved a grant of two hundred thousand dollars (soon matched by the Mellon Foundation) for the construction of the theater and for preparatory costs of the opening season in 1955; the following year the foundation made an additional hundred-thousand-dollar grant.

Langner graciously gave Lincoln the entire credit for getting the enterprise off the ground: "Had it not been for you," he wrote him that spring, "there would be no Shakespeare Festival Theatre . . . we were nothing but a floundering group . . . you gave me the key to the whole success of our project." Lincoln had not only persuaded Langner that he had to buy the land, build the theater, and obtain quarters for the allied academy, but himself became strenuously (he knew no other mode) involved in nearly every phase of the work that followed. All of which delighted John Marshall and the other Rockefeller Foundation officers, unaware of the cost of such total immersion to Lincoln's health. They were especially pleased when he persuaded the producer Joseph Verner Reed to join the festival's board. Reed would prove a mainstay once the festival began to run into difficulties.

In the period preceding the opening of the festival, Lincoln did everything from vetting the plans of the architects (the theater was more or less modeled on London's Globe), to persuading the French government to donate enough teakwood to cover the theater's exterior, to arranging for gold acoustical drapes for the stage, to championing the appointments of the Englishmen John Burrell to run the academy, a school for training young actors in the classical mode, and Denis Carey of the Old Vic to direct the plays. *Julius Caesar* and *The Tempest* were chosen for the inaugural program.

"I am not in control of it, yet," an exultant Lincoln wrote Wystan Auden in late April 1955, shortly before his breakdown, "but I have sufficient authority to determine about half of it now, and later will have the rest." Even though the completed theater didn't entirely please him, he felt it was acoustically fine and "capacious, like a provincial opera house" (it seated fifteen hundred, boasted a ninety-two-foot apron and a forty-five by thirty-three stage opening). Lincoln's hopes for the Shakespeare Festival were no less expansive: "Conditions will be favorable outside of New York to do unlikely things." He hoped for a twelve-week summer season at Stratford, followed by a national tour of educational institutions throughout the country and, above all, for the development of a repertory company of actors (rare in the United States) trained in Burrell's academy and able to avoid the demoralizing blackmail of the standard make-or-break Broadway-Hollywood formula.

Lincoln's breakdown and hospitalization in mid-May took him out of the fray—but not for nearly as long as his doctors advised or his actual condition warranted; even from his hospital bed he was sending off detailed, entirely coherent letters by mid-June. And when opening night arrived on July 12, Lincoln was there (the house in Weston was only twenty minutes from the theater), reading cables from, among others, Winston Churchill.

Julius Caesar, unfortunately, was no match for the cablegrams. It was, in Lincoln's own words, "a terrible flop; the most miserable two days I've spent in twenty three years in the theater . . . a nightmare." Typically, Lincoln felt guilty that he hadn't been able to be on the spot during most of the rehearsal period, thereby leaving a vacuum in leadership and coordination. He felt the critics were entirely justified in panning the production, though he couldn't help wincing (and writing a mild reply) to the murderous review ("a wretched piece of work") that appeared in *The Nation* by the respected critic Harold Clurman.

The poor notices deeply affected the morale of the company, though the second production, *The Tempest*, fared somewhat better. Lincoln was determined that the disaster of the first season not be repeated, and he turned to his sometime friend, the celebrated director John Houseman, to take over as artistic director for Stratford's second season in 1956. Houseman accepted the offer.

The ballet, in the meantime, was on several levels prospering, despite renewed internal tensions within the company. Before leaving on April 1, 1955, for its fourth European tour, the company had had a successful five-week season at City Center, offering two new Balanchine ballets, *Roma* and *Pas de Trois II*. Lincoln felt that Tanny Le Clercq had in particular "made big strides ahead" and that Jacques d'Amboise had become a "sensational" dancer.[3]

If anything, the company was even better received in Europe than before. In Paris every performance was sold out, and scalper tickets went for exorbitant prices. An extended tour of Italy and Germany followed, ending at the Holland Festival. From there the company flew to Los Angeles for six weeks of performing on the West Coast, where critical praise and box office clamor continued to reign. But the long tour, however successful, created its stresses and strains, perhaps in part because the company was traveling without a ballet master.

Betty Cage, for one, was "tired, discouraged and bored." Tanny Le Clercq, though having starred in *Roma* and having grown ever more prominent within the company, remained somehow fearful of Tallchief, even though Maria, now remarried, was pregnant (despite bed rest, she miscarried) and absent from the company for a good part of the tour. Lincoln thought the overriding problem was that NYCB was "at a certain dangerous peak of reputation and effectiveness which is not easy to maintain. The fight up," he wrote Newbold Morris, "is easier often than mere maintenance; the dancers are overworked and underpaid," and there was no large new ballet in the works that might revive their enthusiasm. Certainly Balanchine had no lack of ideas for such a work, but City Center remained in its usual financial doldrums, and given Baum's hard feelings (though carefully disguised) about Lincoln's abrupt departure, what funds existed weren't likely to be allocated to the ballet. Lincoln, as often in the past, would have to search for independent financing if Balanchine was to be able to create new works and thereby sustain his commitment to the company.

An additional problem was the relationship between Robbins and Balanchine. Robbins had long suggested a ballet based on S. Ansky's play *The Dybbuk*, with Leonard Bernstein composing the score. But neither Lincoln nor Balanchine cared for Bernstein's music, and Lincoln didn't care for the man. "Lennie doesn't know if he is a boy or a man," Lincoln wrote Robbins, though he "has half a suspicion that if he is not God, he is some sort of god." His limitations as a person, in Lincoln's opinion, limited the quality of his music. He showed real power in conducting past works of genius, but his own compositions had little of that quality. They had no character at all, in Lincoln's opinion, except for "the dynamism of his compulsive approbation-hunt."

The rejection of *The Dybbuk* angered Robbins, who wrote Lincoln that he was "shocked and surprised." He felt particularly annoyed at Balanchine's "apparent distrust in my ability to convert the material into dance terms suitable to our company." Since "at least four ballets which I have suggested over the past couple of years," Robbins went on, "have been turned down, criticized, or dismissed for one reason or another . . . this gets to be a little insecure making."

Lincoln immediately replied and pulled no punches: "I think it is a great mistake on your part," he began, "to resent Balanchine as profoundly as you do. His admiration of you is the most he has for anyone, besides himself . . . [and] you must admit that he has encouraged you in every way possible to do your best work." Whereas "you have never been very generous about him. . . . He was hurt last summer when, in your interview in Los Angeles, you had said that de Mille, [Michael] Kidd and you were responsible for the new attitude to ballet in musical comedy, completely ignoring his historical contribution in the Rodgers and Hart years from 1935 to 1942."

In general, Lincoln continued, "I feel that it is your fault, not ours, that you are not closer to us in planning our future and in discussion . . . you feel unloved and undesired and not sufficiently appreciated by us. It is not true, but as you know, George has never been a flatterer and I am not a flirt. Nor will I now reaffirm my admiration for your best work, because it is unnecessary. Either you know it, or you never will believe me."

Following this exchange of letters, Lincoln and Robbins got together in person to talk things over. Superficially the meeting went well enough; Lincoln gave Jerry a painting as a present and thanked him "for all his wonderful work with the company." The compliments probably helped to prevent Robbins's permanent alienation, and he even promised to do a pas de deux for NYCB's new season. But the two men would never really get along. When Jerry barked at the dancers, which he did with some frequency, Lincoln would bark at Jerry, confirming his view of Lincoln as "a rich Jew" (Lincoln's words) beating up on "a poor Jew like him." Lincoln continued to deplore Robbins's political capitulation to HUAC, and equally deplored his commercial work on Broadway. He felt Robbins was wasting "a God-given talent" and was, overall, "sadistic and mean"— "quite a detestable character."

Despite "the Robbins Problem," NYCB remained in sound health, though given Lincoln's need to worry, he could always locate a site of concern: Balanchine seemed "tired"; Eglevsky was dancing off the mere "residue of a prestige" no longer warranted; Todd Bolender's choreographic talent was "microscopic" (though Lincoln admitted to liking his new ballet, *Souvenirs*); Melissa Hayden's husband was being "extremely inconvenient" in his attempts to dictate whom she would or would not dance with, and the like. Despite all of which the NYCB's winter season at City Center, its seventeenth, came off well. Balanchine choreographed (to music from Glazunov's *Raymonda*) an admired new *Pas de Dix*, and as a result seemed "fine, completely recovered."

The season also saw the debut of a young black dancer named Arthur Mitchell. Lincoln, as a visiting "dignitary," had initially seen Mitchell dance at the High School of Performing Arts and, without even meeting him, had sent word offering a full scholarship to the School of American Ballet (which had moved to new quarters at Eighty-second Street and Broadway). Mitchell accepted the offer with alacrity, fully aware of the odds of a black man making it in classical ballet. Two other African Americans, Betty Nichols and Janet Collins, had already been enrolled at SAB and one, Louis Johnson, had appeared as a guest soloist in Robbins's *Ballade* a few years earlier. (As for Latinos, Chita Rivera had also studied at the school, and both Moncion and Magallanes were, of course, established principals at NYCB.)

After studying at SAB for three years, Mitchell saw Roland Petit's ballet when it came to New York and noted that the company had several black dancers. He decided he'd have a better chance of becoming a soloist by going to Europe and, as a result, joined the tour of John Butler's American Dance Theater. While in Europe, he received a telegram from Lincoln inviting him to return and to join the corps de ballet with a union contract that called for a salary of ninety dollars a week.

Mitchell accepted at once and, in something of a miracle of timing, joined the company in November 1955: Balanchine immediately picked him to replace d'Amboise (who was filming *Seven Brides for Seven Brothers*) as Tanny Le Clercq's partner in one of the ballets; according to Mitchell, Balanchine initially referred to him as a "Nubian" until Arthur asked him not to. The parents of a few dancers in the corps protested at having their daughters dance with a "Negro"—leading Balanchine and Lincoln immediately to remove those girls from the corps. As Mitchell later commented, "The thing that is so amazing is that I had two of the greatest geniuses of the twentieth century behind me, willing to take the flack from anybody to give me an opportunity because they believed in my talent." Lincoln was pleased with Mitchell's debut, describing him to Pavlik as "very elegant."

Another four-week season for NYCB followed in March 1956 and included the world premiere of Balanchine's *Allegro Brillante* (with Arthur Mitchell dancing as a principal—a remarkably rapid rise from the ranks), and the New York premiere of *Divertimento No. 15*. Soon after, Lincoln signed a "spectacular" contract with NBC to film *Nutcracker* and then, during the summer of 1956, the company toured Europe for three months. By that time, NYCB already had additional invitations in its pocket to go to Japan, Southeast Asia, and Australia during the spring and summer of 1957, with the Department of State as the company's official sponsor—meaning that for once transportation costs wouldn't be a problem; but meaning, too, that NYCB would be serving as a kind of cultural shill for government cold-war policies that Balanchine vigorously approved and Lincoln—though far removed from the political activism of his youth—impassively disapproved.

Lincoln was once again, as he exultantly wrote Pavlik, "insanely busy"; it was the state of being that best suited his temperament and most threatened his health. Not only was he centrally involved with the comings and goings of NYCB (though he didn't go to Europe, which he now considered "a museum," if "a marvelous one"), but as well had begun to participate in a proliferating round of planning sessions for what would become Lincoln Center.

All of which should have been enough to keep even a driven man sated. But Lincoln was driven far beyond the ordinary—which can be understood as an index to his suffering as well as to his energy. He also kept on his plate a hectic social schedule, tedious lunches with potential donors, and an ongoing effort to salvage the Shakespeare Festival following its disastrous first season.

Soon after the critics drew blood, Lincoln's original colleagues at Stratford had second thoughts: Lawrence Langner resigned the presidency of
the board, and Denis Carey and John Burrell left (the latter after Lincoln
undiplomatically described him as being more interested in directing than
in teaching). Lincoln also submitted his resignation to the new president,
Joseph Verner Reed, but in his case it seems to have been more of a power
play to gain additional control over festival proceedings.

Reed, who was overcommitted and neither an intellectual nor a Shakespeare devotee, was more than happy to give him control. He responded
to Lincoln's resignation by refusing it, and got the board to agree to the
appointment of Lincoln's choice, John Houseman (who, among much
else, had run the Mercury Theatre with Orson Welles) as artistic director
for the 1956 summer season. Lincoln was also allowed to hire Rouben
Ter-Arutunian, the scenic and costume designer with whom he'd worked
at City Center, to design the two plays Houseman chose to direct, *King
John* and *Measure for Measure*. But Lincoln did fail to get his young Harvard friend Robert Chapman appointed the new head of the academy;
everyone liked Chapman well enough but he wasn't a Shakespeare specialist and had little experience training actors.[4]

The second Stratford season marked a considerable advance. *King John*
was thought rather an esoteric choice for an essentially middlebrow audience, but the production of *Measure for Measure* was much admired, and
Lincoln thought Arutunian's theater design "breathtaking." Just a few
years before, he'd denounced Rouben to Cadmus as "awful"—which was
typical of the way Lincoln's opinions about individuals, and their talents,
often careened back and forth; similarly, Lincoln would blow up and walk
away from someone, then reappear the next day or month and start chatting away as if the prior incident had never taken place. Since *he* regarded
truthful expressions of opinion, however vehemently delivered or inconsistent, as desirable or at least forgivable, he expected everyone else to.
Often they did not. Most of his close associates became uncomfortably
used to his unpredictable behavior and would minimize or ignore it, but
others became permanently alienated.

In gratitude for the turnabout in the festival's fortunes, Reed wrote
Lincoln, "You are responsible for our 'giant step.' After all, you found
Houseman and by and large you have steered or engineered every worthwhile thing we have done. And more than anyone connected with the
enterprise you have been as nearly selfless as it is possible to be." Reed had
it exactly right: Lincoln had become his ideal, the "suffering servant,"
devoting the bulk of his time and energy to fostering the work of those
he felt were more creative than himself, and forgoing self-promotion.
Throughout this period of his life, he continued to do some occasional
writing, but much less than earlier; only later in life would he produce a

significant body of written work, most of it (again) consecrated to heightening the reputations of artists he'd long since championed.

In the mid-fifties that was above all Pavel Tchelitchev. He was currently again living in Europe, and his reputation, never far reaching, had of late declined. But not in Lincoln's eyes; he regarded Pavlik as one of the great masters of the age, and he continued to push his work and to advise him about how best to restore his standing. Lincoln was no less generous with younger, less-established artists, though he no longer haunted the galleries and studios (now dominated by abstract expressionism, which he abhorred) as he once had. But the work of the young American Honoré Sharrer had early on caught his eye. She'd been represented in MoMA's 1946 show, *Fourteen Americans;* Lincoln had bought one of her paintings and, as early as 1950, had written favorably about her work. He was also greatly taken with the Canadian painter Alex Colville, who, like Sharrer, Cadmus, Tooker, Wyeth, and Jared French, worked primarily in egg tempera and shared as well an "off-center" yet representational subject matter that has led all six to be lumped together (along with Ben Shahn and others) as "magic realists." Colville and Sharrer, like most artists bracketed under a label, any label, objected to it. Colville thought it had at least some value in emphasizing "a sort of mysterious awareness of the value and authority of things," but felt it was a *dis*service when taken to imply that the painters so labeled were merely "clever and amusing conjurers . . . only good for a moment's entertainment."[5]

As with other living artists he admired and knew, Lincoln was unsparing, and often acute, in his criticism of their work. Though he thought his brother-in-law, Paul Cadmus, "a matchless draughtsman, comparable to anyone in the past, with real mastery," Lincoln hadn't hesitated in sending him a blistering critique of one of the paintings *(Lust)* in Paul's *Seven Deadly Sins* series. The same outspokenness held true with Andy Wyeth, whom Lincoln knew much less well and was therefore taking a greater risk with; After Wyeth sent him a photograph of his 1955 painting *Nicholas,* Lincoln expressed concern that the painter's "photographic eye betrays you by flattening out the forms to a coppery, or even papery thinness"; even more generally he warned Wyeth that his mastery of mood too often endangered a fullness of form, which then in turn made the mood "transparently or luminously vacant."

Of the artists closest to home, Fidelma still attempted though rarely completed an occasional drawing. Jensen, who'd initially done some work for the Morgan Library in his capacity as a member of the flourishing Pippin Press, then learned how to prepare vellum manuscripts, repair drawings under the microscope, and the like; he'd demonstrated great aptitude and in 1956 was promoted to full-time employment as a conservator. He continued to paint, but his spare time was limited. Lincoln campily wrote Glenway Wescott that Jensen "has quit Bohemia, gynecological illustration and Boys Town"—but he did manage to buy a new red motorcycle, thereby retaining at least marginal membership. In his note to Glenway, Lincoln added that Jensen "wears a tie and gets to work by ten. You may well imagine this is a great satisfaction to Fido and me"—the lost intonation floating somewhere between camp and a genuinely poignant bit of pseudo-parental pride.

On October 25, 1955, six powerful men gathered for lunch at the Century Club to discuss the possibility of creating a new "musical arts center" from the ground up. Two of the six, Charles Spofford and Anthony Bliss, were, respectively, the chair and the president of the Metropolitan Opera Association. Two others, Floyd Blair and Arthur Houghton, Jr., represented the New York Philharmonic Symphony Society. The remaining two seats were filled by the architect Wallace K. Harrison and the financier John D. Rockefeller III, who contributed start-up funds of half a million dollars. Lincoln knew, with varying degrees of intimacy, all of the men except Floyd Blair, probably the least prominent of the six.[6]

Two months later three more movers and shakers were added to the lunch gatherings, Lincoln being one of them. The other two were Devereux Josephs, chairman of New York Life Insurance, and Robert E. Blum, president of the Brooklyn Institute of Arts and Sciences and a close friend of the urban-renewal czar Robert Moses, chair of the Committee on Slum Clearance, whose bulldog motto was: The Best Way to Get Rid of Slums Is to Level Them.

It was determined early on that the site of the new center—a seventeen-block area on Manhattan's West Side that ran from Sixty-second to Seventieth Streets—would be razed to the ground. The Lincoln Square (later changed to Center) planning committee saw the area as essentially "decayed"; it was indeed run down and did contain many small apartments and crowded rooming houses, but such a large-scale demolition would also destroy many viable family units, a number of post–Civil War buildings of architectural significance, and what some would claim was a coherent neighborhood community.

Lincoln was close enough to John D. Rockefeller III to send him in the summer of 1956 a lengthy memo suggesting "answers" to certain presumed queries from the *New York Times*, including a suggested response to the question, "Do you anticipate serious trouble over the relocation of the present tenants?" Lincoln's suggested answer put him squarely in the Robert Moses camp even as it revealed the distance he'd traveled from his earlier concern with social issues: displacing tenants, he wrote, was an "inevitable" part of "the normal change and expansion . . . of a great city. . . . Certainly we hope to help the present tenants move with the minimum of inconvenience and hardship . . . however, if this were a binding consideration, the city would have changed little in the last fifty years."

In the years ahead, as families in the neighborhood were offered measly cash bonuses ranging from $270 to $500 and relocation only to vacant apartments in public-housing units, the amount of "inconvenience"—and protest—would come as a considerable surprise to the group of prominent and powerful men used to having their own way. Late in 1958 a reporter on the *World-Telegram and Sun* found that scores of families still living on the site were freezing in unheated apartments. When they complained to the buildings' management, they were given a simple instruction: "Move."

Lincoln became very involved, though he never had anything like a determining voice, in the many planning sessions that decided not only the fate of the neighborhood but also which architects would work with Wally Harrison, and which arts groups Lincoln Square would house. "I have no real strength as you know," Lincoln wrote Anthony Bliss, "being on the Lincoln Square project through the tolerance of John [Rockefeller] . . . there are those who have never hidden their curiosity as to why I was there, since I represent little power towards deficit-financing, have a comparatively short history and not a large personal fortune." But Lincoln did view the construction of the center as "the most important architectural opportunity of our century," and he was concerned (as he privately confided to Rockefeller) that Wally, though "a master of political strategy," had as yet put nothing "on paper for us which gives me any confidence in an ultimate masterpiece. For whatever I can judge of his talents, they are in the realm of organization, not of design."

The one area in which Lincoln's voice and influence did carry significant weight with the Lincoln Square planners was in regard to the ballet itself. It had been decided early on that since the visual arts in New York were already well served, Lincoln Square would be confined to the performing arts. But which arts, and represented by which organizations? The Metropolitan Opera and the Philharmonic Symphony Orchestra were from the beginning assumed to be participating units that would have their own new buildings, and both institutions were quick to sign on.

That was the easy part. Decisions about the components of drama and ballet were more complex and potentially explosive. The ballet became an issue from the start. As early as October 1956 Lucia Chase's son, Alexander Ewing, in his capacity as executive secretary of Ballet Theatre Foundation, was writing politely urgent letters to Rockefeller and others protesting the rumor that the New York City Ballet was the presumptive choice for the ballet slot. "We are asking," Ewing wrote Rockefeller, "that the company [Ballet Theatre] be given an equal opportunity in the center"; otherwise, he argued, "no conceivable effort by the Ballet Theatre will be able to counteract this single nod of preference." Rockefeller sent Ewing a bit of partial reassurance, subtly enough worded to avoid any actual commitment: "The completion of the hall for ballet is probably several years ahead. It seems to us that the wisest course to follow during this planning stage is to keep in touch with all of the various organizations which may eventually participate in one way or another." The reply mollified Ballet Theatre for the time being; Ewing wrote back that "concern about being overlooked" had been reduced.[7]

It was not Ewing but Lincoln who unexpectedly upended the working committee's generally shared assumption that the New York City Ballet would be the designated company for dance. Lincoln wasn't at all sure that NYCB would be more secure if it left City Center in favor of Lincoln Square—and he let everyone from John Marshall to John Rockefeller know his views. Yes, he wrote Marshall, NYCB was "miserably housed" at City Center, performing on a small stage basically unsuited to ballet and especially to the large-scale works that Balanchine longed to create. But the company over the years had built up a lively, growing and committed audience, and Lincoln feared that the initial Lincoln Square plan to put the ballet in a house that seated only a thousand people and at ticket prices that would exclude much of the devoted "white-collar audience of cultivated people who have steady but very modest incomes."

Wally Harrison, the chief architect, initially told Lincoln that it was "unthinkable" to build an additional three-thousand-seat hall in Lincoln Square, to which Lincoln responded, "It would be equally unthinkable for the ballet, with its increasing dynamism of audience appeal . . . to penalize itself out of existence." An "agonizing reappraisal" then followed, during which Lincoln argued that the Philharmonic had been assigned its own building, even though, unlike NYCB, it had been "listless and passive" for years, with a leadership neither competent nor steady and performing a repertory that was "in desuetude." By 1957 Lincoln had managed to convince Harrison that the seating needs of the various performance groups did need re-appraising.

Even as Lincoln declared his reluctance to move the New York City Ballet to Lincoln Center (as it began to be called), he also let it be widely known, through a series of memos and conversations, that any thought of inviting Ballet Theatre to fill the dance slot would be a grave mistake. In one such memo he characterized Lucia Chase as someone "who will rarely brook interference, even though her own taste and information are sometimes incomplete . . . no new choreographer has emerged from her company; no dancer of much promise." Lest Lincoln Center's movers and shakers give any thought to representing modern dance, Lincoln let his sword descend with authoritative injustice: "The style of the so-called 'Modern' dance was invented for dancers-come-lately, who created works trimmed to their own inadequacy but rendered saleable by powerful individual performances—as in the case of Martha Graham, Charles Weidman, Doris Humphrey, José Limón, Hanya Holm, Valerie Bettis . . . their dancing days are all about over . . . there is no second generation."

Most of Lincoln Center's planning committee knew Lincoln well enough to discount his penchant for overstatement; as John Marshall put it in an inter-office Rockefeller Foundation memo, Lincoln's "position that he is not sure that the New York City Center company should move into the Center . . . may be a passing opinion on his part and held to in part to demonstrate his disinterestedness as a member of the Lincoln Center Board." Perhaps. But Lincoln repeated his doubts about moving to Lincoln Center often enough and to enough people to make it likely that he was engaged in something more than a cunning charade.

The NYCB company was in fact in crisis. During its European tour, Tanny Le Clercq suddenly fell ill in Copenhagen with polio—as cruel a fate for a dancer as any imaginable. Initially the doctors thought she might die; she didn't, but was permanently paralyzed from the waist down. When he heard the news in New York, Lincoln wrote Glenway Wescott, "We are all destroyed as a result of Tanny's polio. Sweet are the uses of adversity but will He please explain this one." Balanchine remained devotedly at his wife's side for the next five months, doing what he could to bolster her spirits, remaining determinedly optimistic about a full recovery.

They returned to New York in March 1957, and Tanny was taken by ambulance to Lenox Hill Hospital; there the doctors made clear that the paralysis would be permanent. Balanchine had exhausted most of his own funds in Copenhagen, where Tanny had to be turned from one side to another every hour and had required three nurses. In New York, Lincoln picked up the considerable tab for the costs of Tanny's stay at Lenox Hill. After a time she and George left for Warm Springs, Georgia, the center FDR had founded for treating polio; the doctors there were disapproving of the treatment she'd had both in Copenhagen and at Lenox Hill, and a new regimen was begun. Lincoln reported to Pavlik that George remained "very cheerful" but had aged a great deal; he was "full of talk about the future, but when the future starts I really don't know."

Even during the five months that George and Tanny had been in Copenhagen, Lincoln, for the first time since 1935, had had to plan an entire ballet season without any input from Balanchine; that including everything from trying to commission a few "novelties" to working out programs and assigning roles. The responsibility had come at a time when City Center was again floundering financially and when the company itself was tired out from its long European tour. Tanny's illness was coupled with Herbie Bliss, long a company mainstay, having another incapacitating bout of "melancholia" and not being reliably available to dance.

On top of that Lincoln felt that in general "a gradual revolution" was going on in NYCB's ranks: "there is now an older and a younger generation and as a result a delicate balance" had to be found. Among the new dancers, Allegra Kent had caught Balanchine's eye, and she would soon have a meteoric rise. It seemed to Lincoln that both Tallchief and Eglevsky (whom Lincoln had never valued highly) were no longer as keen as they once were to dance (he was wrong about Tallchief; she did leave the company for a time to have her daughter but then returned).

The turmoil and uncertainty made Lincoln feel "grim and lonely"; yet with the vital support of Betty Cage and Eddie Bigelow, the company not only held together but ended up having a strong eleven-week season—the second longest of its career. Lincoln raised enough money (mostly out of his own stock portfolio) to present three new works, Menotti's *The Unicorn*, choreographed by John Butler; Moncion's first work, *Pastorale* (featuring Allegra Kent); and Todd Bolender's *The Masquers*. The Menotti-Butler work proved the most popular, and ten performances were added to meet popular demand.

On other fronts, meanwhile, prospects were encouraging. For its third season, in the summer of 1957, the Shakespeare Festival was finally able (as Lincoln sardonically put it in a letter to Alex Colville) to enlist the kind of "stars they always wanted"—including Katharine Hepburn. Lincoln wasn't convinced that this was "the way to build a company," though he recognized that in the celebrity-oriented United States, where government subsidies for the arts ranged from minimal to nonexistent, it was probably the only way to build a paying clientele. And flock they did to see Hepburn in *The Merchant of Venice*, though Lincoln himself thought Ter-Arutunian's sets were "expensively tacky" and Hepburn's performance "a bravura demonstration of Katharine Hepburn . . . sort of a well-bred Connecticut debutante of the 1930s." With sell-out crowds, a profit for the season of more than a hundred thousand dollars, and a promise from Hepburn to tour in *Much Ado About Nothing* in 1958, the Shakespeare Festival seemed well on its way and Lincoln reduced his commitment to it of time and energy.[8]

The ongoing meetings of the Lincoln Center planning Board also seemed to be taking a promising turn. In January 1957 an "exploratory committee on the dance" was formed, led by George Stoddard, dean of the School of Education at NYU, with the dance critics John Martin and Walter Terry serving as consultants. Stoddard's first step was to inquire tentatively whether Kirstein and Lucia Chase would consider merging their two companies. Both parties turned down the suggestion as a threat to the survival of their very different artistic styles.[9]

Following this failure at "compromise," Stoddard's committee recommended to the board that the New York City Ballet Company be given the nod as the sole unit representing the dance. But the board, embroiled in a host of other matters, temporarily deferred taking action on the recommendation. Seeing which way the wind was blowing, Lucia Chase now signaled her willingness to consider some sort of accommodation for joint representation. Stoddard then suggested that Ballet Theatre and NYCB become dual performing companies under a single corporation—that they join under one board of trustees but not merge. Chase proved willing but Lincoln not. Stoddard reported back to his committee that Kirstein "is deeply concerned about the restraining influence of *any* board upon the ballet as a fine art, and the thought of being joined in any fashion to another company, however excellent, is not presently to his taste."

And there the matter rested for another full year. Which may have been fine with Lincoln, since he knew that Stoddard's committee had at least once recommended that NYCB be chosen as the sole ballet company at Lincoln Center, and was therefore likely to do so again at a later date. He was certainly emphatic in re-emphasizing his reluctance about leaving City Center. "It should be made clear," Lincoln wrote John Rockefeller III, "that as far as the New York City Ballet Company goes, it would not be devastated by its non-selection as a constituent member of Lincoln Square." He seems to have meant it; if not, he was playing a risky high-stakes game of bluffing.

In any case he refocused his attention, as a Lincoln Center board member, on critiquing in general emerging site plans and architectural renderings. Late in 1957 he wrote Edgar Young (a close associate of John III's) of his distress that "after two years of planning, there is neither a basic site plan nor a distinguishing silhouette nor an over-mastering style of design . . . either Lincoln Square is a great design opportunity or it isn't; such projects are not created out of the lowest-common-denominator . . . a master-plan is the work of a master." To a friend he succinctly summed up his complaints: he wanted "some luxurious bubbles to come up between the chinks in the thermo-crete"—not mere shelter but "splendor."

Lincoln took a brief time-out to celebrate a personal milestone: his fiftieth birthday. "I feel older than Methuselah," he wrote Carl Van Vechten in response to his good wishes, "or younger than a kitten, frequently at the same time, and sometimes I just feel fifty." Two weeks later Lincoln was given the National Institute of Arts and Letters Award for "distinguished service to the arts." In presenting the award Glenway Wescott spoke of Lincoln as "a creative man in his own right, a poet and narrator [who] . . . has gradually sacrificed his personal talents, while furthering others' creativity. He has the artist's temperament in every respect except the pride and the selfishness."

Lincoln left no record of his reaction to Glenway's words, but his long-standing doubts about the messenger likely carried over into his estimate of the patronizing message. He'd in fact given up, as Glenway well knew, neither poetry nor "narration," though both had taken a temporary back-seat to other creative enterprises—whether critiquing an architectural rendering or suggesting the design for a ballet. Glenway hit the mark in one respect at least: Lincoln continued to further the creativity of others; "service," as his father had instilled in him long ago, continued to guide his many-faceted and discreet generosities; as Alex Colville justly wrote him the following year, after Lincoln had taken Andy Wyeth to see Colville's paintings, "I really feel that whatever recognition I have received has been due mostly to your appreciation . . . and to your 'kind representations.' "

As for "pride and selfishness," Lincoln was no fool: he knew both qualities were near-universal ingredients of personality, and never claimed their absence from his own.

Japan

(1958–1960)

BALANCHINE'S RETURN TO the company in late 1957 was marked by a remarkable burst of creativity. In the period of a few months he created four new works of astonishing range: the gently pleasing *Gounod Symphony* (much loved by Lincoln), the kinetic *Square Dance*, the sparkling *Stars and Stripes*, and—outshining all but a handful of his ballets—the masterpiece *Agon*, to music by Stravinsky. Balanchine and Stravinsky had worked on *Agon*, off and on, for four years, and the premiere on December 1, 1957, demonstrated beyond debate that the seventy-five-year-old Stravinsky and the long-absent Balanchine were still in full, daring command of their powers. Despite the intricate difficulty of both music and choreography, *Agon* was that rare original: it was hailed at once by critics and public alike.[1]

Less than two months after the great success of that winter season, the company, sponsored by the President's Exchange Program of the State Department, departed for an extended tour of Japan and Australia. Because Balanchine refused to leave Tanny, Lincoln reluctantly decided to go along with the troupe for the four-week Japan leg of the tour (but to skip the four-month stay in Australia that followed). Fidelma stayed behind in Weston; she'd been drawing a bit of late and hoped to be able to work while Lincoln was away and the house quiet.[2]

The company was in the hands of the Japanese managers who had paid the guarantee, and Lincoln learned that the theater they'd booked in Tokyo was "a criminal disaster"—meaning it hadn't enough space for even elementary scenery and special effects, and its footlights were neon tubes. It's "too discouraging," Lincoln wrote his recent acquaintance Donald Richie, the thirty-three-year-old American writer who'd been living in Japan since 1947.

With the poor theater as omen, Lincoln expected the trip to be a catastrophe, but it proved to be a critical (though not a commercial) success for the company, and for Lincoln personally, a milestone event, his initial reluctance turning into astonished, lasting awe. Within a week of arriving, he was already writing to Alex Colville that he was "in a state of emotional exhaustion, psychic impotence and extreme strain imposed by the full impact of this peculiar, wonderful and terrible country." The wonder would grow, the exhaustion—and most assuredly the impotence—recede.

But before the splendors of the country, and its men, came to overwhelm him, Lincoln saw clearly the shocking contradictions of a recently occupied and Americanized country. As he wrote Colville, it was "an orderly feudalism not exactly in desuetude in the middle of the worst corruptions of industrial democracy; the most charming domestic objects side by side with pornographic Hollywood horror, rubber-goods and Rouault, lovely straw-work, pottery, toys and lacquer next to an all girlie revue with pink paper ones competing with the no less real pink cherry-blossoms . . . the most beautiful contemporary textiles and the most sensible classic dress next to bluejeans and pony-tail hair-dos; Shinto shrines and Ex Lax ads, etc."

Donald Richie was at the time (he would later marry the novelist Mary Richie Smith) sharing a seventeenth-century farmhouse that his friend Tex Wetherby, an ex-diplomat who ran an English-language publishing house, had had imported into Tokyo. Both men proved attentive hosts, as did Wetherby's current boyfriend, a Japanese man Lincoln described as "that crazy full-brown tiger Tamotzu," who'd been captain of the university wrestling team and was now an architect. Richie thought Lincoln looked "particularly Western in Japan—the large nose, the black eyebrows, the big body—a seagoing New England prophet, or maybe a schoolmaster out of Dickens. . . . At the same time a natural, massive gentleness. He is here in Japan even more gentle, as though his big hands might poke holes in the *shoji*, as though his large feet might stomp holes in the *tatami*. Tall, he apologetically curls under lintels. Heavy, he tries out floors with a smile of trepidation. His is the gentleness of very strong people . . ."

The splendor of Japanese Kabuki and Noh theater were among the early experiences that left Lincoln so dazzled that he wondered if he'd ever be able to look at Western theater again. He saw the Kabuki first and wrote Bob Chapman that "any idiot who thinks that Broadway is theater should come here, and see an audience entirely in tears at the end of the first (of ten) acts of *The Forty-Seven Ronin* (the most famous Kabuki play)." Noh theater was a very different sort of experience for him: "a grave, intensely serious ceremonial rite . . . the visual aspects are glorious, like the sheen of a celadon vase, the reverse of Kabuki stridency, melodrama and quick violence . . . and don't think it isn't a crippling, riveting bore for a corrupt westerner, because about three quarters of it is."

Lincoln was also stunned at the beauty of Japanese gardens and architecture (already an avid gardener at Weston, he'd attempt, on returning home, to start a Japanese garden, laying down 140 feet of flat stones imprinted with decidedly non-Japanese kitty paws and lined with miniature conifers). Lincoln was astonished, too, at the beauty of Japanese men;

he waxed euphoric about them to Bob Chapman: "an unlimited supply of very dignified, very vital, very beautiful, very unmercenary" young males—"it's a relief to see an ugly one." He himself took up with the bantamweight champion of Chuyo University, who gratifyingly became "a ballet maniac." Yet, as Lincoln later wrote Richie, he "wasn't ever . . . able to get a real hard-on in Japan; to me the boys are like the food, beautiful, but you cannot eat it."

As taken as he was with Japan, Lincoln was primarily occupied with the needs of the large NYCB troupe of sixty-five dancers and six technicians. Betty Cage and Ed Bigelow, as usual, did most of the grunt work, but Lincoln saw to it that the troupe got moved to a better theater, attended nearly nightly, and helped to negotiate the four televised performances that were broadcast nationwide. The Tokyo reviews of the company were overwhelmingly positive ("exceptionally refined and sophisticated . . . ," and so on), though an occasional critic found the speed with which the dancers performed "vulgar."

When the company left for Australia, Lincoln returned home, but his obsession with Japan continued unabated. He devoured books on Japanese history, art, and theater and, as he wrote Richie, wore his kimono— "shyly, but I wear it. I wish you would send me two proper gentlemen's fans for summer gesticulation." He also asked Richie to take pictures of one of his young male friends, "nude with his peter floating in the bath; this is a serious request; also please send me enlarged pictures, from the negative of the nude of him."

Lincoln was already in the long-standing habit of exchanging nude and seminude photographs of attractive young men with Bob Chapman and other friends. The habit was innocent enough—Lincoln compared it to boys exchanging duplicates from their stamp collections—but in the current cultural climate the practice was in fact dangerous. Only a year or two later, the prominent literary critic Newton Arvin, along with several of his younger colleagues at Smith College, would be arrested under a recent Massachusetts statute simply for showing each other such beefcake magazines of the day as *Physique Pictorial* and *Body Beautiful*. Lincoln and his friends were actually passing material through the mails, which potentially opened them up to *federal* charges; they were probably unaware of how serious the consequences might be, though Lincoln, for one, sometimes found an erotic appeal in danger.

Lincoln's fascination with Japan, and his determination to return there quickly and often, was one factor in divesting himself of some of his now-peripheral commitments. John Houseman had succeeded in salvaging the reputation of the Shakespeare Festival, and the summer season of 1958, which featured *The Winter's Tale* and Fritz Weaver's *Hamlet*, had been a considerable success. But success, as Lincoln acutely noted, "merely releases me into a depth-criticism of everything we have done . . . it is nowhere near as good as it could or should be, and after the Noh and even the Kabuki, it is naive, inelegant, inconsistent and tiresome."[3]

Besides, Houseman was threatening to resign due to the "suspended animation" of the festival's slumberous trustees, who seemed incapable of certifying the 1959 summer program. Donald Richie urged Lincoln to do likewise, to stop wasting his time "knitting away at Stratford" when he should be entirely focused on the ballet and on writing more. Mina also urged him to give up Stratford: "You have really done what you can there and it is too wearing to be involved full time in so many responsibilities." (Of recent years Mina and Lincoln had seen each other only in hurried, glancing visits; Mina had been spending long stretches of time in France researching her new book on Bizet, besides which, her commanding ways frightened Fidelma and annoyed Lincoln.)

Lincoln did, by the spring of 1959, reduce his involvement with the Shakespeare Festival, but for a number of years thereafter, during a lull in his other enterprises, he'd reinvolve himself in an advisory capacity. This was especially true during the spring-summer season of 1961 which featured *Macbeth*, *As You Like It*, and *Troilus and Cressida*. He thought the company "the best we have ever recruited," but believed that Jessica Tandy had been woefully miscast as Lady Macbeth (she "is no more Lady Macbeth than Blanche du Bois was, but maybe she will be less high teacup and more hysterical by the time we open"). That season Lincoln often attended rehearsals, and was responsible for the idea of placing *Troilus* in Ole Virginny. It apparently worked well; Lincoln, at least, thought it was "the best thing we have done."

Along with reducing the Shakespeare Festival to a sideline event in his life, Lincoln resigned from the planning committee for Lincoln Center. The motives behind this second divestment are more mysterious, with artistic, political, and personal considerations all playing a role. "I shall never write or speak about the reasons for my resignation," Lincoln assured one committee member, and he seems to have held pretty firmly to that decision. Still, enough fragmentary references exist to piece together the outlines of an explanation.

One important ingredient in the mix was Lincoln's growing unease about being "window dressing"—the one person on the board who "had won any prestige in the actual performing arts"—for what was otherwise a gentlemen's club of "the very rich," united in their conservative enthusiasm for "slum-clearance" and their treatment of artists as "hired hands who are had in to make reports on the same level as plumbers are called in to fix the sink."[4]

The more Lincoln sat among his fellow board members, the more his left-wing sympathies rose from dormancy. At one committee meeting Lincoln argued that any theater for the dance must "eliminate class distinction as to entrances, lounge, bar, or promenade spaces." He also spoke up in behalf of having a series of free Sunday matinees "divided among the great New York charities to show teen-age, underprivileged children the ballet."

Lincoln feared that what had recently happened at the Shakespeare Festival could easily develop at Lincoln Center. At Stratford the banker Eugene Black and other wealthy men had threatened to withhold all support unless the stage manager (Bernie Gersten, later Joe Papp's right-hand man at the Public Theater), who'd invoked the Fifth Amendment under questioning by a congressional committee, was fired and blacklisted. The threat had split the Stratford board, leading it to call in the FBI and to a delay in future planning for more than six months.

Lincoln increasingly felt that he could not "afford as a working theater man to be associated with the people constituting the [Lincoln Center] board," and he officially resigned in May 1959. Lincoln emphasized that he was not doing so in "momentary pique" or because of any action either taken or not taken by the board in regard to the future affiliation of the New York City Ballet with Lincoln Center; rather he characterized his resignation as the culmination of a long period of "reflection about the principles, patronage and direction of the project."

In supporting his brother's action, George Kirstein, now the publisher of *The Nation*, also sounded a left-wing note: "Essentially," he wrote Lincoln, "neither you nor I have any business on these fancy boards with their black-tie manners and their pompous mouthings which are essentially for the purpose of exchanging legal fees or real estate commissions within a small and select group." Donald Richie, for his part, was pleased on literary grounds. He congratulated Lincoln on giving up "missionary work among the very rich . . . their general shitiness will be responsible for your doing what you really ought and must: the ballet and the memoirs" (Lincoln had threatened, half seriously, to devote himself to a five-volume autobiography).

But if political conviction played a central role in Lincoln's resignation, other ingredients were part of the mix. At the board meeting that preceded his resignation, he apparently indulged in a furious outburst, specific content unknown, aimed directly at John Rockefeller III. At the time Lincoln's emotional state in general was precarious. Two months before, in late March, Cadmus had written Jere and Margaret French that Lincoln was "in a rather nervous, unable to sleep state, but not extreme. Fido is somewhat anxious however." Two weeks after that, Cadmus had reported that "Goosie seems better, but excitable. He told someone that he wants to spend half his time in Japan. He told me, 'I've HAD it.' " He apparently avoided a full-blown manic episode, but his raw nerve endings played a role in his outburst of anger in early May at John Rockefeller III.

Both Rockefeller and his close associate Edgar Young took Lincoln's eruption in stride, though both were mystified by it. John, a reticent, reserved man, was the temperamental opposite of his ebullient younger brother Nelson. Even so, he went out of his way (as did Young) to coax Lincoln back onto the Lincoln Center board or, at the very least, to press him to detail his discontent to them over lunch. Lincoln turned down all invitations to reconsider or elucidate, and did so with astonishing brusqueness. When John politely suggested that "people are bound to have differences of opinion from time to time," and Edgar Young informed him that the board hoped he'd reconsider his resignation, Lincoln insisted that Young didn't "realize the full extent of my bitterness. . . . If I spoke to you with [candor] . . . I should say things which you would find hard to pardon. I prefer to leave them unsaid." In the "soft" version he provided Young, he merely announced that Lincoln Center was "a venture which has neither principle, policy nor patronage."

But to John Rockefeller, who continued, in near-supplicant fashion, to plead for an explanatory lunch, Lincoln finally let go full blast: "Four years taught me: the criterion is manipulation of real-estate sweetened by the education-business. Your associates are not inimical to art; to them it is not real. Their habit is compulsive charity to maintain dynastic prestige. . . . For me and my kind, Lincoln Square frames that moral vacuum which makes Europe and Asia wary of American pragmatism." John Rockefeller did not issue another invitation to lunch.

Lincoln, on the other hand, was soon acting as if nothing untoward had happened between them; even as he continued to send John III a series of remarkably frank letters critiquing the architectural plans for the center, among other things, as "heartless, soulless and without a focus," he was warmly offering him and his wife, Blanchette, their choice of ballet tickets. This love-hate behavior was something of a pattern with Lincoln. After his break in the thirties with Philip Johnson for his pro-fascist views, for instance, Lincoln was, by the forties, having the occasional lunch or dinner with him, and by the fifties was recommending him to John D. Rockefeller III as the only architect in the conglomeration of architects currently working on plans for Lincoln Center who was capable of a master design that might give the disparate parts a coherent focus.

Lincoln's dispute with John III and his resignation from the board had no effect on his friendship with Nelson, who'd become a far more powerful figure than his older brother. In the November 1958 race for governor of New York, Nelson ran on the Republican ticket and outpolled his rival by more than half a million votes. During the campaign Lincoln lent his name to the efforts of Democrats for Rockefeller, and within weeks of the election Nelson wrote to thank him for his participation. Lincoln subsequently sent him certain "thoughts" he had about needed cultural programs for the state, and Nelson used them in part when delivering his first annual message to the legislature. Soon after, Nelson and his wife Mary

Tod dined en famille with the Kirsteins and then went with them to the ballet performance that celebrated the tenth anniversary of the formation of the New York City Ballet and the twenty-fifth of Lincoln and Balanchine beginning their work together.

After the NYCB company returned from Japan and Australia, there was something of a "purge" in the ranks. Lincoln put it this way: "Half the company has been replaced and it's been awkward, but we have done pretty well and are on the verge of a great period of creativity." The replacements took place largely within the corps; among the lead dancers, there were few changes. The one new principal added to the roster was the French-born star Violette Verdy, who'd been dancing for a year with Ballet Theatre (and before that, starting at age eleven, with Roland Petit's company). Verdy reacted with "extreme surprise" when Balanchine invited her to join New York City Ballet; she'd taken classes from time to time at the School of American Ballet, but because she was small and didn't have the long, thin physique that typified the female Balanchine dancer, she'd never expected an invitation to join the company. When she first met Lincoln, he frightened her; like so many others, she mistook his scowling face and hulking presence as indicative of the man within. But before long the sophisticated, insightful Verdy came to think of Lincoln as "the great dark eagle" who could be "so gentle"—there was "something amazingly touching, really, about him." For his part Lincoln considered Verdy his "idea of perfection in a performing artist; like a Swiss watch, in action, but with the most sensitive awareness of music and movement."[5]

Verdy's first starring role with the company was in the May 1959 premiere of Balanchine's portion of the two-part *Episodes*, to music by Webern. What also made the premiere a major event was that the other half of the evening was choreographed and performed by Martha Graham. The invitation to Graham had raised a multiplicity of eyebrows, with Balanchine archly telling Lincoln that the company motto should henceforth be "Chock Full of Nuts." But Lincoln insisted that the joint performance was "politically useful," and it was certainly well received; Dick Pleasant, who'd run Ballet Theatre in its first years, wrote to say that the evening had been "so wonderful it hurts." On the other hand, Agnes de Mille years later expressed outrage (as was her wont) that neither Balanchine nor Kirstein went backstage afterwards to congratulate Martha.

Graham herself wrote Lincoln to say that the lack of communication from him "can only mean that in some way I failed your dream and it haunts me and hurts me." No, no, Lincoln hastened (politically) to reassure her: "There is deep satisfaction at an attempt that turned out more as an achievement than an experiment." But in fact he thought Martha's contribution to the evening had been dismal. Among her miscalculations, in Lincoln's view, was that she should have danced the role of Elizabeth, not (at age sixty-six) the "sex pot" Mary, Queen of Scots. Besides, he thought her piece wasn't about sex at all but about authority—or should have been. In any case he felt that Martha had shown "her innate silliness, a fact I have well known for 25 years"—a statement that typifies the way Lincoln could blithely transform the past to suit some present impulse; in truth he'd at one point, and over a considerable period of time, admired and encouraged Graham's work. And Graham remembered that, even if Lincoln chose not to; "I have accepted with joy and love," she wrote him late in 1959, "your curious 'belief' (call it this for want of another word) in me over many years. I have given you the same although at times I might have liked to kick you."

Lincoln was determined to bring at least one of the classical Japanese theaters—Kabuki, Noh, or Gagaku (the dancers and musicians of the Imperial Palace)—to the United States. The obstacles were formidable, and Lincoln flew back to Japan in February 1959 to try to make arrangements. He quickly settled on Gagaku as the most easily transportable troupe, the one that the Japanese authorities would be most likely to release and that the Americans, with their "low tolerance of attentiveness to the unfamiliar," would be most likely to appreciate. Gagaku dated back to the eighth century and was the oldest known dance troupe. Lincoln knew that many Japanese currently held Gagaku in contempt, associating it with their feudal past. But the so-called Black Party, a powerful group of Imperial Household functionaries, believed that Gagaku was a precious inheritance in need of preservation.[6]

It was the Black Party's influence and its belief that "a success in New York would enhance their fading prestige at home" that made it possible for Lincoln to succeed in getting permission for the Gagaku dancers and musicians to leave Japan. But to do so he had to sign "an instrument of understanding" in which he personally took full responsibility for the company. The signing was accompanied by an elaborate ceremony in which Lincoln was driven to the Yosikune Shrine in a palace automobile and shown by a Shinto priest "the God who lives in a large polished silver mirror"; Lincoln bowed before it three times and swore always to honor the emperor's interests.

That turned out to be the easy part. Though the Japanese Foreign Office was willing to pay transportation costs for Gagaku's performers, costumes, and instruments, Lincoln had to sign an agreement, which he reluctantly did, accepting personal indemnity and swearing "moral responsibility" for possible engagements of the company in other American cities. For that signing ceremony, two of the most famous geishas were flown in from Kyoto to perform a dance narrating the relationship between Townsend Harris, the first U.S. envoy to Japan, and O-kichi, the professional geisha spy sent to observe him by the shogun.

Lincoln in general had "a glorious time" on the trip, but he became more aware than ever of the triumph in Japan of "creeping American business aims and ideals and . . . a rather ugly Fascist-type Nationalist retrograde spiritual attitude, which is embittered, desperate and unreal . . . the surface is lovely & should be seen." By mid-March he'd seen enough of it, and "suddenly got acutely home-sick for Fido and Nanook" (their beloved cat).

He was back in New York by the third week in March, and got caught up immediately in making the American arrangements for Gagaku. The Japan Society wanted to be listed as a sponsor, but didn't want to contribute any time or money. The Japanese at the UN and those at the Washington embassy were barely on speaking terms. The Rockefeller Foundation refused to help in any way. "I have had to do all sorts of tricks about money," Lincoln wrote Richie, "and it's too boring and exhausting." But he raised enough (eighteen thousand dollars) for Gagaku to perform, after New York, in Boston, Seattle, Los Angeles, San Francisco, and in the gardens of Dumbarton Oaks in Washington, DC.

On top of preparing for the Gagaku visit, Lincoln had to see to the needs of the Kyoto sculptor Kobashi, whose visit Lincoln had personally subsidized; he described Kobashi to Nelson Rockefeller, whose patronage for him he sought, as "the single most talented plastic artist in Japan, possibly in the last fifty years." Lincoln arranged a gallery show for Kobashi, and also introduced his work to Blanchette Rockefeller. It was Kobashi who made the platform on which the Gagaku dancers performed. (The platform, which cost six thousand dollars, was paid for by Nancy Lassalle; she'd earlier studied at the School of American Ballet and would become its devoted lifelong patron and volunteer.) Kobashi made the platform as close as possible to the one in the Imperial Palace, except that to Lincoln's eye the lacquer was slightly brownish rather than the desired red.

Gagaku had four sold-out performances at City Center and one at the UN (thanks to Lincoln's acquaintance with Dag Hammarskjöld, the secretary-general). The troupe proved a great success, and a personal triumph for Lincoln; Blanchette Rockefeller, for one, wrote him that she was "full of admiration for your own incomparable courage and vision." Of course for Lincoln the perfectionist—oh, if only the lacquer had been a true red!—the Gagaku success didn't gratify (let alone appease) him for long, but instead drove him on to conjure up additional projects. He soon decided that what he now most wanted was to bring Japan's ritual athletics—sumo, kendo, judo, karate, archery—to the States.

What he managed to see and emphasize in such sports was a magnification of what were the only remaining trace elements from Japan's feudal past: "Here is presented a philosophy of the human body in action governed by psychological and spiritual criteria, immaculate presentation, FOR ITSELF alone, plus the ethical elevation of the participant." Lincoln contrasted this philosophy to the ethic of sport in the United States, where competition, breaking records, and moneymaking were the primary fixations. Lincoln also linked "the kind of disciplinary spirit" of Japanese sports with the potential production of great dancers. He gave serious thought to starting a school for ballet in Japan, and even made some preliminary arrangements to that end, though they never came to fruition.

Lincoln confessed to Richie that he was now in the grips of a "hideous obsession with Japan, which I take to be neurotic. . . . I am in love with the IDEA, and maybe the fact of Japan . . . the more clearly I try to think about it, the harder it becomes for me; but it is like the passion I once had for someone like Lew Christensen, 25 years ago: ideal, shining, a potential to be done something about." Lincoln might just as well have compared his newest fixation with his past passion for Nadelman, say, or El Greco. He was a zealous man and seized on a person, a work of art, or even an entire country with a blind hunger that minimized faults, accentuated virtues, and, in its arduous insistence on an unattainable perfection, could thoroughly frighten the object of his attention. "Idealist"—sighting and fighting for perceived potential, a better state of being—is an emotional state of mind that needs no apology, in Lincoln or anyone else, except, that is, when the enthusiasm becomes delirious, the foretaste or fact of mania and its imminent destructiveness.

In regard to Japan's ritual athletics, with its suggestively interwoven associations of religion, militaristic discipline, and sex, Lincoln's ardor, as he himself was aware, does seem to have spiraled into a kind of frenzy. He declared Japan's ritual sport "more alive than any Mass I have ever heard" and insisted that industrial civilization in Japan is just a convenient varnish under which a spirit hides itself to exist. . . . It may be a mad romanticizing, but I see in the dancer, the athlete and the priest, all of whom have the support of a shadow-military society as the rock-bottom salvation of Japanese prestige." Richie tried in advance of Lincoln's next pending visit to calm his obsessive state, writing him that the sports were easily enough seen, but he doubted whether they were really exportable. Among other problems was the fact that Japan had no professional athletes: "The main practitioners are amateurs all of whom have jobs and duties elsewhere." The only athletes likely to make the trip to the States were college students with time to kill during summer vacation.

But Richie's cautionary advice fell on deaf ears. Lincoln decided on a third visit to Japan in September 1959 in order to see more of Japan's ritual sports and to begin to arrange for their transport to the United States. He wrote Richie that Fidelma considered Japan "a man's country and she prefers me to have fun alone and unrestricted, and our house needs painting and she says she will prefer doing it alone." Fidelma's wish to be "alone" for a while rings true enough, but the rest of Lincoln's assessment reeks powerfully of projection. Fidelma may have said it; more likely Lincoln thought it.

Lincoln stayed in Japan for four weeks and traveled around the country more than he previously had. He also had his usual share of sexual adventures, this time featuring a young Zen priest in the Nanzenji monastery and the captain of the basketball team at Kyoto University. But he kept his main mission in the foreground: to see as large a variety of martial sports as possible. He was impressed with the way the inherent violence of most of the sports was contained within "elaborate ritual bows, self-composure and a series of breathtaking postures and movement." The description was not inapt as self-characterization, and—along with his sense of the "self" as powerfully irregular, the chaotic barely contained—helps to explain Lincoln's outsize fascination with martial arts as a metaphor for the human state.

Lincoln had an intense capacity to believe that what he wanted to happen *would* happen; it was part of his heritage of having grown up as an "entitled" child. That capacity carried him far, often enabling him to achieve unlikely goals—as his decades of tenacious struggle to establish a national ballet company well illustrates. Yet Lincoln had his failures, and his passion to bring Japanese ritual athletics to the United States would be—just as Richie had predicted—one of them. Resistance on the part of certain Japanese authorities, in combination with the reluctance of American foundations and donors to lend support, forced cancellation of the project.

Lincoln's driving need to become embroiled in a scheme both intrinsically worthy and inherently difficult to pull off prevented him from wallowing in defeat. Ritual athletics, he told himself, would be some day secured; for now, he would focus on introducing the Kabuki theater to the United States on the occasion of the centennial anniversary of Japan's signing its first trade agreements with the West (if "trade" should prove too dull a matter, Lincoln was quite prepared to substitute some sexier historical event; the important thing was to keep moving).

Within a matter of weeks after giving up on ritual athletics, and with "little to go on except a feeling of urgent necessity" (he meant the approaching centennial, not his inner demons), Lincoln was firing off lengthy, detailed memos to Matsuo Tanaka, the Japanese consul general in New York, and to the Rockefeller and Ford Foundations, soliciting official and financial support for the Kabuki dancers. The memos were full of visionary details: there would be a cross-continental tour, tie-in exhibitions of Meiji art, displays of Kabuki dresses in the major department store windows, banners all along Fifth Avenue, showcases full of calligraphic manuscripts at the New York Public Library, and so on.[7]

It would be a mistake to ascribe plans of such exalted scope to a manic seizure—even if mania (which should never be romanticized as "admirable energy," or the like) may have played some role. But if Lincoln's high-flown schemes for the Kabuki did, to some unknowable degree, reflect a dangerously overexcited state, they reflected, too, his ability to push beyond the limits of acceptable, "reasonable," expectations, to seek out the edge, to soar beyond the formulaic. Sometimes, to be sure, his fantasies were merely preposterous, unaligned with anything conceivably "do-able." But more often they proved genuinely visionary—like formulating the need and possibility for an encompassing performing arts center a full decade before Lincoln Center began to be talked about. And Lincoln's capacity to dream large was, after all, what had made him believe that a company devoted to classical ballet—an art form that itself pushes beyond ordinary limitations and accepted physical boundaries—might succeed in a country largely blind to its appeal.

In regard to Lincoln's plans for the Kabuki, the Ford and Rockefeller Foundations quickly turned him down. But the Japanese Foreign Office did offer a subsidy of seventy-five thousand dollars, which amounted to three-quarters of Lincoln's initial budget. Suddenly it all looked possible, maybe even easy, and Lincoln was off and running. He made immediate plans for a trip to Japan to conclude negotiations in early February 1960, and he hoped to bring with him on the mission an instant committee that included Burt Martinson, the coffee king, David Hays, the scenic designer, David Bouverie (the widower of Alice Astor), Faubion Bowers, the author of *Japanese Theater*; and, as his personal assistant, Eddie Bigelow. Lincoln swore in advance to Richie that "I do not intend to buy a single object, except books, and I will not fuck a single boy."

On arrival in Tokyo, Lincoln ran headlong into a far more leisurely pace and intricate set of demands than he expected or liked. Negotiations would in fact go on for a protracted period of some four months, and the first round in Tokyo during February 1960 was beset with frustration. Matsuo Tanaka proved "belligerent" (he'd recently published a series of anti-American articles about his tenure in New York as consul general), and he refused to offer Lincoln any of the first-rate Kabuki performers, claiming that "he could not deprive [the] Tokyo public of their best loved artists." Lincoln accused Tanaka of behaving "in vile faith," and employed his standard set of theatrical tactics, revised to include Japanese gestures, to win compliance: when a meeting was going badly, he'd get up, bow stiffly, sweep out grandly.

It didn't work. All it produced was a polite suggestion from one of the other Japanese negotiators that Lincoln try "not to be so short tempered." That wasn't workable either. Lincoln preferred staying (in his own words) "curt and unyielding," and in a grandstand play, he left suddenly for a "holiday" in Kyoto. That did produce results. Or seemed to. The Foreign Office intervened and invited Lincoln back to Tokyo for talks that excluded Tanaka. By the time Lincoln returned to the States several days later, he thought he'd closed on arrangements pretty much to his liking. But no. By early March, Lincoln was writing Richie that he was "sad and gloomy; no deal yet with Kabuki; programs all fucked up; the ones they want seem too long or too short."

Yet all was not lost. The Japanese Diet voted to double the budget to one hundred and fifty thousand dollars, thus removing any financial risk for Lincoln or any need to find foundation support to bring the Kabuki troupe to the States. Even so the road wouldn't be easily traversed, nor considerable stumbling avoided. The Diet soon clarified its terms: neither representations of prostitution nor of seppuku (ritual suicide) would be permitted on the stage. This would have ruled out *The Forty-Seven Ronin (Chushingura)* and most of the important roles for female impersonators, who fascinated Lincoln.

"I flipped; I screamed; I shat," Lincoln later wrote Richie. His calculated hysteria produced a compromise: *Chushingura* was allowed back onto the program, but a lesser work, *Kagatsurube*, which also depicted suicide and prostitution, was not. The Kabuki troupe of sixty members left Tokyo for New York on May 27, 1960, and returned on July 27. The seven weeks of performances included New York, Boston, Chicago, San Francisco, Los Angeles, and Seattle. The troupe did much less well, financially, on the West Coast than elsewhere. According to Jerry Robbins, Balanchine was unimpressed: he "thinks they're just a lot of old men standing around." Later in the year Japan awarded Lincoln the "Fourth Class Order of the Sacred Treasure" in recognition of his "outstanding contributions to cultural exchange between our two countries."

During this period of primary absorption in all things Japanese, Lincoln nonetheless made time for other projects, and for friends. Dan Maloney, for one, had again left Ed Hewitt, returned to New York, stayed for several weeks with Lincoln and Fidelma, and had what Lincoln called "a very brilliant opening of his show," which sold out. Jensen Yow, for his part, had become a well-established conservator at the Morgan Library, and after seven years of living with the Kirsteins moved into his own apartment, while continuing to be a source of great comfort to them.[8]

Dan and Jens, along with Paul Cadmus and Wystan Auden, constituted the Kirsteins' innermost circle (the "Goosies" and "Poozas"). Pavlik, who had also been a close confidant, died in 1957, after a period of declining health; to Lincoln's surprise he was named executor of Tchelitchev's estate. Among the rest—Lincoln's vast network of acquaintances—a few people, like Cartier-Bresson ("a marvelous person") and Andy Wyeth, were, through the years, deeply though distantly admired as both artists and men but never became intimates. Others were pressed close to the bosom for a time, then, gently or brusquely (or sometimes, like a revolving door, both) discarded as "no longer promising," humanly or artistically. The painter Bernard Perlin was one such case in point, as was the writer Laurens van der Post. George Platt Lynes was yet another.

Lynes, one of the great photographers of ballet, had known Lincoln since boarding school in 1922, and as young men they saw each other with some regularity. But by the 1950s contact between them was infrequent. Lincoln found Lynes increasingly "silly"—an "idiot-child" who thought "he is irresistible when he is not suicidal . . . people to him are in two categories: pimps and customers, and it's slowly merging into one." When Lynes died of lung cancer in 1955 at the age of forty-eight, Lincoln partook of the usual obsequies (though he skipped the all-male gang-bang given in Lynes's honor). He arranged for a memorial show of Lynes's work at the City Center gallery, and decades later, when a volume of Lynes's portraits was published, Lincoln, then in his eighties, wrote an admiring introduction that stressed Lynes's achievements and said nothing of his personal shortcomings.

With the exception of Auden, whom Lincoln viewed as the "greatest" living poet as well as a person of immense stature and insight ("sort of a pilot for me"), Lincoln's earlier enthusiasm for various English friends waned with the years, though he continued to see most of them on a "passing through" basis. He still found Isherwood an entertaining companion, but "less sympathetic than previously." On his side Isherwood, too, had complaints; "we seem to have become friends," he wrote Lincoln, "almost at long range, by tele-empathy; because nearly always when we are together, the one or both of us are preoccupied."

Lincoln's enthusiasm for Spender, earlier bordering on adoration, took a more precipitous dive. As early as 1951, he'd decided that Auden had been right about Spender all along "when he said he should have stuck to autobiographical prose." He no longer admired Spender the poet and essayist and thought that as a man he'd become "desperately envious and silly." Even as Lincoln himself moved more deeply into the inner sanctums of cultural power in the United States, he blamed Spender for having become "*sincere* and official." By 1958 Spender had been dropped down a hole: "I have no respect for Spender as poet or person," Lincoln summarily wrote Donald Richie.

But his disappointment with Spender was as nothing compared to the unaccented aversion he felt from the first for Leonard Bernstein, whose talents and personality he despised in equal measure. Lincoln reduced Bernstein's gifts to mere "assimilative energies"—which was akin to accusing him of pouncing and gorging on other people's creations. "That he CAN write musical comedies (not very good ones) and symphonies (not very good ones) is what at once pleases and tortures him," Lincoln wrote Jerry Robbins, Bernstein's collaborator and friend. "He is not a very advanced type of human being."

Lincoln could be recklessly impatient with people, bluntly and hurt-fully saying what he felt at the moment, but he was at bottom a bad hater; he would secretly do an important favor for someone he wasn't speaking to, would loan money to an acquaintance whose talent he'd lost confi-dence in, or would "forget" two weeks after a shouting match that it had ever taken place, casually embracing the person who'd recently been his fierce antagonist. "To gratuitously hurt people's feelings is something I try not to do," Lincoln once wrote, "as I hate it when people hurt mine, and increasingly I am a Jewish-Christian and/or a Christian-Jew." Donald Richie put his finger on an essential part of Lincoln's being: "You are a very moral person. . . . I think of Seneca for comparison. . . . It is precisely for this reason that you are understood badly . . . people will not—do not want to—believe that in this world of slipping and slithering and sliding standards there are some which remain inviolate . . . you stand for these and observe them. . . ."

Lincoln's loyalty to certain perceived standards remained strongly in evi-dence as he and John Rockefeller III gradually resumed their relationship and their discussion of the place of the dance at Lincoln Center. By the fall of 1959 the Juilliard School of Music had, along with the Philharmonic and the Metropolitan Opera, become the third constituent group at Lin-coln Center. Both Juilliard and the Metropolitan had (bad) ballet schools, and that became a complicating factor in considering whether there should also be a resident dance company, and if so, which one.

The Juilliard School had had a dance department for some years, with Antony Tudor supervising ballet and Martha Hill modern dance. The well-endowed department hadn't been successful, its resources (in Lin-coln's view) "wastefully bungled," and William Schuman, president of Juilliard, had wanted Balanchine to take over. But Balanchine, of course, already had his own School of American Ballet, which was widely recog-nized as preeminent for a professional career in ballet, and he'd shown no interest in Schuman's proposal. Besides, Balanchine was convinced that the Metropolitan, with its vast financial resources, was intent on creating a significant ballet company of its own.[9]

Lincoln reiterated both to Schuman and to John III that neither he nor Balanchine felt any urgent need to become part of Lincoln Center. As he told Schuman (and wrote John III), "The slot is more a token than a real-ity. At present we have a home [City Center], a credit structure, a reper-tory, an audience [the mailing list had grown to 85,000] and a deficit which, due to the size of the popular-priced auditorium, manages to per-mit an existence. . . . Balanchine and I will not separate ourselves from the City Center." Awaiting further developments, Lincoln set about applying to various foundations and approaching wealthy individuals in an effort to establish a minimum capital fund of three hundred thousand dollars which, over the next five years, would make it possible permanently to establish the NYCB as a "self-perpetuating organism."

In the meantime the company continued to perform, and Balanchine to create; Lincoln saw to that, in the process running himself ragged, as usual. Of the major ballets of 1959–60, one was a failure, the other a triumph. *Pan America*, the work of several choreographers, premiered in January 1960 and was based on music by Carlos Chávez and other Latin American composers, music Lincoln felt Balanchine "could not control." The ballet found little favor, though its guest star, the Danish *premier danseur* Erik Bruhn, was greatly admired—except by Lincoln, who found him "smooth, cold and hard as steel."

The reception of Balanchine's Persian-themed *The Figure in the Carpet*, performed for the first time during the spring season of the same year, was quite different. "I have never seen Balanchine so interested in putting a work over on this scale," Lincoln wrote Baum, "and with all the underlying layers of meaning." To finance the expensive production, Ed Bigelow and Betty Cage mortgaged their country homes and Lincoln his Nineteenth Street town house. Their risk-taking paid off: *Figure* was widely hailed as a masterwork, with even the notoriously rigorous critic B. H. Haggin praising its "richly varied invention."

The drive to create a capital fund was much less successful. Though NYCB had achieved international renown by 1960, with many critics rating it second only to the Kirov and Bolshoi companies, it still lacked the financial security to guarantee a future. Despite Balanchine's revolutionary transfiguration of the classical ballet, and despite dozens of his brilliant creations, NYCB had (unlike the Russian companies) no financial support from the government and no permanent home. Morton Baum had saved the company from likely extinction in the late 1940s, but City Center's wretched stage and its unpredictable finances had by 1960 become a millstone, inhibiting Balanchine from creating the large-scale works he longed to do and failing to draw support from those wealthy individuals who saved their gift-giving for socially certified, gilded institutions.

The situation was about to change. On June 28, 1960, over George Balanchine's signature, Lincoln wrote a lengthy letter to Nelson Rockefeller, now governor of New York, about the state of the arts in this country. He pointed out that people interested in or connected to the arts now formed "a large and dedicated section of the public," a section, he cleverly emphasized, that had great political power "most political personages don't try to reach." Politicians, Lincoln argued, were careful to enlist the support of unions, yet "union members are outnumbered by people interested in the arts" (a factoid Lincoln seems to have conjured out of thin air, through the steady growth of "consumers of culture" in this period is undeniably true).[10]

Lincoln further suggested that although our country fed "the whole world materially, most of our children are starved spiritually and mentally whether they are rich or poor." He cited the recent matinee series he'd inaugurated for "underprivileged" children: the performances "were a revelation to the children whose surprise and enthusiasm knew no bounds." Now came the punch line: only a state-supported theater could guarantee that such a program would have a continuous life, even as it would assure ongoing sustenance for the arts.

Nelson had long since demonstrated both his profound interest in the arts and his intense loyalty to Lincoln; in any celestial accounting, his patronage would rank next to that of Lincoln's own parents. Nelson personally needed no persuading about the importance of a state-sponsored theater, but he did need a gimmick for publicly proposing it. For that he turned to the upcoming 1964 World's Fair at Flushing Meadow, New York. As the state's contribution to that celebration, Nelson decided to propose funds for the erection of a state theater as part of the advancing Lincoln Center complex.

By early October 1960, Lincoln was able to confide to a few people that the state would be spending $17,500,000 to erect a dance theater. It would be designed by Philip Johnson and seat twenty-six hundred people. The city of New York would undertake to maintain the building at an annual cost of about two hundred and fifty thousand dollars, and the New York City Ballet Company would be the principal tenant of the theater.

It had, astonishingly, happened. After nearly thirty dogged years of hand-to-mouth begging, determined improvisation, and alternating periods of despair and euphoria, the New York City Ballet would finally have a permanent home and a guaranteed future. The *Nutcracker* had proved predictive: The Sugar Plum Fairy would remain all smiles. Well, for a while anyway.

The State Theater

(1961–1963)

E ARLY ON THE morning of January 16, 1961, Lincoln received a telegram—the same telegram sent to some 140 other artists and intellectuals—inviting him to attend the inauguration of President-elect John F. Kennedy. Auden had also been invited, and he soon phoned Lincoln to say that "this was not an invitation but a command; if they had made the effort, we should." Lincoln had voted for Kennedy, but reluctantly; "I can't distinguish between our two (un)-distinguished presidential gifts," he'd written Alex Colville. "They tell me the 'men around' Kennedy are better, but it's hard for me to think so by their public statements." But the incoming administration did signal a new climate sympathetic to cultural needs. With Nelson Rockefeller installed as governor of New York, there seemed genuine ground for hope that the United States would at last begin to match Western Europe in lending financial and moral support to the arts.[1]

Despite a snowstorm, Lincoln (but not Fidelma) dutifully attended a wide variety of ceremonies that surrounded the inauguration. He drew excellent grandstand seats for the parade and a special label card (PRE-FERRED STANDING ROOM) for the swearing-in ceremony. He went to Walter Lippmann's cocktail party; sat through a long, tedious concert by the National Symphony Orchestra featuring Randall Thompson's *Testament of Freedom* ("a work," Lincoln laconically put it, "not in the first category of American compositions"); heard Marian Anderson sing two verses of *The Star-Spangled Banner* ("her lapidary diction made the verse sound like poetry"); and watched painfully as Robert Frost tried to deliver a poem with the sun shining in his eyes and blurring his vision.

"I am deeply and sincerely in love with Jack Kennedy," Lincoln wrote Andrew Wyeth after returning to New York. "So far he has not reciprocated, but it's only a question of time. . . . All kidding aside, he is the first President since the 2nd Roosevelt, who is interested in the MIND. . . . I don't think abstract art will appear on our coins or postage-stamps." Lincoln expanded his love feast to include Jackie Kennedy, when, less than a week after the inauguration, she invited Balanchine to tea (NYCB was currently performing in Washington) and word went out on radio and television that he was the first official visitor to the White House. Two months later Jackie appeared at an NYCB performance in New York accompanied by Adlai Stevenson, and went backstage afterward to chat with members of the company.

Reciprocal love of a sort did arrive some six months later: The White House, in September 1961, invited Lincoln to serve on the Advisory Committee for the National Cultural Center (which eventually became known as the Kennedy Center) currently being planned for the capital. Lincoln felt "pleased and honored" and accepted. Soon after, the Shakespeare Festival was asked to perform selections from *Troilus* and *Macbeth* at a White House gala. Lincoln accompanied the Stratford troupe and had "a very amusing time." He liked the assistant assigned to him (Bob Hope's son, Tony Hope), found the sexy security staff "pure mad dream heaven," and "got pissed on champagne in the bomb-shelter" (with the security staff?). After returning home, Lincoln learned that Letitia "Tish" Baldrige, Jackie Kennedy's social secretary, had written someone at NYCB saying that Lincoln had "left a great many fans in The White House behind him—in fact, everyone with whom he came in contact."

Lincoln's connection to the emerging Kennedy Center in Washington was a marginal one, in no way comparable to his involvement with Lincoln Center in New York. By late March 1961 he was engaged both with Nelson Rockefeller and his brother John in hammering out plans for Lincoln Center's "State Theater." Lincoln wanted the entirety of City Center and its various units (opera, light opera, drama, ballet) to find housing in the new theater, with the New York City Ballet as the chief tenant. But he feared that the powerful Metropolitan Opera would thwart his plans; in Lincoln's view the Met had long been dedicated to the destruction of City Center "since it cannot tolerate the discrepancy of a low-priced house with a dynamic philosophy next to a conservative luxury theatre; it must control all artists contracts and all time of playing."

The Met's mechanism for accomplishing this, Lincoln wrote Nelson, was to get the state to deed the lease of its new building to Lincoln Center, a private corporation with interlocking boards consisting of a handful of bankers, lawyers, and real estate operators. The New York City Ballet was, by contrast (in Lincoln's words), "an amorphous organization partly financed by myself, and partly through the City Center; it has no corporate entity and its real properties are in confusion since financing has always been informal, hysterical and inadequate." Should the state of New York give a direct lease to Lincoln Center, then the Met, having the most powerful, rich, and active board, would control "the costs, playing-time, scheduling and policy" of the City Center. And should that come to pass, Lincoln warned Nelson, he and Balanchine "will withdraw those dancers who wish to stay with us and find funds to operate elsewhere."

In a second letter Lincoln contradicted Nelson's assertion that the planned buildings will be "the greatest cultural Center ever built," by emphasizing instead that it will merely "reflect the dominant powers in American society at this moment," and with an overall architectural scheme that "is the lowest common denominator of temporizing and improvising." The center that was about to rise, Lincoln insisted, "has a poor public image" and "no popular support from intellectuals, artists or writers beyond those directly involved."

Nelson may not have entirely agreed, and in any case could not have said so publicly, but in the many discussions that followed, he did throw his weight on the side of making City Center a full-fledged constituent of Lincoln Center, sparing it the Met's control. Nelson argued that constituent status would encourage the city to contribute to the costs of upkeep and would dilute the notion that Lincoln Center existed solely for the social and financial elite that could afford its ticket prices. Newbold Morris and Morton Baum, as chief officers of City Center, carried the major share of the negotiations, and they arrived at a formula that gave New York State ownership of the theater during the two years of the world's fair (1964–65), and New York City ownership thereafter. Rockefeller persuaded New York City's Board of Estimate to put four hundred thousand dollars annually at the disposal of the State Theater for maintenance costs.

The compromise formula wasn't ideal from Lincoln's perspective. Nor was the fact that at this same time, John D. Rockefeller III, whose power and protectorship had earlier enabled Lincoln to have a voice in Lincoln Center's proceedings, began to pull back from involvement. Lincoln had frequently lunched with John and in the interims between had sent him lengthy, candid letters about Lincoln Center policies. In mid-December 1960 Lincoln apparently overstepped the mark when he yet again castigated the planners to John as having no notion "of what it takes to create a work of art. . . . In a word [Lincoln Center] lacks a soul."[2]

The diffident John, uncomfortable with expressing anger, responded with what for him was a resounding rebuke. "You are right in your assumption that you can be most helpful to me by being frank," he wrote Lincoln. "I have to admit, however, that sometimes your comments are a little devastating in their sweep and all-inclusiveness." Lincoln got the message and hastened to make amends: "In spite of what I have said, in fact completely against myself," Lincoln replied, "I feel that these buildings, soulless, undirected, unpoliced as they may NOW be, will be a stupendous addition, not to New York City alone, but to the country and the world."

That was not only laying it on a bit thick, but also a bit incoherently: it was difficult to envision (or applaud) a "stupendous addition" of "soullessness." Additionally Lincoln had made himself sound indifferent to the architecture of Lincoln Center (which he certainly wasn't). He further muddled matters with a complete reversal: "Do not worry about the inclusion of artists on your Board," he now advised John. "The Board is no place for them. Just get the buildings up; the artists will take them over and run them . . ." Meaning what?—surely not that artists, notoriously inept at all matters administrative, would determine what went on in the buildings. Lincoln was clearly flustered. In his haste to repair any damage in his relationship with John III, whose friendship and trust he needed, he'd made himself sound vaguely inept. Chasing after the coattails of power wasn't something he did with particular grace or logic—a function, perhaps, of his essential dignity.

Both the friendship and the theater would ultimately be secured, but in 1961 Lincoln turned most of his attention to the affairs of the New York City Ballet. Balanchine was for the moment exhausted; he'd done a colossal amount of work during the November 1960–January 1961 season at City Center, creating no fewer than five new ballets, including his masterful *Liebeslieder Walzer*. Balanchine also had to undergo a series of painful dental operations to reshape his bite, so the spring 1961 season wouldn't include much that was new.

Besides, George Kirstein, who managed Lincoln's financial affairs, put his brother on notice that for the time being he couldn't dip any further into his own money to pay for new NYCB ballets. The stock market had been down during 1960, and Lincoln's losses were compounded by his several invasions of principal during the year. Two of his trust funds were unbreakable, but George warned Lincoln that his ongoing withdrawals from trusts emanating from their parents' wills left that money "pretty well milked out." That didn't mean, George emphasized, that Lincoln and Fidelma "won't eat regularly in the years ahead," but it did mean, in George's view, that Lincoln would have to exercise "increased restraint . . . on ballet projects."

Lincoln seemed to take his brother's admonitions to heart. Yet he and Balanchine had already had discussions about a major new ballet for early 1962: *A Midsummer Night's Dream*. And their advance plans were large-scale and elaborate, potentially costing more money than even *Nutcracker* had. And so, as always, Lincoln set to work to find it, hating every minute of the inevitable solicitations. This time, though, he got lucky close to home. Between Nancy Lassalle, the ex-SAB dance student turned NYCB mainstay; Burt Martinson, the coffee king who'd been part of Lincoln's Japanese ventures; his sister, Mina; and—somehow, and doubtless over George Kirstein's near-dead body—himself, Lincoln raised seventy-five thousand of the needed hundred thousand dollars by May 1961.

As plans for the new ballet moved forward, one of Lincoln's earlier and seemingly moribund projects suddenly emerged into the foreground. Aware that Seattle would be hosting a world's fair in the spring and summer of 1962, Lincoln had proposed to the city's coordinator of special events, that one hundred young Japanese athletes be brought to Seattle to demonstrate the ritual disciplines of traditional Japanese sports. The coordinator liked the idea and invited Lincoln to undertake negotiations with the Japanese Foreign Office. He'd heard rumors that John Rocke-feller III "is already making trouble for me," purportedly fearing that if the Japanese government sent a group to Seattle they would refuse to do so for the New York World's Fair of 1964. Whether or not the rumors were true, Lincoln decided to move as quickly as possible.[3]

In late December 1961 he left for Japan (with Fidelma to follow), stop-ping off at Seattle to inspect the fairgrounds, talk with officials, and get a general sense of the scope and quality of the planned event. After sizing it all up he wrote enthusiastically to Donald Richie that "the Fair will be perfectly marvelous; it is done with a maximum of taste, intelligence, brightness and chic. I am sure I can bring this all off." Lincoln also wrote Richie that he'd had a "revelation" about the intrinsic meaning, "the essential ethic and aesthetic" at the heart of Japanese ritual sports. It was despair: "The opponent is merely a symbol for the shut world which has to be maintained in some sort of stasis, but which is essentially inimical"; the rituals were designed "to hold hell off at arms length with beautiful manners and a sense of personal well-being." To Alex Colville, he offered a variant description of the essence of ritual sport: "stoicism and a suicidal integrity combining devotion and treachery."

Lincoln may well have intuited an important aspect of Japanese sport; he certainly presented a penetrating insight into his own interior world. Donald Richie, more than anyone—including Lincoln—saw clearly why the country and the person were so close a match. Both thought money had value only for its "buying potential." Both thought people were to be valued for what they do, and were to be invested in for the promise of what they might do. Both combined, confused and concealed great strength with great gentleness.[4]

Richie was now a recently married man. He'd earlier written Lincoln enthusiastically about Mary Evans, a Fulbright scholar living in Japan and teaching a course at a Tokyo university. On first learning the news, Lin-coln had heartily congratulated Richie: "No one not in the situation can possibly understand how wonderful women are for man's weakness; par-ticularly when wives are large enough to know that they cannot change their men; they can only love them." In that pre-feminist age, Lincoln (like most men of the day, and probably most men still) said nothing about what wives might get out of such arrangements, but he did say that he was sure Mary and Fidelma "will get on well."

Certainly he took to Mary immediately, describing her to Betty Cage as "a ravishingly beautiful tall blonde girl . . . with money . . . [and] brains . . . she is a lovely person." Mary, in turn, thought highly of Fidelma, but was less certain about Lincoln. She found Fidelma remarkably beautiful "in a kind of Virginia Wolff way," and also "very, very fragile." The contrast with the charismatic Lincoln who "exuded confidence and energy" was startling, and Mary was relieved that he seemed "so proud and protective" of his wife.

Mary realized that it was her job to show Fidelma around Tokyo while Donald and Lincoln made their rounds to various officials at the Foreign Office, the Shochiku Entertainment Combine, and the Imperial Household offices. She put considerable time into planning outings for Fidelma, but the more she did for her, the more Fidelma seemed to withdraw, leaving Mary bewildered. Several years later, after Mary and Donald divorced, Fidelma revealed that during the Tokyo trip she'd felt that Mary had been assigned to keep her busy in order to give Lincoln an unobstructed amount of time with his adored "athletes." The revelation stunned Mary. She'd known about Donald's multiple male escapades prior to her decision to marry him. She'd also assumed that "we knew all too much about one another's situations" to discuss them. Mary herself had taken lovers after her sex life with Donald had dwindled to nothing and then, after four years of marriage, had decided on divorce.

But Fidelma lacked Mary's unfeigned acceptance of reality and was unwilling, or unable, to do anything comparable. She deeply loved Lincoln and chose to center her life on his needs. This may not have been "good" for her, as adjudged by certain models of "health," but affairs and divorce might have been—given her fragility—far worse. Still, as her suspicion and resentment of Mary's chaperonage demonstrates, Fidelma wasn't—even twenty years into married life with Lincoln—wholly at ease with or indifferent to his "second life" (Jensen recalls a "terrific row" some years earlier over one of Lincoln's boyfriends, as well as a sardonic reference by Fidelma to Lincoln having "one of his homeless boys' nights").

As Lincoln learned only later, Fidelma had been having symptoms of depression before she left for Japan, and should never have made the arduous trip. When Donald Richie first met her he thought her a "desperately unhappy woman . . . her mind was always flitting about like a caged bird, unable to rest." Her conflicted reaction to "Lincoln and the athletes" could have triggered a deeper despair, but the causes of a major depressive episode are always somewhat mysterious and its course difficult to chart. Within days of arriving, Fidelma had lapsed into a severe depression, and Lincoln made the immediate decision to bundle her up and take her back to the States. The official explanation he gave out was that his wife had "influenza with a high fever."

It's a curious but fortunate fact that throughout their long relationship Lincoln and Fidelma were almost never incapacitated at the same time; one was always available to help care for the other. And once back home,

Fidelma did slowly begin to recover, though it was (in Lincoln's words) "a long and hard pull." Nearly six months after her breakdown she was "much better," though still "not one hundred percent . . . she does go out some and sees people."

As Fidelma recuperated, Lincoln was attentive, but various events crowded his schedule. Balanchine's *A Midsummer Night's Dream* opened at City Center on January 17. There had been some stormy moments during the rehearsal period. Another money crisis had threatened to weaken production values, a problem made worse by Balanchine's "livid" rejection of David Hays's drawings for the sets; Lincoln thought they were "lovely," but Hayes dutifully went back to the drawing board. In fact the ballet was a resounding success and marked, in Lincoln's view, the emergence to stardom of Edward Villella: he "seems to have opened up in all ways," Lincoln wrote a friend, "and his dancing has accordingly greatly improved." Villella's pyrotechnical power would make him, in short order, the company's leading male dancer—and an enormous popular favorite.

A startling prospect suddenly loomed: the chance for the New York City Ballet to perform in the Soviet Union during the summer of 1962. The American State Department had for nearly a year dodged all inquiries from Betty Cage about the prospects for such a tour, and the Soviets, in turn, were still smarting from Rudolf Nureyev's 1961 defection. It seemed unlikely that attitudes would change in 1962. But it may have helped NYCB's case that Balanchine neither paid court to Nureyev nor showed any interest in inviting him to join the company. Lincoln felt the same: he initially disliked Nureyev personally (though on better acquaintance felt quite differently), thought he was too old to learn Balanchine's technique and repertory, and believed that any attempt to integrate him into the company would prove too great a shock all around.[5]

Balanchine himself, having defected in the 1920s from the revolution, was hardly keen on returning to his homeland. As negotiations picked up in 1962 and a tour seemed increasingly likely, Balanchine said he would go only if given a Marine guard and a diplomatic passport. The Russian authorities, for their part, wanted to embargo certain ballets they considered "erotic"—including *Orpheus* and *Agon*—the very works that Balanchine particularly wanted the Russian public to see, the ballets that had transformed the classical idiom.

Sol Hurok, whose prior relations with NYCB had been shadowed by failed negotiations and recrimination, was, ironically, the person who most helped tip the balance in favor of a tour. With his clever adroitness and his legion of contacts (he'd been many times to the Soviet Union and had handled the Bolshoi's triumphal visit to the United States in 1959) Hurok smoothed the waters all around. The State Department withdrew its objections, the Russians agreed to Balanchine's choice of repertory, and Balanchine foreswore the Marine guard (though not, understandably, the diplomatic immunity). According to Lincoln, Balanchine nervously predicted that "we will have the biggest failure since the 4th 5 year plan."

According to terms drawn up in May 1962, the State Department agreed to pay City Center $432,000 to cover preparatory costs and operating expenses for eight weeks in the Soviet Union and five in Western Europe. The Soviet Union agreed to supply transportation from the last city of the tour back to New York, and to pay for all food and lodging—no small commitment for a company of ninety people, including two mothers (one girl in the company was only fifteen, and one boy sixteen), plus a doctor. Mina also came along.

The European tour of five weeks preceded the Soviet visit, and passed off successfully, though d'Amboise was hit by a streetcar in Hamburg and couldn't dance for a number of weeks. One striking sideline both for Lincoln and Balanchine came in Vienna, where they spent considerable time watching the white Lipizzaner stallions in their daily class. Lincoln was utterly smitten: the horses were to him "not circus-acrobats; they are ballet-dancers, quadruped *danseurs nobles* in the pure baroque tradition." His interest in the stallions would be ongoing.[6]

When the troupe reached Moscow in October, the newly arrived U.S. ambassador, Foy Kohler, and his wife, took the company under their wing, smoothing their way wherever possible. The company was decidedly on edge, not least Balanchine himself, who consistently wore pegged pants and a cowboy shirt embroidered in silver—as if loudly to declare his Americanness and to distance himself as far as possible from his past. He did, after more than forty years, get to spend time—a mixed blessing, apparently—with his brother, Andrei, a well-known Georgian composer.

The Bolshoi Theatre, in which the company was to perform, was elegant, raked, and enormous. City Center's stage was not raked and was about one-quarter the size of the Bolshoi's. All sorts of adjustments had to be made, and NYCB's technical staff had to exercise considerable ingenuity in making the company's lights and drapes look good on the huge stage. By pre-arrangement NYCB would, after its initial two performances, transfer to the new Palace of Congresses, a formidable building seating 6,500 people.

Opening night at the Bolshoi was heavily loaded with officialdom, their presence, as Lincoln later put it, "required by protocol, not by passion, the hardest audience in the world to melt." The program opened with *Serenade*, based on Tchaikovsky's *Serenade for Strings* and familiar to a Russian audience. Yet as Mina described its reaction to Fidelma (who wisely did not make the trip), the ballet "was received with nothing but polite, meager applause." Balanchine's *Western Symphony* and Jerome

Robbins's *Interplay* (to Morton Gould's pop-jazz score) followed next and, surprisingly, had a warmer reception—"polite-plus" is how Lincoln characterized it.

Then, with fingers crossed, it was *Agon*'s turn. "Oddly enough," as Lincoln put it, "the Bolshoi audience accepted it promptly, with all its strangeness, or rather because of it, since it was not to be compared with anything they had previously seen, since it had neither decoration, costumes, melody, nor narrative . . . it was absorbed as dance, and no greater compliment could have been paid." After the curtain came down, the younger, student segment of the audience rushed to the front of the auditorium and started the kind of unison clapping considered the greatest possible tribute. At the American ambassador's reception that followed, more than five hundred people attended, including Khrushchev's son-in-law, which was taken as a marked compliment.

All twenty-four performances in Moscow sold out; and though prices were high, it was students and intellectuals who filled the huge auditorium. After every performance their rhythmic clapping and the chant "Bal-an-chine" went on and on until he appeared before the curtain, thanked the audience, and said the dancers had to go to bed now. Possibly the greatest sensation of all was *Episodes*, choreographed to Webern's difficult, unfamiliar music, the performances additionally handicapped by a Soviet orchestra that consisted of older musicians wholly unfamiliar with a twelve-tone score. To the Americans' amazement, the young Soviet audiences loved the piece.

In the months before the tour, Betty Cage and whoever happened to be in her office would play a game called Disaster: "what would happen if . . ." If, for example, on the first night Jacques d'Amboise would twist his ankle (he *was* hit by that Hamburg tram). Or: what would happened if Melissa Hayden would literally knock herself out (as had actually occurred during a 1950 performance when she did slip a back disk in Zurich and had to be hospitalized). The ultimate game would always be: what would happen if the Soviet Union and the United States were to declare war during the company's engagement? And the answer would always be: we'd be sent to Siberia.

As it came to pass, war was very nearly declared—giving a far higher predictive batting average to the players of Disaster than anyone cared to boast. The diplomatic crisis came near the end of the Moscow visit, when the Kennedy administration decided to call Khrushchev's bluff about Soviet missile placements in Cuba. When war was averted at almost literally the last minute, the exceedingly nervous company (to say nothing of the rest of the world) drew a collective sigh of relief and moved on to its next set of engagements in Leningrad, Balanchine's hometown.

There, unlike in Moscow, the company enjoyed an unalloyed triumph, and Balanchine was smothered in adulation. But Lincoln saw clearly that the acclaim was "absolutely meaningless to him," that he "has hated every moment of his stay here", as the "steely coldness of his manners during all the flower-throwing and praise" clearly demonstrated; his return to the Soviet Union has been "a kind of crucifixion." According to one of the company's new principal dancers, Patricia Neary, Balanchine "couldn't sleep at night; he told me the phone would ring at four o'clock in the morning, and the radio would go on suddenly. He got thinner and thinner . . ." Lincoln wasn't at all surprised when, after the two-week engagement in Leningrad was over, Balanchine went back to New York for a week's respite.

Though he himself no longer wanted to stay, Lincoln remained with the company. The terrifying days of the missile crisis, plus the accumulated stress over their reception, had taken a real toll on the company; the dancers, Lincoln reported back, "are tired and cracking up," and he felt the obligation to remain with them and to provide Betty Cage with support until Balanchine returned. When the tour had begun in early October, Lincoln was (so Mina reported to Fidelma) "calm, balanced, drinking hardly at all." By the end of November, after the company had left Leningrad and was playing the provinces, Lincoln "got the *volupté de partir*, to such a degree" that one day he abruptly decided to leave for home, canceling a planned stop-off in London.

Much had been accomplished; even Lincoln felt that for the first time he fully understood the dimensions of Balanchine's achievement by seeing the ballets performed night after night in proper-size houses rather than on the cramped City Center stage. Yet overall he summed up the eight weeks in the Soviet Union as "miserable," as an experience "too traumatic for badinage." The comment centrally related to the matrix that lay between politics and art. Since his left-wing orientation was essentially intact, Lincoln hated sounding like a John Bircher or "an anti-Shostakovitch commissar," but he hated, too, the products of so-called "revolutionary" art. While in the Soviet Union he claimed to have seen not one "fantasy or oddity or queerity or anything exportable." Yet his distress extended beyond Soviet art; Pavlik's sister reported to a friend that she'd "received a long letter from Lincoln telling me all his disillusions with Soviet Russia."

But if Lincoln had seen nothing of value—nothing "exportable"—the fault lay not with the socialist values held by the Bolsheviks at the start of the revolution but with Stalinism, which stifled creativity and stamped out dissent of any kind. In equating Bolshevism and Stalinism rather than separating and opposing them (as historical accuracy would have required), Lincoln, like so many other leftists then and now, was driving himself into needless negativism. And the negativism went deep; as he wrote Donald and Mary Richie after returning to the States: "We have not recovered yet and I don't think Balanchine ever will; it [the tour] corroborated his worst [conservative] fears and it shattered my greatest [left-wing] hopes." Lincoln's disappointment went so deep that he even insisted the Russian people "don't want to be liberated . . . they want to be left alone, to stew in their own . . . national neurosis." Khrushchev himself would soon prove him wrong.

After returning home Lincoln began to devote more of his time to writing projects—as friends had long been urging. He was particularly eager to get his poems about life as a GI during World War II collected into a volume, but the response of American publishers was uniformly negative. Some objected to the poems' vernacular, including slang and "obscenities," and some to the quality of the verse (decently high if one valued Kipling and Robert Service); others cited the lack of a market for poetry in general. Lincoln himself thought the problem was "not so much the obscenities . . . [but] the attitude. It's, well, deeply un- or anti-patriotic. . . . The one thing you can't be about a national-sacrifice is unsolemn."[7]

In their rejection letters none of the publishers cited what may have been an additional factor: the poetry was centrally autobiographical and did make several oblique references to homosexuality (both daring and alarming in those pre-Stonewall years); one long poem, "Gloria," was put into the mouth of a charmingly campy transvestite ("Gloria Ivanovna" was one of many playful, and quirky, pseudonyms—"Pussypants," "Natasha," and "Paddy Paws," were others—that Lincoln himself used in letters to like-minded intimates).

When Lincoln's loyal friend Wystan Auden responded to a *New York Times* query, "What books have you read in the last year that you most liked?" Auden replied that the only verse he thought well of was an unpublished manuscript—and named Lincoln's *Rhymes of a PFC*. Auden also tried to peddle the book to Faber & Faber in London, promising that he would do a foreword, but Faber's T. S. Eliot "absolutely loathed" the poems. But James Laughlin of New Directions did decide to bring the book out in the States.

Lincoln's literary friends rallied round him with a fusillade of praise. The poet Bill Meredith found the poems "irresistibly readable." Marianne Moore broadened the context: "Your unmixed passion for what a thing should be, Lincoln—heart-rending Lincoln—stirs me to the soul." And Auden, perhaps responding to the sentiment that "in good friends, it is loyalty, not eyesight, that counts," gave the published version a resounding rave in the *New York Review of Books*: "As a picture of the late war, *Rhymes of a Pfc* is by far the most convincing, moving, and impressive book I have come across."

There wasn't, in the early sixties, a lot of time for literary pursuits. These were the climactic years for the construction of Lincoln Center in general and Philip Johnson's New York State Theater in particular, and a crucial set of interlocking issues absorbed Lincoln's time. At the close of 1962 the Lincoln Center board formally extended an invitation to the New York City Center to become, by degrees, a constituent partner in the new complex, with NYCB participating from the start and being officially regarded as Lincoln Center's primary ballet tenant, and the center's opera company designated to perform at some point thereafter—though the Metropolitan would remain Lincoln Center's primary unit in the field of opera. City Center's other two units, light opera and drama, were considered too shaky and undefined for the time being to share in the invitation; Richard Rodgers's New York Music Theater would, for at least two years, become the tenant for musical comedy and operetta.[8]

The City Center board, guided by Baum and Newbold Morris, accepted the invitation after getting guarantees that ticket prices would not exceed five dollars and that Lincoln Center would advance two hundred thousand dollars for the creation of new ballets during the period of the 1964 World's Fair. It was further agreed that the New York City Ballet would, in 1964, inaugurate the State Theater—though Balanchine and Lincoln insisted on linking that event to a guarantee that for the next three to five years, NYCB would be allocated at least twenty weeks of work in the theater; they won a guarantee of two years, after which contracts would be negotiated.

Lincoln had additional concerns about the pending alliance of NYCB and Lincoln Center. To Baum he insisted that New York City, rather than Lincoln Center, become the State Theater's permanent lessor; after all, he claimed (the terms of insult familiar), Lincoln Center's board members thought "that all dance is the same: José Limón, Martha Graham, Ballet Theater, etc." To W. MacNeil ("Mac") Lowry, a high-ranking officer at the Ford Foundation whom Lincoln had been cultivating and who'd become a personal friend, Lincoln expanded on his theme: the Lincoln Center people were "essentially conservative," interested only in "a known repertory, with only barely improvised novelties"; he denounced Bill Schuman, president of Lincoln Center's board, as a "hard-working charlatan," and Edgar Young, chairman of the building committee, as "just hard-working." If anyone "had an ounce of sense," Lincoln cheerfully ranted, they'd give Balanchine sole control over both opera and ballet at the State Theater—but of course the powers that be knew nothing about "an aristocracy of merit."

As the State Theater rose from the debris of what had once been thousands of people's homes and neighborhood businesses, Lincoln no longer complained about privileged aristocracies and their gross control over the lives of others. Nor did he have more than an occasional word of criticism (delivered in a nosegay of praise) for the theater designed by Philip Johnson—the man he'd once denounced for his fascist leanings. He did acknowledge, however, that the "promenade" space had a too-empty feeling to it, and to correct that imperfection he decided to place two enlarged (from five to nineteen feet high) Nadelman sculptures at either end. There was a slight problem: the theater walls had already gone up. Undeterred, Lincoln had holes smashed in the side of the theater—"a great escapade," in his view—to allow the two overblown figures to be hauled into place. And there they have stood ever since, looking, in their bovine vacuity, like a child's overblown soap carvings.

That small defect corrected, Lincoln managed to find all sorts of wondrous design elements to hail in the State Theater— a building that many architectural critics have subsequently scorned. He praised the superb sight lines—but never had to sit in the top ring. He declared himself "thrilled" with the "unparalleled grandeur and luxury"of the space, calling the theater "the architectural sleeper of all time"—though others have thought that its maroon-and-gold interior with large, gaudy crystals on the boxes resembles a 1950s ladies' powder room, and its exterior a mausoleum (though not one any sensible nonfascist would have erected). Even Philip Johnson would later say that the outside of the theater had "never been satisfactory" to him.

Yet no sooner did George Balanchine step on the theater's stage for the first time than he knew at once that changes, significant changes, were necessary. The orchestra pit was much too small; the concrete flooring would be miserably hard on the dancers; the normal points of entry from the wings would be blocked by light towers; the acoustics and the maroon-colored linoleum (chosen to match, like a handbag in a ladies' ensemble of the day, Johnson's overall color scheme) reflected onto the dancers and their costumes. There was plenty of time—opening night wasn't scheduled until April 1964—to remedy these defects, but the alterations were made at considerable cost. Lincoln now adopted a new line: "The theater is divine, the stage is not."

In the meantime his brother, George, had tired of his connection with *The Nation* and offered to turn it over to Lincoln. Lincoln's plate was more than full. But he was like the tightrope walker who adds one more chair to his load—and plunges off balance to the floor. Urged on by his penchant for dangerous excess, Lincoln initially accepted George's offer. He had a number of what he called "radical notions" for the magazine, including unsigned reviews (long the standard at England's *TLS*) and doubling the number of pages devoted to covering books and the arts. But even Lincoln recognized within a few months that *The Nation* required and deserved more or less full attention, and he withdrew his offer to run the magazine.

The withdrawal may have been triggered by feelings of mounting exhaustion that were finally, in the spring of 1963, diagnosed as hepatitis. His case was severe, and he was hospitalized for nearly a month; only sheer will power, apparently, had been allowing him to push through his fatigue and continue to function. Enforced idleness was the only kind of respite Lincoln could usually manage, and once his energy began to return, he found hospital life rather enjoyable. He was soon reporting to Betsy and Andy Wyeth that "the Porto Ricans and Black Muslims," who mostly comprised the hospital staff, were so overworked and underpaid "that the laboratory reports run four or five days behind what one would normally think of as prompt reportage." He discovered that he "adored" TV and when finally discharged "hated to go home and face life . . . like everything else . . . [the hospital] was very educational."[9]

Mid-1963 was a period of significant arrivals and departures in Lincoln's life. After completing a two-year fellowship he'd won in Indonesia, Dan Maloney returned to the States and again moved in for a time with the Kirsteins. Lincoln also found a new young man, Fred Maddox, to absorb his attention. This was opportune and comforting, since Jensen had recently bought a house in New Jersey and was spending much of his spare time fixing it up; he kept a room on the top floor of the Kirsteins' home where he sometimes worked and slept, but he wasn't around as frequently as in the 1950s, when Nineteenth Street had been his sole residence.[10]

There were also comings and goings at the New York City Ballet. It was in 1963 that Jacques d'Amboise, at the height of his powers as a dancer, also began a second life as a choreographer. Lincoln wrote the Canadian painter Alex Colville that after the fall 1963 season, d'Amboise "was declared by Balanchine and me the heir-apparent." Beyond Colville, did they say that to anyone other than each other? Did it constitute an informal agreement between them, subject to the usual vicissitudes of time and change? Exactly twenty years later, the ramifications of "heir-apparent" would prove weighty.

Lincoln was clear from the start about the stupendous gifts of a seventeen-year-old newcomer, a girl named Roberta Sue Ficker—the name soon changed to Suzanne Farrell. When she was still in the corps, he described her, quite simply, as "the greatest talent we have ever had . . ." In 1963 Farrell took over the lead role from a pregnant Diana Adams in the new Stravinsky-Balanchine ballet, *Movements for Piano and Orchestra.* The debut proved a sensation, Farrell's rise thereafter meteoric.

The company was at its brilliant height. Among its leading female principals were Suzanne Farrell, Melissa Hayden, Allegra Kent, Patricia McBride, and Violette Verdy; among the male dancers, it could boast (along with Magallanes and Moncion, nearing the end of their careers), d'Amboise, Villella, and Arthur Mitchell. And it was a company in depth. There were at least a dozen other highly capable dancers, among them Gloria Govrin, Kay Mazzo, Mimi Paul, Suki Schorer, Anthony Blum,

Conrad Ludlow, John Prinz, and Kent Stowell. Many of these dancers, moreover, had been trained at the School of American Ballet—now universally acknowledged as the finest in the country—and had come up through the ranks.

Moreover, Eugenie Ouroussow, the director of SAB, had in 1962 supervised a national survey on the state of ballet instruction and performance in the United States. Perhaps it should have come as no great surprise, therefore, when "Mac" Lowry of the Ford Foundation (whom Lincoln had long been cultivating, even taking him often to Betty Cage's intimate and exclusive Monday-night dinners), announced a grant in the fall of 1963 for the staggering sum of 6.5 million dollars (roughly the equivalent of some 30 million today). The grant, specifically designed to strengthen the teaching of ballet in the United States, was divided between five companies but the bulk of the Ford money went to the New York City Ballet. True to the stated mission of the grant, NYCB did thereafter send out its principal dancers and scouts to visit regional ballet schools and pick out the most promising youngsters for scholarships either to SAB or to another grantee, the San Francisco Ballet School.

But none of the Ford money went to Ballet Theatre or to any exponents of modern dance. That created huge resentment and an explosion of indignation (even though Ballet Theatre would soon after get a large grant of its own). People stopped Lincoln on the street to accuse him of having taken bread out of their mouths. Martha Graham phoned him to (in Lincoln's words) "sweetly inform me that I was but a common thief," added that she would never speak to him again—and hung up. Publicly, Lincoln said little, but privately he rejected the terms of debate as formulated by his antagonists. He felt the grant was in part the logical result of thirty years of apprenticeship and the deserved recognition of Balanchine's unique accomplishment. Besides, the large sum wasn't designated solely to SAB or NYCB; the bulk of it would go toward supporting local companies across the country, nurturing gifted teachers and students otherwise cut off from access to the resources of the large cities.

True, no part of the grant would go to "modern" dance, but Lincoln claimed that no one any longer knew what that designation amounted to; individuals like Martha Graham, Agnes de Mille, Merce Cunningham, José Limón, and Paul Taylor shared neither repertory, technique, nor method of instruction. "Modern Dance," Lincoln argued, had essentially been a phenomenon of the 1930s, when ballet in the United States was scarcely known; "thirty-five years later, the situation is different and many young dance students who would have been Modern Dancers are now attracted by the virtuosity and glamour of the academic ballet." Practitioners of modern dance did (and still would), of course, take issue with every aspect of Lincoln's analysis, insisting that they were, despite their separate identities, a coherent, vital movement of contemporary opposi-tion to traditional forms of dance, preeminently the ballet.

As the new State Theater neared completion, the interlocking set of rela-tionships between the New York City Ballet, Lincoln Center, City Center, and the city of New York remained murky—to some extent deliberately so, since the future was too full of uncertainty to allow for firm long-term commitments. It *was* agreed that during the two years (1964–66) of the world's fair, NYCB would not be responsible for operating expenses in the State Theater. But if the company (or its umbrella agent, City Center) then went on to become a constituent member of Lincoln Center, it would have to assume various fixed costs and maintenance fees. Lincoln found that prospect "terrifying." At City Center such costs devolved on Morton Baum and the governing board, and NYCB's primary responsi-bility was for expenditures surrounding the production of new ballets. To keep his options open, Lincoln asked Baum to reserve twenty-four weeks of work back at City Center for 1966–67. "We are working towards mov-ing" into Lincoln Center, Lincoln wrote Donald Richie, but "in an agony of apprehension, disquiet and calm."[11]

The company officially opened the State Theater in April 1964, with a gala performance featuring a trumpet fanfare (courtesy of Stravinsky) to draw the crowd into the theater, and a performance of Balanchine's *A Midsummer Night's Dream*. Despite the glamour of the occasion, Lincoln was more, not less, grim about future prospects. As he (accurately) saw it, Nelson Rockefeller's basic motive in making state funds available for erecting the theater had been to provide the New York City Ballet with a permanent home. But after protracted negotiations, the city of New York became the official owner and leased the theater to Lincoln Center for a period of fifty years. The Lincoln Center board, in turn, chose to regard City Center and the NYCB for the time being as tenants, not con-stituents; by fall 1964 other groups had already been booked into the State Theater, among them the Bayanihan Philippine Dance Company, Ballet Theatre, and José Limón.

By the spring of 1965 Bill Schuman, president of Lincoln Center, was busy exploring constituency status at Lincoln Center in the field of mod-ern dance, to be housed in the smaller recital hall in the Juilliard building. Lincoln claimed to have foreseen all this, since he'd learned early on that Lincoln Center "is only interested in money," but it nevertheless came as "rather a blow." As he wrote Van Vechten, "I doubt if we will remain long in Lincoln Center; they really hate us, and musical-comedy, after all, is the great American art-form. Or something."

None of these shifting maneuvers proved permanent. Yet it wasn't until the very end of 1965 that the Lincoln Center board, and Bill Schuman, finally gave way. It accepted the New York City Ballet, under the sponsorship of the City Center, as a constituent member of Lincoln Center, allowing it to inaugurate its first subscription series and giving it control over the State Theater's schedule. It isn't clear how much if any pressure Nelson Rockefeller applied in order to achieve these goals, but Lincoln obviously felt he'd played a considerable role. On December 24, 1965, the day after the lease with Lincoln Center was signed, Lincoln wrote Nelson that "only you realize the bitterness and the long strife which this involved . . . our gratefulness to you is all the more in this season of ritual good-will." As a gesture of appreciation Lincoln gave Nelson a small Nadelman figure.

PART SIX

Decline

Breakdowns/Writings

(1964–1975)

$\mathbf{B}$Y THE MID-SIXTIES the United States was a very different place from what it had been a decade before. The black civil rights movement that had begun to gather force in the 1950s had become a tidal wave of protest. It coincided and commingled with a mounting insurgency against the war in Vietnam and a countercultural insurgency against established authority in general. Following Kennedy's assassination late in 1963, Lyndon B. Johnson had ascended to the presidency and had lent his weight to "victory" both in the civil rights struggle and in Vietnam. His stance would lead to the passage of federal civil rights legislation in 1964–65— and to American defeat in the war overseas.[1]

During this politically charged period, one of the high points came with the historic second march from Selma to Montgomery, Alabama, to protest the police assault a few days earlier on those trying to present a petition of grievances to Governor Wallace; they'd "beaten people unmercifully," as Lincoln put it, "for trying to be people." His left-wing energies resurgent, Lincoln decided to join those going to Alabama to protest what had happened. Accompanying him were Dan Maloney and a young writer named Ken.

Along the route of the march, the three men took turns carrying on their shoulders a small black boy who'd gotten tired on the walk. All along the lines of the march were groups of angry-looking white men, state troopers, and what Lincoln assumed were FBI men (though he didn't know it, the FBI had opened a file on him, a rather thin, innocuous one). At one point a gang, in Lincoln's words, "of snake-faced, fox-faced, pig-faced and rat-faced delinquents howled at Dan Maloney, who was holding the hands of two nine or ten year old kids: 'Ah those yah daddy's black bastards?' A feeble provocation, but it was an intense little spray of hate, and if they could have killed Dan, they would have." It made Lincoln think about what might await Martin Luther King: "How long is God giving Martin Luther King? If, and when he is assassinated, and no power within the range of temporal authority in these United States can prevent it, it will not be in Selma, Montgomery nor Jackson. He will be on a speaking engagement in Portland, Oregon or Lowell, Massachusetts."

The march was deeply moving for Lincoln—like nothing, he wrote,

that he'd "ever experienced in this world." He found the civil rights movement in general inspiring—"really wonderful, the first time since the 30s
there is a real feeling of focus." In his excitement he came up with "a big
plan to do a Civil Rights exhibition in Harlem." It would include a history
of African slavery, a show of African art, and (not exactly one of Harlem's
priority items) "a hall of fame of white civil rights crusaders who have
helped the negro." The focus of the exhibition, though, would be on "the
Negro as ARTIST, and show what he is capable of, which has never been
shown."

But the exhibition never got off the ground, possibly because within a
week after returning from Montgomery, Lincoln was scheduled to leave
(with Dan and Fred Maddox, the latest addition to the Kirstein circle) on
a trip abroad. Fidelma hadn't wanted to join them, and it was the first
opportunity in some time when she could safely be left. In the closing
months of 1964 she'd gone through a difficult time. "Fido is rather nervous," Lincoln wrote her brother, Paul. "The future worries me." She'd
remained "out of sorts" for a longer period than her previous bouts of
depression, but by winter 1965 she seemed stabilized.[2]

The first stop of the trip was Tokyo, where Dan picked up with an air-
line mechanic, Lincoln with a married young architect, and Fred with
assorted ladies of the night, returning to sleep, as Lincoln put it, "innocently, whatever that means . . . like two spoons under the same futon . . .
in my arms." The next stop was Kyoto, a city Lincoln found endlessly fascinating: "For me it is the most marvelous place to see and visit and each
time I find new things in the old things." From there Dan and Fred went
off to explore the region surrounding the Inland Sea, and Lincoln returned to Tokyo further to pursue his amateur diplomacy ("I'm actually
quite good at it"). He had talks about the return of the ballet to Tokyo and
of Gagaku to the States. He also made one more stab at trying to import
Japan's traditional ritual sports. No sale—though everyone was most
polite.

The trio went next to Thailand, where Lincoln found the people "so
amiable and obliging" that he began "to long for a little Japanese violence." From there it was on to India, which Lincoln profoundly disliked;
he thought the inhabitants "hate each other more than foreigners, which
is a new low," but he loved the architectural sights. In two consecutive
days they saw the Taj Mahal and then, after a flight to Istanbul, Hagia
Sophia.

Lincoln returned home to find that Fidelma's improvement had been
temporary: she "was quite hysterical on our arrival." It turned out that she
resented Fred and—unlike his predecessors Jensen and Dan—"fears I
will ask him to live here, which neither he nor I have any intention of
considering." Fred would in fact soon be out of the picture, though he'd
later reappear on the scene, again close to Lincoln. It was Mina more

than Fred, though, who consistently frightened Fidelma, sometimes treating her with disdain and once insensitively telling her that she should be institutionalized.

Though the future relationship of the New York City Ballet to the State Theater remained uncertain, the company was meanwhile enjoying the posh new facilities and working hard with Balanchine to reconfigure some of the more expansive ballets, like *Symphony in C,* to suit the much larger stage. In the midst of these readjustments Balanchine also managed in 1965 to create two major new ballets: *Harlequinade* and *Don Quixote* (at the latter's gala preview, he himself, age sixty, danced the lead role opposite Suzanne Farrell, with whom he was by this point obsessed), and then, in 1967, the astonishing *Jewels.* In line with the Ford grant, Balanchine spent a great deal of time traveling the country giving counsel and recommendations to local ballet schools and companies.[3]

NYCB was also enjoying heightened prestige and security. Both in 1964 and 1965 the company toured Europe, performing in the best theaters of the most important cities. During its seasons at the State Theater, the company played to roughly 70 percent of capacity and for a seven- to eight-week season grossed between four and five hundred thousand dollars. For the spring 1966 season, the first subscription series went into effect and nearly twenty thousand subscribers signed up, thus guaranteeing advance security of almost $350,000. Salaries for the dancers also rose. In 1965 Melissa Hayden and Jacques d'Amboise were the highest-paid members of the company, each making five hundred dollars a week. Yet NYCB still—unlike some other major ballet companies in the world— had no pension plan in place and no guarantee, after retirement, of some sort of employment with the company.

As NYCB in the mid-late sixties came into far greater possession of assurance and institutionalization than it had known, Lincoln—without ever losing his central focus on the fortunes of the company—began to reinvolve himself in writing and to find time to cultivate a few new friendships. When he accompanied the NYCB to London in 1965, for example, Lincoln (through Dickie Buckle) met the sculptor Astrid Zydower. He immediately liked her work and also took to her personally. He was moved, too, by her history. Born of Jewish parents near Posen (where Rose Kirstein's grandmother had once been a wet nurse), Astrid was sent out of harm's way in 1939 to live with a couple in Sheffield, England. She never saw her parents again; they died in the gas chambers. On that 1965 trip, Lincoln bought Astrid's bust of Shakespeare for the Stratford Festival and the following year invited her over (Dickie Buckle horning in on the invitation) for its installation.[4]

Astrid was at least as taken with Lincoln. On their very first meeting she was enchanted by his "creative energy . . . he was so *amazing*, because he seemed bigger than life. . . . He was almost like an electric current or wire." When she came to New York in 1966, he took her to all the major museums and art galleries, and she was dazzled by the range of his knowledge: "a dimension beyond the ordinary sort of intellect." He "made everything into a marvelous adventure" and constantly came up with the unexpected illuminating description—looking at ducks one day, Lincoln referred to how "beautifully tailored" they were.

Dinners at home with the Kirsteins could be somewhat trying, though. Astrid adored Dan Maloney, and especially admired the way he'd take over when Lincoln was tired (he sometimes even fell asleep at the table), telling enchanting anecdotes. But Fidelma cast a worrisome pall over things. She'd spend all day nervously concerned about what to serve the guests that night; once, when the water supply went off in the midst of her preparations, she had (in her own words) "a few minutes of sheer panic" until it came back on. During dinner itself Fidelma usually made only an occasional comment, though now and then she'd become abruptly animated, falling into what Lincoln labeled "acute hysteria." At the time they were both seeing the same psychiatrist, a Dr. Arthur Foxe, and when making a repetitive point, Fidelma would say over and over, "Oh, Dr. Foxe wouldn't want me—or Lincoln—to do *that*." Lincoln would grow impatient but would try hard not to show it, instead leaving the room when he felt one of her outbursts coming on.

When not obsessed with menus, Fidelma, in the country especially, would worry about the well-being of the birds and animals on their property. She'd put out walnuts in little saucers for the mice and would over-feed the winter-starved sparrows "to restore the balance of nature." The result was that mice were soon coming indoors, and occasionally at night Lincoln was awakened by one of them scurrying on or near his bed. He could regard with tenderness Fidelma spending her whole morning feeding the squirrels and bluejays in Gramercy Park but could become irritated at her "taking a week to get herself packed" for Weston.

Nor, a few years later, could he understand her refusal to have the trees, infested with caterpillars, sprayed out of fear "it may poison the birds." If the trees lost their leaves and died, Lincoln patiently pointed out, the birds would have "nothing to live in." As Fidelma grew older her gentle spirit edged closer to the bizarre: she closed down several of the bathrooms in Weston so that spiders living in the drains wouldn't be constantly disturbed.

During these same two years of 1965–66, Lincoln drew closer to Andrew and Betsy Wyeth's young son, Jamie. He'd known him since childhood, but, now in his early twenties, Jamie looked (in Lincoln's description) "golden-wheat-colored, fuzzy and clean like honey on the best bread." He thought Jamie "beautiful, charming . . . hard as nails . . . as cynical as an experienced ambassador," and "the best young painter in this country," better than his father, "less papery." Jamie had dropped out of school to paint and asked Lincoln to pose for a portrait. He agreed without realizing that Jamie was a meticulous perfectionist and that many hours of his time would be consumed in that most difficult of feats for Lincoln: being still. Remarkably, he did manage several six-hour sessions (a testament, undoubtedly, to his fondness for Jamie), and before the rather somber and severe portrait was completed early in 1966, sat for an astonishing total of 165 hours.[5]

The summer of 1966 saw the arrival on the scene of Lincoln's latest young man, one Clint Kisner, an undergraduate studying architecture at the University of Virginia, whom Lincoln found "a more satisfactory companion" than the recently departed Fred Maddox. Lincoln described Clint as "rather small, and like some odd creature out of a 19th century child's book, 'the Secret Garden', or Stevenson." He found Clint "extremely beautiful, although in no obvious sense."[6]

Clint had a boyfriend named Bob, a marine with a body that Lincoln described to Astrid as "absolutely staggering," musculated like a bronze by Giovanni da Bologna. As with all his young men, Lincoln accepted, even took for granted, that they would be sexually drawn to other young men— and want to act on the attraction. For himself, nearly sixty, Lincoln seemed primarily interested in affectionate cuddling and fondling, coupled with companionship, with him playing the role of older brother-father. According to Clint, Lincoln never once had an orgasm with him and referred vaguely to some sort of "prostatic problem." They did go to the steam baths together once—Dan Maloney would give Clint a more complete tour—but Lincoln seemed more interested in watching than in participating. Clint asked him one day if he had sex with Fidelma. "Well of course," Lincoln replied, but Clint took the answer to mean during the early years of their marriage only.

As with Astrid, Lincoln showed Clint around the museums, filling his head with welcome information. He also, and without the slightest hesitation, brought the nineteen-year-old along to various events, among them the summer 1966 opening of the Arts Center at Saratoga Springs, New York (which would serve as a summer home base for NYCB). All he asked in return from Clint was that "if he didn't mind too much," to take Fidelma shopping now and then in order to give her an outing. He'd stuff hundreds of dollars into Clint's hand and suggest "somewhere like Henri Bendel," her favorite store. Fidelma would dutifully go along on the planned excursion but could never find anything that she liked well enough to buy. She preferred garments from the 1940s—clothes that were distinctly out of style but may have represented to her, in fantasy, a time when she was far more happily alive.

When Lincoln took Clint to Mina's house, she ignored him, as she usually did Fidelma; neither was a "proper" companion for her important brother. Mina was now over seventy, and starchier than in her youth. She bought herself a maroon-colored Rolls-Royce limousine and would sit in the back dressed in silk brocade and sables. For one of Lincoln's galas—the 1972 Stravinsky Festival, say—she would throw elaborately elegant parties—beluga caviar, Russian vodka frozen in blocks of ice, the finest champagne. Arriving at one such occasion at the Stanhope Hotel in New York (where she kept an apartment), Mina came up to Clint and said, "Oh, I didn't know you were here"—and promptly walked away. Clint protested the mistreatment to Lincoln. Well, Lincoln said, "she's a tigress," and when Clint said he didn't want to be around her, Lincoln benignly told him that that was just fine.

Lincoln's return to writing included several plays. One of them—which eventually came to be titled *White House Happening* and was about Abraham Lincoln—he sent to Bob Chapman, whose position at Harvard as a tenured professor in charge of the well-equipped Loeb Theater Lincoln had (through his friendship with Harry Levin) largely been responsible for. Whether out of a sense of obligation or because he genuinely admired the play (or some combination thereof), Chapman worked with Lincoln on several sets of revisions during the latter part of 1966 and into 1967. During the process Lincoln went through the writer's usual discouragements and elations. At one point he felt confident that Menotti would want the script for the Spoleto Festival in 1968; at another he felt "pulverized and paralyzed" and thought the script "quite hopeless."[7]

He finally felt the play was in good-enough shape—"better than [John] Drinkwater's 'Abraham Lincoln' and [Robert] Sherwood's piece"— to show it to a few other friends. Nobody raved, but nobody told him to bury it either—and that included Auden and Dickie Buckle. Even Harry Levin, as astute a critic as anyone plying the trade, wrote back that he "was deeply interested by the play—it has life and fire," though he did think the second half "overwritten." This was encouragement enough to set up a reading in early June 1967 and, following that, a summer production at the Loeb, with its semiprofessional repertory company.

The members of the company that summer included Kathryn Walker (currently getting an MA in Celtic); John Lithgow, who'd graduated from Harvard two months before; Tommy Lee Jones, still an undergraduate; Laurence Senelick, who would become a scholar and professor of drama; and Paul Michael Glaser, later famous in the TV series *Starsky and Hutch*. The auditioning, Senelick recalls, was "unnerving . . . not a muscle of Kirstein's face moved. He resembled a bald eagle following the darting of a salmon he meant to have for dinner."

Neither Senelick nor Glaser was cast, but the others, all gifted future stars, were (Lithgow as Lincoln, Walker as Mary Todd, Jones as John Hay). Lincoln himself paid to have Karinska design costumes for the two women in the play, and he brought along John Braden, who'd done work for the New York City Ballet, to design the production. Lincoln decided to direct himself, a mistake on several grounds: objectivity, inexperience (he'd directed operas but not plays), and stress. At the beginning of rehearsals, as is usually the way, all was conviviality, with Lincoln joining the cast for postmortems over ouzo.

But Lincoln as a director left something to be desired. Once the actors put aside their scripts and began to "play" the scenes, it became obvious that several were merely didactic and that others needed work. Rather than fix the script—it had gone stale for him by this point—Lincoln took to giving the actors lectures about the historical context of the play, with just enough side allusions to the affinity between himself and the martyred president to alert the cast that something had gone seriously awry.

Before long Lincoln was drinking heavily, openly carrying around a bottle of vodka, and making heavy-handed moves on Tommy Lee Jones. He also brought in sheets of Lincoln stamps, distributing them to the cast and advising the actors to "meditate" on them. According to Clint Kisner, who'd accompanied him to Cambridge, Lincoln would also lick the stamps on the street and stick them on passerbys' foreheads—"advertising," he'd mutter. His emotional deterioration climaxed when he came at John Braden with a pineapple in one hand and a knife in the other. He threw the pineapple, and Braden caught it and threw it back, not knowing if it was all a joke. But then Lincoln looked as if he was going to come at him with the knife, and Braden fled the theater, hiding for three hours in a nearby church. There was also a terrible scene in Lincoln's hotel when he walked into the wrong room and urinated on a woman asleep in the bed.

A week before the play was due to open, with national press coverage expected, Lincoln was committed to Baldpate Sanitarium in Georgetown, outside Boston. Bob Chapman took over last-minute direction of the play. It *was* widely reviewed—in publications as varied as the *San Francisco Chronicle, Newsweek,* the *Boston Globe,* and the *New York Times*—but with the verdict uniform: "an often embarrassing evening." The *Times* kindly settled for what was mostly a plot summary, plus an offhanded compliment to John Lithgow as capable of having "a future in the theatre." No reviewer suggested a comparable future for Lincoln.

His breakdown was the most serious to date and his suffering the most acute. Lincoln wanted neither Fidelma nor Dan Maloney to witness it and instead asked Clint Kisner to move to Massachusetts and serve as his contact with the outside world. Lincoln's stay at Baldpate would last a full seven weeks, but his resilience was remarkable; within a short time after the breakdown, Clint was able to take him, on some days, for drives in the country; once they stopped at Walker Evans's studio at Annisquam, at another time, at Hyatt Mayor's country house.

By August 19 (the play had opened August 7), Lincoln was writing an entirely coherent letter, and in his own distinctive style, to Morton Baum to tell him that he'd "been seriously ill again. This is a cause of great distress for me. Each time I say: it can't happen again. Each time it is worse. But at least this time I have expert care and I am now well on the road to recovery." He was writing Baum primarily to inform him of two interlocking decisions that he'd made: "I am going to resign as *active* director of the ballet company as soon as is practical. I want Jacques d'Amboise in a strong position. . . . I will be around, of course, but Jacques has to take hold, and the succession must be *apparent* and *inevitable*." It remained to be seen whether Lincoln would stick to his resolve or change his mind about Jacques's suitability to become his heir apparent.

Dan Maloney brought Lincoln home on September 22. As much from reflex as from any intrinsic interest, he was within days trying to come up with new projects, great and small, to remobilize his energies: a dance history for Praeger, a monograph on Tchelitchev's *Hide-and-Seek* for MoMA, a revision of an earlier play on Gurdjieff for whoever would take it (no one would). The wheels were spinning but wanted oil. Two months after returning home he still lacked the energy and concentration needed for any genuinely new undertaking. As for the old—the ballet—he confessed to Alex Colville that his work in that regard went on "as maintenance rather than creation, and I look on it more as duty and habit than any real satisfaction. In the meantime, I fill my time with dark thoughts."

To Clint Kisner he wrote a sweet confessional, essentially begging off from any deep involvement: "It does no good in burdening other people with private problems which they have no real chance of lightening or solving. . . . I know I am difficult and unstable, and as time goes on, possibly more and more remote . . . you aren't set yet; you are still quite open . . . in any case, be a good boy, and don't take pot more than ten times a week; no LSD. Casual fucking for fun: that's the ticket."

But Clint persisted, and Lincoln sometimes talked to him on the phone and occasionally allowed a visit. He tried to explain that basically he was seeing no one, that he was living "a hospital-life in my own home," and that "Fidelma is the only one willing or able to cope with me, except Dan who can cope with everything." It didn't help that their beloved cat Nanook had to be put to sleep ("a real blow and I never want to have another cat"—though he was to have many) or that workmen, because of trouble with the pipes, were constantly tramping through the house, interrupting the peace and quiet. "I am no fun," Lincoln wrote Clint, "I feel old and mean, cranky and unsympathetic and I hate to be seen as I have difficulty with my walking, due to the drugs the doctor thinks I have to take." A little later, though, after some sort of argument with a returned Fred Maddox, Lincoln again picked up with Clint as a companion.

Lincoln gradually began to improve and to find enough preoccupying work to take his mind off the worrisome possibility of a recurrence. Through much of the next year he stayed mostly at home, devoting himself to compiling the pictures and writing the accompanying text for the book that became *Movement and Metaphor.* As he put it to Andy and Betsy Wyeth, "I don't go out much and apart from the theater where I work, keep to myself and write history, looking over to see what has happened of use in the ballet in the last four hundred years."

The book came into being almost accidentally. Nancy Reynolds, a young editor at Praeger, had for five years been in the NYCB corps and had then gone on to study art history at Columbia. Praeger was known for its art books, but Fred Praeger, learning of Nancy's background, suggested a series of books on dance. Nancy called Alex Schierman, Lincoln's new secretary, to ask her to suggest some names and topics; Alex phoned back to say that Lincoln himself had a book in mind that he'd been wanting for years to write. Thus was born *Movement and Metaphor,* Nancy Reynolds's very first edited book (she would go on to become a distinguished dance historian).

The book would take almost three years to complete, though Lincoln was doing other things at the same time (SAB, for example, went through a major move into the Juilliard building). The book as shaped wasn't designed for the general reader but (as Lincoln put it) "for those who, self-chosen, enjoy ballet. Enjoyment may be sharpened if they learn, in some depth, what they watch, through some of its history." After a fifty-page introduction describing the integral elements of ballet production (choreography, music, decor, et al.), Lincoln chose fifty ballets spanning 1573 to 1968 that "define tradition at a given period or extend it through some crucial enlargement."[8]

He well understood that every masterwork, however original or shocking at first viewing, contains "echoes or memories" from the past and contributes to a recognizable continuity of tradition. He also understood the built-in limitations of writing about the phenomenon of movement, even when the reader was familiar with the music employed and even in combination with illustrations (of which *Movement and Metaphor* had many). Lincoln's aim was not to write about actual performance—the dance itself—but to set the art of dance in the historical context of a given period.

For the years 1928–68, Lincoln chose only six ballets as sufficiently seminal to warrant inclusion. Three of the six were by Balanchine (*Apollon Musagète, Agon,* and, added belatedly, *Orpheus*), one (*Jardin aux Lilas*) by Tudor, one *(Fancy Free)* by Robbins—the latter a late addition ("Which is his KEY work? There is none; he stopped before he started," Lincoln wrote Buckle in 1968)—and one the very recent (October 1968) Freddie Ashton ballet *Enigma Variations* (which almost didn't make the cut, Lincoln worrying over and over whether any of Ashton's work could be said to have "changed history").

Nancy Reynolds had heard stories about Lincoln's moods and blow-ups, and she steeled herself for at least one major eruption. But none ever came. Throughout the working process she found Lincoln "so generous, so kind, so interested in me"; though they never became actual friends, she credits him with being responsible for her interest in dance history and her own subsequent career. As Lincoln worked on the book during 1968 and into 1969, he kept changing his mind—typical of writers, not to mention manic-depressives—about whether he'd written "the best book about the dance ever done" or had, "due to my ignorance, lack of consideration and sheer education," produced a useless piece of rubbish. He wrote each essay some five times, and in the process began to lose perspective: "I don't know what to cut; maybe the whole book," he told Nancy Reynolds at one point.

When *Movement and Metaphor* finally appeared in print in 1970, Lincoln complained to Praeger that the book was being "shabbily merchandised." He himself spent some fifteen thousand dollars on ads, but even so sales and reviews were minimal—all but inevitable for a monographic, scholarly work aimed at a specialized audience. Of the few reviews that did appear, all were highly favorable, with the prestigious *Times Literary Supplement* calling the book "absolutely essential."

February 1968 saw the unexpected death of Morton Baum at the relatively young age of sixty-three. A benevolent tyrant, Baum had done more than any other individual to hold City Center together and to provide a reliable if frugal home for the New York City Ballet. As Lincoln wrote Astrid Zydower, "We lost the man who has been supporting us for twenty years." City Center found itself near bankruptcy just as its twenty-fifth anniversary season was approaching. On top of that, the ballet orchestra demanded a substantial pay raise and the musicians' union threatened a strike. Lincoln reported to Alex Colville that he'd been working "three times as hard to keep things from flying apart. Fortunately, habit is stronger than volition."[9]

Despite these troubles NYCB was more secure than ever as the chief occupant of the State Theater, even though Lincoln Center eschewed any financial obligation for new productions. That remained the responsibility of NYCB itself, and it continued to rely primarily, in lieu of many wealthy donors, on the box office. Fortunately the audience for ballet continued to grow, and in 1968 alone enough money was forthcoming to allow for four new Balanchine ballets. One of them, *Metastasis and Pithoprakta*, Lincoln regarded with bemused detachment; "as far as I can judge," he wrote Astrid, "it's about marijuana, heroin and the effects of LSD on the human body."

The ballet featured Suzanne Farrell and Arthur Mitchell. Lincoln's early admiration for Mitchell had somewhat soured; "he is spoiled, silly and won't work," Lincoln complained to Astrid. "Balanchine said if he wasn't colored, no one would look at him." Whether Balanchine ever said such a thing—Lincoln was quite capable of inventing or exaggerating other people's remarks to suit some immediate purpose—Lincoln's own feelings about Mitchell would shift again; he was soon calling him "a black Balanchine" and helping him get the Dance Theater of Harlem, which he referred to as "the first mutation out of Balanchine's work," off the ground. It's worth noting, too, that when the dance historian Olga Maynard interviewed a number of Mitchell's dancers, she concluded that the School of American Ballet "and ONLY SAB (according to these Negro dancers) gave a true and unprejudiced ballet education."

Lincoln was much more taken with two of Balanchine's other ballets during 1968: *Requiem Canticles* and a new version of *Slaughter on Tenth Avenue*. (It had originally appeared in the Rodgers and Hart musical *On Your Toes* in 1936.) Martin Luther King, Jr.'s assassination had greatly upset both Lincoln and Balanchine, and the *Canticles*, a solemn ceremonial to music by Stravinsky, was meant as a tribute to the black leader. As for *Slaughter*, Lincoln found it an "absolutely amazing" period piece.

Though he continued to feel "excessively nervous about our future," Lincoln was encouraged by the emergence, with Balanchine's encouragement, of other choreographic talent within the company. John Clifford, a principal dancer, seemed especially promising, and when Clive Barnes, the newly appointed dance critic of the *New York Times*, panned one of Clifford's early efforts, Lincoln protested angrily; Barnes was gracious in reply, but the two would tangle off and on for years to come. "I almost had a reconciliation with Clive Barnes," Lincoln wrote to Buckle in 1968, "but avoided it at the last moment."

The brilliant dancing of Suzanne Farrell was another source of comfort to Lincoln as he struggled to find the money for new ballets that would feature her. She became everything to Balanchine, a source of inspiration and a consuming object of adoration. In 1968 Farrell starred in three of his four new ballets, and offstage she and Balanchine were constantly in one another's company, creating considerable resentment among NYCB's other ballerinas. Balanchine moved out of the apartment he'd shared with Tanny Le Clercq, now permanently paralyzed from the waist down, and then obtained a Mexican divorce from her. But Farrell had by then fallen in love with another young dancer, Paul Mejia, and to Balanchine's great distress, married him. Mejia's career had been on the rise, but Balanchine now denied him roles. A crisis point was reached when Mejia failed to be cast in the third movement of *Symphony in C* and Farrell sent Balanchine an ultimatum that they would both resign if Paul didn't dance the part. Balanchine ignored the ultimatum and substituted *Stars and Stripes* for *Symphony in C.* Farrell abruptly left the company.

Some of the other ballerinas quietly rejoiced, but Farrell's departure had a seismic effect on the company as a whole, leading to a slew of recastings and sensationalistic press coverage. Lincoln was in England at the time and felt "horribly upset" at the news that they'd lost "the best dancer we have ever had." "I have no sympathy for him," Lincoln wrote Jerry Robbins. The company's chief lighting designer, Ron Bates, "got good and drunk" with Balanchine one night, and Bates reported to Lincoln that Balanchine "said he had behaved abominably and would of course let Paul [Mejia] stay and he should not have behaved this way anyway." "You can imagine what a relief that news was to everybody," Lincoln reported to Fidelma, "not the least I think to him [Balanchine], as he was being consumed by it. Anyway, we all hope he will stick to what he said."

He didn't. Mejia was not invited back. Lincoln stayed out of the controversy, though privately he referred to Farrell and Mejia as "two deluded children." They joined Maurice Béjart's company for a time; when it danced in New York in 1971 Lincoln found the performances "pretentious and boring" and felt that Farrell "floundered about like a lovely bird in an empty cage."[10]

The distressing departure of Farrell aside, Lincoln had, that month of April 1969, the most enjoyable vacation he'd had in years. With Dan Maloney and Fidelma as companions, he avoided seeing anyone in England other than Astrid Zydower and Dickie Buckle. Instead he went constantly to the ballet and theater. He found Olivier's staging of *Love's Labours Lost* "truly magnificent" and thought his friend John Gielgud's *Forty Years On* was "unadulterated raving genius from beginning to end"—whereas Nicol Williamson's Hamlet was "sheer shit from beginning to end." But best of all was Danny La Rue, "the greatest female impersonator since Mae West," in *Passionella*—"the CLOTHES, the KINDNESS, the humor, and the LACK of sick sex" ("sick" going undefined).

As for the ballet, Lincoln was merciless about the hugely heralded partnership of Rudolf Nureyev and Margot Fonteyn, declaring the couple, with high-spirited hyperbole, "the worst thing that ever happened to British Ballet." He thought the Royal Ballet's Anthony Dowell "danced Nureyev off the stage" (Rudi "works his ass off, too, but chiefly at the Vauxhall Baths"). As for Fonteyn, Lincoln felt certain that her "great affection for Rudi in the Nudi" had demoralized the whole company. He was all for firing Margot, exiling Rudi, and "searching the colonies" for real talent.

In the meantime he offered an equally hyperbolic opinion of Karel Reisz's film *Isadora*. He declared it "the best ever produced about a performing artist" and—contrary to his reputation for despising and denouncing all forms of "modern dance"—characterized Duncan as "a genius who used her body to open up hitherto undreamed of possibilities in theatrical movement," despite her disdain for ballet and her refusal to let her pupils so much as enter the Bolshoi Theatre lest they be tainted.

As for Vanessa Redgrave, who played Duncan in the film, Lincoln declared that she "dances better in her little finger than Margot ever did." Not only was she "physically glorious, but she dances with a virtuosity, freedom, largeness of gesture and supreme pathos that one has not seen in free-dance since Martha Graham was a girl." Lincoln partly credited Redgrave's performance with the fact that she'd once studied with Marie "Mim" Rambert, a pioneering figure in English ballet, and soon, in her old age, to become a dear friend of Lincoln's.

His marvelous vacation in London was immediately followed by an NYCB spring 1969 season that had no new Balanchine ballets but featured *Dances at a Gathering*, a premiere by the long-absent Jerome Robbins. The ballet, done to piano pieces by Chopin, was a great triumph with critics and audiences alike; Lincoln thought it "magnificent." He reported to Buckle that Balanchine had told Jerry that he was "a GREAT choreographer . . . he really admires Jerry more than anyone." None of which made Lincoln like Jerry any better as a person, but he delighted in his return to the company, and wrote to tell him so.

In response Jerry thanked him "so very deeply for your support and interest and belief. I'm very happy and comfortable over at the State Theatre, and you have played quite a major part in making me feel so." Despite Jerry's declaration that he was "deeply interested and concerned with the City Ballet," Lincoln doubted the extent of his commitment; "he says he will spend a fortnight in Saratoga [NYCB's summer home], but I bet 'Fiddler On The Roof' [the recent, hugely successful Broadway musical, for which Robbins did the choreography] will be staged for Ulan Bator or Brisbane, first." But no, Robbins followed through in short order with two more highly successful ballets: *In the Night* and *The Goldberg Variations* (which Lincoln described as "a well-deserved triumph").

During the early seventies the basic patterns and commitments of Lincoln's life held firm. A few events—the second trip to the Soviet Union and the extraordinary Stravinsky Festival in 1972—stood out, but the external outlines remained constant. He slept little, rose early, consistently saw a small contingent of intimate "Goosies"—Fidelma, Cadmus, and Jon Anderson (as of the mid-sixties, Paul's genial, sociable companion), Dan Maloney, and Jensen Yow—and when he wasn't attending to the assorted needs of the ballet company, contented himself with various writing projects.[11]

That general pattern still allowed for plenty of variation. Any number of guests crossed the thresholds of the houses in Weston and at Nineteenth Street. Unexpected projects would periodically loom, be enthusiastically explored or quickly negated, have long lives, single viewings, or no life at all. New faces came on the scene—dancers, painters, sculptors, photographers (or even just Lads)—and were received according to the uniqueness of their carriage or wares, to Lincoln's moral state or his lithium level, to the degree they stirred up poignant memories of Muriel Draper or Tom Mabry. How each was treated and judged could vary unpredictably from brusque dismissal to great kindness—or, yet more typically, one could be embraced on Monday, cut dead on Tuesday, casually hailed on Wednesday, reembraced on Thursday. Unless one was a preestablished Goosie, to place oneself in the line of Lincoln's gaze was tantamount to spinning the revolver chamber for Russian roulette.

Thus when the painter Barnett Newman, who wanted to do decor for the ballet, announced in the *New York Times* that the Louvre was a mess of junk and Ingres couldn't draw, Lincoln (by his own account) "rather ostentatiously refused to be introduced to him." One "can't afford to be seen with such people," he chirpily wrote Alex Colville. After Buckle, in a memoir, published some of Lincoln's remarks without getting his permission, he refused for four years to see him; Dickie, Lincoln wrote Marie Rambert, "seems to be striving for all the negative virtues and the more boring vices." Yet even as he cut him, Lincoln blithely proposed to Buckle that "we can still be mutually useful to each other, and isn't that as good a base for an occasional contact as anything else?"

A profoundly serious man who claimed to find nothing funny, Lincoln had a biting wit and could keep sparkling pace with the best of the campy ironists; his letters to Dickie Buckle, for example, are an epistolary triumph of hilarious, scintillating mockery. His increasing distaste for large parties that specialized in bite-size hors d'oeuvres and conversation didn't hold for entirely mute encounters at the Turkish baths. Small-scale dinners featuring the eminent or notorious were also welcome, and he and Fidelma hosted a significant number of them—like the dinner for Patricia and George Harewood that included Maria Callas ("a professional star, working at it twenty-five hours a day," was Lincoln's judgment, "but with a warmth that even dulls her steel-razor will. A sacred monster, but a sympathetic one").

His opinions of people could veer off spectacularly. After years of praising Andrew Wyeth's work, he privately characterized him in 1972 as "the Sir Joshua Reynolds of the Nixonian Era" and added, "I do not think his role as innocent gets any more attractive. Every so often he manages something good . . . [he is] now cocooned . . . in a self-perpetuating prestige factory." He could even abruptly shift gears about whole countries. In 1970 he praised England as "the best run country in the world, with the highest sense of public and private service," and in the next breath denounced it as "a feudal society in desuetude, with no real re-structuring since the Norman Conquest and none likely in the future."

Lincoln would weep unabashedly at funerals, yet in public generally presented himself as the reincarnation of a stoic, scowling Roman senator. This easy cohabitation and acceptance of traditionally opposing qualities within himself is part of what makes him feel like a contemporary figure; he was, to risk a non sequitur, what we might call a "postmodern" person, though the term (if not the temperament) had not yet come into being. When Lincoln denounced those who championed "self-expression" in the arts, he was at base articulating the conviction that the much-vaunted Self—regnant attribute in this (purported) land of the "individual"—was a suspect category, our "selves" being no more than mere kaleidoscopes of shifting, highly contingent fragments, inchoate shards of experience and memory.

Still, on some matters Lincoln was single-minded, his opinion unshaded and unwavering through time. He considered the "hideous" war in Vietnam, for example, "disgusting" from start to finish. As regarded City Center, he consistently tried to preserve its "basic community and social purpose": high-quality performances at "ticket prices within the economic reach of the whole community." As regarded dance, he never wavered in his insistence on the superiority of ballet over other forms, dismissing most of the current dance scene as trivial. Paul Taylor was the one major exception; Lincoln not only admired his work (though with some peripheral complaints) but felt close to him personally and helped him from time to time financially.

But most contemporary choreographers got short shrift. He airily assured Marie Rambert, for example, that the heralded Eliot Feld, "is the poor-man's version of Jerome Robbins, who himself is the rich-man's version of Balanchine." Feld got off rather lightly in comparison with some other touted dancer-choreographers of the day: Lincoln dismissed Béjart as "merely an exploiter of previous innovation" and Alvin Ailey as "having a big success with rather flashy popular numbers which have a sort of tasteless vitality." He thought the Joffrey company "has some good dancers, and a brash style which can be rather appealing," but he "never felt Joffrey had much of a mind." As for Merce Cunningham, whom Lincoln liked personally, and John Cage, Lincoln banished them as "minor anarchs, suicidally inclined and self-restricted." And he and Mim Rambert competed in their correspondence in denigrating Agnes de

Mille—"Agony de Mille" or "Ag the Hag"; Mim called her "envious, self-admiring and even self-exalting"; Lincoln dismissed her "vicious, resentful temperament."

What these disparate dancers had in common, in Lincoln's stern view, was their fatuous insistence on "self-expression" and their inability to see that the profession of dance contains for a faithless culture "the last vestiges of a priesthood." "I am increasingly mystical," Lincoln wrote Astrid in 1971, "about the vocation of the dancer; it is one of the last ways open to Western man, to realize the Self, without selfishness." He felt that he himself was " 'doomed' yet 'chosen' "—meaning, he had a mission and would be allowed to fulfill it, but at a high price.

As Lincoln became more and more involved in the early seventies in his own writing projects, he multitasked with a vengeance. On the same day he could send off a batch of letters ranging from a query to a professor at Chandigarh University about whether a book reference to "Dorgieff" could in fact be Gurdjieff, to a lengthy enumeration to director Tony Richardson of the minimal requirements for his planned film on Nijinsky. From 1971 to 1974 he worked simultaneously on several books at once, books that would be published during the two-year period 1973–75: a history of the New York City Ballet in the form of diary entries (newly composed) with commentary; a massive work on Nadelman; a slender picture book and accompanying essay on the Augustus Saint-Gaudens monument in Boston to Robert Gould Shaw and the black troops he commanded during the Civil War (produced to appear simultaneously with a Saint-Gaudens exhibition at the Metropolitan Museum of Art); and a major work, complete with many previously unknown photographs, on Nijinsky that would establish the dancer as a choreographic genius as well. On top of all that Lincoln turned out the occasional article for publications ranging from *The Nation* to the *New York Review of Books* on topics as diverse as "Musical Life in Soviet Russia," "The Photographs of Thomas Eakins," and "On Stravinsky."[12]

Elie Nadelman, gorgeously published in 1973 (the year of Lincoln's sixty-fifth birthday) by the Eakins Press, represented the culmination of twenty-five years "involved in salvaging, studying and promulgating" Nadelman's work. Before the appearance of Lincoln's impressive study, based on a considerable amount of original research, only a few articles had appeared in English about the Polish sculptor, and there had been no retrospective of his work since MoMA's limited show in 1948. In both his lengthy foreword and his hundred-page "Life and Work" essay, Lincoln tackled the intricacies of Nadelman's lyrical, ironic sculpture and the mysteries of his public reputation, with weighty scholarship and in a lucid style that suffered only occasionally from lapses into the arcane or the overly compressed.

Lincoln emphasized that Nadelman's art was rooted in continuities, that his "bravura elegance and technical virtuosity" reworked rather than rejected tradition—in contrast to current pop, op, minimalist, or mixed media practitioners who self-consciously repudiated historical precedent. But like, he might have added, Balanchine's reworking of the classical tradition in ballet. That emphasis on the importance, the necessity even, of historical continuity reflected Lincoln's own set of values and priorities and goes some way toward accounting for his having been drawn to Nadelman's work in the first place. (One problem with Lincoln's text, in fact, is that it isn't always clear whether a given opinion—the statement, say, that the sculpture represents glosses "on man's fall from grace"—is Nadelman's or Kirstein's). The book, like the sculptor, received little attention when it appeared, but it did share the 1974 College Art Association Mather Award for criticism.

Soon after *Nadelman*, Lincoln published *The New York City Ballet* (which Knopf would reissue five years later, in 1978, as the expanded *Thirty Years: The New York City Ballet*). The book consisted of invented (though Lincoln presented them as "real") diary entries which he used as takeoff points for discussing selected moments in the history of the company he and Balanchine had founded. Lincoln emphasized that part of NYCB's history of which he was most proud: the ballets in which he himself had a direct hand, and the determination from the start to create a distinctly American company. At once highly subjective, opinionated, brilliant, and unreliable, *New York City Ballet* is a stimulating brew and fun to read ("haute vulgarization," was Lincoln's own characterization of it).

While still getting the Nadelman and NYCB books to press, Lincoln was invited by Knopf to write an account of Nijinsky's life that would include photographs, drawings, and paintings. Lincoln needed no persuading. The known representations of Nijinsky—and Lincoln would dig up many that were unknown—had never been collected into a single book and few had been properly reproduced. Along with commentary by Lincoln, the volume would reprint as appendixes two famous essays on Nijinsky by Edwin Denby and Jacques Rivière.[13]

Lincoln plunged strenuously into preparing the Nijinsky book, surveying all the known representations of him and reading all the published literature written about him. He concluded that many of the dance sequences, particularly those done by Baron de Meyer in 1911, when properly laid out (as they hadn't been before) in logical sequence, were able to give a real sense of Nijinsky's movement while dancing. As for the prose commentary on his life, Lincoln decided—again stressing his belief in the continuity of art production—that *Faune*, though indeed full of "fantastically original and revolutionary implications," did nonetheless derive from "something other than a virginal inspiration." He thought two sources for Nijinsky's ballet were especially important: Alexander Gorsky's production of *La Fille du Pharaon* in 1905–6, and Fokine's *Cléo-*

pâtre, in which Nijinsky had danced. Their work was not in itself "wildly important," but Nijinsky's awareness and incorporation of it went a long way toward proving that he was "a man of thought, an analytical intelligence" and not simply a "genius" who relied on "inspiration."

Unlike Fokine, whose innovations, Lincoln maintained, "were far more stylistic than spatial—he ransacked one period after another, as far as the history of costume and decoration went"—Nijinsky had "an underlying sense of Superior Order, which was not rhetorical or decorative." Unlike Fokine and Gorsky, moreover, Nijinsky took the revolutionary step toward "dance autonomy and imagining new dimensions of measuring space by time (in steps)"; that achievement, in Lincoln's view, put him in the ranks of the great innovators ("like Joyce, Brancusi, Picasso, etc.").

In 1972 Mim Rambert, who'd been part of Diaghilev's company and had known Nijinsky well, published her autobiography, *Quicksilver*; in it she'd written that Nijinsky, "more than anyone else," had "revolutionized the classical ballet and was fifty years ahead of his time." Lincoln agreed with that estimate but not with Mim's contention that Nijinsky "introduced completely new principles." He and Mim, then eighty-six but with a keen memory, were already friends, and he gave her half (one thousand dollars) of his advance to serve as a consultant to him while he worked to complete the Nijinsky book (Lincoln gave the other thousand to the Dance Library).

Both in June and October 1973, he spent a week in London so he could talk with Mim on a daily basis. They'd spend mornings together, Lincoln taking notes (which survive) of their conversations; afterward Mim would lie down for a rest, while Lincoln, energized, would race back to his hotel (usually the plush Connaught) to type up her comments and conversation. Mim's net impression of Nijinsky was of "an intelligent, simple, non-verbal but extremely conscious person, with a considerable depth of feeling, but naive." Lincoln infused that estimate with his own ardor. He even decided that Balanchine's work was "a logical marriage of Petipa AND Nijinsky." He felt that Balanchine recognized only Petipa as his "teacher and master because he never saw a Nijinsky work, and only *Faune* in a later recension not well danced." But Lincoln now became convinced that "without Nijinsky's work with Stravinsky, Balanchine's own repertory would never have come into being."

Lincoln talked very little with Mim about Nijinsky's sexuality; he thought she was "too prim" to take on the subject. Besides, Lincoln was determined to avoid gossip in his book, and in any case didn't think Nijinsky's homosexuality was "really important." Lincoln viewed him as a "polytrop, capable in all situations," definitely attracted to women, and with the barest sense of guilt about sex of any kind (except for masturbation), a man who put up with but didn't enjoy Diaghilev's physical attentions. Lincoln interpreted Nijinsky's ballet *Jeux* as "an attempt at determining an objective, mature, and simple sexual acceptance of any-and every-thing." Unlike Nureyev, who promulgated a single role—himself—Nijinsky was psychically advanced enough to become "a genius of personification, not of impersonation or personality. He had no personality, as such."

As Lincoln labored away on the Nijinsky book during much of 1972 and 1973, he was fortunate in being able to rely for his ordinary needs on his inner circle of fellow "Goosies." Each of the "Goosies," except Fidelma, had professional lives of their own and were available on a part-time basis only; yet within those limits, each was devoted. And Fidelma regarded tending to Lincoln's daily needs as her main reason for staying alive.[14]

Her brother Paul, well-known as a painter but not well off, had settled into domesticity with Jon Anderson, a singer and actor (and the model for most of Paul's later drawings). In 1974 Lincoln decided to build them a house just below his on the large parcel of land he owned in Weston. Lovely as the house (designed by Clint Kisner) was, Lincoln never turned over the deed, leaving Paul and Jon feeling somewhat insecure and dependent (though he did leave Paul the house in his will). The proximity of the two homes also meant that Fidelma became their responsibility when Lincoln wasn't in residence (and when he was, he usually leaned on Paul and Jon to prepare meals over the weekend). Paul enjoyed cooking, but not *having* to cook; "those two-day weekends," he complained to a friend, "are by no means vacations. . . . The menus are . . . problematic; there are so few things that Lincoln likes." Actually, except for preferring fish, Lincoln was largely indifferent to food and usually gobbled down whatever was put in front of him.

Fidelma, too, sometimes cooked, but she would worry so about whether the spinach was sufficiently washed or the fish properly boned that she made everyone else anxious or impatient. Going back and forth from country to city was also a protracted ordeal; in October 1973 Fidelma finally got packed up to move back from the country at 2:30 a.m.—and then took six weeks to unpack. To deal with her increasing periods of "nervousness," with worrying herself ragged about minor matters, her psychiatrist advised her to get out of the house as much as possible, even if only to take a walk. In the city she continued with fair frequency to go with Lincoln to ballet premieres and other events of importance to him, her pronounced devotion overcoming her own anxious reluctance to socialize.

Dan Maloney remained close to both Lincoln and Fidelma. He accompanied Lincoln on two of his trips to England in the early seventies and worked several days a week in the studio the Kirsteins fixed up for him by consolidating two rooms and putting in a skylight at the top of the Nineteenth Street house. As for Jensen, he commuted daily from his home in New Jersey to the Morgan Library, where he'd become chief conservator. Jens was highly thought of at the Morgan; it was he who was entrusted with taking a large-scale show of manuscripts to the Royal Library in Stockholm and who became part of the team of American specialists that helped to save books in the aftermath of the Florence floods in 1967. Despite his full life, Jens never neglected his relationship with Lincoln and Fidelma; indeed, after Dan decided to give up the top-floor studio in the Nineteenth Street house, Jens took it over.

While working on his Nijinsky book, Lincoln received word on September 19, 1973, that W. H. Auden, the friend he'd come consistently to admire above all others, had died at age sixty-six (Lincoln's exact age). Lincoln wrote Alex Colville that Auden had been "the strongest influence in my life since 1937" (before that date, he would probably have named his father, Mina, Muriel Draper, and Gurdjieff). Yet he felt no grief at Auden's death, certain that his friend "did not want to live." Auden had recently expressed the fear that he'd die alone in his ramshackle New York apartment and had returned to Oxford, where he'd promptly been robbed. If his end was sad, Lincoln felt certain that "the glory of his verse and the wisdom of his presence" would survive: "He was a magician who continually rehabilitated the commonplace. He undercut pomposity by his common-sense and no-nonsense candor."

Lincoln finished his Nijinsky book in December 1973 and gave it the title *Nijinsky Dancing*. The book would be large enough (a foot square) to allow sequences of photographs actually to "breathe on the page," and would be expensive (thirty-five dollars—all but unprecedented at the time for a single volume). Publication was planned for the fall of 1974, but Lincoln was late in returning corrected proofs and since spring was thought a bad time to publish a "picture" book, *Nijinsky Dancing* was postponed.

The year spanning 1974–75 marked a set of significant developments for Lincoln personally and for NYCB as a company. After yet another nerve-racking crisis over City Center finances, NYCB received an eight-hundred-thousand-dollar grant from the New York State Arts Council in the spring of 1974, easing most fears of cutbacks and closures (even though the Ford Foundation grant wasn't renewed on quite the same generous terms of ten years earlier). At the same time Balanchine, who turned seventy in January 1974, was "full of beans"; on top of his recent 1973 ballet *Cortège Hongrois*, he was at work in 1974 on a host of choreographic projects. The year had begun with the premiere of his *Variations pour une porte et un soupir* to an electronic score by Pierre Henri; Lincoln thought it "a tremendous and very frightening work" suggestive of a chaotic world and of nature's revenge—"the door is shut on our miserable sighs." Then, in mid-1974, Balanchine, working with Alexandra Danilova, who remembered well the Maryinsky version, presented a revised *Coppélia*, which won great favor. Still full of energy, he decided on a Ravel Festival for spring 1975—a festival for which he would create no fewer than eight new ballets.[15]

By then, at her initiative, Suzanne Farrell (but not her husband) had rejoined the company, dancing better than ever and again providing inspiration for Balanchine's genius. Farrell's return marked a minor revolution in the company ("a certain amount of ruffled feathers," as Lincoln put it to Mim Rambert), some of it circumstantial. With Edward Villella in traction from an injury and Violette Verdy suffering from stubborn tendinitis (inflammation of the Achilles tendon), Balanchine had promoted several young dancers to principal roles. At the same time (1975), greater institutional clarification took place. SAB's small board was expanded to allow for more aggressive fund-raising, and the ballet company, previously under the aegis of City Center, created a board of its own. Thereafter, school and company operated independently, in terms of finances and governance, though with obvious artistic linkages.

All of which again put Lincoln to thinking about the issue of the succession. Robbins had recently behaved so badly during rehearsals— "self-indulgent, wasteful of time, indecisive as to taste"—that Lincoln wrote Mim, "I promise you he will never inherit our company. . . . Jacques d'Amboise will. . . . Jacques is at the end of his career as a dancer, but only at the start as a teacher, choreographer and school director; he is purely a product of Balanchine for thirty years, and has absorbed his analysis and style. . . . Balanchine estimates that Jacques is the single classic choreographer for whom he has real respect that has ever been associated with us." Firm as Lincoln (and Balanchine) sounded, many uncertainties remained— not least whether d'Amboise would prove his worth as a choreographer.

There was also a "turnover," as it were, on the personal side. After a number of years with Clint Kisner, Lincoln became involved with another young man, Alex Nixon. They met in late fall 1973 and over the next few months saw each other for dinner and the ballet; then, early in 1974, Lincoln rather formally asked if they could become lovers. Alex said yes. "I have been sent another of those young men," Lincoln wrote Mim, "with whom God provides me at critical points in my life." Lincoln was sixty-six at the time and Alex had just turned twenty-two; but he was more fully formed, conscious of his tastes and ambitions, than Clint had been. A young banker who specialized in analyzing the financial status of independent telephone companies, Alex also had a gift for building and playing pipe organs and harpsichords. "He looks like a child," Lincoln wrote Mim, "but he behaves as if he were my older brother."[16]

His affair with Alex was interrupted, though not ended, by a medical event: early in February 1975 Lincoln was hospitalized with what the doctors described as a mild heart attack. A week after being discharged, he had a second, this time massive, attack that led to a month-long hospital stay. Among the cherished teachings he'd learned from Gurdjieff was an emphasis on "existing while being consumed" and on *conscious* suffering, using disaster against itself. And so, typically, Lincoln was soon writing witty letters from the hospital and laying plans to subvert his doctors' instructions.

"I have been told," he wrote Buckle (with whom, in their seesaw relationship, he was once again speaking), "to 'give up' the Ballet. I have been told a lot of other things and if you think I am interested in a half-ass sort of survival, you don't know me as well as I think you do. 'A little too much is just enough for me' . . . as my ancestor, Le Duc de Kirschstein zum und zu Mecklenberg-Chasid used to say. I have been told I must *never* drink hard liquor agaaaain. Well, dearie . . ." The medical news out of the way, Lincoln filled most of that letter with denouncing the Joffrey's heralded new choreographer, Gerald Arpino, and the *Times* critic, Clive Barnes (whom Lincoln had been instrumental in bringing to New York from London); and relaying juicy tidbits about Alex Nixon.

During his prolonged hospital stay, Fidelma, devoted and courageous (given her own fragility), took turns with Alex visiting every other day. Balanchine came by once or twice and, though absorbed as he was with the upcoming Ravel Festival and with his recent (awful) experience at the Paris Opéra, gave Lincoln inordinate pleasure: he'd long concealed his deep hurt at the way Balanchine—horrified at his operatic outbursts and messy breakdowns—had coolly distanced himself from personal contact.

Dickie Buckle kept Lincoln amused via long-distance mail, the two figuratively giggling over Isherwood (in Lincoln's phrase) having "come out fearlessly, proclaiming himself an 'homosexual'; not a minute too soon." One of Buckle's letters, signed "Alf," ended with these lines: "Well sir, what you done to me in the subway station the other night was not right but I enjoyed it. Do not be afraid that I will let on to Mum and Dad but a new motor-bike would be welcome. Meanwhile my lips are sealed."

Lincoln was home by early April—thirty pounds lighter. He wrote Mim that he was "as energetic as a dying jelly-fish" and felt "rather at a loss to know what to DO, since I am not supposed to Worry; which means I must choose carefully what to worry ABOUT." What he chose, of course, was the ballet company, trying to get used to the notion that it could survive for extended periods without him and to the realization "that I also have been a weight and drive people mad." The company was currently playing in Washington, DC, and when he learned that all the "great ones who have made such a horror of Southeast Asia" had attended the opening, he felt grateful that he "didn't have to be polite to Kissinger." Balanchine, he realized, would have no such problem: "No one can say Balanchine is very enlightened politically, from the liberal point of view.

He was brought up as a servant to the Tsar, and in many ways still remains one."

Given Lincoln's continuing symptoms and weakness, his doctors finally decided that double bypass surgery was necessary. He returned yet again to the hospital and was operated on in mid-May 1975. The surgery went well, and Lincoln was back home in two weeks. But his four-month ordeal was still not over. It wasn't until the second week in June that he was able, twice daily, to walk around nearby Gramercy Park, and even in late July, having gone to Weston to complete his recovery, he continued to feel "rather demoralized, with boring side effects from the surgery; I can't close my left hand or use it much, and my right leg keeps going to sleep . . . it is all hampering and tiresome." In writing Jerry Robbins about ballet business, he called himself "the world's most impatient patient," and confessed that he felt "far away from both School and Company, which I dare say will pass in time but it is rather like living in limbo." All that summer he tired easily and accused himself of being "surly and irascible."

By the early fall he was improved enough to come into the city several days a week and had just enough energy to start issuing firm opinions again on a host of subjects. He announced that the art world was so dreary, he'd never write about it again. His estimate of Andy Wyeth, for one, fell still further; his recent nudes, Lincoln wrote Colville, were "rather antiseptic . . . neat and hygienic." Lincoln was also put off by Wyeth's politics, by what he called his "acceptance of Nixon's flattery and his defense of that crook"; it all "rather cooled me, as far as seeing him often." His displeasure carried over to Jamie Wyeth, whom Lincoln now saw as "a chip off the old block; a remarkable hand and eye, but with a sensibility oddly hard and dry." Lincoln even became more critical of his brother-in-law, Paul Cadmus; he admired his highly finished chalk drawings of the male nude (mostly of his companion Jon Anderson) but thought his recent painting depicting the horrors of the Manhattan subway "not my dish."

The fall of 1975 finally saw the publication of *Nijinsky Dancing*. It gave a jump start to Lincoln's erratic recovery.

CHAPTER THIRTY

Succession

(1976–1985)

FROM THE *New York Times* to the *New York Review of Books*, Lincoln's volume on Nijinsky was saluted ("we are all in debt," and the like) rather than evaluated, since few could cope with the scholarship involved. Still, Lincoln was pleased with the positive reception, and even more so by the nomination that followed later in the year for the National Book Award. But being pleased wasn't exactly a full-time occupation, nor could yesterday's absorbing work help fill the emptiness in today's schedule. Keeping busy, frantically busy, was the only strategy Lincoln had ever developed for holding at bay the demons at the door. But six months after surgery he still felt, as he wrote Mim, "rather disoriented as far as writing goes." He spent what energy he had on trying to raise money for the company and the school, though such work continued to provide little pleasure or satisfaction.[1]

For a time, he thought of preparing a sort of pictorial history of three centuries of dance in the United States; he even had a working title, *See America, Dancing!* But within a month of starting the book, he gave it up: there weren't enough pictures for most of the three centuries and as regarded the contemporary scene, he couldn't face "being polite about the Modern Dance." He next tried to persuade Balanchine to work with him on "a text book with photographs," but as Lincoln himself realized, Balanchine had "little time to spend on anything that boring and concentrated." Lincoln thought of doing the book himself, but soon gave up that project too. In 1977 the idea of working together on "a big Balanchine book of POSITIONS AND PRINCIPLES," which would be Balanchine's "technical testament," again came up, and was again soon shelved.

To a greater degree than ever before, Lincoln turned his attention more to the needs of the school than the company. Eugenie Ouroussow, who'd been the chief administrator at the school since 1934, died in 1975. The essential "two Natalies" (Molostwoff and Gleboff) remained on staff and helped pick up the slack, but there was more need than before for Lincoln to pay detailed attention to the school's workings in general and its finances in particular. Housed in the Juilliard School at Lincoln Center, SAB had an enrollment in 1975 of some four hundred students; out of about a thousand who applied each year, only about sixty or so, after regional auditions, were accepted. Of those about a third were on scholarship, but since the school had no dormitory facilities, many students banded together to meet the cost of an apartment, or lived at the YMCA or YWCA, or stayed at the Professional Children's School on West Sixtieth Street.

The company during these years received aid from the New York State Arts Council and the National Endowment for the Arts. The school, however, had no expectations of assistance from either federal or state governments; its yearly expenditure of some six hundred thousand dollars was mostly raised through events and donors. The earlier Ford Foundation grant had by this point run out, but the foundation gave the school a new matching grant specifically earmarked for learning how to fund-raise and how to gather an endowment. In this regard Nancy Lassalle, who'd once been a student in the school, and her advisory council, would provide yeoman service. Mary Porter, who'd recently come on board as Lincoln's secretary, would also increasingly shift her attention to development work, with Roswell Perkins, president of the Harvard Club and a NYCB board member, as her helpful guide. John Samuels III, the new president of the ballet board, devoted himself to stabilizing the school's corporate identity.

None of this would prove easy in the midst of economic recession—and national disgrace. Nixon's secret and indiscriminate bombings of Cambodia, followed by the scandal of Watergate, further divided a country already suffering from budgetary freezes and from a powerful backlash against the black struggle for equality. President Gerald Ford followed Nixon in his lock-step vetoing of any legislative initiative that threatened to help the black poor. Lincoln viewed the 1976 presidential election that pitted Jimmy Carter against Ford as "the choice . . . between two frightened, inadequate and rather dishonest politicians for whom a large part of the electorate, including me, will exercise the right of not voting." Carter won, but he seemed, like his predecessors, to have no interest in promoting the arts, and no plan for ending the economic recession.

Lincoln was driven toward a heightened involvement in SAB's affairs out of a fierce sense of duty in combination with personally feeling at loose ends and wanting to be of some use—not out of any profound interest in finances or "arts management." Mim Rambert was indignant on his behalf. "I think it is a tragedy that you, who by nature have been made the soul of generosity," she wrote him in 1976, "should have to go with a begging bowl to all the millionaires—what an undeserved humiliation." The following year she focused her gunsights: "It really is a cruel mockery of fate that your work for Balanchine consists of the horrible job of begging. I wonder whether he realizes what a heroic deed you are performing—and at the same time how alone you are in the deepest understanding of him."

While taking on more administrative tasks, Lincoln kept himself nourished by frequent attendance at NYCB performances and by sitting in on Balanchine's advanced "company classes" two or three times a week. "They are a revelation of the guts of dance," he reported to Mim. "He springs about like a ten-year old at seventy-three and screams and rages at our overfed, underbrained dancers. But we have a half-a-dozen girls and boys who have the sense to take all this to heart and mind. . . . I do wish you could see what his accent and emphasis are; how he *shows*." Lincoln's enthusiasm was further rekindled by the premiere in January 1976 of Balanchine's reworked ballet *Chaconne* (from Gluck's *Orpheus and Eurydice*) for Suzanne Farrell, which was rapturously received.

By the new year Lincoln was markedly reviving. In February 1976, he accompanied the troupe to Washington for an engagement at the Kennedy Center, and in March, he used the occasion of Mim's birthday celebration to make yet another trip to London. He wrote the London trip off as "semi-official," since he did confer with Covent Garden's director, John Tooley, with whom he got along well, about a possible NYCB engagement. But Lincoln spent most of his time seeing, among others, Astrid, Mim, the dance critic Mary Clarke, and Dickie Buckle, and attending theater, ballet, and opera. He saw Nureyev dance Balanchine's *Apollo* at Covent Garden, and the performance only further convinced him that Nureyev was no match for Mikhail Baryshnikov, with his "fantastic surfeit of technique" and his inherent decency (even if, in Lincoln's view, Baryshnikov had "no understanding of hysteria, no tragic aura, no analytical intelligence").

Another sign of recovery was the return in Lincoln's letters of the camp tone that had been absent for so long: "Courage, patience, as my old Nanny used to say when she found me wanking. What is the origin of WANK (Anglo-Wanxon?)"; "I can rarely get a hard-on, and then only at the thought of Buckle singing My Little Pussy"; "I have fallen deeply and sincerely in love with Vanessa Redgrave. We are rarely out of each other's arms. . . . I am supporting a Trotskyite, pro-Mao meeting with the man who did DOG DAY AFTERNOON."

Lincoln's spirits may have revived, but he was still without an absorbing project and still filling in his time with ill-fitting chores; while in London, for example, he shopped for antique furniture to equip the State Theater's Green Room. Not having a new book of his own to work on, he settled for accepting (which he'd vowed never again to do) requests to write short introductions to other people's books, and also to self-publishing his poetry. He wrote touchingly that "the time I have given to the indulgence of verse-writing rather neatly equals whatever facility I may have." Yet self-deprecating as he could be about his poetry, he felt hurt that it was so entirely omitted from academic discourse and consideration.

By the spring of 1976 a number of unexpected developments required that Lincoln—to his relief—again play a more hands-on role with the company. Balanchine was hospitalized and put into traction for five weeks to treat intense pain from a sciatic nerve. When released he was able to take rehearsals but no classes, and felt (in Lincoln's view) "rather demoralized." It looked unlikely that aside from his nearly completed Bicentennial tribute to the British, *Union Jack*, he'd be making many additions to the repertory in the upcoming season.[2]

Simultaneously NYCB was threatened with the likely prospect of another musicians' strike—this just at the time when the company was in the middle of its big moneymaker, the annual *Nutcracker* season, was performing brilliantly and with, as Lincoln put it, "a bevy of the best young dancers we have had in years, particularly male: smashers!" During the next few months various efforts at negotiation with the union failed, and at the end of 1976 the musicians went out on strike. Lincoln called it "the worst thing to hit us in forty years," and it lasted about a month. The new contract finally agreed upon gave the orchestra members $330 per week for seven performances, making it the highest-paid ballet orchestra in the country (but still below what was paid musicians in the more prestigious Philharmonic and Metropolitan Opera orchestras). In contrast NYCB corps dancers had a beginning salary of $150 per week, going up after four years to $275. To pay for the hike in the musicians' salaries, as well as the falling off of box office receipts due to the economic recession, the decision was made to raise ticket prices—a decision Lincoln opposed.

In the immediate aftermath of the strike, the company performed resplendently in the *Bournonville Divertissements* and in Balanchine's *Vienna Waltzes;* the spring of 1977, too, was marked by the continuing triumph of Suzanne Farrell and the increasing emergence of the Danish-born dancer Peter Martins. He had been with NYCB for a number of years, and Lincoln now saw in him not only the company's best male dancer, but the possibility of "a real director of the company—not as a choreographer, but as a model-dancer and captain."

The most serious development by far during these difficult few months was the one closest to home: just as Lincoln was at last feeling fully recovered from his surgery, Fidelma had a hideous breakdown, complete with terrifying delusions and hysteria, and had to be hospitalized. Lincoln initially tried to care for her, with the help of a nurse, at home, but she was so seriously ill and improved so little that after two months he moved her to a small hospital near their house in Weston to begin what would be a slow, protracted—and only partial—recovery.

"This of course brings up all sorts of considerations," Lincoln wrote Mim Rambert. "What might have been done differently—what one's responsibility is—to whom and to what. . . . I feel I could have handled this, but I have failed and, in a way, she is a sacrifice to the company, in which she has never had a part. . . . Prayer is about the sole recourse one has, and it is not everyone who can or should place much hope in prayer; besides, prayer is not about asking for relief. . . . I feel you know how hard it is to love someone and yet be forced to put work first. I have no regrets, but sometimes I have doubts."

This may strike one as somewhat self-serving (the difference between "regrets" and "doubts" remains obscure and therefore a bit suspect). But within his acknowledged limits and his admitted "failure," it's difficult to fault Lincoln's handling of a tragic situation. Fidelma did very slowly improve in the small hospital, but it wasn't until June that he was allowed to take her home for dinner two or three times a week. By then she was still unable to care for herself, and given her dislike of having a home attendant, it wasn't at all clear what sort of long-range solution could be managed.

By the time Fidelma was released in September, she agreed to let a local woman, a Mrs. Ida Benson, be in the house from 9 a.m. to 6 p.m. five days a week. Ida seemed kind and willing, drove a car, and took Fidelma, who was afraid of using the stove, to shop for TV dinners and frozen pies. But she wouldn't let Ida do the dishes, afraid she might be a "breaker." By October, Fidelma was noticeably better, though (in her brother's words) "of course on somewhat stupefying medication."

By then, in their incredible my-turn, your-turn pattern, Lincoln was once again, in Cadmus's words, "wildly worse." His downward spiral was swift and profound, leading to a prolonged outburst of what he himself later called "hysterical confusion." His behavior during that confusion was bizarre in the extreme. Both Fidelma and Paul phoned Dan Maloney to warn him that Lincoln had assumed the identity of Othello and was denouncing Danny as Iago; Lincoln was livid, moreover, about "a terrible scene" they'd had at a dinner that never took place. They also told Dan that Lincoln had loaded up his car with ten heavy cartons of books and was on his way to the city, with an expected arrival time of about ten that evening. On his best days Lincoln was a reckless driver, paying only occasional attention to the road, but there was no way to stop him from leaving Weston.[3]

Somewhat later Dan got two calls from Mina saying that Lincoln had arrived at his brother George's house in Mamaroneck, had made a terrible scene, and was indeed on his way to New York. Dan was staying nearby with his girlfriend, Christine Pieters, on East Seventeenth Street, and he said he'd go to the Nineteenth Street house to help Lincoln unload the books and to see if he could calm him down. After waiting until 11:45, Dan was about to leave when he saw Lincoln, without car or books, walking toward the house and looking (in Dan's later words) "extremely angry and mad." When Dan asked him where the books were, Lincoln snapped, "I've read those books." Dan tried to explain that he had to leave briefly to pick up his dog, but that he'd be back shortly.

When he did return soon after, Dan was confronted by a completely darkened house, with even the stair lights turned out. He of course had a key to the house and groped his way in the dark up to his third-floor studio. The following morning, when he came downstairs, Dan saw that the lights were on in the living room, and he went out, as usual, to get the *Times* for Lincoln, thinking that routine gesture might help to calm him. But when he returned, Lincoln was gone and on the living room floor was a hammer and a smashed porcelain cat Dan had made, bits and pieces scattered everywhere. Dan called Cadmus and Lincoln's earlier psychiatrist, Dr. Foxe, and both advised him to stay away for a few days.

When Dan next returned to Nineteenth Street to pick up some clothes and shaving equipment, he discovered that Lincoln had hammered whiskey bottles into smithereens all over the living room floor and had torn up many of Dan's etchings. He'd also put a paper collar around a wooden sculpture Dan had made, dripped blood (his own presumably) on it, and placed the broken head of a porcelain Chinese cat on top. He'd turned some of Dan's paintings to the wall and smeared a torn-up picture of Abraham Lincoln with blood. Dan heard Lincoln in the cellar hammering away, and quickly left.

The following morning Dan asked his girlfriend (and, later, wife) Christine to phone Lincoln. He answered and told her that she needed to come over right away. Rushing to the house, she met Lincoln on the street. Near tears, he said he had something terrible to tell her, then broke down and sobbed in anguish on her shoulder. He told her that Dan had gone mad and was on his way to Kentucky to kill his sister, and he asked Christine to come inside and see what Dan had done to his studio. She refused, but a day or two later, after Lincoln had returned to Weston, Dan himself entered the studio. Lincoln had destroyed nearly everything in it, even including Dan's eyeglasses. He'd taken eggs and milk out of the refrigerator and thrown them, along with baby powder, over everything from clothes to paintings. Distraught, Dan left the house, never to return.

Lincoln refused admission to Gracie Square Hospital and had to be entrapped during intermission at the State Theater by paramedics and a group of police in mufti; as he was being forcibly removed, he looked over sadly at Barbara Horgan and said, "I'm sorry, honey." Once in the hospital, he was given a course of ECT (Electric Convulsive Shock Treatment), which had been successful once before. He was also put on new medication; he responded positively to both. By the end of November, his remarkable resilience to the fore, he was again writing letters and planning trips. But his treatment of Dan had more prolonged consequences. Lincoln refused to make any sort of apology or restitution—could Gurdjieff's "never explain, never apologize" ever have been given so extreme an application? It could perhaps be claimed—as some of his intimates did—that being out of his head, it wasn't "Lincoln" who'd caused the damage. Lincoln well and Lincoln sick, Mina wrote Dan, were two differ-ent people. True, but two people in communication. In the name of a valu-able twenty-year-old friendship and in the name of trying to restore it, Lincoln—who after all was well off—could have at least volunteered to recompense Dan, so far as that was possible (his several paintings and pieces of pottery were beyond salvage).

This was especially urgent for Dan, since—thanks to Lincoln—he was currently jobless. He'd worked for years at the Birch Wathen School, becoming head of its art department and earning what was then the decent salary of $6,500 a year. Lincoln had consistently badgered him about teaching being a "waste of time," and he'd long promised to provide Dan with the equivalent of his yearly salary if he'd agree to quit. "To keep peace between us," Dan had finally resigned from Birch Wathen.

Lincoln not only refused to pay compensation of any kind but also put a ban on Dan's name ever being uttered in his presence. Even Lincoln's defenders have been hard put to come up with a rationale for that behav-ior. Did the ban result from an excess of guilt? But then why not discharge it, at least in part, through a cash settlement? Was Lincoln still suffering from the lingering effects of his "Iago" fantasy? Perhaps—but why had the loyal Dan, of all people, become the object of Lincoln's hallucinatory rage in the first place? Did Lincoln always carry within such an excess of grief and chaos that, when unwell, he discharged it randomly? Possibly—but then why, once "well," didn't he at least make a stab at identifying the rea-sons for his bottled-up wildness, or if he eschewed any further in-depth analysis, why not at least apologize to a person who had proved himself a devoted friend over and over again?

Several intimates have resorted to a different, more psychologically straightforward explanation, suggesting that Lincoln permanently exiled Dan because he'd broken a pledge never to speak to a reporter about Lin-coln's emotional problems. Conceivably—but no concrete evidence has ever surfaced that Dan did betray Lincoln in that way. Besides, twenty years earlier Lincoln had done something similar to Jensen Yow—and no one has ever accused Jens of revealing confidences to the press. Lincoln's episodes of "disturbance," moreover, had already been witnessed by a number of people and were the subject of common gossip among numer-ous others; a reporter hardly required confirmation from a Dan Maloney.

In the face of Lincoln's adamant rejection, Dan thought for a time of taking legal action. He wrote at length to Lincoln's lawyer, John Freeman, outlining what had happened and asking for financial compensation total-ing $9,325. Freeman reported back to Dan that Lincoln refused to pay him one penny in damages, and Freeman advised him to drop any thought of a suit. Though "inconsolably sad" (as he wrote Mina), Dan for a time thought he'd probably proceed legally; he wanted Lincoln to have to "face me in court and try to justify his assault. . . . I have always put him and our friendship above my own interests and safety." But he finally decided against going through with a lawsuit, unwilling to open the wound again: "I don't want to be upset. I couldn't work under the conditions that suing would cause."

The only explanation Dan himself could ever come up with for Lincoln's behavior was that in "a Machiavellian coup," he was trying to get Dan out of the top-floor studio in order to move Fred Maddox, recently restored to favor, into it (the relationship with Alex Nixon having faded away). But all Lincoln had to do was ask, since (as Dan put it) "he knows me well enough to know I would never stay where I was not welcomed." Fred, now thirty-five and a struggling architect, did move into the house (though Jensen got the studio). Lincoln reported to Mim that "the Welsh boy" (Fred) he'd gone "around the world" with sixteen years earlier and had then disengaged from because "I felt I was bad for him," was back in favor and "we seem to fit together like 2 spoons."

Fidelma had been deeply fond of both Jensen and Dan, but she disliked Fred intensely (as did a number of Lincoln's friends). Fortunately, she rarely came into the city these days; its agitated pace was simply too much for her. Though a good deal better, she remained withdrawn, spending more and more time in the country house in Weston. Lincoln, too, as he began his own climb back to health, found the country, and especially working in his garden, a great solace. He'd spend long hours, stark naked, sitting on a little stool, tinkering and trimming the plants that wove down from the house along a path to the pond. He and Fidelma both delighted in the mallards and teals that gathered on their pond, and the families of raccoons, woodchucks, and possums in the surrounding area. Fidelma saw to it that all were exceedingly well fed.

Though no longer gripped by terror and delusions—at her worst Fidelma had thought both Lincoln and her brother were intent on killing her—she would, from this point on, live a subdued and low-key life; once, when friends were visiting at Weston, she went off alone for a walk in the woods, leading one guest to confide to another that "one day she won't come back." Lincoln, in contrast, rebounded quickly from his latest bout, though he still had trouble concentrating. Though aware that a new writing project was essential to his well-being, to feeling functional and useful, he had a difficult time finding and sticking to a topic.

For a time he thought he might do a book on the life portraits of Abraham Lincoln; then Bob Gottlieb (who'd edited Lincoln's last two books, *New York City Ballet* and *Nijinsky Dancing*) suggested he do a book on Isadora Duncan similar to the Nijinsky volume—but Lincoln soon decided there wasn't enough of a pictorial record to carry the project through. Gottlieb next suggested a volume tentatively titled *Ballet Basics: The School of Balanchine*, a big photographic work that would include some twelve hundred pictures as well as text. In essence it was the same book

Lincoln had earlier tried to interest Balanchine in coauthoring, and it was hoped, as the book advanced, that he could be enticed into cooperating (he couldn't). While mulling over the photographic book, Lincoln set to work on a long essay, "Auden in America," for a memorial volume. The distinguished Auden scholar Edward Mendelson praised the finished product as full of brilliant insights—"I found myself almost gasping with admiration now and then"—and Lincoln finally felt that he was still capable of making a useful contribution.[4]

On March 15, 1978, Balanchine suffered a mild heart attack, an event that marked the onset of various physical disabilities. He was at work at the time on a new ballet, *Tricolore*, to music by Georges Auric, a work that had to be taken over by a trio of choreographers, Peter Martins, Jean-Pierre Bonnefous, and Jerome Robbins, and was generally judged unsuccessful. But the company was dancing extremely well, and a whole new wave of young soloists were performing major roles for the first time.

Shortly before his heart attack, Balanchine had told a reporter that there was no place for the defected Russian star, Baryshnikov, in the company ("we have nothing for him"). But Balanchine soon changed his mind, deciding, after all, that (as Lincoln put it) "he himself, Nureyev and Baryshnikov come from the same school, and that the strength of the line lies in their responsibility—elegance and virtuosity." Lincoln was pleased at Balanchine's change of mind; he thought Baryshnikov would be "an inspiration" for the new generation of dancers coming up. Mim Rambert believed that Baryshnikov's presence in the company would stimulate Balanchine "to write for men, and I am sure it will be good for him, too; he has exploited the female material quite enough."

By the summer of 1978 Balanchine seemed recovered, and Baryshnikov joined the company as a full-time principal and began learning a number of Balanchine ballets, including *Stars and Stripes*, *The Prodigal Son*, and the "Rubies" segment of Balanchine's brilliant 1967 ballet *Jewels*. It was a struggle; besides the difficulty at age thirty of adjusting to Balanchine's style, Baryshnikov developed rather bad tendinitis and for a month early in 1979 couldn't dance at all. Lincoln was full of sympathy for "the poor boy." He thought that Balanchine, though liking and admiring Baryshnikov, had generally grown "rather short-tempered" since his heart attack. Besides, Balanchine "demands a kind of personal annihilation" that Lincoln felt Baryshnikov "seems to crave, but doesn't yet understand." Once Baryshnikov started to perform, Lincoln wrote Mim Rambert, he also had to face NYCB's "schooled audience," which was devoted to the repertory but trained to be cool to "stars"—a fact that Baryshnikov, despite his international stature, accepted without question.

By the spring of 1979 Balanchine's health had again deteriorated, and he was periodically disabled with severe bouts of angina. On June 19 he

finally underwent triple bypass surgery, which was successful. After a prolonged rest over the summer—for the first time he missed the company's
Saratoga season—Balanchine again seemed his energetic self; he'd made,
Lincoln reported to Mim, "one of his miraculous recoveries." Lincoln
recalled the time in 1933 when the doctors had told him that Balanchine
would die within three years; Romola Nijinsky had consulted her trance
medium, who gave her the precise date of death in a sealed envelope; the
date had come and gone—and Balanchine's health had steadily improved.[5]

By the time Balanchine returned full-time to the company, Baryshnikov had already decided to accept an offer to become artistic director of
American Ballet Theatre, though his contract allowed him to continue
dancing with NYCB for another year. Many of his friends had thought it
a mistake from the beginning to affiliate with NYCB, that Balanchine
would never do any choreography on him, or any other male superstar.
The prediction, in fact, proved accurate, though it's impossible to say what
might have happened had illness and surgery not intervened.

Lincoln, in any case, had never regarded Baryshnikov as likely to
remain with the company for long or to become a candidate to succeed
Balanchine. And after further contact he hadn't found him personally
sympathetic; Baryshnikov, Lincoln wrote Mim, is "sad, gloomy, thoughtful—not like Nureyev, bouncy and self-absorbed." Lincoln's attentions by
then had come to focus instead on a young dancer named Joseph Duell.
"Joe" had been preceded by his older brother, Daniel Duell, who'd started
at SAB back in 1969. When Joe arrived in the early fall of 1972, the brothers moved into a studio apartment together, which they shared for the
next five years.[6]

By that point Lincoln had lost confidence in Jacques d'Amboise as a
possible successor to Balanchine. D'Amboise, for his part, felt respect and
gratitude toward Lincoln, writing him in 1976, at the close of an eight-
page letter, "You are a marvelous man and responsible for my being a
dancer instead of a petty criminal. . . . I owe you an enormous, unpayable
debt." But by then the sentiment was no longer mutual. In a memo written three years earlier, Lincoln had already soured on d'Amboise, referring to him as "a moral schizophrenic with a very powerful sexual drive
[and] a body enfeebled by weak ankles for so large a frame. . . . I (personally) neither like nor trust him. Once, a long time ago, I loved what I
thought he could have become."

His hopes for d'Amboise now became invested in Joe Duell. He felt
that Joe as a dancer "is one of the few boys who permits himself, or is
somehow allowed, the very rare sense of ecstasy." Though young, he'd
been through quite a lot in his short life, including a botched surgery and
a severe nervous breakdown. Lincoln thought Joe's suffering had "made
him wise beyond his years," and found him lively, inquisitive, and charming. He saw Daniel as less talented and interesting, more conventional,

but recognized that he had a certain valuable "gravity" and was "deeply and powerfully important to Joe."

Lincoln never said anything specific to the brothers about considering them, singularly or together, for the "succession." But certain hints were dropped: "After more preparation . . . more seasoning," and so on. In response the brothers wrote Lincoln as early as 1976 that "large choreographic and managerial assignments obviously do require the competence of trained or eminently knowledgeable people, which we aren't. Some sort of education is indeed in order."

By 1979 Lincoln was ready to acknowledge (to Dickie Buckle) several things: that he was deeply in love with Joe Duell, and that he "regarded him as the white hope, not only as principal dancer, but as eventual successor to Balanchine." Joe, like his brother, Daniel, was a declared heterosexual, and he had a girlfriend in the company, Maria Caligari. Maria, too, has the clearcut recall that Lincoln "wanted to anoint Joe as the successor," wanted him "to take over." Bobby La Fosse, another young principal at the time, also recalls that Lincoln "thought very highly of Joseph . . . as someone to take over the company."

When the NYCB performed at Covent Garden that September, Balanchine was in attendance, but Lincoln was not; dreading a repeat of the disastrous reception of 1950, and eager to avoid the tedious business of official receptions, he stayed home. But he made a point of asking Astrid Zydower to introduce Joe Duell to Mim, describing him as "our succession, together with Peter Martins. I think our future depends on these two." For a time he sounded content to let it rest on Martins alone; "we have such a strong and talented character in Peter Martins," Lincoln wrote Mim Rambert in February 1980, "that George and I would put him in charge tomorrow." That comment marks the moment when Martins formally and favorably entered into Lincoln's calculations for the future, though he'd been in Balanchine's mind for some time. Martins was unmistakably (Lincoln might have said "unavoidably") ahead of Joe in the succession sweepstakes, both as an established *danseur noble* and as a choreographer (audiences and critics alike had applauded his first ballet, *Calcium Night Light*, and later *Sonate di Scarlatti*).

Joe was considerably younger, but Lincoln was convinced that "he will be a choreographer one day." As a dancer he wasn't "flashy," but his "remarkable" personality shone through; Balanchine, according to Lincoln, "promises a big future for him." By the winter 1979–80 season, Balanchine began to make good on that promise; he gave Joe important roles in *La Valse* and *Coppélia*, and anointed him "choreographer of the year" for the annual SAB workshop performance in May; Joe did a piece for two male dancers, aged fifteen and sixteen, that Balanchine "liked . . . very much" and that Lincoln, perhaps predictably, thought "brilliant."

For the spring season of 1980 Balanchine had, in Lincoln's view, "pushed him [Joe] into everything a first-dancer does," including partnering Suzanne Farrell, despite the addition to the company of Ib Anderson, the greatly gifted Danish dancer. Balanchine also asked Joe to do *La Création du Monde* for the school, telling him that if it worked, the ballet would be performed by the company. By the end of 1980 Lincoln was writing Astrid Zydower that Joe was dancing like "a ball of fire" and that Balanchine "has taken him under his wing and has pushed him as a choreographer."

Lincoln's willingness in 1979–80 to settle for the dual succession of Duell and Martins, or of Martins alone, accurately reflected current realities. But Joe's girlfriend, Maria Caligari, sensed that as time went by and Joe became more prominent, Lincoln's support of Martins weakened—though he wavered constantly, at one point flatly referring to Martins as "the successor." Still, "Lincoln could talk to Joe, but not to Peter." Besides, Lincoln's hypersensitive antennae had picked up what he thought was a certain amount of contempt on Peter's part toward him, something more than the generalized arrogance several others had complained about. Humanly Lincoln didn't like Peter. He loved Joe.

During the early months of 1980, Fidelma took a turn for the worse. On one level she still seemed functional, spending a great deal of time in the kitchen obsessing over this or that detail of a given meal. And she rarely complained—though her condition in itself, Lincoln felt, "is a complaint." She would occasionally say, usually when asked, that "everything hurts," not as an accusation or lament but more as a flat, almost theological, statement. Lincoln's breakdowns were galvanic affairs, full of bizarre theatrics and wild display. Fidelma's were silent, terrified retreats, vacant separations. "She gets so little pleasure out of life," Lincoln wrote Astrid Zydower. "She is prey to every sort of apprehension" and would rarely leave their Weston house. He didn't know what, if anything, could bring Fidelma relief. Neither drugs nor therapists seemed to help, though both were tried. With Fidelma, at seventy-six, locked in a web of anxiety, there were scant grounds for hopeful change.[7]

When her hired companion, Ida Benson, wanted to move in with the Kirsteins, Lincoln set himself against the idea; he could barely stand having her around as it was, let alone all the time. In turning down the idea he felt like a brute, an unfeeling monster, and made sure that he never spent less than three days a week in Weston. In case of emergency, Paul and Jon lived right down the hill, but Lincoln still felt haunted by guilt (he'd always felt thus haunted; only the focus had changed). Sometimes he'd go to a bar late at night in a seamy section of Norwalk and hang out with the locals, drinking too much but never getting into any hassle (or, apparently, any sexual situation).

His four days a week in New York were far happier. There he had the built-in companionship of Fred Maddox and, more irregularly, Jens Yow; now an unthinkable fifty-five, Jens had left the Morgan Library and set up for himself on the third floor of the Kirsteins' house as a highly successful conservationist, a consultant in paper works for both Christie's and Sotheby's. There was also an addition to the household: painting away in a back room when he could find the free time was, as of early 1982, one David Langfitt, part-time art student, part-time night guard at Lincoln Center, whose father was a prominent Philadelphia neurosurgeon. Lincoln had indirectly learned that one of the security guards hoped to become a painter and had asked to see his work. Impressed, Lincoln commissioned him to do a portrait of him in his World War II khaki uniform (the same one he sometimes wore, when "high," to the ballet).

Lincoln spent most of his time when in New York dealing with the affairs of the School of American Ballet, where the administrative and funding challenges rose in direct proportion to the success of the enterprise. Gaining entrance to SAB was now highly coveted, with only one out of every ten applicants winning admittance. For the first time boys were auditioning in significant numbers, and Balanchine, at age seventy-seven, "abruptly manifested" (in Lincoln's words) an interest in them—"not carnally, professionally"; he chose eleven already enrolled boys aged twelve to fifteen who showed unusual promise and made them work for three hours a day with the fabled teacher Stanley Williams.

The school was also in better shape financially than it had ever been; by the end of 1981 it had an endowment of some three and a half million—with a drive under way to increase it to fifteen million. A second drive was launched to provide for a school residency. Interested local families and friendly YMCAs were no longer considered adequate for housing pupils whose parents were reluctant to let them live away from home at the tender age best suited for beginning ballet classes.

The company itself had long since become well established and Balanchine, despite mounting symptoms of ill health, continued to create new ballets for it. "Pressed by mortality," Lincoln wrote Mim in 1980, "he rather behaves as if each day is his last. He has been rehearsing a lot, and changing sacred steps so that the so-called critics are in a rage that they have to look at the changes and not recall what it *used* to be." In a comparable way Balanchine split up some long-paired dancing partners, a gesture to "break habit" that Lincoln applauded but that "makes some people nervous and others irritated." And he went right on creating ballets. For the June 1981 mini–Tchaikovsky Festival he created several new ballets as well as creating a new version of *Mozartiana* for Farrell, which was received as a masterpiece—Balanchine's last. The festival had its ups and downs, but Lincoln thought Balanchine "outdid himself."

With George Balanchine. ABOVE: *Early 1950s*
BELOW: *Late 1960s*

ABOVE: From left to right: *Eugenie Ouroussow, Balanchine, Lincoln, and Natalie Molostwoff at the School of American Ballet, early 1950s* BELOW: From left to right: *Charles Laskey, unidentified woman, Vladimir Dimitriev, and Kathryn Mullowny, late 1930s*

ABOVE: *Betty Cage* BELOW: *Lincoln, Gisella Caccialanza, Antony Tudor, Marie-Jeanne, and José Fernández on board ship prior to sailing to South America with the American Ballet in* 1941

School of American Ballet, 1930s

ABOVE: *Classroom at 637 Madison Avenue, the home of the school from 1933 to 1956; Pierre Vladimiroff conducting a men's class with Roy Tobias (first at barre) and Arthur Mitchell (third at barre)* BELOW: *Murial Stuart conducting a girls' class*

Among those watching George Balanchine and Alexandra Danilova staging Coppélia, *1974:* far left, *Marilee Stiles;* second from left, *James Bogan;* third, *Kevin Tyler;* fourth, seated on floor, *Edward Gorey;* fifth, *John Clifford;* seventh, *Robert Gottlieb;* ninth, *Lincoln;* tenth, *Balanchine;* eleventh, *Danilova;* twelfth, *Mina;* thirteenth, *Leo Lerman;* reflected in mirror, from left to right (starting from center): *James Brusock, Hugo Fiorato, Rosemary Dunleavy, Eddie Bigelow*

In Japan, late 1950s. ABOVE: *With young boxer in front of Mount Fuji*
BELOW: *With Donald Richie in Nara*

ABOVE: *Montgomery, Alabama, freedom march,* 1965 BELOW: *Lincoln's play,* White House *Happening, at Loeb Theater, Harvard,* 1967; far right, *John Lithgow as Lincoln*

ABOVE: *Mayor Edward Koch and Jerome Robbins presenting the Handel Medallion to Lincoln, 1987*
BELOW: *With Lew Christensen, 1960s*

Lincoln's eightieth birthday, onstage, The New York State Theater. Back row (left to right): *Kyra Nichols, Darci Kistler, Heather Watts, Alexander Proia, Patricia McBride, Damien Wertzel, Stephanie Saland, Valentina Kozlova, Deborah Wingert*

Peter Martins and Eddie Bigelow scattering Lincoln's ashes on the pond at Weston

In May 1981 Lincoln received word that he'd been named the recipient of the prestigious Benjamin Franklin Medal, given each year by London's Royal Society of Arts to that citizen, alternately of the United States or the United Kingdom, who had notably "forwarded the cause of Anglo-American understanding." Among past recipients were Paul Mellon, William Fulbright, Lincoln's old friend Henry-Russell Hitchcock, and acquaintances Harold Macmillan and Margot Fonteyn. As a welcome relief from sickrooms and administrative tasks, Lincoln decided to accept the medal in person. The trip to London did him good; he went to museums and the theater and saw only Astrid, Mim, Dickie Buckle.

He also made, through Astrid, a new friend in the artist Michael Leonard, whose "realist" paintings he'd earlier seen in reproduction and had found "extremely interesting." Lincoln thought Leonard successfully avoided the realist tendency to lapse into the merely illustrative or to "run over into anecdote," unlike those Americans who, in rebellion against abstract expressionism, were now jumping feet first on the bandwagon of realism—creating, in Lincoln's opinion, "simply another formula, maybe more tidy but just as tiresome." (He always exempted Cadmus, of course, who at seventy-five had developed a loyal clientele, though not an academic following.) Lincoln also liked Michael Leonard as a person, finding him modest and shyly self-enclosed. Michael's recessed temperament neatly complemented Lincoln's unpredictable, volcanic one, and he was soon describing Leonard as part of "the family."[8]

Michael made fairly frequent trips to New York to confer with agents or galleries and to attend shows. In the years ahead, he never failed on these trips to spend time, often a great deal of time, with Lincoln, who'd sweep him up on his daily rounds (still fairly hectic in the early eighties). On April 22, 1982, for example, after enthusiastically viewing transparencies of Michael's work in the morning, the two caught a cab up to Lincoln Center, Lincoln talking "vividly" all the way. Once at SAB, Michael had to hurry to keep pace with Lincoln's swift progress down the hall. They'd pop into one of the large studios that lined the corridor, and alight quietly on a back wall bench to watch the work in progress. During a break the students would come up to say hello; "clearly," in Michael's opinion, "Lincoln is adored by the students . . . they would come smilingly to talk with him, exchange banter, small talk, but with evident delight. . . . I can see that Lincoln needs a daily shot of drinking them in."

After an hour or so of watching classes, the two men would go out for lunch, usually at a Chinese restaurant. The conversation might then take a darker turn, Lincoln confiding to Michael one day that he felt "haunted by a strange sense of terrible evil in the world, evil that makes him feel helpless, powerless and frightened. He is half taken up with Catholicism," though without being a fully paid-up (baptism and confession) member.

Letting Michael know about these feelings, Lincoln said, made him feel better; "the evil cloud" was still there, but describing it "had given him a slightly less despairing outlook, he said."

Though Lincoln never would become "a fully paid-up" Catholic, the Mass, for a time, became "increasingly the center of my thought, even of my life." Still endlessly curious at age seventy-six, he read with particular interest the writings of the radical Catholic authors Father Karl Rahner, Edward Schillebeeckx, and Hans Küng. They gave him "a lot of hope that First Century Christianity is neither dead nor buried." When he read a newspaper article about the declining number of Catholic priests, he regarded that as "good news . . . this means the redundancy of the number who go into the Church as a vocation."

Lincoln also read some fiction—he worked hard, for example, at understanding Joyce's *Finnegans Wake*—and a great deal of American history (the complete edition of Henry Adams's letters; a multiplicity of biographies and books on the Civil War, and so on). He enjoyed announcing that he himself "was born in the 107th year of the 19th century"—the implication being that in many senses he felt an outsider in his own time.

After lunch, Lincoln would usually retreat to his office to confer with his secretary–development officer, Mary Porter, to work at his desk on administrative matters, to write ten letters, and to make twenty phone calls. When the company was performing, Lincoln went almost every night. When it wasn't, he often had dinner guests at his house. There was the now-omnipresent Fred Maddox (whom Michael Leonard found "taciturn and sort of diffident," and who seemed "to switch off all decision-making when he's around Lincoln"). The guests varied from Joe Duell and Maria Caligari to Nancy Lassalle and Ed Bigelow to the arthritic and frail Jesuit priest Father William Lynch and the gallery owner Bob Isaacson.

Lincoln's behavior during dinner varied unpredictably. He was usually keenly alert, full of curiosity and dazzling conversation. Other times he'd get up in the middle of a meal to announce that he was going to bed (sometimes he'd just go). Occasionally he'd fall asleep right at the table, his massive, slumped form snoring away as guests tried to keep up a semblance of talk—especially difficult when Lincoln would periodically awake to shout (in Michael's words) "loud but quite irrelevant and nonsensical remarks . . . it was most unnerving." Yet Michael, like so many others, was enthralled by him; as he wrote in his diary at one point, "although I may carp about the difficulties of being around Lincoln, he is lovable, very formidable, a giant of a man whose warmth toward me has been consistent and whose company is exciting."

The Fall of 1982 proved a difficult time. It began with the death in August of Lincoln's beloved Mim Rambert of a stroke at age ninety-four; writing

Lincoln about her last days, Astrid told him that Mim had "thought you were the greatest human being she had ever met." That was small comfort in the face of the deterioration as well of both Fidelma and Balanchine. After suffering steady loss of energy and a number of falls, Balanchine was admitted to Roosevelt Hospital for a series of tests. He would never leave, though the nature of his illness, Creutzfeldt-Jakob disease, wasn't known until later, after an autopsy. One of Balanchine's last letters, written a month before his hospitalization, was to a schoolgirl who'd written to tell him that her teacher had said "people who have influence over other people are the most powerful people in the world" and had given Balanchine as an example. He replied to the schoolgirl on October 1, just before going into the hospital: "I do not think of myself as a 'powerful' man. I choreograph ballets, because that is what I do. God made me a choreographer. Only God is powerful and we are his servants." Servants. Servants to a higher order—the central, guiding concept that Lincoln and Balanchine, otherwise so different in temperament, shared.[9]

The same month that Balanchine was admitted to the hospital, Fidelma was put in the Putnam-Weaver Nursing & Convalescent Home in Greenwich, Connecticut. Of late she'd needed two nurses around the clock, and there'd been an episode when, knife in hand, she seemed about to threaten her brother and Jon Anderson. The incident led Lincoln to conclude that it wasn't any longer feasible to care for her at home. But she was, in Lincoln's own estimate, "desperately unhappy" in the nursing facility. She became convinced that it was "permanently filthy" and rarely left her tiny room for fear she'd be out of reach of a bathroom.

It was a life in limbo, in "a grey, negative world." Lincoln visited her briefly almost every weekend, keeping up all the while a low-key, one-sided conversation. There were those who doubted just how deep at this point his devotion to Fidelma really was. Fidelma had recently told Mary Porter that Lincoln "had taken her away from what she loved"—the ocean, sky, open air, and sun—"and put her in the woods." Mary thought a small house on the shore somewhere would have done more for Fidelma's sanity and happiness than all the nursing homes and medications combined. Perhaps that was simplistic; no one can say. But locked away, Fidelma kept repeating that she wanted to die, that her continuing existence was only a burden to Lincoln and Paul.

Balanchine's long death rattle ended on April 30, 1983. When the company dancers were told the news the following morning, many of them wept, and continued to weep during rehearsal for that day's matinee performance. Just before the curtain went up, Lincoln appeared in front of it and in a voice that trembled slightly told the hushed audience that Balanchine "is with Mozart, Tchaikovsky, and Stravinsky" now. "I do want to tell you," he added, "how much he valued this audience, this marvelous audience . . . you kept us going fifty years, and will another fifty. One thing he didn't want was that this be interrupted. We will proceed . . ."

Inescapably, gossiping and maneuvering over the succession accelerated almost at once. Joe Duell, Lincoln's version of an ideal heir, had been dancing brilliantly and had made a new ballet, *La Création du Monde;* but Joe was still in his twenties and entirely lacked managerial experience. Five years later Lincoln might bullheadedly have pushed Joe's candidacy, but in 1983 he knew better. Peter Martins seemed the obvious choice as the successor, though Balanchine, while still conscious, had refrained from any formal designation. By mid-March, however, with the spring season in the offing, the NYCB board, nervously trying to avoid controversy, named both Martins and Jerry Robbins as ballet masters in chief, with Martins empowered to make daily artistic decisions, and Robbins serving as general adviser.[10]

No other candidates were actively considered, though Jacques d'Amboise felt he should have been, and Dickie Buckle from a distance championed the choreographer and ballet master John Taras. D'Amboise had earlier been encouraged to view himself as the heir apparent, and although he'd faded as a dancer and failed for the most part as a choreographer, he behaved as if he hadn't noticed and for a time let his hurt and anger at being passed over be known. Taras had periodically choreographed for NYCB and behind the scenes had modestly served as a sort of Balanchine lieutenant, occasionally (mainly in Paris and Berlin) taking on the role of ballet master for the company. But Taras had limited public stature and lacked, as well, the authoritative presence to command the company's fealty. Buckle was Taras's sole champion and claimed that he was surely "not the only person to whom Balanchine spoke of Taras as his successor." At the very least, Buckle urged Lincoln to appoint Taras as his own second-in-command, a sort of deputy general director.

Lincoln slyly pretended to Buckle that he'd ceased to understand NYCB's inner workings, and (this part was closer to the truth) that he no longer had much power in making decisions relating to the company: "I don't need a deputy, as I am already little more than that myself." Yet he also told Buckle that it had taken "the greatest of tact" to forestall "a severe break" between Robbins and NYCB. Buckle was well aware of Lincoln's disdain for Robbins, but he knew nothing of Betty Cage's outright dislike for Peter Martins. It was Betty, during the board's discussions about the succession, who'd telephoned Robbins and fueled his outrage at the prospect of being passed over. The reasons for Betty's anger at Martins are unknown, but it was profound; she detested him. Betty had recently had a series of health problems, had talked of retiring, and probably had stayed on only out of loyalty to Lincoln, but she wasn't at all happy with the new guard now taking charge (she also disliked the ambitious Mary

Porter). Having been at the center of the company's operations for so long, Betty was facing marginalization.

As was Lincoln, her idol. The board hadn't made even a token gesture in his direction, hadn't once gone through the formal pretext of consultation before arriving at its decision to name Peter and Jerry. Lincoln in fact thought the board had acted precipitously and should have waited until the fall, though he couldn't cite any concrete reason for delay. True, he felt that Peter was untried as an administrator and that Jerry was "committed to nobody and nothing." But he had no better candidate to offer. Lincoln's wish to hold off was probably, at bottom, the perfectly human wish to hold back the dawn, to somehow escape the mortal lot of being superseded, put out to pasture—the wish not to turn over his baby to a pack of ungrateful youngsters who'd never had to shoot the rapids or pinch enough nickels to get to the next town. By ignoring Lincoln the board had confirmed that he no longer had any role with the company and was confined to a school already skillfully administered by others and where he had to rustle up busywork. The board had simply called things by their rightful name— but it hurt like hell to have the words spoken out loud.

It must have seemed part and parcel of the cheerless climate when the rest home called to tell Lincoln that Fidelma's nurses had tried to overcome her inertia by getting her to walk to the common room and watch a movie, but that she'd tripped on the way, fallen, and broken her pelvis. To prevent her feet from "twisting," they'd made her wear a brace, which added to the torture. Soon after that she gave up trying to feed herself. "If I felt badly about it," Lincoln stoically concluded, "I could do nothing else."

With regard to NYCB, Lincoln decided to take as his working motto This Is the Way It Is. Accept the situation (or appear to accept it) and attempt to be helpful (or simulate helpfulness) to those named to run the show. He decided that his appropriate role was neither to butter up nor to sabotage the new proprietors, but to see to it that every effort be made to preserve the past without embalming it. After all, he had long bent his energies toward ensuring that the *institution* would survive. There was triumph in that—and to hell with the heartache.

Lincoln, in short, was going to play ball, to be seen as someone lending his weight toward producing a smooth succession. This was particularly true with regard to Peter Martins. Lincoln started to meet with Peter for a half hour or so several nights a week before a performance—though he made no comparable approach to Jerry Robbins, intuiting that he'd never stick. "You have no idea," he wrote Buckle, in midsummer 1983, "of the tiresomeness of Jerry's negative energy, how it wears one down, how it is unproductive in its consistent inconsistency."

Still, Lincoln could backslide now and then. Six months after Balanchine's death he wrote Michael Leonard that "the whole principle" had changed: "I won't say for the worse, but in a way I can't and don't even want to try to control." That July, without anyone's authorization, Lincoln wrote Paul Findlay of England's Royal Opera House, sounding him out about becoming "General Administrator of the New York City Ballet," complementing, not replacing, Martins (in whom "I have every confidence"), who would remain artistic director.

The letter to Findlay, written at 2:00 a.m., may well have been the product of a manic state: it reeks of wild overstatement. Lincoln dismissed Robbins in the letter as "a hack and a shit" whose "usefulness to us [is] absolutely at an end," and he attacked as well the indispensable Barbara Horgan, who'd long been Balanchine's loyal personal assistant and was both his executor and one of his heirs. Lincoln even managed, in passing, to insult Betty Cage (whom he loved), castigating her as "a slightly black witch." Findlay, a sensible man, politely turned Lincoln down.[11]

For more than two years subterranean plots and maneuvers rumbled on, while Martins struggled to learn the ropes, maintain his balance, and try to ignore the constant criticism that *any* successor to Balanchine would have drawn. For his part, Robbins appeared and disappeared according to his, not NYCB's, needs, and the long-in-place team of skilled second-tier staff—especially Ed Bigelow and Barbara Horgan—saw to it that the nuts and bolts remained tight. Lincoln accurately summed matters up during the first year following Balanchine's death: "So far, no seams have been allowed to show and we proceed much as if he [Balanchine] had been alive, except without his authority or the knowledge that the repertory will be permanently enriched." At the end of the second anniversary of Balanchine's death, Lincoln wrote the Harewoods that he was "having a difficult time trying to keep things from getting nasty. It's not about money at all, but the disgusting way our 'Bored' [*sic*] protects their own preposterous turf."

The reference was to the first public rip in the NYCB seam, which centrally involved the school. Lincoln believed, or claimed, that Sid and Anne Bass were the chief players in what became a major organizational rupture; the Basses, according to Lincoln, had given large sums of money to NYCB and wanted a corresponding amount of power in return. Anne Bass had become a close friend of Mary Porter's (as well as of Peter Martins) and, Lincoln believed, had encouraged Mary to spread certain allegations against him, implying that age and emotional instability made him unfit to continue as head of the school. The next step in this alleged plot was for Mary to present herself as a candidate to run the school—a candidacy Anne would then push through the board. According to Michael Leonard, Lincoln became so "infuriated by this act of presumption and disloyalty that he fired Mary on the spot."

But Ed Bigelow, Barbara Horgan, and Mary herself have significantly different versions of what happened. According to Ed, Lincoln had overindulged Mary, letting her do whatever she wanted and not overseeing her activities with sufficient care; further, Ed (and others) claim that Mary, knowing she'd done a good job as development director, now wanted to expand her role at the school, becoming the counterpart of Peter at the company—and indeed had started to "brag" that she would soon replace Lincoln as head of the school. Mary herself corroborates much of Ed's version, at least in outline; having gotten a master's degree in business and public administration at NYU, she'd come to feel that "all of this"—playing second fiddle to a variably functioning Lincoln—"was too small for me."

Barbara Horgan, for her part, recalls that on a trip to Washington, DC, with Lincoln, he suddenly turned to her on the plane and blurted out, "I'm going to fire Mary." Shocked, Barbara asked why. "Insubordination," was Lincoln's curt reply. "Insubordination?" Barbara persisted, "What kind of insubordination? What has she done?" Lincoln mumbled something in reply and Barbara told him flat out, "You can't fire her unless you have something really specific." "Well, we'll see about that," Lincoln answered.

At the time, Mary was out on the road raising money; she'd just gotten a hundred-thousand-dollar gift from Procter & Gamble and was feeling proud of herself when Lincoln called in a rage and told her point-blank that she was fired. Stunned—Lincoln had never gotten angry at her at work, never once yelled at her—Mary asked him why. "Because you think you're omnipotent," Lincoln insufficiently replied. Pressed further by Mary, who'd recently survived cancer, Lincoln shouted, "Because you killed cancer! It's destroyed your personality and you now think you're bigger than life!" And that's the only explanation Lincoln would offer.

But if he thought Mary would quietly accept her fate, he'd misread her. She told Lincoln that he could fire her as his secretary but not as development director—that was a board decision. In trying to reach it, the board went through a series of racking and protracted meetings. Anne Bass led the charge to keep Mary, but a number of Lincoln loyalists, especially the retired Ford Foundation executive MacNeil Lowry, John Lockwood (Nelson Rockefeller's lawyer), and Nancy Lassalle, the longtime donor and mainstay of SAB, continually parried her moves and proved more than a match, in the end, for Bass and Porter. (In the middle of the struggle, and doubtless adding to his prestige, Lincoln was named one of the honorees of the National Medal of Arts in the first year it was awarded.)

At the start of the prolonged board struggle, Peter Martins gathered the faculty and staff of the school and asked them to remain neutral. Since rumors had already spread that most of them were on Lincoln's side (Mary had a number of detractors), Martins's move could be read as a partisan effort to dampen down support for Lincoln—not a suggestion of "neutrality" at all, but a rather bluntly prejudicial one in favor of his friends Anne Bass and Mary Porter. The teachers and staff, in any case, refused to be silenced. They got up a petition to the board declaring that "any action taken damaging to Lincoln Kirstein" would have an effect "devastating to the prestige and best interests of the School." Among the more than twenty signatories (including the entire full-time faculty) were the influential Muriel Stuart, Kay Mazzo, Alexandra Danilova, Suki Schorer, and Stanley Williams. The universally admired Williams let it be known that if Kirstein departed, he would follow. Three board members, moreover, who'd been dancers or ballet masters—Arthur Mitchell, John Taras, and Kent Stowell (as well as Edward Villella)—also spoke up strongly in Lincoln's defense.

Nor did Lincoln himself pretend to neutrality. He worked actively behind the scenes to influence the outcome of the board's deliberations, conferring often with allies like Nancy Lassalle and using his media contacts to release information to the press, and particularly to Anna Kisselgoff, dance critic for the *New York Times*. Starting in early May 1985, a flurry of press reports appeared that left the overall impression that Lincoln alone was the aggrieved party, that a now-hallowed New York institution was being subject to yet another "Texas Takeover"—a reference not only to the wealthy Bass family of Fort Worth but to Anne Bass's purported threat (which she denied making) to "rethink," should Mary not be reinstated, a major pledge she'd made toward building new and larger SAB facilities. In a series of articles, Kisselgoff made a point of noting that "the key factor is the role of Peter Martins, who has not been available to the press for comment—and who has not been counted among Mr. Kirstein's supporters," and this despite the fact, Kisselgoff wrote, that until now Kirstein has "unstintingly" sung Martins's praises.

The upshot was that the board affirmed Lincoln's right to fire his director of development, Lincoln offered to resign in two years (by his eightieth birthday), and the eight-member executive committee of the board voted unanimously to affirm Mary Porter's dismissal. The full board went along, adding a resolution expressing "great appreciation for the outstanding accomplishments" of Mary Porter as development director.

After an interval of several years had passed, Lincoln and Mary's paths once again crossed. Lincoln flew to Houston to attend the opening of its new opera house—and who should be there but Mary Porter, who now lived in that city. Lincoln acted as if nothing had ever happened and greeted her warmly. According to what he told Michael Leonard, Mary "apologized for her past behavior and kissed him." They saw each other a number of times after that and would sit and talk about things that were happening at the school as if Mary had never worked there—or been fired. Gurdjieff's "never explain, never apologize" must have been ringing in Lincoln's ears, if not clogging them. As for Mary, she went on to a highly successful business career and has never lost her conviction, despite having felt mistreated by him, that Lincoln "was a wonderful man . . . a great man. He loved me; I know that. And I loved him very much." (In the circles surrounding Lincoln, people did not fight or love in ordinary, predictable ways.)

Of the thirty board members only four were absent from the critical meeting in May 1985 that had approved the executive committee's resolutions. One of the four was Peter Martins. He may well have thought, as the new boy in town, that the safest strategy was to remove himself from the controversy. But silence is a form of speech, and trying to silence others is an active form of censorship. Martins may not have intended it, but the way he played his hand throughout the crisis was widely interpreted as anti-Lincoln. Certainly Lincoln himself felt that way, and it turned him from an ally into a (temporary) enemy.

He continued to meet regularly with Peter for a drink before curtain time, and continued to praise him publicly, but he also started meeting with a new board member, the business executive Ted Rogers, who would soon become its chair. Ted had his own problems with Peter, and over the next few years they multiplied. In 1985 the board hired Charles "Chip" Raymond as a replacement for Betty Cage, whose deteriorating health had eventuated in a heart attack. Chip was personable but, as soon became apparent, lacked managerial skills. The board decided that Chip should be fired, and Peter was instructed to do so.[12]

But Chip had become Peter's close friend and tennis partner, and he delayed acting on the board's instructions. It became clear to Ted Rogers, as time passed, that Peter might never get on with the matter, and he summoned him to his office. Peter wasn't one to be "summoned" and he let Ted know, on arriving, that he had no intention of taking orders from him. At one point (when Ted accused him of lying) Peter shouted, "How dare you talk to me like that?!" For a passing moment Ted thought the encounter might become physical, but he held his ground. Yet Peter never did fire Chip; the board had to step in and do it. Two other managers then followed, both of whom failed at the job. Ted blamed those failures on the climate of personal intrigue and backbiting that had set in, and felt that Peter lacked the skill to mediate personal disagreements. He'd also come to believe that although Peter quickly proved himself adept at raising money, he wasn't good at managing it; uninterested in balance sheets and budgets, he lacked Balanchine's concern that funds be carefully allocated. Peter, of course, was new at his multifaceted and demanding job and entitled to the benefit of the doubt as he grew into it. What worried Ted, and Lincoln, was that what they called "Peter's arrogance" would interfere with his growth.

That fear seemed confirmed by a new development—during a bitter argument with his wife, Darci Kistler, a principal dancer in the company, Peter had apparently roughed her up and she called the police. When the story hit the newspapers, Ted Rogers convened a high-level meeting of prominent people, a number of whom weren't connected to NYCB (like Keith Reinhardt, the head of the advertising agency DDB Worldwide, and Marilyn Lowry, senior vice president of communications for AT&T). This ad hoc body urged that Peter make a public statement in which he admitted to the domestic violence, apologized for it, and agreed to seek counseling and treatment. When Peter heard the recommendations, he angrily refused to comply. Ted told him that he had no choice in the matter—short of resigning, that is—and Peter finally, reluctantly, went along; and by then, Darci had dropped the charges. Lincoln phoned him to say that if there was ever again such an incident, he'd never again speak to him.

Several years into Peter's tenure, a quite different set of grievances against him gained currency—that as a result of his leadership, or lack thereof, Balanchine's legacy was in danger of being diluted if not lost. Practices were being missed, teaching days canceled, and in general the discipline needed to maintain the steps as Balanchine had devised them had given way to a sloppy, slipshod approach. Lincoln was among those expressing concern.

Every few weeks he'd ask Ted Rogers to have lunch. And usually it was to discuss the same agenda: Peter was a bad choreographer and a bad manager, and he had to be gotten rid of before he destroyed Balanchine's legacy. But who would replace him? Ted asked. Did Lincoln have a candidate in mind? These repetitive meetings went on for some six months. The only concrete names that Lincoln ever suggested as replacements for Peter were Helgi Tomasson and Edward Villella—but he honorably admitted that he couldn't be sure they would be any better at the job than Peter. Given the stalemate, Ted finally stopped making himself available for lunch.

Peter became aware of what was going on. He consulted with various allies, including Barbara Horgan, Balanchine's executor and head of the Balanchine Trust. "Lincoln is trying to get rid of me," he said to her one day. "What would you do if he succeeded?" "I'd take Mr. Balanchine's intellectual property," Barbara remembers telling him, "and I would leave with you, and I don't mind who you tell that to." Barbara's strong backing carried weight. Peter's advisers in general urged him to lie low; with Lincoln himself then under attack by Anne Bass and other board members as "unstable," he probably wasn't thinking clearly, and besides, he wasn't likely to remain a significant factor for much longer. Peter took the advice and, refusing all interviews, wisely let the turmoil run its course.

But he did play an active role in getting one influential board member, Bob Gottlieb, to resign. By that time, Gottlieb—Lincoln's editor at Knopf and currently editor of *The New Yorker* (and, as it happens, editor of this book)—had been on the board for a decade, having back in the seventies agreed to Lincoln's request that he serve. Indeed Gottlieb had, for the better part of a decade, been handling various important managerial tasks, including programming the company's seasons and overseeing its marketing. In the process he'd gotten to know Peter well and had become something of a confidant. When word reached Peter that Bob, too, had been voicing concerns over Balanchine's legacy, Peter felt betrayed.

A critical juncture was reached after Arlene Croce wrote a sharply negative review of Martins's stewardship of the company in Gottlieb's *New Yorker*. He was indignant that Gottlieb hadn't killed the Croce piece, and he called Barbara Horgan at home to vent his anger. Barbara pointed out that there was something called First Amendment rights, that although Gottlieb may have regretted Croce's review, he'd rightly refrained from censoring it. But Peter would have none of it; already inflamed by reports that Gottlieb was "trashing" him, he exploded in anger at him on the phone: "You not only published Arlene's piece, you agree with it!" Soon after, when Gottlieb's term was up, he left the board. Lincoln, who'd earlier told Gottlieb, "You have to look after Peter—I'm too old," stood aside.

At the close of 1985, Mina, in her eighty-ninth year, died. Having bravely decided to undergo open-heart surgery, she'd succumbed a week later to a stroke. In recent years Mina had moved closer to Weston, and Lincoln, grousing all the way, had gone for lunch at her house on most weekends. He'd grumble about Mina "playing Sarah Bernhardt" and exaggerating her infirmities, but the two had deep historical roots, inseparably intertwined over time, and he felt her loss. A year after Mina's death, his brother, George, also died. Unlike Mina, George had never been particularly close to Lincoln, but as the keeper of the family fortune, he'd been a steady part of his life, sounding the note of fiduciary caution as an annoyed Lincoln would struggle against being reined in.

But the death that shook Lincoln most was the suicide on February 16, 1986, of his beloved Joe Duell, aged twenty-nine. Severely depressed, Joe had jumped from a window to his death. The night before, he'd rehearsed Balanchine's *Who Cares?* and then worked with his brother, Daniel, preparing a script for a Ballet Guild luncheon. Daniel could sense that his brother was disturbed but, even twenty years later, he considers Joe's death "a mystery." As it was to everyone who knew him, given that his career, social life, and physical health all seemed enviably upbeat. But depression *is* an enigma (even as treatments for it advance), and its wretched stepchild, suicide, a profound conundrum. Lincoln wasn't one to verbalize his pain, but as he wrote Michael Leonard, "You will realize what a dreadful time we have all been enduring. So great a mystery, in its capacity for being allowed to happen, tests one's firmest faith."[13]

Four years later, Lincoln gave thought to building a chapel in memory of Joe Duell and went so far as to commission Philip Johnson to draw up preliminary plans. But he never followed through on the idea, perhaps realizing that getting enmeshed in creating a memorial could further prolong and intensify his agony.

Old Age

(1986–1996)

I N NEW YORK CITY on one of his periodic visits, Michael Leonard phoned Lincoln at home on the morning of May 18, 1987, and asked him how he felt. "Dull," was the monosyllabic reply. "Apprehensive?" Michael asked, guessing at the reason. "Yes," Lincoln answered emphatically. And with some reason. It was the morning of the planned gala (Nancy Lassalle being planner in chief) to be held that evening at the State Theater in celebration of Lincoln's eightieth birthday. Lincoln was sure the whole thing would be "perfectly awful."[1]

It wasn't—not even for Lincoln. The curtain rose at 6:15 p.m. to reveal the orchestra onstage. It proceeded to play excerpts from *Swan Lake*, Robert Irving conducting, followed by the appearance of Peter Martins holding a microphone. Given the recent tensions with Lincoln, Peter did magnanimously well by him. It had been very difficult selecting a present for Lincoln, Peter told the audience: first of all, he had everything; second, he didn't really want anything; and third, he likes almost nothing. But Lincoln *had* long talked about his desire for the company to do *The Sleeping Beauty*, Martins went on, and (here a screen dropped down on cue) it was hoped that this would be a suitable, pleasing gift. What then followed was a short film showing preliminaries for the planned production—set models by David Mitchell and costume designs by Patricia Zipprodt.

The film finished, a spotlight picked out Lincoln in his customary first-ring seat, and Suzanne Farrell appeared on stage, with ballet mistress Rosemary Dunleavy, to toast him. As if by magic, Lincoln was handed his own glass of vodka and downed it in one gulp. Next followed a performance of Jerry Robbins's *Circus Polka* with ringmaster Mikhail Baryshnikov figuratively cracking the whip as three dozen little girls from SAB danced their hearts out, eventually forming the letters *L* and *K*.

Lincoln was then escorted out of his seat and onto the stage, to be greeted by Mayor Ed Koch, in top comic form. Asking what could be done to honor a man who had "accomplished so much in so many fields," the mayor thought that "possibly you could name a great complex after him"—but thought maybe that had already been done with Lincoln Center. Well, Koch mockingly brooded, perhaps Kirstein could be awarded the Handel Medallion, the city's highest cultural award. Oh, my, it seemed Kirstein had already been given that way back in 1973. But—and here the mayor brightened up—there had been no public ceremony at the time, and so saying, he presented the medallion to Lincoln (who quickly dropped it into his suit pocket).

Lincoln himself then made a short speech, mostly devoted to thanking the "267 people" without whom he would have done nothing. Eddie Warburg, his co-conspirator of fifty years earlier, was in the audience that night, and he later charmingly chided Lincoln for his "usual modesty and generosity in giving others credit for those ideas that they never knew they had until you gave them to them." Eddie added fondly, "We have experienced or witnessed some unimagined wonders and yours is a unique record. O.K. So deny it! It still remains a fact."

As a final touch to the evening, a huge cake was wheeled onstage, as the American flag backdrop from *Stars and Stripes* was unveiled behind it. Lincoln took the one lighted candle off the cake and handed it to one of the SAB children, who blew it out. Flowers and balloons then cascaded down. Lincoln picked up bunches of the flowers, handed them to the children, waved and smiled to the audience—and was gone.

Or almost gone. He thought about making his departure from NYCB abrupt and complete, but decided that would amount to a dereliction. Too much still remained in flux, and in particular the question of who would succeed him as head of the school. Lincoln feared that the board, divided and (in his view) ineffectual, would grab at "an instant president with first thought to his preeminence or name or connections or whatever." Lincoln thought his successor should be an experienced ballet professional "with conscious and up-to-date intimacy in current training and performance realities." He came up with what he thought was the ideal candidate: Robert Lindgren, director of the North Carolina School of the Arts, which Lincoln regarded as (next to SAB) "the most important ballet training institution in the United States." The board went along with Lincoln's recommendation and gave Lindgren the nod. But it quickly became clear that he was the wrong person for the job, not least because he and Peter Martins had trouble finding common ground. Even Lincoln eventually saw that he'd made a mistake, and Lindgren was let go early in 1991.[2]

One of Peter Martins's early-on brainstorms also came a cropper. He had the stirringly democratic idea of inviting choreographers from across the United States to present a season of new works at the State Theater. Jerry Robbins angrily opposed the idea; Jerry ordinarily preferred to evade his responsibilities as "co–ballet master" (and would soon resign the post altogether), but in this instance he chose vigorously to oppose Martins, arguing that such an event would simply "open the doors to a bunch of rank amateurs." The board backed Peter—only to have Robbins proved right. Perhaps the weeding-out process was insufficiently thorough and the wrong choreographers chosen, but whatever the reasons, "the American Music Festival" was commonly viewed as a disaster. Lincoln called it "unproductive and exasperating."

The company itself, in Lincoln's view, was performing "even better than when Balanchine was alive." His latest candidate for "this year's white hope" was the young male dancer Damian Woetzel—who would in fact go on to a long and brilliant career. The downside for Lincoln was the lack of new pieces in the company's repertory. To take up the slack he himself commissioned the composer, Todd Levin, and the principal dancer Bobby La Fosse, to do a ballet based on *Puss in Boots*. To encourage La Fosse, Lincoln—his penchant for hyperbole still operative—told him that he was "the most gifted dancer AND choreographer of your generation."

Lincoln was also disappointed in the school's workshop performance of Fokine's *Les Sylphides*, and annoyed that some of the students resentfully approached it as a boring exercise ("They have no sense of any style other than today's," he lamented). But there was nothing he could do about it, and his ceaseless worry machine focused less on the kids at SAB than on "the kids" at home. That meant primarily Freddie Maddox, David Langfitt, and a newcomer, Nicholas "Nick" Jenkins, a charming, bright Englishman completing his doctorate on Auden, whom Lincoln, on first meeting, had immediately taken to. Nick, in turn, came to understand Lincoln as few people ever had: he was a man, Nick would write in a *New Yorker* article published after Lincoln's death, who "was in two distinct places at once—because he wanted to be, and because he couldn't help being. He sought to be retiring, but he was all the more noticeable as he tried to be invisible. . . . He was a promulgator of order who was fascinated and energized by the ubiquity of disorder. He was a shy individual who never backed away from conflict," and he could turn on people "a fierce and stressful degree of kindness."

Nick had recently married the painter Siri Huntoon, whom Lincoln was also fond of and whom Jensen employed for a time in his restoration work. Lincoln offered Nick, a lively, discerning presence well-liked by everyone (except for Fred Maddox), the job of helping him with his current writing projects. Nick proved of great help to Lincoln in turning out two books, an anthology, *By With To & From: A Lincoln Kirstein Reader* (1991), and *Mosaic* (1994)—an autobiography of variable accuracy that ran up through Lincoln's twenty-sixth year; Nick and Siri were co-dedicatees of the book.

When Nick happened to mention offhandedly that their cramped studio apartment in the East Village was making it difficult for him to write, Lincoln promptly—to Nick's astonishment—had a storage area in the basement of the Nineteenth Street house wired and lit so that Nick could use it as an office. It was a prime example of Lincoln's "fierce and stressful degree of kindness."[3]

As for David Langfitt, he made the decision in 1989 to go to law school and to confine his painting to two days a week. Lincoln strongly disapproved; he thought David had been making real progress and deplored sacrificing talent to security. But David wanted to settle down and have children without having to turn to his surgeon father for help.

As for Fred Maddox, Michael Leonard (like many others) found him an enigmatic figure, a surprisingly sluggish, remote companion for Lincoln to have chosen in his old age. After one visit to Lincoln, Michael wrote in his diary, "we spent quite a lot of the time listening to [Freddie's] recounting of his architectural training . . . and an immodest assessment of his own originality and brilliance. The combination of self-justification and his repetitive and inarticulate way of getting across to us is not very attractive. Lincoln looked at him strangely during these episodes, a look in which there was a high degree of tolerance and affection mixed with a sort of resigned exasperation. There's no doubt they are deeply fond of each other." Perhaps at bottom, it was Fred's sheer ordinariness that accounted for his appeal. For himself, Lincoln had detested being put on a pedestal, treated like a revered cultural monument to whom homage had to be paid and due deference accorded. With Fred he could be one of the guys, hanging out with another guy.

There are those who thought of Fred as a sort of glorified valet. Yet his opinions did sometimes carry weight with Lincoln. According to Paul Cadmus and Jon Anderson, for instance, Fred "was instrumental in ousting Stevie Lonsdale"—a young man who in the mid-eighties served as a kind of part-time secretary for Lincoln—despite the fact that Paul and Jon considered Stevie's "demeanor and general behavior to have been model. He was apparently popular with everyone except Fred." On balance, and despite his reservations, Michael decided that "Freddie is good for the old man, who has many trials to cope with and needs support."

Having Paul and Jon right down the hill from his own house in Weston was another important source of sustenance. In the early eighties Lincoln felt that he and Paul "seem to be less and less close as we grow older; something like exhausting an ancient intimacy that had less warmth than mutual curiosity." That assessment may have reflected a passing mood; Lincoln tended to pound on the keyboard every time he felt ill or well about someone, whereas most adults wait to see whether a feeling becomes lasting before giving voice to it. Not only did Paul (who was five years older than Lincoln) and Jon cook for Lincoln in his own home almost every Saturday night, but on Sundays Lincoln usually had brunch at their place as well.[4]

Cadmus had a modest resurgence in reputation in the early eighties, including a retrospective exhibition in three regional museums (no gallery in New York wanted to participate). At the same time Lincoln decided— doubtless during one of those moods when he felt warm and fuzzy toward

Paul—to do a book about his old friend. He ended up rewriting it some five times, never finding it satisfactory and not finding a publisher for it until 1992 when a private press (Chameleon) finally brought it out.

None of which is to suggest that Lincoln burrowed into his den and became a stay-at-home hermit following his eightieth birthday. Compared with his younger years, he did curtail going to parties or busying himself with SAB's affairs, but he continued to go out and about a good deal. Nick Jenkins, for one, felt Lincoln maintained his "intellectual vibrancy and rigor" right up to the very last few months of his life. During the ballet season he went constantly, almost nightly, to performances (even if he did sometimes fall asleep or leave at the intermission), and he also continued to go fairly regularly to the major art exhibits. He was madly enthusiastic about the Caravaggio show at the Met ("it beggars description"), and madly infuriated at MoMA's renovated building "with triple their original space and six-times the horror of postmodern art. It's like a great super-market." Now and then, Lincoln was even up to promoting the work of a newer artist, like the traditional sculptor George Kelley *and* the avant-garde sculptor Scott Burton. Lincoln had always been more eclectic in his taste than he let on publicly (he greatly admired, for example, the poetry of Frank O'Hara). In art he *did* particularly cherish the "realist" tradition, but as Nick Jenkins has put it, Lincoln showed, even into old age, a willingness "to subvert his own long-maintained orthodoxies, to remain open to novelty, to exhibit Whitmanesque abilities both to contradict himself and to acknowledge with a cheery insouciance that he was doing so."

One day, Nick arrived at the Nineteenth Street house expecting to be bawled out, or even banished—he'd just published a lengthy piece in the *TLS* on the conceptual artist Bruce Nauman. And sure enough, the first thing Lincoln said to him, the tone icy, was, "You realize that Paul Cadmus will never speak to you again." Nick shrugged in resignation and said simply, "It's what I think." Lincoln stared at him in silence, then broke into "a broad, mischievous smile" and proceeded to compliment Nick on his article.

The two men would often talk about art, and on another occasion, Lincoln gleefully told Nick that Tchelitchev used to "refer dismissively" to Picasso as Pot-cassé ("Broken pot"). Nick wasn't amused and asked impatiently (yes, Lincoln intimates *could* be impatient with him without being savaged), "Do *you* think that's right?" Taken by surprise, Lincoln "grinned puckishly." "*Sometimes,*" he said, with a chuckle.

Lincoln also continued to be generous with his donations of money, ranging from fifteen thousand dollars to the National Academy of Design to renovate its foyer to twenty-seven hundred dollars to the Russian Holy Fathers Church (Father Adrian, Balanchine's spiritual adviser, was connected to the Fathers) to repair its sidewalk. He gave money to Daniel Duell's Ballet Chicago, to Paul Taylor's Dance Company, and to Jacques d'Amboise's National Dance Institute. And in 1988 alone, he gave several thousand dollars to AIDS organizations, as well as serving as a sponsor for the AIDS Walk. That in no sense meant that Lincoln had enlisted in the gay liberation brigade. He didn't deplore those who became politically active, but he claimed not to find common ground for identification, for affixing a reductive label to himself that failed to describe his own varied sexual-affectionate history. More important, Lincoln was of a generation for whom sexual behavior in general was not considered the central stuff of public discourse—let alone the central ingredient in one's identity— even if privately he'd long been remarkably open about whom and what he desired.

The donation to Paul Taylor in 1988 was one of several Lincoln gave to his company over the years, and Taylor was grateful for Lincoln's support of a "modern" dancer. Nor, according to Taylor, did Lincoln "want to be credited for it . . . it wasn't to put a plaque up with his name on it, or one of the seats in the theater, like some people do." He backed Taylor morally as well as financially. Back in 1959 Taylor had been a guest performer in NYCB's *Episodes*, and after it Balanchine had had him learn several other dances and asked him to join the company. Taylor decided instead to go out on his own. Lincoln later told him how right he thought the decision had been: "What you have done . . . is so much stronger than it would have been under any other dispensation . . . the strength of your vision prevents much 'collaboration,' which is what has preserved you. Your special quality . . . is something I wished to appropriate for my own purposes, but it proved too powerful to use or borrow."

At Taylor's invitation, Lincoln came to see the dress rehearsal of a new work, *Last Look*, and Taylor sat next to him during the performance. It was a dance about alienation and depression (Paul, too, had had his share), and when the curtain came down, he looked over and saw that tears were streaming down Lincoln's face. "I wish," Taylor later said, "I'd saved them in a little bottle. It was one of the best compliments I ever had."[5]

Admiring Paul the way he did, Lincoln felt the moral responsibility always to speak his mind to him. In 1980, for example, when Taylor was feeling troubled, Lincoln suggested that he was "confused by the presence and pressure of a success which you doubt if you deserve or can sustain. Success is always much harder, and more dangerous than the gripes of failure." He then candidly went on to say that "your sense of confusion and inadequacy sometimes leads you into a style which I have to call silliness. The ridiculous is very appealing, but in my aesthetics there are only three valid styles: the ironic, the tragic and the lyric. The pratfall is not a situation; it's a gag. The ridiculous pleases the public, but it should be used like pepper."

Lincoln had spoken his mind to the right person. Taylor treated the "admonition" as, "considering Lincoln's aesthetics . . . extremely kind and generous." He confessed to Lincoln that "one of the missing parts of my life has been a guide, a father. In my imagination for a long time you have filled that gap. Hope you do not mind me telling you such a personal thing." Later he added, "I *thank* you, I *revere* you, I feel totally *legalized* by you."

For the first time in his life, Lincoln, at age eighty two, felt able to describe himself as "wildly successful and rather rich. . . . I don't have to worry about supporting the ballet-school or company. Both are success-fully funded and have feasible futures." In fact, at the end of 1989, SAB was about to move into splendid new quarters in the Juilliard building—four floors and six large studios, including, at last, a dormitory for students. Like most moves, unexpected costs surfaced and Lincoln met them himself by selling off a fair number of paintings from his art collection, including a Lucian Freud and an Henri Gaudier-Brzeska.[6]

If Lincoln continued regularly to attend NYCB performances, he no longer served either the company or school in any significant capacity. He finally had enough time to write—or, put more accurately, he had fewer reasons not to. Though no longer racing around as he once had to meet an overbooked appointment diary—he was now, after all, in his early eighties—Lincoln still went out fairly often to lunches and dinners and still had people in at Nineteenth Street. When Michael Leonard saw him in 1989, Lincoln gave him a breakfast of grapefruit juice and half a melon and launched into an enthusiastic account of the current Velázquez show at the Met—" 'the best thing ever' "—urging Michael not miss it.

Michael then brought the subject around to Catholicism. Was Lincoln still going to Mass every day? Less frequently, Lincoln answered. He felt that "the Pope and the Church were full of wrong-headedness, though there were a lot of bright, enlightened young minds among the clergy." When, at another time, Michael brought up the significant number of gay Catholic priests who were being denounced and defrocked, Lincoln called it "tragic hypocrisy."

Whatever the cause, Lincoln no longer suffered from extreme mood swings, even though his prominence had subsided and despite the fact that old age is often accompanied by depression. In the years that Nick Jenkins knew him, he only once witnessed any out-of-the-ordinary behavior: in a restaurant Lincoln started talking to an empty seat—but then quickly reverted to normal.

He also still regularly went up to Weston on weekends—and still drove in erratic, hair-raising style. Lincoln seemed to think the car had a will of its own; he told Paul Cadmus that when driving he wasn't "entirely in charge of it, you know. It goes by itself. I love it so much I don't want to hurt its feelings." The daredevil in Lincoln hadn't wholly subsided. He once fell asleep at the wheel, and only the thick toughness of his old car saved him from serious injury or death. Still, he had to go to court, armed with a letter from his doctor to the effect that his drowsiness was due to a new drug he was taking.

In New York, Lincoln continued to give small dinner parties. In 1990, Rudi Nureyev was a guest at one of them. It wasn't until after nine that they sat down for dinner in the small area at the end of the gallery room. The only light came from candles, and the table was beautifully laid with chrysanthemum heads in glass dishes. Talk mostly revolved around the ballet. Rudi refused to be offended when Lincoln attacked Erik Bruhn, who'd been Nureyev's lover and remained his friend. Rudi said at one point that Balanchine was the most important thing to happen to ballet in the twentieth century, and asked what would happen to the New York City Ballet now that he was gone. "He's dead," Lincoln replied. "We have moved on." Lincoln asked Rudi if, as rumored, he was going to resign as director of the Paris Opéra Ballet, and Rudi said he was. "Why don't you train up an assistant if you can't manage the job alone?" Lincoln asked. Rudi responded with a campy non sequitur: "I do not work with anyone who does not go horizontal for me." He never referred to his depleted energy, made no acknowledgment that he was ill with the HIV virus that, three years later, would kill him.

Between 1987 and 1994, from Lincoln's eightieth to his eighty-seventh year, he published—depending on one's definition of a "book"—an astonishing five volumes. They included his collected poetry, *The Poems of Lincoln Kirstein* (1987); the 1989 *Memorial to a Marriage* (dedicated to Joseph Duell), an essay-length accompaniment to Jerry L. Thompson's photographic album of Saint-Gaudens's memorial to Marian Hooper Adams in Washington, DC's Rock Creek cemetery; the eight-hundred-word *Puss in Boots* (1992), an illustrated childlike tale about a heroic cat; *Tchelitchev* (1994), a 110-page study, with illustrative plates; and (with Nick Jenkins's noteworthy help) *Mosaic* (1994), a memoir up through the year 1933.

Memorial to a Marriage, though slim, is noteworthy for the empathy it reveals for the plight of women in a male-dominated society. In speculating on the suicide of Marian ("Clover") Hooper, the wife of Henry Adams, Lincoln wrote, "One senses that beneath her natural warmth, charm, and wit lay a resentment toward a society that assigned women formal courtesy while holding them firmly in bondage." Lincoln deplored Henry Adams's "self-satisfied complacency in assuming that women were incapable of much 'exercise of the mind.' " If this was belated expiation on Lincoln's part for Fidelma's truncated life, if he saw any parallel between her and Marian Hooper, he would have considered any such direct reference flat-footed and vulgar.

Though Lincoln's trips to Weston became less frequent over time, whenever he was there he went to see Fidelma. On one such occasion he took Nick Jenkins with him, and Nick has vividly described the visit: "There she was, a small, slender, very tidily presented and very elegant old woman, sitting beautifully erect on the side of the bed. . . . She looked a bit like a shy bird perched unruffled on a branch." Fidelma said not a single word during the visit, but Lincoln talked quietly to her as he went around the room watering the plants, being careful, in his clumsy way, his hands beginning to shake with age, not to spill any drops onto the window ledge. The chore completed, the three sat for a while in silence, until Lincoln got up and gently said to Fidelma that it was time to go, but that he would see her again the following week.

Two years after Lincoln published *Memorial to a Marriage*, Fidelma, on November 5, 1991, died in her rest-home prison. She was cremated, but Lincoln, instead of keeping her ashes, chose to deliver them to her brother, Paul; his companion, Jon Anderson, saw to it that they were buried in Fidelma's beloved outdoors, under a flowering shrub.

In his book on Tchelitchev—based on his earlier writings about the artist and relying especially on the catalog he'd done for the 1964 retrospective at Huntington Hartford's short-lived Gallery of Modern Art—Lincoln made his intentions clear in the very first line: "This book aims to revive interest in an artist who, so far, has found small mention in [the] annals of contemporary art." *Tchelitchev* is less a biography than an essay in art criticism. In a prose style uncharacteristically straightforward, free of curliqued, complexly mannered digression, Lincoln traced the contrast between contemporary indifference to Tchelitchev's work and the international reputation he'd enjoyed from the 1920s to the 1950s.

Deeply informed by his own friendship with the artist, *Tchelitchev* did incidentally manage to settle a few ancient scores—like singling out Alfred Barr's "Fantastic Art: Dada, Surrealism" (1936) for making "no mention of him [Tchelitchev] even among artists cited as 'independent of surrealism.' " Nor did Lincoln spare Pavlik himself; he made it clear that his friend's volatile, ferocious personality kept more than one patron away. Lincoln also was quick to praise. He described Pavlik's dealer, Julien Levy, whom he'd never much liked, as "long-suffering," and despite his off-and-on-again friendship with Monroe Wheeler, Lincoln portrayed him as "selfless, with a sunny nature" and applauded his "lasting support" for Tchelitchev's work.

Of the five "books," only the memoir *Mosaic* received significant press coverage. Published by the eminent house of Farrar, Straus & Giroux, it was widely, even reverentially reviewed, both in the States and abroad. In England, for example, the *Times Literary Supplement* ended a lengthy review thus: "He has proved himself a writer distinctive enough to fuse, in ordered lucidity, the strife of his life and heart of his art." *Mosaic* is, despite inaccuracies deliberate and otherwise, characterized by the qualities that define Lincoln's best non-fiction: broad knowledge, trenchant sophistication, elegant compression (occasionally over-compression), and witty understatement.

Favorable though the reviews were, they shared two shortcomings: an unawareness of the book's occasional unreliability (in a number of instances, the fantasist and trickster in Lincoln overpowered the historical stickler), and a tendency to regard NYCB's anxiety-ridden history as somehow destined to eventuate in success. Lincoln was particularly disappointed, even irritated, at the review by Arlene Croce (one of the few dance critics he admired) in *The New Yorker.* Though full of complicated praise for *Mosaic,* the review nowhere recognized that the survival of the New York City Ballet had been touch-and-go for decades, not merely years, and a stable outcome hardly foreordained. To pretend otherwise was, after all, tantamount to minimizing the painful uncertainties, the constant crises, doubts, and fears that made the Balanchine/Kirstein commitment all the more remarkable and their eventual triumph all the more breathtaking. Lincoln didn't enjoy being treated referentially as some sort of impenetrable, iconic figure. Yet the formidable exterior he'd developed early on to conceal his pain had always made it difficult to discern the suffering man within.

David Langfitt used the studio these days only on weekends; during the week Jensen would take over the space, then return to his home in New Jersey on weekends. With Nick Jenkins also around, and Lincoln's secretary, Alex Schierman, stopping by often, he had built-in companionship without ever having to leave the house—which in fact he did less and less often with each passing year. But in the early nineties Lincoln still made plenty of exceptions. In the winter of 1991, for example, as NYCB began work on *The Sleeping Beauty,* Lincoln would often go to the State Theater to sit in on rehearsals. (Thanks to two half-million-dollar gifts from board members, the production would be lavish.) And he was of course present on January 30, 1991, when the students first occupied the new dormitory. Interviewed for the occasion by the *New York Times,* Lincoln, true to type, managed to sound the worrywart note: "Physically it couldn't be better. . . . But we have no idea what the maintenance costs are going to be. . . . So I'm grateful, but not cheerful."[7]

Along with occasionally helping out with fund-raising, Lincoln kept several projects on a low burner. He and Jerry L. Thompson talked about doing a follow-up volume to *Quarry,* the photographic book, with text, on the Kirsteins' Nineteenth Street house. The new work, which they jokingly referred to as "Son of Quarry," would do the same sort of job on the house in Weston, even though it contained many fewer art works than Nineteenth Street. From September 1990 to June 1991, Thompson went weekly to Connecticut to photograph. But Lincoln gradually lost interest in the project, and it never came to completion.

He also commissioned Robert La Fosse to choreograph a children's ballet for SAB based on *Puss in Boots*. According to La Fosse, Lincoln actively contributed ideas for the project and sat in on rehearsals. When performed at SAB, the ballet was warmly received, but was never taken into the company's repertory, perhaps because La Fosse and Peter Martins had something of an adversarial relationship, La Fosse not bothering to conceal his distaste for what he saw as Peter's "arrogance."

Lincoln might have been more active still, but he knew perfectly well that certain key donors on the board, led by Anne Bass, simply didn't want him around anymore. Their justifications ran from "Lincoln is too crazy and unreliable" to the more benign "He doesn't know how to manage a modern organization." Jensen Yow distinctly remembers one night at the ballet when Anne Bass told Lincoln to his face, "You just don't know how to run things." Enraged, Lincoln turned around without a word and walked away. On another occasion several people recall a shouting match between the two of them, with Lincoln giving at least as good as he got. ("Wealthy, powerful women" was hardly a category that called out automatic disputation: Agnes Gund and Brooke Astor were among Lincoln's great favorites.) But Lincoln did feel deeply hurt at the attempt by Anne Bass (and others) to put him out to pasture, a hurt compounded by his antagonists' lack of historical understanding of the struggles and setbacks that had finally brought NYCB to its current international status.

Lincoln may still have been dreaming up projects, but with far less sound and fury as he moved into his late eighties. One sign of his growing disengagement was his refusal to deal with the gradual deterioration of the Nineteenth Street house. He would worry about it to Jensen, but would then shrug his shoulders when Jens made practical proposals for repair. The major problem was leakage from the old drainpipes. Lincoln's bathroom, which was right over the front door, was the first to go; he simply shifted to another bathroom. Then the gold fabric started to peel from the living room walls, becoming water-streaked in the process.

Finally persuaded that a plumber should have a look, Lincoln then vetoed the man's proposal for a major renovation. When the bathroom in Fidelma's old room (now Fred's) began to leak into the kitchen, Lincoln continued to ignore the deterioration, which was tantamount to making the statement: "I'll go before the house will, so why bother?"—a sentiment perhaps more realistic than all the practical plans for refurbishment. Which didn't mean that Lincoln's last years were spent in a "Grey Gardens" environment, surrounded by stench and decay, with assorted Collyer brothers hiding behind stacks of yellowing newspapers. Much of the Nineteenth Street house looked as it had before: elegant in its amenities, exquisite in its furnishings and art. The casual guest would have seen nothing of the mounting decay that lay behind some of the moldering walls.

And right up until the last few months of his life, Lincoln would still have treated those guests to a cascade of probing questions and provocative opinion ("Everybody [sic] agrees that Mark Morris is the new Balanchine, save *me*!!!"). Still reading voraciously in the early years of the nineties, he still had clear-cut favorites; he thought Lynn Garafola's book about the Ballets Russes, which in some quarters had been attacked, "very good," and he raved to everyone about John Richardson's *Picasso*. As late as December 1992, at eighty-five, Lincoln was also still occasionally going to the galleries. He was outraged that George Tooker's "handsome" one-man show had been "slammed" by the critics as "affected and retrograde." And he was equally outraged when the critics cheered a retrospective of René Magritte's work, which he found "formularized and coarsely painted."[8]

By the mid-nineties Lincoln had basically stopped going out, yet he continued, with effort, occasionally to attend the ballet (yes, the ballet would of course be the last to go). Once, with Jensen's help, he made it to the outside of the State Theater, but felt too weak to go in; Lincoln started to cry, while Jensen held his hand and the two hid behind the columns to prevent being seen. Yet when he did summon the energy to attend a performance, Lincoln was still capable of strong opinions about it; pleased as he was that the Balanchine Festival in spring 1993 caused "a great international splash," he thought *Orpheus* "was not well done at all." Arlene Croce (still Lincoln's favorite critic, despite her *Mosaic* review) thought the entire festival had been poorly executed and announced that Balanchine's genius had been lost under the now-ten-year-old Martins regime. But Lincoln himself had come around to accepting the view that "there's nobody better around." He might still express displeasure, privately, to an intimate, but in public he now unfailingly supported Martins and, mantra-like, told naysayers, "Balanchine is dead. Martins has made a go of it, has expanded the endowment, opened new quarters, successfully dealt with the unions, held the organization together."

The 1990s saw the simultaneous disappearance of Lincoln as Ogre and Lincoln as Proteus. People like Jerry Thompson, David Langfitt, and Michael Leonard, who first got to know him in the late eighties and early nineties, knew only an affectionate, gentle, brilliant man, disinterested in his own achievements, with a limited amount of energy and a kindly disposition; they expressed disbelief when told the tales of the assaultive, erratic Lincoln of earlier times, of rude eruptions, quicksilver disappearances, and irrational rages. Was it the years that had burned all that away, leaving an essential core of soft-hearted tenderness? Or did his explosive side succumb to his medications (though he kept "forgetting" to take them), suggesting that underlying emotional illness had been the primary cause of his earlier outbursts and anger? It could as well be argued that Lincoln's wrathful, vehement side disappeared *despite* his medications, yielding inescapably to the inroads age makes on energy and the need for combat.

Some days were decidedly better than others. When one visitor asked him how he was doing, Lincoln replied, "I'm getting senile." "What's that like for you?" the guest asked. "It's not so bad," Lincoln said. "It's a little like being your own pet." When Michael Leonard arrived from London for his one-man show in March 1992, Lincoln turned up for the opening on the wrong day and "all in all seemed bleak." Yet when Michael returned in November, Lincoln seemed in "excellent form" and the in-house clan gathered for what turned into an affectionate, campy, "extremely jolly" evening.

And so it went, at least until 1995, when Lincoln developed a debilitating series of physical problems: phlebitis, bedsores, and an enlarged prostate that led to surgery. He was eating badly—mostly Chinese takeout—getting no exercise, and often just lying on his bed in a darkened house, sometimes reading, usually not. Paul Cadmus suggested that he start going to Weston again, that the country might do him good. When he mentioned that a hired limo would make the trip easy, Lincoln's frightened response was, "Oh, no. I might have to talk to the driver."

His appointment diary, once stuffed with projects and ideas for projects that littered the sidewalks of New York for half a century, now became a scratched-up toy for the five cats in residence. When Michael visited on May 16, 1995, he asked Lincoln how he was doing. "Oh, it's a half life," Lincoln replied. "I've got no energy." Michael showed him a few photos of his recent work, and Lincoln seemed to perk up a bit with interest. But there were lapses of silence, and after some twenty or so minutes Lincoln simply said, "Well, I think I'll go up now. Thank you for coming. Thank you for coming." That same spring of 1995, Lincoln gave Nick Jenkins a similar message: "You better go now, Nick." The implication was clear. (Even earlier, when feeling well, Lincoln almost never said "goodbye"; the word seemed too painfully definitive, foreclosing the prospect of another meeting).

Jensen was still in the house during the week, working in his studio, and he frequently checked on Lincoln; Alex Schierman and Paul Cadmus also came by often. In the evenings, Fred Maddox was there. Though no one doubted Maddox's loyalty to Lincoln, Jensen and others very much doubted whether his "closed-off" personality allowed him to provide much emotional comfort. As Lincoln took to his bed and began to sleep more and more, a male nurse was hired to attend to his basic needs. When Jensen, at one point, tried to show Lincoln some art books that he'd especially enjoyed in the past, he turned toward Jensen and quietly said, "I don't care any more."

As the weather warmed up that summer of 1995, Lincoln was moved from his bedroom, which fronted on the street and was noisy at night, to a daybed in the first-floor sitting room, where it was somewhat cooler (the house wasn't air-conditioned) and where Lincoln could be surrounded by some of his favorite paintings. Though he no longer received visitors, an exception was made when a group of five or six NYCB people dropped by; Lincoln briefly rallied at their appearance, but the visit was kept short. By late fall, Lincoln was rarely responsive. He lay in the dark on his bed, asleep most of the time.

On the evening of January 5, 1996, Jensen received a call from Fred Maddox: Lincoln had died. As Jensen put it, "He simply faded away . . . his heart must have given out."

According to Paul Cadmus, Lincoln had been *very* clear that he wanted no religious service following his death, and Paul was furious when Father Adrian pronounced a benediction as Lincoln's ashes were scattered over the pond in Weston. Only about a dozen people were there that day, and each flung from a seashell a portion of the ash across the pond. The wind blew some of the ash back into the faces of the mourners—it had been that kind of a life—and the rest floated on the surface of the pond, some of it blown away by the wind, the rest of it gradually sinking below the water's surface.

ACKNOWLEDGMENTS

I've cited (in "Sources and Abbreviations") the many Kirstein friends and associates who've allowed me to interview them, as well as the owners of privately held materials who've shared Kirstein correspondence and documents with me. Here, I'd like to add my appreciation for various other kinds of assistance.

For help with translation, transcription, and research: Eva Borsook, Emma Robertson (England), Susan Shumaker and, especially, the hardworking Stephen Amico and the resourceful Meghan Horvath. For other kinds of support, leads, and favors: Lynne Adrian, Randall Bourscheidt, Rita Weill Byxbe, Richard Cluster, Elaine Edelman, Catharine Fedeli, Clive Fisher, Olive Fisher, Eric Foner, Lynn Garafola, Melissa Goldstein, Sue Grand, Jan Griscom, Kelli Griscom, Stu Hample, Barbara Horgan, John Howard, Katherine Hourigan, Donna Jensen and Chug Holmes, Arthur Hughes, Deborah Jowitt, Anna Kisselgoff, Ann Kitz, Nicholas Latimer, Stacy Morgan, Claudia Roth Pierpont, Philis Raskind, James E. Siegel, Mary Richie Smith, Joyce Hill Stoner, Steven Watson. My special thanks to Sue Llewellyn for her thoughtful copyedit of the book. I'm especially grateful to Alena Graedon of Knopf for brilliantly executing a thousand tasks during the production phase of this book.

Among the many archivists who've contributed their knowledge and skill, I want to single out Charles Perrier of the Dance Division, NYPL, for the considerable time and energy he spent familiarizing me with the vast Lincoln Kirstein Archives, hunting up various materials and meeting my ever-multiplying requests for photocopies. I also want to give special thanks to the cordial, dedicated Mary Marshall Clark at Columbia's Oral History Project and to the amazingly helpful Amy Fitch at the Rockefeller Archive Center—henceforth my model for what a truly dedicated archivist can do for the meandering, fuzzy scholar.

Other archivists whom I want to single out for going the extra mile are: Beth Alvarez at the University of Maryland; Kyle De Cicco Carey at the Harvard University Archives; Susan Clermont and Jeff Flannery at the Library of Congress; Steven Crook and Diana Burnham at The Berg Collection, NYPL; Eric Frazier at The Boston Public Library; Eugene R. Gaddis and Eric Zafran at the Hartford Atheneum; Susan Halpert and

Sarah Hutcheon at The Schlesinger Library at Radcliffe; Michelle Harvey at MoMA Archives; Heather Heckman at Ballet Society Archives; Stephen Jones at Yale's Beinecke Library; Peter Kayafas at the Eakins Press Foundation; Mary Adams Landa of the privately held Wyeth Collection; L. Rebecca Johnson Melvin at the University of Delaware; Jane Pritchard at the Marie Rambert Archives (England); Sheril Redmon at the Sophia Smith Library; Abigail G. Smith at Harvard University Art Museums Archives (the Fogg); Sandra Stelts, Special Collections, Penn State; Jessica Weidenhorn at the Oral History Project, Columbia University; and Trina Yeckley at the Smithsonian Archives of American Art.

I owe a considerable debt to the four people who read this book in manuscript and gave me the benefit of their insight and expertise: my loyal, indefatigable agent Frances Goldin; my loving if painfully honest partner Eli Zal; my extraordinary editor Bob Gottlieb, whose legendary reputation I now fully understand and whose profound knowledge of the world of ballet has saved me from a number of exquisite missteps; and Professor Nicholas Jenkins, the literary executor of the Lincoln Kirstein Estate, who sent me a comprehensive set of detailed notes on the manuscript of this book, comments remarkable for their acuity—they deeply informed my revisions. I additionally want to thank Nick Jenkins for deciding that I was the "right" person to do Kirstein's biography, and for opening up the treasure trove of his diaries and correspondence for my unconditional use.

SOURCES AND ABBREVIATIONS

DANCE DIVISION, NEW YORK PUBLIC LIBRARY FOR THE PERFORMING ARTS AT LINCOLN CENTER

1. LK/DD: Lincoln Kirstein Papers (see chap. I, n. 1, for full description)
2. DCS/DD: Douglas Coudy Scrapbook
3. RC/DD: Robert Chapman Papers (uncataloged as of 2005)
4. JY/DD: Jensen Yow Papers (uncataloged as of 2005)
5. ABTR/DD: American Ballet Theatre Records
6. BRMC/DD: Records of the Ballets Russes de Monte Carlo
7. LC/DD: Lucia Chase Papers
8. assorted photographic albums (*MGZEB 99–1221; 00–71; *MGZEB 123, folders 198–99; American Ballet Caravan; Family Albums, etc.
9. Interviews: John Gruen with Virgil Thomson, etc.
10. RP/DD: Ruth Page Papers
11. MB/DD: Morton Baum Collection, including his unpublished history of City Center
12. ADM/DD: Agnes de Mille Collection
13. LM/DD: Lillian Moore Papers

BEINECKE LIBRARY, YALE UNIVERSITY

1. EP/BL: Ezra Pound Papers
2. ATP/BL: The Leonie Adams and William Troy Papers
3. MD/BL: Muriel Draper Papers
4. PT/BL: Pavel Tchelitchev Papers
5. MW/BL: Monroe Wheeler Papers
6. GW/BL: Glenway Wescott Papers
7. GPL/BL: George Platt Lynes Diaries
8. VV/BL: Carl Van Vechten Papers
9. AT/BL: Alan Tanner Papers

10. MM/BL: Margaret Marshall Papers
11. JP/BL: James Purdy Papers
12. GSAT/BL: Gertrude Stein/Alice Toklas Papers

MUSIC LIBRARY, YALE UNIVERSITY

VT/YML: Virgil Thomson Papers

SPECIAL COLLECTIONS, PRINCETON UNIVERSITY

1. RB/PU: Richard Blackmur Papers
2. AT/PU: Allen Tate Papers
3. JDC/PU: John Day Co. Archives
4. PB/PU: John Peale Bishop Papers
5. CG/PU: Caroline Gordon Papers
6. EA/PU: Elmer Adler Papers
7. SK/PU: Stanley Kunitz Papers
8. SP/PU: *New Review* correspondence of Samuel Putnam
9. RF/PU: Russell A. Fraser Correspondence
10. MRO/PU: Maria Rosa Oliver Papers

FOGG MUSEUM, HARVARD UNIVERSITY

1. AM/Fogg: Agnes Mongan Papers
2. PS/Fogg: Paul J. Sachs Papers
3. JC/Fogg: John Coolidge Papers
4. EF/Fogg: Edward Forbes Papers

THEATRE COLLECTION, HARVARD UNIVERSITY

BA: Balanchine Archive

UNIVERSITY ARCHIVES, HARVARD UNIVERSITY

1. LK/HUA: assorted Lincoln Kirstein material
2. LK/Mongan: Agnes Mongan Correspondence (as of 2003 mostly uncataloged)

HOUGHTON LIBRARY, HARVARD UNIVERSITY

1. VO/HL: Victoria Ocampo Papers
2. NDP/HL: New Directions Corporation Papers
3. ES/HL: Eric Schroeder Papers

BAKER LIBRARY, HARVARD BUSINESS SCHOOL

LEK/BLH: Louis E. Kirstein Papers

LIBRARY OF CONGRESS

1. FF/LC: Felix Frankfurter Papers
2. EJ/LC: Ernest Jones Papers
3. AC/LC: Aaron Copland Papers
4. DF/LC: David Finley Papers
5. AM/LC: Archibald MacLeish Papers
6. LB/LC: Leonard Bernstein Collection

ARCHIVES OF AMERICAN ART (MoMA)

1. AB/AAA (MoMA): Alfred Barr Papers
2. WA/AAA (MoMA): Winslow Ames Papers
3. LK/Hawkins (MoMA): Frances Hawkins Papers
4. EM/AAA (MoMA): Elizabeth McCausland Papers
5. LK (LOC) MoMA: Lincoln Kirstein Papers
6. HS/AAA (MoMA): Henry Schnakenberg Papers
7. JS/AAA (MoMA): James Thrall Soby Papers
8. HSF/AAA (MoMA): Henry Sayles Francis Papers
9. HM/AAA (MoMA): H. C. Merillat Papers

ARCHIVES OF AMERICAN ART (SMITHSONIAN)

1. WE/SAAA: 1971 interview with Walker Evans
2. EW/SAAA: Paul Cummings May 13, 1971, interview with Edward Warburg
3. BS/SAAA: Ben Shahn Papers
4. WA/SAAA: Webster Aiken Papers
5. AP/SAAA: Alton Pickens Papers

ORAL HISTORY RESEARCH OFFICE, COLUMBIA UNIVERSITY

COH: transcripts of interviews with Schuyler Chapin, Aaron Copland, Philip Johnson, Fred Lazarus, Jr., Jay Leyda, Paul J. Sachs, John Marshall, John D. Rockefeller III, Carl Van Vechten, David Vaughan

SOPHIA SMITH LIBRARY, SMITH COLLEGE

MCP/SS: Mina Curtiss Papers

BERG COLLECTION, NEW YORK PUBLIC LIBRARY AT FORTY-SECOND STREET BC/NYPL

1. MC/DG/Berg: Mina Curtiss/David Garnett Correspondence
2. T/S/Berg: Tchelitchev/Edith Sitwell Correspondence

ROCKEFELLER ARCHIVE CENTER, POCANTICO, NY NAR/RAC

1. RB/RAC: Nelson Rockefeller Papers
2. EY/RAC: E. B. Young Papers
3. Rockefeller Family Associates & other groupings not listed separately from RB/RAC

HARRY RANSOM CENTER, UNIVERSITY OF TEXAS AT AUSTIN

RB/UT: Richard Buckle Papers, including, along with his extensive correspondence, his unpublished ms. "History of a Friendship"; LK correspondence uncataloged as of 2004.

BSA: Ballet Society Archives, NYC

EPF: Eakins Press Foundation Archives, NYC

JL/TL: Jay Leyda Papers, Tamiment Library, NYU

EM/UD: Elva de Pue Matthews Papers, University of Delaware

GRI: Getty Research Institute, Special Collections

KB/PS: Kenneth Burke Papers, Penn State University

JL/ND: James Laughlin Papers, New Directions Archives

JBW/BU: John Brooks Wheelwright Papers, Brown University

KAP/UM: Katherine Anne Porter Papers, University of Maryland

EJ/MOA: Edward Johnson Correspondence, Metropolitan Opera Archives

NO/GU: Ned O'Gorman Papers, Georgetown University

WM/CC: William Meredith Collection, Connecticut College

MRF: Marie Rambert Papers, Rambert Foundation (UK)

JRRT: Jerome Robbins Papers, Jerome Robbins Rights Trust

GE/UH: Gavin Ewart Papers, University of Hull (UK)

PRIVATELY HELD MANUSCRIPT COLLECTIONS

"Letters" signifies less than a dozen. "Correspondence" signifies more than a dozen.

Jon Anderson (Paul Cadmus correspondence with LK, Fidelma, and Jared and Margaret French)

Alex Colville (LK to Colville correspondence)

Robert Gottlieb (LK to Gottlieb letters)

Clint Kisner (LK to Kisner letters)

Jim Klosty (LK to Merce Cunningham letters)

Lynne Robbins Knox (early LK diary and MC's variant ms. "Slices of Life")

Robert La Fosse (LK to La Fosse letters)

Michael Leonard (LK to Leonard correspondence; Michael Leonard diaries)

Barnabas McHenry (LK to McHenry letters)

Alex Nixon (LK to Nixon letters)

Claudia Roth Pierrepont (assorted interviews)

Marie Rambert Estate (LK to Rambert correspondence)

Nancy Reynolds (LK to Reynolds letters)

Donald Richie (diaries; personal recollections)

Laurence Senelick (personal acct. of "White House Happening")

Paul Taylor (LK to Taylor letters)

Steven Watson (notes from his two interviews with LK, plus his interviews with Paul Draper and William Koshland)

Andrew and Betsy Wyeth (LK to Andy and Betsy Wyeth correspondence)

Jamie Wyeth (LK to Jamie Wyeth letters, plus JW/LK tape, late 1970s)

Perez Zagorin (LK letters to Honoré Sharrer)

Astrid Zydower (LK to Zydower correspondence)

Single LK letters: David Vaughan, Frederick Wile

INTERVIEWS

Jon Anderson
Albert Bellas
Ed Bigelow
Ruthanna Boris
Randall Bourscheidt
John Braden
Vida Brown
Maria Caligari
Daniel Duell
James Duff
John Freeman
Robert Gottlieb
Barbara Horgan

Nicholas Jenkins

Clint Kisner

Anna Kisselgoff

Lynne Robbins Knox

Robert La Fosse

David Langfitt

Nancy Lassalle

Michael Leonard

Annabelle Lyon

Davie Lerner

Elsa (Mrs. MacNeil) Lowry

Francis Mason

Arthur Mitchell

Alex Nixon

Ned O'Gorman

Genevieve Oswald

Claudia Roth Pierpont

Mary Porter

James Radich

Nancy Reynolds

Donald Richie

Ted Rogers

Tom Schoff

Mary Richie Smith

Paul Taylor

Jerry Thompson

George Tooker

Violette Verdy

David Vaughan

Frances Whitney

Jamie Wyeth

Jensen Yow

Perez Zagorin

Astrid Zydower

In addition I've utilized the extensive oral history collections at the Columbia Oral History Project, Columbia University, and those at the Dance Division of the New York Public Library.

NOTES

Because this biography is written largely from primary sources, I've kept the citations fairly full (especially in regard to direct quotations), so that future scholars can more easily locate the areas of their special interest. When a footnote number appears at the end of a given paragraph in the text, the accompanying citations are for that paragraph itself *plus* a specified amount of the text following the footnote.

CHAPTER ONE: GROWING UP (1907–1926)

1. For this opening section about the Stein and Kirstein families the most significant archival sources have been the Lincoln Kirstein Papers (henceforth LK/DD) housed at the Dance Division, the New York Public Library for the Performing Arts at Lincoln Center. His papers consist of two main collections, each called the "Lincoln Kirstein Letters," but with separate call numbers, *MGZMD 97 and *MGZMD 123 (the latter contains his diaries for 1919–37). Also important for this opening section are the extensive Louis Kirstein Papers at the Baker Library, Harvard (henceforth LEK/BLH), and the Mina Curtiss Papers at the Sophia Smith Library, Northampton, Massachusetts (henceforth MCP/SS), which includes her unpublished memoir, "The Past and I." I'm indebted to Mina Curtiss's executor, Lynne Robbins Knox, for allowing me to read Mina's "Slices of Life," a variant memoir in her possession; it contains a number of important details not found in "The Past and I."

2. For this and the following two paragraphs: Curtiss, "Past," MCP/SS, 9; LEK speech, June 17, 1915, "Kernwood Country Club," LEK/BLH; LEK to MC, Sept. 25, 27, 30, 1913; MC, "Chosen?" *Massachusetts Review* (1983); LK, "Cut of Kind," LK/DD. As an adult, LK would usually say he'd been named for Abraham Lincoln, but he'd sometimes say he'd been named after Lincoln Filene (and given his middle name, Edward, after Filene's older brother of that name: e.g., LK to Buckle, July 30, 1983, Richard Buckle Papers at The Ransom Center, the University of Texas, henceforth RB/UT).

3. For this and the following two paragraphs: Leon Harris, *Merchant Princes* (Berkley Books, 1980), and George E. Berkley, *The Filenes* (International Pocket Library, 1998). Both studies contain useful material, but need to be used with caution, the Harris book being the less reliable of the two. A brilliantly researched study by Susan Porter Benson, *Counter Cultures: Saleswomen, Managers, and Customers in American Department Stores, 1890–1940* (University of Illinois Press, 1986) contains a significant amount of material on Filene's; see esp. 37, 64, 145, 158 ("the progressive Filene store"), 165, 209, 232.

    The lengthy 1965 interview with Fred Lazarus, Jr., who was closely associated with Louis Kirstein in Federated Department Stores, is filled with unique insights into his personality and business skills (Oral History Research Office, Columbia University, henceforth COH).

4. For this and the following four paragraphs: MC, "Past," MCP/SS, 62–63, 78–80; Louis to Mina, Sept. 25, 27, 30, 1913, LK, *Mosaic* (Farrar, Straus & Giroux, 1994), passim; MC, "Chosen?" *Massachusetts Review* (1983), MCP/SS.

5. For this and the following four paragraphs: MC, "Past," MCP/SS, 8, 26, 40; LK, *Mosaic*, 19 (Rose's decorating); MC to LEK, Sept. 21, 1920, LEK to MC, Sept. 26, 1920, MCP/SS.

6. For this and the following ten paragraphs: LK, "Cut," LK/DD, 23–29, 32; LK, *Mosaic*, 28,

48–51; MC, "Past," 25; LK, *Thirty Years* (henceforth *Thirty*), expanded edition (Knopf, 1978) 3–6; LK, ms. "Foreword," Jan. 1, 1972, LK/DD.

7. For this and the following four paragraphs: LK, *Mosaic*, 32, 33; MC, "Past," 113–14, 124–29, MCP/SS; Lazarus, Jr., interview, COH.

8. For the section on Camp Timanous, the main sources have been: LK, 1919–20 diaries, LK/DD; LK, *Thirty*, 4 (rhythmic); LK, *Mosaic*, 38–40; A. E. ("Chief") Hamilton to LK, Feb. 17, 1920. For an example of Louis's relationship with his difficult brother, Henry: Louis to Henry, Oct. 24, 1912, LEK/BLH. In 1922, at Camp Timanous, LK had a play of his produced, as well as published (badly, in his view): 1922 diary, Feb. 14, 22, Mar. 1, 23, LK/DD.

9. Exeter: LEK to Ford, July 8, Dec. 1, 1921 (Exeter trial); Cape to LEK, Mar. 2, 1922, LEK/BLH; LK, *Mosaic*, 52–58 (Doughty); LK Diary, April 20, 27, Feb. 28 (sissy), May 14 (spoiled), Aug. 30 (bum/self-disgust); LK, 1922 diary, LK/DD. For LK's passion for the arts, and dislike of gym, see especially his 1920 diary for Jan. 2–3, 17, 24–25, Feb. 5, Mar. 5, 9, Apr. 6, 9, 16, 19, 24, 27, 29, May 5, 8, 28–29, June 3–4, 18, 20, Nov. 12, 14; LK 1922 diary: Jan. 1–Aug. 2, especially June 25, July 10; LK, 1922–23 diary: Oct. 10–July 5, LK/DD; LEK to LK, Dec. 1, 1921, Feb. 21, 1922, Hamilton to LEK, July 19, 1921, Mabel Fletcher (tutor) to LEK, Jan. 20, Feb. 17, 1922, Cape to Louis, Dec. 16, 1921—all LEK/BLH.

10. The main sources for LK's experiences at the Berkshire School: LK to "Dearest [Mina]," Sept. 30, n.d. [1922] ("rock"), Oct. 5 [1922] (Babbitt), Nov. 25, 1922 (appendectomy), Mar. 4, 16, May 5 (Dickens), 18, 31, Feb. 1 (plus 3 others n.d. re: Buck), 18 (drag performance), 20, 1923 (favorite artists; "halfway"; good time, election, self-critical), n.d. [1924] ("go crazy"); LK to parents, Sept. 28, 1922 (Chopin; room; football; "deplorable"), May 2, 1923—all in LK/DD; Louis to Mina, Oct. 31 (appendectomy), Nov. 20 ("world"), 1922, Apr. 12, 1923; Louis to Lincoln, Jan. 13, 30, Feb. 17 (Buck), Nov. 17, 1923 (berating), Louis to Mina, Aug. 11, 1924 (education), Louis to George, Aug. 11 (service), Nov. 14, Dec. 10, 1924 (finish), LEK/BLH; LK Diary LK/DD: July 20, 1922 (corset, underwear), Jan. 15 (Klan; body), Jan. 16[?] (conceit), Jan. 22, Feb. 6, Apr. 19, 25 (Lynes), 23 (affected), Mar. 5 (naked), 6 (Chopin), Mar. 25 (morbid), Apr. 6 (Ball), 18 (irritable), May 4 (great artist), 14 (petulant), 18, 20 (Blake), 25 (never great), 1923. "Sneering little bitch" is from a small LK diary, courtesy Lynne Robbins Knox. In his diary entry of July 31, 1922, Lincoln wrote, "Re-reading my diary . . . a good many times I have been scared to put down what I actually thought." In another entry, Oct. 21, 1922, he wrote, "I have often made up stories [he doesn't say which] to put in [the diary] which might have easily happened, but didn't." He vowed, henceforth, "to keep an honest record." But to what extent he then did so has been difficult to evaluate.

There's reason to distrust much of the chapter in *Mosaic* about the Berkshire School; it focuses almost entirely on an "evil" classmate called Clayton Turner, but a check in the school's archives reveals no such student in attendance while Lincoln was there; "Turner" may have been an invention, a composite, or a pseudonym.

11. For the section that follows on Europe and Bloomsbury: Boxes 7–8, LK/DD; Boxes 15 and 45, LEK/BLH; MC, "Past," 59–67; LK, *Thirty*, 1–9 (Keynes, Lopokova); George K. to LEK, July 30, 1924, LEK to George, Aug. 11, 1924, LEK/BLH. In *Thirty* (7) LK writes of Keynes taking him to a Gauguin exhibition; in *Mosaic* (62), he discusses their attendance at a Cézanne show. I've assumed that both occasions happened, rather than that Lincoln in his later book, *Mosaic*, corrected "Gauguin" to "Cézanne"—though (since he was a fabulist) that remains a distinct possibility. The quotations from Garnett's letters to Mina are from the extensive correspondence in the Berg Collection, New York Public Library at Forty-second St. (henceforth BC/NYPL).

Mina's lesbian affair with Henrietta Bingham has been confirmed by her secretary of the final years of her life, Lynne Robbins Knox (interview Apr. 17, 2004), by LK to Michael Leonard, as recorded in the latter's diary for May 16, 1984, courtesy Leonard; and finally, by Henrietta's niece, Sallie Bingham, in her *Passion and Prejudice: A Family Memoir* (Random House, 1990), esp. pp. 192–96. Both the young women went to Freud's colleague Ernest Jones for psychoanalysis. At the same time Mina was being romanced by David Garnett, Henrietta was sleeping both with John Houseman (who would later become a lover of Mina's) and with Lytton Strachey's mainstay, Dora Carrington.

CHAPTER TWO: HARVARD (1927)

1. For the introductory section, and for "the Jewish Question" at Harvard in the 1920s, two secondary works have been of special value: Leonard Baker, *Brandeis and Frankfurter* (New York University Press, 1984), and Nitza Rosovsky, *The Jewish Experience at Harvard and Radcliffe* (exhibition catalog, Harvard Semitic Museum, Sept. 1986), especially 8–26 (distributed by the Harvard University Press). For Kirstein and Brandeis, see LEK to his brother, Henry, Feb. 14, June 18, 1912, LEK to Mina, Oct. 17 (Mack), Nov. 20, 1922, Jan. 30, 1923, LEK to LK, Oct. 28 (Eliot), Apr. 12 (victory), 1923, LEK/BLH; LEK to LK Nov. 17, 1923 (Coolidge), LEK to GK, April 7, 1924, Dec. 9, 1925 (service), LEK to Mina, Dec. 1, 1922 (Mack), MCP/SS; LK Diary, Jan. 24, 1923, LK/DD; *The Gadfly* 2, no. 1 (May 1926), Harvard University Archives.

2. For Harry Curtiss: MC, "The Past and I," MCP/SS, and MC, "Chosen?" *Massachusetts Review* (1983); HK to LEK, May 19, 1926, LEK/BLH; LK Diary, Jan. 23, Feb. 17, Apr. 16, 19, 20, 1927, LK/DD.

3. For LK's room: LK Diary, June 9, 1927, LK/DD. For LK's erotic attractions and adventures: LK diary, Jan. 4, 5 (harassment), 7 (hunter), 8, 10, 15, 31, Feb. 2, 14 (sailors), 16, 20 (rapport), 22, 24, 28 (fondle), Mar. 5, 6, 9 (affected), 11, 17, 21, 23, 26, Apr. 1–2 (bound; Bill), 5 (evil), 6, 9, 13, 16, May 7 (marines), 12, June 7 (touchstone), June 21 (letters), 1927, LK/DD; LK, *Mosaic*, 92 (Lads); Mabry to LK, Apr. 14, 1925, plus two additional letters, undated (but from internal evidence, 1925–26), LK/DD. If LK's letters to Mabry exist, their whereabouts are unknown. As late as 1949, Mabry wrote to LK: "I would do it all again, only more so this time" (Mabry to LK, Nov. 30, 1949, LK/DD).

4. For Varian Fry: LK Diary, Jan. 6, 7, 13, 16, 28, Feb. 12 (nuts), Mar. 26, 28 (aristocratic), 30, Apr. 9 (affected), 12 (like), 13, May 4 (tense), 17 (sex), 18–20, 23, 31 (crumble), June 4 (officious), 5, 21 (Queen), 23, Sept. 8 (Mina), 1927; Andy Marino, *A Quiet American* (St. Martin's, 1999); Marino's excellent biography is skimpy on Fry's Harvard years and wrongly states that the Kirstein/Fry friendship proved "enduring."

5. "The Complete Whifflepink," *Advocate*, Jan. 1927; "March from the Ruins of Athens," *Harvard Advocate*, Dec. 1926; LK to GK, Jan. 25, 1927, LK/BLH, Box 45, folder 8 *(Crimson)*; LK, *Mosaic*, 103 (strident; *Waste Land*). When still a freshman, LK was ordering books by Eliot and Ezra Pound from Shakespeare & Company in Paris (LK to Sylvia Beach, Jan. 19, 1927, Beach Papers, Box 209, Princeton University Special Collections).

   For *Hound and Horn*: LK Diary, Jan. 13 (invaluable), March 7 (Damon; Aiken), 9 (Frankenstein; writers), 24 (Kunitz), 30 (empire), Apr. 2, 20 (Arvin), 6 (fatal), 7 (sedative), 9 (reorganized), 25 (slaving; wrecks; Kunitz), 27 (enjoy), 28, May 1 (innate), 2 (sweat), 4 (Kunitz), 7 (tea), 24 (Cerf), June 14–15 (Grosser), Dec. 18 (Hitchcock), 1927, LK/DD. LK gave Damon's book, *Astrolabe: Infinitudes and Hypocrisies*, a highly favorable review in the *Crimson Bookshelf* (Apr. 11, 1927), even though he hadn't much liked the book and had originally planned to "rip it up as unoriginal"; but he changed the review once he understood that Damon "expected things of me" (LK Diary, Apr. 5, 1927, LK/DD).

   Leonard Greenbaum, *The Hound and Horn* (Mouton & Co. [The Hague], 1966), a careful piece of scholarship, remains the only full-scale history of the magazine throughout its entire run (1927–34), and although partly superseded by the surfacing of additional manuscript materials, is still useful. For background on earlier "little magazines," see especially Walter Sutton, ed., *Pound, Thayer, Watson and THE DIAL* (University Press of Florida, 1994).

   For Wheelwright: John Brooks Wheelwright Papers, Brown University Library (henceforth JBW/BU), especially three LK to JB letters, n.d. [1928?]; LK Diary, June 15 (sonnet), Sept. 30, Oct. 2 (Cézanne), 5 (grotesque), 8 (ballet), 25, Nov. 17 (comic), Dec. 21 (list), 1927, LK/DD; LK, *Mosaic*, 86–88. According to LK (*Mosaic*, 87), Wheelwright was "slain in his early forties by a drunken truck-driver."

   Lincoln greatly admired Mower as "the finest kind of academician," and thought his "mastery of technique complete." He admired Mower less as a painter ("Not adventurous, not substantial"), but willingly sat for a portrait at Mower's request (LK Diary, Apr. 3, May 18, June 1, 9, 14, 1927). For more on Mower, see LK, *Mosaic*, 164–69. For *much* more on

Hound and Horn, see Mitzi Berger Hamovitch, *The Hound & Horn Letters*, with a foreword by LK (University of Georgia Press, 1982); although Hamovitch didn't have access to the Kirstein Papers and was denied other material as well, her book has been indispensable.

6. For Lincoln's relationship with his parents: LK Diary, Feb. 14 (African), 15 (gutless; easily), Mar. 27 (stuff), April 7 (casual), May 14, 26, June 5 (horrible), 7, 13 (flattery; newspaper), 16, 22 (cranky), LK/DD. For Warburg: Jan. 21, 26, Feb. 15 (washouts; sporty), 16, Mar. 11, May 21, 1927, LK/DD; McNeil Lowry's two-part "Conversation" with LK, *The New Yorker*, Dec. 22, 1986 (often away).

CHAPTER THREE: *HOUND AND HORN* (1927)

1. For LK's time in London during June–July: Garnett to Mina, n.d. [summer 1927], BC/NYPL; LK Diary, June 27 (extreme), 29 (superb), July 1 (homosexual year), July 2–3 (galleries; laugh), 4 (ballet), 5 (Grant), 6 (Sokolova), 7 (irritates), 8–9 (catty/mean; Buggers; Westie), 12 (much good; Dobree), 14–17, 20 (Mortimer), 20–26 (Dobree), LK/DD. The "deeply addicted" and "La Chatte" quotes are from an unidentified fragment in LK/DD.

2. For Payson Loomis, see LK, *Mosaic*, 113–51, 156–58. For Gurdjieff, I'm again following the chronology in LK's diary, which recounts only the briefest glimpse of Gurdjieff in 1927, rather than his later autobiographical writings (*Mosaic*, 122–58, and LK, *By With To & From: A Lincoln Kirstein Reader*, Nicholas Jenkins, ed. [Farrar, Straus & Giroux, 1991], henceforth *BWTF*, 66–67), which seem to jumble together the 1927 glimpse with his more extended later visits.

3. For LK's trip to Spain: LK Diary, Aug. 1–15, 1927, LK/DD. For the actual quotations: Mar. 17 (glance), Aug. 5 (Prado), 6, 15 (bullfights), 8 (Escorial), 9 (Goya), 5–8 (Velázquez), 11 (small churches), 13 (go home; vests), 25 (Tom), 27–29 (unsystematized; traveling; Escorial; alone), 30 (painter), 31 (lottery), Sept. 1 (train wreck), 1927.

   For Sacco-Vanzetti: LK Diary, Apr. 19, Aug. 26, 1927, LK/DD; Louis to LK, July 14, Aug. 8, 1927, LEK/BLH.

   For North Africa: LK Diary, Aug. 16–22, 1927, LK/DD. I've omitted the story in *Mosaic* (122) about LK's "near-conversion" experience in Marrakech with a mullah; there is no corroboration at all for it in LK's diary—and contemporary accounts are usually more reliable than later recollections.

   For LK in Paris and London during Sept. 1927: LK Diary, Sept. 2 (Manet), 3 (Beach), 5 (Gurdjieff, Loomis), 6 (Loomis), 7 (cubism; Dobree; Eliot), 8 (Turner), 9 (Rembrandt), 10 (Cuyp), 13 (house; ballet), 15 (Rembrandt; Barr), 17, 21 (leaving), 22 (docking), 23 (Tom), 1927, LK/DD. LK's letter to Eliot, "September 1927," is printed in Hamovitch, *H&H Letters*, 65–67; his comment on Eliot's authority is in LK's introduction to Hamovitch, xvi. Barr's letter to Sachs is in COH (Sachs), 3927–28. Kirstein and Sachs had had at least one previous meeting: Foster Damon took Lincoln to see the new Fogg Museum, which—thanks to the prodigious fundraising of Sachs and the Fogg's director, Edward W. Forbes—had opened in 1927; they'd run into Sachs, who was reluctant to let them in but finally did (LK Diary, May 21, 1927, LK/DD).

4. LK's return to Cambridge: LK Diary, Sept. 23 (Tom), 24 (*H&H*), 25 (*Crimson*), 27 (selling), Oct. 3 (*Crimson*), Oct. 19 (painting), Oct 26 (*Advocate*), Nov. 10 (Parker), Dec. 25 (George), 1927, LK/DD; *New York Times*, Oct. 10, 1927; "Bad taste," uncited, is from Russell Fraser's fine biography of R. P. Blackmur, *A Mingled Yarn* (Harcourt Brace Jovanovich, 1979), 60.

   Varian Fry: LK Diary, Oct. 3, 16, 17, Nov. 1, 1927; *H&H* business manager: LK Diary, Oct. 5, 13, 16; Tom Mabry: Sept. 28, Oct. 11, 17, Nov. 22, 23, 28, Dec. 2, 7, 8, 12, 14, 18, 19, 21, 22, 29, 1927, LK/DD.

   Mina and Harry: LK Diary, Sept. 23, Oct. 14, Dec. 3, 4, 1927, LK/DD.

   LK's sexuality: Diary, Feb. 20, Sept. 30, Oct. 11 (Bryan), Mar. 11 (queer rumor), June 11, 12, Sept. 28, Oct. 15, 22, 23, Nov. 4, 5, 6, 25 (Dick; "complete desirability . . . heat"), Oct. 6, 8, 10, 19 (Philip), Oct. 17 (nervous energy), Nov. 18 (Terry), Nov. 24 (Paul), Dec. 5 (Johnny), Dec. 5 (casual), 1927, LK/DD; Ernest Jones to Mina, Dec. 11, 1927, Aug. 19 [1931], Ernest Jones Papers, Library of Congress. For more detail on the shifting sexual ideology of the day, see George Chauncey, *Gay New York* (Basic Books, 1994), esp. 119–27, Ann Douglas, *Terrible Honesty* (Farrar, Straus & Giroux, 1995), esp. 122–29, 143–55, and John Loughery, *The Other Side of Silence* (Henry Holt, 1998), esp. 113–34.

Hound and Horn: LK, foreword (reprinted in *BWTF*), and Hamovitch, introduction, passim, to *H & H Letters;* LK Diary, Sept. 25, Oct. 1, 3, 4 (intrigue), 5, 8, 13, 19, 20 (mania), 21, 24, 25, 28, Nov. 8–11 (Varian; advertising), 16, 19, 21, 28–30 (Varian), Dec. 6–8 (Varian), 13, 15, 18, 21, 27 (Fry contribution), 1927, LK/DD; LK to LEK, Feb. 2, 1928, LEK/BLH. Sean O'Faoláin, whom *Hound and Horn* published early on, has left a description of the *H&H* office and the "eager zest" of its young editors, "arguing hotly about literature," in *Vive Moi!* (Sinclair-Stevenson, 1963, reprint 1993).

5. Harry Curtiss's death: George to parents, n.d. [1928], LEK to George, Jan. 18, Feb. 18, 1928, LEK/BLH; the one poem by LK is untitled and undated, a second, entitled "Évocation des Ancêtres," is dated May 15, 1928; both were found in Mina's papers: MCP/SS.

CHAPTER FOUR: BRAHMIN BOSTON (1928)

1. For Blackmur and Bandler: Richard P. Blackmur Papers, Princeton University Archives (henceforth RB/PU); LK letters to Blackmur, 1927–37, are in Series II, Box 5, folder 4, Bandler's to Blackmur are in Box 1, folder 12; LK to Russell Fraser (Blackmur's biographer), May 27, June 28, Sept. 21, 1976, Jan. 21, 1977, Nov. 16, 1981, Russell A. Fraser Collection, Princeton; LK Diary, Oct. 5, 1927 (poetical judgment). Among secondary sources Russell Fraser, *Mingled Yarn,* esp. 36–64, has been invaluable; also useful: Isabel Bayley, ed., *Letters of Katherine Anne Porter* (Atlantic Monthly Press, 1990).

2. For LEK and Filene's: George E. Berkley, *The Filenes* (International Pocket, 1998), esp. chap. 10 and 262–63; Fred Lazarus interview, COH; Felix Frankfurter Papers, Library of Congress (henceforth FF/LC). LEK's financial support: LK to LEK, "Tuesday," n.d., May 23, 1928, July 17, 1930, LEK to LK, July 29, 1930, LEK/BLH. On his course work: LK to Russell Fraser, June 28, 1976, Fraser Papers, Princeton University Archives.

3. For Lincoln's social life: LK Diary, June 10, Sept. 29, Oct. 11, 13, 14, 27, 29, 30, Nov. 3–4, 12, 15, 20, 26, Dec. 8, 18, 23, 24, 26, 28, 1927; Oct. 26, Nov. 10, 14 (sex with Alice), 24 (Naushon), 1930; LK, "Cut of Kind," 3–4, LK/DD; *Mosaic,* 96–100. During the period of his Brahmin socializing, Lincoln formed a passionate crush on Eric Schroeder, who married Marn Forbes in 1930. LK's 1932 novel, *Flesh Is Heir,* is dedicated to "E. S." [i.e., Schroeder], who figures in the book as the character "Alex Coronado." Schroeder later became an Islamic scholar and the Keeper of Islamic Art at the Fogg Museum, 1948–1969 (LK Diary, early 1930s, passim; Arthur Hughes to me, May 24, 2006, containing considerable information on Schroeder and the Forbes family).

4. The Harvard Society for Contemporary Art: Barr to Sachs, Dec. 16, 1928, is in COH, p. 3993, of a lengthy interview with Sachs; incorporation papers and catalogs of shows are in LK/DD; *Harvard Crimson,* Dec. 13, 1928; LK, *Mosaic,* 159–75; John Walker, *Self-Portrait with Donors* (Atlantic Monthly Press, 1969), 21–28; Sybil Gordon Kantor, *Alfred H. Barr, Jr.* (MIT Press, 2002). In November 1930 LK met Charles Demuth at Muriel Draper's and found him "a delightful, friendly man" (LK Diary, Nov. 24, 1930, LK/DD).

5. For the European summer of 1929: LK to Blackmur, July 17, 21, Aug. 30, 1929, RB/PU; LK Diary, Nov. 18, 1930 (Gurdjieff); for the importance of *Apollon Musagète,* see the remarkable *No Fixed Points: Dance in the Twentieth Century* (Yale University Press, 2003), 69, by Nancy Reynolds and Malcolm McCormick (henceforth Reynolds and McCormick, *Fixed*). LK's essay, "The Diaghilev Period," which contains an account of Diaghilev's funeral, is reprinted in Jenkins, *BWTF,* 103–29 (the quotes about Balanchine are on 123–25, about Diaghilev on 106). In his Aug. 30, 1929, letter to Blackmur, Lincoln predicted that he wouldn't like the article: "1. it's rhapsodic 2. it's too long. 3. It has nothing to do with America & would be of no use to our readers."

For T. S. Eliot: Hamovitch, *H&H Letters,* 65–70; LK to Blackmur, July 17 (Pound; T. E. Lawrence), 21, Aug. 30, 1929, RB/PU. Eliot did later send an essay and a poem for *Hound and Horn:* "Second Thoughts on Humanism," vol. 2, no. 4; and "Difficulties of a Statesman," vol. 6, no. 1.

For LK's religious leanings: LK Diary, April 21, 1923 (Berkshire), Jan. 17–20, Aug. 1, Sept. 26, Nov. 21, 1927, LK/DD. For Gurdjieff: LK to Blackmur, July 17, 1929 ("mysterious"; "hindrances"), RB/PU; LK Diary, Nov. 18 (sheep skull; disintegration), 24 (slavery),

1930, LK/DD; LK to Alex Nixon, Aug. 6, 1974, courtesy Nixon; Loomis to LK, Dec. 2, 1948, LK/DD; LK, "Cut of Kind" (small way; readied), LK/DD; LK, "A Memoir: The Education" (philosophy; magician), *Raritan* (Fall 1982); LK's *Mosaic*, 113–58, from which the majority of quotations come, especially in the section 151–55 in which he summarizes Gurdjieff's "concepts" and "rules." *Mosaic*, however, unaccountably places the 1929 experiences recounted in his diary in the year 1927 instead; as before, I've followed the chronology in the diary rather than the autobiography, on the assumption that the original document is likely to be the more reliable one. I've been encouraged in this decision by LK's executor, Nicholas Jenkins, who helped LK write *Mosaic* (Jenkins to me, June 4, 2004). I've only sampled the vast secondary literature on Gurdjieff; the most accessible book I've found is John Shirley, *Gurdjieff* (Tarcher/Penguin, 2000). LK himself thought Fritz Peters "has written best about him as a man" (LK, "A Memoir: The Education").

For Pound: LK, *Mosaic*, 147–49, 155–57; LK, "A Memoir: The Education" (tyrannical; hangers-on); Hamovitch, *H&H Letters*, 24–64; LK's remark about "head nor tale" [*sic*] is in the book's foreword, xv. Hamovitch has published a significant amount of the correspondence between *Hound and Horn*'s editors and Pound. But an additional treasure trove of letters, much of it from LK, is in the Ezra Pound Papers at Yale University's Beinecke Library, especially in Series I: General Correspondence (henceforth EP/BL); similarly Hamovitch has reproduced only five (two of which are excerpted) of the twenty-eight LK letters to Allen Tate from his papers at Princeton (henceforth AT/PU).

CHAPTER FIVE: NEW YORK (1929–1931)

1. LK to Mongan (& her sister Betty), Aug. 8, Sept. 10, 1929, Agnes Mongan Papers, Fogg Museum, Harvard University (henceforth AM/Fogg); LK to Blackmur, Aug. 30, 1929, RB/PU. I'm greatly indebted to Abby Smith, archivist at the Fogg, for alerting me in Apr. 2003 to the museum's acquisition (from the Audubon Society) of a new batch of LK letters to Mongan, including the two cited above, and for allowing me access before they were cataloged.

For the discussion of Ezra Pound and *Hound and Horn*, Leonard Greenbaum, *The Hound and Horn*, has, of the secondary sources, been the most useful (the "Cherrystein" quote is on 121). But nearly all the discussion derives from primary sources, and especially from three: (*a*) LK Diary, LK/DD: Bandler, Oct. 21 (disarming), Nov. 12 (incompetent), 24, 1930; Jan. 31 (shortcomings), Feb. 23, 1931; (*b*) the Pound letters published in Hamovitch, *H&H Letters*, 24–64; direct quotations in this section are from: EP to LK, Feb. 8, 1930 (*Dial*), EP to *H&H*, Feb. 26, 1930 (Huxley, Josephson, Wilson, Seldes, Major), EP to *H&H*, March 1, 8, 1930 (MacLeish), EP to *H&H*, Apr. 17, 1930 (More, Babbitt, Lippmann; "slop"; McAlmon), EP to LK, Aug. 3 (Diaghilev; malediction), 30 (Perse), 1930, EP to LK, Oct. 22 (Mortimer, Wheelwright), 26 (Lewis), 1930, EP to LK, March 20 (Fitts), July 8 (kiss-off), Aug. 6 (LK's reply), 1931; and (*c*) the LK letters, EP/BL, especially Series I, Box 8, folder 188, Box 27, folders 1151, 1152; direct quotations in this section are from: LK to Pound, Jan. 17 (don't care; Bunting), Feb. 20 (circumscribed; *Conquistador*), 27 (utmost, Lewis), March 25 (payments), April 4, May 1 (great deal, McAlmon), June 16 (U.S.), July 5 (McAlmon), July 15, 19 (Houghton), Nov. 10 (Lewis; Mortimer; U.S.), 1930, Mar. 4 (advice), June 27 (Cocteau), 1931; Bandler to Pound, Nov. 7, 1930. It isn't clear whether MacLeish ever submitted poetry to *H&H*, but in any case none appeared; his essay "Stephen Spender and the Critics," however, *was* published in *H&H*. In writing that MacLeish was "too sensitive," LK doubtless had in mind the furious letter Archie had written to him (Dec. 17, 1928, Hamovitch, *H&H Letters*, 110) in response to Blackmur's negative review in *H&H*'s Winter 1929 issue ("As a poet Mr. MacLeish has no life of his own") of *The Hamlet of A. MacLeish*; MacLeish had responded: "The review . . . constitutes an attack upon my personal life, my literary honesty and my integrity." MacLeish sent the review to Hemingway, along with a note that referred to "Kirstein's Jewish Harvard Monthly"; Hemingway told him the poem was "wonderful" and to ignore "The Bitch and Bugle." By the mid-thirties MacLeish had changed his views and was writing against anti-Semitism in *Fortune*—even as he continued to minimize its influence in American life (Scott Donaldson, *Archibald MacLeish: An American Life* [Houghton Mifflin, 1992], 185–86, 243–44); *Letters of Archibald MacLeish*, R. H. Winnick, ed. (Houghton Mifflin, 1983), 220, 258–59.

2. *H&H* and personal finances: LK's financial records are scattered in various manuscript depositories, but the yearly summaries, along with a great deal of correspondence, are in the Ballet Society Archives (henceforth BSA) in New York City; LK to Pound, Jan. 17 (monthly), Feb. 27 (reprints), May 1 (bad way), Oct. 28, 30 (books), Nov. 10 (lousy), 19, 1930, Mar. 4, ($4,000), 1931, EP/BL.

Louis Kirstein: Frankfurter to "Lou," Apr. 25, May 29, June 20, 1930, FF/LC. The Frankfurter-Kirstein relationship was ongoing. On Feb. 3, 1939, Frankfurter wrote to him, "I shan't say any of the things that are in my heart for your own will be able to hear them without any utterance"; Hillman to Louis, Sept. 19, 1929 (thanks), LEK/BLH; LEK's speeches are in Box 9, LEK/BLH. For Filene's policies on unionization, see Berkley, *The Filenes*, especially 264–65; according to Berkley (266) Louis marched into Lincoln Filene's office one day in 1933 and said, "Lincoln, you are now a Jew. Hitler has made you one"—but Berkley gives no citation.

Society for Contemporary Art: LK to Austin, July 28, 1930, Austin Papers, Wadsworth Atheneum, Hartford (henceforth CA/WAH); Eugene R. Gaddis, *Magician of the Modern* (Knopf, 2000), esp. 138–42; LK Diary, Nov. 26 (Sachs), Dec. 16, 23–24, 1930, LK/DD.

3. Postgraduation, 1930–31:
(*a*) LK's social life and friendships: LK Diary, Oct. 14, 16, 21 (F. C. Lowell), 23 (fine time), Nov. 4 (Chanler), 10 (Lyman; Marga), 18 (gaga), 24; Dec. 23 (Mina), 1930, LK/DD; LK to Pound, May 1, 1930 (400 percent), EP/BL. For Roger Sessions: LK Diary, April 15, 23, 24, 1927; Oct. 19, Nov. 10, 1930, LK/DD. For Hitchcock: LK Diary, Oct. 28, 1930, Feb. 4, 6, 1931, LK/DD. For Aline Bernstein: LK Diary, Nov. 12, 1930, Jan. 28, 31, Mar. 24, 1931, LK/DD. For Mina: LK Diary, Nov. 24, Dec. 23, 30, 1930; Jan. 19, 28, Feb. 10, 11, 12, 14, 1931, LK/DD. For Warburg: LK Diary, Oct. 26–Nov. 14, 1930, LK/DD. For George Kirstein: LK Diary, Dec. 23, 30, 1930, LK/DD; in the Louis Kirstein Papers at the Harvard Business School (Box 45, folder 9), there's a batch of correspondence between George, Louis, Sarnoff, and various studio officials relating to George entering the motion picture industry (LEK's characterization of Sarnoff is in a letter to Schnitzer, May 25, 1931, George's in a letter to Louis, Mar. 19, 1932, and Lincoln's in his diary, LK/DD, for Dec. 1, 1930, and Jan. 28, 1931). For Mabry: LK Diary, Nov. 24–Dec. 23, 1930, Jan. 19, 31, Feb. 10, 12, Mar. 27 (Mabry tiring of Clifford now that his "education sentimentale" was, after two years, complete, and his "reciprocated loyalty" established), 1931, LK/DD. For Philip Johnson: LK Diary, Dec. 5, 1930, Jan. 19, 31, Mar. 24 (apartment), 1931, LK/DD; for more on Johnson and Mies, see Franz Schulze, *Philip Johnson: Life and Work* (University of Chicago Press, 1994; henceforth Schulze, *Johnson*). For Lyman Paine: LK Diary, Nov. 10 (drunk), 18 (kiss), 24 (terrific; Muriel; Tom; friend), Dec. 23, 1930, Jan. 19, 28 (Mina), Feb. 11, 23, Mar. 31, Apr. [n.d.], Apr. 15, 21, 22, 1931, LK/DD. For Margot: LK Diary, Feb. 23, Apr. 27, 1931, LK/DD.

(*b*) Walker Evans: LK Diary, Nov. 1, 18, Dec. 23, 1930, Jan. 19, 31, Feb. 10, 14, Mar. 24, 26 (mistake), Apr. 22 (Cagney), June 3, 13 (gnat), 1931, LK/DD; the forty-six-page transcript of the 1971 interview with Evans is in the Smithsonian Archives of American Art (SAAA); *Walker Evans American Photographs* (MoMA, 1938; reprint 1988); Julien Levy, *Memoir of an Art Gallery* (Putnam, 1977). Though I've profited from two fine books about Walker Evans (James R. Mellow, *Walker Evans* [Basic Books, 1999], and Jerry L. Thompson, *The Last Years of Walker Evans* [Thames & Hudson, 1997]), I clearly diverge from some of their evaluations. For a detailed, reliable account of LK's many efforts to promote Evans's work, see Belinda Rathbone, *Walker Evans* (Houghton Mifflin, 1995).

(*c*) LK's writing: LK Diary, Nov. 26 (poem), Nov. 25–Dec. 5 (moral tragedy), 1930; *Flesh*: Dec. 5, 30, 1930, Jan. 31 (Louis), Feb. 4 (dope), 1931, LK/DD.

(*d*) Muriel Draper: Her own *Music at Midnight* (Harper & Brothers, 1929); Carl Van Vechten, *The Splendid Drunken Twenties*, edited by Bruce Kellner (University of Illinois Press, 2003) (New Year's Eve is in his daybook entry for Dec. 31, 1928, p. 230); Steven Watson, *Pre-*

pare for Saints (University of California Press, 1998); LK, *Mosaic;* LK, *Thirty,* 12 (dominant). The "bailiffs" quote is from LK to Wheelwright, n.d. [1928/29?], JBW. LK's own diary is filled with stories about MD; the direct quotes are from June 24 (barriers), 1927, Nov. 23, 24 (NYC; Mina), Oct. 23 (Bentley), Dec. 23 (Mina), 1930, Jan. 19, 1931 (New Year's), LK/DD.

4. LK Diary, Dec. 23 (Muriel; Tobey), 1930; Jan. 31, March 5 (frantic; Payson; bored), 1931. Gurdjieff: Jan. 19, Feb. 14, 22, 23, 1931, LK/DD. For Gurdjieff's second visit, starting in November 1931: LK Diary, Oct. 19, Nov. 10, Dec. 7, 9, 16, 18, 1931, Jan. 13, 19, 1932, LK/DD. Lachaise: LK Diary, Oct. 19, 22, Nov. 3, Dec. 7, 10, 1931, LK/DD.

5. *Hound and Horn,* 1930–32:

(a) Bandler: LK Diary, Nov. 25, 1930, March 5, 28, May 9, 11, 13, June 3, 11, 1931, LK/DD; LK to Wheelwright, n.d. [1931?], JBW/BU; Bandler to Blackmur, n.d. [1931?], RB/PU.

(b) Yvor Winters: YW to LK, Feb. 1 (Crane), Mar. 4 (Babbitt), May 9, 17, 23 (Porter; LK offered at one point to send her money), 1930; Feb. 1, 1931; May 4, 1932 (MacLeish—see also YW to LK, June 29, 1930); June 24, Sept. 5, Oct. 21 (Auden and Spender), July 23 (film), 1933; YW to Tate, Dec. 29, 1930—all as printed in R. L. Barth, *The Selected Letters of Yvor Winters* (Swallow Press/Ohio University Press, 2000); LK to Tate, Dec. 8, 1932, May 8, 1933 (on Winters), AT/PU. Jay Leyda's comments are from a 1981 interview on deposit at COH.

(c) A. Hyatt Mayor: LK Diary, Nov. 18, 24, 1930, Jan. 31, Feb. 14, 23, Mar. 3, 4, 1931, LK/DD; LK to Pound, Nov. 10, 1930, June 3, 1931, EP/BL.

(d) Allen Tate and Caroline Gordon: There are more than two dozen mss. letters from LK to Tate (and several to his wife, Caroline Gordon) in the Allen Tate Papers at Princeton University (AT/PU), only five of which have been printed in whole or part in Hamovitch, *H&H Letters.* Among the most important are: LK to Tate, Feb. 20 (admires his poetry), Dec. 8 (Pelham), 1932, Feb. 6 (Pelham), May 8 (Negro), 1933. For the quotations from Tate's side of the correspondence, as well as for the general description of his views on race, I've relied heavily on Thomas A. Underwood's fine biography, *Allen Tate, Orphan of the South* (Princeton University Press, 2000), esp. 256 (Gordon), 291–92 (Mabry), 402, 405–6. There are also a half dozen LK letters to Gordon in the Caroline Gordon Papers at Princeton (CG/PU), Box 33, folder 9; the Penhally remark is in LK to CG, Sept. 5, 1931. LK's comments on agrarianism in general (damn; notions) are in his foreword to the Hamovitch volume, xvii; the comment about "really terrifying" is from LK's diary, Nov. 12, 1930, LK/DD.

(e) The controversy over "nigger": LK/Tate correspondence in AT/PU and in Underwood, *Tate;* LK's diaries, passim. It should also be noted that at one point Lincoln considered (but then abandoned) the idea of commissioning an article to argue that the Northern Abolitionists had a "complete misunderstanding of the South" (LK to Tate, Feb. 16, 1933, AT/PU). There were a few exceptions to the general condemnation of Van Vechten in the black community, but only a few: James Weldon Johnson had some kind words for *Nigger Heaven*'s literary merit, and Paul Robeson, later to become a militant socialist and anticolonialist, sent Van Vechten a telegram calling the book "amazing in its absolute understanding and deep sympathy" (Martin Duberman, *Paul Robeson* [Knopf, 1989], 100). Of additional help in trying to understand the complexities of the use of "nigger" have been Bruce Kellner, ed., *The Letters of Carl Van Vechten* (Yale University Press, 1987), Bruce Kellner's edition of Van Vechten's daybooks from 1922 to 1930, *The Splendid Drunken Twenties* (University of Illinois Press, 2003), 24, for the pre-1926 comment, David Levering Lewis, *The Fight for Equality* (Holt, 2000), and Emily Bernard, *Remember Me to Harlem: The Letters of Langston Hughes and Carl Van Vechten, 1925–1964* (Knopf, 2001): Van Vechten used the word "nigger" in corresponding with his friend Langston Hughes, and without rebuke. For me the most helpful discussion of the issue is Randall Kennedy, *Nigger: The Strange Career of a Troublesome Word* (Vintage, 2002), in which Kennedy argues that given Van Vechten's long history of resisting racial prejudice and in forwarding the careers of black artists—"against this backdrop of achieved trust"—Langston Hughes and other black artists "rightly permitted Van Vechten to use *nigger* as so many African Americans have used it—as an ironic, shorthand spoof on the absurdity of American race relations" (43). LK had not, at that point in his life, earned a comparable trust.

CHAPTER SIX: MUSEUM OF MODERN ART (1929–1932)

1. LK Diary, Feb. 3 (Herzog), 22 (begging), Mar. 24 (office), Apr. 27 (Louis), 1931; Feb. 22, 23 (begging), 31 (Russia), 1932; LK to John Walker III, Dec. 14, 1931 (123–75), LK/DD; LK to LEK, n.d. [1931], Jan. 14, 1932, LEK/BLH; LK to Sachs, May 19, 1931, Paul J. Sachs Papers, Fogg Museum, Harvard (henceforth PS/Fogg); LK Diary, Apr. 1, 1932 (chicanery), LK/DD; Paul J. Sachs Oral History, COH. Louis's breakdown: LK Diary, Sept. 10, 11, 21, Oct. 2, 24 (reproductions), 1931, LK/DD.

On the economic depression and Louis's progressive stance during it, I've relied most on Robert S. McElvaine, *The Great Depression* (Times Books, 1993); also useful have been Michael A. Bernstein, *The Great Depression* (Cambridge University Press, 1987), Charles H. Trout, *Boston, The Great Depression, and the New Deal* (Oxford University Press, 1977), and J. Joseph Huthmacher, *Massachusetts People and Politics: 1919–1933* (Harvard University Press, 1959); Louis Kirstein's own papers (LEK/BLH) contain additional material, including LK's Sept. 28, 1932, letter congratulating his father, and a copy of "Mind Your Own Business," *Atlantic Monthly*, Oct. 1932.

LK's comment on GK (greed) is in LK Diary, Oct. 9, 1931, LK/DD. Harvard's Baker Library (LEK/BLH) contains a substantial correspondence between George and his father, especially for the early thirties, the years George spent in Hollywood; the letters do reveal a man who loved sports, moneymaking, and women, but show as well a decent, considerate, politically progressive side to him not sufficiently appreciated by his brother; George's last companion, Frances Whitney, confirmed to me in a telephone interview that George, all his life, felt aggrieved that Lincoln undervalued and underappreciated him, especially since he successfully managed most of Lincoln's money.

Flesh Is Heir: LK's own doubts: Dec. 5, 1930, Jan. 31 ("grave fears as to its excellence"), 1931. Friends' reactions: LK to Jack Wheelwright, Apr. 20, 1932, JBW/BU; LK Diary, Mar. 4 (Lyman), 31 (Muriel), Apr. 22 (Loomis), 1931, LK/DD; family reactions: LK Diary, June 31, 1931; Feb. 15 (Louis), Feb. 13 (Rose), 14, 15 (MacLeish; Mina; Muriel), Mar. 20 (Hitchcock), Mar. 10, Apr. 3, 13 (Mina), Apr. 17, 26–27 (Forbes), 1932, LK/DD. Publishers' rejections: LK to LEK, n.d. [1931], 19 (Perkins), Oct. 22 (Brewer), Sept. 21, 1931, Mar. 5, 26, 27, 31 (Dahlberg), 1932. Mina had not only begun to write, but as early as 1931 was published in the *Atlantic Monthly* (LK Diary, Feb. 11, 1931, LK/DD). The cited reviews: *Boston Evening Transcript*, Mar. 23, 1932 (LK's reaction, Diary, Mar. 25), the *Sun*, Mar. 12, 1932 (LK on Munson: LK Diary, Mar. 16–18, 29, May 16), *New York Times*, Mar. 12, 1932, *The Nation* (Dahlberg) 134, no. 3483; Garnett to Mina, Apr. 27, 1937, BC/NYPL.

Flesh Is Heir was reissued in 1977 as part of the Popular Library's series Lost American Fiction. In LK's afterword for that edition, he stressed his inability to "invent three-dimensional characters in any satisfactory depth" as the main reason he decided that he wasn't suited to being a novelist. Not that he didn't continue, for a time, to try. He worked on at least three other novels during the thirties (one of them, *Choice of Weapons*, was based on the life of one of his heroes, T. E. Lawrence), but each time he gave up on the project. The 1977 afterword is also the source of LK's inaccurate comment that "the book was ignored" (250–52). His remark about "bad job" is from a letter to Blackmur, June 4, 1932, RB/PU.

Lincoln would also make a number of attempts, continuing as late as the 1960s, to write plays. One of his earliest, *Hero* (about Charles Lindbergh), he coauthored with Dick Blackmur, who in the thirties was intent on becoming a playwright; LK, being typically helpful to a friend, unsuccessfully tried to get one of Blackmur's plays produced by Herman Shumlin (LK Diary, Feb. 4 [Shumlin], June 1, 3, 1931, LK/DD). But that form, too, proved unsuitable to Lincoln's gifts, and neither *Hero* nor any of his other early theatrical efforts saw production. Starting in the 1940s, Lincoln would have some considerable success as a writer of light verse, but it would later be in his numerous nonfiction volumes, most of them devoted to art criticism and ballet, that he would ultimately find his distinctive voice.

He did, in the 1940s, publish one other "narrative"—he resisted calling it a novel because it was based so closely on the story of Lincoln's then-lover, José Martínez, a dancer of working-class Mexican origins. E. M. Forster, by then a good friend of LK's, was chiefly responsible for the book's publication. He urged his friends, including Leonard Woolf, at the distinguished Hogarth Press in England, to publish *For My Brother*. Well received in England, the entire edition of *Brother* was destroyed in a warehouse by Hitler's bombs. The book has never been reprinted, though it is a far more engaging read than *Flesh Is Heir*.

2. There's been some controversy as to whether any of the three women who founded MoMA had ever actually visited the Harvard Society for Contemporary Art (Kantor, *Barr*, 415 n. 25). In the draft of a letter from Eddie Warburg to Renata Adler, Dec. 18, 1986 (AM/Fogg, in the set of documents acquired 4/03, and uncataloged when I read them), he states unequivocally that Abby Rockefeller and Lillie Bliss, accompanied by Conger Goodyear, "came up and looked at one of our shows."

   For MoMA, the Barrs, and Jere Abbott: LK Diary, Nov. 10 (melancholy), 17, Dec. 14 (money), 25 (tight), 1930, Jan. 19 (Abbott), Feb. 4, 6 (Hitchcock), 10 (Marga), 22 (Abbott), 23 (Lachaise), Mar. 31, June 3 (Abbott), June 24 ("I can't remember when I have felt I was so hard up"), 1931, LK/DD.

   For the discussions of MoMA, Rockefeller Center, and the assorted personalities involved, several secondary works have been especially helpful: Kantor, *Barr*; Bernice Kert, *Abby Aldrich Rockefeller* (Random House, 1993); Russell Lynes, *Good Old Modern* (henceforth Lynes, *Modern*), Atheneum, 1973; Daniel Okrent, *Great Fortune: The Epic of Rockefeller Center* (henceforth Okrent, *Fortune*), Viking, 2003; Cary Reich, *The Life of Nelson A. Rockefeller: Worlds to Conquer, 1908–1958* (henceforth Reich, *Nelson*), Doubleday, 1996; and Schulze, *Johnson*.

3. The 1932 Mural Show: LK Diary, Jan. 12, 14, 19, 21 (Nelson), Feb. 5–9, 24–25, Mar. 2, 22, Apr. 4, 6–7, 14–16, 19–23, 28, 30, May 2–3, 11–12, 14, 25, June 1, 3–5, 1932, LK/DD; Hugo Gellert, "We Capture the Walls!," *New Masses*, June 1932 (in his article Gellert also charged that "photographs in the possession of the Museum were withheld from newspapers. Photographing was forbidden. Only the insistence of the writer won for a cameraman permission to take pictures"). On the day of the mural show's official opening, May 3, 1932, Van Vechten, according to Lincoln, "with his Leica camera stood on the steps and photographed O'Keeffe, Demuth, myself and others as they came in" (LK Diary, May 3, 1932, LK/DD); LK, "Contemporary Mural Painting in the United States, *Hound & Horn*, July–Sept. 1932; LK to Agnes Mongan, May 22 (mural show), Edward W. Forbes to LK, June 27 (Shahn), 1932, AM/Fogg—from that part of the collection acquired in Apr. 2003, and then uncataloged. O'Keeffe: LK Diary, Feb. 24, Apr. 14, 1932, LK/DD. Trustees' objections: LK Diary, Apr. 14–15, 1932, LK/DD. Wiborg: LK Diary, Feb. 10, 1932 (nastiest); in 1921 Paul Robeson had starred opposite Mrs. Patrick Campbell in the London production of Mary Hoyt Wiborg's *Taboo*, a silly play about voodoo (see Duberman, *Robeson*, 43–45). The Forbes letter to LK (June 27, 1932, LK/DD) was a furious one; focusing on Ben Shahn's mural, it characterized Sacco and Vanzetti as "clearly convicted criminals" and said that "the disgusting, bloated caricatures of Mr. Morgan and Mr. Rockefeller were an outrage."

   Lachaise refused Lincoln's request to bring Noguchi to his studio, on the grounds that "he was arriviste, slick, no good"; Lincoln told Lachaise that he was "wrong" (LK Diary, Dec. 5, 1931, LK/DD). But Lincoln expressed some negative views of his own about Noguchi's work (LK Diary, Jan. 21, 1932), describing Noguchi's bust of him as "a weak, attenuated pre-adolescent thing; its only appeal is its silhouette" (LK Diary, Jan. 27, 1932, LK/DD). Soon after, LK's opinion of Noguchi as an artist became more admiring.

4. Badger and Loines: LK Diary, Mar. 26–28, Apr. 27, June 11, July 23 (Badger), Sept. 21, 24 (wife), Oct. 19 (marriage), Oct. 24, 27 (Wheelwright), 1931, Jan. 1, 31, Feb. 6, Apr. 28 (physical), May 13 (Muriel), 1932, LK/DD. Margot also told him that his manners were "horrible," that he always went first into an elevator, never helped a lady on with her coat, and would never be a good dancer unless he danced more "loosely." Lincoln, in turn, complained in his diary (June 11, 1931) that "it's a pity Margot isn't finer-grained or older or more grown up."

   For LK and politics: LK, "Films," *Arts Weekly*, Mar. 11, 1932 ("Road"); LK's column, "Books and Characters," for the *Boston Evening American*, a total of nearly three dozen articles, ran from Feb. 26, 1932, through Dec. 23, 1932; the ones with the most significant political content are in the issues of Mar. 11 (Trotsky), 18, May 6, 20 (revolution), 27, July 8, 15, and Nov. 11, 1932. LK was paid twenty-five dollars a column by the *Evening American*; in LK's opinion its publisher, Carl Dreyfus, offered him the column because "he thinks father is going to give him more advertising for Filenes, which he is not, and when he finds out that he is not—I'll be dropped" (LK Diary, May 10, 1932).

LK Diary, June 8, 24, 29, July 20 (Gold), 1931, Feb. 29 *(Fortune)*, May 23 (Dos Passos), 24 (Foster), 1932, LK/DD. As early as Sept. 1931, Muriel told Lincoln "how she was really tired of this country for the first time [and] could leave it with no qualms" (LK Diary, Sept. 9, 1931). I'm grateful to Eric Foner and Lynn Garafola for a copy of LK's six-page FBI file; in addition to the few "calls" and letters cited, Lincoln did, in the mid-forties, serve on the board of People's Songs, Inc., which HUAC declared "subversive." Matthew Josephson, *Infidel in the Temple* (Knopf, 1967), Edward P. Johanningsmeier, *Forging American Communism* (Princeton University Press, 1994), 265–66 *(Soviet)*, and Michael Denning, *The Cultural Front* (Verso, 1996), have been exceptionally useful in providing contextual material on left-wing, modernist intellectuals in the 1930s. The contents of Dos Passos's letters are in Denning, 62, 197; as Denning points out, a significant number of modernist intellectuals indulged in anti-Semitic feelings and remarks, including Theodore Dreiser and Lincoln's friend Archie MacLeish.

5. The 1932 Democratic Convention: LK Diary, Feb. 19 (Wright), Mar. 26–31 (Johnson), June 27–30 (Convention), 1932, LK/DD; Louis to George Kirstein, July 5, Oct. 4, 21, Nov. 7, 11, 15, 1932, LEK/BLH; LK, "Books and Characters," *Boston Evening American*, July 8, 15, Nov. 11 (Foster), 1932. As an example, perhaps, of how Louis tried to cover all political bases, he participated, after the convention but before the election, in a one-day "Business and Industrial Conference" in Washington called by President Hoover; in LEK's papers at BLH there's a short letter from Hoover to Louis, dated Aug. 31, 1932, reading, in its entirety, "I am deeply appreciative of the public service rendered to the whole nation by the conference of last Friday, and I thank you warmly for your personal contribution to its value" (LEK/BLH).

In regard to the actor James Cagney, LK had, at the time of the convention, just published his own article, "James Cagney and the American Hero," in *Hound and Horn* (Apr.–June 1932); in it LK called Cagney "as finished and flexible an artist as there is in the talkies today"; a more personally revealing comment in the essay, one that perhaps locates the heart of Cagney's appeal to LK, is: "No one expresses more clearly in terms of pictorial action the delights of violence, the overtones of a semi-conscious sadism, the tendency towards destruction, towards anarchy which is the basis of American sex-appeal." Some useful details on the convention can be found in Steve Neal, *Happy Days Are Here Again* (Morrow, 2004), and in J. Joseph Huthmacher, *Massachusetts People and Politics* (Harvard University Press, 1959), especially 228–56.

A decade later, when the FBI raided a male brothel on Pacific Street in Brooklyn, the manager, under threat of a prison term, provided a list of names of regular patrons; among them was bachelor Senator Walsh, then chair of the Naval Affairs Committee in the Roosevelt administration. After considerable pressure was brought to bear on the manager, he declared himself mistaken about Senator Walsh, whose reputation never recovered. The composer Virgil Thomson, by then a good friend of Lincoln's, also happened to be at the brothel when the raid took place; Thomson was arrested, briefly detained, and badly shaken; but thanks to influential friends no charges were brought against him.

CHAPTER SEVEN: NIJINSKY (1931–1933)

1. Muriel Draper, *Music at Midnight* (Harper & Brothers, 1929), 190. For details on Fokine's career see Reynolds and McCormick, *Fixed*, and Lynn Garafola, *Diaghilev's Ballets Russes* (henceforth Garafola, *Russes*), Oxford University Press, 1989, passim. For LK's lessons, conversations with, and opinions about Fokine: LK, *Fokine* (British-Continental Press, 1934); LK, four-page ms. "Introduction," BSA; LK Diary, esp. Nov. 13, 15, 19, 20, 26, Dec. 3, 10, 28 (Nijinsky), 1932, Feb. 1, 3, 8, 13 (whistling), Mar. 2, 1933; LK, *Thirty*, 14–16. In the four-page ms. introduction, LK wrote that perhaps what Fokine "contributed most to the classical vocabulary was a renovation of the plasticity of arms and upper portion of the body"; others have claimed that in this regard he'd been profoundly affected by Isadora Duncan, but Fokine denied that to Lincoln; Lincoln also gave as his summary opinion that "Fokine was

something of an archeologist . . . he had a kind of museum-taste, but absolutely no interest in the contemporary scene." For background information on various dance figures like Harriet Hoctor, and dance companies, my indispensable guide has been Reynolds and McCormick, *Fixed*. LK's memoir, *Mosaic*, 212–15, contains some additional details about his youthful experiences of classical ballet, though a few of the datings and recollections are inaccurate.

When Lincoln told Muriel that he'd begun ballet lessons, she asked him to take her son Paul along with him. Lincoln wasn't fond of Paul ("God's vainest boy") but did as she wished. Paul "looked awkward" in class, and Lincoln didn't think he "really gave a damn about dancing as such." But he did introduce him to the well-known ballerina Patricia Bowman (whom, Paul confided, he "wants to screw"); Lincoln found her "common & unimaginative," if "very beautiful" (LK Diary, Dec. 10, 1932, LK/DD).

LK Diary, Jan. 14 (Kreutzberg: "completely unrewarding . . . one is so starved for decent dancing"), May 13, Dec. 5 (Graham), 1931, Feb. 14, Apr. 12, Nov. 21 (Graham), Jan. 17, Mar. 1 (John Martin), May 7, 25, Aug. 6, Oct. 22 (Weidman), 11 (Hoctor), Dec. 2 (first meeting, Romola), 1932, LK/DD. In a diary entry marked "March, 1931," Lincoln wrote, after seeing his old hero, Massine, dance at the Roxy Theater, that he "seemed tired, dull, uninterested; it was sad to be here." In LK's first major article on the dance, "The Diaghilev Period" (*Hound and Horn* July–September, 1930, reprinted in Jenkins, *BWTF*, 103–29), LK had made clear his admiration for Massine's earlier work. LK, "Dance Chronicle," *Hound and Horn* no. 4 (Summer 1931) (Wigman); in this same article LK also dismissed Ruth St. Denis and Ted Shawn ("one can little respect their taste and lack of selection") and Harald Kreutzberg ("a very negligible phenomenon"). The John Martin quote about Martha Graham is from Reynolds and McCormick, *Fixed*, 147. For Gerald Warburg: Ron Chernow, *The Warburgs* (Random House, 1993), especially 243–45, 335–42. In 1983 LK wrote a brief introduction, "Sour Grapes: A Gracious Postscript," to *Ballet: Bias and Belief* (Dance Horizons, 1983), ix–xii, a collection of some of his dance writings, which was also introduced, with commentary, by Nancy Reynolds. In his own introduction, LK referred to his early pieces on Martha Graham as "inked in vitriol"; later, he wrote, he came at least to appreciate "her huge theatrical attraction and longed to partake of it." Still he insisted that he never wavered from his core belief that "everything emanating from her particular genius was pernicious heresy, rooting in self-limiting solipsis." He included "a lot of nasty paragraphs about minor figures and events. . . . I was a naughty show-off with *arriviste* bad manners. Such childishness should have been spanked."

2. Much of my discussion of Frances Flynn Paine and her assorted projects with LK, including the controversy over the Diego Rivera mural, derives primarily from two manuscript sources: LK's Diary, Sept. 4, Dec. 5, 7, 30 (Rivera) 1931, Jan. 14, 26 (Chávez), Feb. 6, 8, 14, 15, 16, 19 *(Billy Budd)*, Mar. 12 (Wilson), Apr. 14, July 16, Oct. 8, 22, 26, 30, Nov. 3 (Nelson), 1932; and the considerable correspondence between Paine and others in the manuscript holdings at the Rockefeller Archive Center (RAC) in Sleepy Hollow, New York. That material is too voluminous to cite in detail, but almost all the important Paine sources are concentrated in the Nelson Aldrich Rockefeller (NAR) Papers, especially Record Group 4, "NAR Personal," Record Group 2, "Business Interests," "RFAM/OMR" and "Family OMR." For LK's relationship in the early thirties with Nelson Rockefeller, LK's diary is the key source; again there are too many references to cite in full, but among the most important entries are: June 25, 26 (Pocantico), July 6, 17, Sept. 8, 9, Oct. 30, 1932, Jan. 12, Mar. 10, 19, 24, Apr. 19 (Renaissance-like), 21 (Paine), 23 (Muriel), 25 (Warburg), 27, 29, May 4 (exceeded), 8 (John Brown), 9 (Charlot), 10 (Paine; strike; Trotskyist), 12 (Frida), 15, 18, 1933, LK/DD. Some information on Frances Paine does exist in secondary sources, especially in Bernice Kert's fine biography, *Abby Aldrich Rockefeller* (Random House, 2003, paperback), henceforth Kert, *Abby*, 346–65; there's also a limited amount of material in Patrick Marnham, *Dreaming with His Eyes Open: A Life of Diego Rivera* (University of California Press, 1998). Some of the details regarding Rockefeller Center are drawn from Okrent, *Fortune*. All three books, as well as Reich, *Nelson*, have been helpful in providing context for the controversy over Rivera's mural in the RCA lobby. For Lincoln's involvement in that controversy, his own diary has been central; the most important entries are: Oct. 31, Nov. 19, 1932, Apr. 19–21, 23–24, 27, May 4, 8–12, 15, 18, 24, 1933, LK/DD. In a letter (Dec. 14, 1931, LK/DD, 123–25) to his

old HSCA associate John Walker III, then assisting Berenson at Villa I Tatti in Florence, LK wrote that "Rivera . . . strikes me as an able follower of the Gioteschi and rather little else. I think his big one-man show [at MoMA] will give him far too much eminence." LK's comments on Raymond Hood are in LK to LEK, Jan. 14, 1932, LEK/BLH. For Selznick, LEK to GK, Nov. 23, 1932, LEK/BLH. For the Film Society, the significant LK Diary entries are: Jan. 12–13, 29, Mar. 23, 1933, LK/DD; see also Julien Levy, *Memoir of an Art Gallery* (Putnam, 1977), esp. pp. 151–55. For the Bryn Mawr visit and LK's comments on Eddie Warburg: LK Diary, Apr. 25, 26, 1933, LK/DD. For Chick Austin: LK Diary, May 13–14, 1933, LK/DD.

One curious sidebar to LK's relationship with Nelson Rockefeller at this time involves Harry Hopkins's plan to set up an agency for unemployed artists; LK thought Nelson was "the irresistible man" for the job, and when he told his friend about it Nelson got into "a white heat of excitement" at the prospect; he said "he'd do it in a second . . . he wants political power [and this would be] the perfect job for him" (LK Diary, Apr. 19, 21, 1933). But in the event, Hopkins chose to put the whole matter in the hands of the Commission of Education. Nearly simultaneously, Lincoln and Nelson thought of collaborating with Philip Johnson and Alan Blackburn of MoMA in creating a high-end "postcard business" located on the roof of "Building #1" at Rockefeller Center. Lincoln warned Johnson that "should Nelson find out we were queer, how quick he'd drop us," and he got Johnson to promise "to live more discreetly" (LK Diary, May 3, 1933). In the process of pursuing the idea, Lincoln introduced Nelson to his father, and the two liked each other a great deal; Louis encouraged Lincoln to pursue the idea, but even before it fell through, LK had had a kind of epiphany about Nelson: "I felt suddenly released from responsibility to [him]. . . . I felt a certain tie snap," perhaps "part of it was guilt for my having raised his hopes so high in relation to Hopkins," perhaps "because I didn't want him to think I wanted anything out of him," perhaps because "I have no fundamental interest in" Nelson (LK Diary, Apr. 25, 27, May 4, 8, 15–19, 1933). When Nelson gave the postcard concession to someone else, and the original collaboration collapsed, Lincoln did feel that Nelson had "sold us down the river"—yet Lincoln and Nelson had ahead of them a long series of achievements and of continuing respect.

3. Eisenstein: Dec. 3, 1931 "Memorandum re: Mrs. Frances F. Paine," RAC; LK Diary, Mar. 8, 13, 19, Apr. 2, 5, 11 (rushes), 14, 18 (lowlife tour), 22, 27, May 6–7 (Sarnoff), July 6, 21, 22, 30 (Wilson), Aug. 4 (Potamkin), 11, 12, 31, Sept. 8, 30, Oct. 8 (Potamkin), 28, Nov. 23 (LK tried to enlist David Selznick), 1932, Feb. 8, 19, 1933 (Warburg), LK/DD; LK, *"Que Viva Mexico!," Arts Weekly*, Apr. 30, 1932 (staggering loss). A large secondary literature exists on Eisenstein's art and life; I found Ronal Bergan, *Eisenstein: A Life in Conflict* (Overlook Press, 1999), 216–40, and Oksana Bulgakowa, *Sergei Eisenstein* (Potemkin Press, 2001), translated by Anne Dwyer, especially helpful in understanding the context in which *Que Viva Mexico!* was made, and unmade, though Bergan makes no mention either of LK or Frances Paine; Bulgakowa does briefly refer once to LK but also says (57) that the NYC premiere of *Thunder* went off "without incident." The story of the protest at the showing of *Thunder*, and the detailed planning that preceded it, is in LK's Diary, Sept. 7, 13–18, 1933, LK/DD; also, *Boston Traveler* (Sept. 9, 1933). "Rough treatment" is from Leon Harris, *Upton Sinclair* (Crowell, 1975, 282); Harris, to a limited degree, manages to modify the indictment against Sinclair (see chap. 22); but in my view he's way off base in claiming (289) that "the most pettish and censorious outbursts [against Sinclair] came from shrill and occasionally epicene worshipers of Eisenstein, some obviously psychotic." His further claim that "none of Sinclair's attackers ever raised a dollar to take over the film from him and save it" (291) is unfair, given Lincoln's appeal (for one) to Sarnoff.

The year before Eisenstein's "lowlife" tour, Lincoln had gone with Tom Mabry to the same Sand Street YMCA behind the Brooklyn Navy Yard in search of a new "dive" they'd heard about. The evening had proved something of a comic disaster. In a downpour of rain, they finally located the place, and saw sailors going in and out. But they made the mistake, due to what Lincoln humorously called their "certified bravado," of barging up and knocking on the door, when they should have rung the bell—and were denied admittance. Lincoln had been told that the place was under the protection of Al Capone, but a drunken sailor outside told them there'd been a raid just the week before. Lincoln decided that "the best technique for low-life is complete naturalness"; but the problem was that "if one feels one is too rich-looking and young, it's hard to be natural." Given his interest in "slumming," he thought he should probably take up boxing (LK Diary, June 3, 1931, LK/DD). For more of LK's adventures at queer speakeasies and in the life, see LK Diary, Jan. 17, Apr. 1, 1932.

In his memoir, *Mosaic*, LK devotes the better part of a long chapter (187–210) to Carl Carlsen, another of his "lowlife" friends. But the name is a pseudonym and the photograph of "Carlsen" a fake, though none of that was hinted at when LK published part of the chapter in *Raritan*. Some of the actual events and interactions between LK and "Carlsen"—whose real name was Tommy Thompson—can be found in LK's Diary (for example, July 15, 20, Aug. 31, 1932, LK/DD). Why Kirstein, so late in life (1994), and after he'd publicly "come out," would bother with such subterfuges is a mystery—unless, which seems highly unlikely (since he was older than LK), Thompson was still alive.

4. Romola Nijinsky: LK to Romola Nijinsky (henceforth RN), Dec. 20, 1932, Romola's hand-written "will," dated Mar. 18, 1933, Ballet Society Archives (henceforth BSA). The only formal agreement I've been able to find is also in BSA: a two-page document dated Apr. 5, 1933, it relates solely to a thousand-dollar loan from LK to RN, which she agrees to repay "out of the first moneys realized by her" from the book's royalties; for more on the thousand-dollar loan, see LK Diary, May 1, 1933, LK/DD. For "great fun": LK, *Thirty*, 16–17. In *Mosaic*, 217, LK places his first meeting with RN as having taken place at the home of Mrs. William K. Vanderbilt.

Passport extension: LK to LEK, Feb. 17, LEK to LK, Feb. 18, Frankfurter to LEK, Feb. 19, telegram Beverly to Rosenbluh, Feb. 20, telegram LK to LEK, Feb. 21 (Ellis Island trip), LK to Frankfurter, Feb. 20, telegram, LK to LEK, Feb. 21, LEK to Walsh, Feb. 25—all 1933, all in LEK/BLH. Frankfurter passed LK's request for Romola's passport extension directly to James Grafton Rogers, Secretary of State Stimson's right-hand man. From BSA: LK to Frankfurter, Feb. 14, 1933, LK to Anne Morgan, Feb. 18, 1933; the letter to Morgan was an attempt to secure Mrs. William K. Vanderbilt's vacation address; Mrs. Vanderbilt, who'd given money over a long period of time for Vaslav's care, and had been kind to Romola, refused further help.

Alice Lowell, to whom Lincoln had once proposed marriage and was now a psychoanalyst, had known Romola well in Paris for several years; she told Lincoln that Romola "was a fiend about money, and she really killed Frederika" (LK Diary, Apr. 30, 1933, LK/DD).

During one of their trips to Ellis Island, an immigration officer sent Lincoln from the room, and Romola later reported that he "tried to make love to her and she very cleverly made out as if it was all just paternal interest . . . what are six kisses," she told Lincoln, "to be allowed to stay 6 weeks more" (LK Diary, Jan. 18, 1933, LK/DD).

Writing *Nijinsky*: LK to Tate, Feb. 6, 1933, AT/PU; LK Diary, Dec. 7 (notations; Romola told LK that the notations had been "transcribed by a French scholar from the Russian, dated Madrid 1917"), 12, 14, 16, 21, 29, 1932, Jan. 2, 5, 8 (Shankar; Rasputin; Mesmer), 9 (Diaghilev), 10–12, 13 (sanitarium), 15, 17, 18 (Ellis Island), 19, 23 (Karsavina), 26–28, 31, Feb. 2, 6 (psychic power), 10, 11, 12 ("I despair of the book ever turning out at all"), 14 (Gavrilov), 17 (Vanderbilt), 18–20 (notations; "amazing"; Vaslav "saint"; animals; Ellis Island), 21, 26, March 2, 3 (notations), 4 (Viking), 5–7, 9 (Muriel; spiritualism; Harry Curtiss), 12 (Woodlawn), 15–18 (hopeless to revive), 19 (Woodlawn; ruins), 21 (notations), 13, 21–22 (publishers), 23, 25–26 (Muriel on "lies"; USSR state ballet), 27 (Vanderbilt), 29 (oxygen), 31, Apr. 1 (de Mille), May 1 (lawsuit), 2, 5 (farewell), 1933. The "Stepanov" and "roared with laughter" quotes are from LK, *Mosaic*, 221–22; and for additional details on Nijinsky's notational system, see Peter Ostwald, *Vaslav Nijinsky* (Robson Books, 1999), 130–31.

When LK was shopping the book around, an editor at Dutton did get excited about the notations, declaring them as important as "Arezzo's innovation of the musical staff in the ninth century" (LK Diary, Mar. 22, 1933, LK/DD). But Lincoln had already been warned by Alexandre Gavrilov, once a Diaghilev soloist, to whom Romola had introduced him, that "Vaslav's notation was only a curiosity—could never be used" (LK Diary, Mar. 3, 1933, LK/DD). Through the well-known balletomane Arnold Haskell, who further edited Romola's manuscript, the book was published in London in 1933, and then, in 1934, by Simon & Schuster in New York. It long served as the central source for information about

Nijinsky, but Bronislava Nijinska's *Early Memoirs* (1981; reprint, Duke University Press, 1992), finally exposed its many factual errors and challenged some of its central interpretations, in the process casting a good deal of suspicion, mostly phrased guardedly, on Romola's character. Another valuable recent addition to the Nijinsky literature, Ostwald, *Vaslav Nijinsky*, argues persuasively in an appendix (348–50) that recent shifts in diagnostic terminology would, in today's usage, make "Schizoaffective Disorder in a Narcissistic Personality" a more accurate description of Nijinsky's condition than the simple term "schizophrenic."

CHAPTER EIGHT: BALLET (1933)

1. Kirstein finances and charitable work: LEK to GK, July 8 (Mina), 13, 25, Aug. 1 (ballyhoo), 8, 10, 18, Sept. 12, 22 (sleeping), Oct. 9, 17, 27, Nov. 20, 28, Dec. 3, 10, 19, 1932, Jan. 7 (fortunate), 20, 25, Feb. 2, 11, 1933; GK to LEK, Sept. 18, Oct. 21 (Rolls), Nov. 27, 1932, Jan. 14 (sick to stomach), 1933; LEK to Fishel, May 27, 1932 (Adath); LK Diary, May 16 (Schacht), 19 (Harvard degree) 1933, LEK/BLH.

2. Muriel Draper appears so often in LK's diaries in the early thirties that any full citation would be pointless. Among the most important entries (and those from which most of the quotes come) are: LK Diary, Feb. 10 (talking about), 14 (Deserta), 23 (sex), Mar. 3, 4 (sex; laughed), May 11 (Ruth Draper), May 13, Nov. 10 (Loomis), June 8 (sex), Aug. 10 (abortion), Sept. 25 (organizer), Dec. 10 (debts; sex), 1931, Jan. 11 (Gurdjieff), 18 (Deserta), Feb. 1 (writing), 3 (moods), 11 (guesses), Mar. 1 (Paul), 4 (deference; inertia), 15 (bravery), Apr. 3 (on LK), 17 (moods), 18, 24 (distance), 25 (chilled), May 2 (on LK), 15 (ordinary), Oct. 1 (Ruth Draper), 8 (responsibility), 1932, May 26, 1933, LK/DD. There is also a great deal in LK's diary about Esther Strachey (too much to cite, given that she was a peripheral figure in LK's life); there's also some material on her brother and sister-in-law, the famed Gerald and Sara Murphy (see especially LK Diary, Nov. 8, 1932). Though primarily lesbian, Esther was briefly married (they divorced in 1932) to the Englishman John Strachey, a Marxist intellectual who became a leading figure in the Labour Party. Esther's second marriage, to Chester Alan Arthur III, the gay grandson of an American president, would fare no better. For more on Esther Strachey, see Amanda Vaill, *Everybody Was So Young* (Houghton Mifflin, 1998), and Hugh Thomas, *John Strachey* (Harper & Row, 1973).

   E. E. Cummings: LK Diary, Feb. 26 (Anne), Mar. 10 (Paul), 23 (Keershtine), Apr. 20 (check), 23 (conversation; Muriel), May 25 (Muriel), 26 (spoiled), 31 (Dos Passos; Art), June 7 (Archie), 14 (hate), 22 (Schmeling; etc.), 23 (LK & homosexuality), July 16 (Archie), Sept. 28 (army), 30 (genius), Nov. 13 (Bandler), 1932, Jun. 7, 10, 12, Aug. 18, 1933, LK/DD. For more on Cummings, see Richard S. Kennedy, *Dreams in the Mirror* (Liveright, 1980), and Christopher Sawyer-Laucanno, *E. E. Cummings: A Biography* (Sourcebooks, 2004).

3. For Virgil Thomson: LK Diary, Apr. 18 (wicked), Dec. 7, 1932 (deprecatory), June 4, 6–8, 10–11, 13, 15 (Grosser), 16, 18–19 (lecture), 24, 26, 28, 1933, LK/DD; LK to VT, May 17, 1933, 123–25, LK/DD; LK, "Virgil Thomson" (serpentine; malice), three-page draft ms., BSA. For more on Thomson, see Anthony Tommasini's excellent *Virgil Thomson: Composer on the Aisle* (W. W. Norton, 1997).

   For Romaine Brooks, Natalie Barney, Dolly Wilde, and others involved in the 20 Rue Jacob salon, the key source is Shari Benstock, *Women of the Left Bank* (University of Texas Press, 1986), which I've relied on for a number of details about Brooks and the Temple d'Amité. For Bérard: LK Diary, June 8, 17, 22, 24, 1933, LK/DD. For Barney: Mar. 8, 1932, June 7, 9, 10, 19, 20, 1933, LK/DD. LK's letters to his parents (LK/DD) have also been important for this section.

   It's essential to emphasize that the excerpts from LK's diary from June 3 to Aug. 8, 1933, first published in *Dance Perspectives* 54 (Summer 1973) and then republished in *BWTF*, 130–58, are not transcripts of LK's actual diary entries. The printed versions are essentially rewritten paraphrases, with a great deal added, omitted or changed, including some of the most important material in the original diaries housed at LK/DD. All the quotations in this book are from the original diaries, never from the published bowdlerized versions. The same caution applies to LK's *Thirty*, where the boldfaced introductions are dated (e.g., "July, 1933:

Paris"), thereby suggesting that they are direct excerpts from LK's diaries, which they are not.

For Wescott: LK Diary, June 10, 21 (chi-chi), 27 (boy), LK/DD. For Wheeler: LK Diary, June 16, 21 (Marx; row), 27, Aug. 16–17 (Stein), 1933, LK/DD. LK had met Wheeler more than a year earlier at Joella and Julien Levy's. Wheeler was already a partner in Harrison of Paris, and LK tried to interest him in drawings by Bill Littlefield (who'd painted LK's undergraduate portrait). When Wheeler didn't care for them, LK wrote in his diary (Mar. 22, 1932): "I was griped and crossed him off my interest. He is very set, smug & arrogant." But in fact, the two became good friends, at least for a time.

For Katherine Anne Porter: LK Diary, June 14, 21, 24, Aug. 10, 14; also Isabel Bayley, ed., *Letters of Katherine Anne Porter* (henceforth Bayley, *Porter*), Atlantic Monthly Press, 1990, 18 (by far); and Hamovitch, *H&H Letters*, 127–38 (Porter), 186 (Doomsday). The Mather chapter ("A Bright Particular Faith, A.D. 1700") was published in the *H&H* issues of Jan.–Mar. 1933.

For Hart Crane: LK Diary, Apr. 28 (Hurricane; sickening), May 4, May 13 (MacLeish), 1932, May 8 (Tunnel), 1933, LK/DD; also LK, *Mosaic*, esp. 187–92, 199–203, 207–10; Barth, *Winters*, 92 (greatest), 138, 186 (great). Winters had never been an uncritical admirer of Crane's, and, judging from Barth's edition of Winters's letters, doesn't seem to have modified his views much over time. Possibly it was the mixed review Winters gave *The Bridge* that had made Crane feel he'd turned his back on him. For Tommy Thompson: LK Diary, Jan. 12, Mar. 12, 1932, May 4, 1933, LK/DD.

There are only two letters (and those copies) from LK to Romola for 1933 (both in LK/DD), but BSA has ten letters from Romola to LK, dated June 16 through Aug. 22, 1933; the request for money is in Romola to LK, July 4, 1933. LK Diary, June 15, 17 (Virgil), 1933, LK/DD.

4. For background on the 1931–33 ballet scene, I've relied particularly on Garafola, *Russes*, Reynolds and McCormick, *Fixed*, chapter 2, and Bernard Taper, *Balanchine* (Times Books, 1984), see 144–45 for the reception of the two ballet companies. A few details are from Doris Hering's 1976 interview with Roman Jasinski, a leading dancer in Blum's company (*MGZMT 3–593, esp. 25–30), DD/NYPL. In *Thirty*, 19, LK makes the curious statement—"curious" for one so knowledgeable—that it was Balanchine and Kochno who "invited" Massine "to join them"; this stands the known evidence on its head. For LK's assorted ballet experiences, his own diary is the chief source: LK Diary, June 2 (Levy), 3 (whores), 7 (fever; opening), 8, 9, (rehearsal), 10–11, 12 (Barr), 13 (Lifar), 13, 17 (Nazis), 15 (Kochno; Romola; Flanner), 16 (Wheeler; Tchelitchev; *Les Sylphides*), 17 (high standards), 18 *(Dame)*, 19 (Lifar; Bérard; Kochno; *Errante*), 21, 24 (Tchelitchev), 23 (Flanner; Massine), 24 (Lifar; Kochno; Nouvel; Jasinski; Balanchine; Virgil on sex), July 3 (Lifar), 4 (Haskell), 5 (boat-train; Fry), 6 (Tamara; *Les Sylphides*), 7 (Romola; Haskell), 8 (Epstein; Balanchine), 11, 13, 16 (Balanchine), 1933, LK/DD; LK to LEK, Feb. 11, 1939 (Johnson), BSA.

For Barr's negotiations with LK about the *Hound and Horn* articles: Barr to LK, Sept. 29, Oct. 3 (anonymity), LK to Barr, Oct. 27, 1933, Barr Papers, Archives of American Art, Museum of Modern Art (henceforth AB/AAA [MoMa]).

For more on Tchelitchev: LK Diary, Mar. 31, 1931, LK/DD; LK, *Mosaic*, 234–35. In later years LK would write a good deal about Tchelitchev; those citations appear in their chronological order. The key biographical work is Parker Tyler's eccentric *The Divine Comedy of Pavel Tchelitchev* (Weidenfeld & Nicolson, 1967); for more on Losch's "green train," see 367–68.

Holland: LK Diary, June 26 (fed up), June 28–July 1, July 5 (money), 7 (Romola arrives; Haskell), 1933, LK/DD; LK to parents, June 30, 1933, LK/DD. As late as the 1970s Romola was haranguing Lincoln with claims that she'd been the "midwife" of NYCB (e.g., Romola to LK, May 24, 1973, BSA).

5. LK Diary, Apr. 2–13 (Virginia); July 5 (Bloomsbury); July 21, 23, 25, Aug. 1: Quennell; July 4, 8, 20, 25: Haskell, 1933, LK/DD. On their way to Virginia, LK and Mina had called on her friends Dean and Alice Acheson (Mina found him attractive, Lincoln thought his wife "a fool"). They also had tea at Justice Brandeis's house; he had "a sweet look," Lincoln thought, and seemed like "a dazed lion." He held Lincoln's hand so long that Lincoln

thought "he'd forgotten, in his abstraction, what it was"; but when he finally withdrew it, the justice "looked hurt."

CHAPTER NINE: BALANCHINE (1932–1933)

1. LK Diary, July 10 (Lifar), 11 (Spender), 12 (Massine; Bloomsbury), 13 (van der Post), 14 (Bloomsbury), 15, 16, 17 (Spender), 19, 20, 22–24, 27 (Spender), 24 (Ackerley), 25 (Forster; *Blackshirt*), 26 (Chick), 27 (Plomer), 28–30 *(The Mint)*, 1933, LK/DD; LK to Austin, July 16, Aug. 2 (Isherwood; Auden), 8 (Forster), 11, 1933, the Wadsworth Atheneum (henceforth WA); LK, *Mosaic*, 249–50 (optimistic); "memo" fragment, July 22, 1973, LK/DD. In Massine's memoir, *My Life in Ballet* (St. Martin's, 1968), Balanchine is mentioned only a few times, always neutrally or favorably, though never with truly enthusiastic praise; "creative inventiveness" (278) is about the limit of it.

   On the history of ballet, LK's own book, *Dance: A Short History of Classic Theatrical Dancing* remains worth consulting. Originally published in 1935, it was reissued in 1942 with a new last chapter, "Dancing in North America: 1519–1942," which is still useful, especially for its insights into LK's own tastes and opinions. After being out of print for twenty years, the book was, in 1969, again reissued, though unrevised (except for an introductory two-page "Apology" by LK), as a Dance Horizons Republication.

   For a detailed account of Chick Austin's life, see Eugene R. Gaddis, *Magician of the Modern* (Knopf, 2000); and for more on the history of ballet in the United States, see Reynolds and McCormick, *Fixed*, chap. 4. For Spender, see David Leeming, *Stephen Spender* (Henry Holt, 1999), and John Sutherland, *Stephen Spender* (Oxford, 2004).

   For William Plomer: LK Diary, July 17, 20, 24, 25 ("The Temple"), 28, Aug. 3 (suppressed), 4, 8, 9, 1933, LK/DD. LK's other recent South African friend, Laurens van der Post, agreed with Spender that "all the passion" had gone out of Plomer's work and went on to denounce him to Lincoln as "intolerably egotistical" and "eagerly promiscuous" (LK Diary, Aug. 8, 1933); but van der Post kept changing his opinion of Plomer, and besides (as his recent biographer, J. D. F. Jones, has revealed in his *Teller of Many Tales* (Carroll & Graf, 2002), was an inveterate liar; later in life he became a close friend to Prince Charles and an adviser to Margaret Thatcher. Plomer could be charming and engaging, though, which contributed to Lincoln's misjudgment of him as "a sweet character" with "a curious deep innocence" (LK Diary, Aug. 8, 1933). Plomer's *Turbott Wolfe* was reissued by the Modern Library in 2003, with an introduction by Nadine Gordimer, in which she wrote (xix): "It is an inexplicable lapse on the part of literary scholars and critics that *Turbott Wolfe* is not recognized as a pyrotechnic presence in the canon of renegade colonialist literature along with Conrad."

2. LK, *Mosaic*, 252–57; Gaddis, *Magician*, 207–12; LK Diary, Aug. 1, 3 (Muriel), 4 (Austin), 5, 6, 7 (Muriel), 10–16 (Balanchine), 16 (consulate), 17 (Wheeler), 18 (Gurdjieff), 28 (*H&H*/postcards), 1933, LK/DD; LK to Austin, Aug. 11, 1933, WA; Romola to LK, July 29, Aug. 1, 4, 22 (plus four undated), BSA; Balanchine telegram to LK, n.d. [1933], Balanchine Archive, Harvard University Theater Collection (henceforth BA/HTC).

CHAPTER TEN: BALANCHINE (1933)

1. George told Lincoln that their father had "railroaded" him into the retail store business (LK Diary, June 31, 1932). In his diary entry for July 21, 1933, LK had written while still in Europe: "Didn't mention my Balanchine plan to him [Virgil] as he might think I was militating against Chick's producing his Opera at Hartford: which I am." LK Diary, Aug. 28 (Mina; Johnson), 29 (Warburg), 30 (Balanchine/Nelson), 31 (Hartford), Sept. 1 (Dimitriev/Warburg), 2, 3 (family), 4 (Johnson), 5, 11, 15, 17 (Nelson), 1933, LK/DD; LK to Louis, Sept. 11, 1933 (blackmail), LEK/BLH.

2. Five telegrams from LK to Balanchine, undated [1933], in BA/HTC re: various arrangements; LK Diary, Sept. 5, 6 (MacLeish), 15 (Toumanova), 19, 20, 21 (passports), 22, 23 (Barr; cowboy), Oct. 1 (Hartford), 2 (Balanchine wire), 3–10 (Blackburn; Art, Inc.), 8 (MacLeish),

1933, LK/DD; Romola to LK, Sept. 8, 11, 25 (Bandler), 26 ("our"/nice girl), Oct. 3 (Bullitt—also LK Diary for Apr. 16, May 29, 30, 1927), 15 (Diaghilev), n.d. [November], 1933; LK to Romola, Sept. 8 (money/Balanchine), 22 (terrible), Oct. 4, 31 (issue/dearie), Nov. 7 (something regular), 14 (Fadiman), 1933; LK to Fadiman, Nov. 17, 1933—all in BSA.

For the Bourman book: John Day Co. [no signature] to LK, Nov. 20, Dec. 1, 1933, John Day Co. Archives (henceforth JDA/PU), Princeton University. The Bourman book, *The Tragedy of Nijinsky*, did get published four years later in England, after Lincoln himself helped to edit it (LK to Romola, May 11, 1934, BSA); it was reprinted in 1970 by the U.S. firm, Greenwood Press. Romola's biography "has been almost continually in print ever since" its 1933 publication (Reynolds and McCormick, *Fixed*, 756, n. 53.)

3. LK Diary, Oct. 17–18, 19–21, 24, 27 (Hartford), 21–22 (Ashfield), 23–24, Nov. 4 (Louis/discouraged), 23–24 (Warburg), 26 (Bullitt), 28–29 (Boston), 30 (Barr), 31 (difficile), Nov. 1 (Jooss), 2 (miners), 3 (tuition), 5 (Lifar), 6 (MacLeish), 7 (simple & deep), 4, 8, 17 (Vladimiroff), 10–16 (Balanchine's illness and character), 12, 15 (Warburg), 15 (sex-starved; Fadiman), 19 (Diaghilev), 20 (Geva; Harkness; FDR), 21 (Moe), 30 (Louis), Dec. 1 (misdated "Nov. 1"; Balanchine/Diaghilev), 2 (misdated "Nov. 2"; wet dreams), 5 (beast), 23 (Haskell), 1933, LK/DD. The comments on Misia Sert putting up the money and Balanchine being "wild" about Lifar are from LK to Romola, Nov. 7, 1933, BSA. LK's comments on Lifar are in *Vogue*, Nov. 1, 1933. For Tamara Geva: LK Diary, Oct. 11, 12, 1933, LK/DD; Tamara Geva, *Split Seconds* (Harper & Row, 1972), 351–57.

The exchange of letters between Doris Levine, LK, and Romola—DL to Romola, Jan. 13, 1934, LK to Romola, Mar. 5, May 11, Romola to LK, Apr. 23, 1934, plus an undated [Feb. 1934?] LK telegram to Romola threatening a lawsuit over Dodge's photographs—are all in BSA. Lincoln had a jointly signed agreement with Romola, dated Apr. 5, 1933, in which she'd promised to repay "out of the first net profits of the book," the thousand dollars Lincoln had borrowed from Eddie Warburg in order to rescue her from what she'd claimed was "poverty" (a copy of the agreement, along with a draft of it, is in BSA). But when the book came out in the United States and sold well, Romola never sent him the money. Lincoln, already furious at her, wrote to Fadiman that he was "putting this matter in the hands of my attorney," though whether he ever got the money back is unknown (LK to Fadiman, Apr. 4, 1934, BSA). The dozen later telegrams and letters between LK and Romola, running from 1935 to 1938, then picking up again from 1946 to 1948, are all in BSA; Romola's letters contain some rose-colored details about Vaslav's life and his insulin-shock treatments with Dr. Manfred Sakel, inventor of the technique, as well as pleas for assistance (to which LK did sometimes respond).

4. Ruthanna Boris: multiple telephone interviews 2003–6, plus the unpublished chapters of her memoir which she kindly sent me. Her initial exchange of letters with LK is described in her ms. "Prologue," as is the information that Ruthanna's mother had earlier written to John Martin of the *New York Times* asking for advice on where her daughter, "afflicted with an insatiable appetite for dancing," might study. Martin had sent several suggestions, *not* including the American School of Ballet (though he'd earlier made encouraging remarks on the proposal LK had given him: LK to Fadiman, Apr. 4, 1934, BSA).

Eddie Warburg had a quite different view of Dimitriev, calling him "a wretched man": "Balanchine was easy but his business manager just put on a sit-down strike every two minutes in order to get more money out of us" (Paul Cummings's interview with Warburg, May 13, 1971, SAAA). Balanchine, in turn, characterized Eddie to Lincoln as "gentil," coolly adding that he himself "detested good taste" (LK Diary, Oct. 23, 1933, LK/DD). In regard to MoMA's sponsorship, LK wrote in his diary (Oct. 24) that the suggestion had "raised a hornet's nest"; Philip Johnson said he "won't give any cash: it's got around town . . . [that Lincoln had] made use of Chick" and that "it's all off."

Dimitriev at one point (LK Diary, Nov. 18, 1933) went even further in denouncing Balanchine to Lincoln, claiming that "one must always act as if any idea were Balanchine's first, as he appropriates them all anyway," and that he was "bitter against Massine" because he felt the latter had "copped many of his ideas." Vladimiroff (LK Diary, Dec. 5, 1933) also told stories about how Balanchine, "playing the old man with a long beard in *Petrouchka*, once made up his nose like a penis, and another time his face like an Xmas tree," and that Diaghilev had been "furious."

5. Fokine: LK, *Fokine*, introduction by Arnold Haskell (British-Continental Press, 1934); LK Diary, Oct. 13 (bitter), 22, Nov. 7, 18, 19, 28, Dec. 5, 1933, LK/DD. For more on Fokine's character, see Garafola, *Russes*, esp. 44–45, 196–97.

6. *Hound and Horn:* LK to Scott, Oct. 25, 1933, LK to Wheelwright, Nov. 28, 1933, JBW/BU; LK to Rukeyser, Feb. 27, 1933, BC/NYPL; LK Diary, Dec. 31, 1933, Jan. 2 (guilt), 1934, LK/DD; LK to Troy, Leonie Adams and William Troy Papers, Beinecke Library, Yale University (henceforth ATP/BL); Barr to LK, Oct. 25, 1933, AB/AAA (MoMA). For additional evidence of LK's continuing, if irregular, commitment to the Left, see his article "The Hound & Horn, 1927–1934," *Harvard Advocate* 12 no. 2 (Christmas 1934). In that piece LK wrote, "I realize now [1934] that had the magazine continued it would have been definitely left." He also recalls making plans with Stephen Spender during the summer of 1933 "for internationalizing the magazine as an agency against reaction in every form." At the time, however, Lincoln seems to have accepted Bandler's advice to keep the magazine free of politics (see LK to Tate, Oct. 17, 1933, AT/PU).

The Henry James issue (Apr.–June 1934) included James manuscripts that Bandler had bought at an auction of George Harvey's effects in 1931, as well as a distinguished group of articles by such well-known figures as Marianne Moore, Edmund Wilson, Francis Fergusson, Stephen Spender, and Newton Arvin. Gertrude Stein had agreed to contribute a piece but was unable to finish in time; and T. S. Eliot finally decided he had nothing to say (LK, *Advocate* 121, no. 2—also the source for letters of regret and schemes to resuscitate; Wheeler's interest is from LK Diary, Jan. 23, 1934, LK/DD).

CHAPTER ELEVEN: SCHOOL OF AMERICAN BALLET (1934)

1. For problems with the workmen, Philip Johnson, and students: LK Diary, Dec. 9 (bitterly), 16–19, 21, 23–24 (paychecks; Johnson), 26–28, Dec. 4, 9, 14, 16–17, 19, 22 (Dollar), 23–24, 26–28, 1933, Jan. 4 (Dollar), 1934. For the Ballets Russes de Monte Carlo: LK, "The Dance: The Persistence of Ballet" (Ballets Russes), Jan. 31, *The Nation;* LK, "The Dance: The Music Hall: Reviews: the Movies" (Bowman), *The Nation*, Mar. 14, 1934; LK Diary, Dec. 7, 15, 17–18, 22 (Laskey), 25–26, 27 (Bérard), 28 (Hurok/Laskey), 1933, Jan. 12 (Haskell), 23 (Martin), 1934.

2. For Balanchine's health: LK Diary, Jan. 7, 16, 19, 1933, Feb. 2 (Geyelin), 1934, LK/DD. For immigration problems: LK to Bullitt, Jan. 15, 1934, BSA; LK Diary, Jan. 11, 19, Feb. 8, 19, 1934, LK/DD; LK to Louis, Feb. 26, May 11, 1934, LEK/BLH.

3. For Warburg: LK Diary, Nov. 20, Dec. 7, 23, 29, 31, 1933, Jan. 1 (male sex), 5 (doubts/soulless), 7 (amorous), 25, 1934. Eddie had earlier confessed to Lincoln (LK Diary, Nov. 20, 1933) that "he cares for nothing in the world . . . has no interest, is terrified that I'll ask him to do something in the school"; even his new apartment already "bores him." Dimitriev told Lincoln that he thought Eddie lived in "a prison de luxe" (LK Diary, Nov. 23, 1933). In several of our phone interviews (Sept. 16 and Nov. 22, 2003) and her letter to me of Nov. 9, 2003, Ruthanna Boris said that she and others at the school—in particular the "Dorothie Littlefield dancers," who "loved to gossip about sex" knew that Eddie "had gay experiences"; his distressed father, in fact, called the school "a whore house" and "feared that his son was a homosexual." In her letter of Nov. 9, 2003, Ruthanna Boris contrasted Eddie and LK this way: "Where Lincoln's attitude was serious, concerned, responsible, Warburg played the friendly, playful role with us (the dancers), brought friends to visit our classes and rehearsals [actually, so did Lincoln, though not as often, especially after Dimitriev reprimanded him for defiling "our temple"] and, with them acted the genial host of a private party." For Zilboorg, see Ron Chernow, *The Warburgs* (Random House, 1993), 333–34, 346–47; Chernow's account of Eddie's involvement with Lincoln and the June 1934 performance at Woodlands (344–46) is not entirely accurate.

4. For money matters: the projected 1934 school budget, undated [1934?] is in BSA, along with LK's various income and expense statements that (except for the total of his allowance) are

difficult to decipher with any assurance. For Louis Kirstein: LK Diary, Dec. 17 (Rose), 27, 1933, Jan. 4, 10, 18 (sculptor), 1934; Trout, *Boston*, 247; LK to Louis, April 9, 1934 (no idea), BSA; LK to Louis, Jan. 22, 1934 (broke), E. R. Beverley (sec. to Louis) to Lincoln, May 26, June 5, 1934, Lincoln to Beverley, June 2, 1934, all in LEK/BLH. Mina's allowance from her father in 1933 came to $4,400; I didn't find any figures for George. In a letter from Doris Levine to Beverley (Jan. 20, 1934, BSA), she wrote that LK in 1933 had given a total of $324 "to help out certain deserving artists"; Louis had told him that he was only entitled to give away money he himself had earned; Lincoln, suspiciously, claimed to have earned exactly $324 for articles he'd written for various publications.

For Dimitriev: LK to Romola, Nov. 7, 1933 (darling), BSA; LK Diary, Nov. 23 (Gurdjieff), 28, Dec. 13–14, 23 (Haskell), 26, 1933; multiple phone interviews with Boris, plus her unpublished memoir, courtesy Boris.

For various ideas for ballets and demonstrations: LK Diary, Nov. 19, Dec. 2–4, 13, 19, 22, 1933; Feb. 11 (Rover Boys), 1934, LK/DD.

School crisis: LK Diary, Nov. 23 (perform first); Dec. 13, 1933/Jan. 6, 8, 1934 (Radio City); Dec. 31 (Dimitriev), 1933, Jan. 9 (water), 14 (Dimitriev), 16 (Warburg), 18, 22 (Balanchine), 27 (cursed), 28 (dangerous; flattery), 30 (bitterness), 31 (emollient), Feb. 9 (Warburg/desire to live), 10 (apology), 1934, LK/DD.

5. The new students: phone interview with Annabelle Lyon (Nov. 23, 2003); multiple phone interviews with Ruthanna Boris; LK Diary, Jan. 13 (fresh), 15, 16 (Laskey), 22, 29, Feb. 1, 8 (Haakon), 1934, LK/DD; Richard Buckle (in collaboration with John Taras), *George Balanchine, Ballet Master* (henceforth Buckle, *Balanchine*); Random House, 1988, 85–6; Jennifer Dunning, *But First a School* (Viking, 1985); LK's remarks on Ouroussow, who had recently died, are from the program of the *Tenth Annual Workshop Performances of the School of American Ballet*, May 21, 1975, LK/DD; LK to Louis, May 11, 1934, LEK/BLH.

For Bowles and Harry Dunham: LK Diary, Jan. 5, 6, 20–27, Feb. 23, 24, Apr. 4, June 4, 7, 11, 18, 20, 21, 25, 27, 28, July 6, 1934, LK/DD. In 1935 Dunham joined the Nazi youth movement under Baldur von Schirach, then returned to New York and promptly joined the Communist Party; he made films for Earl Browder's 1936 campaign for the presidency. These details and more are in Jeffrey Miller, ed., *In Touch: The Letters of Paul Bowles* (Farrar, Straus & Giroux, 1994), Paul Bowles, *Without Stopping* (Putnam, 1972), and Virginia Spencer Carr, *Paul Bowles* (Scribner, 2004). In regard to Balanchine, who found Bowles's music "not danceable," Bowles wrote a friend (Bruce Morrisette, Mar. 1934, Miller, *In Touch*, 133) that the ballet *Dreams*, which Balanchine was currently doing with George Antheil, contained "the 3rd movement of my Sonata included practically verbatim as to the first theme!" When Bowles brought the matter up to Antheil, he purportedly "blushed and stammered about, and said he had forgotten my piece; which incidentally he was very fond of . . . and played over and over."

For Muriel Draper: LK Diary, Dec. 11–12, 17, 22, 31, 1933, Jan. 1, 7, 10, 15, 21, 24–25, 31, Feb. 3, 6, 11, 12, 14, 28, Mar. 7, 8, Apr. 20, 1934, LK/DD. For Margot: Dec. 24, 26, 1933, Jan. 9, 20, 29 (kiss), Feb. 3, 4, Mar. 4, 1934, LK/DD. Spender on Gurdjieff: Apr. 29, 1934, LK/DD.

6. For Balanchine: LK Diary, April 20 (murderer), May 9 (contempt), 1934; for Antheil and Fergusson: Jan. 25, 26, Feb. 1, 2 (suggestible), 5, 7, 11, 14, 23, 28, Mar. 1, 2, 6, 26 (jazz), 1934, LK/DD. Privately Fergusson was "nasty about Balanchine" to Lincoln, saying among other things that "he was nothing as [a] teacher" (LK Diary, Feb. 3, 1934).

LK's grunt work: LK Diary, Feb. 6, 17, 19, Mar. 2, 3 *(Harper's)*, 13–14 (Montreal), 20 (consul), 22 (precarious), 26–27 (Vladimiroff), Apr. 3 (pederasts), 1934, LK/DD. Among the many testimonials to Vladimiroff's excellence as a teacher: Annabelle Lyon in *I Remember Balanchine*, edited by Francis Mason (Doubleday, 1991), 142; and Ruthanna Boris (multiple phone interviews, 2003–6).

Money issues: LK Diary, Mar. 11 (lid), 17 (Rose), 20, 21, Apr. 14, 15, 1934, LK/DD; Louis to Frankfurter, Jan. 15, 1934 (business better), LK to Louis, Jan. 22, 23, May 17, 1934, LEK/BLH; LK to Louis, Apr. 9, 1934, BSA (which also has various budgets and balance sheets for the school).

CHAPTER TWELVE: THE WARBURGS (1934)

1. LK Diary, June 3 (Gellert), 1932, Feb. 11, Apr. 9, May 14 (Nelson), 13 (Edmonston), 15 (map), June 29 (Nelson), 1934, LK/DD; ms., "Cut of Kind" (gentile), LK/DD; Leonard Baker, *Brandeis and Frankfurter* (NYU Press, 1986), 291 (doomed); correspondence between Frankfurter and Louis Kirstein, along with a number of Louis's speeches (Box 11) on the Jewish crisis, are in LEK/BLH; Reich, *Nelson Rockefeller*, especially 138–40.

   For Philip Johnson: LK Diary, Mar. 6 (Machine Art/decorator), 8, May 1 (parade), 6, 7, 15–17, 20, 22, Aug. 20, 21, Nov. 6 (lunch), 1934, LK/DD; Schulze, *Johnson*, esp. 108 (Mies remark), 121, 127–146 (135, *Mercury*); LK to Barr, n.d. [1934], AB/AAA, (MoMA); Robert A. M. Stern 1985 interview with Johnson, COH; LK to *The Nation*, written Nov. 15, 1934, published in the Dec. 5 issue. In a brilliant op-ed piece (Jan. 31, 2005) in the *New York Times*, Mark Stevens showed how Johnson's political history is linked to the lack of a "particular center" in his architecture.

2. Phone interview with Annabelle Lyon, Nov. 23, 2003 (congenial); Ruthanna Boris to me, Nov. 23 (planting), 2003, plus multiple phone interviews, 2003–6; LK Diary, Mar. 29 (angelic), Apr. 1 (Mannes), Apr. 24, May 1, 19 (Hawkins), 14 (pals), 26 (Howard), June 20 (Laskey), 1934, LK/DD. Ruthanna Boris (in the letter cited above) recalls Lincoln setting up a shelf of some dozen books for the students and telling them " 'This is your history. This is your library'—read the books and for God's sake, put them back when you are finished." For more on Hawkins, see Agnes de Mille, *Martha: The Life and Work of Martha Graham* (Random House, 1991), esp. 225–330, in which de Mille describes his manner as "almost disdainful," "haughty and extremely aggressive." Despite the many insights in *Martha*, the biography contains, in my view, a number of dubious interpretations (as noted in this book's later chapters).

3. Preparations for the June performance: Balanchine: LK Diary, March 14 (pray), 21 (Dimitriev/Thomson), 26 (Riabouchinska), 1934, LK/DD; *Serenade:* Ruthanna Boris to me, Nov. 7, 2003; phone interview with Annabelle Lyon, Nov. 22, 2003; LK Diary, Mar. 15, May 16–17 (Virgil), Mar. 16, 21 (Marie-Jeanne), Apr. 3, 10, May 5, 8, 11 (Mielziner), May 17, 23 (Stettheimer), 20, June 6 (Bloomingdale's), 1934, LK/DD; *Songes:* LK Diary, Apr. 14, May 1, 9, 14, 21, 31, 1934, LK/DD; *Mozartiana:* LK Diary, Mar. 15, May 5, 11, 31, 1934; *Dreams:* May 21, 31, June 10, 1934, LK/DD; Eddie Warburg: LK Diary, May 29, 31, June 19–20, 27, 1934, LK/DD. For Lincoln's poetry: Diary, June 22, 1934; a month before (Diary, May 24), he'd also stopped work on his novel, *The Leader*, "struck by its entire artificiality."

   For Cummings and *Tom:* LK Diary, Apr. 16, 17, May 17 (Watkins), Apr. 28, May 7, 8, 16 (Virgil), 20, 23, June 1, 30, July 10, 12, Aug. 5 (Muriel), 18, 1934, LK/DD; for additional details (not always accurate in regard to Lincoln), see Sawyer-Laucanno, *E. E. Cummings*. Virgil wanted to use Florine Stettheimer, who'd done the sets for his *Four Saints*, for *Tom*, but Lincoln wasn't interested. He thought her paintings were "quite O.K." but "the chi-chi is too feminine for me. She is inordinately pleased with them" (LK Diary, May 17, 23, 1934, LK/DD). In fact Lincoln hadn't been much taken, either, with *Four Saints*; he thought "there were many moments of curious loveliness" but found "much of it was monotonous and repetitious" (LK Diary, Feb. 24, 1934, LK/DD).

4. Gurdjieff: LK Diary, Apr. 18 (Virgil), 1932, Nov. 20, 23, 24, 29, Dec. 3, 12, 15, 21, 1933, Jan. 21, April 23, 26, 28, May 2, 3, 5, 8, 11, 13, 22, June 5, 1934, LK/DD.

   For the Woodlands performances: LK Diary, Apr. 27, May 18 (Austin), June 8–10, 1934, LK Diary, LK/DD; LK to Austin, "Friday" [1933], Nov. 4, 1933, June 20, 1934, WA. Eddie Warburg's account of the event in Mason, *I Remember Balanchine*, 125, is largely inaccurate; unfortunately it has been reprinted as gospel in Chernow, *The Warburgs*, 345, which makes the further error of suggesting that *Alma Mater* was part of the event. Even LK's own brief version in *Thirty*, 42–43, unaccountably contradicts his diary entries by including *Les Songes* as part of the program, and by making the "pleasant feast" and festive surroundings of the garage appear far more attractive than in his 1934 description—and Dimitriev as alone in feeling insulted. For *Alma Mater:* LK Diary, May 5, 22, 23, 1934, LK/DD; Vicki Ohl, *Fine & Dandy: The Life and Work of Kay Swift* (Yale University Press, 2004).

CHAPTER THIRTEEN: THE LEFT (1934)

1. LK Diary, June 13, 14, 19–21, 25, 28, 29, July 2, 6, Aug. 27–8, 1934, LK/DD; Dimitriev to Louis, Sept. 15, 1934, LK to Louis, Sept. 7 [Nov./Dec. 1934], BSA (scholarships). Eddie to Muriel, Dec. 15, 1934, the Muriel Draper Papers, Beinecke Library, Yale (henceforth MD/BL); LK to parents, Sept. 7, 1934, LK to Louis, Sept. 17 (Eddie abroad), 1934, both BSA.
   Balanchine's attack and its aftermath: LK Diary, July 12–22, 29, 31, Aug. 2, 5, 9, 10–19, 23, 27, 31, Sept. 13, Oct. 1, 4, 11, 1934, LK/DD. Muriel's opinions and departure: LK Diary, July 20, Aug. 2, 5, 7, 8, 1934, LK/DD.

2. LK Diary, Aug. 29, Sept. 10–12 (Revenge), Sept. 6 (Balanchine), 7 (Merovich), 11, 14, 26 (Louis), 12 (Dimitriev), 13 (Virgil), 18–20 (Company; de Basil), Sept. 22 (Austin), 26 (guilt), 1934, LK/DD; LK to parents, Sept. 7 (money), Dimitriev to Louis, Sept. 15, 1934, Louis to LK, Sept. 17, Dec. 4, 15, LK to Louis, Sept. 17, 20 [Nov.–Dec.], Kaplan (lawyer) to Louis, Sept. 21, Reinfeld (accountant) to Louis, Oct. 2—all 1934, all in BSA. LK, "Revolutionary Ballet Forms," *New Theatre*, Oct. 1934. In regard to LK's cosmic sense of "guilt," at another time he wrote in his diary (June 9, 1934), "I have a guilt obsession of some sort which takes itself out in various shynesses: i.e. I'm not a professional, etc. I hate to read the theatrical sections of the papers for fear it might say something derisive."

3. LK and the Left: LK Diary, July 29, Aug. 1, 2, 8 (apocalyptic), 31 *(New Theatre)*, Sept. 1, 3 (textile), 5 (Mayor), 7 (Evans) (revolution), Oct. 3 (Loomis), 9 (ILD), 14, Nov. 16 (Louis), 16 *(New Theatre)*, Oct. 16, 19, 25, 27, Nov. 2, 5 *(Red Hydra)*, 20 (Balanchine), 23 (Reisman), 24–25 *(New Masses)*, 28 (Rose), Nov. 5 (Ocko), 2, 8 (Shahn), 16 (Mina), 22 (Procession), 1934, LK/DD. Hurwitz, who did cartoons for the *Daily Worker*, would soon turn to films, forming the left-wing "Frontier Films" in the late thirties and himself directing the famous documentary *Native Land* (with voice-over narration by Paul Robeson); the film reenacted scenes of civil liberties violations—and the FBI promptly labeled it "obviously a Communist project" (Duberman, *Robeson*, 261). For more on Philip Reisman (and also Ben Shahn), see Bram Dijkstra, *American Expressionism: Art and Social Change 1920–1950* (Harry N. Abrams, 2003). LK, *Portrait of Mr. B* (Viking, 1984), 18 (relief; vests).
   For early planning on the Avery performances: LK Diary, Sept. 28, 30, Oct. 2 (useless), 4, 1934, LK/DD. Draper to Strachey, Aug. 6, 1932, MD/BL.
   For Wirt Taylor: LK Diary, Oct. 9, 12, 15, 18, 19, 26 (happy), 31 *(Southern Worker)*, Nov. 2, 6, 10, 19, 29, Dec. 10, 12, 16, LK/DD; also, John Williams, "Struggle of the Thirties in the South," in Bernard Sternsher, ed., *The Negro in Depression and War* (Quadrangle, 1969), and Robin D. G. Kelley, *Hammer and Hoe: Alabama Communists During the Great Depression* (University of North Carolina Press, 1990). Lincoln wrote two poems about Wirt Taylor, "The Linesman," and "The Burner," but included neither in *The Poems of Lincoln Kirstein* (Eakins Press, 1987).

CHAPTER FOURTEEN: HARTFORD (1935)

1. LK Diary, Oct. 21 (NYC series), 23 (Balanchine; Watkins), 24 25, 29, Nov. 1, 3 (Balanchine), 23 (sadism), 24 (tickets), 26 (Eddie), Dec. 1 (sadism), 3 (tyrannical), 1934, Jan. 5 (sadism), 11 (Gisella), 16, 17 (Dollar), 18 (Laskey), 19 (sadism; Vilzak), 23 (morale/Vilzak), 1935, LK/DD. A number of people—especially Lucia Davidova, Francisco Moncion, Leon Barzini, William Weslow, and Janet Reed—comment on Balanchine's "coldness" and his "streak of cruelty" in Mason, ed., *I Remember Balanchine*.
   In his diary entry for Jan. 16, Lincoln describes Eddie Warburg as "in a panic" when Dollar twisted his ankle; Eddie "at once took him to his apartment. Had the best doctor, etc. On account of his analysis he couldn't make a pass at him. But they had a nice talk. Bill denied he was queer." But the very next day Dollar told Lincoln that "he wanted to find a rich man to keep him" (LK Diary, Jan. 17, 1935).

2. Hartford: LK Diary, Oct. 9, 12, Nov. 5, 9 *(Transcendence)*, 16 (tickets), 27 (Hawkins), Dec. 2 (dress parade/Hawkins), 4 (bus), 5 (crew), 6–8, 1934, LK/DD; LK to Winslow Ames, Nov. 5, 1934, Winslow Ames Papers, Archives of American Art (MoMA) (henceforth

WA/AAA [MoMA]); Warburg to Draper, Dec. 15, 1934, MD/BL; LK to Louis, Dec. 3, 1934, LK to Goetz, Dec. 12, 1934, BSA; LK to Soby, Dec. 11, 1934, Durlacher Papers, Getty (henceforth DPG), Box 2, folder 19 (in thanking Soby for the party, Lincoln—a notoriously bad speller—wrote to "Sobey").

When Lincoln spoke of being "broke," he was referring, of course, to immediately available cash, which mostly derived from an allowance ($4,085 for the year 1934, and gifts from his mother to pay for assorted expenses [$8,390 in 1934]). Beyond that Lincoln was steadily (thanks to his parents) accumulating assets, though Louis still refused to allow him direct access to them. At the end of 1935, Lincoln had nearly $24,000 in some half dozen savings accounts, as well as various investments in stocks and bonds; the latter had earlier been purchased at a cost of some $23,000, but due to the Depression had fallen by the end of 1935 to a worth of some $13,000. (These figures derive from various accounting statements in BSA, as well as from Reinfeld [accountant] to Beverley, Mar. 1, 1935, BSA.)

Balanchine had the week before made changes in Franklin Watkins's costume designs, which had filled Lincoln "with fear," apparently because he thought Watkins's sets—which he'd initially had to talk the painter into doing—would likewise be altered; but in fact they were greeted with admiration and enthusiasm by everyone (LK Diary, Nov. 26, 1934, LK/DD). Although the notices were generally good, the dandyish man-about-town, Lucius Beebe, whom Lincoln had met earlier (and dismissed as "insolent, snobbish and energetic"), wrote a piece in the *New York Herald Tribune* (Dec. 9, 1934) that was full of arch comments about the audience and the "opulent lunacy" of the occasion, without ever describing or analyzing the ballets themselves. Beebe's article made Lincoln "furious."

3. Post-Hartford: LK Diary, Oct. 26, Nov. 16, 17 (Tchelitchev), 29, Dec. 10–12, 14, 16, 18–21, 25, 1934, Jan. 2, 3, 5, 7–9, 14, 16, Feb. 2, 4, 1935, LK/DD; Louis to Frankfurter, Jan. 15, 1934, Louis to Henry [his brother], Jan. 21, 1935, LEK/BLH. For an example of Cummings's anger over *Tom*, see his exchange of letters with Ezra Pound: Barry Ahearn, *Pound/Cummings: The Correspondence of Ezra Pound and E. E. Cummings* (University of Michigan Press, 1996), 50, 92–93. The composer David Diamond did write a score for Cummings's *Tom*, but it was never staged (Sawyer-Laucanno, *Cummings*, 407–8).

Balanchine had once asked Lincoln how he knew "the fascists were any worse than the Communists." When Lincoln decided he'd try to put over the idea of a ballet about a strike, left-wing friends advised him to work through Dimitriev and Tchelitchev and "*around* Balanchine" (LK Diary, Oct. 20, Nov. 6, 1934). Felix Warburg deprecated Eddie's involvement in the ballet; after visiting the school he characterized it as "more a whore house" than anything else (LK Diary, Oct. 13, 1934).

4. Lincoln had been helping to support and promote Lachaise for some time, working hard to get him commissions and, when the sculptor was down and out, giving him money: LK to Winslow Ames, Apr. 4, 16, June 12, July 31, 1934, WA/AAA; LK to Agnes Mongan, Apr. 1, 1934, AM/Fogg; LK to Chick Austin, May 2, 21, 1934, CA/WAH. In regard to the MoMA retrospective, Lachaise was his usual difficult self, threatening to stop the show unless Barr followed his instructions about which pieces to include; throughout the process, Lincoln served as intermediary. When the show was finally mounted, Lincoln thought it seemed "somehow monotonous, too large in one way and too small in another for a life's work." Though seventeen thousand people saw the show, Lachaise failed to sell a single piece, and to survive, was soon back to borrowing small sums from Lincoln: LK Diary, Dec. 20, 1934, Jan. 14 (stop show), 24, 26, Feb. 2 (mounted), 5, 14, 26 (sales), 1935, LK/DD.

Lincoln was modest about his poetry, usually preferring to call it "verse"; in preparing *Low Ceiling* for publication, he wrote, "It's not as if they are so damned good they can wait indefinitely to be printed." Among his more significant articles from 1934–35 was a review (*Direction* [Apr.–June 1935]) of his friend Stephen Spender's long poem *Vienna*. The English reviews, in contrast to the splendid earlier critical reception of Spender's *Poems 1933*, had been all but uniformly negative (see John Sutherland, *Stephen Spender,* 173–74). But Lincoln, while finding some fault with *Vienna*, in general hailed it as "remarkable." He went so far as to write, "More than Auden or Day Lewis . . . Spender has a power of human, sweet energy, which is neither rhetorical, brilliant, or arrogant as Auden, nor worthy and flaccid as Day Lewis." Lincoln was soon to meet Auden and would become his intimate friend and great admirer. In another article, "The Dance: Some American Dancers" (*The Nation,* Feb. 27, 1935), Lincoln attacked (some not for the first time) many of the pioneering figures in "modern dance," including Mary Wigman, Martha Graham, Charles Weidman, Doris Humphrey; and Helen Tamiris. The latter struck back angrily (*The Nation,* Mar. 20, 1935), characterizing Lincoln's article as "petty, abusive, envious, sneering, supercilious. . . . There is no need for Mr. Kirstein to substitute insulting condescension for his mislaid critical faculty."

A mutual acquaintance had reported to Lincoln that Muriel herself had "gotten off very much on the wrong foot" at an American Embassy lunch in Moscow by "usurping conversation," and that Bill Bullitt, the American ambassador, was very "griped" about it (LK Diary, Mar. 8, 13 [Muriel], 26 [sickle], 1935, LK/DD).

Lectures: LK Diary, Jan. 4, 16, Feb. 18, 21, 23 (Barnum), Mar. 16 (Mayor), 8, 15, 22, 29–31, Feb. 4, 26, 1935; Jan. 17, Feb. 6, 18 (verse), 1935; lessons with Hawkins: LK Diary, Jan., Feb., 1935, passim; "Joe": Dec. 28, 30, 1934, Jan. 8, 27, Feb. 17, 19, 20, 22, 26–28, Mar. 2, 3, 5–8, 12, 13, 17, 22, June 15, Aug. 4, 1935; Eugene Loring: July 10, Oct. 11, 1934, Jan. 10, 13, 1935; Margot Loines: LK Diary, Sept. 13, 24–25, Nov. 12, Dec. 2, 28, 1934, Jan. 14, 20, Feb. 6, 26, Mar. 9, 23, Apr. 8, 12, 25, 27, May 9, 13, 1935, LK/DD. The "gas station attendant" was someone named Ray, whom Lincoln occasionally stopped off to see.

Despite their occasional difficulties, four decades later Hawkins would tell Lincoln, "I just want you to know that I do appreciate your vision and your making this wonderful training [with Balanchine] available to me" (Hawkins to LK, July 31, 1974, BSA).

5. Bryn Mawr: LK Diary, Feb. 7, 8, 10, 12 (Vosseler), Feb. 23, 28 (Geva); Feb. 3, 13, 18, 20 (Soudeikine); Jan. 28–31, Feb. 1, 20 (Balanchine's illness); Feb. 14 (Tchelitchev); Feb. 20 (courage); Dec. 30, 1934, Jan. 18, 28, 30, Feb. 18, 24 (joy), 26 (Geyelin), 1935 (Haakon); Feb. 13, 14, 23, 28, 1935, LK/DD. Among other sources of Lincoln's dislike of Geva was his conviction that she'd been responsible for Balanchine removing Heidi Vosseler from her role in *Serenade* (after she'd rehearsed it for a year), so that Geva could dance it instead (LK Diary, Feb. 12, 13, 1935). *Dreams:* LK Diary, Feb. 17 (Antheil); *Errante:* LK Diary, Nov. 20, 22 (flung), 1933, Dec. 14 (James), 1934, Jan. 27, Feb. 13, 14 (Pavlik), 1935, LK/DD. For Margot's subsequent life: Internet Broadway Database (www.ibdb.com); *New York Times,* June 18, 1937, Aug. 12, 1991.

Though Lincoln would become one of the great champions of Tchelitchev's art, when he saw his show at Julien Levy's gallery late in 1934, he did buy one "lovely drawing" as a gift for Balanchine but thought "the rest of the paintings curious and corrupt, and I don't care a lot for them" (LK Diary, Dec. 12, 1934, LK/DD). Lincoln soon changed his mind and throughout his lifetime wrote extensively and enthusiastically about Pavlik's art, culminating in his magisterial *Tchelitchev* (Twelvetrees Press, 1994). For a listing of LK's articles on Tchelitchev, see *Lincoln Kirstein: The Published Writings, 1922–1977: A First Bibliography* (Yale University Library, 1978), compiled by Harvey Simmonds, Louis H. Silverstein, and Nancy Lassalle. The volume has now been updated and expanded: *Lincoln Kirstein: A Bibliography of Published Writings,* Peter Kayafus, ed. (Eakins Press Foundation, 2007). In addition, the short essays LK regularly wrote for NYCB handbills have now been collected: *Lincoln Kirstein: The Program Notes* (working title as of 2006), Randall Bourscheidt, ed. (Eakins Press Foundation, 2007). In my own view LK's three most important articles on Tchelitchev are his twenty-two-page introduction to *Pavel Tchelitchew Drawings* (H. Bittner, 1947; reprint, Hacker Art Books, 1971); "The Interior Landscapes of Pavel Tchelitchew," *Magazine of Art* (Feb. 1948); and "Pavel Tchelitchew," in *Pavel Tchelitchew: An Exhibition in the Gallery of Modern Art* (Gallery, 1964). LK himself thought highly of James Thrall Soby's catalog for MoMA's 1942 Tchelitchev retrospective and Parker Tyler's biography, *The Divine Comedy of Pavel Tchelitchew* (Weidenfeld & Nicolson, 1967). For Tchelitchev's homoerotic art, see David Leddick, *The Homoerotic Art of Pavel Tchelitchev* (Elysium Press, 1999).

6. LK Diary, Feb. 19 (Dimitriev), 20 (Volodin/Dollar/courage), 21, 23 (Tchelitchev/nervous/bulwark), family: Feb. 22, 24 (Mina), 27 (George), 28 (Rose), 25 (cocktail rehearsal), 26 (Balanchine), 27 (orchestra), 28 (Martin), 28, Mar. 2 (Fokine), Mar. 1 (opening), 1935, LK/DD. Toward the end of the run at the Adelphi Theatre, Balanchine discovered most of the Godard music, "superbly orchestrated by Godard himself," at Schirmer's; in Lincoln's view, Brand "obviously never even looked" (LK Diary, Mar. 12, 1935, LK/DD).

John Martin, Graham, and de Mille: Martin to LK, Nov. 21, 1933, BSA; LK Diary, Oct. 16, 21, Nov. 16 (antagonist), Dec. 16, 30 (de Mille), 1934, Jan. 15 (de Mille), 18, 30 (Graham), Feb. 3 (de Mille), 6 (unaccountable), 10 (certain talent), 11 (trust), 20 (de Mille), Mar. 6, 13, 14, 1935, LK/DD; LEK to LK, Dec. 17, 1934, LEK/BLH; *New York Times*, Dec. 16, 1934 (open letter), Aug. 18, 25, Dec. 15, 1935; LK, "The Dance," *The Nation*, Feb. 27, 1935 (Graham). Lincoln's father also thought John Martin's open letter "favorable . . . by far the best article I have seen on the subject" and urged his son to send Martin "a nice note" (LEK to LK, Dec. 17, 1934, LEK/BLH). Also: Edward Burns, ed., *The Letters of Gertrude Stein and Carl van Vechten, 1913–1946* (henceforth Burns, *Letters*), Columbia University Press, 1986, 402–3 (delightful); LK, *Thirty*, 50–1 *(Reminiscence)*; Agnes de Mille, *Dance to the Piper* (Little Brown, 1951), 168 (blistering); Martha Graham, *Blood Memory* (Doubleday, 1991); de Mille, *Martha*; Russell Freedman, *Martha Graham: A Dancer's Life* (Clarion, 1998), 51 (original). Despite his resentments and disagreements with John Martin, Lincoln twice wrote and spoke movingly about his gifts as a critic and his invaluable services to modern dance ("In Appreciation: John Martin," "Sept. 1962," no source given, LK/DD, folder 123-22; and the transcript of LK speech at the John Martin reception at the Dance Collection, NYPL, June 6, 1974, LK/ DD).

Post–opening night: LK Diary, Mar. 3, 5 (*Dreams*/Watkins/Lowell/Haakon), 5 (Sokolow/Horst/Graham), 6, 9 (Martin), 6 (Tchelitchev/de Mille), 3, 17 (Howard), 4, 8 (Hurwitz, Ocko), 5 (Lindbergh), 7 (Balanchine), 10 (Geva/Balanchine on Graham/Stravinsky/Bankhead, etc.), 5, 6, 11 (Balanchine), 12 (Hawkins), 13 (Lyon), 14 (de Mille), 17 (final performance), 1935, LK/DD. At lunch with Anne Lindbergh a few days later (LK Diary, Mar. 16, 1935, LK/DD), Lincoln found her "quite sweet." He sensed that he seemed "to faze her by my intensity on the ballet," which he tried to repress for the occasion, especially since she made it clear that "she couldn't allow herself an interest in the ballet as she hasn't much energy and has carefully apportioned her life, some to making Charles happy, some to being a good mother, some to writing a little."

CHAPTER FIFTEEN: THE METROPOLITAN OPERA (1935)

1. LK Diary, Mar. 10 (teaching/codirector), Mar. 13, 14 (Dimitriev & co.), 14, 16 (Merovich), Mar. 20, 21, 25, Apr. 9, 10, 25 (contracts), Mar. 20 (amicable/vacation), 21, 22 (Vanderbilt/*Jardin*/Shahn), Mar. 22, Apr. 10 (Ford), Mar. 22 (Massine), 24 (force), 26 (Deutsch/potbelly), April 12 (vacation), 13 (restudying/less impatient), 17 (*Dance*), 18, 21 (*Low Ceiling*), 28 (Dimitriev), May 6 (Company), 9, 11 (vaguely), 1935, LK/DD; LK to Winslow Ames, June 13, 1935 (*Dance*), WA/AAA. For Muriel Stuart: LK Diary, March 25, 27 (appreciated), 29; Tobi Tobias interview with Stuart, NYPL; after having taught a few classes, Stuart told Lincoln that the dancers seemed to her "like sticks—dry and juiceless" (LK Diary, April 9, Nov. 21, 1935). *Low Ceiling: Herald Tribune*, May 26, 1935. Spender reassured Lincoln that he found the poems quite independent of any influence of his, and admired them a good deal. Muriel Draper, too, liked Lincoln's poems better than he thought she would (LK Diary, May 31, 1935). Anne Lindbergh, on the other hand, "tried to explain that she'd read my poems and didn't understand them all" (LK Diary, June 16, 22 [Spender], 1935, LK/DD).

In preparing his book *Dance*, Lincoln found Paul Magriel "of enormous aid to me." Magriel was at work as an archivist in the Library of Congress, preparing "a very remarkable bibliography of all books relating to dancing," and Lincoln leaned heavily on him for reference materials; he also seems to have helped Magriel, who was living in poverty, with a bit of money (LK to Louis, July 5, 1935, BSA; LK Diary, Apr. 18, 1935, LK/DD).

For Tchelitchev: For a listing of LK's many writings on Tchelitchev, see Simmonds et al., *A First Bibliography*; in addition there's a thirteen-page typescript (1949), "Pavel Tchelitchev," signed by LK in the Tchelitchev Papers, Beinecke Library, Yale University (PT/BL) that contains some valuable commentary; LK Diary, Mar. 22, 24, Apr. 26–28 (Dimitriev), May 2 (Muriel/Dimitriev/capacities/Communists), 5 (position); *Medea*: Mar. 24, 31, Apr. 6, 9, 10, 27, May 3, 10, 17, 1935, LK/DD; LK to Jay Leyda, Sept. 21, 1935, Jay Leyda Papers, Tamiment (henceforth JL/TL); what is apparently LK's four-page scenario for *Medea* is in PT/BL.

The hard-to-please Virgil Thomson had (in 1933) originally introduced Lincoln to Tche-litchev, whom Thomson later characterized in an interview as "a man of considerable brains and sensitivity" (John Gruen interview with Thomson, Dance Collection, NYPL, *(S) MGZMT 5-344). For Charles Henri Ford, see especially Steven Watson's fine introduction to the reissue of *The Young and Evil* (Gay Presses of New York, 1989), and James Dowell, "Charles Henri Ford Was There," *Gay & Lesbian Review* (Nov.–Dec. 2001), as well as the documentary film Dowell made with John Kolomvakis about Ford's life, *Sleep in a Nest of Flames*.

2. LK Diary, Apr. 5 (Balanchine/Littlefield), 6 *(Medea)*, 8 (injection/Geva), 15, 16 (Fokine), 1935, LK/DD. Bronia Nijinska: LK Diary, Mar. 13, Apr. 12, 17 (Hart), 25 (prospectus), May 1, 2, 1935, LK/DD; see also Drue Fergison, "Bringing *Les Noces* to the Stage," Lynn Garafola and Nancy Van Norman Baer, eds., *The Ballets Russes and Its World* (Yale University Press, 1999). Nijinska's *Early Memoirs*, translated and edited by Irina Nijinska and Jean Rawlinson (Holt, Rinehart & Winston) wasn't published until 1981. In 1935 Elizabeth Arden also expressed an interest in having Lincoln write her biography (LK Diary, Aug. 15, 1935, LK/DD).

3. LK, *Dance: A Short History of Classic Theatrical Dancing* (G. P. Putnam's Sons, 1935), 321, 357–58 (Balanchine), 323 (Massine), 350, 354–55 (Humphry, Weidman, Graham, and others), 352 (St. Denis/Shawn). Reprinted and revised in 1942, under the title *The Book of the Dance*, it was reissued again by Dance Horizons in 1987, with "An Appreciation" by Nancy Reynolds. See also Reynolds's entry on Lincoln in the *International Encyclopedia of Dance* (Oxford University Press, 1998), in which she characterizes *Dance* as "a densely written tour de force . . . much of the material, such as dance in the United States during the nineteenth century, had scarcely been previously researched" (vol. 4, 27).

    LK to Winslow Ames, Nov. 27, 1935 ("bitterly"), WA/AAA; LK Diary, Oct. 7 (awk-wardly), Nov. 10 (judgments). He worried particularly that he "didn't know nearly enough about music" (May 16). Among the many diary references that attest to Lincoln's hard work on *Dance*, see Mar. 11, Apr. 17, May 21, July 23, Aug. 4, 7, 22, Sept. 11, 17 (the day he fin-ished), 20, 24, Oct. 2, 3, 7, 1935, LK/DD. Lincoln found that he worked particularly well on the book when at Mina's home, Ashfield (Aug. 6, 12). Once again Hyatt Mayor was a great help to him as he worked on the book (June 4, Sept. 4). Lincoln had wanted 150 illustrations, but the publisher cut the number to below 100 (July 10); on the other hand the publisher had asked for a "short" book of some 35,000 words and Lincoln delivered 135,000 words—and threatened to take it to another publisher if they asked for broad cuts (Diary, Sept. 27).

4. Dimitriev to LEK, July 3, 1935, BSA; LK to Blackmur, Sept. 28, 1935, RB/PU; LK Diary, May 12, 23, 1935, LK/DD. Production Company/School: LK Diary, June 5, 11, 13, 14, 19, 24, 26, 28, 29, Aug. 15, Sept. 4, 1935, LK/DD.

    "Tour": Paul Cummings interview with Eddie Warburg, May 13, 1971 (lawsuits, etc.), SAAA; LK to Louis, Nov. 15, 1935, LEK/BLH; LK Diary, Sept. 28, 30 (White Plains), Oct. 3 (Balanchine), 4, 9, 16 (Vilzak), 7 (Merovich), 15, 17 (New Haven), 18, 21–23 (Scran-ton), Nov. 4, 6 (Merovich), 1935, LK/DD. In his diary entry of Oct. 16 Lincoln wrote, as examples of Schollar's nastiness, that when Vilzak said he thought Caccialanza was "a good dancer," Schollar said, "Soldat"; and when he praised Leda Anchutina, she spat out, "Dwarf!"

    Sol Hurok was among those who gloated over the failed tour; that made Lincoln espe-cially angry because Hurok, who'd represented de Basil's Ballets Russes de Monte Carlo since 1933, had recently persuaded Margaret Marshall, *The Nation*'s literary editor, not to allow Lincoln to review the Ballets Russes' performances. In reaction Lincoln announced he would no longer write for *The Nation* at all. But in her reply (LK Diary, Oct. 1, 4, 1935) Mar-garet Marshall persuasively pointed out that "logic is on the side of having the ballet reviewed by someone whom Mr. Hurok nor any one else can charge with having, so to speak, a vested interest" (the exchange is in Box 15, LEK/BLH).

5. The Met: LK, *Thirty*, 52–57; LK Diary, Dec. 30, 1934 (sweet), Feb. 5 (Page), Apr. 11, May 20, 22 (Fisher), 24 (Johnson meeting), 28, 31 (Dimitriev), June 3 (Eddie), July 24 (de Mille), Aug. 6, 11 (papers), 15, 19, 22 (auditions), 24, Sept. 4, 14, 25, (Fisher), Oct. 10, 13, 24, 25, 26, 29 (Schelling), 29 (Johnson), 1935, LK/DD; *Time*, Aug. 19, 1935; *The New York Times*, Aug. 16 (Martin), 26 (LK), 1935; LK to Louis, Nov. 15, 1935, LEK/BLH. Agnes de Mille

had let Lincoln know that she wanted to do the choreography for the Met's production of Smetana's *The Bartered Bride*, and he told her he'd "see what I can do" (LK Diary, Nov. 7, 1935). Mina's pregnancy and abortion: LK Diary, May 23 (George), 27 (Mt. Morris), 30, June 1; Wirt Taylor: LK Diary, June 25/Sept. 11/Oct. 17; Hyatt Mayor: Nov. 16; Lachaise: Oct. 12—all 1935, all LK/DD. Taper's *Balanchine* (164–75) contains an especially fine and reliable discussion of the American Ballet's experience at the Met.

Another dramatic upheaval during these same months came in July 1935, when Mina's old friend Aline Bernstein, the set designer (and Tom Wolfe's former lover), again attempted suicide. Mina and Lincoln rushed down from Ashfield to the White Plains hospital, where they found that Aline's despairing family members had given up hope and were discussing funeral arrangements. Mina, too, thought Aline would succumb, and suddenly recalled a promise she'd made to her years before that in case of her death Mina would immediately contact Tom Wolfe's editor, Maxwell Perkins, and retrieve Aline's letters so they could never be published. But to everyone's surprise Aline somehow pulled through (LK Diary, July 23, 1935, LK/DD; Mina Curtiss, ms. "The Past and I," MCP/SS). In that unpublished memoir Mina identified herself as the model for the character "Lily Mandell" in Wolfe's *Of Time and the River*; Lily was described in the novel as "a tall and sensual-looking Jewess [Wolfe was a pronounced anti-Semite] . . . with smoldering and arrogant glances."

Muriel Draper: LK Diary, Aug. 4, 5, Sept. 29, Dec. 8 (press); Lyman Paine: Oct. 13; Sept. 30 (syphilis/Hamburg), Oct. 2, 3 (*New Theatre*), 4 (Browder), 8, Nov. 20 (long talk), 16 (*Southern Worker*), 1935, LK/DD; T. E. Lawrence: LK Diary, May 14 (standard), June 17, 1935.

Lachaise: May 29, June 11, Oct. 16 (shattered), 17, 19 (son), Nov. 1, 18, 1935, LK/DD; LK to Winslow Ames (Lyman Allen Museum), Oct. 23, 1935, Dec. 21, 28 (dispossess), Ames to LK, Oct 24, 1935, WA/AAA (MoMA). Nelson Rockefeller phoned Lincoln to ask if there was anything more he could do for Lachaise's widow; Lincoln asked him to provide the funds to rescue a large group of figures molded in clay that he'd just discovered were in danger of falling to pieces if not fixed in plaster or cast in bronze; Nelson agreed to undertake the job. Lincoln also consulted with Alfred Barr about turning Lachaise's sketches for a Philadelphia assignment into a finished piece (LK Diary, Oct. 22, 1935, LK/DD).

6. Elaine Kendall interview with Annabelle Lyon, Dance Division, NYPL, (S)* MGZMT 3-1861 (transcript); Carolyn Watts interview with Phyllis W. Manchester, 1975, Dance Division, NYPL, (S) *MGZMT 5-503 (transcript).

Vladimiroff: LK Diary, May 12, July 29, Aug. 29, Oct. 14 (bastard), 16 (love), 18 (Cuba), 21 (Stuart), Nov. 15 (compromise), Dec. 3 (Balanchine), 6 (de Basil), 1935, LK/DD. *Tom:* LK Diary, Sept. 19, Oct. 1, 7, 9, 11 (Nabokov), 14, 16, 26, Nov. 4, 6, 18 (Muriel), 28, Dec. 1, 24, 1935, LK/DD. Josephine Baker: LK Diary, Oct. 29, 1935, LK/DD.

7. LK Diary, Nov. 17 (frail), 21 (*Carmen*), 26 (apprehension), 28/29 (Tchelitchev/Ford), 30 (costumes/trustees), Dec. 1–4 (Tchelitchev), 4–6 (*Lakmé*), 16 (opening night), Jan. 16, 1936 (Doc/*Follies*), Dec. 19–20 (illness, Mools, Mead, and so on), 22 (*Aida*; backstage), 25, 31, Jan. 3 (LK more active), 7, 8 (Pelletier), 9 (Dimitriev), 12 (Vilzak), 16, 17 (Eddie/Johnson/Balanchine), 18 (Erskine), 27 (criticism), 1935, LK/DD. *Orpheus:* LK Diary, Jan. 21, 24–25 (letter), Feb. 7 (youthful), 20, 25, Mar. 4, 6, 9, 10, 12, 13, 1936, LK/DD.

CHAPTER SIXTEEN: BALLET CARAVAN (1936)

1. LK to Johnson, Jan. 14, 23, 1936, EJ/MOA; LK Diary, Mar. 2 (meeting), 6 (Johnson), 9/10 (own season), 1936, LK/DD; LK to Louis, Mar. 13, 15 (flight), 16–21 (LA), 1936, LEK/ BLH; de Mille, *Dance to the Piper,* 179 (sick). While in Hollywood, Lincoln tried to interest several producers in doing a film with a ballet theme but got nowhere. He himself wrote a twenty-seven-page scenario for such a film, which, after LK's return to New York, Monroe Wheeler sent on to Richard Halliday at Paramount. He initially expressed some interest ("if we ever get the right framework") but then "indefinitely postponed" the picture (Halliday to Wheeler, April 30, 1936, Halliday to LK, Sept. 23, 1936, plus LK's scenario, entitled "IDEA FOR A STORY FOR A FILM WHICH WOULD USE THE AMERICAN BAL-LET," BSA).

Coudy: LK Diary, Nov. 26, Dec. 4, 19 (courting), 23 (warm), 29, 1935, Jan. 1, 11, 13 (personal), 17, 19, 24 (kids), Feb. 7 (power), 10, 28, Mar. 3, 29, Apr. 6, 8, 23 (Loring), 28, 30, May 8 (Loring), 24 (manly), 26, 28, June 6, 16, 1936, LK/DD. In one of my phone interviews with Ruthanna Boris (Nov. 22, 2003), she told me that she'd had "a terrible crush" on Coudy and described him as "tall, dark and good-looking"; he was "a good, but not a great dancer." Boris further reported that Coudy told her that one day when he was attending services at Saint Patrick's Cathedral in New York, a "young priest named Spellman had approached him and they had sex behind a pillar."

Christensen: LK Diary, Jan. 25, Feb. 7, 18 (angel), 20, 25, Mar. 6 (flash), 29, Apr. 14 (Ashfield), 28 (Balanchine), May 5 (tenderness), 6 (firm), 24, 26, 28, 1936, LK/DD. Coudy tried to persuade Lincoln that Harold Christensen had a "much better character" than his brother, Lew; and now and then Lincoln himself felt Lew was not quite the paragon he thought him—e.g.: "Lew is really too much of a kid. I guess it's the cold meat and potatoes of the Nordic seas" (LK Diary, May 24, 26, 1936, LK/DD).

Orpheus: Garnett to Mina, June 28, 1936, BC/NYPL; LK, *Thirty,* 54–57; LK Diary, May 8 (Tchelitchev), 21–24 (union), 24 (opening), 25 *(The Bat),* 1936, LK/DD; LK to Ames, May 25, 1936, WA/AAA (MoMA); *New York Times,* May 23, 1936; *Time,* June 1, 1936. William Dollar had lately, according to Lincoln, "been behaving vilely: dances like a pig, horrid temper and nasty atmosphere he gives off. No one seems to know why. Mools suggested he dopes. I doubt it. . . . Balanchine counts on him less and less" (LK Diary, May 25, 1936). Though Lincoln was temporarily down on Hyatt Mayor, and had always had mixed feelings about Glenway Wescott (much preferring the company of his lover Monroe Wheeler), both men strongly defended *Orpheus,* and Wescott wrote a letter to Edward Johnson singing the ballet's praises (LK Diary, May 25, 1936).

2. Ballet Caravan: LK to Mongan, June 16, 1936, AM/Fogg; LK to Louis, June 17 and n.d. [late June 1936], BSA; LK to Louis, July 9, 1936, LEK/BLH; LK Diary, May 27, May 28, June 17, Sept. 25 (Balanchine & Caravan), June 4 (letters/resentment), 24, July 2 (Balanchine & Met), [misdated "June 2"] May 29, June 4, 11, 16 (Frances H.), 9 (Carter/morale/Eddie/Erick H./Loring), 11, 16, 19, 24 (Erick), 25 (Stuart/Balanchine), July 2, 4 (Erick), 9 (Carter/Dollar), 15 (Carter/*Pocahontas*), 24, 28 (Balanchine spoiled), Aug. 1, 7, 13 (Easthampton), 29 (Keene/separate), Sept. 25 (Ogunquit), 1936, LK/DD; John Martin, "The Dance: A New Troupe," *New York Times,* June 28, 1936. The Caravan dancers included Ruthanna Boris, Gisella Caccialanza, Annabelle Lyon, and Charles Laskey (LK to Ames, June 10, 1936, WA/AAA).

Lincoln's notion that Massine and Balanchine might combine forces wasn't some bizarre fantasy of his own creation; in the fall of 1936, Massine did suggest to Balanchine that the two "go into a big international company combining our best dancers." When Balanchine told Lincoln, he said that in his view it wasn't "very interesting to go on with the same old line of Fokine and Massine." Within the same week Boris Kochno tried to persuade Balanchine "to come back to Basil as he is afraid Massine will leave, and they will have no choreographer but Lichine." Two months later, Balanchine had yet another offer: René Blum asked him to stage "whatever he wants" for the upcoming Paris Exposition (LK Diary, Massine: Nov. 19 (1936)/Jan. 24 (1937), Nov. 24 (Kochno), 1936, Jan. 19 (Blum), 1937, LK/DD.

In the programs of the American Ballet performances at the Met, Coudy, along with continuing to dance, is listed several times as stage manager (Douglas Coudy Scrapbook, Dance Division Archives, NYPL: *MGZRS 00-1604); that experience might have contributed to LK appointing him company manager for the Caravan. *Hartford Courant,* Dec. 2, 1936. Coudy and Rabanna Hasburgh danced the leads in *Soldier and Gypsy;* it was the only ballet Coudy danced that first summer. When *Soldier* was performed in New York City that fall, the *New York Sun* (Nov. 2, 1936) called it "the most ambitious . . . and also the most colorful" of the ballets offered but felt it was "clever rather than distinctive." The following year, 1937, Coudy danced extensively: in Dollar's *Promenade,* Christensen's *Encounter* and *Filling Station,* Erick Hawkins's *Show Piece,* and the Loring-Bowles ballet, *Yankee Clipper.* In 1939 Coudy joined the Catherine Littlefield Ballet as a soloist, danced at the Met from 1940 to

1942, then worked as a stage manager (for American Concert Ballet) and, in 1944, dance director for shows starring Jimmy Durante and (at the Copacabana) Sophie Tucker.

3. The first Caravan tour: Marilyn Hunt interview with Eugene Loring, Mar. 11, 1976 (unfriendly), (*[S] MGZMT 5-704); Rose Anne Thom interview with Bessie Schonberg (*[S] MGZMT 5-1018); Marilyn Hunt interview with Eugene Loring, Mar. 11, 1976 (*[S] MGZMT 5-704)—all in Dance Division Archives (DD), NYPL; de Mille, *Martha*, 228 (backstage); LK Diary, July 24 (Graham/Harold), 28, Aug. 1 (Balanchine), 7, 13, Aug. 1/29 (Coudy), Sept. 25, 1936, LK/DD; LK to Louis, July 9 (Langner), 23, 1936, LEK/BLH; Louis to LK, July 23, 1936, LK/DD; Louis to Mina, July 23, 1936, MCP/SS; LK Diary, Apr. 30 (Graham), 1935, LK/DD. Despite feeling well treated at Bennington, Lincoln continued to write articles denigrating "modern dance" (e.g., "Ballet and the Modern Dance Today," *Dance* [Oct. 1936]: "The modern dance is primarily a cerebral creation," and so on). From a later period there are several recollections by company members of Lincoln "treating us with such respect" and "always being very nice to us": Hiromi Sakamoto 1998 interview with Roberta Meier (transcript: MGZMT 3-2152) and Goldschmidt's 1999 interview with Lynn Stetson (transcript: MGZMT 3-2168), DD/NYPL.

4. John Martin, the *New York Times*, Sept. 13, 1936; LK to Beverley, Oct. 13, 1936 (Louis), BSA; LK to Louis, Nov. 4 (YMHA), 1936, LEK/BLH; LK Diary, Oct. 2 (school), June 19, 24, 25, 29 (Vladimirov), Oct. 8 (Vilzak), Aug. 1, 29, Sept. 25, Oct. 17, Nov. 13 (Stravinsky), Sept. 25 *(Clipper)*, Nov. 3, 10, 13 (Audubon), Oct. 17, Nov. 15 (Muriel), 1936, LK/DD. Caravan: LK Diary, Oct. 24 (Smith), 29 (de Mille), Nov. 3 (nasty), 10, 18 (Danbury), 24, Dec. 5 (Hartford), 1936, Jan. 19 (Vilzak), 1937. Martha Graham: LK Diary, Oct. 2, 8, Dec. 22 (personally), 1936; Jan. 26 (Dollar), Feb. 14 (afire), Mar. 19 (George), 1937, LK/DD; LK, "Ballet: Record and Augury," *Theatre Arts* (Sept. 1940), 654; LK to Beverley, Sept. 11, 1936, Levine to Beverley, Nov. 26, 1936, BSA. WPA: LK Diary, Nov. 12 (Barnes), 13, 17, 27, Dec. 5, 10, 18, 22, 29, 31 (Tamiris), 1936, Jan. 5, 7, 19 (dreadful), 1937, LK/DD; LK to Louis, Dec. 22, 1936, LEK/BLH.

5. LK Diary, Nov. 24 (boxing), Dec. 5, 18 (Mina), 1936, Jan. 21 (Barnum), Feb. 1 (Beaton), 1937; phone interview with Frances Whitney, George's last companion.

Cadmus: LK Diary, Dec. 10, 29, 1936, Jan. 5 (stroking), 26, Feb. 6 (Pavlik), 10, Mar. 3, 22 (sadistic), Apr. 4, 12, 18/30 (Jere), May 7, 1937, LK/DD.

José Martínez: LK Diary, Mar. 20 (angel), Apr. 4, 16 (Mabry), 25, 28, May 1, 5 (capricious), 1937, LK/DD.

CHAPTER SEVENTEEN: BALLET CARAVAN (1937–1938)

1. Stravinsky Festival: *Stravinsky: Selected Correspondence*, vol. 2, edited and with commentaries by Robert Craft (henceforth Craft, *Stravinsky*, 2); Knopf, 1984, esp. 314–21. Craft points out (316, n. 2) that Stravinsky insisted that *Jeu* was *not* commissioned: " 'I simply sold the performance rights for the period of a year and for America, without exclusivity' "); Nancy Reynolds, *Repertory in Review*, Dial, 1977, *(Musagète)*; LK, "Working with Stravinsky" (prodigality; Sharaff), *Modern Music* (Mar./Apr. 1937); reprinted in Minna Lederman, ed., *Stravinsky in the Theatre* (Pellegrini & Cudahy, 1949), and in Jenkins, ed., *By With*, 159–63; LK, *Blast at Ballet* (Marstin Press, 1938), henceforth LK, *Blast*, 35 (midair), 38–41; LK Diary, Sept. 13, 1934 (cuckoos), Dec. 5 (abortion), 10 (investigation), 1936, Jan. 19 (heavenly), 21, Feb. 3 (Chaney), Jan. 22, Feb. 1, 11 (Stettheimer/Pavlik), Feb. 9/Apr. 19 (Halicka), Feb. 13, 14, 20, Apr. 21 (Sharaff), Mar. 16/23 (Chaney set), 23 *(Jeu)*, 31 (collaboration/bore), Apr. 22 (Hawkins), 26 (Vanderbilt), 27–29 (performances), 1937, LK/DD; for more on Florine Stettheimer and her sisters, see Seven Watson's admirable *Strange Bedfellows: The First American Avant-Garde* (Abbeville, 1991); multiple phone interviews with Ruthanna Boris, 2003–06; Cummings interview with Warburg, May 13, 1971, EW/SAAA (a warning: EW sometimes confuses the receptions of *Orpheus* and the Stravinsky gala); LK to Blackmur, Feb. 23, 1937, RB/PU; *New York Times*, Apr. 28, 1937 (Martin), *Time*, May 10, 1937 (sophisticated).

2. LK to Frances Hawkins, Mar. 22, 25 (enthusiastic), 29 (dance theater), Apr. 1 (Houseman),

12, 13 (Martin), Hawkins to LK, Apr. 7, Louis to Dimitriev, May 3—all 1937, all BSA; Taper, *Balanchine*, 183–90 (Goldwyn); LK, *Thirty*, 70–71 (leadership); LK to Louis, May 6 (accompanied by salary scales and itemized budget), 10, June 10 (permanent), Louis to LK, May 8, Levine to Louis, June 23—all 1937, all BSA; LK Diary, Feb. 22, 26 (Louis), Apr. 9, May 2 *(Chronicle)*, 4 (Marie Jeanne), 6/10 (Laskey), 1937, LK/DD; Feb. 6, 10, 16, 24, Apr. 12 (impetuous/Shawn), Apr. 15, May 5, 12 (collaborative evenings). LK's review of *American Document* is in *The Nation* (Sept. 3, 1938); he additionally gave Graham high praise in the article he wrote in 1937 for Merle Armitrage's *Martha Graham* and in his 1938 pamphlet *Blast at Ballet*, 90–93. A 7-pp. outline (n.d.) for the collaborative evenings, complete with budgets and artists, is in BSA. For a time Lincoln flirted with MoMA as a possible sponsor for the collaborative evenings; both the president, Conger Goodyear, and Nelson Rockefeller were "very much interested," and Tom Mabry tried to lobby for it, but Alfred Barr saw mostly difficulties in the connection. Both Nelson and Wallace Harrison "intimated" a willingness to provide some funding (LK to Louis, June 10, 1937, LEK/BLH; LK to Goodyear, Sept. 16, 1937, AB/AAA [MoMA]).

3. LK Diary, Jan. 7, 24, Feb. 8 (Bowles), May 12 (Wescott), 1937, LK/DD; Paul Bowles, *Without Stopping* (Putnam, 1972), 192, 204–5 (orchestration); Sawyer-Laucanno, *Cummings*, 179–180; *Bombs:* Jan. 24, 26, Feb. 6 (literary), 1937, LK/DD; Katherine Anne Porter to Wescott, Nov. 16, 1938 (Audubon), KAP/UM. Lincoln himself went to see the reigning doyenne of the Stadium concerts, Mrs. Charles "Minnie" Guggenheim, who told him she didn't feel the Caravan had "enough of a name" yet to draw in an audience for an evening-long performance of its own; Lincoln decided she was a "very naive woman." (LK Diary, Apr. 27, 1937, LK/DD).

4. Louis to Mina, July 15, 1937, MCP/SS; Louis to Frankfurter, Apr. 3, 1939 (United Jewish Appeal); LEK/BLH (Boxes 10 and 38 contain a number of documents, speeches, and transcripts that testify to LEK's ongoing energy, commitment, and socially progressive, though not radical views. As an example: [We need] "a recognition of the rights of men to some protection in an insecure society"—Box 10, folder 2). As an example of Louis's urgent involvement in the plight of European Jewry: "We have just finished our Associated Jewish Philanthropies' campaign with the largest amount ever received" (Louis to LK, Nov. 12, 1938, BSA). In Nov. 1938, President Roosevelt invited Louis to the White House to discuss "the Jewish situation—he is terribly concerned about what is happening in Palestine," Louis reported to his son (LEK to LK, Nov. 4, Dec. 24, 1938, LEK/BLH). In 1938 Louis was also given an honorary Doctorate of Commercial Science by Boston University.

1937 Caravan summer tour: Doug Coudy Scrapbook, DD/NYPL; Levine to Kirsteins, July 19 (Smallens), 1937, LK to parents, July 21 (Philadelphia), LK to Louis, Oct. 4 (investment; Europe), Levine to Beverley, Aug. 2 (expenses), 24 (cash receipts; salaries), LK to Beverley, Aug. 9—all 1937, all BSA. LK's articles on the dance for *The Nation* included "The Monte Carlo Season" (Nov. 13, 1937), a high-spirited attack on de Basil's recent revival of Fokine's *Coq d'Or* ("infantile, tiresome and old-fashioned"), in which he publicly and boldly put himself at odds with John Martin, who'd favorably reviewed the revival. Lincoln devoted a second *Nation* article ("The Critic's Lexicon," Feb. 5, 1938), entirely to challenging Martin's dance vocabulary and attitude ("To hate the ballet is his privilege, but . . . he must find some new terms to cover it"); as Lincoln wrote his parents (Feb. 5, 1938, BSA), the article "created a considerable amount of comment, most of it favorable". Also in 1937 Lincoln did pieces for *Modern Music* ("Working with Stravinsky"), *Arts and Decoration* ("Homage to Stravinsky"), *Town and Country* ("To Dance"), and he both wrote for and served as the monthly dance editor of *Dance Observer*—though forced to resign in 1938 as a result of his attack on John Martin (LK, *Blast at Ballet*, 73); when *Blast* was published in 1938, Lincoln extended his critique of Martin still further. Probably Lincoln's most significant article that year was "Crisis in the Dance," *North American Review* (Spring 1937), 81–103, in which he wrote of Diaghilev as "a purveyor of artistic hors d'oeuvres," analyzed Massine's recent "symphonic ballets," revised upward his opinion of Mary Wigman's work, and made some trenchant contrasts between Diaghilev's "classic" ballet and contemporary versions of it, and as well deliberately blurred some of the assumed distinctions between ballet and modern dance ("ballet dancers can make more legible use of 'modern' movement as a stylistic expression than many modernists," and so on). Lincoln also continued to write occasional poetry (LK to Wheelwright, Apr. 1, June 2, 1938, JBW/BU), and began work on a short book, which would be published as *Blast*, in 1938.

5. LK to parents, Oct. 29, 1937, LK to Louis, Dec. 16, 1937, Hawkins to Levine, Nov. 5, 1937—all BSA; Louis to LK, Dec. 6, 17, 1937, Mar. 29 (Federated), 1938, LEK/BLH.

   Dimitriev stock: LK to parents, Oct. 29, 1937, LK to Louis, Mar. 30, Apr. 6, 13, Leonard Wallstein, Jr. (lawyer), to Louis, June 17, 21, Sept. 2, Oct 7 (storm), Louis to LK, Apr. 7, Sept. 7—all 1938, BSA. At Dimitriev's insistence changes were made in the agreement as late as June 1940 (Morris Fish to Louis, June 6, 1940, BSA).

   Some of LK's financial records, mostly in summary form for income tax purposes, are in BSA. Assuming their accuracy (they appear to have been prepared either by an accountant and/or Doris Levine), they provide at least a rough estimate of LK's income and expenses for 1938. His main assets (stocks, bonds, savings accounts, and so on) had a market value of about $47,000. His income for the year came to nearly $11,000 (plus roughly $3,000 from the school); his royalties from *Dance* and *Low Ceiling* came to just over $67. His household and "personal" expenses, excluding books ($863), came to nearly $8,000. His father's accumulated contributions from 1927 to 1938 (*Hound and Horn*, School of American Ballet and Ballet Caravan) came to more than $150,000; these are listed not as gifts to LK but as sums he "owes" his father, though this should be seen as a technical distinction since LK hadn't nearly the personal resources to pay back such a sum. Among LK's "contributions" for the year it's noteworthy that he paid the hospital bills of two "very poor people," one a student at the school, the other a former wardrobe mistress for the Caravan.

6. The Met: LK to Louis, Apr. 13 (newspapers), 1938 (Met), BSA; LK, *Blast*, 30–36. Though the papers tended to assume that Balanchine had resigned, the Met had in fact made the decision not to rehire the company; and though Lincoln publicly supported Balanchine's complaints against the Met, he in fact thought "both are seriously at fault" (LK to Louis, March 28, 1938, LEK/BLH).

   The Caravan: LK to Louis, Oct. 29, Dec. 16 (Sarnoff), 1937 (Nelson), Jan. 31, Feb. 7 (paying), Mar. 18 (absorption/Nelson), 28, 30, Apr. 1 (never go), 13, Sept. 6, 12, 1938, LK to parents, Dec. 21 (Sarnoff), 1937, LK to Beverley, May 27, 1938, Louis to LK, Dec. 17 (Hawkins), 1937, Jan. 11, Feb. 9, Mar. 29, Apr. 7, Sept. 7, 1938, Louis to Levine, Apr. 7 (optimistic), 1938, Hawkins to Lincoln, May 31 (Stoes), Sept. 12, 1938, Hawkins to Levine, Nov. 5, 1937, Hawkins to Louis, Feb. 9 (Haakon), 21, May 13 (20 percent), 1938—all BSA or LEK/BLH; LK to Austin, Jan. 11, 1938, CA/WAH; Gaddis, *Magician*, 324–25; LK to Copland, Sept. 19, 1938, AC/LC. NBC and CBS: LK to parents, Jan. 10, Feb. 5, Apr. 25, Hawkins to LK, Mar. 27—all 1938, all BSA or LEK/BLH. *Filling Station:* Gruen interview with Virgil Thomson, DD/NYPL; LK, *Thirty*, 71–72; LK, *Blast*, 45–46 (representative).

7. This composite description of Lincoln's life on the road with the Caravan derives mostly from a series of nine letters from LK to "Dear Ones" (Paul Cadmus and Jared and Margaret French) or to Paul himself; I'm greatly indebted to the owner of the Cadmus Papers, Cadmus's longtime companion, Jon Anderson, for allowing me to photocopy and quote from this series, as well as from a great many more LK/Cadmus letters in his possession. The Eugene Loring quotes are from Marilyn Hunt's Mar. 11, 1976, interview with Loring (DD/NYPL, MGZMT 5-704). A few additional details (e.g., "irksome") in this composite description come from LK's two-part "Transcontinental Caravan," *Dance* (Feb.–Mar., 1939), (Austin/Fayetteville/Edmonton/Toronto/Dallas), from LK, "Popular Style in American Dancing," Apr. 16, 1938 (Americanism) *The Nation*, and from Louis to LK, Nov. 12 (San Francisco), Hawkins to LK, Oct. 18 (Detroit and Chicago reviews), 26, 31 (Milwaukee), Nov. 23 (LA), 1938, BSA. Along with Leda Anchutina, another newcomer to the troupe during the Caravan's third year was the then-unknown Todd Bolender. *Billy the Kid* was Copland's second ballet commission; Ruth Page had given him his first, which resulted in the 1935 *Hear Ye! Hear Ye!* For CBS, NBC, Hurok: LK to parents (2): n.d.; Nov. 20, 1938, LEK/BLH. After the Caravan's successful four performances under the sponsorship of the American Lyric Theatre in New York City in April 1939, Lincoln renewed discussions with Mark Levine, Sol

Hurok's right-hand man, about a possible arrangement between them: LK to Louis, Jan. 12, 1940, BSA. For additional details on CBS, NBC, and Hurok, see Harlow Robinson, *The Last Impresario* (Viking Penguin, 1994), especially 271–72.

Billy the Kid: LK, "About 'Billy the Kid,' " *Dance Observer,* Oct. 1938; LK, *Thirty,* 77–78; Hawkins to LK, Oct. 26, 1938, BSA; Hunt interview with Loring, 1976, DD/NYPL; LK to "Dear Ones," n.d. [1938], Oct. 27, 1938, courtesy Anderson; LK to Copland, Sept. 19, 1938, AC/LC; LK to parents, Oct. 6 (dress), 1938, BSA. Pete Martínez: LK Diary, Mar. 24 (wise), Apr. 2, 18, 1937, LK/DD; LK to "Dear Ones" series (unqueer; marines), courtesy Anderson.

Lincoln apparently flirted for a time with some kind of a tie-in with the San Francisco Ballet, but Frances Hawkins rebuked him: "There is no reason why the San Francisco Ballet should capitalize on any of the Caravan's publicity. . . . You are so generous that you just want to work with everybody." She took him to task in a similar way when he requested pictures of Catherine Littlefield's *Café Society* and Ruth Page's *Frankie and Johnny* for an article he was writing: "Look, Lincoln, I don't think you ought to give them such publicity—mention Littlefield and Page if you must—but pictures, no! . . . I know that you are writing to advance the *American* cause—but can't you do it . . . [without] giving publicity gratis to the Caravan's competitors?" (Hawkins to LK, twice: one n.d., the other Nov. 4, 1938, BSA).

8. LK to Balanchine, May 20, 1939, BSA; LK to Tchelitchev, Jan. 9, 1939, PT/BL; LK to Louis, Sept. 14, 1939 ("I have seen Balanchine quite a lot"), BSA. I've seen no reference to the proposal in the May 20, 1939, letter elsewhere, nor any written response from Balanchine in the various archival collections I've researched. Lincoln himself makes no further reference to it in his correspondence and writings, though a few months after sending his letter to Balanchine, he did put out feelers in various directions in an attempt to save the Caravan or to merge it with "other established companies"; he even approached Denham's Monte Carlo: LK to parents, July 12, Nov. 3 (combine), 8 (Monte Carlo/Columbia), 1939, LK to Louis, Sept. 15, 1939, BSA. Since LK's proposal to Balanchine was never taken up, I assume that Balanchine turned it down during a personal meeting with Lincoln, though the possibility remains that a written reply from Balanchine might yet appear. For Balanchine's career at this point and his marriage to Vera Zorina, see Taper, *Balanchine,* 190–97, and Robert Gottlieb, *George Balanchine,* HarperCollins, 2004; (henceforth Gottlieb, *Balanchine*), 91–99. For Ballet Theatre: Reynolds and McCormick, *Fixed,* 271–75; LK to Chase, telegram Feb. 1, 1940, American Ballet Theatre Records, Dance Division, NYPL (henceforth ABTR/DD, NYPL). Balanchine, to Lincoln's delight, was back teaching mornings at the School in Sept. 1939 (though he left for Hollywood again in late November), and taught every grade (LK to Rose, Sept. 21, 1939, BSA.)

According to Frances Hawkins (Hawkins to LK, Nov. 10, 1938), the Mordkin Ballet, though it had twenty-six engagements that year, couldn't get even a hundred-dollar guarantee. Richard Pleasant, the guiding force behind Ballet Theatre's first season, had already contacted and met with Lincoln to discuss the current agitation to unionize ballet dancers; Pleasant to LK, Feb. 28, LK to Pleasant, Mar. 2, 1939, American Ballet Theatre Records (ABTR), (S) *MGZMD 49–3846, DD/NYPL; Richard Buckle, *George Balanchine,* Random House, 1988, 123 ($200,000), henceforth Buckle, *Balanchine.* Caravan: LK to Cadmus, n.d., courtesy Jon Anderson; LK to Nelson, Dec. 12, 1939, NAR Personal, Rockefeller Archive Center (henceforth NAR/RAC).

World's Fair: LK to Louis, Sept. 6, Louis to LK, Sept. 7, 1938, BSA; Lincoln helped put together for the fair a "Wright/Griffith/Steiglitz exhibit" (Barr to LK, July 17, 1939, AB/AAA [MoMA]). The Ford Pavilion: LK to Frances, Apr. 16, May 2, 14 (sold out)—all 1940, all BSA; see also LK, *Thirty,* 79–80.

When giving his theater and dance library to MoMA on a trial basis, Lincoln paid half the $1,560 annual salary of the librarian (Paul Magriel): LK to Beverley, Aug. 11, Levine to Beverley, Oct. 27, both 1939, Beverley to Louis, n.d. [Aug. 1940?], Barr to LK, Apr. 21, June 2, LK to Barr, Apr. 27, Beaumont to Barr, June 7, Abbott to LK, Oct. 9—all 1939, all AB/AAA (MoMA); interview with Genevieve Osborne, 6/29/03.

The school: LK to Louis, Dec. 30, 1938, Sept. 14, 1939, Levine to Beverley, Feb. 12, 1940 (better), LK to Hawkins, Apr. 16, 1940 (Graham)—all BSA; Lincoln stopped taking a salary as of June 1939. For his attempts to cut personal expenses: Levine to Beverley, Oct. 27,

1939, Feb. 6, Oct. 1, 1940, LK to Beverley, Dec. 16, 1939, LK to Louis, Feb. 16 (impossible), Aug. 2, 1940, Louis to LK, Feb . 12 (Dimitriev), 1940—all BSA. George Kirstein, apparently at his father's request, had tried to get Lincoln to economize, but had to throw up his hands ("I cannot seem to make any impression on him"): George to Louis, Sept. 7, 10, Louis to George, Sept. 8, 1938, BSA.

Reception of *Blast:* Levine to Beverley, Oct. 17, 20 (self-published; 2,000), Nov. 23, Hawkins to LK, Oct. 26—all 1938, all BSA; LK to "Dear Ones," courtesy Anderson; *The Nation,* Dec. 17, 1938 (Barzun). Politics: LK to Louis, Mar. 18, 28, 1938, Mar. 6, 1939, BSA; LK, "The English," *The Nation,* Mar. 3, 1938; LK to Leyda, Apr. 4, 1939, JL/TL. Edmund Wilson, for one, took Muriel sharply to task for her refusal to see that "the Stalin regime in its present phase is pretty hopelessly reactionary and corrupt" (Wilson to Draper, Nov. 14, 1938, MD/BL).

CHAPTER EIGHTEEN: SOUTH AMERICA: BALLET (1939–1941)

1. Multiple interviews with Jon Anderson, Paul Cadmus's life partner of many decades; interview with George Tooker, July 12, 2003. I'm grateful to Jon Anderson for allowing me to photocopy letters in his possession from Fidelma to her brother during the early 1930s; the only dated one (July 3, 1932) contains the contents of Egbert Cadmus's letter to his daughter. For the Afghan puppy: Hawkins to LK, May 21, July 5, 1940, LK to Hawkins, May 14, 24, 1940, BSA. Some additional details about the Cadmus family are from Justin Spring, *Paul Cadmus, The Male Nude* (Universe/Rizzoli, 2002), LK's *Paul Cadmus* (Pomegranate Art books, 1992), David Leddick, *Intimate Companions* (St. Martins, 2000), and especially his two interviews with Paul Cadmus, June 23, Oct. 21, 1999 (transcripts courtesy Claudia Roth Pierpont).

2. Caravan: LK to parents, Nov. 3 (eventuality), 1939, Hawkins to LK, Nov. 17, 29 (notices), Dec. 6, 1939, July 5, 1940 (Graham teaching), Levine to Beverley, July 10, 1940—all BSA; LK, "Ballet: Record and Augury," *The Arts,* Sept. 1940 (legacy). The quotes from Graham to Lincoln are from a half dozen undated [probably 1939–40] letters in LK/DD; also LK to Hawkins, May 2, 1940, BSA. An ongoing life for *Billy the Kid* began almost immediately when Ballet Theatre, early in 1940, opened negotiations with Lincoln for its showing; they were protracted and sometimes testy (e.g., LK to Richard Pleasant, Nov. 4, 1940: "I apologize to you for my initial burst of good feeling"). The various telegrams and letters are in the Records of the American Ballet Theatre, DD/NYPL (S) *MGZMD-49, folder 3846; also, LK to Hawkins, Apr. 16, 1940, BSA; LK to Copland, Nov. 11, 1940, AC/LC.

   Another of LK's important contributions to the field of dance in these same years (1939–40) was the publication of his seventy-page pamphlet in 1939, *Ballet Alphabet: A Primer for Laymen* (with drawings by Paul Cadmus), reprinted in LK, *Ballet: Bias and Belief* (Dance Horizons, 1983), with an introduction and commentary by Nancy Reynolds. The short book is a guide to the technique and practice of the dance. LK's original manuscript ran to some hundred thousand words, but his publisher forced him, as per their original agreement, to cut it nearly in half (LK to Louis, Sept. 15, 1939, LK to Rose, Sept. 18, 1939, BSA).

3. Reynolds and McCormick, *Fixed,* 117–40, for the general ballet picture in 1940; Denham to LK, Nov. 13, 1939, June 26, 28, 1940, LK to Denham, June 18, 1940, Records of the Ballet Russe de Monte Carlo, DD/NYPL, ZBD-492, folders 2775–77 (henceforth BRMC/DD); LK, letter to *PM Weekly,* Dec. 1, 1940 (in which LK referred to Fokine's recent *Le Coq d'Or* as "a large bore"); and "Ballet Blitz," *Town and Country,* Oct. 1940 (attack). In the same article Lincoln referred to Ballet Theatre as "that brash baby of the ballet world, that liberal democracy of lavish waste and possibilities, that curious phenomenon of the success story and the museum." In a second article, "Home Team: The Ballet Theatre," *Decision* (Apr. 1941), Lincoln made additional negative comments on BT: "Freshness is never enough . . . it did not mean outrageously brilliant novelties, nor outstanding dancers, nor in fact any ideas or artistic distinction at all." *Balustrade:* Taper, *Balanchine,* 197.

4. LK to Louis, Feb. 11, Nov. 3 (South America), 1939, BSA; I'm indebted to Reich, *Nelson Rockefeller,* 174–209, for background details on NR's South American appointment; LK to Ouroussow, June 12, 1941 (in charge), LK to parents, June 9 (school), 17 (Barbour), 1941,

Levine to Beverley, June 30, 1941 (Mabry), Somkin to Levine, Apr. 1, 1941 (lesion)—all BSA. Ruth Page and her husband Tom Fisher had tried to talk Lincoln into turning the tour into a joint venture, but he politely declined (LK to Page, Mar. 31, 1941, Fisher to LK, Apr. 2, 1941, LK/DD.) Lincoln's proposals to Nelson (two versions), the tentative tour itinerary and LK's "General Report to the Coordinator" (June 12, 1941), which includes lists of company members, ballets, choreographers, musicians, and designers, as well as a 2-pp. memo from LK to the entire company, Mar. 25, 1941, are all in BSA.

5. The South American tour: LK to parents, June 27, July 3, 11, 20, Aug. 4, 18, 27, Levine to Beverley, July 1, 3, Louis to LK, July 1, 28, LK to Louis, Dec. 5, 1941, Hawkins to LK, Aug. 1, LK to Witherspoon, Sept. 5, LK to Harrison, Sept. 16, Ouroussow to Beverley, Oct. 16—all 1941, all BSA; LK to Chavez, Aug. 21, 1941, LK/DD; LK to Virgil, July 26, Aug. 14, 1941, Jan. 12, 1942, VT/YML; LK to Lynes/Wescott/Wheeler, July 7, 1941, Nelson to LK, Aug. 21, 1941, WW/BL; LK to Hawkins, July 8, 13, 14, Aug. 3, LK/Hawkins, LK to Hawkins, Aug. 3, 1941, LK to Moffitt, July 30, 1942, MoMA; LK to McCausland, Sept. 10, 1941, EM/AAA (MoMA); LK to Maria Rosa Oliver (2), n.d. [1941], Fidelma to Oliver, n.d. [1941?], MRO/PU; LK to Lucia Chase, Sept. 18, 1941, LC/DD; LK to Paul Cadmus, July 27, 28, courtesy Anderson; LK to Nelson, June 26, July 2, 1941, LK to Jones, July 8, 27, Arthur Jones to Nelson, July 28, Aug. 7, Warner to Miller, Aug. 26, Da Silva to Miller, Aug. 26, Miller to Nelson, Sept. 3, 8, Smith to Harrison, Sept. 16—all 1941, all NAR/RAC; also in NAR/RAC are Carleton Sprague Smith's 2-pp. report to Harrison (Sept. 16, 1941) and LK's two different summary reports to Nelson, neither dated—the first one, twenty-six pages long, describes tour conditions through August; the other, eleven pages in length, covers the entire tour through November.

Through the courtesy of the Librarian of Congress, the company was given recording apparatus to take along with them; two folklore specialists, Seamus Doyle and Preston Corsa, were put in charge of this side project and eventually collected more than 250 original songs on acetate and aluminum discs, which were then deposited in the Library of American Folk Song of the Music Division of the Library of Congress.

LK printed excerpts from a so-called travel diary (the original of which, if it existed, has not turned up in any of the archival sources researched) in the *American Dancer* (Sept.–Dec. 1941), and were then reprinted in LK, *Ballet: Bias & Belief*, 77–95. Originally published while the company was still in South America, or soon after its return, these "excerpts" are sanitized versions of LK's actual views and experiences and should be used with great caution. A case in point is his visit to Brazil's leading musical figure, Heitor Villa-Lobos, which he simply notes in the *American Dancer* excerpts as having taking place, entirely omitting his negative reaction: "Villa-Lobos has lapsed into a kind of outraged eccentricity and cultivates being difficult . . . he practically threw me out of the room"; LK to Virgil Thompson, July 26, 1941, VT/YML.

CHAPTER NINETEEN: SOUTH AMERICA: MOMA (1942)

1. Dance Archives: Interview with Genevieve Oswald, June 29, 2003; Barr to Nelson Rockefeller, Feb. 23, 1940, along with budget proposal, LK to Barr, Apr. 5, 1940, excerpts from the June 15, 1939, and Mar. 6, 1940, minutes of the MoMA Board of Trustees, Magriel to LK, May 9, 1940, AB/AAA (MoMA); LK to Hawkins, Mar. 7, 1940, BSA; *Dance Observer* (Apr. 1940); *New York Times*, Mar. 10, 1940. In 1940–41 Magriel curated several small shows of selections from the archives for exhibitions at MoMA (e.g., *New York Times*, Oct. 27, 1940); LK to Martha Graham, Oct. 18, 1940, LK/DD. *Dance Index*: LK to Van Vechten, Nov. 27, Dec. 1, 1941, Oct. 3, 1942, VV/BL; Burns, *Letters*, vol. 2, 757; the "Shiva" comment is from Nicholas Jenkins, "Notes on Duberman ms.," 2006. By Dec. 1942 the editors of *Dance Index* had become Lincoln and Donald Windham; by March 1943 Windham was sole editor, but by the Feb. 1946 issue, LK was once again coeditor. Joseph Cornell did montage covers for *Dance Index* as well as the cover for the first issue, "The Painter's Birthday."

When Magriel was drafted into the army in 1942, the Dance Archives remained uncataloged, and tended to be neglected; contained within the body of MoMA's Library, Lincoln wrote that "it ekes out a rather miserable existence." As a result, he began to dispense some of the more valuable materials to Harvard and to the New York Public Library (LK to Barr, Nov. 16, 1942, AB/AAA [MoMA]; LK to Doubs, Dec. 23, 1942, LK to John Marshall, Feb. 17, 1943, LK [LOC] MoMA).

Serge Denham: LK to Denham, Nov. 26, 1941 (including a seven-page draft "agreement"), Michael Horwitz (artist manager) to David Libidins (business manager, Ballet Russe), Dec. 30, 1941, Feb. 4, 1942 (3), Horwitz to Denham, n.d., folders 1775–2777, BRMC/DD/NYPL; on Denham's interest in Americana, see Reynolds and McCormick, *Fixed*, esp. 287–89; Massine, *Ballet*, 220–22; Reich, *Nelson*, 208–9, chap. 15 passim, LK telegram to Nelson, Feb. 25, 1942 (deferment), LK (LOC)/ MoMA.

Draft deferment: Lockwood (Rockefeller General Counsel) to Local Board #44, Feb. 20, LK to Lockwood, Mar. 12, Lockwood to LK, Mar. 16, LK telegram to Nelson, Feb. 25, Nelson telegram to LK, Mar. 18, Nelson to General Hershey (head of draft), Feb. 28, LK to Clark, Mar. 19, 26, Clark to LK, Mar. 25—all 1942, all in NAR/RAC.

2. South American Politics: LK to Nelson, n.d. [late 1941], Nelson to Abbott, Apr. 4, 1942, LK to Nelson, Mar. 23, May 24, 27, June 14, July 21 (dullards, *En Guardia*), 27, Aug. 3, 1942, NAR/RAC; LK to Nelson, Aug. 15, 1942 ("not sent"), LK to parents, Sept. 19, 1942 (Mexico), BSA; LK to Glenway, n.d. [May 1942], May 28 (Naval Academy), GW/BL; LK to Monroe, May 21, 1942, MW/BL; LK to Dick Abbott, n.d. [May 1942], LK (LOC) MoMA; LK to Laughlin, April 28, 1942, NDP/HL; LK to Major Sherlock Davis (military attaché, U.S. Embassy, Buenos Aires), Aug. 1, 1942, LK (LOC) MoMA; LK to Harding, Oct. 27, 1942, enclosing his 15-pp. "General Political Conclusions," NAR/RAC (a near-duplicate draft version of seventeen pages, entitled "Memorandum of Trips to Latin America Illustrating Previously Stated Political Conclusions: May–October 1941–42, is in BSA; it contains somewhat more information on Friele, Riesman, Caffery, jail, and so on.) Lincoln sent Nelson detailed critiques of two of his most prominent operatives, Berent Friele and Philip Riesman. He called Friele a man "of charm if slight energies"—no match at all for the wily U.S. Ambassador Jefferson Caffery; Friele, in Lincoln's view, had shown "little imagination" in setting up the sort of unique, desirable services that the U.S. Embassy itself failed to supply. In Rio, for example, the coordinator's office sponsored a radio program that was, in Lincoln's view, "ineffective," and its designedly independent press program had come under the control of the American Embassy. As for Phil Riesman, an executive vice president of RKO, Lincoln described him as all at once "careless and inefficient," ignorant of the public relations of which he was presumably a specialist—and more than a little sinister. Riesman decided that Lincoln was "a Communist," and he may have had a hand in Lincoln being arrested at the airport when he arrived in São Paulo from Rio. So far as Lincoln knew his papers were entirely in order, but the arresting officer told him that he'd failed to register with the police in Rio—no one having bothered to tell him that the procedure was necessary. He was fined four hundred dollars and released. Orson Welles: LK to Wescott, May 28 (cry-baby), GW/BL; LK to Nelson, May 24, 27, Aug. 3 (Sarnoff), NAR/RAC.

3. South American art: LK to Hawkins, May 21, Sept. 8, 1942, LK (Hawkins) MoMA; LK to Paul Cadmus, May 27, June 7, Aug. 23 (Siqueiros; Fidelma; Spanish), 1942, courtesy Anderson; LK telegram to Soby, June 10, 1942, LK (LOC), MoMA; LK to Caffery, June 14, 1942, NAR/RAC; LK to Wheeler, June 14 (lonely), July 15, Aug. 7 (Taylor; MoMA prestige; Siqueiros), Sept. 23, Wheeler to LK, May 21, 29, July 3, 15, 29, telegram Aug. 14 (Chillán), 18 (Santiago), Sept. 4 (Chillán) 1942, MW/BL; LK to Barr, June 19 (prices), 22 (Butler), July 8, 1942, LK to Abbott, Sept. 1 (Ecuador; Taylor), LK drafts and reports on setting up Department of Latin American Art at MoMA, plus d'Harnoncourt's response, Oct. 17, LK (LOC) MoMA; LK to Mongan, June 29, 1942, AM/Fogg. A number of Lincoln's quoted opinions about individual artists are taken from his catalog for MoMA's 1943 show, Latin-American Collection of the Museum of Modern Art; a copy of the catalog is in LK/DD. LK's comment on "not a source but a tributary" is in a June 18, 1943, letter (LK [LOC] MoMA) to Grace Morley, director of the San Francisco Museum of Art, and probably the country's leading specialist in Latin American art; she agreed with his opinion and while feeling that his choice of purchases had been "just, fair and representative," expressed disappointment that he "had not discovered more new and better artists and works that had been unknown to me" (Morley to LK, Aug. 5, 1943, AB/AAA [MoMA]). During 1943–44 Lincoln published

several articles on Siqueiros: "La Reciente Obra Mural de Siqueiros en el Conjunto del Muralismo Mexicano," *Hoy*, June 26, 1943; "Siqueiros in Chillán," *Magazine of Art*, Dec. 1943; "Siqueiros: Painter and Revolutionary," *Magazine of Art*, Jan. 1944; Siqueiros sent Lincoln a rather grandiose letter of instructions about his pending exhibition at MoMA: Siqueiros to LK, Dec. 17, 1942 (LK [LOC] MoMA). For the Chilean antifascist publication *Forma* (Oct. 1942), Lincoln also wrote "Through an Alien Eye," which referred to Siqueiros's Chillán murals as "the most important new synthesis of plastic elements since the Cubist Revolt in 1911." LK's brief historical survey, "South American Painting," includes discussions of, among others, Portinari, Segal, and Horacio Butler (*Studio*, Oct. 1944).

4. Balanchine: LK to Nelson, Mar. 23 (handsomely), July 21 (invited back), Aug. 3 (crabbing), 1942, NAR/RAC; LK to Hawkins, July 8, 1942, LK (Hawkins) MoMA; LK to Wheeler, June 21 (Pavlik), 1942, MW/BL; LK to Moffitt, July 30 (augmented), 1942, LK (LOC) MoMA; Ouroussow to LK (overwhelmed; banquet), Aug. 27, 1942, BSA, LK to Ocampo, April 15 *(Estancia)*, 1942, VO/HL. Lincoln wrote an article, "Latin American Music for Ballet," *Theatre Arts*, May 1942, that included discussions of Ginastera's and Mignone's work. In Chile, Lincoln purchased the rights for choreographic performance to Domingo Santa Cruz's *Five Small Pieces for Strings*, which on hearing, Balanchine very much liked. After their return to the States, Lincoln assisted Balanchine in his mounting of several ballets for Mrs. Lytle Hull's New Opera Company, and they intended to hire Matta to do sets and costumes for a new ballet using Santa Cruz's music. But there wasn't enough time, since Balanchine was called to Hollywood to direct the dance sequences for the film *Lady in the Dark*. In regard to music Lincoln also worked hard, but unsuccessfully, to get a production of the Brazilian composer Camargo Guarneri's opera *Malazarte*. [LK to Wolff, Nov. 6, 24, LK to Jorge di Castro, Nov. 11, LK to Alfred Frankenstein (music and art critic for the *San Francisco Chronicle*), Nov. 23, 1942, LK to Charles Seeger (Pan-American Union), Dec. 16, 1942/LK to Carlos Chávez, Jan. 8; LK to Steiner, Jan. 23, 1943 (Guarneri), LK (LOC) MoMA].

5. Wheeler to LK, July 3, 1942 (Tchelitchev), LK to Wheeler, Sept. 4, 1942, MW/BL; d'Harnoncourt to LK, Oct. 17, 1942, BSA. LK to Wasson, Feb. 16, 1943 (folk art); LK to Maria Rosa Oliver, Dec. 29, 1942; LK to Saslawsky, Jan. 28, 1943; LK to Urruchua, Mar. 5, 1943; Amalia Polleri de Viana, Feb. 17, 1943, LK to Nelson, Feb. 17, 1943 (Urruchua), Wheeler to Barr & Kirstein, Jan. 21, 1943, LK to Wheeler & Barr, Jan. 22, 1943 (Siqueiros); LK to Horacio Butler, Feb. 25, 1943—all in LK (LOC) MoMA; "Preliminary Draft . . . for the Formation of a Department of Latin American Art . . ." plus "Objectives" plus "The Permanent Collection . . ." plus "Latin Americans at the Museum of Modern Art"—all in LK (LOC) MoMA. There are also dozens and dozens of letters in LK (LOC) MoMA from Lincoln to a wide assortment of people that document his tumultuous activities in the fall of 1942, including his work on behalf of individual Latin American artists and cultural figures; above I've documented several of the most important, but the rest are far too numerous to list here.

6. For sample obits: *Boston Evening Standard*, Dec. 10, 1942, *Women's Wear Daily*, Dec. 10, 1942, *Boston Globe*, Dec. 14, 1942; Frankfurter to Mina, Jan. 28, Feb. 19 (biography), 1943, MCP/SS; La Guardia telegram to Rose, Dec. 10, 1942, FDR to Rose, Dec. 11, 1942, John A. Roosevelt to Rose, Jan. 25, 1943 (Louis had given John his first job in 1938 as a stock clerk in the basement store of Filene's; John later became a manager in a branch shop in Winchester, not leaving Filene's until May 1941)—all in LEK/BLH, which also has a dozen short notes from FDR to Louis dating back to 1929, when Roosevelt was governor of New York; Rose to Julius Marx, Dec. 28, 1942, LK/DD. After going to Washington at FDR's request in July 1941, Louis reported to Lincoln, "I had quite a chat with the President. . . . He says both he and Churchill are very much surprised that Hitler went into Russia—they cannot understand why he did not grab the Mediterranean and Suez Canal especially when he had a chance to do it (Louis to LK, July 28, 1941, BSA). Louis, perhaps due to his declining health, had, during the months before his death, been sounding a somewhat sharper, more disapproving note toward Lincoln than recently: "You will have to get along on what you earn" (Louis to Lincoln, Apr. 25, 1942, BSA); "His father . . . has very little confidence in any plans that he may have" (Beverley to Levine, Apr. 30, 1942, BSA).

Lincoln's shrinkage of projects: LK to Schurz, Dec. 16, 1942 (South American painting), LK to Stephen Clark, Jan. 18, 1943 (lectures), "Program for the First Year 1943–44," LK to Robert C. Smith, Jan. 25, Feb. 2 (catalog), 1943—all LK (LOC) MoMA; Barr to LK, Mar. 24, 1943, AB/AAA (MoMA); LK to Ouroussow, Feb. 20, Oct. 8 (Fidelma), 1943, BSA; LK to Moe, Feb. 17, 1943 (Graham), LK (LOC) MoMA. Several months later Ouroussow reported to Lincoln that Balanchine "is *violently* opposed" to their plan for having a six- to eight-year-old children's group at the school: "says it will undermine our professional reputation and considers it useless. Says we will turn into a kindergarten" (Ouroussow to LK, June 18, 1943, BSA). *For My Brother:* LK to Blanche Knopf, Jan. 11, LK to Lehmann, Jan. 18, 1942, LK (LOC) MoMA; LK to Draper, "Saturday," n.y. MD/BL; Lehmann to LK, May 18, Isherwood to LK, Mar. 29, Apr. 11, August 28 (reviews; second impression)—all 1943, all LK/DD; *New Statesman*, Sept. 25, 1943. There's some question as to whether Lincoln had himself conceived the book as a novel; he sent Lehmann an actual portrait of Pete for inclusion, suggesting that he meant *Brother* to be taken literally, as a work of nonfiction; it was Lehmann who decided the portrait was a "mistake" because "as cut and made into a continuous narrative by Christopher [Isherwood], the book had to go into the novel class and the portrait would have been slightly inappropriate" (Lehmann to LK, May 18, LK/DD).

CHAPTER TWENTY: THE ARMY (1943–1945)

1. LK to Schnakenberg, Mar. 15, 1943, HS/AAA (MoMA); LK to Wheeler, May 31, 1943, GW/BL; LK to Barr, Mar. 8, 1943, Aug. 11, AB/AAA (MoMA); Isherwood to LK, Mar. 29, Apr. 11, May 1, LK to Paul and Fidelma, "Thursday," n.d.—all 1943, all LK/DD; LK to Abbott, May 17, LK to Hawkins (6), all simply "Monday," etc., 1943, LK (LOC) MoMA; LK to MacLeish, Apr. 23, May 1, 1943, AM/LC; LK to Leyda, Aug. 23, 1943, JL/TL. George Platt Lynes's diaries document Lincoln's reappearance in New York, in uniform, as early as Mar. 31, 1943, GPL/BL; Pete Martínez to LK, Mar. 21, "July '43", plus an undated letter from "Kitze" (one of Pete's nicknames) to LK, telling him that he'd "give anything to see you. I love you very much and miss you more then [*sic*] ever."

2. American Battle Art: Varga *(Life)* to LK, Sept. 7, LK to Kerr, Sept. 22 *(Life)*, Soby to LK (MoMA), Oct. 12, 18 (West Point), LK to Ogden, Oct. 16 (book), LK to Wheeler, Oct. 18, LK to Munson (Bobbs-Merrill), Oct. 19, LK to Cummings, Oct. 29, Nov. 9 (book), Cummings to LK, Nov. 3, Margot Johnson (LK's agent) to LK, Nov. 3, LK to Major Johnson, Nov. 6 (West Point), LK to Captain Sackas, Nov. 17/24 (War College, and so on)—all 1943, all LK/DD; LK to McCausland, Nov. 1, 9, 1943, Mar. 18, 1944, McCausland to LK, Nov. 6, 1943, Garrett to McCausland, March 27, 1944, EM/AAA (MoMA); LK to Walker, Feb. 10, 1944 (National Gallery of Art, MoMA), LK to Major Johnson (West Point), March 18, 1944, LK/DD; LK to Finley, March 7, 17, 22, 30, Apr. 1, 10, 1944, Finley to LK, Mar. 11, 30, LK to MacLeish, Mar. 22, Finley to Clark—all 1944, all DF/LC; LK to Wheeler, Feb. 19, 1944 (book), GW/BL; LK to Sachs, Feb. 14, Mar. 7, Sachs to LK, Mar. 10, 1944, EF/Fogg; LK to Barr, Mar. 4, 13, Barr to LK, Mar. 13, 21—all 1944, all AB/AAA (MoMA); Mongan to LK, Apr. 12, 1944 (staggered), AM/Fogg; LK, 59-pp. catalog, *American Battle Painting, 1776–1918* (National Gallery of Art, MoMA); LK, "American Battle Art: 1588–1944," published in three parts, Mar.–May 1944, *Magazine of Art*; LK's 7-pp. proposal for the War Museum is included in LK to Barr, Mar. 24, 1944 (AB/AAA (MoMA), a longer (thirteen-pp.) version of the proposal is in LK to Mongan, Apr. 19, 1944 (AM/Fogg).

3. LK to Barr, Mar. 4, 1944, AB/AAA (MoMA); LK to Soby, Apr. 16, 1944, DPG; LK to Soby, Apr. 16 (Pvt. Parts), June 14, 1944, GRI; Isherwood to LK, May 1 (medium), Aug. 31 (verse), Nov. 18 (communication), LK to Isherwood, Sept. 17 (Choura; Paris), Oct. 17, Cadmus to LK, n.d. [1944], LK to Cadmus, Aug. 25, Sept. 17 (Isherwood), Oct. 7, Feb. 17 [1945], George Kirstein to LK, June 13, Tchelitchew to LK, Sept. 11 (Fidelma), LK to Rorimer, Sept. 20, LK to Mina, Sept. 23 (Wystan; Archie), LK to Cairns, Oct. 13 (insulting), Cairns to LK, Nov. 17, Finley to LK, Nov. 17—all 1944, all LK/DD; LK to Virgil Thomson, Oct. 4 (scandals), 1944, Nov. 9 (Lifar; synagogue), VT/YML; LK to MacLeish, Sept. 12 (thrilling;

Patton), 17 *(classe moyenne)*, MacLeish to LK, Oct. 11, Nov. 1, 1944, LK to MacLeish, Dec.
16 (Cairns; play), 1944, AM/LC; LK to Wheeler, Aug. 14 (pipe dream), 23 *(Jeu de Paume)*,
1944, Jan. 16 (Choura), 1945, GW/BL; LK to Hawkins, Nov. 9 (muzzle), [1944], LK
(Hawkins) MoMA; LK to Margaret Marshall, Feb. 8, Mar. 20, 1945, MM/BL; LK, "Letter
from France" (Paris theater), *The Nation*, Jan. 27, 1945, LK, *Rhymes of a PFC* (henceforth
Rhymes); New Directions, 1964; LK to Thomson, Nov. 12, 1944, Feb. 2 (Nancy), 1945,
VT/YML; interview with Davie Lerner and Jim Radich (who knew LK somewhat in the
army and describes him as "always friendly and nice"—and eager to maintain his anonymity),
June 26, 2003 (desk, and so on). Pete Martínez: Isherwood to Cadmus, Sept. 29, 1944, courtesy Anderson; LK to Hawkins, Nov. 9 [1944], LK (Hawkins), MoMA; LK to Isherwood,
Nov. 12, 1944, LK to Cadmus [n.d., Nov. 1944], LK/DD. Glenway Wescott tended to agree
with Isherwood about LK's poetry: in the draft of a letter (May 20, 1946, GW/BL) to Lincoln, and perhaps never sent, Wescott writes, "Let me make a sort of plea for prose"; he characterized LK's verse, with some but hardly entire justice, as "over-educated pastiche with
under-disciplined technique." I'm greatly indebted to Professor Nicholas Jankins for leading
me toward at least a partial appreciation of LK's poetry and for pointing out its valuable autobiographical content.

For background on SHAEF, the Monuments Commission, and the recovery of art, I'm
indebted to Lynn H. Nicholas, *The Rape of Europa* (Knopf, 1994); and Elizabeth Simpson,
ed., *The Spoils of War* (Harry N. Abrams, 1997). According to the *New York Times* (Feb. 27,
2003), as many as one hundred thousand pieces of plundered art are still missing, with
mounting pessimism that most will ever be recovered. After his return to the States, Lincoln
continued to protest, as he'd already done when in Europe, the transfer of the holdings of the
Prussian state museums into the custody of the National Gallery in Washington, DC; Lincoln held John Walker, who he felt had blown up and over-publicized his own limited role in
the recovery effort, directly responsible (e.g., LK to Stout, n.d. [fall 1945], BSA).

Polymath that he was, Lincoln was not only sending Virgil Thomson a ton of information on musical life in Paris (Virgil wrote Lincoln that he was "better than any other source
of information"—VT to LK, Aug. 2, 1945, VT/YML), but was simultaneously giving Aaron
Copland a rundown on the musical scene preparatory to his possible visit (LK to Copland,
Mar. 23, 1945, AC/LC), writing an encyclopedic article ("French Films During the Occupation") for the *MoMA Bulletin*, Jan. 1945 (he was the only American in the audience for the
first showing of the documentary *Paris se libère*), and providing Soby and Barr with detailed
accounts of emerging French painters and sculptors, along with detailed recommendations
for which ones to buy (LK to Soby, Mar. 15, 1945, JS/AAA [MoMA]). He also wrote a three-
part series of articles, "Art in the Third Reich—Survey, 1945," that so impressed Barr and
others at MoMA that the museum's *Magazine of Art* published in Oct. 1945 as a special
issue, along with Barr's own 1933 series on Nazi Art (LK to Barr, Jan. 5, 1945, Barr to LK,
June 29, July 17, 31, 1945, Barr to Morse, June 29, 1945, AB/AAA [MoMA]). As Barr wrote
Lincoln in the June 29 letter, "I never get over wondering at your prodigiousness."

Tchelitchev: Tchelitchev to Tanner, June 28, Aug. 28, Sept. 25 (denunciation), Oct. 5—
all 1944, all AT/BL; Tchelitchev to LK, Oct. 3 (Fidelma), 1944, LK to Cadmus, Sept. 17,
1944, Cadmus to LK, n.d. [1944], LK/DD; Martha Graham to David Zellmer, Jan. 16,
May 20 (devil), July 24, Sept. 11, 1944, (S) *MGZMD 117, DD/NYPL; in the May 20 letter,
Graham went on to say that "purposeless homosexuality bores me," and in her July 24 letter to
Zellmer added "Quite frankly I am getting a little tired of the boys. They are so mercurial."

4. Germany: LK to Groozle [Fidelma], March 24 (miss), to Grooslie [Fidelma], May 6, LK to
Cadmus, Jan. 22 (comb), Feb. 17, April 29 (Tanagra), May 6/7 (beauty-tost), 1945, LK/DD;
LK to MacLeish, Dec. 16, 1944 (worse), Feb. 24, 1945 (official list), AM/LC; LK to "Glen,"
April 4 (Mauriac), 1945, GW/BL; Mina to Goosie [LK], Apr. 13, 1945, LK to Rose and
Fidelma, Apr. 13, 1945 (FDR), 1945, LK/DD; LK to Marshall, Apr. 24 (notion of defeat),
1945, LK/DD; LK to Mongan, n.d. [1945], HUA; LK to Sharrer, June 12, 1945, courtesy
Zagorin. A poem LK wrote ("Arts & Monuments") about his encounter with the countess is
in LK, *Rhymes*, 148–54. LK wrote a number of articles about his work in Germany: "War
Uncovers a Ghost of Gothic Fresco" [Mont Saint Martin], *Art News*, May 1–14, 1945;

"Monuments of Old Germany" (Posey), *The Nation*, Sept. 1, 1945; "The Reichsmarschall's Retreat" (Göring's house), *Town and Country;* "A Visit to Der Stuermer" (Julius Streicher), *The Nation*, June 30, 1945 and, most importantly, "The Quest of the Golden Lamb" (Alt Aussee), *Town and Country*, Sept. 1945. LK's correspondence with Margaret Marshall explores plans for his *Nation* articles: LK to MM, May 27, June 1, 20, July 2, 22, 1945, MM/BL. LK wrote a poem, "Siegfriedslage," about meeting up with Auden; see LK, *The Poems of Lincoln Kirstein* (Atheneum, 1987). Much of the detail about the recovering of the Van Eyck altarpiece comes from the "Quest" article, as well as from Nicholas, *Rape of Europa*, and several of Lincoln's letters: LK to Mongan, n.d., AM/Fogg; LK to Fidelma, May 13 (strafed; future), LK to Fidelma[?] May 22 (Stout; intolerant), June 12 (Kafka; Auden), 1945, Mina to LK, Aug. 21 [1945?], LK/DD; 6 letters Fidelma to Paul (painting; Wellfleet; Fire Island, and so on)—all n.d. [1944–45], all courtesy Anderson.

5. LK to Paul, May 26, June 23, 1945, LK/DD; Isherwood to Paul, Nov. 30, 1944, Aug. 2, 1945, courtesy Anderson; LK to Barr, n.d. [1945], AB/AAA (MoMA); LK to Thompson, May 25, 1945, VT/YML; LK to Marshall, July 2 (Auden; boring), 1945, MM/BL; LK to Nelson, July 24, 1945, Nelson to LK, Sept. 22, 1945, NAR/RAC; LK to Paul, Nov. 30 (ballet), 1944, May 26, 1945, LK/DD; LK to George Stout (Rose), n.d. [fall 1945], BSA; LK to Copland, June 16, 1945, AC/LC; Tchelitchev to Tanner, Sept. 27, 1945, AT/BL; Argentina protest: SCHW: #757; Foreman to LK, May 17, 1946, BSA.

CHAPTER TWENTY-ONE: BALLET SOCIETY (1946–1947)

1. LK to George Stout, n.d. [1945], Stephen C. Clark to LK, April 1, 1946 (MoMA), Parsner [?] to LK, Jan. 18 *(Tribune)*, 1946, BSA. Art texts: Mongan to LK, May 2, 13, June 11, 1946, Sachs to LK, June 4, BSA; LK to Sachs, June 6 (Walker), 1946, EF/Fogg. Lincoln's articles in 1946 included "Pedro Figari," *Magazine of Art*, Mar. 1946; a throwaway piece, "Seeing Things" for *Mademoiselle*, Oct. 1946, which he did (or so he claimed) in order to afford to buy a painting by the youthful George Tooker, Cadmus's most recent lover (LK to "Paul and Mr. Tooker", July "Twentysomething," [1946]), courtesy Anderson; the first of many articles he would write on Henri Cartier-Bresson, a recent acquaintance who would become a longtime friend (*New York Times Magazine*, Feb. 2, 1947); and the forty-four-page catalog essay for the Whitney Museum's show on Rimmer, Nov. 5–27, 1946.

George Kirstein to LK, May 10, GK to Beverly, May 27 (money), 1946, BSA; Mme. Lachaise to LK, n.d. [1946], LK to Lachaise, n.d. [1946], Nelson to LK, May 6 (loyalty), 13, 1946, LK to Kerr (Knoedler's), May 10, 1946, BSA; LK to Lachaise, Nov. 19, 1946, LK/DD; Petrov to LK, Aug. 13, Nelson to LK, July 1 (initial), Oct. 16 (family), LK to Nelson, May 2 (generous), Aug. 15 (patina), Nov. 10 (Knoedler's)—all 1946, all NAR/RAC; LK to Nelson, Jan. 19 (Knoedler's), 20, 1947, NAR/RAC; LK to Lynes, "Sunday before Xmas," 1946, GW/BL. In terms of having a full plate, Lincoln even suggested ("I am quite serious") to Jay Leyda that they start a new magazine called *Humana*, designed to be "in the forefront of creative work in this country for the next decade" (LK to Leyda, Dec. 31, 1946, HDP/HL). Lachaise biography: LK to McCausland, May 6, 23, July 12, Aug. 5 (privacy), Sept. 12, Nov. 25, McCausland to LK, May 20, 25, July 9, 13, Aug. 8—all 1946, all EM/AAA (MoMA); LK to Mme. Lachaise, Nov. 19, 1946, LK to Fisher, Dec. 15, 1946 (new ending), Basil [Petroff of Knoedler's] to LK, Feb. 5, 1947 (reception of show: "Even Madame is pleased"), LK/DD; Lachaise to LK, n.d., BSA. McCausland, Alfred Barr, and Agnes Mongan were among those who failed to share Lincoln's enthusiasm for the Lachaise installation, feeling that the dramatic lighting was overemphatic (McCausland to LK, Apr. 3, 1947, LK/DD; Mongan to LK, Feb. 6, 1947 ("that hushed silence did make me a bit uncomfortable"), LK/HUA, uncataloged as of May 20, 2003.

2. William Rimmer: LK to Mongan, Feb. 14, Apr. 4 (Eakins; sensuality), 12 (cranky), 15 (plus one n.d.—"Lion in the Arena"), 1944, AM/Fogg; Mongan to LK, Feb. 16, Apr. 12, May 11, 13, 1944, LK to Cadmus, n.d. (KAMP), [1944–45], LK/DD; LK to John Aldrich, July 8, 1946, JBW/BU; LK to Forbes, Apr. 4, 1944, EF/Fogg; LK to Cadmus and Tooker, July 12, 1946, courtesy Anderson. In the course of his research Lincoln learned that at an earlier

point, Edward Forbes of the Fogg Museum had refused the offer of Rimmer's papers, diaries, and notes, which were subsequently lost; "it seems to me hair-raising," Lincoln wrote George Stout "that the Fogg could not even give storage room to these papers" (LK to Stout, n.d., BSA). Along with his 44-pp. catalog, *William Rimmer, 1816–1879*, for the Whitney and Boston Fine Arts exhibits, Lincoln also wrote a short piece on the artist, "The Rediscovery of William Rimmer" (Rodin, expressionists) in the *Magazine of Art*, Mar. 1947; however, Lincoln never did write the full-length book on Rimmer that he'd initially intended.

3. Ballet Society: LK to Thomson, Aug. 11, 1946, enclosing LK's eight-page proposal for Ballet Society, VT/YML; Caccialanza to LK, n.d. [1945?], LK to Denham, Nov. 8, Denham to LK, Nov. 25, LK to Mrs. Le Clercq, Nov. 8, LK to Denham, Nov. 8 (brilliant), LK to Tanaquil Le Clercq, Nov. 20, Robert Vernon to LK, Nov. 30 (Seligmann), LK to Seligmann, Nov. 23, LK to Beverley, Nov. 22—all 1946, all BSA; Martha Graham to LK, n.d. [1946], Lévi-Strauss to LK, Nov. 20, 1946, LK to Fisher, Nov. 11, 1946 (expensive), LK/DD; LK to Lucia Chase, Nov. 14 (difficult), 1946, ABTR/DD; LK to Virgil, Nov. 10 [misdated "Dec. 10"], 24 (Pavlik; Bernstein; betrayal), Dec. 11, Virgil to LK, Dec. 5—all 1946, all VT/YML. Ballet Society mixed seasoned dancers with advanced students from SAB, a practice that Virgil Thomson, for one, thought ill advised, confusing everyone's performance level. Lincoln also refused to provide free tickets to the critics, arguing that their reviews would have no effect on the society's fortunes, since performances were rarely repeated and since they had no intention of touring; many of the critics took out their own subscriptions, but the only prominent review of (for example) the very first performance was in the *Herald Tribune* (LK to Tom Fisher, Dec. 15, 1946, LK/DD). The wisdom of Lincoln's attitude toward the critics is certainly arguable; a string of favorable reviews might have led to a very different outcome when he unsuccessfully tried to book Ballet Society performances in other East Coast cities. For fine, detailed descriptions of *Four Temperaments*, see Reynolds and McCormick, *Fixed*, 297, and of *Orpheus*, 299.

   On LK's finances: George Kirstein to LK, Mar. 12 (prudence), 1947, GK to Casner, April 23 (SAB "self-supporting"), 1947, LK/DD; GK to Rose, Apr. 28, 1947, BSA. Ruth Page was eager to get Lincoln to produce her ballet *Billy Sunday*. Though he told her, in his blunt way, "I now feel that I really don't believe in it—either the form or the subject," she and her husband, the equally tenacious Tom Fisher, continued to press him and to conjure up other schemes for possible collaboration (Ruth "is burning up to work with you on some future project"); Lincoln held them off, but the exchange, on both sides, sometimes became testy (LK to Ruth, Jan. 25, Feb. 15, Mar. 12 (Billy), Apr. 2, 14, LK to Tom and Ruth, Mar. 16, Fisher to LK, Mar. 14 (burning), 26—all 1947, all RP/DD. In 1950, Lincoln described Page as "a silly girl, but not a bad one; I like her much better than [José] Limón"; he also described Tom Fisher as "a fascinating gangster-type"—one of Lincoln's higher compliments (LK to Buckle, May 17, 1950, Richard Buckle Papers, The Ransom Center, The University of Texas, henceforth RB/UT). In 1952, it again looked as if NYCB might do a Ruth Page ballet (probably *Revenge*). But hearing the rumor, Jerry Robbins insisted that if it did come to pass, a note be inserted into the program to the effect that "all the directors have not agreed" (Cage to LK, June 16, 1952, *MGZMD 38, DD/NYPL). Balanchine finally decided that Page's ballet was "very bad" (GB to LK, Aug. 4, 1952, LK/DD) and it was not put into NYCB's roster.

4. How much of his available assets Lincoln did end up spending on Ballet Society remains obscure; in a letter to Virgil Thomson (Mar. 10, 1947, VT/YML), Lincoln claimed to have spent in the first year "all the money I have been given by my mother for two years"—yet it's unclear whether he meant Rose's twenty-thousand-dollar gift or the much larger trust fund she'd set up for him. Lincoln's curtailment of Ballet Society activities was in part involuntary: he was unable, as originally planned, to organize subscription performances in Boston, Washington, DC, Hartford, and elsewhere (LK to Fisher, Dec. 30, 1946, LK/DD). The curators of the December 1946 event were George Amberg, head of MoMA's department of dance and theatre design, and Iris Barry, director of the museum's film library. Among the works shown were Baron de Meyer's 1913 photographs of Nijinsky and Steichen, Arnold

Genthe's of Isadora Duncan, a Van Vechten Kodakchrome series of contemporary dancers (including Martha Graham), "native dances" filmed by the U.S. Signal Corps in Japan, Tibet, and China, and a group of performance films of the Monte Carlo, Ballet Theatre, and de Basil companies.

LK to Stravinsky, May 7, 1946, "Excerpts From the Stravinsky-Kirstein Correspondence," (S) *MGZMD 97–402, DD/NYPL; LK to Thomson, Dec. 11, 1946, VT/YML; LK to Lynes, Jan. 16, 1947 [misdated "1946"], GW/BL. It seems likely, but not certain, that the programs on Jan. 13 and 14 were somewhat different. There's reference in some of LK's correspondence, as part of "the second program," to a solo performance by the dancer Iris Mabry (LK to Lynes, Jan. 7, 1947) and to the "stunning and exciting" Balanchine *Divertimento*, music by Alex Haieff (Vernon, Jr., to LK, Jan. 15, 1947, BSA); yet it's been generally thought (Taper, *Balanchine*, 405, is an exception; he puts the premiere on Jan. 13) that *Divertimento* was first given at Ballet Society's sixth performance, Feb. 6, 1948 [as seemed confirmed by LK to Lucia Chase, June 27, 1947, (S) *MGZMD 49–3847, DD/NYPL]. Along with Virgil, Pavlik, too, denounced Lincoln for "throwing money away" on *Highland Fling*, "another idiotic ballet on the scotch men 'war'!!"; he blamed Balanchine's baleful influence: "The ideas of poor Geo B. are appalling, the poor man is completely intellectually dead—stupid and polluted by Zorina" (Pavlik to LK, Aug. 7, 1947, LK/DD). Talley Beatty: LK to Virgil Thomson, June 1, 1947, VT/YML.

Pete, Fidelma, and Tooker: Interview with Tooker, July 12, 2003 (Fidelma, Jared and Margaret French, Cadmus, and others); LK to Cadmus, Nov. 30, 1944 (kind), LK to Cadmus and Tooker, July 12, 1946, courtesy Anderson; LK to Stout (tempera), n.d., plus a May 28, 1946, postcard, sender not identified (chic), plus LK to "Kee-yuds [kids]," n.d. BSA; LK to Lynes, Aug. 20 (Fidelma; Isherwood), Nov. 19 (queens), plus a third, n.d. (Forster), 1947, GW/BL; Morgan [E. M. Forster] to LK, July 3, 1947, LK/DD; Fidelma to Paul, July 18, 1946 (Mina), Isherwood to Cadmus, July 2, 27, Aug. 19, 1947, courtesy Anderson. Occasionally Fidelma would also spend time alone at Mina's place, Ashfield: "I behaved well for once, since for once I felt wanted," she wrote her brother after one such visit (Fidelma to Paul, n.d. [June 1944?], courtesy Anderson). Mina, who could sometimes play the dictatorial grande dame, was also given to periodic bursts of envy at Lincoln's growing prominence, a position she very much coveted for herself. For more on Tooker: Thomas H. Garver, *George Tooker* (Pomegranate, 1992). Lincoln described Tooker's work during these early years as "REMARKABLE" (LK to Lynes, Oct. 27, 1947, GW/BL), and (of a self-portrait) "sensational" (LK to Lynes, Aug. 20, 1947).

According to David Langfitt (interview, Apr. 27, 2003), Lincoln regarded Jared as "unstable" and feared he might end up destroying himself and/or his paintings. About Donald Windham, Lincoln had decidedly mixed feelings. Early on in their acquaintance, Lincoln wrote, "I hope he [Windham] survives his youth" (LK to Cadmus, Nov. 30, 1944, LK/DD). In regard to his editorship of *Dance Index*, he credited Windham at one point with "very good ideas," yet at another time described him as "absolutely, hopelessly uninterested on any very serious plane" (LK to Fidelma [?], Aug. 1, 1945, LK to Levine, May 19, 1945, BSA). When Windham left *Dance Index*, LK wrote Denby that he'd "retired on his ill gotten gains" (LK to Denby, Jan. 16, 1946, BSA).

For LK's high opinion of Sharrer: LK to Cadmus and Tooker, July 12, 1946, courtesy Anderson. As an example of Sharrer's gratitude to him: Sharrer to LK, Sept. 2, 1947, LK/DD, in which she thanks Lincoln (as she did again in 1949 and 1951) for all his help—for his recommending her to the Guggenheim Foundation, submitting to them a painting that he owned, getting her connected to the Knoedler's gallery. LK's behind-the-scenes work in Sharrer's behalf is yet another example of the quiet support and encouragement he gave to many artists.

The great costumer, Karinska, who would have a long history with the New York City Ballet and had already done work with Balanchine and Ballet Theatre, executed many of the costumes designed by others for Ballet Society, including *Four Temperaments*, *Renard*, and *Orpheus* (see Toni Bentley, *Costumes by Karinska* [Harry N. Abrams, Inc., 1995]).

Pippin Press: LK to Lynes, Aug. 20 (good boy), Oct. 27, Nov. 19, 1947, GW/BL; LK to

Whitney, Dec. 23, 1947, LK to Nelson, n.d. [1947], LK/DD; LK to Nelson, Dec. 30, 1947, NAR/RAC. As Lincoln's letters to Whitney and Nelson suggest, Pippin Press, by late 1947, was in serious financial trouble but later became successful.

5. Tchelitchev drawings: LK to Mongan, Feb. 3, 20, Mar. 3, Apr. 22, Nov. 4, 13, Mongan to LK, Feb. 6, March 1, April 15, Nov. 8, Mongan to Sachs, Feb. 5—all 1947, all LK/HUA (uncataloged as of May 5, 2003); LK to Lynes, Jan. 7, 1946, GW/BL; Tchelitchev to LK, July 14 (smiles), Aug. 24 (anemia), 1946, n.d. [1947], LK/DD; LK to Barr, Apr. 1, 1947, Barr/MoMA; LK to Soby, Feb. 25 (ballet drawings), 27, Mar. 3 (enclosing draft of LK's intro-duction), 12, 1947, June 23 (lack of public; earlier articles), 1950, Soby/MoMA. The book, *Tchelitchev's Drawings*, was published by H. Bittner & Co., with the reproductions done in collotype plates by the expert Harold Hugo of Meriden Gravure Co. Lincoln had " a horror" of his introduction sounding pretentious and he got Soby, Barr, and Agnes Mongan to read over his drafts. Even so he continued to feel that his essay was "too thick and pretentious" and ended up cutting out all historical references and confining himself to a discussion of the drawings themselves (LK to Mongan, Mar. 3, Apr. 22, 1947, LK/HUA, uncataloged as of Mar. 3, 2005). Nonetheless his essay got a mixed reception. The Harvard critic Harry Levin (a friend of both Lincoln's and Mina's) thought the introduction "one of the best pieces of critical writing that I have seen from your pen" (Levin to LK, Aug. 18, 1946, LK/DD). But as Lincoln wrote Alice Toklas (who was helping him get started on his incipient Elie Nadel-man project), "A lot of people do not like the Tchelitchev introduction" (LK to Toklas, Dec. 1, 1947, GSAT/BL). The grounds for complaint centered on the essay's abstract discus-sion of the nature of drawing, and its relative lack of comment on the specific Tchelitchev pieces in the book. Pavlik himself, however, did—unprecedentedly—like Lincoln's preface "very much" (Pavlik to LK, Sept. 12, 1947, LK/DD).

Yet another project Lincoln took on in this same period was Gian Carlo Menotti's revised version for Broadway of his two chamber operas, *The Medium* and *The Telephone*. Bal-let Society had originally performed *The Medium*, and it had proved such a success that Lin-coln was encouraged to proceed to Broadway, hoping the production would serve as a significant source of income for Ballet Society. Oliver Smith had originally designed *The Medium*, but Lincoln didn't like his production and a new one was installed. The double bill opened in April 1947. Though produced for a moderate fifteen thousand dollars (despite having fourteen stagehands), and though it got an excellent set of critical notices and had a decent run of more than 225 performances, it failed to make any money. Lincoln's original budget had been seven thousand dollars, and the additional costs "since I am alone in all this, is quite a sizeable blow" (LK to Virgil, Feb. 24, 1947, VT/YML). But in the fall of 1947 *The Medium* was due to go on the road, at least as far as Philadelphia and Boston, and Lincoln still hoped he'd earn some money from it (LK to Virgil, Oct. 8, 1946, Feb. 24 (Oliver Smith), Mar. 10, Oct. 23, 1947, VT/YML; LK to Ruth Page, Jan. 25, Mar. 16, 1947, LK to Fisher, Oct. 16, 1947, RP/DD; Pavlik to LK, Aug. 7, 1947, LK/DD; LK to Lynes, Feb. 29, Aug. 20, 1947, Sept. 11, GW/BL).

6. Balanchine and Tallchief to LK, April 17 (Paris; centuries), Balanchine to LK, May 9 (Chase), June 7 (critics; devote all time), 21—all 1947, all BSA; Balanchine to LK, n.d. [1947] (elaborate corporation), courtesy Barbara Horgan. In a letter to Stravinsky, Lincoln added more details about Balanchine's unhappiness: "He could never get to see Hirsch, the director of the National Theatres; he was forced to use students in the school for *Serenade*" (LK to Stravinsky, July 15, 1947, LK/DD). Mina to LK, Apr. 2 (disheartened; Balanchine), 11 (money; Toumanova), 14 (scores), 24, 1947, Mina to Rose, Mar. 2, 12, 19, 1947, MCP/SS. For *Ballets des Champs-Élysées:* Reynolds and McCormick, *Fixed*, 223–24; LK to Ruth Page, Mar. 12, LK to Ruth and Tom, Mar. 16, 1947, RP/DD. I've relied heavily on *Fixed* for back-ground on African Americans in dance (339–46) and for information on Cage and Cunning-ham (354–57).

Mina's book, *The Letters of Marcel Proust*, would be published in 1949. Her correspon-dence with the Harvard scholar Harry Levin about Proust (and other matters) is in MCP/SS. Mina had been forging a considerable career for herself over the past decade. From 1935–39 she'd worked with Orson Welles and John Houseman producing scripts for the Mercury Theater of the Air. During World War II she worked for the Office of War Information in

Washington for a time and also created a radio program featuring the letters soldiers sent back home; from that emerged a book, *Letters Home*, published in 1944. After the war she'd decided not to return to teaching at Smith, devoting herself to a career as a writer.

7. LK and Lucia Chase: LK to Virgil, Feb. 24, Mar. 10, Sept. 12 (Committee; Paris), 1947, VT/YML; LK to Page & Fisher, Dec. 15, 30 (unsuited), 1946, Jan. 25, Feb. 15 (chew), Mar. 16, 1947, LK/DD; LK to Lawrence, Aug. 20, 1946, LK to Latham, May 26 (service), 1947, LK to Chase, Nov. 7, 14, 1946, June 27 (*Divertimento*; Cuevas), Aug. 6, 1947, Aug. 2, 10, Oct. 15, Nov. 18, 1948, Chase to LK, Aug. 6, 1947—all ABTR/DD; Chase to Lincoln, Aug. 9, 1947, Nov. 22, 1948, LK/DD; Balanchine to LK, June 21 (*Divertimento*), 1947, BSA; Stravinsky to LK, July 18, 1947, Taras to LK, Sept. 14, 1947, LK to Amberg, Aug. 29, 1947 LK/DD; LK to Lynes, Aug. 20 (thin), 1947, plus n.d. [1947], GW/BL; Reynolds and McCormick, *Fixed*, 271–76, 286–87.

8. LK to Lynes, Aug. 20 (Hawkins), 1947, Nov. 19 (Mountbatten), GW/BL; LK to Thomson, Jan. 18 (lectures), Mar. 10, Sept. 12 (Hindemith), 1947 (Met), VT/YML; LK to Fisher, Oct. 16, 1947 (*Concertante*; pigs), RP/DD; Hawkins to George Kirstein, Apr. 16, GK to Hawkins, Apr. 16 (LK resources), 1948, LK/DD; LK, *Thirty Years*, 96 (LK on Baum). Lincoln gave a number of lectures during this period, including a whole series at Fordham; he always turned over his lecture fees to Ballet Society. A number of details about City Center, and especially organizational ones, are drawn from Morton Baum's lengthy unpublished history of the place (DD/NYPL *MGZMB 85–1040).

9. Kirstein to Stravinsky, May 20, July 22 (Pavlik), Oct 16, Dec. 16, Stravinsky telegram to LK, May 25, July 18, 1947, LK to Stravinsky, Jan. 4, Oct. 23, 28, 1948—all in typed "Excerpts From The Stravinsky-Kirstein Correspondence" (henceforth "Excerpts"), LK/DD, 97–402; Pavlik to LK, July 12, Aug. 7, 19, Sept. 3 (nonsense), 1947, LK/DD; Dorothea Tanning to LK, Sept. 26, 1946, Sept. 3, 10, 12, Oct. 31, 1947, BSA; Tanning to LK, Mar. 4, May 23, Aug. 18, 26, Dec. 10, n.d. [1948–1952], LK/DD; LK to Virgil, Oct. 23, 1947, VT/YML.

CHAPTER TWENTY-TWO: THE ART WORLD (1948)

1. McFadden and Martínez to LK, "July 6," n.d., McFadden to LK, n.d. [1948–49], plus program for the Ennis Studios ballet demonstration of Apr. 20, 1949, BSA; Yow to Cadmus, Dec. 13, 1946, January 31 (Pavlik), [1947], courtesy Anderson; multiple interviews with Jensen Yow (for Pippin Press & Melton, in particular, the interview of Apr. 12, 2003); LK to Joseph Verner Reed, Mar. 15 (Pippin), 1948, BSA; LK to John Coolidge, Nov. 7, 1957 [1947?], JC/Fogg.

   Elie Nadelman: LK to Lynes, n.d. (Wheeler), [1948], GW/BL; LK to Toklas, Sept. 4, 15, Nov. 1, Dec. 1, 1947, Jan. 4 (selfless; savage), 18 (Gallup), Feb. 1 (suicide), Mar. 28, June 3 (Van Vechten), GSAT/BL; LK to Dudley Easby, Sept. 15, 1947, Easby to LK, Oct. 21, 1947, LK to Wheeler, June 15, 1948, Wheeler to LK, July 14, 1948, Levin to LK, Nov. 4, 1948, Meyer Schapiro to LK, Aug. 24, 1948, Barr to LK, June 16 (discredited), Sept. 2 (thirties), Oct. 25 ($2,500), 1948, LK/DD; Bernard Berenson to LK, Jan. 18, "March 1948," Nov. 18, 30, Barr to LK, Jan. 27 (Amberg), 1948, LK to Barr, Aug. 29, 1947 (dazzled), Jan. 23 (desperate; Tchelitchev), plus one with n.d. [1948], Oct. 19, 1948, AB/AAA (MoMA); LK to Nelson, Feb. 16 (figurines), 1949, BSA; LK to Mongan, Feb. 3 (Barr), 1948, AM/HUA. Despite Meyer Schapiro's doubts about Nadelman, Lincoln was a great admirer; in 1949 in fact, he took Schapiro's "manuscript course" at Columbia, which "thrilled" him: "He goes on a bit, but one learns so much and this opens one's eyes to everything else."

   Though Nadelman had turned down the offer to exhibit at the Harvard Society for Contemporary Art, they succeeded in borrowing a marble from his fellow Pole, the cosmetician Helena Rubinstein, who'd bought out Nadelman's entire London show in 1911 (LK to Barr, n.d. [1948]), AB/AAA (MoMA). Among the large number of secondary sources on Nadelman, the standout is Barbara Haskell's *Elie Nadelman: Sculptor of Modern Life* (Harry N. Abrams, 2003), published on the occasion of the Whitney Museum's 2003 retrospective; Haskell gives Lincoln full credit for his "seminal importance" and "extreme sensitivity" (200) to Nadelman's work, but accurately points out that the uncovering of new information since LK's own *Elie Nadelman* (Eakins Press, 1973) has cast doubt on some of his facts and interpretations. Viola Nadelman's letters to LK in LK/DD make it abundantly clear that she relied on him for advice on everything from real estate to castings to income—and was hugely grateful to him: "I did not know . . . that there existed such kindness and such generous giving of self, as you have shown to me" (Viola Nadelman to LK, June 1, 1950, LK/DD). For the inner workings of MoMA during these years: Lynes, *Modern*, passim. Among the more important of LK's eight earlier articles on Nadelman is: "Elie Nadelman: Sculptor of the Dance," *Dance Index*, Nov. 6, 1948, and his exhibition catalog for the MoMA show of 1948; also useful is "Mr. Harper," article in *Harper's Magazine*, Apr. 1948, about a visit with LK to the Nadelman house.

2. LK, "The State of Modern Painting," *Harper's Magazine*, Oct. 1948; Braden to Nelson, Sept. 23, 1948, NAR/RAC; Mongan to LK, March 16, Nov. 13, 1948, Soby to LK, Dec. 12, 1948, LK to Carlos Chávez, Jan. 20, 1949, LK/DD; Sachs to LK, Nov. 8, LK to Sachs, Nov. 10, 1948, JC/Fogg; MacAgy to *Harper's*, Oct. 22, 1948; LK to Plaut, Mar. 8, 1948, LK to Mongan, Jan. 11, Feb. 3 (Schreyer), 1948, AM/Fogg; LK to Barr, Oct. 19, 23, 1948, AB/AAA (MoMA). For my discussion of LK's eclectic tastes I'm greatly indebted to Nicholas Jenkins's "comments on Duberman manuscript." Others who wrote approving letters to *Harper's* included Stravinsky, David Finley, Eugene Berman, and Bernard Berenson. One of Nelson Rockefeller's young associates, Tom Braden, reported that "Lincoln is not being vicious," though he felt the piece "slightly dishonest" since he'd criticized MoMA's permanent collection without specifically naming the artists he admired and felt should be included (Braden to Nelson, Sept. 23, 1948, NAR/RAC). Lincoln's current antagonism toward MoMA was also fed by the trustees' treatment of Richard McLanathan of the Boston Museum of Fine Arts. The highly qualified McLanathan was one of two finalists (and Lincoln's choice) in 1947–48 to head MoMA's department of painting and sculpture; but the trustees were so reluctant and dilatory about giving him sufficient power to "clean house," which Lincoln thought necessary, that McLanathan withdrew (McLanathan to LK, Nov. 25, Dec. 5, 19 [twice], 1947, Jan. 22, 1948, Jan. 2, Apr. 25, 1949, LK/DD).

   As difficult as Lincoln could sometimes be with Barr and MoMA, he leapt to their defense when Boston's Institute of Modern Art, which had been organized in 1938 as a branch of MoMA, decided to substitute "Contemporary" for "Modern" in its title, and in the process issued a manifesto that sharply attacked, among much else, MoMA's "sensationalism." Lincoln wrote a letter of ice-cold fury to James Plaut, director of the Boston Institute and a man Lincoln had known—and disliked—in the army, accusing him of "self-righteousness" and of making misguided charges in the manifesto that MoMA was somehow suffering from intellectual fatigue, or even corruption. And he specifically defended Barr, declaring that "the only people who are in a position" to attack him . . . are those in an equivalent position of background, proven work and intellectual rigor"—implying that he, Lincoln, was but Plaut wasn't. Still, Lincoln wrote Carlos Chávez (Jan. 20, 1949, LK/DD) that "I am no longer close to the activities of the Museum of Modern Art," where, in LK's view, he was considered "a traitor" for his *Harper's* article.

   The article had originally been written for a 1948 *Time-Life* round table on art, which LK had agreed to participate in (along with, among others, Kirk Askew, Clement Greenberg, Aldous Huxley, Raymond Mortimer, Meyer Schapiro, and Francis Henry Taylor). But Lincoln withdrew from the conference just days before it was due to start, belatedly deciding that the panel was overly "political"—which probably meant weighted against his views on abstract expressionism—included no working artist, and was insufficiently qualified ("Huxley is a well-known literary figure, but his distinction in the field of art is unrecorded"). In bowing out, Lincoln also cited the *Time-Life* tendency "to oversimplify for the sake of a preconceived formula . . . the great part of the *Time-Life* art stories . . . have that tone of patronage and tolerant amusement which . . . [is] one of the strongest factors for Philistine confusion in our whole artistic situation" (Brennan to LK, May 24, June 9, LK to Brennan, June 9, LK to Davenport, June 10, Davenport to LK, June 10—all 1948, all LK/DD).

   Lincoln devoted much of his inaugural *New Republic* (Mar. 28, 1949) column, "Public Mask and Private Sorrows," to a rather (for Lincoln) diplomatic critique of the Metropolitan Museum of Art, contrasting its policies and presentations unfavorably with those of the National Gallery in Washington, DC, and the Boston Museum, and concluding that "recent attacks against the Metropolitan are to the good." LK's review of Berenson's *History and Aesthetics in the Visual Arts* is in the *New Republic* issue of Jan. 10, 1949; comments on the piece: Mongan to LK, Mar. 25, Oct. 27, Berenson to LK, Nov. 30, LK to Mongan, Dec. 14, Berenson to LK, Jan. 28, 1949, LK/DD; LK to Mongan, Apr. 15 (tacky), May 3, 1949, AM/HUA. LK's other *New Republic* pieces are in the issues of Apr. 18 (Weber), May 23, Sept. 26, Dec. 12, 1949, Feb. 27, Dec. 11, 1950, Apr. 2, Sept. 10, Dec. 10, 1951. Hatch to LK, Jan. 25, Apr. 27 (blind alley), May 3, July 26 (sour), 1949, Goodrich to Straight, Apr. 18, LK to Goodrich, Apr. 25, Goodrich to LK, May 5, 1949, LK/DD.

3. Morton Baum's unpublished "history of city center," passim, DD/NYPL; Joan Peyser, *Bernstein* (Morrow, 1987), 153–54 (Thomson review). New York City did provide City Center with some indirect subsidies: it pegged the Center's yearly rental fee at only ten thousand dollars (it could have gotten sixty on the open market); it maintained upkeep on the building; and it installed at city expense both air-conditioning and a motion picture projection booth (John Marshall internal memo to Rockefeller Foundation staff, Feb. 2, 1949, NAR/RAC). Behind the scenes Lincoln also continued to work on behalf of a number of artists whose work he admired. He pressed Nelson Rockefeller, for example, to see Henry Koerner's one-man show at the Midtown Gallery and William Brice's at the Downtown; as well, he highly recommended that Nelson purchase Bernard Perlin's large tempera *The Garden* (LK to Nelson, Jan. 10, Feb. 16, 1949, NAR/RAC). Also, through his friendship with Agnes Mongan, he tried to get the Fogg Museum both to give Tchelitchev a one-man show and to accept Pavlik's preferred gift of some of his sketchbooks—but ran up against the Fogg's policy not to give shows to living artists (Mongan to LK, Jan. 17, 1949, LK to Mongan, Feb. 13, 16, 1949, AM/HUA). Most of Tchelitchev's twenty-six sketchbooks eventually went to Yale, not the Fogg (LK to Mongan, Apr. 15, 1949, AM/HUA).

4. LK to Lynes, Feb. 23 (free love; Woody), 1948, GW/BL; LK to Nelson, Jan. 29, Hawkins to Nelson, Mar. 3, 1948, NAR/RAC; Anatole Chujoy, *New York City Ballet*, Da Capo: 1982, 190–193 (Mar. 22 program); Nelson to LK, Mar. 2, June 3, 1948, LK/DD; de Mille to LK, Jan. 28, 1948 (*Far Harbour*), Hawkins to Sapiro, Feb. 19 ($750), 1948, LK/DD; Robert Craft, ed., *Stravinsky: Selected Correspondence*, LK to Stravinsky, Jan. 4 (*Far Harbour*), 1948, Knopf: 1982, vol. 1, 271; Marshall to LK, Jan. 23, 1948, NAR/RAC: Hawkins to Bouverie, Mar. 17, 1948, BSA; LK to Toklas, June 3 (lectures), 1948, GSAT/BL. Lincoln embarked on a second lecture tour in 1949; one of his engagements was at the Ringling Museum of Art in Sarasota, now headed by Chick Austin (Hawkins to Hines, Mar. 1, 1949, LK to Austin, Apr. 12, 1949, LK/DD; Mongan to LK, Apr. 21, 1949, AM/HUA; LK to Andrew Wyeth, Apr. 27, 1949 [contents of lectures], courtesy Wyeth).

5. Taper, *Balanchine*, 219–25; Chujoy, *Ballet*, 194–201; Gottlieb, *Balanchine*, 112–13; LK, *Thirty Years*, 99–103; LK to Stravinsky, Apr. 29, Stravinsky to LK, Oct. 23, 1948 (Craft, *Stravinsky*, vol. 1, 271–72); LK to Baum, May 3, 1948, Wescott to LK, Aug. 12, 1948 (ruinously), LK/DD; LK to Baum, May 8, 1948, Hawkins to Baum, n.d. [1948], July 1, 1948 (Abbott), MB/DD; LK to Wescott, May 29, 1948, GW/BL; LK to Nelson, May 30 (Thomson), June 4, 11 (Marshall), memo to Nelson, Oct. 5, 1948, NAR/RAC; Hawkins to McDonald, July 15/n.d. (San Francisco), LK to Marshall, Sept. 13 (Moe), Marshall to LK, Sept. 16 (trustees), 1948, LK to Nelson, Oct. 29, 1948, BSA; Hawkins to Fisher, Oct. 21 (inheritance), 1948, RP/DD. The Argentine literary figure Maria Rosa Oliver, who'd become one of LK's most trusted friends, expressed her pleasure at the success of *Orpheus* but wrote him that although she admired Stravinsky the artist, she "dislike[d him] as a man. I know he is intelligent and witty, but he is mean" (Oliver to LK, Aug. 11, 1949, LK/DD). De Cuevas had at one point offered the International Theatre in Columbus Circle, on which he'd taken a six-year lease, free of charge to Lincoln and Balanchine for whatever purposes they wished—but had then returned to Europe without mentioning the matter again (LK to Nelson, Apr. 4, May 30, 1948, NAR/RAC; *New York Times*, June 3, 1948).

6. *Newsweek*, Oct. 25, 1948; LK to Chase, Oct. 15, 1948, ABTR/DD; LK to Nelson, Oct. 29 (SAB), Nov. 5 (Marshall), Nelson to LK, Nov. 3 (twice), Baum internal memo, Nov. 4, 1948, NAR/RAC; Baum to LK, Nov. 23 (future), 1948, MB/DD; Fisher to LK, Nov. 1, 1948, RP/DD; LK to Chase, Nov. 18, 24, Chase to LK, Nov. 22, 1948, LC/DD; Edith Sitwell to LK, Sept. 15, 1948, Mar. 5, Apr. 7, 1949, Osbert Sitwell to LK, May 8, July 30, 1949, Horner

to LK, Dec. 6, 20, 1948, Gallup to LK, Nov. 28 (Pavlik/Edith), 1949, LK/DD. For the Sitwell tour and David Horner: LK to Mongan, Dec. 14, 1948, LK/DD; Philip Ziegler, *Osbert Sitwell* (Knopf, 2000); Charles Henri Ford, *Water from a Bucket: A Diary, 1948–1957* (henceforth Ford, *Bucket*); Turtle Point Press, 2001, 16–21 (Sitwells).

7. Hawkins to Nelson, Nov. 30, 1948, LK to Nelson, Jan. 10 (rehearsals), Aug. 24 (Hawkins), Balanchine to Nelson, Feb. 14, 1949, NAR/RAC; Hawkins to Rose Kirstein, Dec. 7, 1948, LK to Chávez, Jan. 20, 1949 (overwhelming; aged), Hawkins to Baum, Mar. 15 (Cage; $600), 1949, LK to Austin, Apr. 12 (hard up), 1949, Mar. 15, 1949, Hawkins to LK, Oct. 15 (cancer), 1951, LK/DD; Baum, unpublished history, passim, DD/NYPL; Balanchine-signed form letter, Feb. 16, 1949, contains the Baum letter (original not located); LK to Markevitch, Apr. 26, 1949, Hawkins to Chandler Cowles, Feb. 10, Hawkins to Bouverie, Feb. 21, Balanchine to Marshall, Feb. 10, 1949, BSA; LK to Marshall, Mar. 18, Apr. 5, 26, Marshall to LK, Mar. 29, Apr. 18, Balanchine to Nelson, Feb. 14, Boyer to Balanchine, Feb. 17, Baum to Nelson, Apr. 22 (new ballets), Jones to Packard, May 6, Packard to Nelson, May 10—all 1949, all NAR/RAC. *The Classic Ballet: Basic Technique and Terminology* (Knopf, 1952) detailed the system of positions, movements, and techniques practiced at SAB; Carlus Dyer designed the short book, and Muriel Stuart was the primary author; both Balanchine and Lincoln wrote brief introductory notes to it. Lincoln glancingly acknowledged David Vaughan, but his role in writing the book was in fact considerable (Interview with David Vaughan, Aug. 3, 2005; Lynn Garafola, "Dollars for Dance," *Dance Chronicle* 25(1), n. 103).

8. Deborah Jowitt, *Jerome Robbins: His Life, His Theater, His Dance* (henceforth Jowitt, *Robbins*); Simon & Schuster, 2004, 143–53; Amanda Vaill, *Somewhere: The Life of Jerome Robbins* (henceforth Vaill, *Robbins*), Broadway Books, 2006; Chujoy, *Ballet*, 212–19; Michael Kidd telegram to LK, Jan. 20, 1949, LK/DD; LK to Barr, Oct. 19 (anxiety), 1948, AB/AAA (MoMA); LK to Robbins, Sept. 6, 1951, courtesy Jerome Robbins Rights Trust (JRRT). LK and Blitzstein had a minor financial disagreement over the cost of orchestrating Blitzstein's score for *The Guests*, but it didn't permanently damage the friendship (Blitzstein to LK, June 24, Cage to Blitzstein, July 6, LK to Blitzstein, Aug. 29, 1949, BSA).

Illness: LK to "Dear Ones," May 10 (Fidelma), LK to Cadmus, July 31, 1949, LK to "Kidsies," n.d. (ballet) [1949], courtesy Anderson; LK to Nelson, June 24 (enforced; crab), Nelson to LK, Aug. 18, 1949, NAR/RAC; Pavlik to LK, June 26, Maria Rosa Oliver to LK, July 16, 1949, Lincoln to Moore, June 23, July 11, Moore to LK, July 3 (exhibit), LK to Beaton, July 27, 1949, Forster to LK, July 16, 1949 (very ill), LK/DD; Mina to LK, n.d. [1949–50?], MCP/SS; LK to Blitzstein, June 23 (Fidelma), 1949, BSA; Garnett to Mina, March 16, 1950, T/S/Berg; Oliver to LK, Aug. 11, 1949, LK/DD; LK to Soby, Aug. 16 (Nadelman), 1949, JS/AAA (MoMA); Burns to Mina, Dec. 25, 1949, MCP/SS; LK to "Dear Ones," Aug. 22 (Naushon), 1949, courtesy Anderson; Oliver to LK, Sept. 6 (the "boys"), Mabry to LK, Nov. 30 (marriage), 1949, LK/DD; LK to Buckle, Mar. 12 (angel), 1950, RB/UT. The ever-ungenerous Pavlik Tchelitchev, on his part, wrote his dear—when he wasn't denouncing her—friend Edith Sitwell, that "Linc is not in his right mind. . . . He says things that have no reality"—though surely Pavlik wasn't thinking of Lincoln's constantly reiterated claim that he, Pavlik, was the most consequential contemporary painter (Pavlik to Sitwell, Sept. 3, 1949, Aug. 20, 28, 1950, T/S/Berg). Lincoln's early lover, Tom Mabry, who had also married, had a different take on their somewhat comparable situations: "We pay much for being married. . . . I think the responsibility of Fidelma has been more than anyone can ever imagine. That in your opinion you have not properly fulfilled it is neither here nor there. The weight of it is there. The need for air is there" (Mabry to LK, Nov. 30, 1949, LK/DD).

CHAPTER TWENTY-THREE: CITY CENTER (1948–1950)

1. Politics: LK to Mongan, May 3, 1949 (shrieked), AM/HUA; Mina to Garnett, Mar. 10, 1947, MCP/SS; GK to Mina (with a copy to LK), Sept. 19, 1949 (Hiss), LK/DD; LK to "Dear Ones," Aug. 22, 1949, courtesy Anderson. The following year Lincoln unambiguously wrote Maria Rosa Oliver that in regard to Hiss, "my brother is convinced [he] is entirely innocent"; in a second letter referring to politics, he wrote her, "I must say the situation is awfully grim,

but somehow I keep a curious basis of stubborn optimism" (LK to Maria Rosa Oliver, June 2 [Hiss], Aug. 31 [optimism], 1950, MRO/PU). For background on the period, see Marty Jezer, *The Dark Ages: Life in the United States 1945–1960* (South End Press, 1982), esp. 259–74.

Buckle's letters to LK are in LK/DD; LK's to Buckle are at the Ransom Center of the University of Texas (RB/UT) at Austin (uncataloged as of 2005). Their extensive correspondence, running more than thirty years (1949–81), is far too large to list by individual items; but in the case of a direct quote from the correspondence, the given letter *will* be cited: LK to Buckle, Sept. 10, Oct. 10 (Fonteyn; Ashton; Balanchine's "genius"), 13 (Helpmann; Somes; LK party); 21 (Lambert, Ashton, Balanchine, Helpmann; "twenty years," "sad," "popular interest"), Nov. 6 *(Illuminations)*, 1949, Mar. 12, (ANYBODY), 18 "cruising into intimacy," 1950, RB/UT. Buckle to LK, Sept. 26 (de Valois; Webster), 1949, LK/DD; A few snippets from the correspondence appear in Buckle's *The Adventures of a Ballet Critic* (henceforth Buckle, *Critic*); Cresset Press, 1953, as part of the chapter "A Pen-Friend" (166–89), in which Buckle writes, with some inaccuracy and acidity, about the friendship. Lincoln had refused to give permission for broader quotation from the correspondence; he'd repeatedly warned Buckle to "remember, I adjure you, that this correspondence is between US, alone" (LK to Buckle, Oct. 13, 29 [Robbins; Webster], Dec. 2 [Karinska], 1949, RB/UT).

2. 1949 NYCB seasons: Baum, unpublished "history," DD/NYPL; Chujoy, *Ballet*, 220–29; Robins, *Hurok* (Penguin, 1994); Toni Bentley, *Karinska* (Harry N. Abrams, 1995); Christensen to LK, May 24, 1949, LK to Stravinsky, Nov. 28 (Tallchief), Dec. 2 *(Firebird;* Feb. season), Stravinsky to LK, Dec. 2 *(Jinx; Firebird)*, 1949, Pavlik to Cage, Mar. 9, 1950, "New York City Ballet Program: Fall Season 1949," LK/DD; LK to "Dear Ones," Aug. 22, 1949, courtesy Anderson; LK to Buckle, Sept. 10 (sports), Dec. 2 (ten new ballets; de Valois), 1949, RB/UT; Pavlik to Edith Sitwell, Feb. 28, 1950, PT/ES, Berg; LK to Thomson, Sept. 28, 1949, VT/YML; LK to Nelson, Nov. 17 (advance), 1949, NR/RAC.

3. Feb. 1950 season: Stravinsky telegram to LK, Dec. 23, 1949, LK to Alice Bouverie, Dec. 19, 1949, LK/DD; LK to Nelson, Feb. 21 (advance), 1950, NR/RAC; Jowitt, *Robbins*, 169–71; Chujoy, *NYCB*, 237–45; "A Conversation with Lincoln Kirstein," *W. H. Auden Society Newsletter* 7, Oct. 1991 (Auden hated); multiple interviews with Ed Bigelow, 2003–6; LK to Buckle, Jan. 17 (Balanchine; *Jones Beach*), 27 *(Anxiety; Jones Beach)*, Feb. 3 (awe), 16 (sensational), 21 (remarkable; Magallanes), Buckle to LK, Feb. 17 (success), 1950, RB/UT; LK to Robert Chapman, Mar. 12 (hated; Irish), 1950, RC/DD (uncataloged as of 2005).

For Lincoln's two-part article and its aftermath: LK, "Balanchine and American Ballet," *Ballet* (May–June 1950); LK to Cage, Apr. 1 (English dancing), 1950, LK/DD. As examples of the respect and appreciation many members of the company felt for Lincoln, see the taped interviews at NYPL/DD with, among others, Marlene Mesavage DeSavino, Joysanne Sidimus, Muriel Stuart, Jillana, Ruth Gilbert, Phyllis Manchester, and Lynn Stetson; and my own interviews with, among others, Ed Bigelow, Nancy Lassalle, Violette Verdy, Paul Taylor, Vida Brown. As Ruth Gilbert put it in her interview: "Lincoln Kirstein was a humble man. He stayed in the background."

4. London 1950: LK, *Thirty*, 113 (alien); Chujoy, *NYCB*, 246–64; LK to Van Vechten, March 20, 1950, VV/Yale; LK to Buckle, Feb. 3 (odd), Mar. 20 (warning), Apr. 20 (grunts), May 10 (Pavlik), May 31/June 5 (dancers angry), RB/UT; LK to Cage, Apr. 1 (chaos; lunatic), LK to Baum (Webster), Mar. 28, Apr. 8 (terms; Hurok, 1950, Auden to LK, Aug. 30, 1950, LK/DD; LK to Maria Rosa Oliver, June 2 (Forster), 1950, MRO/PU; Forster to Margaret French, Mar. 27, 1950, courtesy Anderson. Buckle's response to LK's warning letter, along with some of the details of the March–April visit, are in RB's unpublished manuscript, "The History of a Friendship" (henceforth RB/HF/UT), which is part of his collected papers at the University of Texas. Harold Nicolson, in a May 30, 1950, letter to LK (LK/DD), confirmed that David Webster "has a reputation of being a most cantankerous fellow." The April Waldorf ball: Hawkins to Jones, Mar. 23, Goeller to Nelson R., Mar. 27, 1950, NR/RAC; LK to Buckle, Apr. 20 (poor), May 1, 1950, RB/UT.

5. LK to Buckle, Apr. 20 (share house), 31 (twenty guineas), May 16–17 (Institute), Buckle to "Dearest of Jeep-Drivers," n.d. (house), 1950, RB/UT; phone interview with Perez Zagorin

(Sharrer's husband), 2005; LK to Betsy and Andrew Wyeth, July 24, Aug. 17, 1950, courtesy Andrew and Betsy Wyeth.

On the reception of Symbolic Realism: Ewan Phillips to LK, May 8 (institute), 1950, LK/DD; *Time*, Aug. 21 (*Observer* quote), 1950; Gorer's article is in *The Listener*, Aug. 3, Lincoln's reply, Aug. 24, 1950; Auden to LK, Aug. 12, 1950, LK/DD; Rothenstein to LK, July 21 (Tate), 1950, BSA. Alton Pickens, a fellow artist in the show, hardly shared Gorer's high opinion of Cadmus: "I find the moralizing [in *Sloth* and *Envy*] pompous," Pickens wrote Lincoln, "and also a feeble justification for, in reality, saying—'but it [is] too terrible that we are all human—and with bodies too' " (Pickens to LK, Sept. 22, 1950, LK/DD). In something of a double exaggeration, Lincoln wrote Nelson Rockefeller (who'd lent two paintings to the show) that it had been "ferociously received by the Press, and enthusiastically by the public" (LK to Nelson, Aug. 30, 1950, NR/RAC). Lincoln did come to know Pickens personally, and before that, had a considerable correspondence with him about art; LK's side of it, some dozen letters, is in Pickens, AAA/Smithsonian.

Covent Garden: LK to Buckle, May 25 (program), June 5 (Sodome), Buckle to LK, "Sunday," n.d. (mistake), Sept. 1 (tour), 1950, RB/UT; Baum, "history," DD/NYPL; LK to Cadmus, July 3 (Freud), Aug. 31 (Forster; EXHAUST), 1950, courtesy Anderson; Chujoy, *NYCB*, 253–64 (reviews; *The Witch*); LK, *Thirty*, 113–16; Buckle, *Adventures*, 179–89 (move to hotel, and so on); Buckle, HF/RB/UT; T. S. Eliot to LK, July 19, 1950, BC/NYPL; LK to Stravinsky, Aug. 23 (provincialism; tour), 1950, LK/DD; LK to Rothermere, July 24, 1950, BSA; Cage to LK, Aug. 30 (tour), 1950, LK/DD; Cage to Baum, Aug. 19, Sept. 2 (tour), 1950, LK memo accompanying Cage to Baum, Sept. 2 (paratrooper), 1950, MB/DD. A young balletomane, Clive Barnes, later the *New York Times* dance critic, also wrote Lincoln a complimentary letter (July 19, 1950, LK/DD) to say he'd been "lucky enough" to be present during his address to the London Ballet Circle, and found it "wonderful to hear someone stand up and declare their belief in the dance."

Fidelma's cards and letters to her brother (courtesy Jon Anderson) are almost never dated and rarely show postmarks; sometimes the contents of a given letter (or the rare postmark) will reveal the date, but since this material is, at the same time, privately held, I won't attempt individual citations.

Ashton: LK to Stravinsky, Aug. 23 (Harewood; Eliot; Ashton "livid"; press), 1950, LK/DD; LK to Buckle, May 1, 10 (Ninette), 16, Buckle to "Jeep," n.d., "Sunday (buffeted)," n.d., Sept. 20 (prediction), 1950, RB/UT; Cranko to LK, Oct. 30, 1950, BSA; Sadler's Wells manager to LK, May 23 (Cranko), LK to Osbert, Aug. 1 (Forster), 1950, LK/DD; Ashton to LK, May 1, n.d. plus 4 n.d. [1950], LK/DD; in one of these earlier letters (n.d.), Ashton had written of Fidelma, "I love her real sympathy, real understanding . . . real goodness." LK's letter to the *Times* is reproduced in Chujoy, *NYCB*, 256–57. LK's worsening depression and behavior: LK to Osbert Sitwell, Aug. 1 (novels), 18 (Aberconway; Freud; Forster; charwoman), LK to Harewood, Aug. 19, LK to Forster, Aug. 19, 1950, LK/DD.

CHAPTER TWENTY-FOUR: A HOME (1951–1952)

1. Fire Island: LK to "Dear Ones," Aug. 31 (bright), Sept. 22, 1950, courtesy Anderson; LK to Cage, Aug. 25 (untamed), 1950, LK/DD; Auden to LK, Aug. 27, 1950, BC/NYPL; LK to Buckle, Oct. 20 (cats), 1950, RB/UT; Fidelma to Paul, n.d., Lincoln to Paul, Sept. 14, 22 (Buster), courtesy Anderson.

2. LK to the Stravinsky, Aug. 23, Sept. 22, Stravinsky to LK, Aug. 25, Sept. 16, 1950, LK/DD; LK to Maria Rosa Oliver, Aug. 31/Sept. 24 (Teatro), Oliver to LK, Oct. 4, 1950, MRO/PU; LK to Rothenstein, Aug. 26, Rothenstein to LK, Sept. 7, 1950, BSA; LK to Edith Sitwell, Aug. 27, Sitwell to LK, Aug. 30, 1950, LK/DD; LK to Nelson, Oct. 21 (Colón), 1950, NR/RAC; LK to Buckle, Nov. 9 (*Macbeth*), 1950, RB/UT; LK to Maria Rosa Oliver, Nov. 11 (Sitwells), 1950, MRO/PU; LK to "Dear Ones," n.d. (re-avert), courtesy Anderson.

3. LK to Cage, Sept. 1, 1950, LK/DD; Baum, "history," DD/NYPL; LK to Buckle, Sept. 15, Oct. 20 (finished), Buckle to LK, Sept. 20, 1950, RB/UT; LK to Stravinsky, Sept. 22, Stravinsky to LK, Sept. 26, 1950, LK to Osbert Sitwell, Aug. 18 (Bliss), 1950, LK/DD; LK to John

Marshall, Oct. 31 (no season), 1950, NR/RAC; LK to Buckle, Nov. 30/Dec. 2 season, 1950, RB/UT.

4. NYC Ballet, Feb.–June 1951 New York season, plus Chicago: LK to Buckle, Feb. 3 (*La Valse;* Kaye), 1950, Jan. 10, Feb. 25 (displacing), 28 (Tudor; snake), Mar. 13 (profit; Kaye/Robbins), 22 (*cabrioles*), Apr. 5 (painting), Apr. 10, May 11 (Chicago), June 6 (butt), July 7 (*Cage*), 10 (Hurok), Aug. 1, 3 (Leonidoff), 1951, RB/UT; LK to Blevins Davis, Feb. 6 (Chase), LK/DD; LK to Nelson, Mar. 12 (gross), 1951, NR/RAC; LK to "Dear Ones" (Cadmus and others), Nov. 5 (Bolender), 1950, Feb. 26, 1951, LK to Cadmus, Feb. 4 (Kaye), 1951, courtesy Anderson; Jowitt, *Robbins*, 187–90 (*Cage*); Chujoy, *NYC Ballet*, 287–92 (June season), LK, *Thirty*, 118–19 (tour), Baum, unpublished "history," NYPL/DD; Cage to Leonidoff, July 26, 1951, BSA; Janet Reed and Todd Bolender danced the leads in *Jeu de Cartes;* though Lincoln admired the performances of both artists, on a personal level he developed considerable distaste for Bolender, finding him "quite hysterical . . . when it comes down to anything definite, he is never there" (LK to "Dear Ones," Nov. 5, 1950, courtesy Anderson).

5. *The Classic Ballet:* interview with David Vaughan, Aug. 3, 2005; Vaughan to LK, Mar. 4, 1952, courtesy Vaughan; LK to Buckle, July 19, 1951, Mar. 1 (press), 1952, RB/UT; LK to Cage, Aug. 25, Sept. 1, LK to Osbert Sitwell, Aug. 18, LK to Forster, Aug. 19, LK to Edith Sitwell, Aug. 27—all 1950, all LK/DD; Vaughan to LK, Mar. 4, 1952, LK/DD; LK to Marshall, Aug. 31, 1950, NR/RAC. Referring to Lincoln's introduction to *The Classic Ballet*, his friend, the poet Marianne Moore, wrote him that she "never could have imagined that discussion of a subject could so personify it" (Moore's letters to LK are in LK/DD).

6. LK to Buckle, Sept. 8 (advance), Nov. 21, Dec. 2, 1951, RB/UT; LK to Cadmus, Dec. 10 (Piper), 31, 1950, Sept. 11 (Bolender), Dec. 2, 1951, courtesy Anderson; Chujoy, *NYCB*, 299–317; LK, *Thirty*, 121–24; Baum, unpublished "history," MB/DD.

7. Nineteenth Street house: LK to Cadmus, Dec. 1951, courtesy Anderson; LK to Buckle, March 1, Apr. 4, 1952, Buckle, unpublished ms., "History of a Friendship," RB/UT; LK to Chapman, May 9, 14, 21, 1952, Chapman correspondence (henceforth RC/DD); LK to Wheeler, Oct. 20, 1052, GW/BL; LK to Cadmus, May 28, June 24, 27, Aug. 6, courtesy Anderson; LK to Pavlik, Aug. 10, 1952, BT/BL.

Jensen Yow: LK to Buckle, Feb. 3, May 11 (south'n sweet), 1951, RB/UT; Yow to LK, Feb. 27, "July 28" [1951?], one n.d., LK/DD; LK to Cadmus, one undated [Nov. 1950?] (temperament/*Jealousy*), Dec. 31 (incorporated; mother type), 1950, Jan. 3 (angle; Nadelman; kind), 13 (Nadelman), 17 (Wescott), 19 (dewlaps), 27 (Pavlik), 31, Feb. 26 (Lynes), Aug. 9, 17, 30 (Mina), Sept. 11/17 (Weslow), Dec. 2, 10—all 1951, all courtesy Anderson; LK to Yow, Jan. 11, 17, 26, Feb. 7, 13, Apr. 6, May 4, July 4, 24, 30, 31 (likeness), Aug. 6, Lynes to Cadmus, Sept. 14 (Weslow)—all 1951, all courtesy Yow (who has now deposited his LK correspondence with DD/NYPL, as well as LK's letters to Bob Chapman, both uncataloged as of 2005).

Pavlik: Edith Sitwell to LK, Dec. 27, 1949, Jan. 14, Feb. 6, May 24 (genius), 1950, LK to Sitwell, Aug. 27, 1950, Pavlik to Lincoln and Fidelma, Dec. 18, 1950, LK/DD; Pavlik to Edith Sitwell, May 16, Aug. 20 (Balanchine), 1950, T/S/Berg; LK to Soby, JS/AAA/MoMA; LK to Buckle, Oct. 20, Nov. 9 (magnificent), 1950, RB/UT; LK to Cadmus, Nov. 27, 1950, Jan. 13, 27, 31, 1951, courtesy Anderson; LK to Oliver, Jan. 23, 1951, MRO/PU; LK to Chapman, Mar. 25 (Levin), 1952, RC/DD. Pavlik did at least have the grace, after he was feeling better, to apologize to Lincoln and Fidelma for being "a thankless pig . . . I still feel that we have been now for more than 15 years *going together somewhere.*"

8. Halasz: LK to Newbold Morris, Jan. 16, 24, LK to Center Board, Jan. 23, Morris to LK, Jan. 18, 1952, BSA; LK to John Marshall, Feb. 4, 1952, NR/RAC. Halasz took the matter to court, where he won a small monetary settlement. *Amahl* was a success, even though LK felt it was "hurriedly directed, over-set and under-considered" (LK to Chapman, n.d. [spring, 1952], RC/DD). Feb/March 1952 season: Baum, unpublished "history," MB/DD; Jowitt, *Robbins*, 208–10 (*Ballade*); attendance and financial figures are from a document in BSA; telegram LK to Ashton, Feb. 1, 1952, BSA; LK to Cage and Balanchine, July 24 (*Bayou*), 1952, LK/DD; LK to Chapman, Jan. 24 (Tudor), Feb. 8 (*Ballade*), 23 (Ashton), Mar. 18, 1952, RC/DD; LK to Buckle, Feb. 23 (d'Amboise; *Caracole*), Mar. 1 (Ashton; Tudor), 9 (Robbins), 1952, RB/UT; LK to Baum, Mar. 18 (*Gloire*), MB/DD. Rose Kirstein: George to Mina, Sept. 19, 1949, Mina to LK, Sept. 2, 1950, LK/DD.

9. 1952 European tour: LK, *Thirty*, 125 (depoliticized); Jowitt, *Robbins*, 213–31; Chujoy, *NYCB*, 334–63; Baum, unpublished "history," MB/DD; *New York Tribune*, May 21, 1952 (Morris); LK to Cadmus, Dec. 10 (heartless), 1951, courtesy Anderson; LK to Baum, May 15 (Betty), Cage to Baum, Apr. 17 (Webster), n.d. (idiot), May 8 (Balanchine/Barcelona), July 8 (Hurok), Cage to LK, "Good Friday," May 11 (Leonidoff)—all 1952, all MB/DD; Wescott to LK, May 12 (Paris), LK to Wescott, July 15 (London), 1952, GW/BL; LK to Webster, May 8, Balanchine to Boris, June 16, telegram, June 14, Boris to Balanchine, June 19, Boris to Cage, June 20, BSA; Cage to Baum, May 25 (Webster/Florence), July 1 (Hurok), Cage to LK, n.d. (one), May 11 (complaints/Paris), 17 (Florence), 20 (Baum), June 2 (Balanchine), 12 (School)/Baum/Paris), 29 (The Hague/Paris/Kaye/Robbins), July 8, 9 (Cage), 11 (London), 15 (Kaye), 18, 22, 26 (Franklin), 28 (Kaye/Robbins/Hayden), 31 (Hayden), Aug. 2, 9 (Leonidoff), 25, Chujoy to LK, June 18, July 4, 9 (London/programs), 22, 31 (Kaye/Hayden/de Valois/Rambert), telegram July 8, LK to Cage, Apr. 26, May 19 (Webster/praise), 21 (gang), 27, 28, June 17 (praise), July 16, 23 (Robbins)/Franklin, 24 (Robbins), 28 (managing director/Kaye), Aug. 3 (Robbins/Kaye), 18, 20 (Robbins), Balanchine to LK, n.d. (angry), LK to Balanchine, July 30, Aug. 10 *(Revenge)*, Robbins to Cage, July 18 (Kaye) Balanchine to LK, Aug. 4, LK to Britten, Sept. 9—all 1952, all LK/DD; LK to Buckle, May 18, June 27 (Kaye), 1952, RB/UT; LK to Robbins, Sept. 6, 1951, Jerome Robbins Trust (JRRT).

10. Rose's death: the many letters of condolence are in LK/DD; LK to Pavlik, Aug. 10 (clear; upset), 1952, PT/BL; Mina to LK, Nov. 27 (frightfully), 1952, LK to Balanchine, July 30, 1952, LK/DD; LK to Oliver, Feb. 12 (Fidelma; advance guard), 1952, MRO/PU; Mina's unpublished "Slices of Life" (gallantry), MCP/SS.

Muriel's death: *New York Herald Tribune*, Aug. 27, 1952; LK to Pavlik, Sept. 1 (wildly), 30, 1952, PT/BL; LK to Oliver, June 2, 1950 (obsessed), MRO/PU; LK to Cadmus, Aug. 10, 1952, courtesy Anderson; LK to Wakehurst, Sept. 29, 1952 (Lincoln), LK/DD; Amster et al. to LK, Jan. 17, 1952, Paul Draper to LK (2) n.d. [Sept. 1952], MD/BL; LK to CVV, May 11, 1963, VV/BL, courtesy Olive Fisher.

CHAPTER TWENTY-FIVE: MANAGING DIRECTOR (1953–1954)

1. The primary source materials that inform my analysis of LK's tenure as managing director of City Center are too voluminous to cite in any detailed, comprehensive way. The bulk of the relevant material is in BAS, LK/DD, and NAR/RAC; some of the information also derives from scattered collections in other depositories or in private hands, as well as from several interviews, especially those with Jensen Yow, George Tooker, and Ed Bigelow. Wherever the text contains an actual quotation, I *do*, however, cite the source; in this first paragraph, for example, the John Marshall quote is from an interoffice memo of Aug. 5, 1952, NAR/RAC.

2. LK to Britten, Sept. 9, 1952, LK memo, Oct. 7, 1952 to Center board, LK/DD. In its article on LK's appointment, the *New York Times* (Oct. 2, 1952) had also announced that he would "coordinate adjuncts of the Center"—that is, the opera, ballet, and drama divisions. LK to Cadmus, Oct. 28, 1952, courtesy Anderson; Moore to LK, Feb. 16, 1953, BSA; LK to "Dear Kids" (the Wyeths), Oct. 15, 1953, courtesy Andrew and Betsy Wyeth; LK to Fahs, Nov. 14 (shaky), 1952, NAR/RAC; Theatre: LK to Wheeler, Oct. 26, 1952, GW/YL; LK to Buckle, Jan. 2, 1953, RB/UT; LK to Pavlik, Mar. 24, 1953, PT/BL.

3. A few weeks after canceling the drama season, the trustees also suspended plans for a film festival at City Center (LK to d'Harnoncourt, Dec. 2, 1952, LK/DD). The ballet's cash position wasn't strong enough for Lincoln to give the go-ahead to Agnes de Mille for the planned production of her *Rib of Eve*—or at least so he claimed: When writing to her to cancel, he expressed "severe disappointment," but he expressed quite different sentiments to Dickie Buckle: "I had to cancel de Mille's RIB OF EVE, which hurt not at all; her HARVEST ACCORDING for Ballet Theatre was a big meretricious bore." Lincoln did, however, think de Mille's autobiography, *Dance to the Piper*, had "great charm" and he gave the book a generous blurb (LK to de Mille, Nov. 14, 23, 1952, ADM/DD; LK to Buckle, Nov. 15, 1952, RB/UT).

The critic Edwin Denby, whom Lincoln greatly respected, at first disliked *Scotch Sym-*

phony, but later developed a more favorable view. Lincoln characterized *Metamorphoses* as a "sort of mellow-world Balanchine, wildly symphonic like a visual gamelan-orchestra" (LK to Buckle, Nov. 22, 1952, RB/UT). To Pavlik, who had always had mixed feelings about Balanchine, Lincoln expressed agreement that the choreographer lacked "visual imagination. He has a musical imagination . . . color is uninteresting to him, and he would prefer to have as little décor as possible. . . . Hence, our success is attributive entirely to the *dance* elements in theatrical-dance" (LK to Pavlik, PT/BL). Virgil Thomson went beyond Pavlik in his criticism of Balanchine: His "musical tastes are even less courageous [compared to Diaghilev], being pretty strictly confined to Stravinsky and his diminishing circle. . . . I just don't think that the ballet as an esthetic spectacle has shown a rising curve in 35 years" (VT to LK, Jan. 26, 1950, VT/YML).

4. LK to Buckle, Jan. 8 (Tanny), 1953, RB/UT; LK to Morris, Mar. 30, 1953, BSA; Baum, unpublished "history" (accusations against LK), MB/DD; LK to Morris, Mar. 30, 31, 1953, BSA; LK to Buckle, Jan. 2 (Napoleon), 1953, RC/UT. For a sample of the venomous feelings between Lincoln and Rosenstock, see LK to Rosenstock, Mar. 27, 1953, BSA. For a sample of the Baum/LK hostility, see LK to Baum, Apr. 14, 1953, LK/DD.

5. Multiple interviews with Jensen Yow; LK to Cadmus, Oct. 5 (lovely), 1952, courtesy Anderson; interview with Yow (overwhelmed); Leo Lerman to Gray Foy, Nov. 12 ("worshipped"), 1952; LK to Wyeth, Dec. 28, 1953, courtesy Andrew and Betsy Wyeth. Fidelma to Paul, a number of undated letters (the internal references place them around 1953), courtesy Anderson.

6. LK to Pavlik, June 1 (stupid/star), 1953, PT/BL; Jowitt, *Robbins,* 228 (critics). Lincoln apparently had another of his "nervous difficulties" in late March–early April, but bounced back more quickly than usual (Mina to Lincoln, "Easter Sunday," 1953; LK to Pavlik, Aug. 3, 1953, PT/BL; May 15 press release canceling *Fanfare,* LK/DD; LK to Baum, May 14, 20, 1953, LK/DD; Baum, unpublished "history," MB/NYPL.

7. LK memo to Newbold Morris, May 14 (notification), 1953, BSA. The key documents regarding Lincoln's role in getting the grant and the foundation's internal process regarding it are: John Marshall's memos, Apr. 2, 15, May 14, LK to Nelson Rockefeller, May 27, LK to Boyer, June 2 (LK's gifts to Center)—all 1953; LK to Rosenstock (designer/*Show Boat*), Feb. 15, 1954, NAR/RAC. Similarly Lincoln "urged" Joseph Rosenstock "should you want foundation funds involved in this production" to drop his choice (Leopold Sachse) of designer for *Die Frau ohne Schatten.* Initially "outraged," Rosenstock eventually backed down (LK to Leopold Sachse, Feb. 12, 1954, LK to Rosenstock [production], Feb. 15, 1954, Marshall internal memo [outraged], NAR/RAC).

　　A memo in RAC records the gist of a telephone conversation during which Wally Harrison warned the foundation that "the chief trouble with Kirstein was that he tends to make plans so large that they cannot be carried out . . . be sure that Kirstein is not expanding too fast if the grant should be made . . . there should be an opportunity for review at stated periods." A friend of Lincoln's, Harrison meant him no harm, and Marshall and others were also aware of Lincoln's "expansionist" tendencies; the result was that annual budgets were incorporated as part of the grant in order to ensure the necessary safeguards.

8. The most important primary materials used in describing LK's activities August–October 1953 in this and the following paragraphs are: LK to Copland, Aug. 19, 1953, AC/LC; Marshall memos of discussions with LK, Aug. 7 (art gallery), 18, 19, 25, Sept. 18, some with enclosures relating to budgets and projects sent him by LK, LK to Boyer, July 21, 1953 (tour), LK to Nelson, Aug. 28—all 1953, all NAR/RAC; LK telegram to Nelson, Aug. 24, Betty Cage to LK, Sept. 6, 10, Oct. 20 plus three n.d., telegram Oct. 4, telegram LK to Cage, Oct 12, postcard Le Clercq to LK Oct. 30[?], Nelson to LK, Oct. 2, Ed Bigelow to LK, Sept. 15, Oct. 3—all 1953, all LK/DD; LK to Virgil Thomson, Aug. 18, 1953, VT/YML; Marshall to LK, Aug. 28, 1953, BSA; LK to Cadmus, Sept. 13, 22, Oct. 4, 1953, courtesy Anderson; d'Harnoncourt's views are in Edgar Young to General Files, Dec. 1, 1953, NAR/RAC, in which the MoMA director is also described as saying, "Kirstein is a very difficult person, hard to get along with, has many simply crazy ideas, but nevertheless has the spirit that makes City Center a vital enterprise." Lincoln was closer to Kallman during this period than he would be

subsequently; there are some dozen witty, campy letters from Kallman to LK from the fifties (including a reference to Stravinsky as "the mighty anal") in the Berg Collection/NYPL.

9. For this and the following three paragraphs: LK to Pavlik, Jan. 19, 1954, PT/BL; Marshall internal memos, Sept. 18/Nov. 6 (LK on theatre), NAR/RAC; LK to Morris, Oct. 19, 1953, BSA (expediency); LK to Chapman, Oct. 8, 23 (Hollywood/spend), Nov. 11 (advance), 1953, RC/DD. The opera season (*The Trial* and *Hansel and Gretel*) was also a financial success, moving "the whole picture" at the Center "from despair six months ago, to slight affluence today [which] is nothing short of miraculous" (LK to Nelson, Nov. 4, 1953, NAR/RAC). Ferrer's season cleared $87,000 for the Center, which allowed for the start-up of *Center* magazine, edited by Richard Hatch, as well as the reinvigoration of Friends of the City Center, in both of which Lincoln was active (LK to Nelson, Nov. 29, 1953, NAR/RAC). The surplus also made it possible to raise the basic rehearsal pay of the ballet company (LK to John D. Rockefeller III, Dec. 21, 1953, NAR/RAC), and to establish the Center Light Opera Company; its first season (*Fledermaus, Show Boat*, and *Carousel*) began in May 1954 (JM notes on lunch with LK, Jan. 12, 1954, NAR/RAC). John Marshall agreed with Lincoln that the one "serious" offering of the drama season, *Richard III*, came off badly; in Marshall's words, "Margaret Webster, the Director . . . turned the cast into automata [and]. . . Ferrer is certainly not up to acting a Shakespearean role" (JM internal memo to Rockefeller officials, Dec. 10, 1953, NAR/RAC).

10. For this and the following three paragraphs: LK to Chapman, Oct. 23, 1953 (Harvard student) RC/DD; LK to Buckle, July 10, 1951 (Auden); interviews with Yow and Tooker. His once-close relationship with George Tooker took a bad turn in the early fifties, when Lincoln commissioned a table from Tooker's live-in lover, Bill Christopher, but thought the finished project "just awful" and returned it; that deeply angered the mild-mannered Tooker and seems permanently to have altered his feelings toward Lincoln (interview with Tooker; LK to Cadmus, Oct. 5 [awful], 26, 1952, courtesy Anderson). Nonetheless Lincoln remained an admirer and promoter of Tooker's art. On Jensen: LK to Chapman, Dec. 10, 1952, RC/DD; LK to Cadmus, Apr. 21, Oct. 28, 1952, courtesy Anderson; LK to Wyeth, Dec. 28, 1953, courtesy Wyeths. Pippin Press: LK to Pavlik, Apr. 29, 1954; *The New Yorker*, Aug. 27, 1955 (positive review); LK to Casner, May 24 (LK's $15,000 investment in press), 1954, BSA. On Maloney: LK to Buckle, June 6, 1951, RB/UT; LK to Cadmus, Dec. 2 (truck drivers), 1951, Feb. 18, Mar. 12, 28, Apr. 5, Aug. 31, 1952, courtesy Anderson; LK to Osbert, Aug. 18, 1950, LK/DD; LK to Pavlik, Mar. 24, 1953/Dec. 17, 1954 (Osbert), PT/BL. Lincoln was a good deal less fond of Hewitt: e.g., "Ed doing nothing [in London] except guardsmen and wasting his money and my time and interest" (LK to Cadmus, Mar. 12, 1952, courtesy Anderson). Maloney had his first show at the Hewitt Gallery in Nov. 1953. The catalog, for which Lincoln wrote a brief introduction, is in LK/DD. That Lincoln's admiration for Dan's work was genuine is confirmed in his private comments; e.g., LK to Pavlik, Apr. 5, 1952, courtesy Anderson: Dan "has learned to handle water-color *very* well"; LK to Andrew Wyeth, Dec. 28, 1953, courtesy Wyeths: "Maloney had a very good show indeed . . . The pictures were very small but extremely brilliant and accomplished."

11. NYCB: "JM's diary on Walter Terry," Mar. 2, 1954, Marshall inter-office memo, Feb. 3, 1954, NAR/RAC; LK to Tom Fisher [Ruth Page's husband], Jan. 13, 1954, LK/DD; LK to Chapman, Feb. 9, 18, 1954, RC/DD. Balanchine had been on the cover of *Time* magazine (Jan. 25, 1954) the week before *Nutcracker* opened. After seeing the premiere, Cole Porter wired Lincoln, IT MADE ME PROUD OF NEW YORK. ALL MY CONGRATULATIONS (Feb. 5, 1954), and Marianne Moore wrote him, "This is glittering perfection . . . with the ecstatic after-sense of everything right without a flaw," LK/DD. SAB had to move into new quarters in 1954 after being forced out of the Tuxedo Building at 637 Madison Avenue.

12. *Tender* and *The Saint:* LK to Chavez, Mar. 13, 1954, LK/DD; Robbins to LK, Apr. 5, 1954, BSA; *New York Times*, Apr. 2, 1954; LK to Copland, June 4, 1954, AC/LC; LK to Baum, June 7 (*Saint*), 1954, BSA; JM interoffice memo, June 21, 1954, LK to JM, June 24, 1954, NAR/RAC.

  John D. Rockefeller III: LK to JR III, May 10, Aug. 24, 1954, LK to Morris, Jan. 23 (balance of power), 1955, BSA; JR III memo, June 18 (survey, and so on), JR III to Baum, June 22, LK to JR III, June 25, July 9, Dana Creel to JR III, July 21 (Kirstein artist, and so on), Edgar Young memos of Dec. 31 conversations with Delaney and Reis—all 1954, all NAR/RAC.

For Lincoln's resignation: LK to Morris, Jan. 5, Morris to Lincoln, Jan. 24, 1955, BSA; LK to JR III, Jan. 24, Edgar Young to JR III, Jan. 6, 1955, NAR/RAC; LK to Pavlik, Mar. 28, 1955 (bored), PT/BL; LK to Morris, Mar. 26, 1956, BSA. Both the *New York Times* (Jan. 28, 1955) and *Variety* (Feb. 2, 1955) wrote up the resignation as a clash between Lincoln, the forward-looking artist, and a stodgy commercial-minded management.

CHAPTER TWENTY-SIX: LINCOLN CENTER (1955–1957)

1. LK's hospitalization: LK to Pavlik, June 30 (ECT, Jensen), 1955, PT/BL; LK to Chávez, July 9 (psychiatry), 1955, LK/DD; LK to Robbins, Oct. 31, 1954, JRRT; Sitwell to LK, Nov. 8, 1956, LK/DD; LK to Hammarskjöld, Oct. 22 (psychiatry), 1954, BSA; multiple interviews with Jensen Yow. In my *Paul Robeson* (Knopf, 1989), I discuss at some length the treatment options of the time and the controversy surrounding ECT; see especially 743–45. Two lines in a letter from David Garnett to Mina (May 13, 1955, MC/DG/Berg) provide a glimpse of how wild Lincoln became: "What is left ambiguous in your letter is whether he tried to kill Fido or George's wife. I gather from his wrecking his own house that it was Fido." What needs factoring in, of course, is Mina's penchant, similar to Lincoln's own, for theatrical exaggeration, as well as her deeply ambivalent love-hate relationship with him.
2. The key documents for the Shakespeare Festival have been John Marshall's interview at COH; LK, "Shakespeare and the Theatre of Style," *Center* (Aug.–Sept. 1954); LK to Chapman, Mar. 2 (Burrell), 26 (drapes), Apr. 13 (Carey), RC/DD; LK to Pavlik, Mar. 28 (capacious), 1955, PT/BL; LK to Auden, Apr. 27, 1955, LK to Langner, Apr. 30, 1955, Langner to LK, June 10 (floundering), 1955, BSA; LK to Yow (flop), July 16 (Fine), 18 (guilt), 1955, courtesy Yow; *The Nation*, Aug. 8, 1955.
3. NYCB: LK to Pavlik, Mar. 28 (Tanny), Apr. 16 (Cage), Oct. 19 (recovered; Europe), 1955, Jan. 25 (tired), Feb. 14, Mar. 7 (elegant), 1956, PT/BL; LK to Baum, June 22 (fear), 1955, MB/DD; LK to Morris, June 30, 1955, LK to Craft, Sept. 19 (radically), 1957, BSA; LK to Robbins [1954?] (on Bernstein), Robbins to LK, Nov. 11 (shocked), 1954, LK to Robbins, Nov. 14 (resent), 1954, JRRT; LK to "George, Edith [Tanny's mother] and Tanny," Jan. 2 (Robbins; Eglevsky, and others), 1956, BSA; LK to Buckle, Dec. 19 (*Souvenirs*), 1955, RC/UT; my interview with Arthur Mitchell, Sept. 25, 2003 (history/geniuses), and Vida Brown, Apr. 27, 2004 (Tanny); Joan Kramer's interview with Rouben ter-Arutunian, DD/NYPL; LK's telegram to Mitchell, Aug. 24, 1955, is in LK/DD; Allegra Kent, *Once a Dancer* . . . (St. Martin's, 1997), chaps. 6–8; Maria Tallchief with Larry Kaplan, *Maria Tallchief: America's Prima Ballerina* (Henry Holt, 1997), chap. 13–14. Even at this point in its history, NYCB didn't have clear sailing financially. Late in 1955 City Center once again got into serious trouble due to the other units losing a ton of money: Orson Welles's *King Lear* was a critical flop and lost $75,000, and the opera $125,000. Baum canceled the ballet's four-week rehearsal period, putting the season in jeopardy. As Lincoln wrote Andy and Betsy Wyeth, "I had to raise $16,000 overnight," and to do so he had to sell one of Andy Wyeth's paintings (LK to Wyeths, Feb. 14, 1956, courtesy Wyeths; also Henry Morgenthau III to Cage, Oct. 18, Cage to Baum, Oct. 4, Cage to LK, Oct. 13—all 1956, all BSA). Lincoln's distaste for Robbins was mutual; Robbins wrote Tanaquil Le Clercq, for example, that Lincoln "screws up everything. . . . Not only that, but he's going around telling everybody I'm a son of a bitch for not working with the company" (Dec. 3, 12, 1956, Jan. 22, 1957, JRRT).

   In late 1956 Newbold Morris took the initiative in trying to get Lincoln to return to City Center. He proved willing, even eager, to return if certain non-negotiable requirements were met: that he be appointed artistic administrator with "complete authority to revise the whole policy and direction of the New York City Opera Company" from a Central European to an Italian-French orientation. He also required an administrative assistant who would serve as business manager. Morris was so certain that the board would agree to Lincoln's terms that he named a specific date (Dec. 7, 1956) for the public announcement and in the interim urged Lincoln to enter into assorted discussions with people like Anthony Bliss at the Metropolitan Opera. But it was not to be. Lincoln had required the unanimous agreement of the board, and neither Baum nor Jean Dalrymple would agree to his conditions. Lincoln refused any further negotiation and withdrew his offer to return. The key documents outlining this episode are: LK to Morris, Nov. 3, Dec. 4, LK to Claire Reis, Nov. 13, LK memo to Bliss, Nov. 26, LK to Marshall, Nov. 27, LK to Bliss, Dec. 2, LK to Rudolph Bing, Dec. 14—all 1956, all BSA.

4. Shakespeare Festival: LK to Chapman, Oct. 4, 1955, RC/DD; LK to Reed, Mar. 1, 16, 17, 3-pp. memo LK to Reed, Mar. 17, 23, Reed telegram to LK, Mar. 17, 6-pp. letter Mar. 27—all 1956, all BSA; LK to Pavlik, Nov. 2, May 3 (Arutunian), 1955, PT/BL; Joan Kramer interview with ter-Arutunian, DD/NYPL; LK to Wescott, Apr. 28, 1956, GW/BL; LK to Cadmus, Oct. 4, 18 (awful), 1953, courtesy Anderson; *The Nation,* July 21, 1956. In the midst of all this Lincoln also joined Norris Houghton and T. Edward Hambleton in co-producing on two consecutive Monday evenings at the Phoenix Theatre, the Virgil Thomson–Gertrude Stein opera *The Mother of Us All* (LK to Pavlik, Mar. 7, 1956, PT/BL; LK to Reed, Mar. 23, 1956, BSA).

5. Helping artists: LK to Pavlik, Mar. 28 (prints), Dec. 30 (Knoedler's), 1955, Jan. 25 (Harrison), 1956, PT/BL; LK to Wescott, Apr. 23, 1956, GW/BL; interview with Tooker (table). Sharrer: Sharrer to LK, 15 items, LK/DD; LK to Sharrer, Mar. 6, 1958, LK/DD; LK, exhibition catalog, *Symbolic Realism in American Painting, 1940–1950* (Institute of Contemporary Arts, 1950), LK to Robert Beverley Hale, Apr. 30 (pushing Sharrer), 1956; Spanierman Gallery, *Honoré Sharrer,* 2002, telephone interview with Perez Zagorin (Sharrer's husband), 2004, Zagorin to me, June 4, 2005 (magic realism), Apr., 2006. Though Lincoln *did* admire Cadmus's work, he also wrote: "Cadmus is a renegade Catholic with a terrible sense of positive evil. . . . I think he is a physical snob. He is anti-intellectual . . . he adores the human body as such—and his Sins [the paintings] are deformations of an adoration: a kind of black Mass, a negative celebration." (LK to Alton Pickens, Oct. 3, 1950, AP/SAAA). Colville: phone interview with Colville, Jan. 19 (Fidelma), 2004; LK, "Alex Colville," *Canadian Art* (Aug. 1958) [Colville thought the article "very good"—AC to LK, Apr. 8, 1958]; LK's introduction to Helen J. Dow, *The Art of Alex Colville;* AC's side of the correspondence with Lincoln is in LK/DD (the quotes on magic realism are from his letters of Oct. 7, Nov. 5, 1954); Lincoln's letters are in Colville's possession and he kindly photocopied them for me. I'm likewise indebted to Andrew and Betsy Wyeth, who had their archivist Mary Adams Landa send me photocopies of all of Lincoln's many letters to them; LK's comments on Cadmus are in LK to Betsy and Andy Wyeth, Nov. 9, 1956, and his comments on Wyeth's lack of form are in LK to Andy, Nov. 17, 1956 (courtesy Andrew and Betsy Wyeth).

    When Ed Hewitt and Dan Maloney went to Japan for an extended stay in 1957, Lincoln took charge of Hewitt's gallery on East Sixty-fifth Street, hiring Robert Isaacson to run it. For openers Lincoln organized a group show of eighteen artists including Tooker, Maloney, Colville, and Jared French that ran from June 3 to July 3, 1957.

6. Beginnings of Lincoln Center: Edgar B. Young, an associate of John D. Rockefeller III and a participant in every phase of the planning and building of Lincoln Center, has written a still useful insider's book (though Lincoln thought it wildly partisan), *Lincoln Center: The Building of an Institution* (NYU Press, 1980). For understanding Lincoln's participation in the first few years, the crucial documents have been: LK memo to John III, Aug. 2, Oct. 6, LK to Edgar Young, Nov. 6, Dec. 13, LK to Marshall and Fahs, Nov. 10—all 1956, all NAR/RAC; LK to Pavlik, Dec. 30, 1955, May 3, 1956, PT/BL; LK to Bliss, Nov. 16, 1956, LK Nov. 27 memo of Nov. 26 conversation with Anthony Bliss, BSA; *World-Telegram and Sun,* Dec. 1, 2, 1958.

7. Ballet at Lincoln Center: Edgar Young memos to Rockefeller, Oct. 25, Dec. 7, 1956, Ewing to Rockefeller, Nov. 26, 1956, Jan. 21, 1957, Rockefeller to Ewing, Dec. 7, 1956, Jan. 3, 1957, Stoddard memo to committee, Sept. 17, 1957—all NAR/RAC. LK's doubts about moving: LK to Marshall, Nov. 10, 1956, LK to John Rockefeller III, Jan. 1 (audience), 1957, LK to Edgar Young, Jan. 3 (Harrison), 7, 10 (Philharmonic), 1957, LK "draft statement" (11 pp.) on "Dance as a Performing Art in Lincoln Square," Feb. 7 (Ballet Theatre), 1957, John Marshall interoffice memo, Feb. 18 (Ballet Theatre), 1957—all NAR/RAC. Le Clercq's polio: LK to Wescott, Nov. 10, 1956, GW/BL; Cage to LK, Oct. 31, 1956, BSA; LK to Pavlik, Nov. 20, 1956, Feb. 4 (revolution), Apr. 2 (Lenox), 1957, PT/BL. According to Jerome Robbins (Rob-

bins to Le Clercq, Feb. 6, 1957, JRRT), it was Menotti who insisted on using John Butler, who in turn insisted on hiring a non-NYCB dancer, making Lincoln so angry that he slapped Menotti and walked out.

8. Stratford: LK to Craft, June 12, 1957, LK to Langner, Sept. 18, 1957, Langner to LK, Sept. 20, 1957, BSA; LK to Cadmus, July 6, 1957, courtesy Anderson; LK to Jensen, Sept. 5, 1957, courtesy Yow; LK to Colville, July 1, Sept. 13, 1957, courtesy Colville.

9. Lincoln Center (ballet: 1957–58): Edgar Young, *Lincoln Center*, 58–60; Marshall interoffice memo of LK conversation, Apr. 4, LK to Young, Apr. 5, LK to Rockefeller III, May 16, June 3, Nov. 29 (devastated), Young to "Directors of Lincoln Center," June 13, 5-pp. memo—all 1957, all NAR/RAC. Lincoln Center (architecture: 1957): LK to Marshall, Feb. 19, 1957, NAR/RAC; LK to Young, Nov. 1 (site), 1957, BSA; LK to Colville, May 9 (splendor), 1957, Nov. 6 (recognition), 1958, courtesy Colville; LK to Van Vechten, May 15, 1957, VV/BL. Wyeth thought Colville was "the most interesting painter he has seen in a very long time" (LK to Colville, Oct. 28, 1958, courtesy Colville).

Early in 1958 the Advisory Committee on the Dance was formed to discuss the unresolved status of dance at Lincoln Center. Among the dozen members were Lucia Chase, Martha Graham, Lincoln Kirstein, William Schuman, and Edgar Young. Its first meeting was held on Jan. 13, 1958, and it met monthly thereafter. Judging from the official minutes of the meetings (which are, along with incidental letters from participants, in RFA-EY), little was accomplished during 1958 in regard to specific resolutions or actions. Materials relating to the National Institute Award are in GW/BL.

CHAPTER TWENTY-SEVEN: JAPAN (1958–1960)

1. LK to Stravinsky, Aug. 24, 1954, BSA, LK to Pavlik, Dec. 17, 1954, PT/BL; LK, "Igor Stravinsky," *The Nation*, June 15, 1957.

2. NYCB 1958 tour: Japan: LK to Richie, Nov. 12, Dec. 22, 1957 (theater), Oct. 24 (return), 1958, Apr. 17 (hard-on), 1959, Richie to LK, Dec. 16, 1957, LK/DD; LK to Cadmus, Mar. 26 (Tamotzu), 1958, courtesy Anderson; LK to Chapman, Mar. 20 (ugly), Apr. 1 (Chuyo), 2 (theater), 1958, RC/DD; LK to Colville, Mar. 26/July 6 (young men), 1958, courtesy Colville. In a typical gesture of generosity, Lincoln sent Alex Colville, then a struggling young painter, an expensive set of Japanese papers and brushes. While in Japan, Lincoln, through the publisher Tex Wetherby, met Mishima and liked him personally. But he thought *Confessions of a Mask* wasn't "much of anything" compared to Genet (LK to MacGregor [?], Sept. 3, 1958, ND/YH); on the other hand he thought Mishima's novel *Golden Pavilion* "terrific" (LK to Richie, June 9, 1959, LK/DD; Richie to me, July 15, 29, Aug. 3, 2003). As an offshoot of his intense reading about Japan, LK wrote an article for *The Nation* (Jan. 31, 1959) evaluating books about the country (especially those issued by Tuttle).

Australia: LK to Cadmus, May 17 (Australia), 1958, courtesy Anderson; LK to Richie, Apr. 18 (peter), May 1, 1958, courtesy Richie; Cage to LK, Apr. 19, May 5, 10, BSA. The company's notices in Australia were good, but it did mediocre business, partly because Eglevsky left early and Tallchief didn't go at all (Cage to Eglevsky, May 5, 1958, BSA; Cage to Baum, May 5, 1958, MB/DD). There was also a significant amount of hurt feelings and anger on the part of Melissa Hayden and Patricia McBride when Balanchine, via cable, asked Allegra Kent instead of them to understudy Diana Adams in *Swan Lake*; Cage thought Balanchine "is being very stubborn and unfair" (Cage to LK, May 27, 1958, BSA).

3. Stratford: Houseman to LK, Jan. 4, 27, 1959 (animation), BSA; Mina to LK, Apr. 15, 1959, LK/DD; LK to Richie, June 16, July 6 (success), 1958, Richie to LK, Feb. 9, 1959, LK/DD. When Houseman resigned as artistic director, Lincoln denounced him as "petty and unfair" (LK to St. Denis, July 22, 1959, BSA). With the benefit of hindsight, Houseman took a more temperate view in his memoir *Unfinished Business* (Applause Books, 1972). LK's involvement in 1961: LK to Richie, May 14 (Tandy), LK/DD; Lincoln to Wescott, June 7, 1961, GW/BL; LK to Meredith, Aug. 21 (Troilus), 1961, WM/CC. Lincoln took a less kindly view of Hepburn's performance in *Antony and Cleopatra* in 1960: Her "virginal egotism and metallic vigor defeated the first notion of Cleopatra" (LK to Colville, Oct. 20, 1960, courtesy Colville). He

later summarized his entire experience with the Stratford Festival, as having gone "far to prove that Americans cannot speak or act the Bard on any level past the preparatory school" (LK to Ewart, Nov. 4, 1979, GE/UH).

4. Lincoln Center: LK to Reginald Allen, May 6 (resignation), 1959, minutes of meeting of Advisory Committee on the Dance, March 6, 1958, RAC; George Kirstein to LK, May 7, 1959, LK to Bliss, May 15 (FBI), BSA; Richie to LK, May 22 (shitiness), LK/DD; Cadmus to Jerry and Margaret French, Mar. 21, Apr. 6, 21, 1959, courtesy Anderson; JDR III to LK, May 13, 18, July 1, Oct. 6, 20, LK to JDR III, May 14, 24, July 7 (real estate), Aug. 26, Oct. 1 (heartless), 27 (City Center), 29, Nov. 9 (sink), Young to LK, May 26, June 3, 16, LK to Young, June 4 (bitterness), 18 (principle)—all 1959, all RAC; Bliss to LK, May 20, 1959, LK to Heyman, Oct. 19 (matinees), 1959, BSA. Nelson: NR to LK, Nov. 24, 1958, BSA; LK to NR, Nov. 27, NR to LK, Dec. 3, 1958, NAR/RAC; NR to LK, Jan. 6, 1959, BSA (includes Rockefeller's message to the legislature, with the paragraphs marked that contain LK's suggestions). Lincoln attended Nelson's inauguration, and the NYCB performed at his inaugural ball (LK to Colville, Jan. 3, 1959, courtesy Colville).

5. NYCB 1958–59: LK to Richie, Sept. 24 (awkward), 1958, LK/DD; LK to Colville, Apr. 16 (Verdy), 1960, courtesy Colville; interview with Violette Verdy, Feb. 21 (surprised; eagle), 2004; Maria Tallchief with Larry Kaplan, *Maria Tallchief* (Henry Holt, 1997), esp. 252–56; Pleasant to LK, May 15, 1959, BSA; Agnes de Mille, *Martha*, 348; LK memo to Betty Cage, May 18, Graham to LK, Oct. 14 (kick), 1959; Graham to LK, May 26, LK to Graham, May 31, 1959, BSA. Lincoln wrote Richie (May 17, 1959, LK/DD) that "the Webern notices only hint at the splendor Balanchine hath wrought; the Graham part is silly and old-fashioned . . . he wiped her out. But the public thinks, natch, she is Very Great; she ain't, dear . . . she is, finally, a silly lonely woman, with a sort of heroic tenacity." Additional examples of Lincoln initially frightening some dancers are interviews in DD/NYPL with Yvonne Mounsey, a principal, and Carol Sumner, a soloist. Of the five other Balanchine premieres during 1958–59, the most notable was probably *Seven Deadly Sins*, with Auden and Kallman translating Kurt Weill's libretto and Lotte Lenya singing the role of Anna. The ballet was, in Lincoln's words, "a stupendous success," with double the number of performances added (LK to Richie, Dec. 1, 16 (stupendous), 1958, LK/DD).

6. Gagaku and ritual sports: LK memo to Young, Apr. 20 (attentiveness; Yosikune), 1959, MB/DD; LK to Richie, Feb. 11, 1959, May 17 (Fidelma), 1959, June 13 (Gagaku tour; sports), LK/DD; LK to Jensen, Feb. 27 (house), 1959, courtesy Yow; LK to Cadmus (students), Feb. 28, 1959, courtesy Anderson; LK to Chapman, Mar. 10, 1959 (fascist); Weatherby to LK, July 5/Aug. 13 (Japan Society), 1959, LK/DD; Mina to Leyda, July 30, 1959, JL/TL. Kobashi: LK to Richie, Jan. 20., Apr. 17 (neurotic; IDEA), 1959, LK/DD; LK to Nelson, Apr. 28, 1959, NAR/RAC; LK to Colville, June 14 (Mass), Sept. 30 (broadsword), 1959, courtesy Colville. Lincoln accompanied Gagaku on its sold-out tour, staying in Los Angeles with Isherwood and his new, long-lasting lover, the youthful Don Bachardy, whom Lincoln thought "adorable"; Isherwood "hated" Gagaku, and Lincoln "honestly" couldn't figure out why. Lincoln in turn thought Hollywood "horrid. . . . Chris [Isherwood] likes the artificiality, the atmosphere of a lurid country-club which is really a cemetery, and a cemetery which is certainly a country-club" (LK to Richie, June 13, 1959, LK/DD). Ritual athletics: LK to Richie, June 13, July 1, 12 (ballet), 21 (ballet), Richie to LK, May 22, July 6, Aug. 3, LK/DD.

7. Kabuki: LK to consul general, Dec. 22, 1959, Marshall interoffice memo Dec. 21, 1959, RAC; LK to Fahs, Feb. 24 (urgent; committee), 1960, Fahs to LK, Dec. 22, 1959, LK to Fahs, Jan. 6, 1960, Fahs interoffice memo, Mar. 24, 1960 (Chushingura), RAC; LK to Shepard Stone (Ford Foundation), Jan. 7, 1960, LK to Doolittle, Feb. 18, 1960, BSA; Stone to LK, Jan. 21, 1960, LK to Richie, Dec. 27 (Diet), 1959, Feb. 2, 4 (books), Mar. 6 (gloomy), 26 (flipped), 1960, LK/DD; Robbins to Le Clercq, June 12, 1960, JRRT.

8. Social circle: LK to Richie, July 6, 1958 (greatest), Apr. 24, 1959 (Dan's show), LK/DD; LK to Chapman, Feb. 18, 27 (Lynes suicidal), RC/DD; LK to Cadmus, Dec. 2 (Lynes), 1951, courtesy Anderson; LK to PT, June 30, Nov. 2, 20 (Lynes show), Dec. 9, 30 (gang bang), 1955, Feb. 4 (Cartier-Bresson), 1957, PT/BL; LK introduction to *Portrait: The Photographs of*

George Platt Lynes (Twin Palms, 1994); LK to Colville, Mar. 7 (pilot), 1957, courtesy Colville. Isherwood: CI to LK, Dec. 30, 1951 (fun), Mar. 31, 1952 (empathy), LK to Cadmus, Dec. 2 (entertaining), 1951, Mar. 12 (less sympathetic), 1952, courtesy Anderson. Sitwells: LK to Pavlik, Mar. 28 (huge), 1955, PT/BL. Spender: LK to Buckle, May 11 (prose), 1951, RB/UT; LK to Richie, Aug. 1 (respect), 1958, Nov. 17 (moral), 1959, LK/DD; LK to Robbins, Oct. 31, 1954, JRRT. Lincoln nonetheless tried to interest Bernstein in the work of the Japanese composer Mayezumi (LK to Bernstein, Apr. 12, 1960), LB/LC.

9. NYBC and Lincoln Center: LK memo to John III, Oct. 15, 27, Nov. 9 (Schuman/Balanchine/subsidy), 1959, RAC; Bliss to LK, Aug. 7 (Met), 1959, BSA; John III to LK, Oct. 6, 20, 1959, RAC; Schuman to LK, Mar. 9, 1960, LK to Schuman, Mar. 10, 1960, BSA; LK to John Barrett (Old Dominion Foundation), Apr. 23, 1960, MB/DD. *Pan America* and *Figure:* LK to Baum, Mar. 8, 1960, MB/DD; LK to Richie, Dec. 3, 1959, Apr. 7, 10, May 2 (mortgage), 1960, LK to Chávez, Dec. 6 (Bruhn), 1959, LK/DD; Cage to Lenya, Apr. 30 (mortgage), 1960, BSA; minutes of Ballet Society meetings of May 24, 1960 (capital fund), BSA; B. H. Haggin, *Hudson Review*, May 1960 (117: Bruhn), July 1960 (invention). Some half dozen letters from Lincoln to potential donors (Winslow Ames, Donald Engle, and others) in MB/DD (Box l) demonstrate his hands-on effort to solicit funds.

10. State Theater: LK to Nelson, June 28, 1960, LK to Barrett (Old Dominion Foundation), Oct. 3, 1960, BSA.

CHAPTER TWENTY-EIGHT: THE STATE THEATER (1961–1963)

1. Many of the details and all of the quotes regarding Kennedy's inauguration are from LK's "The New Augustan Age," *The Nation*, Feb. 4, 1961; LK to Colville, Oct. 20 (vote), 1960, courtesy Colville; LK to Wyeth, Feb. 4, 1961, courtesy Andrew and Betsy Wyeth; Cage to Leonidoff, Jan. 26 (tea), Mar. 25 (Adlai), 1961, BSA; LK to Nelson, Mar. 28, 1961, MB/DD; LK to Nelson, n.d. (public image), BSA; Young, Center, 118–121. White House: Dutton to LK, Sept. 11, 1961; LK to Dutton, Sept. 18, 1961, BSA; LK to Chapman, Oct. 5, 1961, RC/DD; Baldrige to Tanner, Oct. 12, 1961, BSA; LK to William Meredith, Oct. 17, 1961, WM/CC.

2. LK to JDR III, Dec. 12, 1960, Jan. 31 (distress), 1961, JDR III to LK, Dec. 23, 1960, RAC; COH interview with JDR III, and Robert A. M. Stern's 1985 interview with Philip Johnson (also COH).

3. LK to Baum, Jan. 7, 1961 (spring 1961); GK to LK, Mar. 21 (finances), 1961, BSA. Seattle World's Fair/Japan: LK to Colville, Feb. 4 (treachery), 1962, courtesy Colville; LK memo to Harold Shaw, Dec. 5, 1961, LK to Japanese cultural attaché DC, Dec. 3, 1961, LK to Dean Rusk, Jan. 12, 1962, LK telegram to Shaw, Mar. 28, 1962, BSA; LK to Richie, Dec. 24 (Seattle/despair), 1961; interview with Mary Richie Smith (Fidelma; Tokyo), Sept. 25, 2003; Donald Richie, *Japan Journals 1947–2004* (Stone Bridge Press, 2004); LK to Cage, et al., Jan. 27 (Mary), 1962, BSA; LK to Richie, Apr. 10, 1962 (pull), LK to Richie, June 25 (100 percent), LK/DD. Early in 1963, the idea of importing a small group of athletes again arose, but again failed to take hold (LK to Richie, Jan. 19, 1963, LK/DD).

4. LK to Tsushima, Jan. 29, 1962, LK/DD; LK to Richie, Oct. 5 (Hayes), 1961, LK/DD; LK to William Meredith, "Wednesday," n.d. [Jan. 1962], WM/CC; LK to Mary and Donald, Feb. 13 (vanity), March 27 (return), 1962, Richie to LK, Feb. 20, 1962, LK/DD; Richie to me, July 15 (Fidelma), 29, Aug. 3, 2003.

5. Soviet Union: Cage to Grigorieff, May 2, Leonidoff to Cage, July 26, Aug. 19, Oct. 5, Cage to Leonidoff, Oct. 28—all 1961, all BSA; Diane Solway, *Nureyev: His Life* (Morrow, 1998), 221–22; LK to Buckle, Apr. 18 (Nureyev; five year), 1962, RB/UT; LK to Richie, May 10 (Marine), 1962, LK/DD; Cage to Bowman (State Dept.), May 7 (terms), 1962, MB/DD. According to Lincoln, Balanchine called Nureyev "the female Mephistopheles" (LK to Richies, Apr. 21, 1963, LK/DD).

6. 1962 tour to Europe and the Soviet Union: LK, "Cultural Confrontation" (Lipizzaner), unpublished ms., LK/DD; LK to John and Blanchette Rockefeller, Oct. 29, 1962, RAC; Mina to Fidelma, Oct. 10, 1962, MCP/SS; *I Remember Balanchine*, 464 (Neary); LK to Dean Rusk, Nov. 8 (Kohler), 1962, LK to Lowry, Nov. 5 (Balanchine), 1962, BSA; LK to Richies,

Dec. 18 (badinage/hopes), 1962, LK/DD; LK to Buckle, Nov. 27 (volupté), 1962, RB/UT; LK to Meredith, Jan. 6 (miserable; exportable), 1963, WM/CC; Zaoussailoff to Tanner, Feb. 12 (disillusions), 1963, AT/BL.

7. *Rhymes of a PFC:* LK to Young, July 23, 1962, BSA; LK to Laughlin, Jan. 23 (Weatherby), Laughlin to LK, Feb. 5, 1963, ND/YH; LK to Buckle, Feb. 27 (Gloria), May 2 (unpatriotic/ Auden/Eliot), RB/UT; Meredith to LK, Nov. 2, 1964, Moore to LK, Dec. 8, 1964, Auden to LK, June 20, 1964, plus one n.d., LK/DD. When New Directions did go ahead with publication of *Rhymes of a Pfc,* Auden wrote an astonishingly laudatory review. There's no evidence that Auden's friendship for Lincoln mandated his glowing opinon of *Rhymes,* though it could have heightened it. (Auden, "Private Poet," *New York Review of Books,* Nov. 5, 1964). During this same period, Lincoln wrote Buckle, "Have you read the Collected Letters of Oscar Wilde . . . what a marvelous book and what a great saint and martyr" (LK to Buckle, Aug. 6, 1962, RB/UT).

8. Lincoln Center: LK to Lowry (Schuman/Young), Nov. 5, LK to Baum, Nov. 16 (conservative), 1962, Morris to Schuman, Jan. 21 (modifications), 1963, MB/DD; LK to Young, July 23, 1962 (20 weeks), Young to LK, Aug. 8 (lessee), 1963, BSA; LK to Richies, Jan. 19 (grandeur), 1963; Robert A. M. Stern 1985 interview with Philip Johnson (outside), COH; LK to Buckle, Feb. 27, 1963, RB/UT.

9. *The Nation:* LK to Richie, Apr. 21, 1963, LK/DD; Cage to Leonidoff, June 10/July 24 (hepatitis), 1963, BSA; LK to Nelson, July 2, 1963, NAR/RAC; Cadmus to Aitken, Aug. 7, 1963; LK to Wheeler, April 9, 1963, GW/BL; LK to Cadmus, Aug. 12 *(Nation),* 1963, courtesy Anderson.

10. Mid-1963: LK to Richie, Aug. 31 (Maloney), 1963, LK/DD; LK to Colville, Oct. 7 (heir), 1963, courtesy Colville; LK to Betsy and Andy Wyeth, July 30, 1963, courtesy Wyeths.

    Ford grant: LK to Buckle, Dec. 10, 1963, RB/UT; LK, *Thirty,* 180–83; LK to Schuman, Dec. 26 (modern dance), LK to Lowry, Dec. 27, 1963, BSA; interview with Nancy Reynolds, Aug. 28, 2003; Jenkins's "comments on Duberman ms." (Graham); LK to Van Vechten, Jan. 6, 1964, LK to Chávez, Jan. 14 (vilification), 1964, LK/DD; LK to Colville, Jan. 22 (thief), 1964, courtesy Colville.

11. Institutional status: Young to Morris, May 19, 1964, MB/DD; LK to Richie, Feb. 16, 1964, LK/DD; LK to Chapman, Sept. 2, 1964, RC/DD; LK to Buckle, Aug. 4 (blow), 18 (money), 1964, RB/UT; LK to Van Vechten, Aug. 27 (art-form), 1964 VV/BL; Schuman to Morris, Dec. 4, 1964, MB/DD; *Herald Tribune,* Dec. 12, 1964; Craft to LK, March 23 (fanfare), 1964, LK/DD; Schuman to Baum, June 14 (Juilliard), 1965, MB/DD; LK to Nelson, Dec. 24, 1965, NAR/RAC .

CHAPTER TWENTY-NINE: BREAKDOWNS/WRITINGS (1964–1975)

1. Most of the details and all the quotes regarding Lincoln's participation in the March are from an unpublished (the article was rejected by *The Nation*) piece, "On the March: Montgomery," LK/DD. I've been unable to establish the identity of "Ken," but Lincoln had recently recommended him to the poet Bill Meredith both for the skill of his verse and for his insider knowledge of the famed Mount Morris Baths (which Ken referred to as the "Ethiopian Embassy"), located at the corner of 125th Street and Madison Avenue—baths that Lincoln characterized as "a rendezvous" for "notorious homosexuals, deviated preverts, and merchant semen." "Many is the time," he'd written Meredith, "when the well-known Director of the New York City Ballet is caught there, having his cock sucked or vice versa, often vera vice." Ken and the Mount Morris Baths are in LK to Meredith, WM/CC; LK to Leyda, n.d. (focus), JL/TL. As a further example of how Lincoln's left-wing commitments were recharged during this period, he contributed five hundred dollars to the Harvard radical newspaper *Old Mole,* suggested a list of people for the organizers to send sample copies to, and set up several meetings between members of the Mole collective and influential sympathizers like Lillian Hellman (Dick Cluster to me, Mar. 14, 2003). LK to Zydower, Jan. 11 (Harlem), 1965, courtesy Zydower. Thanks to Lynn Garafola, who petitioned for it, I've been able to read Lincoln's (surprisingly short) FBI file. Fidelma's depression: LK to Cadmus, Aug. 27, 1964, courtesy Anderson; LK to Fania [Marinoff, wife of Van Vechten], Sept. 18, 1964, VV/BL.

2. 1965 trip: LK to Fidelma, Apr. 9, 20, 1965, LK/DD; LK to Cadmus and Anderson, Apr. 15, 20 (futon), 25, May 6, 1965, courtesy Anderson; LK to Jensen, Apr. 15 plus one n.d., May 7, Yow/DD; LK to Buckle, Apr. 10, 1965, RB/UT; LK memo to Takio Enna, Apr. 22, 1965, "The Traditional Ritual Sports . . ." BSA; LK to Zydower, May 27 (hysterical), 1965, courtesy Zydower.

3. NYCB: LK to Buckle, Aug. 18, 1964, RB/UT; Leonidoff to Cage, Jan. 19, 1965, BSA; Hayden to Cage, Oct. 28, 1965, Cage to Baum, Nov. 1, 1965, MB/DD.

4. Zydower: I'm grateful to Astrid Zydower for allowing me to photocopy Lincoln's letters to her (1965–91). Her unexpected death in 2005 and the disordered state of her papers have now made the whereabouts of the original letters problematic. See the citations for quoted letters in notes 1–2; in this section "sparrows" is from LK to Zydower, Dec. 5, 1966. I'm also grateful to Zydower for her willingness to sit for an interview in London (Feb. 19, 2004) with Stephen Amico (LK's intellect; ducks, and so on). Lincoln's poem, "Kristallnacht" (*The Poems of Lincoln Kirstein* [Eakins Press, 1987], 252–54), is partly based on Zydower's childhood, with variations.

    Thanks to Jon Anderson, I've been able to read a batch of Fidelma's letters, mostly undated, to her brother Paul. From internal evidence, the letter containing the "sheer panic" quote is from August 1969.

5. Jamie Wyeth: interview with Jamie Wyeth, Jan. 8, 2004; LK to Zydower, Oct. 15, 1965, Aug. 23, Dec. 5 (attacked), 1966, courtesy Zydower; LK to Colville, Oct. 21 (Knoedler's), Nov. 8, Dec. 3, 1965, Jan. 19, 1966, Aug. 11 (cynical; best), 1969, courtesy Colville; LK to Betsy Wyeth, Apr. 3, 1966, courtesy Andrew and Betsy Wyeth. Jamie had his first one-man show (at Knoedler's) in November 1966, and it got an exceptionally savage reception, most of the complaints aimed at his "outmoded" realistic portraiture, the arrogant attempt of a very young man to ignore or set back the "ongoing stream of modern art." Lincoln encouraged Jamie to go on painting in exactly the same way he had been.

6. Kisner: interview with Kisner, June 7, 2004; LK to Zydower, Aug. 23 (Bob), 1966, Sept. 24 (Maddox), 1969, courtesy Zydower; Jenkins's "notes on Duberman manuscript" (fantasy). In our interview Kisner claimed that the only time he had an orgasm with Lincoln was through "mind control"; that is, using some sort of "Gurdjieffian" technique, Lincoln made Clint come without touching himself or being touched by Lincoln.

7. "White House Happening": LK to Chapman, March 1 (Menotti), 13 (hopeless), 29 (Karinska), Apr. 7 (odd), RC/DD; Levin to LK, Apr. 29 (overwritten), May 17, 1967, Chapman to LK, Oct. 12, Nov. 4–5, 16, 1966, May 24 (reading), 1967, LK/DD; LK to Buckle, June 28 (Beaton), Aug. 27 (London), 1967, RB/UT; LK to Baum, Aug. 19 (resignation; d'Amboise), 1967, courtesy Frederic Wile; Laurence Senelick to me, Feb. 26 (rehearsals; breakdown), 2003; LK to Schroeder, Sept. 26, 1967 (Gurdjieff); interviews with Kisner (July 6, 2004) and Braden (June 9, 2003); LK to Colville, Nov. 15 (ballet), 1967, courtesy Colville; LK to Kisner, Nov. 29 (fun), 1967, May 1969 (house), June 3 (drugs), 10 (Fidelma), 14, July 3, 1968, courtesy Kisner. Maddox told Astrid Zydower that the break with Lincoln had been "traumatic and that it took him years & years to get over. It completely shattered him" (Zydower to LK, undated fragment [1970s?]), LK/DD. Maddox has refused my requests for an interview. A copy of LK's Gurdjieff play, *Magic Carpet*, is in GW/BL. Lincoln stayed in touch for a time with both Tommy Lee Jones and John Lithgow; he wrote Bob Chapman (Aug. 21, 1970, RC/DD), "Tommy Lee Jones, my favorite anti-lover has landed in the Big Time. . . . I find him irresssssssistibbbble. So does he."

8. *Movement and Metaphor:* LK to Buckle, Aug 10, Sept 7, 1968, RB/UT; interview with Nancy Reynolds, Aug. 28, 2003; LK to Reynolds, Feb. 28, Mar. 19 (ignorance), 28 (cut), Sept. 5 (hate), 1969, Mar. 23, 1970, Reynolds to LK, Apr. 28, 1969, LK to Ellyn Childs (Praeger), Apr. 1 (shabbily), 1971, Aldor to Johnson, Apr. 9, 14 (sales), 1971—all courtesy Reynolds; TLS, Jan. 1972. Lincoln saw Ashton's *Enigma Variations* on his 1969 trip to England, some six months after the ballet's premiere. He "adored" it and decided to add it to *Movement and Metaphor*, even though he'd finished the book. He found (weak) justification for including *Variations* as "a seminal work" in its purported use of "The Composer [Elgar] as First-Dancer" (Buckle, ms. autobiography, UT). His alternate justification for including Ashton focused not on innovation but continuity: "Fred continues the English traditional gift of nar-

rative pantomime and domesticity; his big influence is not Balanchine but Sarah Bernhardt." Lincoln also justified omitting both Massine ("he was a wonderful dancer and an unchoreographer") and Fokine ("Fokine, the eclectic, could and did everything, manipulating the language like a master, but was not, in terms of movement, as such, an innovator in the analysis of action—like Nijinsky, who is, for my money, the greatest inventor in the medium" (LK to Buckle, n.d. [1970], RB/UT).

9. LK to Buckle, Oct. 5, 1965 (Mitchell), Mar. 14 (Clifford), Apr. 18 *(Canticles; Slaughter)*, June 22 (Barnes), July 3 (Baum), 11 (nervous), Sept. 7 (bankrupt), 1968, RB/UT; LK to Colville, March 28 (habit), 1968, courtesy Colville; LK to Zydower, Dec. 20 *(Metastaseis)*, 1967, Jan. 11 (20 years), 1969, courtesy Zydower; Barnes to LK, May 21, 1968, LK/DD; Olga Maynard to Ouroussow, Jan. 25 (mutation), Feb. 8 (SAB), 1970, BSA; LK to Robbins, n.d. [1969], JRRT. SAB's move into new quarters in the Juilliard School is fully described in LK, *Thirty Years*, 205–8. For the spat with Clive Barnes: LK to *New York Times*, May 31, June 2, Mar. 23, 1970. Yet Barnes devoted one of his columns in its entirety to a penetrating appreciation of Lincoln's character and contributions (*New York Times*, May 30, 1971); fifteen years later Barnes again wrote a strongly pro-Kirstein piece (*New York Post*, May 21, 1985). Cecil Beaton wrote Lincoln (Jan. 29, 1972, LK/DD) that "the best thing to happen to the English stage was that Clive Barnes has taken out Naturalization papers." In regard to the Dance Theater of Harlem, Lincoln was himself a donor, chaired its board of directors, and successfully solicited a grant of $375,000 for the company from Mac Lowry at the Ford Foundation (e.g., LK to Lowry, Oct. 15, 1969, BSA; interview with Mitchell, Sept. 25, 2003). Lincoln went to London with Dance Theater in July 1974 "in order to orchestrate" its debut there (LK to Rambert, May 16, 1974, MRE). Eugenie Ouroussow, however, cautioned the dance historian Olga Maynard to take the expression "a black Balanchine" with "a large grain of salt." "I asked Lincoln," she wrote Maynard, "about this and he quite agreed & said that he wouldn't like to be quoted on this" (Ouroussow to Maynard, Feb. 4, n.d. [1975?], BSA).

10. LK to Fidelma, Apr. 1 (Bates), 1969, LK/DD; LK to Buckle, Apr. 7 (theater), 12 (Rudi and Margot), 18, 25, 1969, RB/UT; LK to Chapman, April 10 (La Rue), RC/DD; LK to Colville, April 22, 1969, courtesy Colville; unidentified LK "letter to the editor" [*Life?*], Apr. 18 (Isadora), 1969; LK to Rambert, Mar. 15, Béjart), 1971, MRF. Nearly thirty years earlier, Lincoln had in fact devoted the very first issue (January 1942) of his magazine *Dance Index* to Duncan.

Robbins: LK, *Thirty Years*, 195–98; LK to Buckle, Apr. 25, May 15 (Farrell), 1969, RB/UT; LK to Cadmus, May 16, 1969, courtesy Anderson; LK to Robbins, May 23, 1969, LK/DD; Robbins to LK, May 24, 1969, JRRT. When an article in the *New York Times* (June 27, 1971) tried to exempt Robbins's work from recent "trivial" offerings at NYCB, Robbins went so far as to protest in a letter to the editor that his "own recent ballets are as deeply rooted in that organization as they can possibly be." Lincoln and Balanchine successfully discouraged him from sending the letter.

11. LK to Colville, Apr. 22 (feudal), July 23 (Newman), 1969, June 25 (England), 1970, Oct. 20 (Wyeth), 1972, courtesy Colville; LK to Neil and Tony [Richardson], Apr. 23 (Nijinsky), 30 (Self), 1970; Rambert to LK, Mar. 20 (de Mille), 1973, Feb. 26 (de Mille), 1974, LK/DD; LK to Buckle, Feb. 12, 1969, Feb. 20 (Tyler), May 4 (contact), 1970, RB/UT; LK statement on the 1970 strike, Apr. 21, 1970, BSA. The orchestra strike in 1970 went on for four weeks of the scheduled eight-week ballet season, with a compromise settlement (Cage to Leonidoff, July 10, 1970, BSA); LK to Rambert, Nov. 16/22 (Feld), 1970, Feb. 3 (Béjart; Ailey; Vietnam), May 1 (Joffrey; Buckle), 7 (Goldberg), Dec. 30, 1971, Jan. 30/Feb. 12, 1974 (de Mille), MRE; Jenkins's "comments on Duberman manuscript" (seriousness); LK to Klosty, Feb. 28 (Cunningham/Cage), 1971, LM/DD; LK to Zydower, Mar. 19 (Vietnam; Callas), July 17 (Fidelma), 1971, courtesy Zydower; "Music and Musical Life in Soviet Russia: 1917–1970," *New York Times Book Review*, Apr. 16, 1972; "Aid and Comfort to Eakins," *The Nation*, May 15, 1972; "On Stravinsky," *New York Review of Books*, June 29, 1972. Two years after the original publication of *Rhymes* in 1964, New Directions issued *Rhymes and More Rhymes of a PFC*, some thirty-five pages longer. Lincoln intended to expand *Lay This Laurel* into a full-scale work, *Saint-Gaudens and the Civil War*, but that never happened (Leslie Katz to LK, June 5, 1974, BSA).

A decade later, when de Mille sought to reestablish contact, Lincoln wrote her one of the classic kiss-off letters: "You and I are old enough not to beat about the bush or mince words. . . . I really don't see that anything can be gained in our seeing one another. Whatever might have transpired years ago is gone, and I have neither the strength nor the will to start new matters. If this sounds churlish, it's a risk I have to take. I wish you well, but there's an end to it" (LK to de Mille, Dec. 6, 1982, LK/DD).

Yet another example of Lincoln's about-faces is his sharp shift of opinion about Lorca Massine (the estranged son of Léonide). When Lorca joined NYCB in 1970 as a dancer-choreographer, Lincoln thought (and Balanchine agreed with him) that he "has more talent than anyone we have found since Robbins." But by the following year he'd decided that Lorca was "badly trained, cannot dance very well," and lacked enough confidence to become a first-rate choreographer (LK to Rambert, Nov. 16, 22, 1970, Dec. 30, 1971, MRE). Lincoln even had a temporary disenchantment with Jamie Wyeth and for a time stopped seeing him altogether: Jamie "became even more so in the same direction and it's a cold hearted career, but by no means may impede him from doing excellent work. It simply does not magnetize me as a way of life" (LK to Colville, Oct. 20, 1972, courtesy Colville).

The second tour of the Soviet Union in 1972 lasted twenty-four days and encompassed twenty-seven performances in four cities. Even though Moscow's Palace of Congresses held some six thousand people, the theater was sold out and the crush for tickets enormous. The critics were favorable, but less enthusiastic than the audiences (*Izvestia*, Oct. 14, 1972; Bigelow [?] to LK, Oct. 1, 1972, LK/DD). The tour was handled (badly) by the State Department, which refused to let the always reliable Leonidoff participate as manager (Leonidoff to Cage, Nov. 8, 1972, Cage to Leonidoff, Nov. 17, 1972, BSA; LK, *Thirty Years*, 224–25).

The Stravinsky Festival is fully covered in LK, *Thirty Years*, 214–23. Stravinsky had died the year before and Lincoln had attended the church service ("It was very touching to see Balanchine on his knees, but after all he is a very God-fearing man": LK to Rambert, May 1, 1971, MRE). The week-long festival included thirty ballets, twenty-one of them brand new; Balanchine choreographed seven of the ballets and Robbins four. Getting ready for the Festival was, according to Lincoln, "like preparations for a battle." He thought two of Balanchine's new works "masterpieces": *Violin Concerto* and *Duo Concertant*, and Robbins's *Requiem Canticles* "noble and elegant" (LK to Rambert and Zydower, July 1, 1972, MRE).

12. Interview with Paul Taylor, June 11, 2003; assorted letters LK to Taylor, courtesy Taylor. *Nadelman:* While writing the book, Lincoln went through a roller coaster of emotions; "I have been . . . in despair about it," he wrote Alex Colville at one point. "I fear it is overwritten and over-wrought"—and here and there it was (LK to Colville, Feb. 16, 1971, courtesy Colville); LK to Zydower, Mar. 23 (Met), 1973, courtesy Zydower; LK to Buckle, Dec. 27, 1973 (haute), RB/UT. The book had been turned down by several publishers before being accepted by Leslie Katz (publisher of the Eakins Press); he and his wife, the poet Jane Mayhall, were to become close friends of Lincoln's. Katz characterized the book as "a study of concentrated brilliance and exuberant vitality" (Katz to LK, Sept. 21, 1970, LK/DD). The book was printed at the famed Oficina Bodoni in Verona, which accounts for its sumptuous appearance. Hilton Kramer, the *New York Times* critic, read a section of the book in an early draft and felt "it contains some of the best writing on art I have ever read" (Kramer to LK, Feb. 13, 1971, BSA). In his Jan. 1, 1979, "Art View" column in the *New York Times*, he called LK's *Nadelman* "a masterpiece of modern criticism." Among the few other substantial reviews was Sanford Schwartz's brilliant critique in *The New Yorker*, Oct. 20, 1975. Among much else, Schwartz characterizes LK's *Nadelman* as "cranky, demonic, magisterial" and tellingly refers to Lincoln's two dominant writing modes in the book as "rhapsodic" and "combative." Lincoln thought Nadelman's son, Jan, "a creep" who "hated his father" and they got into a bad row when Jan "had the nerve to make terrible bronze casts of the WOODEN figures, all scaled up; disgusting" (LK to Buckle, May 1, 1974, RB/UT).

13. Nijinsky: LK to Rambert, Mar. 28 (Gorsky; Fokine), Apr. 29 (Bronia), Aug. 20 (Balanchine), Sept. 23, 1973, Jan. 4 (Gottlieb), 9, 1974, MRE; LK to Zydower; Dec. 11, 1973, courtesy Zydower; "Notes on Conversations with Madame Rambert," Buckle to LK, Jan. 2, 1974, LK to Craft, Oct. 21 (naive), 1973, LK/DD; LK to Buckle, Dec. 27, 1973, Jan. 21 (homosexuality; prim), 23, Oct. 8 (proofs), 1974, RB/UT; Rambert, *Quicksilver* (Macmillan, 1972), 60–61.

Dickie Buckle offered to help Lincoln, and that generous gesture had led to the renewal of their friendship; he lent Lincoln photographs and gave the completed manuscript a thorough critique (Buckle to LK, Jan. 2, Mar. 12, 1974, LK/DD; LK to Buckle, Jan. 13, Feb. 14, Mar. 18, 1974, RB/UT; LK to Rambert, Mar. 19, 1974, MRE). Lincoln was delighted with his editor on *Nijinsky Dancing*, Bob Gottlieb (he "tells me when I get too high-flown and fancy"), and pleased that the publisher, Knopf, was committed to high-quality reproductions. Buckle had published his own book on Nijinsky in 1971, which Lincoln thought was "decent but boring and very little about Nijinsky"; but he gave the book a positive blurb: "the best biography of a dancer in the language" (LK to Zydower, Dec. 1971, courtesy Zydower).

14. The "Goosies": Cadmus to Aitken, April 25 (cooking), 1974, courtesy Anderson. Fidelma: Margaret French to Jared French, Dec. 13, n.d. [1972?], LK to Margaret French, May 18, 1971, courtesy Anderson; LK to Zydower, Feb. 29, 1972, Dec. 11 (moving), 1973, courtesy Zydower. Dan Maloney: Cadmus to Jerry French, June 8, 1970, courtesy Anderson, LK to Astrid, Sept. 9 (studio), Oct. 19 (teaching; better and better), 1970, Mar. 19, 1971, courtesy Zydower; LK to Margaret French, May 18, 1971; LK to Colville, Oct. 5 (Auden), 1973, courtesy Colville.

15. LK to Rambert, Jan. 4 *(Soupir)*, May 16/June 1 (d'Amboise), Sept. 17 (beans), Nov. 8, 1974, Jan. 13 (ruffled), 1975, MRE; LK to Buckle, Oct. 8, 1974, RB/UT; LK to Nelson, Sept. 10, 1974, LK to Schuyler Chapin, Sept. 17, 1974, BSA. Jerome Robbins's *The Dybbuk* also premiered in spring 1974, but failed to satisfy the choreographer or anyone else. Lincoln found Robbins "very difficult" but still felt that aside from Balanchine, "he is better than anyone else" (LK to Buckle, Jan. 21, 1974, RB/UT).

16. Several phone interviews with Alex Nixon, plus correspondence; as well, Nixon has generously given me a number of letters from Lincoln, Fidelma, and several other people. Since these letters are currently in my possession, I'll omit citations from them. The description of Nixon is in LK to Rambert, May 16, 1974, MRE. Heart attacks and surgery: LK to Buckle, n.d. (medical report) [Feb. 1975], Aug. 18 (Ravel; Croce), RB/UT; LK to Rambert, "March 5 or 6 or 7," (Fidelma), Apr. 4 (jellyfish), 24 (Kissinger), June 10 (demoralized), 1975, MRE; LK to Zydower, Mar. 7 (Balanchine), Maloney to Zydower, May 31, 1975, courtesy Zydower; Jenkins's "comments on Duberman ms" (hurt); Porter to Rambert, May 19, 1975, BSA; LK to George Kirstein, Mar. 23 (Balanchine), 1974, LK/DD; LK to Katz, June 10 (walks), 1975, EPF; LK to Robbins, June 18 (limbo), July 2 (surly), 1975, JRRT; LK to Colville, Aug. 19 (Wyeths; Cadmus), 1975, courtesy Colville. Lincoln brought up to Betsy Wyeth her husband's "obsession with a common thief like Nixon," dismissing it as "a charming peccadillo"—but not before comparing it to Lindberg's fascination with Göring and Ezra Pound's with Mussolini—adding, as well, the insulting comment, "You don't have to have a great mind to be a great painter" (LK to Betsy Wyeth, Mar. 23, 1975, courtesy Andrew and Betsy Wyeth).

CHAPTER THIRTY: SUCCESSION (1976–1985)

1. *New York Times*, Dec. 13, 1975, *New York Review of Books*, Apr. 15, 1976; LK to Rambert, Nov. 4 (new book), Dec. 15 (fund-raising), 29 (surfeit), 1975, Jan. 28 (company class), Nov. 18 (Carter), 1976, MRE; Rambert to LK, June 3, Sept. 22, 1975, Jan. 3 (cruel), Feb. 10 (begging), June 5, July 16, 1976, May 27, Dec. 11, 1977, Balanchine to Nelson, April 5 (finances), 1977, BSA; LK to Buckle, Dec. 2 (polite), 1975, Apr. 12 (camp), 1976, RB/UT; LK to John Samuels, Feb. 13 (sample fund-raising), 23 (textbook), Apr. 20 (furniture), Aug. 11 (fund-raising), 1976, BSA; LK, *Thirty*, 250–54 (SAB); Mary Clarke to LK, Mar. 31, 1976 (London), Wheeler to LK, May 18 (intro), 1976, Tooley to LK, Aug. 5, 1976, LK/DD; LK to Ewart, July 26 (Ballads), Oct. 14 (choice), 1976, GE/UH; LK to Chapman, Mar. 26 (Baryshnikov), 1976, RC/DD. In January 1977 NYCB was awarded a million-dollar challenge grant by the National Endowment for the Arts; that meant having to raise six million on their own—which they did by late 1979 (LK to "Dear Friend," Nov. 23, 1979, BSA; interview with Albert Bellas, Nov. 10, 2006). Through membership on the Anglo-American Bicentennial Citizens Commission, Lincoln had spent considerable time, and had involved Lord Harewood, in arranging a ballet-opera exchange; but with Watergate, the project collapsed (e.g., LK to Nelson, March 16, 1976, BSA). In 1975 NYCB's budget was roughly six million dollars.

Lincoln worked hard, if apologetically, to get *Rhymes of a Pfc* reissued, and finally, as a present to himself for his seventieth birthday, paid James Laughlin of New Directions three thousand dollars to reprint the book, with some dozen new poems included (LK to Laughlin, Aug. 16, Sept. 2, Oct. 12, Dec. 29 [three thousand], JL to LK, Aug. 26, Oct. 6, Dec. 28, 1976, ND). The poems were published in paperback, with a print run of fifteen hundred. LK to Ewart, Aug. 13, 1976, GE/UH. When Ewart edited *The Penguin Book of Light Verse*, he included Lincoln's poem "Double Date." Lincoln doesn't appear in some half dozen other standard poetry anthologies of the twentieth century that I checked, but one of his poems is printed in David Lehman and John Graham, eds., *The Oxford Book of American Verse* (Oxford Univ. Press, 2006), and Paul Fussell does discuss LK's poems both in *The Great War and Modern Memory* (Oxford Univ. Press, 1975) and in *Wartime* (Oxford Univ. Press, 1989). *Rhymes* was finally published in England by David R. Godine in 1981, and received a glowing anonymous review in *The Observer* (Dec. 13, 1981) that ranked Lincoln with the very best poets of World War II (Keith Douglas, Roy Fuller, Randall Jarrell, Vernon Scannell, and Alun Lewis).

2. LK to Rambert, July 29 (Balanchine), Dec. 13 (Martins), 1976; LK to Chapman, July 29 (smashers), 1976; LK to Buckle, Jan. 26 (strike), 1977, RB/UT. Fidelma: multiple interviews with Jon Anderson; LK to Rambert, Mar. 7, May 11, July 11, Nov. 30 (confusions), 1977, MRE; LK to Zydower, May 11, 1977, courtesy Zydower; Cadmus to Aiken, Sept 24 (Benson), Oct. 5, Nov. 14 (wildly), WA/SAAA; LK to Ewart, Dec. 12 (recur), 1977, GE/UH.

3. Lincoln's breakdown: phone conversations and emails with Alex Nixon; Nixon to George Kirstein, Nov. 17, 1977, courtesy Nixon; interview with John Freeman, 2004; interview with Barbara Horgan, May 29, 2003 (Gracie Square); Dan Maloney's quoted words are from Maloney to John Freeman, Nov. 11, 1977. Four other letters piece out the story: Maloney to Mina, Feb. 23, June 28, Aug. 1, 1978, Mina to Dan, July 14, 1978 (the letters are under seal in MCP/SS, and I am hugely grateful to Mina's executor, Lynne Robbins Knox, and to Smith's archivist, Sherrill Redmon, for allowing me access). Mina, by this point in her early eighties and suffering from severe arthritis, responded warmly to Dan's letters, and even sent him fifteen hundred dollars "because of my appreciation of what you are, and of your kindness to me . . . [the money] is in no way an attempt to settle even partially any past or future dealings you may have with my brother."

After Jens moved out of the Nineteenth Street house in the late fifties, Lincoln had destroyed about a hundred of his paintings that had been stored in the basement; in "one of his rages" he threw them all into the street. Deciding Lincoln had been "out of his head," Jensen forgave him: "I thought he was more important to me than the pictures." The matter was never again mentioned between them (interview with Yow, April 12, 2003). Yet a third such incident involved Nick Jenkins's wife, the painter Siri Huntoon. Siri had stored some of her paintings in the basement of the Nineteenth Street house and shortly after Lincoln's death, when she and Nick were moving out of New York, they went to get the pictures. Nothing had as yet been disturbed in the house, due to the various protocols attached to Lincoln's will. Though they searched everywhere, Siri's paintings were not to be found. Either Lincoln or—less likely—someone else had thrown them out. Siri, needless to add, was—like Dan and Jensen—enormously upset over the loss.

4. LK to Spark, Dec. 2 (Lincoln), 1977, LK to Mim, July 11, Nov. 30 (Maddox), 1977, July 29 (Isadora), 1978, MRE; Gottlieb to LK, Dec. 29, 1977, LK/DD; Abbott to Thomson, Feb. 5 (LK better), 1978, VT/YML; LK to Ewart, Nov. 15 (Auden), 1978, GE/UH. In the spring term of 1978, Lincoln gave a series of lectures at Yale on arts management (Brustein to LK, May 12, 1978, BSA); Mendelson to LK, Mar. 15, 24, May 24, 1978, Aug. 4 (admiration), LK/DD; LK to Rambert, May 24, 1978, to Rambert and Astrid, Nov. 29 (Baryshnikov), 1978, MRE; LK to Buckle, Sept. 1 (inspiration), 1978, RB/UT; Taper, *Balanchine*, 353–56. Given his interest in life portraits of Abraham Lincoln, LK glowingly reviewed James Mellow's *The Face of Lincoln* in the *New York Review of Books*, Aug. 14, 1980. This may have marked the beginning of Lincoln's acquaintance with Mellow and his agreement to let Mellow be his biographer—the biography aborted by Mellow's premature death.

5. LK to Mim, March 4 (1933), 1979, MRE; Paul Taylor to LK, June 7 (Misha), 1979, LK/DD. Shortly before Balanchine's surgery, Nureyev had danced with the company in the poorly

received *Le Bourgeois Gentilhomme*. As Lincoln saw more of Nureyev, he liked him a great deal better, finding him "intelligent and funny and cosy," though "professionally deformed; he simply cannot imagine a role in which he does not play RUDOLPH [*sic*] NUREYEV" (LK to Zydower, Apr. 23, 1979, courtesy Zydower). Oppositely, he found Baryshnikov, on further contact, sometimes "gloomy and . . . often surly" (LK to Buckle, June 21, 1979, RT/UT); LK to Rambert, Nov. 11 (bouncy), 1979, MRE.

6. The Duells: interviews with Daniel Duell (Feb. 15, 2004), Maria Caligari (June 20, 2003), Robert La Fosse (June 27, 2003), and Arthur Mitchell (Sept. 25, 2003); LK memo to NW[?], July 22 (d'Amboise), 1973, Duells to LK, April 5, 1976, LK/DD; Zydower to LK, Dec. 8, 1979, LK/DD; LK to Buckle, Apr. 8, Aug. 18 (Martins/Duell), 1979, Jan. 20 (large parts), Mar. 10 (Workshop), Apr. 19 (brilliant), May 14 (first dancer), Oct. 14 (*La Création*), 1980, May 18 (Duell), July 1 (Martins), RB/UT; LK to Zydower, Aug. 19 (breakdown), 1979, Dec. 24 (ball of fire), 1980, Joe Duell to Zydower, Sept. 25, 1979, courtesy Zydower; LK to Rambert, Feb. 18 (Martins), 1980, MRE.

    The Covent Garden engagement, NYCB's first in fourteen years, had a mixed reception. Many of the same complaints made in 1950 were repeated: too much "showbiz" and "abstraction," not enough attention to synthesizing (à la Diaghilev) the arts (*New York Times*, Oct. 7, 1979; Mary Clarke, "The Return of New York City Ballet," *Dancing Times*, Oct. 1979).

7. Fidelma: interviews with Jon Anderson (Norwalk); LK to Rambert, Feb. 18, 1980, LK to Rambert and Zydower, Sept. 2 (companion), 1980, MRE; LK to Zydower, Dec. 24 (hurts), 1980, Mar. 10, July 20 (drugs, doctors), 1981, courtesy Zydower; LK to Wyeth, Mar. 30, 1980, courtesy Wyeths; LK to Buckle, July 1, 1981, RB/UT.

    SAB: LK to Astrid, March 10 (boys), 1981, courtesy Zydower; LK to Rambert, Nov. 20 (carnally), 1981, MRE; LK to John Freeman, Dec. 1 (endowment), 1981, BSA. Tchaikovsky Festival: LK to Zydower, July 20, 1981, courtesy Zydower; LK to Rambert, Aug. 23, 1981, MRE.

8. Interviews with David Langfitt and Michael Leonard; LK to Leonard, June 15, 1980, June 10 (Kung), 16 (priests), 1982, courtesy Leonard; Leonard to LK, May 25, June 23, July 13, 1982, LK/DD; Michael Leonard, Diary, Apr. 21, 1982. I'm enormously grateful to Michael Leonard for taking the time (and finding the patience!) to read his diary entries about Lincoln into a tape recorder. Most of the details of Michael's Apr. 1982 visit come directly from his diary.

9. Interview with Mary Porter, July 30, 2003; Zydower to LK, Aug. 6, 1982, courtesy Zydower; Poerio to Balanchine, Sept. 22, 1982, Balanchine to Poerio, Oct. 1, 1982, DD/NYPL; LK to Leonard, Nov. 2, 18, 1982, courtesy Leonard. According to Mina's secretary and executor, Lynne Robbins Knox (phone interview, Apr. 17, 2004), Mina, too, felt that Lincoln "left Fidelma alone too much . . . neglected her." Fall 1982: Taper, *Balanchine*, 386–87; Cadmus to Zydower, Sept. 7, 1982, LK to Zydower, Dec. 28 (unhappy), 1982, Feb. 10 (bathroom), 1983, courtesy Zydower; LK to Leonard, Oct. 3 (nurses), 1982, courtesy Leonard; interviews with Jon Anderson (knife).

10. Interviews with Barbara Horgan, Mary Porter, Robert La Fosse, Nancy Lassalle, Daniel Duell, Albert Bellas, Bob Gottlieb, Ed Bigelow, and Ted Rogers have been of critical importance in narrating the issues relating to the succession; to avoid recriminations I've deliberately refrained from assigning particular opinions or quotations to any one individual among the nine. Edward Villella, in his autobiography *Prodigal Son* (Univ. of Pittsburgh Press, 1998), remarks (on p. 281) that d'Amboise had long "supported the rumor that he was the heir apparent."

    Buckle telegram and letter to LK, Mar. 29, LK to Buckle, Mar. 25, Apr. 7, 20, July 30 (Robbins), 1983, RB/UT; LK to Rambert, Oct. 15 (nobody), 1976, MRE. For Robbins's actions and reactions, see Jowitt, *Robbins*, 459–63; Vaill, *Robbins*, 482–4; *New York Times*, May 1, 1983 (curtain); interview with Randall Bourscheidt, June 7, 2006. Fidelma: LK to Leonard, May 31, July 5, Nov. 11 (control), 1983, courtesy Leonard; LK to Zydower, Aug. 9, Dec. 4, 1983, courtesy Zydower. In Apr. 1985, Lincoln tripped on a grating when coming out of a theater, fell to the sidewalk, and got a "huge gash" in his head; the incident fed opposition to him as "unstable" (interview with David Langfitt, Apr. 27, 2003).

There's a long-standing controversy about when and if Balanchine actually did name Peter Martins as his successor. Martins himself, in an Oct. 29, 1998, interview (with Ellen Sorrin, DD/NYPL), claims that Balanchine, a full ten years before his death, offered him the post and he accepted the offer. Others (including Barbara Horgan) place the event in Balanchine's hospital room, toward the end of Balanchine's life, when he called Gillian Atfield and Orville Schell, respectively president and chair of the board, to his bedside to let his wishes be known. Still others deny that Balanchine ever specifically designated anyone.

11. Interviews with Horgan, Porter, Bigelow; LK to Findlay, July 4, 1983, BSA; Orville Schell to LK, Apr. 9 (presently), 1984, BSA; LK to Zydower, Mar. 28 (seams), 1984, courtesy Zydower. Lincoln told Michael Leonard that he'd wanted Findlay to become his successor at the school, and to share artistic control with Martins, but that Peter had emphatically turned down the suggestion (Michael Leonard Diary, Oct. 19, 1983, courtesy Leonard). A year later Lincoln came up with another candidate, Nigel Redden, to serve as a "general administrator" combining the functions of "personnel, development, the Board, public-relations and finance," and he chastised the board's failure to fill such a post as "self-indulgence" (LK to Orville Schell, Oct. 16, Schell to LK, Oct. 25, 1984, BSA). According to Buckle, around this same time the board gave Betty Cage her notice, "and Kirstein had not spoken up for her" (RB/HF/UT); Anna Kisselgoff, May 7, 22, June 9, 1985, *New York Times.* Lassalle to Winterer, May 5, 1985; Buckle ms. autobiography, RB/UT; *New York Times,* May 8 (Williams), 15, 24; Perkins to LK, May 22, 1985; Villella to board, May 19, LK/DD; Frances Schreuder to LK, Aug. 10, 1986, LK/DD; Michael Leonard Diary, May 10 (Porter), 1987, courtesy Leonard. LK to Leonard, Mar. 6 (ballet good), 1985, courtesy Leonard; Bok (Harvard) to LK, Dec. 10, 1984, BSA. "Chip" Raymond: Schell to Robbins, Jan. 16, 1985, LK to Anne and Sid Bass (Robbins), Jan. 31, 1985, BSA; interview with Ted Rogers, Feb. 16, 2005. In 1985 Lincoln was also awarded a doctorate of humane letters from Harvard.

12. Interviews with Ted Rogers (Feb. 16, 2005) and Robert Gottlieb (July 22, 2006). The NYCB board had been operating with limited financial information. Ted Rogers brought in Marcia Thompson and the Ford Foundation's "Arts Stabilization Model" based on "balance sheet management" that required the board to understand its assets and its liabilities and how they changed from year to year.

13. LK to Zydower, June 15 (Fidelma), 1987, courtesy Zydower. Joe Duell's death: interview with Daniel Duell, Feb. 15, 2004; LK to Leonard, Feb. 20 (mystery), 1986; Jenkins's "comments on Duberman ms." (chapel). *Dance Magazine,* Apr. 1986, published a touching tribute to Duell by Marilyn Hunt.

CHAPTER THIRTY-ONE: OLD AGE (1986–1996)

1. Michael Leonard Diary, May 18, 1987, courtesy Leonard; *New York Times,* May 20, 1987; Warburg to LK, n.d., LK/DD. Farrell had earlier (Oct. 31, 1986, LK/DD) put her sentiments in a letter to Lincoln: "I just wanted . . . to thank you for all you've done for all of us."

2. LK to Ingersoll, Apr. 29 (Lindgren), 1987, BSA; LK memo to Chief Executive Officer, Jan. 13 (opinion of board), 1986 [possibly not sent], LK to Laughlin, Feb. 8 (company), 1987, JL/ND; Leonard diary, May 17 (Woetzel), 1987, courtesy Leonard; interview with Ted Rogers (Festival), Feb. 16, 2005; LK to Leonard, Aug. 3 (unproductive), Sept. 4 (new), 1988, courtesy Leonard. Martins has described the initial division of power with Robbins, and also Robbins's decision early on to stick to his own ballets and leave the rest to Peter (Martins interview with Ellen Sorrin, Oct. 28, 1998, DD/NYPL); Nicholas Jenkins, "The Great Impresario," *The New Yorker,* April 13, 1998.

3. Interviews with Jensen Yow, Robert La Fosse, and David Langfitt; LK to Laughlin, Feb. 8 (company), 1987, JL/ND; Jenkins to me, Nov. 22, 2006; LK to Leonard, June 20, 1988, courtesy Leonard; LK to La Fosse, Nov. 12, 1988, courtesy La Fosse; Leonard Diary, May 17 (Woetzel), 1987, Oct. 19 (Fred), 1987, Oct. 23 (Jenkins), 29 (privacy), 1989, courtesy Leonard.

4. PR to Leonard, June 10 (closer), 1982, Mar. 14 (Abrams), Aug. 27 (MoMA), 1984, Mar. 6 (Caravaggio), Nov. 8 (Kelley), 1985, courtesy Leonard; LK to Colville, Sept. 2 (Cadmus),

1982, courtesy Colville; LK to Chapman, Apr. 10 (Cadmus), 1983, RC/DD; Jenkins to me, Nov. 22, 2006.

5. Interview with Paul Taylor, June 6, 2003 (plaque; generous; *Look*); Taylor to LK, Oct. 8, 1976, BSA; Taylor to LK, May 31, June 7, 1979 (father), Apr. 24, 1980, May 24, 1986, May 14, 1987, Mar. 1, 1992, LK/DD; LK to Taylor, June 5, 1979, Apr. 28, May 1, 14, 1980, courtesy Taylor; Leonard Diary, May 7, 1987; LK, "The Monstrous Itch" (review of Taylor's *Private Domain* [Knopf, 1987], *New York Review of Books*, June 11, 1987).

6. LK to Leonard, July 14 (SAB), 1989, courtesy Leonard; LK to Zydower, Dec. 2 (costs), 1989, courtesy Zydower; Leonard Diary, Oct. 23, 28, Nov. 6, 1989, Nov. 9, 1990, courtesy Leonard; Arlene Croce, "Citizen Kirstein," *The New Yorker*, June 13, 1994.

7. LK to Buckle, Jan. 30 (*Beauty*), 1991; *New York Times*, Jan. 9, 1991; interview with Robert La Fosse, June 27, 2003; LK to La Fosse, June 14, 1991, courtesy La Fosse; interview with Jensen Yow, Apr. 12, 2003 (Bass; deterioration); interview with Jerry L. Thompson, July 16, 2003. According to Michael Leonard, Lincoln found *Quarry* "as unsatisfactory as I did"; apparently no one edited the error-filled text (Leonard Diary, Apr. 30, 1987).

8. Leonard Diary, May 1 (Richardson), 1990, Mar. 5, 12 (opening), Nov. 15 (form), 1992, Oct. 20, 22 (country), 31, 1993, May 16 (dialogue), 1995, courtesy Leonard; LK to Buckle, Jan. 16 (Garafola), 1991, July 1, 1993 (Martins), RB/UT; LK to Leonard, Dec. 21 (Tooker/Magritte), 1992, courtesy Leonard; interviews with Jensen Yow and Nicholas Jenkins; Steven Watson "notes" (pet) on two interviews with LK, courtesy Watson.

INDEX

PHOTOGRAPHIC CREDITS

A NOTE ON THE TYPE

This book was set in Janson, a typeface long thought to have been made by the Dutchman Anton Janson, who was a practicing typefounder in Leipzig during the years 1668–1687. However, it has been conclusively demonstrated that these types are actually the work of Nicholas Kis (1650–1702), a Hungarian, who most probably learned his trade from the master Dutch typefounder Dirk Voskens. The type is an excellent example of the influential and sturdy Dutch types that prevailed in England up to the time William Caslon (1692–1766) developed his own incomparable designs from them.

Composed by Creative Graphics, Allentown, Pennsylvania
Printed and bound by Berryville Graphics, Berryville, Virginia
Book design by Robert C. Olsson